To my grandchildren: Jacob, Jason, Ruth, Eliana, Natalie, Rachel, and Leo. My hope is that your capacity for empathy and compassion will help make the world a better place.

—E.A.

To my family, Deirdre Smith, Christopher Wilson, and Leigh Wilson

—T.D.W.

To my mentor, colleague, and friend, Dane Archer

—R.M.A.

To my students—past, present, and future—for making coming to work each morning fun, educational, and unpredictable.

—S.R.S.

Brief Contents

1 Introducing Social Psychology   21

2 Methodology: How Social Psychologists Do Research   43

3 Social Cognition: How We Think About the Social World   71

4 Social Perception: How We Come to Understand Other People   104

5 The Self: Understanding Ourselves in a Social Context   139

6 The Need to Justify Our Actions: The Costs and Benefits of Dissonance Reduction   177

7 Attitudes and Attitude Change: Influencing Thoughts and Feelings   208

8 Conformity: Influencing Behavior   246

9 Group Processes: Influence in Social Groups   289

10 Interpersonal Attraction: From First Impressions to Close Relationships   323

11 Prosocial Behavior: Why Do People Help?   364

12 Aggression: Why Do We Hurt Other People? Can We Prevent It?   395

13 Prejudice: Causes, Consequences, and Cures   433

Social Psychology in Action 1   Using Social Psychology to Achieve a Sustainable and Happy Future   475

Social Psychology in Action 2   Social Psychology and Health   496

Social Psychology in Action 3   Social Psychology and the Law   516

Social Psychology

Ninth Edition

Global Edition

Elliot Aronson

Timothy D. Wilson

Robin M. Akert

Samuel R. Sommers

Pearson

Columbus • Indianapolis • New York City • San Francisco Amsterdam • Cape Town • Dubai • London • Madrid • Milan • Paris • Montréal • Toronto • Delhi • Mexico City • São Paulo • Sydney • Hong Kong • Seoul • Singapore • Taipei • Tokyo

VP, Product Development: Dickson Musslewhite
Senior Acquisitions Editor: Amber Chow
Editorial Assistant: Luke Robbins
Executive Development Editor: Sharon Geary
Project Development: Piper Editorial
Senior Acquisitions Editor, Global Edition: Sandhya Ghoshal
Editor, Global Edition: Punita Kaur Mann
Director, Project Management Services: Lisa Iarkowski
Project Management Team Lead: Denise Forlow
Project Manager: Shelly Kupperman
Content Producer: Isha Sachdeva
Program Management Team Lead: Amber Mackey
Program Manager: Diane Szulecki
Director of Field Marketing: Jonathan Cottrell
Senior Product Marketing Manager: Lindsey Prudhomme Gill

Executive Field Marketing Manager: Kate Stewart
Marketing Assistant, Field Marketing: Paige Patunas
Marketing Assistant, Product Marketing: Frank Alarcon
Operations Manager: Mary Fischer
Operations Specialist: Diane Peirano
Associate Director of Design: Blair Brown
Interior Design: Kathryn Foot
Cover Design: Lumina Datamatics, Inc.
Cover Art: Topform/Shutterstock
Digital Media Editor: Christopher Fegan
Digital Media Project Manager: Pamela Weldin
Media Editor, Global Edition: Naina Singh
**Full-Service Project Management
  and Composition:** Lumina Datamatics, Inc.
Text Font: Palatino LT Pro 9.5/13

Credits and acknowledgments borrowed from other sources and reproduced, with permission, in this textbook appear on the appropriate page within the text or on pages 587–592.

Pearson Education Limited
KAO Two
KAO Park
Harlow
CM17 9NA
United Kingdom

and Associated Companies throughout the world

Visit us on the World Wide Web at: www.pearsonglobaleditions.com

© Pearson Education Limited 2018

ISBN 10: 1-292-18654-2
ISBN 13: 978-1-29-218654-2

20 19 18 17
5 4 3 2 1

British Library Cataloguing-in-Publication Data
A catalogue record for this book is available from the British Library

Typeset in Palatino LT Pro 9.5/13 by Lumina Datamatics, Inc.
Printed in Malaysia (CTP-VVP)

Contents

Preface 11
About the Authors 17
Special Tips for Students 19

1 Introducing Social Psychology 21

Defining Social Psychology 23
TRY IT! How Do Other People Affect Your Values? 23
Social Psychology, Philosophy, Science,
and Common Sense 24
How Social Psychology Differs from Its Closest Cousins 26
TRY IT! Social Situations and Behaviors 27

The Power of the Situation 29
The Importance of Explanation 30
The Importance of Interpretation 32

Where Construals Come From: Basic Human Motives 35
The Self-Esteem Motive: The Need to Feel Good
About Ourselves 36
SUFFERING AND SELF-JUSTIFICATION
The Social Cognition Motive: The Need to Be Accurate 37
EXPECTATIONS ABOUT THE SOCIAL WORLD
Summary 40 • Test Yourself 41

2 Methodology: How Social Psychologists Do Research 43

Social Psychology: An Empirical Science 44
**TRY IT! Social Psychology Quiz:
What's Your Prediction?** 45
Formulating Hypotheses and Theories 45
INSPIRATION FROM EARLIER THEORIES
AND RESEARCH • HYPOTHESES BASED
ON PERSONAL OBSERVATIONS

Research Designs 47
The Observational Method: Describing Social Behavior 48
ETHNOGRAPHY • ARCHIVAL ANALYSIS • LIMITS
OF THE OBSERVATIONAL METHOD
The Correlational Method: Predicting Social Behavior 50
SURVEYS • LIMITS OF THE CORRELATIONAL METHOD:
CORRELATION DOES NOT EQUAL CAUSATION
**TRY IT! Correlation and Causation:
Knowing the Difference** 53
The Experimental Method: Answering Causal Questions 54
INDEPENDENT AND DEPENDENT VARIABLES • INTERNAL
VALIDITY IN EXPERIMENTS • EXTERNAL VALIDITY
IN EXPERIMENTS • FIELD EXPERIMENTS • REPLICATIONS
AND META-ANALYSIS • BASIC VERSUS APPLIED RESEARCH

New Frontiers in Social Psychological Research 62
Culture and Social Psychology 63
The Evolutionary Approach 63
Social Neuroscience 64

Ethical Issues in Social Psychology 65
Summary 68 • Test Yourself 69

3 Social Cognition: How We Think About the Social World 71

On Automatic Pilot: Low-Effort Thinking 73
People as Everyday Theorists: Automatic
Thinking with Schemas 74
Which Schemas Do We Use? Accessibility and Priming 76
Making Our Schemas Come True: The Self-Fulfilling
Prophecy 78

Types of Automatic Thinking 81
Automatic Goal Pursuit 82
Automatic Decision Making 83
Automatic Thinking and Metaphors
About the Body and the Mind 83
Mental Strategies and Shortcuts: Judgmental Heuristics 85
HOW EASILY DOES IT COME TO MIND? THE AVAILABILITY
HEURISTIC • HOW SIMILAR IS A TO B? THE
REPRESENTATIVENESS HEURISTIC
TRY IT! Reasoning Quiz 89
PERSONALITY TESTS AND THE REPRESENTATIVENESS
HEURISTIC

Cultural Differences in Social Cognition 90
Cultural Determinants of Schemas 90
Holistic versus Analytic Thinking 91

Controlled Social Cognition: High-Effort Thinking 93
Controlled Thinking and Free Will 93
**TRY IT! Can You Predict Your (or Your Friend's)
Future?** 96
Mentally Undoing the Past: Counterfactual Reasoning 96
Improving Human Thinking 97
TRY IT! How Well Do You Reason? 98
Watson Revisited 99
Summary 100 • Test Yourself 102

4 Social Perception: How We Come to Understand Other People 104

Nonverbal Communication 106
TRY IT! Using Your Voice as a Nonverbal Cue 107
Facial Expressions of Emotion 107
EVOLUTION AND FACIAL EXPRESSIONS • WHY IS DECODING
SOMETIMES DIFFICULT?
Culture and the Channels of Nonverbal
Communication 110

First Impressions: Quick but Long-Lasting 113
The Lingering Influence of Initial Impressions 114
Using First Impressions and Nonverbal
Communication to Our Advantage 115

Causal Attribution: Answering the "Why" Question   117

The Nature of the Attribution Process   117

TRY IT! Listen as People Make Attributions   118

The Covariation Model: Internal versus
External Attributions   118

The Fundamental Attribution Error: People
as Personality Psychologists   121

THE ROLE OF PERCEPTUAL SALIENCE IN THE FUNDAMENTAL
ATTRIBUTION ERROR • THE TWO-STEP ATTRIBUTION
PROCESS

Self-Serving Attributions   126

The "Bias Blind Spot"   128

Culture and Social Perception   129

Holistic versus Analytic Thinking   130

SOCIAL NEUROSCIENCE EVIDENCE

Cultural Differences in the Fundamental
Attribution Error   131

Culture and Other Attributional Biases   133

Summary   135 • Test Yourself   137

5   The Self: Understanding Ourselves
in a Social Context   139

The Origins and Nature of the Self-Concept   140

Cultural Influences on the Self-Concept   142

**TRY IT! A Measure of Independence
and Interdependence**   143

Functions of the Self   144

Knowing Ourselves Through Introspection   145

Focusing on the Self: Self-Awareness Theory   145

**TRY IT! Measure Your Private Self-
Consciousness**   147

Judging Why We Feel the Way We Do:
Telling More Than We Can Know   147

The Consequences of Introspecting About Reasons   148

Knowing Ourselves by Observing Our Own Behavior   150

Intrinsic versus Extrinsic Motivation   151

Mindsets and Motivation   154

Understanding Our Emotions: The Two-Factor
Theory of Emotion   154

Finding the Wrong Cause: Misattribution of Arousal   157

Using Other People to Know Ourselves   159

Knowing Ourselves by Comparing Ourselves
to Others   160

Knowing Ourselves by Adopting Other
People's Views   161

Knowing Our Future Feelings by Consulting
Other People   163

Self-Control: The Executive Function of the Self   164

Impression Management: All the World's a Stage   166

Ingratiation and Self-Handicapping   167

Culture, Impression Management,
and Self-Enhancement   169

Self-Esteem: How We Feel About Ourselves   170

Summary   173 • Test Yourself   175

6   The Need to Justify Our Actions:
The Costs and Benefits of Dissonance
Reduction   177

The Theory of Cognitive Dissonance   178

When Cognitions Conflict   178

WHY WE OVERESTIMATE THE PAIN OF DISAPPOINTMENT

Dissonance and the Self-Concept   182

Decisions, Decisions, Decisions   183

DISTORTING OUR LIKES AND DISLIKES • THE PERMANENCE
OF THE DECISION

TRY IT! The Advantage of Finality   185

CREATING THE ILLUSION OF IRREVOCABILITY •
THE DECISION TO BEHAVE IMMORALLY

Dissonance, Culture, and the Brain   187

DISSONANCE IN THE BRAIN • DISSONANCE ACROSS
CULTURES

Self-Justification in Everyday Life   189

The Justification of Effort   189

TRY IT! Justifying What You've Done   191

External versus Internal Justification   191

COUNTERATTITUDINAL ADVOCACY

Punishment and Self-Persuasion   193

THE LASTING EFFECTS OF SELF-PERSUASION •
NOT JUST TANGIBLE REWARDS OR PUNISHMENTS

The Hypocrisy Paradigm   196

Justifying Good Deeds and Harmful Acts   197

THE BEN FRANKLIN EFFECT: JUSTIFYING ACTS OF KINDNESS

TRY IT! The Internal Consequences of Doing Good   199

DEHUMANIZING THE ENEMY: JUSTIFYING CRUELTY

Some Final Thoughts on Dissonance:
Learning from Our Mistakes   201

POLITICS AND SELF-JUSTIFICATION •
OVERCOMING DISSONANCE

Summary   205 • Test Yourself   206

7   Attitudes and Attitude Change:
Influencing Thoughts and Feelings   208

The Nature and Origin of Attitudes   210

Where Do Attitudes Come From?   210

COGNITIVELY BASED ATTITUDES • AFFECTIVELY BASED
ATTITUDES

TRY IT! Affective and Cognitive Bases of Attitudes   212

BEHAVIORALLY BASED ATTITUDES

Explicit versus Implicit Attitudes   213

When Do Attitudes Predict Behavior?   215

Predicting Spontaneous Behaviors   216

Predicting Deliberative Behaviors   216

SPECIFIC ATTITUDES • SUBJECTIVE NORMS • PERCEIVED
BEHAVIORAL CONTROL

How Do Attitudes Change?   219

Changing Attitudes by Changing Behavior:
Cognitive Dissonance Theory Revisited   219

Persuasive Communications and Attitude Change   220

THE CENTRAL AND PERIPHERAL ROUTES
TO PERSUASION • THE MOTIVATION TO PAY
ATTENTION TO THE ARGUMENTS • THE ABILITY TO PAY
ATTENTION TO THE ARGUMENTS • HOW TO ACHIEVE
LONG-LASTING ATTITUDE CHANGE

Emotion and Attitude Change   225
FEAR-AROUSING COMMUNICATIONS • EMOTIONS
AS A HEURISTIC • EMOTION AND DIFFERENT TYPES
OF ATTITUDES

Attitude Change and the Body   229

The Power of Advertising   230

How Advertising Works   231

Subliminal Advertising: A Form of Mind Control?   232
DEBUNKING THE CLAIMS ABOUT SUBLIMINAL
ADVERTISING • LABORATORY EVIDENCE FOR SUBLIMINAL
INFLUENCE

TRY IT! Consumer Brand Attitudes   **235**

Advertising, Stereotypes, and Culture   235
GENDER STEREOTYPES AND EXPECTATIONS •
CULTURE AND ADVERTISING

Resisting Persuasive Messages   239

Attitude Inoculation   239

Being Alert to Product Placement   239

Resisting Peer Pressure   240

When Persuasion Attempts Backfire:
Reactance Theory   241
Summary   243 • Test Yourself   244

8   Conformity: Influencing Behavior   **246**

Conformity: When and Why   248

Informational Social Influence:
The Need to Know What's "Right"   250

The Importance of Being Accurate   253

When Informational Conformity Backfires   254

When Will People Conform to Informational
Social Influence?   255
WHEN THE SITUATION IS AMBIGUOUS • WHEN THE SITUATION
IS A CRISIS • WHEN OTHER PEOPLE ARE EXPERTS

Normative Social Influence: The Need
to Be Accepted   256

Conformity and Social Approval:
The Asch Line-Judgment Studies   258

The Importance of Being Accurate, Revisited   261

The Consequences of Resisting Normative
Social Influence   263

**TRY IT! Unveiling Normative Social Influence
by Breaking the Rules**   **264**

When Will People Conform to Normative
Social Influence?   264
WHEN THE GROUP GROWS LARGER • WHEN THE GROUP IS
IMPORTANT • WHEN ONE HAS NO ALLIES IN THE GROUP •
WHEN THE GROUP'S CULTURE IS COLLECTIVISTIC

Minority Influence: When the Few Influence
the Many   268

Strategies for Using Social Influence   269

The Role of Injunctive and Descriptive Norms   270

Using Norms to Change Behavior:
Beware the "Boomerang Effect"   272

Other Tactics of Social Influence   273

Obedience to Authority   276

The Role of Normative Social Influence   279

The Role of Informational Social Influence   280

Other Reasons Why We Obey   281
CONFORMING TO THE WRONG NORM • SELF-JUSTIFICATION •
THE LOSS OF PERSONAL RESPONSIBILITY

The Obedience Studies, Then and Now   283
IT'S NOT ABOUT AGGRESSION
Summary   286 • Test Yourself   287

**9   Group Processes: Influence
in Social Groups**   **289**

What Is a Group?   290

Why Do People Join Groups?   290

The Composition and Functions of Groups   291
SOCIAL NORMS • SOCIAL ROLES • GROUP
COHESIVENESS • GROUP DIVERSITY

Individual Behavior in a Group Setting   295

Social Facilitation: When the Presence of
Others Energizes Us   296
SIMPLE VERSUS DIFFICULT TASKS • AROUSAL
AND THE DOMINANT RESPONSE • WHY THE PRESENCE
OF OTHERS CAUSES AROUSAL

Social Loafing: When the Presence of
Others Relaxes Us   299

Gender and Cultural Differences in Social Loafing:
Who Slacks Off the Most?   300

Deindividuation: Getting Lost in the Crowd   301
DEINDIVIDUATION MAKES PEOPLE FEEL LESS
ACCOUNTABLE • DEINDIVIDUATION INCREASES
OBEDIENCE TO GROUP NORMS • DEINDIVIDUATION
ONLINE

Group Decisions: Are Two (or More)
Heads Better Than One?   303

Process Loss: When Group Interactions
Inhibit Good Problem Solving   304
FAILURE TO SHARE UNIQUE INFORMATION •
GROUPTHINK: MANY HEADS, ONE MIND

Group Polarization: Going to Extremes   307

Leadership in Groups   309
LEADERSHIP AND PERSONALITY • LEADERSHIP
STYLES • THE RIGHT PERSON IN THE RIGHT
SITUATION • GENDER AND LEADERSHIP • CULTURE
AND LEADERSHIP

Conflict and Cooperation   313

Social Dilemmas   313

TRY IT! The Prisoner's Dilemma   **315**
INCREASING COOPERATION IN THE PRISONER'S DILEMMA

Using Threats to Resolve Conflict   316
EFFECTS OF COMMUNICATION

Negotiation and Bargaining   318
Summary   320 • Test Yourself   321

10 Interpersonal Attraction: From First Impressions to Close Relationships 323

What Predicts Attraction? 325

The Person Next Door: The Propinquity Effect 326

TRY IT! Mapping the Effect of Propinquity in Your Life 326

Similarity 328
OPINIONS AND PERSONALITY • INTERESTS AND EXPERIENCES • APPEARANCE • GENETICS • SOME FINAL COMMENTS ABOUT SIMILARITY

Reciprocal Liking 330

Physical Attractiveness 331
WHAT IS ATTRACTIVE? • CULTURAL STANDARDS OF BEAUTY • THE POWER OF FAMILIARITY • ASSUMPTIONS ABOUT ATTRACTIVE PEOPLE

Evolution and Mate Selection 336
EVOLUTION AND SEX DIFFERENCES • ALTERNATE PERSPECTIVES ON SEX DIFFERENCES

Making Connections in the Age of Technology 340

Attraction 2.0: Mate Preference in an Online Era 341

The Promise and Pitfalls of Online Dating 343

Love and Close Relationships 345

Defining Love: Companionship and Passion 345

TRY IT! Passionate Love Scale 347

Culture and Love 347

Attachment Styles in Intimate Relationships 349

This Is Your Brain . . . in Love 351

Theories of Relationship Satisfaction: Social Exchange and Equity 352
SOCIAL EXCHANGE THEORY • EQUITY THEORY

Ending Intimate Relationships 358

The Process of Breaking Up 358

The Experience of Breaking Up 359
Summary 361 • Test Yourself 362

11 Prosocial Behavior: Why Do People Help? 364

Basic Motives Underlying Prosocial Behavior: Why Do People Help? 365

Evolutionary Psychology: Instincts and Genes 366
KIN SELECTION • THE RECIPROCITY NORM

TRY IT! The Dictator Game 367
GROUP SELECTION

Social Exchange: The Costs and Rewards of Helping 368

Empathy and Altruism: The Pure Motive for Helping 369

Personal Qualities and Prosocial Behavior: Why Do Some People Help More Than Others? 373

Individual Differences: The Altruistic Personality 374

TRY IT! Empathic Concern 374

Gender Differences in Prosocial Behavior 375

Cultural Differences in Prosocial Behavior 375

Religion and Prosocial Behavior 377

The Effects of Mood on Prosocial Behavior 377
EFFECTS OF POSITIVE MOODS: FEEL GOOD, DO GOOD • FEEL BAD, DO GOOD

Situational Determinants of Prosocial Behavior: When Will People Help? 379

Environment: Rural versus Urban 379

Residential Mobility 380

The Number of Bystanders: The Bystander Effect 381
NOTICING AN EVENT • INTERPRETING THE EVENT AS AN EMERGENCY • ASSUMING RESPONSIBILITY • KNOWING HOW TO HELP • DECIDING TO IMPLEMENT THE HELP

Effects of the Media: Video Games and Music Lyrics 386

How Can Helping Be Increased? 388

Increasing the Likelihood That Bystanders Will Intervene 388

Increasing Volunteerism 390

Positive Psychology, Human Virtues, and Prosocial Behavior 391
Summary 392 • Test Yourself 393

12 Aggression: Why Do We Hurt Other People? Can We Prevent It? 395

Is Aggression Innate, Learned, or Optional? 396

The Evolutionary View 397
AGGRESSION IN OTHER ANIMALS

Culture and Aggression 398
CHANGES IN AGGRESSION ACROSS TIME AND CULTURES • CULTURES OF HONOR

Gender and Aggression 401
PHYSICAL AGGRESSION • RELATIONAL AGGRESSION

TRY IT! Do Women and Men Differ in Their Responses? 403

Learning to Behave Aggressively 403

Some Physiological Influences 405
THE EFFECTS OF ALCOHOL • THE EFFECTS OF PAIN AND HEAT

Social Situations and Aggression 407

Frustration and Aggression 408

Provocation and Reciprocation 409

TRY IT! Insults and Aggression 410

Weapons as Aggressive Cues 410

Putting the Elements Together: The Case of Sexual Assault 411
MOTIVATIONS FOR RAPE • SEXUAL SCRIPTS AND THE PROBLEM OF CONSENT • PUTTING THE ELEMENTS TOGETHER

Violence and the Media 414

Studying the Effects of Media Violence 414
EXPERIMENTAL STUDIES • LONGITUDINAL STUDIES

The Problem of Determining Cause and Effect 417

How to Decrease Aggression 419
Does Punishing Aggression Reduce Aggression? 419
USING PUNISHMENT ON VIOLENT ADULTS
Catharsis and Aggression 421
THE EFFECTS OF AGGRESSIVE ACTS ON SUBSEQUENT
AGGRESSION • BLAMING THE VICTIM OF OUR
AGGRESSION
What Are We Supposed to Do with Our Anger? 423
VENTING VERSUS SELF-AWARENESS
TRY IT! Controlling Your Anger **424**
TRAINING IN COMMUNICATION AND PROBLEM-SOLVING
SKILLS • COUNTERING DEHUMANIZATION
BY BUILDING EMPATHY
Disrupting the Rejection-Rage Cycle 426
Summary 428 • Test Yourself 431

13 Prejudice: Causes, Consequences,
and Cures 433

Defining Prejudice 434
The Cognitive Component: Stereotypes 435
FROM CATEGORIES TO STEREOTYPES
TRY IT! Stereotypes and Aggression **437**
WHAT'S WRONG WITH POSITIVE STEREOTYPES? •
STEREOTYPES OF GENDER
The Affective Component: Emotions 440
TRY IT! Identifying Your Prejudices **441**
The Behavioral Component: Discrimination 441
RACIAL DISCRIMINATION • GENDER DISCRIMINATION •
THE ACTIVATION OF PREJUDICE
Detecting Hidden Prejudices 447
Ways of Identifying Suppressed Prejudices 447
Ways of Identifying Implicit Prejudices 448
The Effects of Prejudice on the Victim 450
The Self-Fulfilling Prophecy 450
Stereotype Threat 451
Causes of Prejudice 454
Pressures to Conform: Normative Rules 454
Social Identity Theory: Us versus Them 456
ETHNOCENTRISM • IN-GROUP BIAS • OUT-GROUP
HOMOGENEITY • BLAMING THE VICTIM • JUSTIFYING
FEELINGS OF ENTITLEMENT AND SUPERIORITY
Realistic Conflict Theory 460
ECONOMIC AND POLITICAL COMPETITION
Reducing Prejudice 462
The Contact Hypothesis 463
When Contact Reduces Prejudice 465
WHERE DESEGREGATION WENT WRONG
Cooperation and Interdependence:
The Jigsaw Classroom 467
WHY DOES JIGSAW WORK?
TRY IT! Jigsaw-Type Group Study **469**
THE GRADUAL SPREAD OF COOPERATIVE
AND INTERDEPENDENT LEARNING
Summary 471 • Test Yourself 473

Social Psychology in Action 1
Using Social Psychology
to Achieve a Sustainable
and Happy Future 475

Applied Research in Social Psychology 478
Capitalizing on the Experimental Method 479
ASSESSING THE EFFECTIVENESS OF
INTERVENTIONS • POTENTIAL RISKS OF SOCIAL
INTERVENTIONS
Social Psychology to the Rescue 481
Using Social Psychology to Achieve
a Sustainable Future 481
Conveying and Changing Social Norms 482
**TRY IT! Reducing Littering with
Descriptive Norms** **483**
Keeping Track of Consumption 484
Introducing a Little Competitiveness 485
Inducing Hypocrisy 485
Removing Small Barriers to Achieve
Big Changes 487
Happiness and a Sustainable Lifestyle 489
What Makes People Happy? 489
SATISFYING RELATIONSHIPS • FLOW: BECOMING
ENGAGED IN SOMETHING YOU ENJOY • ACCUMULATE
EXPERIENCES, NOT THINGS • HELPING OTHERS
TRY IT! Applying the Research to Your Own Life **492**
Do People Know What Makes
Them Happy? 492
Summary 493 • Test Yourself 494

Social Psychology in Action 2
Social Psychology and Health 496

Stress and Human Health 497
Resilience 498
Effects of Negative Life Events 499
TRY IT! The College Life Stress Inventory **500**
LIMITS OF STRESS INVENTORIES
Perceived Stress and Health 501
Feeling in Charge: The Importance
of Perceived Control 502
INCREASING PERCEIVED CONTROL IN
NURSING HOMES • DISEASE, CONTROL, AND
WELL-BEING
Coping with Stress 506
Gender Differences in Coping
with Stress 507
Social Support: Getting Help from Others 507
TRY IT! Social Support **508**
Reframing: Finding Meaning in
Traumatic Events 509
Prevention: Promoting Healthier Behavior 511
Summary 513 • Test Yourself 514

Social Psychology in Action 3

Social Psychology and the Law   516

Eyewitness Testimony   518

Why Are Eyewitnesses Often Wrong?   518
ACQUISITION • STORAGE • RETRIEVAL

Judging Whether Eyewitnesses Are Mistaken   523
RESPONDING QUICKLY • THE PROBLEM WITH
VERBALIZATION • POST-IDENTIFICATION
FEEDBACK

TRY IT! The Accuracy of Eyewitness Testimony   526

The Recovered Memory Debate   526

Juries: Group Processes in Action   529

How Jurors Process Information
During the Trial   529

Confessions: Are They Always What They Seem?   530

Deliberations in the Jury Room   532
Summary   533 • Test Yourself   534

Glossary   536

References   542

Credits   587

Name Index   593

Subject Index   608

Answer Key   619

Preface

When we began writing this book, our overriding goal was to capture the excitement of social psychology. We have been pleased to hear, in many kind letters and e-mail messages from professors and students, that we succeeded. One of our favorite responses was from a student who said that the book was so interesting that she always saved it for last, to reward herself for finishing her other work. With that one student, at least, we succeeded in making our book an enjoyable, fascinating story, not a dry report of facts and figures.

There is always room for improvement, however, and our goal in this, the ninth edition, is to make the field of social psychology an even better read. When we teach the course, there is nothing more gratifying than seeing the sleepy students in the back row sit up with interest and say, "Wow, I didn't know that! Now *that's* interesting." We hope that students who read our book will have that same reaction.

What's New in This Edition?

We are pleased to add new features to the ninth edition that we believe will appeal to students and make it easier for them to learn the material. Each chapter begins with some learning objectives, which are repeated in the sections of the chapter that are most relevant to them and in the chapter-ending summary. All major sections of every chapter now end with review quizzes. Research shows that students learn material better when they are tested frequently, thus these section quizzes, as well as the test questions at the end of every chapter, should be helpful learning aids. Every chapter now has several writing prompts that instructors can decide to assign or not. In addition, we have retained and refined features that proved to be popular in the previous edition. For example, many of the Try It! exercises, which invite students to apply specific concepts to their everyday behavior, have been revised or replaced.

We have updated the ninth edition substantially, with numerous references to new research. Here is a sampling of the new research that is covered:

- A signature of our book continues to be Chapter 2, "Methodology: How Social Psychologists Do Research," a readable, student-friendly chapter on social psychology research methods. This chapter has been updated for the ninth edition with new references and examples.

- Chapter 3, "Social Cognition: How We Think About the Social World," has been reorganized to make the structure clearer to students. There are now four major sections: On Automatic Pilot: Low-Effort Thinking; Types of Automatic Thinking, Cultural Differences in Social Cognition, and Controlled Social Thinking. There are also new sections on automatic goal pursuit and decision making. Finally, the chapter has been updated with numerous new references.

- Chapter 4, "Social Perception: How We Come to Understand Other People," now includes a new section on "First Impressions: Quick but Long-Lasting," with new coverage of thin-slicing, belief perseverance, and the use of nonverbal communication to personal advantage (e.g., in the form of power posing). The chapter also presents updated research and conclusions regarding the universality of emotional expression, and new popular media examples from programs such as *Breaking Bad*, *Duck Dynasty*, and the podcast *Serial*.

- Chapter 5, "The Self: Understanding Ourselves in a Social Context," has been reorganized into seven major sections instead of five, which should make the material clearer to students. We also revised the opening example, added a section on affective forecasting, reorganized some of the other sections (e.g., on culture and the self and on mindsets), added two new figures, and deleted or consolidated two other figures. Nearly 50 references to recent research have been added.

- Chapter 6, "The Need to Justify Our Actions," now includes a revised definition of cognitive dissonance and two dozen new references. These updates include studies examining dissonance and cheating, hypocrisy and its consequences for self-justification, the justification of kindness in very young children, and a field study of justification of effort among participants in a religious ritual in Mauritius.

- Chapter 7, "Attitudes and Attitude Change: Influencing Thoughts and Feelings," includes some reorganization of section order in response to reviewer suggestions and an updated analysis of advertising, stereotypes, and culture. New Try It! exercises have also been added regarding the role of automatic thought processes in consumer-related attitudes.

- Chapter 8, "Conformity: Influencing Behavior," now boasts a new section on tactics of social influence, including the foot-in-the-door and door-in-the-face technique. We have also added review of the Bond et al. (2012) election study in which the appearance of an "I Voted" button on Facebook was found to influence users' own likelihood of voting. This chapter also discusses the role of normative social influence in the polar plunge trend and the ALS ice bucket challenge that went viral on social media in 2014.

- Chapter 9, "Group Processes: Influence in Social Groups," includes a new section on the relationship between group diversity, morale, and performance. The discussion of deindividuation has also been updated to consider the tendency as it is manifested in on-line contexts.

- Chapter 10, "Interpersonal Attraction: From First Impressions to Close Relationships," has a new opening vignette focusing on Tinder and other dating-related apps/websites. We have expanded the treatment of fertility and attraction in response to reviewer feedback, and also added new research on the relationship between genetic similarity and attraction.

- In Chapter 11, "Prosocial Behavior: Why Do People Help?" we substantially revised the sections on religion and prosocial behavior and on positive psychology. We now discuss recent research by van den Bos on appraisal and bystander intervention and recent media examples, such as a mention of the movie *Kick Ass*.

- Chapter 12, "Aggression: Why Do We Hurt Other People? Can We Prevent It?," has undergone significant organizational changes across the entire chapter for clarity and narrative flow. The first section now unifies various answers to the question of the origins of aggression—evolutionary, cultural, learned, physiological influences—with special attention to gender and aggression (similarities as well as the familiar differences). We have also added a section, "Putting the Elements Together: The Case of Sexual Assault." Here we not only updated the references but also added the latest studies about causes of rape and sexual assault; sexual scripts; and a 2015 review of research on sexual miscommunications.

- In Chapter 13, "Prejudice: Causes, Consequences, and Cures," we have added more on the Implicit Association Test (IAT) as it relates to measuring implicit bias. The chapter also now includes more social neuroscience research on social categorization and expands its discussion of the effects of prejudice on its targets. Several new glossary entries have been added to reflect these updates.

- Social Psychology in Action chapters—"Using Social Psychology to Achieve a Sustainable and Happy Future," "Social Psychology and Health," and "Social Psychology and the Law"—have been updated with many references to new research, but remain shorter chapters. When we teach the course, we find that students are excited to learn about these applied areas. At the same time, we recognize that some instructors have difficulty fitting the chapters into their courses. As with the previous edition, our approach remains to maintain a shortened length for the applied chapters to make it easy to integrate these chapters into different parts of the course in whatever fashion an instructor deems best. SPA1, "Using Social Psychology to Achieve a Sustainable and Happy Future," has a new opening example about the effects of climate change on U.S. cities and a new discussion of how experiences make people happier than material things. In SPA2, "Social Psychology and Health," we revised the sections on perceived control, "tend and befriend" responses to stress, and behavioral causes of health problems. SPA3, "Social Psychology and Law," has updated information on the role of post-identification feedback on eyewitness confidence and revised conclusions regarding the repressed memory debate.

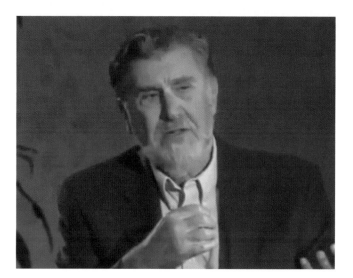

This edition of *Social Psychology* offers a variety of video types including interviews, as shown here with our lead author Elliot Aronson; news segments; and original lab experiment re-enactments directed by the authors and filmed at Tufts University.

Teaching and Learning Resources

A really good textbook should become part of the classroom experience, supporting and augmenting the professor's vision for the class. *Social Psychology* offers a number of supplements that enrich both the professor's presentation of social psychology and the students' understanding of it.

MyPsychLab®

- **MyPsychLab** combines proven learning applications with powerful assessment to engage students, assess their learning, and help them succeed.

- **An individualized study plan for each student**, based on performance on chapter pre-tests, helps students focus on the specific topics where they need the most support. The personalized study plan arranges content from less complex thinking—like remembering and understanding—to more complex critical-thinking skills—like applying and analyzing—and is based on Bloom's taxonomy. Every level of the study plan provides a formative assessment quiz.

- **Media assignments** for each chapter—including videos with assignable questions—feed directly into the gradebook, enabling instructors to track student progress automatically.

- **The Pearson eText** lets students access their textbook anytime and anywhere, and in any way they want, including listening online.

- Designed to help you develop and assess concept mastery and critical thinking, the Writing Space offers a single place to create, track, and grade writing assignments, provide resources, and exchange meaningful, personalized feedback with students, quickly and easily. Thanks to assisted-graded and create-your-own assignments, you decide your level of involvement in evaluating students' work. And because of integration with Turnitin®, **Writing Space** can check students' work for improper citation or plagiarism.

Instructor Resources

We know that instructors are "tour guides" for their students, leading them through the exciting world of social psychology in the classroom. As such, we have invested tremendous effort in the creation of a world-class collection of instructor resources that will support professors in their mission to teach the best course possible.

For this edition, new coauthor Sam Sommers guided the creation of the supplements package. Here are the highlights of the supplements we are pleased to provide:

PRESENTATION TOOLS AND CLASSROOM ACTIVITIES

- **MyPsychLab Video Series for Social Psychology** Current and cutting edge, the new *MyPsychLab Video Series* for social psychology features videos covering the most recent research, science, and applications. Watch clips from ABC's wildly popular *What Would You Do?* series and discover how real people in real-world scenarios bring to life classic concepts in social psychology.

- **Social Psychology PowerPoint Collection** The PowerPoints provide an active format for presenting concepts from each chapter and incorporating relevant figures and tables. Instructors can choose from three PowerPoint presentations: a lecture presentation set that highlights major topics from the chapters, a highly visual lecture presentation set with **embedded videos**, or a PowerPoint collection of the complete art files from the text. The PowerPoint files can be downloaded from www.pearsonglobaleditions.com/aronson.

- **Instructor's Resource Manual** The Instructor's Manual includes key terms, lecture ideas, teaching tips, suggested readings, chapter outlines, student projects and research assignments, Try It! exercises, critical thinking topics and discussion questions, and a media resource guide. It has been updated for the ninth edition with hyperlinks to ease facilitation of navigation within the IM.

ASSESSMENT RESOURCES

- **Test Bank** Each of the more than 2,000 questions in this test bank is page-referenced to the text and categorized by topic and skill level. Each question in the test bank was reviewed by several instructors to ensure that we are providing you with the best and most accurate content in the industry.

LEARNING CATALYTICS

- **Learning Catalytics**™ is an interactive, student-response tool that uses students' smartphones, tablets, or laptops to engage them in more sophisticated tasks and thinking. Now included with MyLab & with eText, Learning Catalytics enables you to generate classroom discussion, guide your lecture, and promote peer-to-peer learning with real-time analytics. Instructors, you can:

  - Pose a variety of open-ended questions that help your students develop critical thinking skills.

  - Monitor responses to find out where students are struggling.

  - Use real-time data to adjust your instructional strategy and try other ways of engaging your students during class.

  - Manage student interactions by automatically grouping students for discussion, teamwork, and peer-to-peer learning.

Acknowledgments

Elliot Aronson is delighted to acknowledge the collaboration of Carol Tavris in helping him update this edition. He would also like to acknowledge the contributions of his best friend (who also happens to be his wife of 60 years), Vera Aronson. Vera, as usual, provided inspiration for his ideas and acted as the sounding board for and supportive critic of many of his semiformed notions, helping to mold them into more-sensible analyses.

Tim Wilson would like to thank his graduate mentor, Richard E. Nisbett, who nurtured his interest in the field and showed him the continuity between social psychological research and everyday life. He also thanks the many students who have taken his course in social psychology over the years, for asking fascinating questions and providing wonderful examples of social psychological phenomena in their everyday lives. Lastly, he thanks the many graduate students with whom he has had the privilege of working for joining him in the ever-fascinating discovery of new social psychological phenomena.

Robin Akert is beholden to Jonathan Cheek, Julie Donnelly, Nan Vaida, Melody Tortosa, and Lila McCain for their feedback and advice, and to her family, Michaela and Wayne Akert, and Linda and Jerry Wuichet; their enthusiasm and boundless support have sustained her on this project as on all the ones before it. Finally, she wishes to express her gratitude to Dane Archer—mentor, colleague, and friend—who opened the world of social psychology to her and who has been her guide ever since.

Sam Sommers would like to acknowledge, first and foremost, the lovely Sommers ladies, Marilyn, Abigail, and Sophia, for being patient with round-the-clock revision sessions, for tolerating the constantly expanding mass of papers and books on the floor of the study (he promises to clean them up before work starts on the tenth edition), and for frequently providing excellent real-life examples that illustrate social psychological concepts. He also gives special thanks to all of his teachers of social psychology, for introducing him to the field, for continued support, and for serving as role models as instructors, mentors, researchers, and writers.

No book can be written and published without the help of many people working with the authors behind the scenes, and our book is no exception. We would like to thank the many colleagues who read one or more chapters of this edition and of previous editions of the book.

Reviewers of the Ninth Edition

Jim Allen, *State University of New York, College at Geneseo*; Kathryn Anderson, *Our Lady of the Lake University*; Anila Bhagavatula, *California State University–Long Beach*; Amy Bradshaw-Hoppock, *Embry-Riddle Aeronautical University*; Ngoc Bui, *University of La Verne*; Bernardo Carducci, *Indiana University Southeast*; Alex Czopp, *Western Washington University*; Keith Davis, *University of South Carolina*; Michael Dudley, *Southern Illinois University Edwardsville*; Heidi English, *College of the Siskiyous*; Joe Ferrari, *DePaul University*; Christine Floether,

Centenary College; Krista Forrest, *University of Nebraska at Kearney*; Allen Gorman, *Radford University*; Jerry Green, *Tarrant County College*; Dana Greene, *University of North Carolina*; Donnell Griffin, *Davidson County Community College*; Lisa Harrison, *California State University, Sacramento*; Gina Hoover, *Ohio State University*; Jeffrey Huntsinger, *Loyola University Chicago*; Alisha Janowsky, *University of Central Florida*; Bethany Johnson, *University of Nebraska–Omaha*; Deborah Jones, *Columbia University*; Suzanne Kieffer, *University of Houston*; Marvin Lee, *Tennessee State University*; Alexandra Luong, *University of Minnesota Duluth*; Robyn Mallett, *Loyola University Chicago*; Brian Meier, *Gettysburg College*; Andrea Mercurio, *Boston University*; Lori Nelson, *University of Iowa*; Darren Petronella, *Nassau Community College*; Jennifer Rivers, *Elms College*; Kari Terzino, *Des Moines Area Community College*; T. Joel Wade, *Bucknell University*; Angela Walker, *Quinnipiac University*; Chrysalis Wright, *University of Central Florida*; Garry Zaslow, *Nassau Community College*; Jie Zhang, *University at Buffalo*

Reviewers of Past Editions

Jeffrey B. Adams, *Saint Michael's College*; Bill Adler, *Collin County Community College*; John R. Aiello, *Rutgers University*; Charles A. Alexander, *Rock Valley College*; Sowmya Anand, *Ohio State University*; Nathan Arbuckle, *Ohio State University*; Art Aron, *State University of New York, Stony Brook*; Danny Axsom, *Virginia Polytechnic Institute and State University*; Joan W. Baily, *Jersey City State College*; Norma Baker, *Belmont University*; Austin Baldwin, *University of Iowa*; John Bargh, *New York University*; William A. Barnard, *University of Northern Colorado*; Doris G. Bazzini, *Appalachian State University*; Arthur Beaman, *University of Kentucky*; Gordon Bear, *Ramapo College*; Susan E. Beers, *Sweet Briar College*; Kathy L. Bell, *University of North Carolina at Greensboro*; Leonard Berkowitz, *University of Wisconsin–Madison*; Ellen S. Berscheid, *University of Minnesota*; John Bickford, *University of Massachusetts, Amherst*; Thomas Blass, *University of Maryland*; C. George Boeree, *Shippensburg University*; Lisa M. Bohon, *California State University, Sacramento*; Jennifer Bosson, *The University of Oklahoma*; Chante C. Boyd, *Carnegie Mellon University*; Peter J. Brady, *Clark State Community College*; Kosha Bramesfeld, *Pennsylvania State University*; Kelly A. Brennan, *University of Texas, Austin*; Richard W. Brislin, *East-West Center of the University of Hawaii*; Jeff Bryson, *San Diego State University*; Melissa Burkley, *Oklahoma State University*; Amy Bush, *University of Houston*; Amber Bush Amspoker, *University of Houston*; Brad Bushman, *Iowa State University*; Thomas P. Cafferty, *University of South Carolina, Columbia*; Melissa A. Cahoon, *Wright State University*; Frank Calabrese, *Community College of Philadelphia*; Michael Caruso, *University of Toledo*; Nicholas Christenfeld, *University of California, San Diego*; Margaret S. Clark, *Carnegie Mellon University*; Russell D. Clark, III, *University of North Texas*; Susan D. Clayton, *Allegheny College*; Megan Clegg-Kraynok, *West Virginia University*; Brian M. Cohen, *University of Texas, San Antonio*; Florette Cohen, *Rutgers University*; Jack Cohen, *Camden County College*; Steven G. Cole, *Texas Christian University*; Eric J. Cooley, *Western Oregon State University*; Diana Cordova, *Yale University*; Traci Craig, *University of Idaho*; Jack Croxton, *State University of New York, Fredonia*; Keith E. Davis, *University of South Carolina, Columbia*; Mary

Ellen Dello Stritto, *Ball State University*; Dorothee Dietrich, *Hamline University*; Kate Dockery, *University of Florida*; Susann Doyle, *Gainesville College*; Steve Duck, *University of Iowa*; Michael G. Dudley, *Southern Illinois University Edwardsville*; Karen G. Duffy, *State University of New York, Geneseo*; Valerie Eastman, *Drury College*; Tami Eggleston, *McKendree College*; Timothy Elliot, *University of Alabama–Birmingham*; Steve L. Ellyson, *Youngstown State University*; Cindy Elrod, *Georgia State University*; Kadimah Elson, *University of California, San Diego/Grossmont College*; Rebecca S. Fahrlander, *University of Nebraska at Omaha*; Alan Feingold, *Yale University*; Edward Fernandes, *East Carolina University*; Phil Finney, *Southeast Missouri State University*; Susan Fiske, *University of Massachusetts*; Robin Franck, *Southwestern College*; Denise Frank, *Ramapo College of New Jersey*; Timothy M. Franz, *St. John Fisher College*; William Rick Fry, *Youngstown State University*; Russell Geen, *University of Missouri*; Glenn Geher, *State University of New York at New Paltz*; David Gersh, *Houston Community College*; Frederick X. Gibbons, *Iowa State University*; Cynthia Gilliland, *Louisiana State University*; Genaro Gonzalez, *University of Texas*; Jessica Gonzalez, *Ohio State University*; Sara Gorchoff, *University of California, Berkeley*; Beverly Gray, *Youngstown State University*; Gordon Hammerle, *Adrian College*; H. Anna Han, *Ohio State University*; Judith Harackiewicz, *University of Wisconsin–Madison*; Elaine Hatfield, *University of Hawaii, Manoa*; Vicki S. Helgeson, *Carnegie Mellon University*; Joyce Hemphill, *Cazenovia College*; Tracy B. Henley, *Mississippi State University*; Ed Hirt, *Indiana University*; Harold Hunziker Jr., *Corning Community College*; David E. Hyatt, *University of Wisconsin–Oshkosh*; Marita Inglehart, *University of Michigan*; Carl Kallgren, *Behrend College, Pennsylvania State University, Erie*; Stephen Kilianski, *Rutgers University*; Bill Klein, *Colby College*; James D. Johnson, *University of North Carolina, Wilmington*; Lee Jussim, *Rutgers University*; Stephen Kilianski, *Rutgers University*; Fredrick Koenig, *Tulane University*; Alan Lambert, *Washington University, St. Louis*; Emmett Lampkin, *Kirkwook Community College*; Elizabeth C. Lanthier, *Northern Virginia Community College*; Patricia Laser, *Bucks County Community College*; G. Daniel Lassiter, *Ohio University*; Dianne Leader, *Georgia Institute of Technology*; John Lu, *Concordia University*; Stephanie Madon, *Iowa State University*; John Malarkey, *Wilmington College*; Andrew Manion, *St. Mary's University of Minnesota*; Allen R. McConnell, *Michigan State University*; Adam Meade, *North Carolina State University*; Joann M. Montepare, *Tufts University*; Richard Moreland, *University of Pittsburgh*; Dave Nalbone, *Purdue University–Calumet*; Carrie Nance, *Stetson University*; Todd D. Nelson, *Michigan State University*; Elaine Nocks, *Furman University*; Matylda Osika, *University of Houston*; Cheri Parks, *Colorado Christian University*; W. Gerrod Parrott, *Georgetown University*; David Peterson, *Mount Senario College*; Mary Pritchard, *Boise State University*; Cynthia K. S. Reed, *Tarrant County College*; Dan Richard, *University of North Florida*; Neal Roese, *University of Illinois*; Darrin L. Rogers, *Ohio State University*; Joan Rollins, *Rhode Island College*; Paul Rose, *Southern Illinois University Edwardsville*; Lee D. Ross, *Stanford University*; Alex Rothman, *University of Minnesota*;

M. Susan Rowley, *Champlain College*; Delia Saenz, *Arizona State University*; Brad Sagarin, *Northern Illinois University*; Fred Sanborn, *North Carolina Wesleyan College*; Connie Schick, *Bloomsburg University*; Norbert Schwartz, *University of Michigan*; Gretchen Sechrist,*University at Buffalo*; Richard C. Sherman, *Miami University of Ohio*; Paul Silvia, *University of North Carolina at Greensboro*; Randolph A. Smith, *Ouachita Baptist University*; Linda Solomon, *Marymount Manhattan College*; Janice Steil, *Adelphi University*; Jakob Steinberg, *Fairleigh Dickinson University*; Mark Stewart, *American River College*; Lori Stone, *The University of Texas at Austin*; JoNell Strough, *West Virginia University*; T. Gale Thompson, *Bethany College*; Scott Tindale, *Loyola University of Chicago*; David M. Tom, *Columbus State Community College*; David Trafimow, *New Mexico State University*; Ruth Warner, *St. Louis University*; Anne Weiher, *Metropolitan State College of Denver*; Gary L. Wells, *Iowa State University*; Jackie White, *University of North Carolina at Greensboro*; Paul L. Wienir, *Western Michigan University*; Kipling D. Williams, *University of Toledo*; Tamara Williams, *Hampton University*; Paul Windschitl, *University of Iowa*; Mike Witmer, *Skagit Valley College*; Gwen Wittenbaum, *Michigan State University*; William Douglas Woody, *University of Northern Colorado*; Clare Zaborowski, *San Jacinto College*; William H. Zachry, *University of Tennessee, Martin*; Leah Zinner, *University of Wisconsin–Madison*

We also thank the wonderful editorial staff of Pearson for their expertise and professionalism, including Dickson Musslewhite (Editorial Director), Diane Szulecki (Program Manager), Lindsey Prudhomme Gill (Product Marketing Manager), Luke Robbins (Editorial Assistant), Christopher Fegan (Digital Product Manager), and Shelly Kupperman (Project Manager). We would especially like to thank Mary Piper Hansen (Developmental Editor), who provided expert guidance with constant good cheer and insight even through barrages of e-mail exchanges and attachments, and Amber Chow (Executive Editor), whose smart vision for the book, and commitment to making it as good as it can be, have truly made a difference. Finally, we thank Mary Falcon, but for whom we never would have begun this project.

Thank you for inviting us into your classroom. We welcome your suggestions, and we would be delighted to hear your comments about this book.

Elliot Aronson
elliot@cats.ucsc.edu

Tim Wilson
tdw@virginia.edu

Robin Akert
rakert@wellesley.edu

Sam Sommers
sam.sommers@tufts.edu

Global Edition Acknowledgments

Pearson would like to thank the following people for their work on the content of the Global Edition:

Albert Lee Kai Chung, *Nanyang Technological University*
Ashum Gupta
Alizeh Batra Merchant, *New York University Abu Dhabi*
Pooja Thakur
Elizabeth Wright, *Murdoch University*

About the Authors

Elliot Aronson

When I was a kid, we were the only Jewish family in a virulently anti-Semitic neighborhood. I had to go to Hebrew school every day, late in the afternoon. Being the only youngster in my neighborhood going to Hebrew school made me an easy target for some of the older neighborhood toughs. On my way home from Hebrew school, after dark, I was frequently waylaid and roughed up by roving gangs shouting anti-Semitic epithets.

I have a vivid memory of sitting on a curb after one of these beatings, nursing a bloody nose or a split lip, feeling very sorry for myself and wondering how these kids could hate me so much when they didn't even know me. I thought about whether those kids were taught to hate Jews or whether, somehow, they were born that way. I wondered if their hatred could be changed—if they got to know me better, would they hate me less? I speculated about my own character. What would I have done if the shoe were on the other foot—that is, if I were bigger and stronger than they, would I be capable of beating them up for no good reason?

I didn't realize it at the time, of course, but eventually I discovered that these were profound questions. And some 30 years later, as an experimental social psychologist, I had the great good fortune to be in a position to answer some of those questions and to invent techniques to reduce the kind of prejudice that had claimed me as a victim.

Elliot Aronson is Professor Emeritus at the University of California at Santa Cruz and one of the most renowned social psychologists in the world. In 2002, he was chosen as one of the 100 most eminent psychologists of the twentieth century. Dr. Aronson is the only person in the 120-year history of the American Psychological Association to have received all three of its major awards: for distinguished writing, distinguished teaching, and distinguished research. Many other professional societies have honored his research and teaching as well. These include the American Association for the Advancement of Science, which gave him its highest honor, the Distinguished Scientific Research award; the American Council for the Advancement and Support of Education, which named him Professor of the Year of 1989; the Society for the Psychological Study of Social Issues, which awarded him the Gordon Allport prize for his contributions to the reduction of prejudice among racial and ethnic groups; and the William James Award from the Association for Psychological Science. In 1992, he was named a Fellow of the American Academy of Arts and Sciences. A collection of papers and tributes by his former students and colleagues, The Scientist and the Humanist, *celebrates his contributions to social psychological theory and its application to real-world problems. Dr. Aronson's own recent books for general audiences include* Mistakes Were Made (but not by ME), *with Carol Tavris, and a memoir,* Not by Chance Alone: My Life as a Social Psychologist.

Tim Wilson

One day when I was 8, a couple of older kids rode up on their bikes to share some big news: They had discovered an abandoned house down a country road. "It's really neat," they said. "We broke a window and nobody cared!" My friend and I hopped onto our bikes to investigate. We had no trouble finding the house—there it was, sitting off by itself, with a big, jagged hole in a first-floor window. We got off of our bikes and looked around. My friend found a baseball-sized rock lying on the ground and threw a perfect strike through another first-floor window. There was something exhilarating about the smash-and-tingle of shattering glass, especially when we knew there was nothing wrong with what we were doing. After all, the house was abandoned, wasn't it? We broke nearly every window in the house and then climbed through one of the first-floor windows to look around.

It was then that we realized something was terribly wrong. The house certainly did not look abandoned. There were pictures on the wall, nice furniture, books in shelves. We went home feeling frightened and confused. We soon learned that the house was the home of an elderly couple who were away on vacation. Eventually, my parents discovered what we had done and paid a substantial sum to repair the windows. For years, I pondered this incident: Why did I do such a terrible thing? Was I a bad kid? I didn't think so, and neither did my parents. How, then, could a good kid do such a bad thing? Even though the neighborhood kids said the house was abandoned, why couldn't my friend and I see the clear signs that someone lived there? How crucial was it that my friend was there and threw the first rock? Although I didn't know it at the time, these reflections touched on several classic social psychological issues, such as whether only bad people do bad things, whether the social situation can be powerful enough to make good people do bad things, and the way in which our expectations about an event can make it difficult to see it as it really is. Fortunately, my career as a vandal ended with this one incident. It did, however, mark the beginning of my fascination with basic questions about how people understand themselves and the social world—questions I continue to investigate to this day.

Tim Wilson did his undergraduate work at Williams College and Hampshire College and received his PhD from the University of Michigan. Currently Sherrell J. Aston Professor of Psychology at the University of Virginia, he has published numerous articles in the areas of introspection, attitude change, self-knowledge, and affective forecasting, as well as a recent book, Redirect: The Surprising New Science of Psychological Change. *His research has received the support of the National Science Foundation and the National Institute for Mental Health. He has been elected twice to the Executive Board of the Society for Experimental Social Psychology and is a Fellow in the American Psychological Society and the Society for Personality and Social Psychology. In 2009, he was named a Fellow of the American Academy of Arts and Sciences. In 2015 he received the William James Fellows Award from the Association for Psychological Science. Wilson has taught the Introduction to Social Psychology course at the University of Virginia for more than 30 years. In 2001 he was awarded the University of Virginia All-University Outstanding Teaching Award, and in 2010 was awarded the University of Virginia Distinguished Scientist Award.*

Robin Akert

One fall day when I was about 16, I was walking with a friend along the shore of the San Francisco Bay. Deep in conversation, I glanced over my shoulder and saw a sailboat capsize. I pointed it out to my friend, who took only a perfunctory interest and went on talking. However, I kept watching as we walked, and I realized that the two sailors were in the water, clinging to the capsized boat. Again I said something to my friend, who replied, "Oh, they'll get it upright—don't worry."

But I *was* worried. Was this an emergency? My friend didn't think so. And I was no sailor; I knew nothing about boats. But I kept thinking, "That water is really cold. They can't stay in that water too long." I remember feeling very confused and unsure. What should I do? Should I do anything? Did they really need help?

We were near a restaurant with a big window overlooking the bay, and I decided to go in and see if anyone had done anything about the boat. Lots of people were watching but not doing anything. This confused me too. Meekly, I asked the bartender to call for some kind of help. He just shrugged. I went back to the window and watched the two small figures in the water. Why was everyone so unconcerned? Was I crazy?

Years later, I reflected on how hard it was for me to do what I did next: I demanded that the bartender let me use his phone. In those days before "911," it was lucky that I knew there was a Coast Guard station on the bay, and I asked the operator for the number. I was relieved to hear the Guardsman take my message very seriously.

It had been an emergency. I watched as the Coast Guard cutter sped across the bay and pulled the two sailors out of the water. Maybe I saved their lives that day. What really stuck with me over the years was how other people behaved and how it made me feel. The other bystanders seemed unconcerned and did nothing to help. Their reactions made me doubt myself and made it harder for me to decide to take action. When I later studied social psychology in college, I realized that on the shore of the San Francisco Bay that day, I had experienced the "bystander effect" fully: The presence of other, apparently unconcerned bystanders had made it difficult for me to decide if the situation was an emergency and whether it was my responsibility to help.

Robin Akert graduated summa cum laude from the University of California at Santa Cruz, where she majored in psychology and sociology. She received her PhD in experimental social psychology from Princeton University. She is currently a Professor of Psychology at Wellesley College, where she was awarded the Pinanski Prize for Excellence in Teaching early in her career. She publishes primarily in the area of nonverbal communication, and recently received the AAUW American Fellowship in support of her research. She has taught the social psychology course at Wellesley College for nearly 30 years.

Sam Sommers

I went to college to major in English. I only found myself in an Intro to Psychology course as a second-semester freshman because, well, it just seemed like the kind of thing you did as a second-semester freshman. It was when we got to the social psychology section of the course that a little voice in my head starting whispering something along the lines of, *Hey, you've gotta admit this is pretty good stuff. It's a lot like the conversations you have with your friends about daily life, but with scientific data.*

As part of the class, we had the opportunity to participate in research studies for course credit. So one day I found myself in an interaction study in which I was going to work on solving problems with a partner. I walked in and it was clear that the other guy had arrived earlier—his coat and bag were already hanging on the back of a chair. I was led to another, smaller room and shown a video of my soon-to-be partner. Then I was given a series of written questions about my perceptions of him, my expectations for our upcoming session together, and so forth. Finally, I walked back into the main area. The experimenter handed me a chair and told me to put it down anywhere next to my partner's chair, and that she would go get him (he, too, was presumably completing written questionnaires in a private room).

So I did. I put my chair down, took a seat, and waited. Then the experimenter returned, but she was alone. She told me the study was over. There was no other participant; there would be no problem-solving in pairs. The video I had watched was of an actor, and in some versions of the study he mentioned having a girlfriend. In other versions, he mentioned a boyfriend. What the researchers were actually studying was how this social category information of sexual orientation would influence participants' attitudes about the interaction.

And then she took out a tape measure.

The tape measure was to gauge how close to my partner's chair I had placed my own chair, the hypothesis being that discomfort with a gay partner might manifest in terms of participants placing their chairs farther away. Greater comfort with or affinity for the partner was predicted to lead to more desire for proximity.

And at that, I was hooked. The little voice in my head had grown from a whisper to a full-throated yell that this was a field I could get excited about. First of all, the researchers had tricked me. That, alone, I thought was, for lack of a better word, *cool.* But more important, they had done so in the effort to get me and my fellow participants to reveal something about our attitudes, preferences, and tendencies that we never would have admitted to (or perhaps even would have been aware of) had they just asked us directly. Here was a fascinatingly creative research design, being used in the effort to study what struck me as an incredibly important social issue.

Like I said, I was hooked. And I look forward to helping to introduce you to this field that caught me by surprise back when I was a student and continues to intrigue and inspire me to this day.

Sam Sommers earned his BA from Williams College and his PhD from the University of Michigan. Since 2003 he has been a faculty member in the Department of Psychology at Tufts University in Medford, Massachusetts. His research examines issues related to stereotyping, prejudice, and group diversity, with a particular interest in how these processes play out in the legal domain. He has won multiple teaching awards at Tufts, including the Lerman-Neubauer Prize for Outstanding Teaching and Advising and the Gerald R. Gill Professor of the Year Award. He was also inducted into the Tufts Hall of Diversity for his efforts to promote an inclusive climate on campus for all students. He has testified as an expert witness on issues related to racial bias, jury decision-making, and eyewitness memory in criminal trial proceedings in seven states. His first general audience book on social psychology was published in 2011, titled Situations Matter: Understanding How Context Transforms Your World. *His next book, titled* Your Brain on Sports, *is coauthored with L. Jon Wertheim of* Sports Illustrated *and will be published in early 2016.*

Special Tips for Students

"There is then creative reading as well as creative writing," said Ralph Waldo Emerson in 1837, and that aptly sums up what you need to know to be a proficient student: Be an active, creative consumer of information. How do you accomplish that feat? Actually, it's not difficult. Like everything else in life, it just takes some work—some clever, well-planned, purposeful work. Here are some suggestions about how to do it.

Get to Know the Textbook

Believe it or not, in writing this book, we thought carefully about the organization and structure of each chapter. Things are presented as they are for a reason, and that reason is to help you learn the material in the best way possible. Here are some tips on what to look for in each chapter.

Key terms are in boldface type in the text so that you'll notice them. We define the terms in the text, and that definition appears again in the margin. These marginal definitions are there to help you out if later in the chapter you forget what something means. The marginal definitions are quick and easy to find. You can also look up key terms in the alphabetical Glossary at the end of this textbook.

Make sure you notice the headings and subheadings. The headings are the skeleton that holds a chapter together. They link together like vertebrae. If you ever feel lost, look back to the previous heading and the headings before it—this will give you the "big picture" of where the chapter is going. It should also help you see the connections between sections.

The summary at the end of each chapter is a succinct shorthand presentation of the chapter information. You should read it and make sure there are no surprises when you do so. If anything in the summary doesn't ring a bell, go back to the chapter and reread that section. Most important, remember that the summary is intentionally brief, whereas your understanding of the material should be full and complete. Use the summary as a study aid before your exams. When you read it over, everything should be familiar. When you have that wonderful feeling of knowing more than is in the summary, you'll know that you are ready to take the exam.

Be sure to do the Try It! exercises. They will make concepts from social psychology concrete and help you see how they can be applied to your own life. Some of the *Try It!* exercises replicate social psychology experiments. Others reproduce self-report scales so you can see where you stand in relation to other people. Still others are short quizzes that illustrate social psychological concepts.

Watch the videos. Our carefully curated collection of interviews, news clips, and research study reenactments is designed to enhance, and help you better understand, the concepts you're reading. If you can see the concept in action, it's likely to sink in a little deeper.

Just Say No to the Couch Potato Within

Because social psychology is about everyday life, you might lull yourself into believing that the material is all common sense. Don't be fooled. The material presented in this book is more complicated than it might seem. Therefore, we want to emphasize that the best way to learn it is to work with it in an active, not passive, fashion. You can't just read a chapter once and expect it to stick with you. You have to go over the material, wrestle with it, make your own connections to it, question it, think about it, interact with it. Actively working with material makes it memorable and makes it your own. Because it's a safe bet that someone is going to ask you about this material later and you're going to have to pull it out of memory, do what you can to get it into memory now. Here are some techniques to use:

- Go ahead and be bold—use a highlighter! If you highlight important points using the highlighting tool in your toolbar, you will remember those important points better and can scroll back through them later.

- Read the chapter before the applicable class lecture, not afterward. This way, you'll get more out of the lecture, which will likely introduce new material in addition to what is in the chapter. The chapter will give you the big picture, as well as a lot of detail. The lecture will enhance that information and help you put it all together. If you haven't read the chapter first, you may not understand some of the points made in the lecture or realize which points are most important.

- Here's a good way to study material: Write out a key concept or a study in your own words, without looking at the book or your notes. Or say it out loud to yourself—again in your own words, with your eyes closed. Can you do it? How good was your version? Did you omit anything important? Did you get stuck at some point, unable to remember what comes next? If so, you now know that you need to go over that information in more detail. You can also study with someone else, describing theories and studies to each other and seeing if you're making sense.

- If you have trouble remembering the results of an important study, try drawing your own version of a graph of the findings (you can use our data graphs for an idea of how to proceed). You will probably find that you remember the research results much better in pictorial form than in words. Draw the information a few times and it will stay with you.

- Remember, the more you work with the material, the better you will learn and remember it. Write it in your own words, talk about it, explain it to others, or draw visual representations of it.

• Last but not least, remember that this material is a lot of fun. You haven't even started reading the book yet, but we think you're going to like it. In particular, you'll see how much social psychology has to tell you about your real, everyday life. As this course progresses, you might want to remind yourself to observe the events of your daily life with new eyes—the eyes of a social psychologist—and try to apply what you are learning to the behavior of friends, acquaintances, strangers, and, yes, even yourself. Make sure you use the *Try It!* exercises and visit the Web site. You will find out how much social psychology can help us understand our lives. When you read the news, think about what social psychology has to say about current events and behaviors; we believe you will find that your understanding of daily life is richer. If you notice a news article that you think is an especially good example of "social psychology in action," please send it to us, with a full reference to where you found it and on what page. If we decide to use it in the next edition of this book, we'll list your name in the Acknowledgments.

We realize that ten years from now you may not remember all the facts, theories, and names you learn now. Although we hope you will remember some of them, our main goal is for you to take with you into your future a great many of the broad social psychological concepts presented herein—and, perhaps more important, a critical and scientific way of thinking. If you open yourself to social psychology's magic, we believe it will enrich the way you look at the world and the way you live in it.

Chapter 1
Introducing Social Psychology

 ## Chapter Outline and Learning Objectives

Defining Social Psychology

1.1 **What is social psychology, and how is it different from other disciplines?**

Social Psychology, Philosophy, Science, and Common Sense

How Social Psychology Differs from Its Closest Cousins

The Power of the Situation

1.2 **Why does it matter how people explain and interpret events—and their own and others' behavior?**

The Importance of Explanation

The Importance of Interpretation

Where Construals Come From: Basic Human Motives

1.3 **What happens when people's need to feel good about themselves conflicts with their need to be accurate?**

The Self-Esteem Motive: The Need to Feel Good About Ourselves

The Social Cognition Motive: The Need to Be Accurate

It is a pleasure to be your tour guides as we take you on a journey through the world of social psychology. The four authors of your book, combined, have taught this course for almost 100 years, so we know the terrain pretty well. As we embark on this journey, our hope is to convey our excitement about social psychology—what it is and why it matters. Not only do we enjoy teaching this stuff, we also love contributing to the growth and development of this field—for, in addition to being teachers, each of us is a scientist who has contributed to the knowledge base that makes up our discipline. In effect, not only are we leading this tour, we also helped create some of its major attractions. We will travel to fascinating and exotic places like prejudice, love, propaganda, education, the law, aggression, compassion, . . . all the rich variety and surprise of human social life. Ready? OK, let's go!

Let's begin with a few examples of the heroic, touching, tragic, and puzzling things that people do:

- After two brothers set off a bomb at the finish line of the Boston Marathon in 2013, killing three people and severely injuring 170 others, citizens of Boston raced to the rescue. Many, in spite of the risk to themselves, ran straight to the site of the bombing to help the injured, putting tourniquets on bleeding wounds until ambulances could arrive. "We're a strong city," said the mayor. "Boston will overcome."

- Kristen has known Martin for 2 months and feels that she is madly in love with him. "We're soul mates!" she tells her best friend. "He's the one!" "What are you thinking?" says the BF. "He's completely wrong for you! He's as different from you as can be—different background, religion, politics; you even like different movies." "I'm not worried," says Kristen. "Opposites attract. I know that's true; I read it on Wikipedia!"

- Janine and her brother Oscar are arguing about fraternities. Janine's college didn't have any, but Oscar is at a large state university in the Midwest, where he has joined Alpha Beta. He went through a severe and scary hazing ritual to join, and Janine cannot understand why he loves these guys so much. "They make the pledges do such stupid stuff," she says. "They humiliate you and force you to get sick drunk and practically freeze to death in the middle of the night. How can you possibly be happy living there?" "You don't get it," Oscar replies. "Alpha Beta is the best of all fraternities. My frat brothers just seem more fun than most other guys."

- Abraham Biggs Jr., age 19, had been posting to an online discussion board for 2 years. Unhappy about his future and that a relationship had ended, Biggs announced on camera that he was going to commit suicide. He took an overdose of drugs and linked to a live video feed from his bedroom. None of his hundreds of observers called the police for more than 10 hours; some egged him on. Paramedics reached him too late, and Biggs died.

- In the mid-1970s, several hundred members of the Peoples Temple, a California-based religious cult, immigrated to Guyana under the guidance of their leader, the Reverend Jim Jones, where they founded an interracial community called Jonestown. But within a few years some members wanted out, an outside investigation was about to get Jones in trouble, and the group's solidarity was waning. Jones grew despondent and, summoning everyone in the community, spoke to them about the beauty of dying and the certainty that everyone would meet again in another place. The residents willingly lined up in front of a vat containing a mixture of Kool-Aid and cyanide, and drank the lethal concoction. (The legacy of this massacre is the term "drinking the Kool-Aid," referring to a person's blind belief in an ideology that could lead to death.) A total of 914 people died, including 80 babies and the Reverend Jones.

Why do many people rush into danger and discomfort to help strangers in trouble? Is Kristen right that opposites attract or is she just kidding herself? Why did Oscar come to love his fraternity brothers in spite of the hazing they had put him through? Why would people watch a troubled young man commit suicide in front of their eyes, when, by simply flagging the video to alert the Web site, they might have averted a tragedy? How could hundreds of people be induced to kill their own children and then commit suicide?

All of these stories—the good, the bad, the ugly—pose fascinating questions about human behavior. In this book, we will show you how social psychologists go about answering them.

Defining Social Psychology

1.1   What is social psychology, and how is it different from other disciplines?

The task of the psychologist is to try to understand and predict human behavior. Different kinds of psychologists go about this task in different ways, and we want to show you how social psychologists do it. **Social psychology** is the scientific study of the way in which people's thoughts, feelings, and behaviors are influenced by the real or imagined presence of other people: parents, friends, employers, teachers, strangers—indeed, by the entire social situation (Allport, 1985). When we think of social influence, the kinds of examples that readily come to mind are direct attempts at persuasion, whereby one person deliberately tries to change another person's behavior or attitude. This is what happens when advertisers use sophisticated techniques to persuade us to buy a particular brand of toothpaste, or when our friends try to get us to do something we don't really want to do ("Come on, have another beer—everyone is doing it"), or when the schoolyard bully uses force or threats to get smaller kids to part with their lunch money.

The study of direct attempts at **social influence** is a major part of social psychology and will be discussed in our chapters on conformity, attitudes, and group processes. To the social psychologist, however, social influence is broader than attempts by one person to change another person's behavior. It includes our thoughts and feelings as well as our overt acts, and takes many forms other than deliberate attempts at persuasion. We are often influenced merely by the *presence* of other people, including perfect strangers who are not interacting with us. Other people don't even have to be present: We are governed by the imaginary approval or disapproval of our parents, friends, and teachers and by how we expect others to react to us. Sometimes these influences conflict with one another, and social psychologists are especially interested in what happens in the mind of an individual when they do. For example, conflicts frequently occur when young people go off to college and find themselves torn between the beliefs and values they learned at home and the beliefs and values of their professors or peers. (See the Try It!)

Social Psychology

The scientific study of the way in which people's thoughts, feelings, and behaviors are influenced by the real or imagined presence of other people

Social Influence

The effect that the words, actions, or mere presence of other people have on our thoughts, feelings, attitudes, or behavior

TRY IT!
How Do Other People Affect Your Values?

Think of the major values that govern people's lives: love, money, sex, religion, freedom, compassion for others, security, children, duty, loyalty, and so on. Make three lists of the 10 values that are most important to (1) you, (2) your parents, and (3) your closest friends in college. If there are differences in your lists, how do they affect you? Are some of your values conflicting with those of your parents or friends, and if so do you find yourself rejecting one set of values in favor of the other? Are you trying to find a compromise between the two?

Our thoughts, feelings, and actions are influenced by our immediate surroundings, including the presence of other people—even mere strangers.

We will spend the rest of this introductory chapter expanding on these issues, so that you will get an idea of what social psychology is, what it isn't, and how it differs from other, related disciplines.

Social Psychology, Philosophy, Science, and Common Sense

Throughout history, philosophy has been a major source of insight about human nature. Indeed, the work of philosophers is part of the foundation of contemporary psychology. Psychologists have looked to philosophers for insights into the nature of consciousness (e.g., Dennett, 1991) and how people form beliefs about the social world (e.g., Gilbert, 1991). Sometimes, however, even great thinkers find themselves in disagreement with one another. When this occurs, how are you supposed to know who is right? Are there some situations where Philosopher A might be right, and other situations where Philosopher B might be right? How would you determine this?

We social psychologists address many of the same questions that philosophers do, but we attempt to look at these questions scientifically—even questions concerning that great human mystery, love. In 1663, the Dutch philosopher Benedict Spinoza offered a highly original insight. In sharp disagreement with the hedonistic philosopher Aristippus, he proposed that if we fall in love with someone whom we formerly

British soldiers stand near burning vehicles in Kabul, Afghanistan, after a suicide car bomber killed soldiers on a NATO-led peacekeeping mission. What causes a person to become a suicide bomber? Popular theories say such people must be mentally ill, alienated loners, or psychopaths. But social psychologists would try to understand the circumstances and situations that drive otherwise healthy, well-educated, bright people to commit murder and suicide for the sake of a religious or political goal.

hated, that love will be stronger than if hatred had not preceded it. Spinoza's proposition was beautifully worked out, with impeccable logic. But how can we be sure that it holds up? Does it always hold up? What are the conditions under which it does or doesn't? These are *empirical* questions, meaning that their answers can be derived from experimentation or measurement rather than by personal opinion (Aronson, 1999; Aronson & Linder, 1965).

Now let's take another look at the examples that opened this chapter. Why did these people behave the way they did? One way to answer would simply be to ask them. We could ask the people who observed Abraham Biggs's suicide why they didn't call the police; we could ask Oscar why he enjoys fraternity life; we could ask the Boston rescuers why they ran headlong into a potentially dangerous situation. The problem with this approach is that people are often unaware of the reasons behind their own responses and feelings (Gilbert, 2008; Nisbett & Wilson, 1977; Wilson, 2002). People might come up with plenty of justifications for not calling the police to rescue Biggs, but those justifications might not be the *reason* they did nothing.

After the mass suicide at Jonestown, everyone had an explanation:

- Jones used hypnotism and drugs to weaken the resistance of his followers.
- Jones attracted people who were already clinically depressed.
- Only mentally ill or emotionally disturbed people join cults.

These were the leading "common sense" answers, but they are mistaken. Moreover, if we rely on commonsense explanations of one particular tragic event, we don't learn much that helps us understand other, similar ones.

Thus, in explaining a tragedy like Jonestown—or any other topic of interest—social psychologists would want to know which of many possible explanations is the most likely. To do this, we have devised an array of scientific methods to test our assumptions, guesses, and ideas about human social behavior, empirically and systematically rather than by relying on folk wisdom, common sense, or the opinions and insights of philosophers, novelists, political pundits, and our grandmothers. Doing experiments in social psychology presents many challenges, primarily because we are attempting to predict the behavior of highly sophisticated organisms in complex situations. As scientists, our goal is to find objective answers to such questions as: What are the factors that cause aggression? What causes prejudice, and how might we reduce it? What variables cause two people to like or love each other? Why do certain kinds of political advertisements work better than others?

To answer questions like these, the first task of the social psychologist is to make an educated guess, called a *hypothesis*, about the specific situations under which one outcome or the other would occur. Just as a physicist performs experiments to test hypotheses about the nature of the physical world, the social psychologist performs experiments to test hypotheses about the nature of the social world. The next task is to design well-controlled experiments sophisticated enough to tease out the situations that would result in one or another outcome. This method allows us to make accurate predictions once we know the key aspects of the prevailing situation. (See Chapter 2.)

Social psychologists are not opposed to folk wisdom—far from it. The primary problem with relying entirely on such sources is that, like philosopher A and philosopher B, they often disagree with one another. Consider what folk wisdom has to say about the factors that influence how much we like other people. We know that "birds of a feather flock together." Of course, we say, thinking of the many examples of our pleasure in hanging out with people who share our backgrounds and interests. But folk wisdom also tells us—as it persuaded lovestruck Kristen—that "opposites attract." Of course, we say, thinking of all the times we were attracted to people with different backgrounds and interests. Well, which is it? Similarly, are we to believe that "out of sight is out of mind" or that "absence makes the heart grow fonder"?

Social psychologists would suggest that there are some conditions under which birds of a feather do flock together, and other conditions under which opposites do attract. Similarly, in some conditions absence does make the heart grow fonder, and in others "out of sight" does mean out of mind. But it's not enough to say both proverbs can be true. Part of the job of the social psychologist is to do the research that specifies the *conditions* under which one or another is most likely to take place.

How Social Psychology Differs from Its Closest Cousins

If you are like most people, when you read the examples that opened this chapter, you assumed that the individuals involved had some weaknesses, strengths, and personality traits that led them to respond as they did. Some people are leaders and others are followers; some people are public-spirited and others are selfish; some are brave and others are cowardly. Perhaps the people who failed to get help for Abraham Biggs were lazy, timid, selfish, or heartless. Given what you know about their behavior, would you loan them your car or trust them to take care of your new puppy?

Asking and trying to answer questions about people's behavior in terms of their traits is the work of personality psychologists, who generally focus on *individual differences*, the aspects of people's personalities that make them different from others. Research on personality increases our understanding of human behavior, but social psychologists believe that explaining behavior primarily through personality traits ignores a critical part of the story: the powerful role played by social influence.

Consider again the tragedy at Jonestown. Remember that it was not just a handful of people who committed suicide there, but almost 100 percent of them. It is highly improbable that they were all mentally ill or had the same constellation of personality traits. If we want a richer, more thorough explanation of this tragic event, we need to understand what kind of power and influence a charismatic figure like Jim

Personality psychologists study qualities of the individual that might make a person shy, conventional, rebellious, and willing to wear a turquoise wig in public or a yellow shirt in a sea of blue. Social psychologists study the powerful role of social influence on how all of us behave.

Jones possessed, the nature of the impact of living in a closed society cut off from other points of view, and other factors that could have caused mentally healthy people to obey him. In fact, as social psychologists have shown, the social conditions at Jonestown were such that virtually anyone—even strong, nondepressed individuals like you or us—would have succumbed to Jones's influence.

Here is a more mundane example. Suppose you volunteer for a charity event at your university's campus and see a fellow student you have been hoping to get to know better. The student is not being helpful. The student is playing on his/her phone while everyone else is setting up and working. You decide that you're not so interested. This person seems quite lazy and not helpful, even selfish. A few weeks later, you see this student again, now helping an elderly man carry his groceries. So what is this person "really" like? Helpful and friendly or lazy and selfish? All of us are capable of being helpful in some situations and unhelpful in others. A much more interesting question is: What factors were different in these two situations that had such a profound effect on the student's behavior? That is a social psychological question. (See the Try It!)

TRY IT!
Social Situations and Behaviors

1. Think of reasons due to which someone can appear to be helpful and prosocial in one situation and unhelpful, lazy, or selfish in another. Can you think of an example of this from your friends, family, or even yourself?

2. What kind of situations do you think would be most likely to elicit helpful behavior from this person? Which situations would lead them to being unhelpful?

3. Can you think of examples of how others might perceive you differently in different situations? For example, are you confident speaking in front of a small group of friends but nervous giving a presentation to a large group of strangers?

4. Why do you think we tend to judge someone's personality based on how they are acting in one particular situation?

Social psychology is related to other disciplines in the social sciences, including sociology, economics, and political science. Each examines the influence of social factors on human behavior, but important differences set social psychology apart—most notably in their level of analysis. For biologists, the level of analysis might be genes, hormones, or neurotransmitters. For personality and clinical psychologists, the level of the analysis is the individual. *For the social psychologist, the level of analysis is the individual in the context of a social situation.* For example, to understand why people intentionally hurt one another, the social psychologist focuses on the psychological processes that trigger aggression in specific situations. To what extent is aggression preceded by frustration? Does frustration always precede aggression? If people are feeling frustrated, under what conditions will they vent their frustration with an aggressive act and under what conditions will they restrain themselves? What are other causes of aggression? (See Chapter 12.)

Other social sciences are more concerned with social, economic, political, and historical factors that influence events. Sociology, rather than focusing on the individual, focuses on such topics as social class, social structure, and social institutions. Of course, because society is made up of collections of people, some overlap is bound to exist between the domains of sociology and those of social psychology. The major difference is that in sociology, *the level of analysis is the group, institution, or society at large.* So while sociologists, like social psychologists, are interested in causes of aggression, sociologists are more likely to be concerned with why a particular society (or group within a society) produces different levels of violence in its members. Why is the murder rate in the United States so much higher than in Canada or Europe? Within the United States, why is the murder rate higher in some geographic regions than in others? How do changes in society relate to changes in aggressive behavior?

Social psychology differs from other social sciences not only in the level of analysis, but also in what is being explained. *The goal of social psychology is to identify properties of human nature that make almost everyone susceptible to social influence, regardless of social class or culture.* The laws governing the relationship between frustration and aggression, for example, are hypothesized to be true of most people in most places, not just members of one gender, social class, culture, age group, or ethnicity.

However, because social psychology is a young science that developed mostly in the United States, many of its findings have not yet been tested in other cultures to see if they are universal. Nonetheless, our goal is to discover such laws. And increasingly, as methods and theories developed by American social psychologists are adopted by European, Asian, African, Middle Eastern, and South American social psychologists, we are learning more about the extent to which these laws are universal, as well as cultural differences in the way these laws are expressed (see Chapter 2). *Cross-cultural research* is therefore extremely valuable, because it sharpens theories, either by demonstrating their universality or by leading us to discover additional variables that help us improve our understanding and prediction of human behavior. We will offer many examples of cross-cultural research in this book.

In sum, social psychology is located between its closest cousins, sociology and personality psychology (see Table 1.1). Social psychology and sociology share an interest in the way the situation and the larger society

The people in this photo can be studied from a variety of perspectives: as individuals or as members of a family, a social class, an occupation, a culture, or a region. Sociologists study the group or institution; social psychologists study the influence of those groups and institutions on individual behavior.

Table 1.1 Social Psychology Compared to Related Disciplines

Sociology	Social Psychology	Personality Psychology
The study of groups, organizations, and societies, rather than individuals.	The study of the psychological processes people have in common that make them susceptible to social influence.	The study of the characteristics that make individuals unique and different from one another.

influence behavior. Social psychology and personality psychology share an interest in the psychology of the individual. But social psychologists work in the overlap between those two disciplines: They emphasize the psychological processes shared by most people around the world that make them susceptible to social influence.

REVIEW QUESTIONS

1. The question of the individual differences that lead one teenage boy to commit violent acts and his brother to rarely commit them would be most interesting to
   a. sociologists.
   b. personality psychologists.
   c. social psychologists.
   d. biologists.

2. If a teenage girl is caught shoplifting, what would social psychologists want to study about her?
   a. Whether or not her friends also shoplift and if this influenced her decision to do so
   b. What grades she is getting in school
   c. How her brain structure might be different from the brain structure of other girls her age
   d. How much money her parents earn and whether or not she has a part-time job to earn her own income

3. Which of the following statements is true about both social psychology and sociology?
   a. Sociologists focus on individual differences while social psychologists focus more on personality.
   b. Sociologists focus more on groups while social psychologists focus more on society as a whole.

   c. Sociologists focus more on society as a whole while social psychologists focus more on how society influences individuals.
   d. Both social psychology and sociology mainly focus on social class, economic status, and social institutions.

4. What is the "level of analysis" for a social psychologist?
   a. The individual in the context of a social situation.
   b. The social situation itself.
   c. A person's level of achievement.
   d. A person's level of reasoning.

5. Most social psychologists gather most of their information about why people act the way they do from sources and methods such as
   a. folk wisdom and common sense.
   b. asking people their opinion.
   c. conducting experiments.
   d. interpreting a culture through its news, art, images, and music.

See page 619 for the answers.

The Power of the Situation

1.2 Why does it matter how people explain and interpret events—and their own and others' behavior?

Suppose you stop at a roadside restaurant for a cup of coffee and a piece of pie. The server comes over to take your order, but you are having a hard time deciding which pie you want. While you are hesitating, she impatiently taps her pen against her notepad, rolls her eyes toward the ceiling, scowls at you, and finally snaps, "Hey, I haven't got all day, you know!" Like most people, you would probably think that she is a nasty or unpleasant person.

But suppose, while you are deciding whether to complain about her to the manager, a regular customer tells you that your "crabby" server is a single parent who was kept awake all night by the moaning of her youngest child, who was terribly sick; that her car broke down on her way to work and she has no idea where she will find the money to have it repaired; that when she finally arrived at the restaurant, she learned that her coworker was too drunk to work, requiring her to cover twice the usual number of tables; and that the short-order cook keeps screaming at her because she is not picking up the orders fast enough to please him. Given all that information, you might now conclude that she is not a nasty person but an ordinary human under enormous stress.

This small story has huge implications. Most Americans will explain someone's behavior in terms of personality; they focus on the fish, and not the water the fish swims in. The fact that they fail to take the situation into account has a profound impact on how human beings relate to one another—such as, in the case of the server, whether they feel sympathy and tolerance or impatience and anger.

The Importance of Explanation

Fundamental Attribution Error

The tendency to overestimate the extent to which people's behavior is due to internal, dispositional factors and to underestimate the role of situational factors

Thus, the social psychologist is up against a formidable barrier known as the **fundamental attribution error:** the tendency to explain our own and other people's behavior entirely in terms of personality traits and to underestimate the power of social influence and the immediate situation. We are going to give you the basics of this phenomenon here, because you will be encountering it throughout this book. Understanding that people's behavior is often not caused by their personalities but by the situations they are in is central to social psychology.

Explaining behavior in terms of personality can give us a feeling of false security. When people try to explain repugnant or bizarre behavior, such as suicide bombers or the people of Jonestown taking their own lives and killing their own children, they find it tempting and, in a strange way, comforting to write off the victims as flawed human beings. Doing so gives them the feeling that it could never happen to them. Ironically, this way of thinking actually increases our vulnerability to destructive social influences by making us less aware of our own susceptibility to them. Moreover, by failing to fully appreciate the power of the situation, we tend to oversimplify the problem, which can lead us to blame the victim in situations where the individual was overpowered by social forces too difficult for most of us to resist, as in the Jonestown tragedy.

To take a more everyday example, imagine a situation in which two people are playing a game and they must choose one of two strategies: They can play competitively and try to win as much money as possible and make sure their partner loses as much as possible, or they can play cooperatively and try to make sure they both win some money. How do you think each of your friends would play this game?

Few people find this question hard to answer; we all have a feeling for the relative competitiveness of our friends. Accordingly, you might say, "I am certain that my friend Jennifer, who is a hard-nosed business major, would play this game more competitively than my friend Anna, who is a soft-hearted, generous person." But how accurate are you likely to be? Should you be thinking about the game itself rather than who is playing it?

To find out, Lee Ross and his students conducted the following experiment (Liberman, Samuels, & Ross, 2004). They described the game to resident assistants (RAs) in a student dorm and asked them to come up with a list of undergrads whom they thought were either especially cooperative or especially competitive. As expected, the RAs easily identified students who fit each category. Next, Ross invited these students to play the game in a psychology experiment. There was one added twist: The researchers varied a seemingly minor aspect of the social situation—what the game was called. They told half the participants that they would be playing the

---

Figure 1.1 Why the Name of the Game Matters

In this experiment, when the name of the game was the "Community Game," players were far more likely to behave cooperatively than when it was called the "Wall Street Game"—regardless of their own cooperative or competitive personality traits. The game's title conveyed social norms that trumped personality and shaped the players' behavior.

(Data from Liberman, Samuels, & Ross, 2004)

Wall Street Game and the other half that they would be playing the Community Game. Everything else about the game was identical. Thus, people who were judged as either competitive or cooperative played a game that was called either the Wall Street Game or the Community Game, resulting in four conditions: cooperative people playing the Wall Street Game, cooperative people playing the Community Game, competitive people playing the Wall Street Game, or competitive people playing the Community Game.

Again, most of us go through life assuming that what really counts is an individual's personality, not something about the individual's immediate situation and certainly not something as trivial as what a game is called, right? Not so fast! As you can see in Figure 1.1, the name of the game made a tremendous difference in how people behaved. When it was called the Wall Street Game, approximately two-thirds of the students responded competitively; when it was called the Community Game, only a third responded competitively. The name of the game sent a powerful message about how the players should behave. But a student's alleged personality trait made no measurable difference in the student's behavior. The students labeled *competitive* were no more likely to adopt the competitive strategy than those who were labeled *cooperative*. We will see this pattern of results throughout this book: Aspects of the social situation that may seem minor can overwhelm the differences in people's personalities (Ross & Ward, 1996).

If merely assigning a name to the game has an important impact on the behavior of the players, what do you think the impact would be of changing the atmosphere of the classroom to reflect the nature of the game being played? Suppose you are a seventh-grade history teacher. In one of your classes, you structure the learning experience so that it resembles the situation implied by the term "Wall Street Game." You encourage competition, you tell your students to raise their hands as quickly as possible and to jeer at any incorrect answers given by other students. In your other class, you structure the learning situation such that the students are rewarded for cooperating with one another, for listening well, for encouraging one another and pulling together to learn the material. What do you suppose the effect these different situations might have on the performance of your students, on their enjoyment of school, and on their feelings about one another? Such an experiment will be discussed in Chapters 12 and 13 (Aronson & Patnoe, 2011).

Of course personality differences do exist and frequently are of great importance, but social and environmental situations are so powerful that they have dramatic effects on almost everyone. This is the domain of the social psychologist.

The Importance of Interpretation

It is one thing to say that the social situation has profound effects on human behavior, but what exactly do we mean by the social situation? One strategy for defining it would be to specify the objective properties of the situation, such as how rewarding it is to people, and then document the behaviors that follow from these objective properties.

Behaviorism

A school of psychology maintaining that to understand human behavior, one need only consider the reinforcing properties of the environment

This is the approach taken by **behaviorism**, a school of psychology maintaining that to understand human behavior, one need only consider the reinforcing properties of the environment: When behavior is followed by a reward (such as money, attention, praise, or other benefits), it is likely to continue; when behavior is followed by a punishment (such as pain, loss, or angry shouts), it is likely to become extinguished. Dogs come when they are called because they have learned that compliance is followed by positive reinforcement (e.g., food or petting); children memorize their multiplication tables more quickly if you praise them, smile at them, and paste a gold star on their foreheads following correct answers. Behavioral psychologists, notably the pioneering behaviorist B. F. Skinner (1938), believed that all behavior could be understood by examining the rewards and punishments in the organism's environment.

Behaviorism has many strengths, and its principles explain some behavior very well. (See Chapter 10.) However, because the early behaviorists did not concern themselves with cognition, thinking, and feeling—concepts they considered too vague and mentalistic and not sufficiently anchored to observable behavior—they overlooked phenomena that are vital to the human social experience. Most especially, they overlooked the importance of *how people interpret their environments*.

Construal

The way in which people perceive, comprehend, and interpret the social world

For social psychologists, the relationship between the social environment and the individual is a two-way street. Not only does the situation influence people's behavior; people's behavior also depends on their interpretation, or **construal**, of their social environment (Griffin & Ross, 1991; Ross & Nisbett, 1991). For example, if a person approaches you, slaps you on the back, and asks you how you are feeling, your response will depend not on what that person has done, but on how you *interpret* that behavior. You might construe these actions differently depending on whether they come from a close friend who is concerned about your health, a casual acquaintance who is just passing the time of day, or an automobile salesperson attempting to be ingratiating for the purpose of selling you a used car. And your answer will vary also, even if the question about your health were worded the same and asked in the same tone of voice. You would be unlikely to say, "Actually, I'm feeling pretty worried about this kidney pain" to a salesperson, but you might tell your close friend.

Gestalt Psychology

A school of psychology stressing the importance of studying the subjective way in which an object appears in people's minds rather than the objective, physical attributes of the object

The emphasis on construal has its roots in an approach called **Gestalt psychology**. First proposed as a theory of how people perceive the physical world, Gestalt psychology holds that we should study the subjective way in which an object appears in people's minds (the *gestalt*, or whole) rather than the way in which the objective, physical attributes of the object combine. For example, one way to understand how people perceive an overall image of a painting would be to break it down into its individual elements, such as the exact amounts of primary colors applied to the different parts of the canvas, the types of brushstrokes used to apply the colors, and the different geometric shapes they form. According to Gestalt psychologists, however, it is impossible to understand how an object is perceived only by studying these building blocks of perception. The whole is different from the sum of its parts. One must focus on the phenomenology of the perceivers—on how an object appears to them—instead of on its objective components.

The Gestalt approach was formulated by German psychologists in the first part of the twentieth century. In the late 1930s, several of these psychologists fled to the United States to escape the Nazi regime. Among the émigrés was Kurt Lewin, generally considered the founding father of modern experimental social psychology. As a young German Jewish professor in the 1930s, Lewin experienced the anti-Semitism rampant in Nazi Germany. The experience profoundly affected his thinking, and once he moved to the United States, Lewin helped shape American social psychology, directing it toward a deep interest in exploring the causes and cures of prejudice and ethnic stereotyping.

As a theorist, Lewin took the bold step of applying Gestalt principles beyond the perception of objects to social perception. It is often more important to understand how people perceive, comprehend, and interpret the social world, he said, than it is to understand its objective properties (Lewin, 1943). "If an individual sits in a room trusting that the ceiling will not come down," he said, "should only his 'subjective probability' be taken into account for predicting behavior or should we also consider the 'objective probability' of the ceiling's coming down as determined by engineers? To my mind, only the first has to be taken into account."

Kurt Lewin (1890–1947).

Social psychologists soon began to focus on the importance of how people construe their environments. Fritz Heider, another early founder of social psychology, observed, "Generally, a person reacts to what he thinks the other person is perceiving, feeling, and thinking, in addition to what the other person may be doing." We are busy guessing all the time about the other person's state of mind, motives, and thoughts. We may be right—but often we are wrong.

That is why construal has major implications. In a murder trial, when the prosecution presents compelling evidence it believes will prove the defendant guilty, the verdict always hinges on precisely how each jury member construes that evidence. These construals rest on a variety of events and perceptions that often bear no objective relevance to the case. During cross-examination, did a key witness come across as being too remote or too arrogant? Did the prosecutor appear to be smug, obnoxious, or uncertain?

Fritz Heider (1896–1988).

A special kind of construal is what Lee Ross calls "naïve realism," the conviction that we perceive things "as they really are." If other people see the same things differently, therefore, it must be because *they* are biased (Ehrlinger, Gilovich, & Ross, 2005; Pronin, Gilovich, & Ross, 2004; Ross, 2010). Ross has been working closely with Israeli and Palestinian negotiators. These negotiations frequently run aground because of naïve realism; each side assumes that other reasonable people see things the same way they do. "[E]ven when each side recognizes that the other side perceives the issues differently," says Ross, "each thinks that the other side is biased while they themselves are objective and that their own perceptions of reality should provide the basis for settlement." So both sides resist compromise, fearing that their "biased" opponent will benefit more than they.

In a simple experiment, Ross took peace proposals created by Israeli negotiators, labeled them as Palestinian proposals, and asked Israeli citizens to judge them. The Israelis liked the Palestinian proposal attributed to Israel more than they liked the Israeli proposal attributed to the Palestinians. Ross concludes, "If your own proposal isn't going to be attractive to you when it comes from the other side, what chance is there that the *other* side's proposal is going to be attractive when it comes from the other side?" The hope is that once negotiators on both sides become fully aware of this phenomenon and how it impedes conflict resolution, a reasonable compromise will be more likely.

You can see that construals range from the simple (as in the question "How are you feeling?") to the remarkably complex (international negotiations). And they affect all of us in our everyday lives. Imagine that Jason is a college student who admires Maria from afar. As a budding social psychologist, you have the job of predicting

Research by social psychologists on construal shows why negotiation between nations can be so difficult: Each side thinks that it sees the issues clearly but that the other side is "biased."

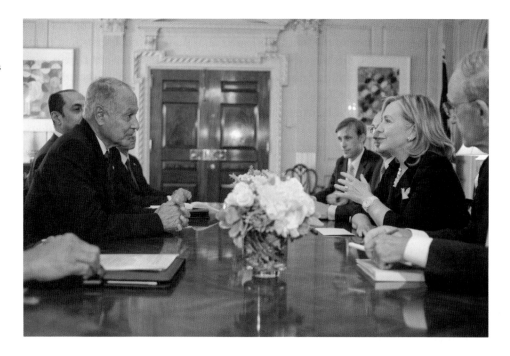

whether or not Jason will ask Maria to have dinner with him. To do this, you need to begin by viewing Maria's behavior through Jason's eyes—that is, by seeing how Jason interprets her behavior. If she smiles at him, does Jason construe her behavior as mere politeness, the kind of politeness she would extend to any of the dozens of nerds and losers in their class? Or does he view her smile as an encouraging sign that inspires him to ask her out? If she ignores him, does Jason figure that she's playing hard to get, or does he take it as a sign that she's not interested in him? To predict what Jason will do, it is not enough to know Maria's behavior; we must know how Jason interprets her behavior.

Now suppose that after class one day, Maria impulsively kisses Jason on the cheek as she says goodbye. Again, how he responds will depend on how he construes that act: Does he interpret that kiss as a sign of romantic interest on Maria's part, clear evidence that she's hot for him? Or does he see it as a sisterly signal that Maria wants to be friends but isn't really into him? Were Jason to misinterpret the situation, he might commit a serious blunder: He might turn his back on what could have been the love of his life, or he might express his own passionate feelings inappropriately. In either case, social psychologists would say that the best strategy for understanding Jason's reaction would be to find a way to determine his construal of Maria's behavior rather than to dissect the objective nature of the kiss itself (its length, degree of pressure, etc.). But how are these construals formed? Stay tuned.

REVIEW QUESTIONS

1. The *fundamental attribution error* is best defined as the tendency to
  a. explain our own and other people's behavior entirely in terms of personality traits, thereby underestimating the power of social influence.
  b. explain our own and other people's behavior in terms of the social situation, thereby underestimating the power of personality factors.
  c. believe that people's group memberships influence their behavior more than their personalities.
  d. believe that people's personalities influence their behavior more than their group memberships.

2. Which of the following statements are examples of "Naive Realism"?
  a. "Ninety-seven percent of scientists from relevant academic disciplines agree that global climate change is real and is caused by humans."
  b. "People who deny global climate change disagree with these experts."

c. "My opinion on global climate change is the most correct."

d. "People who disagree with my opinion about global climate change are biased."

3. Andre's manager, Liz, conducts his annual performance evaluation. According to social psychologists, Andre's positive or negative reaction to Liz's feedback will most likely depend on

a. whether or not he likes his manager.

b. how he construes the feedback.

c. whether or not he receives an increase in his salary.

d. how ambitious Andre is in his career goals.

4. Social psychology had its origins in

a. Gestalt psychology.

b. Freudian psychology.

c. behavioral psychology.

d. biological psychology.

5. "Naïve realism" refers to the fact that

a. most people are naïve (uneducated) about psychology.

b. few people are realistic.

c. most people would rather be naïve than accurate.

d. most people believe they perceive things accurately.

See page 619 for the answers.

Where Construals Come From: Basic Human Motives

1.3 **What happens when people's need to feel good about themselves conflicts with their need to be accurate?**

How will Jason determine why Maria kissed him? If it is true that subjective and not objective situations influence people, we need to understand how people arrive at their subjective impressions of the world. What are people trying to accomplish when they interpret the social world? Are they concerned with making an interpretation that places them in the most positive light (e.g., Jason's deciding that "Maria is ignoring me just to make me jealous") or with making the most accurate interpretation, even if it is unflattering (e.g., "Painful as it may be, I must admit that she would rather go out with a sea slug than with me")? Social psychologists seek to understand the fundamental laws of human nature, common to all, that explain why we construe the social world the way we do.

We human beings are complex organisms. At any given moment, various intersecting motives underlie our thoughts and behaviors, including hunger, thirst, fear, a desire for control, and the promise of love, favors, and other rewards. (See Chapters 10 and 11.) Social psychologists emphasize the importance of two central motives: *the need to feel good about ourselves* and *the need to be accurate*. Sometimes, each of these motives pulls us in the same direction. Often, though, these motives tug us in opposite directions, where to perceive the world accurately requires us to admit that we have behaved foolishly or immorally.

Leon Festinger, one of social psychology's most innovative theorists, realized that it is precisely when these two motives pull in opposite directions that we can gain our most valuable insights into the workings of the mind. Imagine that you are the president of the United States and your country is engaged in a difficult and costly war. You have poured hundreds of billions of dollars into that war, and it has consumed tens of thousands of American lives as well as thousands more lives of innocent civilians. The war seems to be at a stalemate; no end is in sight. You frequently wake up in the middle of the night, bathed in the cold sweat of conflict: On the one hand, you deplore all the carnage that is going on; on the other hand, you don't want to go down in history as the first American president to lose a war.

Some of your advisers tell you that they can see the light at the end of the tunnel, and that if you intensify the bombing or add thousands more troops, the enemy will soon capitulate and the war will be over. This would be a great outcome for you: Not only will you have succeeded in achieving your military and political aims, but history will consider you to have been a great leader as well. Other advisers, however,

Leon Festinger (1919–1989) wrote: "If the empirical world looks complicated, if people seem to react in bewilderingly different ways to similar forces, and if I cannot see the operation of universal underlying dynamics, then that is my fault. I have asked the wrong questions; I have, at a theoretical level, sliced up the world incorrectly. The underlying dynamics are there, and I have to find the theoretical apparatus that will enable me to reveal these uniformities." Finding and illuminating those underlying dynamics is the goal of social psychology.

This is Edward Snowden, a former computing contractor for the National Security Agency. Snowden's release in 2013 of thousands of classified documents related to the U.S. government's surveillance programs led the Department of Justice to charge him with espionage. Some have argued that Snowden is a spy, a traitor, and a criminal who should be brought back to the United States from his asylum in Russia to face trial. Others view him as a whistleblower, a patriot, and a hero fighting to protect privacy rights and inform the American public of what its government is up to (in fact, here you see him pictured receiving a German peace prize, a prize he was only able to accept via Skype). Each side is sure that they are right. Where do differing construals come from, and what are their consequences?

believe that intensifying the bombing will only strengthen the enemy's resolve; they advise you to sue for peace.

Which advisers are you likely to believe? President Lyndon Johnson faced this exact dilemma in the 1960s, with the war in Vietnam; so did George W. Bush in 2003, when the war in Iraq did not end in six weeks as he had predicted; so did Barack Obama, in deciding in 2009 whether to invest more troops in the war in Afghanistan. (See Chapter 6.) Most presidents have chosen to believe their advisers who suggest escalating the war, because if they succeed in winning, the victory justifies the human and financial cost; but withdrawing not only means going down in history as a president who lost a war, but also having to justify the fact that all those lives and all that money have been spent in vain. As you can see, the need to feel good about our decisions can fly in the face of the need to be accurate, and can have catastrophic consequences (Draper, 2008; McClellan, 2008; Woodward, 2011). In Johnson's case, the decision to increase the bombing *did* strengthen the enemy's resolve, thereby prolonging the war in Vietnam.

The Self-Esteem Motive: The Need to Feel Good About Ourselves

Self-Esteem

People's evaluations of their own self-worth—that is, the extent to which they view themselves as good, competent, and decent

Most people have a strong need to maintain reasonably high **self-esteem**—that is, to see themselves as good, competent, and decent (Aronson, 1998, 2007; Baumeister, 1993; Tavris & Aronson, 2007). Given the choice between distorting the world to feel good about themselves and representing the world accurately, people often take the first option. They put a slightly different spin on the matter, one that puts them in the best possible light. You might consider your friend Roger to be a nice guy but an awful slob—somehow he's always got stains on his shirt and empty food cartons all over his kitchen. Roger, though, probably describes himself as being casual and noncompulsive.

Self-esteem is obviously a beneficial thing, but when it causes people to justify their actions rather than learn from them, it can impede change and self-improvement. Suppose a couple gets divorced after 10 years of a marriage made difficult by the husband's irrational jealousy. Rather than admitting the truth—that his jealousy and possessiveness drove his wife away—the husband blames the breakup of his marriage on her; she was not responsive enough to his needs. His interpretation serves a purpose: It makes him feel better about himself (Simpson, 2010). The consequence of this distortion, of course, is that learning from experience becomes unlikely. In his next marriage, the husband will probably recreate the same problems. Acknowledging our deficiencies is difficult, even when the cost is seeing the world inaccurately.

SUFFERING AND SELF-JUSTIFICATION Let's go back to one of our early scenarios: Oscar and the hazing he went through to join his fraternity. Personality psychologists might suggest that only extroverts who have a high tolerance for embarrassment would want to be in a fraternity. Behavioral psychologists would predict that Oscar would dislike anyone or anything that caused him pain and humiliation. Social psychologists, however, have found that the major reason that Oscar and his fellow pledges like their fraternity brothers so much was the degrading hazing ritual itself.

Here's how it works. If Oscar goes through a severe hazing to become a member of the fraternity but later discovers unpleasant things about his fraternity brothers, he will feel like a fool: "Why did I go through all that pain and embarrassment to live in a house with a bunch of jerks?" To avoid feeling like a fool, he will try to justify his decision to undergo the hazing by distorting his evaluation of his fraternity brothers. He will try to put a positive spin on his experiences.

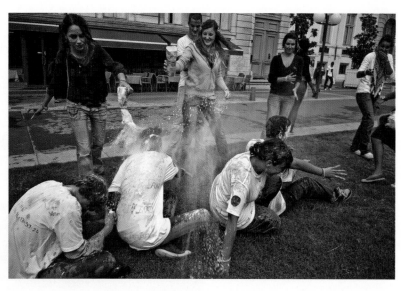

An outside observer like his sister Janine, however, can see the downside of fraternity life more clearly. The fraternity dues make a significant dent in Oscar's budget, the frequent parties take a toll on the amount of studying he can do, and consequently his grades suffer. But Oscar is motivated to see these negatives as trivial; indeed, he considers them a small price to pay for the sense of brotherhood he feels. He focuses on the good parts of living in the fraternity, and he dismisses the bad parts as inconsequential.

These first-year students are being "welcomed" to their university by seniors who subject them to hazing. Hazing is sometimes silly, but it is often dangerous as well (and even fatal), leading college campuses to crack down on the practice. One difficulty faced by such efforts is that for all of its downsides, hazing can also build group cohesiveness.

Does this explanation sound far-fetched? In a series of laboratory experiments, social psychologists investigated the psychological consequences of hazing. The experimenters held constant everything in the situation, including the precise behavior of the fraternity members; the only thing they varied was the severity of the hazing that the students underwent to become members. The results demonstrated that the more unpleasant the procedure the participants underwent to get into a group, the more they liked the group—even though, objectively, the group members were the same people behaving the same way for everyone (Aronson & Mills, 1959; Gerard & Mathewson, 1966). (See Chapter 6.)

The take-home message is that human beings are motivated to maintain a positive picture of themselves, in part by justifying their behavior, and that under certain specifiable conditions, this leads them to do things that at first glance might seem surprising or paradoxical. They might prefer people and things for whom they have suffered to people and things they associate with ease and pleasure.

The Social Cognition Motive: The Need to Be Accurate

Even when people are bending the facts to see themselves as favorably as they can, most do not live in a fantasy world. We might say they bend reality but don't completely break it. But the ways in which human beings think about themselves and the social world influence what they do. Many social psychologists therefore specialize in the study of **social cognition**: how people select, interpret, remember, and use information to make judgments and decisions (Fiske & Taylor, 2013; Markus & Zajonc, 1985; Nisbett & Ross, 1980). Researchers who investigate processes of social cognition begin with the assumption that all people try to view the world as accurately as possible. They regard human beings as amateur sleuths who are doing their best to understand and predict their social world.

Just as the need to preserve self-esteem can occasionally run aground, so too does the need to be accurate. Unfortunately, we often make mistakes in that effort to understand and predict, because we almost never know all the facts we need to judge a given situation accurately. Whether it is a relatively simple decision, such as which breakfast cereal offers the best combination of healthfulness and tastiness, or a slightly more complex decision, such as our desire to buy the best car we can

Social Cognition

How people think about themselves and the social world; more specifically, how people select, interpret, remember, and use social information to make judgments and decisions

We rely on a series of expectations and other mental short-cuts in making judgments about the world around us, from important life decisions to which cereal to buy at the store, a conclusion with which advertisers and marketers are very well aware.

for under $12,000, or a much more complex decision, such as choosing a partner who will make us deliriously happy for the rest of our lives, it is usually impossible to gather all the relevant information in advance. Moreover, we make countless decisions every day. No one has the time and stamina to gather all the facts for each of them.

Does this sound overblown? Aren't most decisions fairly easy? Let's take a closer look. Which breakfast cereal is better for you, Lucky Charms or Quaker Oats 100% natural granola with oats, honey, and raisins? If you are like most of our students, you answered, "100% Natural." After all, Lucky Charms is a kids' cereal, full of sugar and cute little marshmallows, with a picture of a leprechaun on the box. Quaker Oats cereal boxes have pictures of healthy granola and wheat, and doesn't *natural* mean "good for you"? If that's the way you reasoned, you have fallen into a common cognitive trap: You have generalized from the cover to the product. A careful reading of the ingredients in small print will reveal that, per one cup serving, Quaker Oats 100% Natural has 420 calories, 30 grams of sugar, and 12 grams of fat; *Men's Health* magazine rated it the worst packaged cereal in America. In contrast, a cup of Lucky Charms has 142 calories, 14 grams of sugar, and 1 gram of fat. Even in the simple world of cereals, things are not always what they seem.

EXPECTATIONS ABOUT THE SOCIAL WORLD   To add to the difficulty, sometimes our expectations about the social world interfere with perceiving it accurately. Our expectations can even change the *nature* of the social world. Imagine that you are an elementary school teacher dedicated to improving the lives of your students. At the beginning of the academic year, you review each student's standardized intelligence test scores. Early in your career, you were pretty sure that these tests could gauge each child's potential; now you are certain that they do. Almost invariably, the kids who got high scores on these tests are the ones who did the best in your classroom, and the kids who got low scores performed poorly.

This scenario doesn't sound all that surprising, except for one thing: You might be wrong about the validity of the intelligence tests. It might be that the tests were not accurate but that you unintentionally treated the kids with high scores and the kids with low scores differently. This is exactly what Robert Rosenthal and Lenore Jacobson (1968/2003) found in their investigation of a phenomenon called the *self-fulfilling prophecy*: You expect that you or another person will behave in some way, so you act in ways to make your prediction come true. (See Chapter 3.) The researchers went into elementary school classrooms and administered a test. They then informed each teacher that, according to the test, a few specific students were "bloomers" who were about to take off and perform extremely well. In actuality, the test showed no such thing. The children labeled as bloomers were chosen at random by drawing names out of a hat and thus were no different, on average, from any of the other kids. Lo and behold, on returning to the classroom at the end of the school year, Rosenthal and Jacobson found that the bloomers were performing extremely well. The mere fact that the teachers were led to expect them to do well caused an improvement in their performance. This striking phenomenon is no fluke; it has been replicated a number of times in many different schools (Rosenthal, 1994).

Although this outcome seems almost magical, it is embedded in an important aspect of human nature. If you were one of those teachers and were led to expect two or three specific students to perform well, you would be more likely to treat them in special ways: paying more attention to them, listening to them with more respect, calling on them more frequently, encouraging them, and trying to teach them more challenging material. Your attention and attitude would, in turn, almost certainly make these students feel happier, more respected, more motivated, and smarter—and, *voilà*, the prophecy is fulfilled. Thus, even when we are trying to perceive the social world as accurately as we can, there are many ways in which we can go wrong, ending up with the wrong impressions.

REVIEW QUESTIONS

1. Which of the following is true about social cognition?
   a. Most people would rather completely ignore reality and feel better about themselves.
   b. Most people try to have an accurate view of the world but often do not have enough information to make accurate judgments.
   c. Most people try to have an accurate view of the world, and most people's view of the world is close to 100% accurate.
   d. Most people are not concerned with having accurate information when they make decisions or interpret a situation.
2. Which of the following is most true about people with high self-esteem?
   a. Most people interpret events in ways that help to preserve their self-esteem.
   b. Few people care about maintaining their high self-esteem.
   c. Most people will do things that are against their morals or against the law in order to preserve their self-esteem.
   d. Most people prefer to see the world accurately, even if this means damaging their self-esteem.
3. Which of the following statements demonstrate(s) a self-fulfilling prophecy?
   a. "The test will be postponed."
   b. "That student of mine is unlikely to clear next week's test."
   c. "That student of mine is likely to top next week's test."
   d. "The test results don't matter since I'm confident about myself."

See page 619 for the answers.

We defined social psychology as the scientific study of social influence. But why do we want to understand social influence in the first place? What difference does it make whether our behavior has its roots in the desire to be accurate or to bolster our self-esteem?

The basic answer is simple: We are curious. Social psychologists are fascinated by human social behavior and want to understand it on the deepest possible level. In a sense, all of us are social psychologists. We all live in a social environment, and we are all more than mildly curious about such issues as how we become influenced, how we influence others, and why we fall in love with some people, dislike others, and are indifferent to still others. You don't have to be with people literally to be in a social environment. Facebook is a social psychologist's dream laboratory because it's all there: love, anger, bullying, bragging, affection, flirting, wounds, quarrels, friending and unfriending, pride and prejudice.

Today, social psychologists' interest in how people think, feel, and act in social environments leads to research designed to study behavioral tendencies on Facebook, Twitter, and across other platforms, sites, and apps.

Social psychology can help us study social problems and find ways to solve them. Social psychologists might study whether children who watch violence on television become more aggressive themselves—and, if so, what kind of intervention might be beneficial.

Many social psychologists have another reason for studying the causes of social behavior: to contribute to the solution of social problems. This goal was present at the founding of the discipline. Kurt Lewin, having barely escaped the horrors of Nazi Germany, brought to America his passionate interest in understanding how the transformation of his country had happened. Ever since, social psychologists have been keenly interested in their own contemporary social challenges, as you will discover reading this book. Their efforts have ranged from reducing violence and prejudice to increasing altruism and tolerance (Chapters 11 and 13). They study such pressing issues as how to induce people to conserve natural resources like water and energy, practice safe sex, or eat healthier food (Chapter 7). They study the effects of violence in the media (Chapter 12). They work to find effective strategies to resolve conflicts within groups—whether at work or in juries—and between nations (Chapter 9). They explore ways to raise children's intelligence through environmental interventions and better school programs, and reduce the high school dropout rate of minority students. They study happier topics, too, such as passion, liking, and love—and what sustains them (Chapter 10).

Throughout this book, we will examine many other examples of the application of social psychology to real-world problems. For interested readers, we have included three final chapters on health, the environment, and law. We hope that by understanding the fundamental causes of behavior as social psychologists study them, you will also be better able to change your own self-defeating or misguided behavior, improve your relationships, and make better decisions.

We are now ready to begin our tour of social psychology in earnest. So far, we have been emphasizing the central theme of social psychology: the enormous power of most social situations. As researchers, our job is to ask the right questions and to find a way to capture the power of the social situation and bring it into the laboratory for detailed study. If we are adept at doing that, we will arrive at truths about human behavior that are close to being universal. And then we may be able to bring our laboratory findings into the real world—for the ultimate betterment of our society.

Summary

1.1 What is social psychology, and how is it different from other disciplines?

- **Defining Social Psychology** Social psychology is defined as the scientific study of the way in which people's thoughts, feelings, and behaviors are influenced by the real or imagined presence of other people. Social psychologists are interested in understanding how and why the social environment shapes the thoughts, feelings, and behaviors of the individual.

  - **Social Psychology, Philosophy, Science, and Common Sense** Social psychologists approach the understanding of **social influence** differently from philosophers, journalists, or the layperson. Social psychologists develop explanations of social influence through *empirical methods*, such as experiments in which the variables being studied are

carefully controlled. The goal of the science of social psychology is to discover universal laws of human behavior, which is why *cross-cultural research* is often essential.

- **How Social Psychology Differs from Its Closest Cousins** When trying to explain social behavior, personality psychologists explain the behavior in terms of the person's individual character traits. Although social psychologists would agree that personalities vary, they explain social behavior in terms of the *power of the social situation* to shape how one acts. *The level of analysis for social psychology is the individual in the context of a social situation.* In contrast, the level of analysis for sociologists is the group, institution, or society at large. Social psychologists seek to identify universal properties of human nature that make everyone susceptible to social influence regardless of their social class, gender, or culture.

1.2 Why does it matter how people explain and interpret events—and their own and others' behavior?

- **The Power of the Situation** Individual behavior is powerfully influenced by the social environment, but many people don't want to believe this.

  - **The Importance of Explanation** Social psychologists must contend with the **fundamental attribution error**, the tendency to explain our own and other people's behavior entirely in terms of personality traits and to underestimate the power of social influence. But social psychologists have shown time and again that social and environmental situations are usually more powerful than personality differences in determining an individual's behavior.

  - **The Importance of Interpretation** Social psychologists have shown that the relationship between individuals and situations is a two-way street, so it is important to understand not only how situations influence individuals, but how people *perceive and interpret* the social world and the behavior of others. These perceptions are more influential than objective aspects of the situation itself. The term **construal** refers to the world as it is interpreted by the individual.

1.3 What happens when people's need to feel good about themselves conflicts with their need to be accurate?

- **Where Construals Come From: Basic Human Motives** The way in which an individual construes (perceives, comprehends, and interprets) a situation is largely shaped by two basic human motives: *the need to feel good about ourselves* and *the need to be accurate*. At times these two motives tug in opposite directions; for example, when an accurate view of how we acted in a situation would reveal that we behaved selfishly.

  - **The Self-Esteem Motive: The Need to Feel Good About Ourselves** Most people have a strong need to see themselves as good, competent, and decent. People often distort their perception of the world to preserve their self-esteem.

  - **The Social Cognition Motive: The Need to Be Accurate** Social cognition is the study of how human beings think about the world: how they select, interpret, remember, and use information to make judgments and decisions. Individuals are viewed as trying to gain accurate understandings so that they can make effective judgments and decisions that range from which cereal to eat to whom they marry. In actuality, individuals typically act on the basis of incomplete and inaccurately interpreted information.

Test Yourself

1. Social psychology is the study of

   a. the real or imagined influence of other people.

   b. social institutions, such as the church or school.

   c. social events, such as football games and dances.

   d. psychological processes, such as dreaming.

2. The question of why one person becomes a murderer and his/her neighbor does not would be most interesting to researchers in the field of

   a. biology.

   b. sociology.

   c. social psychology.

   d. personality psychology.

3. Which of these studies about cults would be suited to a social psychologist?

   a. Why one society has more cults than another

   b. Factors that influence "normal" people to join a cult

   c. The number of cults in each society

   d. How the organization of one cult differs from another

4. Which of the following is/are true about the fundamental attribution error?

   a. Most people's behavior is due to the situation they are in, not their personalities.

   b. "My behavior is entirely based on my personality."

   c. We tend to explain other people's behavior in terms of their personality traits and to give less importance to the influence of the situation.

   d. We tend to explain other people's behavior in terms of the situation they are in and give less importance to the influence of personality traits.

5. What are the main differences between what social psychologists and personality psychologist examine?

   a. Social psychology focuses on what makes one person unique, while personality psychology focuses on the shared features that make cultures different or similar to each other.

   b. Social psychology focuses on individual differences; personality psychology looks at how most people would behave in a situation.

c. Social psychology examines similarities in the ways that social influences can affect most people, whereas personality psychology examines the differences between individuals.

d. Social psychology focuses on personality traits whereas personality psychology examines the reasons that these personality traits came to be.

6. Which of the following statements about self-esteem is false?

a. Most people have very low self-esteem.

b. Most people interpret events in ways that help to preserve their self-esteem.

c. Most people will act in ways that seem irrational or counterintuitive in order to maintain their self-esteem.

d. Most people have trouble admitting their own weaknesses and will interpret events inaccurately in order to portray themselves in a more flattering manner.

7. Which of these is an example of "Naive Realism"?

a. Seventy percent of voters said they will cast their ballot for Candidate X while 20% said they plan to vote for Candidate Y.

b. "I'm voting for Candidate X because she seems like a better leader, while Candidate Y seems naive."

c. "I'm voting for Candidate Y because he has values similar to mine."

d. "Supporters of Candidate Y don't see him for what he really is. Only supporters of Candidate X and I can see what a terrible leader Candidate Y would be."

8. What was the main contribution of Gestalt psychology to social psychology?

a. It added an understanding of how the brain works.

b. It emphasized how people perceive the physical world.

c. It showed that the whole is larger than the sum of its parts.

d. It added historical perspective to the study of behavior.

9. What two central motives influence the way we construe the world?

a. The need to feel our opinions are right.

b. The need to maintain reasonably high self-esteem.

c. The need to feel superior to others.

d. The need to be accurate in our perceptions and decisions.

e. The need for self-expression.

10. To get people to change self-destructive behavior, social psychologists would be likely to

a. persuade them by offering useful information.

b. scare the living daylights out of them.

c. threaten them with punishment.

d. all of the above.

e. none of the above.

See page 619 for the answers.

Chapter 2
Methodology
How Social Psychologists Do Research

 ## Chapter Outline and Learning Objectives

Social Psychology: An Empirical Science

2.1 **How do researchers develop hypotheses and theories?**

Formulating Hypotheses and Theories

Research Designs

2.2 **What are the strengths and weaknesses of various research designs that social psychologists use?**

The Observational Method: Describing Social Behavior
The Correlational Method: Predicting Social Behavior
The Experimental Method: Answering Causal Questions

New Frontiers in Social Psychological Research

2.3 **What impact do cross-cultural studies, the evolutionary approach, and social neuroscience research have on the way in which scientists investigate social behavior?**

Culture and Social Psychology
The Evolutionary Approach
Social Neuroscience

Ethical Issues in Social Psychology

2.4 **How do social psychologists ensure the safety and welfare of their research participants, while at the same time testing hypotheses about the causes of social behavior?**

In this information age, when pretty much anything can be found on the Internet, pornography is more available than ever before. One study found that 25% of all search engine requests were pornography related (Carroll et al., 2008). Another found that a quarter of all employees who have access to the Internet visit porn sites during their workdays ("The Tangled Web of Porn," 2008). It is thus important to ask whether exposure to pornography has harmful effects. Is it possible, for example, that looking at graphic sex increases the likelihood that men will become sexually violent?

There has been plenty of debate on both sides of this question. Legal scholar Catharine MacKinnon (1993) argued that "Pornography is the perfect preparation—motivator and instruction manual in one—for . . . sexual atrocities" (p. 28). In 1985, a group of experts, appointed by the attorney general of the United States, voiced a similar opinion, concluding that pornography is a cause of rape and other violent crimes. But in 1970, another commission reviewed much of the same evidence and concluded that pornography does *not* contribute significantly to sexual violence. Who are we to believe? Is there a scientific way to determine the answer? We believe there is, and in this chapter we will discuss the kinds of research methods social psychologists employ, using research on pornography as an example.

Social Psychology: An Empirical Science

2.1   How do researchers develop hypotheses and theories?

A fundamental principle of social psychology is that many social problems, such as the causes of violence, can be studied scientifically (Reis & Gosling, 2010; Reis & Judd, 2000; Wilson, Aronson, & Carlsmith, 2010). Before we discuss how social psychological research is done, we begin with a warning: The results of some of the experiments you encounter will seem obvious because social psychology concerns topics with which we are all intimately familiar—social behavior and social influence (Richard, Bond, & Stokes-Zoota, 2001). This familiarity sets social psychology apart from other sciences. When you read about an experiment in particle physics, it is unlikely that the results will connect with your personal experiences. We don't know about you, but we have never thought, "Wow! That experiment on quarks was just like what happened to me while I was waiting for the bus yesterday," or "My grandmother always told me to watch out for positrons and antimatter." When reading about the results of a study on helping behavior or aggression, however, it is quite common to think, "Come on. I could have predicted that. That's the same thing that happened to me last Friday."

The thing to remember is that, when we study human behavior, the results may appear to have been predictable—in retrospect. Indeed, there is a well-known human tendency called the **hindsight bias**, whereby after people know that something occurred, they exaggerate how much they could have predicted it before it occurred (Calvillo, 2013; Davis & Fischhoff, 2014; Fischhoff, 2007; Nestler, Blank, & Egloff, 2010). After we know the winner of a political election, for example, we begin to look for reasons why that candidate won. After the fact, the outcome seems inevitable and easily predictable, even if we were quite unsure who would win before the election. The same is true of findings in psychology experiments; it seems like we could have easily predicted the outcomes—after we know them. The trick is to predict what will happen in an experiment before you know how it turned out. To illustrate that not all obvious findings are easy to predict, take the Try It! quiz that follows.

Hindsight Bias

The tendency for people to exaggerate, after knowing that something occurred, how much they could have predicted it before it occurred

TRY IT!

Social Psychology Quiz: What's Your Prediction?

Answer the following questions, each of which is based on social psychological research.

1. Suppose an authority figure asks college students to administer near-lethal electric shocks to another student who has not harmed them in any way. What percentage of these students will agree to do it?

2. If you give children a reward for doing something they already enjoy doing, they will subsequently like that activity (a) more, (b) the same, or (c) less.

3. When a business or governmental agency is faced with an important choice it is always better to have a group of people make the decision, because "two heads are better than one": (a) true (b) false.

4. Repeated exposure to a stimulus—such as a person, a song, or a painting—will make you like it (a) more, (b) the same, or (c) less.

5. You ask an acquaintance to do you a favor—for example, to lend you $10—and he or she agrees. As a result of doing you this favor, the person will probably like you (a) more, (b) the same, or (c) less.

6. Who do think would be *least* likely to help a stranger who drops a bunch of papers all over the ground? Some who is in a (a) good mood (b) neutral mood, or (c) bad mood?

7. In the United States, female college students tend not to do as well on math tests as males do. Under which of the following circumstances will women do as well as men: (a) when they are told that there are no gender differences on the test, (b) when they are told that women tend to do better on a difficult math test (because under these circumstances they rise to the challenge), or (c) when they are told that men outperform women under almost all circumstances?

8. Which statement about the effects of advertising is most true? (a) Subliminal messages implanted in advertisements are more effective than normal, everyday advertising; (b) normal TV ads for painkillers or laundry detergents are more effective than subliminal messages implanted in ads; (c) both types of advertising are equally effective; or (d) neither type of advertising is effective.

9. What effect, if any, does playing violent video games have on how likely people are to act aggressively in everyday life? (a) playing the games increases the likelihood that they will act aggressively; (b) they become less aggressive because the games "get it out of their system"; (c) playing the games has no effect on how aggressive people are.

10. Students walking across campus are asked to fill out a questionnaire on which they rate the degree to which student opinion should be considered on a local campus issue. Which group do you think believed that students should be listened to the most? (a) Those given a light clipboard with the questionnaire attached; (b) those given a heavy clipboard with the questionnaire attached; (c) the weight of the clipboard made no difference in people's ratings.

See page 619 for the answers.

Formulating Hypotheses and Theories

How, then, do social psychologists come up with the ideas for their studies? Research begins with a hunch, or hypothesis, that the researcher wants to test. There is lore in science that holds that brilliant insights come all of a sudden, as when Archimedes shouted, "Eureka! I have found it!" when the solution to a problem flashed into his mind. Although such insights do sometimes occur suddenly, science is a cumulative process, and people often generate hypotheses from previous theories and research.

INSPIRATION FROM EARLIER THEORIES AND RESEARCH   Many studies stem from a researcher's dissatisfaction with existing theories and explanations. After reading other people's work, a researcher might believe that he or she has a better way of explaining people's behavior. In the 1950s, for example, Leon Festinger was dissatisfied with the ability of a major theory of the day, behaviorism, to explain why people change their attitudes. He formulated a new approach—cognitive dissonance theory—that made specific predictions about when and how people would change their attitudes. As we will see in Chapter 6, other researchers were dissatisfied with Festinger's explanation of the results he obtained, so they conducted further research to test other possible explanations. Social psychologists, like scientists in other

I love games. I think I could be very happy being a chess player or dealing with some other kinds of games. But I grew up in the Depression. It didn't seem one could survive on chess, and science is also a game. You have very strict ground rules in science, and your ideas have to check out with the empirical world. That's very tough and also very fascinating.

—LEON FESTINGER, 1977

disciplines, engage in a continual process of theory refinement: A theory is developed; specific hypotheses derived from that theory are tested; based on the results obtained, the theory is revised and new hypotheses are formulated.

HYPOTHESES BASED ON PERSONAL OBSERVATIONS Social psychology also deals with phenomena we encounter in everyday life. Researchers often observe something in their lives or the lives of others that they find curious and interesting, stimulating them to construct a theory about why this phenomenon occurred—and to design a study to see if they are right. In the early 1960s, for example, a tragic murder was committed in the Queens section of New York City that led to a major research area in social psychology. Kitty Genovese, a young woman returning to her apartment late one night in 1964, was brutally killed in an attack that lasted 45 minutes. The *New York Times* reported that 38 apartment residents either saw the attack from their windows or heard Genovese's screams, and that no one attempted to help her, not even by calling the police. Although we know now that the *Times* exaggerated the number of eyewitnesses who did nothing (Cook, 2014; Pelonero, 2014), the story vividly captured public fears and, for its time, "went viral." There is no doubt that bystanders often fail to help in emergencies (as we will see in Chapter 11), and the Genovese murder triggered a great deal of soul searching as to why. Some concluded that living in a metropolis dehumanizes us and leads inevitably to apathy, indifference to human suffering, and lack of caring.

Bibb Latané and John Darley, two social psychologists who taught at universities in New York, had another idea. Instead of focusing on "what was wrong with New Yorkers," Latané and Darley thought it would be more interesting and important to examine the social situation in which Genovese's neighbors found themselves. Maybe, they thought, the more people who witness an emergency, the less likely it is that any given individual will intervene. Genovese's neighbors might have assumed that someone else had called the police, a phenomenon Latané and Darley (1968) called the *diffusion of responsibility.* Perhaps the bystanders would have been more likely to help had each thought he or she alone was witnessing the murder. How can we tell whether this hypothesis is true? In science, idle speculation will not do; researchers must collect data to test their hypotheses. Let's look at how different research designs are used to do just that.

In October of 2011, a 2-year-old girl was struck by two vans in a row. A dozen people walked or rode past her. Why didn't they stop to help?

REVIEW QUESTIONS

1. Why do some social psychology research findings seem like we could have predicted the results?
   a. Because we are not predicting. These studies are famous and it is likely that we heard about them in the news and then forgot about them.
   b. Because most people have an advanced understanding of how human societies function, allowing them to predict such findings.
   c. Because hindsight bias suggests that we tend to exaggerate how easily we could have predicted something.
   d. Because they tap into the collective unconscious.

2. Which of the following suggest (s) why social psychologists often come up with new ideas that are based on previous theories and research?

   a. Previous experts in the field know best.
   b. They might think that they have a better way of explaining the same behavior.
   c. Older theories and research can always be refined and improved.
   d. Newer social psychologists are unoriginal.

3. Which of the following suggests why social psychologists often come up with theories that are based on phenomena that they or others encounter in real life?
   a. To give their experiments more realism
   b. To try and answer why a real-life event occurred
   c. To get more attention from the media
   d. None of the above

See page 619 for the answers.

Research Designs

2.2 **What are the strengths and weaknesses of various research designs that social psychologists use?**

Social psychology is a scientific discipline with a well-developed set of methods for answering questions about social behavior, such as the one about the causes of violence with which we began this chapter, and the one about reactions to violence that we just discussed. There are three types of methods: the *observational method*, the *correlational method*, and the *experimental method* (see Table 2.1). Any of these methods could be used to explore a specific research question; each is a powerful tool in some ways and a weak tool in others. Part of the creativity in conducting social psychological research involves choosing the right method, maximizing its strengths, and minimizing its weaknesses.

Here we discuss these methods in detail and try to provide you with a firsthand look at both the joy and the difficulty of conducting social psychological studies. The joy comes in unraveling the clues about the causes of interesting and important social behaviors, just as a sleuth gradually unmasks the culprit in a murder mystery. Each of us finds it exhilarating that we have the tools to provide definitive answers to questions philosophers have debated for centuries. At the same time, as seasoned researchers, we have learned to temper this exhilaration with a heavy dose of humility, because there are formidable practical and ethical constraints involved in conducting social psychological research.

Table 2.1 A Summary of Research Methods

Method	Focus	Question Answered
Observational	Description	What is the nature of the phenomenon?
Correlational	Prediction	From knowing X, can we predict Y?
Experimental	Causality	Is variable X a cause of variable Y?

The Observational Method: Describing Social Behavior

There is a lot to be learned by being an astute observer of human behavior. If the goal is to describe what a particular group of people or type of behavior is like, the **observational method** is very helpful. This is the technique whereby a researcher observes people and records measurements or impressions of their behavior. The observational method may take many forms, depending on what the researchers are looking for, how involved or detached they are from the people they are observing, and how much they want to quantify what they observe.

ETHNOGRAPHY One example of observational learning is **ethnography**, the method by which researchers attempt to understand a group or culture by observing it from the inside, without imposing any preconceived notions they might have. The goal is to understand the richness and complexity of the group by observing it in action. Ethnography is the chief method of cultural anthropology, the study of human cultures and societies. As social psychology broadens its focus by studying social behavior in different cultures, ethnography is increasingly being used to describe different cultures and generate hypotheses about psychological principles (Fine & Elsbach, 2000; Flick, 2014; Uzzel, 2000).

Consider this example from the early years of social psychological research. In the early 1950s, a small cult of people called the Seekers predicted that the world would come to an end with a giant flood on the morning of December 21, 1954. They were convinced that a spaceship from the planet Clarion would land in the backyard of their leader, Mrs. Keech, and whisk them away before the apocalypse. Assuming that the end of the world was not imminent, Leon Festinger and his colleagues thought it would be interesting to observe this group closely and chronicle how they reacted when their prophecy was disconfirmed (Festinger, Riecken, & Schachter, 1956). To monitor the hour-to-hour conversations of this group, the social psychologists found it necessary to become members and pretend that they too believed the world was about to end. On the fateful morning of December 21, 1954, with no flood waters lapping at the door and no sign of a spaceship, they observed a curious thing: Rather than admitting that she was wrong, Mrs. Keech "doubled down" on her beliefs, announcing that God had spared Planet Earth because of the Seekers' faith, and that it was now time for the group to go public and recruit more members. Based on his observations of Mrs. Keech's tenacious adherence to her beliefs, Festinger formulated one of the most famous theories in social psychology, cognitive dissonance, which we discuss in Chapter 6.

The key to ethnography is to avoid imposing one's preconceived notions on the group and to try to understand the point of view of the people being studied. Sometimes, however, researchers have a specific hypothesis that they want to test using the observational method. An investigator might be interested, for example, in how much aggression children exhibit during school recesses. In this case, the observer would be systematically looking for particular behaviors that are concretely defined before the observation begins. For example, aggression might be defined as hitting or shoving another child, taking a toy from another child without asking, and so on. The observer might stand at the edge of the playground and systematically record how often these behaviors occur. If the researcher were interested in exploring possible sex and age differences in social behavior, he or she would also note the child's gender and age. How do we know how accurate the observer is? In such studies, it is important to establish **interjudge reliability**, which is the level of agreement between two or more people who independently observe and code a set of data. By showing that two or more judges independently come up with the same observations, researchers ensure that the observations are not the subjective, distorted impressions of one individual.

Observational Method

The technique whereby a researcher observes people and systematically records measurements or impressions of their behavior

Ethnography

The method by which researchers attempt to understand a group or culture by observing it from the inside, without imposing any preconceived notions they might have

Interjudge Reliability

The level of agreement between two or more people who independently observe and code a set of data; by showing that two or more judges independently come up with the same observations, researchers ensure that the observations are not the subjective, distorted impressions of one individual

ARCHIVAL ANALYSIS   The observational method is not limited to observations of real-life behavior. The researcher can also examine the accumulated documents, or archives, of a culture, a technique known as an **archival analysis** (Mullen, Rozell, & Johnson, 2001; Oishi, 2014). For example, diaries, novels, suicide notes, popular music lyrics, television shows, movies, magazine and newspaper articles, advertising, social media, and the ways in which people use the Internet all tell us a great deal about human behavior. One study, for example, analyzed millions of Twitter messages sent in 84 countries to examine daily rhythms in people's mood. Judging by the content of the messages they send, most people's positive moods appear to peak at two different times of the day: In the morning, soon after they get up, and late in the evening, before they go to bed (Golder & Macy, 2011). Researchers have also used archival data to answer questions about pornography usage. For example, do you think that people who live in some areas of the United States are especially likely to look at on-line pornography? Perhaps you guessed that it is those who live in more liberal "blue" states that are the biggest consumers, given that liberals tend to have more permissive attitudes toward social issues. To address this question, a researcher examined credit card subscriptions to Internet pornography sites (Edelman, 2009). Although he was not given access to the names of people who subscribed, he did know their zip codes, which enabled him to estimate regional variations. As it turned out, residents of "blue" states and "red" were equally likely to subscribe to pornography sites (residents of Utah came in first).

LIMITS OF THE OBSERVATIONAL METHOD   The study that analyzed Twitter messages revealed interesting daily patterns, but it did not say much about *why* moods peak in the morning and at night. Furthermore, certain kinds of behavior are difficult to observe because they occur only rarely or only in private. You can begin to see the limitations of the observational method. Had Latané and Darley chosen this method to study the effects of the number of bystanders on people's willingness to help a victim, we might still be waiting for an answer, given the infrequency of emergencies and the difficulty of predicting when they will occur. And, archival data about pornography, while informative about who is accessing it, tells us little about the effects on their attitudes and behavior of doing so. Social psychologists want to do more than just describe behavior; they want to predict and explain it. To do so, other methods are more appropriate.

Archival Analysis

A form of the observational method in which the researcher examines the accumulated documents, or archives, of a culture (e.g., diaries, novels, magazines, and newspapers)

Researchers use archival analyses to test psychological hypotheses. One study, for example, analyzed millions of Twitter messages to see how people's moods varied over the course of a day.

The Correlational Method: Predicting Social Behavior

A goal of social science is to understand relationships between variables and to be able to predict when different kinds of social behavior will occur. What is the relationship between the amount of pornography people see and their likelihood of engaging in sexually violent acts? Is there a relationship between the amount of violence children see on television and their aggressiveness? To answer such questions, researchers frequently use another approach: the correlational method.

Correlational Method

The technique whereby two or more variables are systematically measured and the relationship between them (i.e., how much one can be predicted from the other) is assessed

With the **correlational method**, two variables are systematically measured, and the relationship between them—how much you can predict one from the other—is assessed. People's behavior and attitudes can be measured in a variety of ways. Just as with the observational method, researchers sometimes make direct observations of people's behavior. For example, researchers might be interested in testing the relationship between children's aggressive behavior and how much violent television they watch. They too might observe children on the playground, but here the goal is to assess the relationship, or correlation, between the children's aggressiveness and other factors, such as TV viewing habits, which the researchers also measure.

Correlation Coefficient

A statistical technique that assesses how well you can predict one variable from another—for example, how well you can predict people's weight from their height

Researchers look at such relationships by calculating the **correlation coefficient**, a statistic that assesses how well you can predict one variable from another—for example, how well you can predict people's weight from their height. A positive correlation means that increases in the value of one variable are associated with increases in the value of the other variable. Height and weight are positively correlated; the taller people are, the more they tend to weigh. A negative correlation means that increases in the value of one variable are associated with decreases in the value of the other. If height and weight were negatively correlated in human beings, we would look very peculiar; short people, such as children, would look like penguins, whereas tall people, such as NBA basketball players, would be all skin and bones! It is also possible, of course, for two variables to be completely unrelated, so that a researcher cannot predict one variable from the other (see Figure 2.1).

Surveys

Research in which a representative sample of people are asked (often anonymously) questions about their attitudes or behavior

SURVEYS   The correlational method is often used in **surveys**, research in which a representative sample of people are asked questions about their attitudes or behavior. Surveys are a convenient way to measure people's attitudes; for example, people can be telephoned and asked which candidate they will support in an upcoming election or

Figure 2.1 The diagrams below show three possible correlations in a hypothetical study of watching violence on television and aggressive behavior in children. The diagram at the left shows a strong positive correlation: The more television children watched, the more aggressive they were. The diagram in the middle shows no correlation: The amount of television children watched is not related to how aggressive they were. The diagram at the right shows a strong negative correlation: The more television children watched, the less aggressive they were.

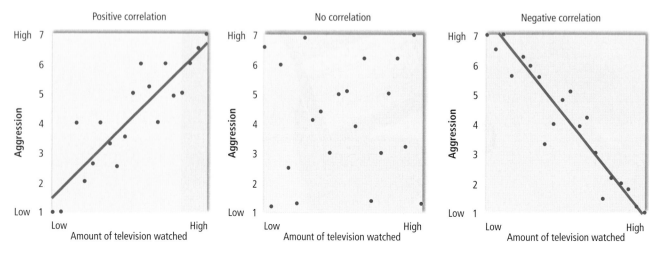

how they feel about a variety of social issues. Psychologists often use surveys to help understand social behavior and attitudes—for example, by seeing whether the amount of pornography men say they read is correlated with their attitudes toward women.

Surveys have a number of advantages, one of which is allowing researchers to judge the relationship between variables that are difficult to observe, such as how often people engage in safer sex. The researcher looks at the relationship between the questions asked on the survey, such as whether people who know a lot about how HIV is transmitted are more likely than other people to engage in safer sex.

Another advantage of surveys is the capability of sampling representative segments of the population. Answers to a survey are useful only if they reflect the responses of people in general—not just the people actually tested (called the *sample*). Survey researchers go to great lengths to ensure that the people they test are typical. They select samples that are representative of the population on a number of characteristics important to a given research question (e.g., age, educational background, religion, gender, income level). They also make sure to use a **random selection** of people from the population at large, which is a way of ensuring that a sample of people is representative of a population by giving everyone in the population an equal chance of being selected for the sample. As long as the sample is selected randomly, we can assume that the responses are a reasonable match to those of the population as a whole.

There are famous cases of surveys that yielded misleading results by failing to sample randomly. In the fall of 1936, for example, a weekly magazine called *The Literary Digest* conducted a large survey asking people which candidate they planned to vote for in the upcoming presidential election. The magazine obtained the names and addresses of its sample from telephone directories and automobile registration lists. The results of its survey of 2 million people indicated that the Republican candidate, Alf Landon, would win by a landslide. Of course, you know that there never was a President Landon; instead, Franklin Delano Roosevelt won every state in the Union but two. What went wrong with *The Literary Digest* poll? In the depths of the Great Depression, many people could not afford telephones or cars. Those who had them were doing well financially; most well-to-do voters were Republican and overwhelmingly favored Alf Landon. However, the majority of the voters were not well off—and

Random Selection

A way of ensuring that a sample of people is representative of a population by giving everyone in the population an equal chance of being selected for the sample

In the fall of 1936, a magazine called the *Literary Digest* predicted that the Republican candidate for present would win by a landslide, based on a poll they conducted. Instead, Franklin Roosevelt won every state but two, as seen in the map below. What went wrong with the *Literary Digest* poll?

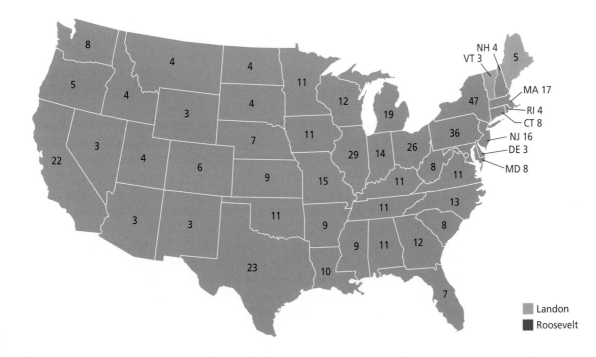

Landon
Roosevelt

overwhelmingly supported the Democratic candidate, Roosevelt. By using a list of names that excluded the less affluent members of the population, *The Literary Digest* surveyed a nonrepresentative sample. (*The Literary Digest* never recovered from this methodological disaster and went out of business shortly after publishing its poll.)

Modern political polls are not immune from such sampling errors. Many polling companies only contact people on their home phones (landlines), because of the difficulty of obtaining directories of cell phone numbers. They do so at their peril, because research shows that Americans who rely solely on cell phones are more likely to vote for Democratic candidates. Indeed, polls that didn't try to reach cell phones, in the weeks preceding the 2012 presidential election, tended to underestimate the margin of President Obama's victory (Silver, 2012).

Another potential problem with survey data is the accuracy of the responses. Straightforward questions, regarding who people intend to vote for or what they typically do, are relatively easy to answer. But asking survey participants to predict how they might behave in some hypothetical situation or to explain why they behaved as they did in the past is an invitation to inaccuracy (Schuman & Kalton, 1985; Schwarz, Groves, & Schuman, 1998). Often people simply don't know the answer—but they think they do. Richard Nisbett and Tim Wilson (1977) demonstrated this "telling more than you can know" phenomenon in a number of studies in which people often made inaccurate reports about why they responded the way they did. Their reports about the causes of their responses pertained more to their theories and beliefs about what should have influenced them than to what actually influenced them. (We discuss these studies at greater length in Chapter 5.)

LIMITS OF THE CORRELATIONAL METHOD: CORRELATION DOES NOT EQUAL CAUSATION   The major shortcoming of the correlational method is that it tells us only that two variables are related, whereas the goal of the social psychologist is to identify the *causes* of social behavior. We want to be able to say that A causes B, not just that A is correlated with B.

If a researcher finds that there is a correlation between two variables, it means that there are three possible causal relationships between these variables. For example, researchers have found a correlation between the amount of violent television children watch and how aggressive they are (similar to the pattern shown in the graph on the left side in Figure 2.1, though not quite as strong; see Eron, 1987). One explanation of this correlation is that watching TV violence causes kids to become more violent themselves. It is equally probable, however, that the reverse is true: that kids who are violent to begin with are more likely to watch violent TV. Or there might be no causal relationship between these two variables; instead, both TV watching and violent behavior could be caused by a third variable, such as having neglectful parents who do not pay much attention to their kids. (Experimental evidence supports one of these causal relationships; we will discuss which one in Chapter 12.) When using the correlational method, it is wrong to jump to the conclusion that one variable is causing the other to occur. *Correlation does not prove causation.*

Unfortunately, forgetting this adage is one of the most common methodological errors in the social sciences. Consider a study of birth control methods and sexually transmitted diseases (STDs) in women (Rosenberg, Davidson, Chen, Judson, & Douglas, 1992). The researchers examined the records of women who had visited a clinic, noting which method of birth control they used and whether they had an STD. Surprisingly, the researchers found that women who relied on condoms had significantly more STDs than women who used diaphragms or contraceptive sponges. This result was widely reported in the popular press, with the conclusion that the use of diaphragms and sponges caused a lower incidence of disease. Some reporters urged women whose partners used condoms to switch to other methods.

Can you see the problem with this conclusion? The fact that the incidence of disease was correlated with the type of contraception women used is open to a number of causal

A study conducted in the early 1990s found a correlation between the type of birth control women used and their likelihood of getting a sexually transmitted disease (STD). Those whose partners used condoms were more likely to have an STD than were women who used other forms of birth control. Does this mean that the use of condoms caused the increase in STDs? Not necessarily—see the text for alternative explanations of this research finding.

interpretations. Perhaps the women who used sponges and diaphragms had sex with fewer partners. (In fact, condom users were more likely to have had sex with multiple partners in the previous month.) Perhaps the partners of women who relied on condoms were more likely to have STDs than were the partners of women who used sponges and diaphragms. There is simply no way of knowing. Thus, the conclusion that the birth control methods protected against STDs cannot be drawn from this correlational study.

As another example of the difficulty of inferring causality from correlational designs, let's return to the question of whether pornography causes aggressive sexual acts against women, such as rape. In one study, male college students at a large midwestern university completed an anonymous survey on which they indicated whether they had ever engaged in sexually coercive behavior as well as the frequency with which they viewed various forms of pornography (Carr & VanDeusen, 2004). The researchers found a small but statistically significant correlation, such that the more pornography the students reported using, the greater the likelihood that they had committed sexual violence (Hald, Malamuth, & Yuen, 2010). Another study found, in a nationally representative sample of women in the United States, that the more the women reported looking at pornography on the Internet, the higher the number of sexual partners they had had (Wright & Arroyo, 2013).

As suggestive as these findings are, they do not establish that using pornography made the male students more likely to commit sexual violence or that looking at Internet porn made the women want to have sex with many partners. Can you think of alternative explanations for these correlations? It is possible that men who are aggressive toward women are more interested in pornography; that is, it is their aggression causing their attraction to pornography, and not the pornography causing their aggression (Malamuth et al., 2000). Alternatively, there could be some third variable, such as something in a man's upbringing or subculture, that makes him more likely to commit sexual violence and look at pornography. Similarly, women who want to have sex with multiple partners could be more interested in looking at Internet porn, rather than the other way around. Other examples of the difficulty of inferring causality from correlational studies are shown in the following Try It!

TRY IT!
Correlation and Causation: Knowing the Difference

It can be difficult to remember that, when two variables are correlated, it doesn't necessarily mean that one caused the other; correlation does *not* allow us to make causal inferences. For each of the following examples, think about why the correlation was found. Even if it seems obvious which variable was causing the other, are there alternative explanations?

1. A study found that elderly people who were never married or who are widowed who have a pet dog live longer, on an average, than those who do not have a pet dog. In other words, there is a positive correlation between pet ownership and life expectancy. Can pets replace medical interventions such as medicines and surgeries to increase lifespan?

2. Imagine that a study found a negative correlation in university students' number of Instagram followers and average grades. Could students improve their grades by reducing their Instagram followers or deleting their accounts?

3. Posting selfies on Instagram correlates positively with being an extrovert. Can introverts change their personalities by posting more pictures of themselves through their social media accounts?

4. A study found that there are more students diagnosed with learning disabilities such as dyslexia in private rather than public schools. Could the teaching methods in private schools be causing students to develop learning disabilities?

5. A positive correlation was found between people who use one type of web browser over another and being convicted of murder. Could authorities decrease the homicide rate by banning this browser?

6. A study found a positive correlation between people who are frequently late and being more creative and successful. Could arriving to work late help our careers rather than hurt them?

7. There is a negative correlation between following the practices of certain Eastern religions that favor a vegetarian

diet and heart attacks. Could people who are at risk of a heart attack reduce their risk by converting to these religions?

8. A well-known correlation is that of global warming and pirates. There is a negative correlation between annual average global temperatures and the number of pirates sailing the seas. Could we reverse the effects of climate change by adding more pirates to international waters?

9. Parent groups found out that the perpetrators of a school shooting frequently played a certain first-person shooter video game. Should authorities ban these kinds of games

to prevent other young people from picking up guns and murdering their peers?

10. A study found that people who are more intelligent tend to swear more and have messier and more cluttered desks. Could people increase their intelligence by swearing like a sailor and tidying their workspaces less often?

See page 619 for the answers.

Experimental Method

The method in which the researcher randomly assigns participants to different conditions and ensures that these conditions are identical except for the independent variable (the one thought to have a causal effect on people's responses)

Independent Variable

The variable a researcher changes or varies to see if it has an effect on some other variable

The Experimental Method: Answering Causal Questions

The only way to determine causal relationships is with the **experimental method**. Here, the researcher systematically orchestrates the event so that people experience it in one way (e.g., they witness an emergency along with other bystanders) or another way (e.g., they witness the same emergency but are the sole bystander). The experimental method is the method of choice in most social psychological research, because it allows the experimenter to make causal inferences.

INDEPENDENT AND DEPENDENT VARIABLES To illustrate how this is done, let's return to our earlier example of Bibb Latané and John Darley, the two social psychologists who came up with the hypothesis that the more people who witness an emergency, the less likely it is that any one of them will intervene. As with any experiment, they needed to vary the critical aspect of the situation that they thought would have a causal effect, in their case the number of people who witnessed an emergency. This is called the **independent variable**, which is the variable a researcher changes or varies to see if it has an effect on some other variable. The researcher then observes whether the independent variable (e.g., the number of bystanders) has the predicted effect on the outcome of interest, namely the **dependent variable**, which is the variable a researcher measures to see if it is influenced by the independent variable—in this case whether people who help in an emergency (see Figure 2.2).

Sound simple? Actually, it isn't. Staging an experiment to test Latané and Darley's hypothesis about the effects of group size involves severe practical and ethical difficulties. What kind of emergency should be used? Ideally (from a scientific perspective), it should be as true to the Genovese case as possible. Accordingly, you would want to stage a murder that passersby could witness. In one condition, you could stage the murder so that only a few onlookers were present; in another condition, you could stage it so that a great many onlookers were present.

Obviously, no scientist in his or her right mind would stage a murder for unsuspecting bystanders. But how could the researchers arrange a realistic situation that is upsetting enough to be similar to the Genovese case without it being too upsetting? In addition,

Figure 2.2 Researchers vary the independent variable (e.g., the number of bystanders people think are present) and observe what effect that has on the dependent variable (e.g., whether people help).

Independent Variable	Dependent Variable
The variable that is hypothesized to influence the dependent variable. Participants are treated identically except for this variable.	The response that is hypothesized to depend on the independent variable. All participants are measured on this variable.

Example: Latané and Darley (1968)	
The number of bystanders	**How many participants helped?**
Participant + Victim	85%
Participant + Victim + Two others	62%
Participant + Victim + Four others	31%

how could they ensure that each bystander experienced the same emergency except for the independent variable whose effect they wanted to test—namely, the number of bystanders?

Let's see how Latané and Darley (1968) dealt with these problems. Imagine that you are a participant in their experiment. You arrive at the scheduled time and find yourself in a long corridor with doors to several small rooms. An experimenter greets you and takes you into one of the rooms, mentioning that five other students, seated out of view in the other rooms, will be participating with you. The experimenter leaves after giving you a pair of headphones with an attached microphone. You put on the headphones, and soon you hear the experimenter explaining to everyone that he is interested in learning about the kinds of personal problems college students experience.

To ensure that people will discuss their problems candidly, he explains that each participant will remain anonymous and each will stay in his or her separate room and communicate with the others only via the intercom system. The experimenter further says that the discussion will be recorded, but to encourage openness, he will not listen to it "live." Finally, the experimenter asks participants to take turns presenting their problems, each speaking for 2 minutes, after which each person will comment on what the others have said. To make sure this procedure is followed, he says, only one person's microphone will be turned on at a time.

The group discussion begins. You listen as the first participant admits that he has found it difficult to adjust to college. With some embarrassment, he mentions that he sometimes has seizures, especially when under stress. When his 2 minutes are up, you hear the other four participants discuss their problems; then it is your turn. When you have finished, the first person speaks again. To your astonishment, he soon begins to experience one of the seizures he mentioned earlier:

> I—er—um—I think I—I need—er—if—if could—er—er—somebody er—er—er—er—er—er—er—give me a little—er—give me a little help here because—er—I—er—I'm—er—er—h—h—having a—a—a real problem—er—right now and I—er—if somebody could help me out it would—it would—er—er s—s—sure be—sure be good . . . because—er—there—er—er—a cause I—er—I—uh—I've got a—a one of the—er—sei—er—er—things coming on and—and—and I could really—er—use some help so if somebody would—er—give me a little h—help—uh—er—er—er—er c—could somebody—er—er—help—er—uh—uh—uh (choking sounds) . . . I'm gonna die—er—er—I'm . . . gonna die—er—help—er—er—seizure—er (chokes, then quiet). (Darley & Latané, 1968, p. 379)

What would you have done in this situation? If you were like most of the participants in the actual study, you would have remained in your room, listening to your fellow student having a seizure, without doing anything about it. Does this surprise you? Latané and Darley kept track of the number of people who left their cubicle to find the victim or the experimenter before the end of the victim's seizure. Only 31% of the participants sought help in this way. Fully 69% of the students remained in their cubicles and did nothing—just as Kitty Genovese's neighbors failed to offer assistance in any way.

Does this finding prove that the failure to help was due to the number of people who witnessed the seizure? How do we know that it wasn't due to some other factor? We know because Latané and Darley included two other conditions in their experiment. In these conditions, the procedure was identical to the one we described, with one crucial difference: The size of the discussion group was smaller, meaning that fewer people witnessed the seizure. In one condition, the participants were told that there were three other people in the discussion group besides themselves (the victim plus two others), and in this case, helping behavior increased to 62%. In a third condition, participants were told that there was only one other person in their discussion group (the victim), and in that case, nearly everyone helped (85%; see Figure 2.2).

> Theory is a good thing, but a good experiment lasts forever.
> —Peter Leonidovich Kapista

Dependent Variable

The variable a researcher measures to see if it is influenced by the independent variable the researcher hypothesizes that the dependent variable will depend on the level of the independent variable

These results indicate that the number of bystanders strongly influences the rate of helping, but it does not mean that the size of the group is the only cause of people's decision to help. After all, when there were four bystanders, a third of the participants still helped; conversely, when participants thought they were the only witness, some of them failed to do so. Obviously, other factors influence helping behavior—the bystanders' personalities, their prior experience with emergencies, and so on. Nonetheless, Latané and Darley succeeded in identifying one important determinant of whether people help: the number of bystanders that people think are present.

INTERNAL VALIDITY IN EXPERIMENTS   How can we be sure that the differences in help across conditions in the Latané and Darley seizure study were due to the different numbers of bystanders who witnessed the emergency? Could something else have produced this effect? This is the beauty of the experimental method: We can be sure of the causal connection between the number of bystanders and helping, because Latané and Darley made sure that everything about the situation was the same in the different conditions *except* for the independent variable—the number of bystanders. Keeping everything but the independent variable the same in an experiment is referred to as *internal validity*. Latané and Darley were careful to maintain high internal validity by making sure that everyone witnessed the same emergency. They prerecorded the supposed other participants and the victim and played their voices over the intercom system so that everyone heard exactly the same thing.

You may have noticed, however, that there was a key difference between the conditions of the Latané and Darley experiment other than the number of bystanders: Different people participated in the different conditions. Maybe the observed differences in helping were due to characteristics of the participants instead of the independent variable. The people in the sole-witness condition might have differed in any number of ways from their counterparts in the other conditions, making them more likely to help. Maybe they were more likely to know something about epilepsy or to have experience helping in emergencies. If either of these possibilities is true, it would be difficult to conclude that it was the number of bystanders, rather than something about the participants' backgrounds, that led to differences in helping.

Fortunately, there is a technique that allows experimenters to minimize differences among participants as the cause of the results: **random assignment to condition**. This is the process whereby all participants have an equal chance of taking part in any condition of an experiment; through random assignment, researchers can be relatively certain that differences in the participants' personalities or backgrounds are distributed evenly across conditions. Because Latané and Darley's participants were randomly assigned to the conditions of their experiment, it is very unlikely that the ones who knew the most about epilepsy all ended up in one condition. Knowledge about epilepsy should be randomly (i.e., roughly evenly) dispersed across the three experimental conditions. This powerful technique is the most important part of the experimental method.

Even with random assignment, however, there is the (very small) possibility that different characteristics of people did not distribute themselves evenly across conditions. For example, if we randomly divide a group of 40 people into two groups, it is possible that those who know the most about epilepsy will by chance end up more in one group than in the other—just as it is possible to get more heads than tails when you flip a coin 40 times. This is a possibility we take seriously in experimental science. The analyses of our data come with a **probability level (*p*-value)**, which is a number, calculated with statistical techniques, that tells researchers how likely it is that the results of their experiment occurred by chance and not because of the independent variable. The convention in science, including social psychology, is to consider results *significant* (trustworthy) if the probability level is less than 5 in 100 that the results might be due to chance factors rather than the independent variables studied. For example, if we flipped a coin 40 times and got 40 heads, we would probably assume that this was very unlikely to have occurred by chance and that there was something

Random Assignment to Condition

A process ensuring that all participants have an equal chance of taking part in any condition of an experiment; through random assignment, researchers can be relatively certain that differences in the participants' personalities or backgrounds are distributed evenly across conditions

Probability Level (*p*-value)

A number calculated with statistical techniques that tells researchers how likely it is that the results of their experiment occurred by chance and not because of the independent variable or variables; the convention in science, including social psychology, is to consider results *significant* (trustworthy) if the probability level is less than 5 in 100 that the results might be due to chance factors and not the independent variables studied wrong with the coin (we might check the other side to make sure it wasn't one of those trick coins with heads on both sides!). Similarly, if the results in two conditions of an experiment differ significantly from what we would expect by chance, we assume that the difference was caused by the independent variable (e.g., the number of bystanders present during the emergency). The p-value tells us how confident we can be that the difference was due to chance rather than the independent variable.

To summarize, the key to a good experiment is to maintain high **internal validity**, which we can now define as making sure that the independent variable, and *only* the independent variable, influences the dependent variable. This is accomplished by controlling all extraneous variables and by randomly assigning people to different experimental conditions (Campbell & Stanley, 1967). When internal validity is high, the experimenter is in a position to judge whether the independent variable causes the dependent variable. This is the hallmark of the experimental method that sets it apart from the observational and correlational methods: Only the experimental method can answer causal questions, such as whether exposure to pornography causes men to commit violent acts.

For example, researchers have tested whether pornography causes aggression by randomly assigning consenting participants to watch pornographic or nonpornographic films (the independent variable) and measuring the extent to which people acted aggressively toward women (the dependent variable). In a study by Donnerstein and Berkowitz (1981), males were angered by a female accomplice and then were randomly assigned to see one of three films: violent pornography (a rape scene), nonviolent pornography (sex without any violence), or a neutral film with no violence or sex (a talk show interview). The men were then given an opportunity to act aggressively toward the woman who had angered them, by choosing the level of electric shock she would receive in an ostensibly unrelated learning experiment (the accomplice did not really receive shocks, but participants believed that she would). The men who had seen the violent pornography administered significantly more-intense shocks to the woman than did the men who had seen the nonviolent pornography or the neutral film, suggesting that it is not pornography per se that leads to aggressive behavior, but the violence depicted in some pornography (Mussweiler & Förster, 2000). We review this area of research in more detail in Chapter 12.

EXTERNAL VALIDITY IN EXPERIMENTS   For all the advantages of the experimental method, there are some drawbacks. By virtue of gaining enough control over

Internal Validity

Making sure that nothing besides the independent variable can affect the dependent variable; this is accomplished by controlling all extraneous variables and by randomly assigning people to different experimental conditions

A good deal of social psychological research takes place in laboratory settings. How do social psychologists generalize from the findings of these studies to life outside the laboratory?

the situation so as to randomly assign people to conditions and rule out the effects of extraneous variables, the situation can become somewhat artificial and distant from real life. For example, it might be argued that Latané and Darley strayed far from the original inspiration for their study, the Kitty Genovese murder. What does witnessing a seizure while participating in a laboratory experiment in a college building have to do with a brutal murder in a densely populated urban neighborhood? How often in everyday life do we have discussions with other people through an intercom system? Did the fact that the participants knew they were in a psychology experiment influence their behavior?

These are important questions that concern **external validity**, which is the extent to which the results of a study can be generalized to other situations and other people. Note that two kinds of generalizability are at issue: the extent to which we can generalize from the situation constructed by an experimenter to real-life situations, referred to as generalizability across *situations*, and the extent to which we can generalize from the people who participated in the experiment to people in general, referred to as generalizability across *people*.

When it comes to generalizability across situations, research in social psychology is sometimes criticized for being conducted in artificial settings that cannot be generalized to real life—for example, psychological experiments at a university. To address this problem, social psychologists attempt to increase the generalizability of their results by making their studies as realistic as possible. But this is hard to do in a laboratory setting in which people are placed in situations they would rarely, if ever, encounter in everyday life, such as occurred in Latané and Darley's group discussion of personal problems over an intercom system. Instead, psychologists attempt to maximize the study's **psychological realism**, which is the extent to which the psychological processes triggered in an experiment are similar to psychological processes that occur in everyday life (Aronson, Wilson, & Brewer, 1998). Even though Latané and Darley staged an emergency that in significant ways was unlike those encountered in everyday life, was it psychologically similar to real-life emergencies? Were the same psychological processes triggered? Did the participants have the same types of perceptions and thoughts, make the same types of decisions, and choose the same types of behaviors that they would in a real-life situation? If so, the study is high in psychological realism and we can generalize the results to everyday life.

Psychological realism is heightened if people feel involved in a real event. To accomplish this, experimenters often tell participants a **cover story**—a disguised version of the study's true purpose. Recall, for example, that Latané and Darley told people that they were studying the personal problems of college students and then staged an emergency. It would have been a lot easier to say to people, "Look, we are interested in how people react to emergencies, so at some point during this study we are going to stage an accident, and then we'll see how you respond." We think you'll agree that such a procedure would be very low in psychological realism. In real life, we never know when emergencies are going to occur, and we do not have time to plan our responses to them. If participants knew that an emergency was about to happen, the kinds of psychological processes triggered would have been quite different from those of a real emergency, reducing the psychological realism of the study.

Social psychologists are also concerned with generalizability across people. Latané and Darley's experiment, for example, documented an interesting, unexpected example of social influence whereby the mere knowledge that others were present reduced the likelihood that people helped. But what have we learned about people in general? The participants in their study were 52 male and female students at New York University who received course credit for participating in the experiment. Would the study have turned out the same way if a different population had been used? Would the number of bystanders have influenced helping behavior had

External Validity

The extent to which the results of a study can be generalized to other situations and to other people

Psychological Realism

The extent to which the psychological processes triggered in an experiment are similar to psychological processes that occur in everyday life

Cover Story

A description of the purpose of a study, given to participants, that is different from its true purpose and is used to maintain psychological realism the participants been middle-aged blue-collar workers instead of college students? Midwesterners instead of New Yorkers? Japanese instead of American?

The only way to be certain that the results of an experiment represent the behavior of a particular population is to ensure that the participants are randomly selected from that population. Ideally, samples in experiments should be randomly selected, just as they are in surveys. Increasingly, social psychologists are conducting research with diverse populations and cultures, some of it over the Internet (e.g., Lane, Banaji, & Nosek, 2007). But, unfortunately, it is impractical and expensive to select random samples for most social psychology experiments. It is difficult enough to convince a random sample of Americans to agree to answer a few questions over the telephone as part of a political poll, and such polls can cost thousands of dollars to conduct. Imagine the difficulty Latané and Darley would have had convincing a random sample of Americans to board a plane to New York to take part in their study, not to mention the cost of such an endeavor. Even trying to gather a random sample of students at New York University would not have been easy; each person contacted would have had to agree to spend an hour in Latané and Darley's laboratory.

Of course, concerns about practicality and expense are not good excuses for doing poor science. Many researchers address this problem by studying basic psychological processes that make people susceptible to social influence, assuming that these processes are so fundamental that they are universally shared. In that case, participants for social psychology experiments don't really have to come from all over the country or world. Of course, some social psychological processes are likely to be quite dependent on cultural factors, and in those cases, we'd need diverse samples of people. The question then is, how can researchers tell whether the processes they are studying are universal?

FIELD EXPERIMENTS   One of the best ways to increase external validity is by conducting **field experiments**. In a field experiment, researchers study behavior outside the laboratory, in its natural setting. As in a laboratory experiment, the researcher controls the occurrence of an independent variable (e.g., group size) to see what effect it has on a dependent variable (e.g., helping behavior) and randomly assigns people to the different conditions. Thus, a field experiment has the same design as a laboratory experiment, except that it is conducted in a real-life setting rather than in the relatively artificial setting of the laboratory. The participants in a field experiment are unaware that

Field Experiments

Experiments conducted in natural settings rather than in the laboratory

the events they experience are in fact an experiment. The external validity of such an experiment is high, because, after all, it is taking place in the real world, with real people who are more diverse than a typical college student sample.

Many such field studies have been conducted in social psychology. For example, Latané and Darley (1970) tested their hypothesis about group size and bystander intervention in a convenience store outside New York City. Two "robbers" (with full knowledge and permission of the cashier and manager of the store) waited at the checkout counter until there were either one or two other customers approaching to get in line. They then asked the cashier to retrieve the most expensive beer the store carried. The cashier said he would have to check in the back to see how much of that brand was in stock. While the cashier was

Social psychologists are interested in how generalizable their findings are to different kinds of people. What are the challenges in doing so? What approaches do social psychologists take?

gone, the robbers picked up a case of beer in the front of the store, declared, "They'll never miss this," put the beer in their car, and drove off.

Because the robbers were rather burly fellows, no one attempted to intervene directly to stop the theft. The question was, when the cashier returned, how many people would help by telling him that a theft had just occurred? As it turned out, the number of bystanders had the same inhibiting effect on helping behavior as in the laboratory seizure study: Significantly fewer people reported the theft when there was another customer-witness in the store than when they were alone.

It might have occurred to you to ask why researchers conduct laboratory studies at all, given that external validity is so much better with field experiments. Indeed, it seems to us that the perfect experiment in social psychology would be one that was conducted in a field setting with a sample randomly selected from a population of interest and with extremely high internal validity (all extraneous variables controlled, people randomly assigned to the conditions). Sounds good, doesn't it? The only problem is that it is very difficult to satisfy all these conditions in one study, making such studies virtually impossible to conduct.

There is almost always a trade-off between internal and external validity—that is, between being able to randomly assign people to conditions and having enough control over the situation to ensure that no extraneous variables are influencing the results, and making sure that the results can be generalized to everyday life. We have the most control in a laboratory setting, but the laboratory may be unlike real life. Real life can best be captured by doing a field experiment, but it is very difficult to control all extraneous variables in such studies. For example, the astute reader will have noticed that Latané and Darley's (1970) beer theft study differed from laboratory experiments in an important way: People could not be randomly assigned to the alone or in-pairs conditions. Were this the only study Latané and Darley had performed, we could not be sure whether the kinds of people who prefer to shop alone, as compared to the kinds of people who prefer to shop with a friend, differ in ways that might influence helping behavior. By randomly assigning people to conditions in their laboratory studies, Latané and Darley were able to rule out such alternative explanations.

The trade-off between internal and external validity has been referred to as the **basic dilemma of the social psychologist** (Aronson & Carlsmith, 1968). The way to resolve this dilemma is not to try to do it all in a single experiment. Most social psychologists opt first for internal validity, conducting laboratory experiments in which people are randomly assigned to different conditions and all extraneous variables are controlled; here there is little ambiguity about what is causing what. Other social psychologists prefer to maximize external validity by conducting field studies. And many social psychologists do both. Taken together, both types of studies meet the requirements of our perfect experiment.

REPLICATIONS AND META-ANALYSIS Replications are the ultimate test of an experiment's external validity. Only by conducting studies in different settings, with different populations, can we determine how generalizable the results are. Often, though, when many studies on one problem are conducted, the results are somewhat variable. Several studies might find an effect of the number of bystanders on helping behavior, for example, while a few do not. How can we make sense of this? Does the number of bystanders make a difference or not? Fortunately, there is a statistical technique called **meta-analysis** that averages the results of two or more studies to see if the effect of an independent variable is reliable. Earlier we discussed p-values, which tell us the probability that the findings of one study are due to chance or to the independent variable. A meta-analysis essentially does the same thing, except that it averages the results of many different studies. If, say, an independent variable is found to

Basic Dilemma of the Social Psychologist

The trade-off between internal and external validity in conducting research; it is very difficult to do one experiment that is both high in internal validity and generalizable to other situations and people

Replications

Repeating a study, often with different subject populations or in different settings

Meta-Analysis

A statistical technique that averages the results of two or more studies to see if the effect of an independent variable is reliable have an effect in only 1 of 20 studies, the meta-analysis will tell us that that one study was probably an exception and that, on average, the independent variable is not influencing the dependent variable. If an independent variable is having an effect in most of the studies, the meta-analysis is likely to tell us that, on average, it does influence the dependent variable.

Most of the findings you will read about in this book have been replicated in several different settings, with different populations; we know, then, that they are reliable phenomena, not limited to the laboratory or to college sophomores. For example, Anderson and Bushman (1997) compared laboratory studies on the causes of aggression with studies conducted in the real world. In both types of studies, violence in the media caused aggressive behavior. Similarly, Latané and Darley's original findings have been replicated in numerous studies. Increasing the number of bystanders inhibited helping behavior with many kinds of people, including children, college students, and future ministers (Darley & Batson, 1973; Latané & Nida, 1981); in both small towns and large cities (Latané & Dabbs, 1975); in a variety of settings, such as psychology laboratories, city streets, and subway trains (Harrison & Wells, 1991; Latané & Darley, 1970; Piliavin & Piliavin, 1972); and with different kinds of emergencies, such as seizures, potential fires, fights, and accidents (Latané & Darley, 1968; Shotland & Straw, 1976; Staub, 1974), as well as with less-serious events, such as having a flat tire (Hurley & Allen, 1974). Many of these replications took place in real-life settings (e.g., on a subway train) where people could not possibly have known that an experiment was being conducted. We will frequently point out similar replications of the major findings we discuss in this book (Wilson, 2011).

BASIC VERSUS APPLIED RESEARCH   You may have wondered how people decide which specific topic to study. Why would a social psychologist decide to study helping behavior, cognitive dissonance theory, or the effects of pornography on aggression? Is he or she simply curious? Or does the social psychologist have a specific purpose in mind, such as trying to reduce sexual violence?

The goal in **basic research** is to find the best answer to the question of why people behave as they do, purely for reasons of intellectual curiosity. The researchers aren't trying to solve a specific social or psychological problem. In contrast, **applied research** is geared toward solving a particular social problem. Here, building a theory of behavior is usually secondary to solving the specific problem, such as alleviating racism, reducing sexual violence, or stemming the spread of AIDS.

In social psychology, the distinction between basic and applied research is fuzzy. Even though many researchers label themselves as either basic or applied scientists, the endeavors of one group are not independent of those of the other group. There are countless examples of advances in basic science that at the time had no known applied value but later proved to be the key to solving a significant applied problem. As we will see later in this book, for example, basic research with dogs, rats, and fish on the effects of feeling in control of one's environment has led to the development of techniques to improve the health of elderly nursing home residents (Langer & Rodin, 1976; Richter, 1957; Schulz, 1976; Seligman, 1975).

Most social psychologists would agree that, to solve a specific social problem, we must understand the psychological processes responsible for it. Indeed, Kurt Lewin (1951), one of the founders of social psychology, coined a phrase that has become a motto for the field: "There is nothing so practical as a good theory." He meant that to solve such difficult social problems as urban violence or racial prejudice, one must first understand the underlying psychological dynamics of human nature and social interaction. Even when the goal is to discover the psychological processes underlying social behavior, the findings often have clear applied implications, as you'll see throughout this book.

Basic Research

Studies that are designed to find the best answer to the question of why people behave as they do and that are conducted purely for reasons of intellectual curiosity

Applied Research

Studies designed to solve a particular social problem

There is nothing so practical as a good theory.
—KURT LEWIN, 1951

REVIEW QUESTIONS

1. Which kind of study is best suited to ethnography?
   a. A study of what factors cause Green Peace activists to be committed to their ideals.
   b. A study to see if violent videogames cause children to act more violently.
   c. A study to see if people are more likely to litter in a place that has already been littered.
   d. A study examining people's posts on Twitter to see how moods fluctuate throughout the day.

2. Why is it important to establish interjudge reliability in an observational study?
   a. To make sure the observations are less empirical
   b. To make sure the observations are subjective
   c. To make sure the observations are not subjective and have not been distorted by one person
   d. To resolve disputes between researchers

3. Social psychology uses three main methods for answering questions about social behavior. These methods are
   a. observational, ethnographical, and experimental.
   b. correlational, observational, and archival analysis.
   c. correlational, observational, and surveys.
   d. correlational, observational, and experimental.

4. What are some of the limits of the observational method?
   a. Some kinds of behavior happen only rarely or happen mostly in private settings.
   b. Most participants in experiments refuse to be observed.
   c. It can only be carried out in the lab.
   d. It allows us to describe behavior but not to predict or explain it.

5. Imagine that a researcher finds a negative correlation in adults in the relationship between years of education and denial of global climate change. Which of the following is the most reasonable conclusion one can draw from the study?
   a. People who are more educated know more scientists and thus are more likely to know someone who has conducted research on this topic.
   b. Based on how many years of education an adult has completed, you can reasonably predict how likely they are to believe global climate change.
   c. People who are less educated probably know how to interpret information from scientific studies and the news media.
   d. People who have less money and less education are not as informed about global issues.

6. Which of the following is the basic dilemma of social psychology research?
   a. The interest in creating an experiment that is generalizable across different people and situations.
   b. The difficulty in studying controversial issues such as murder and pornography.
   c. The difficulty in establishing both high internal and external validity.
   d. The difficulty in knowing if the dependent variable is actually being affected by the independent variable or whether some other variable could be causing the effect.

7. Which of the following is the best way to increase the external validity of a study?
   a. Make sure it is low in psychological realism.
   b. Conduct the study in the laboratory instead of the field.
   c. Replicate the study with a different population of people in a different setting.
   d. Make sure you have at least two dependent variables.

8. Social psychologists often do experiments in the laboratory, instead of the field, to
   a. increase internal validity.
   b. increase external validity.
   c. conduct a meta-analysis.
   d. decrease psychological realism.

See page 619 for the answers.

New Frontiers in Social Psychological Research

2.3 **What impact do cross-cultural studies, the evolutionary approach, and social neuroscience research have on the way in which scientists investigate social behavior?**

Social psychologists are always looking for new ways of investigating social behavior, and in recent years some exciting new methods have been developed.

These methodological advances have been spurred on by new questions about the origins of social behavior, because new questions and new methods often develop hand in hand.

Culture and Social Psychology

Social psychology largely began as a Western science, conducted by Western social psychologists with Western participants. This raises the question of how universal the findings are. To study the effects of culture on social psychological process, social psychologists conduct **cross-cultural research** (Cohen, 2014; Gelfand, Chiu, & Hong, 2014; Heine, 2010; Kitayama & Cohen, 2007; Miller & Boyle, 2013; Nisbett, 2003). Some findings in social psychology are culture-dependent, as we will see throughout this book. In Chapter 3, for example, we will see that Westerners and East Asians rely on fundamentally different kinds of thought to perceive and understand the social world. In Chapter 5, we'll discuss cultural differences in the very way people define themselves. Whether we emphasize personal independence or social interdependence reflects our cultural values (Henrich, Heine, & Norenzayan, 2010).

Conducting cross-cultural research is not simply a matter of traveling to another culture, translating materials into the local language, and replicating a study there (Heine et al., 2002; van de Vijver & Leung, 1997). Researchers have to guard against imposing their own viewpoints and definitions, learned from their culture, onto another culture with which they are unfamiliar. They must also be sure that their independent and dependent variables are understood in the same way in different cultures (Bond, 1988; Lonner & Berry, 1986).

Suppose, for example, that you wanted to replicate the Latané and Darley (1968) seizure experiment in another culture. Clearly, you could not conduct the identical experiment somewhere else. The tape-recorded discussion of college life used by Latané and Darley was specific to the lives of New York University students in the 1960s and could not be used meaningfully elsewhere. What about more subtle aspects of the study, such as the way people viewed the person who had the seizure? Cultures vary considerably in how they define whether or not another person belongs to their social group; this factor figures significantly in how they behave toward that person (Gudykunst, 1988; Triandis, 1989). If people in one culture view the victim as a member of their social group but people in another culture perceive the victim as a member of a rival social group, you might find very different results in the two cultures—not because the psychological processes of helping behavior are different, but because people interpreted the situation differently. It can be quite daunting to conduct a study that is interpreted and perceived similarly in dissimilar cultures. Cross-cultural researchers are sensitive to these issues, and as more and more cross-cultural research is conducted carefully, we will be able to determine which social psychological processes are universal and which are culture-bound (Heine, 2010). For example, there is substantial evidence that playing violent video games makes people act in more aggressive ways and makes them less likely to help others. But is this true just in Western countries? A recent review of the literature compared studies of video games in the United States and Japan. As it happened, the deleterious effects of violent video games were the same in both countries (Anderson et al., 2010).

The Evolutionary Approach

Evolutionary theory was developed by Charles Darwin (1859) to explain the ways in which animals adapt to their environments. Central to the theory is **natural selection**, the process by which heritable traits that promote survival in a particular environment are passed along to future generations, because organisms with those traits are more likely to produce offspring. A common example is how giraffes came to have long necks. In an environment where food is scarce, giraffes that happened to have

Cross-Cultural Research

Research conducted with members of different cultures, to see whether the psychological processes of interest are present in both cultures or whether they are specific to the culture in which people were raised

Some basic psychological processes are universal, whereas others are shaped by the culture in which we live. For example, are people's self-concepts shaped by cultural rules of how people must present themselves, such as the requirement by the Taliban regime in Afghanistan that women cover themselves from head to toe? Cross-cultural research is challenging but necessary for exploring how culture influences the basic ways in which people think about and interact with others.

Evolutionary Theory

A concept developed by Charles Darwin to explain the ways in which animals adapt to their environments

Natural Selection

The process by which heritable traits that promote survival in a particular environment are passed along to future generations; organisms with those traits are more likely to produce offspring long necks could feed on foliage that other animals couldn't reach. These giraffes were more likely to survive and produce offspring than were other giraffes, the story goes, and the "long neck" gene thus became common in subsequent generations.

In biology, evolutionary theory is used to explain how different species acquired physical traits such as long necks. But what about social behaviors, such as the tendency to be aggressive toward a member of one's own species or the tendency to be helpful to others? Is it possible that social behaviors have genetic determinants that evolve through the process of natural selection, and, if so, is this true in human beings as well as animals? These are the questions posed by **evolutionary psychology**, which attempts to explain social behavior in terms of genetic factors that have evolved over time according to the principles of natural selection. The core idea is that evolution occurs very slowly, such that social behaviors that are prevalent today, such as aggression and helping behavior, are due at least in part to adaptations to environments in our distant past (Buss, 2005; Durrant, Ellis, Nelson, Mizumori, & Weiner, 2013; Neuberg, Kenrick, & Schaller, 2010). We will discuss in upcoming chapters how evolutionary theory explains social behavior (e.g., Chapter 10 on interpersonal attraction, Chapter 11 on prosocial behavior, and Chapter 12 on aggression). Here, in our chapter on research methods, it is important to note that a lively debate has arisen over the testability of evolutionary hypotheses. Because current behaviors are thought to be adaptations to environmental conditions that existed thousands of years ago, psychologists make their best guesses about what those conditions were and how specific kinds of behaviors gave people a reproductive advantage. But these hypotheses are obviously impossible to test with the experimental method. And just because hypotheses sound plausible does not mean they are true. For example, some scientists now believe that giraffes did not acquire a long neck in order to eat leaves in tall trees. Instead, they suggest, long necks first evolved in male giraffes to gain an advantage in fights with other males over access to females (Simmons & Scheepers, 1996). Which of these explanations is true? It's hard to tell. On the other hand, evolutionary approaches can generate novel hypotheses about social behavior that can be tested with the other methods described in this chapter.

Evolutionary Psychology

The attempt to explain social behavior in terms of genetic factors that have evolved over time according to the principles of natural selection

Social Neuroscience

As we have seen, social psychology is concerned with how people's thoughts, feelings, and behaviors are influenced by the real or imagined presence of other people. Most research studies in social psychology, then, study just that—thoughts, feelings, and behaviors. Human beings are biological organisms, however, and social psychologists have become increasingly interested in the connection between biological processes and social behavior. These interests include the study of hormones and behavior, the human immune system, and neurological processes in the human brain. To study the brain and its relation to behavior, psychologists use sophisticated technologies, including electroencephalography (EEG), in which electrodes are placed on the scalp to measure electrical activity in the brain, and functional magnetic resonance imaging (fMRI), in which people are placed in scanners that measure changes in blood flow in their brains. Social psychologists take these measurements while participants think about and process social information, allowing them to correlate different kinds of brain activity with social information processing. This kind of research promises to open up a whole new area of inquiry into the relationship of the brain to behavior (Cacioppo & Cacioppo, 2013; Chiao et al., 2010; Lieberman, 2013; Ochsner, 2007).

Social psychologists are studying the brain and its relation to behavior. They use technologies such as electroencephalography (EEG) and functional magnetic resonance imaging (fMRI).

REVIEW QUESTIONS

1. What is the goal of cross-cultural research in social psychology?
   a. To find out which social psychological processes are dictated by culture and which are universal.
   b. To answer questions like whether violent video games are destroying cultures.
   c. To rank or compare cultures.
   d. To find out if all social psychological processes are dictated by culture.

2. What can evolutionary psychology help explain?
   a. Physical changes in a species, such as the long neck of a giraffe, which resulted in a reproductive advantage in a given environment.
   b. Physical changes in humans, such as why some people grow wisdom teeth and others do not.
   c. How certain kinds of human behaviors could be partially due to adapting to a particular environment in our ancestors' past.

   d. How certain kinds of human behaviors could be partially due to adapting to our present environment.

3. What is the goal of social neuroscience?
   a. To legitimize social psychology as a science through the use of machines such as EEGs and fMRIs
   b. To settle debates in social psychology, such as whether a social process is caused by brain structure or culture
   c. To explore how different kinds of brain activity correlate with social information processing by having participants think about a social situation and seeing which parts of the brain are involved.
   d. To see if social processes can happen without other people being present. This is achieved by having participants think about a social situation and measuring which parts of the brain are involved.

See page 619 for the answers.

Ethical Issues in Social Psychology

2.4 **How do social psychologists ensure the safety and welfare of their research participants, while at the same time testing hypotheses about the causes of social behavior?**

As you read this chapter, did it bother you to learn that researchers sometimes mislead people about the true purpose of their study or that, in Latané and Darley's seizure study, people were put in a situation that might have been upsetting? In their quest to create realistic, engaging situations, social psychologists frequently face ethical dilemmas. For scientific reasons, we want our experiments to resemble the real world as much as possible and to be as sound and well controlled as we can make them. But we also want to avoid causing our participants stress, discomfort, or unpleasantness. These two goals sometimes conflict as the researcher goes about the business of creating and conducting experiments.

Above all, researchers are concerned about the health and welfare of the individuals participating in their experiments. Researchers are also in the process of discovering important information about human social behavior, such as bystander intervention, prejudice, conformity, aggression, and obedience to authority. Many of these discoveries are bound to benefit society. Indeed, given the fact that social psychologists have developed powerful tools to investigate such issues scientifically, many scholars feel it would be immoral not to conduct experiments to explore them. To gain insight into such critical issues, however, researchers must create vivid events that are involving for the participants. Some of these events might make the participants uncomfortable, such as witnessing someone having a seizure. We can't resolve the

"DON'T TELL ME THIS NONSENSE DOESN'T VIOLATE THE CODE OF BIOETHICS."

ScienceCartoonsPlus.com

Informed Consent

Agreement to participate in an experiment, granted in full awareness of the nature of the experiment, which has been explained in advance

Deception

Misleading participants about the true purpose of a study or the events that will actually transpire

Debriefing

Explaining to participants, at the end of an experiment, the true purpose of the study and exactly what transpired

Institutional Review Board (IRB)

A group made up of at least one scientist, one nonscientist, and one member not affiliated with the institution that reviews all psychological research at that institution and decides whether it meets ethical guidelines; all research must be approved by the IRB before it is conducted

dilemma by making pious claims that participants never experience discomfort in an experiment or by insisting that all is fair in science and then forging blindly ahead. Clearly, some middle ground is called for.

The dilemma is less problematic if researchers can obtain **informed consent** from their participants prior to their participation. To obtain informed consent, the researcher explains the nature of the experiment to participants before it begins and asks for their permission to participate. If participants are made fully aware of the kinds of experiences they are about to undergo and state that they are willing to participate, the ethical dilemma is resolved. In many social psychology experiments, this sort of description is feasible—and where it is feasible, it is done. But sometimes it is impossible. Suppose Latané and Darley had told their participants that a seizure was about to be staged, that it wouldn't be a real emergency, and that the point was to see if they offered help. Such a procedure would be bad science. In this kind of experiment, it's essential that the participant experience contrived events as if they were real; this is called a *deception experiment*. **Deception** in social psychological research involves misleading participants about the true purpose of a study or the events that transpire. Note that not all research in social psychology involves deception. Note further that there is a difference between the use of deception in psychology experiments and tricking people for entertainment purposes, as happens on television shows such as *Punk'd*. Psychologists use deception only if it is the only way in which they can test a hypothesis about social behavior.

When deception is used in a study, the postexperimental interview, called the debriefing session, is crucial. **Debriefing** is the process of explaining to the participants, at the end of an experiment, the true purpose of the study and exactly what transpired. If any participants have experienced discomfort, the researchers attempt to undo and alleviate it. During debriefing too the participants learn about the goals and purpose of the research. The best researchers question their participants carefully and listen to what they say, regardless of whether or not deception was used in the experiment. (For a detailed description of how debriefing interviews should be conducted, see Aronson et al., 1990.)

In our experience, virtually all participants understand and appreciate the need for deception, as long as the time is taken in the postexperimental debriefing session to review the purpose of the research and to explain why alternative procedures could not be used. Several investigators have gone a step further and assessed the impact on people of participating in deception studies (e.g., Christensen, 1988; Epley & Huff, 1998; Finney, 1987; Gerdes, 1979; Sharpe, Adair, & Roese, 1992). These studies have consistently found that people do not object to the kinds of mild discomfort and deceptions typically used in social psychological research. In fact, some studies have found that most people who participated in deception experiments reported learning more and enjoying the experiments more than did those who participated in nondeception experiments (Smith & Richardson, 1983). For example, Latané and Darley (1970) reported that, during their debriefing, the participants said that the deception was necessary and that they were willing to participate in similar studies in the future—even though they had experienced some stress and conflict during the study.

To ensure that the dignity and safety of research participants are protected, the American Psychological Association (2010) has published a list of ethical principles that govern all research in psychology (see Figure 2.3). In addition, any institution (such as a university) that seeks federal funding for psychological research is required to have an **institutional review board (IRB)** that reviews research before it is conducted. The board, which must include at least one scientist, one nonscientist, and one person who is not affiliated with the institution, reviews all research proposals and decides whether the procedures meet ethical guidelines. Any aspect of the experimental procedure that this committee judges to be overly stressful or upsetting must

Figure 2.3 The American Psychological Association, a professional organization that represents psychology in the United States, has established ethical guidelines that psychological researchers are expected to follow. Some of them are listed here.

(Adapted from APA Ethical Principles of Psychologists and Code of Conduct, 2010)

Selected Ethical Principles of Psychologists in the Conduct of Research

1. Psychologists seek to promote accuracy, honesty, and truthfulness in the science, teaching, and practice of psychology.
2. Psychologists respect the dignity and worth of all people, and the rights of individuals to privacy, confidentiality, and self-determination.
3. When psychologists conduct research in person or via electronic transmission or other forms of communication, they obtain the informed consent of the individual.
4. When obtaining informed consent psychologists inform participants about (1) the purpose of the research, expected duration, and procedures; (2) their right to decline to participate and to withdraw from the research once participation has begun; (3) the foreseeable consequences of declining or withdrawing; (4) reasonably foreseeable factors that may be expected to influence their willingness to participate such as potential risks, discomfort, or adverse effects; (5) any prospective research benefits; (6) limits of confidentiality; (7) incentives for participation; and (8) whom to contact for questions about the research and research participants rights.
5. Psychologists have a primary obligation and take reasonable precautions to protect confidential information obtained through or stored in any medium.
6. Psychologists do not conduct a study involving deception unless they have determined that the use of deceptive techniques is justified by the studys significant prospective scientific, educational, or applied value and that effective nondeceptive alternative procedures are not feasible.
7. Psychologists explain any deception that is an integral feature of the design and conduct of an experiment to participants as early as is feasible.
8. Psychologists provide a prompt opportunity for participants to obtain appropriate information about the nature, results, and conclusions of the research, and they take reasonable steps to correct any misconceptions that participants may have of which the psychologists are aware.

be changed or deleted before the study can be conducted. Note that some of the research described in later chapters was conducted before IRBs were required in the early 1970s. You will need to decide whether you would have approved these studies if you were on an IRB that judged them.

REVIEW QUESTIONS

1. Which of the following is true about obtaining participants' informed consent for an experiment?
   a. It can be done before or after an experiment.
   b. It does not need to explain the nature of the experiment, as this would give away too many details.
   c. Participants should be told what kind of experiences they are agreeing to undergo.
   d. It is not necessary unless the experiment involves some sort of deception.

2. Which of the following is the most important priority in designing psychology experiments?
   a. To be as close to the real world as possible
   b. To be as controlled as possible in order to increase validity

   c. To maintain the health and welfare of the participants
   d. To find out the answers to important issues affecting society, such as aggression and prejudice

3. Which of the following is/are true of the post-experimental interview known as debriefing?
   a. If the participants experienced anything that made them feel uncomfortable, the researchers try to counteract this.
   b. It is not necessary to debrief participants if they gave their informed consent.
   c. The researchers inform the participants about the goals and purpose of the research and explain any deception.
   d. All of the above.

See page 619 for the answers.

Summary

2.1 How do researchers develop hypotheses and theories?

- **Social Psychology: An Empirical Science** A fundamental principle of social psychology is that social influence can be studied scientifically.

    - **Formulating Hypotheses and Theories** Social psychological research begins with a hypothesis about the effects of social influence. Hypotheses often come from previous research findings; researchers conduct studies to test an alternative explanation of previous experiments. Many other hypotheses come from observations of everyday life, such as Latané and Darley's hunches about why people failed to help Kitty Genovese.

2.2 What are the strengths and weaknesses of various research designs that social psychologists use?

- **Research Designs** Social psychologists use three research designs: the observational method, the correlational method, and the experimental method.

    - **The Observational Method: Describing Social Behavior** The **observational method**, whereby researchers observe people and systematically record their behavior, is useful for describing the nature of a phenomenon and generating hypotheses. It includes **ethnography**, the method by which researchers attempt to understand a group or culture by observing it from the inside, without imposing any preconceived notions they might have. Another method is **archival analysis**, whereby researchers examine documents or archives, such as looking at photographs in magazines to see how men and women are portrayed.

    - **The Correlational Method: Predicting Social Behavior** The **correlational method**, whereby two or more variables are systematically measured and the relationship between them assessed, is very useful when the goal is to predict one variable from another. For example, researchers might be interested in whether there is a correlation between the amount of violent television children watch and how aggressive they are. The correlational method is often applied to the results of surveys in which a representative group of people are asked questions about their attitudes and behaviors. To make sure that the results are generalizable, researchers randomly select survey respondents from the population at large. A limit of the correlational method is that *correlation does not equal causation.*

- **The Experimental Method: Answering Causal Questions** The only way to determine causality is to use the **experimental method**, in which the researcher randomly assigns participants to different conditions and ensures that these conditions are identical except for the independent variable. The **independent variable** is the one researchers vary to see if it has a causal effect (e.g., how much TV children watch); the **dependent variable** is what researchers measure to see if it is affected (e.g., how aggressive children are). Experiments should be high in **internal validity**, which means that people in all conditions are treated identically, except for the independent variable (e.g., how much TV children watch). **External validity**—the extent to which researchers can generalize their results to other situations and people—is accomplished by increasing the realism of the experiment, particularly its psychological realism (the extent to which the psychological processes triggered in the experiment are similar to those triggered in everyday life). It is also accomplished by **replicating** the study with different populations of participants. As in any other science, some social psychology studies are basic research experiments (designed to answer basic questions about why people do what they do), whereas others are applied studies (designed to find ways to solve specific social problems).

2.3 What impact do cross-cultural studies, the evolutionary approach, and social neuroscience research have on the way in which scientists investigate social behavior?

- **New Frontiers in Social Psychological Research** In recent years, social psychologists have developed new ways of investigating social behavior.

    - **Culture and Social Psychology** To study the ways in which culture shapes people's thoughts, feelings, and behavior, social psychologists conduct cross-cultural research. This is not simply a matter of replicating the same study in different cultures; researchers have to guard against imposing their own viewpoints and definitions, learned from their culture, onto another culture with which they are unfamiliar.

    - **The Evolutionary Approach** Some social psychologists attempt to explain social behavior in terms of genetic factors that have evolved over time according to the principles of natural selection. Such ideas are hard to test experimentally but can generate novel hypotheses about social behavior that can be tested with the experimental method.

- **Social Neuroscience** Social psychologists have become increasingly interested in the connection between biological processes and social behavior. These interests include the study of hormones and behavior, the human immune system, and neurological processes in the human brain.

2.4 **How do social psychologists ensure the safety and welfare of their research participants, while at the same time testing hypotheses about the causes of social behavior?**

- **Ethical Issues in Social Psychology** Social psychologists follow federal, state, and professional guidelines to ensure the welfare of their research participants. These include having an **institutional review board** approve their studies in advance, asking participants to sign **informed consent** forms, and **debriefing** participants afterwards about the purpose of the study and what transpired, especially if there was any deception involved.

Test Yourself

1. How do most researchers in social psychology devise new ideas for what to study?

  a. By drawing on earlier theories

  b. By drawing on earlier research and refining it

  c. By basing it on something in their own lives or events they came across in the news

  d. All of the above

2. Suppose a researcher found a strong negative correlation between college students' grade point average (GPA) and the amount of alcohol they drink. Which of the following is the best conclusion from this study?

  a. Students with a high GPA study more and thus have less time to drink.

  b. Drinking a lot interferes with studying.

  c. If you know how much alcohol a student drinks, you can predict his or her GPA fairly well.

  d. People who are intelligent get higher grades and drink less.

3. Which of the following would be the best way to improve the external validity of an experiment about whether or not people are more likely to help a disabled person open a door when they are in a good mood?

  a. Make sure the experiment uses the observational method.

  b. Make sure it uses the correlational method to measure if mood correlates with helping behavior.

  c. Make the experiment as realistic as possible and conduct it in a real-life setting instead of in a lab.

  d. Give the participants a good cover story.

4. Which of the following is true of cross-cultural research?

  a. It is a good way to increase the internal validity of a study.

  b. A study must be replicated in at least three cultures to be considered valid.

  c. Because social psychology began as a Western science, most experimenters within it are not overly concerned with generalizing their results to non-Western cultures.

  d. Its conducted to study the effects of culture on social psychological process.

5. Which of the following is not true about field experiments?

  a. They take place in real-life settings instead of inside a laboratory.

  b. They use the same kinds of designs as laboratory experiments.

  c. They use an independent variable but not a dependent variable.

  d. They tend to be high in external validity because they are conducted in the real world.

6. Suppose an experiment is designed such that male undergraduate university student participant groups are split in half at random. One group plays a violent video game and another plays a neutral game. Immediately afterwards, the participants have someone "accidentally" bump into them. The experimenter is measuring whether or not the participants react aggressively to the person who bumped into them. Which of the following are true about this experiment?

a. It has high external validity because it uses a heterogeneous sample.

b. The independent variable is how participants react and the dependent variable is which video game group they were assigned to.

c. The dependent variable is how participants react and the independent variable is which video game group they were assigned to.

d. It meets the condition of "random assignment to condition" because each participant was equally likely to be assigned to the violent or non-violent video game condition.

7. Let's suppose that the same experiment's (as in Question 6) procedures were repeated using a wider range of participants who vary in age, gender, occupation, and ethnicity. What is this process called and what is its purpose?

a. Random assignment to condition; increase generalizability

b. A meta-analysis; to increase internal validity

c. Replication; to increase external validity

d. Replication; to increase internal validity

8. Imagine a researcher is examining the relationship between people who regularly eat a certain kind of food and obesity. Which of the following could be true?

a. A positive correlation suggests that people who eat lots of that food are more likely to be obese.

b. No correlation suggests that there is no relationship between eating this kind of food and obesity.

c. No correlation suggests that people who eat this food are more likely to be overweight but not obese.

d. A negative correlation suggests that people who eat this kind of food are less likely than the general population to be obese.

9. An experiment that takes place in a lab is designed to determine if the number of people watching makes one more patient with being asked annoying questions. The experiment uses some deception. Which of the following is/are true?

a. The experimenter must obtain informed consent of each participant before the experiment and must debrief them afterwards.

b. Because the experiment involves some deception, no consent is necessary, only debriefing.

c. During debriefing, the experimenter is not obliged to tell the participants about the real nature of the study lest they should tell participants in the waiting room on their way out.

d. During debriefing, the experimenter must tell the participants about the real nature of the study.

10. What is the purpose of an Institutional Review Board?

a. To approve studies in advance to make sure that they have a strong validity

b. To approve studies in advance to make sure that they can later be easily replicated in order to increase external validity

c. To approve studies in advance to make sure that they follow ethical guidelines and will not cause any undue harm to the participants

d. To meet with participants after an experiment to conduct debriefing and see if all the participants gave their informed consent

See page 619 for the answers.

Chapter 3
Social Cognition
How We Think About the Social World

 ## Chapter Outline and Learning Objectives

On Automatic Pilot: Low-Effort Thinking

3.1 What is automatic thinking, and how are schemas an example of that kind of thought? What are the advantages and disadvantages of schemas?

People as Everyday Theorists: Automatic Thinking with Schemas

Which Schemas Do We Use? Accessibility and Priming

Making Our Schemas Come True: The Self-Fulfilling Prophecy

Types of Automatic Thinking

3.2 What are other types of automatic thinking and how do they operate?

Automatic Goal Pursuit

Automatic Decision Making

Automatic Thinking and Metaphors About the Body and the Mind

Mental Strategies and Shortcuts: Judgmental Heuristics

Cultural Differences in Social Cognition

3.3 How does culture influence social thinking?

Cultural Determinants of Schemas

Holistic Versus Analytic Thinking

Controlled Social Thinking: High-Effort Thinking

3.4 What are some of the drawbacks of controlled thinking, and how can we improve its effectiveness?

Controlled Thinking and Free Will

Mentally Undoing the Past: Counterfactual Reasoning

Improving Human Thinking

Watson Revisited

It was an epic match on *Jeopardy!*, the television quiz show on which contestants are given an answer and have to provide the correct question. Two of the three contestants were among the best players of all time, namely, Ken Jennings, who held the record for the longest winning streak on the show (74 consecutive games), and Brad Rutter, who was the all-time money winner. What about the third contestant? Who would dare match his or her wits against these formidable opponents? Actually, it wasn't a "he" or "she," but an "it": a supercomputer named Watson, developed by IBM and named after that company's founder, Thomas J. Watson.

The match was nip and tuck at first, but by the third and last day Watson had built an insurmountable lead. Time after time, the supercomputer gave correct responses to esoteric clues. In the category, Legal 'Es', for example, Watson listened to the clue, "This clause in a union contract says that wages will rise or fall depending on a standard such as cost of living" and correctly responded, "What is escalator?" Ken Jennings, who described himself as "the Great Carbon-Based Hope against a new generation of thinking machines," conceded defeat by writing on his video screen, "I, for one, welcome our new computer overlords," paraphrasing a line from an episode of *The Simpsons* (Jennings, 2011; Markoff, 2011).

This was not the first time an IBM computer had outwitted human beings. In 1997, Gary Kasparov, the reigning chess champion of the world, conceded defeat in the sixth and decisive game against an IBM computer named Big Blue. But what was especially impressive about Watson's victory was that the supercomputer did not simply look up answers in a vast memory bank. The IBM researchers deliberately chose to compete in the game *Jeopardy!* because, to win, you have to understand natural language, with all its subtleties and double meanings. Watson had to figure out, for example, that the term "Legal 'Es'" was a pun on the word *legalese*, meaning that the answers would involve legal terms but that they would all begin with the letter *e*. The fact that it could do so, faster and more accurately than the best human beings ever to play the game, was impressive indeed.

Should we all feel a little less smart, like the commentator who remarked, after Big Blue defeated Gary Kasparov that he felt "a twinge of IQ loss and an increase in hairiness" (Dunn, 1997)? Well, computers are getting smarter and smarter, but they have a long way to go before they can match the human brain. When the field of artificial intelligence began in the 1950s, computer scientists believed that in a short amount of time they would produce machines that could outthink human beings in every way. But as powerful as computers are, and as good as they are at games like chess and *Jeopardy!*, there are key areas in which they don't come close to matching humans. For example, human beings are much better than computers at understanding the nuances of people's behavior and decoding their intentions, wishes, and desires. Because of this, computers fail miserably at games in which it is crucial to figure out what is going on inside people's heads and understand things from their point of view, such as poker (C. Wilson, 2011). Perhaps computers will get there, as in the futuristic movie *Her*, in which computer operating systems have become so sophisticated that they have minds of their own and understand their users astutely—so much so that people fall in love with them. But as for now, the human brain far outperforms the fastest computer in the key task of thinking about other people. In this chapter we will see how.

The human brain has evolved to be a powerful, finely tuned instrument for understanding other people (Liebeman, 2013). More generally, people are extremely good at **social cognition**, which, as we saw in Chapter 1, refers to the ways in which people think about themselves and the social world, including how they select, interpret, remember, and use social information. No computer can match us in this

Social Cognition

How people think about themselves and the social world; more specifically, how people select, interpret, remember, and use social information to make judgments and decisions kind of thinking. That's not to say people are perfect social thinkers. Social psychologists have uncovered some fascinating mistakes to which we are prone, despite our uncanny cognitive abilities. In this chapter, we will see both the power and limits of social cognition.

To understand how people think about their social worlds and how accurate their impressions are likely to be, we need to distinguish between two different kinds of social cognition. One kind of thought is quick and automatic. When we meet someone for the first time, we often form lightning-quick impressions of him or her, without consciously deliberating about it. Similarly, we often make decisions "without thinking," such as jamming on the brakes of our car when we see a child step into the road (Bargh, Schwader, Hailey, Dyer, & Boothby, 2012; Dijksterhuis, 2010; Jonas, 2013; Payne & Gawronski, 2010; Wilson, 2002). This is called *automatic thinking*. Other times, of course, people pause and think carefully about the right course of action. You may have spent hours deliberating over important decisions in your life, such as where to go to college, or whether to break up with your boyfriend or girlfriend. This is the second kind of social cognition—*controlled thinking*—which is more effortful and deliberate. Quite often the automatic and controlled modes of social cognition work well together. Think of the automatic pilot that flies modern airplanes, monitoring hundreds of complex systems and adjusting instantly to changes in atmospheric conditions. The autopilot does just fine most of the time, although occasionally it is important for the human pilot to take over and fly the plane manually. Humans too have "automatic pilots" that monitor their environments, draw conclusions, and direct their behaviors. But we can also "override" this automatic type of thinking and analyze a situation slowly and deliberately. We will begin by examining the nature of automatic thinking.

Rodin's famous sculpture, *The Thinker*, mimics controlled thinking, where people sit down and consider something slowly and deliberately. Even when we do not know it, however, we are engaging in automatic thinking, which is nonconscious, unintentional, involuntary, and effortless.

On Automatic Pilot: Low-Effort Thinking

3.1   What is automatic thinking, and how are schemas an example of that kind of thought? What are the advantages and disadvantages of schemas?

People are very good at sizing up a new situation quickly and accurately. They figure out who is there, what is happening, and what might happen next. When you attended your first college class, for example, you probably made quick assumptions about who people were (the person standing at the lectern was the professor) and how to behave. We doubt that you confused the class with a fraternity party. And you probably reached these conclusions without even being aware that you were doing so.

Imagine a different approach: Every time you encounter a new situation, you stop and think about it slowly and deliberately, like Rodin's statue *The Thinker*. When you are introduced to someone new, you have to excuse yourself for

It is the mind which creates the world about us, and even though we stand side by side in the same meadow, my eyes will never see what is beheld by yours.

—GEORGE GISSING, *THE PRIVATE PAPERS OF HENRY RYECROFT*, 1903

Automatic Thinking

Thinking that is nonconscious, unintentional, involuntary, and effortless

15 minutes while you analyze what you have learned and how much you like the person. Sounds exhausting, doesn't it? Fortunately, we form impressions of people quickly and effortlessly, without much conscious analysis of what we are doing. We do these things by engaging in an automatic analysis of our environments, based on our past experiences and knowledge of the world. **Automatic thinking** is thought that is nonconscious, unintentional, involuntary, and effortless. Although different kinds of automatic thinking meet these criteria to varying degrees (Bargh et al., 2012; Hassin, 2013; Jonas, 2013; Moors & De Houwer, 2006), for our purposes we can define automaticity as thinking that satisfies all or most of them.

People as Everyday Theorists: Automatic Thinking with Schemas

Automatic thinking helps us understand new situations by relating them to our prior experiences. When we meet someone new, we don't start from scratch to figure out what he or she is like; we categorize the person as "an engineering student" or "like my cousin Helen." The same goes for places, objects, and situations. When we walk into a fast-food restaurant we've never visited, we know, without thinking, not to wait at a table for a waiter and a menu. We know that we have to go to the counter and order, because our past experience automatically tells us that this is what we do in fast-food restaurants.

Schemas

Mental structures people use to organize their knowledge about the social world around themes or subjects and that influence the information people notice, think about, and remember

More formally, people use **schemas**, which are mental structures that organize our knowledge about the social world. These mental structures influence the information we notice, think about, and remember (Bartlett, 1932; Heine, Proulx, & Vohs, 2006; Markus, 1977). The term *schema* is very general; it encompasses our knowledge about many things—other people, ourselves, social roles (e.g., what a librarian or an engineer is like), and specific events (e.g., what usually happens when people eat a meal in a restaurant). In each case, our schemas contain our basic knowledge and impressions that we use to organize what we know about the social world and interpret new situations. For example, if you watch the television show *The Bachelor* or *The Bachelorette*, you have probably developed schemas for different types of contestants, such as "the snide backstabbing villain" and the "naïve one whose heart will be broken."

Schemas are very useful for helping us organize and make sense of the world and to fill in the gaps of our knowledge. Think for a moment what it would be like to have no schemas at all. What if everything you encountered was inexplicable, confusing, and unlike anything else you've ever known? Tragically, this is what happens to people who suffer from a neurological disorder called Korsakov's syndrome. People with this disorder lose the ability to form new memories and must approach every situation as if they were encountering it for the first time, even if they have actually experienced it many times before. This can be so unsettling—even terrifying—that some people with Korsakov's syndrome go to great lengths to try to impose meaning on their experiences. Neurologist Oliver Sacks (1987) gives the following description of a Korsakov patient named Thompson:

Theory helps us to bear our ignorance of facts.

—George Santayana,
The Sense of Beauty, 1896

> He remembered nothing for more than a few seconds. He was continually disoriented. Abysses of amnesia continually opened beneath him, but he would bridge them, nimbly, by fluent confabulations and fictions of all kinds. For him they were not fictions, but how he suddenly saw, or interpreted, the world. Its radical flux and incoherence could not be tolerated, acknowledged, for an instant—there was, instead, this strange, delirious, quasi-coherence, as Mr. Thompson, with his ceaseless, unconscious, quick-fire inventions, continually improvised a world around him . . . *for such a*

patient must literally make himself (and his world) up every moment. (pp. 109–110; emphasis in original)

In short, having continuity, being able to relate new experiences to our past schemas, is so important that people who lose this ability invent schemas where none exist.

Schemas are particularly useful when we are in confusing situations, because they help us figure out what is going on. Consider a classic study by Harold Kelley (1950) in which students in different sections of a college economics class were told that a guest lecturer would be filling in that day. To create a schema about what the guest lecturer would be like, Kelley told the students that the economics department was interested in how different classes reacted to different instructors and that the students would thus receive a brief biographical note about the instructor before he arrived. The note contained information about the instructor's age, background, teaching experience, and personality. One version said, "People who know him consider him to be a very warm person, industrious, critical, practical, and determined." The other version was identical except that the phrase "a very warm person" was replaced with "a rather cold person." The students received one of these personality descriptions at random.

The guest lecturer then conducted a class discussion for 20 minutes, after which the students rated their impressions of him. Given that there was some ambiguity in this situation—after all, the students had seen the instructor for only a brief time—Kelley hypothesized that they would use the schema provided by the biographical note to fill in the blanks. This is exactly what happened. The students who expected the instructor to be warm gave him significantly higher ratings than the students who expected him to be cold, even though all the students had observed the exact same teacher behaving in the same way. The students who expected the instructor to be warm were also more likely to ask him questions and to participate in the class discussion. Has this happened to you? Have your expectations about a professor influenced your impressions of him or her? Did you find, oddly enough, that the professor acted just as you'd expected? Ask a classmate who had a different expectation about the professor what he or she thought. Do the two of you have different perceptions of the instructor based on the different schemas you were using?

Of course, people are not totally blind to what is actually out there in the world. Sometimes what we see is relatively unambiguous and we do not need to use our schemas to help us interpret it. For example, in one of the classes in which Kelley conducted his study, the guest instructor was quite self-confident, even a little arrogant. Given that arrogance is a relatively unambiguous trait, the students did not need to rely on their expectations to fill in the blanks. They rated the instructor as arrogant in both the

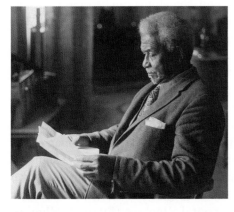

People who know him consider him a rather cold person, industrious, critical, practical, and determined.

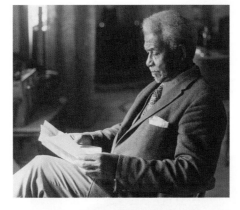

People who know him consider him a very warm person, industrious, critical, practical, and determined.

warm and cold conditions. However, when they rated this instructor's sense of humor, which was less clear-cut, the students relied on their schemas: The students in the warm condition thought he was funnier than the students in the cold condition did. The more ambiguous our information is, then, the more we use schemas to fill in the blanks.

It is important to note that there is nothing wrong with what the students in Kelley's study did. As long as people have reason to believe their schemas are accurate, it is perfectly reasonable to use them to resolve ambiguity. If a stranger comes up to you in a dark alley and says, "Take out your wallet," your schema about such encounters tells you that the person wants to steal your money, not admire pictures of your family. This schema helps you avert a serious and perhaps deadly misunderstanding.

I know that often I would not see a thing unless I thought of it first.
—NORMAN MACLEAN,
A River Runs Through It

Accessibility

The extent to which schemas and concepts are at the forefront of people's minds and are therefore likely to be used when making judgments about the social world

Is this man a diligent student who is exhausted from working too hard or is he lazy and shirking his responsibilities by sleeping? The way we judge others can be influenced by schemas that are accessible in our memories. If your friend had just texted you to say that she was partying all night and was going to skip class to take a nap, you might be more likely to perceive this stranger as an irresponsible student.

Which Schemas Do We Use? Accessibility and Priming

The social world is full of ambiguous information that is open to interpretation. Imagine, for example, that you are riding on a city bus and a man gets on and sits beside you. He mutters incoherently to himself and rocks back and forth in his seat. At one point, he starts singing an old Nirvana tune. How would you make sense of his behavior? You have several schemas you could use. Should you interpret his behavior with your "alcoholic" or "mentally ill person" schema? How will you decide?

The schema that comes to mind and guides your impressions of the man can be affected by **accessibility**, the extent to which schemas and concepts are at the forefront of the mind and are therefore likely to be used when making judgments about the social world (Chaxel, 2014; Higgins, 1996a; Wheeler & DeMarree, 2009; Wyer & Srull, 1989). Something can become accessible for three reasons. First, some schemas are chronically accessible due to past experience (Chen & Andersen, 1999; Coane & Balota, 2009; Schlegel et al., 2009). This means that these schemas are constantly active and ready to use to interpret ambiguous situations. For example, if there is a history of alcoholism in your family, traits describing a person with alcoholism are likely to be chronically accessible to you, increasing the likelihood that you will assume that the man on the bus has had too much to drink. If someone you know has a mental illness, however, thoughts about how people with mental illnesses behave are likely to be more accessible than thoughts about someone with alcoholism, leading you to interpret the man's behavior very differently.

Second, something can become accessible because it is related to a current goal. The concept of mental illness might not be chronically accessible to you, but if you are studying for a test in your abnormal psychology class and need to learn about different kinds of mental disorders, this concept might be temporarily accessible. As a consequence, you might be more likely to notice the man on the bus and interpret his behavior as a sign of a mental disorder—at least until your test is over and you no longer have the goal of learning about mental illnesses (Eitam & Higgins, 2010; Martin & Tesser, 1996; Masicampo & Ambady, 2014).

Lastly, schemas can become temporarily accessible because of our recent experiences (Bargh, 1996; Higgins & Bargh, 1987; Oishi, Schimmack, & Colcombe, 2003). This means that a particular schema or trait happens to be primed by something people have been thinking or doing before encountering an event. Suppose that right before the man on the bus sat down, you were reading *Girl, Interrupted*, Susanna Kaysen's memoir about her time in a psychiatric hospital. Given that thoughts about psychiatric patients were accessible in your mind, you would probably assume that the man had a mental illness. If, however, you had just looked out the window and seen a man leaning against a building drinking from a paper bag, you would probably assume that the man on the bus was drunk (see Figure 3.1). These are examples of **priming**, the process by which recent experiences increase the accessibility of a schema, trait, or concept. Reading *Girl, Interrupted* primes certain traits, such as those describing people with mental illnesses, making it more likely that these traits will be used to interpret a new event, such as the behavior of the man on the bus, even though this new event is completely unrelated to the one that originally primed the traits.

The following classic experiment illustrates the priming effect (Higgins, Rholes, & Jones, 1977). Research participants were told that they would take part in two unrelated studies. In the first, a perception study, they would be asked to identify different colors while at the same time memorizing a list of words. The second was a reading comprehension study in which they would read a paragraph about a man named Donald and then give their impressions of him. This paragraph is shown in Figure 3.2. Take a moment to read it. What do you think of Donald?

You might have noticed that many of Donald's actions are ambiguous—interpretable in either a positive or a negative manner—such as the fact that he piloted a boat without knowing much about it and that he wants to sail across the Atlantic. You might put a positive spin on these acts, deciding that Donald has an admirable sense of adventure. Or you could give the same behavior a negative spin, assuming that Donald is reckless and impulsive.

How did the participants interpret Donald's behavior? As expected, it depended on whether positive or negative traits were primed and accessible. In the first study, the researchers randomly divided people into two groups and gave them different words to memorize. People who had first memorized the words *adventurous, self-confident, independent,* and *persistent* later formed positive impressions of Donald, viewing him as a likable man who enjoyed new challenges. People who had first memorized *reckless, conceited, aloof,* and *stubborn* later formed negative impressions of Donald, viewing him as a stuck-up person who took needlessly dangerous chances.

But it was not just memorizing any positive or negative words that influenced people's impressions of Donald. In other conditions, research participants memorized words that were also positive or negative, such as *neat* or *disrespectful*. However, these

Figure 3.1 How We Interpret an Ambiguous Situation

The role of accessibility and priming.

Priming

The process by which recent experiences increase the accessibility of a schema, trait, or concept

Figure 3.2 Priming and Accessibility

In the second of a pair of studies, people were asked to read this paragraph about Donald and form an impression of him. In the first study, some of the participants had memorized words that could be used to interpret Donald in a negative way (e.g., reckless, conceited), while others had memorized words that could be used to interpret Donald in a positive way (e.g., adventurous, self-confident). As the graph shows, those who had memorized the negative words formed a much more negative impression of Donald than did those who had memorized the positive words.

(Based on data in Higgins, Rholes, & Jones, 1977)

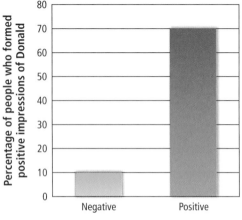

Words memorized in the first study

Description of Donald

   Donald spent a great deal of time in his search of what he liked to call excitement. He had already climbed Mt. McKinley, shot the Colorado rapids in a kayak, driven in a demolition derby, and piloted a jet-powered boat—without knowing very much about boats. He had risked injury, and even death, a number of times. Now he was in search of new excitement. He was thinking perhaps he would do some skydiving or maybe cross the Atlantic in a sailboat. By the way he acted one could readily guess that Donald was well aware of his ability to do many things well. Other than business engagements, Donald's contacts with people were rather limited. He felt he didn't really need to rely on anyone. Once Donald made up his mind to do something it was as good as done no matter how long it might take or how difficult the going might be. Only rarely did he change his mind even when it might well have been better if he had.

traits didn't influence their impressions of Donald because the words did not apply to Donald's behavior. Thoughts, then, have to be both *accessible* and *applicable* before they will act as primes, exerting an influence on our impressions of the social world. Priming is a good example of automatic thinking, because it occurs quickly, unintentionally, and unconsciously. When judging others, people are usually not aware that they are applying concepts or schemas that they happened to be thinking about earlier.

Making Our Schemas Come True: The Self-Fulfilling Prophecy

Self-Fulfilling Prophecy

The case wherein people have an expectation about what another person is like, which influences how they act toward that person, which causes that person to behave consistently with people's original expectations, making the expectations come true

People are not just passive recipients of information—they often act on their schemas in ways that change the extent to which these schemas are supported or contradicted. In fact, people can inadvertently make their schemas come true by the way they treat other people (Madon et al., 2011; Rosenthal & Jacobson, 1968; Scherr et al., 2011; Stinson et al., 2011; Willard, Madon, Guyll, Scherr, & Buller, 2012). This **self-fulfilling prophecy** operates as follows: People have an expectation about what another person is like, which influences how they act toward that person, which causes that person to behave consistently with people's original expectations, making the expectations come true. Figure 3.3 illustrates the sad self-perpetuating cycle of a self-fulfilling prophecy.

   In what has become one of the most famous studies in social psychology, Robert Rosenthal and Lenore Jacobson (1968) demonstrated the self-fulfilling prophecy in an elementary school. They administered a test to all the students in the school and told the teachers that some of the students had scored so well that they were sure to "bloom" academically in the upcoming year. In fact, this was not necessarily true: The students identified as "bloomers" were chosen at random by the researchers. As we discussed in Chapter 2, the use of random assignment means that, on average, the students designated as bloomers were no smarter or more likely to bloom than any of the other kids. The only way in which these students differed from their peers was in

Figure 3.3 The Self-Fulfilling Prophecy

A sad cycle in four acts.

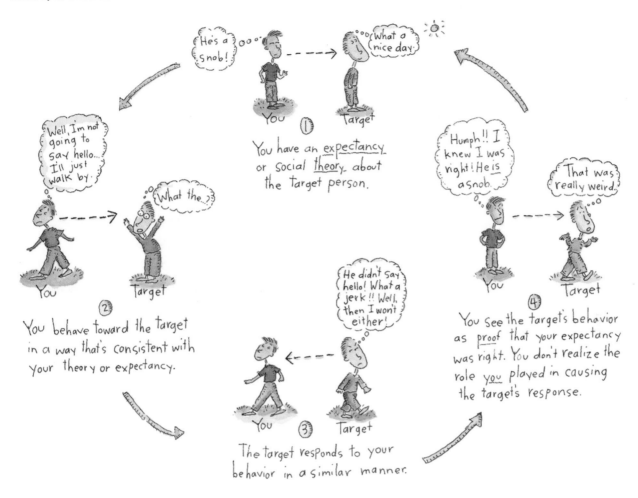

the minds of the teachers (neither the students nor their parents were told anything about the results of the test).

After creating the expectation in the teachers that certain students would do especially well, Rosenthal and Jacobson waited to see what would happen. They observed the classroom dynamics periodically, and, at the end of the school year, they gave all of the children an IQ test. Did the prophecy come true? Indeed it did. The students in each class who had been labeled as bloomers showed significantly greater gains in their IQ scores than the other students did (see Figure 3.4). The teachers' expectations had become reality. Rosenthal and Jacobson's findings have since been replicated in a number of both experimental and correlational studies (Jussim, 2012; Madon et al., 2003; 2008; 2011; Natanovich & Eden, 2008; Sorhagen, 2013).

What happened in the classrooms studied by Rosenthal and Jacobson (1968)? Did the teachers callously decide to give more attention and encouragement to the bloomers? Not at all. Most teachers are very dedicated and would be upset to learn that they favored some students over others. Far from being a conscious, deliberate act, the self-fulfilling prophecy is instead an example of automatic thinking (Chen & Bargh, 1997). Interestingly, the teachers in the Rosenthal and Jacobson study reported that they spent slightly less time with the students who were labeled as bloomers. In subsequent studies, however, teachers have been found to treat bloomers (the students they expect to do better) differently in four critical ways: They create a

Prophecy is the most gratuitous form of error.

—George Eliot
(Mary Ann Evans Cross), 1871

Figure 3.4 The Self-Fulfilling Prophecy: Percentage of First and Second Graders Who Improved on an IQ Test Over the Course of the School Year

Those whom the teachers expected to do well actually improved more than the other students.

(Figure adapted from Rosenthal & Jacobson, 1968. Reprinted with permission of R. Rosenthal.)

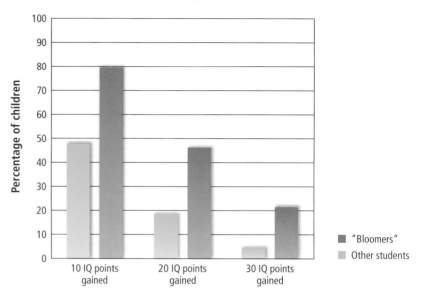

warmer emotional climate for bloomers, giving them more personal attention, encouragement, and support; they give bloomers more material to learn and material that is more difficult; they give bloomers more and better feedback on their work; and they give bloomers more opportunities to respond in class and give them longer to respond (Brophy, 1983; Rosenthal, 1994; Snyder, 1984).

In real life, of course, psychologists do not give teachers false expectations about how well their students will do. But teachers are only human, and they may acquire faulty expectations about their students based on the students' gender, race, social class, or family history. Any one of these factors could instill expectations in the minds of the teachers and lead to self-fulfilling prophecies, just as in the Rosenthal and Jacobson study. In fact, there is evidence that teachers in actual classrooms are especially likely to act in ways that confirm their low expectations of minority and disadvantaged students (Madon, Jussim, & Eccles, 1997; McKown & Weinstein, 2008). One study, for example, found that if first grade teachers had overly low expectations of their students, those students did worse on standardized tests of math, reading, and vocabulary 10 years later—especially if those children came from poor families (Sorhagen, 2013). That is, teachers who think a child from a low-income family doesn't have what it takes to succeed in school inadvertently acted in ways that made that child do more poorly in school. The magnitudes

Teachers can unintentionally make their expectations about their students come true by treating some students differently from others.

of these effects were small, amounting to a few points on standardized tests, indicating that low expectations do not doom students to be at the bottom of the class. Nonetheless, self-fulfilling prophecies are real and can make it harder for capable students to perform up to their true abilities. And, we should note, the same thing can happen outside the classroom, such as in the workplace, where bosses might influence their employees' behavior via self-fulfilling prophecies.

To summarize, we have seen that the amount of information we face every day is so vast that we have to reduce it to a manageable size. In addition, much of this information is ambiguous or difficult to decipher. One way we deal with this "blooming, buzzing confusion"—in William James's words—is to rely on schemas, which help us reduce the amount of information we need to take in and help us interpret ambiguous information. These schemas are applied quickly, effortlessly, and unintentionally; in short, they are one form of automatic thinking. But schemas are only one of several examples of how we automatically process information about the social world, as we will see next.

> It is a capital mistake to theorize before you have all the evidence. It biases the judgment.
> —Sherlock Holmes (Sir Arthur Conan Doyle), 1898

REVIEW QUESTIONS

1. Which of the following is the best summary of the function of schemas?
   a. Schemas usually result in erroneous judgments because of the self-fulfilling prophecy.
   b. Schemas are always beneficial because they help people organize the world and fill in the gaps in their knowledge.
   c. Schemas are very useful in helping people organize information about the world, but they are problematic when they result in self-fulfilling prophecies.
   d. Schemas are useful for helping us organize information about other people but not about events such as what we should do when eating in a restaurant.

2. Which of the following is *not* a way in which schemas can become accessible in people's minds?
   a. The more negative in content a schema is, the more likely it is to be accessible.
   b. Schemas can be accessible because of people's past experiences.
   c. Schemas can become temporarily accessible because of priming.
   d. Schemas can be accessible if they are related to our current goals.

3. Which of the following is the best example of a self-fulfilling prophecy?
   a. A teacher believes that boys are better at math than girls, but boys in his class do worse than girls in math.
   b. Bob thinks that members of the Alpha Beta Psi sorority are unfriendly and snobby. Whenever he meets members of this sorority, they are friendly toward him.
   c. Sarah is worried that her son is not gifted in music, but he does better at his piano lessons than she expected.
   d. Jill thinks her daughter is not a very good reader and doesn't spend much time reading to her. As a result her daughter falls behind in reading at school.

4. Suppose you're driving home from watching a scary movie about a hitchhiker who was a murderer when you see someone talking loudly with a friend. Because you saw the movie, you assume that you are witnessing an argument that will probably end in a fight. This is an example of
   a. priming.
   b. base rate information.
   c. belief perseverance.
   d. controlled thinking.

5. Rob is definitely not the most attractive guy in the dorms, but he is extremely confident about who he is and how he looks. He is convinced that most women find him to be very attractive, and he in fact usually gets dates with women who are much more attractive than he is. What is the best explanation of Rob's success?
   a. Self-affirmation theory
   b. Self-fulfilling prophecy
   c. The representativeness heuristic
   d. Holistic thinking

See page 620 for the answers.

Types of Automatic Thinking

3.2 **What are other types of automatic thinking and how do they operate?**

There are several other forms of automatic thinking that help us interpret the social world and make decisions, without necessarily intending to do so.

Automatic Goal Pursuit

When it comes to setting goals for ourselves, such as what career path to follow, we often do so carefully and consciously, deliberating for some time about what we want to do. That's not the only way, however, that we choose what goals to follow. In our everyday lives there are often competing goals, and the choice of which one to follow can happen automatically. Suppose, for example, that you are taking a difficult math course in which the professor grades on a curve, guaranteeing that only a few people will get As. A classmate you don't know very well tells you he is having difficulty with some of the material and asks whether you can have coffee and go over your class notes with him. On the one hand, you want to be helpful, satisfying your goal to be a caring, compassionate person. On the other hand, you want to satisfy your goal of doing well in the class and are hesitant to hurt your chances by raising someone else's grade. Which goal do you act on? You could mull this over for a while, consciously weighing your options. Often, however, it is our nonconscious minds that choose the goal for us, basing the decision in part on which goal has been recently activated or primed (Aarts & Elliot, 2012; DeMarree et al., 2012; Förster, Liberman, & Friedman, 2007; Hassin, 2013; Loersch & Payne, 2011; Marien, Custers, Hassin, & Aarts, 2012).

Social psychologists have tested this hypothesis by priming people's goals in a subtle way and then seeing if it influences their behavior. In a study by Azim Shariff and Ara Norenzayan (2007), for example, participants were asked to make sentences out of sets of provided words—such as *felt*, *she*, *eradicate*, *spirit*, and *the*—from which they could make a sentence like "She felt the spirit." Next, as part of what was supposedly a different study, participants played an economic game in which they were given ten $1 coins and asked to divide them up between themselves and the next participant. Only the next participant would know what they decided, and that participant wouldn't know who they were. Think for a moment what you would do in this situation. Here's an opportunity to make a quick 10 bucks, and there is a definite temptation to pocket all the coins. But you might feel a little guilty hoarding all the money and leaving nothing for the next person. This is one of those situations in which there is a devil on one of our shoulders ("Don't be a fool—take it all!") and an angel on the other ("Do unto others as you would have them do unto you"). In short, people want the money, but this conflicts with their goal to be nice to others. Which goal wins out?

It depends in part on which goal has been recently primed. Remember the sentence-unscrambling task people did first? For some participants, the words people were given had to do with God (spirit, divine, God, sacred, and prophet), which were designed to prime the goal of acting kindly to one's neighbor. In the control condition, people got neutral words. An important detail is that participants did not make a connection between the sentence-making task and the economics game—they thought the two tasks were completely unrelated. Even so, the people who made sentences out of the words having to do with God left significantly more money for the next participant ($4.56 on average) than did people who got the neutral words ($2.56 on average). And it turned out that it was not just words about God that primed the goal of being more altruistic. In a third condition, the sentence task contained nonreligious words that had to do with fairness to others, such as *civic* and *contract*. People in this condition left nearly as much money for the next person as did people primed with God words ($4.44 on average). Studies such as this one show that goals can be activated and influence people's behavior without their knowing it,

Research has found that people's goals can be activated unconsciously by their recent experiences. For example, someone who walks by a church might have the "Golden Rule" activated without knowing it, making him or her more likely to give money to a homeless person.

because people didn't realize that the words they got in the first task had anything to do with their decision about how to divide the money in the second task. The moral? Your decision about whether to help your classmate in your math class might depend on which goals have recently been primed. If you had just walked by your place of worship, for example, or read a book in which people were kind to others, you might be especially likely to help your classmate.

> Outside consciousness there rolls a vast tide of life which is perhaps more important to us than the little isle of our thoughts which lies within our ken.
>
> —E. S. Dallas (*1866*)

Automatic Decision Making

What about when you have an important decision to make, such as which apartment to rent or what car to buy? Here again, we often approach such decisions slowly and deliberately, weighing the alternatives carefully. Sometimes, though, we might be better off letting our automatic minds get involved. Suppose, for example, that you are hunting for an apartment and have looked at a dozen alternatives. You've gathered a lot of information—the rents, their size, where they're located, which ones have free Internet access, who your neighbors would be, and so on. It's time to make a decision so you sit down to sift through all of the information so that you can analyze it and make the best choice. But is that the best way to proceed? Consider this alternative: Instead of consciously thinking about the apartments, what if you distracted yourself by doing something completely unrelated, such as doing some homework, and then seeing which apartment feels like the right choice?

Research shows that too much conscious reflection about a choice can get in the way of a good decision, and that sometimes a period of distraction actually helps us make the best choice (Bargh, 2011; Bos & Dijksterhuis, 2012; Creswell, Bursley, & Satpute, 2013; Dijksterhuis & Nordgren, 2006; Nordgren et al., 2011; Wilson, 2002). We are not recommending, however, that you give up conscious thought altogether. First, for distraction to improve a decision, people must have a conscious goal to make a good choice. That is, consciousness enters into the process at the beginning by setting the agenda, such as trying to choose the best apartment. Second, conscious thought is superior when the decision requires a series of simple rules. For example, if we asked you to compute the product of 143×657, it would not help you to distract yourself by doing your homework. When there are a clear set of rules to follow, such as how to multiply two numbers, it is best to follow those rules consciously and deliberately.

Distraction helps the most when the decision requires people to integrate a lot of complex information, such as comparing the pros and cons of a dozen apartments. In this case our unconscious minds often do a better job of sifting through the information and figuring out the best alternative. In everyday life, of course, decisions often involve both of these processes—sifting through complex information (which is best done unconsciously) but also following simple rules, such as "whatever else, the apartment has to have free Internet access" (which is best done consciously). The best approach, then, is to utilize both parts of our mind. Indeed, one study found that people made the best choice of apartments when they spent 2 minutes thinking consciously about the alternatives and then 2 minutes distracting themselves by solving anagrams (Nordgren, Bos, & Dikksterhuis, 2011). Participants in this condition picked better apartments than did participants who engaged only in conscious thought alone or only did the anagram task.

Automatic Thinking and Metaphors About the Body and the Mind

Suppose that, as you are leaving a store one day, a stranger approaches you and says that her purse was just stolen and asks if you could spare a couple of dollars so that she could take the bus home. On the one hand, the woman could be telling the truth and really need someone to help her out, but on the other, she could be making the whole thing up in order to get money to buy drugs or alcohol. Will you decide to help her? As we have just seen, when faced with ambiguous situations such as this one, people rely on schemas and that are accessible in their minds. If the schema of helpfulness was just primed—maybe you just saw a clerk in the store go out of her way to help someone—you will be more likely to help the stranger.

But what if we told you that your decision will also depend on whether you just smelled something fresh and clean? Suppose, for example, that some window washers were cleaning the glass outside the store and that you could smell the citrusy aroma of the cleaning solution they were using. As preposterous as it may sound, research shows that that the scent of cleanliness increases the degree to which people trust strangers and their willingness to help others (Helzer & Pizarro, 2011; Meier, Schnall, Schwarz, & Bargh, 2012).

It turns out that it is not just schemas that can be primed and influence people's judgments and decisions. The mind is connected to the body, and when we think about something or someone, we do so with reference to how our bodies are reacting. Sometimes this is pretty straightforward; if we are tired, for example, we might interpret the world more negatively than if we are feeling peppy and full of energy. What is less obvious is that metaphors about the body and social judgments also influence our judgments and decisions (Barsalou, 2008; Lakoff & Johnson, 1999; Zhong & Liljenquist, 2006). For example, cleanliness is usually associated with morality, and dirtiness with immorality, as seen by such phrases as "washing away our sins" and "dirty thoughts." These are just metaphors, of course—thoughts aren't literally dirty. But priming metaphors about the relationship between the mind and the body influence what we do and think (Landau, Meier, & Keefer, 2010).

Will this person's answers to the questionnaire be influenced by how heavy the clipboard is? Why or why not?

In one study, for example, participants sat down in a room that had just been sprayed with citrus-scented Windex or in a room with no odor. As the researchers predicted, those who were in the room that smelled clean were more trusting of a stranger and more likely to donate time and money to a charity (Liljenquist, Zhong, & Galinsky, 2010). In another study, participants who held a cup of hot coffee thought that a stranger was friendlier than did participants who held a cup of iced coffee. Holding the hot or cold beverage seems to have activated the metaphor that friendly people are "warm" and unfriendly people are "cold," thereby influencing people's impression of the stranger (Williams & Bargh, 2008). In yet another study, college students who filled out a survey attached to a heavy clipboard thought that student opinion should be given more consideration on a local campus issue than did students who filled out the survey attached to a light clipboard. Why? There is a metaphor that associates weight with importance, as indicated by the phrases, "carries weight" and "adding weight to the argument." Apparently, feeling the weight of the heavy clipboard primed this metaphor, causing participants to believe that student opinion should be given more weight (Jostmann, Lakens, & Schubert, 2009).

In each of these studies, a physical sensation (smelling something clean, feeling a hot beverage, holding something heavy) activated a metaphor that influenced judgments about a completely unrelated topic or person. This research shows that it is not just schemas that can be primed in ways that influence our judgments and behavior; priming metaphors about the relationship between the mind and the body can too (IJzerman & Semin, 2010).

Mental Strategies and Shortcuts: Judgmental Heuristics

Another form of automatic thinking is to apply specific rules and shortcuts when thinking about the social world. These shortcuts are, for the most part, extremely useful, but they can sometimes lead to erroneous inferences about the world. For example, think back to your decision of where to apply to college. One strategy you might have taken was to investigate thoroughly every one of the more than 3,000 colleges and universities in the United States. You could have read every catalog from cover to cover, visited every campus, and interviewed as many faculty members, deans, and students as you could find. Getting tired yet? Such a strategy would, of course, be prohibitively time-consuming and costly. Instead of considering every college and university, most high school students narrow down their choices to a small number of options and find out what they can about these schools.

This example is like many other decisions and judgments we make in everyday life. When deciding which job to accept, what car to buy, or whom to marry, we usually do not conduct a thorough search of every option ("OK, it's time for me to get married; I think I'll consult the Census Bureau's list of unmarried adults in my town and begin my interviews tomorrow"). Instead, we use mental strategies and shortcuts that make the decisions easier, allowing us to get on with our lives without turning every decision into a major research project. These shortcuts do not always lead to the best decision. For example, if you had exhaustively studied every college and university in the United States, maybe you would have found one that you liked better than the one where you are now. Mental shortcuts are efficient, however, and usually lead to good decisions in a reasonable amount of time (Gigerenzer, 2008; Gilovich & Griffin, 2002; Griffin & Kahneman, 2003; Kahneman, 2011; Nisbett & Ross, 1980).

What shortcuts do people use? One, as we have already seen, is to use schemas to understand new situations. Rather than starting from scratch when examining our options, we often apply our previous knowledge and schemas. We have many such schemas, about everything from colleges and universities (e.g., what Ivy League colleges and big Midwestern universities are like) to other people (e.g., teachers' beliefs about the abilities of students from a low-income family). When making specific kinds of judgments and decisions, however, we do not always have a ready-made schema to apply. At other times, there are too many schemas that could apply, and it is not clear which one to use. What do we do?

At times like these, people often use mental shortcuts called **judgmental heuristics** (Gigerenzer, 2008; Shah & Oppenheimer, 2008; Tversky & Kahneman, 1974). The word *heuristic* comes from the Greek word meaning "discover"; in the field of social cognition, heuristics are the mental shortcuts people use to make judgments quickly and efficiently. Before discussing these heuristics, we should note that they do not guarantee that people will make accurate inferences about the world. Sometimes heuristics are inadequate for the job at hand or are misapplied, leading to faulty judgments. In fact, a good deal of research in social cognition has focused on just such mistakes in reasoning; we will document many such mental errors in this chapter. As we discuss the mental strategies that sometimes lead to errors, however, keep in mind that people use heuristics for a reason: Most of the time, they are highly functional and serve us well.

Judgmental Heuristics
Mental shortcuts people use to make judgments quickly and efficiently

HOW EASILY DOES IT COME TO MIND? THE AVAILABILITY HEURISTIC   Suppose you are sitting in a restaurant with several friends one night when it becomes clear that the waiter has made a mistake with one of the orders. Your friend Alphonse ordered the veggie burger with onion rings but instead got the veggie burger with fries. "Oh, well," he says, "I'll just eat the fries." This starts a discussion of whether he should have sent back his order, and some of the gang accuse Alphonse of not being assertive enough. Suppose he turns to you and asks, "Do you think I'm an unassertive person?" How would you answer?

One way, as we have seen, would be to call on a ready-made schema that provides the answer. If you know Alphonse well and have already formed a picture of how assertive he is, you can recite your answer easily and quickly: "Don't worry, Alphonse, if I had to deal with a used-car salesman, you'd be the first person I'd call." Suppose, though, that you've never really thought about how assertive Alphonse is and have to think about your answer. In these situations, we often rely on how easily different examples come to mind. If it is easy to think of times Alphonse acted assertively (e.g., the time he stopped someone from cutting in line in front of him at the movies), you will conclude that Alphonse is a pretty assertive guy. If it is easier to think of times Alphonse acted unassertively (e.g., the time he let a salesperson talk him into an expensive cell phone plan), you will conclude that he is pretty unassertive.

This mental rule of thumb is called the **availability heuristic**, which is basing a judgment on the ease with which you can bring something to mind (Caruso, 2008; Pachur, Hertwig, & Steinmann, 2012; Schwarz & Vaughn, 2002; Tversky & Kahneman, 1973). There are many situations in which the availability heuristic is a good strategy to use. If you can easily recall several instances when Alphonse stood up for himself, he probably is an assertive person; if you can easily recall several times when he was timid or meek, he probably is not. The trouble with the availability heuristic is that sometimes what is easiest to remember is not typical of the overall picture, leading to faulty conclusions.

When physicians are diagnosing diseases, for example, it might seem relatively straightforward for them to observe people's symptoms and figure out what disease, if any, they have. Sometimes, though, symptoms might be a sign of several different disorders. Do doctors use the availability heuristic, whereby they are more likely to consider diagnoses that come to mind easily? Several studies of medical diagnoses suggest that the answer is yes (Weber, 1993).

Consider Dr. Robert Marion's diagnosis of Nicole, a 9-year-old girl who came to his office one day. Nicole was normal in every way except that once or twice a year she had strange neurological attacks characterized by disorientation, insomnia, slurred words, and strange mewing sounds. Nicole had been hospitalized three times, had seen over a dozen specialists, and had undergone many diagnostic tests, including CT scans, brain-wave tests, and virtually every blood test there is. Still, the doctors were stumped. Within minutes of seeing her, however, Dr. Marion correctly diagnosed her problem as a rare inherited blood disorder called acute intermittent porphyria (AIP). The blood chemistry of people with this disorder often gets out of sync, causing a variety of neurological symptoms. It can be controlled with a careful diet and by avoiding certain medications.

How did Dr. Marion diagnose Nicole's disorder so quickly when so many other doctors failed to do so? He had just finished writing a book on the genetic diseases of historical figures, including a chapter on King George III of England, who—you guessed it—suffered from AIP. "I didn't make the diagnosis because I'm a brilliant diagnostician or because I'm a sensitive listener," Dr. Marion admitted. "I succeeded where others failed because [Nicole] and I happened to run into each other in exactly the right place, at exactly the right time" (Marion, 1995, p. 40).

In other words, Dr. Marion used the availability heuristic. AIP happened to come to mind quickly because Dr. Marion had just read about it, making the diagnosis easy. Although this was a happy outcome of the use of the availability heuristic, it is easy to see how it can go wrong. As Dr. Marion says, "Doctors are just like everyone else. We go to the movies, watch TV, read newspapers and novels. If we happen to see a patient who has symptoms of a rare disease that was featured on the previous night's 'Movie of the Week,' we're more likely to consider that condition when making a diagnosis" (Marion, 1995, p. 40). That's fine if your disease happens to be the topic of last night's

Availability Heuristic

A mental rule of thumb whereby people base a judgment on the ease with which they can bring something to mind

Physicians have been found to use the availability heuristic when making diagnoses. Their diagnoses are influenced by how easily they can bring different diseases to mind.

movie. It's not so good if your illness isn't available in your doctor's memory, as was the case with the 12 doctors Nicole had seen previously.

Do people use the availability heuristic to make judgments about themselves? It might seem as if we have well-developed ideas about our own personalities, such as how assertive we are, but we often lack firm schemas about our own traits (Markus, 1977). We thus might make judgments about ourselves based on how easily we can recall examples of our own behavior. To see if this is true, researchers performed a clever experiment in which they altered how easy it was for people to remember examples of their own past behaviors (Schwarz et al., 1991). In one condition, they asked people to think of 6 times they had acted assertively. Most people readily thought of times they turned down persistent salespeople and stood up for themselves. In another condition, the researchers asked people to think of 12 times they had acted assertively. These participants had to try very hard to think of this many examples. All participants were then asked to rate how assertive they thought they really were.

The question was, did people use the availability heuristic (the ease with which they could bring examples to mind) to infer how assertive they were? As seen on the left side of Figure 3.5, they did. People asked to think of six examples rated themselves as relatively assertive because it was easy to think of this many examples. People asked to think of 12 examples rated themselves as relatively unassertive because it was difficult to think of that many. Other people were asked to think of 6 or 12 times they had acted unassertively, and similar results were found; those asked to think of six examples rated themselves as relatively unassertive, whereas those asked to think of 12 examples had trouble doing so and thus rated themselves as relatively assertive (see the right side of Figure 3.5). In short, people use the availability heuristic when making judgments about themselves and other people (Caruso, 2008). Recently, a devious college professor used this technique to improve his course evaluations. He asked his students to list either 2 or 10 ways that the course could be improved and then to rate their overall impression of the course. Who gave the course the highest ratings? Those asked to list 10 ways it could be improved, because they found it hard to think of that many examples and thus thought, "If I can't come up with that many criticisms, it must be a great course!" (Fox, 2006).

Figure 3.5 Availability and Assertiveness

People asked to think of 6 times they had behaved assertively found it easy to do so and concluded that they were pretty assertive people. People asked to think of 12 times they had behaved assertively found it difficult to think of so many examples and concluded that they were not very assertive people (see the left-hand side of the graph). Similar results were found among people asked to think of 6 or 12 times they had behaved unassertively (see the right-hand side of the graph). These results show that people often base their judgments on availability, or how easily they can bring information to mind.

(Based on Schwarz et al., 1991)

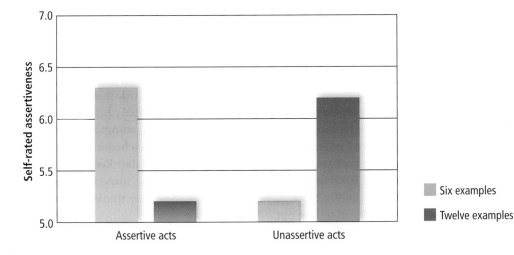

Representativeness Heuristic

A mental shortcut whereby people classify something according to how similar it is to a typical case

Base Rate Information

Information about the frequency of members of different categories in the population

HOW SIMILAR IS A TO B? THE REPRESENTATIVENESS HEURISTIC   Suppose you attend a state university in New York. At the student union one day, you meet a student named Brian. Brian has blond hair and a deep tan, seems to be very mellow, and likes to go to the beach. What state do you think Brian is from? Because Brian matches a common stereotype for Californians, you might guess that that is his home state. If so, you would be using the **representativeness heuristic**, which is a mental shortcut we use to classify something according to how similar it is to a typical case—such as how similar Brian is to your conception of Californians (Kahneman & Frederick, 2002; Kahneman & Tversky, 1973; Lonsdale & North, 2012; Spina et al., 2010).

Categorizing things according to representativeness is often a perfectly reasonable thing to do. If we did not use the representativeness heuristic, how else would we decide where Brian comes from? Should we just randomly choose a state, without making any attempt to judge his similarity to our conception of students from New York State versus out-of-state students? Actually, there is another source of information we might use. If we knew nothing about Brian, it would be wise to guess that he was from New York State, because at state universities there are more in-state than out-of-state students. If we guessed New York State, we would be using what is called **base rate information**, information about the relative frequency of members of different categories in the population (e.g., the percentage of students at New York state universities who are from New York).

What do people do when they have both base rate information (e.g., knowing that there are more New Yorkers than Californians at a university) and contradictory information about the person in question (e.g., knowing that Brian is blond and mellow and likes to hang out at the beach)? Kahneman and Tversky (1973) found that people do not use base rate information sufficiently, paying most attention to how representative the information about the specific person is of the general category (e.g., Californians). Although this is not a bad strategy if the information about the person is very reliable, it can get us into trouble when the information is flimsy. Given that the base rate of Californians attending state universities in New York is low, you would need to have very good evidence that this person is a Californian before ignoring the base rate and guessing that he is one of the few exceptions. And given that it is not that unusual to find people from eastern states who have blond hair, are laid-back, and like to go to the beach, you would be wise to use the base rate in this instance.

We don't mean to imply that people totally ignore base rate information (Koehler, 1993, 1996). Baseball managers consider the overall likelihood of left-handed batters getting a hit off of left-handed pitchers when deciding whom to send up as a pinch hitter, and birdwatchers consider the prevalence of different species of birds in their area when identifying individual birds ("That probably wasn't a bay-breasted warbler, because they've never been seen in this area"). The point is that people often focus too much on individual characteristics of what they observe ("But it did seem to have a chestnut-colored throat; hmm, maybe it was a bay-breasted warbler") and too little on the base rates.

Throughout history, for example, people have assumed that the cure for a disease must resemble—be representative of—the symptoms of the disease, even when this wasn't the case. At one time, eating the lungs of a fox was thought to be a cure for asthma, because foxes have a strong respiratory system (Mill, 1843). Such a reliance on representativeness may even impede the discovery of the actual cause of a disease. Around the turn of the twentieth century, an editorial in a Washington newspaper denounced the foolhardy use of federal funds to research far-fetched ideas about the causes of yellow fever, such as the absurd contention of one Walter Reed that yellow fever was caused by, of all things, a mosquito (which, of course, turned out to be the cause; Nisbett & Ross, 1980). How do heuristics influence your thinking? Take the quiz in the following Try It! to find out.

TRY IT!

Reasoning Quiz

Answer each of the following questions.

1. Consider the letter *r* in the English language. Do you think this letter occurs more often as the first letter of words (e.g., *rope*) or more often as the third letter of words (e.g., *park*)?
   a. More often as the first letter
   b. More often as the third letter
   c. About equally often as the first and as the third letter

2. Which of these do you think cause more fatalities in the United States?
   a. Accidents
   b. Strokes
   c. Accidents and strokes in approximately equal numbers

3. Suppose you flipped a fair coin six times. Which sequence is more likely to occur: HTTHTH or HHHTTT? (H = heads, T = tails)?
   a. HTTHTH is more likely.
   b. HHHTTT is more likely.
   c. Both sequences are equally likely.

4. After flipping a coin and observing the sequence TTTTT, what is the probability that the next flip will be heads?
   a. Less than .5
   b. .5
   c. Greater than .5

See page 620 for the answers.

PERSONALITY TESTS AND THE REPRESENTATIVENESS HEURISTIC   Suppose you took a personality test, such as one of the many that are available online, and received the following feedback:

> You have a need for other people to like and admire you, and yet you tend to be critical of yourself. While you have some personality weaknesses, you are generally able to compensate for them. You have considerable unused capacity that you have not turned to your advantage. Disciplined and self-controlled on the outside, you tend to be worrisome and insecure on the inside. At times you have serious doubts as to whether you have made the right decision or done the right thing. You prefer a certain amount of change and variety and become dissatisfied when hemmed in by restrictions and limitations. You also pride yourself as an independent thinker and do not accept others' statements without satisfactory proof. But you have found it unwise to be too frank in revealing yourself to others. At times you are extroverted, affable, and sociable, while at other times you are introverted, wary, and reserved. Some of your aspirations tend to be rather unrealistic. Security is one of your major goals in life.

"Wow," you might think. "This test is amazing; it is uncanny how well it captured who I am." If so, you are not alone. Bertram Forer (1949) gave this feedback to a group of students and asked them to rate how well it described them, on a scale from 0 = very poor to 5 = excellent. The average rating was 4.26—a phenomenon that has come to be known as the "Barnum effect" after the circus owner and showman P. T. Barnum.

Why do most people believe that this personality description describes them so well? One culprit is the representativeness heuristic: The statements are vague enough that virtually everyone can find a past behavior that is similar to (representative of) the feedback. Consider the statement, "At times you have serious doubts as to whether you have made the right decision or done the right thing." All of us can think of times this was true of us—that is, of examples that are representative of this statement. Who hasn't second-guessed themselves about an important decision, such as where to go to college or what major to choose? Similarly, all of us can think of times when we were independent thinkers and times when we revealed too much about ourselves. The reason the feedback seems to describe us so well is that we do not go beyond the representative examples that come to mind and think, "Actually, there are just as many times when I didn't feel or act this way." So, be wary of magazine quizzes and horoscopes that give generic feedback, which could apply to just about anyone.

REVIEW QUESTIONS

1. Which of the following is the best summary of research on automatic goal pursuit?
   a. People can only select which goals to work toward using controlled thinking.
   b. People often pursue goals that have been recently primed, without realizing that that is why they are pursuing the goal.
   c. People often pursue goals that have been recently primed, but only if they are consciously aware that the goal has been primed.
   d. People never choose their goals consciously; they only pursue automatically primed goals.

2. Suppose you are buying a new home and have looked at several different houses. According to research on automatic decision making, what would be the best way for you to make up your mind about which one to buy?
   a. Distract yourself by working on puzzles and then choose a house.
   b. Think consciously about the alternatives and then make up your mind.
   c. Spend a few minutes thinking consciously about the alternatives and then several minutes distracting yourself by working on puzzles.
   d. Get a good night's sleep and then choose a house when you first wake up in the morning.

3. Suppose you have invited a new acquaintance over to your apartment and want to make a good impression; in other words, you want this person to like you. Which of the following should you do?

   a. Serve the person a warm drink and hope that he or she holds it in their hands while you are talking to him or her.
   b. Serve the person a cold drink and hope that he or she holds it in their hands while you are talking to him or her.
   c. Bake some bread before the person comes over so that the apartment smells nice.
   d. Serve the person a snack on a very heavy plate.

4. Over Thanksgiving break, your parents ask you if you can think of 12 reasons why your college is better than its archrival. You find it hard to come up with many reasons and end up thinking, "Hmm, maybe the schools aren't all that different." Which of the following mental strategies did you probably use to reach this conclusion?
   a. The representativeness heuristic
   b. Base rate information
   c. The anchoring and adjustment heuristic
   d. The availability heuristic

5. According to research in social psychology, why do many people believe that their horoscopes are accurate descriptions of who they are and what is likely to happen to them?
   a. Horoscopes are written in a vague way so that most people view them as representative of their personalities and past behaviors.
   b. Horoscopes trigger automatic decision making.
   c. People find it difficult to bring to mind examples that are similar to the horoscope.
   d. Horoscopes automatically prime people's life goals.

See page 620 for the answers.

Cultural Differences in Social Cognition

3.3   How does culture influence social thinking?

It may have occurred to you to wonder whether the kinds of automatic thinking we have been discussing are present in all people throughout the world, or whether they are more common in some cultures than in others. If so, you are in good company; social psychologists have become increasingly interested in the influence of culture on social cognition.

Cultural Determinants of Schemas

Although everyone uses schemas to understand the world, the *content* of our schemas is influenced by the culture in which we live. One researcher, for example, interviewed a Scottish settler and a local Bantu herdsman in Swaziland, a small country in southeastern Africa (Bartlett, 1932). Both men had been present at a complicated cattle transaction that had occurred a year earlier. The Scottish man needed to consult his records to recall how many cattle were bought and sold and for how much. The Bantu man promptly recited from memory every detail of the transaction, including from whom each ox and cow had been bought, the color of each animal, and the price of each transaction. The Bantu people's memory for cattle is so good that they do not bother to brand them; if a cow happens to wander away and gets mixed up with a neighbor's herd, the owner simply goes over and takes it back, having no trouble distinguishing his animal from the dozens of others.

Clearly, an important source of our schemas is the culture in which we grow up. Cattle are a central part of the Bantu economy and culture, and therefore the Bantu have well-developed schemas about cattle. To an American, one cow might look like any other, though this person might have well-developed schemas, and hence an excellent memory, for transactions on the New York Stock Exchange or the latest contestants on *The Voice*. Schemas are a very important way by which cultures exert their influence—namely, by instilling mental structures that influence the very way we understand and interpret the world. In Chapter 5, we will see that people in different cultures have fundamentally different schemas about themselves and the social world, with some interesting consequences (Wang & Ross, 2007). Here we point out that the schemas our culture teaches us strongly influence what we notice and remember about the world.

Holistic versus Analytic Thinking

Culture influences social cognition in other fundamental ways. An analogy that is often used is that the human mind is like a toolbox filled with specific tools to help people think about and act in the social world. All humans have access to the same tools, but the culture in which they grow up can influence the ones they use the most (Norenzayan & Heine, 2005). If you live in a house that has screws instead of nails, you will use your screwdriver more than a hammer, but if your house contains nails and not screws, the screwdriver won't get much use.

By the same token, culture can influence the kinds of thinking people automatically use to understand their worlds. Not *all* kinds of thinking, mind you. The kinds of automatic thinking we have discussed so far, such as unconscious thinking and the use of schemas, appear to be used by all humans. But some basic ways in which people typically perceive and think about the world *are* shaped by culture. To illustrate these differences, take a quick look at the top picture on this page. Okay, now take a quick look at the picture right beneath it: Did you notice any differences between the two pictures? Your answer might depend on the culture in which you grew up. Richard Nisbett and his colleagues have found that people who grow up in Western cultures tend to have an **analytic thinking style**, a type of thinking in which people focus on the properties of objects without considering their surrounding context. For example, Westerners are most likely to focus on the planes because they are the main objects in the pictures. They are thus more likely to notice differences in these objects, such as the fact that the passenger plane has more windows in the second picture than in the top one (Masuda & Nisbett, 2006). People who grow up in East Asian cultures (e.g., China, Japan, or Korea) tend to have a **holistic thinking style**, a type of thinking in which people focus on the overall context, particularly the ways in which objects relate to each other (Miyamoto, 2013; Nisbett, 2003; Norenzayan & Nisbett, 2000).

For example, East Asians are more likely to notice differences in the backgrounds of the pictures, such as the fact that the shape of the control tower changes from one to the other. (Note that in the actual study, people saw 20-second videos of these scenes and tried to find all the differences between them. The pictures on the

Analytic Thinking Style

A type of thinking in which people focus on the properties of objects without considering their surrounding context; this type of thinking is common in Western cultures

Holistic Thinking Style

A type of thinking in which people focus on the overall context, particularly the ways in which objects relate to each other; this type of thinking is common in East Asian cultures (e.g., China, Japan, and Korea)

Take a quick look at these two photos and see if you notice any differences between them. As discussed in the text, the differences you notice may have to do with the culture in which you grew up.

previous page are the last scenes from these two videos.) In Chapter 4, we will see that these differences in thinking styles also influence how we perceive emotions in other people. Suppose, for example, that you ran into a classmate who was surrounded by a group of friends. If you grew up in the West, you would likely focus only on your classmate's face (the object of your attention) to judge how he or she is feeling. If you grew up in East Asia, you would likely scan everyone's faces in the group (the overall context) and use this information to judge how your classmate is feeling (Ito, Masuda, & Li, 2013; Masuda, Ellsworth, & Mesquita, 2008).

Where do these differences in holistic versus analytic thinking come from? Richard Nisbett (2003) suggests that they are rooted in the different philosophical traditions of the East versus West. Eastern thought has been shaped by the ideas of Confucianism, Taoism, and Buddhism, which emphasize the connectedness and relativity of all things. Western thought is rooted in the Greek philosophical tradition of Aristotle and Plato, which focuses on the laws governing objects, independent of their context. Recent research suggests, however, that the different thinking styles might also stem from actual differences in the environments in the different cultures. Yuri Miyamoto, Richard Nisbett, and Takahiko Masuda took photographs in randomly chosen locations in cities in Japan and the United States. They matched the scenes as best they could; for example, the sizes of the cities were equivalent, as were the buildings that were photographed in each city (e.g., hotels and public elementary schools). The researchers hypothesized that the scenes in the Japanese cities would be "busier"—that is, they would contain more objects that competed for people's attention—than the scenes in the American cities. They were right. The Japanese scenes contained significantly more information and objects than the American scenes.

Could this be one reason why Americans focus more on a foreground object, whereas East Asians focus more on the overall context? To find out, Miyamoto and her colleagues did a second study in which they showed the pictures of American or Japanese cities to a sample of American and Japanese college students. The students were asked to imagine that they were in the scene depicted in each picture, with the idea that the Japanese pictures would prime holistic thinking, whereas the American pictures would prime analytic thinking. Then the students completed the same airplane picture task described above, in which they tried to detect the differences between two similar pictures. As predicted, the people who saw the photos of Japanese cities were more likely to detect changes in the *background* of the test pictures, whereas people who saw the pictures of the American cities were more likely to detect changes in the *main object* of the pictures. This finding suggests that people in all cultures are capable of thinking holistically or analytically (they have the same tools in their mental toolbox), but that the environment in which people live, or even which environment has been recently primed, triggers a reliance on one of the styles (Boduroglu, Shah, & Nisbett, 2009; Cheung, Chudek, & Heine, 2011; Norenzayan, Choi, & Peng, 2007; Varnum et al., 2010).

REVIEW QUESTIONS

1. Which of the following is true of the holistic thinking style?
   a. It involves a focus on the properties of objects without considering their surrounding context.
   b. People living in the West can think holistically if they are primed with pictures taken in Japan.
   c. The holistic style of thinking has a genetic basis.
   d. It may have its roots in the Greek philosophic traditions of Aristotle and Plato.

2. Which of the following is true about cultural differences in social thinking?
   a. Although everyone uses schemas to understand the world, the content of those schemas is influenced by the culture in which they live.
   b. Schemas influence what people notice in the world but have no influence on what they remember.

c. Schemas influence what people remember but have no influence on what they notice in the world.

d. Culture has no influence on automatic thinking.

3. Which is the definition of analytic thinking?
   a. A type of thinking in which people focus on the overall context, particularly the ways in which objects relate to each other.
   b. A type of thinking in which people focus on the properties of objects without considering their surrounding context.
   c. Thinking that is conscious, intentional, voluntary, and effortful.
   d. Thinking that is nonconscious, unintentional, involuntary, and effortless.

4. Where do differences in holistic versus analytic thinking come from?
   a. Genetic differences between Asians and non-Asian Westerners
   b. Different educational systems in the East versus the West
   c. Different weather patterns in the East versus the West
   d. Different philosophical traditions of the East versus the West

5. Researchers took photographs in randomly chosen locations in cities in Japan and the United States. They found that on average, city scenes in Japan contained more:
   a. businesses and advertisements.
   b. people and residences.
   c. objects that competed for people's attention.
   d. buildings and concrete.

See page 620 for the answers.

Controlled Social Cognition: High-Effort Thinking

3.4 **What are some of the drawbacks of controlled thinking, and how can we improve its effectiveness?**

It may have struck you as odd that we have spent so much of this chapter on automatic thinking, when controlled thinking is one of the hallmarks of what it is to be human. We are the only species (as far as we know) that has the ability to engage in conscious reflection about ourselves and the outside world, and we often use that ability to great purpose, solving difficult problems and planning for the future. After all, we are the species that has discovered the cures for fatal diseases, built architectural wonders, and put people on the moon. And we did so at least in part with **controlled thinking**, which is defined as thinking that is conscious, intentional, voluntary, and effortful. People can usually turn this on or turn off at will and are fully aware of what they are thinking. Further, this kind of thought is effortful in the sense that it requires mental energy. People have the capacity to think in a conscious, controlled way about only one thing at a time; they cannot be thinking about what they will eat for lunch today at the same time they are thinking through a complex math problem (Weber & Johnson, 2009).

So why so much emphasis on automatic thinking? The reason is that in the past few decades, social psychologists have discovered that this kind of thinking is much more powerful and prevalent than previously believed. As we saw earlier in this chapter, people's ability to think quickly and nonconsciously is quite impressive and is critical to our survival. Nonetheless, some social psychologists believe that the pendulum has swung too far in favor of automatic thinking and that we have underestimated the value and power of controlled thinking (Baumeister & Masicampo, 2010; Baumeister, Masicampo, & Vohs, 2011). A lively debate has ensued over the relative importance of each type of thought.

Controlled Thinking

Thinking that is conscious, intentional, voluntary, and effortful

My first act of free will shall be to believe in free will.

—WILLIAM JAMES

Controlled Thinking and Free Will

One focus of this debate is on the age-old question of free will (Knobe et al., 2012). Do we really have control over our actions, such that we can freely choose what to do at any given point in time? Maybe not as much as we think, if our behavior is under the control of automatic thought processes of which we are unaware.

"Well," you might reply, "I know that I have free will because I can decide right now whether to scratch my head, close this book, or stand up and dance like a chicken." Are you done with your chicken dance now? If so, consider this: Although it certainly seems like our ability to choose what we do demonstrates the existence of free will, it turns out that it is not that simple. Daniel Wegner (2002, 2004; Ebert & Wegner, 2011) demonstrated that there can be an *illusion* of free will that is very much like the "correlation does not equal causation" problem we discussed in Chapter 2. Your thought "I think I'll do the chicken dance now" and your subsequent behavior (flapping your arms and hopping around the room) are correlated, making it seem like the thought caused the action. But they might actually have been produced by a third variable—namely, an unconscious intention that caused both the conscious thought and the behavior.

Perhaps an example other than chicken dancing will make this clearer. Suppose you are sitting on the couch watching television and have the thought, "A bowl of ice cream sure would taste good right now." So you get up and go to the freezer and scoop out a serving of your favorite flavor. But maybe, as you were watching television, the desire for ice cream arose unconsciously first (perhaps primed by something you saw in a commercial). This unconscious desire led both to the conscious thought that you wanted ice cream and to your decision to get up and go to the freezer. In other words, the conscious thought "I want ice cream" was a consequence of an unconscious process, and was not the cause of your decision to go to the freezer. After all, sometimes people find themselves on the way to the refrigerator *without* having had the conscious thought that it was time for a snack. Their unconscious desire triggered the action without any intervening conscious thought. As another example, people who are able to choose their lottery numbers are more confident that they will win than people who are assigned numbers, even though the probability is the same (Langer, 1975). And what sports fans haven't felt that they have helped their favorite team by crossing their fingers or donning their lucky hat at a key moment in the game?

As these examples show, people sometimes believe that they are exerting more control over events than they really are. But it can also work the other way: People can actually be controlling things more than they realize. A number of years ago, a new technique called facilitated communication was developed to allow communication-impaired people, such as those with autism and cerebral palsy, to express themselves. A trained facilitator held the fingers and arm of a communication-impaired client at a computer keyboard to make it easier for the client to type answers to questions. This technique caused great excitement, because it seemed that people who had been unable to communicate with the outside world suddenly were able to do so, voicing all sorts of thoughts and feelings with the aid of the facilitator. Parents were thrilled by the sudden opportunity to communicate with their previously silent children.

Sadly, facilitated communication was soon discredited when it became clear that it was not the communication-impaired person who was doing the typing but, unwittingly, the facilitator. In one well-designed study, researchers asked separate questions over headphones of the facilitator and the communication-impaired person. The facilitator might have heard, "How do you feel about today's weather?" while the communication-impaired person heard, "How did you like your lunch today?" The answers that were typed matched the questions the facilitator heard (e.g., "I wish it were sunnier"), not the ones posed to the communication-impaired client (Mostert, 2010; Wegner, Fuller, & Sparrow, 2003; Wegner, Sparrow, & Winerman, 2004; Wheeler et al., 1993). The facilitators were not deliberately faking it; they genuinely believed that it was the communication-impaired person who was choosing what to type and that they were simply helping them move their fingers on the keyboard—but in fact, it was the facilitators doing the typing.

Facilitated communication was developed to allow communication-impaired people to express themselves. Unfortunately, it appears to be the case that the facilitators were unwittingly controlling the communications.

These examples illustrate that there can be a disconnect between our conscious sense of how much we are causing our own actions and how much we really are causing them. Sometimes we overestimate the amount of control we have, as when we believe that wearing our lucky hat will help our favorite sports team score a goal. Sometimes we underestimate the amount of control we have, as was the case with the facilitators who thought it was the client choosing what to type when they were unconsciously doing it themselves (Wegner, 2002).

Why does it matter what people believe? It turns out that the extent to which people believe they have free will has important consequences (Bargh, 2013; Clark et al., 2014; Dar-Nimrod & Heine, 2011). The more people believe in free will, for example, the more willing they are to help others in need and the less likely they are to engage in immoral actions such as cheating (Baumeister, Masicampo, & Dewall, 2009). In one study, college students either read a series of statements that implied the existence of free will, such as "I am able to overcome the genetic and environmental factors that sometimes influence my behavior," or a series of statements that implied the absence of free will, such as "Ultimately, we are biological computers—designed by evolution, built through genetics, and programmed by the environment" (Vohs & Schooler, 2008, p. 51). Next, all participants took a test composed of items from the Graduate Record Exam (GRE), scored their own tests, and paid themselves $1 for every correct answer. At least that is what participants were supposed to do. The question was, did some participants cheat and take extra money, beyond what they had actually earned? It turned out that people cheated significantly more when they read the statements implying that there is no free will than when they read the statements implying that there is free will. Why? When experiencing temptation, people who believe that they can control their actions probably exert more effort to do so, thinking, "I could easily steal some money, but I can control what I do, so it's up to me to be strong and do the right thing." In contrast, people who believe that there is no free will think, "I want the money, and I'm not really in control of my actions, so I might as well just go with that impulse." Thus, regardless of how much free will human beings *really* have, it is in society's best interest for us all to *believe* that we have it. (See the Try It! below for a demonstration of how much free will people think they have compared to other people.)

TRY IT!

Can You Predict Your (or Your Friend's) Future?

A. Please answer the following questions about *yourself*. In each row, circle *one* of the three possible options, according to which one best captures the genuine possibilities for what might happen during the year after you graduate from college.

1. have an exciting job or be in an exciting graduate program	have a boring job or be in a boring graduate program	both are possible
2. live in a really nice apartment or house	live in a really crappy apartment or house	both are possible
3. be in a long-term relationship	be single	both are possible
4. travel to Europe	not travel to Europe	both are possible
5. do something useful	waste time	both are possible
6. keep in close contact with my college friends	not keep in close contact with my college friends	both are possible

B. Please answer the following questions about *a college friend of your choosing*. In each row, circle *one* of the three possible options, according to which one best captures the genuine possibilities for what might happen during the year after he or she graduates from college.

1. have an exciting job or be in an exciting graduate program	have a boring job or be in a boring graduate program	both are possible
2. live in a really nice apartment or house	live in a really crappy apartment or house	both are possible
3. be in a long-term relationship	be single	both are possible
4. travel to Europe	not travel to Europe	both are possible
5. do something useful	waste time	both are possible
6. keep in close contact with his or her college friends	not keep in close contact with his or her college friends	both are possible

See page 620 for an explanation of how to interpret your answers.

Mentally Undoing the Past: Counterfactual Reasoning

Counterfactual Thinking

Mentally changing some aspect of the past as a way of imagining what might have been

Another important question about controlled thinking is when people do it. When do we go off automatic pilot and think about things more slowly and consciously? One circumstance is when we experience a negative event that was a "close call," such as failing a test by just a point or two. Under these conditions, we engage in **counterfactual thinking**, which is mentally changing some aspect of the past as a way of imagining what might have been (Markman et al., 2009; Roese, 1997; Schacter, Benoit, De Brigard, & Szpunar, 2013; Tetlock, 2002; Wong, Galinsky, & Kray, 2009). "If only I had answered that one question differently," you might think, "I would have passed the test."

Counterfactual thoughts can have a big influence on our emotional reactions to events. The easier it is to mentally undo an outcome, the stronger the emotional reaction to it (Camille et al., 2004; Miller & Taylor, 2002; Zhang & Covey, 2014). One group of researchers, for example, interviewed people who had suffered the loss of a spouse or child. As expected, the more people imagined ways in which the tragedy could have been averted, by mentally undoing the circumstances preceding it, the more distress they reported (Branscombe et al., 1996; Davis et al., 1995).

Sometimes the emotional consequences of counterfactual reasoning are paradoxical. For example, who do you think would be happier: an Olympic athlete who won a silver medal (came in second) or an Olympic athlete who won a bronze medal (came in third)? Surely the one who got the silver, because they did better! Actually it is the reverse, because the silver medal winner can more easily imagine having won the event and therefore engages in more counterfactual reasoning. To test these hypotheses, Medvec, Madey, and Gilovich (1995) analyzed videotapes of the 1992 Olympics. Both immediately after their event and while they received their medals, silver medal winners appeared less happy than bronze medal winners. And during interviews with reporters, silver medal winners engaged in more counterfactual reasoning by saying things like, "I almost pulled it off; it's too bad." The moral seems to be that if you are going to lose, it is best not to lose by a slim margin.

Who do you think would be happier: someone who won a silver medal at the Olympics or someone who won a bronze? Surprisingly, research shows that silver medalists are often less happy, because they can more easily imagine how they might have come in first and won a gold.

Earlier we described controlled thinking as conscious, intentional, voluntary, and effortful. But like automatic thinking, different kinds of controlled thought meet these requirements to different degrees. Counterfactual reasoning is clearly conscious and effortful; we know we are obsessing about the past, and this kind of thinking often takes up so much mental energy that we cannot think about anything else. It is not, however, always intentional or voluntary. Even when we want to stop dwelling on the past and move on to something else, it can be difficult to turn off the kind of "if only" thinking that characterizes counterfactual reasoning (Andrade & Van Boven, 2010; Goldinger et al., 2003).

This is not so good if counterfactual thinking results in rumination, whereby people repetitively focus on negative things in their lives. Rumination has been found to be a contributor to depression (Lyubomirsky, Caldwell, & Nolen-Hoeksema, 1993; Watkins, 2008; Watkins & Nolen-Hoeksema, 2014). Thus, it is not advisable to ruminate constantly about a bad test grade to the point where you can't think about anything else. Counterfactual thinking can be useful, however, if it focuses people's attention on ways they can cope better in the future. Thinking such thoughts as "If only I had studied a little harder, I would have passed the test" can be beneficial, to the extent that it gives people a heightened sense of control over their fate and motivates them to study harder for the next test (Nasco & Marsh, 1999; Roese & Olson, 1997).

Improving Human Thinking

One purpose of controlled thinking is to provide checks and balances for automatic thinking. Just as an airline captain can turn off the automatic pilot and take control of the plane when trouble occurs, controlled thinking takes over when unusual events occur. How successful are people at correcting their mistakes? How can they be taught to do better?

> The greatest of all faults, I should say, is to become conscious of none.
> —THOMAS CARLYLE

One approach is to make people a little more humble about their reasoning abilities. Often we have greater confidence in our judgments than we should (Buehler, Griffin, & Ross, 2002; Juslin, Winman, & Hansson, 2007; Merkle & Weber, 2011; Vallone et al., 1990). Teachers, for example, sometimes have greater confidence than is warranted in their beliefs about the abilities of boys versus girls. Anyone trying to improve human inference is thus up against an **overconfidence barrier** (Metcalfe, 1998). One approach, then, might be to address this overconfidence directly, getting people to consider the possibility that they might be wrong. This tack was taken by one team of researchers (Lord, Lepper, & Preston, 1984). They found that when asked to consider the opposite point of view to their own, people realized there were other ways to construe the world than their own way; consequently, they made fewer errors in judgment (Anderson, Lepper, & Ross, 1980; Hirt, Kardes, & Markman, 2004; Mussweiler, Strack, & Pfeiffer, 2000).

Overconfidence Barrier

The fact that people usually have too much confidence in the accuracy of their judgments

Another approach is to directly teach people some basic statistical and methodological principles about how to reason correctly, with the hope that they will apply these principles in their everyday lives. Many of these principles are already taught in courses in statistics and research design, such as the idea that if you want to generalize from a sample of information (e.g., a group of welfare mothers) to a population (e.g., all welfare mothers), you must have a large, unbiased sample. Do people who take such courses apply these principles in their everyday lives? Are they less likely to make the kinds of mistakes we have discussed in this chapter? A number of studies have provided encouraging answers to these questions, showing that people's reasoning processes can be improved by college statistics courses, graduate training in research design, and even brief onetime lessons (Crandall & Greenfield, 1986; Malloy, 2001; Nisbett et al., 1987; Schaller, 1996).

Richard Nisbett and his colleagues (1987), for example, examined how different kinds of graduate training influenced people's reasoning on everyday problems involving statistical and methodological reasoning—precisely the kind of reasoning we have considered in this chapter, such as people's understanding of how to generalize from small samples of information (see the Try It! below for sample questions). The researchers predicted that students in psychology and medicine would do better on the statistical reasoning problems

TRY IT!
How Well Do You Reason?

The following two questions assess methodological and statistical reasoning. For each question, choose the answer that is correct based on principles of methodology or statistics.

1. The city of Middleopolis has had an unpopular police chief for a year and a half. He is a political appointee who is a crony of the mayor, and he had little previous experience in police administration when he was appointed. The mayor has recently defended the chief in public, announcing that in the time since he took office, crime rates have decreased by 12%. Which of the following pieces of evidence would most deflate the mayor's claim that his chief is competent?
   a. The crime rates of the two cities closest to Middleopolis in location and size have decreased by 18% in the same period.
   b. An independent survey of the citizens of Middleopolis shows that 40% more crime is reported by respondents in the survey than is reported in police records.
   c. Common sense indicates that there is little a police chief can do to lower crime rates. These are for the most part due to social and economic conditions beyond the control of officials.
   d. The police chief has been discovered to have business contacts with people who are known to be involved in organized crime.

2. After the first 2 weeks of the major league baseball season, newspapers begin to print the top 10 batting averages. Typically, after 2 weeks, the leading batter has an average of about .450. Yet no batter in major league history has ever averaged .450 at the end of a season. Why do you think this is?
   a. A player's high average at the beginning of the season may be just a lucky fluke.
   b. A batter who has such a hot streak at the beginning of the season is under a lot of stress to maintain his performance record. Such stress adversely affects his playing.
   c. Pitchers tend to get better over the course of the season as they get more in shape. As pitchers improve, they are more likely to strike out batters, so batters' averages go down.
   d. When a batter is known to be hitting for a high average, pitchers bear down more when they pitch to him.
   e. When a batter is known to be hitting for a high average, he stops getting good pitches to hit. Instead, pitchers "play the corners" of the plate because they don't mind walking him.

See page 620 for the answers.

than students in law and chemistry would, because graduate programs in psychology and medicine include more training in statistics than programs in the other two disciplines do.

As Figure 3.6 shows, after 2 years of graduate work, students in psychology and medicine improved on the statistical reasoning problems more than students in law and chemistry did. The improvement among the psychology graduate students was particularly impressive. Interestingly, the students in the different disciplines performed equally well on sample items from the Graduate Record Exam, suggesting that they did not differ in overall intelligence. Instead, the different kinds of training they had received appeared to influence how accurately and logically they reasoned on everyday problems (Nisbett et al., 1987). Thus, there are grounds for being optimistic about people's ability to overcome the kinds of mistakes we have documented in this chapter. And you don't have to go to graduate school to do it. Sometimes it helps simply to consider the opposite, as participants in the Lord and colleagues' (1984) study did. Beyond this, formal training in statistics helps, at both the graduate and undergraduate levels. So if you were dreading taking a college statistics course, take heart: It might not only satisfy a requirement for your major, but improve your reasoning as well!

Figure 3.6 Performance on a Test of Statistical Reasoning Abilities by Graduate Students in Different Disciplines

After 2 years of graduate study, students in psychology and medicine showed more improvement on statistical reasoning problems than students in law and chemistry did.

(Figure from Nisbett, Fong, Lehman, Cheng, 1987. Reprinted with permission of AAAS.)

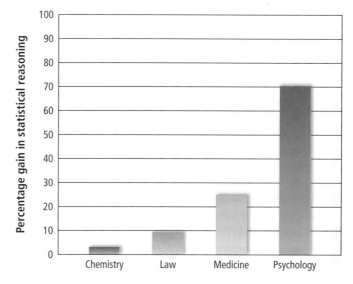

Watson Revisited

By now we have seen two very different modes of social cognition: one that is effortless, involuntary, unintentional, and unconscious (automatic thinking) and another that is more effortful, voluntary, intentional, and conscious (controlled thinking). As we mentioned at the beginning of the chapter, these two kinds of thought, in combination, are extremely powerful, particularly when it comes to understanding the social world. The IBM computer Watson may have succeeded on the TV show *Jeopardy!*, but we wouldn't recommend that you ask Watson to find you a romantic partner, raise your children, or help you negotiate a difficult business deal.

But as we've seen in this chapter, social cognition is by no means perfect. People make mistakes in reasoning, even to the point of unintentionally acting in ways to make their faulty theories come true (the self-fulfilling prophecy). How can we reconcile the fact that human beings have amazing cognitive abilities that have resulted in dazzling cultural and intellectual achievements but at the same time are prone to making consequential mental errors like the ones documented in this chapter?

The best portrait of the social thinker is this: Whereas people are very sophisticated social thinkers who have amazing cognitive abilities, there is also plenty of room for improvement. The shortcomings of social thinking can be quite significant, as demonstrated by examples in this chapter and in later ones (e.g., racial prejudice— see Chapter 13). An apt metaphor for human thinking is that people are like "flawed scientists," brilliant thinkers who are attempting to discover the nature of the social world in a logical manner but who do so imperfectly. People are often blind to truths that don't fit their schemas and sometimes treat others in ways that make their schemas come true—something good scientists would never do.

REVIEW QUESTIONS

1. Sam is playing a carnival game challenging him to guess which of the 20 cups is hiding the red ball. Unfortunately, he picked the cup directly to the *left* of the winning cup and thus did not win the stuffed donkey he wanted. According to social psychological research, he is most likely to
   a. experience cognitive dissonance.
   b. engage in counterfactual thinking.
   c. blame his mistake on the noise of the crowd.
   d. subsequently avoid similar games.

2. Which of the following is true about research on free will?
   a. People rarely overestimate the amount of control they have over their behavior.
   b. Sometimes people underestimate the amount of control they have over their behavior.
   c. Studies have shown that people have free will over almost everything they do.
   d. The more people believe in free will, the more likely they are to engage in immoral actions such as cheating.

3. Which of the following is the best description of facilitated communication?
   a. It is a promising new way of letting communication-impaired people, such as those with autism, express their thoughts.
   b. The facilitators, who hold the fingers and arm of communication-impaired people on a keyboard, are deliberately faking the answers.

c. The facilitators believe that communication-impaired people are choosing what to type, but they are probably wrong and unknowingly determining the answers themselves.
   d. Facilitated communication helps people with mild versions of autism to communicate but does not help those with severe cases.

4. Enrolling in which of the following graduate programs would be most likely to improve your statistical reasoning ability about problems in everyday life?
   a. Psychology
   b. Medicine
   c. Law
   d. Chemistry

5. According to this chapter, which is the best analogy to describe people's thinking abilities?
   a. People are cognitive misers.
   b. People are motivated tacticians.
   c. People are skilled detectives.
   d. People are flawed scientists.

See page 620 for the answers.

Summary

3.1 What is automatic thinking, and how are schemas an example of that kind of thought? What are the advantages and disadvantages of schemas?

- **On Automatic Pilot: Low-Effort Thinking** People are extremely good at **social cognition**, which refers to the ways in which people think about themselves and the social world. Although no computer can match us in this kind of thinking, we are not perfect social thinkers. Social psychologists have uncovered some fascinating mistakes to which we are prone, despite our uncanny cognitive abilities. A great deal of social cognition—how people think about themselves and the social world—involves **automatic thinking**, which is nonconscious, unintentional, involuntary, and effortless.

  - **People as Everyday Theorists: Automatic Thinking with Schemas** An important part of automatic thinking is using our past knowledge to organize and interpret new information. More specifically, people use **schemas**, mental structures for organizing their knowledge about the social world around themes or subjects and for influencing what they notice, think about, and remember. Schemas are extremely useful tools for reducing ambiguity about the social world.

- **Which Schemas Do We Use? Accessibility and Priming** Sometimes a situation is ambiguous and it is not clear what schema applies. Schemas are most likely to be used if they are high in **accessibility**, which means they are at the forefront of our minds. Schemas can be accessible because we have used them a lot in the past, because they are related to our current goals, or because of **priming**, which is the process by which recent experiences increase the accessibility of a schema.

- **Making Our Schemas Come True: Self-Fulfilling Prophecies** Schemas are problematic when they cause self-fulfilling prophecies, whereby a schema or expectation about another person influences how we act toward that person, which causes that person to behave consistently with our expectation.

3.2 What are other types of automatic thinking and how do they operate?

- **Types of Automatic Thinking** There are several other forms of automatic thinking that help us interpret the social world and make decisions, without necessarily intending to do so.

    - **Automatic Goal Pursuit** In our everyday lives there are often competing goals, and the one we choose to follow can happen automatically. People often act on goals that have been recently primed.

    - **Automatic Decision Making** People's unconscious minds often help them make good decisions. A good procedure is to analyze all the alternatives, spend some time analyzing the options consciously, and then distract oneself to allow unconscious processes to operate.

    - **Automatic Thinking and Metaphors About the Body and the Mind** In addition to using schemas to reduce ambiguity about the world, people use metaphors about the mind and the body. Physical sensations (e.g., holding a heavy clipboard) can **prime** a metaphor (e.g., that important thoughts "have weight"), which then influences people's judgments (e.g., that student opinion should be given more weight on a campus issue).

    - **Mental Strategies and Shortcuts: Judgmental Heuristics** Another form of automatic thinking is the use of **judgmental heuristics**, which are mental shortcuts people use to make judgments quickly and efficiently. Examples are the **availability heuristic**, whereby people base a judgment on the ease with which they can bring something to mind, and the **representativeness heuristic**, whereby people classify something according to how similar it is to a typical case. Heuristics are extremely useful and often produce accurate judgments, but can be misused, producing faulty judgments.

3.3 How Does Culture Influence Social Thinking?

- The human mind is like a toolbox filled with specific tools to help people think about and act in the social world. All humans have access to the same tools, but the culture in which they grow up can influence the ones they use the most.

    - **Cultural Determinants of Schemas** Although everyone uses schemas to understand the world, the *content* of our schemas is influenced by the culture in which we live.

    - **Holistic versus Analytic Thinking** Western cultures tend to have an **analytic thinking style**, a type of thinking in which people focus on the properties of objects without considering their surrounding context. People who grow up in East Asian cultures tend to have a **holistic thinking style**, a type of thinking in which people focus on the overall context, particularly the ways in which objects relate to each other.

3.4 What are some of the drawbacks of controlled thinking, and how can we improve its effectiveness?

- **Controlled Social Thinking** Not all social cognition is automatic; we also engage in **controlled thinking**, which is conscious, intentional, voluntary, and effortful.

    - **Controlled Thinking and Free Will** There can be a disconnect between our conscious sense of how much we are causing our own actions and how much we really are causing them. Sometimes we overestimate the amount of control we have, and sometimes we underestimate the amount of control we have. But the more people believe in free will, the more willing they are to help others in need and the less likely they are to engage in immoral actions such as cheating.

    - **Mentally Undoing the Past: Counterfactual Reasoning** One form of controlled thinking is **counterfactual reasoning**, whereby people mentally change some aspect of the past as a way of imagining what might have been.

    - **Improving Human Thinking** In this chapter, we documented several ways in which social cognition can go wrong, producing faulty judgments. Research shows that some kinds of thinking, such as statistical reasoning, can be improved dramatically with training—such as by taking a course in statistics.

    - **Watson Revisited** Human beings are very sophisticated social thinkers who have amazing cognitive abilities. But we are also capable of consequential mistakes, such as self-fulfilling prophecies. People are like "flawed scientists"—brilliant thinkers who are attempting to discover the nature of the social world in a logical manner but do so imperfectly.

Test Yourself

1. Which of the following is the best summary of research on automatic thinking?

   a. Automatic thinking is vital to human survival, but it is not perfect and can produce mistaken judgments that have important consequences.

   b. Automatic thinking is amazingly accurate and rarely produces errors of any consequence.

   c. Automatic thinking is a problem because it usually produces mistaken judgments.

   d. Automatic thinking works best when it occurs consciously.

2. Jennifer and Nate are walking along the street when they see a man walk out of a convenience store clutching a bag. The owner of the store runs out and shouts for the man to stop and come back. Jennifer immediately assumes that there has been a robbery, whereas Nate immediately assumes that the man forgot to get his change and that the store owner wants to give it to him. What is the best explanation for why Jennifer and Nate interpreted this event differently?

   a. Jennifer and Nate were engaged in controlled thinking that resulted in different assumptions about what was going on.

   b. Jennifer and Nate have different personalities.

   c. Jennifer and Nate fell prey to the self-fulfilling prophecy.

   d. Different schemas were accessible in Jennifer and Nate's minds, perhaps because they had different recent experiences that primed different schemas.

3. Which of the following is true about the use of schemas?

   a. Schemas are an example of controlled thinking.

   b. When people have an incorrect schema, rarely do they act in a way to make it come true.

   c. Although schemas can lead to errors, they are a very useful way of organizing information about the world and filling in gaps in our knowledge.

   d. The schema we use is influenced only by what information is chronically accessible and not by our goals or by what has been primed recently.

4. Tiffany has a hard time trusting her friends because she believes they are irresponsible. Accordingly, when she makes dinner plans with one friend, she also makes backup plans with someone else, and she goes to one or the other. Her friends soon in turn begin to "blow off" their arrangements with Tiffany, because they are never sure whether she will show up. Tiffany thinks to herself, "See, I was right, my friends are irresponsible." Which of the following best explains why Tiffany made this conclusion?

   a. Accurate social perception due to controlled processes

   b. A self-fulfilling prophecy

   c. Holistic thinking

   d. Accurate social perception due to automatic processes

5. Suppose you wanted your friend Stephan to feel like a more assertive person. According to research on _____, you should ask him to think of _____ times in the past when he acted in an unassertive manner.

   a. Representativeness heuristic; 12

   b. Availability heuristic; 3

   c. Representativeness heuristic; 3

   d. Availability heuristic; 12

6. Which one of the following involves the *least* amount of automatic thinking?

   a. acting according to goals that have been primed

   b. using metaphors about the body to make judgments

   c. counterfactual reasoning

   d. self-fulfilling prophecies

7. Which of the following is true?

   a. All human beings have the same cognitive "tools" that they can use.

   b. When people move from one culture to another they generally do not learn to think like people in the new culture.

   c. East Asians tend to think more holistically and Westerners tend to think more analytically because of genetic differences between East Asians and Westerners.

   d. American college students were more likely to notice changes in the background of a picture whereas Japanese college students were more likely to notice changes in the main objects in the foreground of the picture.

8. Research on controlled thinking and free will shows that:

   a. There is a disconnect between our conscious sense of how much we are causing our actions and how much we are really causing our actions.

   b. It doesn't really matter whether or not people believe that they have free will.

   c. Some primates have just as much free will as human beings.

   d. People definitely do not have free will.

9. Suppose you are trying to raise money for your favorite charity and you set up a table in the lobby of a campus building. Which of the following is likely to increase the likelihood that passersby will donate money?

    a. Give them a very light clipboard with information about your charity.

    b. Ask people to hold a cold bottle of water while they listen to what you have to say.

    c. Show them pictures of Japanese cities so that they think holistically.

    d. Spray some citrus-scented cleaning solution on the table.

10. Based on everything you've read in this chapter, what is the best conclusion about social cognition?

    a. People would be better off if we could turn off automatic thinking and rely solely on controlled thinking.

    b. Whereas people are very sophisticated social thinkers who have amazing cognitive abilities, there is also plenty of room for improvement.

    c. Social cognition is pretty much the same throughout the world in all cultures that have been studied.

    d. One purpose of controlled thinking is to set goals for ourselves; that cannot be done with automatic thinking.

See page 620 for the answers.

Chapter 4
Social Perception
How We Come to Understand Other People

 ## Chapter Outline and Learning Objectives

Nonverbal Communication

4.1 How do people use nonverbal cues to understand others?

Facial Expressions of Emotion

Culture and the Channels of Nonverbal Communication

First Impressions: Quick but Long-Lasting

4.2 How quickly do first impressions form, and why do they persist?

The Lingering Influence of Initial Impressions

Using First Impressions and Nonverbal Communication to Our Advantage

Causal Attribution: Answering the "Why" Question

4.3 How do people determine why others do what they do?

The Nature of the Attribution Process

The Covariation Model: Internal versus External Attributions

The Fundamental Attribution Error: People as Personality Psychologists

Self-Serving Attributions

The "Bias Blind Spot"

Culture and Social Perception

4.4 What role does culture play in processes of social perception and attribution?

Holistic versus Analytic Thinking

Cultural Differences in the Fundamental Attribution Error

Culture and Other Attributional Biases

Other people are not easy to figure out. Why are they the way they are? Why do they do what they do? The frequency and urgency with which we pose these questions are clear in a touching story, sent in years ago by a reader to the *New York Times*. The reader explains that a female friend who had recently ended a relationship had decided to throw away a bag containing her ex's love letters, cards, and poems. She was stunned when her former boyfriend called the next day to ask why she had done this. How had he found out? It turns out that a homeless man found the letters while going through the garbage, read the correspondence, and became curious about how the two lovers' relationship had come to such an end. He went to a pay phone and called the boyfriend to find out, after finding his number in one of the letters. "I would have called you sooner," he told the former boyfriend, "but this was the first quarter I was given today" (De Marco, 1994).

The homeless man was down on his luck—no home, no money, reduced to rifling through garbage cans—and yet that endless fascination with the human condition still asserted itself. He needed to know why the couple broke up. He even spent his only quarter to find out.

We all have a fundamental fascination with explaining other people's behavior. But the reasons why people behave as they do are usually hidden from us. Unfortunately, we can't read other people's minds. All we have to go on is observable behavior: what people do, what they say, their facial expressions, gestures, and tone of voice. We rely on subtle cues and first impressions, putting together these puzzle pieces as best we can, hoping they will lead to reasonably accurate and useful conclusions.

Our desire to understand other people is so fundamental that it carries over into our hobbies and recreational lives. We go to movies, read novels, eavesdrop on conversations, and watch people flirt at bars because thinking about the behavior even of strangers and fictional characters fascinates us (Weiner, 1985). This basic aspect of human cognition has been exploited brilliantly by reality television producers, who cast television shows with real people, not actors, and film them as they go about their lives. You can watch *Teen Mom* or *Real Housewives*, *Keeping Up with the Kardashians*, or *The Bachelor*. Why are these shows so popular? Because we enjoy trying to figure people out. Consider *Duck Dynasty*, the hugely popular show depicting daily exploits of the Robertsons, a colorful, bearded clan from the Louisiana bayou whose family business making hunting products has led to a real-life rags-to-riches story. Or the NPR podcast *Serial*, which by the end of 2014 was attracting over a million listeners per week tuning into the latest in the unfolding investigation of the death of Hae Min Lee, the murder conviction of her ex-boyfriend Adnan Syed, and the nuanced relationships of those in their former social circle. As we watch and listen to shows such as these, with characters both similar and very different from ourselves, we form impressions of the individuals in question. We make attributions about them; that is, we reach conclusions about who we think they are and why they do what they do. These attributions help us understand their motivations, choices, and behavior—all of which are topics in this chapter.

And it isn't just reality television that seeks to capture this obsession we have with the characters around us. More "traditional" forms of television have also become grittier and driven by more complex characters in recent years (Martin, 2013). Who can forget the frenzy surrounding the final episodes of *Breaking Bad* in 2013? Whether they had been watching the series all along or had to binge on Netflix to catch up, it seemed like most of America had little more on their minds than the enthralling saga of chemistry-teacher-turned-druglord Walter White. Some of the questions that literally kept viewers up at night were plot driven, as we waited to find out what would happen to Walter, his family, and various criminal associates. But the truly fascinating and even polarizing aspects of the show were character related: Had mild-mannered Mr. White undergone a total transformation to become Heisenberg, the crystal meth king of New Mexico, or had those tendencies for calculated deception and ruth-lessness been simmering underneath all along? Who in Walter's inner circle was an innocent casualty of his turn toward crime, and who was just as culpable as he was? And just whom were we supposed to be rooting for anyway? If you have any doubt that the *Breaking Bad* phenomenon owed a tremendous debt to our fascination with what makes other people tick, look no further than the experience of Anna Gunn, the actress who played Skyler, Walter's wife. Gunn's character became such a controver-sial flash point for viewers—some empathizing with her plight, many others exco-riating her as the show's true villain—that she felt moved to publicly sort through these increasingly heated viewer reactions in an op-ed piece titled "I Have a Character Issue" (Gunn, 2013).

You don't have to be a fan of any of the shows we just mentioned—or watch television at all—to appreciate that there's a basic human fascination with the complex and contradictory characters around us. From "people watching" out in public to first impressions about a new professor on the first day of class to late-night conversations with friends about why so-and-so just acted the way he did, much of our daily mental energy is devoted to analyzing other people. Why? Because thinking about other individuals and their behavior helps us understand and predict our social universe (Heider, 1958; Kelley, 1967). This effort to make sense of the social world around us is the focus of this chapter. Specifically, we will discuss **social perception**—the study of how we form impressions of other people and how we make inferences about them. We'll start with one particularly important source of information used in thinking about others: nonverbal communication, such as people's facial expressions, body movements, and tone of voice.

Social Perception

The study of how we form impressions of and make inferences about other people

Nonverbal Communication

4.1 How do people use nonverbal cues to understand others?

In the course of daily interaction, so much of what we have to say to other people doesn't require us to actually *say* anything at all. Our nonverbal expressions provide others with a wealth of information about us; we use these same nonverbal cues to learn about them (Gifford, 1991; Hall, Gunnery, & Andrzejewski, 2011; Hall, Murphy, & Schmid Mast, 2007). **Nonverbal communication** refers to how people communicate, inten-tionally or unintentionally, without words. Facial expressions, tone of voice, gestures, body positions and movement, the use of touch, and eye gaze are the most frequently used and most revealing channels of nonverbal communication (Knapp, Hall, & Horgan, 2014).

Nonverbal cues serve a variety of functions in communication. They help us to express our emotions, our attitudes, and our personality (and to perceive those same characteristics in others). For example, you express "I'm angry" by narrowing your eyes, lowering your eyebrows, and setting your mouth in a thin, straight line. You communicate your personality traits, such as being an extravert, with broad gestures and frequent changes in voice pitch and inflection (Knapp et al., 2014). Just think about how difficult it can sometimes be to convey the true meaning and tone of your message when communicating on email or via text. There's a reason why emoticons and now emojis are so popular; they help fill in gaps created by the lack of nonverbal cues in such communications. You can explore how you use one aspect of nonverbal communication—your voice—in the Try It! on the next page.

Nonverbal Communication

The way in which people communicate, intentionally or unintentionally, without words; nonverbal cues include facial expressions, tone of voice, gestures, body position and movement, the use of touch, and gaze

When the eyes say one thing, and the tongue another, a practiced man relies on the language of the first.

—Ralph Waldo Emerson, *The Conduct of Life*

TRY IT!

Using Your Voice as a Nonverbal Cue

A student new to English was listening to an English radio station and was very confused when the radio jockeys Jen and Stephanie laughed in joy after Jen told Stephanie "I totally hate you." What type of cue did the student miss out on? Imagine yourself to be in Jen's position and repeat what she said. Make guesses about the words that might have been emphasized by Jen and the tone she might have used.

Sierra's mother asked her how her siblings were doing after Sierra had been on the phone with her sisters. Sierra responded, "Abigail and Janice said they are doing fine, and both made many positive comments about their current life. However, I doubt Janice is doing as fine as she says." Why do you think she has interpreted the same message given by both of her siblings differently?

Try saying saying out loud "I don't know her" so that it communicates each of the emotions listed below. Experiment with the pitch of your voice (high or low), the speed with which you speak, the loudness or softness of your voice, and which words you stress.

- You're angry.
- You're being sarcastic.
- You're scared.
- You're surprised.
- You're disgusted.
- You're very happy.

Now try this exercise with a friend. Turn your back to your friend as you repeat the sentence; you want your friend to have to rely on your voice as the only cue, without help from any facial expressions. How well does he or she guess the emotions you are expressing? Have your friend try the exercise too. Can you understand his or her nonverbal vocal cues? If you don't always correctly identify the emotions in each other's voices, discuss what was missing or confusing in the voice. In this way, you'll be able to figure out, for example, what a "disgusted" voice sounds like as compared to an "angry" or "scared" voice.

Social psychologists are not the only ones to recognize the importance of nonverbal communication. Today it seems like every political debate or high-profile press conference is inevitably followed by a panel of pundits who analyze what was said but also *how* it was said. Indeed, on today's cable news channels, the title "body language expert" appears to be just as common as "political correspondent." Some of these analyses are more informed than others. The best ones draw on an extensive scientific literature concerning nonverbal communication. Interestingly, though, nonverbal forms of communication have typically been studied individually, in their separate "channels." In other words, some studies examine eye gaze, others investigate gestures, and still others explore the role of body posture in social perception. But in everyday life, nonverbal cues of many kinds occur all at the same time in a quite dazzling orchestration of simultaneous information (Archer & Akert, 1980; Knapp et al., 2014). Let's focus on the research concerning a few of these channels now before turning to how we interpret the full symphony of nonverbal information as it occurs naturally.

Facial Expressions of Emotion

The crown jewel of nonverbal communication is the facial-expressions channel. This aspect of communication has a long history of research, beginning with Charles Darwin's book *The Expression of the Emotions in Man and Animals* (1872). Its primacy is due to the exquisite communicativeness of the human face (Becker, Kenrick, Neuberg, Blackwell, & Smith, 2007; Fernández-Dols & Crivelli, 2013; Kappas, 1997; Wehrle, Kaiser, Schmidt, & Scherer, 2000). Look at the photographs on page 108. We bet you can figure out which emotions these expressions convey with very little effort.

EVOLUTION AND FACIAL EXPRESSIONS   Darwin's research on facial expressions has had a major impact on the field in many areas. We will focus on his belief that the primary emotions conveyed by the face are universal: the argument that all humans **encode**, or express, these emotions in the same way and that all humans can **decode**, or interpret them, with comparable accuracy. Darwin's interest in evolution led him to believe that nonverbal forms of communication were species specific and not culture specific. He proposed that facial expressions were vestiges of once-useful

Encode

To express or emit nonverbal behavior, such as smiling or patting someone on the back

Decode

To interpret the meaning of the nonverbal behavior other people express, such as deciding that a pat on the back was an expression of condescension and not kindness physiological reactions. For example, if early hominids ate something that tasted terrible, they would have wrinkled their noses in displeasure and expelled the food from their mouths. Research by Joshua Susskind and his colleagues (2008) offers support for Darwin's view. They studied the facial expressions of disgust and fear and found, first, that the muscle movements of each emotion were completely the opposite of the other. Second, they found that the "fear face" enhances perception, while the "disgust face" decreases it. For fear, the facial and eye muscle movements increase sensory input, such as widening the visual field, increasing the volume of air in the nose, and speeding up eye movements—all useful responses to something that is frightening. In contrast, for disgust, the muscle movements decrease input from these senses: Eyes narrow and less air is breathed in, which are useful reactions to something that smells or tastes disgusting (Susskind et al., 2008).

Was Darwin right that facial expressions of emotion are universal? The answer seems to be yes, for the most part, for six major emotional expressions: anger, happiness, surprise, fear, disgust, and sadness. For example, in a particularly well-designed study, Paul Ekman and Walter Friesen (1971) traveled to New Guinea, where they studied the decoding ability of the South Fore, a preliterate tribe that, until that time, had had no contact with Western civilization. They told the Fore people brief stories with emotional content and then showed them photographs of American men and women expressing the six emotions; the Fores' job was to match the facial expressions of emotion to the stories. The Fores were as accurate as Western subjects. The researchers then asked the Fore people to demonstrate, while being photographed, facial expressions that would match the stories they were told. These photographs, when later shown to American research participants, were also decoded accurately. This research yielded considerable evidence that the ability to interpret the six major emotions is cross-cultural—part of being human and not a product of people's particular cultural experiences (Biehl et al., 1997; Ekman, 1993; Ekman et al., 1987; Elfenbein & Ambady, 2002; Haidt & Keltner, 1999; Izard, 1994; Matsumoto & Wilingham, 2006).

These photographs depict facial expressions of the six major emotions. Can you guess the emotion expressed on each face?

Top row answers (L to R): anger, fear, disgust. Bottom row (L to R): happiness, surprise, sadness.

Why do we say that evidence has supported universal emotional expression, but only "for the most part"? Well, for decades, textbooks such as this one have offered an unqualified "yes" to the question of universality. But recent research paints a more complicated picture. Studies have found that individuals from Western cultures maintain more rigid boundaries between the six major emotions when applying them to faces, whereas Asian respondents show overlap in their use of these categories (Jack, Garrod, Yu, Caldara, & Schyns, 2012). Other research has supported universality when asking participants from across cultures to match emotional labels to faces but found evidence of cross-cultural differences when allowing people to freely sort faces into their own grouping system (Gendron, Roberson, van der Vyver, & Barrett, 2014). Clearly, cultural variation in encoding and decoding remains an open research question among contemporary social psychologists.

Beyond these six emotions, are there other emotional states that are communicated with distinctive and readily identifiable facial expressions? Researchers are exploring just this question for emotions such as contempt, anxiety, shame, determination, envy, and embarrassment (Ekman, O'Sullivan, & Matsumoto, 1991; Harmon-Jones, Schmeichel, Mennitt, & Harmon-Jones, 2011; Harrigan & O'Connell, 1996; Keltner & Shiota, 2003; van de Ven, Zeelenberg, & Pieters, 2011). For example, research has indicated that the emotion of *pride* exists cross-culturally. Pride is a particularly interesting emotional display because it involves a facial expression as well as body posture and gesture cues. Specifically, the prototypical pride expression includes a small smile, the head tilted back slightly, a visibly expanded chest, and arms raised above the head or hands on hips (Tracy & Robins, 2004). Photographs of pride expressions were accurately decoded by research participants in the United States and Italy, as well as individuals from a preliterate, isolated tribe in Burkina Faso, West Africa (Tracy & Robins, 2008). Jessica Tracy and David Matsumoto (2008) explored pride and its opposite, *shame*, by coding the spontaneous expressions of judo athletes at the 2004 Olympic and Paralympic Games. Sighted and blind athletes from 37 countries were coded on their nonverbal behavior just after they had won or lost a match. The pride expression was associated with winning for both sighted and blind athletes around the world. Shame, expressed by slumped shoulders and a sunken chest, was significantly associated with losing for all the athletes except one group—sighted athletes from highly individualistic cultures, such as those of the United States and Western Europe. In individualistic cultures, shame is a negative, stigmatized emotion that one tends to hide rather than display (Robins & Schriber, 2009).

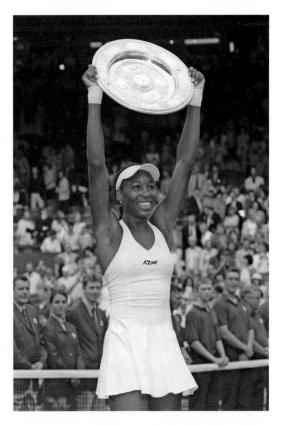

The nonverbal expression of pride, involving facial expression, posture, and gesture, is encoded and decoded cross-culturally.

President Barack Obama and 2012 U.S. Olympic gymnast McKayla Maroney show off their matching "McKayla is not impressed" faces. Recent research suggests that beyond the six major emotion expressions, other expressions may also be universally recognized.

Affect Blends

Facial expressions in which one part of the face registers one emotion while another part of the face registers a different emotion

WHY IS DECODING SOMETIMES DIFFICULT?   Decoding facial expressions accurately is more complicated than we have indicated, however, for multiple reasons. First, people frequently display **affect blends** (Du, Tao, & Martinez, 2014; Ekman & Friesen, 1975): One part of their face registers one emotion while another part registers a different emotion. Take a look at the accompanying photographs and see if you can tell which two emotions are being expressed in each face. An affect blend is the sort of expression you might display if a person told you something that was

Often, people express more than one emotion at the same time. Can you tell which emotions these people are expressing? The answers are printed below.

(The Paul Ekman Group, LLC)

Answers: The man is expressing a blend of anger (the eye and eyebrow region) and disgust (the nose and mouth region). The woman is expressing a blend of surprise (eyes and eyebrows) and happiness (mouth). (It may help to cover half of the photograph with your hand to see each emotional expression clearly.)

Display Rules

Culturally determined rules about which nonverbal behaviors are appropriate to display

both horrible and inappropriate—you'd be disgusted with the content and angry that the person told you. A second complication is that aspects of the same facial expression can have different implications based on context and other cues (Barrett, Mesquita, & Gendron, 2011; Hassin, Aviezer, & Bentin, 2013; Parkinson, 2013). For example, studies indicate that decoding of facial displays varies depending on eye gaze (Adams et al., 2010; Ulloa, Puce, Hugueville, & George, 2014). For an approach-oriented emotion like anger, decoding is quickest when a face stares right at you, presumably alerting you that you are the target of the anger and might need to prepare for confrontation. But for avoidance-oriented emotions like fear, decoding is easiest when a face displays an averted gaze—the eyes looking over to the side reveal to you the exact location of the scary object, signaling to you that you should also be fearful of whatever is off in that direction (Adams & Kleck, 2003). And yet a third reason why decoding facial expressions can be challenging has to do with culture.

Culture and the Channels of Nonverbal Communication

For decades, Paul Ekman and his colleagues have studied the influence of culture on the facial display of emotions (Ekman & Davidson, 1994; Ekman & Friesen, 1971; Matsumoto & Ekman, 1989; Matsumoto & Hwang, 2010). They have concluded that **display rules** are particular to each culture and dictate what kinds of emotional expressions people are supposed to show. As we saw in our discussion of athletes' spontaneous expressions at the Olympics and Paralympics (Tracy & Matsumoto, 2008), the display rules of more individualistic cultures discourage the expression of shame in front of others, while the display rules of more collectivistic cultures allow (or even encourage) it.

Here is another example: American cultural norms typically discourage emotional displays in men, such as grief or crying, but allow the facial display of such emotions in women. In comparison, in Japan, traditional cultural rules dictate that women should not exhibit a wide, uninhibited smile (Ramsey, 1981). Japanese women will often hide a wide smile behind their hands, whereas Western women are allowed—indeed, encouraged—to smile broadly and often (Henley, 1977; La France, Hecht, & Paluck, 2003). Japanese norms lead people to cover up negative facial expressions with smiles and laughter and, in general, to display fewer facial expressions than are displayed in the West (Argyle, 1986; Aune & Aune, 1996; Gudykunst, Ting-Toomey, & Nishida, 1996; Richmond & McCroskey, 1995).

There are, of course, other channels of nonverbal communication besides facial expressions. These nonverbal cues are strongly shaped by culture. Eye contact and gaze are particularly powerful nonverbal cues, as alluded to above. In American culture, people often become suspicious when a person doesn't "look them in the eye" while speaking, and they find it disconcerting to speak to someone who is wearing dark sunglasses. However, as you can see in Figure 4.1, in other parts of the world, direct eye gaze is considered invasive or disrespectful.

Another form of nonverbal communication is how people use personal space. Imagine that you are talking to a person who stands too close to you or too far away; these deviations from "normal" spacing will affect your impressions of that person. Cultures vary greatly in what is considered normative use of personal space (Hall, 1969; Hogh-Olesen, 2008). For example, most Americans like to have a bubble of open space, a few feet in radius, surrounding them. In comparison, in some other cultures it is normal for strangers to stand right next to each other, to the point of touching; someone who stands apart may be considered odd or suspicious.

Figure 4.1

Cultural Differences in Nonverbal Communication

Many forms of nonverbal behavior are specific to a given culture. Not only do some of the nonverbal behaviors of one culture mean nothing in another, but the same nonverbal behavior can exist in two cultures but have very different meanings in each. Such nonverbal differences can lead to misunderstanding when people from different societies interact. Some of these cultural differences are noted here.

Eye contact and gaze

In American culture, direct eye contact is valued; a person who won't "look you in the eye" is perceived as being evasive or even lying. However, in many parts of the world, direct eye contact is considered disrespectful, especially with superiors. For example, in Nigeria, Puerto Rico, and Thailand, children are taught not to make direct eye contact with their teachers and other adults. Cherokee, Navajo, and Hopi Native Americans use minimal eye contact as well. Japanese use far less direct eye contact than Americans do. In contrast, Arabs use a great deal of eye contact, with a gaze that would be considered piercing by people from some other cultures.

Personal space and touching

Societies vary in whether they are high-contact cultures, where people stand close to each other and touch frequently, or low-contact cultures, where people maintain more interpersonal space and touch less often. High-contact cultures include Middle Eastern, South American, and southern European countries. Low-

contact cultures include North American, northern European, Asian, Pakistani, and Native American peoples. Cultures also differ in how appropriate they consider same-sex touching among friends. For example, in Korea and Egypt, men and women hold hands, link arms, or walk hip to hip with their same-sex friends, and these nonverbal behaviors carry no sexual connotation. In the United States, such behavior is much less common, particularly between male friends.

Hand and head gestures

The "OK" sign: The OK sign is formed by making a circle with your thumb and index finger, with your three other fingers extended upward. In the United States, this means "okay." However, in Japan, this hand gesture means "money." In France, it means "zero"; in Mexico, it means "sex." In Ethiopia, it means "homosexuality." Finally, in some South American countries, such as Brazil, it is an obscene gesture, carrying the same meaning as the American "flipping the bird" sign, where the middle finger is the only one extended.

The thumbs-up gesture: In the United States, raising one thumb upward with the rest of the fingers in the fist means "OK." Several European countries have a similar meaning for this gesture; for example, in France it means "excellent!" However, in Japan, the same gesture means "boyfriend," while in Iran and Sardinia, it is obscene.

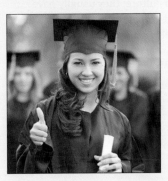

The "hand-purse" gesture: This gesture is formed by straightening the fingers and thumb of one hand and bringing them together so the tips touch, pointing upward. This gesture has no clear meaning in American culture. However, in Italy, it means "What are you trying to say?"; in Spain, it means "good"; in Tunisia, it means "slow down"; and in Malta, it means "you may seem good, but you are really bad."

Nodding the head: In the United States, nodding one's head up and down means "yes" and shaking it from side to side means "no." However, in some parts of Africa and India, the opposite is true: nodding up and down means "no," and shaking from side to side means "yes." To complicate this situation even more, in Korea, shaking one's head from side to side means "I don't know" (which in the United States is communicated by a shrug of the shoulders). Finally, Bulgarians indicate disagreement by throwing their heads back and then returning them to an upright position—which is frequently mistaken by Americans as meaning agreement.

Emblems

Nonverbal gestures that have well-understood definitions within a given culture; they usually have direct verbal translations, such as the OK sign

Gestures of the hands and arms are also a fascinating means of communication. Americans are very adept at understanding certain gestures, such as the OK sign, in which one forms a circle with the thumb and forefinger and curves the rest of the fingers above the circle, or "flipping the bird," in which one bends all the fingers down at the first knuckle except the longest, middle finger. Gestures such as these, which have clear, well-understood definitions, are called **emblems** (Archer, 1997a; Ekman & Friesen, 1975). The important thing to keep in mind about emblems is that they are not universal; each culture has devised its own emblems, and these are not necessarily understandable to people from other cultures (see Figure 4.1). Thus, "flipping the bird" will be a clear communicative sign in American society, whereas in some parts of Europe you'd need to make a quick gesture with a cupped hand under your chin to convey the same message. On one occasion when President George H. W. Bush used the "V for victory" sign (forming a V shape with his fingers), he did it backward—with the palm of his hand facing him instead of the audience. Unfortunately, he flashed this gesture to a large crowd in Australia, and in Australia this emblem is the equivalent of "flipping the bird" (Archer, 1997a)!

To summarize, people's nonverbal communication can tell us a lot about their attitudes, emotions, and intentions. In some instances, as with the expression of major emotions, the conclusions people draw from these bits of social data are fairly consistent across cultures. In other instances, as with eye contact, personal distance, and gestures, the same nonverbal information is interpreted very differently by people in different parts of the world. But regardless of where you're from, it's clear that much of what you pick up on in the course of social interaction is conveyed nonverbally. In short, much of what is said in daily conversations takes place before anyone actually *says* anything at all.

REVIEW QUESTIONS

1. Joshua Susskind et al. (2008) studied the facial expressions of disgust and fear. What major conclusion did they arrive at?
   a. The muscle movements of disgust and fear emotions were exactly the same.
   b. The "fear face" decreases perception, while "disgust face" enhances perception.
   c. For fear, less air is breathed in and eye movements are slower, in contrast, for disgust, eyes widen and more air is breathed in.
   d. The muscle movements of disgust and fear emotions were completely the opposite of the other.

2. The research by Paul Ekman and Walter Friesen (1971) indicated that the ability to interpret six major emotions is
   a. a product of people's particular cultural experiences.
   b. a result of an individual's predispositions.
   c. cross-cultural.
   d. highly individualistic.

3. In the case of pride, research has indicated that
   a. photographs of pride expressions could not be accurately decoded by participants from the United States.
   b. the prototypical pride expressions included slumped shoulders and a sunken chest.
   c. photographs of pride expressions were accurately decoded by participants from the United States.
   d. pride expressions were not associated with winning around the world.

4. A large number of researches have indicated that decoding facial expressions accurately is complicated because
   a. one part of people's face registers one emotion while another part registers a different emotion.
   b. aspects of the same facial expression have similar implications irrespective of the context and other cues.
   c. display rules are not particular to each culture and do not dictate what kinds of emotional expressions people are supposed to show.
   d. eye gaze has nothing to do with decoding of facial expressions in case of approach-oriented emotions like anger and avoidance-oriented emotions like fear.

5. Which of the following is true about emblems?
   a. Each culture has devised its own emblems.
   b. Emblems are understandable to people across cultures.
   c. Emblems do not tell us about the sender's intentions.
   d. Emblems are a clear form of verbal communication.

See page 620 for the answers.

First Impressions: Quick but Long-Lasting

4.2   How quickly do first impressions form, and why do they persist?

What do we know about people when we first meet them? We know what we can see and hear. And even though we also know we should not "judge a book by its cover," we do form impressions of others based on the slightest of cues. For example, Sam Gosling has conducted research on "what your stuff says about you," as presented in his book *Snoop* (2008). Is your room messy or orderly? What posters are on your wall? What objects are on your desk and shelves? All of these possessions can be used by observers (potential snoopers) as clues to what you are really like. For example, consider what we might learn from an individual whose office or car doesn't have much decoration in the form of personal objects or photos. One possibility, Gosling suggests, is that this is the mark of a person who wants to establish a clear separation between his or her private self and his or her work/public self. Another is that this is someone low on the personality trait of extraversion: extraverts tend to decorate public spaces more, making them inviting to other people and sparking conversations with passersby. When you think about your own room, what cues do you think it provides to others about your personality? What can you learn about your friends from their rooms and their "stuff"?

This is Kenneth "Babyface" Edmonds, American musical performer and producer. Research suggests that the same characteristics that earned him his nickname might also lead perceivers to jump to the conclusion that he is friendly, honest, and gullible.

Of course, as you now know, another factor that plays a major role in first impressions is nonverbal communication. What we have not reviewed yet is just how quickly such communication takes place. Research indicates that we form initial impressions of others based solely on their facial appearance in less than 100 milliseconds (Bar, Neta, & Linz, 2006; Willis & Todorov, 2006). That's less than 1/10 of one second! And recent research indicates that we show signs of this tendency to consistently infer character from faces when we're as young as 3 years old (Cogsdill, Todorov, Spelke, & Banaji, 2014).

One example of these quick snap judgments is that people who have "baby faces"—features that are reminiscent of those of small children, with big eyes, a small chin and nose, and a high forehead—tend to be perceived as having childlike traits as well, such as being naive, warm, and submissive (Livingston & Pearce, 2009; Zebrowitz & Montepare, 2008). Obviously, these impressions are not always correct, but there is some evidence that we can make accurate judgments about others simply based on facial appearance. As another example, after brief glances at photographs of men's and women's faces, research participants are able to judge sexual orientation at above-chance levels of accuracy, suggesting that there may indeed be a scientific basis to the notion of "gaydar" (Rule, Ambady, Adams, & Macrae, 2008; Rule, Ambady, & Hallett, 2009). Or in another set of studies, American participants rated the faces of Canadian political candidates (with whom they were totally unfamiliar) on the dimensions of powerfulness and warmth. Their first-impression ratings correlated with actual election results: The more powerful the candidates looked, the more likely they were to have won their election; the warmer they looked, the less likely they were to have won (Rule & Ambady, 2010; Todorov, Said, Engell, & Oosterhof, 2008). Just think about this for a moment—all the time, money, and effort candidates expend to try to win elections, and in the end, the simple question of how powerful their face looks emerges as a significant predictor of success. Perhaps we were too dismissive earlier of the importance of "body language experts"!

Indeed, it is amazing just how limited an exposure to other people is enough for us to form meaningful first impressions about their abilities or personalities. Nalini Ambady and her colleagues have referred to such social perception based on extremely brief snippets of behavior as **thin-slicing** (Ambady & Rosenthal, 1992; Rule, Krendl, Ivcevic, & Ambady, 2013; Slepian, Bogart, & Ambady, 2014). In one study, they examined an instance of social perception familiar to most readers of

Thin-Slicing
Drawing meaningful conclusions about another person's personality or skills based on an extremely brief sample of behavior

Much like TV's Dr. Cal Lightman, many of us find it professionally (and personally) useful to be able to accurately detect when other people are being dishonest.

this book (not to mention its authors): how college students form impressions of their professors (Ambady & Rosenthal, 1993). For the study, the researchers videotaped more than a dozen instructors while teaching and then selected three random 10-second clips from each one. After removing the audio track, they showed the silent video clips to students who had never before taken a class with these instructors. Students were asked to rate the teachers on a series of variables including how competent, confident, and active they appeared to be. Not surprisingly, participants had little trouble coming up with ratings—as we've discussed, first impressions come to us quickly. But recall that Ambady's prediction was that thin-sliced impressions would be *meaningful*, not just fast. To test this, she compared the ratings made by her participants—whose only exposure to the instructors came in the form of brief, silent video clips—with the end-of-semester teaching evaluations these instructors received from their actual students. The result was a strong correlation: the thin-sliced impressions were incredibly similar to the perceptions of students who spent an entire semester with the instructors. In fact, even when shorter, 6-second silent clips were used, participants were still able to accurately predict who the highest-rated teachers were (Ambady & Rosenthal, 1992).

Similar findings have been observed outside the classroom. Patients draw informative first impressions based on thin-slice exposures to doctors; clinicians do the same with their patients (Ambady, LaPlante, Nguen, Rosenthal, & Levinson, 2002; Slepian et al., 2014). Our ability to extract meaningful information from very limited encounters has also captured the attention of authors and television producers. The research of Ambady and colleagues plays a central role in Malcolm Gladwell's best-selling *Blink* (2005). And some of you are likely familiar with the work of the fictional Dr. Cal Lightman, deception detection expert and lead character of the television show *Lie to Me*. If Lightman's mantra, "the truth is written all over our faces," seems to you like it was ripped right out of a social psychology textbook, there's good reason: His character was based on Paul Ekman, the psychologist responsible for the faces you see on page 108 as well as a scientific consultant to the show. That said, to date there has been little in the way of published scientific data to support the idea that people can effectively use microexpressions—involuntary facial movements—to reliably determine deception as accurately as Lightman does on television.

It is clear, then, just how quickly first impressions happen. But do they last? If first impressions faded from view as quickly as they came into focus, then first impressions might not matter much when it comes to social perception. But it turns out they do matter. Let's look at just how important and long-lasting first impressions really are.

The Lingering Influence of Initial Impressions

As we saw in Chapter 3, when people are unsure about the nature of the social world, they use their schemas to fill in the gaps. A schema is a mental shortcut: When all we have is a small amount of information, our schemas provide additional information to fill in the gaps (Fiske & Taylor, 2013; Markus & Zajonc, 1985). Thus, when we are trying to understand other people, we can use just a few observations of a person as a starting point and then, using our schemas, create a much fuller understanding. This idea suggests that our initial impressions have staying power—that they color the way we interpret the information we learn next.

As an example, consider a hypothetical individual you've never met before. Let's call him Keith. We want you to mull over your impressions of Keith as we tell you the following about him: Keith is an interesting guy. People who know him say he's intelligent. Another word often used to describe him is industrious. Keith can also be

I think the first reading of a poem is a true one, and after that we delude ourselves into the belief that the sensation, the impression, is repeated.

—JORGE LUIS BORGES,
THIS CRAFT OF VERSE

impulsive as well as critical. Still others have described him as stubborn and envious. Based on this information, what's your impression of Keith at this point?

Now consider another hypothetical stranger. We'll call him Kevin. Kevin is an interesting fellow as well. People who know him have called him envious. Also stubborn. And you know what, it just so happens that other descriptors that people use when talking about Kevin are critical, impulsive, industrious, and intelligent.

By now, you've likely sensed the pattern. Keith and Kevin are being described the same way. Or, at least, the content of what you've been told about them is the same; the order of the descriptors has been switched around. What conclusions do you think people would draw about Keith versus Kevin? When Solomon Asch (1946) ran this very study, describing hypothetical individuals with the same descriptors you read above, he found that order made a big difference. Participants formed a more positive impression of someone described as intelligent-industrious-impulsive-critical-stubborn-envious (Keith, in our example), compared to someone described as envious-stubborn-critical-impulsive-industrious-intelligent (Kevin, in our case). Why? Because first impressions are powerful. In this instance, Keith's positive traits of being intelligent and industrious create a filter—a schema—through which subsequent traits are viewed. After learning that he is smart and hardworking, perhaps you also perceived "impulsive" and "critical" in a positive light—as in, sure, Keith may make quick decisions and critique the work of others, but that can be productive for someone who's intelligent. Kevin, on the other hand? You already know he's envious and stubborn. This makes it easy to see those same traits of critical and impulsive as negatives, bringing them in line with the initial expectations you have for him.

Asch's study demonstrates that there's a **primacy effect** in social perception: What we learn first about another person colors how we see the information we learn next. In addition to primacy effects, we also have schemas regarding which traits tend to appear together in clusters. That is, we use a few known characteristics to determine what other characteristics a person likely has (Sedikides & Anderson, 1994; Werth & Foerster, 2002; Willis & Todorov, 2006). For example, a capable, can-do person is also seen as powerful and dominant, whereas an incompetent person is seen as the opposite (Fiske, Cuddy, & Glick, 2006; Todorov et al., 2008; Wojciszke, 2005). Or consider physical attractiveness. We often presume that "what is beautiful is good"—that people with physical beauty will also have a whole host of other wonderful qualities (Dion, Berscheid, & Walster, 1972; Eagly, Ashmore, Makhijani, & Longo, 1991; Jackson, Hunter, & Hodge, 1995).

But primacy effects and schemas about which characteristics go together aren't the only reasons why first impressions have lasting effects. When it comes to social perception, we also have a tendency for **belief perseverance**, or standing by initial conclusions even when subsequently learned information suggests we shouldn't. In dozens of studies over several decades, research participants have opted to stick by their original impressions even once the basis for their that judgment is contradicted or revealed as erroneous (Anderson, 1995; Ross, Lepper, & Hubbard, 1975). Indeed, belief perseverance has been cited to explain why jurors have a hard time disregarding evidence ruled inadmissible or why scientists are slow to discount published research conclusions that turn out to be based on fabricated data (Greitemeyer, 2013; Lilienfeld & Byron, 2013). As Chapter 6 will detail, we find inconsistent thoughts unpleasant and uncomfortable. Once we make up our minds, we're inclined to keep them made up. And so first impressions, once formed, can prove pretty hard to shake.

Primacy Effect

When it comes to forming impressions, the first traits we perceive in others influence how we view information that we learn about them later

Belief Perseverance

The tendency to stick with an initial judgment even in the face of new information that should prompt us to reconsider

Using First Impressions and Nonverbal Communication to Our Advantage

There are clear implications of the research on first impressions: When trying to win people over, there's no overemphasizing how important it is to start off on the right foot.

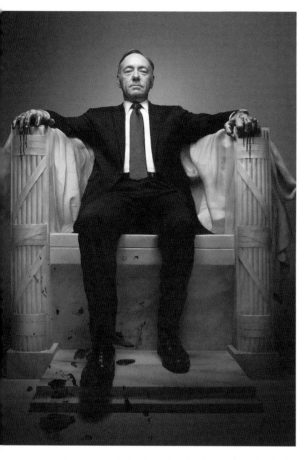

To watch the Machiavellian (and at times, bloodied) politician Francis Underwood in an episode of *House of Cards* is to witness Kevin Spacey putting his character through a series of high-status postures and poses. Research on power posing demonstrates that simply adopting a body posture typically associated with high-status can make us feel or act more powerful as well.

Getting ready for public speaking? Make sure the opening moments of your presentation are your most polished, as that thin-slice will set an influential tone. Going on a job interview? How you dress, whether you maintain eye contact, your body posture—these are immediately apparent factors that may shape how others evaluate the rest of your visit. Even the simplest of introductory actions, like the way you shake hands, can have a dramatic effect: Research indicates that perceptions of handshake quality are significantly related to assessments of personality and even final hiring recommendations in an interview setting (Chaplin, Phillips, Brown, & Clanton, 2000; Stewart, Dustin, Barrick, & Darnold, 2008).

Interestingly, you can also capitalize on the importance of nonverbal communication by using your own body language to change how you yourself think, feel, and act. This is the provocative idea demonstrated by research that Dana Carney, Amy Cuddy, and Andy Yap (2010) conducted on what they refer to as "power posing." In one study, participants were asked to assume different nonverbal body postures for a total of 2 minutes. In one condition, these were high-power poses, such as standing behind a table, leaning forward with hands planted firmly on its surface; in the other condition, these were low-power poses, such as standing with feet crossed and arms wrapped around one's own torso. Immediately after holding the high-power poses, participants reported feeling more powerful. They adopted a riskier strategy on a gambling task. Saliva analysis indicated that they even experienced a surge in testosterone compared to the low-power posers, who also felt less powerful and became more risk averse (Carney et al., 2010). These findings identify yet another potential strategy for your next job interview: spend a few minutes before you get there striking superhero poses in the bathroom mirror. You may just psych yourself into a more emboldened, impressive performance. Or, as the study authors put it, "fake it 'til you make it." That something so simple as body posture could have such profound effects is an idea that has clearly struck a nerve with the general public: Cuddy's 2012 TED talk describing this research already has been viewed by 25 million people and counting.

REVIEW QUESTIONS

1. Research indicates that which of the following candidates would be most likely to win a political election?
   a. Denise, whose face other people often perceive as indicating a warm personality
   b. Theo, who many people believe is gay based only on his facial appearance
   c. Vanessa, who has large eyes, a high forehead, and a small, child-like nose
   d. Rudy, whose face is usually seen by others as indicating a cold, calculating, and powerful personality

2. Ambady and colleagues were able to conclude that the thin-sliced impressions formed by their participants were based on meaningful information because
   a. their ratings based on 30-second clips were little different than their ratings based on 6-second clips.
   b. their ratings of the silent video clips corresponded strongly with the ratings that the instructors received from their actual students at the end of the semester.
   c. ratings were similar for silent video clips and for the same video clips when shown with audio.
   d. while the thin-sliced video clips were brief, it took participants a relatively long amount of time to come up with ratings of the instructors they viewed.

3. Asch's (1946) research on person perception provided evidence for which of the following conclusions?
   a. There is a primacy effect in social perception.
   b. First impressions serve as a filter through which subsequently learned information is interpreted.
   c. Even when the content of information conveyed about two individuals remains the same, the order in which we learn it can have a powerful effect on our impression.
   d. All of the above.

4. Belief perseverance can help explain which of the following?

   a. Why people who watch news programs that refer to climate change as a hoax remain convinced of that conclusion even in the face of scientific evidence to the contrary.

   b. Why during jury deliberations it is easier to convince fellow jurors to change their votes from guilty to not guilty than it is to change their minds in the opposite direction.

   c. Why weather forecasters are better at predicting rainfall totals than snowfall totals.

   d. All of the above.

5. Which of the following statements regarding the Carney et al. (2010) power-posing research is true?

   a. Standing in a closed posture with one's arms wrapped around one's own torso tends to be a high-power pose.

   b. While participants who previously had posed in a high-power posture exhibited evidence of increased testosterone, their self-report responses indicated that they did not feel more powerful after the manipulation.

   c. Participants who posed in a high-power posture adopted riskier strategies on a subsequent gambling task.

   d. Participants were less willing to adopt low-power poses compared to high-power poses.

See page 620 for the answers.

Causal Attribution: Answering the "Why" Question

4.3   How do people determine why others do what they do?

We have seen that when we observe other people, we have a rich source of information—their nonverbal behavior—on which to base our impressions. However, nonverbal behavior and other components of first impression formation are not fail-safe indicators of what a person is really thinking or feeling. If you meet an acquaintance and she says, "It's great to see you!" does she really mean it? Perhaps she is acting more thrilled than she really feels, out of politeness. Perhaps she is outright lying and really can't stand you. The point is that even though nonverbal communication is sometimes easy to decode and first impressions are quick to form, there is still substantial ambiguity as to what a person's behavior really means (Ames & Johar, 2009; DePaulo, 1992; DePaulo, Stone, & Lassiter, 1985).

Why did that acquaintance behave as she did? To answer this "why" question, we will use our immediate observations to form more elegant and complex inferences about what people are really like and what motivates them to act as they do. How we go about answering these questions is the focus of **attribution theory**, the study of how we infer the causes of other people's behavior.

The Nature of the Attribution Process

Fritz Heider (1958) is frequently referred to as the father of attribution theory. His influential book defined the field of social perception, and his legacy is still very much evident in current research (Crandall, Silvia, N'Gbala, Tsang, & Dawson, 2007; Kwan & Chiu, 2014). Heider discussed what he called "naive," or "common-sense," psychology. In his view, people were like amateur scientists, trying to understand other people's behavior by piecing together information until they arrived at a reasonable explanation or cause (Surian, Caldi, & Sperber, 2007; Weiner, 2008).

One of Heider's most valuable contributions is a simple dichotomy: When trying to decide why people behave as they do—for example, why a father has just yelled at his young daughter—we can make one of two attributions. One option is to make an **internal attribution**, deciding that the cause of the father's behavior was something about him—his disposition, personality, attitudes, or character—an explanation that assigns the causes of his behavior internally. For example, we might decide that

In the beginning was not the word, not the deed, not the silly serpent. In the beginning was why? Why did she pluck the apple? Was she bored? Was she inquisitive? Was she paid? Did Adam put her up to it? If not, who did?

—John Le Carré,
The Russia House, 1989

Attribution Theory

A description of the way in which people explain the causes of their own and other people's behavior

Internal Attribution

The inference that a person is behaving in a certain way because of something about the person, such as attitude, character, or personality

External Attribution

The inference that a person is behaving a certain way because of something about the situation he or she is in; the assumption is that most people would respond the same way in that situation

the father has poor parenting skills and disciplines his child in inappropriate ways. Alternatively, we might make an **external attribution**, deciding that something in the situation, not in the father's personality or attitudes, caused his behavior. If we conclude that he yelled because his daughter had just stepped into the street without looking, we would be making an external attribution for his behavior.

Notice that our impression of the father will be very different depending on the type of attribution we make. For this particular example, if we make an internal attribution, we'll form a negative impression. If we make an external attribution, we won't learn much about the father—after all, most parents would have done the same thing if their child had just disobeyed them by stepping into the street. Quite a difference!

This internal/external attribution dichotomy plays an extraordinarily important role in even the most intimate parts of our lives. Indeed, spouses in happy, satisfied marriages make very different attributions about their partners than spouses in troubled, distressed marriages. Satisfied spouses tend to make internal attributions for their partners' positive behaviors (e.g., "She helped me because she's such a generous person") and external attributions for their partners' negative behaviors (e.g., "He said something mean because he's so stressed at work right now"). In contrast, spouses in distressed marriages tend to display the opposite pattern: Their partners' positive behaviors are chalked up to external causes (e.g., "She helped me because she wanted to impress our friends"), while negative behaviors are attributed to internal causes (e.g., "He said something mean because he's a self-centered jerk"). When an intimate relationship becomes troubled, this second pattern of attributions about one's partner only makes the situation worse and can have dire consequences for the future of the relationship (Bradbury & Fincham, 1991; Fincham, Bradbury, Arias, Byrne, & Karney, 1997; McNulty, O'Mara, & Karney, 2008).

TRY IT!

Listen as People Make Attributions

Forming attributions is a major part of daily life, and you can watch the attribution process in action! All you need to do is find a group of friends and an interesting topic to discuss. Perhaps one of them starts telling you about something that happened to her that day, or perhaps the group is discussing another person whom everybody knows. As they talk, pay very close attention to what they say. They will be trying to figure out why the person being discussed did what she did or said what he said. In other words, they will be making attributions. Your job is to try to keep track of their comments and label the attributional strategies they are using.

In particular, are they making internal attributions (about a person's character or personality), or are they making situational attributions (about all the other variables that make up a person's life)? Do your friends seem to prefer one type of attribution to the other? If their interpretation is internal, what happens when you suggest another possible interpretation, one that is external? Do they agree or disagree with you? What kinds of information do they offer as "proof" that their attribution is right? Observing people when they are making attributions in real conversations will show you just how common and powerful this type of thinking is when people are trying to understand each other.

The Covariation Model: Internal versus External Attributions

The first, essential step in the process of social perception is determining how people decide whether to make an internal or an external attribution. Harold Kelley's major contribution to attribution theory was the idea that we notice and think about more than one piece of information when forming such judgments (Kelley, 1967, 1973). For example, let's say you ask your friend to lend you her car, and she says no. Naturally, you wonder why. What explains her behavior? Kelley's theory, called the **covariation model**, says that you will examine multiple behaviors from different times and situations to answer this question. Has your friend refused to lend you her car in the past? Does she lend it to other people? Does she normally lend you things when you ask her?

Kelley, like Heider before him, assumed that when we are in the process of forming an attribution, we gather information, or data. The data we use, according to Kelley, are about how a person's behavior "covaries," or changes, across time and place and depending on the target of the behavior. By discovering covariation in people's behavior (e.g., your friend refuses to lend you her car, but she agrees to lend it to others), you can reach a conclusion about what causes their behavior.

According to Fritz Heider, we tend to see the causes of a person's behavior as internal. For example, when we see a driver exhibiting signs of "road rage," we are likely to assume that he is at fault for losing his temper. If we knew the person's situation–perhaps he is rushing to the hospital to check on a family member and another driver has just cut him off–we might come up with a different, external attribution.

When we are forming an attribution, what kinds of covariation information do we examine? Kelley (1967) identified three key types: *consensus*, *distinctiveness*, and *consistency*. Suppose that you are working at your part-time job at the mall and you observe your boss yelling at another employee, Hannah. Automatically, you ask that attributional question: "Why is the boss yelling at Hannah and being so critical? Is it something about the boss, something about Hannah, or something about the situation that surrounds and affects him?"

How would Kelley's (1967, 1973) model of covariation assessment answer this question? **Consensus information** refers to how other people behave toward the same stimulus—in this case, Hannah. Do other people at work also yell at or criticize Hannah? If so, perhaps something about Hannah's job performance is responsible for the interaction you witnessed; if not, you become more confident that your boss is to blame. **Distinctiveness information** refers to how the actor (the person whose behavior we are trying to explain) responds to other stimuli. Is Hannah the only employee whom your boss criticizes publicly? If so, we wonder what it is about her that seems to set him off; if not, we again start to think that he's responsible for the confrontation. **Consistency information** refers to the frequency with which the observed behavior between the same actor and the same stimulus occurs across time and circumstances. Does the boss criticize Hannah regularly and frequently, whether the store is filled with customers or empty?

According to Kelley's theory, when these three sources of information combine into one of two distinct patterns, a clear attribution can be made. People are most likely to make an internal attribution (deciding that the behavior was due to something about the boss) when the consensus and distinctiveness of the act are low but its consistency is high (see Figure 4.2). We would be pretty confident that the boss yelled at Hannah because he is an impatient or vindictive person if we knew that no one else yells at Hannah, that the boss yells at other employees, and that the boss yells at Hannah every chance he gets. People are likely to make an external attribution (in this case, about Hannah) if consensus, distinctiveness, and consistency are all high. Finally, when consistency is low, we cannot make a clear internal or external attribution, so we resort to a special kind of external or situational attribution, one that assumes that something unusual or peculiar must have happened in this particular circumstance—for example, the boss just received very upsetting news that day and uncharacteristically lost his temper with the first person he saw.

Covariation Model

A theory that states that to form an attribution about what caused a person's behavior, we systematically note the pattern between the presence or absence of possible causal factors and whether the behavior occurs

Consensus Information

Information about the extent to which other people behave the same way toward the same stimulus as the actor does

Distinctiveness Information

Information about the extent to which one particular actor behaves in the same way to different stimuli

Consistency Information

Information about the extent to which the behavior between one actor and one stimulus is the same across time and circumstances

Figure 4.2 The Covariation Model

Why did the boss yell at his employee Hannah? To decide whether a behavior was caused by internal (dispositional) factors or by external (situational) factors, people use consensus, distinctiveness, and consistency information.

Why did the boss yell at his employee Hannah?			
People are likely to make an *internal attribution*—it was something about the boss—if they see this behavior as	*low* in consensus: The boss is the only person working in the store who yells at Hannah	*low* in distinctiveness: The boss yells at all the employees	*high* in consistency: The boss yells at Hannah almost every time he sees her
People are likely to make an *external attribution*—it was something about Hannah—if they see this behavior as	*high* in consensus: All of the employees yell at Hannah too	*high* in distinctiveness: The boss doesn't yell at any of the other employees	*high* in consistency: The boss yells at Hannah almost every time he sees her
People are likely to think it was something peculiar about the particular circumstances in which the boss yelled at Hannah if they see this behavior as	*low or high* in consensus	*low or high* in distinctiveness	*low* in consistency: This is the first time that the boss has yelled at Hannah

The covariation model assumes that people make causal attributions in a rational, logical way. People observe the clues about consensus, distinctiveness, and consistency and then draw a logical inference about why the person did what he or she did. Research has confirmed that people often do make attributions in this way (Forsterling, 1989; Gilbert, 1998a; Hewstone & Jaspars, 1987; Hilton, Smith, & Kim, 1995; Orvis, Cunningham, & Kelley, 1975; White, 2002)—with two exceptions. Studies have shown that people don't use consensus information as much as Kelley's theory predicted; they rely more on consistency and distinctiveness when forming attributions (McArthur, 1972; Wright, Lüüs, & Christie, 1990). Also, people don't always have the relevant information they need on all three of Kelley's dimensions. For example, you may not have consistency information because this is the first time you have ever asked your friend to borrow her car. In these situations, research has shown that people proceed with the attribution process using the information they do have and, if necessary, making guesses about the missing data (Fiedler, Walther, & Nickel, 1999; Kelley, 1973).

To summarize, the covariation model portrays people as master detectives, deducing the causes of behavior as systematically and logically as Sherlock Holmes would. However, people aren't always logical or rational when forming judgments about others. Sometimes they distort information to satisfy their need for high self-esteem (see Chapter 6). At other times they use mental shortcuts that, although often helpful, can lead to inaccurate judgments (see Chapter 3). Unfortunately, the attributions we make are sometimes just plain wrong. In the next section, we will discuss some specific errors or biases that plague the attribution process. One shortcut is very common: the idea that people do what they do because of the kind of people they are, not because of the situation they are in.

The Fundamental Attribution Error:
People as Personality Psychologists

One day in December 1955, a Black seamstress in Montgomery, Alabama, refused to give up her seat on the city bus to a White man. At the time, segregationist "Jim Crow" laws in the South relegated African Americans to second-class status in all aspects of everyday life. They could sit in the middle section if it was empty, but they had to give up their seats to White people when the bus got full; the front 10 rows were always reserved for White people only (Feeney, 2005). That day in 1955, Rosa Parks broke the law and refused to give up her seat. Later, she said, "People always say I didn't give up my seat because I was tired, but that wasn't true. I was not tired physically. . . . No, the only tired I was, was tired of giving in" (Feeney, 2005, pp. A1, B8). Ms. Parks was convicted of violating the segregation laws and fined. In response, African Americans boycotted the Montgomery buses for over a year and mounted a legal challenge that led to a successful Supreme Court decision in 1956 outlawing segregation on buses. Rosa Parks's brave act was the precipitating event of the American civil rights movement (Shipp, 2005).

On October 24, 2005, Rosa Parks died at the age of 92. To commemorate her, the American Public Transportation Association called for December 1 to be the "Tribute to Rosa Parks Day." Buses in major cities across the country designated that one seat, behind the driver, be kept empty for the day in her honor. To alert riders, signs were posted on the windows adjacent to the seat, with Rosa Parks's photograph and the small caption "It all started on a bus" (Ramirez, 2005).

A New York City journalist rode the buses that day to see if people would honor the request—after all, an empty seat on a crowded city bus is a coveted item. He found that the vast majority of riders did so, even during rush hour, when just finding a place to stand is difficult. However, some people did sit in the special seat (Ramirez, 2005). Now this was an interesting development, both to the journalist and to his fellow travelers. Why did they do it? It seemed to be a flagrant act of disrespect. How could one not honor Rosa Parks? Were these "sitters" prejudiced, even racist? Were they selfish or arrogant, believing that their personal needs were more important than anything else? In short, negative dispositional attributions were being made about these sitters.

Being a good reporter, the journalist began asking the sitters why they chose to sit in this special seat. Lo and behold, a situational explanation emerged. They hadn't seen the sign. In fact, the small signs were badly placed and easy to miss in the midst of scheduling announcements (Ramirez, 2005). After the sign was pointed out to sitters, they reacted swiftly. One man "read it quickly, shuddered, then uttered a loud profanity in dismay. He scooted out of the seat. 'I didn't realize it was there. . . . It's history. . . . It means freedom'" (Ramirez, 2005, p. B1). Another rider, a Black man, began to sit down but stopped halfway when he saw the sign. He said to another rider, a Black woman, "'But people were sitting here.' The woman said gently, 'They couldn't see the sign.' 'Well,' the man said, peeling away the sign and moving it to the edge of the seat, 'they will now'" (Ramirez, 2005, p. B1). Thus, many on the bus were making the wrong attribution about the sitters. The other riders believed that their behavior was due to the kind of people they were (bad ones) instead of due to the situation—in this case, a too small, poorly located sign.

Rosa Parks, sitting at the front of the bus, after the Supreme Court ruled that bus segregation is illegal.

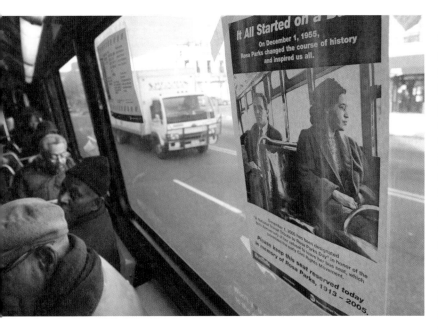

Buses across the United States posted a sign like this one, asking riders to keep one seat empty to honor Rosa Parks.

Fundamental Attribution Error

The tendency to overestimate the extent to which other people's behavior is due to internal, dispositional factors and to underestimate the role of situational factors

The fundamental theory or schema most of us have about human behavior is that people do what they do because of the kind of people they are, not because of the situation they are in. When thinking this way, we are more like personality psychologists, who see behavior as stemming from internal dispositions and traits, than like social psychologists, who focus on the impact of social situations on behavior. As we saw in Chapter 1, this tendency to overestimate the extent to which other people's behavior is due to internal, dispositional factors, and to underestimate the role of situational factors is called the **fundamental attribution error** (Heider, 1958; Jones, 1990; Ross, 1977; Ross & Nisbett, 1991). The fundamental attribution error has also been called the *correspondence bias* (Gilbert, 1998b; Gilbert & Jones, 1986; Gilbert & Malone, 1995; Jones, 1979, 1990).

There have been many empirical demonstrations of the tendency to see people's behavior as a reflection of their dispositions and beliefs rather than as influenced by the situation (Arsena, Silvera, & Pandelaere, 2014; Gawronski, 2003a; Miller, Ashton, & Mishal, 1990; Miller, Jones, & Hinkle, 1981). For example, in a classic study, Edward Jones and Victor Harris (1967) asked college students to read an essay written by a fellow student that either supported or opposed Fidel Castro's rule in Cuba and then to guess how the author of the essay really felt about Castro (see Figure 4.3). In one condition, the researchers told the students that the author freely chose which position to take in the essay, thereby making it easy to guess how he really felt. If he chose to write in favor of Castro, clearly he must be sympathetic to Castro. In another condition, however, the students learned that the author had been assigned the position as a participant in a debate. One should not

Figure 4.3 The Fundamental Attribution Error

Even when people knew that the author's choice of an essay topic was externally caused (i.e., in the no-choice condition), they assumed that what he wrote reflected how he really felt about Castro. That is, they made an internal attribution from his behavior.

(Based on Jones & Harris, 1967)

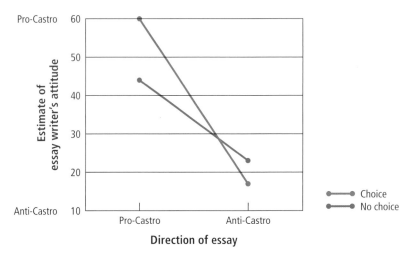

assume, then, that the writer believed what he wrote. Yet the participants in this study (and in dozens of others like it) assumed that the author really believed what he wrote, even when they knew he had no choice as to which position to take. As you can see in Figure 4.3, people ratcheted down their guesses a little bit—there was not as much difference between their estimates of the author's attitude in the pro-Castro and anti-Castro conditions as there was in the choice condition—but they still assumed that the content of the essay reflected the author's true feelings to some extent.

Why is the fundamental attribution error so fundamental? It is not always wrong to make an internal attribution; clearly, people sometimes do what they do because of the kind of people they are. However, considerable evidence indicates that social situations can strongly affect behavior; indeed, the major lesson of social psychology is that these influences can be extremely powerful. The point of the fundamental attribution error is that people often tend to underestimate external influences when explaining other people's behavior. Even when the influence of the situation on behavior is obvious, as in the Jones and Harris (1967) experiment, people persist in making internal attributions (Li, Johnson, Cohen, Williams, & Knowles, 2012; Newman, 1996; Ross, Amabile, & Steinmetz, 1977; Ross & Nisbett, 1991).

THE ROLE OF PERCEPTUAL SALIENCE IN THE FUNDAMENTAL ATTRIBUTION ERROR   Why do people fall prey to the fundamental attribution error? One reason is that when we try to explain someone's behavior, our focus of attention is usually on the person, not on the surrounding situation (Baron & Misovich, 1993; Heider, 1944, 1958; Jones & Nisbett, 1972). In fact, the situational causes of another person's behavior are practically invisible to us (Gilbert, 1998b; Gilbert & Malone, 1995). If we don't know what happened to someone earlier in the day (e.g., she received an F on her midterm), we can't use that situational information to help us understand her current behavior. And even when we know her situation, we still don't know how she interprets it (e.g., the F may not upset her because she's planning to drop the course anyway). If we don't know the meaning of the situation for her, we can't accurately judge its effects on her behavior.

If information about the situational causes of behavior is unavailable or difficult to interpret, what does that leave us with? Although the situation may be close to invisible, the individual is "perceptually prominent"—our eyes and ears notice people. And what we notice seems like the reasonable and logical cause of the observed behavior (Heider, 1958). We can't see the situation, so we overlook its importance. People, not the situation, have **perceptual salience** for us; we pay attention to them, and we tend to think that they alone cause their behavior (Heider, 1958; Lassiter, Geers, Munhall, Ploutz-Snyder, & Breitenbecher, 2002).

Several studies have confirmed the importance of perceptual salience—especially an elegant one by Shelley Taylor and Susan Fiske (1975). In this study, two male students engaged in a "get acquainted" conversation. (They were actually both accomplices of the experimenters and followed a script during their conversation.) At each session, six actual research participants also took part. They sat in assigned seats, surrounding the two conversationalists (see Figure 4.4). Two sat on each side of the actors; they had a clear, profile view of both individuals. Two observers sat behind each actor; they could see the back of one actor's head but the face of the other. Thus, the conversationalist who was visually salient—that is, the individual the participants could see better—was cleverly manipulated.

After the conversation, participants were asked questions about the two men—for example, Who had taken the lead in the conversation? Who had chosen the topics to be discussed? What happened? The person they could see better was the person they

Be not swept off your feet by the vividness of the impression, but say, "Impression, wait for me a little. Let me see what you are and what you represent."

—EPICTETUS, *Discourses*

Perceptual Salience

The seeming importance of information that is the focus of people's attention

Figure 4.4 Manipulating Perceptual Salience

This is the seating arrangement for two actors and the six research participants in the Taylor and Fiske study. Participants rated each actor's impact on the conversation. Researchers found that people rated the actor they could see more clearly as having the larger role in the conversation.

(Based on Taylor & Fiske, 1975)

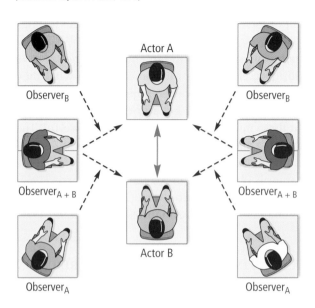

thought had more impact on the conversation (see Figure 4.5). Even though all the observers heard the same conversation, those who faced student A thought he had taken the lead and chosen the topics, whereas those who faced student B thought he had taken the lead and chosen the topics. In comparison, those who could see both students equally well thought both were equally influential.

Perceptual salience plays a role in how we view higher-stakes conversations as well. Consider a police interrogation in which investigators question a potential suspect for an unsolved crime. G. Daniel Lassiter and his colleagues (2007; Lassiter, 2010) presented 21 courtroom judges and 24 police officers with a videotape of an individual confessing to a crime. These judge and police participants were shown one of three different versions of the videotape: (a) the camera's focus was on the suspect only, (b) the camera's focus was on the detective only, or (c) there was equal camera focus on the suspect and the detective. Participants were asked to rate how "voluntary" the confession was, as opposed to "coerced." For both the judge and the police respondents, the videotape that focused only on the suspect produced significantly higher ratings of "voluntariness" than the other two videotape versions (Lassiter et al., 2007). In other words, the perceptual salience of the suspect, when shown alone, triggered a fundamental attribution error, making him appear guiltier than when he was less perceptually salient. These results are worrisome because videotaping the suspect only is standard operating procedure in many real criminal investigations. In fact, one country, New Zealand, has adopted a rule of "equal focus" camera perspective (suspect + detective) for videotaped interrogations, in direct response to concerns about just such attributional bias (Lassiter, Ratcliff, Ware, & Irvin, 2006).

Research indicates that the viewpoint from which a police interrogation is videorecorded can influence how jurors perceive it. In the image above, both the officer and the suspect are depicted. How might this same interaction be interpreted differently if only the suspect was visible to observers?

Figure 4.5 The Effects of Perceptual Salience

These are the ratings of each actor's causal role in the conversation. People thought that the actor they could see better had more impact on the conversation.

(Based on Taylor & Fiske, 1975)

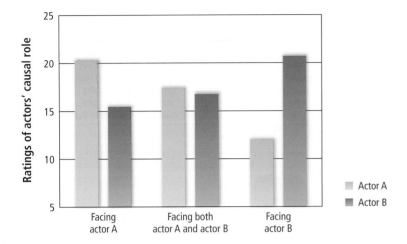

Our visual point of view, or perceptual salience, helps explain why the fundamental attribution error is so widespread. We focus our attention more on the person than on the surrounding situation because the situation is so hard to see or know. So we hear someone argue strongly in favor of Castro's regime in Cuba, and our first inclination is to explain this in dispositional terms: "This person must be a socialist." But we are capable of realizing that this explanation might not be the whole story. We certainly have the mental sophistication to think, "On the other hand, I know he was assigned this position as part of a debate," adjusting our attributions more toward a situational explanation. However, the problem is that people often don't adjust their judgments enough. In the Jones and Harris (1967) experiment, participants who knew that the essay writer did not have a choice of topics nevertheless thought that what he had written told them *something* about his true attitudes. They adjusted insufficiently from the most salient information—the position taken in the essay (Quattrone, 1982).

THE TWO-STEP ATTRIBUTION PROCESS In sum, we go through a **two-step attribution process** when we make attributions (Gilbert, 1989, 1991, 1993; Krull, 1993). We make an internal attribution, assuming that a person's behavior was due to something about that person. We then sometimes attempt to adjust this attribution by considering the situation the person was in. It's just that we often don't make enough of an adjustment in this second step. Indeed, when we are distracted or preoccupied, we often skip the second step altogether, making an internal attribution in the extreme (Gilbert & Hixon, 1991; Gilbert & Osborne, 1989; Gilbert, Pelham, & Krull, 1988). Why? Because the first step (making the internal attribution) occurs quickly and spontaneously, whereas the second step (adjusting for the situation) requires more effort and conscious attention (see Figure 4.6). Indeed, recent brain-imaging studies provide evidence at a neural level that our tendency to spontaneously consider the internal, mental states of actors often leaves us less likely to think later about potential situational explanations for their actions (Brosch, Schiller, Mojdehbakhsh, Uleman, & Phelps, 2013; Moran, Jolly, & Mitchell, 2014).

When do we engage in this second step of attributional processing? If and when we consciously slow down and think carefully before reaching a judgment. If we are cognitively alert and motivated to make as accurate a judgment as possible. Or if we are suspicious about the behavior of the target person—for example, believing that he or she has ulterior motives (Hilton, Fein, & Miller, 1993; Risen & Gilovich, 2007;

Two-Step Attribution Process

Analyzing another person's behavior first by making an automatic internal attribution and only then thinking about possible situational reasons for the behavior, after which one may adjust the original internal attribution

Figure 4.6

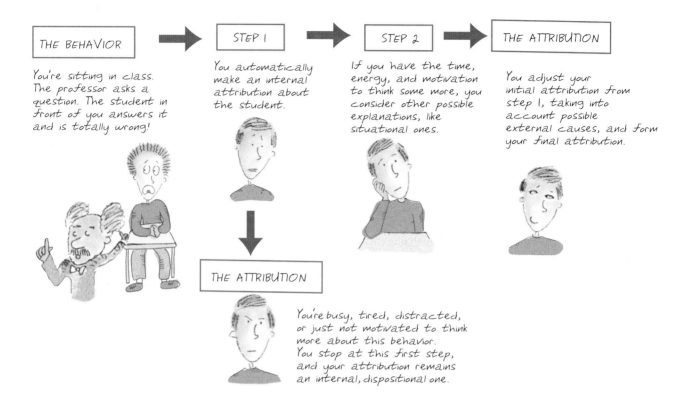

THE TWO-STEP PROCESS OF ATTRIBUTION

THE BEHAVIOR
You're sitting in class. The professor asks a question. The student in front of you answers it and is totally wrong!

STEP 1
You automatically make an internal attribution about the student.

STEP 2
If you have the time, energy, and motivation to think some more, you consider other possible explanations, like situational ones.

THE ATTRIBUTION
You adjust your initial attribution from step 1, taking into account possible external causes, and form your final attribution.

THE ATTRIBUTION
You're busy, tired, distracted, or just not motivated to think more about this behavior. You stop at this first step, and your attribution remains an internal, dispositional one.

Webster, 1993). Of course, this two-step model of attribution may be less applicable to individuals in cultures in which internal attributions are not a default response (Mason & Morris, 2010), as discussed in the final section of this chapter.

Self-Serving Attributions

Imagine that Imani goes to her chemistry class one day feeling anxious because she's getting her midterm grade back. The professor returns her exam. Imani turns it over and sees that she has received an A. What will Imani think explains her grade? As you might guess, people tend to take personal credit for their successes: Imani is likely to think that her success was due to the fact that she's good at chemistry and just plain smart. But what if she got a bad grade? Here, she is more likely to blame external events beyond her control, such as the professor for giving an unfair test. When our self-esteem is threatened, we often make **self-serving attributions**. Simply put, these attributions refer to people's tendency to take credit for their successes by making internal attributions but to blame the situation (or others) for their failures by making external attributions (Kestemont et al., 2014; McAllister, 1996; Miller & Ross, 1975; Pronin, Lin, & Ross, 2002; Robins & Beer, 2001).

A particularly interesting arena for studying self-serving attributions is sports. When explaining their victories, athletes and coaches both point overwhelmingly to aspects of their own teams. In fact, an analysis of professional athletes' and coaches' explanations for their team's wins and losses found that 80% of the attributions for wins were to such internal factors. Losses were more likely to be attributed to external causes, outside of the team's control, such as bad luck or the superior play of the other team (Lau & Russell, 1980). Roesch and Amirkhan (1997) further wondered if an athlete's skill, experience, and type of sport predicted attributional tendencies. They found that less experienced athletes were more likely to make self-serving

Self-Serving Attributions

Explanations for one's successes that credit internal, dispositional factors and explanations for one's failures that blame external, situational factors attributions than experienced ones; experienced athletes realize that losses are sometimes their fault and that they can't always take full credit for wins. They also found that athletes in solo sports made more self-serving attributions than those in team sports. Solo athletes, such as tennis players, know that winning and losing rests on their shoulders.

Why do we make self-serving attributions? Most people try to maintain their self-esteem whenever possible, even if that means distorting reality by changing a thought or belief. (We will discuss this concept at length in Chapter 6.) Here we see a specific attributional strategy that can be used to maintain or raise self-esteem: just locate "causality"—the reason something happened—where it does you the most good (Greenberg, Pyszczynski, & Solomon, 1982; Shepard, Malone, & Sweeny, 2008; Snyder & Higgins, 1988). We are particularly likely to engage in self-serving attributions when we fail at something and we feel we can't improve at it. The external attribution truly protects our self-esteem, as there is little hope we can do better in the future. But if we believe we can improve, we're more likely to attribute our current failure to internal causes and then work on improving (Duval & Silvia, 2002). Another, related reason has to do not with how we see ourselves but rather with how we present ourselves to others (Goffman, 1959). We want people to think well of us. Telling others that our poor performance was due to some external cause can be a way to put a "good face" on failure.

Yet one more reason individuals make self-serving attributions has to do with our earlier discussion about the kind of information that is available to people. Let's imagine the attributional process of another student in Imani's chemistry class, Ron, who did poorly on the midterm. Ron knows that he studied very hard for the midterm, that he typically does well on chemistry tests, and that in general he is a good student. The D on the chemistry midterm comes as a surprise. The most logical attribution Ron can make is that the test was unfair—the D grade wasn't due to a lack of ability or effort. The professor, however, knows that some students did well on the test and some did poorly; given the information available to her, it is logical for the professor to conclude that Ron, not the difficulty of the test, was responsible for his poor grade (Miller & Ross, 1975; Nisbett & Ross, 1980).

People also alter their attributions to deal with other kinds of threats to their self-esteem. One of the hardest things to understand in life is the occurrence of tragic events such as random attacks, terminal diseases, and fatal accidents. Even when they happen to strangers we have never met, they can be upsetting. They remind us that if such tragedies can happen to someone else, they could happen to us. So we take steps to deny this fact. One example is the belief that bad things happen only to bad people—or, at least, only to people who make stupid mistakes or poor choices. This allows us to rest assured that bad things won't happen to us because we won't be that careless. Melvin Lerner (1980, 1998) has called this the **belief in a just world**—the assumption that people get what they deserve and deserve what they get (Aguiar, Vala, Correia, & Pereira, 2008; Hafer, 2000; Hafer & Begue, 2005).

The just-world belief has some sad and even tragic consequences. For example, suppose a female student on your campus was the victim of a rape by a male student. How do you think you and your friends would react? Would you wonder if she'd done something to trigger the rape? Ask if she had been acting suggestively earlier in the evening or whether she had invited the man into her room? All of these questions are examples of a defensive attribution process by which people might try to make themselves feel better about the attack by placing some of the blame onto the victim (Burger, 1981; Lerner & Miller, 1978; Stormo, Lang, & Stritzke, 1997; Walster,

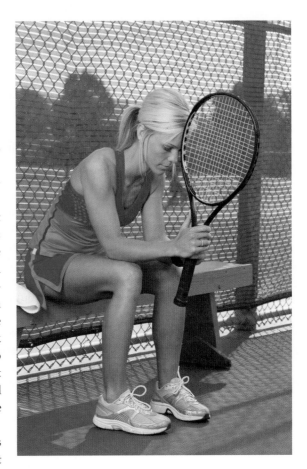

One domain in which self-serving biases may be particularly common is the world of sports, especially among solo athletes, for whom the entire weight of winning or losing rests on their shoulders.

Belief in a Just World

A form of defensive attribution wherein people assume that bad things happen to bad people and that good things happen to good people

1966). Indeed, research has found that the victims of crimes or accidents are often seen as contributing to their own fate. For example, people often believe that victims of rape and domestic abuse are to blame for the crimes others have committed against them (Abrams, Viki, Masser, & Bohner, 2003; Bell, Kuriloff, & Lottes, 1994; Summers & Feldman, 1984). By using this attributional bias, the perceiver does not have to acknowledge that there is a certain randomness to becoming a victim, that an accident or criminal may be waiting just around any corner. The belief in a just world keeps anxiety-provoking thoughts about one's own safety at bay.

The "Bias Blind Spot"

By now, we've discussed a number of attributional biases. Can you recall times when your thinking has reflected the fundamental attribution error or a self-serving attribution? What about other people? Do you think they fall prey to such biases more often than you do? Emily Pronin and colleagues have studied just this question and found evidence for a **bias blind spot**: We tend to think that others are more susceptible to attributional biases than we are, indicating a "blind spot" when reflecting on our own thought processes (Hansen, Gerbasi, Todorov, Kruse, & Pronin, 2014; Pronin, Gilovich, & Ross, 2004; Pronin, Lin, & Ross, 2002).

In order to study the bias blind spot, these researchers presented participants with descriptions of a number of biases. We will focus on two here: self-serving attributions and victim blaming. The descriptions the participants read never used the word "bias" (which makes it sound like a bad thing); instead, they were described as "tendencies" to think a certain way, which were then explained. Participants were asked to rate how susceptible they thought they were to each of these thought tendencies, using a scale ranging from "not at all" to "strongly." Next, participants made the same ratings for how susceptible they thought the average American was to these tendencies. The results indicated a striking difference: Participants felt they were only "somewhat" susceptible to self-serving attributions, while the average American was rated as much more susceptible, an ironically self-serving belief in its own right (see Figure 4.7). Similarly, participants felt they rarely committed the "blaming the victim" attribution, but again,

Bias Blind Spot

The tendency to think that other people are more susceptible to attributional biases in their thinking than we are

Figure 4.7 Perceived Susceptibility to Attributional Biases for Self and the Average American

Research participants rated their own susceptibility to two attributional biases and that of the "average American." They believed that others were significantly more likely to engage in biased thinking than they themselves were.

(Based on Pronin, Lin, & Ross, 2002)

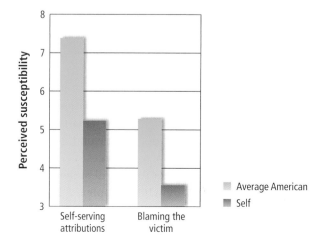

the average American was judged as much more likely to do so (see Figure 4.7). Thus, it appears that we realize that attributionally biased thinking can occur—in other people— but we're not so good at spotting it in ourselves. Our own thoughts seem rational and sensible, but other people, hey, they're susceptible to biases! These findings suggest that we often need to reflect more carefully on our judgment processes, check our conclusions, and remind ourselves that a bias blind spot may be lurking.

REVIEW QUESTIONS

1. Kelley assumed that when we are in the process of forming an attribution,
   a. we do not bother to gather information from any source regarding a person's behavior.
   b. we try to gather information to understand how a person's behavior changes across time and place.
   c. we reach a conclusion about causes of people's behavior based on our feelings.
   d. we do not give importance to change in a person's behavior across time.

2. The frequency with which the observed behavior between the same person and the same stimulus occurs across time and situations is called
   a. discriminative information.
   b. observed information.
   c. consensus information.
   d. consistency information.

3. Fundamental attribution error refers to the
   a. tendency to overestimate the extent to which other people's behavior is due to the situation they are in.
   b. tendency to underestimate other people's behavior as a reflection of their internal, dispositional factors.
   c. tendency to overestimate other people's behavior as a reflection of their dispositional beliefs and situational factors.
   d. tendency to overestimate the extent to which other people's behavior is due to dispositions and beliefs and to underestimate the role of situational factors.

4. Which of the following is the most accurate conclusion based on the Jones and Harris (1967) Castro essay study?
   a. When a target's behavior is forced, perceivers do not attribute it to any sort of internal cause.
   b. We are less generous with ourselves when making attributions for negative events than we are when others are the actors.
   c. We are more likely to make an internal attribution for a chosen action versus a forced action.
   d. We are more likely to make an internal attribution when the actor in question is perceptually salient.

5. Who of the following individuals is most likely to make a self-serving attribution?
   a. Rory, a golfer in the very early stages of his career
   b. Mariano, a baseball player who has won multiple championships in the past
   c. LeBron, a basketball player who has been playing since he was very young
   d. Roger, a professional tennis player with over a decade of experience

See page 620 for the answers.

Culture and Social Perception

4.4   What role does culture play in processes of social perception and attribution?

Social psychologists are focusing more and more on the role of culture in many aspects of social perception. Beyond our discussion of nonverbal communication and emblems above, does the culture in which we grow up influence how we perceive other people and try to make sense of their behavior? Let's look at the evidence.

North American and some other Western cultures stress individual autonomy. A person is perceived as independent and self-contained; his or her behavior reflects internal traits, motives, and values (Markus & Kitayama, 1991). The intellectual history of this cultural value can be traced from the Judeo-Christian belief in the individual soul and the English legal tradition of individual rights (Kitayama et al., 2006; Menon, Morris, Chiu, & Hong, 1999). In contrast, East Asian cultures such as those in China, Japan, and Korea tend to stress group autonomy. The individual is more likely to derive his or her sense of self from the social group. The intellectual history of this belief derives from the Confucian tradition—for example, the "community man" (*qunti de fenzi*) or "social being" (*shehui de renge*)—as well as from Taoism and Buddhism (Menon et al., 1999, p. 703; Zhu & Han, 2008).

Holistic versus Analytic Thinking

Research has indicated that these differing cultural values predict the kind of information that people notice and pay attention to. As we discussed in Chapter 3, the values inherent in individualistic Western cultures cause people, as they grow up, to develop more of an *analytic thinking style*. This style involves focusing on the properties of objects (or people) while paying much less attention, if any, to the context or situation that surrounds that object. In contrast, the values of collectivistic cultures, such as those of East Asia (e.g., China, Korea, and Japan), cause people to develop more of a *holistic thinking style*. Here, people focus on the "whole picture"—that is, the object (or person) and the context that surrounds that object as well as the relationships that exist between them (Nisbett, 2003; Nisbett & Masuda, 2003). We don't mean to suggest that these are either/or differences, that all people in one culture think one way and all people in another culture think another way; obviously, a great deal of variability exists within cultures as well. But these generalized differences in thinking styles do predict how we perceive other people.

For example, imagine that you are talking to a group of friends. The expression on one friend's face catches your attention. She's frowning, and her mouth is set in a tight line. What is she feeling? The analytic thinking style suggests that you would focus on her face alone and reach a decision. The holistic thinking style suggests that you would scan the faces of the others in the group, compare them to hers, and then reach a decision.

Takahiko Masuda and colleagues (2008) conducted a study much like this example. They presented research participants in the United States and Japan with cartoon drawings of people in groups. One person in each cartoon was the central figure, shown in the foreground. This person had a facial expression that was happy, sad, angry, or neutral. The other people in the group had facial expressions that either matched the central figure or were different. The participants' task was to judge the central person's emotion on a 10-point scale. The researchers found that the facial expressions of the other group members' faces had little effect on Americans' ratings of the central figure. If the central figure was smiling broadly, he received a high rating for "happy." It didn't matter what the rest of the group was expressing.

What emotion do you think the central person (the one in the middle) is experiencing in each of these cartoons? Your answer might depend on whether you live in a Western or East Asian culture (see the text as to why).

In comparison, the facial expressions of the other group members had a significant effect on Japanese participants' ratings of the central figure. A broad smile was interpreted as very happy if the group members were also smiling; the same broad smile was interpreted as less happy if the other group members looked sad or angry. In short, the meaning of the cartoon character's facial expression depended on his "context"— what the other cartoon characters standing next to him were feeling (Masuda et al., 2008). The researchers also measured the eye-tracking movements of the participants as they looked at the cartoons. The Japanese spent more time looking at the cartoon characters in the background than did the Americans. Both groups began by looking at the central character, but after 1 second, the Japanese started to scan over the other characters significantly more than did the Americans (Masuda et al., 2008).

SOCIAL NEUROSCIENCE EVIDENCE   The eye-tracking results in the study by Masuda and colleagues (2008) suggest that something very interesting is going on, at a physiological level, in people as they engage in analytic versus holistic thinking. Beyond eye movements, other researchers have explored how differences in cultural thinking styles predict how the brain responds to social stimuli (Knowles, Morris, Chiu, & Hong, 2001; Mason & Morris, 2010). Trey Hedden and colleagues (2008) used functional magnetic resonance imaging (fMRI) to examine where in the brain cultural experience predicts perceptual processing. Their participants, East Asians and Americans, underwent fMRI brain scans while making judgments about the length of lines inside boxes. Some participants were told to ignore the box around each line ("ignore context"), and some were told to pay attention to the box around each line ("attend to context"). Although participants from the two cultures were equally accurate at judging the lengths of the lines, they showed significantly more brain activity when they had to follow the instructions that were the opposite of their usual cultural thinking style. That is, American participants showed greater activation in higher-order cortical regions (frontal and parietal areas) when told to pay attention to the context, while East Asian participants showed greater activity in the same brain regions when told to ignore context. Greater cortical activation means that the participant had to exert more attention (in a sense, had to work harder cognitively) when asked to perceive objects in a way that was not typical (Hedden et al., 2008).

Other researchers have used event-related potentials (ERPs) to measure brain activity among individuals from different cultures (Goto, Ando, Huang, Yee, & Lewis, 2010; Goto, Yee, Lowenberg, & Lewis, 2013). While fMRI indicates which brain regions are active, ERPs provide a more fine-grained analysis of the onset and offset of neural firing by measuring electrical activity through sensors placed on the scalp. In one study, researchers presented participants with a series of simple perceptual tasks that involved visual information about "targets" and context (Lewis, Goto, & Kong, 2008). In an interesting twist, their participants were all Americans who had grown up in American culture but were of two different ethnic backgrounds: European American or East Asian American. The pattern of ERPs indicated that the European American participants paid more attention to the targets, while the East Asian American participants paid more attention to the context surrounding the targets.

Cultural Differences in the Fundamental Attribution Error

Earlier we saw that people often commit the fundamental attribution error, overestimating the extent to which people's behavior is due to internal, dispositional factors and underestimating the role of situational factors. Is the fundamental attribution error stronger in Western than Eastern cultures?

As it turns out, people in individualist cultures do prefer dispositional attributions about others, relative to people in collectivist cultures, who prefer situational attributions (Newman & Bakina, 2009; Tang, Newman, & Huang, 2014).

For example, Joan Miller (1984) asked people of two cultures—Hindus living in India and Americans living in the United States—to think of various examples of their friends' behaviors and to explain why those behaviors occurred. The American participants used more dispositional explanations for the behaviors. In contrast, Indian participants gravitated toward situational explanations for their friends' behaviors. But, you might be thinking, perhaps the Americans and Indians generated different kinds of examples. Perhaps the Indians thought of behaviors that were really situationally caused, whereas the Americans thought of behaviors that were really dispositionally caused. To test this alternative hypothesis, Miller (1984) took some of the behaviors generated by the Indian participants and gave them to Americans to explain. The attributional difference remained: Americans still found internal, dispositional causes for the behaviors that the Indians had thought were caused by the situation.

Remember our earlier discussion of the role of evolution in the display of facial expression? Well, Miller's (1984) cross-cultural findings serve as an important reminder that environmental forces—in this case cultural experiences—play a major role in social perception processes as well. In fact, some of the most interesting findings from Miller's (1984) research come from the American and Indian children she examined. In addition to comparing the attributional tendencies of adults from the two cultures, Miller also analyzed the attributions of 8-, 11-, and 15-year-olds. Unlike the significant differences she observed among the adults, children from the United States and India were more or less indistinguishable in terms of how they explained their friends' behaviors. In short, cross-cultural differences in social perception do not appear to be inborn; rather, we arrive in this world with a flexibility of thinking style that is molded over time by cultural (and other) influences.

A fascinating look at this flexibility is provided by Ying-Yi Hong and colleagues (2003), who investigated the fundamental attribution error among Hong Kong Chinese college students. These students were bicultural—deriving their identity not only from their Hong Kong Chinese culture but also from Western culture, to which they had had a great deal of exposure. The participants were first shown a series of images and asked brief questions about them. The purpose of the photographs was to activate, or prime, one aspect of their bicultural identity. Half the participants saw images representing American culture, such as the American flag and the U.S. Capitol building. The other half saw Chinese images, such as a Chinese dragon and the Great Wall. Participants in the control condition saw geometric figures, which did not prime either culture. Next, in a supposedly unrelated task, participants were shown a photograph of a fish swimming in front of a school of other fish. They were asked to make an attribution: Why was this fish swimming in front of the others? Their responses were coded for dispositional reasons (e.g., "The fish is leading the other fish") and situational reasons (e.g., "The fish is being chased by the other fish"). The researchers found that about 30% of the control group made situational attributions about the central fish. However, participants primed with thoughts of one culture or the other showed markedly different patterns. Those primed with Chinese cultural images were more likely to make situational attributions about the fish (nearly 50% of the participants), while those primed with American cultural images were less likely to make situational attributions (about 15% of

> Resemblances are the shadows of differences. Different people see different similarities and similar differences.
>
> —VLADIMIR NABOKOV, *PALE FIRE*

Research has shown that when forming attributions, people in collectivistic cultures such as Japan are more likely to take situational information into account than are people in individualistic cultures.

Bicultural research participants were first "primed" with images from one of their cultural heritages: either images evoking American culture or images evoking Chinese culture, like these.

the participants), instead making dispositional attributions (Hong, Chiu, & Kung, 1997; Hong, Morris, Chiu, & Benet-Martinez, 2000).

Thus, it appears that Western cultures prompt people to think more like personality psychologists, viewing behavior in dispositional terms. In contrast, Eastern cultures seem to prompt people to think more like social psychologists, considering the situational causes of behavior. However, it would be a mistake to think that members of collectivist cultures don't *ever* make dispositional attributions. Of course they do—it's just a matter of degree. Recent research indicates that a tendency to think dispositionally about others is prevalent in many cultures. However, members of collectivistic cultures are more aware of how the situation affects behavior and more likely to take situational effects into account (Choi, Dalal, Kim-Prieto, & Park, 2003; Choi & Nisbett, 1998; Choi, Nisbett, & Norenzayan, 1999; Krull et al., 1999; Miyamoto & Kitayama, 2002). Thus, the difference is that people in collectivist cultures are more likely to go beyond dispositional explanations and consider information about the situation as well.

Culture and Other Attributional Biases

Continuing to explore the link between culture and attributional biases, social psychologists have examined the self-serving bias and found a strong cultural component to it as well. In a recent meta-analysis of 266 studies conducted all over the world, Amy Mezulis and her colleagues (2004) found that the self-serving bias is strongest in the United States and some other Western countries—Canada, Australia, and New Zealand. It is also prevalent in Africa, Eastern Europe, and Russia. Within the United States, samples of participants who were of White, Asian, African, Hispanic, and Native American descent did not differ significantly from each other in the degree of self-serving bias. On the other hand, some Asian cultures displayed a markedly low or even absent level of self-serving bias: Japan, the Pacific Islands, and India (Mezulis et al., 2004).

In many traditional Asian cultures, the values of modesty and harmony with others are highly valued. For example, Chinese students are expected to attribute their success to other people, such as their teachers or parents, or to other aspects of the situation, such as the high quality of their school (Bond, 1996; Leung, 1996). Their cultural tradition does not encourage them to attribute their success to themselves

Next, these research participants were asked to make an attribution about the behavior of the fish in the front of the pack. Would they make dispositional or situational attributions about the fish's behavior, given the cultural priming they had experienced earlier?

Sports competitors often make very different attributions for their outcomes based on whether they win or lose as well as cross-cultural variability in attributional tendencies.

(such as to their talent or intelligence), as it does in the United States and other Western countries. As you might expect, Chinese research participants took less credit for their successes than U.S. participants did (Anderson, 1999; Lee & Seligman, 1997). Instead, Chinese students attributed their success to aspects of their situation, reflecting the values of their culture.

Do individualistic and collectivistic cultures differ in how they explain Olympic gold-medal success? Prior research has indicated that "cultural products" such as advertising, song lyrics, television shows, and art have content that reflects their culture's values: more individualistic content in Western cultures and more collectivistic content in countries such as Japan, Korea, China, and Mexico (Morling & Lamoreaux, 2008). Hazel Markus and her colleagues (2006) found that this applies to television and newspaper sports commentary as well. They coded Japanese and American media accounts of their countries' gold medal–winning athletes. They found that U.S. media described the performance of American gold medalists in terms of their unique abilities and talents. In comparison, Japanese media described the performance of Japanese gold medalists in much broader terms, including the individual's ability but also encompassing his or her past experiences of success and failure and the role of other people such as coaches, teammates, and family in his or her success. Finally, American coverage focused more on positive aspects than negative ones (e.g., "[his] strength keeps him in the running"), consistent with a self-serving attributional style, while Japanese coverage focused more equally on positive and negative aspects (e.g., "Her second Olympics is a regrettable one. She was almost at the top, but she didn't have a perfect performance"; Markus et al., 2006, pp. 106–107). The following two quotes from gold medalists summarize the different ways in which culture influences how one explains one's own behavior:

> I think I just stayed focused. It was time to show the world what I could do. . . . I knew I could beat [her], deep down in my heart I believed it . . . the doubts kept creeping in . . . but I just said, "No, this is my night." (Misty Hyman, American gold medalist in the women's 200-m butterfly). (Markus et al., 2006, p. 103)

> Here is the best coach in the world, the best manager in the world, and all of the people who support me—all these things were getting together and became a gold medal. So I think I didn't get it alone, not only by myself (Naoko Takahashi, Japanese gold medalist in the women's marathon). (Markus et al., 2006, p. 103)

What about failure? Remember that in individualistic cultures such as the United States, people tend toward the self-serving bias, looking outside of themselves—to the situation—to explain failure. In collectivist cultures such as Chinese, the reverse is true: People often attribute failure to internal causes, not to external ones (Anderson, 1999; Oishi, Wyer, & Colcombe, 2000). In fact, in some Asian cultures such as Japan and Korea, self-critical attributions are a common and important "glue" that holds groups together. In response to self-criticism, others offer sympathy and compassion, which strengthens the interdependence of the group members (Kitayama & Uchida, 2003).

Finally, recall that the belief in a just world is a defensive attribution that helps people maintain their vision of life as safe, orderly, and predictable. Is there a cultural component to this as well? Adrian Furnham (1993) argues that in a society where most people tend to believe the world is a just place, economic and social inequities are considered "fair." In such societies, people believe that the poor and disadvantaged have less because they deserve less. Thus, the just-world attribution can be used to explain and justify injustice. Preliminary research suggests that, indeed, in cultures with extremes of wealth and poverty, just-world attributions are more common than in cultures where wealth is more evenly distributed (Dalbert & Yamauchi, 1994; Furnham, 1993; Furnham & Procter, 1989). For example, research participants in India and South Africa received higher scores on the just-world belief scale than participants in the United States, Australia, Hong Kong, and Zimbabwe, who had scores in the middle of the scale.

REVIEW QUESTIONS

1. Research has indicated that the values inherent in an individualistic culture cause people to develop more of an analytic thinking style that involves
   a. paying more attention to the context or situation rather than to the properties of the person or object.
   b. paying more attention to the properties of the person or object rather than to the context or situation.
   c. paying equal attention to the context or situation as well as to the properties of the object or person.
   d. paying attention to all the others in the group and judging the person.

2. Event-related potentials (ERP) research measuring patterns among individuals from different ethnic backgrounds indicated that
   a. European American participants paid more attention to the context surrounding the targets rather than the targets while East Asian Americans paid less attention to the context surrounding the targets and paid more attention to the target.
   b. no significant difference was found between European American participants and East Asian American participants in terms of attention paid to the targets.
   c. East Asian American participants paid more attention to the context surrounding the targets while European American participants paid more attention to the targets.
   d. no significant difference was found between European American participants and East Asian American participants in terms of attention paid to the context surrounding the targets.

3. Individualistic and collectivist cultures have been found to differ in explaining failure. Which of the following is true?

   a. In individualistic cultures such as in the United States, people have a tendency toward self-serving bias. They tend to explain failure by looking outside of themselves, attributing it to the situation.
   b. In collectivistic cultures such as the Chinese, people attribute failure to external causes as they want to defend themselves.
   c. In most collectivistic cultures, it is common to attribute failure to internal as well as external causes.
   d. In some Asian cultures, such as Korea and Japan, it is common to attribute failure to the situation and other external causes. Self-critical attributions are considered to weaken the interdependence of the group members.

4. Preliminary research on just-world attributions compared cultures with extremes of wealth and poverty and cultures where wealth is more evenly distributed. According to the research, in which cultures are just-world attributions more common?
   a. Cultures where wealth is evenly distributed.
   b. Cultures with extremes of wealth and poverty.
   c. Cultures that are very wealthy and there is no poverty.
   d. Cultures that are extremely poor.

5. Belief in a just world is _____ that helps people maintain their vision of life as _____.
   a. an internal attribution; unpredictable
   b. a self-serving bias; unsafe
   c. an internal attribution; safe
   d. a defensive attribution; predictable

See page 621 for the answers.

Summary

4.1 **How do people use nonverbal cues to understand others?**

- **Nonverbal Communication** Nonverbal communication is used to express emotion, convey attitudes, and communicate personality traits. People can accurately decode subtle nonverbal cues.

  - **Facial Expressions of Emotion** The six major emotions are universal, encoded and decoded similarly by people around the world; they have evolutionary significance. **Affect blends** occur when one part of the face registers one emotion and another part registers a different emotion. Mirror neurons are involved in emotional encoding and decoding and help us experience empathy.

- **Culture and the Channels of Nonverbal Communication** Other channels of nonverbal communication include eye gaze, touch, personal space, gesture, and tone of voice. **Display rules** are particular to each culture and dictate what kinds of emotional expressions people are supposed to show. **Emblems** are gestures with well-defined meanings and are culturally determined.

4.2 How quickly do first impressions form, and why do they persist?

- **First Impressions: Quick but Long-Lasting** We form impressions of other people based on their facial structure, possessions, attire, and a variety of other cues, and this process begins within milliseconds. Research on **thin-slicing** indicates that these snap judgments are not just quick; they also pick up on meaningful information and converge with the impressions formed by perceivers with even longer exposure to the target in question.

  - **The Lingering Influence of Initial Impressions** Once formed, impressions remain influential because the **primacy effect** demonstrates that the first traits we perceive in another person influence our interpretation of subsequently learned information. We also tend toward **belief perseverance**, or clinging to conclusions even in the face of evidence that seems to indicate we should change our minds.

  - **Using First Impressions and Nonverbal Communication to Our Advantage** Knowing what influences social perception can allow us to manage how others see us and to use our own bodily posture to gain self-confidence.

4.3 How do people determine why others do what they do?

- **Causal Attribution: Answering the "Why" Question** According to **attribution theory**, we try to determine why people do what they do in order to uncover the feelings and traits that are behind their actions. This helps us understand and predict our social world.

  - **The Nature of the Attribution Process** When trying to decide what causes people's behavior, we can make one of two attributions: an **internal**, or dispositional, attribution or an **external**, or situational, attribution.

  - **The Covariation Model: Internal versus External Attributions** The **covariation model** focuses on observations of behavior across time, place, actors, and targets of the behavior. It examines how the perceiver chooses either an internal or an external attribution. We make such choices by using **consensus**, **distinctiveness**, and **consistency** information.

  - **The Fundamental Attribution Error: People as Personality Psychologists** In making attributions, people also use various mental shortcuts, including schemas and theories. One common shortcut is the **fundamental attribution error**, the tendency to believe that people's behavior corresponds to (matches) their dispositions. A reason for this bias is that a person's behavior has greater **perceptual salience** than does the surrounding situation. The **two-step attribution process** states that the initial and automatic attribution tends to be dispositional, but it can be altered by situational information at the second step.

- **Self-Serving Attributions** People's attributions are also influenced by their personal needs. **Self-serving attributions** occur when people make internal attributions for their successes and external attributions for their failures. The **belief in a just world**, where we believe that bad things happen to bad people and good things happen to good people, allows us to avoid thoughts about our own mortality.

- **The "Bias Blind Spot"** The **bias blind spot** indicates that we think other people are more susceptible to attributional biases in their thinking than we are.

4.4 What role does culture play in processes of social perception and attribution?

- **Culture and Social Perception** Social psychologists have increasingly begun to consider cross-cultural differences in how people interpret the world around them.

  - **Holistic versus Analytic Thinking** In individualistic cultures like the United States, people tend to pay more attention to the properties of objects. In collectivistic cultures like those of East Asia, people focus more on the whole picture, including context and the relationships between objects, as demonstrated by **social neuroscience evidence** from fMRI and ERP studies.

  - **Cultural Differences in the Fundamental Attribution Error** Although people from both individualistic and collectivistic cultures demonstrate the fundamental attribution error, members of collectivist cultures are more sensitive to situational causes of behavior as long as situational variables are salient.

  - **Culture and Other Attributional Biases** There is also evidence for cross-cultural differences in self-serving attributions and belief in a just world. Typically, these differences, too, occur between Western, individualistic cultures and Eastern, collectivistic cultures.

Test Yourself

1. According to Darwin's research on facial expressions, how do humans encode primary emotions?

a. All humans encode primary emotions in the same way.

b. Humans make a lot of effort to convey primary emotions.

c. Expression of primary emotions is culture specific.

d. Humans learn to encode primary emotions through the process of learning.

2. According to research studies, individuals from which culture maintain more rigid boundaries between the six major emotions when applying them to faces?

a. Western

b. Indian

c. Chinese

d. Japanese

3. During her three-month visit to the United States, Rose had an opportunity to meet people from diverse cultures. She was very fond of analyzing their facial expressions while meeting them on various occasions. She observed that _____women often tried to hide a wide smile behind their hands whereas _____women smiled broadly without hesitation.

a. African American; Indian

b. Japanese; British

c. Japanese; Western

d. African American; Australian

4. Which of the following best illustrates the primacy effect in social perception?

a. Joseph was introduced to his class as someone who is rigid, jealous, inquisitive, and very brilliant. His classmates formed a very positive impression of him and wanted to make him their friend.

b. Mike entered a room filled with lots of people. He was introduced by his best friend as someone who is very brilliant, creative, rigid, and jealous. Everybody in the room formed a very positive impression of him.

c. When Chris met Joe for the first time, he found Joe to be very knowledgeable and wise. Later, on other occasions, Chris discovered that Joe was a fake and regarded him as stupid.

d. Wendy was smart and assertive during her adolescence and continued to be the same as a grown-up and was appreciated by everybody.

5. You visited a close friend after a long time and wanted to have a good time together. All of a sudden her brother came out of his room and started yelling at her. You wondered what was wrong with her brother. Is he crazy? Doesn't he know how to behave with people? He seemed like a very impatient and ill-mannered person. You felt very bad for your friend, who started crying. What kind of attribution were you making about your friend's brother?

a. External attribution

b. Self-serving attribution

c. Internal attribution

d. Fundamental attribution

6. Suppose a certain student, Jake, falls asleep during every chemistry class. Further suppose that Jake is the only one who falls asleep in this class and he falls asleep in all of his other classes. According to Kelley's covariation theory of attribution, how will people explain his behavior?

a. It is due to something unusual about this particular class because his behavior is low in consensus, high in distinctiveness, and high in consistency.

b. Chemistry is really a boring class because Jake's behavior is high in consensus, high in distinctiveness, and high in consistency.

c. It is due to something unusual about Jake because his behavior is low in consensus, low in distinctiveness, and high in consistency.

d. It is due to something peculiar about the circumstances on a particular day because his behavior is high in consensus.

7. Imagine that you are in Hong Kong reading the morning news and you notice a headline about a double murder that took place overnight. A suspect is in custody. Which of the following headlines is most likely to accompany the story?

a. Dispute over Gambling Debt Ends in Murder

b. Crazed Murderer Slays Two

c. Homicidal Maniac Stalks Innocents

d. Bloodthirsty Mobster Takes Revenge

8. Ming is from China; Jason is from the United States. Both participate in an experiment in which they take a test, are given feedback, and are told that they did very well. They are then asked to make attributions for their performance. Based on cross-cultural research on the self-serving bias, you would expect that

   a. Jason but not Ming will say that he succeeded due to his high ability.

   b. neither Ming nor Jason will say that they succeeded due to their high ability.

   c. both Ming and Jason will say that they succeeded due to their high ability.

   d. Ming but not Jason will say that he succeeded due to his high ability.

9. Which of the following statements best describes cultural differences in the fundamental attribution error?

   a. Members of collectivist cultures rarely make dispositional attributions.

   b. Members of Western cultures rarely make dispositional attributions.

   c. Members of collectivist cultures are more likely to go beyond dispositional explanations, considering information about the situation as well.

   d. Members of Western cultures are more likely to go beyond dispositional explanations, considering information about the situation as well.

10. It is 10:00 A.M. and Jamie, an American college student, is dragging himself to his next class to turn in a paper for which he pulled an all-nighter. Through a haze of exhaustion, on the way to class he sees a student slip and fall down. How would Jamie be most likely to interpret the cause of the student's behavior?

    a. Jamie's attribution will most heavily be influenced by his own personality.

    b. Given what we know about Jamie's current cognitive capacity and cultural background, he will likely assume that the student fell because he or she was clumsy.

    c. Jamie would probably attribute the cause to the situation, such as the fact that it was raining and the sidewalks were slippery.

    d. Jamie would be so tired that he would not make any causal attributions.

See page 621 for the answers.

Chapter 5
The Self
Understanding Ourselves in a Social Context

 ## Chapter Outline and Learning Objectives

The Origins and Nature of the Self-Concept

5.1 What is the self-concept, and how does it develop?

Cultural Influences on the Self-Concept

Functions of the Self

Knowing Ourselves Through Introspection

5.2 To what extent do people know themselves through introspection, and what are the consequences of introspection?

Focusing on the Self: Self-Awareness Theory

Judging Why We Feel the Way We Do: Telling More Than We Can Know

The Consequences of Introspecting About Reasons

Knowing Ourselves by Observing Our Own Behavior

5.3 In what ways do people come to know themselves by observing their behavior?

Intrinsic versus Extrinsic Motivation

Mindsets and Motivation

Understanding Our Emotions: The Two-Factor Theory of Emotion

Finding the Wrong Cause: Misattribution of Arousal

Using Other People to Know Ourselves

5.4 In what ways do people use others to know themselves?

Knowing Ourselves by Comparing Ourselves to Others

Knowing Ourselves by Adopting Other People's Views
Knowing Our Future Feelings by Consulting Other People

Self-Control: The Executive Function of the Self

5.5   **When are people likely to succeed at self-control, and when are they likely to fail?**

Impression Management: All the World's a Stage

5.6   **How do people portray themselves so that others will see them as they want to be seen?**

Ingratiation and Self-Handicapping
Culture, Impression Management,
   and Self-Enhancement

Self-Esteem: How We Feel About Ourselves

5.7   **What are the pros and cons of having high self-esteem?**

Great athletes are born and not made—or so it seems. "She's a natural," we hear, or "he's one in a million." Talent is important to athletic success, of course, which is why one of your authors became a psychologist instead of a professional baseball player. But is talent everything? Consider Mia Hamm, who in her prime was the best women's soccer player in the world. When she was 10, she talked herself onto an 11-year-old boys' team and eventually led them in scoring. In college she didn't think she was that good, but as she played against the top players in the country, she found herself "improving faster than I had ever dreamed possible" (Hamm, 1999, p. 4). After playing on teams that won the World Cup and an Olympic gold medal, here is what Hamm said about people who called her the best player in the world: "They're wrong. I have the potential, maybe, but I'm still not there" (Hamm, 1999, p. 15). Or consider Derek Jeter, the all-star major league shortstop who played for the New York Yankees for 19 seasons. When he was a kid in Kalamazoo, Michigan, few people thought he had the talent to become a professional baseball player. His reaction? "You know, I love it when people doubt me. It makes me work harder to prove them wrong." It's all about effort, he says: "When it's all said and done, the worst thing you can say is, 'Ah, well, I could've been better if I'd worked a little harder'" (Zimmerman, 2008).

The point of these stories is not just that "practice makes perfect"; it's about the importance of how we see ourselves and our abilities. Some people view athletic talent as a gift you either have or you don't—the "one in a million" theory. The problem is that when such people do poorly, as every athlete does on occasion, it is a devastating sign that they don't have it. "I'm *not* one in a million, and nothing can change that," they think. "So why bother practicing? Maybe I should take a psychology class instead." Others, such as Mia Hamm and Derek Jeter, view athletic performance as a skill that can be improved. Failure is a sign that they need to work harder, not that they should give up. As we will see in this chapter, how people view their own abilities and interpret the reasons for their behavior can be crucial determinants of their success. But how do people come to know themselves? More generally, what is the nature of the self, and how do people discover it? These are the questions to which we turn.

The Origins and Nature of the Self-Concept

5.1   **What is the self-concept, and how does it develop?**

Who are you? How did you come to be this person you call "myself"? A good place to begin is with the question of whether we are the only species that has a "self." Although it is doubtful that other species can think of themselves as unique beings in the same way that we do, some fascinating studies suggest that other species have at least a rudimentary sense of self (Gallup, 1997). To study whether animals have a self-concept, researchers placed a mirror in an animal's cage until the mirror became a familiar object. The animal was then briefly anesthetized, and an odorless red dye was painted on its brow or ear. What happened when the animal woke up and looked in the mirror? Members of the great ape family, such as chimpanzees and orangutans, immediately touched the area of their heads marked with the red spot, whereas lesser apes, such as gibbons, did not (Suddendorf & Butler, 2013).

These studies suggest that chimps and orangutans have a rudimentary sense of self. They realize that the image in the mirror is themselves and not another animal, and they recognize that they look different from how they looked before (Gallup, Anderson, & Shillito, 2002; Heschl & Burkart, 2006; Posada & Colell, 2007). What about other animals? Individual members of other species have passed the mirror test, including two dolphins, one Asian elephant, and two magpies, but no other nonhuman species regularly passes the test other than the great apes (Anderson & Gallup, 2011; Suddendorf & Butler, 2013).

Researchers have examined whether other species have a self-concept, by seeing whether individuals recognize that an image in a mirror is them and not another member of their species. The same procedure has been used with human infants.

Wondering when a sense of self develops in humans, researchers used a variation of the red-dye test with toddlers and found that human self-recognition develops at around 18 to 24 months of age (Hart & Matsuba, 2012; Lewis & Ramsay, 2004). Then, as we grow older, this rudimentary sense of self develops into a full-blown **self-concept**, defined as the overall set of beliefs that people have about their personal attributes. One way psychologists have studied how people's self-concept changes from childhood to adulthood is by asking people of different ages to answer the simple question "Who am I?" Typically, a child's self-concept is concrete, with references to clear-cut, easily observable characteristics like age, sex, neighborhood, and hobbies. A 9-year-old answered the question this way: "I have brown eyes. I have brown hair. I have brown eyebrows. . . . I'm a boy. I have an uncle that is almost 7 feet tall" (Montemayor & Eisen, 1977, p. 317).

Self-Concept

The overall set of beliefs that people have about their personal attributes

As we mature, we place less emphasis on physical characteristics and more on psychological states (our thoughts and feelings) and on considerations of how other people judge us (Hart & Damon, 1986; Livesley & Bromley, 1973; Montemayor & Eisen, 1977). Consider this 12th-grade high school student's answer to the "Who am I?" question:

> I am a human being. . . . I am a moody person. I am an indecisive person. I am an ambitious person. I am a very curious person. I am not an individual. I am a loner. I am an American (God help me). I am a Democrat. I am a liberal person. I am a radical. I am a conservative. I am a pseudoliberal. I am an atheist. I am not a classifiable person (i.e., I don't want to be). (Montemayor & Eisen, 1977, p. 318)

Clearly, this teenager has moved well beyond descriptions of her hobbies and appearance (Harter, 2003). What do we see as key attributes of "the self" when we are adults? To answer that question, imagine that you had a good friend when you were 25 but lost track of this person and didn't see him or her again until 40 years later. You notice that your friend has changed in certain ways, and the question is, how do these changes alter your view of the person's "true self"? A recent study asked participants this question and found that some changes, such as physical declines, minor cognitive deficits, and new preferences, don't change people's basic view of who someone is. If our friend Bob now needs prescription eyeglasses, doesn't recall things as well as he used to, and has become a vegetarian, we still see him as the same old Bob (with some minor

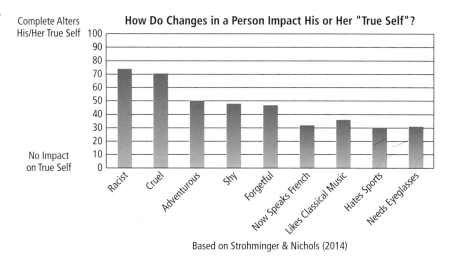

How Do Changes in a Person Impact His or Her "True Self"?

Complete Alters His/Her True Self — 100

No Impact on True Self — 0

(Categories: Racist, Cruel, Adventurous, Shy, Forgetful, Now Speaks French, Likes Classical Music, Hates Sports, Needs Eyeglasses)

Based on Strohminger & Nichols (2014)

Figure 5.1 What Do We See as Key Attributes of Other People's Selves?

Participants were asked to imagine that they saw an old friend that they knew when they were 25 years old but had not seen in 40 years. They were given a list of ways in which their friend had changed and rated each one according to how much it would alter their view of their friend' true self, on a scale that went from 0% ("this change has no impact on his/her true self") to 100% (this change completely alters his/her true self"). People thought that changes in their friend's morality (e.g., how cruel he/she was) would alter his/her true self more than other changes. People thought that changes in perceptual abilities (e.g., changes in vision) would have the smallest impact on their friend's true self.

(Data from Strohminger & Nichols, 2014)

changes). But if an old friend has undergone a moral transformation—for example, if Bob shows signs of cruelty when he used to be kind or racist when he used to be egalitarian—we hardly recognize him as the same person (see Figure 5.1). In short, morality is viewed as central to the self-concept, more so than cognitive processes or desires (Goodwin, Piazza, & Rozin, 2014; Strohminger & Nichols, 2014).

Cultural Influences on the Self-Concept

An important influence on our self-concepts is the culture in which we grew up. Consider Masako Owada, the crown princess of Japan. When she married Crown Prince Naruhito in June 1993, at age 29, she was a brilliant career diplomat in the Foreign Ministry, educated at Harvard and Oxford. She spoke five languages and was on the fast track to a prestigious job as a diplomat. Her decision to marry the prince surprised many observers because it meant she would have to give up her career. Indeed, she gave up any semblance of an independent life, becoming subservient to the prince and the rest of the royal family and spending much of her time participating in rigid royal ceremonies. Although some people hoped that she would modernize the monarchy, "the princess has not changed the imperial family as much as it has changed her" ("Girl Born to Japan's Princess," 2001).

How do you feel about Masako's decision to marry the prince? Your answer may say something about the nature of your self-concept and the culture in which you grew up. In many Western cultures, people have an **independent view of the self**, which is a way of defining oneself in terms of one's own internal thoughts, feelings, and actions and not in terms of the thoughts, feelings, and actions of others (Kitayama & Uchida, 2005; Markus & Kitayama, 1991, 2010; Nisbett, 2003; Oyserman & Lee, 2008; Triandis, 1995). Consequently, many Western observers were mystified by Masako's decision to marry the crown prince. They assumed that she was coerced into the marriage by a backward, sexist society that did not properly value her worth as an individual with an independent life of her own.

In contrast, many Asian and other non-Western cultures have an **interdependent view of the self**, which is a way of defining oneself in terms of one's relationships to other people and recognizing that one's behavior is often determined by the thoughts, feelings, and actions of others. Here, connectedness and interdependence between people are valued, whereas

Independent View of the Self

A way of defining oneself in terms of one's own internal thoughts, feelings, and actions and not in terms of the thoughts, feelings, and actions of other people

---

The squeaky wheel gets the grease.

—AMERICAN PROVERB

The nail that stands out gets pounded down.

—JAPANESE PROVERB

When Harvard-educated Masako Owada abandoned her promising career to marry Crown Prince Naruhito of Japan and assumed the traditional roles required of her, many Western women questioned her decision. At issue for many was cultural interdependence versus independence of the self.

independence and uniqueness are frowned on. For example, when asked to complete sentences beginning with "I am," people from Asian cultures are more likely to refer to social groups, such as their family or religious group, than people from Western cultures are (Bochner, 1994; Triandis, 1989). To many Japanese and other Asians, Masako's decision to give up her career was not at all surprising and was a natural consequence of her view of herself as connected and obligated to others, such as her parents and the royal family. What is viewed as positive and normal behavior by one culture may be viewed very differently by another.

Ted Singelis (1994) developed a questionnaire that measures the extent to which people view themselves as interdependent or independent. Sample items from this scale are given in the Try It! given below. Studies generally show that people who live in East Asian countries agree more with the interdependence items, whereas those who live in Western countries agree more with the independence items (Taras et al., 2014).

Interdependent View of the Self

A way of defining oneself in terms of one's relationships to other people, recognizing that one's behavior is often determined by the thoughts, feelings, and actions of others

TRY IT!

A Measure of Independence and Interdependence

Instructions: Indicate the extent to which you agree or disagree with each of these statements.

	Strongly Disagree						Strongly Agree
1. My happiness depends on the happiness of those around me.	1	2	3	4	5	6	7
2. I will sacrifice my self-interest for the benefit of the group I am in.	1	2	3	4	5	6	7
3. It is important to me to respect decisions made by the group.	1	2	3	4	5	6	7
4. If my brother or sister fails, I feel responsible.	1	2	3	4	5	6	7
5. Even when I strongly disagree with group members, I avoid an argument.	1	2	3	4	5	6	7
6. I am comfortable with being singled out for praise or rewards.	1	2	3	4	5	6	7
7. Being able to take care of myself is a primary concern for me.	1	2	3	4	5	6	7
8. I prefer to be direct and forthright when dealing with people I've just met.	1	2	3	4	5	6	7
9. I enjoy being unique and different from others in many respects.	1	2	3	4	5	6	7
10. My personal identity, independent of others, is very important to me.	1	2	3	4	5	6	7

Note: These questions are taken from a scale developed by Singelis (1994) to measure the strength of people's interdependent and independent views of themselves. The actual scale consists of 12 items that measure interdependence and 12 items that measure independence. We have reproduced five of each type of item here: The first five are designed to measure interdependence, and the last five are designed to measure independence. For scoring instructions, turn to page 621. (Adapted from Singelis, 1994.)

We do not mean to imply, however, that every member of a Western culture has an independent view of the self and that every member of an Asian culture has an interdependent view of the self. In the United States, for example, people who live in states that were settled more recently by European Americans, such as Oklahoma and Utah, tend to have more of an independent view of the self than do people who live in more "settled" East Coast states, such as Massachusetts and Connecticut. One sign of this, according to a recent study, is that babies born in recently settled states have more unusual names than babies born in other states. That is, one sign of an independent self-construal is giving your baby an unusual name, and parents are more likely to do that in states such as Oklahoma than they are in states such as Connecticut (see Figure 5.2). The same difference was found in recently settled versus older areas of Canada (Varnum & Kitayama, 2011).

Figure 5.2 Date of Statehood and Frequency of Popular Baby Names

This graph shows selected U.S. states and the year they attained statehood. It can be seen that the more recently a state became part of the union, the less likely parents were to give their children popular names. Researchers view this as evidence that residents of these states have a more independent self-view

(Based on Varnum & Kitayama, 2011)

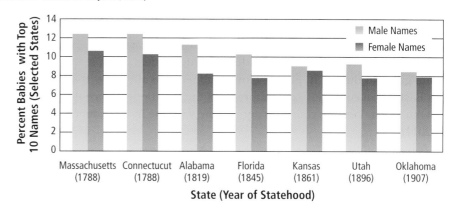

Nonetheless, the difference between the Western and Eastern sense of self is real and has interesting consequences for communication between the cultures. Indeed, the differences in the sense of self are so fundamental that it is very difficult for people with independent selves to appreciate what it is like to have an interdependent self and vice versa. After giving a lecture on the Western view of the self to a group of Japanese students, one psychologist reported that the students "sighed deeply and said at the end, 'Could this really be true?'" (Kitayama & Markus, 1994, p. 18). To paraphrase William Shakespeare, in Western society the self is the measure of all things. But however natural we consider this conception of the self to be, it is important to remember that it is socially constructed and therefore may differ from culture to culture.

Functions of the Self

What exactly does the self do? There are four main functions: *self-knowledge* is the way we understand who we are and formulate and organize this information; *self-control* is the way we make plans and execute decisions, such as your decision to read this book right now instead of going out for ice cream; *impression management* is the way we present ourselves to other people and get them to see us the way we want to be seen; and *self-esteem* is the way in which we try to maintain positive views of ourselves. In the remainder of the chapter, we will discuss all four of these functions.

REVIEW QUESTIONS

1. Which of the following is *least* likely to pass the "mirror" test suggesting they have at least a rudimentary self-concept?
   a. An orangutan
   b. A chimpanzee
   c. A 12-month-old human infant
   d. A 3-year-old human child

2. When thinking about other people, which of the following will we see as most central to their self-concept?
   a. Their morals

   b. Their preferences and attitudes
   c. Their physical attributes
   d. Their memories

3. Which is the best definition of an *independent* view of the self?
   a. Defining oneself in terms of one's relationships to other people
   b. Defining oneself in terms of one's own internal thoughts, feelings, and actions

c. Someone who enjoys activities such as dancing and team sports

d. Someone who enjoys activities such as reading and writing poetry

4. Which is the best definition of an *interdependent* view of the self?

    a. Defining oneself in terms of one's relationships to other people

b. Defining oneself in terms of one's own internal thoughts, feelings, and actions

c. Someone who enjoys activities such as dancing and team sports

d. Someone who enjoys activities such as reading and writing poetry

See page 621 for the answers.

Knowing Ourselves Through Introspection

5.2 **To what extent do people know themselves through introspection, and what are the consequences of introspection?**

We've seen that the culture in which people grow up helps shape their self-concept. But how exactly do we come to know who we are and why we do what we do? One way is with **introspection**, which is looking inward to examine the "inside information" that we—and we alone—have about our thoughts, feelings, and motives. Have you ever stopped for a moment to think about how you really felt about something, such as what you want to major in? Or wondered why you do what you do, such as why you binge watched the latest *Netflix* drama instead of studying for your psychology test? If so, you were using introspection. One of the most amazing things about the human mind is that we can use it to examine ourselves.

As useful as introspection can be, however, it is by no means perfect. For one thing, it is not always pleasant to be thinking about ourselves, and for another, the reasons for our feelings and behavior can be hidden from conscious awareness. Let's take a look at some of the consequences and limits of introspection.

Introspection

The process whereby people look inward and examine their own thoughts, feelings, and motives

Introspection is difficult and fallible . . . the difficulty is simply that of all observation of whatever kind.
—WILLIAM JAMES, 1890

Focusing on the Self: Self-Awareness Theory

Sometimes our thoughts naturally turn inward, and we think about ourselves. At other times this happens because of external circumstances, such as seeing ourselves in a mirror or in a video that a friend just took of us on her smartphone. When this happens, we are in a state of self-awareness. According to **self-awareness theory**, when this happens, we evaluate and compare our current behavior to our internal standards and values (Carver, 2003; Duval & Silvia, 2002; Duval & Wicklund, 1972; Morin, 2011; Phillips & Silvia, 2005). In short, we become self-conscious in the sense that we become objective, judgmental observers of ourselves, seeing ourselves as an outside observer would.

Let's say that you feel you should quit smoking, and one day you catch an image of yourself in a store window smoking a cigarette. How do you think you will feel? Seeing your reflection will likely highlight the disparity between your behavior and your internal standards. If you can change your behavior to match your internal guidelines (e.g., quit smoking), you will do so. If you feel you can't change your behavior, being in a state of self-awareness will be uncomfortable because you will be confronted with disagreeable feedback about yourself (Duval & Silvia, 2002). This seems to happen pretty frequently. In one study, researchers asked 365 high school juniors (in two American cities) what they were thinking about at random points in their day and found that the more often people said they were thinking about themselves, the more likely they were to be in a bad mood (Mor et al., 2010). Figure 5.3 illustrates how self-awareness makes us conscious of our internal standards and directs our subsequent behavior.

Self-Awareness Theory

The idea that when people focus their attention on themselves, they evaluate and compare their behavior to their internal standards and values

Figure 5.3 Self-Awareness Theory: The Consequences of Self-Focused Attention

When people focus on themselves, they compare their behavior to their internal standards.

(Based on Carver & Scheier, 1981)

① You come across a self-focusing cue in the environment (eg, a mirror, a camera, or an audience).

② This cue creates a state of self-awareness... You become aware of and think about yourself...

③ You compare your current thoughts or behavior to your internal standards or expectations for yourself. Do they match?

4a If NO... uh-oh! (either) what to do?

4b If YES... everything's fine!

5a Change your behavior so it matches your standard for yourself. Feel great!

5b If you can't or won't change your behavior... Feel terrible! Flee from a state of self-awareness as quickly as possible!

But as I looked into the mirror, I screamed, and my heart shuddered: for I saw not myself but the mocking, leering, face of a devil.

—FRIEDRICH NIETZSCHE, *THUS SPAKE ZARATHUSTRA*

I swear to you . . . that to be overly conscious is a sickness, a real, thorough sickness.

—FYODOR DOSTOEVSKY, *NOTES FROM UNDERGROUND*, 1864

When people are in a negative state of self-awareness, they often try to escape this state by, for example, avoiding looking at pictures of themselves on their friends' Facebook pages. Sometimes people go even further in their attempt to escape the self. Abusing alcohol, for example, temporarily diverts negative thoughts about oneself and even binge eating and sexual masochism can be effective, albeit dangerous, ways of turning off one's internal spotlight (Baumeister, 1991). The fact that people regularly engage in such dangerous behaviors, despite their risks, is an indication of how aversive self-focus can be (Hull, Young, & Jouriles, 1986; Leary & Tate, 2010).

Not all means of escaping the self, however, are so damaging. Many forms of religious expression and spirituality are also effective means of avoiding self-focus (Baumeister, 1991; Leary, 2004a). Further, self-focus is not always aversive. If you have just experienced a major success, focusing on yourself can be pleasant indeed because it highlights your positive accomplishments (Greenberg & Musham, 1981; Silvia & Abele, 2002). Self-focus can also be a way of keeping you out of trouble by reminding you of your sense of right and wrong. For example, several studies have found that when people are self-aware (e.g., in front of a mirror), they are more likely to follow their moral standards, such as avoiding the temptation to cheat on a test (Beaman, Klentz, Diener, & Svanum, 1979; Diener & Wallbom, 1976; Gibbons, 1978). Self-awareness, then, is particularly aversive when it reminds people of their shortcomings, and under these circumstances (e.g., right after doing poorly on a test), people try to avoid it. At other times, however—such as when that little devil is on your shoulder pushing you into temptation—a dose of self-awareness is not such a bad thing because it makes you more aware of your morals and ideals. How self-aware do you tend to be? Complete the Try It! given below to find out.

I have often wished I had time to cultivate modesty. . . . But I am too busy thinking about myself.

—DAME EDITH SITWELL

TRY IT!

Measure Your Private Self-Consciousness

How much do you focus on yourself when you are alone? The following questions are taken from a scale developed by Fenigstein, Scheier, and Buss (1975) to measure private self-consciousness—the consistent tendency to be self-aware.

Instructions: Answer the following questions as honestly as possible on a scale from 1 to 5, where

1 = extremely uncharacteristic (not at all like me)
2 = somewhat uncharacteristic
3 = neither characteristic nor uncharacteristic
4 = somewhat characteristic
5 = extremely characteristic (very much like me)

1. I'm always trying to figure myself out.	1	2	3	4	5
2. Generally, I'm not very aware of myself.	1	2	3	4	5
3. I reflect about myself a lot.	1	2	3	4	5
4. I'm often the subject of my own fantasies.	1	2	3	4	5
5. I never scrutinize myself.	1	2	3	4	5
6. I'm generally attentive to my inner feelings.	1	2	3	4	5
7. I'm constantly examining my motives.	1	2	3	4	5
8. I sometimes have the feeling that I'm off somewhere watching myself.	1	2	3	4	5
9. I'm alert to changes in my mood.	1	2	3	4	5
10. I'm aware of the way my mind works when I work through a problem.	1	2	3	4	5

For scoring instructions, turn to page 621. (Adapted from Fenigstein, Scheier, & Buss, 1975)

Judging Why We Feel the Way We Do: Telling More Than We Can Know

Another function of introspection is trying to figure out why we feel the way we do. The problem is that knowing why is not so easy. Imagine trying to decide why you love someone. Being in love typically makes you feel giddy, euphoric, and preoccupied; in fact, the ancient Greeks thought love was a sickness. But what causes you to feel this way? Exactly what is it about your sweetheart that made you fall in love? We know it is something about our loved one's looks, personality, values, and background. But precisely what? How can we possibly describe the special chemistry that exists between two people? A friend of ours once told us he was in love with a woman because she played the saxophone. Was this really the reason? The heart works in such mysterious ways that it is difficult to tell.

Unfortunately, it's not just love that is difficult to explain. As we saw in Chapter 3, many of our basic mental processes occur outside of awareness (Vazire & Wilson, 2012; Wilson, 2002; Wilson & Dunn, 2004). This is not to say that we are thinkers without a clue—we are usually aware of the final result of our thought processes (e.g., that we are in love) but often unaware of the cognitive processing that led to the result. It's as if the magician pulled a rabbit out of a hat: You see the rabbit, but you don't know how it got there. How do we deal with this rabbit problem? Even though we often don't know why we feel a certain way, it seems we are always able to come up with an explanation. We are the proud owners of the most powerful brain to evolve on this planet, and we certainly put it to use. Unfortunately, it didn't come with an owner's manual. Introspection may not lead us to the true causes of our feelings and behavior, but we'll manage to convince ourselves that it did. Richard Nisbett and Tim Wilson referred to this phenomenon as "telling more than we can know" because people's explanations of their feelings and behavior often go beyond what they can reasonably know (Nisbett & Ross, 1980; Nisbett & Wilson, 1977; Wilson, 2002).

In one study, for example, college students recorded their daily moods every day for 5 weeks (Wilson, Laser, & Stone, 1982). The students also kept track of things that might predict their daily moods, such as the weather, their workload, and how much sleep they had gotten the night before. At the end of the 5 weeks, the students estimated how much their moods were related to these other variables. An analysis of the data showed that in many cases people's estimates were wrong. For example, most people believed that the amount of sleep they got predicted how good a mood they were in the next day when in fact this wasn't true: The amount of sleep was unrelated to people's moods. People weren't clueless; most knew, for example, that how well they were getting along with their friends was a good predictor of their mood. But overall, people weren't all that accurate in knowing what predicted their moods (Johansson, Hall, Skiström, & Olsson, 2005; Wegner, 2002; Wilson, 2002).

> We can never, even by the strictest examination, get completely behind the secret springs of action.
>
> —IMMANUEL KANT

Why not? It turned out that participants were relying on their **causal theories** about mood. People have many theories about what influences their feelings and behavior (e.g., "My mood should be affected by how much sleep I got last night") and often use these theories to help them explain why they feel the way they do (e.g., "I'm in a bad mood; I'll bet the fact that I got only 6 hours of sleep last night has a lot to do with it"). We learn many of these theories from the culture in which we grow up—ideas such as "absence makes the heart grow fonder" and that people are "blue" on Mondays. The only problem is that, as discussed in Chapter 3, our schemas and theories are not always correct and thus can lead to incorrect judgments about the causes of our actions.

Causal Theories
Theories about the causes of one's own feelings and behaviors; often we learn such theories from our culture (e.g., "absence makes the heart grow fonder")

We do not mean to imply that people rely solely on their causal theories when introspecting about the reasons for their feelings and behaviors. In addition to culturally learned causal theories, people have a great deal of information about themselves, such as how they have responded in the past and what they happen to have been thinking about before making a choice (Andersen, 1984; Wilson, 2002). The fact remains, however, that introspecting about our past actions and current thoughts does not always yield the right answer about why we feel the way we do (Hassin, 2013; Wilson & Bar-Anan, 2008).

> The truth is, we never know for sure about ourselves. . . . Only after we've done a thing do we know what we'll do. . . . [That] is why we have spouses and children and parents and colleagues and friends, because someone has to know us better than we know ourselves.
>
> —RICHARD RUSSO, *STRAIGHT MAN*, 1997

The Consequences of Introspecting About Reasons

In the first season of the television show *30 Rock*, Liz Lemon, Tina Fey's character, has broken up with her boyfriend, Dennis, after he botched a home repair job in her apartment and brought home a Great Dane (knowing that she was allergic to dogs). But then Dennis came into the office and bared his soul in front of the whole gang, telling Liz that he would always love her. Should she get back together with him? Liz isn't sure, so she decides to make a list of Dennis's pros and cons. She draws a line down the middle of the paper and has no trouble filling up both sides. On the pro side, for example, she writes, "takes good care of his feet," "is funny when he goofs on his friends," and "has already seen me throw up two times." On the con side, she writes, "dental hygiene," "wears acid wash denim," and "has already seen me throw up."

When Liz gets home that evening, she finds that Dennis has cleaned up her apartment, built bookshelves, and mounted the television on the wall. So she takes out her list and adds to the pro side "fixed TV." The next day, her boss, Jack (Alec Baldwin's character), says something nice about Dennis, prompting Liz to add yet another entry to the pro side: "Jack likes Dennis." But things quickly fall apart when Dennis stops by again that evening. When she throws him out again, he slams the door, and the newly installed bookshelves and wall-mounted television come crashing down. As Liz surveys the wreckage on her floor, she takes out her list, adds Dennis's latest misadventure to the con list, and emphatically folds it up for the last time.

30 Rock is a fictional comedy, of course, and the episode just described is a spoof on a common activity, namely, making a list of pros and cons about an important decision. But does putting reasons down on paper really clarify our thoughts, making it easier to decide what we really want? Actually, no. Tim Wilson and his colleagues found that analyzing the reasons for our feelings is not always the best strategy and in fact can make matters worse (Wilson, 2002; Wilson, Dunn, Kraft, & Lisle, 1989; Wilson, Hodges, & La Fleur, 1995; Yamada et al., 2014).

As we saw in the previous section, it is hard to know exactly why we feel the way we do about something, especially in an area as complicated as romantic relationships. Some of the very same things Liz Lemon had on the pro side of her list, for example, also appeared on the con side. And some things are easier to put into words (e.g., "wears acid wash denim") than others (e.g., the special chemistry that can exist between two people). The problem is that we often convince ourselves that the reasons we generate reflect how we actually feel, even if they just happen to occur to us at the moment. One would think that Liz Lemon would know how she felt about Dennis; after all, she had been dating him for a while. But once she starting making her list of reasons, her feelings seemed to swing back and forth, depending on the latest entry on her list.

Research has confirmed this process of **reasons-generated attitude change**, which is attitude change resulting from thinking about the reasons for your attitudes. This happens because, when people analyze the reasons for their attitudes, they (a) bring to mind reasons that don't really reflect how they feel and (b) talk themselves into believing that this is how they feel. In a study by Wilson and Kraft (1993), for example, college students involved in relationships wrote down why things were going the way they were with their dating partner—much like Liz Lemon did. This caused them to change their minds about how their relationship was going; if they wrote down positive reasons, they became more positive, but if they wrote down negative reasons, they became more negative. Over time, though, the effects of analyzing reasons tends to wear off, and people's original "hard to explain" attitudes return. Thus, if people make important decisions right after analyzing reasons—such as deciding whether to break up with their boyfriend or girlfriend—they might make a decision they later regret. This is because right after analyzing reasons, people tend to focus on the things that are easy to put into words (e.g., those acid-wash jeans) and ignore feelings that are hard to explain (e.g., that special chemistry). But it is the hard-to-explain feelings that often matter in the long run (Halberstadt & Levine, 1997; Sengupta & Fitzsimons, 2004; Wilson, Lindsey, & Schooler, 2000).

In an episode of the TV program *30 Rock*, Liz Lemon (played by Tina Fey) made a list of the reasons why she liked and disliked her boyfriend Dennis (played by Dean Winters). According to research on self-generated attitude change, the act of making this list might have changed her mind about how she felt, at least temporarily.

Reasons-Generated Attitude Change

Attitude change resulting from thinking about the reasons for one's attitudes; people assume that their attitudes match the reasons that are plausible and easy to verbalize

In sum, it is often difficult for people to know exactly why they feel the way they do, and it can be dangerous to think too much about one's reasons. If introspection has its limits, how else might we find out what sort of person we are and what our attitudes are? We turn now to another source of self-knowledge: observations of our own behavior.

REVIEW QUESTIONS

1. When people focus attention on themselves, they
   a. evaluate and compare their behavior to their internal standards and values.
   b. are less likely to drink alcohol or engage in binge eating.
   c. are less likely to follow their moral standards.
   d. almost always like what they see about themselves.

2. Suppose that your friend Meghan says, "If I get less than 8 hours of sleep, I'm in a terrible mood the next day." Based on research in social psychology, what is the best conclusion about her statement?
   a. She is probably right because people generally know why they feel the way they do.
   b. She is probably wrong because people rarely know why they feel the way they do.

   c. She is likely to be right only if she first made a list of all the reasons why she is in a good mood or bad mood on a typical day.
   d. Her statement is probably based on a causal theory that may or may not be true.

3. Which of the following is *true*?
   a. When deciding whether to break up with a romantic partner, it is a good idea to make a list of the pros and cons of the relationship.
   b. People generally know why they feel the way they do.
   c. It can be dangerous to think too much about the reasons why we feel the way we do about a romantic partner.
   d. People who analyze the reasons for their feelings generally have a clearer idea of how they really feel.

See page 621 for the answers.

Knowing Ourselves by Observing Our Own Behavior

5.3 In what ways do people come to know themselves by observing their behavior?

Suppose that a friend of yours asks you how much you like classical music. You hesitate because you never listened to classical music much when you were growing up, but lately you have found yourself listening to symphonies every now and then. "Well, I don't know," you reply. "I guess I like some kinds of classical music. Just yesterday I listened to a Beethoven symphony on the radio while I was driving to work." If so, you used an important source of self-knowledge: observations of one's own behavior—in this case, what you chose to listen to.

Self-perception theory argues that when our attitudes and feelings are uncertain or ambiguous, we infer these states by observing our behavior and the situation in which it occurs (Bem, 1972). Let's consider each part of this theory. First, we infer our inner feelings from our behavior only when we are not sure how we feel. If you've always known that you love classical music, you do not need to observe your behavior to figure this out (Andersen, 1984; Andersen & Ross, 1984). Maybe, though, your feelings are murky; you've never really thought about how much you like it. If so, you are especially likely to use your behavior as a guide to how you feel (Chaiken & Baldwin, 1981; Wood, 1982).

Second, people judge whether their behavior really reflects how they feel or whether it was the situation that made them act that way. If you freely choose to listen to the classical music station—no one makes you do it—you are especially likely to conclude that you listen to that station because you like classical music. If it is your spouse and not you who turned to the station playing Beethoven, you are unlikely to

I've always written poems . . . I never know what I think until I read it in one of my poems.

—Virginia Hamilton Adair

Self-Perception Theory

The theory that when our attitudes and feelings are uncertain or ambiguous, we infer these states by observing our behavior and the situation in which it occurs conclude that you listen to classical music in your car because you like it.

Sound familiar? In Chapter 4, we discussed attribution theory—the way in which people infer someone else's attitudes and feelings by observing that person's behavior. According to self-perception theory, people use the same attributional principles to infer their own attitudes and feelings. For example, if you were trying to decide whether a friend likes classical music, you would observe her behavior and explain why she behaved that way. You might notice, for example, that she is always listening to classical music in the absence of any situational pressures or constraints—no one makes her play Mozart on her smartphone. You would make an internal attribution for her behavior and conclude that she likes Mozart. Self-perception theory says that we infer our own feelings in the same way: We observe our behavior and explain it to ourselves; that is, we make an attribution about why we behaved that way (Critcher & Gilovich, 2010; Laird, 2007; Olson & Stone, 2005; Wilson, 2002). In fact, it is not only attitudes and preferences that we infer from our behavior—we also infer how motivated we are to do something, as we will now see.

Intrinsic versus Extrinsic Motivation

Imagine that you are an elementary school teacher who wants your students to develop a love of reading. Not only do you want your students to read more, but you also want them to develop a love of books. How might you go about accomplishing this? It is not going to be easy because so many other things compete for your students' attention, such as television, video games, and social media.

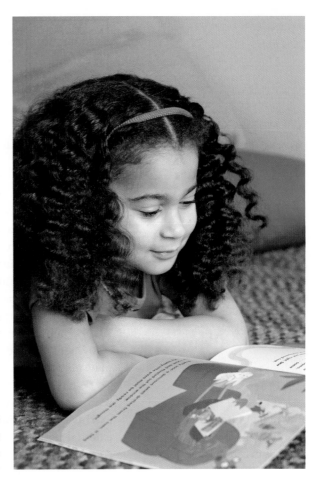

Many programs try to get children to read more by rewarding them. But do these programs increase or decrease a child's love of reading?

If you are like many educators, you might decide that a good approach would be to reward the children for reading. Maybe that will get them to put down those game controllers and pick up a book—and develop a love of reading in the process. Teachers have always rewarded kids with a smile or a gold star on an assignment, but recently they have turned to more powerful incentives, such as candy, brownies, and toys (Perlstein, 1999). A chain of pizza restaurants is also encouraging kids to read more, offering elementary school students a certificate for a free pizza if they read a certain number of books (see "Book It!" at www.bookitprogram.com). One school district has taken this a step further by rewarding high school students with cash prizes if they do well on advanced placement exams (Hibbard, 2011).

There is no doubt that rewards are powerful and that pizzas and money will help to motivate kids. One of the oldest and most fundamental psychological principles, called positive reinforcement, says that giving a reward each time a behavior occurs will increase the frequency of that behavior. Whether it be a food pellet delivered to a rat pressing a bar or a free pizza given to a child for reading, rewards can change behavior.

But people are not rats, and we have to consider the effects of rewards on what's inside—people's thoughts about themselves, their self-concept, and their motivation to read in the future. Does being paid to read, for example, change people's ideas about *why* they are reading? The danger of reward programs such as Book It! is the very self-perception process we have just discussed. Kids may infer that they are reading to earn something, not because they find reading to be an enjoyable activity in its own right. When the reward programs end and pizzas are no longer forthcoming, children may actually read less than they did before.

Intrinsic Motivation

The desire to engage in an activity because we enjoy it or find it interesting, not because of external rewards or pressures

Extrinsic Motivation

The desire to engage in an activity because of external rewards or pressures, not because we enjoy the task or find it interesting

Overjustification Effect

The tendency for people to view their behavior as caused by compelling extrinsic reasons, making them underestimate the extent to which it was caused by intrinsic reasons

This is especially likely to happen to children who already liked to read. Such children have high **intrinsic motivation**: the desire to engage in an activity because they enjoy it or find it interesting, not because of external rewards or pressures (Harackiewicz & Elliot, 1993, 1998; Harackiewicz & Hulleman, 2010; Hirt, Melton, McDonald, & Harackiewicz, 1996; Hulleman, Schrager, Bodmann, & Harackiewicz, 2010; Lepper, Corpus, & Iyengar, 2005; Ryan & Deci, 2000; Vansteenkiste et al., 2010). Their reasons for engaging in the activity have to do with themselves—the enjoyment and pleasure they feel when reading a book. In other words, reading is play, not work.

What happens when the children start getting rewards for reading? Their reading, originally stemming from intrinsic motivation, is now also spurred by **extrinsic motivation**, which is people's desire to engage in an activity because of external rewards or pressures, not because they enjoy the task or find it interesting. According to self-perception theory, in such situations people often assume that they are motivated by the rewards and not their intrinsic interest. That is, children who liked to read at the outset now assume that they are cracking open books only to get the reward. The unfortunate consequence is that rewards can make people lose interest in activities they initially enjoyed. This is called the **overjustification effect**, which results when people view their behavior as caused by compelling extrinsic reasons, such as a reward, making them underestimate the extent to which their behavior was caused by intrinsic reasons (Deci, Koestner, & Ryan, 1999a, 1999b; Harackiewicz, 1979; Lepper, 1995; Lepper, Henderlong, & Gingras, 1999; Warneken & Tomasello, 2008).

In one study, for example, fourth- and fifth-grade teachers introduced four new math games to their students, and during a 13-day baseline period they noted how long each child played each math game. As seen in the leftmost line in Figure 5.4, the children initially had some intrinsic interest in the math games in that they played them for several minutes during this baseline period. For the next several days, a reward program was introduced. Now the children could earn credits toward certificates and trophies by playing the math games, and as we might expect, the amount of time they spent on the math games increased (see the middle line in Figure 5.4).

The key question is, what happened after the reward program ended and the kids could no longer earn rewards for playing the games? As predicted, an overjustification effect occurred in that the children spent significantly less time on the math games than they had initially, before the rewards were introduced (see the rightmost line in Figure 5.4). The researchers determined, by comparing these results to those of a control condition, that it was the rewards that made people like the games less and not the fact that everyone became bored with the games as time went by. In short, the rewards destroyed the children's intrinsic interest in the games so that by

Figure 5.4 The Overjustification Effect

During the initial baseline phase, researchers measured how much time elementary school students played math games. During the reward program, they rewarded the children with prizes for playing with the games. When the rewards were no longer offered (during the follow-up phase), the children played with the games even less than they had during the baseline phase, indicating that the rewards had lowered their intrinsic interest in the games.

(Adapted from Greene, Sternberg, & Lepper, 1976)

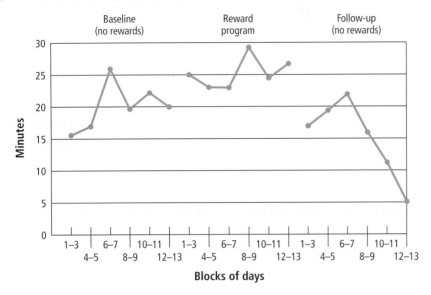

the end of the study, they were hardly playing the games at all (Greene, Sternberg, & Lepper, 1976).

What can we do to protect intrinsic motivation from the dangers of society's reward system? Fortunately, there are conditions under which overjustification effects can be avoided. Rewards will undermine interest only if interest was initially high (Calder & Staw, 1975; Tang & Hall, 1995). If a child has no interest in reading, then getting him or her to read by offering rewards is not a bad idea because there is no initial interest to undermine.

Also, the type of reward makes a difference. So far, we have discussed **task-contingent rewards**, meaning that people rewarded simply for doing a task, regardless of the quality of their performance. In the pizza program, for example, kids get reward for the number of books they read, not how well they read them. Sometimes **performance-contingent rewards** are used, whereby the reward depends on how well people perform the task. An example is giving students cash prizes for doing well on advanced placement exams, not simply for taking the exams. This type of reward is less likely to decrease interest in a task—and may even increase interest— because the earned reward conveys the message that you are good at the task (Deci & Ryan, 1985; Pulfrey, Darnon, & Butera, 2013). Thus, rather than giving kids a reward simply for playing math games—a task-contingent reward—it is better to give them a reward for doing *well* in math—a performance-contingent reward. Performance-contingent rewards must be used with care, however, because they too can backfire. Even though they convey positive feedback, these types of rewards can put pressure on people by making them feel evaluated, which makes it harder for them to do well and lowers their intrinsic interest in the activity (Harackiewicz, 1989; Harackiewicz, Manderlink, & Sansone, 1984). The trick is to convey positive feedback without

> I remember that the game [of basketball] lost some of its magical qualities for me once I thought seriously about playing for a living.
>
> —BILL RUSSELL, 1979

Task-Contingent Rewards

Rewards that are given for performing a task, regardless of how well the task is done

Performance-Contingent Rewards

Rewards that are based on how well we perform a task

putting extra pressure on people by making them feel nervous and apprehensive about being evaluated.

Mindsets and Motivation

Fixed Mindset

The idea that we have a set amount of an ability that cannot change

Growth Mindset

The idea that our abilities are malleable qualities that we can cultivate and grow

There is another way in which people's self-perceptions influence their motivations, and that is the way in which they perceive their own abilities. Some people believe that their abilities are set in stone; they either have them or they do not. Psychologist Carol Dweck (2006) calls this a **fixed mindset**—the idea that we have a set amount of an ability that cannot change. According to this view, we have a fixed amount of intelligence, athletic ability, musical talent, and so on. Other people, like Mia Hamm and Derek Jeter, believe that abilities are the result of hard work, which Dweck calls a **growth mindset**—the belief that our abilities are malleable qualities that we can cultivate and grow. Research shows that the mindset people have is crucial to their success: People with the fixed mindset are more likely to give up after setbacks and are less likely to work on and hone their skills; after all, if they fail, it must be a sign that they simply don't have what it takes. People with the growth mindset—again, think of Mia Hamm and Derek Jeter—view setbacks as opportunities to improve through hard work (Cury, Da Fonseca, Zahn, & Elliot, 2008).

Mindsets are important not only to athletic performance but also to how we view any ability, including how good we are at academics. Most students hit a bump in the road when they start college; for you, maybe it was a lower grade than you expected on a psychology or math test. How did you react to your disappointing grade? Dweck's research shows that students who have a fixed mindset about intelligence are more likely to give up and do poorly on subsequent tests, whereas those with growth mindsets are more likely to redouble their efforts and do better on subsequent tests. Research also shows that the mindsets can change; people with fixed views can learn to adopt the growth view (Yeager, Pauneska, Walton, & Dweck, 2014). Thus, the next time you experience a setback—be it on the athletic field, in your classes, or in your personal relationships—you might want to view it as an opportunity to work harder and improve rather than as a sign that you "don't have what it takes."

Understanding Our Emotions: The Two-Factor Theory of Emotion

How do you know which emotion you are experiencing at any given time? Is it fear or elation? This question probably sounds kind of silly: Don't we know how we feel

Sally is trying to give her daughter encouragement before she takes her final exams. But, according to research on fixed and growth mindsets, did she say the right thing? As discussed in this chapter, it is better for parents to convey to their children that their abilities are malleable qualities that can grow with hard work (the growth mindset) rather than communicate the idea that abilities are fixed quantities that you either have or do not have.

without having to think about it? Not necessarily. The way in which we experience emotions has a lot in common with the kinds of self-perception processes we have been discussing.

Stanley Schachter (1964) proposed a theory of emotion that says we infer what our emotions are in the same way we infer what kind of person we are or what we like. In each case, we observe our behavior and then explain to ourselves why we are behaving that way. The only difference in these types of inferences is the kind of behavior we observe. Schachter says we observe our internal behaviors—how physiologically aroused we feel. If we feel aroused, we then try to figure out what is causing this arousal. For example, suppose you go for a 3-mile run one day and are walking back to your apartment. You go around a corner and nearly walk right into an extremely attractive person from your psychology class whom you are just getting to know. Your heart is pounding, and you feel a little sweaty. Is it because love is blossoming between you and your new friend or simply because you just went for a run?

Schachter's theory is called the **two-factor theory of emotion** because understanding our emotional states requires two steps: We must first experience physiological arousal, and then we must seek an appropriate explanation or label for it. Because our physical states are difficult to label on their own, we use information in the situation to help us make an attribution about why we feel aroused (see Figure 5.5).

Two-Factor Theory of Emotion

The idea that emotional experience is the result of a two-step self-perception process in which people first experience physiological arousal and then seek an appropriate explanation for it

Figure 5.5 The Two-Factor Theory of Emotion

People first experience physiological arousal and then attach an explanation to it.

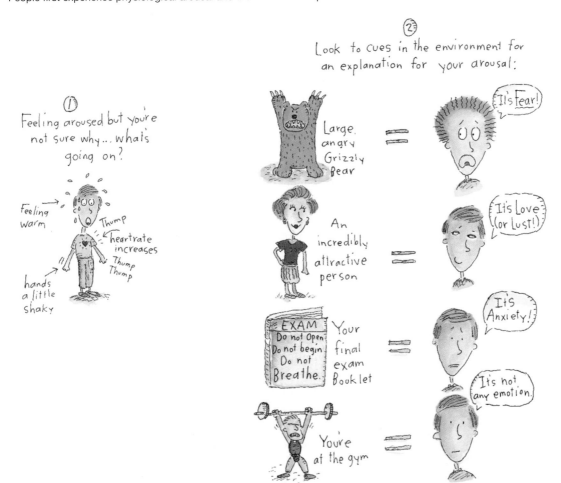

Imagine that you were a participant in a classic study by Stanley Schachter and Jerome Singer (1962) that tested this theory. When you arrive, the experimenter tells you he is studying the effects that a vitamin compound called Suproxin has on vision. After a physician injects you with a small amount of Suproxin, the experimenter asks you to wait while the drug takes effect. He introduces you to another participant who, he says, has been given some of the same vitamin compound. The experimenter gives each of you a questionnaire to fill out, saying he will return in a little while to give you the vision tests.

You look at the questionnaire and notice that it contains some highly personal and insulting questions. For example, one question asks, "With how many men (other than your father) has your mother had extramarital relationships?" (Schachter & Singer, 1962, p. 385). The other participant reacts angrily to these offensive questions, becoming more and more furious, until he finally tears up his questionnaire, throws it on the floor, and stomps out of the room. How do you think you would feel? Would you feel angry as well?

As you've probably guessed, the real purpose of this experiment was not to test people's vision. The researchers set up a situation in which the two crucial variables— arousal and an emotional explanation for that arousal—would be present or absent, and then they observed which, if any, emotions people experienced. The participants did not really receive an injection of a vitamin compound. Instead, some participants received epinephrine, a hormone produced naturally by the human body that causes arousal (body temperature and heart and breathing rates increase), and the other half received a placebo that had no physiological effects.

Imagine how you would have felt had you received the epinephrine: As you read the insulting questionnaire, you begin to feel aroused. Remember, the experimenter didn't tell you the shot contained epinephrine, so you don't realize that the injection is making you feel this way. The other participant—who was actually an accomplice of the experimenter—reacts with rage. You are likely to infer that you are feeling flushed and aroused because you too are angry. You have met the conditions Schachter (1964) argues are necessary to experience an emotion: You are aroused, you have sought out and found a reasonable explanation for your arousal in the situation that surrounds you, and so you become furious. This is indeed what happened: The participants who had been given epinephrine reacted much more angrily than did participants who had been given the placebo.

A fascinating implication of Schachter's theory is that people's emotions are some- what arbitrary, depending on what the most plausible explanation for their arousal happens to be. Schachter and Singer (1962) demonstrated this idea in two ways. First, they showed that they could prevent people from becoming angry by providing a nonemotional explanation for why they felt aroused. They did this by informing some of the people who received epinephrine that the injection would increase their heart rate, make their face feel warm and flushed, and cause their hands to shake slightly. When people actually began to feel this way, they inferred that it was not because they were angry but because the drug was taking effect. As a result, these participants did not react angrily to the questionnaire.

Second, Schachter and Singer showed that they could make participants expe- rience a very different emotion by changing the most plausible explanation for their arousal. In another condition, participants received the epinephrine but did not get the insulting questionnaire, and the accomplice did not respond angrily. Instead, the accomplice acted in a euphoric, devil-may-care fashion, playing basketball with rolled-up pieces of paper, making paper airplanes, and playing with a hula hoop he found in the corner. How did the participants respond? Now they inferred that they must be feeling happy and euphoric and often joined in on the fun.

The Schachter and Singer experiment has become one of the most famous studies in social psychology because it shows that emotions can be the result of a self-perception process: People look for the most plausible explanation for their arousal. Sometimes the most plausible explanation is not the right one, and so people end up experiencing a mistaken emotion. The people who became angry or euphoric in the Schachter and Singer (1962) study did so because they felt aroused and thought this arousal was due to the obnoxious questionnaire or to the infectious, happy-go-lucky behavior of the accomplice. The real cause of their arousal, the epinephrine, was hidden from them, so they relied on situational cues to explain their behavior.

> I could feel all the excitement of losing the big fish going through the transformer and coming out as anger at my brother-in-law.
> —Norman Maclean,
> *A River Runs Through It*, 1976

Finding the Wrong Cause: Misattribution of Arousal

Do people form mistaken emotions in their everyday lives in the same way as participants did in the Schachter and Singer (1962) study? In everyday life, one might argue, people usually know why they are aroused. If a mugger points a gun at us and says, "Give me your wallet!" we feel aroused and correctly identify this arousal as fear. If our heart is thumping while we walk on a deserted moonlit beach with the man or woman of our dreams, we correctly label this arousal as love or sexual attraction.

In many everyday situations, however, there is more than one plausible cause for our arousal, and it is difficult to identify how much of the arousal is due to one source or another. Imagine that you go to see a scary movie with an extremely attractive date. As you are sitting there, you notice that your heart is thumping and you are a little short of breath. Is this because you are wildly attracted to your date or because the movie is terrifying you? It is unlikely that you could say, "Fifty-seven percent of my arousal is due to the fact that my date is gorgeous, 32 percent is due to the scary movie, and 11 percent is due to indigestion from all the popcorn I ate." Because of this difficulty in pinpointing the precise causes of our arousal, we sometimes misidentify our emotions. You might think that most of your arousal is a sign of attraction to your date when in fact a lot of it is due to the movie (or maybe even indigestion).

If so, you have experienced **misattribution of arousal**, whereby people make mistaken inferences about what is causing them to feel the way they do (Anderson, Siegel, White, & Barrett, 2012; Bar-Anan, Wilson, & Hassin, 2010; Hütter & Sweldens, 2013; Oikawa, Aarts, & Oikawa, 2011; Rydell & Durso, 2012; Zillmann, 1978). Consider how this worked in a field experiment by Donald Dutton and Arthur Aron (1974). An attractive young woman asked men visiting a park in British Columbia if they would fill out a questionnaire for her as part of a psychology project looking at the effects of scenic attractions on people's creativity. When they had finished, she said that she would be happy to explain her study in more detail when she had more time. She tore off a corner of the questionnaire, wrote down her name and phone number, and told the participant to give her a call if he wanted to talk with her some more. How attracted do you think the men were to this woman? Would they telephone her and ask for a date?

Misattribution of Arousal

The process whereby people make mistaken inferences about what is causing them to feel the way they do

This is a hard question to answer. Undoubtedly, it depends on whether the men were involved with someone else, how busy they were, and so on. It might also depend, however, on how they interpreted any bodily symptoms they were experiencing. If they were aroused for some extraneous reason, they might mistakenly think that some of the arousal was the result of attraction to the young woman. To test this idea, Dutton and Aron (1974) had the woman approach males in the park under two very different circumstances.

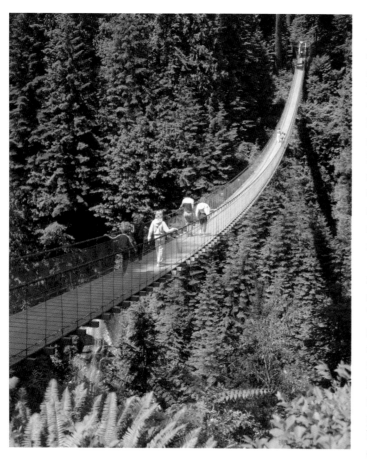

When people are aroused for one reason, such as occurs when they cross a scary bridge, they often attribute this arousal to the wrong source—such as attraction to the person they are with.

In one condition, the men were walking across a 450-foot-long suspension bridge that spanned a deep canyon. The bridge was made of wooden planks attached to wire cables, and as they walked across, they had to stoop to hold on to the low handrail. A little way out over the canyon, the wind tended to catch the bridge and make it wobble from side to side. This is a scary experience, and most people who cross the bridge become more than a little aroused—their heart pounds against their chest, they breathe rapidly, and they begin to perspire. It was at this point that the attractive woman approached a man on the bridge and asked him to fill out her questionnaire. How attracted do you think the men in this condition felt toward her?

In another condition, the woman waited until men had crossed the bridge and rested for a while on a bench in the park before approaching them. They had a chance to calm down—their hearts were no longer pounding, and their breathing rate had returned to normal. They were peacefully admiring the scenery when the woman asked them to fill out her questionnaire. How attracted were these men to the woman? Schachter's two-factor theory would predict that the men approached on the bridge would be considerably more aroused than the men sitting on the bench and might mistakenly think that some of this arousal was the result of attraction to the beautiful woman. That is exactly what happened. A large proportion of the men approached on the bridge telephoned the woman later to ask her for a date, whereas relatively few of the men approached on the bench telephoned the woman (see Figure 5.6). This type of misattribution of arousal has been found in numerous subsequent studies in both men and women (e.g., Meston & Frohlich,

---

Figure 5.6 Misattribution of Arousal

When a woman approached men on a scary bridge and asked them to fill out a questionnaire, a high percentage of them were attracted to her and called her for a date. When the same woman approached men after they had crossed the bridge and had rested, relatively few called her for a date.

(Based on Dutton & Aron, 1974)

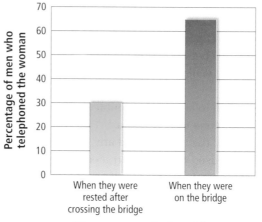

Woman approached participants

2003; Zillmann, 1978). The moral is this: If you encounter an attractive person and your heart is going thump-thump, think carefully about why you are aroused—or you might fall in love for the wrong reasons!

To sum up this section, one way that people learn about themselves—including their attitudes, motives, and emotions—is to observe their behavior and the conditions under which that behavior occurs. This includes observations of their outward behavior (e.g., whether they are reading a book and whether they are being rewarded for doing so) as well as their bodily responses (e.g., whether their heart is thumping when talking with a stranger). We turn now to another important source of self-knowledge, namely, other people.

REVIEW QUESTIONS

1. Which of the following statements best illustrates self-perception theory?
   a. "I might not know why, but I know what I like."
   b. "I often don't know what I like until I see what I do."
   c. "I like classical music because my wife is always playing it."
   d. "I get a warm feeling inside when I listen to my favorite songs."

2. Suppose you are a parent and want your children to do well in school. Which of the following is likely to work the best?
   a. Tell them that they were born with a lot of academic talent.
   b. Tell them that academic ability is something that they can cultivate and grow if they work hard.
   c. When they are young, give them money for every book they read.
   d. Tell them that intelligence is inherited and that there is a lot of it in your family.

3. Under which of the following conditions is overjustification effect most likely to occur?
   a. Tom was very keen to learn French. He joined French classes and spent a lot of time studying French.
   b. Neel was hardly interested in learning French but his parents forced him to join French classes. He started taking an interest in learning French when a credit system was introduced.
   c. Jesica joined French classes as she was very keen to learn French. Later, when a credit system was introduced, she started taking more interest in her French classes. When the credit system was withdrawn, her interest in learning French declined significantly.
   d. John joined French classes as most of his friends were attending the same. However, later, he gave up learning French as he could not cope up with the syllabus.

4. Which of the following is an example of growth mindset?
   a. Alice's parents believe that Alice has limited intellectual capacity. It will remain the same as she grows.
   b. Jim believes that if he works hard, he can be a far better athlete.
   c. Joy thought that success and belief in oneself do not go together.
   d. Michael realized that even if he worked hard, he continued to get poor marks. He gave up working hard as he thought he did not have the ability to get good marks.

See page 621 for the answers.

Using Other People to Know Ourselves

5.4   In what ways do people use others to know themselves?

The self-concept does not develop in a solitary context but is shaped by the people around us. If we never interacted with other people, our own image would be a blur because we would not see ourselves as having selves distinct from those of others. Remember the mirror and red-dye test we discussed earlier, used to determine if animals have a self-concept? Variations of this test have been used to show that social contact is indeed crucial to the development of a self-concept. Gordon Gallup (1997) compared the behavior of chimpanzees raised in normal family groupings with that of chimps who were raised alone in complete social isolation. The socially experienced chimps "passed" the mirror test; after red dye was put on their foreheads and they looked at themselves in a mirror, they immediately used their mirrored image to explore the red areas of their heads. However, the socially isolated chimps did not react to their reflections at all; they did not recognize themselves in the mirror, suggesting that they had not developed a sense of self.

There is little satisfaction in the contemplation of heaven for oneself if one cannot simultaneously contemplate the horrors of hell for others.

—P. D. James,
The Children of Men, 1992

Knowing Ourselves by Comparing Ourselves to Others

How do we use others to define ourselves? One way is to measure our own abilities and attitudes by seeing how we stack up against other people. Suppose you work in an office that subscribes to a charity fund. You can deduct from your monthly paycheck whatever you want and have it go to worthy organizations. You decide to donate $50 a month. How generous is this? Should you be feeling particularly proud of your philanthropic nature? One way to answer this question is to compare yourself to others. If you know that your friend Hannah donated only $10 per month, you are likely to feel that you are a very generous person who cares a lot about helping others. If you find out, however, that Hannah donated $100 per month, you probably will not view yourself as quite so generous.

This example illustrates **social comparison theory**, originally formulated by Leon Festinger (1954) and refined by many others (Bruchmann & Evans, 2013; Buunk & Gibbons, 2013; Hoorens & Van Damme, 2012; Lockwood, Shaughnessy, Fortune, & Tong, 2012; Suls & Wheeler, 2000). The theory holds that people learn about their own abilities and attitudes by comparing themselves to others and revolves around two important questions: When do people engage in social comparison? And with whom do they choose to compare themselves? The answer to the first question is that people socially compare when there is no objective standard to measure themselves against and when they are uncertain about themselves in a particular area (Suls & Fletcher, 1983; Suls & Miller, 1977). If the office donation program is new and you are not sure what amount would be generous, you are especially likely to compare yourself to others.

As to the second question—with whom do people compare themselves?—the answer depends on whether your goal is to get an accurate assessment of your abilities, to determine what the top level is so that you know what to strive for, or to feel better about yourself. To illustrate why these goals matter, suppose that it is the first day of your college Spanish class and you are wondering about your abilities and how well you will do in the class. With whom should you compare yourself: a student who mentions that she lived in Spain for 2 years, a student who says she took the course on a lark and has never studied Spanish before, or a student who has a similar background to yours? If your goal is to get the most accurate assessment of your abilities, then it makes sense to compare yourself to others who have a similar background in the area in question (Goethals & Darley, 1977; Miller, 1982; Suls, Martin, & Wheeler, 2000). That is, comparing yourself to a student with a very similar background in Spanish—the one who, like you, took Spanish in high school but has never traveled to a Spanish-speaking country—will be most informative. If that student is doing well in the class, you probably will too (Thornton & Arrowood, 1966; Wheeler, Koestner, & Driver, 1982).

If your goal is to know what excellence is—the top level to which you can aspire—you are likely to engage in **upward social comparison**, which is comparing yourself to people who are better than you are with regard to a particular trait or ability (Johnson, 2012). That is, if you want to know the "best of the best" so that you can dream of getting there someday, then clearly you should compare yourself to the student who lived in Spain and see how well she is doing in the class. A problem with upward social comparison, however, is that it can be dispiriting, making us feel inferior. We'll never learn the language like that student who studied in Spain! (Beer, Chester, & Hughes, 2013; Chan & Sengupta, 2013; Normand & Croizet, 2013; Ratliff & Oishi, 2013). If our goal is to feel good about ourselves and boost our egos, then we are better off engaging in **downward social comparison**—comparing ourselves to people who are worse than we are with regard to a particular trait or ability

Social Comparison Theory

The idea that we learn about our own abilities and attitudes by comparing ourselves to other people

Upward Social Comparison

Comparing ourselves to people who are better than we are with regard to a particular trait or ability

Downward Social Comparison

Comparing ourselves to people who are worse than we are with regard to a particular trait or ability

(Aspinwall & Taylor, 1993; Bauer & Wrosch, 2011; Brakel, Dijkstra, & Buunk, 2012; Chambers & Windschitl, 2009; Guenther & Alicke, 2010; Wehrens, Kuyper, Dijkstra, Buunk, & Van Der Werf, 2010). That is, if you compare your performance in the class to that of the student who is taking Spanish for the first time, you will likely feel good about your own abilities because you will surely have her beat. As another example, when interviewed by researchers, the vast majority of cancer patients spontaneously compared themselves to other patients who were more ill than they were, presumably as a way of making themselves feel more optimistic about the course of their own disease (Wood, Taylor, & Lichtman, 1985).

Another way we can feel better about ourselves is to compare our current performance with our own past performance. In a sense, people use downward social comparison here as well, though the point of comparison is a "past self," not someone else. In one study, people made themselves feel better by comparing their current self with a past self who was worse off. One student, for example, said that her "college self" was more outgoing and sociable than her "high school self," who had been shy and reserved (Ross & Wilson, 2003; Wilson & Ross, 2000).

In short, the nature of our goals determines who we compare ourselves to. When we want an accurate assessment of our abilities and opinions, we compare ourselves to people who are similar to us. When we want information about what we can strive toward, we make upward social comparisons, though doing so can make us feel inferior. When our goal is to make ourselves feel better, we compare ourselves to those who are less fortunate (including our past selves); such downward comparisons make us look better.

> Most people are other people. Their thoughts are someone else's opinions, their lives a mimicry, their passions a quotation.
> —OSCAR WILDE, 1905

Knowing Ourselves by Adopting Other People's Views

As we just saw, sometimes we use other people as a measuring stick to assess our own abilities. When it comes to our views of the social world, however, often we adopt the views our friends hold. Have you ever noticed that people who hang out together tend to see the world in the same way? Maybe the roommates in the apartment across the hall all support Democratic candidates for president and enjoy watching *The Good Wife* together, whereas the roommates in the apartment next door are Libertarians and big fans of *Game of Thrones*. One explanation for people holding common views, of course, is that "birds of a feather flock together"—that is, people who have similar views are attracted to each other and are more likely to become friends than are people who have dissimilar views. In Chapter 10, we will see evidence for this "birds of a feather" hypothesis (Newcomb, 1961).

But it is also true that people adopt the views of the people they hang out with, at least under certain conditions. Charles Cooley (1902) called this the "looking glass self," by which he meant that we see ourselves and the social world through the eyes of other people and often adopt those views. According to recent research, this is especially true when two people want to get along with each other (Hardin & Higgins, 1996; Huntsinger & Sinclair, 2010; Shteynberg, 2010; Sinclair & Lun, 2010; Skorinko & Sinclair, 2013). If a close friend thinks that *The Good Wife* is the best television show ever made, you will probably like it as well.

Perhaps it seems obvious that friends influence what each other thinks. What is surprising, however, is that such **social tuning**—the process whereby people adopt another person's attitudes—can happen even when we meet someone for the first time, if we want to get along with that person. And social tuning can happen unconsciously. Imagine, for example, that you were a participant in a study by Stacey Sinclair and her colleagues (Sinclair, Lowery, Hardin, & Colangelo, 2005). When you arrive,

Social Tuning

The process whereby people adopt another person's attitudes

the experimenter acts in either a likable or an unlikable manner. In the likable condition she thanks you for participating and offers you some candy from a bowl, whereas in the unlikable condition she pushes the bowl of candy to the side and exclaims, "Just ignore this; some of the experimenters in my lab like to give subjects candy for their participation, but I think you are lucky just to get credit" (Sinclair et al., 2005, p. 588). You then sit at a computer and complete a simple task in which you press one key every time the word *good* appears on the screen and another whenever the word *bad* appears.

Unbeknownst to you, the computer task is a measure of automatic prejudice. A photograph of a White or Black face is flashed very rapidly right before the word *good* or *bad* appears. The faces are flashed so quickly that you do not consciously see them, and the computer measures how long it takes you to respond to the words. Previous research has shown that such subliminal flashes can influence people under controlled laboratory conditions (see Chapter 7 for a discussion of this research). In the present study, the assumption was that if people were prejudiced toward Black people, then they should respond relatively quickly to *bad* when it was preceded by a Black face and relatively slowly to *good* when it was preceded by a Black face.

To see if people "tuned" their views to the experimenter, the researchers altered one other thing: In half of the sessions the experimenter wore a T-shirt that expressed antiracism views ("eracism"), and in half of the sessions she did not. The question was, did people unconsciously adopt the experimenter's antiracist views more when she was likable than when she was not? As seen in Figure 5.7, the answer is yes. When the experimenter was likable, participants showed less automatic prejudice when she was wearing the antiracism T-shirt than when she was not. Without even knowing it, they "tuned" their views toward hers. What about when she was unlikable? As seen in Figure 5.7, participants seemed to react against

---

Figure 5.7 Social Tuning to a Likable Experimenter

Participants took a test of automatic prejudice toward Black people, after interacting with an experimenter who was likable or unlikable and wore an antiracism T-shirt or a blank T-shirt. When the experimenter was likable, participants showed less automatic prejudice when she was wearing the antiracism T-shirt than when she was not (the higher the number on the scale, the more the anti-Black prejudice). When the experimenter was unlikable, participants reacted against her views: They showed more automatic prejudice when she was wearing the antiracist T-shirt than when she was not. These results show that people tend to automatically adopt the views of people they like, but automatically reject the views of people they do not.

(Adapted from Sinclair, Lowery, Hardin, & Colangelo, 2005)

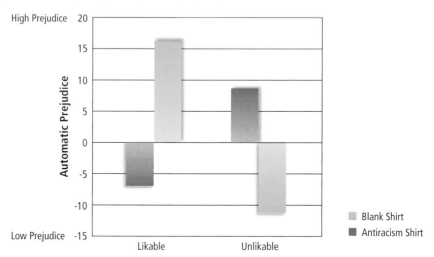

her views: They showed more automatic prejudice when she was wearing the anti-racist T-shirt than when she was not. These results show that we tend to automatically adopt the views of people we like but automatically reject the views of people we do not.

Knowing Our Future Feelings by Consulting Other People

What if we are trying to predict how we will feel about something in the future, such as the latest summer blockbuster movie or a first date with someone? Should we rely on how other people felt about these things when making **affective forecasts**, which are people's predictions about how they will feel in response to a future emotional event? Suppose, for example, that you are single and have the opportunity to go out with someone you've never met. Let's say you came across this person on a dating Web site, and he or she seems to be nice and good-looking. We'll call this Condition A. Now suppose that you don't know anything about the person—no dating profile—but you know that a friend likes him or her. We'll call this Condition B. Would you rather see the profile or get your friend's recommendation? That is, would you rather be in Condition A or B?

If you are like most people, you would rather see the dating profile (Condition A) because you have more information about that person and thus can form your own judgment about how much your potential date. In Condition B the person is more of an unknown quantity and thus seems like a riskier choice. Sure, your friend likes him or her, but who knows whether you will feel the same way as your friend? Research shows, however, that this would not necessarily be the best choice. Trusting other people's reactions (in this case, your friend's opinion) can be a wise approach.

In one study, researchers asked a group of college women to look at a profile of a male student that included his photograph and information about his age, height, weight, favorite book, favorite movie, and so on and to predict how much they would enjoy a 5-minute speed date with him (Gilbert, Killingsworth, Eyre, & Wilson, 2009). This condition was essentially Condition A in our example above. Another group of college women weren't given any information about the male student, but they were told how much one other female student had enjoyed a 5-minute speed date with him and based their prediction on that information. This was essentially Condition B from our example above. All the women from both groups then had a speed date with the man and rated how much they enjoyed it. Who made better predictions about how much they would enjoy the date—those who read the man's profile or those who found out how much someone else had liked him? As it happened, it was the second group of women who made the better predictions. They based their affective forecasts on how much another student had liked the man, and this turned out to be a good source of information. After all, if the man in the dating experiment was arrogant and self-centered, most women would pick up on that on the speed date, and finding out how they felt about him would tip us off that we wouldn't like him either. Similarly, if the man was incredibly charming, funny, and warm—Hugh Grant comes to mind—then most women would like him, and knowing that would also be a good predictor of how we would feel. What about the women who read the man's profile? A small amount of information about what someone is like can be faulty; the man's profile probably didn't accurately capture what he was like in person. Thus, although other people's reactions to things like first dates and movies and books are rarely perfectly aligned with others, knowing their reactions can be very useful information when predicting how we will feel, even better than knowing a little bit about that thing (Eggleston, Wilson, Lee, & Gilbert, 2014).

Affective Forecasts

People's predictions about how they will feel in response to a future emotional event

REVIEW QUESTIONS

1. Elina's parents wanted her to be one of the top students in her class. They always told her to compare herself with those students who were performing far better than her. But Elina felt inferior by doing so. She wanted to feel good about herself. To boost her ego, she engaged in

   a. upward social comparison.

   b. same-level social comparison.

   c. downward social comparison.

   d. "best of the best" social comparison.

2. Which of the following is true about social tuning?

   a. People decide consciously about whether to agree with someone else's attitudes.

   b. People will adopt someone else's attitudes only if they largely agree with that position to start with.

   c. People are especially likely to adopt someone else's attitudes when they want to get along with that person.

   d. Members of Western cultures are more likely to engage in social tuning than members of East Asian cultures.

3. Which of the following is an example of "looking glass self"?

   a. We see ourselves and others according to our own views and resist the views of others. We just need to look within us to know what abilities we have.

   b. We see ourselves and others around us in accordance with the situation. We may or may not adopt the views of others.

   c. We see ourselves and others around us through the eyes of other people and often adopt those views. This is especially true when we want to get along with each other.

   d. We adopt the views of another person even if we don't want to get along with each other.

See page 621 for the answers.

Self-Control: The Executive Function of the Self

5.5 When are people likely to succeed at self-control, and when are they likely to fail?

Lijiao has vowed to take the high road with her ex-boyfriend, Brandon, by not rehashing all of the hurtful things he did when they were together. "What's done is done," she thinks. "Time to move on." One night she runs into Brandon at a party, and, wouldn't you know it, there he is with her friend Meghan, whom Brandon swore he wasn't interested in. Lijiao is tempted to make a scene and lay into both of them, but she grits her teeth, puts on her best smile, and acts as if she couldn't care less. She is proud of herself, but a little while later she finds herself devouring a bowl of potato chips, even though she had promised herself to eat a healthy diet. In this example, Lijiao is doing something familiar to us all—trying to exert self-control. She succeeds in one respect—by suppressing her desire to tell off her ex-boyfriend—but fails in another—by not sticking to her healthy diet. What determines how successful we are at exerting self-control?

An important function of the self is to be the chief executive who makes choices about what to do, both in the present and in the future (Baumeister, Schmeichel, & Vohs, 2007; Carver & Scheier, 1998; Higgins, 1989, 2005; Vohs & Baumeister, 2011). We appear to be the only species, for example, that can imagine events that have not yet occurred and engage in long-term planning, and it is the self that does this planning and exerts control over our actions (Gilbert, 2006; Gilbert & Wilson, 2007). Regulating our behavior and choices in optimal ways, of course, can be easier said than done, as anyone who has been on a diet or tried to quit smoking knows.

One form of self-control that does not work very well (and often backfires) is *thought suppression*, whereby we try to push thoughts out of our minds. Often, the more we try not to think about something, such as an ex-boyfriend or the chips on the buffet table, the more those very thoughts keep coming to mind (Baird, Smallwood, Fishman, Mrazek, & Schooler, 2013; Wegner, 1992, 1994, 2011). A better strategy is to go ahead and think about the forbidden topic while trying to exert willpower when it comes to acting on those thoughts. We are likely to have the most willpower when we have plenty of energy while trying to control our actions (Baumeister & Hetherington, 1996; Schmeichel & Baumeister, 2004). But, because self-control requires energy, spending this energy on one task limits the amount that can be spent on another task, just as going for a 5-mile run makes it difficult to immediately play a game of basketball. This explains why Lijiao ate the potato chips—she had used up her "self-control" energy on being nice to her ex-boyfriend.

To test this idea, researchers asked participants to exert self-control on one task to see if this reduced their ability to exert control on a subsequent and completely unrelated task. In one study, for example, people who were instructed to suppress a thought (don't think about a White bear) were worse at trying to regulate their emotions on a second task (try not to laugh while watching a comedy film) as compared to people who did not first have to suppress their thoughts (Muraven, Tice, & Baumeister, 1998). Although the tasks were quite different, the researchers suggest that the first one depleted the resource that people use to control their behaviors and feelings, making it difficult to engage in a subsequent act of self-control.

Another example of this "depletion effect" is that people often have more energy to engage in self-control in the morning than they do in the afternoon because by the afternoon they are mentally depleted. For example, suppose you were tempted to do something dishonest, such as downloading music illegally, which you know you shouldn't do. Would you be more likely to give into the temptation and do it in the afternoon or the morning? Recent studies show that people are more likely to act dishonestly in the afternoon because they have less mental energy to resist temptation later in the day (Kouchaki & Smith, 2014).

Research, also suggests, however, that this "depletion effect" is not inevitable and that indeed people have some control over how much willpower they can muster in any given situation (Egan, Hirt, & Karpen, 2012). For example, simply believing that willpower is an unlimited resource can help: Those who hold this belief are better able to keep going and avoid being depleted by a difficult task, as long as the task is not too demanding (Job, Dweck, & Walton, 2010; Vohs, Baumeister, & Schmeichel, 2012).

Another approach is to engage in prayer. This was shown in a recent study that randomly assigned participants to pray or not pray before engaging in a task that required a lot of energy (Friese & Wänke, 2014). Those in the prayer condition were asked to spend 5 minutes praying or thinking about "a person, a group of persons, their hopes and wishes, something they were currently concerned with, or anything else they wished in whatever manner they wished to do so" (Friese & Wänke, 2014, p. 57). Note that this was worded in such a way that nonreligious people could do it too. All participants then performed a difficult task (suppressing their emotions and facial expressions while watching comedy films), followed by another difficult cognitive task. Everyone had enough energy to do the first task, regardless of whether they had prayed or not. But those who prayed were better able to muster the energy to do well on the second task as well. That is, they were better able to keep going and perform well on the second task, whereas those who didn't pray showed the usual depletion effect, doing poorly on the second task. Why did prayer help? Perhaps it convinced people that they had the resources and willpower to keep going; as we saw, that very belief can increase people's willpower. Thus, if Lijiao had spent a few minutes praying before the party or simply reminding herself that she was a strong person who had a lot of willpower, she would have been able to ignore her ex-boyfriend and avoid the potato chips as well.

What else can people do to increase their self-control? It helps to form specific implementation intentions in advance of a situation in which you will need to exert self-control (Gollwitzer & Oettingen, 2011; Oettingen, 2012). That is, instead of saying to yourself, "I'm going to study a lot for the next test in my psychology class," make specific "if-then" plans that specify how and when you will study and how you will avoid temptations. For example, you might make these plans: "I'm going to the library right after class on Thursday, and if my roommate texts me and says I should join her at a party that night, I'll tell her that I'll meet up with her after I'm done studying."

REVIEW QUESTIONS

1. Soha was not able to get her thoughts off her boyfriend, who she thought was going around with another girl simultaneously. She needed to complete some difficult assignments on time. Under which of the following conditions would Soha be most likely to meet her deadline?
   a. Soha needs to force herself to suppress her thoughts and then concentrate on her assignments.
   b. Soha may spend time thinking about her boyfriend in the morning but she must exercise self-control and focus on her assignments in the evening.
   c. Soha may go out with her friends during the day and get back to her assignments when she is in the mood.
   d. Soha may pray for sometime before beginning the task to muster energy for performing the task.

2. Eduardo is tempted to eat some of his roommate's cookies, even though his roommate told him not to. Under which of the following conditions would Eduardo be mostly likely to resist the temptation to eat the cookies?
   a. It's the afternoon, and Eduardo has had a busy morning.

   b. Eduardo believes that willpower is fixed resource and that people have a limited amount of it.
   c. Eduardo went to the gym that morning and had a good workout.
   d. Eduardo had spent a few minutes praying earlier in the day.

3. Tarek needs do his laundry but has been very busy. Under which of the following conditions is he most likely to his laundry in the next few days?
   a. He says to himself, "I'll do my laundry at 7:00 P.M. tomorrow, and if my roommate says we should play video games then, I'll ask him if we can do that later."
   b. He vows to do it at some point the next day.
   c. He vows to do it sometime in the next 2 days.
   d. He vows not to think about video games the next day so that he doesn't spend time doing that instead of doing his laundry.

See page 621 for the answers.

Impression Management: All the World's a Stage

5.6   How do people portray themselves so that others will see them as they want to be seen?

In 1991, David Duke decided to run for governor of Louisiana as a mainstream conservative Republican. He had some obstacles to overcome in convincing people to vote for him because for most of his adult life he had been a White supremacist and an anti-Semite who in 1989 had sold Nazi literature from his office (Applebome, 1991). To improve his appeal, he claimed that he no longer supported Nazi ideology or the Ku Klux Klan, of which he had been a leader (or "grand wizard") in the 1970s. He also tried to improve his appearance by undergoing facial cosmetic surgery. Duke's campaign rhetoric didn't fool too many Louisiana voters. They perceived the same racist message disguised in new clothes, and he was defeated by the Democratic candidate Edwin Edwards. In 2003, he was sentenced to 15 months in federal prison for allegedly using funds raised from supporters for personal investments and gambling (Murr & Smalley, 2003).

Keep up appearances whatever you do.
—Charles Dickens, 1843

Impression management in action: In the 1970s, David Duke was a leader in the Ku Klux Klan; in 1991, he ran for governor of Louisiana as a mainstream conservative Republican. A remarkable change occurred in Duke's presentation of self during this time.

Though few politicians attempt as extreme a makeover as David Duke did, managing public opinion is hardly a new concept in politics. The public knew that President Franklin Roosevelt had suffered from polio, but the extent of his disability was kept secret. He used a wheelchair in private but never in public. Instead, he made speeches standing at a podium, supported by an aide to his side. More recently, numerous politicians have tried to revamp their public image after being caught in scandals, some more successfully than others. Congressman Anthony Weiner, for example, resigned in 2011 after it became public that he was "sexting" with several women (texting them explicit messages and pictures) after denying that he had done so. Two years later he attempted a comeback in a run for the mayorship of New York City, claiming that his sexting days were behind him. But after it came out that he was still sending explicit texts to women under the alias "Carlos Danger," he garnered only 5% of the vote in the Democratic primary.

These are extreme examples of **impression management**, which is the attempt by people to get others to see them the way they want to be seen (Gibson & Poposki, 2010; Goffman, 1959; Ham & Vonk, 2011; Phelan & Rudman, 2010; Schlenker, 2003; Uziel, 2010). Just as politicians try to put the best possible spin on their actions and manage the impressions others have of them, so do we in our everyday lives. As Erving Goffman (1959) pointed out, we are all like stage actors who are trying our best to convince the "audience" (the people around us) that we are a certain way, even if we really are not.

Impression Management

The attempt by people to get others to see them as they want to be seen

Ingratiation and Self-Handicapping

People have many different impression management strategies (Jones & Pittman, 1982). One is **ingratiation**—using flattery or praise to make yourself likable to another, often a person of higher status (Jones & Wortman, 1973; Proost, Schreurs, De Witte, & Derous, 2010; Romero-Canyas et al., 2010). We can ingratiate through compliments, by agreeing with another's ideas, by commiserating and offering sympathy, and so on. If your boss drones on at a staff meeting, nearly putting the entire office to sleep, and you say, "Great job today, Sue. Loved your presentation," you are probably ingratiating. Ingratiation is a powerful technique because we all enjoy having someone be nice to us—which is what the ingratiator is good at. However, such a ploy can backfire

Ingratiation

The process whereby people flatter, praise, and generally try to make themselves likable to another person, often of higher status

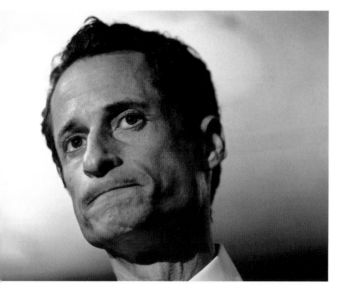

Sometimes politicians do not succeed in remaking their image to the public, such as Anthony Weiner's unsuccessful bid for mayor of New York City, after resigning from the U.S. Congress.

Self-Handicapping

The strategy whereby people create obstacles and excuses for themselves so that if they do poorly on a task, they can avoid blaming themselves

if the recipient of your ingratiation senses that you're being insincere (Jones, 1964; Kauffman & Steiner, 1968).

Another strategy and the one that has attracted the most research attention is **self-handicapping**. In this case, people create obstacles and excuses for themselves so that if they do poorly on a task, they can avoid blaming themselves. Doing poorly or failing at a task is damaging to your self-esteem. In fact, just doing less well than you expected or than you have in the past can be upsetting, even if it is a good performance. How can you prevent this disappointment? Self-handicapping is a rather surprising solution: You can set up excuses before the fact, just in case you do poorly (Arkin & Oleson, 1998; Jones & Berglas, 1978; Schwinger, Wirthwein, Lemmer, & Steinmayr, 2014; Snyder, Malin, Dent, & Linnenbrink-Garcia, 2014).

Let's say it's the night before the final exam in one of your courses. It's a difficult course, required for your major, and one in which you'd like to do well. A sensible strategy would be to eat a good dinner, study for a while, and then go to bed early and get a good night's sleep. The self-handicapping strategy would be to pull an all-nighter, do some heavy partying, and then wander into the exam the next morning bleary-eyed and muddle-headed. If you don't do well on the exam, you have an excuse to offer to others to explain your performance, one that deflects the potential negative internal attribution they might otherwise make (that you're not smart). If you ace the exam, well, so much the better—you did it under adverse conditions (no sleep), which suggests that you are especially bright and talented.

There are two major ways in which people self-handicap. In its more extreme form, called *behavioral self-handicapping*, people act in ways that reduce the likelihood that they will succeed on a task so that if they fail, they can blame it on the obstacles they created rather than on their lack of ability. The obstacles people have been found to use include drugs, alcohol, reduced effort on a task, and failure to prepare for an important event (Deppe & Harackiewicz, 1996; Lupien, Seery, & Almonte, 2010). Interestingly, research shows that men are more likely to engage in behavioral self-handicapping than are women (Hirt & McCrea, 2009; McCrea, Hirt, & Milner, 2008).

The second type, called *reported self-handicapping*, is less extreme. Rather than creating obstacles to success, people devise ready-made excuses in case they fail (Baumgardner, Lake, & Arkin, 1985; Hendrix & Hirt, 2009). We might not go so far as to pull an all-nighter before an important exam, but we might complain that we are not feeling well. People can arm themselves with all kinds of excuses: They blame their shyness, test anxiety, bad moods, physical symptoms, and adverse events from their past.

A problem with preparing ourselves with excuses in advance, however, is that we may come to believe these excuses and hence exert less effort on the task. Why work hard at something if you are going to do poorly anyway? Self-handicapping may prevent unflattering attributions for our failures, but it often has the perverse effect of causing the poor performance we feared to begin with. Further, even if self-handicappers avoid unflattering attributions about their performance (e.g., people thinking they aren't smart), they risk being disliked by their peers. People do not like others whom they perceive as engaging in self-handicapping strategies (Hirt, McCrea, & Boris, 2003; Rhodewalt et al., 1995). Women are particularly critical of other people who self-handicap. Thus, as we saw earlier, women are less likely to engage in the kind of self-handicapping in which they put obstacles in their own way, and they are more critical of others who do so (Hirt & McCrea, 2009; McCrea, Hirt, & Milner 2008). Why? Research shows that women place more value on trying hard to achieve something than men do and thus are more critical of people who seem not to try hard and then make up excuses for doing poorly.

> To succeed in the world, we do everything we can to appear successful.
> —FRANÇOIS DE LA ROCHEFOUCAULD, 1678

Culture, Impression Management, and Self-Enhancement

People in all cultures are concerned with the impression they make on others, but the nature of this concern and the impression management strategies people use differ considerably from culture to culture (Lalwani & Shavitt, 2009). We have seen, for example, that people in Asian cultures tend to have a more interdependent view of themselves than people in Western cultures do. One consequence of this identity is that "saving face," or avoiding public embarrassment, is extremely important in Asian cultures. In Japan, people are very concerned that they have the "right" guests at their weddings and the appropriate number of mourners at the funerals of their loved ones—so concerned, in fact, that if guests or mourners are unavailable, they may go to a local "convenience agency" and rent some. These agencies (*benriya*) have employees who are willing to pretend—for a fee—that they are your closest friends. A woman named Hiroko, for example, worried that too few guests would attend her second wedding. No problem—she rented six, including a man to pose as her boss, at a cost of $1,500. Her "boss" even delivered a flattering speech about her at the wedding (Jordan & Sullivan, 1995). Although such impression management strategies might seem extreme to Western readers, the desire to manage public impressions is just as strong in the West (as exemplified by David Duke's attempts to change the way the public viewed him).

REVIEW QUESTIONS

1. Amanda is at a team picnic with her coach and fellow soccer players. Which of the following is the best example of ingratiation?
   a. Amanda tells her coach that the quinoa salad he made was delicious, even though she thinks it tasted like dirt.
   b. Amanda tells her coach that he might want to consider taking cooking lessons.
   c. Amanda tells the 10-year-old brother of one her teammates that she likes his sneakers, which she thinks look great.
   d. The coach tells Amanda that she is a good player but should keep practicing to improve her skills.

2. Ben is worried that he will do poorly on his psychology test. Which of the following is the best example of *behavioral* self-handicapping?
   a. He spends a couple of extra hours studying, and right before the test, he tells his friends that he studied really hard.
   b. Instead of studying the night before, he stays up late watching movies on his computer. Right before the test, he tells his friends that he saw some great movies instead of studying.
   c. He spends a couple of extra hours studying. Then, right before the test, he tells his friends that he isn't feeling very well.
   d. Right before the test, Ben tells the professor that her class is the best one he's ever taken.

3. Ben is worried that he will do poorly on his psychology test. Which of the following is the best example of *reported* self-handicapping?
   a. He spends a couple of extra hours studying, and right before the test, he tells his friends that he studied really hard.
   b. Instead of studying the night before, he stays up late watching movies on his computer. Right before the test, he tells his friends that he saw some great movies instead of studying.
   c. He spends a couple of extra hours studying. Then, right before the test, he tells his friends that he isn't feeling very well.
   d. Right before the test, Ben tells the professor that her class is the best one he's ever taken.

See page 621 for the answers.

Self-Esteem: How We Feel About Ourselves

5.7   **What are the pros and cons of having high self-esteem?**

As part of its "Real Beauty Sketches" campaign, the Dove soap company released a video designed to boost women's self-esteem. In the video, a sketch artist draws two pictures of the same woman without seeing her—based on the woman's descriptions of herself and the other based on a friend's description of her. Invariably, to the women's surprise, the portrait based on her friend's description is more attractive than the portrait based on her own description, leading to the tagline "You are more beautiful than you think." This prompted an Internet spoof about what would happen if men were the participants. In this video, the drawings based on men's descriptions of themselves looked like George Clooney or Brad Pitt, whereas the drawings based on their friends' descriptions looked like deformed creatures from a Disney movie—leading to the tagline "You might not be as good looking as you think" (www.snotr.com/video/10987/Dove_Commercial_Parody__Guy_Version).

The Dove company says it made its video because it is committed to "building positive self-esteem and inspiring all women and girls to reach their full potential" (http://realbeautysketches.dove.us). But is it true that women need such a boost in **self-esteem**, defined as people's evaluation of their own self-worth—that is, the extent to which they view themselves as good, competent, and decent? Probably not because when it comes to feeling good about ourselves, most of us are doing just fine. True, a recent meta-analysis did find that men have more positive views of their physical appearance than women do, but this same study found that women have higher self-esteem in some areas (e.g., their perception of their moral and ethical qualities) and that women and men have equally high self-esteem in other areas, such as academics and social acceptance (Gentile et al., 2009).

Putting gender differences aside, we might ask a more basic question: Should everyone strive to achieve as much self-esteem as possible, showering themselves with praise as much as they can? Well, it is certainly true that we should try to avoid low self-esteem, which is a very unpleasant state that is associated with depression and the feelings that we are ineffective and not in control of our lives (Baumeister, Campbell, Krueger, & Vohs, 2003). What's more, high self-esteem protects us against thoughts about our own mortality. This is the basic tenet of **terror management theory**, which holds that self-esteem serves as a buffer, protecting people from terrifying thoughts about death (Greenberg, Solomon, & Pyszczynski, 1997; Pyszczynski, Greenberg, Solomon, Arndt, & Schimel, 2004; Schimel & Greenberg, 2013). That is, in order to protect themselves from the anxiety caused by thoughts of their own deaths, people embrace cultural worldviews that make them feel like they are effective actors in a meaningful, purposeful world. People with high self-esteem are thus less troubled by thoughts about their own mortality than people with low self-esteem are (Schmeichel et al., 2009).

Another advantage of evaluating ourselves positively is that it motivates us to persevere when the going gets rough. In fact, it may even make us exaggerate how good we are at things and be overly optimistic about our futures, motivating us to try harder when we encounter obstacles in our path (Taylor & Brown, 1988). To illustrate this, consider two students who are thinking about their postgraduation job prospects. "I don't know," the first one thinks. "The economy isn't doing so well, and I don't think I have what it takes to compete with all those talented young people entering the job market. I'd say that there is only a 20% chance that I'll get my dream job right out of school." The second student thinks, "Yes, it's a tough market, but I think my prospects are great if I work hard and do well in school. I'm good enough

Self-Esteem

Peoples evaluations of their own self-worth—that is, the extent to which they view themselves as good, competent, and decent

Terror Management Theory

The theory that holds that self-esteem serves as a buffer, protecting people from terrifying thoughts about their own mortality

In Greek mythology, Narcissus fell in love with his own reflection in a pool of water and was so fond of his own image that he couldn't leave and eventually died. Today, narcissism refers to the combination of excessive self-love and a lack of empathy toward others.

to get my dream job." Now, for the sake of the argument, let's suppose that Student 1 is more correct than Student 2; it *is* a tough economy, after all, and few students land their first choice of job right away. But which student will work harder to achieve that goal? And which one is more likely to achieve it? Research shows that people who are optimistic—even unreasonably so—try harder, persevere more in the face of failure, and set higher goals than do people who are not (Nes & Segerstrom, 2006; Scheier, Carver, & Bridges, 2001; Shepperd, Klein, Waters, & Weinstein, 2013). Obviously, Student 2 shouldn't exaggerate his or her prospects too much; people who believe that they will be the next winner of *The Voice* when they can't carry a tune are destined for failure and heartbreak. But a dose of optimism and confidence is a good thing to the extent that it makes people work harder to achieve their goals.

What happens when that dose is too large? There is a form of high self-esteem that is unhealthy, namely, **narcissism**, which is the combination of excessive self-love and a lack of empathy toward others (Furnham, Richards, & Paulhus, 2013; Schriber & Robins, 2012; Twenge & Campbell, 2009). Narcissists are extremely self-centered, concerned much more with themselves than with other people. On the Narcissistic Personality Inventory, a commonly used questionnaire measure, narcissists endorse such items as "I wish somebody would someday write my biography" and "I find it easy to manipulate people" (Raskin & Terry, 1988). That is, narcissists go far beyond optimists in their high opinions of themselves.

If you were born after 1980, you might want not want to hear this, but narcissism has been increasing among college students in recent years. Jean Twenge and her colleagues (Twenge, Konrath, Foster, Campbell, & Bushman, 2008; Twenge & Foster, 2010) tracked down studies that administered the Narcissistic Personality Inventory to college students in the United States between the years 1982 and 2008. As seen in Figure 5.8, there has been a steady increase in scores on this test since the mid-1980s. And there is some evidence that narcissism is more prevalent in America than in other cultures (Campbell, Miller, & Buffardi, 2010; Foster, Campbell, & Twenge, 2003).

Why the increase in narcissism? Nobody knows, though Twenge and colleagues (2008) speculate that American culture at large has become increasingly self-focused. To illustrate this, researchers coded the lyrics of the 10 most popular songs of the year between 1980 and 2007. They counted the number of first-person singular pronouns in the lyrics (e.g., "I," "me") and found a steady increase over time (see Figure 5.8; DeWall, Pond, Campbell, & Twenge, 2011). True, the Beatles released a song called "I, Me, Mine"

Narcissism

The combination of excessive self-love and a lack of empathy toward others

Figure 5.8 Are People Becoming More Narcissistic?

The top (red) line shows average scores for college students on the Narcissistic Personality Inventory (NPI), a common measure of narcissism, from the years 1980 to 2008. The bottom (blue) line shows the percentage of first-person pronouns (e.g., I, me, mine) in the lyrics of the 10 most popular songs of the year from 1980 to 2007. As you can see there has been a steady increase on both measures over time, suggesting that narcissism may be increasing.

(Based on Twenge & Foster, 2010)

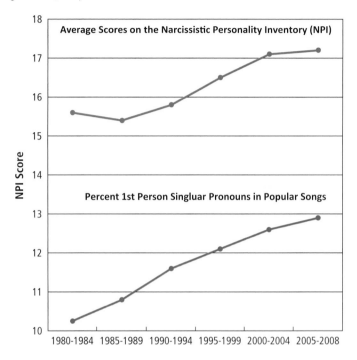

in 1970, but such self-references have become even more common, such as John Legend's "All of Me" or Avicii's "Wake Me Up." This trend has spawned many spoofs, such as the song "Selfie" by the Chainsmokers, in which the singer keeps interrupting her monologue to take another picture of herself, and MadTV's parody of a Coldplay music video called *The Narcissist*. This pattern toward self-reference is also true in books. Using the Google Books ngram database, researchers searched books published between the years 1960 and 2008 and found that first-person singular pronouns ("I," "me") increased by 42% over that time period (Twenge, Campbell, & Gentile, 2013). Although the reasons are not entirely clear, Americans seem to become more focused on themselves. (Perhaps we should pause for a moment here so that we can all take selfies.)

Well, you might ask, why is it a problem to be so self-focused? Won't that increase the chances of getting what we want in life? Actually, no. Narcissists do less well academically than others, are less successful in business, are more violent and aggressive, and are disliked by others, especially once people get to know them (Bushman & Baumeister, 2002; Twenge & Campbell, 2009).

Many young people are not so self-focused, of course, and devote countless hours to helping others through volunteer work. Ironically, in so doing they may have hit upon a way to become happier than by taking the narcissistic route. Imagine that you were in a study conducted by Dunn, Aknin, and Norton (2008). You are walking across campus one morning when a researcher approaches you and gives you an envelope with $20 in it. She asks you to spend it on yourself by 5:00 P.M. that day, such as by buying yourself a gift or paying off a bill. Sounds pretty nice, doesn't it? Now imagine that you were randomly assigned to another condition. Here you also get $20, but the researcher asks you to spend it on someone else by 5:00 P.M., such as by taking a friend out for lunch or donating it to a charity. How would that make you feel? It turns out that when the researchers contacted people that evening and asked how happy they were, those assigned to the "spend it on others" condition were happier than those asked to spend the money on themselves. A little less self-focus and a little more concern with others can actually make us happier.

To recap, having high self-esteem is generally a good thing to the extent that it makes people optimistic about their futures and work harder for what they want in life. There is a form of high self-esteem, however, that is quite problematic—namely, narcissism—which, as we have seen, is extreme high self-regard combined with a lack of empathy toward others. The best combination is to feel good about ourselves but also to look out for and care about others.

REVIEW QUESTIONS

1. Which of the following is most true about self-esteem?
   a. It's good to have low self-esteem because that motivates people to improve.
   b. In general, women have lower self-esteem than men.
   c. People who are optimistic try harder, persevere more in the face of failure, and set higher goals than do people who are not.
   d. The higher a person's self-esteem, the better off he or she is.

2. The basic tenet of terror management theory is that
   a. people are becoming increasingly narcissistic.
   b. it is important for governments to protect its citizens from terrorist attacks.
   c. people are less terrified of dying if they are religious.
   d. self-esteem protects people against thoughts about their own mortality.

3. Which of the following is most true about narcissism?
   a. In general, college students are becoming less narcissistic.
   b. It is characterized by excessive self-love and a lack of empathy toward others.
   c. People who are narcissistic do better academically than those who are not.
   d. People who are narcissistic have more friends and a better social life than those who are not.

See page 621 for the answers.

Summary

5.1 What is the self-concept, and how does it develop?

- **The Origins and Nature of the Self-Concept** Studies show that great apes such as chimpanzees and orangutans have a rudimentary sense of self because they pass the mirror self-recognition test, whereas lesser apes do not. In humans, self-recognition develops at around 18 to 24 months of age, and by adolescence the self-concept becomes much more complex. As people grow older, their sense of self develops into a full-blown **self-concept**, defined as the overall set of beliefs that people have about their personal attributes. In adulthood, people view morality is viewed as central to the self-concept, more so than cognitive processes or desires.

  - **Cultural Differences on the Self-Concept** People who grow up in Western cultures tend to have an independent view of the self, whereas people who grow up in Asian cultures tend to have an interdependent view of the self.

  - **Functions of the Self** The self serves four functions: *self-knowledge*, our beliefs about who we are and the way in which we formulate and organize this information; *self-control*, the way in which

we make plans and execute decisions; *impression management*, how we present ourselves to other people; and *self-esteem*, the way we feel about ourselves.

5.2 To what extent do people know themselves through introspection, and what are the consequences of introspection?

- **Knowing Ourselves Through Introspection** One way we attempt to learn about our own feelings, motives, and emotions is with **introspection**, which is looking inward to examine the "inside information" that we—and we alone—have about our thoughts, feelings, and motives.

  - **Focusing on the Self: Self-Awareness Theory** When people focus on themselves, they evaluate and compare their current behavior to their internal standards and values.

  - **Judging Why We Feel the Way We Do: Telling More Than We Can Know** When people introspect about why they feel the way they do, they often use causal theories, many of which are learned from one's culture.

- **The Consequences of Introspecting About Reasons** When people think about the reasons for their attitudes, they assume that their attitudes match the reasons that are plausible and easy to verbalize, leading to reasons-generated attitude change.

5.3 In what ways do people come to know themselves by observing their behavior?

- **Knowing Ourselves by Observing Our Own Behavior** People also gain self-knowledge by observing their own behavior. **Self-perception theory** argues that when our attitudes and feelings are uncertain or ambiguous, we infer these states by observing our own behavior and the situation in which it occurs.

  - **Intrinsic versus Extrinsic Motivation** An **over-justification effect** occurs when people focus on the extrinsic reasons for their behavior and underestimate their intrinsic reasons.

  - **Mindsets and Motivation** Some people have a **fixed mindset** about their abilities, which is the idea that they have a set amount of the ability that cannot change. Others have a **growth mindset**, the idea that their abilities are malleable qualities that they can cultivate and grow. People with a fixed mindset are more likely to give up after setbacks and are less likely to work on and hone their skills, whereas people with a growth mindset view setbacks as opportunities to improve through hard work.

  - **Understanding Our Emotions: The Two-Factor Theory of Emotion** Emotional experience is often the result of a two-step self-perception process in which people first experience arousal and then seek an appropriate explanation for it.

  - **Finding the Wrong Cause: Misattribution of Arousal** Sometimes people make mistaken inferences about what is causing them to be aroused.

5.4 In what ways do people use others to know themselves?

- **Using Other People to Know Ourselves** Our self-concepts are shaped by the people around us.

  - **Knowing Ourselves by Comparing Ourselves to Others** According to **social comparison theory**, we learn about our own abilities and attitudes by comparing ourselves to other people.

  - **Knowing Ourselves by Adopting Other People's Views** In addition, people tend to automatically adopt the attitudes of those they like and want to interact with.

- **Knowing Our Future Feelings by Consulting Other People** When making **affective forecasts**, which are people's predictions about how they will feel in response to a future emotional event, it is useful to know how other people reacted to that event.

5.5 When are people likely to succeed at self-control, and when are they likely to fail?

- **Self-Control: The Executive Function of the Self** In general, exerting energy on one task limits people's ability to exert self-control on a subsequent task. However, simply believing that willpower is an unlimited resource can help people exert more self-control, as can praying in advance of a task and forming implementation intentions.

5.6 How do people portray themselves so that others will see them as they want to be seen?

- **Impression Management: All the World's a Stage** People try to get others to see them as they want to be seen.

  - **Ingratiation and Self-Handicapping** People have many different **impression management** strategies. One is **ingratiation**—using flattery or praise to make yourself likable to another, often a person of higher status. Another is **self-handicapping**, whereby people create obstacles and excuses for themselves so that if they do poorly on a task, they can avoid blaming themselves.

  - **Culture, Impression Management, and Self-Enhancement** The desire to manage the image we present to others is strong in all cultures, although the kinds of images we want to present depend on the culture in which we live.

5.7 What are the pros and cons of having high self-esteem?

- **Self-Esteem: How We Feel About Ourselves** Most of us have high self-esteem, which has the benefits of avoiding depression, allowing us to persevere in the face of failure, and, as shown by research on of **terror management theory**, protecting us from thoughts about our own mortality. There is a form of high self-esteem, however, that is quite problematic—namely, **narcissism**—which is extreme high self-regard combined with a lack of empathy toward others. The best combination is to feel good about ourselves but also to look out for and care about others.

Test Yourself

1. Which of the following statements is *least* true, according to research on self-knowledge?

a. The best way to "know thyself" is to look inward, introspecting about ourselves.

b. Sometimes the best way to know ourselves is to see what we do.

c. We often try to figure out ourselves by comparing ourselves to others.

d. One way we know ourselves is by using theories we learn from our culture.

2. Which is the following is *not* a function of the self?

a. Self-knowledge

b. Self-control

c. Impression management

d. Self-criticism

3. At David's home no one smoked. He also never liked the idea of smoking. While making friends in high school, although he was very cautious, he discovered that all his friends smoked whenever they got together. None of them thought there was anything wrong with smoking. On several occasions, because of their pressure, he smoked. Which of the following would be the best way for David to deal with the situation?

a. He can try to be more self-focused. This will remind him of his sense of right and wrong.

b. He may stop meeting these friends so as to not fall prey to their pressure.

c. He may think of changing his internal standards and values so that he can enjoy the company of his friends.

d. He can avoid being self-aware so as to not feel terrible about violating his values.

4. Which of the following statements is an example of causal theories about feelings and behavior?

a. I work as hard as possible to feel good. My teachers and parents are very happy with me.

b. I will find time to give company to my parents to convey that I care for them. This will make them very happy.

c. I shall pursue a course of study that is popular. This will help me choose an appropriate profession later.

d. I yelled angrily at my friend today. I think my disturbed sleep last night has a lot to do with my outburst this morning.

5. Observing her deep passion for playing the piano, Dolly's school principal decided to give her a cash prize if she topped piano events in which she represented the school. This is an example of

a. task-contingent reward.

b. intrinsic reward.

c. performance-contingent reward.

d. fixed-reward.

6. Catherine did very well on her math test. Which of the following statements should her mother tell her to increase the chances that Catherine will not give up on math if it later becomes more difficult for her?

a. "You really worked hard for this test, and your hard work paid off!"

b. "You are such a smart kid, you excel in everything you do!"

c. "You are so good in math, you obviously have a gift for this!"

d. "I'm so glad to see you are doing better than all your classmates!"

7. Your friend Jane is interning at a law firm. When you ask her how it's going, she says, "I'm feeling good about it because I'm doing much better than the intern who started a month after me." What kind of social comparison is Jane making?

a. Upward social comparison

b. Downward social comparison

c. Impression comparison

d. Self-knowledge comparison

8. Which of the following is most true about learning about our own attitudes, motives, and emotions?

a. We learn about our attitudes, motives, and emotions by observing our behavior.

b. We learn about our attitudes, motives, and emotions by observing the conditions under which our behavior takes place.

c. We get to understand ourselves better by observing the role models we follow and the environment in which they live.

d. Both a and b are true.

9. Elise wants to increase her ability at self-control, such as by spending more time studying. Which of the following is *most* likely to work?

a. When she is studying, she should try hard to suppress thoughts about the party she could have gone to.

b. Just before it is time for her to study, she should do something that requires a lot of concentration, such as a difficult puzzle.

c. She should eat a small, sugary snack before studying.

d. She should adopt the belief that willpower is an unlimited resource.

10. Which of the following is the best strategy for increasing self-control?

a. I have the willpower and I know I will complete my work today itself.

b. I am really going to study hard for my history test this week.

c. I am going to study till late night. If my friend calls asking me to accompany him for a movie, I shall tell him that I will go with him the next time.

d. Before sitting down to study, I will pray for some time so as to feel more energetic to study.

See page 621 for the answers.

Chapter 6
The Need to Justify Our Actions
The Costs and Benefits of Dissonance Reduction

 ## Chapter Outline and Learning Objectives

The Theory of Cognitive Dissonance

6.1 **What is cognitive dissonance, and how do people avoid dissonance to maintain a positive self-image?**

When Cognitions Conflict
Dissonance and the Self-Concept
Decisions, Decisions, Decisions
Dissonance, Culture, and the Brain

Self-Justification in Everyday Life

6.2 **How does cognitive dissonance operate in everyday life, and what are some constructive ways of reducing it?**

The Justification of Effort
External versus Internal Justification
Punishment and Self-Persuasion
The Hypocrisy Paradigm
Justifying Good Deeds and Harmful Acts
Some Final Thoughts on Dissonance: Learning from Our Mistakes

It was shocking news: 39 people were found dead at a luxury estate in Rancho Santa Fe, California, participants in a mass suicide. All were members of an obscure cult called Heaven's Gate. Each body was laid out neatly, feet clad in brand-new Black Nikes, face covered with a purple shroud. The cult members died willingly and peacefully, leaving behind videotapes describing their reasons for suicide: They believed that the Hale-Bopp Comet, a recently discovered comet streaking across the night skies, was their ticket to a new life in paradise. They were convinced that in Hale-Bopp's wake was a gigantic spaceship whose mission was to carry them off to a new incarnation. To be picked up by the spaceship, they first needed to rid themselves of their current "containers." That is, they needed to leave their own bodies by ending their lives. Alas, no spaceship ever came.

Several weeks before the mass suicide, some members of the cult purchased an expensive, high-powered telescope. They wanted to get a clearer view of the comet and the spaceship that they believed was traveling behind it. A few days later, they returned the telescope and politely asked for their money back. When the store manager asked them if they had problems with the scope, they replied, "Well, gosh, we found the comet, but we can't find anything following it" (Ferris, 1997). Although the store manager tried to convince them that there was nothing wrong with the telescope and that nothing was following the comet, they remained unconvinced. Given their premise, their logic was impeccable: We know an alien spaceship is following behind the Hale-Bopp Comet. If an expensive telescope has failed to reveal that spaceship, then there is something wrong with the telescope.

Their thinking might strike you as strange, irrational, or stupid, but, generally speaking, the members of the Heaven's Gate cult were none of those things. Neighbors who knew them considered them pleasant, smart, and reasonable. What is the process by which intelligent, sane people can succumb to such fantastic thinking and self-destructive behavior? In this chapter, we will show you why their behavior is not mysterious after all. It is simply an extreme example of a normal human tendency: the need to justify our actions and commitments.

The Theory of Cognitive Dissonance

6.1 What is cognitive dissonance, and how do people avoid dissonance to maintain a positive self-image?

During the past half-century, social psychologists have discovered that one of the most powerful determinants of human behavior stems from our need to preserve a stable, positive self-image (Aronson, 1969, 1998). Most people believe they are above average—more ethical and competent, better drivers, better leaders, better judges of character, and more attractive than the majority (Brown, 2012; Fine, 2008; Gilovich, 1991). But if most of us see ourselves as reasonable, moral, and smart, what happens when we are confronted with information implying that we have behaved in ways that are unreasonable, immoral, or stupid? That is the subject of this chapter.

When Cognitions Conflict

Many years ago, Leon Festinger (1957) developed and investigated the precise workings of what is arguably social psychology's most important and most provocative theory: the theory of **cognitive dissonance**. He defined dissonance as the discomfort that is caused when two cognitions (beliefs, attitudes) conflict, or when our behavior conflicts with our attitudes. Cognitive dissonance always produces discomfort, and in response we try to reduce it. But unlike the ways we satisfy other uncomfortable feelings—for example, reducing hunger or thirst by eating or drinking—the path to reducing dissonance is not always simple or obvious. In fact, it can lead to fascinating

Cognitive Dissonance

The discomfort that people feel when two cognitions (beliefs, attitudes) conflict, or when they behave in ways that are inconsistent with their conception of themselves changes in the way we think about the world and the way we behave. How can we reduce dissonance? There are three basic ways (see Figure 6.1):

- By changing our behavior to bring it in line with the dissonant cognition.
- By attempting to justify our behavior through changing one of the dissonant cognitions.
- By attempting to justify our behavior by adding new cognitions.

To illustrate each of these, let's look at something that millions of people do several times a day: smoke cigarettes. If you are a smoker, you are likely to experience dissonance because you know that smoking significantly increases the risks of lung cancer, emphysema, and earlier death. How can you reduce this dissonance? The most direct way is to change your behavior and give up cigarettes. Your behavior would then be consistent with your knowledge of the link between smoking and cancer. Although many people have succeeded in quitting, it's not easy; many have tried and failed. What do these people do? It would be wrong to assume that they simply swallow hard, light up, and prepare to die. They don't. Researchers studied the behavior and attitudes of heavy smokers who attended a smoking cessation clinic but then relapsed. What do you suppose the researchers discovered? Heavy smokers who tried to quit and failed managed to lower their perception of the dangers of smoking. In this way, they could continue to smoke without feeling terrible about it (Gibbons, Eggleston, & Benthin, 1997).

A study of more than 360 adolescent smokers found the same thing: the greater their dependence on smoking and the greater the trouble they had quitting, the more justifications they came up with to keep smoking (Kleinjan, van den Eijnden, &

Figure 6.1 How We Reduce Cognitive Dissonance

There are three basic ways of reducing dissonance: change your behavior, change your cognition, or add a new cognition.

Teenagers who smoke usually justify their actions with such cognitions as "Smoking is cool"; "I want to be like my friends"; "in movies, everyone smokes"; "I'm healthy; nothing is going to happen to me"; or "adults are always on my back about stuff I do."

Self-Affirmation

In the context of dissonance theory, a way of reducing dissonance by reminding oneself of one or more of one's positive attributes

Engels, 2009). And smokers can come up with some pretty creative justifications. They say that smoking is worth the risk of cancer and emphysema because it is so enjoyable, and besides it relaxes them and reduces nervous tension and in this way actually improves their health. Some add a cognition that allows them to focus on the vivid exception: "Look at my grandfather. He's 87 years old, and he's been smoking a pack a day since he was 12. That proves it's not always bad for you." Some smokers, even pregnant women who hear warnings all the time, convince themselves that the data linking nicotine to cancer are inconclusive, or if they just cut down, the chance of harm is reduced (Naughton, Eborall, & Sutton, 2012). Smokers' self-justifications like these turn up in studies all over the world (Fotuhi et al., 2013).

Another popular way of reducing dissonance through adding a new cognition is **self-affirmation**, in which a person focuses on one or more of his or her good qualities to lessen the dissonant sting caused by doing something foolish: "Yeah, I feel pretty stupid to still be smoking, but boy am I a good cook. In fact, let me tell you about this new recipe . . ." (McConnell & Brown, 2010; Steele, 1988). These justifications may sound silly to the nonsmoker, but that is our point. As the smokers' rationales show, people experiencing dissonance will often deny or distort reality to reduce it.

When you understand dissonance, you will see it in action all around you. Here are three diverse examples.

- Which comes first—thinking that binge drinking is fun or going to a party and getting wasted? Does the attitude about drinking cause the behavior or does the behavior cause the attitude? A longitudinal study of college students found it is the latter, thanks to dissonance. Suppose that students who think it's pretty stupid to get sick drunk every weekend are cajoled into a night of binge drinking by their friends. Not wanting to admit to themselves that they are wimpy conformists, they reduce the dissonance between their attitude and their action by convincing themselves that binge drinking is good fun. Their attitudes about it change (van der Zwaluw et al., 2013).

- What happens to the people who predict the end of the world, sell their possessions and await doomsday at the top of a mountain, and who then, fortunately, turn out to be wrong? Notice how few of them admit they were foolish to be so gullible? Instead, they usually reduce dissonance by saying something like, "Our prediction was accurate; we just used numbers from the wrong chapter of the Bible."

- How do people resolve the dissonance when two central aspects of their identity conflict? In one study, researchers wondered how gay men who were strongly identified with their Christian church dealt with anti-gay pronouncements from their ministers. One way to resolve dissonance would be to change their behavior—that is, to change their church or even leave their religion. But those who decide to stay in the church resolve dissonance by focusing on the shortcomings of the minister; for example, they say, "It's not my religion that promotes this prejudice—it's the bigotry of this particular preacher" (Pitt, 2010).

In short, understanding dissonance explains why so much of human thinking is not rational, but *rationalizing*. No matter how smart they are, people who are in the midst of reducing dissonance are so involved with convincing themselves that they are right that they frequently end up behaving irrationally and maladaptively (Stanovich, West, & Toplak, 2013). Sometimes, of course, we pursue new information because we want to be accurate in our views or make the wisest decisions. But once we are committed to our views and beliefs, most of us distort new information in a way that confirms them (Hart et al., 2009; Ross, 2010). People who don't want to give up scientifically discredited ideas (such as the mistaken belief that vaccines cause autism), or who receive bad news about their health can be equally "creative" in denying evidence and reducing their discomfort (Aronson, 1997; Croyle & Jemmott, 1990; Pratarelli, 2012).

For example, suppose you have strong feelings about whether or not the death penalty deters people from committing murder. We now give you a series of arguments on both sides of the issue; some of those arguments are plausible and others are silly. Which arguments will you remember best? If you are thinking rationally, you should remember the plausible arguments best and the implausible arguments least, regardless of your own position. But what does dissonance theory predict? A silly argument that supports your own position arouses some dissonance because it raises doubts about the wisdom of that position or the intelligence of people who agree with it. Likewise, a sensible argument on the other side of the issue also arouses some dissonance because it raises the possibility that the other side might be smarter or more accurate than you had thought. Because these arguments arouse dissonance, we try not to think about them. This is exactly what researchers have repeatedly found. People remember the plausible arguments agreeing with their own position and the *implausible* arguments agreeing with the *opposing* position (Biek, Wood, & Chaiken, 1996; Edwards & Smith, 1996; Hart et al., 2009; Jones & Kohler, 1959).

WHY WE OVERESTIMATE THE PAIN OF DISAPPOINTMENT The process of reducing dissonance is largely unconscious; it hums along below awareness, keeping our attitudes in harmony without our thinking about it.

Imagine that you have just interviewed for the job of your dreams. You expect to be disappointed if you don't get the job. Then, to your utter amazement, you *don't* get the job. How long do you think your disappointment will last? The answer is: It depends on how successfully you reduce the dissonance caused by not getting the job. When you first get the bad news, you will be disappointed; however, more than likely you will soon put a spin on it that makes you feel better. It was a dead-end job anyway. And that interviewer was a jerk.

Interestingly, people often do not anticipate how successfully they will reduce dissonance. When people think about how they will react to future negative events, they show an **impact bias**, whereby they overestimate the intensity and duration of their negative emotional reactions. For example, people overestimate how dreadful they will feel following a romantic breakup, loss of a job, or not getting into the dorm they wanted (Dunn, Wilson, & Gilbert, 2003; Gilbert & Ebert, 2002; Mellers & McGraw, 2001; Wilson & Gilbert, 2005). They fail to realize that dissonance reduction will eventually save them from future anguish—seeing to it that they realize how much better off they are without that difficult partner, how lousy that job really was, and how great the people are in the dorm they originally thought was unappealing.

Given that people have successfully reduced dissonance in the past, why is it that they are not aware that they will do so in the future? Again, because dissonance reduction is largely unconscious; in fact, it works better that way (Gilbert & Ebert, 2002). It is not effective to hear ourselves say, "I'll try to make myself feel better by

Impact Bias

The tendency to overestimate the intensity and duration of one's emotional reactions to future negative events

When we think about the future, we overestimate how bad negative events, like the end of a romantic relationship, will make us feel. What we fail to recognize is that dissonance reduction often helps us back bounce quickly.

convincing myself that the person who just rejected me is an idiot." It is more effective if we unconsciously transform our view of the interviewer; we feel better believing that anyone could see that he is an idiot (Bem & McConnell, 1970; Goethals & Reckman, 1973).

Dissonance and the Self-Concept

In Leon Festinger's original formulation, any two cognitions could be dissonant. He was correct, but his student Elliot Aronson showed that dissonance is most painful, and we are most motivated to reduce it, when one of those cognitions is about the self: when our self-concept or self-esteem is threatened by the cognition that we have done something that violates our view of ourselves (Aronson, 1969).

This advance on the theory led to important and nonobvious discoveries. Who do you think feels the greatest dissonance after doing something cruel, foolish, or incompetent: a person with high self-esteem or low self-esteem? The answer is: the people with the highest self-esteem. They experience the most dissonance when they behave in ways that are contrary to their high opinion of themselves, and they will work harder to reduce it than will those with average levels of self-esteem. In contrast, when people who have low self-esteem commit a stupid or immoral action, they do not feel as much dissonance, because the cognition "I have done an awful thing" is consonant with the cognition "I am a loser; I'm always doing awful things." Psychopaths also are fairly immune from dissonance: the cognition "I just treated that person in a cold and heartless way" is consistent with "I'm really good at manipulating all those stupid people who can't see through me" (Murray, Wood, & Lilienfeld, 2012).

In a classic experiment, Aronson and David Mettee (1968) predicted that individuals who had been given a boost to their self-esteem would be less likely to cheat, if given the opportunity to do so, than individuals who had a lower opinion of themselves. After all, if you think of yourself as an honest person, cheating would be dissonant with that self-concept. However, people who have had a temporary blow to their self-esteem, and thus are feeling low and worthless, might be more likely to cheat at cards, kick their dog, or do any number of things consistent with having a low opinion of themselves. In this experiment, the self-esteem of college students was temporarily modified by giving the subjects false information about their personalities. After taking a personality test, one-third of the students were given positive feedback; they were told that the test indicated that they were mature, interesting, deep, and so forth. Another third of the students were given negative feedback; they were told that the test revealed that they were relatively immature, uninteresting, shallow, and the like. The remaining one-third of the students were not given any information about the results of the test. Immediately afterward, the students were scheduled to participate in an experiment conducted by a different psychologist who had no apparent relation to the personality inventory. As part of this second experiment, the participants played a game of cards against some of their fellow students. They were allowed to bet money and keep whatever they won. In the course of the game, they were given a few opportunities to cheat and thereby win a sizable sum of cash. The findings confirmed the prediction of dissonance theory: The students who had gotten the positive feedback were *least* likely to take the opportunity to cheat; the students who had gotten the negative feedback were *most* likely to cheat; and the control group fell in between. The positive feedback had virtually inoculated them against cheating.

In a more recent set of experiments, researchers found that people were less likely to cheat (to claim money they weren't entitled to from the experimenter) when

Both salvation and punishment for man lie in the fact that, if he lives wrongly, he can befog himself so as not to see the misery of his position.
—LEO TOLSTOY

their self-concept of "not being a cheater" was invoked. Some students read instructions that focused on their identity ("Please don't be a cheater"), whereas others read instructions that focused on the action ("Please don't cheat"). The "Please don't be a cheater" group was far less likely to cheat, because that would have created dissonance with their self-concept of being good and honest. The second group, which was asked to simply refrain from the behavior of "cheating," however, claimed more than twice as much money as people who were asked not to be "cheaters," and this difference occurred in a face-to-face situation as well as when it was done privately online (Bryan, Adams, & Monin, 2013).

If high self-esteem can serve as a buffer against dishonest or self-defeating behavior because people strive to keep their self-concepts consonant with their actions, this research has wide-ranging applications. For example, many African American children believe that they "don't have what it takes" to succeed academically, so they don't work hard, so they don't do as well as they might—all of this perfectly, if tragically, consonant. A team of social psychologists conducted a simple intervention, which they replicated three times with three different classrooms (Cohen et al., 2009). They bolstered African American children's self-esteem by having them do structured, self-affirming writing assignments. The children had to focus their attention on their good qualities in areas outside of academics and their most important values (e.g., religion, music, or love for their family). This self-affirmation raised their general self-esteem, which in turn reduced their academic anxiety, resulting in better performance. The lowest-achieving Black students benefited the most, and the benefits persisted in a follow-up study two years later. Thus, changing the students' negative self-perceptions had long-term benefits both on self-esteem and performance on objective exams.

Still, we must be cautious in generalizing from these results. Bolstering self-esteem can't be done in an artificial way. Otherwise, as dissonance theory would predict, self-affirmation can backfire. Two experiments found that among people with low self-esteem, repeating positive self-statements (such as "I'm a lovable person") and asserting how true they were ("that's really me!") actually made them feel worse, compared to people who did not repeat the statements or who focused on how the statements were both true and not true (Wood, Perunovic, & Wood, 2009). Similarly, when children who have low self-esteem are given inflated praise ("You made an *incredibly* beautiful drawing!"), that praise often backfires, discouraging them from taking on new challenges that they fear they won't be able to meet (Brummelman et al., 2014). To be effective, self-affirmation must be grounded in reality (Kernis, 2001); the person has to focus on his or her actual strengths, positive values, and good qualities and then strive to make them consonant with his or her actions.

Decisions, Decisions, Decisions

Every time we make a decision, we experience dissonance. How come? Suppose you are about to buy a car, but you are torn between a van and a subcompact. You know that each has advantages and disadvantages: The van would be more convenient. You can sleep in it during long trips, and it has plenty of power, but it gets poor mileage and it's hard to park. The subcompact is a lot less roomy, and you wonder about its safety: but it is less expensive to buy, it's a lot zippier to drive, and it has a pretty good repair record. Before you decide, you will probably get as much information as you can. You go online and read what the experts say about each model's safety, gas consumption, and reliability. You'll talk with friends who own a van or a subcompact. You'll probably visit automobile dealers to test-drive the vehicles to see how each one feels. All this predecision behavior is perfectly rational.

Let's assume you decide to buy the subcompact. We predict that your behavior will change in a specific way: You will begin to think more and more about the number of miles to the gallon as though it were the most important thing in the world. Simultaneously, you will almost certainly downplay the fact that you can't sleep in your subcompact. Who wants to sleep in their car on a long trip anyway? Similarly, you will barely remember that your new small car can put you at greater risk of harm in a collision. How does this shift in thinking happen?

DISTORTING OUR LIKES AND DISLIKES   In any decision, whether it is between two cars, two colleges, or two potential lovers, the chosen alternative is seldom entirely positive and the rejected alternative is seldom entirely negative. After the decision, your cognition that you are a smart person is dissonant with all the negative things about the car, college, or lover you chose; that cognition is also dissonant with all the *positive* aspects of the car, college, or lover you *rejected*. We call this **postdecision dissonance**. Cognitive dissonance theory predicts that to help yourself feel better about the decision, you will do some unconscious mental work to try to reduce the dissonance.

What kind of work? In a classic experiment, Jack Brehm (1956) posed as a representative of a consumer testing service and asked women to rate the attractiveness and desirability of several kinds of small appliances. Each woman was told that as a reward for having participated in the survey, she could have one of the appliances as a gift. She was given a choice between two of the products she had rated as being equally attractive. After she made her decision, each woman was asked to rerate all the products. After receiving the appliance of their choice, the women rated its attractiveness somewhat higher than they had the first time. Not only that, but they drastically lowered their rating of the appliance they might have chosen but decided to reject.

In this way, following a decision, we reduce dissonance to make ourselves feel better about the choice we made.

THE PERMANENCE OF THE DECISION   The more important the decision, the greater the dissonance. Deciding which car to buy is clearly more important than deciding between a toaster and a coffeemaker; deciding which person to marry is clearly more important than deciding which car to buy. Decisions also vary in terms of how permanent they are—that is, how difficult they are to revoke. It is a lot easier to trade in your new car for another one than it is to get out of an unhappy marriage. The more permanent and less revocable the decision, the stronger is the need to reduce dissonance (Bullens, van Harreveld, Förster, & van der Pligt, 2013).

In a simple but clever experiment, social psychologists intercepted people at a racetrack who were on their way to place $2 bets and asked them how certain they were that their horses would win (Knox & Inkster, 1968). The investigators also approached other bettors just as they were leaving the $2 window, after having placed their bets, and asked them the same question. Almost invariably, people who had already placed their bets gave their horses a much better chance of winning than did those who had not yet placed their bets. Because only a few minutes separated one group from another, nothing real had occurred to increase the probability of winning; the only thing that had changed was the finality of the decision—and hence the dissonance it produced.

Other investigators tested the irrevocability hypothesis in a photography class (Gilbert & Ebert, 2002). In their study, participants were

Postdecision Dissonance

Dissonance aroused after making a decision, typically reduced by enhancing the attractiveness of the chosen alternative and devaluating the rejected alternatives

Life is full of tough choices, like where to attend college. Once we make a decision, we often inflate the importance of positive aspects of our choice (i.e., the college we selected) and minimize the positive aspects of the other alternatives (i.e., the colleges we didn't select).

recruited through an advertisement for students interested in learning photography while taking part in a psychology experiment. Students were informed that they would shoot some photographs and print two of them. They would rate the two photographs and then get to choose one to keep. The other would be kept for administrative reasons. The students were randomly assigned to one of two conditions. In Condition One, students were informed that they had the option of exchanging photographs within a five-day period; in Condition Two, students were told that their choice was final. The researchers found that *prior* to making the choice between the two photographs, the students liked them equally. The experimenters then contacted the students several days after they had made their choice to find out if those who had a choice to exchange photographs liked the one they chose more or less than did those in the no-choice (irrevocable) condition. And, indeed, the students who had the option of exchanging photographs liked the one they finally ended up with less than did those who made the final choice on the first day.

All sales are final. When will these customers be happier with their new car: ten minutes before the purchase or ten minutes after?

Interestingly, when students were asked to predict whether keeping their options open would make them more or less happy with their decision, they predicted that keeping their options open would make them happier. They were wrong. Because they underestimated the discomfort of dissonance, they failed to realize that the finality of the decision would make them happier.

TRY IT!
The Advantage of Finality

Ask five friends who are not in this class the following question: Imagine you are shopping for a particular cell phone and you find it in two stores. The price for the phones is identical, but in Store A you have the option of exchanging the phone within 30 days, while in Store B all sales are final. One week after your purchase, which situation will make you happier with the cell phone: Store A (with the option to return the phone) or Store B (purchase not revocable)?

CREATING THE ILLUSION OF IRREVOCABILITY   The irrevocability of a decision always increases dissonance and the motivation to reduce it. Because of this, unscrupulous salespeople have developed techniques for creating the illusion that irrevocability exists. One such technique is called **lowballing** (Cialdini, 2009; Cialdini et al., 1978; Weyant, 1996). Robert Cialdini, a distinguished social psychologist, temporarily joined the sales force of an automobile dealership to observe this technique closely. Here's how it works: You enter an automobile showroom intent on buying a particular car. Having already priced it at several dealerships and online, you know you can purchase it for about $18,000. You are approached by a personable middle-aged man who tells you he can sell you one for $17,679. Excited by the bargain, you agree to write out a check for the down payment so that he can take it to the manager as proof that you are a serious customer. Meanwhile, you imagine yourself driving home in your shiny new bargain. Ten minutes later the salesperson returns, looking forlorn. He tells you that in his zeal to give you a good deal, he miscalculated and the sales manager caught it. The price of the car comes to $18,178.

Lowballing

An unscrupulous strategy whereby a salesperson induces a customer to agree to purchase a product at a low cost, subsequently claims it was an error, and then raises the price; frequently, the customer will agree to make the purchase at the inflated price

You are disappointed. Moreover, you are pretty sure you can get it a bit cheaper elsewhere. The decision to buy is not irrevocable. And yet in this situation far more people will go ahead with the deal than if the original asking price had been $18,178, even though the reason for buying the car from this particular dealer—the bargain price—no longer exists.

There are at least three reasons that lowballing works. First, although the customer's decision to buy is reversible, a commitment of sorts does exist. Signing a check for a down payment creates the illusion of irrevocability, even though, if the car buyer thought about it, he or she would quickly realize that it is a nonbinding contract. In the world of high-pressure sales, however, even a temporary illusion can have real consequences. Second, the feeling of commitment triggered the anticipation of an exciting event: driving out with a new car. To have had the anticipated event thwarted (by not going ahead with the deal) would have been a big letdown. Third, although the final price is substantially higher than the customer thought it would be, it is probably only slightly higher than the price at another dealership. Under these circumstances, the customer in effect says, "Oh, what the heck. I'm here, I've already filled out the forms, I've written out the check—why wait?" Thus, by using dissonance reduction and the illusion of irrevocability, high-pressure salespeople increase the probability that you will decide to buy their product at their price.

THE DECISION TO BEHAVE IMMORALLY   Of course, decisions about cars, appliances, racehorses, and even presidential candidates are the easy ones. Often, however, our choices involve moral and ethical issues. When is it OK to lie to a friend, and when is it not? When is an act stealing, and when is it just "what everyone does"? We have seen that having high self-esteem can insulate a person from yielding to the temptation to cheat. But sometimes the temptation is too great. How people reduce dissonance following a difficult moral decision has implications for whether they behave more *or less* ethically in the future.

Take the issue of cheating on an exam. Suppose you are a college sophomore taking the final exam in organic chemistry. Ever since you can remember, you have wanted to be a surgeon, and you think that your admission to medical school will depend heavily on how well you do in this course. A key question involves some material you know fairly well, but because so much is riding on this exam, you feel acute anxiety and draw a blank. You happen to be sitting next to one of the best students in the class, and when you glance at her paper you see that she is just completing her answer to the crucial question. You avert your eyes. Your conscience tells you it's wrong to cheat, and yet, if you don't cheat, you are certain to get a poor grade. And if you get a poor grade, you are convinced that there goes medical school.

Regardless of whether or not you decide to cheat, the threat to your self-esteem arouses dissonance. If you cheat, your belief or cognition "I am a decent, moral person" is dissonant with your cognition "I have just committed an immoral act." If you decide to resist temptation, your cognition "I want to become a surgeon" is dissonant with your cognition "I could have nailed a good grade and admission to medical school, but I chose not to. Wow, was I stupid!"

Suppose that after a difficult struggle, you decide to cheat. According to dissonance theory, it is likely that you would try to justify the action by finding a way to minimize its negative aspects. In this case, an efficient path to reducing dissonance would involve changing your attitude about cheating. You would adopt a more lenient attitude toward cheating, convincing yourself that it is a victimless crime that doesn't hurt anybody, that everybody does it, and that, therefore it's not really so bad.

After he cheats, this student will try to convince himself that everybody would cheat if they had the chance.

Suppose, by contrast, after a difficult struggle, you decide not to cheat. How would you reduce your dissonance? Again, you could change your attitude about the morality of the act, but this time in the opposite direction. That is, to justify giving up a good grade, you convince yourself that cheating is a heinous sin, that it's one of the lowest things a person can do, and that cheaters should be rooted out and severely punished.

What has happened is not merely a rationalization of your own behavior, but a change in your system of values. Thus, two people acting in two different ways could have started out with almost identical attitudes toward cheating. One came within an inch of cheating but decided to resist, while the other came within an inch of resisting but decided to cheat. After they had made their decisions, however, their attitudes toward cheating would diverge sharply as a consequence of their actions (see Figure 6.2).

These speculations were tested by Judson Mills (1958) in an experiment he performed in an elementary school. Mills first measured the attitudes of sixth graders toward cheating. He then had them participate in a competitive exam, with prizes awarded to the winners. The situation was arranged so that it was almost impossible to win without cheating. Mills made it easy for the children to cheat and created the illusion that they could not be detected. Under these conditions, as one might expect, some of the students cheated and others did not. The next day, the sixth graders were again asked to indicate how they felt about cheating. Sure enough, the children who had cheated became more lenient toward cheating, and those who had resisted the temptation to cheat adopted a harsher attitude.

Take another look at Figure 6.2 and imagine yourself at the top of that pyramid, about to make any important decision, such as whether to stay with a current romantic partner or break up, use illegal drugs or not, choose this major or that one, do something unethical or be honest. Keep in mind that once you make a decision, you are going to justify it to reduce dissonance, and that justification may later make it hard for you to change your mind . . . even when you should.

Dissonance, Culture, and the Brain

Cognitive dissonance theory has been supported by thousands of studies, some in related areas such as cognition (biases in how the brain processes information), memory (how we shape our current memories to be consonant with our self-concepts), and attitudes. (see Chapter 7.) Investigators are learning what aspects of cognitive dissonance seem to be universal, perhaps hardwired in the brain, and which vary across cultures (Cohen, 2014).

DISSONANCE IN THE BRAIN Experiments with monkeys and chimps support the notion that cognitive dissonance has some built-in, adaptive functions. Remember the study in which homemakers ranked appliances and then, after getting to keep an appliance of their choice, lowered their ranking of the previously attractive appliance they did not choose? Once human beings choose between two options, we are likely to stay with it, even when another option comes along (Arad, 2013). Studies with primates suggest that the reason may be that there is an evolutionary benefit to sticking with a tried-and-true option and rejecting a novel alternative

Figure 6.2 The Cheating Pyramid

Imagine two students taking an exam. Both are tempted to cheat. Initially, their attitudes toward cheating are almost identical, but then one impulsively cheats and the other does not. Their attitudes will then undergo predictable changes.

(Created by Carol Tavris and used with permission)

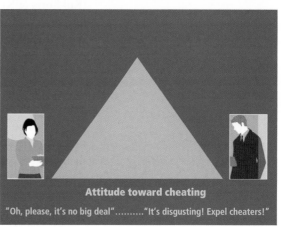

(which, at least in our species' past, could be risky or dangerous). When monkeys and chimps are placed in a similar situation, having to choose between different-colored M&Ms instead of kitchen appliances, they later reduced their preference for the color of M&Ms they had not chosen (Egan, Santos, & Bloom, 2007; see also West et al., 2010). Obviously, monkeys and chimps do not have a self-concept to protect. It seems likely that their preference for holding to a "win-stay" strategy, at least in the selection of food, was evolutionarily adaptive, increasing their ability to survive and procreate.

Neuroscientists have tracked brain activity to discover what parts of the brain are active when a person is in a state of dissonance and motivated to do something to reduce it (Harmon-Jones & Amodio, 2012). Using fMRI technology, they can monitor neural activity in specific areas while people are experiencing various kinds of dissonance: for example, while they are rating their preferences for things they had chosen and those they had rejected, while they are arguing that the uncomfortable scanner experience was actually quite pleasant, or while they are confronted with unwelcome information. The areas of the brain that are activated during dissonance include the striatum and other highly specific areas within the prefrontal cortex, the site prominently involved in planning and decision making (Izuma et al., 2010; Kitayama et al., 2013; Qin et al., 2011).

In a study of people who were trying to process dissonant or consonant information about their preferred presidential candidate, Drew Westen and his colleagues (2006) found that the reasoning areas of the brain virtually shut down when a person is confronted with dissonant information and the emotion circuits of the brain light up happily when consonance is restored. As Westen put it, people twirl the "cognitive kaleidoscope" until the pieces fall into the pattern they want to see, and then the brain repays them by activating circuits involved in pleasure. It seems that the feeling of cognitive dissonance can literally make your brain hurt!

DISSONANCE ACROSS CULTURES   We can find dissonance operating in almost every part of the world (e.g., Beauvois & Joule, 1996; Imada & Kitayama, 2010; Sakai, 1999), but it does not always take the same form, and the *content* of the cognitions that produce it may differ across cultures. In "collectivist" societies, where the needs of the group matter more than the needs of a particular person (as in "individualist" societies), dissonance-reducing behavior might be less prevalent, at least on the surface (Kokkoris & Kühnen, 2013; Triandis, 1995). In such cultures, we'd be more likely to find behavior aimed at maintaining group harmony and less likely to see people justifying their own personal misbehavior—but more likely to see people experiencing dissonance when their behavior shames or disappoints *others*.

Japanese social psychologist Haruki Sakai (1999), combining his interest in dissonance with his knowledge of Japanese community orientation, found that, in Japan, many people will vicariously experience dissonance on the part of someone they know and like. The observers' attitudes change to conform to those of their dissonance-reducing friends. Moreover, in subsequent experiments, Japanese participants justified their choices when they felt others were observing them while they were making their decision, but not later; this pattern was reversed for Americans (Imada & Kitayama, 2010). The perceived privacy or public visibility of the choice being made interacts with culture to determine whether dissonance is aroused and the choice needs to be justified.

Nonetheless, most causes of dissonance are international and intergenerational. For example, in multicultural America, immigrant parents and their young-adult children often clash over cultural values: the children want to be like their peers, but their elders want them to be like them. This conflict often creates enormous dissonance in the children because they love their parents but do not embrace all of their values. In a longitudinal study of Vietnamese and Cambodian adolescents in the United States, those who were experiencing the most cognitive dissonance were most likely to get into trouble, do less well in school, and fight more with their parents (Choi, He, & Harachi, 2008).

REVIEW QUESTIONS

1. Which of the following techniques relating to *post-decision dissonance* could a clothing store use to increase customer satisfaction?
   a. Cut all prices in half.
   b. Ask customers to make a radio ad saying how great the store is.
   c. Charge a membership fee to shop at the store.
   d. Make all sales final.

2. Meghan has been accepted to two top graduate schools. Under which condition will she experience the most dissonance?
   a. When she is thinking about the pros and cons of both programs before making up her mind.
   b. When she is pretty sure which program she wants to attend but has not yet notified the school of her decision.
   c. Right after she decides which program to attend and notifies the school of her decision.
   d. Meghan will experience an equal amount of dissonance in each of the above three circumstances.

3. What was the finding of the experiment conducted by Mills (1958) on attitudes toward cheating?
   a. Children who had cheated indicated that they felt very guilty and promised their teachers that they would never do so again.
   b. Children who had cheated became more lenient toward cheating, while those who had resisted the temptation to cheat adopted a harsher attitude.
   c. Children who had resisted the temptation to cheat indicated that they should have cheated as this was the only way to win prizes.
   d. Children's attitude toward cheating remained the same before and after the exam.

4. Jake's professor tells Jake that if he is caught cheating on an exam, he will be expelled. Amanda's professor tells her that if she is caught cheating, she will have only to write a short paper about why cheating is wrong. If both students don't cheat, dissonance theory would predict that:
   a. Amanda will feel more honest than Jake will.
   b. Jake will feel more honest than Amanda will.
   c. Amanda and Jake will feel equally honest.
   d. Amanda and Jake will feel equally dishonest because were both threatened in advance.

5. Which of the following areas of the human brain have been found to be active during dissonance?
   a. The striatum and other specific areas within the prefrontal cortex
   b. The amygdala and emotional circuits of the brain
   c. The midbrain and specific areas within the parietal cortex
   d. The cerebellum and specific areas within the temporal cortex

See page 621 for the answers.

Self-Justification in Everyday Life

6.2   How does cognitive dissonance operate in everyday life, and what are some constructive ways of reducing it?

Suppose you put in a lot of effort to get into a particular club and it turns out to be a totally worthless organization, consisting of boring, pompous people doing trivial activities. You would feel pretty foolish, wouldn't you? A sensible person doesn't work hard to gain something worthless. Such a circumstance would produce significant dissonance; your cognition that you are a sensible, adept human being is dissonant with your cognition that you worked hard to get into a dismal group. How would you reduce this dissonance?

The Justification of Effort

You might start by finding a way to convince yourself that the club and the people in it are nicer, more interesting, and more worthwhile than they appeared to be at first glance. How can one

The harsh training required to become a marine will increase the recruits' feelings of cohesiveness and their pride in the corps.

Figure 6.3 The Justification of Effort

The more effort we put into becoming members of a group, and the tougher the initiation, the more we will like the group we have just joined—even if it turns out to be a dud.

(Based on Aronson & Mills, 1959)

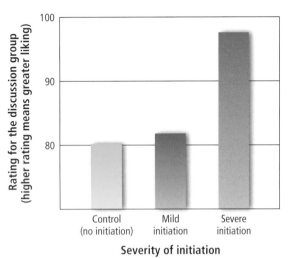

A devotee participates in a ritual as part of the Hindu festival of Thaipusam.

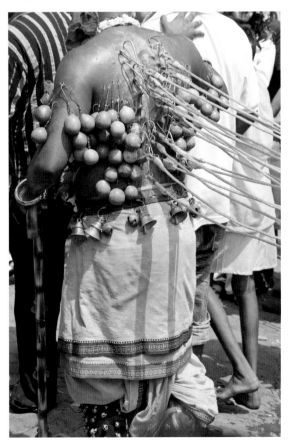

turn boring people into interesting people and a trivial club into a worthwhile one? Easy. Even the most boring people and trivial clubs have some redeeming qualities. Activities and behaviors are open to a variety of interpretations; if we are motivated to see the best in people and things, we will tend to interpret these ambiguities in a positive way. We call this the **justification of effort**, the tendency for individuals to increase their liking for something they have worked hard to attain.

In a classic experiment, Elliot Aronson and Judson Mills (1959) explored the link between effort and dissonance reduction. In their experiment, college students volunteered to join a group that would be meeting regularly to discuss various aspects of the psychology of sex. To be admitted to the group, they volunteered to go through a screening procedure. For one-third of the participants, the procedure was demanding and unpleasant; for another third, it was only mildly unpleasant; and the final third was admitted to the group without any screening at all.

Each participant was then allowed to listen in on a discussion being conducted by the members of the group he or she would be joining. Although the participants were led to believe that the discussion was live, they were listening to a prerecorded tape. The taped discussion was designed to be as dull and bombastic as possible. After the discussion was over, each participant was asked to rate it in terms of how much he or she liked it, how interesting it was, how intelligent the participants were, and so forth.

As you can see in Figure 6.3, participants who expended little or no effort to get into the group did not enjoy the discussion much. They were able to see it for what it was—a dull and boring waste of time. Participants who went through a severe initiation, however, convinced themselves that the same discussion, though not as scintillating as they had hoped, was dotted with interesting and provocative tidbits and was therefore, in the main, a worthwhile experience. These findings have been replicated under a variety of circumstances: people justify the effort they have expended on everything from a worthless self-help program to a course of physical therapy (Coleman, 2010; Conway & Ross, 1984; Cooper, 1980; Gerard & Mathewson, 1966).

A stunning example of the justification of effort comes from an observational study done in the multicultural nation of Mauritius (Xygalatas et al., 2013). Every year, the Hindu festival of Thaipusam includes two rituals: a low-ordeal ritual involving singing and collective prayer, and a severe-ordeal ritual called Kavadi. "Severe" is something of an understatement. Participants are pierced with needles, hooks, and skewers, carry heavy bundles, and drag carts that are attached by hooks to their skin for more than four hours. Then they climb a mountain barefooted to reach the temple of Murugan. Afterward, the researchers gave both the low-ordeal and severe-ordeal participants the opportunity to anonymously donate money to the temple. The severe-ordeal ritual produced much higher donations than the low-ordeal ritual. The greater the men's pain, the greater their commitment to the temple.

We are not suggesting that most people enjoy difficult, unpleasant, painful experiences, nor that people enjoy things that are merely associated with unpleasant experiences. Rather, if a person agrees to go through a demanding or an unpleasant experience in order to attain some goal or object, that goal or object becomes more attractive. Consider the sex discussion group described above: If you were walking to the meeting and a passing car splashed mud all over you, you would not like that group any better. However, if you volunteered to jump into a mud puddle in order to be admitted to a group that turned out to be boring, you *would* like the group better. (See the Try It!)

Justification of Effort

The tendency for individuals to increase their liking for something they have worked hard to attain

---

TRY IT!
Justifying What You've Done

Think about something that you have gone after in the past that required you to put in a lot of effort or that caused you considerable trouble. Perhaps you waited for several hours in a long line to get tickets to a concert; perhaps you sat in your car through an incredible traffic jam in order to connect with someone your friend swears is your perfect match.

1. List the things you had to go through to attain your goal.

2. Do you think you tried to justify all that effort? List some of the ways you might have exaggerated the good things

about the goal and another list of how you might have minimized any negative aspects of the goal.

3. The next time you put in a lot of effort to reach a goal, you might want to monitor your actions and cognitions carefully to see if the goal was *really* worth it or whether there is any self-justification involved.

External versus Internal Justification

Suppose your friend Jen shows you her expensive new dress and asks your opinion. You think it is atrocious and are about to say so, advising her to exchange it before another human being sees her in it, when she tells you that she has already had it altered, which means that she cannot return it. What do you say? Chances are you go through something like the following thought process: "Jen seems so happy and excited about her new dress. She spent a lot of money for it, and she can't take it back. If I say what I think, I'll upset her."

So you tell Jen that you like her dress. Do you experience much dissonance? We doubt it. Many thoughts are consonant with having told this lie, as outlined in your reasoning. In effect, your cognition that it is important not to embarrass or cause pain to people you like provides ample **external justification** for having told a harmless lie.

What happens, though, if you say something you don't believe when there *isn't* a good external justification for being insincere? What if your friend Jen is wealthy and can easily afford to absorb the cost of her ugly new dress? What if she sincerely wanted to know what you thought? Now the external justifications—the reasons for lying to Jen about the dress—are minimal. If you still withhold your true opinion, you will experience dissonance. When you can't find external justification for your behavior, you will attempt to find **internal justification**; you will try to reduce dissonance by changing something about yourself, such as your attitude or behavior.

COUNTERATTITUDINAL ADVOCACY   How can you do this? You might begin by looking harder for positive things about the dress that you hadn't noticed before. Within a short time, your attitude toward the dress will have moved in the direction of the statement you made. And that is how *saying becomes believing*. Its official term is **counterattitudinal advocacy**. It occurs when we claim to have an opinion or attitude that differs from our true beliefs. When we do this with little external justification— that is, without being motivated by something outside of ourselves—what we believe begins to conform more and more to the lie we told.

External Justification

A reason or an explanation for dissonant personal behavior that resides outside the individual (e.g., to receive a large reward or avoid a severe punishment)

Internal Justification

The reduction of dissonance by changing something about oneself (e.g., one's attitude or behavior)

Counterattitudinal Advocacy

Stating an opinion or attitude that runs counter to one's private belief or attitude

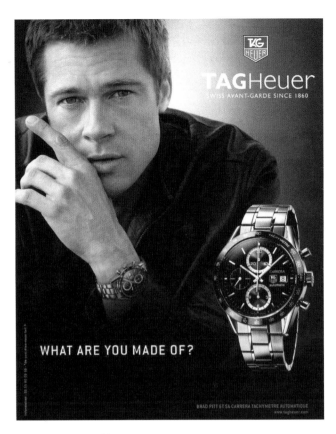

Celebrities are paid huge amounts of money to endorse products. Do you think that Brad Pitt believes the message he is delivering about this expensive watch? Is the justification for his endorsement internal or external?

This proposition was first tested in a groundbreaking experiment by Leon Festinger and J. Merrill Carlsmith (1959). College students were induced to spend an hour performing a series of excruciatingly boring and repetitive tasks. The experimenter then told them that the purpose of the study was to determine whether or not people would perform better if they had been informed in advance that the tasks were interesting. They were each informed that they had been randomly assigned to the control condition—that is, they had not been told anything in advance. However, he explained, the next participant, a young woman who was just arriving in the anteroom, was going to be in the experimental condition. The researcher said that he needed to convince her that the task was going to be interesting and enjoyable. Because it was much more convincing if a fellow student rather than the experimenter delivered this message, would the participant do so? Thus, with his request, the experimenter induced the participants to lie about the task to another student.

Half of the students were offered $20 for telling the lie (a large external justification), while the others were offered only $1 for telling the lie (a small external justification). After the experiment was over, an interviewer asked the lie-tellers how much they had enjoyed the tasks they had performed earlier in the experiment. The results validated the hypothesis: The students who had been paid $20 for lying—that is, for saying that the tasks had been enjoyable—rated the activities as the dull and boring experiences they were. But those who were paid only $1 for saying the task was enjoyable rated the task as significantly more enjoyable. In other words, people who had received an abundance of external justification for lying told the lie but didn't believe it, whereas those who told the lie without much external justification convinced themselves that what they said was closer to the truth.

Can you induce a person to change an attitude about things that matter, such as attitudes toward the police or the legalization of marijuana? Whenever college students have launched demonstrations to protest segregation, sex discrimination, the Vietnam War, tuition increases, or Wall Street greed and lack of corporate accountability, the police have usually reacted with excessive force, using clubs, tear gas, and pepper spray on the students to disperse them. You can imagine how angry that action made the protesters and their supporters. Is it possible to change students' attitudes to make them more understanding of the police? In a different domain, could you change the attitudes of people who believe that marijuana is harmful and should be prohibited?

The answer is yes, and you do it not by offering people large incentives to write a forceful essay supporting the police or the legalization of marijuana, but with small incentives. When Yale University students were offered a large cash reward for writing an essay supporting the excessive force used by the local police, they did not need to convince themselves that they believed what they had written; the external justification was enough. However, when they were induced to write a supportive essay for a *small* reward, they did, in fact, soften their attitudes toward the actions of the police (Cohen, 1962). Another study found the same pattern of results with students at the University of Texas who were opposed to the legalization of marijuana. When they were well paid for writing an essay favoring legalization, their real attitudes did not change. When they were given only a small fee, however, they needed to convince themselves that there was some truth in what they had written, and their attitudes became more prolegalization (Nel, Helmreich, & Aronson, 1969). In these studies, as in many others, the smaller the external incentive, the greater the attitude change.

Experiments on counterattitudinal advocacy have been applied to a wide range of real-world problems, from reducing prejudice to reducing the risk of eating disorders. In the former, White college students were asked to write a counterattitudinal essay publicly endorsing a controversial proposal at their university to double the amount of funds available for academic scholarships for African American students. Because the total amount of funds was limited, this meant cutting by half the amount of scholarship funds available to White students. As you might imagine, this was a highly dissonant situation. How might the students reduce dissonance? As they came up with more and more reasons in writing their essays, they ended up convincing themselves that they believed in that policy. And not only did they believe in it, but their general attitude toward African Americans became more favorable (Leippe & Eisenstadt, 1994, 1998). Later experiments with diverse groups have gotten the same results, including a decrease in White prejudice toward Asian students (Son Hing, Li, & Zanna, 2002) and, in Germany, German prejudice toward Turks (Heitland & Bohner, 2010).

Counterattitudinal advocacy has also been effective in dealing with a far different problem: eating disorders (such as bulimia) and dissatisfaction with one's body. In American society, where super-thin is considered beautiful, many women are dissatisfied with the size and shape of their own bodies, and the internalization of the media's "thin ideal" leads not only to unhappiness but also to constant dieting and eating disorders. In an effort to disrupt this pattern, a team of researchers assigned high school and college women with body-image concerns to either dissonance or control conditions. Women in the dissonance condition had to compose their own arguments against the "thin is beautiful" image they had bought into, by writing an essay describing the emotional and physical costs of pursuing an unrealistic ideal body and by acting out that argument to discourage other women from pursuing the thin ideal. Participants in the dissonance condition showed significant increases in their satisfaction with their bodies, as well as a decrease in chronic dieting, and were happier and less anxious than women in the control conditions. Moreover, their risk of developing bulimia was greatly reduced (McMillan, Stice, & Rohde, 2011; Stice et al., 2006). This intervention has been replicated with 12- and 13-year-old English girls (Halliwell & Diedrichs, 2014) as well as with Latina, African American, and Asian/Hawaiian/Pacific Island women (Rodriguez et al., 2008; Stice et al., 2008).

Punishment and Self-Persuasion

All societies run, in part, on punishment or the threat of punishment. You know, while cruising down the highway at 80 miles an hour, that if a cop spots you, you will pay a substantial fine, and if you get caught often, you will lose your license. So we learn to obey the speed limit when patrol cars are in the vicinity. By the same token, schoolchildren know that if they cheat on an exam and get caught, they could be humiliated by the teacher and punished. So they learn not to cheat while the teacher is in the room, watching them. But does harsh punishment teach adults to want to obey the speed limit? Does it teach children to value honest behavior? We don't think so. All it teaches is to try to avoid getting caught.

Let's look at bullying. It is extremely difficult to persuade children that it's not right or enjoyable to beat up other children. But, theoretically, it is conceivable that under certain conditions they will persuade *themselves* that such behavior is unenjoyable. Imagine that you are the parent of a six-year-old boy who often beats up his four-year-old brother. You've tried to reason with your older son, to no avail. In an attempt to make him a nicer person

Parents can intervene to stop one sibling from tormenting another right at the moment of the incident, but what might they do to make it less likely to happen in the future?

(and to preserve the health and welfare of his little brother), you begin to punish him for his aggressiveness. As a parent, you can use a range of punishments, from the mild (a stern look) to the severe (spanking, forcing the child to stand in the corner for two hours, depriving him of privileges for a month). The more severe the threat, the higher the likelihood the youngster will cease and desist—while you are watching him. But he may hit his brother again as soon as you are out of sight. Just as most drivers learn to watch for the highway patrol while speeding, your six-year-old still enjoys bullying his little brother; he has merely learned not to do it while you are around to punish him. What can you do?

THE LASTING EFFECTS OF SELF-PERSUASION   Suppose that you threaten him with a mild punishment. In either case—under threat of severe punishment or of mild punishment—the child experiences dissonance. He is aware that he is not beating up his little brother, and he is also aware that he would like to beat him up. When he has the urge to hit his brother and doesn't, he implicitly asks himself, "How come I'm not beating up my little brother?" Under severe threat, he has a convincing answer in the form of a sufficient external justification: "I'm not beating him up because, if I do, my parents are going to punish me." This serves to reduce the dissonance.

The child in the mild threat situation experiences dissonance too. But when he asks himself, "How come I'm not beating up my little brother?" he doesn't have a convincing answer, because the threat is so mild that it does not provide a superabundance of justification. This is called **insufficient punishment**. The child is refraining from doing something he wants to do, and while he does have some justification for not doing it, he lacks complete justification. In this situation, he continues to experience dissonance; therefore, the child must find another way to justify the fact that he is not hitting his kid brother. The less severe you make the threat, the less external justification there is; the less external justification, the higher the need for internal justification. The child can reduce his dissonance by convincing himself that he doesn't want to beat up his brother. In time, he can go further in his quest for internal justification and decide that beating up little kids is not fun.

To find out if this is what happens, Elliot Aronson and J. Merrill Carlsmith (1963) devised an experiment with preschoolers. They couldn't very well have young children hitting each other for the sake of science, so they decided to perform their experiment with a more benign goal: attempting to change the children's desire to play with some appealing toys. The experimenter first asked each child to rate the attractiveness of several toys. He then pointed to a toy that the child considered among the most attractive and told the child that he or she was not allowed to play with it. Half of the children were threatened with mild punishment if they disobeyed; the other half were threatened with severe punishment. The experimenter left the room for a few minutes, giving the children the time and opportunity to play with the other toys and to resist the temptation to play with the forbidden toy. None of the children played with the forbidden toy.

Next, the experimenter returned and asked each child to rate how much he or she liked each of the toys. Initially, everyone had wanted to play with the forbidden toy, but during the temptation period, when they had the chance, not one child played with it. Obviously, the children were experiencing dissonance. How did they respond to this uncomfortable feeling? The children who had received a severe threat had ample justification for their restraint. They knew why they hadn't played with the toy, and therefore they had no reason to change their attitude about it. These children continued to rate the forbidden toy as highly desirable; indeed, some even found it more desirable than they had before the threat.

But what about the others? Without much external justification for avoiding the toy—they had little to fear if they played with it—the children in the mild threat condition needed an *internal* justification to reduce their dissonance. Before long,

---

Insufficient Punishment

The dissonance aroused when individuals lack sufficient external justification for having resisted a desired activity or object, usually resulting in individuals devaluing the forbidden activity or object they persuaded themselves that the reason they hadn't played with the toy was that they didn't like it. They rated the forbidden toy as less attractive than they had when the experiment began. The forbidden-toy study was a good example of how self-justification leads to **self-persuasion**. The children who were tempted to play with the forbidden toy but resisted came to believe that the toy wasn't so wonderful after all: they *persuaded themselves* of this belief to justify the fact that by obeying the adults, they had given up something they wanted. Self-persuasion is more permanent than direct attempts at persuasion precisely because the persuasion takes place internally and not because of external coaxing, threats, or pressure.

Moreover, the effects of self-persuasion in young children can be lasting. In a replication of the forbidden-toy experiment, the overwhelming majority of the children who had been mildly threatened for playing with a terrific toy decided, on their own, not to play with it, even when given the chance several *weeks* later; the majority of the children who had been severely threatened played with the forbidden toy as soon as they could (Freedman, 1965). (See Figure 6.4.) Remember these findings when you become a parent! Parents who use punishment to encourage their children to adopt desirable values should keep the punishment mild—barely enough to produce a change in behavior—and the values will follow.

NOT JUST TANGIBLE REWARDS OR PUNISHMENTS   As we have seen, a sizable reward or a severe punishment provides strong external justification for an action. They encourage compliance but prevent real attitude change. So if you want a person to do something or not to do something only once, the best strategy would be to promise a large reward or threaten a severe punishment. But if you want a person to become committed to an attitude or to a behavior, the *smaller* the reward or punishment that will lead to momentary compliance, the *greater* will be the eventual change in attitude and therefore the more permanent the effect.

This phenomenon is not limited to tangible rewards and punishments; justifications can also come in more subtle packages. Take friendship. We like our friends, we trust our friends, we do favors for our friends. Suppose you are at a party at the home of a close friend. Your friend is passing around a strange-looking appetizer. "What is it?" you ask. "Oh, it's a fried grasshopper; you have to try it!" She's a good friend and you don't want to embarrass her in front of the others, so you pick one up and eat it. How much do you think you will like this new snack food? Now suppose you are a guest at the home of a person you don't know well, and he offers you the same appetizer of fried grasshopper. You comply.

The crucial question is: In which of these two situations will you like the taste of the grasshopper better? A common-sense prediction is that the grasshopper would taste better when recommended by a friend, but dissonance theory makes the opposite prediction. Think about why; which condition involves less external justification? In the first case, when you ask yourself, "How come I ate that disgusting insect?" you have ample justification: you ate it because your good friend asked you to. In the second case, you don't have this kind of outside justification, so you must create it. Namely, you must convince yourself that you *liked* the grasshopper.

Although this may seem a rather bizarre example of dissonance-reducing behavior, it's not as far-fetched as you might think. Indeed, in one experiment, army reservists were asked to eat fried

Self-Persuasion

A long-lasting form of attitude change that results from attempts at self-justification

Figure 6.4 The Forbidden Toy Experiment

Children who had received a threat of mild punishment were far less likely to play with a forbidden toy (orange bar) than children who had received a threat of severe punishment (blue bar). Those given a mild threat had to provide their own justification by devaluing the attractiveness of the toy ("I didn't want to play with it anyhow"). The resulting self-persuasion lasted for weeks.

(Based on data in Freedman, 1965)

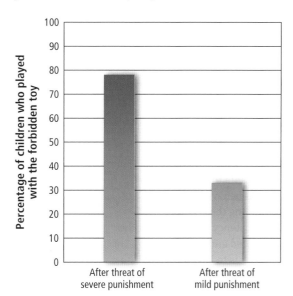

Figure 6.5 External versus Internal Justification

As this graphic summarizes, insufficient punishment or reward leads to self-justification, which in turn leads to self-persuasion and lasting change. Larger rewards or punishments may produce temporary compliance, which rarely lasts.

grasshoppers as part of a research project on survival foods (Zimbardo et al., 1965). Reservists who ate grasshoppers at the request of a stern, unpleasant officer increased their liking for grasshoppers far more than those who ate grasshoppers at the request of a well-liked, pleasant officer. Those who complied with the unfriendly officer's request had little external justification for their actions. As a result, they adopted positive attitudes toward eating grasshoppers to justify their otherwise strange and dissonance-arousing behavior. (See Figure 6.5.)

The Hypocrisy Paradigm

Understanding self-justification helps us explain the fascinating, sometimes amusing, sometimes alarming phenomenon of hypocrisy: A famous minister fulminates against homosexuality, but has a gay lover. A politician wages a high-profile campaign against prostitution and then is caught with a high-priced call girl. A woman ends a relationship because her partner had an affair but somehow doesn't consider her own outside affairs as equally serious.

In a series of studies of what they call the "pot calling the kettle Black" problem, researchers wondered how people reduce the dissonance of being guilty of ethical violations they condemn in others. Can you guess by now? Hypocrites judge *others* more harshly than do people who have not committed the same unethical acts, and they present *themselves* as being more virtuous and ethical than everyone else. That is, they typically polarize their judgments, seeing more evil in others and more righteousness in themselves (Barkan, Ayal, Gino, & Ariely, 2012).

Let's delve a little deeper. It is important to understand how hypocrisy operates because people often behave in ways that run counter to their own beliefs and their best interests. For example, although college students know that sexually transmitted diseases (STDs) are serious problems, only a small percentage of sexually active students use condoms. Not a surprise; condoms are inconvenient and unromantic, and they remind people of disease—the last thing they want to be thinking about in the heat of passion. No wonder that sexual behavior is often accompanied by denial: "Sure, STDs are a problem, but not for *me*."

How do you break through this wall of denial? In the 1990s, Elliot Aronson and his students developed a research design they called **hypocrisy induction** (Aronson, Fried, & Stone, 1991; Cooper, 2010; Stone et al., 1994). They asked two groups of college students to compose a speech describing the dangers of AIDS and other STDs, advocating the use of condoms every time a person has sex. In one group, the students merely composed the arguments. In the second group,

Hypocrisy Induction

The arousal of dissonance by having individuals make statements that run counter to their behaviors and then reminding them of the inconsistency between what they advocated and their behavior. The purpose is to lead individuals to more responsible behavior.

after composing their arguments, they were to recite them in front of a video camera and were told that an audience of high school students would watch the resulting tape. In addition, half of the students in each group were made mindful of their own failure to use condoms by making a list of the circumstances in which they had found it particularly difficult, awkward, or impossible to use them.

The participants in one group experienced the highest dissonance: those who made a video for high school students after the experimenter got them to think about their own failure to use condoms. Why? They were made aware of their own hypocrisy; they had to deal with the fact that they were preaching behavior that they themselves were not practicing. To remove the hypocrisy and maintain their self-esteem, they would need to start practicing what they were preaching. And that is exactly what the researchers found. When they gave each student the chance to buy condoms cheaply, the students in the hypocrisy condition were far more likely to buy condoms than students in any of the other conditions. Moreover, when the researchers phoned the students several months after the experiment, they found that the effects held. People in the hypocrisy condition—the students who would have felt the most cognitive dissonance—reported far higher use of condoms than did those in the control conditions.

Hypocrisy induction—making people aware of the dissonance between what they are doing and what they are preaching to others—has since been applied to a wide array of problems: getting people to quit smoking, apply sunscreen to prevent skin cancer, stop disordered eating, and manage other health concerns (Cooper, 2012; Freijy & Kothe, 2013; Peterson, Haynes, & Olson, 2008). Hypocrisy induction has even been applied to help drivers who fall victim to road rage, which is responsible for thousands of traffic accidents and fatalities each year. An angry driver typically thinks, "Look at that SOB who just cut me off! Selfish jerk! He's about to get what's coming to him!" Seiji Takaku (2006) decided to apply the hypocrisy-induction paradigm to this problem. He used video to simulate a highway situation in which a driver is cut off by another driver, a common incident that frequently causes anger. In the experimental condition, the participants themselves first accidentally cut off another driver, thus being reminded of the fact that we are all capable of making this mistake. Takaku found that when people are reminded of their own fallibility, they are quicker to go from anger to forgiveness than if this reminder is not induced. The reminder reduces their perceived need to retaliate.

You might keep Takaku's method in mind the next time you find yourself fuming in traffic. And, by the way, that anger you feel at *other* cell phone users who drive while texting . . .?

Justifying Good Deeds and Harmful Acts

When we like people, we show it by treating them well. When we dislike people, we also often show it, perhaps by going out of our way to snub them. But it can also work the other way around: our own behavior toward a person affects whether we like or dislike that individual. Whenever we act either kindly or cruelly toward another person, self-justification sees to it that we never quite feel the same way about that person again.

THE BEN FRANKLIN EFFECT: JUSTIFYING ACTS OF KINDNESS   What happens when you do a favor for someone? In particular, what happens when you are subtly induced to do a favor for a person you don't much like; will you like the person more—or less? Dissonance theory predicts that you will like the person more after doing the favor. Can you say why?

Understanding dissonance can help us increase people's likelihood of making healthy, safe choices.

We do not love people so much for the good they have done us as for the good we have done them.
—LEO TOLSTOY, 1869

Figure 6.6 The Justification of Kindness

If we have done someone a personal favor (blue bar), we are likely to feel more positively toward that person than if we don't do the favor (orange bar) or do the favor because of an impersonal request (yellow bar).

(Based on data in Jecker & Landy, 1969)

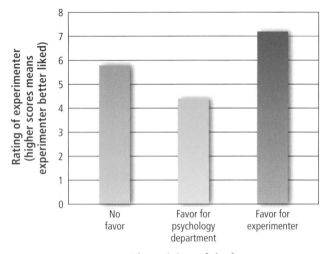

The recipient of the favor

This phenomenon has been a part of folk wisdom for a long time. Benjamin Franklin confessed to having used it as a political strategy. While serving in the Pennsylvania state legislature, Franklin was disturbed by the political opposition and animosity of a fellow legislator. So he set out to win him over. He didn't do it by "paying any servile respect to him," Franklin wrote, but rather by inducing his opponent to do him a favor—namely, lending him a rare book he was eager to read. Franklin returned the book promptly with a warm thank-you letter. "When we next met in the House," Franklin said, "he spoke to me (which he had never done before), and with great civility; and he ever after manifested a readiness to serve me on all occasions, so that we became great friends and our friendship continued to his death. This is another instance of the truth of an old maxim I had learned, which says, 'He that has once done you a kindness will be more ready to do you another than he whom you yourself have obliged'" (Franklin, 1868/1900).

Benjamin Franklin was clearly pleased with the success of his blatantly manipulative strategy. But as scientists, we should not be convinced by his anecdote. We have no way to know whether Franklin's success was due to this particular gambit or to his all-around charm. That is why it is important to design and conduct an experiment that controls for such things as charm. Such an experiment was finally done—240 years later (Jecker & Landy, 1969). Students participated in an intellectual contest that enabled them to win a substantial sum of money. Afterward, the experimenter approached one-third of them, explaining that he was using his own funds for the experiment and was running short, which meant he might be forced to close down the experiment prematurely. He asked, "As a special favor to me, would you mind returning the money you won?" The same request was made to a different group of subjects, not by the experimenter but by the departmental secretary, who asked them if they would return the money as a special favor to the (impersonal) psychology department's research fund, which was running low. The remaining participants were not asked to return their winnings at all. Finally, all of the participants were asked to fill out a questionnaire that included an opportunity to rate the experimenter. Participants who had been cajoled into doing a special favor for him found him the most attractive; they convinced themselves that he was a wonderful, deserving fellow. The others thought he was a pretty nice guy but not anywhere near as wonderful as did the people who had been asked to do him a favor. (See Figure 6.6.)

Think back to the experiment in which White students developed more favorable attitudes toward African Americans after having said publicly that they favored preferential treatment for Black students. Can you see how the "Ben Franklin effect" might apply here, how this act of helping might have contributed to their change in attitudes? (See Try It!) The mechanism starts

Without realizing it, Ben Franklin may have been the first dissonance theorist.

early. In a study of four-year-olds, some children were told to give away some of their playful stickers to a doggie puppet "who is sad today"; others had a choice of how much to share with Doggie. The children who were allowed to choose to be generous to the sad doggie later shared more with a new puppet named Ellie, compared with children who had been instructed to share (Chernyak & Kushnir, 2013). Once children saw themselves as generous kids, they continued to behave generously.

We can see how helping others might change our self-concept and our attitudes. But what if you harmed another person; what then might happen to your feelings?

TRY IT!

The Internal Consequences of Doing Good

Anthony takes the subway to school. During peak hours, he often sees elderly people struggling to find a seat. However, Anthony does not feel compassion for them and has never given up his seat, believing that since they paid the same train fare, he should be as entitled to a seat as anyone else.

Suppose Anthony somehow decides to give up his seat for an elderly person one day. Based on what you know about cognitive dissonance theory, how would Anthony's prosocial action affect his attitude toward helping the elderly in the subway?

DEHUMANIZING THE ENEMY: JUSTIFYING CRUELTY A sad, though universal, phenomenon is that all cultures are inclined to dehumanize their enemies by calling them cruel names and regarding them as "vermin," "animals," "brutes," and other nonhuman creatures. During World War II, Americans referred to the German people as "krauts" and portrayed them as brutes; they called the Japanese people "Japs" and portrayed them as sneaky and diabolical; during the Vietnam War, American soldiers referred to the Vietnamese as "gooks"; after the wars in Iraq and Afghanistan began, some Americans began referring to the enemy as "ragheads" because of the turbans or other headdresses that many Arabs and Muslims wear. The use of such language is a way of reducing dissonance: "I am a good person, but we are fighting and killing these other people; therefore, they must deserve whatever they get, because they aren't fully human like us." The other side, of course, is doing the same thing: for example, the Nazis portrayed the Jews as rats; during the Cold War, the Soviets called the Americans greedy capitalist pigs; after 9/11, anti-American demonstrators called Americans "rabid dogs." Of course, many people have always held negative and prejudiced attitudes toward certain groups, and calling them names might make it easier for them to treat them ruthlessly. How can we be certain that self-justification can *follow* acts of cruelty rather than only cause them? To test this possibility, the social psychologist must temporarily step back from the helter-skelter of the real world and enter the more controlled setting of the experimental laboratory.

In one of the first demonstrations of the way that the need to reduce dissonance can change attitudes toward an innocent victim, experimenters asked students, one at a time, to watch a young man (a confederate of theirs) being interviewed, and then describe their general opinions of him. Next, the students were instructed to

There's nothing people can't contrive to praise or condemn and find justification for doing so.

—MOLIÉRE,
THE MISANTHROPE

As evident in this racist propaganda from an election in Pennsylvania in the 1860's, White efforts to dehumanize Blacks made it easier for them to treat Black people cruelly and justify discrimination and other brutal acts against them. Dehumanization of outgroups, minorities, or enemies is an unfortunately common way of reducing dissonance.

provide the confederate with an analysis of his short-comings as a human being (Davis & Jones, 1960). After telling him things they knew were certain to hurt him—that they thought he was shallow, untrustworthy, and boring—they convinced themselves that he deserved to be insulted this way; why, he really *was* shallow and boring. Their opinion of him had become much more negative than it was prior to saying the hurtful things to him directly.

It may seem a big jump from the laboratory to the battlefield, but dissonance links them. Imagine these two scenes: (1) A soldier kills an enemy combatant in the heat of battle; (2) a soldier kills an innocent civilian who happened to be in the wrong place at the wrong time. Which soldier will experience more dissonance? We predict that it would be the latter. Why? When engaged in combat with an enemy soldier, it is a "you or me" situation; if the soldier had not killed the enemy, the enemy might have killed him. So even though wounding or killing another person is rarely taken lightly, it is not nearly so heavy a burden, and the dissonance not nearly as great, as it would be if the victim were an unarmed civilian, a child, or an old person. Indeed, one of the major causes of PTSD among veterans of the wars in Afghanistan and Iraq is their inability to reduce dissonance over killing children, bystanders, and other innocent civilians—a result of the difficult of fighting a war against counterinsurgents rather than a formal army (Klug et al., 2011).

This prediction, about which soldier will feel the greater dissonance, was supported by the results of an experiment in which volunteers had to administer a supposedly painful electric shock to a fellow student (Berscheid, Boye, & Walster, 1968). As one might expect, these students disparaged their victim as a result of having administered the shock. But half of the students were told that there would be a turnabout: the other student would be given the opportunity to retaliate against them at a later time. Those who were led to believe that their victim would be able to retaliate later did not derogate the victim. Because the victim was going to be able to even the score, there was little dissonance, and therefore the harm-doers had no need to belittle their victim in order to convince themselves that he or she deserved it. The results of these laboratory experiments suggest that, during a war, military personnel are more likely to demean civilian victims (because these individuals can't retaliate) than military victims.

A more dramatic experiment on the justification-of-cruelty effect was done to examine the relationship between torture and blame. Suppose you read that a suspect in a particularly terrible crime has been tortured in an attempt to get him to reveal information. He insists he is innocent, but his interrogators simply increase the pain they are inflicting on him. Do you sympathize with the interrogator and blame the suspect for not confessing, or do you sympathize with the suffering suspect? Dissonance theory predicts that people who are *closest* to the situation—for example, being a prison staffer having to observe the torture—would reduce dissonance by seeing the victim as more likely to be guilty and therefore deserving of the pain inflicted on him. But those who are more distant from the situation—listening to the interrogation on the radio—would be more inclined to see the victim as innocent. And that is just what the experimenters found (Gray & Wegner, 2010). The closer people are to committing acts of cruelty, the greater their need to reduce the dissonance between "I am a good, kind person" and "I am causing another human being to suffer." The easiest route is to blame the victim: he is guilty, he started this, it's all his fault, he's not one of us anyway.

Think of the chilling implications of this research: namely, that people do not perform acts of cruelty and come out unscathed. Success at dehumanizing the victim virtually guarantees a continuation or even an escalation of the cruelty: It sets up an endless chain of violence, followed by self-justification (in the form of dehumanizing and blaming the victim), followed by still more violence and dehumanization (Sturman, 2012).

In this manner, unbelievable acts of human cruelty can escalate, such as the Nazi "Final Solution" that led to the murder of six million European Jews. But all tyrants and oppressors reduce dissonance by justifying their cruelty. This is how they sleep at night. During his four-year trial for war crimes, crimes against humanity, and genocide, Slobodan Milosevic, the "Butcher of the Balkans," justified his policy of ethnic cleansing that caused the deaths of more than 200,000 Croats, Bosnian Muslims, and Albanians. He was not responsible for those deaths, he kept saying at his trial; he was only responding to the aggression *they* perpetrated against the innocent Serbians. Riccardo Orizio (2003) interviewed seven other dictators, including Idi Amin, Jean-Claude "Baby Doc" Duvalier, Mira Markovic (the "Red Witch," Milosevic's wife), and Jean-Bédel Bokassa of the Central African Republic (known as the Ogre of Berengo). Every one of them claimed that everything they did—torturing or murdering their opponents, blocking free elections, starving their citizens, looting their nation's wealth, launching genocidal wars—was done for the good of their country. The alternative, they said, was chaos, anarchy, and bloodshed. Far from seeing themselves as despots, they saw themselves as self-sacrificing patriots. Unfortunately, atrocities are not a thing of the past but are as recent as today's news.

Some Final Thoughts on Dissonance: Learning from Our Mistakes

At the beginning of this chapter, we raised a vital question regarding the followers of Heaven's Gate (as we did in Chapter 1 about the followers of the Reverend Jim Jones): How could intelligent people allow themselves to be led into the apparently senseless behavior of mass suicide? Of course, many factors were operating, including the charismatic power of each of the leaders, the existence of social support for the views of the group from other members, and the relative isolation of each group from dissenting views, producing a closed system—like living in a roomful of mirrors.

Yet, in addition to these factors, one of the single most powerful forces was the existence of a high degree of cognitive dissonance within the minds of the participants. As we have seen, when individuals make an important decision and invest heavily in that decision (in terms of time, effort, sacrifice, and commitment), the result is a strong need to justify those actions and that investment. The more they give up and the harder they work, the greater will be the need to convince themselves that their views are correct. The members of the Heaven's Gate cult made monumental sacrifices for their beliefs: they abandoned their friends and families, left their professions, relinquished their money and possessions, moved to another part of the world, and worked hard and long for the particular cause they believed in—all actions that increased their commitment to the belief.

By understanding cognitive dissonance, therefore, you can understand why the Heaven's Gate people, having bought a telescope that failed to reveal a spaceship, concluded that the telescope was faulty. To have believed otherwise—"There is no spaceship after all!"—would have created too much dissonance to bear. That they went on to commit suicide in the belief that their higher incarnation would get on that spaceship may be bizarre but it is not unfathomable. It is simply an extreme manifestation of a process that we have seen in operation over and over again.

Much of the time, dissonance-reducing behavior can be useful because it allows us to maintain self-esteem. Yet if we were to spend all our time and energy defending our egos, we would never learn from our mistakes, bad decisions, and incorrect beliefs. Instead, we would ignore them, justify them, or, worse still, attempt to turn them into virtues. We would get stuck within the confines of our narrow minds and fail to grow or change. And, in extreme cases, we might end up justifying our own smaller Heaven's Gates—mistakes that can harm ourselves and others.

POLITICS AND SELF-JUSTIFICATION   It's bad enough when ordinary people get caught up in the self-justifying cycle, but when a political leader does so, the consequences can be devastating for the nation and the world (Tavris & Aronson, 2007). In 2003, President George W. Bush wanted to believe that Iraqi leader Saddam Hussein possessed weapons of mass destruction (WMD), nuclear

The members of the Heaven's Gate cult were just plain folks of all races, backgrounds, and walks of life. Yet almost all of them eventually committed suicide because of their commitment to the cult and its beliefs, an extreme result of the mechanism of cognitive dissonance that all of us experience.

and biochemical weapons that posed a threat to America and Europe. He needed this belief to be true to justify his decision to launch a preemptive war, although Iraq posed no immediate threat to the United States and none of its citizens had been involved in the attacks of 9/11. According to White House insider Scott McClellan (2009), this need led the president and his advisers to interpret CIA reports as definitive proof of Iraq's weapons of mass destruction, even though the reports were ambiguous and were contradicted by other evidence (Stewart, 2011; Wilson, 2005).

After the invasion of Iraq, as the months dragged on and still no WMD were discovered, administration officials had to admit that there were none. Now what? How did President Bush and his staff reduce dissonance between "We believed there were WMD that justified this war" and "We were wrong"? By adding new cognitions to justify the war: Now they said that the U.S. mission was to liberate the nation from a cruel dictator and give the Iraqi people the blessings of democratic institutions. Even if things are not going well now, they said, history will vindicate us in 10 or 20 or 50 years. To an uncommitted observer, these justifications are inadequate; after all, there are many brutal dictators in the world, and no one can foresee the long-term results of any war begun for a short-term purpose. But to President Bush and his advisers, the justifications seemed reasonable (Bush, 2010).

Of course we cannot be certain what was going on in George Bush's mind, but some five decades of research on cognitive dissonance suggests that he and his advisers may not have been intentionally deceiving the American people; it is more likely that, like the members of Heaven's Gate, they were deceiving themselves, blinding themselves to the possibility of being wrong. Needless to say, Mr. Bush was not the only leader to engage in this kind of self-justifying behavior. The memoirs of some of our most beleaguered former presidents, Democrat and Republican alike, are full of the kinds of self-serving, self-justifying statements that can best be summarized as "If I had it all to do over again, I would not change much. Actually, I wouldn't change anything except how my opponents treated me unfairly" (Johnson, 1971; Nixon, 1990). Barack Obama has not yet written his memoirs of his presidential decisions; stay tuned.

OVERCOMING DISSONANCE   Few of us will ever wield the power of a world leader or end our lives in a cult waiting for a spaceship to transport us to another planet. But, on a smaller scale, in our zeal to protect our self-concept, we often make foolish mistakes and compound that failure by blinding ourselves to the possibility of learning from them. Is there hope? We think so. Although the process of self-justification is unconscious, once we know that we are prone to justify our actions, we can begin to monitor our thinking and, in effect, "catch ourselves in the act." If we can learn to examine our behavior critically and dispassionately, we stand a chance of breaking out of the cycle of action followed by self-justification followed by more committed action.

After DNA testing proved that he could not have committed the rape he was convicted of, David Lee Wiggins was released from a Texas prison in 2012 after serving 23 years. How might dissonance explain why prosecutors in wrongful conviction cases often have a hard time accepting that the defendant is actually not guilty?

Admittedly, acknowledging our mistakes and taking responsibility for them is easier said than done. Imagine that you are a prosecutor who has worked hard for many years to put "bad guys" in prison. You're the good guy. How will you respond to the dissonant information that DNA testing suggests that a few of those bad guys you put away might be innocent? Will you welcome this evidence with an open mind, because you would like justice to be done, or will you reject it, because it might show that you were wrong? Unfortunately—but not surprisingly for those who understand dissonance theory—many prosecutors in America make the latter choice: They resist and block the efforts by convicted prisoners to reopen their cases and get DNA tests. Their dissonance-reducing reasoning is something like this: "Well, even if he wasn't guilty of *this* crime, he was surely guilty of something else; after all, he's a bad guy."

But at least one prosecutor chose to resolve that dissonance in a more courageous way. Thomas Vanes had routinely sought the death penalty or extreme prison sentences for defendants convicted of horrible crimes. One man, Larry Mayes, served more than 20 years for rape before DNA testing cleared him of the crime. Vanes was sure that the DNA test would confirm Mayes's guilt. "But he was right, and I was wrong," Vanes wrote. "Hard facts trumped opinion and belief, as they should. It was a sobering lesson, and none of the easy-to-reach rationalizations (just doing my job, it was the jurors who convicted him, the appellate courts had upheld the conviction) completely lessen the sense of responsibility—moral, if not legal—that comes with the conviction of an innocent man" (quoted in Tavris & Aronson, 2007).

Throughout our lives, all of us, in our roles as family members, workers, professionals, and citizens, will be confronted with evidence that we were wrong about something important to us—something we did or something we believed. Will you step off the pyramid in the direction of justifying that mistake . . . or will you strive to correct it?

REVIEW QUESTIONS

1. After spending two years of tedious work fixing up an old house themselves, Abby and Brian are even more convinced that they made the right choice to buy the place. Their feelings are an example of
   a. counterattitudinal advocacy.
   b. insufficient punishment.
   c. the Ben Franklin effect.
   d. justifying their effort.

2. Briana undergoes treatment for drug addiction. After she leaves the clinic, Briana is most likely to stay off drugs if the treatment at the clinic was
   a. involuntary (she was ordered to undergo treatment) and a difficult ordeal.
   b. involuntary (she was ordered to undergo treatment) and an easy experience.
   c. voluntary (she chose to undergo treatment) and an easy experience.
   d. voluntary (she chose to undergo treatment) and a difficult ordeal.

3. Your friend Amy asks you what you think of the shoes she just bought. Privately, you think they are the ugliest shoes you have ever seen, but you tell her you love them. In the past, Amy has always valued your honest opinion and doesn't care that much about the shoes, which were inexpensive. Because the external justification for your fib was _____, you will probably _____.
   a. high, decide you like the shoes
   b. high, maintain your view that the shoes are ugly

   c. low, decide you like the shoes
   d. low, maintain your view that the shoes are ugly

4. According to Jecker & Landy (1969), if we do someone a personal favor, how are we likely to feel toward that person as compared to if we don't do the favor?
   a. More negatively
   b. More indifferent
   c. More positively
   d. More biased

5. Which of the following individuals is likely to experience the greatest dissonance?
   a. A soldier who kills a civilian.
   b. A gang member who kills a member of a competing gang.
   c. A soldier who kills 3 enemy troops.
   d. A hit man who kills a stranger for money.

6. Which of the following people is most likely to be able to admit a major mistake?
   a. A prosecutor, because he or she is trained to pursue justice at all costs.
   b. A political leader, because otherwise he or she would be voted out of office.
   c. A member of a religious sect, because he or she can leave at any time.
   d. All of the above will find it hard to admit having been wrong.
   e. The prosecutor and politician will find it easier than most other people to admit being wrong.

See page 621 for the answers.

Summary

6.1   What is cognitive dissonance, and how do people avoid dissonance to maintain a positive self-image?

- **The Theory of Cognitive Dissonance** Most people need to see themselves as intelligent, sensible, and decent folks who behave with integrity. This chapter is about the behavior changes and cognitive distortions that occur when we are faced with evidence that we have done something that is not intelligent, sensible, or decent—the mental effort we expend to maintain that positive self-image.

  - **When cognitions conflict** Cognitive dissonance is the discomfort (dissonance) that people feel when two cognitions (beliefs, attitudes) conflict, or when they behave in ways that are inconsistent with their conception of themselves (self-concept). To reduce the dissonance, people either (1) change their behavior to bring it in line with their cognitions about themselves, (2) justify their behavior by changing one of their cognitions, or (3) attempt to justify their behavior by inventing new cognitions. One common kind of new cognition is *self-affirmation*, focusing on a positive quality to offset feelings of having acted foolishly. When people's self-esteem is temporarily enhanced, they are less likely to cheat or commit other unethical acts, and more likely to work hard to improve their grades, so as to keep their behavior consonant with their self-concept. But people are not good at anticipating how they will cope with future negative events; they show an **impact bias**, overestimating how bad they will feel, because they don't realize that they will be able to reduce dissonance. People often process information in a biased way, one that fits their preconceived notions. We humans prefer to rationalize our actions to avoid dissonance, even at the expense of rational behavior or more accurate beliefs.

  - **Dissonance and the self-concept** Dissonance is most painful, and people are most motivated to reduce it, when information or behavior conflicts with an important part of their self-concept or threatens their self-esteem. People with high self-esteem are more motivated to reduce dissonance caused by a blow to their self-worth than people who have low self-esteem. When people's self-esteem is temporarily enhanced, or when their self-concept of being honest people is invoked, they are less likely to cheat or commit other unethical acts, and more likely to work hard to improve

their grades, so as to keep their behavior consonant with their self-concept.

  - **Decisions, decisions, decisions** Decisions arouse dissonance because they require choosing one thing and not the other. The thought that we may have made the wrong choice causes discomfort—**postdecision dissonance**—because it would threaten our self-image as one who makes good decisions. After the choice is final, the mind diminishes the discomfort through solidifying the case for the item chosen or the course of action taken. That is how dissonance reduction can change a person's values and morality: once an unethical act is committed, the person experiencing dissonance justifies it, thereby increasing the likelihood of committing it again.

  - **Dissonance, culture, and the brain** Dissonance seems to be hardwired in the brain; different parts of the brain are activated when people are in a state of mental conflict or have made a choice. Because postdecision dissonance has been observed in monkeys, it may have an evolutionarily adaptive purpose in primates. However, although cognitive dissonance occurs in non-Western cultures as well as Western ones, the content of what creates dissonant cognitions and the process and intensity of dissonance reduction do vary across cultures, reflecting the difference in cultural norms.

6.2   How does cognitive dissonance operate in everyday life, and what are some constructive ways of reducing it?

- **Self-Justification in Everyday Life** Researchers have studied the forms of dissonance reduction and their application in many spheres of life.

  - **The justification of effort** People tend to increase their liking for something they have worked hard to attain, even if the thing they have attained is not something they would otherwise like. This explains the intense loyalty that initiated recruits feel for their fraternities and military institutions after undergoing hazing.

  - **External versus internal justification** When we perform an action because of the ample external reward to do it, then the action has little or no effect on our attitudes or beliefs. However, if the reward is not big enough to justify the action, we find ourselves experiencing cognitive dissonance because there is little **external justification** for what we did. This activates an **internal**

justification process to justify the action to ourselves. The internal process of self-justification has a much more powerful effect on an individual's long-term values and behaviors than does a situation where the external justifications are evident. When people publicly advocate something that is counter to what they believe or how they behave, called **counterattitudinal advocacy**, they will feel dissonance. Counterattitudinal advocacy has been used to change people's attitudes in many ways, from their prejudices to self-defeating beliefs and harmful practices such as bulimia.

- **Punishment and self-persuasion** Another way of getting people to change is not by administering severe punishment, but **insufficient or mild punishment**, as the forbidden-toy experiment demonstrated. The less severe the threat or the smaller the reward, the less external justification the person has for compliance, and thus the greater the need for internal justification. The resulting **self-persuasion** becomes internalized and lasts longer than temporary obedience to avoid a punishment.

- **The hypocrisy paradigm** Hypocrisy induction is a method of making people face the difference between what they say and what they do. It takes advantage of the need to reduce dissonance to foster socially beneficial behaviors. In the case of an AIDS-prevention experiment, participants videotaped speeches about the importance of using condoms and they were made aware of their own failure to use them. To reduce dissonance, they changed their behavior—they purchased condoms.

- **Justifying good deeds and harmful acts** A clever application of cognitive dissonance theory is to get someone to like you by having them do you a favor. This works because the person needs to internally justify the fact that they did something nice for you. The converse is true as well. If you harm another person, to reduce the threat to your self-image that could come from doing a bad deed, you will tend to justify what you did by denigrating your victim: the person deserved it, or he or she is not "one of us" anyway. In extreme cases such as conflict and war, many people will embrace the cognition that the victim or enemy deserved everything they got because they are less than human.

- **Learning from our mistakes** Dissonance reduction is counterproductive when it solidifies negative values and behaviors, and this applies to everyone from members of small cults to national leaders. Knowing that humans are dissonance-reducing animals can make us more aware of the process. The next time we feel the discomfort of having acted counter to our values, we can consciously pause the self-justification process to reflect on our action.

Test Yourself

1. You know you're eating too much junk food and that it's bad for your energy and health. Which of the following will not reduce your dissonance?

   a. Cutting out your favorite afternoon sweets.

   b. Deciding that all those health warnings are stupid exaggerations.

   c. Admitting you are eating too many sweets but claim that they boost your energy for studying.

   d. Accepting the fact that your attitudes and behavior simply conflict.

2. You are reading a blog by someone whose point of view is really making you angry. Which of her arguments are you most likely to focus on and remember?

   a. Her silliest claims, because she is a silly person.

   b. Her silliest claims, because they are consonant with your opinion that she is a silly person.

   c. Her smartest claims, so that you can contradict them in a post.

   d. Her smartest claims, because they are so unlikely to have come from a silly person.

3. Who is likely to feel the greatest dissonance after making a colossal blunder?

   a. A person with high self-esteem

   b. A person with low self-esteem

   c. A psychopath

   d. A narcissist

4. You are eager to persuade your fellow classmates to vote in an important upcoming election. Which of these ways of persuasion is mostly likely to work?

   a. "Please vote; it's really important."

   b. "You're a voter; don't forget the election is Tuesday."

c. "You're an unpatriotic citizen if you don't vote."

d. "Don't bother voting; your vote won't matter anyway."

5. Post-decision dissonance has been observed

a. in monkeys.

b. in shoppers.

c. in people who've cheated.

d. in people who just bought a car.

e. all of the above.

f. a and d.

6. When does "saying become believing"?

a. When you claim to have an opinion that differs from your true beliefs for no strong reason.

b. When what you say is what you believe.

c. When someone forces you to say something you don't believe.

d. When you're paid a lot of money to lie.

7. What is the "hypocrisy paradigm" in experimental research?

a. Choosing participants who are hypocrites in order to study their rationalizations.

b. Requiring participants to write essays that are critical of hypocrisy.

c. Making participants understand that everyone is a hypocrite.

d. Making participants aware of their own hypocrisy in not practicing what they preach.

8. In terms of dissonance theory, what is the primary reason that "we" (our side) often dehumanizes "them," the enemy, seeing them as animals, brutes, or monsters?

a. The enemy is violent and cruel and deserves whatever we do to them.

b. The enemy started the war.

c. Our side has treated the enemy brutally and needs to justify these actions.

d. Our side is more moral and humane than their side.

9. A group of school students who did not eat healthy were called to be ambassadors for promoting healthy eating habits among the students of the school. They encouraged healthy eating through speeches and posters. Their teachers and close friends reminded them that they themselves usually had junk food. This method is known as

a. inconsistency advocacy.

b. cognitive dissonance.

c. self-persuasion.

d. hypocrisy induction.

e. increasing self-esteem.

f. good health therapy.

10. For years you have believed that eating kumquats is really good for your health. You drink kumquat juice and buy the highest-premium kumquat bars, and you've run a pro-kumquat website for years. Now you learn that a major review of 18 studies has found that kumquats have no benefits and are even potentially harmful. What would be the most constructive way for you to reduce your dissonance caused by this discovery?

a. "The research is biased. I'll wait for a more scientific study."

b. "I must be an incredibly stupid person to have been eating kumquats all these years."

c. "I thought I was doing the right thing, but I'm glad to have better information."

d. "I'm furious and going to start an anti-kumquat blog immediately."

See page 621 for the answers.

Chapter 7
Attitudes and Attitude Change
Influencing Thoughts and Feelings

 ## Chapter Outline and Learning Objectives

The Nature and Origin of Attitudes

7.1 What are the different kinds of attitudes and on what are they based?

Where Do Attitudes Come From?
Explicit versus Implicit Attitudes

When Do Attitudes Predict Behavior?

7.2 Under what conditions do attitudes predict behavior?

Predicting Spontaneous Behaviors
Predicting Deliberative Behaviors

How Do Attitudes Change?

7.3 How do internal and external factors lead to attitude change?

Changing Attitudes by Changing Behavior: Cognitive Dissonance Theory Revisited
Persuasive Communications and Attitude Change
Emotion and Attitude Change
Attitude Change and the Body

The Power of Advertising

7.4 **How does advertising work to change people's attitudes?**

How Advertising Works
Subliminal Advertising: A Form of Mind Control?
Advertising, Stereotypes, and Culture

Resisting Persuasive Messages

7.5 **What are some strategies for resisting efforts at persuasion?**

Attitude Inoculation
Being Alert to Product Placement
Resisting Peer Pressure
When Persuasion Attempts Backfire: Reactance Theory

It sometimes seems like advertising is everywhere we look. Ads that pop up on your computer, on professional sports team jerseys, in public restrooms, on video screens at gasoline pumps, and even on motion sickness bags on airplanes (Story, 2007). But Andrew Fischer, a 20-year-old from Omaha, Nebraska, may just win the prize for advertising innovation. Fischer placed an ad on eBay, offering to wear someone's logo or message on his forehead for 30 days (in the form of a nonpermanent tattoo). The bidding was furious, especially after the national press wrote about Fischer, and was finally won by a company called SnoreStop that makes—you guessed it—products to help people stop snoring. They paid Fischer a whopping $37,375, and he dutifully imprinted their logo on his forehead. "For 40 grand, I don't regret looking like an idiot for a month," reported Fischer (Newman, 2009, p. B3).

It is easy to laugh at the lengths to which advertisers will go, brushing them off as absurd but harmless attempts to influence our attitudes and behaviors. We should keep in mind, though, that advertising can have powerful effects. Consider the history of cigarette ads. In the nineteenth century, most consumer goods, including tobacco products, were made and sold locally. But as the Industrial Revolution led to the mass production of many consumer products, manufacturers sought broader markets. Advertising was the natural result. In the 1880s, cigarettes were being mass-produced for the first time, and moguls such as James Buchanan Duke began to market their brands aggressively. Duke placed ads in newspapers, rented space on thousands of billboards, hired famous actresses to endorse his brands, and gave gifts to retailers who stocked his products. Other cigarette manufacturers soon followed suit (Kluger, 1996).

These efforts were phenomenally successful, as sales of cigarettes skyrocketed in the United States. But there remained a vast untapped market—namely, women. Until the early twentieth century, men bought 99% of cigarettes sold. It was socially unacceptable for women to smoke; those who did were considered to have questionable

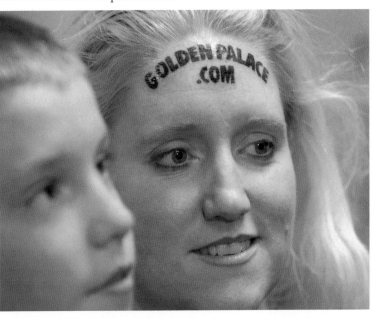

People have begun offering their bodies as venues for advertisers. A Utah woman, shown here, received $10,000 to advertise Golden Palace casino on her forehead. She plans to use the money to send her son to private school.

morals. This began to change with the burgeoning women's rights movement and the fight to achieve the right to vote. Ironically, smoking cigarettes became a symbol of women's emancipation (Kluger, 1996). Cigarette manufacturers were happy to encourage this view by targeting women in their advertisements. Because it was unacceptable for women to smoke in public, early cigarette ads never showed a woman actually smoking. Instead, they tried to associate smoking with sophistication and glamour or convey that cigarettes helped control weight ("Reach for a Lucky instead of a sweet"). By the 1960s, cigarette advertisements were making a direct link between women's liberation and smoking, and a new brand was created (Virginia Slims) specifically for this purpose ("You've come a long way, baby"). Women began to purchase cigarettes in droves.

In 1955, 52% of men and 34% of women in the United States smoked (Centers for Disease Control and Prevention, n.d.). Fortunately, the overall smoking rate has decreased since then, but the gap between men and women has narrowed. As of 2012, 21% of adult men smoked, compared to 16% of adult women (Centers for Disease Control and Prevention, 2014).

To make up for this shrinking market in the United States, tobacco companies now have begun aggressively marketing cigarettes in other countries. The World Health Organization estimates that 50,000 teenagers a day begin smoking in Asia alone, and that smoking may eventually kill *one-quarter* of the young people currently living in Asia (Teves, 2002).

Is advertising responsible for this looming public health crisis? To what extent can advertising really shape people's attitudes and behavior? Exactly what is an attitude, anyway, and through what processes can it be changed? These questions, which are some of the oldest in social psychology, are the subject of this chapter.

The Nature and Origin of Attitudes

7.1 What are the different kinds of attitudes and on what are they based?

Each of us *evaluates* the world around us. We form likes and dislikes of virtually everything we encounter; indeed, it would be odd to hear someone say, "I feel completely neutral toward anchovies, chocolate, Nickelback, and Barack Obama." For most people, at least *one* of those targets should elicit strong attitudes, don't you think? Simply put, **attitudes** are evaluations of people, objects, or ideas (Banaji & Heiphetz, 2010; Bohner & Dickel, 2011; Eagly & Chaiken, 2007; Petty & Krosnick, 2014). Attitudes are important because they often determine what we do—whether we eat or avoid anchovies and chocolate, buy Nickelback songs or change the radio station when they come on, and vote for Barack Obama or his political opponent.

Where Do Attitudes Come From?

One provocative answer to the question of where attitudes come from is that they are linked, in part, to our genes (Dodds et al., 2011; Lewis, Kandler, & Riemann, 2014; Schwab, 2014; Tesser, 1993). Evidence for this conclusion comes from the fact that identical twins share more attitudes than do fraternal twins, even when the identical twins were raised in different homes and never knew each other. One study, for example, found that identical twins had more similar attitudes toward, say, the death penalty and jazz than fraternal twins did (Martin et al., 1986). Now, we should be careful how we interpret this evidence. No one is arguing that there are specific genes that determine our attitudes; it is highly unlikely, for example, that there is a "jazz loving" gene that determines your music preferences. It appears, though, that some attitudes are an indirect function of our genetic makeup. They are related to things such as our temperament and personality, which are directly related to our genes (Olson et al., 2001). People may have inherited a temperament and personality from their parents that make them predisposed to like jazz more than pop music.

Even if there is a genetic component, our social experiences clearly play a major role in shaping our attitudes. Social psychologists have focused on these experiences and how they result in different kinds of attitudes. They have identified three components of attitudes: the *cognitive component*, or the thoughts and beliefs that people form about the attitude object; the *affective component*, or people's emotional reactions toward the attitude object; and the *behavioral component*, or how people act toward the attitude object. Importantly, any given attitude can be based on any one of these components or some combination of them (Zanna & Rempel, 1988).

Attitudes

Evaluations of people, objects, and ideas

That is the way we are made; we don't reason; where we feel, we just feel.
—MARK TWAIN,
A CONNECTICUT YANKEE IN KING ARTHUR'S COURT, 1885

COGNITIVELY BASED ATTITUDES   Sometimes our attitudes are based primarily on the relevant facts, such as the objective merits of an automobile. How many miles per gallon does it get? What are its safety features? To the extent that an evaluation is based primarily on beliefs about the properties of an attitude object, we say it is a **cognitively based attitude**. An attitude of this kind allows us to classify the pluses and minuses of an object so that we can quickly determine whether we want to have anything to do with it. Consider your attitude toward a basic object like a vacuum cleaner. Your attitude is likely to be based on your beliefs about the objective merits of various brands, such as how well they clean up dirt and how much they cost—not on more emotional considerations such as how sexy they make you feel.

AFFECTIVELY BASED ATTITUDES   An attitude rooted more in emotions and values than on an objective appraisal of pluses and minuses is called an **affectively based attitude** (Breckler & Wiggins, 1989; Bülbül & Menon, 2010; Zanna & Rempel, 1988). Sometimes we simply like a car, regardless of how many miles per gallon it gets. Occasionally we even feel strongly attracted to something—such as another person—in spite of having negative beliefs about him or her (e.g., knowing the person is a "bad influence").

As a guide to which attitudes are likely to be affectively based, consider the topics that etiquette manuals will tell you should not be discussed at a dinner party: politics, sex, and religion. People seem to vote more with their hearts than their minds, for example, caring more about how they feel about a candidate than their beliefs about his or her specific policies (Abelson et al., 1982; Westen, 2007). In fact, it has been estimated that one-third of the electorate knows virtually nothing about specific politicians but nonetheless has strong feelings about them (Redlawsk, 2002; Wattenberg, 1987).

If affectively based attitudes do not come from examining the facts, where do they come from? A variety of sources. They can stem from people's values, such as basic religious and moral beliefs. People's feelings about such issues as abortion, the death penalty, and premarital sex are often based more on their sense of value than on a cold examination of the facts. The function of such attitudes is not so much to paint an accurate picture of the world as to express and validate one's basic value system (Maio et al., 2001; Smith, Bruner, & White, 1956; Snyder & DeBono, 1989). Other affectively based attitudes can result from a sensory reaction, such as liking the taste of chocolate (despite its number of calories), or an aesthetic reaction, such as admiring a painting or the shape and color of a car. Still others can be the result of conditioning (Hofmann et al., 2010).

Classical conditioning works this way: A stimulus that elicits an emotional response is accompanied by a neutral, nonemotional stimulus until eventually the neutral stimulus elicits the emotional response by itself. For example, suppose that when you were a child you experienced feelings of warmth and love when you visited your grandmother. Suppose also that her house always smelled faintly of mothballs. Eventually, the smell of mothballs alone will trigger the emotions you experienced during your visits, through the process of classical conditioning (De Houwer, 2011; Walther & Langer, 2010)

In **operant conditioning**, behaviors we freely choose to perform become more or less frequent, depending on whether they are followed by a reward (positive reinforcement) or punishment. How does this apply to attitudes? Imagine that a 4-year-old White girl goes to the playground with her father and begins to play with an African-American girl. Her father expresses strong disapproval, telling her, "We don't play with that kind of child." It won't take

Cognitively Based Attitude

An attitude based primarily on people's beliefs about the properties of an attitude object

Affectively Based Attitude

An attitude based more on people's feelings and values than on their beliefs about the nature of an attitude object

Classical Conditioning

The phenomenon whereby a stimulus that elicits an emotional response is repeatedly paired with a neutral stimulus that does not, until the neutral stimulus takes on the emotional properties of the first stimulus

Operant Conditioning

The phenomenon whereby behaviors we freely choose to perform become more or less frequent, depending on whether they are followed by a reward or punishment

Some attitudes are based more on emotions and values than on facts and figures. Attitudes toward gay marriage may be such a case.

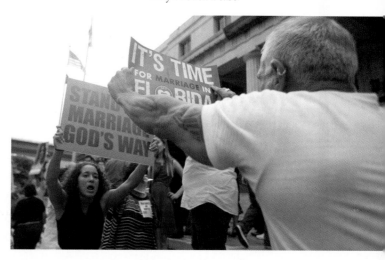

Figure 7.1 Classical and Operant Conditioning of Attitudes

Affectively based attitudes can result from either classical or operant conditioning.

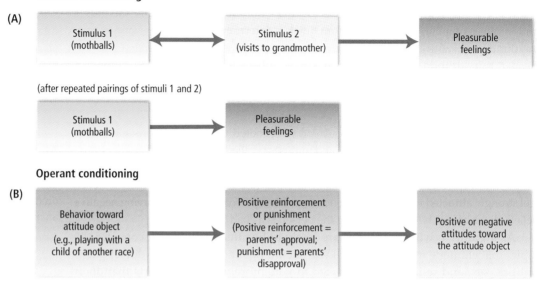

long before the child associates interacting with African Americans with disapproval, and therefore adopts her father's racist attitudes. Attitudes can take on a positive or negative affect through either classical or operant conditioning, as shown in Figure 7.1 (Cacioppo et al., 1992; Kuykendall & Keating, 1990).

Although affectively based attitudes come from many sources, we can group them into one family because they (1) do not result from a rational examination of the issues, (2) are not governed by logic, and (3) are often linked to people's values, so that efforts to change them challenge those values (Katz, 1960; Smith, Bruner, & White, 1956). How can we tell if an attitude is more affectively or cognitively based? See the following Try It! for one way to measure the bases of people's attitudes.

TRY IT!

Affective and Cognitive Bases of Attitudes

Instructions: Fill out this questionnaire to see how psychologists measure the affective and cognitive components of attitudes.

1. Circle the number on each scale that best describes your feelings toward snakes.

hateful	−3	−2	−1	0	1	2	3	love
sad	−3	−2	−1	0	1	2	3	delighted
annoyed	−3	−2	−1	0	1	2	3	happy
tense	−3	−2	−1	0	1	2	3	calm
bored	−3	−2	−1	0	1	2	3	excited
angry	−3	−2	−1	0	1	2	3	relaxed
disgusted	−3	−2	−1	0	1	2	3	acceptance
sorrowful	−3	−2	−1	0	1	2	3	joy

2. Circle the number on each scale that best describes the traits or characteristics of snakes.

useless	−3	−2	−1	0	1	2	3	useful
foolish	−3	−2	−1	0	1	2	3	wise
unsafe	−3	−2	−1	0	1	2	3	safe
harmful	−3	−2	−1	0	1	2	3	beneficial
worthless	−3	−2	−1	0	1	2	3	valuable
imperfect	−3	−2	−1	0	1	2	3	perfect
unhealthy	−3	−2	−1	0	1	2	3	wholesome

Add up the sum of your responses to Question 1 and, separately, your responses to Question 2.

Question 1 measures the affective component of your attitude toward snakes, whereas Question 2 measures the cognitive component of attitudes. Most people's attitudes toward snakes are more affectively than cognitively based. If this is true of you, your total score for Question 1 should depart more from zero (in a negative direction for most people) than your total score for Question 2.

Now go back and fill out the scales again, substituting *vacuum cleaners* for *snakes*. Most people's attitudes toward a utilitarian object such as a vacuum cleaner are more cognitively than affectively based. If this is true of you, your total score for Question 2 should depart more from zero than your total score for Question 1.

BEHAVIORALLY BASED ATTITUDES   A **behaviorally based attitude** stems from people's observations of their own behavior toward an object. This may seem a little odd: How do we know how to behave if we don't already know how we feel? According to Daryl Bem's (1972) *self-perception theory*, under certain circumstances people don't know how they feel until they see how they behave. For example, suppose you asked a friend how much she likes to exercise. If she replies, "Well, I guess I like it, because I always seem to be going for a run or heading over to the gym to work out," we would say she has a behaviorally based attitude. Her attitude is based more on an observation of her behavior than on her cognitions or affect.

As noted in Chapter 5, people infer their attitudes from their behavior only under certain conditions. First, their initial attitude has to be weak or ambiguous. If your friend already has a strong attitude toward exercising, she does not have to observe her behavior to infer how she feels about it. Second, people infer their attitudes from their own behavior only when there are no other plausible explanations available. If your friend believes she exercises to lose weight or because her doctor has ordered her to, she is unlikely to assume that she runs and works out because she enjoys it. (See Chapter 5 for a more detailed description of self-perception theory.)

Behaviorally Based Attitude

An attitude based on observations of how one behaves toward an object

How can I know what I think till I see what I say?
—Graham Wallas,
The Art of Thought, 1926

Explicit versus Implicit Attitudes

Once an attitude develops, it can exist at two levels. **Explicit attitudes** are ones we consciously endorse and can easily report; they are what we think of as our attitude when someone asks us a question like "What is your opinion on affirmative action?" **Implicit attitudes**, on the other hand, are involuntary, uncontrollable, and at times unconscious evaluations (Gawronski & Bodenhausen, 2012; Gawronski & Payne, 2010; Greenwald & Banaji, 1995; Hahn & Gawronski, 2014; Hahn et al., 2014; Wilson, Lindsey, & Schooler, 2000).

Consider Robert, a White college student who genuinely believes that all races are equal and abhors the very idea of any kind of racial bias. This is Robert's explicit attitude, in the sense that it is his conscious evaluation of members of other races that governs how he chooses to act. For example, consistent with his explicit attitude, Robert recently signed a petition in favor of affirmative action policies at

Explicit Attitudes

Attitudes that we consciously endorse and can easily report

Implicit Attitudes

Attitudes that exist outside of conscious awareness

his university. Robert has grown up in a culture in which there are many negative stereotypes about minority groups, however, and it is possible that some of these negative ideas have seeped into him outside of his awareness (Devine, 1989; Xu, Nosek, & Greenwald, 2014). When he is around African Americans, for example, perhaps some negative feelings are triggered automatically. If so, he has a negative implicit attitude toward African Americans, which is likely to influence those behaviors he is not monitoring or attending to, such as whether he makes good eye contact or how nervous he appears to be (Dovidio, Kawakami, & Gaertner, 2002; Greenwald et al., 2009). People can have explicit and implicit attitudes toward virtually anything, not just other racial groups. For example, students can believe explicitly that they hate math yet still have a positive attitude at an implicit level, finding that—in spite of what they claim—they actually enjoy working through a certain type of problem (Galdi, Arcuri, & Gawronski, 2008; Ranganath & Nosek, 2008; Steele & Ambady, 2006). How do we know this? A variety of techniques have been developed to measure implicit attitudes, one of the most popular of which is the Implicit Association Test, or IAT, which we discuss in Chapter 13. But for now, let's focus on the question of where our implicit attitudes come from.

People can have both explicit and implicit attitudes toward the same topic. Social psychologists have been especially interested in people's explicit and implicit attitudes toward members of other races.

Laurie Rudman, Julie Phelan, and Jessica Heppen (2007) have found evidence that implicit attitudes are rooted more in people's childhood experiences, whereas explicit attitudes are rooted more in their recent experiences. In one study, the researchers measured college students' implicit and explicit attitudes toward overweight people. They also asked the students to report their current weight and their weight when they were growing up. Participants' implicit attitudes toward overweight people were predicted by their childhood weight but not their current weight, whereas their explicit attitudes were predicted by their current weight but not their childhood weight. An additional finding from this study was that people whose mother was overweight and were close to their mothers had positive implicit attitudes toward overweight people, even if their explicit attitudes were negative. In short, people can often have different implicit and explicit attitudes toward the same thing, one rooted more in childhood experiences and the other based more on their adult experiences.

In sum, research on implicit attitudes is a relatively young field, and social psychologists are actively investigating the nature of these attitudes, how to measure them, when they converge versus diverge with explicit attitudes, and the degree to which they predict behavior (Briñol & Petty, 2012; Fazio & Olson, 2003; Greenwald et al., 2009; Payne, Burkley, & Stokes, 2008). We will return in Chapter 13 to a discussion of implicit attitudes as they apply to stereotyping and prejudice. The focus in the remainder of this chapter will be on the more general relationship between attitudes and behavior and on the processes through which attitudes change.

REVIEW QUESTIONS

1. Which of the following conclusions is the most consistent with research on the heritability of attitudes?
   a. Our attitudes are shaped by our surroundings and do not seem to have any genetic component to them.
   b. Our attitudes are inherited and dictated by our genetic makeup, with little influence from environmental factors.
   c. We often inherit a temperament or personality that renders us likely to develop similar attitudes to those held by our genetic relatives.
   d. Fraternal twins are just as likely to share attitudes as are identical twins.

2. People's emotional reaction to a target is referred to as the _____ component of attitudes.
   a. affective
   b. behavioral
   c. cognitive
   d. operant

3. Which component of an attitude is most related to the process of examining facts and weighing the objective merits of a target?
   a. Affective
   b. Behavioral
   c. Cognitive
   d. Operant

4. Adults' tendency to experience happy, nostalgia-filled feelings when they hear the music of an ice cream truck can be best explained by the relationship of attitudes to
   a. classical conditioning.
   b. operant conditioning.
   c. self-perception.
   d. values.

5. Newman is currently overweight, but as a child he was quite thin. His current explicit attitude toward the overweight is likely to be more _____ and his current implicit attitude toward the overweight is likely to be more _____.
   a. behaviorally based; cognitively based
   b. cognitively based; behaviorally based
   c. negative; positive
   d. positive; negative

See page 621 for the answers.

When Do Attitudes Predict Behavior?

7.2   Under what conditions do attitudes predict behavior?

Remember our discussion of cigarette advertising? The reason corporations and other groups are willing to spend so much money on ad campaigns is because of a simple assumption: When people change their attitudes (e.g., cigarettes are for women too), they change their behavior as well (e.g., women start smoking). In reality, though, the relationship between attitudes and behavior is not so simple, as shown in a classic (and concerning) study. In the early 1930s, Richard LaPiere embarked on a cross-country sightseeing trip with a young Chinese couple. Prejudice against Asians was common in the United States at this time, so at each hotel, campground, and restaurant they entered, LaPiere worried that his friends would be refused service. To his surprise, of the 251 establishments he and his friends visited, only one refused to serve them (LaPiere, 1934).

Struck by this apparent lack of prejudice, LaPiere decided to explore people's attitudes toward Asians in a different way. After his trip, he wrote a letter to each establishment he and his friends had visited, asking if it would serve a Chinese visitor. Of the many replies, only *one* said it would. More than 90% said they definitely would not; the rest were undecided. Why were the attitudes people expressed in writing the reverse of their actual behavior?

LaPiere's study was not, of course, a controlled experiment. As he acknowledged, there are several reasons why his results may show inconsistency between people's attitudes and behavior. He had no way of knowing whether the proprietors who answered his letter were the same people who had served him and his friends, and even if they were, people's attitudes could have changed in the months between the time they served the Chinese couple and the time they received the letter. Nonetheless, the lack of correspondence between people's attitudes and how they actually acted was so striking that we might question the assumption that behavior routinely follows from attitudes. Indeed, more recent research has also found that people's attitudes can be poor predictors of their behavior (Ajzen & Sheikh, 2013; Fishbein & Ajzen, 2010; Wicker, 1969), including one study in which researchers found results similar to LaPiere's when it came to the willingness of bed-and-breakfast owners to rent a room to two gay men on their honeymoon (Howerton, Meltzer, & Olson, 2012).

> We give advice but we do not influence people's conduct.
> —François de La Rochefoucauld, *Maxims*, 1665

How can this be? Does a person's attitude toward an ethnic group or political candidate or cigarettes really tell us nothing about how he or she will behave? How can we reconcile LaPiere's findings—and other studies like it—with the fact that many times behavior and attitudes *are* consistent? Indeed, attitudes do predict behavior, but only under certain specifiable conditions (DeBono & Snyder, 1995; Glasman & Albarracín, 2006). One key factor is knowing whether the behavior we are trying to predict is spontaneous or planned (Fazio, 1990).

Predicting Spontaneous Behaviors

Sometimes we act spontaneously, thinking little about what we are about to do. When LaPiere and his Chinese friends entered a restaurant, the manager did not have a lot of time to reflect on whether to serve them; he or she had to make a snap decision. Similarly, when someone stops us on the street and asks us to sign a petition, we usually don't stop and think about it for 5 minutes—we decide on the spot whether to sign the petition.

Attitudes will predict spontaneous behaviors only when they are highly accessible to people (Fazio, 1990, 2007; Petty & Krosnick, 2014). **Attitude accessibility** refers to the strength of the association between an object and an evaluation of it, which is typically measured by the speed with which people can report how they feel about the object or issue (Fazio, 2000; Young & Fazio, 2013). When accessibility is high, your attitude comes to mind whenever you see or think about the attitude object. When accessibility is low, your attitude comes to mind more slowly. It follows that highly accessible attitudes will be more likely to predict spontaneous behaviors because people are more likely to be thinking about their attitude when they are called on to act. But what makes attitudes accessible in the first place? One important determinant is the degree of experience people have behaving with the attitude object. Some attitudes are based on hands-on experience, such as a person's attitude toward the homeless after volunteering at a homeless shelter. Other attitudes are formed without much experience, such as a person's attitude toward the homeless that is based on reading stories in the newspaper. The more direct experience people have with an attitude object, the more accessible their attitude will be, and the more accessible it is, the more likely their spontaneous behavior will be consistent with that attitude (Glasman & Albarracín, 2006).

Predicting Deliberative Behaviors

Some decisions and behaviors are less spontaneous, however. We might take our time and deliberate, for example, when it comes to matters such as where to go to college, what courses to register for, or whether to accept a job offer. Under these conditions,

Attitude Accessibility

The strength of the association between an attitude object and a person's evaluation of that object, measured by the speed with which people can report how they feel about the object

Theory of Planned Behavior

The idea that people's intentions are the best predictors of their deliberate behaviors, which are determined by their attitudes toward specific behaviors, subjective norms, and perceived behavioral control

While some behaviors result from spur-of-the-moment, spontaneous decisions, others emerge from more thoughtful processes in which we carefully weigh pros and cons. The theory of planned behavior helps us understand the link between attitudes and these sorts of deliberative behaviors.

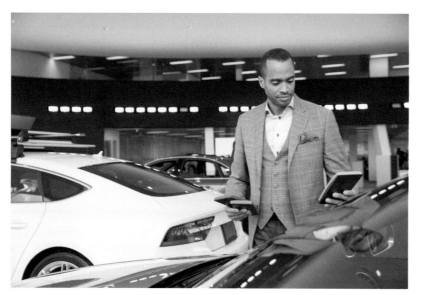

the accessibility of our attitude is less important. Given enough time and motivation to think about an issue, even inaccessible attitudes can be conjured up and influence the choice we make. It is only when we have to decide how to act on the spot, without time to think it over, that accessibility becomes critical (Eagly & Chaiken, 1993; Fazio, 1990).

The best-known theory of when and how attitudes predict deliberative behaviors is the **theory of planned behavior** (Ajzen & Fishbein, 1980; Ajzen & Sheikh, 2013; Fishbein & Ajzen, 2010). According to this theory, when people have time to contemplate how they are going to behave, the best predictor of their behavior is their intention, which is determined by three things: their attitude

Figure 7.2 The Theory of Planned Behavior

According to this theory, the best predictors of people's planned, deliberative behaviors are their behavioral intentions. The best predictors of their intentions are their attitudes toward the specific behavior, their subjective norms, and their perceived behavioral control of the behavior.

(Adapted from Ajzen, 1985)

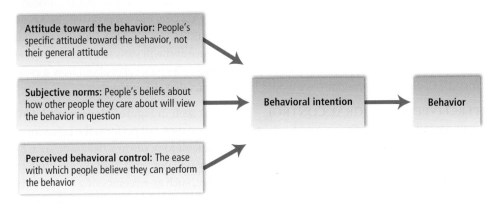

toward the specific behavior, subjective norms, and perceived behavioral control (see Figure 7.2). Let's consider each of these in turn.

SPECIFIC ATTITUDES   The theory of planned behavior holds that the more specific the attitude toward the behavior in question, the better that attitude can be expected to predict the behavior. In one study, researchers asked a sample of married women for their attitudes toward birth control pills, ranging from their general attitude toward birth control to their specific attitude toward using birth control pills during the next 2 years (see Table 7.1). Two years later, they asked the women whether they had used birth control pills at any time since the last interview. As Table 7.1 shows, the general attitudes expressed two years earlier did not predict the women's subsequent use of birth control at all. This general attitude had not taken into account other factors that could influence such a decision, from concern about the long-term effects of the pill to their attitudes regarding other available forms of birth control. The more specific the original question was about the act of using birth control pills, the better the attitude predicted actual behavior (Davidson & Jaccard, 1979).

This study and others like it help explain why LaPiere (1934) found such inconsistency between people's attitudes and behaviors. His question to the proprietors—whether they would serve "members of the Chinese race"—was very general. Had he asked a much more specific question—such as whether they would serve an educated, well-dressed, well-to-do Chinese couple accompanied by a White American college professor—the proprietors might have given an answer that was more predictive of their actual behavior.

> If actions are to yield all the results they are capable of, there must be a certain consistency between them and one's intentions.
>
> —François de La Rochefoucauld, Maxims, 1665

Table 7.1 Specific Attitudes Are Better Predictors of Behavior

Different groups of women were asked about their attitudes toward birth control. The more specific the question, the better it predicted their actual use of birth control over the next two years.

Attitude Measure	Attitude—Behavior Correlation
Attitude toward birth control	0.08
Attitude toward birth control pills	0.32
Attitude toward using birth control pills	0.53
Attitude toward using birth control pills during the next 2 years	0.57

Note: If a correlation is close to 0, it means that there is little to no relationship between the two variables. The closer the correlation is to 1, the stronger the positive relationship between attitudes and behavior.

(Adapted from Davidson & Jaccard, 1979)

SUBJECTIVE NORMS   In addition to measuring attitudes toward the behavior, we also need to measure subjective norms—people's beliefs about how others they care about will view the behavior in question (see Figure 7.2). Knowing these beliefs can be just as important as knowing the person's attitudes when it comes to trying to predict someone's intentions (Hood & Shook, 2014; Park & Smith, 2007). For example, suppose we want to predict whether Deepa intends to go to a violin concert and we know that she doesn't like classical music. We would probably say that she won't go. But suppose we also know that Deepa's best friend, Kristen, is playing in the concert, and that Deepa assumes that Kristen will be disappointed if she is not in the audience and will view her failure to show up as a slap in the face. Knowing this subjective norm—Deepa's belief about how a close friend will view her behavior—we would likely predict that she will go.

PERCEIVED BEHAVIORAL CONTROL   Finally, as seen in Figure 7.2, people's intentions are influenced by the ease with which they believe they can perform the behavior—perceived behavioral control. If people think it is difficult to perform a behavior, such as remembering to use a condom when having sex, they will not form a strong intention to do so. If people think it is easy to perform the behavior, such as remembering to buy milk on the way home from work, they are more likely to form a strong intention to do so.

Considerable research supports the idea that asking people about these determinants of their intentions—attitude specificity, subjective norms, and perceived behavioral control—increases our ability to anticipate how they will act. Specifically, these factors help us predict those behaviors that are planned and deliberative, such as deciding what job to accept, whether to wear a seat belt, whom to vote for, and, yes, whether to use a condom when having sex (Albarracín et al., 2001; Hood & Shook, 2014; Rise, Sheeran, & Hukkelberg, 2010; Manning, 2009).

REVIEW QUESTIONS

1. The major finding of LaPiere's (1934) classic study on attitudes and behavior involving prejudice and hotel/restaurant owners is that
   a. people are more prejudiced than their self-reported attitudes would lead us to believe.
   b. people's attitudes are not always reliable predictors of their behaviors.
   c. the less accessible an attitude is, the more likely it is to shape behavior.
   d. when it comes to racial prejudice, people's attitudes are particularly strong predictors of their behaviors.

2. Attitude accessibility is a particularly good predictor of behavior when
   a. the behavior in question is spontaneous.
   b. the behavior in question is deliberative.
   c. the attitude in question is general.
   d. the attitude in question is an unpopular one.

3. Which of the following is the best example of a deliberative behavior?
   a. Buying a candy bar from the rack next to the check-out line at the grocery store
   b. Telling a salesman who calls you on the phone that you aren't interested in the item he's selling
   c. Deciding at the last minute to skip a class because your friends just told you that they're going to a movie you want to see

   d. Making a decision regarding where you want to travel over your next vacation break

4. Neena plays badminton and is not at all interested in table tennis. Her close friend Simi is participating in a national-level table tennis match being held in their town. Based on subjective norms, what do you think Neena would do?
   a. Neena would likely watch her favorite movie at home.
   b. Neena would likely go and watch the match to avoid disappointing Simi.
   c. Neena would likely avoid Simi till the match is over.
   d. Neena would likely request a common friend to go and watch the match.

5. In trying to predict deliberative behaviors, what three considerations must we evaluate?
   a. Cognitively based attitudes, behaviorally based attitudes, affectively based attitudes
   b. Attitude specificity, subjective norms, perceived behavioral control
   c. Classical conditioning, operant conditioning, self-perception theory
   d. Attitude accessibility, explicit attitudes, implicit attitudes

See page 621 for the answers.

How Do Attitudes Change?

7.3   How do internal and external factors lead to attitude change?

Thus far we have defined different types of attitudes and discussed the circumstances under which attitudes predict behavior. But another important point about attitudes also warrants our attention: Attitudes are not always consistent. They often change. In America, for example, the popularity of the president often rises and falls with surprising speed. Right after President Obama assumed office, in January of 2009, 67% of Americans said they approved of the job he was doing. By November of 2010, as the economic recovery in the United States sputtered, his approval rating had dropped to 47%. Then, right after Osama Bin Laden was killed in a raid by U.S. Navy Seals in May of 2011, his approval rating shot back up to 60%. It stood at 57% in November 2012 at the time of his re-election, but fell back into the 40s by 2014 (AP-GfK Poll, 2014) and started to inch upward in early 2015.

When attitudes change, they often do so in response to social influence. Our attitudes toward everything from a presidential candidate to a brand of laundry detergent can be influenced by what other people do or say. This is why attitudes are of such interest to social psychologists; even something as personal and internal as an attitude is a highly social phenomenon, influenced by the imagined or actual behavior of other people. The entire premise of advertising, for example, is that your attitudes toward consumer products can be influenced by publicity. Remember Andrew Fischer? After he tattooed SnoreStop onto his forehead, Web sales of the product increased by 500%, aided by coverage of Fischer's stunt in the national press (Puente, 2005). But such external influences are not the only forces that shape our attitudes. Let's now take a look at the conditions under which attitudes are most likely to change.

> The ability to kill or capture a man is a relatively simple task compared with changing his mind.
> —Richard Cohen, 1991

> By persuading others, we convince ourselves.
> —Junius

Sometimes attitudes change dramatically over short periods of time. For example, Americans' approval rating of President Obama has gone up and down since he assumed the presidency.

Changing Attitudes by Changing Behavior: Cognitive Dissonance Theory Revisited

We have already discussed one way that attitudes change: when people behave inconsistently with their attitudes and cannot find external justification for their behavior. We refer, of course, to cognitive dissonance theory. As we noted in Chapter 6, people experience dissonance when they do something that threatens their image of themselves as decent, kind, and honest—particularly if there is no way they can explain away this behavior as due to external circumstances.

If you wanted to change your friends' attitudes toward a problematic behavior like smoking, using tanning beds, or texting while driving, one way to succeed might be to get them to give speeches against each practice. An antismoking speech, for example. You would want to make it hard for your friends to find external reasons for giving the speech; for example, you would not want them to justify their actions by saying, "I'm doing it as a special favor for my friend" or "I'm getting paid to do it." That is, as we saw in Chapter 6, the goal is to get your friends to find *internal justification* for giving the speech, whereby they must seek to reduce the dissonance of giving the speech by deciding that they actually believe what they are saying. But what if your goal is to change attitudes on a mass scale? Suppose you were hired by the American Cancer Society to come up with an antismoking campaign that could be used nationwide to counteract the kind of tobacco advertisements we discussed at the beginning of this chapter. Although dissonance techniques are powerful, they are difficult to carry out on a mass scale (e.g., it would be hard to have all American smokers make antismoking speeches under just the right conditions of internal justification). To change as many people's attitudes as possible, you would have to resort to other techniques of attitude change. You would probably construct some sort of **persuasive communication**, such as a speech or television advertisement that advocates a particular side of an issue. How should you construct your message so that it would change people's attitudes?

Persuasive Communication

A message advocating a particular side of an issue

Persuasive Communications and Attitude Change

Suppose the American Cancer Society has given you a six-figure budget to develop your advertising campaign. Should you pack your public service announcement with facts and figures? Or should you take a more emotional approach, including in your message frightening visual images of diseased lungs? Should you hire a movie star to deliver your message or a Nobel Prize–winning medical researcher? Should you take a friendly tone and acknowledge that it is hard to quit smoking, or should you take a hard line and tell smokers to quit cold turkey? You can see the point: Constructing an effective persuasive communication is complicated.

Luckily, social psychologists, beginning with Carl Hovland and his colleagues, have conducted many studies over the years on what makes a persuasive communication effective (Hovland, Janis, & Kelley, 1953). Drawing on their experiences during World War II, when they worked for the United States Army to increase the morale of soldiers (Stouffer et al., 1949), Hovland and his colleagues conducted many experiments on the conditions under which people are most likely to be influenced by persuasive communications. In essence, they studied "who says what to whom," looking at the *source* of the communication (e.g., how expert or attractive the speaker is), the *communication* itself (e.g., the quality of the arguments, whether the speaker presents both sides of the issue), and the nature of the *audience* (e.g., whether the audience is hostile or friendly to the point of view in question). Because these researchers were at Yale University, their approach to the study of persuasive communications remains known as the **Yale Attitude Change approach**.

This approach yielded a great deal of useful information on how people change their attitudes in response to persuasive communications; some of this information is summarized in Figure 7.3. As the research mounted, however, a problem became apparent: Many aspects of persuasive communications turned out to be important, but it was not clear which were more important than others—that is, it was unclear when one factor should be emphasized over another.

For example, let's return to that job you have with the American Cancer Society. The marketing manager wants to see your ad next month. If you were to read the many Yale Attitude Change studies, you might find lots of useful information about who should say what to whom in order to construct a persuasive communication. However, you might also find yourself saying, "There's a lot of information here, and I'm not sure what to emphasize. Should I focus on who delivers the ads? Or should I worry more about the content of the message?"

> Of the modes of persuasion furnished by the spoken word there are three kinds. The first kind depends on the personal character of the speaker; the second on putting the audience into a certain frame of mind; the third on the proof, or apparent proof, provided by the words of the speech itself.
>
> —ARISTOTLE,
> *RHETORIC*

Yale Attitude Change Approach

The study of the conditions under which people are most likely to change their attitudes in response to persuasive messages, focusing on the source of the communication, the nature of the communication, and the nature of the audience

THE CENTRAL AND PERIPHERAL ROUTES TO PERSUASION More recent attitude researchers have asked the same questions: When is it best to stress factors

Figure 7.3 The Yale Attitude Change Approach

Researchers at Yale University initiated research on what makes a persuasive communication effective, focusing on "who said what to whom."

The Yale Attitude Change Approach

The effectiveness of persuasive communications depends on who says what to whom.

Who: The Source of the Communication

- Credible speakers (e.g., those with obvious expertise) persuade people more than speakers lacking in credibility (Hovland & Weiss, 1951; Jain & Posavac, 2000).

- Attractive speakers (whether due to physical or personality attributes) persuade people more than unattractive speakers do (Eagly & Chaiken, 1975; Khan & Sutcliffe, 2014). Attractive agents are more persuasive. *International Journal of Human-Computer Interaction, 30,* 142–150.

- People sometimes remember a message longer than they do information about the message source. In this manner, information from a low-credibility source sometimes becomes more persuasive with the passage of time, a phenomenon referred to as the sleeper effect (Kumkale & Albarracín, 2004; Pratkanis, Freenwald, Leippe, & Baumgardner, 1988).

What: The Nature of the Communication

- People are more persuaded by messages that do not seem to be designed to influence them (Petty & Cacioppo, 1986; Walster & Festinger, 1962).

- It is generally better to present a two-sided communication (one that presents arguments for and against your position) than a one-sided communication (one that presents only arguments favoring your position), especially when you are sure to refute the arguments on the other side of the issue (Cornelis, Cauberghe, & De Pelesmacker, 2014; Igou & Bless, 2003; Lumsdaine & Janis, 1953).

- In terms of speech order, if speeches are to be given back to back and there will be a delay before people have to make up their minds, it is better to go first before the person arguing for the other side. Under these conditions, there is likely to be a primacy effect wherein people are more influenced by what they hear first. If there is a delay between the speeches and people will make up their minds right after hearing the second one, it is better to go last. Under these conditions, there is likely to be a recency effect, wherein people remember the second speech better than the first one (Haugtvedt & Wegener, 1994; Miller & Campbell, 1959).

To Whom: The Nature of the Audience

- An audience that is distracted during the persuasive communication will often be persuaded more than one that is not distracted (Albarracín & Wyer, 2001; Festinger & Maccoby, 1964).

- People low in intelligence tend to be more influenceable than people high in intelligence, and people with moderate self-esteem tend to be more influenceable than people with low or high self-esteem (Rhodes & Wood, 1992).

- People are particularly susceptible to attitude change during the impressionable ages of 18 to 25. Beyond those ages, attitudes are more stable and resistant to change (Krosnick & Alwin, 1989; Sears, 1981.)

---

central to the communication, such as the strength of the arguments? When is it best to stress factors peripheral to the logic of the arguments, such as the credibility or attractiveness of the person delivering the speech (Chaiken, 1980; Chaiken, Wood, & Eagly, 1996; Petty & Wegener, 2014)? The **elaboration likelihood model** of persuasion (Petty, Barden, & Wheeler, 2009; Petty & Cacioppo, 1986), for example, specifies when people will be influenced by what the speech says (i.e., the logic of the arguments) and when they will be influenced by more superficial characteristics (e.g., who gives the speech or how long it is).

The theory states that under certain conditions people are motivated to pay attention to the facts in a communication, which means that the more logically compelling those facts are, the more persuasion occurs. That is, sometimes people elaborate on the messages they hear, carefully thinking about and processing the content of the communication. Petty and Cacioppo (1986) call this the **central route to persuasion**. Under other conditions, people are not motivated to pay attention to the facts; instead, they notice only the surface characteristics of the message, such as how long it is and who is delivering it. Here, people will not be swayed by the logic of the arguments, because they are not paying close attention to what the communicator says. Instead, they are persuaded if the surface characteristics of the message—such as the fact that

Elaboration Likelihood Model

A model explaining two ways in which persuasive communications can cause attitude change: *centrally,* when people are motivated and have the ability to pay attention to the arguments in the communication, and *peripherally,* when people do not pay attention to the arguments but are instead swayed by surface characteristics

Central Route to Persuasion

The case in which people have both the ability and the motivation to elaborate on a persuasive communication, listening carefully to and thinking about the arguments presented

Peripheral Route to Persuasion
The case in which people do not elaborate on the arguments in a persuasive communication but are instead swayed by more superficial cues

it is long or is delivered by an expert or attractive communicator—make it seem like a reasonable one. Petty and Cacioppo call this the **peripheral route to persuasion** because people are swayed by things peripheral to the message itself. For example, if you happen to follow reality TV star Khloe Kardashian on Twitter, you may have seen any of a variety of tweets related to particular products, such as one stating that a particular brand of jeans "makes your butt look scary good." Such a communication is, shall we say, light on factual evidence; if it persuaded anyone to go out and buy this brand of jeans, it is likely to have done so through the peripheral route. Indeed, some companies now reportedly pay celebrities as much as $10,000 per post to tweet about the virtues of various products (Rexrode, 2011).

What determines whether people take the central versus the peripheral route to persuasion? The key is whether they have both the motivation and the ability to pay attention to the facts. When people are truly interested in the topic and thus motivated to pay close attention to the arguments, *and* if people have the ability to pay attention—for example, if nothing is distracting them—they are more likely to take the central route (see Figure 7.4).

THE MOTIVATION TO PAY ATTENTION TO THE ARGUMENTS One thing that determines whether people are motivated to pay attention to a communication is the personal relevance of the topic: How important is the topic to a person's well-being? For example, consider the issue of whether Social Security benefits should be reduced. How personally relevant is this to you? If you are a 72-year-old whose sole income is from Social Security, the issue is extremely relevant; if you are a 20-year-old from a well-to-do family, the issue likely has little personal relevance.

Sometimes attitude change occurs via a peripheral route. For example, we can be swayed more by who delivers a persuasive message than by the strength of the message itself, such as when consumers buy certain products because a celebrity tweets about them.

The more personally relevant an issue is, the more willing people are to pay attention to the arguments in a speech and therefore the more likely they are to take the central route to persuasion. In one study, for example, college students were asked to listen to a speech arguing that all college seniors should be required to pass a comprehensive exam in their major before they graduate (Petty, Cacioppo, & Goldman, 1981). Half of the participants were told that their university was seriously considering requiring comprehensive exams. For these students, the issue was personally relevant. For the other half, it was a "ho-hum" issue—they were told that their university might require such exams, but would not implement them for 10 years.

The researchers then introduced two variables that might influence whether people would agree with the speech. The first was the strength of the arguments presented. Half of the participants heard arguments that were strong and persuasive (e.g., "The quality of undergraduate teaching has improved at schools with the exams"), whereas the others heard arguments that were weak and unpersuasive (e.g., "The risk of failing the exam is a challenge most students would welcome"). The second variable was a peripheral cue—the prestige of the speaker. Half of the participants were told that the author of the speech was an eminent professor at Princeton University, whereas the others were told that the author was a high school student.

Figure 7.4 The Elaboration Likelihood Model

The elaboration likelihood model describes how people change their attitudes when they hear persuasive communications.

When deciding how much to agree with the speaker's position, the participants could use one or both of these different kinds of information; they could listen carefully to the arguments and think about how convincing they were, or they could simply go by who said them and how prestigious that source was. As predicted by the elaboration likelihood model, the way in which persuasion occurred depended on the personal relevance of the issue. The left panel of Figure 7.5 shows what happened when the issue was highly relevant to the listeners. These students were greatly influenced by the quality of the arguments (i.e., persuasion occurred via the central route). Those who heard strong arguments agreed much more with the speech than did those who heard weak arguments. It didn't matter who presented the arguments, the Princeton professor or the high school student. A good argument was a good argument, even if it was written by someone who lacked prestige.

What happens when a topic is of low relevance? As seen in the right panel of Figure 7.5, what mattered then in the comprehensive exam study was not the strength of the arguments but who the speaker was. Those who heard strong arguments agreed with the speech only slightly more than those who heard weak arguments, whereas those who heard the Princeton professor were much more swayed than those who heard the high school student.

I'm not convinced by proofs but signs.

—Coventry Patmore

Figure 7.5 Effects of Personal Relevance on Type of Attitude Change

The higher the number, the more people agreed with the persuasive communication. Left panel: When the issue was highly relevant, people were swayed by the quality of the arguments more than the expertise of the speaker. This is the central route to persuasion. Right panel: When the issue was low in relevance, people were swayed by the expertise of the speaker more than the quality of the arguments. This is the peripheral route to persuasion.

(Based on data in Petty, Cacioppo, & Goldman, 1981)

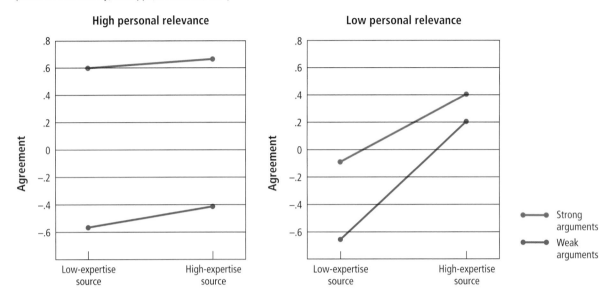

This finding illustrates a general rule: When an issue is personally relevant, people pay attention to the arguments in a speech and will be persuaded to the extent that the arguments are sound. When an issue is not personally relevant, people pay less attention to the arguments. Instead, they will rely upon mental shortcuts, following such peripheral rules as "Prestigious speakers can be trusted" (Chen & Chaiken, 1999; Fabrigar et al., 1998).

THE ABILITY TO PAY ATTENTION TO THE ARGUMENTS   Sometimes even when we want to pay attention to a persuasive communication, it is difficult to do so. Maybe we're tired and sitting in a hot and crowded room, maybe we're distracted by construction noise outside the window, maybe the issue is too complex and hard to evaluate. When people are unable to pay close attention to the arguments, they are swayed more by peripheral cues (Petty & Brock, 1981; Petty et al., 2009). For example, consider the daunting task faced by a jury that has to evaluate a case involving complicated scientific evidence. Perhaps a trial in which the plaintiff is suing because he believes that exposure to a toxic substance at work made him ill. Now, most jurors are not scientists—they don't have the expertise needed to carefully weigh the arguments in such a case, even if they want to.

Indeed, in a study examining this very scenario, Cooper and colleagues (1996) showed mock jurors a video reenactment of a product liability trial. One of the critical witnesses to testify was an expert biologist hired by the plaintiff to persuade the jury that the product in question had caused the plaintiff's illness, and the researchers varied how qualified the expert seemed to be: some mock jurors were told that the expert had published 45 research articles in peer-reviewed journals and his multiple advanced degrees came from prestigious universities; other jurors learned that the expert had published far fewer articles and his degrees came from relatively obscure schools. When his scientific testimony was relatively simple and easy to understand, participants paid little attention to the expert's apparent credentials, instead focusing on the strength of the arguments he offered. Able to understand the persuasive arguments, they engaged in a central route. But when his scientific testimony was complicated and conveyed in jargon that only a molecular biologist could fully grasp, mock jurors relied on the expert's credentials to determine how much stock to place in his testimony. Unable to attend carefully to the persuasive communication, they were influenced by peripheral cues (Cooper et al., 1996).

In short, your own expertise and personal tendencies shape your ability to pay attention to persuasive arguments. As one more example, those of us who are "morning people" are more likely to take central route to persuasion the earlier in the day it is. But those of us who are "evening people" are more likely to take the central route as the hours grow later (Martin & Marrington, 2005).

HOW TO ACHIEVE LONG-LASTING ATTITUDE CHANGE   Now that you know a persuasive communication can change people's attitudes in either of two ways—via the central or the peripheral route—you may be wondering what difference it makes. Does it really matter whether it was the logic of the arguments or the expertise of the source that changed students' minds about comprehensive exams in the Petty and colleagues (1981) study? Given the bottom line—they changed their attitudes—why should any of us care how they got to that point?

If we are interested in creating long-lasting attitude change, we should care a lot. People who base their attitudes on a careful analysis of the arguments will be more likely to maintain this attitude over time, more likely to behave consistently with this attitude, and more resistant to counterpersuasion than people who base their attitudes on peripheral cues (Mackie, 1987; Petty & Briñol, 2012; Petty & Wegener, 1999). In one study, for example, people changed their attitudes either by analyzing the logic of the arguments or by using peripheral cues. When the participants were telephoned 10 days later, those who had analyzed the logic of the arguments were more likely to have maintained their new attitude—that is, attitudes changed via the central route to persuasion lasted longer (Chaiken, 1980).

Emotion and Attitude Change

Now you know exactly how to construct your ad for the American Cancer Society, right? Well, not quite. Before people will consider your carefully constructed arguments, you have to get their attention. If you are going to show your antismoking ad on television, for example, how can you be sure people will watch the ad when it comes on, instead of changing the channel or fast-forwarding through their DVR? One way is to grab people's attention by playing to their emotions.

FEAR-AROUSING COMMUNICATIONS   One way to get people's attention is to scare them—for example, by showing pictures of diseased lungs and presenting alarming data about the link between smoking and lung cancer. This kind of attempt to change attitudes by stirring up fears is called a **fear-arousing communication**. Public service ads often take this approach by trying to scare people into practicing safer sex, wearing seat belts, cutting down on carbon emissions, and staying away from drugs. For example, since January 2001 cigarettes sold in Canada have been required to display graphic pictures of diseased gums and other body parts that cover at least 50% of the outside label. A few years ago the U.S. Food and Drug Administration ruled that all cigarette packs sold in the United States were to contain similar images, but after legal challenges from the tobacco industry, the USFDA abandoned the plan (Felberbaum, 2013).

Do fear-arousing communications work? It depends on whether the fear influences people's ability to pay attention to and process the arguments in a message.

Fear-Arousing Communication

Persuasive message that attempts to change people's attitudes by arousing their fears

The FDA has tried to implement guidelines to require all cigarette packs sold in the United States to display pictures that warn about the dangers of smoking, such as the one shown here. Do you think that this ad would scare people into quitting?

If a moderate amount of fear is created and people believe that listening to the message will teach them how to reduce this fear, then they are more likely to be motivated to analyze the message carefully and their attitudes via the central route (Emery et al., 2014; Petty, 1995; Rogers, 1983).

Consider a study in which a group of smokers watched a graphic film depicting lung cancer and then read pamphlets with specific instructions about how to quit smoking (Leventhal, Watts, & Pagano, 1967). As shown by the bottom line in Figure 7.6, people in this condition reduced their smoking significantly more than people who were shown only the film or only the pamphlet. Why? Watching the film scared people, and giving them the pamphlet reassured them that there was a way to reduce this fear—by following the instructions on how to quit. Seeing only the pamphlet didn't work very well, because there was little fear motivating people to read it carefully. Seeing only the film didn't work very well either, because people are likely to tune out a message that raises fear but does not give information about how to reduce it. This may explain why some attempts to frighten people into changing their attitudes and behaviors fail: They succeed in scaring people but do not provide specific ways to help them reduce that fear (Aronson, 2008; Hoog, Stroebe, & de Wit, 2005; Ruiter, Abraham, & Kok, 2001).

Fear-arousing appeals will also fail if they are so strong that they overwhelm people. If people are terribly frightened, they will become defensive, deny the importance of the threat, and be unable to think rationally about the issue (Feinberg & Willer, 2011; Janis & Feshbach, 1953; Liberman & Chaiken, 1992). So if you have

Figure 7.6 Effects of Fear Appeals on Attitude Change

People were shown a scary film about the effects of smoking, instructions about how to stop smoking, or both. Those who were shown both had the biggest reduction in the number of cigarettes they smoked.

(Adapted from Leventhal, Watts, & Pagano, 1967)

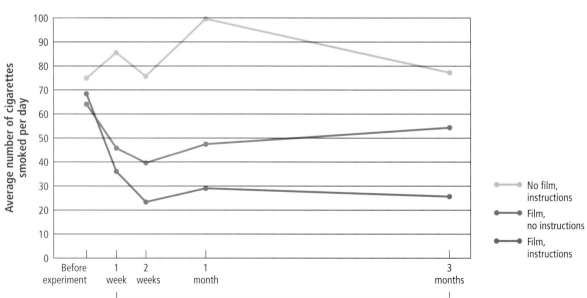

decided to arouse people's fear in your ad for the American Cancer Society, keep these points in mind: Try to create enough fear to motivate people to pay attention to your arguments, but not so much fear that people will tune out what you say. And make sure to include some specific recommendations about how to stop smoking so people will be reassured that paying close attention to your arguments will help them reduce their fear.

EMOTIONS AS A HEURISTIC   Another way in which emotions can cause attitude change is by acting as a signal for how we feel about something. According to the **heuristic–systematic model of persuasion** (Chaiken, 1987), when people take the peripheral route to persuasion, they often use heuristics. Recall from Chapter 3 that heuristics are mental shortcuts people use to make judgments quickly and efficiently. In the present context, a heuristic is a simple rule people use to decide what their attitude is without having to spend a lot of time analyzing every last detail about the topic at hand. Examples of such heuristics are "Experts are always right" and "People who speak quickly must know what they're talking about."

Interestingly, our emotions and moods can themselves act as heuristics to determine our attitudes. When trying to decide what our attitude is about something, we often rely on the "How do I feel about it?" heuristic (Forgas, 2013; Kim, Park, & Schwarz, 2010; Storbeck & Clore, 2008). If we feel good, we must have a positive attitude; if we feel bad, it's thumbs down. Now this probably sounds like a pretty good rule to follow, and, like most heuristics, it is—most of the time. Suppose you need a new couch and go to a furniture store to look around. You see one in your price range and are trying to decide whether to buy it. Using the "How do I feel about it?" heuristic, you do a quick check of your feelings and emotions. If you feel great while you're sitting on the couch in the store, you will probably buy it.

The only problem is that sometimes it is difficult to tell where our feelings come from. Is it really the couch that made you feel great, or is it something completely unrelated? Maybe you were in a good mood to begin with, or maybe on the way to the store you heard your favorite song on the radio. The problem with the "How do I feel about it?" heuristic is that we can make mistakes about what is causing our mood, misattributing feelings created by one source (our favorite song) to another (the couch; see Chapter 5 on misattribution; Claypool et al., 2008). When this happens, you might make a bad decision. After you get the new couch home, you might discover that it no longer makes you feel all that great. It makes sense, then, that retailers strive to create good feelings while presenting their products: salespeople play appealing music and put art on the walls of the showroom; real estate agents bake cookies in the kitchen before staging an open house. Their underlying hope is that people will attribute at least some of the pleasant feelings that ensue to the product they are trying to sell.

More generally, emotions can also influence the way that people think about persuasive messages (Petty & Briñol, 2015). For instance, when we're in a good mood, we tend to relax a bit, comfortable in the assumption that the world is a safe place, which can lead us to be content with heuristic cues like the credibility and apparent expertise of a source. A bad mood, however, often puts on alert, sharpening our skepticism and leading us to pay more attention to message quality. While we may be persuaded by a weak message from an attractive source when we're happy, it usually takes a strong message to sway us when we're sad (Schwarz, Bless, & Bohner, 1991).

Heuristic–Systematic Model of Persuasion

An explanation of the two ways in which persuasive communications can cause attitude change: either systematically processing the merits of the arguments or using mental shortcuts or heuristics

"*While we're waiting for His Honor, may I offer the jury a selection of hand-dipped Swiss chocolates, compliments of my client?*"

Henry Martin/The New Yorker Collection/www.cartoonbank.com

Many advertising campaigns attempt to use emotions to persuade people. How might an ad about climate change that makes use of foreboding weather images such as this one have different effects on people than an ad emphasizing scientific data?

It is useless to attempt to reason a man out of a thing he was never reasoned into.

—JONATHAN SWIFT

EMOTION AND DIFFERENT TYPES OF ATTITUDES The success of various attitude-change techniques also depends on the type of attitude we are trying to change. As we saw earlier, not all attitudes are created equally; some are based more on beliefs about the attitude object (cognitively based attitudes), whereas others are based more on emotions and values (affectively based attitudes). Several studies have shown that it is best to fight fire with fire: If an attitude is cognitively based, your best bet is to try to change it with rational arguments; if it is affectively based, you're better off trying to change it with emotional appeals (Conner et al., 2011; Fabrigar & Petty, 1999; Haddock et al., 2008; Shavitt, 1989).

Consider a study of the effectiveness of different kinds of advertisements (Shavitt, 1990). Some ads stress the objective merits of a product, such as an ad for an appliance that discusses its price, efficiency, and reliability. Other ads stress emotions and values, such as ones for designer jeans that try to associate their brand with sex, beauty, and youthfulness rather than saying anything about the objective qualities of the product. Which kind of ad is most effective? To find out, participants looked at different kinds of advertisements. Some were for "utilitarian products" such as air conditioners and coffee. People's attitudes toward such products tend to be formed after an appraisal of the functional aspects of the products and thus are cognitively based. The other items were "social identity products" such as perfume and greeting cards. People's attitudes toward these types of products tend to reflect a concern with how they appear to others and are therefore more affectively based.

As shown in Figure 7.7, people reacted most favorably to the ads that matched the type of attitude they had. If people's attitudes were cognitively based, the ads

Figure 7.7 Effects of Affective and Cognitive Information on Affectively and Cognitively Based Attitudes

When people had cognitively based attitudes, cognitively based advertisements that stressed the utilitarian aspects of the products worked best. When people had more affectively based attitudes, affectively based advertisements that stressed values and social identity worked best. The higher the number, the more favorable thoughts people listed about the products after reading the advertisements.

(Based on data in Shavitt, 1990)

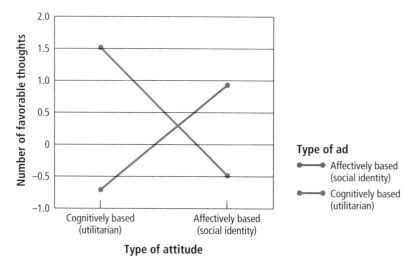

that focused on the utilitarian aspects of these products, such as the energy efficiency of the air conditioner, were most successful. If people's attitudes were more affectively based, the ads that focused on values and social identity concerns were most successful. The graph displayed in Figure 7.7 shows the number of favorable thoughts people had in response to the different kinds of ads. Similar results were found on a measure of how much people intended to buy the products.

Attitude Change and the Body

Although you know a lot by now about how to craft your persuasive message for the American Cancer Society, there is yet one more thing you might want to take into account: what will your audience be doing when they hear it? Reclining comfortably on a living room couch? Sitting in a crowded school auditorium during a required assembly? Our physical environment and even our body posture play surprising roles in the process of attitude change (Briñol & Petty, 2009, 2012). For example, several studies across different cultures have found that being asked to hold an object in one's mouth in a way that forces the brow to furrow and lips to pucker in a frown-like manner leads participants to perceive a cartoon as being less funny; holding an object in one's teeth in a manner that forces the face into a smile makes the cartoon seem *more* humorous (Dzokoto et al., 2014; Strack, Martin, & Stepper, 1998). Sometimes facial expressions change our attitudes rather than vice versa.

Or consider a study by Briñol and Petty (2003) in which participants were asked to test out the durability of some new headphones. Some were asked to shake their heads from side to side while wearing them, whereas others were asked to nod their heads up and down. While doing this, the participants listened to an editorial arguing that all students should be required to carry personal identification cards on campus. One final twist was that half of the participants heard strong, persuasive arguments (e.g., that ID cards would make the campus safer for students) whereas the other half heard weak, unconvincing arguments (e.g., that if students carried the cards, security guards would have more time for lunch).

As you have no doubt gathered, the point of the study was not to test the headphones but to see whether shaking or nodding one's head while listening to a persuasive communication influenced the likelihood of persuasion. The idea was that even though the head movements had nothing to do with the editorial, these actions might influence how confident people felt in the arguments they heard. Nodding one's head up and down, as people do when they say yes, might increase feelings of confidence compared to shaking one's head side to side, as people do when they say no. This is exactly what happened, with interesting consequences. When the arguments in the editorial were strong, people who nodded their heads agreed with them more than did people who shook their heads, because the head-nodders had more confidence in the strong arguments that they heard (see the left side of Figure 7.8). But when the arguments were weak, head nodding had the opposite effect. It gave people more confidence that the arguments they heard were in fact weak and unconvincing, making them *less* convinced than people who shook their heads from side to side (see the right side of Figure 7.8).

Figure 7.8 Effects of Confidence in One's Thoughts on Persuasion

People who nodded their heads up and down, compared to those who shook their heads from side to side, had greater confidence in their thoughts about the message (e.g., "Wow, this is really convincing" when the arguments were strong, and "Wow, this is really dumb" when the arguments were weak).

(Figure adapted from Briñol & Petty, 2003)

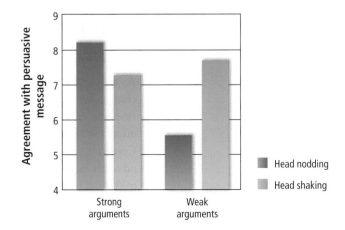

The moral? What people are doing when you try to persuade them makes a difference. Sitting in a soft, cushy chair at the computer store just might make you more comfortable with the idea of spending more on your new laptop than you had originally budgeted. Getting customers to smile even before they hear about your product may get them to transfer positive feelings to the item you're trying to sell them. And anything you can do to increase audience members' confidence in their thoughts about your message will make that message more effective—just as long as your arguments are strong and convincing in the first place.

REVIEW QUESTIONS

1. One way to change someone's attitude is to get that person to give a speech arguing against his or her actual viewpoint. This strategy can lead to attitude change through cognitive dissonance as long as _____ is/are present.
   a. peripheral cues to persuasion
   b. a motivated audience that feels a sense of personal relevance
   c. two-sided arguments
   d. insufficient justification for making the speech

2. Which of the following is *not* one of the three factors considered by the Yale Attitude Change approach?
   a. Nature of the audience
   b. Message source
   c. Fear
   d. Nature of the communication itself

3. A debate breaks out at the town hall meeting over whether local real estate taxes should be raised to pay for a new public school building. Which of the following individuals is most likely to process the persuasive information raised during this debate through the *peripheral* route?
   a. Gob, who has no school-aged children of his own and owns no real estate
   b. Lindsay, whose daughter still has 3 years left of public school
   c. Michael, who is a real estate executive whose business is affected by local tax rates
   d. Buster, a local teacher, who is working in a temporary classroom because the current school building is too small for the number of students enrolled

4. The physical attractiveness of the source of a persuasive communication would be best described as which of the following?
   a. Systematic cue
   b. Central cue
   c. Peripheral cue
   d. Rational cue

5. Fear-arousing persuasive communication is most likely to be effective when
   a. very high levels of fear are induced.
   b. very low levels of fear are induced.
   c. a plan for reducing the fear is provided.
   d. the target of the communication is a utilitarian or functional object.

6. Briñol and Petty (2003) conducted a study in which participants tried on headphones while listening to a persuasive editorial. Half of the participants shook their head side-to-side while listening; the other half nodded up-and-down while listening. Which group of participants expressed the greatest agreement with the arguments expressed in the editorial at the end of the study?
   a. The head-shakers who heard weak arguments in the editorial.
   b. The head-shakers who heard strong arguments in the editorial.
   c. The head-nodders who heard weak arguments in the editorial.
   d. The head-nodders who heard strong arguments in the editorial.

See page 621 for the answers.

The Power of Advertising

7.4   How does advertising work to change people's attitudes?

As alluded to elsewhere in this chapter, many examples of when, why, and how we change our attitudes are provided by considering the influence of advertising. In many respects, advertising is a direct application of social psychology—it's a concerted effort to change the way that consumers think about and act toward a certain product. Consider, for example, this insight into human nature provided by Don Draper, 1960s advertising guru and lead character of the hit TV show *Mad Men*: "People want to be told what to do so badly that they'll listen to anyone."

Is this an exaggeration? Of course it is—you already know from the preceding sections that whether or not people listen depends on factors such as a message's source and the nature of a communication itself. For that matter, should we be taking any psychological advice from Don Draper, a man whose own mental health often seems unstable? Probably not. But there remains a kernel of truth underlying Draper's comment. Advertising *is* powerful, and people are surprisingly susceptible to its influence.

One curious thing about advertising is that most people think it works on everyone but themselves (Wilson & Brekke, 1994). People typically comment, "There is no harm in watching commercials. Some of them are fun, and they don't influence me." It turns out that people are influenced by advertisements more than they think, even when it comes to those annoying on-line pop-up ads (Capella, Webster, & Kinard, 2011; Courbet et al., 2014; Ryan, 1991;

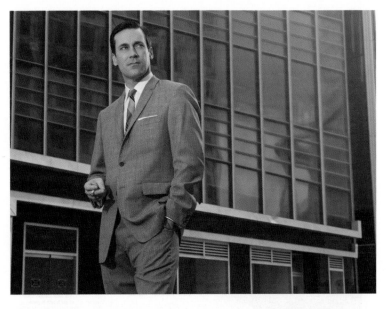

The successful advertiser, like TV's Don Draper, can use social psychological principles of attitude change to make any product seem attractive, personally relevant, useful, and even necessary.

Wells, 1997; Wilson, Houston, & Meyers, 1998). Among the best evidence that advertising works comes from studies using what are called *split cable market tests*. Advertisers work in conjunction with cable companies and grocery stores, showing a target commercial to a randomly selected group of people. They keep track of what people buy by giving potential consumers special ID cards that are scanned at checkout counters; thus, they can tell whether people who saw the commercial for ScrubaDub laundry detergent actually buy more ScrubaDub— the best measure of advertising effectiveness. The results of over 300 split cable market tests indicate that advertising does work, particularly for new products (Lodish et al., 1995).

Further evidence that advertising can change attitudes (and behaviors) is provided by successful public health campaigns. As we've discussed, advertising, product placement, and the behavior of admired figures can have powerful effects on people's behavior, including tobacco and alcohol use (Pechmann & Knight, 2002; Saffer, 2002). This raises an important question: Do public service ads designed to reduce people's use of drugs such as alcohol, tobacco, and marijuana work? A meta-analysis of studies that tested the effects of a media message (conveyed via television, radio, electronic, and print media) on substance use among youths was encouraging (Derzon & Lipsey, 2002). After a media campaign that targeted a specific substance, such as tobacco, kids were less likely to use it. Television and radio messages had even bigger effects than messages in the print media (Ibrahim & Glantz, 2007), providing some hope for the success of media campaigns to promote healthier behavior.

You can tell the ideals of a nation by its advertisements.

—George Norman Douglas, *South Wind*, 1917

How Advertising Works

How does advertising work, and what types of ads work best? The answers follow from our earlier discussion of attitude change. If advertisers are trying to change an affectively based attitude, then, as we have seen, it is best to fight emotions with emotions. Many advertisements take the emotional approach—for example, ads for different brands of soft drinks. Given that different brands of colas are not all that different, and that they have little nutritional value to be touted, many people do not base their purchasing decisions on the objective qualities of the different brands. Consequently, soda advertisements do not stress facts and figures. As one advertising executive noted, "The thing about soda commercials is that they actually have nothing to say" ("Battle for Your Brain," 1991). Instead of presenting facts, soft drink ads play

This ad is one of the most famous in the history of advertising. Although today it is easy to see how sexist and offensive it is, when it appeared in the 1930s it succeeded in making a problem (bad breath) personally relevant by playing on people's fears and insecurities about personal relationships. Can you think of contemporary ads that try to raise similar fears?

to people's emotions, trying to associate feelings of excitement, youth, energy, and sexual attractiveness with the brand.

But for products for which people's attitudes are more cognitively based, we need to ask an additional question: How personally relevant is the issue? Consider, for example, the problem of heartburn. This is not a topic that evokes strong emotions and values in most people—it is more cognitively based. To people who suffer from frequent heartburn, however, the topic clearly has direct personal relevance. In this case, the best way to change people's attitudes is to use logical, fact-based arguments: Convince people that your product will reduce heartburn the best or the fastest and people will buy it (Chaiken, 1987; Petty & Cacioppo, 1986).

What about a cognitively based attitude that is not of direct personal relevance to people? For example, what if you are trying to sell a heartburn medicine to people who experience heartburn only every now and then and do not consider it a big deal? Here you have a problem, because people are unlikely to pay close attention to your advertisement. You might succeed in changing their attitudes via the peripheral route, such as by having attractive movie stars endorse your product. The problem with this, as we have seen, is that such attitude change triggered by peripheral cues does not last long (Chaiken, 1987; Petty & Cacioppo, 1986). So if you have a product that does not trigger people's emotions and is not directly relevant to their everyday lives, you are in trouble.

But don't give up. The trick is to *make* your product personally relevant. Let's take a look at some actual ad campaigns to see how this is done. Consider the case of Gerald Lambert, who early in the twentieth century inherited a company that made a surgical antiseptic used to treat throat infections—Listerine. Seeking a wider market for his product, Lambert decided to promote it as a mouthwash. The only problem was that no one at the time used a mouthwash or even knew what one was. So having invented the cure, Lambert invented the disease. Look at the ad for Listerine, which appeared in countless magazines over the years. Even though today we find this ad incredibly sexist, at the time it successfully played on people's fears about social rejection and failure. The phrase "Often a bridesmaid, never a bride" became one of the most famous in the history of advertising. In a few cleverly chosen words, it succeeded in making a problem—bad breath—personally relevant to millions of people. Don Draper would be proud.

Subliminal Advertising: A Form of Mind Control?

Effective advertising tells consumers what they want, sometimes even before they know they want it. But what happens when we don't even recognize that an attempt at persuasion is underway? This question brings us to the idea of subliminal advertising. For example, in September 2000, during the heat of the U.S. presidential campaign between George W. Bush and Al Gore, a man in Seattle was watching a political advertisement on television. At first the ad looked like a run-of-the-mill political spot in which an announcer praised the benefits of Bush's prescription drug plan and criticized Gore's plan. But the viewer thought that he noticed something odd. He videotaped the ad the next time it ran and played it back at a slow speed, and sure enough, he *had* noticed something unusual. As the announcer said, "The Gore prescription plan: Bureaucrats decide . . ." the word RATS (as in the last four letters of "bureaucrats") flashed on the screen very quickly—for just one-thirtieth of a second. The alert viewer notified officials in the Gore campaign, who quickly contacted the press. Soon the country was abuzz about a possible attempt by the Bush campaign to use subliminal messages to create a negative impression of Al Gore. The Bush campaign denied that anyone had deliberately inserted the word RATS, claiming that it was "purely accidental" (Berke, 2000).

The RATS incident was neither the first nor the last controversy over the use of **subliminal messages**, defined as words or pictures that are not consciously perceived but may influence people's judgments, attitudes, and behaviors. In the late 1950s, James Vicary supposedly flashed the messages "Drink Coca-Cola" and "Eat popcorn" during movies at his theater and claimed that sales at the concession counter skyrocketed (according to some reports, Vicary made up these claims; Weir, 1984). Wilson Bryan Key (1973, 1989) has written several best-selling books on hidden persuasion techniques, which claim that advertisers routinely implant sexual messages in print advertisements, such as the word *sex* in the ice cubes of an ad for gin, and male and female genitalia in everything from butter to the icing in an ad for cake mix. Key (1973) argues that these images are not consciously perceived but put people in a good mood and make them pay more attention to the advertisement. More recently, gambling casinos in Canada removed a brand of slot machines after it was revealed that the machines flashed the winning symbols on every spin, at a speed too fast for the players to see consciously (Benedetti, 2007).

Subliminal messages are not just visual; they can be auditory as well. There is a large market for audiotapes that contain subliminal messages to help people lose weight, stop smoking, improve their study habits, raise self-esteem, and even shave a few strokes off their golf game. But are subliminal messages effective? Do they really make us more likely to buy consumer products or help us lose weight and stop smoking? Most members of the public believe that subliminal messages can shape their attitudes and behaviors (Zanot, Pincus, & Lamp, 1983). Are they right?

DEBUNKING THE CLAIMS ABOUT SUBLIMINAL ADVERTISING   Few of the proponents of subliminal advertising have conducted controlled studies to

Subliminal Messages
Words or pictures that are not consciously perceived but may nevertheless influence judgments, attitudes, and behaviors

During the 2000 U.S. presidential race, George W. Bush aired a television ad about his prescription drug plan, during which the word RATS was visible on the screen for a split second. Do subliminal messages like this one have any effect on people's attitudes?

PEOPLE HAVE BEEN TRYING TO FIND THE BREASTS IN THESE ICE CUBES SINCE 1957.

The advertising industry is sometimes charged with sneaking seductive little pictures into ads.

Supposedly, these pictures can get you to buy a product without your even seeing them.

Consider the photograph above. According to some people, there's a pair of female breasts

hidden in the patterns of light refracted by the ice cubes.

Well, if you really searched you probably *could* see the breasts. For that matter, you could also see Millard Fillmore, a stuffed pork chop and a 1946 Dodge.

The point is that so-called "subliminal advertising" simply

doesn't exist. Overactive imaginations, however, most certainly do.

So if anyone claims to see breasts in that drink up there, they aren't in the ice cubes.

They're in the eye of the beholder.

ADVERTISING
ANOTHER WORD FOR FREEDOM OF CHOICE.
American Association of Advertising Agencies

There is no scientific evidence that implanting sexual images in advertising boosts sales of a product. In fact, subliminal advertising is rarely used and is outlawed in many countries. The public is very aware of the subliminal technique, however—so much so that advertisers sometimes poke fun at subliminal messages in their ads.

back up their claims. Fortunately, many studies of subliminal perception have been conducted, allowing us to evaluate their sometimes-outlandish claims. Simply stated, there is no evidence that the types of subliminal messages encountered in everyday life have any influence on people's behavior. Hidden commands do not cause us to line up and buy popcorn any more than we normally do, and the subliminal commands on self-help tapes do not (unfortunately!) help us quit smoking or lose weight (Brannon & Brock, 1994; Nelson, 2008; Pratkanis, 1992; Theus, 1994; Trappey, 1996). For example, one study randomly assigned people to listen to subliminal self-help recordings designed to improve memory or to one designed to raise their self-esteem (Greenwald et al., 1991). Neither of the recordings had any effect on people's memory or self-esteem. Even so, participants were convinced that they had worked, which explains why you can still today find subliminal self-help audio sold on-line and in bookstores. It would be nice if we could all improve ourselves simply by listening to music with subliminal messages, but this study and others like it show that subliminal audio is no better at solving our problems than visits to a palm reader.

LABORATORY EVIDENCE FOR SUBLIMINAL INFLUENCE   You may have noticed that we said that subliminal messages don't work when "encountered in everyday life." There *is* evidence, however, that people can be influenced by subliminal messages under carefully controlled laboratory conditions (Dijksterhuis, Aarts, & Smith, 2005; Verwijmeren et al., 2011). In one study, for example, Dutch college students saw subliminal flashes of the words "Lipton Ice" (a brand of ice tea) or a nonsense word made of the same letters (Karremans, Stroebe, & Claus, 2006). All the students were then asked whether they would prefer Lipton Ice or a brand of Dutch mineral water to drink. If students were not thirsty at the time, the subliminal flashes had no effect on what they chose. But if students were thirsty, those who had seen the subliminal flashes of "Lipton Ice" were significantly more likely to choose that beverage than were students who had seen subliminal flashes of the nonsense word. Several other laboratory studies have found similar effects of pictures or words flashed at subliminal levels (e.g., Bargh & Pietromonaco, 1982; Bermeitinger et al., 2009; Snodgrass, Shevrin, & Abelson, 2014; Strahan, Spencer, & Zanna, 2002).

Does this mean that advertisers will figure out how to use subliminal messages in everyday advertising? Maybe, but it hasn't happened yet. To get subliminal effects, researchers have to make sure that the illumination of the room is just right, that people are seated just the right distance from a viewing screen, and that nothing else is occurring to distract people as the subliminal stimuli are flashed. Further, even in the laboratory, there is no evidence that subliminal messages can get people to act counter to their wishes, values, or personalities (Neuberg, 1988). Thus, it is highly unlikely that the appearance of RATS in the Bush campaign ad convinced any Gore supporters to vote for Bush. For more on the relationship between automatic thinking and consumer attitudes, check out the following Try It!

TRY IT!

Consumer Brand Attitudes

Here are two exercises to test the role of automatic thought processes in consumer-related attitudes. You can do the exercises on your own, but the first one in particular might be easier to test on a friend.

A. Let's start with a baseline memory assessment. Below are four word pairs. Read each pair aloud to your friend (or to yourself), who should pay close attention and try to remember them—yes, there will be a test!

    i. Blue-duck
    ii. Ocean-moon
    iii. Window-hammer
    iv. Ski-climb

OK, while your friend is rehearsing these four word pairs and trying to remember them, you should read the following questions and ask for immediate, first-instinct responses:

    1. Name the first automobile brand that comes to mind.
    2. Name the first laundry detergent brand that comes to mind.
    3. Name the first soft drink brand that comes to mind.

    Was your friend's laundry detergent Tide? Was the soft drink Mountain Dew? There actually is no memory test here—what we're interested in is whether the word pairs from the first half of the exercise primed particular brand names in the second half. Perhaps *ocean-moon* made your friend more likely to think of Tide, a semantically related brand name. Perhaps learning *ski-climb* made your friend think of a mountain, and therefore Mountain Dew. Information does not have to be subliminal in order to affect how (and how often) we think of particular consumer goods. Priming, as discussed in Chapter 3, can make certain thoughts, concepts, and attitudes more accessible, including those related to the purchases we make.

B. Consider the following eight companies. From this list, see if you can guess the Top 3 in terms of total sales revenue (not profit, but revenue) for 2013:

- Berkshire Hathaway
- Valero Energy
- Cardinal Health
- Archer Daniels Midland
- Microsoft
- Target
- Pepsi
- Amazon.com

Ready? Do you have your Top 3 selected? Keep reading for the correct answers . . .

    The list above is already in the right order. So starting at the top, the companies with highest total sales revenue on the list were Berkshire Hathaway, Valero Energy, and Cardinal Health. Our guess is that these weren't your answers. We know that they wouldn't have been our guesses! For that matter, you may never have heard of some of the companies at the top of this list, and therein lies the explanation for what just happened. Remember the availability heuristic from Chapter 3? Microsoft, Target, Pepsi, Amazon … these are familiar brand names. And the more easily a brand name comes to mind, the more popular, more successful, and even just flat-out better we often assume that brand to be. Of course, there is a wide and complex range of economic factors that contribute to a company's success; such questions are beyond the scope of our present focus. But for our purposes, this example provides yet another reason why advertising may pay off in the long run: we tend to think pleasant thoughts about that which is familiar.

Advertising, Stereotypes, and Culture

Ironically, the hoopla surrounding subliminal messages has obscured the fact that ads are most powerful when people consciously perceive them. For that matter, advertising influences more than just our consumer attitudes. Advertisements transmit cultural stereotypes in their words and images, subtly connecting products with desired images, feelings, and desires. Back to our friend Don Draper again: "Advertising is based on one thing: happiness. And you know what happiness is? Happiness is the smell of a new car. It's freedom from fear. It's a billboard on the side of the road that screams reassurance that whatever you are doing is okay. You are okay."

Advertising both reflects and shapes the biases present in our society, as demonstrated by the divergent responses to this 2013 Cheerios ad featuring an interracial family.

On a less happy note, advertisements can also reflect, reinforce, and perpetuate stereotypical ways of thinking about others. Until recently, most ads tended to depict groups of Whites, heterosexual couples, families that are "traditional" and so on. You would think that divorced families, the middle-aged and the elderly, people of color, lesbians and gay men, the physically disabled, and others just didn't exist. And breaking that mold is not always easy, as General Mills found out in 2013 when a heartwarming Cheerios commercial featuring an interracial couple and their adorable biracial daughter sparked a disturbing Internet backlash of hateful, racist responses. Fortunately, the ad generated a lot of positive reaction as well, and General Mills brought back the family for another Cheerios commercial during the 2014 Super Bowl.

GENDER STEREOTYPES AND EXPECTATIONS Gender stereotypes are particularly pervasive in advertising imagery. The message is often that men are doers and women are observers. Several studies have examined television commercials throughout the world and coded how men and women are portrayed. As seen in Figure 7.9, one review found that women were more likely than men to be portrayed in dependent roles (that is, not in a position of power but dependent on someone else) in every country that was examined (Furnham & Mak, 1999). More recent studies have found that these stereotypical views of women persist in advertising (Conley & Ramsey, 2011; Eisend, 2010; Shaw, Eisend, & Tan, 2014).

Gender Roles

Societal beliefs—such as those conveyed by media and other sources—regarding how men and women are expected to behave

These different depictions of men and women reflect **gender roles**, societal beliefs about how men and women are expected to behave. For example, in many cultures, women are expected to assume the role of wife and mother and have limited opportunities to pursue other careers. In the United States and other countries, these expectations are evolving, and women do have more opportunities than ever before. But conflict can still result when expectations change for some roles but not for others assumed by the

---

Figure 7.9 Portrayals of Women and Men in Television Advertising

The ways in which women and men are portrayed in television commercials have been examined throughout the world. In every country, women were more likely to be portrayed in powerless, dependent roles than men were.

(Based on data in Furnham & Mak, 1999)

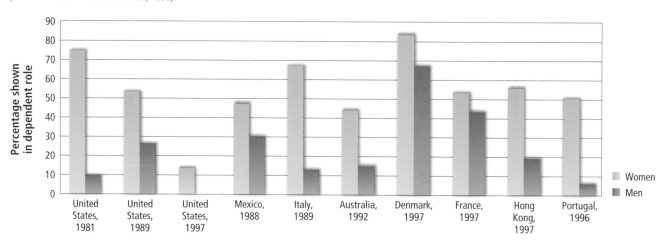

same person. In India, for example, women were traditionally permitted to take only the roles of wife, mother, agricultural laborer, and domestic worker. As their rights have expanded, women are increasingly working at other professions. At home, though, many husbands still expect their wives to assume the traditional role of childrearer and household manager, even if their wives have other careers. Conflict results because many women are expected to "do it all"—maintain a career, raise the children, clean the house, and attend to their husband's needs (Brislin, 1993; Wax, 2008). Such conflicts are not limited to India; many American readers will find this kind of role conflict all too familiar (Eagly & Diekman, 2003; Kite, Deaux, & Haines, 2008; Marks, Lam, & McHale, 2009; Rudman, 1998; Sandberg, 2013). And research suggests that societal roles such as these can be powerful determinants of people's feelings, behavior, and personality (Eagly, Diekman, Johannesen-Schmidt, & Koenig, 2004; Eagly & Steffen, 2000).

Advertising both reflects and shapes the gender roles present in a society. Women in ads are often depicted as wives or mothers–very important roles, of course! But these are usually depictions of women placing the needs of others before their own. Men, on the other hand, are portrayed in a wider range of roles, including many that convey an impression of power over others.

But let's get back to advertising. Because you might be thinking, well, advertisements reflect the stereotypes and expectations of a society, but they play little role in influencing people's attitudes and behavior. Actually, the images conveyed in advertisements are far from harmless. Consider, for example, the unrealistically thin body style for women glamorized by ads and the media more generally. Although many, if not most, world societies throughout history have considered plumpness in females attractive, Western culture, and especially American culture, currently values unrealistic thinness in the female form (Grossbard et al., 2009; Jackson, 1992; Weeden & Sabini, 2005). The women shown in Western advertisements, magazines, and movies are getting thinner all the time, are thinner than women in the actual population, and are often so thin that they would qualify for a diagnosis of anorexia (Fouts & Burggraf, 1999; Wiseman et al., 1992). The message to women and young girls? To be beautiful you must be thin. This message is hitting home: Girls and women in America are becoming increasingly dissatisfied with the way they look (Bearman, Presnell, & Martinez, 2006), a dissatisfaction that is often unrelated to their *actual* body size (Grabe & Hyde, 2006). What's worse, body dissatisfaction has been shown to be a risk factor for eating disorders, low self-esteem, and depression (Slevec & Tiggemann, 2011; Stice et al., 2011). But is there a causal connection between the way women are depicted in the media and women's feelings about their own bodies? It appears that there is. Experimental studies show that women who are randomly assigned to look at media depictions of thin women show a dip in their body self-image (Grabe, Ward, & Hyde, 2008). And a recent meta-analysis of research studies indicates that Americans endorsed the "thin is beautiful" standard for women even more strongly in the 2000s than in the 1990s (Grabe et al., 2008).

What about advertising depictions of attractive *male* bodies? Until recently, there was very little research on this question, but studies conducted of late suggest that men are beginning to come under the same pressure to achieve an ideal body that women have experienced for decades (Cafri et al., 2005; Cafri & Thompson, 2004; Grossbard et al., 2008; Morry & Staska, 2001; Wiseman & Moradi, 2010). Specifically, Harrison Pope and his colleagues (1999) analyzed advertisements starting in 1950 from two women's magazines, *Glamour* and *Cosmopolitan*, for how often male and female models were pictured in a state of undress. For women, the percentage remained at about 20% over the decades, but for men a change was clear. In 1950, fewer than 5% of ads showed men in some state of undress; by 1995, that figure had risen to as much as 35% (Pope, Phillips, & Olivardia, 2000).

Do these presentations of (nearly) naked—and unrealistically idealized—male bodies affect men's perceptions of themselves? Ida Jodette Hatoum and Deborah Belle (2004) investigated this question by focusing on the relationship between media consumption and bodily concerns in a sample of college men. They found that reading male-oriented magazines such as *Maxim, Details, Esquire, Men's Fitness,* and *Men's Health*—all of which consistently present the "hypermuscular" male body— was significantly correlated with negative feelings about one's own body. In addition, these researchers found that the more men were exposed to these male-directed magazines, the more they valued thinness in women as well.

CULTURE AND ADVERTISING Related to issues of gender and advertising is the question of whether there are differences across cultures in the kinds of attitudes people have toward products, perhaps reflecting the differences in self-concept we discussed in Chapter 5. As we saw, Western cultures tend to stress independence and individualism, whereas many Asian cultures stress interdependence and collectivism. Maybe these differences influence the kinds of attitudes people have and hence how advertisements affect those attitudes (Aaker, 2000; de Mooij, 2014).

To examine this possibility, researchers created different print ads for the same product that stressed independence (e.g., an ad for shoes said, "It's easy when you have the right shoes") or interdependence (e.g., "the shoes for your family") and showed them to both Americans and Koreans (Han & Shavitt, 1994). The Americans were persuaded most by the ads stressing independence, and the Koreans were persuaded by the ads stressing interdependence. The researchers also analyzed actual magazine advertisements in the United States and Korea and found that these ads were in fact different as well: American ads tended to emphasize individuality, self-improvement, and benefits of the product for the individual consumer, whereas Korean ads tended to emphasize the family, concerns about others, and benefits for one's social group. In general, then, advertisements, like other forms of persuasive communication, work best if they are tailored to the kind of attitude they are trying to change and the expectations and thinking styles of the target audience.

REVIEW QUESTIONS

1. Research on public service ads designed to promote healthy behavior indicates that such efforts
   a. almost always fail.
   b. are more effective at changing the attitudes of men versus women.
   c. are more effective via television than print ads when their target is young people.
   d. are most effective when they are subliminal.

2. The best way for an advertisement to change an affectively based attitude is to use a _____ appeal.
   a. cognitive
   b. behavioral
   c. affective
   d. fact-filled

3. Research on subliminal influence in advertising demonstrates that subliminal efforts at persuasion are
   a. less effective than people assume them to be.
   b. more effective than people assume them to be.
   c. more effective in individualistic versus collectivistic cultures.
   d. more effective in collectivistic versus individualistic cultures.

4. Women who are randomly assigned to look at media depictions of thin women
   a. always develop eating disorders.
   b. experience a decrease in body self-image.
   c. come to place a greater emphasis on men's physical appearance, particularly how muscular they are.
   d. show an increase in self-esteem.

5. Hatoum and Belle (2004) examined the relationship between media consumption and bodily concerns in a sample of college men. Their research found that
   a. unrealistically idealized presentations of male bodies in the media led the men to join a gym.
   b. reading male-oriented magazines that present the "hypermuscular" male body significantly correlated with negative feelings about one's body.
   c. reading male-oriented magazines that present the "hypermuscular" male body significantly correlated with positive feelings about one's body.
   d. reading male-directed magazines had no relationship with the men valuing thinness in women.

See page 621 for the answers.

Resisting Persuasive Messages

7.5 **What are some strategies for resisting efforts at persuasion?**

By now you very well may be getting nervous (and not just because the chapter hasn't ended yet). With all these clever methods out there designed to change your attitudes, are you ever safe from persuasive communications? Indeed you are, or at least you can be if you use some counterstrategies of your own. Here's how to make sure all those persuasive messages that bombard you don't turn you into a quivering mass of constantly changing opinion.

Attitude Inoculation

One step you can take is to consider the arguments against your attitude before someone attacks it. The more people have thought about pro and con arguments beforehand using the technique known as **attitude inoculation** (Banas & Miller, 2013; Ivanov, Pfau, & Parker, 2009; McGuire, 1964), the better they can ward off attempts to change their minds using logical arguments. The process functions much like a medical inoculation, in which patients are exposed to a small amount of a weakened version of a virus to protect them from developing the full-blown viral disease upon subsequent exposure. Here's how it works for protecting against attitude change: By considering "small doses" of arguments against their position, people become more resistant to later, full-blown attempts to change their attitudes. In other words, having thought about the counterarguments beforehand, people are relatively immune to the effects of the later persuasive communication. In contrast, if people have not thought much about the issue ahead of time—for example, if they formed their attitude via the peripheral route—they are particularly susceptible to an attack on that attitude that uses logical appeals.

Attitude Inoculation
Making people immune to attempts to change their attitudes by initially exposing them to small doses of the arguments against their position

In one study, for example, William McGuire (1964) "inoculated" people by giving them brief arguments against *cultural truisms*, beliefs that most members of a society accept uncritically, such as the idea that we should brush our teeth after every meal. Two days later, people came back and read a much stronger attack on the truism, one that contained a series of logical arguments about why brushing your teeth too frequently is a bad idea. The people who had been inoculated against these arguments earlier were much less likely to change their attitudes than were those in a control group who had not been inoculated. Why? The individuals who were inoculated with weak arguments had time to think about why these arguments were false, making them more able to contradict the stronger attack they heard two days later. The control group, never having thought about how often people should brush their teeth, was particularly susceptible to the strong communication arguing against frequent brushing.

The chief effect of talk on any subject is to strengthen one's own opinions and, in fact, one never knows exactly what he does believe until he is warmed into conviction by the heat of the attack and defense.
—Charles Dudley Warner,
Backlog Studies, 1873

Being Alert to Product Placement

When an advertisement comes on during a TV show, people often decide to press the mute button on the remote control or the fast-forward button on the DVR; we've also all learned to try to ignore pop-up ads and other efforts at persuasion when we're on-line. To counteract these efforts to avoid ads, advertisers look for ways of displaying their wares during the show or movie itself. Many companies pay the producers to incorporate their products into the script (Kang, 2008). If you have ever watched *American Idol*, you've probably noticed that ever-present Coca-Cola cup in front of each judge. Maybe the revolving groups of judges over the years have all genuinely and personally loved Coke. But more likely the Coca-Cola company paid to have their product prominently displayed. They are not alone: By many estimates, more than $3 billion is now spent annually on similar product placements; Heineken

Product placement, in which a commercial product is incorporated into the script of a movie or television show, is becoming more common.

reportedly paid $45 million just for one movie, enough to convince James Bond to abandon his usual penchant for martinis and drink the Dutch beer instead in 2012's *Skyfall* (Olmstead, 2012; Van Reijmersdal, Neijens, & Smit, 2009).

One reason product placement can work is that people do not always realize that someone is trying to influence their attitudes and behavior. Our defenses are down; when we see a character like James Bond drinking a certain brand of beer, we're often more focused on the movie itself than on the fact that someone is trying to influence our attitudes. As a result, we don't generate counter-arguments (Burkley, 2008; Levitan & Visser, 2008; Wheeler, Briñol, & Hermann, 2007). Children are especially vulnerable. One study, for example, found that the more children in grades 5 to 8 had seen movies in which adults smoked cigarettes, the more positive were their attitudes toward smoking (Heatherton & Sargent, 2009; Wakefield, Flay, & Nichter, 2003).

This leads to the question of whether forewarning people that someone is about to try to change their attitudes is an effective tool against product placement, or persuasion more generally. It turns out that it is. Several studies have found that warning people about an upcoming attempt to change their attitudes makes them less susceptible to that attempt. When people are forewarned, they analyze what they see and hear more carefully and as a result are likely to avoid attitude change. Without such warnings, people pay little attention to the persuasive attempts and tend to accept the messages at face value (Sagarin & Wood, 2007; Wood & Quinn, 2003). So before letting kids watch TV or sending them off to the movies, it is good to remind them that they are likely to encounter several attempts to change their attitudes.

Resisting Peer Pressure

A companion's words of persuasion are effective.

—Homer

We've seen that many efforts to shape our attitudes consist of appeals to our emotions. Can we ward off this kind of opinion change technique just as we can ward off the effects of logical appeals? This is an important question, because many critical changes in attitudes and behaviors occur not in response to logic, but via more emotional appeals. Consider the way in which many adolescents begin to smoke, drink, or take drugs. Often they do so in response to pressure from their peers, at an age when they are particularly susceptible to such pressure. Indeed, one study found that the best predictor of whether an adolescent smokes marijuana is whether he or she has a friend who does so (Allen, Donohue, & Griffin, 2003; Yamaguchi & Kandel, 1984).

Think about how this occurs. It is not as if peers present a set of logical arguments ("Hey, Jake, did you know that recent studies show that moderate drinking may have health benefits?"). Instead, peer pressure is linked more to people's values and emotions, playing on their fear of rejection and their desire for freedom and autonomy. In adolescence, peers become an important source of social approval— perhaps the most important—and can dispense powerful rewards for holding certain attitudes or behaving in certain ways, some of which may be positive, but others of which are problematic, such as using drugs or engaging in unprotected sex. What is needed is a technique that will make young people more resistant to attitude change attempts via peer pressure so that they will be less likely to engage in dangerous behaviors.

One possibility is to extend the logic of McGuire's inoculation approach to more affectively based persuasion techniques such as peer pressure. In addition to inoculating people with doses of logical arguments that they might hear, we could also inoculate them with samples of the kinds of emotional appeals they might encounter. Consider Jake, a 13-year-old who is hanging out with some classmates, many of whom are smoking cigarettes. The classmates begin to tease Jake about not smoking, calling him names. One of them even lights a cigarette and holds it in front of Jake, daring him to take a puff. Many 13-year-olds, facing such pressure, would cave in and smoke that cigarette. But suppose that we have immunized Jake from such social pressures by exposing him to mild versions of them ahead of time, and showing him ways to combat these pressures. We might have him role-play a situation where a friend calls him a chicken for not smoking a cigarette and teach him to respond by saying, "I'd be more of a chicken if I smoked it just to impress you." Would this help him resist the more powerful pressures exerted by his classmates?

Several programs designed to prevent smoking in adolescents suggest that it would. In one, psychologists used a role-playing technique with seventh graders, very much like the one we just described (McAlister et al., 1980). The researchers found that these students were significantly less likely to smoke 3 years after the study, compared to a control group that had not participated in the program. This result is encouraging and has been replicated in similar programs designed to reduce smoking and drug abuse (Botvin & Griffin, 2004; Chou et al., 1998).

A number of interventions designed to prevent smoking in adolescents have had some success. Many celebrities have lent their names and pictures to the effort, such as actor Jackie Chan, who was the spokesperson for an anti-smoking campaign in Taiwan.

When Persuasion Attempts Backfire: Reactance Theory

Suppose you want to make sure that your child never smokes. "Might as well err on the side of giving too strong a message," you might think, absolutely forbidding your child to even look at a pack of cigarettes. "What's the harm?" you figure. "At least this way my child will get the point about how serious this is."

Actually, there is harm to administering strong prohibitions: The stronger they are, the more likely they will backfire, actually causing an *increase* in interest in the prohibited activity. According to **reactance theory** (Brehm, 1966), people do not like feeling that their freedom to do or think whatever they want is being threatened. When they feel that their freedom is threatened, an unpleasant state of reactance is aroused, and people can reduce this reactance by performing the threatened behavior (e.g., smoking, dating the person your parents told you to stay away from). Have you ever been at a restaurant and had your server warn you, "careful, that plate is hot," but you decided to touch it anyway? Or done something simply because your parents, teachers, or other authority figures explicitly told you that you couldn't? Well, that's reactance.

In one study, for example, researchers placed one of two signs in the bathrooms on a college campus, in an attempt to get people to stop writing graffiti on the restroom walls (Pennebaker & Sanders, 1976). One sign read, "Do not write on these walls under any circumstances." The other gave a milder prohibition: "Please

Reactance Theory

The idea that when people feel their freedom to perform a certain behavior is threatened, an unpleasant state of resistance is aroused, which they can reduce by performing the prohibited behavior don't write on these walls." The researchers returned 2 weeks later and observed how much graffiti was written after they posted the signs. As predicted, significantly more people wrote graffiti in the bathrooms with the "Do not write . . ." sign than with the "Please don't write..." sign. Similarly, people who receive strong admonitions against smoking, taking drugs, or getting their nose pierced become more likely to perform these behaviors to restore their sense of personal freedom and choice (Erceg, Hurn, & Steed, 2011; Miller et al., 2007). And recent research demonstrates that when service employees specifically ask customers to give them positive evaluations on a post-purchase satisfaction survey, they actually end up getting lower ratings as a result (Jones, Taylor, & Reynolds, 2014). Reactance strikes again!

All of which is to say that despite the long list of attitude change strategies cataloged in this chapter, efforts at persuasion are not always effective. We aren't hopelessly at the mercy of those who would seek to change how we think and act. So the next time you are watching television and an ad comes on for a particular brand of pain relief medicine (or you see a product placement in a movie), you can actively consider what steps you might take to resist the impact of advertising. That is, assuming that you do not want to be at the mercy of the advertising industry—you might not think it is worth the effort to muster your defenses against ads for pain relievers. But what about attempts to get you to vote for a particular political candidate or to develop positive attitudes toward cigarettes? So remember, despite the extensive research literature demonstrating the wide range of factors that can change our attitudes, we are not automatons that must march blindly to the tune of Madison Avenue, Don Draper, or anyone else trying to influence how we think. Sometimes it is worth the cognitive effort to ask ourselves how much we want to be influenced by persuasive communications and then take specific steps to avoid that influence.

REVIEW QUESTIONS

1. The concept of attitude inoculation indicates that we are better able to resist a later attempt to change our attitudes when we are first exposed to arguments that
   a. support our existing attitude.
   b. are weakened versions of arguments we might hear later.
   c. prevent us from considering alternative viewpoints ahead of time.
   d. lead us to pay more attention to peripheral cues.

2. Which of the following is the best explanation for why product placement can be effective at changing attitudes?
   a. It tends to operate via the central route to persuasion.
   b. The audience is often unaware that an effort at attitude change is occurring.
   c. It usually leads to a reactance response.
   d. Cognitively based efforts at persuasion tend to have longer-lasting effects.

3. Peer pressure effects tend to be linked most often to what type of attitude?
   a. Cognitively based attitudes
   b. Affectively based attitudes

   c. Inoculated attitudes
   d. Negative attitudes

4. Which of the following concepts relates to the ironic research finding that the stronger the warning against a certain attitude or behavior, the more people sometimes wish to exhibit it?
   a. Attitude inoculation
   b. Peer pressure
   c. Implicit attitude
   d. Reactance theory

5. Cameron and Mitchell want to convince their daughter to stop leaving her toys scattered all around the floor, so they leave her a sign by her toy box. According to reactance theory, which of the following signs would be most effective?
   a. "Please try to remember to clean up your toys when you are done with them."
   b. "All toys MUST be put away after they are used."
   c. "Do not leave toys lying around!."
   d. "Your job is to clean up after yourself."

See page 621 for the answers.

Summary

7.1 What are the different kinds of attitudes, and on what are they based?

- **The Nature and Origin of Attitudes** An **attitude** is a person's enduring evaluation of people, objects, and ideas.

  - **Where Do Attitudes Come From?** Although some attitudes may have a genetic component, they are based mostly on our experiences. **Cognitively based attitudes** are based mostly on people's beliefs about the properties of the attitude object. **Affectively based attitudes** are based more on people's emotions and values; they can be created through **classical conditioning** or **operant conditioning**. **Behaviorally based attitudes** are based on people's actions toward the attitude object.

  - **Explicit Versus Implicit Attitudes** Once an attitude develops, it can exist at two levels. **Explicit attitudes** are ones we consciously endorse and can easily report. **Implicit attitudes** operate outside of conscious awareness.

7.2 Under what conditions do attitudes predict behavior?

- **When Do Attitudes Predict Behavior?** Under what conditions will people's attitudes dictate how they actually behave?

  - **Predicting Spontaneous Behaviors** Attitudes predict spontaneous behaviors only when they are relatively accessible. **Attitude accessibility** refers to the strength of the association between an object and an evaluation of it.

  - **Predicting Deliberative Behaviors** According to the **theory of planned behavior**, deliberative (nonspontaneous) behaviors are a function of people's attitude toward the specific act in question, subjective norms (people's beliefs about how others view the behavior in question), and how much people believe they can control the behavior.

7.3 How do internal and external factors lead to attitude change?

- **How Do Attitudes Change?** Both internal and external factors influence our attitudes.

  - **Changing Attitudes by Changing Behavior: Cognitive Dissonance Theory Revisited** One way that attitudes change is when people engage in counterattitudinal advocacy for low external justification. When this occurs, people find internal justification for their behavior, bringing their attitudes in line with their behavior.

- **Persuasive Communications and Attitude Change** Attitudes can also change in response to a **persuasive communication**. According to the **Yale Attitude Change approach**, the effectiveness of a persuasive communication depends on aspects of the communicator, or source of the message; aspects of the message itself (e.g., its content); and aspects of the audience. The **elaboration likelihood model** specifies when people are persuaded more by the strength of the arguments in the communication and when they are persuaded more by surface characteristics. When people have both the motivation and ability to pay attention to a message, they take the **central route to persuasion**, where they pay close attention to the strength of the arguments. When they have low motivation or ability, they take the **peripheral route to persuasion**, where they are swayed by surface characteristics, such as the attractiveness of the speaker.

- **Emotion and Attitude Change** Emotions influence attitude change in a number of ways. **Fear-arousing communications** can cause lasting attitude change if a moderate amount of fear is aroused and people believe they will be reassured by the content of the message. Emotions can also be used as heuristics to gauge one's attitude; if people feel good in the presence of an object, they often infer that they like it, even if those good feelings were caused by something else. Finally, the effectiveness of persuasive communications also depends on the type of attitude people have. Appeals to emotion and social identity work best if the attitude is based on emotion and social identity.

- **Confidence in One's Thoughts and Attitude Change** People's confidence in their thoughts about an attitude object affects how much they will be influenced by a persuasive communication. People's confidence can be affected by such things as whether they are nodding or shaking their head while listening to a persuasive message.

7.4 How does advertising work to change people's attitudes?

- **The Power of Advertising** Advertising has been found to be quite effective at changing people's attitudes, as indicated by split cable market tests, where advertisers show different advertisements to different samples of cable subscribers and then look at what they buy.

- **How Advertising Works** Advertising works by targeting affectively based attitudes with emotions, by targeting cognitively based attitudes with facts, and by making a product seem personally relevant.

- **Subliminal Advertising: A Form of Mind Control?** There is no evidence that subliminal messages in advertisements have any influence on people's behavior. Subliminal influences have been found, however, under controlled laboratory conditions.

- **Advertising, Stereotypes, and Culture** In addition to changing people's attitudes toward commercial products, advertisements often transmit societal stereotypes, such as **gender stereotypes and expectations** regarding both women and men. Analyses of **Culture and Advertising** also reveal interesting differences that converge with other cross-cultural findings in social and self-perception.

7.5 What are some strategies for resisting efforts at persuasion?

- **Resisting Persuasive Messages** Researchers have studied a number of ways by which people can avoid being influenced by persuasive messages.

- **Attitude Inoculation** One way is to expose people to small doses of arguments against their position, which makes it easier for them to defend themselves against a persuasive message they hear later.

- **Being Alert to Product Placement** Increasingly, advertisers are paying to have their products shown prominently in TV shows and movies. Forewarning people about attempts to change their attitudes, such as product placement, makes them less susceptible to attitude change.

- **Resisting Peer Pressure** Teaching kids how to resist peer pressure ahead of time can make them less vulnerable to it later on.

- **When Persuasion Attempts Backfire: Reactance Theory** According to **reactance theory**, people experience an unpleasant state called reactance when their freedom of choice is threatened. Attempts to manage people's attitudes can backfire if they make people feel that their choices are limited.

Test Yourself

1. All of the following are true about attitudes *except* one. Which one is false?

   a. Attitudes are related to our temperament and personality.

   b. Attitudes rarely change over time.

   c. Attitudes can be changed with persuasive communications.

   d. Under the right conditions attitudes predict people's behavior.

2. Paige wants to buy a puppy. She does some research and decides to buy an English Springer Spaniel rather than a Great Dane because they are smaller, more active, and good with children. Which type of attitude influenced her decision?

   a. Affectively based attitude

   b. Behaviorally based attitude

   c. Explicitly based attitude

   d. Cognitively based attitude

3. On a survey, Marquel reports that he agrees with wearing a seat belt. According to the theory of planned behavior, which of the following would be the best predictor of whether Marquel will wear a seat belt on a given day?

   a. He generally agrees that safe driving is important.

   b. His best friend, Trevor, who is always talking about how important it is to wear a seat belt, is in the car with him.

   c. His attitude toward seat belts is not very accessible.

   d. Marquel believes that it is hard to remember to wear his seat belt.

4. People will be most likely to change their attitudes about smoking if an antismoking advertisement

   a. uses extremely graphic pictures of how smoke can harm the body and warns of the risks of smoking.

   b. gives people subliminal messages about the risks of smoking as well as recommendations of how to quit.

   c. uses graphic pictures of the damages of smoking on the body and then provides specific recommendations on how to quit smoking.

   d. uses success stories of how people quit smoking.

5. Emilia would be most likely to pay attention to facts about the danger of AIDS during a school assembly *and* remember the facts for a long time if

   a. the speaker emphasized statistical information about AIDS throughout the world.

b. the speaker emphasized how the disease has spread in her community and there isn't anything distracting Emilia from listening.

c. the speaker emphasized how the disease has spread in her community and at the same time Emilia's best friend is whispering to her about a big party that weekend.

d. the speaker is a nationally known expert on AIDS.

6. You are trying to sell a new electronic toothbrush at the airport to busy, distracted travelers. Which of the following strategies is *least* likely to be successful at getting people to buy a toothbrush?

a. Make up a flier that gives convincing reasons why the toothbrush is so good.

b. Make a large sign that says, "9 out of 10 dentists recommend this toothbrush!"

c. Put up a large banner featuring a picture of your friend who looks like Brad Pitt posing with the toothbrush.

d. Stop people and say, "Do you know that this is the toothbrush that is used the most by Hollywood stars?"

7. Under which of the following conditions would people be most likely to vote for a political candidate? They

a. like the candidate's policies but have negative feelings toward him or her.

b. know little about the candidate's policies but have positive feelings toward him or her.

c. see subliminal ads supporting the candidate on national television.

d. see television ads supporting the candidate while they are distracted by their children.

8. Suppose that while you are watching a film at a movie theater the words "Drink Coke" are flashed on the screen at speeds too quick for you to see consciously. According to research on subliminal perception, which of the following is true?

a. You will get up and buy a Coke, but only if other people start to do so first.

b. You will get up and buy a Coke, but only if you prefer Coke to Pepsi.

c. You will be *less* likely to get up and buy a Coke.

d. You will be no more likely to buy a Coke than if the subliminal messages were not flashed.

9. Lara is a teenager who often comes across very thin women in advertisements, magazines, and movies. Which of the following messages is she likely to get from such media exposure?

a. She should be concerned about her health and well-being.

b. She must be thin to be beautiful.

c. The media depicts unrealistically thin women.

d. Women can look very thin from certain angles.

10. Which of these techniques is likely to help adolescents the most in resisting powerful peer pressure?

a. Presenting a set of logical arguments

b. Role-playing situations ahead of time

c. Positive reinforcement

d. Negative reinforcement

See page 621 for the answers.

Chapter 8
Conformity
Influencing Behavior

 ## Chapter Outline and Learning Objectives

Conformity: When and Why

8.1 **What is conformity, and why does it occur?**

Informational Social Influence: The Need to Know What's "Right"

8.2 **How does informational social influence motivate people to conform?**

The Importance of Being Accurate

When Informational Conformity Backfires

When Will People Conform to Informational Social Influence?

Normative Social Influence: The Need to Be Accepted

8.3 **How does normative social influence motivate people to conform?**

Conformity and Social Approval: The Asch Line-Judgment Studies

The Importance of Being Accurate, Revisited

The Consequences of Resisting Normative Social Influence

When Will People Conform to Normative Social Influence?

Minority Influence: When the Few Influence the Many

Strategies for Using Social Influence

8.4 **How can people use their knowledge of social influence to influence others?**

The Role of Injunctive and Descriptive Norms

Using Norms to Change Behavior: Beware the "Boomerang Effect"

Other Tactics of Social Influence

Obedience to Authority

8.5   What have studies demonstrated about people's willingness to obey authority figures?

The Role of Normative Social Influence

The Role of Informational Social Influence
Other Reasons Why We Obey
The Obedience Studies, Then and Now

On April 9, 2004, a man called a McDonald's restaurant in Mount Washington, Kentucky, and identified himself as a police detective to the assistant manager, Donna Jean Summers, 51. He told her she had a problem: One of her employees had stolen from the restaurant. He said he had talked to McDonald's corporate headquarters and to the store manager, whom he named correctly. The policeman gave Ms. Summers a rough description of the perpetrator, a teenage female, and she identified one of her employees (whom we will refer to as Susan, to protect her identity). The police detective told the assistant manager that she needed to search Susan immediately for the stolen money, or else Susan would be arrested, taken to jail, and searched there (Wolfson, 2005).

You might be thinking that this all sounds a bit odd. Ms. Summers said later that she was initially confused, but the caller was very authoritative and presented his information in a convincing manner. And, after all, he was a policeman. We're supposed to obey the police. During the phone call, Ms. Summers thought she heard police radios in the background.

So she called Susan into a small room and locked the door. Susan was 18 and had been a perfect employee to that point. The policeman on the phone told Ms. Summers what to do and what to say. Following his instructions, she ordered Susan to take off her clothing, one item at a time, until she was standing naked. Ms. Summers put all the clothes in a bag and put the bag outside the room, as instructed by the caller. Susan was now crying, fearful of the allegations and humiliated by the strip search. Unfortunately, her nightmare had just begun.

Susan was not the first fast-food employee to be victimized in this manner. Phone calls to restaurant managers, ordering them to abuse their employees, had been occurring around the country for several years. It just took law enforcement time to put the whole picture together. In all, managers of 70 restaurants, representing a dozen different chains in 32 states, received these phone calls and obeyed the caller's instructions (Barrouquere, 2006; Gray, 2004; Wolfson, 2005). The caller, as you have probably guessed, was not a policeman but was perpetrating a horrible hoax.

It was now 6:00 p.m., and Susan had been standing naked in the small, locked room for an hour. Ms. Summers needed to get back to supervising the cooking area, so the "policeman" told her to find someone else to guard Susan. She called her fiancé, Walter Nix Jr., 42, who agreed to come to the restaurant. Mr. Nix locked himself in the room with the naked and increasingly terrified teenager. At this point, the events become even more disturbing. Mr. Nix also believed the caller was who he said he was, and Mr. Nix proved even more obedient. In a series of escalating demands over 3 hours, the "detective" told Mr. Nix to force Susan to acquiesce to various sexual demands. The caller also talked directly to Susan, threatening her with what would happen if she didn't obey. "I was scared because they were a higher authority to me. I was scared for my safety because I thought I was in trouble with the law," she said (Wolfson, 2005, p. 3).

Three hours later, the caller told Mr. Nix to replace himself with another man. Thomas Simms, a 58-year-old employee, was called into the room. As he put it later, he knew immediately "something is not right about this." He refused to obey the man on the phone. He called in Ms. Summers and convinced her something was wrong. "I knew then I had been had," she said. "I lost it. I begged [Susan] for forgiveness.

I was almost hysterical" (Wolfson, 2005, p. 7). At this point, the "detective" hung up the phone. Susan's abuse was finally over.

After an investigation that involved police detectives in several states, a Florida man, David R. Stewart, 38, was arrested and charged as the telephone hoaxer. A married father of five, Stewart worked as a prison guard and was formerly a volunteer sheriff's deputy. At his trial, with only circumstantial evidence against him, the jury returned a verdict of not guilty. There have been no further fast-food hoax phone calls since then (ABC News, 2006). The assistant manager, Donna Summers, and her (no longer) fiancé, Walter Nix Jr., pleaded guilty to various charges. Ms. Summers was sentenced to probation, and Mr. Nix was sentenced to 5 years in prison. Susan, who now suffers from panic attacks, anxiety, and depression, sued the McDonald's corporation for failing to warn employees nationally after the first hoaxes occurred at their restaurants. She was awarded $6.1 million in damages by a Kentucky jury (Barrouquere, 2006; Wolfson, 2005).

In one of the saddest comments on this event, Susan's therapist said that Susan followed orders that night because her experience with adults "has been to do what she is told, because good girls do what they are told" (Wolfson, 2005). Indeed, every day, people try to get us to do what they want—to conform to their influence—sometimes through direct requests and sometimes through more subtle processes. The most powerful form of this social influence produces obedience and occurs when an authority figure gives an order. A more subtle version of conformity is when others indirectly indicate to us what is appropriate, and we come to sense that it is in our best interest to go along with them. In this chapter, we will focus on the potentially positive and negative effects of these social influence processes, beginning with more subtle examples of conformity and moving on to the obedience to authority that made possible the terrible fast-food restaurant hoax described above.

Conformity: When and Why

8.1 What is conformity, and why does it occur?

Do as most do, and [people] will speak well of thee.
— Thomas Fuller

It were not best that we should all think alike; it is difference of opinion that makes horse races.
— Mark Twain

Which one of the two quotations to the left do you find more appealing? Which one describes how you feel about conformity? We wouldn't be surprised if both of your answers are the second quotation, particularly if you're American. This is because American culture stresses the importance of not conforming (Kim & Markus, 1999; Kitayama, Conway, Pietromonaco, Park, & Plaut, 2010; Kitayama, Park, Sevincer, Karasawa, & Uskul, 2009; Markus, Kitayama, & Heiman, 1996). Americans picture themselves as a nation of rugged individualists, people who think for themselves, stand up for the underdog, and go against the tide to fight for what they think is right. This cultural self-image has been shaped by the manner in which the nation was founded, by a system of government, and by this society's historical experience with western expansion—the "taming" of the Wild West (Kitayama et al., 2006; Turner, 1932).

American mythology has celebrated the rugged individualist in many ways. For example, one of the longest-running and most successful advertising campaigns in American history featured the "Marlboro Man." As far back as 1955, the photograph of a lone cowboy on the range was an archetypal image. It also sold a lot of cigarettes. Clearly, it told us something about ourselves that we want and like to hear: that we make up our own minds and that we're not spineless, weak conformists (Cialdini, 2009; Pronin, Berger, & Molouki, 2007). More recently, consider the example of Apple Computer, one of the most valuable publicly traded companies in the world (Rooney, 2012). For several years, Apple's advertising slogan captured a similar sentiment of nonconformity: "Think different."

But are we, in fact, nonconforming creatures? Are the decisions we make always based on what we think, or do we use other people's behavior to help us decide what to do? In spite of Apple's advertising telling customers to "think different," take a careful look around the lecture hall next time you're in class and count how many glowing Apple logos stare back at you from the laptops of your fellow students. The computer of the nonconformist is now everywhere.

On a far more sobering note, as we saw in Chapter 6, the mass suicide of the Heaven's Gate cult members suggests that people sometimes conform in extreme and astonishing ways—even when making as crucial a decision as whether to take their own lives. But, you might argue, surely this is an extremely unusual case. Perhaps the followers of Marshall AppleWhite were disturbed people who were somehow predisposed to do what a charismatic leader told them to do. There is, however, another, more chilling possibility: Maybe many of us would have acted the same way had we been exposed to the same long-standing, powerful conformity pressures as were the members of Heaven's Gate. According to this view, almost anyone would have conformed in these same extreme circumstances.

If this statement is true, we should be able to find other situations in which people, placed under strong social pressures, conformed to a surprising degree. And, in fact, we can. For example, in 1961, activists in the American civil rights movement incorporated Mohandas Gandhi's principles of nonviolent protest into their demonstrations to end segregation. They trained their "Freedom Riders" (so named because they boarded buses and disobeyed "back of the bus" seating rules) in the passive acceptance of violent treatment. Thousands of southern African Americans, joined by a smaller number of northern Whites, many from college campuses, demonstrated against the segregationist laws of the South. In confrontation after confrontation, the civil rights activists adhered to the principles of nonviolence that others had taught them; they remained stoic as they were beaten, clubbed, hosed, whipped, and even killed by southern sheriffs and police (Nelson, 2010; Powledge, 1991). New recruits conformed to the nonviolent responses the existing members modeled, and this contagious commitment to nonviolent protest helped usher in a new era in America's fight for racial equality.

Under strong social pressure, individuals will conform to the group even when this means doing something immoral. In 2004, American soldiers' degrading abuse of Iraqis held at the Abu Ghraib prison sparked an international scandal and a great deal of soul-searching back home. Why did the soldiers humiliate their captives? As you read this chapter, you will see how the social influence pressures of conformity can contribute to decent people committing indecent acts.

But just a few years later, social pressure resulted in a tragic rather than heroic course of events. On the morning of March 16, 1968, American soldiers in Vietnam boarded helicopters that would take them to the village of My Lai. One pilot radioed that he saw enemy soldiers below, and so the Americans jumped off the helicopters, rifles blazing. They soon realized that the pilot was wrong—there were no enemy soldiers, only women, children, and elderly men cooking breakfast over small fires. Inexplicably, the leader of the platoon ordered one of the soldiers to kill the villagers. Other soldiers began firing too, and the carnage spread, ending with the deaths of 450 to 500 Vietnamese civilians (Hersh, 1970). Similar processes of social influence have been implicated in more recent military atrocities, including the humiliating abuse of Iraqi captives at the Abu Ghraib prison starting in 2003 (Hersh, 2004), the killing of thousands of Iraqi civilians and the destruction of tens of thousands of houses in Fallujah in 2004 (Marqusee, 2005), and American soldiers urinating on the corpses of Taliban fighters in Afghanistan in 2011 (Martinez, 2012).

In all these examples, people found themselves caught in a web of social influence. In response, they altered their behavior to conform to the expectations of others (O'Gorman, Wilson, & Miller, 2008). For social psychologists, this is the essence of **conformity**: changing one's behavior due to the real or imagined influence of others (Aarts & Dijksterhuis, 2003; Kiesler & Kiesler, 1969; Sorrentino & Hancock, 2014). As these examples show, the consequences of conformity span a wide range, from bravery to tragedy. But why did these people conform? Some probably conformed because they did not know what to do in a confusing or unusual situation. The behavior of the people around them served as a cue as to how to respond, and they decided to act in a similar manner. Other people probably conformed because they did not wish to be ridiculed or punished for being different from everybody else. They chose to act the way the group expected so that they wouldn't be rejected or thought less of by group members. Let's see how each of these reasons for conforming operates.

Conformity

A change in one's behavior due to the real or imagined influence of other people

---

REVIEW QUESTIONS

1. Which of the following is the most direct and powerful example of social influence?
   a. Complying with a polite request made by a friend
   b. Conforming to a group norm
   c. Obedience to an order from an authority figure
   d. Emotion-based attitudes

2. Which of the following statements is true about conformity?
   a. People continue to behave in a manner they think is right even though the situation is confusing.
   b. People act in accordance with others when they do not fear social rejection.
   c. People conform because they do not bother about the expectations of others.

   d. People change their behavior due to the powerful influence of other people.

3. Conformity always includes
   a. positive and moral behavior.
   b. negative and immoral behavior.
   c. the real or imagined influence of other people.
   d. an authority figure.

See page 621 for the answers.

Informational Social Influence: The Need to Know What's "Right"

8.2   How does informational social influence motivate people to conform?

Life is full of ambiguous and confusing situations. How should you address your psychology professor—as Dr. Aronson, Professor Aronson, Mr. Aronson, or Elliot? How should you vote in the upcoming campus election that would raise your student activity fees? Do you cut a piece of sushi or eat it whole? Did the scream you just heard in the hallway come from a person joking with friends or from the victim of a mugging?

In these and many other scenarios, we feel uncertain about what to think or how to act. We simply don't know enough to make a good or accurate choice. Luckily, we have a powerful and useful source of knowledge available to us—the behavior of other people. Sometimes we simply ask directly about the appropriate way to act. One of your authors remembers fondly the freshman from a few years ago who asked him, "Is college like *Harry Potter*? Do we call you 'Professor'?" (The answer: "Yes, it's *exactly* like *Harry Potter*. Now put your wand down and take out your potions cauldron.") Many times, though, we watch others, observing their behavior to help us achieve a better definition of the situation (Kelley, 1955; Thomas, 1928). When we subsequently act like everyone else, we are conforming, but this doesn't mean we are weak, spineless individuals with no self-reliance. Instead, the influence of others leads us to conform because we see those people as a valuable source of information to guide our behavior. We conform because we believe that others' interpretation of an ambiguous set of circumstances is accurate and will help us choose an appropriate course of action. This is called **informational social influence** (Cialdini & Goldstein, 2004; Deutsch & Gerard, 1955; Kuan, Zhong, & Chau, 2014).

As an illustration of how other people can be a source of information, imagine that you are a participant in the following experiment by Muzafer Sherif (1936). In the first phase of the study, you are seated alone in a dark room and asked to focus your attention on a dot of light 15 feet away. The experimenter asks you to estimate in inches how far the light moves. You stare earnestly at the light, and, yes, it seems to move a little. You say, "about 2 inches," though it is not easy to tell exactly. The light disappears and then comes back; you are asked to judge again. The light seems to move a little more this time, and you say, "4 inches." After several of these trials, the light seems to move about the same amount each time—somewhere in the neighborhood of 2 to 4 inches.

The interesting thing about this task is that the light was not actually moving at all. It looked as if it was because of a visual illusion called the autokinetic effect: If you stare at a bright light in a uniformly dark environment (e.g., a star on a dark night), the light will appear to waver a bit back and forth. This occurs because you have no stable visual reference point with which to anchor the position of the light. The distance that the light appears to move varies from person to person but becomes relatively consistent for each person over time. In Sherif's experiment, all the subjects arrived at their own stable estimate during the first phase of the study, but these estimates differed across people. Some thought the light was moving only an inch or so; others thought it was moving as much as 10 inches.

Sherif chose the autokinetic effect because he wanted a situation that would be ambiguous—where the correct definition of the situation would be unclear to his participants. In the second phase of the experiment, a few days later, the participants were paired with two other people, each of whom had had the same

Informational Social Influence
Relying on other people as a source of information to guide our behavior; we conform because we believe that others' interpretation of an ambiguous situation is correct and can help us choose an appropriate course of action

Eight thousand pumpkins meet the Eiffel Tower. While the holiday is based on ancient British and Irish traditions surrounding All Hallows' Eve, Halloween as we know it is a completely American phenomenon—until October 1997, that is, when "Ah-lo-ween" was introduced to the French public by retailers in an effort to boost consumer spending to spark a sagging French economy (Cohen, 1997). Informational social influence is how the French literally learned what this holiday is about. As of Halloween 1997, they had no idea of what "treek au treeting" was. However, by Halloween 2000, French shops were decorated in Black and orange, carved pumpkins were displayed, and nightclubs held costume competitions.

(Associated Press, 2002)

prior experience alone with the light. Now the situation became a truly social one, as all three made their judgments out loud. Remember, the autokinetic effect is experienced differently by different people: Some see a lot of movement, and some see not much at all. After hearing their partners give judgments that were different from their own, what did people do?

Over the course of several trials as a group, people converged on a common estimate, and each member of the group tended to conform to that estimate. These results indicate that people were using each other as a source of information, coming to believe that the group estimate was the correct one (see Figure 8.1). An important feature of informational social influence is that it can lead to **private acceptance**, when people conform to the behavior of others because they genuinely believe that these other people are right.

It might seem equally plausible that people publicly conformed to the group but privately maintained the belief that the light was moving only a small amount. For example, maybe someone privately believed that the light was moving 10 inches but announced that it had moved 3 inches, the group consensus, to avoid standing out from the crowd or looking foolish. This would be a case of **public compliance**, conforming publicly without necessarily believing in what the group is doing. Sherif cast doubt on this interpretation of his study, however, by asking people to judge the lights one more time, this time back on their own. Even though they no longer had to worry about looking silly in front of other participants, they continued to give the answer the group had given earlier. One study even found that people still conformed to the group estimate when they participated individually a full year later (Rohrer, Baron, Hoffman, & Swander, 1954). These results suggest that people were relying on each other to define reality and came to privately accept the wisdom of the group estimate.

The power of conformity to produce private acceptance has been demonstrated in several areas of life, including energy conservation. In one study, Jessica Nolan and her colleagues (2008) gave a sample of California residents information urging them to conserve electricity. The household members received one of four messages. Three of these presented basic reasons to conserve: to protect the environment, to benefit society, or to save money. The fourth message contained information designed to promote conformity: The participants were told that the majority of their neighbors conserved electrical energy. The researchers then measured actual energy usage from the homes' electrical meters. They found that the fourth message, containing information about the behavior of one's neighbors, caused people to conserve more energy than did the other three messages (Nolan et al., 2008). Similarly, Goldstein, Cialdini, and Griskevicius (2008) managed to increase hotel guests' compliance with a "reuse your bath towels and save energy" request, a widely used hotel management technique that hasn't always proved popular with guests. The researchers found that an informational sign in the bathroom, stating that the majority of guests in this very room had reused their towels, was significantly more effective than the general "Help the Environment" appeal usually used by hotels.

Private Acceptance

Conforming to other people's behavior out of a genuine belief that what they are doing or saying is right

Public Compliance

Conforming to other people's behavior publicly without necessarily believing in what the other people are doing or saying

---

"It's always best on these occasions to do what the mob do." "But suppose there are two mobs?" suggested Mr. Snodgrass. "Shout with the largest," replied Mr. Pickwick.

—Charles Dickens, *Pickwick Papers*

Figure 8.1 One Group's Judgments in Sherif's (1936) Autokinetic Studies

People estimated how far a point of light appeared to move in a dark room. When they saw the light by themselves, their estimates varied widely. When they were brought together in groups and heard other people announce their estimates, people conformed to the group's estimate of how much the light moved, adjusting their private beliefs based on the information other group members provided.

(Data from Sherif, 1936)

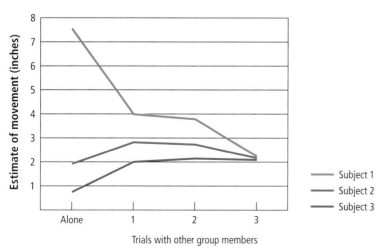

The Importance of Being Accurate

Later research extended Sherif's classic study on informational conformity in interesting ways (Baron, Vandello, & Brunsman, 1996; Levine, Higgins, & Choi, 2000; Muchnik, Aral, & Taylor, 2013). This research employed judgment tasks that are more like real life than the autokinetic effect. It also revealed another variable that affects informational social influence: how important it is to be accurate at the task.

For example, in one study, research participants were given an involving but ambiguous task: eyewitness identification (Baron et al., 1996). Just like eyewitnesses of a real crime, the participants were asked to pick a "perpetrator" out of a lineup, though in this instance they were asked to do it several times. For each of the 13 lineups, the participants were first shown a slide of a man—the perpetrator. Next, they saw a slide of a lineup composed of four men, one of whom was the perpetrator. In the lineup, the perpetrator was sometimes dressed differently than he had been in the prior slide. The participant's job was to pick him out. The task was made difficult (and ambiguous) by presenting the slides extremely quickly: Participants saw each slide for only half a second. The study took place in a group consisting of the participant and three confederates. Each of the four said their answers out loud after viewing each pair of slides. On the critical seven trials, where informational social influence would be measured, the three confederates answered before the participant—and all the confederates gave the same wrong answer.

The researchers also manipulated how important it was to the research participants to be accurate at the task. In the high-importance condition, they were told that the upcoming task was a real test of eyewitness identification ability and that police departments and courts would soon be using it to differentiate good eyewitnesses from poor ones. Participants' scores would therefore establish standards against which future eyewitness performance would be judged. In addition, those who were most accurate at the task would receive a $20 bonus from the experimenters. In contrast, in the low-importance condition, the research participants were told that the study was a first attempt to study eyewitness identification and that the slide task was still being developed. Thus, as the participants began the task, they were in two very different states of mind. Half thought their performance was very important and would have ramifications for real-life legal proceedings. They were motivated to do well (and earn their $20). The other half saw this as just a basic research study like any other. Their performance didn't seem like it was all that important.

The high-importance condition mirrors the concerns of many situations in everyday life—your judgments and decisions have consequences, and you're motivated to "get things right." Does that make you more or less susceptible to informational social influence? The researchers found that it makes you *more* susceptible. In the low-importance condition, participants conformed to the confederates' judgments and gave the same wrong answers on just 35% of the critical trials. In the high-importance condition, participants conformed to the confederates' judgments on 51% of the critical trials.

> Yes, we must, indeed, all hang together or, most assuredly, we shall all hang separately.
>
> —Benjamin Franklin at the signing of the Declaration of Independence, 1776

Even for judgments of the utmost importance—such as when an eyewitness to a crime later tries to identify the culprit—informational social influence influences our perceptions.

But relying on other people as a source of information is a strategy that also comes with risks. In a different eyewitness study, pairs of eyewitnesses each watched separate videos of what they believed to be the exact same event (Gabbert, Memon, & Allan, 2003). Unbeknownst to participants, each member of the pair viewed a slightly different video. Among pairs that were allowed to discuss the video before each eyewitness took an individual memory test, 71% of witnesses went on to mistakenly recall personally having seen items that only their partner had actually seen. This experiment illustrates the major risk of using other people around you for information: What if those other people are wrong? Indeed, this is why most police procedures require that when there are multiple eyewitnesses in a case, each one is to be interviewed individually by investigators and view a lineup individually as well. Informational social influence among eyewitnesses is not welcome in the courtroom (Levett, 2013).

When Informational Conformity Backfires

Ninety-nine percent of the people in the world are fools, and the rest of us are in great danger of contagion.

—Thornton Wilder, *The Matchmaker*

A dramatic form of informational social influence occurs during crises, when an individual is confronted with a frightening, potentially dangerous situation to which he or she is ill equipped to respond (Killian, 1964). The person may have no idea of what is really happening or what he or she should do. When one's personal safety is involved, the need for information is acute—and the behavior of others is very informative.

Consider what happened on Halloween night in 1938. Orson Welles, the gifted actor and film director, and the Mercury Theater broadcast a radio play based loosely on H. G. Wells's science fiction fantasy *War of the Worlds*. Remember, this was the era before television; radio was a primary source of entertainment, and

Orson Welles, renowned actor and director, whose War of the Worlds radio broadcast in 1938 sparked a public scare that spread, in large part, due to informational social influence.

it was the only source for fast-breaking news. That night, the drama that Welles and his fellow actors broadcast—portraying the invasion of Earth by hostile Martians—was so realistic that untold numbers of listeners became frightened and alerted the police; many were so panic stricken that they tried to flee the "invasion" in their cars (Cantril, 1940).

Why were Americans convinced that what they heard was a real news report of an actual invasion by aliens? Hadley Cantril (1940), who studied this real-life "crisis," suggested two reasons. One was that the play parodied existing radio news shows very well, and many listeners missed the beginning of the broadcast (when it was clearly identified as a play) because they had been listening to a popular show on another station. The other culprit, however, was informational social influence. Many people were listening with friends and family. As the *War of the Worlds* scenario became increasingly frightening, they naturally turned to each other, out of uncertainty, to see whether they should believe what they heard. Seeing looks of concern and worry on their loved ones' faces added to the panic people were beginning to feel. "We all kissed one another and felt we would all die," reported one listener (Cantril, 1940, p. 95).

A late-nineteenth-century social scientist Gustav Le Bon (1895) was the first researcher to document how emotions and behavior can spread rapidly through a crowd—an effect he called *contagion* (Dezecache et al., 2013; Hatfield, Cacioppo, & Rapson, 1993; Levy & Nail, 1993). As we have learned, in a truly ambiguous situation, people become more likely to rely on the interpretation of others. Unfortunately, in a truly ambiguous and confusing situation, other people may be no more knowledgeable or accurate than we are. If other people are misinformed, we will adopt their mistakes and misinterpretations. Depending on others to help us define the situation can therefore lead us into serious inaccuracies.

When Will People Conform to Informational Social Influence?

Let's review the situations that are the most likely to produce conformity because of informational social influence.

WHEN THE SITUATION IS AMBIGUOUS   Ambiguity is the most crucial variable for determining how much people use each other as a source of information. When you are unsure of the correct response, the appropriate behavior, or the right idea, you will be most open to influence from others. The more uncertain you are, the more you will rely on others (Allen, 1965; Renfrow & Gosling, 2006; Tesser, Campbell, & Mickler, 1983; Walther et al., 2002). Situations such as the military atrocities discussed above were ambiguous ones for the people involved—ideal circumstances for informational social influence to take hold. Most of the soldiers were young and inexperienced. When they saw other soldiers shooting at the villagers or humiliating prisoners, many of them thought this was what they were supposed to do, and they joined in.

WHEN THE SITUATION IS A CRISIS   Crisis often occurs simultaneously with ambiguity. In a crisis situation, we usually do not have time to stop and think about exactly which course of action we should take. We need to act—immediately. If we feel scared and panicky and are uncertain what to do, it is only natural for us to see how other people are responding and to do likewise. Unfortunately, the people we imitate may also feel scared and panicky and not be behaving rationally.

Captain Chesley "Sully" Sullenberger became a hero in January 2009 when he safely landed USAir flight 1549 on the Hudson River after its engines had shut down. In interviews, "Captain Sully" always has been quick to credit his flight crew for their heroism as well. Informational social influence suggests that the passengers would have looked to the expertise of the flight attendants to figure out what was going on during the mid-air crisis. The crew's ability to remain calm and follow procedure helped keep the passengers calm and safely in their seats during the emergency landing and deplaning.

Soldiers, for example, are undoubtedly on edge during their tours of duty. Further, in many wars, it is not easy to tell who the enemy is. In the Vietnam War, civilians who were sympathizers of the Vietcong were known to have laid mines in the path of U.S. soldiers, fired guns from hidden locations, and thrown or planted grenades. Similarly, in Iraq and Afghanistan, it was (and remains) difficult to tell if people were civilians or combatants, allies or enemies. It is perhaps not surprising, then, that these soldiers often turned to others around them to gauge the proper course of action. Had these individuals not been in the midst of a chronic crisis situation and instead had more time to think about their actions, perhaps tragedy and scandal would have been avoided.

WHEN OTHER PEOPLE ARE EXPERTS   Typically, the more expertise or knowledge a person has, the more valuable he or she will be as a guide in an ambiguous situation (Allison, 1992; Cialdini & Trost, 1998). For example, a passenger who sees smoke coming out of an airplane engine will probably check the flight attendants' reaction rather than their seatmates'; however, experts are not always reliable sources of information. Imagine the fear felt by the young man listening to the *War of the Worlds* broadcast who called his local police department for an explanation, only to learn that the police too thought the events described on the radio were actually happening (Cantril, 1940)!

REVIEW QUESTIONS

1. Informational social influence occurs
   a. when we believe that other people's reactions can help us arrive at an accurate reading of a situation.
   b. through public but not private conformity.
   c. only in a crisis.
   d. autokinetically.

2. Which of the following statements regarding Sherif's (1936) study of perceptions of the autokinetic effect is true?
   a. Participants conformed publicly but not privately.
   b. Participants did conform, but the effects of this conformity were short lived as they reverted to their previous, individually given responses once they were no longer part of a group.
   c. Participants conformed because they were in a group with their friends, and they simply wanted to fit in with the group.
   d. Participants conformed because they believed the other people's responses were accurate.

3. The more important it is to people to make an accurate decision,
   a. the less likely they are to conform to informational social influence.
   b. the more likely they are to conform to informational social influence.

   c. the more they seek to make that decision on their own, uninfluenced by what the people around them have to say.
   d. the more they will prefer public to private conformity.

4. Which of the following statements best captures the relationship between informational social influence and eyewitness performance in legal proceedings?
   a. Because the stakes are so high in a criminal trial, eyewitnesses do not conform to informational social influence.
   b. Eyewitnesses are encouraged to use informational social influence in providing their testimony at trial.
   c. The legal system often takes steps to prevent conformity to informational social influence among eyewitnesses.
   d. Informational social influence always makes eyewitnesses more accurate.

5. Informational social influence is most likely to occur when
   a. a situation is unambiguous and not a crisis.
   b. the other people around are not experts and the situation is not a crisis.
   c. the other people around are experts and the situation is ambiguous.
   d. a situation is a crisis but also unambiguous.

See page 621 for the answers.

Normative Social Influence: The Need to Be Accepted

8.3   How does normative social influence motivate people to conform?

They're called polar plunges, and they started out as charity fund-raisers: sanctioned events in which people take a quick swim in ice-cold water to attract donations and attention to a worthwhile cause. Groups like the Special Olympics carefully planned and organized them, limiting the amount of time people spent in the cold temperatures and making sure that medical personnel were on hand in case of complications. But by early 2014, school districts across New England (and other cold-climate locales) were e-mailing parents to warn them about polar plunge dares that were spreading virally among adolescents via social media (Wilson, 2014). Teenagers were challenging each other to jump into freezing water without life vests, with no adult supervision, and often at night—when temperatures were even lower and visibility was poor. Many accepted the dares, filming their dangerous feats and then posting them on Facebook and YouTube. But some weren't so lucky, with multiple injuries and at least one death reported in New Hampshire, where melting snow increased water levels and the speed of river currents, making a jump into frigid waters a potentially life-threatening leap (Phillip, 2014).

Why do people engage in such risky behavior? Why does anyone follow the group's lead when the resulting behavior is far from sensible and may even be fatal? We doubt that the Facebook polar plungers risked their lives due to informational conformity. It is difficult to argue that a high school student staring at a rushing winter river filled with ice and other debris would say, "Gee, I don't know what to do. I guess

Polar plunges started as sanctioned and carefully planned fund-raisers such as the one depicted here. But when teenagers started daring each other to jump into icy-cold water on their own and post videos of these exploits online, the desire to be accepted and liked by others led to dangerous and even deadly behavior.

jumping in there makes sense." This example suggests that there must be something else besides the need for information that can explain conformity. And there is: We also conform so that we will be liked and accepted by other people (Maxwell, 2002). We conform to the group's **social norms**—implicit (and sometimes explicit) rules for acceptable behaviors, values, and beliefs (Deutsch & Gerard, 1955; Kelley, 1955; Miller & Prentice, 1996; Sanfey, Stallen, & Chang, 2014). Groups have certain expectations about how their members should behave, and members in good standing conform to these rules. Members who do not are perceived as different, difficult, and eventually deviant. In the social media era, these norms are transmitted faster than ever. As one New Hampshire school principal noted in discussing the polar plunge fad, these days "you can start a trend like this very quickly, and it jumps exponentially. I think that's exactly what's happening here" (Wilson, 2014).

Of course, conformity to social norms isn't always dangerous. It isn't even always a bad thing. Consider another recent, even more widespread phenomenon involving icy water, this one resulting in a record-setting effort to *save* lives. As anyone on social media knows, in the summer of 2014, the "ice bucket challenge" went viral. Inspired by online posts from Pete Frates, a former college baseball player battling amyotrophic lateral sclerosis (ALS, or Lou Gehrig's disease as it is also known), Facebook exploded with videos of people dumping ice water on themselves and challenging particular friends to do the same. In one version of the challenge, those who were named were supposed to donate $10 to the ALS Association if they agreed to a public soaking within 24 hours, $100 if they didn't. By August 2014, the ice bucket challenge was everywhere, with celebrities including LeBron James, Bill Gates, Justin Bieber, Kerry Washington, Lady Gaga, and George W. Bush joining in. Some derided the phenomenon as "slacktivism," suggesting that people were more interested in having fun online than saving lives. But it's hard to argue with the numbers: According to the ALS Association (ALSA), donations during the height of the ice bucket craze totaled over $100 million, up from $2.8 million during the same time period the year before, and including over 3 million new donors (ALSA, 2014).

Why is normative conformity like that demonstrated by these Facebook trends so powerful? One reason is that deviant group members—those who go against the flow—are often ridiculed, punished, or even rejected by other group members (Abrams, Palmer, Rutland, Cameron, & Vajn de Vyer, 2014; James & Olson, 2000;

Social Norms

The implicit or explicit rules a group has for the acceptable behaviors, values, and beliefs of its members

Customs do not concern themselves with right or wrong or reason. But they have to be obeyed; one reasons all around them until [one] is tired, but [one] must not transgress them, it is sternly forbidden.

—Mark Twain

Miller & Anderson, 1979). For example, in Japan, a whole class (or even the entire school) will sometimes turn against one student perceived as different, alternately harassing and shunning the individual. In a highly cohesive, group-oriented culture such as Japan, this kind of treatment can have tragic results: Twelve teenage victims of bullying killed themselves in one year (Jordan, 1996). Another social phenomenon in Japan is the *hikikomori*, teenagers (mostly male) who have withdrawn from all social interaction. They spend all their time alone, in their bedrooms in their parents' homes. Some *hikikomori* have remained sequestered for over a decade. Japanese psychologists state that many *hikikomori* were the victims of severe bullying before their withdrawal (Jones, 2006). Recently, researchers in the United States and Great Britain have begun to study cyberbullying in middle and secondary schools. This form of bullying, using cell phones and the Internet, is increasingly frequent, affecting as many as 11% of middle school children (Kowalski, Giumetti, Schroeder, & Lattanner, 2014; Wilton & Campbell, 2011).

We human beings are by nature a social species. Few of us could live happily as hermits, never seeing or talking to another person. Through interactions with others, we receive emotional support, affection, and love, and we partake of enjoyable experiences. Other people are extraordinarily important to our sense of well-being. Research on individuals who have been isolated for long periods of time indicates that being deprived of human contact is stressful, traumatic, and psychologically painful (Baumeister & Leary, 1995; Schachter, 1959; Williams & Nida, 2011).

Given this fundamental human need for social companionship, it is not surprising that we often conform to gain acceptance from others. Conformity for normative reasons occurs in situations where we do what other people are doing, not because we are using them as a source of information but so that we won't attract negative attention, be made fun of, get into trouble, or be rejected. Thus, **normative social influence** occurs when the influence of other people leads us to conform in order to be liked and accepted. This type of conformity results in public compliance with the group's beliefs and behaviors but not necessarily in private acceptance (Cialdini, Kallgren, & Reno, 1991; Deutsch & Gerard, 1955; Nail, McDonald, & Levy, 2000).

You probably don't find it too surprising that people sometimes conform to be liked and accepted by others. You might be thinking, where's the harm? If the group is important to us and wearing the right clothes or using the right slang will gain us acceptance, why not go along? But when it comes to more important kinds of behaviors, such as hurting another person, surely we will resist such conformity pressures. And, of course, we won't conform when we are certain of the correct way of behaving and the pressures are coming from a group that we don't care all that much about. Or will we?

In August 2014, the "ice bucket challenge" exploded on social media, capitalizing on normative conformity to raise unprecedented amounts of money in the battle against ALS. Here, one of millions of participants takes her turn with the challenge, with a little help from an overeager friend and photographer.

Normative Social Influence

Going along with what other people do in order to be liked and accepted by them; we publicly conform with the group's beliefs and behaviors but do not always privately accept them

Conformity and Social Approval: The Asch Line-Judgment Studies

Solomon Asch (1951, 1956) conducted a series of now-classic studies exploring the power of normative social influence. Asch devised the studies assuming that there are limits to how much people will conform. Naturally, people conformed in the Sherif studies (see page 252), he reasoned, because the situation was highly ambiguous—trying to guess how many inches a light was moving. But when a situation was wholly unambiguous, Asch expected that people would act like rational, objective problem solvers. When the group said or did something that contradicted an obvious truth, surely people would resist social pressures and decide for themselves what was going on.

To test his hypothesis, Asch conducted the following study. Had you been a participant, you would have been told that this was an experiment on perceptual judgment and that you'd be taking part with seven other students. Here's the scenario: The experimenter shows everyone two cards, one with a single line on it and the other with three lines labeled 1, 2, and 3. He asks each of you to judge and then announce out loud which of the three lines on the second card is closest in length to the line on the first card (see Figure 8.2).

It is crystal clear that the correct answer is the second line. Not surprisingly, each participant says, "Line 2." Your turn comes next to last, and, of course, you say, "Line 2" as well. The last participant concurs. The experimenter then presents a new set of cards and asks the participants again to make their judgments and announce them out loud. Again, the answer is obvious, and everyone gives the correct answer. At this point, you are probably thinking, "What a waste of time. I've got a paper due tomorrow. I need to get out of here."

As your mind starts to wander, though, something surprising happens. The experimenter presents a third set of lines, and again the answer is obvious—line 3 is clearly the closest in length to the target line. But the first participant announces that the correct answer is line 1! "This guy must be so bored that he fell asleep," you think. Then the second person announces that line 1 is the correct answer. The third, fourth, fifth, and sixth participants all agree; it's now your turn. Startled at this point, you are probably looking at the lines very closely to see if you missed something. But no, line 3 is clearly the right answer. What will you do? Will you stand up for what you believe to be the truth, blurting out, "Line 3," or will you go along with the group and give the obviously wrong answer, "Line 1"?

As you can see, Asch set up a situation to discover if people would conform even when the right answer was absolutely obvious. In each group, all the individuals except for the actual participant were confederates of the research team

Figure 8.2 Asch's Line—Judgment Task

In a series of studies of normative social influence, participants judged which of the three comparison lines on the right was closest in length to the standard line on the left. The correct answer was always obvious (as it is here). However, members of the group (actually confederates) gave the wrong answer out loud. Now the participant faced a dilemma: Give the right answer and go against the whole group, or conform to their behavior and give an obviously wrong answer?

(Adapted from Asch, 1956)

Standard line

Comparison lines

Participants in an Asch line study. The real participant is seated in the middle. He is surrounded by the experimenter's accomplices, who have just given the wrong answer on the line task.

who had been instructed to give the wrong answer on 12 of the 18 trials. What happened? Contrary to what Asch expected, a considerable amount of conformity occurred: Seventy-six percent of the participants conformed and gave an obviously incorrect response on at least one trial. On average, people conformed on about one-third of the trials on which the accomplices gave an incorrect answer (see Figure 8.3).

Why did people conform so much of the time? Participants couldn't have needed information from others to help them make a decision, as they did in the Sherif study, because the situation was not ambiguous. The right answers were so obvious that when people in a control group made the judgments by themselves, they were accurate more than 98% of the time. Instead, normative pressures came into play. Even though the other participants were strangers, the fear of being the lone dissenter was so strong that most people conformed, at least occasionally. One participant explained, "Here was a group; they had a definite idea; my idea disagreed; this might arouse anger . . . I was standing out [like] a sore thumb . . . I didn't want particularly to make a fool of myself . . . I felt I was definitely right . . . [but] they might think I was peculiar" (Asch, 1956).

These are classic normative reasons for conforming: People go along anyway so as not to feel peculiar or look foolish. Notably, in contrast to informational social influence, normative pressures usually result in *public compliance without private acceptance*; people go along with the group even if they think it is wrong or do not believe in what they are doing.

What was especially surprising about Asch's results is that people were concerned about looking foolish even in front of complete strangers. It is not as if the participants were in danger of being ostracized by a group that was important to them. Yet decades of research since the original Asch study have indicated that conformity for normative reasons can occur simply because we do not want to risk social disapproval, even from complete strangers we will never see again (Bond & Smith, 1996; Chen, Wu, Tong, Guan, & Zhou, 2012; Cialdini & Goldstein, 2004).

In a variation of his study, Asch (1957) demonstrated just how powerful social disapproval can be in shaping behavior. As before, the confederates gave the wrong answer 12 out of 18 times, but in this version the actual participants were the only ones allowed to write down their answers on a piece of paper instead of saying them out loud. Now people did not have to worry about what the group thought of them because the group would never find out what their answers were. Conformity dropped dramatically, occurring on an average of only 1.5 of the 12 trials (Insko, Smith, Alicke, Wade, & Taylor, 1985; Nail, 1986). As Serge Moscovici (1985) observed, the Asch studies are "one of the most dramatic illustrations of conformity, of blindly going along with the group, even when the individual realizes that by doing so he turns his back on reality and truth" (p. 349).

Research by Gregory Berns and his colleagues has provided biological evidence for just how unpleasant and uncomfortable it is to resist

> It isn't difficult to keep alive, friends—just don't make trouble—or if you must make trouble, make the sort of trouble that's expected.
>
> —ROBERT BOLT,
> *A MAN FOR ALL SEASONS*

Figure 8.3 Results of the Asch Line—Judgment Study

Participants in the Asch line study showed a surprising level of conformity, given how obvious it was that the group was wrong in its judgments. Seventy-six percent of the participants conformed on at least one trial; only 24% of participants never conformed at all (see bar labeled zero). Most participants conformed on one to three of the 12 trials in which the group gave the wrong answer. However, a sizable number of participants conformed to the group's incorrect response nearly every single time (see the two bars on the right).

(Adapted from Asch, 1957)

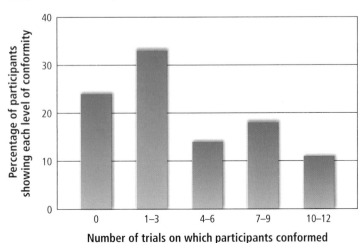

normative social influence (Berns et al., 2005). Berns and his research team used functional magnetic resonance imaging (fMRI) to examine the changes in brain activity of research participants as they either normatively conformed to a group's judgment or maintained their independence and disagreed with the group.

Instead of judgments of line length, the task in this study involved mental rotation. While in the fMRI scanner, participants were shown a three-dimensional figure and then asked if a second figure (rotated in a different direction) was the same as the first figure or different. They indicated their answers by pushing a button. The task was slightly more difficult than Asch's line-judgment task; the baseline error rate, when participants made judgments alone, was 13.8%, compared to Asch's (1951, 1956) baseline error rate of 2%.

Before being placed in the fMRI scanner, participants met and interacted with four other participants who were, as you've probably guessed, actually confederates. These four would be doing the same mental rotation task, but only the participant would have his or her brain activity monitored. During the task, the participant completed one-third of the trials with no knowledge of the answers of the other four people. On the remaining two-thirds of the trials, the participant saw the other four group members' answers on a visual display. Half of the time, the group had all chosen the wrong answer, and the other half of the time, they had all chosen the right answer.

Now, what did the participants do, and, most important, what areas of their brains were more active when they did it? First, as with the original Asch study, participants conformed to the group's wrong answers a fair amount of the time (41% of the trials, to be exact). On the baseline trials, when the participants answered alone, the fMRI results indicated increased activity in the posterior brain areas dedicated to vision and perception. When the participants conformed to the group's wrong answers, activation occurred in the same areas; however, when participants chose to give the right answer and thus disagree with the group's unanimous wrong answer, the visual/perceptual areas of the brain were not activated. Instead, different areas of the brain became more active: the amygdala, an area devoted to negative emotions, and the right caudate nucleus, an area devoted to modulating social behavior (Berns et al., 2005). Thus, more recent brain-imaging research has continued to explore the same issues Asch first examined six decades ago and has provided support for the idea that normative social influence occurs because people feel negative emotions, such as discomfort and tension, when they go against the group (Chen et al., 2012; Shestakova et al., 2013).

The Importance of Being Accurate, Revisited

Now, you may be thinking, "Okay, so we conform to normative social influence, but hey, only when it's something little. Who cares whether you give the right answer on a line-judgment task? It doesn't matter, nothing is at stake—I'd never conform to the group's wrong answer if something important were involved!" And this would be a very good criticism. Recall our discussion of importance in connection with informational social influence; we found that in ambiguous situations, the more important the decision a person has to make, the more the person conforms for informational reasons. What about in nonambiguous situations? Maybe the more important the decision is, the less the person would conform? When it's important to you to be right, are you strong enough to withstand group pressure and disagree with the group?

Recall the first study of eyewitness identification that we discussed earlier, in which Baron and his colleagues (Baron et al., 1996) included experimental conditions that triggered social influence. In the research, participants viewed pairs of slides, one of the perpetrator alone and one of the perpetrator in a lineup. Participants watched the slides in groups with two confederates. When studying informational conformity, the researchers made the task fiendishly difficult and therefore ambiguous—the slides were projected for only half a second. In order to study normative social influence, however, the researchers made the same task ridiculously easy: The participants viewed each slide for a full 5 seconds, and they were shown each pair of slides twice. Now the task becomes analogous to Asch's line-judging task; basically, if you're awake, you'll get the right answer. Baron and colleagues proved that the task was easy by having individuals in a control group each view the slides alone. The controls answered correctly on 97% of the trials.

Baron and colleagues again manipulated the importance of the participants being accurate, in the same ways we discussed earlier. Half were led to believe that it was very important that they give the right answers, and half were told it really didn't matter how they did. Now how did participants respond when the confederates give the obviously wrong answer? Did they conform to the group on at least some of the trials, as the participants in the Asch study did? Or did the participants who believe accuracy is very important give the correct answers every time, standing up to the group and ignoring the normative pressure to agree with them?

The researchers found that participants in the low-importance condition conformed to the group on 33% of the critical trials—very close to the rate in Asch's line-judgment task. What happened to the participants in the high-importance condition? Rather than standing up to the group across the board, they caved in on at least some trials. They did conform less to the obviously wrong answers of the group; on only 16% of the critical trials did they echo the group's blatantly wrong answer. But they still conformed sometimes! These findings underscore the power of normative social influence: Even when the group is wrong, the right answer is obvious, and there are strong incentives to be accurate, some people still find it difficult to risk social disapproval, even from strangers (Baron et al., 1996; Hornsey, Majkut, Terry, & McKimmie, 2003). And as the examples of polar plunging by dare demonstrate, this desire to be accepted can have tragic consequences.

Fads are another fairly frivolous example of normative social influence. By 2007, the Crocs fad was in full force as kids (and parents) everywhere could be found out and about in these plastic clogs with Swiss-cheese holes. Just a few years later, reviews are decidedly more mixed: anti-Croc pages with more than a million followers have sprouted up on Facebook and Twitter.

Normative social influence most closely reflects the negative stereotype of conformity we referred to earlier: the belief that those who conform are spineless and weak. Ironically, while this type of social pressure can be difficult to resist, people are often quick to deny that they've been influenced by normative considerations. Recall the energy conservation study by Nolan and colleagues (2008) described earlier. In this study, researchers assessed the effectiveness of different arguments for reducing electricity use among Californians. The most effective persuasive message was telling consumers that their neighbors were conserving energy. But participants *believed* that this message had little effect on them, especially compared to participants who received information regarding protecting the environment or saving money. As Nolan and her coauthors conclude, we often underestimate the power of normative social influence.

But your denial that normative pressures affect you doesn't stop others from trying to exert influence through such processes. How else to explain why some television producers hire professional laughers to sit in the studio audience to make their comedies seem funnier (Warner, 2011)? Or why some sports teams pay abnormally enthusiastic fans to rile up fellow spectators at their home games (Sommers, 2011)? Clearly, the desire to fit in and be accepted is part of human nature, whether or not we're willing to admit it. Just think of the role normative social influence plays on a day-to-day basis. For example, although few of us are slaves to fashion, we tend to wear what is considered appropriate and stylish at a given time. Men's wide neckties, popular in the 1970s, gave way to narrow ties in the 1980s before widening again in the 1990s and seeing a resurgence of skinny ties today; women's hemlines dropped from mini to maxi and then rose again. Normative social influence is at work whenever you notice a particular look shared by people in a certain group, and, no matter what it is, it will look outdated just a few years later until the fashion industry revives it in a new trend.

The Consequences of Resisting Normative Social Influence

One way to observe the power of normative social pressure is to examine the consequences when people manage to resist it. Indeed, entire television empires have been built around this very premise, that violating norms has consequences, and those consequences can be entertaining—at least when it's someone else suffering them and not you. *Seinfeld, Curb Your Enthusiasm, Louie,* and other shows that inspire a potent mixture of laughter and cringing among viewers have become cult (and sometimes mainstream) classics by mining the comedic landscape that is resisting normative social influence.

In your own life, if a person refuses to do as the group asks and thereby violates its norms, what happens? Think about the norms that operate in your group of friends. Some friends have an egalitarian norm for making group decisions. For example, when choosing a movie, everyone gets to state a preference; the choice is then discussed until agreement is reached. What would happen if, in a group with this kind of norm, you stated at the outset that you wanted to see only *Rebel Without a Cause* and would not agree to watch anything else? Your friends would be surprised by your behavior; they would also be annoyed with you or even angry. If you continued to disregard the friendship norms of the group by failing to conform, two things would most likely happen. First, the group would try to bring you "back into the fold," chiefly through increased communication. Teasing comments and long discussions would ensue as your friends tried to figure out why you were acting so strangely and tried to get you to conform to their expectations (Garfinkle, 1967). If these tactics didn't work, your friends would most likely say negative things to you and about you and start to withdraw from you (Festinger & Thibaut, 1951). Now, in effect, you've been rejected (Abrams, Marques, Brown, & Henson, 2000; Hornsey, Jetten, McAuliffe, & Hogg, 2006; Jetten & Hornsey, 2014; Marques, Abrams, & Serodio, 2001; Milgram & Sabini, 1978).

Stanley Schachter (1951) demonstrated how the group responds to an individual who ignores normative influence. He asked groups of college students to read and discuss a case history of "Johnny Rocco," a juvenile delinquent. Most of the students took a middle-of-the-road position about the case, believing that Rocco should receive a judicious mixture of love and discipline. Unbeknownst to the participants, however, Schachter had planted an accomplice in the group who was instructed to disagree with the group's recommendations. The accomplice consistently argued that Rocco should receive the harshest amount of punishment, regardless of what the other group members argued.

How was the deviant treated? He became the target of the most comments and questions from the real participants throughout most of the discussion, and then, near the end, communication with him dropped sharply. The other group members had tried to convince the deviant to agree with them; when it appeared that it wouldn't work, they started to ignore him altogether. In addition, they punished him. After the discussion, they were asked to fill out questionnaires that supposedly pertained to

> Success or failure lies in conformity to the times.
> —Niccolò Machiavelli, *The Prince*

Whether through stand-up routines in which he explores taboo topics and embarrassing revelations that most of us would never address in public or via his sitcom alterego who once showed up to a Black-tie gala in the Hamptons in a T-shirt and jeans, Louis CK is one contemporary comedian who produces many of his laughs (and cringeworthy moments) by exploring the consequences of norm violation.

future discussion meetings of their group. The participants were asked to nominate one group member who should be eliminated from further discussions if the group size had to be reduced. They nominated the deviant. They were also asked to assign group members to various tasks in future discussions. They assigned the unimportant or boring jobs, such as taking notes, to the deviant. Social groups are well versed in how to bring a nonconformist into line. No wonder we respond as often as we do to normative pressures! You can find out what it's like to resist normative social influence in the following Try It!

TRY IT!
Unveiling Normative Social Influence by Breaking the Rules

One way to find out the norms of a given culture is noticing the reaction of others when you happen to break those norms. For example, standing on the right side of the escalator in Singapore would earn you looks of disdain from others. Reserving your seat using a pack of tissue is relatively common in Singapore, but may seem confusing to others. What are some of the norms common in your culture?

Suppose someone from a relatively different culture has broken the norms you have listed. Would you expect someone in your culture and their culture to react similarly? Why or why not?

Try having a conversation with a friend and stand either too close or too far away (e.g., 1 foot or 7 feet). Have a typical, normal conversation with your friend—only the spacing you use with this person should be different. Note how your friend responds. If you're too close, your friend will probably back away; if you continue to keep the distance small, he or she may act uncomfortable and even end your conversation sooner than usual. If you're too far away, your friend will probably come

closer; if you back up, he or she may think you are in a strange mood. In either case, your friend's response will probably include looking at you a lot, having a puzzled look on his or her face, acting uncomfortable or confused, and talking less than normal or ending the conversation.

You have acted in a nonnormative way, and your conversational partner is, first, trying to figure out what is going on and, second, responding in a way to get you to stop acting oddly. From this one brief exercise, you will get the idea of what would happen if you behaved oddly all the time—people would try to get you to change, and then they would probably start avoiding or ignoring you.

When you're finished, "debrief" your friend, explaining the exercise, so that your behavior is understood. Note the tremendous relief you feel on revealing why you were acting so peculiarly. This is yet one more demonstration of the strength of normative pressure and the challenge inherent to resisting it!

When Will People Conform to Normative Social Influence?

Although conformity is common, people don't always cave in to peer pressure. After all, we certainly do not all agree on many major issues, such as abortion, affirmative action, or same-sex marriage. Exactly when are people most likely to conform to normative pressures? Some answers to this question are provided by Bibb Latané's (1981) **social impact theory**. According to his theory, the likelihood that you will respond to social influence depends on three variables regarding the group in question:

1. *Strength:* How important to you is the group?

2. *Immediacy:* How close is the group to you in space and time during the attempt to influence you?

3. *Number:* How many people are in the group?

Social Impact Theory

The idea that conforming to social influence depends on the group's importance, immediacy, and the number of people in the group

Social impact theory predicts that conformity will increase as strength and immediacy increase. Clearly, the more important a group is to us and the closer group members are to us physically, the more likely we will be to conform to its normative pressures.

Social influence operates differently when it comes to group size. As the size of the group increases, so does the normative pressure it exerts, but each additional person has less of an influencing effect—going from three people to four makes much more of a difference than going from 53 people to 54. If we feel pressure from a group to conform, adding another person to the majority makes a much bigger difference if the group is small rather than large. Latané constructed a mathematical model that captures these hypothesized effects of strength, immediacy, and number and has applied this formula to the results of many conformity studies (Bourgeois & Bowen, 2001; Latané & Bourgeois, 2001; Latané & L'Herrou, 1996; Wolf, 2014).

For example, gay men who live in communities highly involved in AIDS awareness activities (where strength, immediacy, and number would all be high) report feeling more social pressure to avoid risky sexual behavior and stronger intentions to do so than gay men who live in less involved communities (Fishbein et al., 1993). Similarly, a recent study of heterosexual dating couples (a relationship typically high in strength and immediacy) reveals that an individual's own tendency to engage in heavy drinking is significantly predicted by the norm set by his or her partner's drinking tendencies (Mushquash et al., 2011).

Let's see in more detail what social impact theory says about the conditions under which people will conform to normative social pressures.

WHEN THE GROUP GROWS LARGER   At what point does group size stop influencing conformity? Asch (1955) and later researchers found that conformity increases as the number of people in the group increase, but once the group reaches four or five other people, conformity does not increase much (Bond, 2005; Campbell & Fairey, 1989; Gerard, Wilhelmy, & Conolley, 1968)—just as social impact theory suggests (see Figure 8.4). In short, it does not take an extremely large group to create normative social influence, but the larger the group, the stronger the social pressure.

WHEN THE GROUP IS IMPORTANT   Another tenet of social impact theory is that the strength of the group—defined as how important the group is to us—makes a difference. Normative pressures are much stronger when they come from people whose friendship, love, and respect we cherish because there is a large cost to losing this love and respect (Abrams, Wetherell, Cochrane, Hogg, & Turner, 1990; Guimond, 1999; Hogg, 1992; Nowak, Szamrej, & Latané, 1990). One consequence of this conclusion is that it can be dangerous to have policy decisions made by highly cohesive groups because they care more about pleasing each other and avoiding conflict than arriving at the best, most logical decision. We will see several examples of this phenomenon in Chapter 9.

We should note, however, that the very act of conforming normatively to important groups *most* of the time can earn you the right to deviate occasionally without serious consequences. This interesting observation was made by Edwin Hollander (1960, 1985), who stated that conforming to a group over time earns you **idiosyncrasy credits**, much like putting money in the bank to save for future use. It's as if your past conformity allows you, at some point in the future, to deviate

Figure 8.4 Effects of Group Size on Conformity

Asch varied the size of the unanimous majority in his study and found that once the majority numbered four, adding more people had little influence on conformity.

(Based on Asch, 1955)

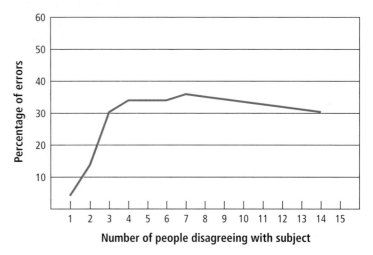

Idiosyncrasy Credits

The tolerance a person earns, over time, by conforming to group norms; if enough credits are earned, the person can, on occasion, deviate from the group without retribution from the group (to "make withdrawals") without getting into too much trouble. Let's say, for example, that your friends are all in agreement that they want to go out for Chinese food. You, however, feel like Mexican food tonight, and rather than simply going along with group consensus, you decide to stick to your guns and lobby for burritos. If you have typically followed their friendship norms in other areas in the past, your friends will be less likely to become upset with you for your current nonconformity, for you've earned the right to deviate from their normative rules in this area on this occasion (Hornsey, Grice, Jetten, Paulsen, & Callan, 2007; Jetten & Hornsey, 2014).

WHEN ONE HAS NO ALLIES IN THE GROUP   Normative social influence is most powerfully felt when everyone in the group says or believes the same thing—for example, when your group of friends all believe that *The Lord of the Rings* was the greatest movie trilogy ever made. Resisting such unanimous social influence is difficult or even impossible, unless you have an ally. If another person disagrees with the group—say, by nominating the original *Star Wars* movies as the best trilogy ever—this behavior will help you buck the tide as well.

To test the importance of having an ally, Asch (1955) conducted another version of his conformity experiment. He had six of the seven confederates give the wrong answer, while one confederate gave the right answer on every trial. The subject was no longer alone. Although still disagreeing with the majority of the group, having one ally dramatically changed the situation, helping the subject resist normative pressures. People conformed on an average of only 6% of the trials in this study, compared to 32% when all of the confederates gave the wrong answer. Several other studies have found that observing another person resist normative social influence emboldens the individual to do the same (Allen & Levine, 1969; Morris & Miller, 1975; Nemeth & Chiles, 1988).

The difficulty of being the lone dissenter is apparent even in the U.S. Supreme Court. After hearing a case, the nine justices first determine, informally, whether they are unanimous or split in their decision. Some justices then write opinion drafts and others decide which draft they will sign. There are informal attempts at influence, and eventually all make a decision. A content analysis of all the Supreme Court decisions from 1953 to 2001 (4,178 decisions, involving 29 different justices) indicated that the most common decision was the 9–0, unanimous one (35% of all decisions). And the least common decision? The one that required one justice to disagree with all of his or her colleagues, the 8–1 split, which accounted for only 10% of decisions over 48 years (Granberg & Bartels, 2005).

WHEN THE GROUP'S CULTURE IS COLLECTIVISTIC   "In America, the squeaky wheel gets the grease. In Japan, the nail that stands out gets pounded down" (Markus & Kitayama, 1991, p. 224). Is it true that the society in which one is raised affects the frequency of normative social influence? Perhaps not surprisingly, the answer is yes. Stanley Milgram (1961, 1977) replicated the Asch studies in Norway and France and found that the Norwegian participants conformed to a greater degree than the French participants did. Milgram (1961, p. 51) describes Norwegian society as "highly cohesive," with "a deep feeling of group identification," while French society, in comparison, shows "far less consensus in both social and political life." In another cross-cultural study of normative social influence, people in Lebanon, Hong Kong, and Brazil conformed to a similar extent (both to each other and to the American sample), whereas participants from the Bantu tribe of Zimbabwe conformed to a much greater degree (Whittaker & Meade, 1967). As the researchers pointed out, conformity has a very high social value in Bantu culture.

Although Japanese culture is more highly conforming than American culture in many areas, two Asch-type studies found that when the group unanimously gave the incorrect answer, Japanese students were less conformist in general than North

Americans (Frager, 1970; Williams & Sogon, 1984). In Japan, cooperation and loyalty are directed to the groups to which one belongs and with which one identifies; there is little expectation that one should conform to the behavior of strangers, especially in such an artificial setting as a psychology experiment. Similarly, conformity was much higher in a British sample when the participants thought the other group members were psychology majors like themselves rather than art history majors (Abrams et al., 1990). Similarly, German research participants have shown less conformity in the Asch experiment than North Americans (Timaeus, 1968); in Germany, conformity to strangers is less valued than conformity to a few well-defined groups (Moghaddam, Taylor, & Wright, 1993).

A more systematic review of the role of culture in conformity is provided by a meta-analysis of 133 Asch line-judgment studies conducted in 17 countries: the United States, Canada, Britain, France, the Netherlands, Belgium, Germany, Portugal, Japan, Hong Kong, Fiji, Zimbabwe, Congo, Ghana, Brazil, Kuwait, and Lebanon (Bond & Smith, 1996). Participants from more collectivistic cultures showed higher rates of conformity on the line task than participants from more individualistic cultures. In collectivistic cultures, conformity is seen as a valued trait, not as a somewhat negative one. Agreeing with others is viewed not as an act of submission or cowardice in collectivist cultures but as an act of tact and sensitivity (Hodges & Geyer, 2006; Smith & Bond, 1999). Because the emphasis is on the group and not the individual, people in collectivistic cultures value normative social influence because it promotes harmony and supportive relationships in the group (Guisinger & Blatt, 1994; Kim, Triandis, Kagitcibasi, Choi, & Yoon, 1994; Markus et al., 1996; Zhang, Lowry, Zhou, & Fu, 2007).

J. W. Berry (1967; Kim & Berry, 1993) explored the issue of conformity as a cultural value by comparing two cultures that had very different strategies for accumulating food. He hypothesized that societies that relied on hunting or fishing would value independence, assertiveness, and adventurousness—traits needed to find and bring home food. He also postulated that societies that were primarily agricultural would value cooperativeness, conformity, and acquiescence—traits that made close living and interdependent farming more successful. Berry used an Asch-type conformity task to compare the Inuit people of Baffin Island in Canada, a hunting and fishing society, to the Temne of Sierra Leone in Africa, a farming society. Consistent with

The extent to which conformity is valued varies across cultures. In the Opening Ceremony of the 2008 Beijing Olympics, a worldwide television audience was mesmerized by the sight of 2,008 drummers performing in perfect synchronization.

Berry's hypothesis, the Temne showed a significant tendency to accept the suggestions of fellow group members in the study, while the Inuit almost completely disregarded them. As one Temne put it, "When the Temne people choose a thing, we must all agree with the decision—this is what we call cooperation"; in contrast, the few times the Inuit did conform to the group's wrong answer, they did so with "a quiet, knowing smile" (Berry, 1967, p. 417).

Minority Influence: When the Few Influence the Many

We shouldn't leave our discussion of normative social influence with the impression that groups affect individuals but the individual never has an effect on the group. As Serge Moscovici (1985, 1994; Moscovici, Mucchi-Faina, & Maass, 1994) says, if groups always succeeded in silencing nonconformists, rejecting deviants, and persuading everyone to go along with the majority point of view, how could change ever be introduced into the system? We would all be little robots, marching along with everyone else in monotonous synchrony, never able to adapt to changing reality. Clearly, this is not the case (Imhoff & Erb, 2009).

Instead, an individual or minority of group members can indeed influence the behavior or beliefs of the majority (Horcajo, Briñol, & Petty, 2014; Moscovici, 1985, 1994; Mucchi-Faina & Pagliaro, 2008; Sinaceur, Thomas-Hunt, Neale, O'Neill, & Haag, 2010). This is called **minority influence**. The key is consistency: People with minority views must express the same view over time, and different members of the minority must agree with one another. If a person in the minority wavers between two different viewpoints or if two individuals express different minority views, the majority will dismiss them as people who have peculiar and groundless opinions. If, however, the minority expresses a consistent, unwavering view, the majority is more likely to take notice and even adopt the minority view (Moscovici & Nemeth, 1974). For example, in the 1970s, a minority of scientists began to call attention to evidence of human-caused climate change. Today, the majority is paying attention, and political leaders from most industrialized nations have met to discuss possible worldwide solutions. As another example, in the 1960s, a minority of feminists began to address women as "Ms." instead of "Miss" or "Mrs." Today, "Ms." is the standard form of address in the workplace and many other contexts (Zimmer, 2009).

In a meta-analysis of nearly 100 studies, Wendy Wood and her colleagues describe how minority influence operates (Wood, Lundgren, Ouellette, Busceme, & Blackstone, 1994). People in the majority can cause other group members to conform through normative influence. As in the Asch experiments, the conformity that occurs may be a case of public compliance without private acceptance. People in the minority can rarely influence others through normative means, however. In fact, majority group members may be hesitant to agree publicly with the minority; they don't want anyone to think that they side with those unusual, strange views. Minorities therefore exert their influence on the group via the other principal method: informational social influence. The minority can introduce new and unexpected information to the group and cause the group to examine the issues more carefully. Such careful examination may cause the majority to realize that the minority view has merit, leading the group to adopt all or part of the minority's view. In short, majorities often obtain public compliance because of normative social influence, whereas minorities are more likely to achieve private acceptance because of informational social influence (De Dreu & De Vries, 2001; Levine, Moreland, & Choi, 2001; Wood, Pool, Leck, & Purvis, 1996).

Minority Influence

The case where a minority of group members influences the behavior or beliefs of the majority

---

Never let anyone keep you contained, and never let anyone keep your voice silent.

—ADAM CLAYTON POWELL

REVIEW QUESTIONS

1. Societal rules regarding acceptable behavior are known as
   a. contagion.
   b. social norms.
   c. minority influence.
   d. convergence.

2. Asch's line-judgment research indicated that
   a. participants demonstrated public conformity without private acceptance.
   b. every single participant conformed at least one time.
   c. conformity was greater when participants wrote down their responses rather than said them aloud.
   d. conformity occurs only on a task that is of personal importance to the individual.

3. Compared to informational social influence, normative social influence
   a. leads to more internalized, private attitude change.
   b. is more consistent across different cultures.
   c. has less to do with being accurate and more to do with fitting in.
   d. is a tendency about which most Americans hold positive attitudes.

4. A 12-person jury is deliberating on a murder trial. Eleven members of the jury want to vote guilty and convict the defendant; only one juror wants to vote not guilty. The holdout juror, Henry, digs in and will not change his mind. According to research, what is the best prediction for how the rest of the group will react to Henry's deviance?
   a. They will eventually come to ignore him and try to punish him by being generally unpleasant toward him.
   b. They will come to appreciate his principled stand the longer he holds out in defiance of their position.
   c. They will seek to change his opinion by using idiosyncrasy credits.
   d. They will try to use minority influence to change his mind.

5. Which of the following conclusions is consistent with the predictions of social impact theory?
   a. Conformity is more likely among groups of strangers than within established groups that are important to us.
   b. Social influence increases in a linear fashion as a group grows in size; in other words, each new member added to a group adds the same amount of social influence as the previous member added.
   c. The more immediate a group is, the more social influence it tends to exert.
   d. Conformity is less prevalent in collectivist cultures than it is in individualistic cultures.

6. The key to minority influence is
   a. normative social pressure.
   b. immediacy.
   c. creativity.
   d. consistency.

See page 621 for the answers.

Strategies for Using Social Influence

8.4 **How can people use their knowledge of social influence to influence others?**

We have seen how informational and normative conformity occurs. Even in a highly individualistic culture such as the United States, conformity of both types is common. Are there ways that we can put this tendency to good, productive use? Can we capitalize on conformity to change behavior for the common good? The answer is a resounding yes.

Consider a "61-million-person" experiment conducted via Facebook during the 2010 U.S. congressional elections (Bond et al., 2012). On Election Day, researchers arranged for millions of Facebook users to receive either an informational or a social message about voting (a control group received no message at all). The informational message appeared at the top of their "News Feed" and provided a link for finding their local polling place as well as an "I Voted" button they could click to update friends with the news that they had voted. The social message included this same information but with one addition: It told users how many of their own Facebook friends had also voted, showing them a randomly selected set of six photos of these voting friends. Compared to the control condition, the informational message had little impact on users' own likelihood of voting. But Facebook users who received

We can capitalize on the tendency to conform to change behavior for the common good, as in the effort to use social media messages to increase voter turnout.

People create social conditions and people can change them.

—Tess Onwueme

Injunctive Norms

People's perceptions of what behaviors are approved or disapproved of by others

Descriptive Norms

People's perceptions of how people actually behave in given situations, regardless of whether the behavior is approved or disapproved of by others

the social message were significantly more likely to vote, as measured by their likelihood of clicking the site's "I Voted" button as well as actual voting records (Bond et al., 2012). These findings highlight just how powerful it can be to learn what others are up to—in fact, Bond et al. (2012) found that even seeing the social message posted to a friend's News Feed (not by one of *your* friends but by someone else your friend knows) was enough to have an indirect influence on a Facebook user's own voting behavior.

The Role of Injunctive and Descriptive Norms

Robert Cialdini, Raymond Reno, and Carl Kallgren have suggested that social norms are particularly useful for subtly inducing people to conform to positive, socially approved behavior (Cialdini, Kallgren, & Reno, 1991; Jacobson, Mortensen, & Cialdini, 2011; Kallgren, Reno, & Cialdini, 2000; Schultz et al., 2007). For example, we all know that littering is wrong. But when we've finished enjoying a snack at the beach or in a park, what determines whether we toss the wrapper on the ground or carry it with us until we come to a trash can? Let's say we wanted to decrease littering (or increase recycling or blood donations or contributions to other worthwhile causes). How would we go about doing it?

Cialdini and colleagues (1991) suggest that first we need to focus on what kind of norm is operating in the situation. A culture's social norms are of two types. **Injunctive norms** have to do with what we *think* other people approve or disapprove of. Injunctive norms motivate behavior by promising rewards (or punishments) for normative (or nonnormative) behavior. For example, an injunctive norm in our culture is that littering is wrong and that donating blood is a good thing to do. **Descriptive norms** concern our perceptions of the way people *actually* behave in a given situation, regardless of whether the behavior is approved or disapproved of by others. Descriptive norms motivate behavior by informing people about what is effective or adaptive behavior. For example, while we all know that littering is wrong (an injunctive norm), we also all know that there are situations when people are likely to do it (a descriptive norm)—for example, dropping peanut shells on the ground at a baseball game or leaving trash at your seat in a movie theater. Descriptive norms also tell us that relatively few people donate blood and that only a small percentage of registered voters actually vote. In sum, an injunctive norm relates to what most people in a culture approve or disapprove of; a descriptive norm relates to what people actually do (Kallgren et al., 2000; White, Smith, Terry, Greenslade, & McKimmie, 2009).

In a series of studies, Cialdini and colleagues have explored how injunctive and descriptive norms affect people's likelihood to litter. For example, in one field experiment, patrons of a city library were returning to their cars in the parking lot when a confederate approached them (Reno, Cialdini, & Kallgren, 1993). In the control group, the confederate just walked by. In the *descriptive norm condition*, the confederate dropped an empty bag from a fast-food restaurant on the ground before passing the participant. By littering, the confederate was subtly communicating that "this is what people do in this situation." In the *injunctive norm condition*, the confederate was not carrying anything but instead picked up a littered fast-food bag from the ground before passing the participant. By picking up someone else's litter, the confederate was subtly communicating that "littering is wrong." These three conditions occurred in one of two environments: Either the parking lot was heavily littered (ahead of time by the experimenters, using paper cups, candy wrappers, and so on), or the area was clean and unlittered (previously cleaned up by the experimenters).

At this point, research participants have been exposed to one of two types of norms about littering (or to no norm at all in a control group). And all this has happened in a littered or a clean environment. How were participants' own littering tendencies affected? When they got back to their cars, they found a large flyer slipped under the driver's side of the windshield. The flyer appeared on all the other cars too (not surprising since the experimenters put them there). The participant had two choices at this point: throw the flyer on the ground, littering, or bring the flyer inside their car to dispose of it later. What did they do? Who refrained from littering?

The control group tells us the baseline of what percentage of people typically litter in this situation. As you can see in Figure 8.5, the researchers found that slightly more than one-third of people threw the flyer on the ground; it didn't matter if the area was already littered or if it was clean. In the descriptive norm condition, the confederate's littering communicated two different messages, depending on the condition of the parking lot. In the littered parking lot, the confederate's behavior reminded participants that people often litter here—the confederate served as just one salient example of the type of behavior that had led to such a messy parking lot in the first place. In the clean parking lot, however, the confederate's behavior communicated a different message. Now, the behavior stood out as unusual—it reminded participants that most

Invoking conformity to social norms can be used in the effort to address societal problems such as littering.

Figure 8.5 The Effect of Injunctive and Descriptive Norms on Littering

The data for the control group (left) indicate that 37% to 38% of people litter a handbill found on their car windshield whether the environment (a parking lot) is littered or clean. When a descriptive norm is made salient, littering decreases significantly only in the clean environment (middle). When an injunctive norm is made salient, littering decreases significantly in both types of environment, indicating that injunctive norms are more consistently effective at changing behavior.

(Adapted from Reno, Cialdini, & Kallgren, 1993)

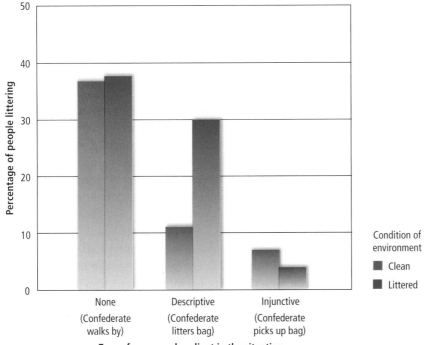

people don't litter in this area, which is why it looked so clean otherwise. Hence, we would expect the confederate's littering behavior to remind participants of a descriptive norm against littering in the clean environment, and this is what the researchers found. Finally, what about the injunctive norm condition? This kind of norm was less context dependent: Seeing the confederate picking up someone else's litter invokes the injunctive norm that littering is wrong in both the clean and the littered environments, thereby leading to the lowest amount of littering in the study (Reno et al., 1993).

In light of studies such as this one, researchers have concluded that injunctive norms are more powerful than descriptive norms in producing desirable behavior (Kallgren et al., 2000). This should not surprise you because injunctive norms tap into normative conformity—we conform (e.g., refraining from littering) because someone's behavior reminds us that our society disapproves of littering. We will look like selfish slobs if we litter, and we will feel embarrassed if other people see us litter. While norms are always present to some extent—we *know* that littering is bad—they are not always *salient* to us (Jonas et al., 2008; Kallgren et al., 2000). To promote socially beneficial behavior, something in the situation needs to draw our attention to the relevant norm. Thus, anything that highlights *injunctive norms*—what society approves and disapproves of—can be used to create positive behavioral change (Bodimeade et al., 2014).

Using Norms to Change Behavior: Beware the "Boomerang Effect"

Efforts to change behavior by using norms have a downside, however. As one example, in recent years, university administrators have tried a new technique for decreasing alcohol binge drinking on their campuses. The idea is that students typically overestimate how much their peers drink (Lewis, Belliveau, Herndon, & Keller, 2007; Perkins, 2007). Thus, telling them that "students at your school, on average, consume only X number of drinks a week" should lead them to decrease their own alcohol intake as they conform to this lower level. But researchers have noted a major problem with this approach: Sometimes, it backfires, or "boomerangs." That is, for students who already drink very little (or not at all), finding out that the average student on campus drinks more than they do leads them to *increase* their own alcohol intake to be more like everyone else! In short, the public service message meant to decrease alcohol consumption can actually have the effect of increasing it (Perkins, Haines, & Rice, 2005). Accordingly, your efforts to change others' behavior through processes of conformity must consider that there are different types of people receiving your message: those performing the undesirable behavior at an *above-average* level (whom you want to convince to decrease the behavior) and those performing the undesirable behavior at a *below-average* level (who you want to continue doing what they're already doing rather than to boomerang by increasing the undesirable behavior).

P. Wesley Shultz and colleagues tested this idea by focusing on a desirable behavior we've already discussed in this chapter: conserving electricity (Shultz et al., 2007). Residents of a California neighborhood agreed to take part in the study. Their baseline energy usage was measured, and they were divided into two groups: those whose energy consumption was above the average for their neighborhood and those whose energy consumption was below the average. The households were then randomly assigned to receive one of two kinds of feedback about their energy usage over several weeks. In the *descriptive norm condition*, they were told how much energy they had used that week, told how much energy the average household in their neighborhood had used (the descriptive norm information), and given suggestions for energy conservation. In the *descriptive norm plus injunctive norm condition*, they received all of the above information plus one subtle but important addition: If they had consumed less energy than the average household, the researcher drew a smiley face next to the information. If they had consumed more energy than the average

❄ **Last Winter Comparison** | You used **5% LESS** natural gas than your efficient neighbors.

Your usage last winter:

*Therms: Standard unit of measuring heat energy

Smiley faces aren't just for kids. In this case, they're part of an effort from a utility company to use injunctive norms to convince consumers to cut down on their energy use.

household, the researcher drew a sad face instead. The happy or sad face communicated the *injunctive* part of the message—the recipients were receiving either approval or disapproval for the amount of energy they had used.

Weeks later, researchers measured energy usage again. Did the messages help convince people to conserve energy? Did those who already used low amounts stray from the path of conservation righteousness and boomerang, deciding that it would not be so bad for them to be a little less efficient just like their wasteful neighbors? First, the results indicated that the descriptive norm message had a positive effect on those who consumed more energy than average; they cut back and conserved. However, the descriptive norm message had a boomerang effect on those who consumed less energy than average. Once they learned what their neighbors were doing (using electricity like crazy), they felt liberated to increase their own usage!

On the other hand, the "descriptive norm plus injunctive norm" message was uniformly successful. Those whose consumption was more than average decreased their usage when they received this message. Most important, those whose consumption was below average to begin with did not boomerang—they maintained their same, low level of energy use as before the study started. The smiley face reminded them that they were doing the right thing, and they kept on doing it (Schultz et al., 2007). This study has had a major impact on energy conservation strategies in the United States. The use of smiley and sad faces to give injunctive norm feedback, combined with descriptive norm energy-usage information, is now being used by utility companies in various major metropolitan areas, including Boston, Chicago, Sacramento, and Seattle (Kaufman, 2009).

Other Tactics of Social Influence

The savvy practitioner of social influence has more than one trick up his or her sleeve. Using norms is not the only way to change other people's behavior. For one, the sequence in which a series of requests is made also contributes to the effectiveness of social influence. Consider the following scenario: You are approached by someone identifying himself as a member of a group called Citizens for Safe Driving. His hope is that you'll be willing to support his group's campaign by placing a sign in your front yard for a week or so. He then shows you a photo of the sign in question. It's huge! It blocks much of the house in the picture, completely concealing the front door. To be honest, it's not a particularly attractive sign either; the "Drive Carefully" lettering even looks a bit crooked. Oh, and did we mention that it will probably require making holes in your lawn?

Our guess is that you aren't too excited at the prospects of adding this sign to your homestead, even on a temporary basis. Indeed, when Jonathan Freedman and

Would you agree to put a big sign in your yard, blocking the front of your house? Research on the door-in-the-face technique suggests that your answer might depend on whether or not you have already agreed to a smaller request first.

Foot-in-the-Door Technique

Social influence strategy in which getting people to agree first to a small request makes them more likely to agree later to a second, larger request

Door-in-the-Face Technique

Social influence strategy in which first asking people for a large request that they will probably refuse makes them more likely to agree later to a second, smaller request

Propaganda

A deliberate, systematic attempt to advance a cause by manipulating mass attitudes and behaviors, often through misleading or emotionally charged information

Scott Fraser (1966) made this very request of home owners in Palo Alto, California, they found just 17% willing to put the sign in their yard. But the researchers also figured out a way to make the same request seem much more agreeable: by first getting people to comply with a smaller request. Specifically, in another condition, the researchers first asked participants if they would place in their window a small, 3-inch sign that read, "Be a safe driver." Then, 2 weeks later, these participants were asked about putting up the larger (and uglier) yard sign, and a whopping 76% now agreed (Freedman & Fraser, 1966). This increase in compliance based on an earlier, smaller request is the **foot-in-the-door technique** in action—so named for the traveling salesman whose underlying strategy is to get at least one foot inside your house so you can't slam the door shut on him.

Why does it work? Think about what happens when you get people to agree to any request, even a small one. They start to see themselves as agreeable people. They feel committed to a helpful course of action. To say no to a follow-up request—even if it comes from a different person—could trigger uncomfortable feelings of inconsistency or dissonance (Burger, 1999; Cialdini, 2009; Pascual, Guéguen, Pujos, & Felonneau, 2013).

Interestingly, the opposite tactic also works. That is, another way to get people to agree to a request is first to ask them for a much larger commitment, one to which you know they'll say no. This is the **door-in-the-face technique**. In one study, Cialdini and colleagues (1975) approached college students and asked if they would be willing to spend 2 hours chaperoning a group of troubled children on a field trip to the local zoo. Only 17% of students agreed to this request. But consider the experience of other participants who were first asked about their willingness to volunteer every week for a minimum of 2 years at a local juvenile detention center. Every single one of the students refused this large request. But when they were then asked about chaperoning the 2-hour zoo trip, 50% agreed.

In short, people are also more likely to agree to the request you really care about when you first hit them up for a bigger favor that forces them to say no. One reason is that the first, bigger request makes the second "ask" seem less daunting by comparison. Another reason has to do with feelings of reciprocity (Chan & Au, 2011; Pascual & Guéguen, 2005). After all, it seems like you—the requestor—have made some concessions here, coming down from your initially huge favor to a more much manageable later request. To the target of your requests, it feels as if the least they can do is negotiate a bit as well, meeting you halfway and agreeing to something smaller. Of course, little do they know that it was this second, smaller request that you really cared about all along.

Are these strategies for social influence ones you can envision using in your own life? Or maybe you bristle at the thought of such conscious efforts to manipulate others? At the very least, newly aware of their existence, perhaps now you'll be on the lookout for those times when other people attempt to use them on you. The ethics of such tactics make for an interesting discussion. Less debatable, though, is the conclusion that social influence *can* be used to pursue illegal, immoral, and unconscionable aims. Consider the extraordinary example of **propaganda**, especially as perfected by the Nazi regime in the 1930s. Propaganda has been defined as "the deliberate, systematic attempt to shape perceptions, manipulate cognitions, and direct behavior to achieve a response that furthers the desired intent of the propagandist" (Jowett & O'Donnell, 1999, p. 6).

Adolf Hitler was well aware of the power of propaganda as a tool of the state. In 1933, he appointed Joseph Goebbels head of the newly created Nazi Ministry of

Popular Enlightenment and Propaganda. It was a highly efficient agency that permeated every aspect of Germans' lives, controlling all forms of media, including newspapers, films, and radio. The Nazis also disseminated their ideology through the extensive use of posters and "spectacles"—lavish public rallies that aroused powerful emotions of loyalty and patriotism among massive crowds (Jowett & O'Donnell, 1999). Nazi propaganda was taught in schools and further promoted in Hitler Youth groups. It always presented a consistent, dogmatic message: The German people must act to protect their racial purity and to increase their *Lebensraum* (living space) through conquest (Staub, 1989).

The concerns with *Lebensraum* led to World War II; the concerns with racial purity led to the Holocaust. How could the German people have acquiesced to the destruction of European Jewry? A major factor was prejudice (which we will discuss further in Chapter 13). Anti-Semitism was not a new Nazi idea; it had existed in Germany and the rest of Europe for hundreds of years. Propaganda is most successful when it taps into an audience's preexisting beliefs. Thus, the German people's anti-Semitism was strengthened and expanded by Goebbels's ministry. Jews were described in the Nazi propaganda as destroyers of Aryan racial purity and thus a threat to German survival. They were "pests, parasites, bloodsuckers" (Staub, 1989, p. 103) and were compared to "a plague of rats that needed to be exterminated" (Jowett & O'Donnell, 1999, p. 242). Still, anti-Semitism alone is not a sufficient explanation for the Holocaust. Germany was initially no more prejudiced against Jews than were its neighbors (or even the United States) in the 1930s, but none of these other countries came up with the genocidal concept of a "final solution" as Germany did (Tindale, Munier, Wasserman, & Smith, 2002).

One answer to the question of what made the Holocaust possible is propaganda, which operated in the form of persuasive messages leading to attitude change, as we discussed in Chapter 7. But the propaganda also initiated social influence processes, persuading many Germans through informational conformity. They learned new "facts" (which were really lies) about the Jews and new solutions to what the Nazis had defined as the "Jewish question." The propaganda did an excellent job of convincing Germans that the Jews were a threat. As we saw earlier, people experiencing a crisis—in this case, runaway inflation and economic collapse in Germany—are more likely to conform to information provided by others.

But surely, you are thinking, there must have been Germans who did not agree with the Nazi propaganda. Yes, there were, but it certainly wasn't easy to be one of them. The Nazi ideology so permeated daily life that children and teenagers in Hitler Youth groups were encouraged to spy on their own parents and report them to the Gestapo if they were not "good" Nazis (Staub, 1989). Neighbors, coworkers, salespeople in shops, or passersby on the street—they could all turn you in if you said or did something that indicated disloyalty. This situation is ripe for normative conformity, through which public compliance can occur even without private acceptance. Rejection, ostracism, and even torture or death were strong motivators for normative conformity, and many ordinary Germans conformed to Nazi propaganda. Whether they did so for informational or normative reasons, their conformity permitted the Holocaust to occur.

Nazi propaganda permeated all facets of German life in the 1930s and 1940s. Here, huge crowds attend the 1934 Nuremberg rally. Such large public gatherings were a technique frequently used by Goebbels and Hitler to promote loyalty and conformity to the Nazi party.

To swallow and follow, whether old doctrine or new propaganda, is a weakness still dominating the human mind.

—CHARLOTTE PERKINS GILMAN

REVIEW QUESTIONS

1. A _____ norm involves perceptions of which behaviors society approves of; a _____ norm involves perceptions of how people actually behave.
   a. public; private
   b. private; public
   c. descriptive; injunctive
   d. injunctive; descriptive

2. _____ norms are most powerful for changing people's behaviors.
   a. Informational
   b. Normative
   c. Injunctive
   d. Descriptive

3. Which of the following provides an illustration of how the use of norms to change behavior can backfire and produce a "boomerang effect"?
   a. Jerry finds out that everyone in his building is conserving water by installing a low-flow shower head, so he decides that he doesn't need to worry about conserving, and he begins taking even longer showers than usual.
   b. Elaine notices that the new, attractive guy at the office brings a reusable cup instead of bottled water, so she goes out of her way to show off her reusable cup whenever he is in the vicinity in order to win his affection.

   c. Kramer finds out that he is using more electricity than most people in the neighborhood, so he cuts down on his usage by shutting off his computer, lights, and hot tub every time he leaves his apartment.
   d. George finds out that all of his neighbors are stealing cable television, so he decides that he will get an illegal cable hookup as well.

4. The foot-in-the-door technique
   a. works only when the second request comes from the same person as the first request.
   b. capitalizes on people's desire for self-consistency.
   c. is an example of propaganda.
   d. works only when the requests come from someone in a position of authority.

5. The door-in-the-face technique
   a. is an example of informational social influence.
   b. illustrates the importance of people's desire to be accurate.
   c. relies at least in part on norms of reciprocity.
   d. is more likely to work during a time of crisis.

See page 621 for the answers.

Obedience to Authority

8.5   What have studies demonstrated about people's willingness to obey authority figures?

This chapter covers some dark territory in its mapping of human nature. We began with the victimization and abuse of an innocent, teenaged fast-food worker. We have progressed to a discussion of propaganda and conformity in the genocide perpetrated by Nazi Germany. One shared aspect of these sordid examples is the role played by a forceful authority figure or leader. Indeed, obedience to authority is the most powerful form of social influence. From a young age, we are socialized to obey authority figures whom we perceive as legitimate (Blass, 2000; Staub, 1989). We internalize this norm of obedience such that we usually conform to rules and laws even when the authority figure isn't present—you stop at red lights even if the cops aren't parked at the corner. However, as you've discovered in this chapter, obedience can have tragic consequences too, as people will obey the orders of an authority figure to hurt or even kill other human beings.

As with many eras, the past century was marked by repeated atrocities and genocides—in Germany, yes, but also the rest of Europe, Armenia, Ukraine, Rwanda, Cambodia, Bosnia, Sudan, and elsewhere. One of the most important questions facing the world's inhabitants, therefore, becomes, where does the role played by social influence end and personal responsibility begin? The philosopher Hannah Arendt (1965) was particularly interested in understanding the causes of the Holocaust. How could Hitler's Nazi regime in Germany carry out the murder of millions based on religion, ethnicity, sexual orientation, physical disability, and political beliefs? Arendt argued that most participants in the Holocaust were not sadists or psychopaths who enjoyed mass murder but rather ordinary citizens subjected to complex and powerful social pressures. As a journalist, she covered the trial of Adolf Eichmann, the Nazi official responsible for the transportation of Jews to the death camps, and concluded that he was not the bloodthirsty monster that many people made him out to be but rather a common bureaucrat who did what he was told without questioning his orders (Miller, 1995).

Our point is not that Eichmann—or the soldiers at My Lai or the Khmer Rouge in Cambodia or the Serbs in Bosnia—should be excused for the crimes they committed. The point is that it is too easy to explain their behavior as the acts of madmen. It is more fruitful—and more frightening—to view much of their behavior as the acts of ordinary people exposed to extraordinary social influence. How can we be sure that these atrocities were not caused solely by evil, psychopathic people but also by powerful social forces operating on people of all types? The way to find out is to study social pressure with an empirical research eye under controlled conditions. We could take a sample of

Victims of the Holocaust from the Bergen-Belsen concentration camp, 1945.

ordinary citizens, subject them to various kinds of social influence, and see to what extent they will conform and obey. Can an experimenter influence ordinary people to commit immoral acts, such as inflicting severe pain on an innocent bystander? Stanley Milgram (1963, 1974, 1976) decided to find out in what has become the most famous series of studies in social psychology.

Imagine that you were a participant in one of Milgram's studies. You answer an ad in the newspaper, asking for participants in a study on memory and learning. When you arrive at the laboratory, you meet another participant, a 47-year-old, somewhat overweight, pleasant-looking fellow. The experimenter, wearing a White lab coat, explains that one of you will play the role of a teacher and the other the role of a learner. You draw a slip of paper out of a hat and discover that you will be the teacher. It turns out that your job is to read to the other participant a list of word pairs (e.g., *blue–box*, *nice–day*) and then test him on his memory for the list. The experimenter instructs you to deliver an electric shock to the learner whenever he makes a mistake because the purpose of the study is to examine the effects of punishment on learning.

You watch as the other participant—the learner—is strapped into a chair in an adjacent room and electrodes are attached to his arm. You are seated in front of a shock generator whose 30 switches deliver varying levels of shock in 15-volt increments, starting at 15 volts and going all the way up to 450 volts. There are labels accompanying these switches, from "Slight Shock" to "Danger: Severe Shock" to an ominous "XXX" next to the highest levels (see the following photos below). The experimenter tells you that the first time the learner makes a mistake, you should give him a shock of 15 volts, and then you will increase that amount by 15 volts for each subsequent mistake he makes. So that you will know what the shocks are like, the experimenter gives you a sample shock of 45 volts, which proves surprisingly painful.

Left: The shock generator used in Milgram's research. *Right:* The learner (an accomplice of the experimenter) is strapped into the chair, and electrodes are attached to his arm.

(Adapted from Milgram, 1974.)

You read the list of word pairs to the learner and then begin the testing phase. After announcing the first word of each pair, you give four possible multiple-choice answers; the learner responds by pressing one of four switches, illuminating a light on the answer box in front of you. Everything begins smoothly as the learner gets the first few right. Then he gets some wrong, and, as instructed, you deliver a shock each time. At this point, you are probably getting concerned about the number and severity of the shocks you will have to give. When you get to the 75-volt level, the learner, whom you can hear over an intercom, emits a painful "Ugh!" Perhaps you pause and ask the experimenter what you should do. "Please continue," he responds without hesitation. As the learner continues to make mistakes, you deliver more shocks. The learner protests, shouting, "Ugh! Experimenter! That's all! Get me out of here!" You look at the experimenter with concern. He tells you calmly, "It is absolutely essential that you continue" (see Figure 8.6).

Figure 8.6 Milgram Transcript and Prompts

Transcript of the learner's protests in Milgram's obedience study and of the prods used by the experimenter to compel people to continue giving shocks.

(Based on Milgram, 1963, 1974)

Learner's Protests

75 volts: Ugh!

90 volts: Ugh!

105 volts: Ugh! (louder)

120 volts: Ugh! Hey this really hurts.

135 volts: Ugh!!

150 volts: Ugh!!! Experimenter! That's all. Get me out of here. I told you I had heart trouble. My heart's starting to bother me now. Get me out of here, please. My heart's starting to bother me. I refuse to go on. Let me out.

165 volts: Ugh! Let me out! (shouting)

180 volts: Ugh! I can't stand the pain. Let me out of here! (shouting)

195 volts: Ugh! Let me out of here. Let me out of here. My heart's bothering me. Let me out of here! You have no right to keep me here! Let me out! Let me out of here! Let me out! Let me out of here! My heart's bothering me. Let me out! Let me out!

210 volts: Ugh! Experimenter! Get me out of here. I've had enough. I won't be in the experiment anymore.

225 volts: Ugh!

240 volts: Ugh!

255 volts: Ugh! Get me out of here.

270 volts: Ugh! (agonized scream) Let me out of here. Let me out of here. Let me out of here. Let me out. Do you hear? Let me out of here.

285 volts: Ugh! (agonized scream)

300 volts: Ugh! (agonized scream) I absolutely refuse to answer anymore. Get me out of here. You can't hold me here. Get me out. Get me out of here.

315 volts: Ugh! (intensely agonized scream) I told you I refuse to answer. I'm no longer part of this experiment.

330 volts: Ugh! (intense and prolonged agonized scream) Let me out of here. Let me out of here. My heart's bothering me. Let me out, I tell you. (hysterically) Let me out of here. Let me out of here. You have no right to hold me here. Let me out! Let me out! Let me out of here! Let me out!

Instructions Used by the Experimenter to Achieve Obedience

Prod 1: Please continue or Please go on.

Prod 2: The experiment requires that you continue.

Prod 3: It is absolutely essential that you continue.

Prod 4: You have no other choice; you must go on.

The prods were always made in sequence: Only if prod 1 had been unsuccessful could prod 2 be used. If the subject refused to obey the experimenter after prod 4, the experiment was terminated. The experimenter's tone of voice was at all times firm but not impolite. The sequence was begun anew on each occasion that the subject balked or showed reluctance to follow orders.

Special prods. If the subject asked whether the learner was likely to suffer permanent physical injury, the experimenter said:

Although the shocks may be painful, there is no permanent tissue damage, so please go on. [Followed by prods 2, 3, and 4 if necessary.]

If the subject said that the learner did not want to go on, the experimenter replied: Whether the learner likes it or not, you must go on until he has learned all the word pairs correctly. So please go on. [Followed by prods 2, 3, and 4 if necessary.]

What would you do? How many people do you think would continue to obey the experimenter, increasing the levels of shock all the way up the shock panel until they had delivered the maximum amount of 450 volts?

When this question was posed to psychology majors at Yale University, they estimated that less than 1% of the population would go to this extreme. A sample of middle-class adults and a panel of psychiatrists made similar predictions. Based on our discussion of conformity thus far, however, perhaps you are not as optimistic. Indeed, most of Milgram's participants succumbed to the pressure of the authority figure. The average maximum shock delivered was 360 volts, and 62.5% of the participants went all the way to the end of the panel, delivering the 450-volt shock. A full 80% of the participants continued giving the shocks even after the learner, who earlier had mentioned that he had a heart condition, screamed, "Let me out of here! Let me out of here! My heart's bothering me. Let me out of here! . . . Get me out of here! I've had enough. I won't be in the experiment any more" (Milgram, 1974, p. 56).

It is important to note that the learner was actually an accomplice of the experimenter who was acting rather than suffering—he did not receive any actual shocks. It is equally important to note that the study was very convincingly done so that people believed they really were shocking the learner. Here is Milgram's description of one participant's response to the teacher role:

> I observed a mature and initially poised businessman enter the laboratory smiling and confident. Within 20 minutes he was reduced to a twitching, stuttering wreck, who was rapidly approaching a point of nervous collapse. He constantly pulled on his earlobe, and twisted his hands. At one point he pushed his fist into his forehead and muttered, "Oh God, let's stop it." And yet he continued to respond to every word of the experimenter, and obeyed to the end. (Milgram, 1963, p. 377)

These research participants ranged in age from the twenties to the fifties and included people with a variety of occupations. While participants in the original 1963 study were all men, in a follow-up Milgram found nearly identical obedience rates among women. Why did so many of these individuals conform to the wishes of the experimenter, to the point where they genuinely believed they were inflicting great pain on another human being? Why were the college students, middle-class adults, and psychiatrists so wrong in their predictions about what people would do? In a dangerous way, each of the reasons that we have explored in this chapter on conformity contributed to cause Milgram's participants to obey—just as many Germans did during the Holocaust and soldiers have done during more recent atrocities in Iraq and Afghanistan. Let's take a close look at how this played out in Milgram's research.

The Role of Normative Social Influence

First, it is clear that normative pressures made it difficult for people in Milgram's studies to refuse to continue. As we have seen, if someone really wants us to do something, it can be difficult to say no. This is particularly true when the person is in a position of authority. Milgram's participants probably believed that if they refused to continue, the experimenter would be disappointed, hurt, or maybe even angry—all of which put pressure on them to continue. It is important to note that this study, unlike the Asch study, was set up so that the experimenter actively attempted to get people to conform, giving commands such as "It is absolutely essential that you continue." When an authority figure is so insistent that we obey, it is difficult to say no (Blass, 1991, 2000, 2003; Hamilton, Sanders, & McKearney, 1995; Meeus & Raaijmakers, 1995; Miller, 1986).

The fact that normative pressures were present in the Milgram study is clear from a variation that he conducted. This time, there were three teachers, two of whom were confederates. One confederate was instructed to read the list of word pairs and the other to tell the learner whether his response was correct. The (real) participant's job was to deliver the shocks, increasing their severity with each error, as in the original study. At 150 volts, when the learner gave his first vehement protest, the first confederate refused to continue despite the experimenter's command that he do so. At 210 volts, the second confederate refused to continue. The result? Seeing their peers disobey made it much easier for the actual participants to disobey too. Only 10% of the participants gave the maximum level of shock in this version of the study (see Figure 8.7). This result is similar to Asch's finding that people did not conform nearly as much when one accomplice bucked the majority.

The Role of Informational Social Influence

Despite the power of the normative pressures in Milgram's original study, they are not the sole reason people complied. The experimenter was authoritative and insistent, but he was hardly pointing a gun at participants and telling them to "conform or else"; the participants were free to get up and leave anytime they wanted to. Why didn't they, especially when the experimenter was a stranger they had never met before and probably would never see again?

As we saw earlier, when people are in confusing circumstances and unsure what they should do, they use other people to help define the situation. Informational social influence is especially powerful when the situation is ambiguous, when it is a crisis, and when the other people in the situation have some expertise. All three of these characteristics describe the situation Milgram's participants faced. The scenario—a study of the effects of punishment on learning—seemed straightforward enough when the experimenter explained it, but it quickly turned into something else altogether. The learner cried out in pain, but the experimenter told the participant that the

---

Figure 8.7 Results of Different Versions of the Milgram Study

In the standard version of Milgram's study, obedience was 62.5%. This rate dropped when the study took place in a nondescript office location rather than the Yale Psychology Department. It dropped further when the teacher had to physically place the learner's hand on a shock plate, when the experimenter issuing commands was located remotely, and when two other "teachers" (actually confederates) refused to continue with the study. Finally, when participants were left to their own to determine the level of shock, almost none of them went to the end of the shock panel. The variation in these bars demonstrates just how context-dependent obedience to authority can be.

(Data from Milgram, 1974)

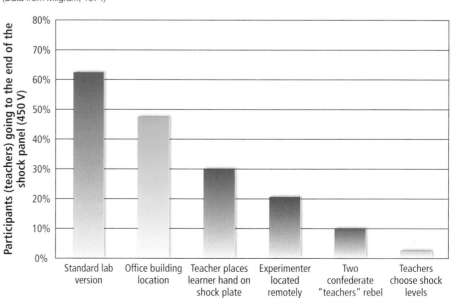

shocks did not cause permanent damage. The participant didn't want to hurt anyone, but he or she had agreed to be in the study and to follow the directions. When in such a state of conflict, it was only natural for the participants to use an expert—the experimenter in the scientific-looking White lab coat—to help them decide what was the right thing to do (Hamilton et al., 1995; Krakow & Blass, 1995; Miller, 1986; Miller, Collins, & Brief, 1995).

Another version of Milgram's study supports the idea that informational influence was operative. This version was identical to the original except for three critical changes: First, the experimenter never said which shock levels were to be given, leaving this decision up to the participant. Second, before the study began, the experimenter received a telephone call and had to leave the room, telling the participant to continue without him. Third, there was a confederate playing the role of an additional teacher, whose job was to record how long it took the learner to respond to each word pair. When the experimenter left, this other "teacher" said that he had just thought of a good system: How about if they increased the level of shock each time the learner made a mistake? He insisted that the real participant follow this procedure.

Note that in this situation, the person giving the commands has no expertise: He was just a regular person, no more knowledgeable than the participants themselves. Because he lacked expertise, people were much less likely to use him as a source of information about how they should respond. As seen in Figure 8.7, in this version, full compliance dropped to only 20%. (The fact that 20% still gave the maximum shock suggests that some people were so uncertain about what to do that they used even a nonexpert as a guide.)

An additional variation conducted by Milgram underscores the importance of authority figures as experts in eliciting such obedience. In this variation, two experimenters gave the real participants their orders. At 150 volts, when the learner first cried out that he wanted to stop, the two experimenters began to disagree about whether they should continue the study. At this point, every single one of the participant-teachers stopped responding. Note that nothing the victim ever did caused all the participants to stop obeying; however, when the authorities' definition of the situation became unclear, the participants broke out of their conforming role.

> When you think of the long and gloomy history of man, you will find more hideous crimes have been committed in the name of obedience than in the name of rebellion.
>
> —C. P. Snow

Other Reasons Why We Obey

Both normative and informational social influences were very strong in Milgram's research; however, these reasons for complying still fall short of fully explaining why people acted in a manner that seems so inhumane. They account for why people initially complied with the experimenter's instructions, but after it became increasingly obvious what was happening to the learner, why didn't participants realize that what they were doing was terribly wrong and stop? Just as the fast-food restaurant managers continued to abuse their employees long after the demands of the "policeman" on the phone shifted from merely bizarre to obviously illegal, many of Milgram's participants pressed the shock levers time after time after time despite the cries of anguish from a fellow human being.

CONFORMING TO THE WRONG NORM   To understand this continued compliance, we need to consider additional aspects of the situation. We don't mean to imply that Milgram's participants were completely mindless or unaware of what they were doing. As video of the sessions clearly shows, all were terribly concerned about the plight of the victim. The problem was that they were caught in a web of conflicting norms, and it was difficult to determine which ones to follow. At the beginning of the study, it was perfectly reasonable to heed the norm that says, "Obey expert, legitimate authority figures." The experimenter was confident and knowledgeable, and the study seemed like a reasonable test of an interesting hypothesis. So why not cooperate and do as you are told?

But, gradually, the rules of the game changed, and this "obey authority" norm became less and less appropriate. The experimenter, who seemed so reasonable before, was now asking people to inflict great pain on their fellow participant. But once people follow one norm, it can be difficult to switch midstream, to realize that this norm is no longer appropriate, or to recognize that another norm, "Do not inflict needless harm on a fellow human being," should be followed. For example, suppose the experimenter had explained, at the outset, that he would like people to deliver possibly fatal shocks to the other participant. How many people would have agreed? Very few, we suspect, because it would have been clear that this violated an important social and personal norm about harming others. Instead, the experimenter pulled a kind of "bait and switch" routine, whereby he first made it look like an "obey authority" norm was appropriate and then only later gradually revealed just how he planned to use his authority in this situation (Collins & Brief, 1995).

It was particularly difficult for people to abandon the "obey authority" norm in the Milgram study because of three key aspects of the situation. First, the study was fast paced, preventing the participants from stopping to reflect on what they were doing. They were busy recording the learner's responses, keeping track of the word pairs, and determining whether the learner's responses were right or wrong. Given that they had to attend carefully to these details and move along at a fast pace, it was difficult for them to realize that the norm guiding their behavior—cooperating with the authority figure—was, after a while, no longer appropriate (Conway & Schaller, 2005; Modigliani & Rochat, 1995). We suspect that if, halfway through the study, Milgram's participants had been told to take a break or had been left in the room by themselves for a period of time, many more would have successfully redefined the situation and refused to continue.

SELF-JUSTIFICATION   A second important aspect of the situation in the Milgram study is that, as alluded to above, the experimenter asked people to increase the shocks in very small increments. The participants did not go from giving a small shock to giving a potentially lethal one. Instead, at any given point, they only faced a smaller decision about whether to increase by a meager 15 volts the amount of shock they had just given. As we saw in Chapter 6, every time a person makes an important or difficult decision, dissonance is produced, along with resultant pressures to reduce it. An effective way of reducing dissonance produced by a difficult decision is to decide that the decision was fully justified. But because reducing dissonance provides a justification for the preceding action, it can make a person vulnerable to further escalating a now-justified activity.

Thus, in the Milgram study, the participants' initial agreement to administer the first shock created internal pressure on them to continue to obey. As the participants administered each successive level of shock, they had to justify it in their own minds. After they had justified a particular shock level, it became very difficult for them to decide on a place where they should draw the line and stop. How could they say, in effect, "Okay, I gave him 200 volts, but not 215—never 215!" Each succeeding shock and its justification laid the groundwork for the next shock and would have been dissonant with quitting; 215 volts is not *that* different from 200, and 230 is not *that* different from 215. Those who did break off the series did so against enormous internal pressure to continue (Darley, 1992; Gilbert, 1981; Miller et al., 1995). The incremental nature of the shock task was essential to the level of obedience Milgram observed, much in the same way that incrementally increasing a series of requests allows the foot-in-the-door technique to operate, as described earlier.

THE LOSS OF PERSONAL RESPONSIBILITY   The third reason why it was difficult for participants to abandon the "obey authority" norm in the Milgram studies is a particularly troubling one. Sometimes when you are the research participant (or the employee) and the other person is a legitimate authority figure (the experimenter, the boss, the military commander, the police officer), you become the "puppet," and they are pulling the strings. They can define what it is you are supposed to do, and they are responsible for the end results—after all, it was their idea, and you were "just following orders." Milgram (1974) stressed that the loss of a sense of personal responsibility for one's actions was a critical component explaining the results of the obedience studies.

When faced with the prospect of acting in unpleasant or unseemly ways, it becomes easier to do so when you can offload personal responsibility for those actions to someone else. An example of a particularly disturbing job is that of prison guards who must carry out a capital punishment sentence. How do these guards respond to a job in which they are told to kill another person? Clearly, they need to reduce their cognitive dissonance. Taking a life is a supremely problematic and disturbing act, so they often need to engage in self-justification in order to do it. Michael Osofsky, Albert Bandura, and Philip Zimbardo (2005) studied guards on the execution teams of three southern state prisons and compared them to their fellow guards who did not conduct executions. All the guards responded anonymously to a questionnaire that asked them to rate their level of agreement with statements such as "Because of the nature of their crime, murderers have lost the right to live" and "Those who carry out state executions should not be criticized for following society's wishes."

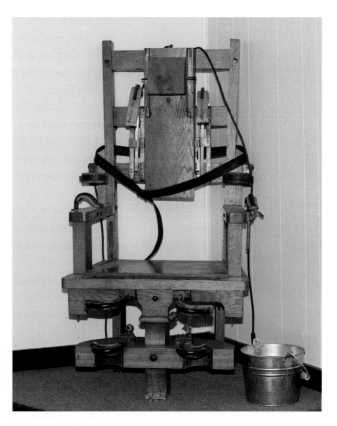

Research indicates that one way prison officials deal with the potential dissonance and distress of having to carry out a death sentence is to morally disengage from their work and deny personal responsibility for the actions in question.

The researchers found a significant difference in the attitudes of the two types of guards. The execution-team guards demonstrated much more "moral disengagement" from their work than did the other guards. The execution-team guards denied all personal responsibility for the executions. They felt they were just implementing orders—in this case, those of a judge and jury. They also engaged in justification in other areas. Compared to the regular prison guards, they dehumanized the prisoners more, seeing them as lacking important human qualities. They perceived the prisoners as more of a threat to society, such that it was necessary that they be killed. All these attitudes helped the execution guards reduce their qualms about the morality of what they did at work. As one guard put it, "I had a job to do, that's what we did. Our job was to execute this man and we were going to do it in a professional manner" (Osofsky, Bandura, & Zimbardo, 2005, p. 386).

The Obedience Studies, Then and Now

Stanley Milgram's study of obedience is widely considered to be one of the most important contributions to the field of psychology (Benjamin & Simpson, 2009). His work, conducted in the early 1960s, was replicated in the following years by researchers in 11 countries, involving approximately 3,000 research participants (Blass, 2000). However, Milgram's research paradigm also ignited a storm of protest (and soul-searching) in the research community over the ethical treatment of research participants.

Milgram's research was criticized by some as unethical for several reasons. First, the study involved *deception*. Participants were told it was a study on memory and learning, when of course it was not; participants were told the electric shocks were real, when of course they were not. Second, there was not fully *informed consent* on the part of participants. When they agreed to be in the study, they were not informed as to its true nature, and thus they never really consented to take part in the scenario they eventually experienced. Third, their role as teacher caused them *psychological distress* during the course of the study. Fourth, it was not made clear to participants that they had the *right to withdraw* from the study at any time; in fact, the experimenter stated the exact opposite—for example, that they "had to continue." Fifth, the participants experienced *inflicted insight*. When the study ended, some of them had learned unpleasant things about themselves that they had not agreed to beforehand (Baumrind, 1964, 1985; Milgram, 1974; Miller, 2009). More recent critiques have focused on disturbing allegations that Milgram misrepresented his debriefing methods in his published papers and that many research participants actually left the study unaware that the learner had been a confederate and the shocks had been fake (Nicholson, 2011; Perry, 2013).

Although the ethical issues surrounding Milgram's study were not, as is often suggested, the reason that formal ethical guidelines for research participants were created in the United States in 1966 (they were created primarily to protect participants in medical research), these new guidelines made conducting obedience research such as Milgram's increasingly problematic (Benjamin & Simpson, 2009). Indeed, decades would pass without researchers conducting follow-up studies of obedience using Milgram's procedure (Blass, 2009), and many students learned in their psychology courses that such studies could never be run again. But that all changed in 2006.

That year, Jerry M. Burger (2009) conducted the first Milgram-style obedience study in the United States in decades. Much had changed in the country during that time. Had the likelihood of being obedient, even to the point of inflicting harm, changed as well? In order to conduct this study under modern ethical guidelines, Burger (2009) made a number of changes to the procedure. First, he reduced the psychological distress experienced by participants by stopping the study after 150 volts, when the learner is first heard yelling that he wants out and refuses to go on. Analysis of data from eight of Milgram's study versions indicated that when disobedience occurred, it was most likely to happen at this point in the study; most previous participants who passed the 150-volt mark tended to go all the way to end of the shock panel anyway (Packer, 2008). Second, participants were prescreened by a clinical psychologist, and those who were identified as even slightly likely to have a negative reaction to the experience were excluded from the study (38% were excluded). Finally, Burger (2009) explicitly and repeatedly told his participants that they could leave the study at any time, as could the learner.

In most respects, though, Burger's (2009) study was like the original. His experimenter used the same basic verbal "prods" that Milgram's used (e.g., "It is absolutely essential that you continue") when participants began to waver. Burger's participants, like Milgram's, were adult men and women recruited through newspaper advertisements and flyers. Their age range of 20 to 81 years was broader than Milgram's, though their average age of about 43 years was similar. They were ethnically more diverse than Milgram's participants, and they were also more highly educated: 40% of Burger's sample had college degrees, and another 20% had advanced degrees. Finally, because the Milgram obedience studies are quite well known, Burger excluded participants who had taken more than two college-level psychology courses.

What did Burger (2009) find? Are people more disobedient today than they were in Milgram's time? After all, during the intervening decades, as large numbers of Americans took part in the civil rights movement and various antiwar movements and other protests, many had accepted the injunctive norm that questioning authority was the right thing to do. Did such cultural experiences translate into newly empowered, disobedient participants? Sadly, the answer is no. Burger (2009) found no significant difference in obedience rates between his participants and Milgram's. After the critical 150-volt shock had been delivered and the learner cried out to be released, 70% of Burger's participants obeyed and were ready to continue (at which point, Burger ended the study). At this same point in the comparable Milgram study, 82.5% were obedient and continued; this difference between 70% and 82.5% is not a statistically significant one.

Note that Burger's ethically necessary changes in methodology also complicate a direct comparison to Milgram's results (Miller, 2009). Some of Burger's changes may have decreased slightly the likelihood of obedience; others may have increased its likelihood. For example, perhaps repeated reminders beforehand that they could withdraw from the study at any time made it easier for participants to ultimately disobey. But the most profound change Burger made was stopping the study after 150 volts. While this makes the procedure more ethical, it means we have no idea how many participants, today, would go all the way to the 450-volt level (Twenge, 2009). Much of the extraordinary power of the Milgram obedience studies came from participants' choices after 150 volts, as they continued step by small step to the last switch on the shock generator. It is during this part of the study that participants felt the most conflicted and anxious. It is here that they revealed their response to a pressing moral conflict (Miller, 2009). This information is lost in the recent replication. And, as such, it reminds us that scientific inquiry has two sometimes competing aims: to discover new knowledge and to do no harm.

IT'S NOT ABOUT AGGRESSION   Before leaving our discussion of Milgram's research, we should mention one other possible interpretation of his results: Did the participants act so inhumanely because there is an inherently evil side to human nature, lurking just below the surface, ready to be expressed with the flimsiest excuse? To test this hypothesis, Milgram conducted another version of his study. Everything was the same except that the experimenter told the participants that they could choose any level of shock they wished to give the learner when he made a mistake. Milgram gave people permission to use the highest levels, telling them that there was a lot to be learned from all levels of shock. This instruction should have allowed any aggressive urges to be expressed unchecked. Instead, the participants chose to give very mild shocks (see Figure 8.7 on page 280). Only 2.5% of the participants gave the maximum shock. Thus, the Milgram studies do not show that most people have an evil streak that eagerly shines through when the surface is scratched (Reeder, Monroe, & Pryor, 2008). Instead, these studies demonstrate that social pressures can combine in insidious ways to make humane people act in an inhumane manner. Let us conclude this chapter with the words of Stanley Milgram himself:

> Even Eichmann was sickened when he toured the concentration camps, but in order to participate in mass murder he had only to sit at a desk and shuffle papers. At the same time the man in the camp who actually dropped [the poison] into the gas chambers is able to justify his behavior on the grounds that he is only following orders from above. Thus there is fragmentation of the total human act; no one man decides to carry out the evil act and is confronted with its consequences. The person who assumes full responsibility for the act has evaporated. Perhaps this is the most common characteristic of socially organized evil in modern society. (Milgram, 1976, pp. 183–184)

REVIEW QUESTIONS

1. Which of the following was a goal of Milgram's obedience research?
  a. To identify the abnormal personality characteristics associated with sadistic behavior
  b. To justify and exonerate the behaviors linked to genocide and other inhuman acts
  c. To better understand the social forces that contribute to destructive and immoral behavior
  d. To identify cultural differences in aggression

2. Which of the following illustrates the role played by normative social influence in the obedience of Milgram's participants?
  a. When other "teachers" (actually confederates) refused to continue with the study, participants' obedience rates declined significantly.
  b. Men and women exhibited similar levels of obedience in the research.

c. The "learner" (actually a confederate) announced before the study began that he had a preexisting heart condition.

d. Many participants showed signs of nervous laughter during the course of the study.

3. Which of the following was *not* one of the instruction prods used by the experimenter in the Milgram studies?
   a. "The experiment requires that you continue."
   b. "Please continue."
   c. "It is absolutely essential that you continue."
   d. "If you do not continue, you will not be paid for your participation."

4. Which of the following is a common ethical concern raised about the Milgram study?
   a. Participants' compensation was low.
   b. Participants were forced to learn unpleasant things about themselves without agreeing to that ahead of time.

c. Participants were never given the chance to serve in the role of learner.

d. Participants had to receive a sample shock of 75 volts before the study began.

5. Which of the following is a change that Burger (2009) made from the original Milgram study when he replicated the research several decades later?
   a. He examined only female participants.
   b. The study was stopped once participants went past 150 volts.
   c. He told participants that the study was part of research on the effects of punishment on learning.
   d. He paid participants for their involvement.

See page 621 for the answers.

Summary

8.1 What is conformity, and why does it occur?

- **Conformity: When and Why** Conformity occurs when people change their behavior due to the real (or imagined) influence of others. There are two main reasons people conform: informational and normative social influences.

8.2 How does informational social influence motivate people to conform?

- **Informational Social Influence: The Need to Know What's "Right"** Informational social influence occurs when people do not know the correct (or best) action to take. They look to the behavior of others as an important source of information, using it to choose appropriate courses of action for themselves. Informational social influence usually results in **private acceptance**, in which people genuinely believe in what other people are doing or saying.

  - **The Importance of Being Accurate** In situations where it is important to be accurate, the tendency to conform to other people through informational social influence increases.

  - **When Informational Conformity Backfires** Using other people as a source of information can backfire when they are wrong about what's going on.

  - **When Will People Conform to Informational Social Influence?** People are more likely to conform to informational social influence when

the situation is ambiguous, when they are in a crisis, or if experts are present.

8.3 How does normative social influence motivate people to conform?

- **Normative Social Influence: The Need to Be Accepted** **Normative social influence** occurs when we change our behavior to match that of others because we want to remain a member of the group in good standing and continue to gain the advantages of group membership. We conform to the group's **social norms**, implicit or explicit rules for acceptable behaviors, values, and attitudes. Normative social influence usually results in **public compliance** but not private acceptance of other people's ideas and behaviors.

  - **Conformity and Social Approval: The Asch Line-Judgment Studies** In a series of classic studies, Solomon Asch found that people would conform, at least some of the time, to the obviously wrong answer of the group.

  - **The Importance of Being Accurate, Revisited** When it is important to be accurate, people are more likely to resist normative social influence and go against the group, giving the right answer. But public conformity still occurs.

  - **The Consequences of Resisting Normative Social Influence** Resisting normative social influence can lead to ridicule, ostracism, and rejection by the group.

- **When Will People Conform to Normative Social Influence?** **Social impact theory** specifies when normative social influence is most likely to occur by referring to the strength, immediacy, and size of the group. We are more likely to conform when the group is one we care about, when the group members are unanimous in their thoughts or behaviors, when the group has three or more members, and when we are members of collectivist cultures. Past conformity gives people **idiosyncrasy credits**, allowing them to deviate from the group without serious consequences.

- **Minority Influence: When the Few Influence the Many** Under certain conditions, an individual (or small number of people) can influence the majority. The key is consistency in the presentation of the minority viewpoint.

8.4   How can people use their knowledge of social influence to influence others?

- **Strategies for Using Social Influence** Knowing about the tendency to conform can inform our strategic efforts to change the behavior of others

  - **The Role of Injunctive and Descriptive Norms** Communicating **injunctive norms**, expectations regarding the behaviors that society approves of, is a more powerful way to create change than communicating **descriptive norms**, expectations regarding how people actually behave.

  - **Using Norms to Change Behavior: Beware the "Boomerang Effect"** One must be careful that descriptive norms do not create a boomerang effect, making an undesirable behavior more likely than it previously was.

  - **Other Tactics of Social Influence** Other efforts to change people's behavior include the **foot-in-the-door technique**, in which the requestor first secures agreement with a small favor before following up with a larger request, and the **door-in-the-face technique**, in which the requester first asks for a large favor that will certainly be rejected before following up with a smaller, second request. **Propaganda**, as utilized in Nazi Germany, is yet another strategy.

8.5   What have studies demonstrated about people's willingness to obey authority figures?

- **Obedience to Authority** In the most famous series of studies in social psychology, Stanley Milgram examined obedience to authority. He found chilling levels of obedience, to the point where a majority of participants administered what they thought were potentially lethal shocks to a fellow human being.

  - **The Role of Normative Social Influence** Normative pressures make it difficult for people to stop obeying authority figures. They want to please the authority figure by doing a good job.

  - **The Role of Informational Social Influence** The obedience studies created a confusing situation for participants, with competing, ambiguous demands. Unclear about how to define what was going on, they followed the orders of the expert.

  - **Other Reasons Why We Obey** Participants conformed to the wrong norm: They continued to follow the "obey authority" norm even when it was no longer appropriate. It was difficult for them to abandon this norm because of the fast-paced nature of the study, the fact that the shock levels increased in small increments, and their loss of a feeling of personal responsibility.

  - **The Obedience Studies, Then and Now** Milgram's research design was criticized on ethical grounds, involving deception, informed consent, psychological distress, the right to withdraw, and inflicted insight. A recent U.S. replication found that the level of obedience in 2006 was not significantly different from that found in the classic study in the 1960s.

Test Yourself

1. All of the following are examples of informational social influence *except*

a. you are running a race, but because you are unsure of the route, you wait to check which of two roads the other runners follow.

b. you've just started work at a new job, and a fire alarm goes off; you watch your coworkers to see what to do.

c. when you get to college, you change the way you dress so that you "fit in" better—that is, so that people will like you more.

d. you ask your adviser which classes you should take next semester.

2. Which of the following is true, according to social impact theory?

a. People conform more to others who are physically close than to others who are physically distant.

b. People conform more if the others are important to them.

c. People conform more to three or more people than to one or two people.

d. All of the above are true.

3. In Asch's line studies, participants who were alone when asked to report the length of the lines gave the correct answer 98% of the time. However, when they were with the confederates who sometimes gave an obviously wrong answer, 76% of participants gave the wrong answer at least once. This suggests that Asch's studies are an illustration of

a. public compliance with private acceptance.

b. public compliance without private acceptance.

c. informational influence.

d. private compliance.

4. Which of the following is most true about informational social influence?

a. When deciding whether to conform, people should ask themselves whether the other people know more about what is going on than they do.

b. People should always try to resist it.

c. People are most likely to conform when others have the same level of expertise as they do.

d. Often, people publicly conform but do not privately accept this kind of influence.

5. In the experiment by Reno, Cialdini, and Kalligren (1983), the confederate's littering behavior was expected to remind participants of a/an _____ norm against littering in the clean environment. Seeing the confederate picking up someone else's litter invoked the _____ norm that littering is wrong in both the clean and littered environments.

a. Social; descriptive

b. Injunctive; descriptive

c. Descriptive; injunctive

d. Informational; injunctive

6. Tom is a new student at his university. During the first week of classes, he notices a fellow student from one of his classes getting on a bus. Tom decides to follow the student and discovers that this bus takes him right to the building where his class meets. This best illustrates what kind of conformity?

a. Obedience to authority

b. Informational social influence

c. Public compliance

d. Normative social influence

7. Which of the following best describes an example of normative social influence?

a. Carrie is studying with a group of friends. When comparing answers on the practice test, she discovers that they all answered the question differently than she had. Instead of speaking up and telling them she thinks the answer is something else, she agrees with their answer because she figures they must be right.

b. Samantha is supposed to bring a bottle of wine to a dinner party she is attending. She doesn't drink wine herself but figures she can just ask the store clerk for advice on what kind to buy.

c. Miranda is out to lunch with her boss and coworkers. Her boss tells a joke that makes fun of a certain ethnic group, and everyone else laughs. Miranda doesn't think the joke is funny but laughs anyway.

d. Charlotte is flying on an airplane for the first time. She is worried when she hears the engine make a strange noise but feels better after she looks at the flight attendants and sees that they are not alarmed.

8. In Milgram's research,

a. participants were informed about the true nature of the study.

b. fully informed consent was obtained from participants.

c. it was made clear to participants that they could withdraw from the study at any time.

d. participants were not informed about the true nature of the study.

9. Which of the following strategies of social influence creates a situation similar to that experienced by Milgram's study in that it relies on requests that increase in severity in incremental fashion?

a. Contagion

b. Foot-in-the-door technique

c. Door-in-the-face technique

d. Descriptive norms

10. Which of the following had the *least* influence on participants' willingness to keep giving shocks in the Milgram studies?

a. Loss of personal responsibility

b. Self-justification

c. Informational social influence

d. Participants' aggression

See page 621 for the answers.

Chapter 9
Group Processes
Influence in Social Groups

 ## Chapter Outline and Learning Objectives

What Is a Group?

9.1 What are groups, and why do people join them?

Why Do People Join Groups?
The Composition and Functions of Groups

Individual Behavior in a Group Setting

9.2 In what ways do individuals perform differently when others are around?

Social Facilitation: When the Presence of Others Energizes Us
Social Loafing: When the Presence of Others Relaxes Us
Gender and Cultural Differences in Social Loafing: Who Slacks Off the Most?
Deindividuation: Getting Lost in the Crowd

Group Decisions: Are Two (or More) Heads Better Than One?

9.3 Are two (or more) heads better than one in decision making, and how do leaders shape group outcomes?

Process Loss: When Group Interactions Inhibit Good Problem Solving
Group Polarization: Going to Extremes
Leadership in Groups

Conflict and Cooperation

9.4 What determines the likelihood that individual or group conflict will escalate or be resolved?

Social Dilemmas
Using Threats to Resolve Conflict
Negotiation and Bargaining

On March 19, 2003, an unseasonably cool spring day in Washington, D.C., President George W. Bush convened a meeting with his top advisers in the Situation Room, the nerve center in the basement of the White House. Months of planning had come down to this moment—final approval of the invasion of Iraq. The president first asked whether any of his advisers had any last thoughts or recommendations. When none did, he asked the staff to establish a secure video link with General Tommy Franks, the commander of all U.S. armed forces in the Middle East. Franks and his senior field commanders, who were at Prince Sultan Air Force Base in Saudi Arabia, gave President Bush a final briefing, after which General Franks concluded, "The force is ready to go, Mr. President." President Bush then gave a prepared statement: "For the peace of the world and the benefit and freedom of the Iraqi people, I hereby give the order to execute Operation Iraqi Freedom. May God bless the troops" (Woodward, 2004, p. 379).

With these words, President Bush set in motion a controversial war that will undoubtedly be debated by historians for decades to come. Social psychologists are fascinated by how the decision to invade Iraq was made—indeed, how important decisions of any kind are made. For example, do groups of experts make better decisions than do individuals? The American government has at its disposal a huge number of talented people with expertise in world affairs, national security, human rights, and military intelligence, and it might seem that drawing on this combined expertise would lead to the best decisions. Groups don't always make good decisions, however—especially when they are blinded by the desire to maintain cohesiveness or to please a dominant leader. In this chapter, we will focus on questions about the nature of groups and how they influence people's behavior, which are some of the oldest topics in social psychology (Forsyth & Burnette, 2010; Kerr & Tindale, 2004; Wittenbaum & Moreland, 2008; Yuki & Brewer, 2014).

What Is a Group?

9.1 What are groups, and why do people join them?

Group

Two or more people who interact and are interdependent in the sense that their needs and goals cause them to influence each other

Six students studying independently at tables in the library are not a group. But if they meet to study for their psychology final together, they are. A **group** consists of two or more people who interact and are interdependent in the sense that their needs and goals cause them to influence each other (Cartwright & Zander, 1968; Lewin, 1948; Turner, 1982). (However, groups are usually larger than two, with two people sometimes referred to as a dyad instead; Moreland, 2010.) Like a president's advisers working together to reach a foreign policy decision, citizens meeting to solve a community problem, or people who have gathered to blow off steam at a party, groups consist of people who have assembled for a common purpose.

Think for a moment of the number of groups to which you belong. Don't forget to include your family, campus groups (such as clubs or political organizations), community groups, sports teams, and more temporary groups (such as your classmates in a small seminar). All of these count as groups because you interact with the other members and you are interdependent: You influence them, and they influence you.

Why Do People Join Groups?

Joining forces with others allows us to accomplish objectives that would be more difficult to meet individually. (Ever try to move to a new dorm room or apartment on your own? Much quicker and less painful if you can get others to help you.) Forming relationships with other people also fulfills a number of basic human needs—so basic, in fact, that there may be an innate need to belong to groups. Some researchers argue that in our evolutionary past, there was a substantial survival advantage to establishing bonds with other people (Baumeister & Leary, 1995; DeWall & Richman, 2011). People who bonded together were better able to hunt for and grow food, find mates, and care for children. Consequently, researchers argue, the need to belong has become entrenched in all societies. Consistent with this view, people in all cultures are motivated to form relationships with other people and to resist the dissolution of these relationships (Gardner, Pickett, & Brewer, 2000; Manstead, 1997). People monitor their status in groups and look for any sign that they might be rejected (Blackhart, Nelson, Knowles, & Baumeister, 2009; Kerr & Levine, 2008; Leary & Baumeister, 2000; Pickett & Gardner, 2005). One study found that people who were asked to recall a time when they had been rejected by others estimated the temperature of the current room they were in to be 5 degrees lower than did people who were asked to recall a time when they were accepted by others (IJzerman & Semin, 2010; Zhong & Leonardelli, 2008). Social rejection can be, literally, chilling.

Groups have a number of benefits. They are an important part of our identity, helping us define who we are, and are a source of social norms, the explicit or implicit rules defining what is acceptable behavior. Groups also help us accomplish goals that we could not complete on our own.

Not only do people have a strong need to belong to social groups, but they also have a need to feel distinctive from those who do *not* belong to the same groups. If you go to a large state university, you might have a sense of belonging, but being a member of such a large collective is unlikely to make you feel distinctive from others. Groups that are relatively small can fulfill both functions by giving us a sense of belonging with our fellow group members and also making us feel special and distinctive. This helps explain why people are attracted to smaller groups within their college environments, such as fraternities or sororities (Brewer, 1991, 2007; Tasdemir, 2011).

Another important function of groups is that they help us define who we are. As we saw in Chapter 8, other people can be an important source of information, helping us resolve ambiguity about the nature of the social world (Darley, 2004). Groups provide a lens through which we can understand the world and our place in it (Hogg, Hohman, & Rivera, 2008). So groups become an important part of our identity—witness the number of times people wear shirts emblazoned with the name of one of their groups (e.g., a campus organization, a sports team, their university or college). Groups also help establish social norms, the explicit or implicit rules defining what is acceptable behavior.

The Composition and Functions of Groups

The groups to which you belong probably vary in size from a few members to several dozen members. Most groups, however, have three to six members (Desportes & Lemaine, 1988; Levine & Moreland, 1998; McPherson, 1983). If groups become too large, you cannot interact with all the members; for example, the college or university that you attend is not a group because you are unlikely to meet and have interdependent goals with every other student. In the sections to follow, we will consider factors that influence how individuals behave within groups and how groups themselves function.

SOCIAL NORMS　As we saw in Chapter 8, social norms are a powerful determinant of our behavior (Hogg, 2010; Kameda, Takezawa, & Hastie, 2005; Sanfey, Stallen, & Chang, 2014). All societies have norms about which behaviors are acceptable, some of which all members are expected to obey (e.g., we should be quiet in libraries) and some of which vary from group to group (e.g., what is appropriate to wear to weddings and funerals). If you belong to a fraternity or sorority, you can probably think of social norms that govern behavior in your group, such as whether alcoholic beverages are consumed and how you are supposed to feel about rival fraternities or sororities.

It is unlikely that your singing group, drama ensemble, or other groups to which you belong share these same exact norms. The power of norms to shape behavior becomes clear when we violate them too often: We are shunned by other group members and, in extreme cases, pressured to leave the group (Jetten & Hornsey, 2014; Marques, Abrams, & Serodio, 2001; Schachter, 1951).

Social Roles

Shared expectations in a group about how particular people are supposed to behave

SOCIAL ROLES Most groups have a number of well-defined **social roles**, which are shared expectations in a group about how particular people are supposed to behave (Ellemers & Jetten, 2013; Hare, 2003). Whereas norms specify how all group members should act, roles specify how people who occupy certain positions in the group should behave. In a business, a boss and an employee occupy different roles and are expected to act in different ways in that setting. Like social norms, roles can be very helpful because people know what to expect from each other. When members of a group follow a set of clearly defined roles, they tend to be satisfied and perform well (Barley & Bechky, 1994; Bettencourt & Sheldon, 2001).

There are, however, potential costs to social roles. People can get so far into a role that their personal identities and personalities get lost. Suppose that you agreed to take part in a 2-week psychology experiment in which you were randomly assigned to play the role of a guard or a prisoner in a simulated prison. You might think that the role you were assigned to play would not be very important; after all, everyone knows that it is only an experiment and that people are just pretending to be guards or prisoners. Philip Zimbardo and his colleagues, however, had a different hypothesis. They believed that social roles can be so powerful that they overwhelm our personal identities to the point that we become the role we are playing.

To test this idea, Zimbardo and colleagues conducted a highly unusual (and controversial) study. They built a mock prison in the basement of the psychology department at Stanford University and paid students to play the role of guard or prisoner (Haney, Banks, & Zimbardo, 1973; Zimbardo, 2007). The role students played was determined by the flip of a coin. Guards were outfitted with a uniform of khaki shirts and pants, a whistle, a police nightstick, and reflective sunglasses. Prisoners were given a loose-fitting smock with an identification number stamped on it, rubber sandals, a cap made from a nylon stocking, and a locked chain attached to one ankle.

The researchers planned to observe the students for 2 weeks to see whether they began to act like real prison guards and prisoners. As it turned out, the students quickly assumed these roles—so much so that the researchers ended the experiment after only 6 days. Many of the guards became abusive, coming up with increasingly creative ways of verbally harassing and humiliating the prisoners. The prisoners became passive, helpless, and withdrawn. Some prisoners, in fact, became so anxious and depressed that they had to be released from the study earlier than the others.

Zimbardo and his colleagues randomly assigned students to play the role of prisoner or guard in a mock prison. The students assumed these roles all too well.

Remember, everyone knew that they were in a psychology experiment and that the prison was only make-believe. But the roles of guard and prisoner were so compelling and powerful that this simple truth was often overlooked. People got so far into their roles that their personal identities and sense of decency somehow got lost. In fact, one major methodological criticism of Zimbardo's study—beyond the obvious ethical questions regarding the treatment of research participants—is that the students quickly figured out what the study was about and role-played in the manner that they thought was expected of them (Banuazizi & Movahedi, 1975; Griggs & Whitehead, 2014).

But what is clear is that it didn't take coercion, bribery, or weeks and weeks of training to prompt these "guards" and "prisoners" to slip easily into their roles and that, in particular, some of the student guards clearly and quickly took things much too far.

Does this sound familiar? As mentioned in Chapter 8, in 2004 it came to light that American military guards had been abusing prisoners in Abu Ghraib, a prison in Iraq (Hersh, 2004). A report written by U.S. major general Taguba, who investigated the claims of abuse, documented numerous cases of physical beatings, sexual abuse, and psychological humiliation. The American public was shocked by pictures of U.S. soldiers smiling as they stood in front of naked Iraqi prisoners, as if they were posing in front of local landmarks for the folks back home. Did a few bad apples happen to end up in the unit guarding the prisoners? Not according to Zimbardo (2007). "What's bad is the barrel," Zimbardo argued. "The barrel is the barrel I created by my prison—and we put good boys in, just as in this Iraqi prison. And the barrel corrupts. It's the barrel of the evil of prisons—with secrecy, with no accountability—which gives people permission to do things they ordinarily would not" (quoted in O'Brien, 2004).

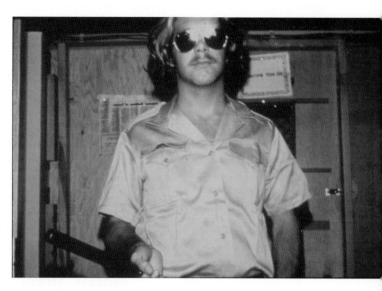

One of the guards from Zimbardo's prison experiment at Stanford.

This is not to say that the soldiers should be excused for their actions. The abuse came to light when 24-year-old Joe Darby, an army reservist at Abu Ghraib, reported what was happening. As in Zimbardo's study, not everyone was caught in the web of their social roles, unable to resist. But as much as we would like to think that we would be one of these heroes, the lesson from the Zimbardo prison study—and Milgram's studies of obedience, discussed in Chapter 8—is that many if not most of us would not fully resist the social influences in these powerful situations and would perhaps perform acts we thought we were incapable of.

GROUP COHESIVENESS   Another important aspect of how a group functions is how cohesive it is. **Group cohesiveness** refers to the qualities of a group that bind members together and promote mutual liking (Dion, 2000; Hogg, 1993; Holtz, 2004; Rosh, Offermann, & Van Diest, 2012). If a group has formed primarily for social reasons, such as a group of friends who like to go to the movies together on weekends, then the more cohesive the group is, the better. This is pretty obvious; would you rather spend your free time with a bunch of people who don't care much for each other or a tight-knit bunch of people who feel committed to you and other group members? As you would expect, the more cohesive a group is, the more its members are likely to stay in the group, take part in group activities, and try to recruit new like-minded members (Levine & Moreland, 1998; Pickett, Silver, & Brewer, 2002; Spink, Ulvick, Crozier, & Wilson, 2014).

Group Cohesiveness

Qualities of a group that bind members together and promote liking between them

If the function of the group is to work together and solve problems, however—as it is for a military unit or sales team at a company—then the story is not quite so simple. Doing well on a task causes a group to become more cohesive (Mullen & Cooper, 1994; Picazo, Gamero, Zornoza, & Peiró, 2014), but is the reverse true? Does cohesiveness cause a group to perform well? It does if the task requires close cooperation between the group members, such as the case of a football team executing a difficult play or a military unit carrying out a complicated maneuver (Casey-Campbell & Martens, 2009; Gully, Devine, & Whitney, 1995). Sometimes, however, cohesiveness can get in the way of optimal performance if maintaining good relations among group members becomes more important than finding good solutions to a problem. Is it possible, for example, that the cohesiveness felt by President Bush and his advisers got in the way of clear thinking about whether to invade Iraq? We will return to this question later in the chapter when we discuss group decision making.

GROUP DIVERSITY   Related to cohesiveness is the matter of how diverse a group's composition is. More often than not, members of a group tend to be alike in age, sex, beliefs, and opinions (Apfelbaum, Phillips, & Richeson, 2014;

George, 1990; Levine & Moreland, 1998). There are at least two reasons for the relative homogeneity of groups. First, many groups tend to attract people who are already similar before they join (Alter & Darley, 2009; Feld, 1982). As we'll see in Chapter 10, people are attracted to others who share their attitudes and thus are likely to recruit fellow group members who are similar to them. Second, groups tend to operate in ways that encourage similarity in the members (Moreland, 1987). This can happen in a number of important ways, some of which we discussed in Chapter 8.

In short, people tend to gravitate toward groups with similar others, and such similarity typically predicts group cohesiveness. Consider a study conducted by McLeod, Lobel, and Cox (1996) in which college students were assigned to brainstorming groups ranging in size from three to five. Half of these groups were comprised entirely of White students. That is, these groups were not diverse at all with regard to race—they were racially homogeneous. The other half of the groups were racially diverse, including White students as well as Asian American, African American, and/or Latino students. All groups, regardless of their diversity, were assigned the same task: to spend 15 minutes brainstorming ideas for how best to attract more tourists to the United States. At the end of each session, participants were asked how much they liked the other members of their group. As you might predict based on the conclusion that homogeneous groups are often cohesive, members of all-White groups reported liking their fellow group members more than did members of diverse groups.

But remember that just because a group is cohesive does not mean it is performing at its optimal level. Indeed, when McLeod and colleagues (1996) analyzed the ideas each group developed for boosting tourism, they found that the diverse groups had come up with more feasible and effective possibilities. Participants may have enjoyed being in a group with similar others, but their performance was strongest when in a diverse group. These findings are consistent with more general conclusions that while diversity—of all types, not just related to race—can sometimes come at the expense of a group's cohesiveness and morale, a diversity of backgrounds or perspectives often predicts improved performance in terms of group creativity, information sharing, and flexible problem solving (De Dreu & Weingart, 2003; Phillips, Mannix, Neale, & Gruenfeld, 2004; Sommers, 2006).

There is no simple answer to the question of how diversity affects groups (Apfelbaum et al., 2014; Mannix & Neale, 2005; van Knippenberg, van Ginkel, & Homan, 2013). For that matter, as we just alluded to, there are many ways to define a group's diversity—in terms of race and other social demographics, sure, but also diversity in terms of experience, education, attitude, and other dimensions. Increasingly, though, a variety of organizations seem to be betting on the positive potential of diversity. There is a reason why institutions such as universities, the military, and Fortune 500 companies currently spend effort and resources to achieve diversity in their ranks: They believe that it will lead to improved performance, whether in terms of learning environment or the corporate bottom line (Herring, 2009; Page, 2008). Figure 9.1 suggests that—in correlational terms at least—they are often right. Similarly, in a more recent experimental study using a stock market simulation, researchers found that traders randomly assigned to an ethnically diverse marketplace made better, more accurate decisions about how to price stocks than did equally experienced traders assigned to a homogeneous market, supporting the conclusion that the friction caused by diversity

> Isn't it amazing that we are all made in God's image, and yet there is so much diversity among his people?
> —DESMOND TUTU, 2010

Figure 9.1 Racial/Gender Diversity and Business Performance

To examine the relationship between a business's performance and its racial and gender diversity, Herring (2009) conducted a correlational study of over 1,000 U.S. workplaces and found a positive association between both types of diversity with (a) sales revenue and (b) number of customers. These results seem to indicate a positive relationship between diversity and a business's bottom line. But as you know, because these data are only correlational, we cannot draw conclusions here regarding one variable causing another.

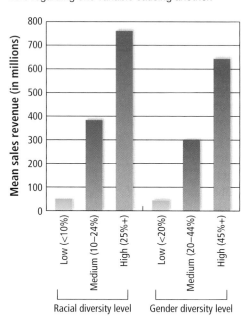

can upend conformity and improve decision making (Levine et al., 2015). And still other research indicates that the threats to cohesiveness and morale posed by diversity are usually short term, lessening over time as group members learn to work with one other and even come to take pride in their group's diversity (Allmendinger & Hackman, 1995; Jehn, Northcraft, & Neale, 1999). In short, while no one ever said navigating diversity would be easy, research findings support the proposition that group diversity often brings with it a variety of long-term performance benefits.

REVIEW QUESTIONS

1. Which of the following is *not* an example of a group?
   a. Six students studying together for an exam
   b. The 12-person cast of a musical theater production
   c. A four-person work team collaborating on a project via Web conferencing
   d. Seven commuters waiting together silently at a bus stop

2. One reason people join groups is to
   a. avoid having to deal with normative social influence.
   b. accomplish objectives that are more difficult or impossible to accomplish alone.
   c. decrease their cohesiveness.
   d. avoid well-defined social roles.

3. Group cohesiveness is particularly important for a group when
   a. the group has formed for primarily social reasons.
   b. the group's primary objective is problem solving.
   c. the group is diverse in terms of gender but not when it is diverse in terms of race.
   d. financial decision making is involved.

4. From an evolutionary perspective, groups
   a. are more productive when they have two or three members as opposed to when they are larger.
   b. help fulfill a basic human need to affiliate and belong with others.

   c. often lead to immoral behavior, such as that observed among abusive prison guards.
   d. are better able than individuals to avoid the influence of social norms.

5. Richard needs a team of highly goal-oriented individuals for a short-term project. The members would be required to work closely with each other and solve issues related to a new product being launched by the company. Can cohesiveness between the team members interfere in the optimal performance of the team?
   a. No, a group is formed mainly for social reasons and cohesiveness is an essential element of every group.
   b. Yes, if maintaining good relations among group members becomes more important than finding solutions to problems.
   c. Yes, a good team is one that remains focused on routine tasks rather than being cohesive.
   d. No, a group that is high on cohesiveness ensures effective decisions from its members.

See page 621 for the answers.

Individual Behavior in a Group Setting

9.2   **In what ways do individuals perform differently when others are around?**

Thus far, we have focused on why people join groups and how groups function. But another question we might ask is, what are the effects of being in a group on the performance of individual people? Do you act differently when others are around? When do we "choke" under the pressure of having people watching us? When does having other people around lead us to raise our game and perform better than usual? Simply being in the presence of other people can have a variety of interesting effects on our behavior. We will begin by looking at how a group affects your performance on something with which you are no doubt very familiar—taking a test in a class.

Social Facilitation: When the Presence of Others Energizes Us

It is time for the final exam in your psychology class. You have spent countless hours studying the material, and you feel ready. When you arrive, you see that the exam is scheduled in a tiny room already packed with students. You squeeze into an empty desk, elbow to elbow with your classmates. The professor arrives and says that if any students are bothered by the close quarters, they can take the test by themselves in one of several smaller rooms down the hall. What should you do?

The question is whether being with other people will affect your performance (Geen, 1989; Guerin, 1993; Zajonc, 1965). The presence of others can mean one of two things: (a) performing a task with coworkers who are doing the same thing you are or (b) performing a task in front of an audience that is not doing anything but observing you. Note that the question is a basic one about the effects of the mere presence of other people, even if they are not part of a group that is interacting. Does the simple fact that other people are around you make a difference, even if you never speak or interact with them in any way?

To answer this question, we need to talk about insects—cockroaches, in fact. Believe it or not, a classic study using cockroaches as research subjects suggests an answer to the question of how you should opt to take your psychology test. Robert Zajonc and his colleagues (Zajonc, Heingartner, & Herman, 1969) built a contraption to see how a cockroach's behavior was influenced by the presence of its peers. The researchers placed a bright light (which cockroaches dislike) at the end of a runway and timed how long it took a roach to escape the light by running to the other end, where it could scurry into a darkened box (see the left side of Figure 9.2). The question was, did roaches perform this simple feat faster when they were by themselves or when they were in the presence of other cockroaches?

> Mere social contact begets . . . a stimulation of the animal spirit that heightens the efficiency of each individual workman.
>
> —Karl Marx, *Das Kapital*, 1867

Figure 9.2 Cockroaches and Social Facilitation

In the maze on the left, cockroaches had a simple task: to go from the starting point down the runway to the darkened box. They performed this feat faster when other roaches were watching than when they were alone. In the maze on the right, the cockroaches had a more difficult task. It took them longer to solve this maze when other roaches were watching than when they were alone.

(Based on data in Zajonc, Heingartner, & Herman, 1969)

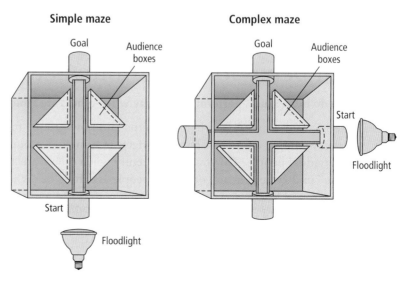

You might be wondering how the researchers managed to persuade other cockroaches to be spectators. They simply placed other roaches in clear plastic boxes next to the runway. These roaches were in the bleachers, so to speak, observing the solitary cockroach do its thing (see Figure 9.2). As predicted, the individual cockroaches performed the task faster when other roaches were there watching than when they were by themselves.

We would not give advice on how you should take your psychology test based only on one study that used cockroaches. But the story does not end here. Dozens of studies have been done on the effects of the mere presence of others, involving human beings as well as other species, such as ants and birds (e.g., Aiello & Douthitt, 2001; Krasheninnikova & Schneider, 2014; Sharma, Booth, Brown, & Huguet, 2010). The findings of these studies are remarkably consistent: As long as the task is a relatively simple, well-learned one—as escaping a light is for cockroaches—the mere presence of others improves performance.

Research on social facilitation finds that people do better on a well-learned task when in the presence of others than when they are alone. If students have studied hard and know the material well, they might be better off taking an exam in a room with lots of other people.

SIMPLE VERSUS DIFFICULT TASKS   Before concluding that you should stay in the crowded classroom to take your exam, we need to consider a different set of findings. Remember that we said that the presence of others enhances performance on *simple, well-learned* tasks, like cockroaches escaping a light. What happens when we give people a more difficult task to do and place them in the presence of others? To find out, Zajonc and his colleagues (1969) included another condition in the cockroach experiment. This time, the cockroaches had to solve a maze that had several runways, only one of which led to the darkened box (see the right side of Figure 9.2). When working on this more difficult task, the opposite pattern of results occurred: The roaches took *longer* to solve it when other roaches were present than when they were alone. Many other studies have also found that people and animals do worse in the presence of others when the task is difficult (e.g., Augustinova & Ferrand, 2012; Bond & Titus, 1983; Geen, 1989).

AROUSAL AND THE DOMINANT RESPONSE   In an influential article, Zajonc (1965) offered an elegant theoretical explanation for why the presence of others facilitates a well-learned response but inhibits a less practiced or new response. He argued that the presence of others increases physiological arousal (i.e., our bodies become more energized). When such arousal exists, it is easier to perform a dominant response (e.g., something we're good at) but harder to do something complex or learn something new. Consider, for example, a behavior that is second nature to you, such as riding a bicycle or writing your name. Arousal caused by the presence of other people watching you should make it even easier to perform these well-learned tasks. But let's say you have to do something more complex, such as learning a new sport or working on a difficult math problem. Now arousal will lead you to feel flustered and do less well than if you were alone (Schmitt, Gilovich, Goore, & Joseph, 1986). This phenomenon became known as **social facilitation**, which is the tendency for people to do better on simple tasks and worse on complex tasks when they are in the presence of others and their individual performance can be evaluated.

WHY THE PRESENCE OF OTHERS CAUSES AROUSAL   Why does the presence of others lead to arousal? Researchers have developed three theories to explain the role of arousal in social facilitation: Other people cause us to become particularly alert and vigilant, they make us apprehensive about how we're being evaluated, and they distract us from the task at hand.

Social Facilitation

When people are in the presence of others and their individual performance can be evaluated, the tendency to perform better on simple tasks and worse on complex tasks

The first explanation suggests that the presence of other people makes us more alert. When we are by ourselves reading a book, we don't have to pay attention to anything but the book; we don't have to worry that the lamp will ask us a question. When someone else is in the room, however, we have to be alert to the possibility that he or she will do something that requires us to respond. Because other people are less predictable than lamps, we are in a state of greater alertness in their presence. This alertness, or vigilance, causes mild arousal. The beauty of this explanation (the one preferred by Zajonc, 1980) is that it explains both the animal and the human studies. A solitary cockroach need not worry about what the cockroach in the next room is doing; however, it needs to be alert when in the presence of another member of its species—and the same goes for human beings.

The second explanation focuses on the fact that unlike cockroaches, people are often concerned about how others are evaluating them. When other people can see how you are doing, the stakes are raised: You feel as if the other people are evaluating you; you will be embarrassed if you do poorly and pleased if you do well. This concern about being judged, called *evaluation apprehension*, can cause arousal. According to this view, then, it is not the mere presence of others but rather the presence of others who are evaluating us that causes arousal and subsequent social facilitation (Blascovich, Mendes, Hunter, & Salomon, 1999; Muller & Butera, 2007).

The third explanation centers on how distracting other people can be (Feinberg & Aiello, 2006; Muller, Atzeni, & Fabrizio, 2004). It is similar to Zajonc's (1980) notion that we need to be alert when in the presence of others, except that it focuses on the idea that any source of distraction—be it the presence of other people or noise from the party going on in the apartment upstairs—will put us in a state of conflict because it is difficult to pay attention to two things at the same time. This divided attention produces arousal, as any college student knows who has ever tried to get work done in the presence of a roommate who is listening to loud music, talking on the phone, or otherwise making it hard to focus. Consistent with this interpretation, nonsocial sources of distraction, such as a flashing light, can cause the same kinds of social facilitation effects as the presence of other people (Baron, 1986).

We have summarized research on social facilitation in the top half of Figure 9.3 (we will discuss the bottom half in a moment). This figure illustrates that there is more than one reason why the presence of other people is arousing. The consequences of this arousal, however, are the same: When you are around other people, you do better on tasks that are simple and well learned, but you do worse on tasks that are complex and require you to learn something new.

Where, then, should you take your psychology exam? We recommend that you stay with your classmates, assuming you know the material well, so that it is relatively simple for you to recall it. The arousal produced by being elbow to elbow with your classmates should improve your performance. But when you study for an exam—that is, when you learn new material—you should do so by yourself, away from other people. In this situation, the arousal caused by others will make it more difficult to concentrate. And, oh yes, it is not only the presence of real people who can influence our behavior—so can the presence of our favorite television characters. In one study, college students performed a simple or complex task while a picture of their favorite television character or some other television character was displayed on a computer screen. When the television character was people's favorite, it was as if a real person was in the room: People did better on the simple task but worse on the complex task. When the television character wasn't people's favorite, their performance was unaffected. And, interestingly, the results were the same for human versus animated characters—social facilitation occurred in the presence of a beloved doctor from *Grey's Anatomy* but also for those participants whose favorite was, say, Stewie from *Family Guy* (Gardner & Knowles, 2008).

Figure 9.3 Social Facilitation and Social Loafing

The presence of others can lead to social facilitation or social loafing. The important variables that distinguish the two are evaluation, arousal, and the complexity of the tasks.

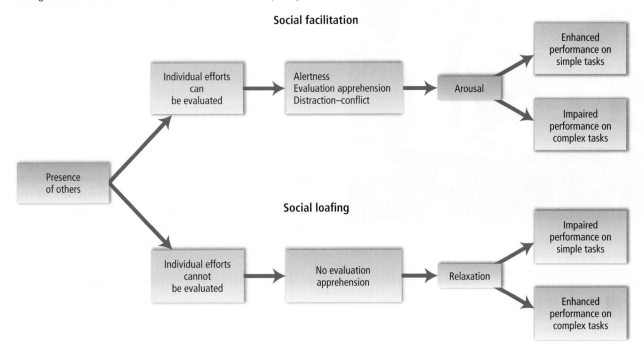

Social Loafing: When the Presence of Others Relaxes Us

When you take your psychology exam, your individual efforts will be evaluated (i.e., you will be graded on the test). This is typical of the research on social facilitation we have reviewed: People are working on something either alone or in the presence of others, and their individual efforts are easily evaluated. Often when you are in the presence of others, however, your individual efforts cannot be distinguished from those of the people around you. Such is the case when you clap after a concert (no one can tell how loudly you as an individual are clapping) or when you play an instrument in a marching band (your instrument blends in with all the others).

These situations are the opposite of the social facilitation settings we have just considered. In social facilitation, the presence of others puts the spotlight on you, making you aroused. But if being with other people means we can merge into a group, becoming less noticeable than when we are alone, we should become relaxed. Because no one can tell how well we are doing, we should feel less evaluation apprehension. What happens then? Will this relaxation produced by becoming lost in the crowd lead to better or worse performance? Again, the answer depends on whether we are working on a simple, unimportant task or a complex task.

Let's first consider simple tasks, such as trying to pull as hard as you can on a rope. The question of how working with others would influence performance on such a basic task was first studied in the 1880s by a French agricultural engineer, Max Ringelmann (1913). He found that when a group of men pulled on a rope, each individual exerted less effort than when he did it alone. In other words, eight individuals pulling on the rope did not exert eight times the force as one person pulling

Which of us . . . is to do the hard and dirty work for the rest—and for what pay?

—*John Ruskin*

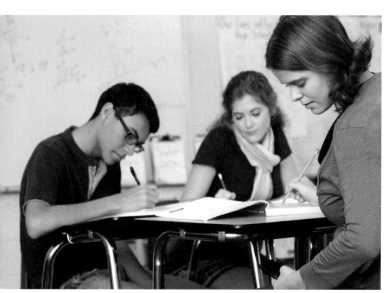

Sometimes being surrounded by others allows us to slack off (or "loaf"), demonstrating that there's not a single, simple answer to the question of how the presence of other people affects individual performance.

Social Loafing

When people are in the presence of others and their individual performance cannot be evaluated, the tendency to perform worse on simple or unimportant tasks but better on complex or important tasks

alone. A century later, social psychologists Bibb Latané, Kipling Williams, and Stephen Harkins (2006) called this **social loafing**, which is the tendency for people to relax when they are in the presence of others and their individual performance cannot be evaluated, such that they do worse on simple tasks that they don't care about but better on complex tasks that are important to them. Social loafing in groups has since been found on a variety of simple tasks, such as clapping your hands, cheering loudly, and thinking of as many uses for an object as you can (Karau & Williams, 2001; Lount & Wilk, 2014; Shepperd & Taylor, 1999).

What about complex tasks? Recall that when performance in a group cannot be identified, people become more relaxed. Recall also our earlier discussion of the effects of arousal on performance: Arousal enhances performance on simple tasks but impairs performance on complex tasks. By the same reasoning, becoming relaxed impairs performance on simple tasks—as we have just seen—but can improve performance on complex tasks (Jackson & Williams, 1985). This process is illustrated on the bottom part of Figure 9.3.

Gender and Cultural Differences in Social Loafing: Who Slacks Off the Most?

Kate and William are working with several classmates on a class project, and no one will be able to assess their individual contributions. Who is more likely to slack off and let the other do most of the work: Kate or William? If you said William, you are probably right. In a review of more than 150 studies of social loafing, the tendency to loaf was found to be stronger in men than in women (Karau & Williams, 1993). Women tend to be higher than men in *relational interdependence*, which is the tendency to focus on and care about personal relationships with other individuals. Perhaps it is this focus that makes women less likely to engage in social loafing when in groups (Eagly, 1987; Wood, 1987).

Research has also found that the tendency to loaf is stronger in Western cultures than Asian cultures, which may be due to the different self-definitions prevalent in these cultures (Karau & Williams, 1993). Asians are more likely to have an *interdependent view of the self*, which is a way of defining oneself in terms of relationships to other people (see Chapter 5). This self-definition may reduce the tendency toward social loafing when in groups. We should not, however, exaggerate these gender and cultural differences. Women and members of Asian cultures do engage in social loafing when in groups; they are just less relatively likely to do so than men or members of Western cultures (Chang & Chen, 1995; Hong, Wyer, & Fong, 2008).

To summarize, you need to know two things to predict whether the presence of others will help or hinder your performance: whether your individual efforts can be evaluated and whether the task is simple or complex. If your performance can be evaluated, the presence of others will make you alert and aroused. This will lead to social facilitation effects, where people do better on simple tasks but worse on complex tasks (see the top of Figure 9.3). If your efforts cannot be evaluated (i.e., you are one cog in a machine), you are likely to become more relaxed. This leads to social loafing effects, where people do worse on simple tasks that they don't care about but better on complex ones (see the bottom of Figure 9.3).

These findings have numerous implications for the way in which groups should be organized. On the one hand, if you are a manager who wants your employees to work on a relatively simple problem, a little evaluation apprehension is not such a bad thing—it may very well improve performance. You shouldn't place your employees in groups where their individual performance cannot be observed because social loafing (lowered performance on simple tasks) is likely to result. On the other hand, if you want your employees to work on a difficult, complex task, then lowering their evaluation apprehension—by placing them in groups in which their individual performance cannot be observed—is likely to result in better performance.

Deindividuation: Getting Lost in the Crowd

The consequences of feeling anonymous can be much more serious than loafing on a group task, however. Being in a group can also cause **deindividuation**, which is the loosening of normal constraints on behavior when people can't be identified (Lea, Spears, & de Groot, 2001). In other words, getting lost in a crowd can lead to an unleashing of behaviors that we would never dream of exhibiting by ourselves. Throughout history, there have been many examples of groups of people committing horrendous acts that no individual would do on his or her own, such as military atrocities; acts of looting, arson, and violence; hysterical fans at rock concerts trampling each other to death; and other examples sometimes referred to more colloquially as resulting from a "mob mentality."

One particularly troubling example in the United States is the shameful history of Whites—often cloaked in the anonymity of hooded robes—lynching African Americans. Brian Mullen (1986) content-analyzed newspaper accounts of 60 lynchings committed between 1899 and 1946 and discovered that the more people there were in the mob in question, the greater the savagery and viciousness with which they killed their victims. Similar results were observed by Robert Watson (1973), who studied 24 cultures and found that warriors who hid their identities before going into battle—for example, by using face and body paint—were significantly more likely to kill, torture, or mutilate captive prisoners than were warriors who did not hide their identities.

DEINDIVIDUATION MAKES PEOPLE FEEL LESS ACCOUNTABLE   Why does deindividuation seem to lead to and exacerbate impulsive (often violent) acts? One reason is that recognizing that there is a reduced likelihood that any individual will be singled out and blamed leaves people feeling less accountable for their actions (Diener, 1980; Postmes & Spears, 1998; Zimbardo, 1970). In Harper Lee's novel *To Kill a Mockingbird*, for example, a mob of White southerners assembled to lynch Tom Robinson, a Black man falsely accused of rape. Here is a classic case of deindividuation: It was night, the men were dressed alike, and it was difficult to tell one from another. But then Scout, the 8-year-old daughter of Robinson's attorney, Atticus, recognized one of the farmers and greeted him by name. She unwittingly performed a brilliant social psychological intervention by making the mob feel more like individuals who were accountable for their actions. And, indeed, the mob then disbanded and went home.

DEINDIVIDUATION INCREASES OBEDIENCE TO GROUP NORMS   In a meta-analysis of more than 60 studies, researchers found that becoming deindividuated also increases the extent to which people obey the group's norms (Postmes & Spears, 1998). Sometimes the norms of a specific group to which we belong conflict with the norms of other groups or of society at large. When these group members are together and deindividuated, they become more likely to act according to the group norms

Deindividuation
The loosening of normal constraints on behavior when people can't be identified (such as when they are in a crowd)

If you can keep your head when all about you are losing theirs . . .
—Rudyard Kipling, "*If*," 1909

The robes and hoods of the Ku Klux Klan cloak its members in anonymity; their violent behavior is consistent with research on deindividuation.

than societal norms. In *To Kill a Mockingbird*, for example, the norms of the lynch mob were to take the law into their own hands, but clearly these norms conflicted with other rules and laws. Because of the conditions promoting deindividuation, they were about to ignore the others and act on the group's norms until Scout stepped in and reminded them that they were individuals. Thus, it is not just that deindividuation reduces the likelihood that one person will stand out and be blamed but also that it increases adherence to the local group's norms.

Consequently, deindividuation does not always lead to aggressive or antisocial behavior—it depends on what the norm of the group is. Imagine that you are at a rowdy college party at which everyone is dancing wildly to very loud music. To the extent that you feel deindividuated—it is dark, and you are dressed similarly to other people—you are more likely to join the group and let loose on the dance floor. Thus, it is the specific norm of the group that determines whether deindividuation will lead to positive or negative behaviors (Hirsh, Galinsky, & Zhong, 2011; Johnson & Downing, 1979). If the group is angry and the norm is to act violently, deindividuation will make people in the group act aggressively. If we are at a party and the norm is to eat a lot, being deindividuated will simply increase the likelihood that we will eat the entire bowl of guacamole.

DEINDIVIDUATION ONLINE   Deindividuation doesn't require face-to-face contact. In fact, it thrives with less physical forms of interaction. Anyone who has ever read the comments section at the bottom of a Web site news article or YouTube clip has witnessed deindividuation at work, whereby people feel less inhibited about what they write because of their anonymity. In many respects, the Internet is ideal terrain for the emergence of deindividuation (Lee, 2004). Given how quickly many Web forums deteriorate into strings of insulting "trolling" or obscene comments, numerous Web sites have moved away from allowing anonymous participation, now requiring users to sign in with a Facebook account or other identifying information before they are allowed to post.

In the pre-Internet era, angry readers and others seeking to stir up debate would have written letters to a newspaper editor or vented their feelings to coworkers at the watercooler. In both cases, their discourse would have likely been more civil, free of the profanities used in many online forums, in large part because people are not anonymous in these older settings. With the onset of new, online ways in which we can communicate anonymously come certain advantages in terms of free and open discussion of difficult topics. But there is also a cost, namely, an apparent reduction in common civility. And one of the chief culprits responsible is deindividuation.

The phenomenon of the internet "troll" is a modern example of deindividuation, made possible by the feelings of anonymity that often go along with being on-line.

REVIEW QUESTIONS

1. The concept of *social facilitation* is so named because of the idea that when the presence of others is arousing,
   a. this arousal facilitates better task performance.
   b. this arousal facilitates a well-learned, dominant response.
   c. hard tasks are facilitated, but easy tasks are impeded.
   d. deindividuation is facilitated.

2. Which of the following is *not* an explanation for why the presence of other people can be arousing?
   a. The presence of other people is distracting and causes conflict, as individuals have to decide what they should pay attention to.
   b. When other people are around, an individual has to be on alert in anticipation of what might happen next.
   c. When other people are around, individuals become more concerned about how they are being evaluated.
   d. Having other people around makes an individual feel less accountable for his or her own actions.

3. Your social psychology professor calls you up to the front of the classroom and asks you to answer a series of course-related questions out loud. Even though you feel the eyes of your classmates on you, you find the questions to be easy. According to the model of _____, you should perform _____ on these questions than you would have if you had been asked them in private, without an audience.
   a. social facilitation; worse
   b. social facilitation; better
   c. social loafing; worse
   d. social loafing; better

4. Women are less likely to engage in social loafing compared to men because they tend to
   a. be lower in relational interdependence.
   b. have no relational interdependence.
   c. be higher in relational interdependence.
   d. know that people will notice them.

5. Individuals experiencing deindividuation
   a. feel increasingly accountable for their actions.
   b. exhibit greater conformity to specific group norms.
   c. are less likely to engage in destructive or immoral behavior.
   d. are unlikely to experience this feeling online, as deindividuation is much less common in virtual environments.

See page 621 for the answers.

Group Decisions: Are Two (or More) Heads Better Than One?

9.3 Are two (or more) heads better than one in decision making, and how do leaders shape group outcomes?

We have just seen that the presence of other people influences individual behavior in a number of interesting ways. We turn now to one of the major functions of groups: making decisions. Most important decisions in the world today are made by groups because it is assumed that groups are better decision makers than individuals. In the American judicial system, for example, most verdicts are determined by groups of individuals (juries), not single individuals (see Social Psychology in Action 3, "Social Psychology and the Law"). The U.S. Supreme Court is made up of nine justices, not just one. Similarly, governmental and corporate decisions are often made by groups of people who meet to discuss the issues; U.S. presidents have a cabinet and the National Security Council to advise them.

> Nor is the people's judgement always true: The most may err as grossly as the few.
>
> —JOHN DRYDEN, *ABSALOM AND ACHITOPHEL*, 1682

Is it true that two (or more) heads are better than one? Most of us assume the answer is yes. A lone individual may be subject to all sorts of whims and biases, whereas several people together can exchange ideas, catch each other's errors, and reach better decisions. We have all taken part in group decisions in which we listened to someone else and thought to ourselves, "Hmm, that's a really good point—I never would have thought of that." In general, groups can perform better than individuals when group members freely contribute independent opinions from a variety of viewpoints, if people are motivated to search for the answer that is best for the entire group and not just for themselves, or when they rely on the individual with the most expertise (De Dreu, Nijstad, & van Knippenberg, 2008; Surowiecki, 2004). Sometimes, though, two or more heads are not better than one—or at least no better than two heads working alone (Hackman & Katz, 2010; Kerr & Tindale, 2004). Several factors can cause groups to make worse decisions than individuals would.

Process Loss: When Group Interactions Inhibit Good Problem Solving

One potential problem is that a group can perform well only if the most expert or talented members can convince the others that they are right. This is not always easy, given that many of us bear a strong resemblance to mules when it comes to admitting we are wrong. You undoubtedly know what it's like to try to convince a group to follow your idea, be faced with opposition and disbelief, and then have to sit there and watch the group make the wrong decision. This is called **process loss**, which is any aspect of group interaction that inhibits good problem solving (Steiner, 1972; Tidikis & Ash, 2013). Process loss can occur for a number of reasons. Groups might not try hard enough to find out who the most competent members are and instead rely on someone who really doesn't know what he or she is talking about. Perhaps the most competent members find it difficult to disagree with everyone else in the group (recall our discussion of normative social pressures in Chapter 8). Other causes of process loss involve communication problems: In some groups, people don't listen to each other; in others, one person is allowed to dominate the discussion while the others tune out (Sorkin, Hays, & West, 2001; Watson, Johnson, Kumar, & Critelli, 1998).

Process Loss

Any aspect of group interaction that inhibits good problem solving

FAILURE TO SHARE UNIQUE INFORMATION   Suppose you are meeting with three other people to decide whether to support a particular candidate for Student Senate president. You all know some of the same things about the candidate, such as the fact that she was president of her sophomore class and is an economics major. But each of you has unique information as well. Maybe you are the only one who knows that she was punished for underage drinking in her first-year dorm, whereas one of the other group members is the only one who knows that she volunteers every week at a local homeless shelter. Obviously, the four of you will make the best decision if you share with each other everything you know about the candidate.

But there is a funny thing about groups: They tend to focus on the information they already share and ignore facts known to only some members of the group (McLeod, 2013; Toma & Butera, 2009; Wittenbaum & Park, 2001). One study, for example, used a situation similar to the one we have just described, in which students decided who among several candidates was most qualified to be student body president (Stasser & Titus, 1985). In the shared information condition, groups of four participants were given the same packet of information to read, which indicated that Candidate A was the best choice for office. Not surprisingly, when the groups met to discuss the candidates, almost all of the members chose Candidate A. In the unshared information condition, each participant in the group received a different packet of information. All participants learned that Candidate A had the same four negative qualities, but each learned that Candidate A also had two unique positive qualities—that is, positive qualities that were different from those listed in other participants' packets. Thus, if the four participants shared with each other the information that was in their packets, they would learn that Candidate A had a total of eight positive qualities and four negative qualities. Instead, most of the groups in the unshared information condition never realized that Candidate A had more good than bad qualities because when they met, they focused on the information they shared rather than on the information they did not. As a result, few of these groups chose Candidate A.

Subsequent research has focused on ways to get groups to focus more on unshared information (Campbell & Stasser, 2006; Scholten, van Knippenberg, Nijstad, & De Dreu, 2007). Unshared information is more likely to be brought up later in the discussion, suggesting that group discussions should last long enough to get beyond what everyone already knows (Fraidin, 2004; Larson, Christensen, Franz, & Abbott, 1998). It also helps to tell group members not to share what their initial preferences are at the outset of the discussion; if they do, they will focus less on unique, unshared information (Mojzisch & Schulz-Hardt, 2010). Another approach is to assign different group members to specific areas of expertise so that they know that they alone are responsible for certain types of information (Stasser, Stewart, & Wittenbaum, 1995; Stewart & Stasser, 1995).

This last lesson has been learned by many couples, who know to rely on each other's memories for different kinds of information. One member of a couple might be responsible for remembering the times of social engagements, whereas the other might be responsible for remembering when to pay the bills. When the combined memory of a group is more efficient than the memory of its individual members, we call it **transactive memory** (Peltokorpi, 2008; Rajaram & Pereira-Pasarin, 2010; Wegner, 1995). By learning to specialize their memories and knowing what their partner is responsible for, couples often do quite well in remembering important information. The same can be true of groups if they develop a system whereby different people are responsible for remembering different parts of a task (Ellis, Porter, & Wolverton, 2008; Lewis, Belliveau, Herndon, & Keller, 2007; Moreland, 1999). In sum, the tendency for groups to fail to share important information known to only some of their members can be overcome if people learn who is responsible for what kinds of information and take the time to discuss these unshared data (Stasser, 2000).

Transactive Memory

The combined memory of a group that is more efficient than the memory of the individual members

GROUPTHINK: MANY HEADS, ONE MIND   Earlier we mentioned that group cohesiveness can get in the way of clear thinking and good decision making. Using real-world events, Irving Janis (1972, 1982) developed an influential theory of group decision making that he called **groupthink**, a kind of thinking in which maintaining group cohesiveness and solidarity is more important than considering the facts in a realistic manner. According to Janis's theory, groupthink is most likely to occur when certain preconditions are met, such as when the group is highly cohesive, isolated from contrary opinions, and ruled by a directive leader who makes his or her wishes known. One of his examples is illustrated in the Bay of Pigs invasion, the decision that President John F. Kennedy and his advisers made to invade Cuba in 1961. This was during the Cold War, when there was a great deal of tension between the Soviet Union and the United States, and the communist revolution in Cuba (with the support of the Soviet Union) was seen as an enormous threat. The idea was to land a small force of CIA-trained Cuban exiles on the Cuban coast who would then instigate and lead a mass uprising against Fidel Castro, the Cuban leader. What looked good on paper to the Kennedy administration turned out to be a fiasco. Soon after the invasion was launched, Castro's forces captured or killed nearly all the U.S.-backed forces. Friendly Latin American countries were outraged that the United States had invaded one of their neighbors, and Cuba became even more closely allied with the Soviet Union. Later, President Kennedy would ask, "How could we have been so stupid?" (Sorenson, 1966).

Groupthink

A kind of decision process in which maintaining group cohesiveness and solidarity is more important than considering the facts in a realistic manner

While there were certainly numerous factors that contributed to this decision, Janis (1982) pointed a finger at groupthink. The decision met many of the circumstances likely to elicit groupthink: Kennedy and his team were riding high on their close victory in the 1960 election and were a tight-knit, homogeneous group. Because they had not yet made any major policy decisions, they lacked well-developed methods for discussing the issues. Moreover, Kennedy made it clear that he favored the invasion, and he only asked the group to consider details of how it should be executed rather than questioning whether it should proceed at all.

"All those in favor say 'Aye.'"
"Aye."
"Aye."
"Aye."
"Aye."
"Aye."

Henry Martin/The New Yorker
Collection/The Cartoon Bank

When these preconditions of groupthink are met, several symptoms appear (see Figure 9.4). The group begins to feel that it is invulnerable and can do no wrong. People exercise self-censorship, failing to voice contrary views because they are afraid of ruining the group's high morale or because they fear being criticized by the others. For example, Arthur Schlesinger, one of Kennedy's advisers, reported that he had severe doubts about the Bay of Pigs invasion but never expressed these concerns during the discussions out of a fear that "others would regard it as presumptuous of him, a college professor, to take issue with august heads of major government institutions" (Janis, 1982, p. 32). If anyone does voice a contrary viewpoint, the rest of the group is quick to criticize, pressuring the person to conform to the majority view. This kind of behavior creates an illusion of unanimity where it looks as if everyone agrees. On the day the group voted on whether to invade, President Kennedy asked all those present for their opinion—except Arthur Schlesinger.

The perilous state of groupthink leads to an inferior decision-making process. As seen at the far right in Figure 9.4, for example, the group does not consider the full range of alternatives, does not develop contingency plans, and does not adequately

---

Figure 9.4 Groupthink: Antecedents, Symptoms, and Consequences

Under some conditions, maintaining group cohesiveness and solidarity is more important to a group than considering the facts in a realistic manner (see "Antecedents"). When this happens, certain symptoms of groupthink occur, such as the illusion of invulnerability (see "Symptoms"). These symptoms lead to defective decision making.

(Based on data in Janis & Mann, 1977)

Antecedents of groupthink	Symptoms of groupthink	Defective decision making
The group is highly cohesive: The group is valued and attractive, and people very much want to be members. **Group isolation:** The group is isolated, protected from hearing alternative viewpoints. **A directive leader:** The leader controls the discussion and makes his or her wishes known. **High stress:** The members perceive threats to the group. **Poor decision-making procedures:** No standard methods to consider alternative viewpoints.	**Illusion of invulnerability:** The group feels it is invincible and can do no wrong. **Belief in the moral correctness of the group:** "God is on our side." **Stereotyped views of out-group:** Opposing sides are viewed in a simplistic, stereotyped manner. **Self-censorship:** People decide not to voice contrary opinions so as not to "rock the boat." **Direct pressure on dissenters to conform:** If people do voice contrary opinions, they are pressured by others to conform to the majority. **Illusion of unanimity:** An illusion is created that everyone agrees—for example, by not calling on people known to disagree. **Mindguards:** Group members protect the leader from contrary viewpoints.	**Incomplete survey of alternatives** **Failure to examine risks of the favored alternative** **Poor information search** **Failure to develop contingency plans**

consider the risks of its preferred choice. Can you think of other governmental decisions that may have been plagued by groupthink? Some have suggested that President Bush's decision to invade Iraq in 2003 was such a case. Bush's former press secretary, Scott McClellan, for example, wrote that once the president made his view known, "it was rarely questioned" because "that is what Bush expected and made known to his top advisers" (McClellan, 2008, p. 128). We leave it to future historians to decide whether this and other important decisions resulted from sound decision-making processes or from groupthink.

Many years have passed since the theory of groupthink was first proposed, and a number of researchers have put it to the test (Packer, 2009; Tetlock, Peterson, McGuire, Chang, & Field, 1992; Turner, Pratkanis, Probasco, & Leve, 2006). The upshot of this research is that defective group decision making may be more common than the original theory assumed. The groupthink theory held that a specific set of conditions had to be met in order for groupthink to occur—namely, the antecedents listed on the left side of Figure 9.4. It now appears that groupthink can occur even when some of these antecedents are missing. It may be enough for people to identify strongly with the group, have clear norms about what the group is supposed to do, and have low confidence that the group can solve the problem (Baron, 2005; Henningsen, Henningsen, Eden, & Cruz, 2006; Mok & Morris, 2010).

We now know that groups and their leaders can take several steps to make groupthink less likely (Flowers, 1977; McCauley, 1989; Zimbardo & Andersen, 1993):

- **Remain impartial.** A leader should not take a directive role but should remain impartial.

- **Seek outside opinions.** The group should invite outside opinions from people who are not members and who are thus less concerned with maintaining group cohesiveness.

- **Create subgroups.** A leader can divide the group into subgroups that first meet separately and then meet together to discuss their different recommendations.

- **Seek anonymous opinions.** A group might also take a secret ballot or ask members to write down their opinions anonymously; doing so ensures that people give their true opinions, uncensored by a fear of recrimination from the group.

Fortunately, President Kennedy learned from his mistakes with the Bay of Pigs decision, and when he encountered his next major foreign policy decision, the Cuban missile crisis, he took many of these steps to avoid groupthink. When his advisers met to decide what to do about the discovery that the Soviet Union had placed nuclear-tipped missiles in Cuba pointed toward the United States, Kennedy often absented himself from the group so as not to inhibit discussion. He also brought in outside experts who were not members of the in-group. That Kennedy successfully negotiated the removal of the Soviet missiles was almost certainly due to the improved methods of group decision making he adopted.

> The only sin which we never forgive in each other is difference of opinion.
> —RALPH WALDO EMERSON, *SOCIETY AND SOLITUDE*, 1870

The concept of groupthink has become widely known in the general culture, and writers and pundits alike have blamed it for many bad decisions. A New York Times article, for example, claimed that experts on the Federal Reserve Board should have predicted the mortgage-based financial crisis of 2007, but didn't because they exhibited symptoms of groupthink (Shiller, 2008).

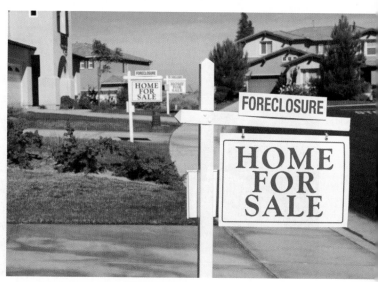

Group Polarization: Going to Extremes

Maybe you are willing to grant that groups sometimes make poor decisions. Surely, though, groups will usually make less risky decisions than a lone individual will. One individual might be willing to bet the ranch on a risky proposition, but if others help make the decision, they will interject reason and moderation. Or will they? In examining the question of whether groups or individuals make riskier decisions, many initial studies found, surprisingly, that groups make riskier decisions than individuals do.

For example, in one study, people were asked to consider the following scenario: A low-ranked participant in a national chess tournament, playing an early match against a highly favored opponent, has the choice of whether to attempt a deceptive but risky maneuver that might lead to quick victory if it is successful or almost certain defeat if it fails. When deciding alone, people said that the chess player should make the risky gambit only if there were at least a 30% chance of success. But after discussing the problem with others in a group, people said that the chess player should go for it even if there were only a 10% chance of success (Wallach, Kogan, & Bem, 1962). Findings such as these became known as the *risky shift*. But further research made clear that such shifts are not the full story. It turns out that groups tend to make decisions that are more extreme in the same direction as the initial predispositions of their members. So if the individual members of a group are already leaning toward a risky decision, group discussion will usually exaggerate that risky tendency. But when people are initially inclined to be conservative, groups tend to make even more conservative decisions than individuals do.

Consider this problem: Roger, a young married man with two children, has a secure but low-paying job and no savings. Someone gives him a tip about a stock that will triple in value if the company's new product is successful but will plummet if the new product fails. Should Roger sell his life insurance policy and invest in the company? Most people recommend a safe course of action here: Roger should buy the stock only if the new product is very certain to succeed. When they talk it over in a group, they become even more conservative, deciding that the new product would have to have a nearly 100% chance of success before they would recommend that Roger buy stock in the company. This tendency for groups to make decisions that are more extreme than the initial inclination of its members—toward greater risk if people's initial tendency is to be risky and toward greater caution if people's initial tendency is to be cautious—is known as **group polarization** (Brown, 1965; Palmer & Loveland, 2008; Rodrigo & Ato, 2002).

Group polarization occurs for two main reasons. According to the *persuasive arguments* interpretation, all individuals bring to the group a set of arguments supporting their initial recommendation. One aspect of being in a group is that you might be exposed to persuasive arguments you hadn't thought of before. For example, in considering Roger's investment strategy, one member of the group might stress that cashing in the life insurance policy is an unfair risk to Roger's children should he die prematurely. Another group member might not have considered this possibility; thus, he or she becomes more conservative as well. A series of studies supports this interpretation of group polarization, whereby each member presents arguments that other members have not considered (Burnstein & Vinokur, 1977; El-Shinnawy & Vinze, 1998).

According to the *social comparison* interpretation, when people discuss an issue in a group, they first check out how everyone else feels. What does the group value: being risky or being cautious? In an effort to fit in and be liked, many people then take a position that is similar to everyone else's but a little more extreme. In this way, the individual supports the group's values and also presents himself or herself in a positive light—as a "good" group member worthy of praise and support. Both

Group Polarization

The tendency for groups to make decisions that are more extreme than the initial inclinations of their members

Joining a group is likely to lead an individual's attitudes to become more extreme through processes of group polarization.

the persuasive arguments and the social comparison interpretations of group polarization have received research support (Boos, Schauenberg, Strack, & Belz, 2013; Brauer, Judd, & Gilner, 1995; Isenberg, 1986).

Leadership in Groups

Another critical issue related to group decision making is the role of a leader in group outcomes. The question of what makes a great leader has intrigued psychologists, historians, and political scientists for some time (Bass, 1998; Chemers, 2000; Fiedler, 1967; Haslam, Reicher, & Platow, 2013; Klenke, 1996; Simonton, 1987). One of the best-known answers to this question is the **great person theory**, which maintains that certain key personality traits make a person a good leader, regardless of the nature of the situation the leader faces.

If the great person theory is true, we ought to be able to isolate the key aspects of personality that make someone an effective leader. Is it a combination of intelligence, charisma, and courage? Is it better to be introverted or extroverted? Should we add a dollop of ruthlessness to the mix as well, as Niccolò Machiavelli suggested in 1513 in his famous treatise on leadership, *The Prince*? Or do highly moral people make the best leaders?

LEADERSHIP AND PERSONALITY People of all different personality types can become successful leaders. Compared to nonleaders, for example, leaders tend to be only slightly more intelligent, extroverted, charismatic, open to new experiences, confident in their leadership abilities, and assertive (Ames & Flynn, 2007; Chemers, Watson, & May, 2000; Judge, Bono, Ilies, & Gerhardt, 2002; Van Vugt, 2006). Surprisingly few personality characteristics correlate strongly with leadership effectiveness, and the relationships that have been found tend to be modest (Avolio, Walumbwa, & Weber, 2009; von Wittich & Antonakis, 2011). For example, Dean Simonton (1987, 2001) gathered information about 100 personal attributes of all U.S. presidents, such as their family backgrounds, educational experiences, occupations, and personalities. Only three of these variables— height, family size, and the number of books a president published before taking office—correlated with how effective the presidents were in office. Tall presidents, those from small families, and those who have published books are most likely to become effective leaders, as rated by historians. The other 97 characteristics, including personality traits, were not related to leadership effectiveness at all.

LEADERSHIP STYLES Although great leaders may not have specific kinds of personalities, they do appear to adopt specific kinds of leadership styles. **Transactional leaders** set clear, short-term goals and reward people who meet them. **Transformational leaders**, on the other hand, inspire followers to focus on common, long-term goals (Bass, 1998; Haslam et al., 2013). So while transactional leaders do a good job of making things run smoothly, it is transformational leaders who think outside the box and inspire their followers to exert themselves to meet big-picture goals.

Interestingly, these leadership styles are not closely linked with personality traits; it is not as if people are "born to be" one type of leader or the other (Judge, Colbert, & Ilies, 2004; Nielsen & Cleal, 2011). Further, these styles are not mutually exclusive; in fact, the most effective leader is one who adopts both styles (Judge & Piccolo, 2004). If no one was minding the day-to-day operation of an organization or people were not being rewarded for meeting short-term objectives, the organization would suffer. At the same time, it is important to have a charismatic leader who inspires people to think about long-term objectives.

There is properly no history, only biography.

—Ralph Waldo Emerson, *Essays, History*, 1841

Great Person Theory

The idea that certain key personality traits make a person a good leader, regardless of the situation

Transactional Leaders

Leaders who set clear, short-term goals and reward people who meet them

Transformational Leaders

Leaders who inspire followers to focus on common, long-term goals

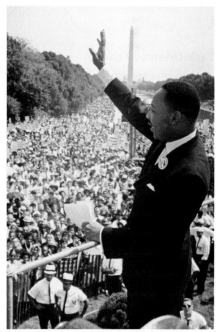

What determines whether someone, such as Martin Luther King, Jr., is a great leader? Is it a certain constellation of personality traits, or is it necessary to have the right person in the right situation at the right time?

THE RIGHT PERSON IN THE RIGHT SITUATION   As you know by now, one of the most important tenets of social psychology is that, to understand social behavior, it is not enough to consider personality traits alone—we must take the social situation into account as well. For example, a business leader can be highly successful in some situations but not in others. Consider the late Steve Jobs, who, at age 21, founded the Apple Computer Company with Stephen Wozniak. Jobs was anything but a traditional suit-and-tie corporate leader. A product of the 1960s counterculture, he turned to computers only after experimenting with LSD, traveling to India, and living on a communal fruit farm. In the days when there were no personal computers, Jobs's offbeat style was well suited to starting a new industry. Indeed, within 5 years, he had become the leader of a billion-dollar company. But Jobs's unorthodox style was ill suited to managing a large corporation in a competitive market. Apple's earnings began to suffer, and in 1985 Jobs was forced out. Undeterred, Jobs cofounded Pixar in 1986, the first major company to make computer-generated animation, and then sold it to the Disney Company in 2006 for $7.4 billion. And in the 1990s, Apple faced some of the same technological challenges it had at its inception, needing to revamp the operating system for its Macintosh computers and regain market share. Whom did Apple hire to lead this new challenge? Steve Jobs, of course, whose ability to think creatively and inspire his workforce to take risks made him the right person to lead these companies in times when a new direction was called for.

A comprehensive theory of leadership thus needs to focus on the characteristics of the leader, the followers, and the situation. The best-known theory of this type is the **contingency theory of leadership**, which argues that leadership effectiveness depends both on how task oriented or relationship oriented the leader is and on the amount of control and influence the leader has over the group (Fiedler, 1967; Yukl, 2011). There are basically two kinds of leaders, the theory argues: **task-oriented leaders**, who are concerned more with getting the job done than with workers' feelings and relationships, and **relationship-oriented leaders**, who are concerned more with workers' feelings and relationships. Task-oriented leaders do well in *high-control work situations*, when the leader's position in the company is clearly perceived as powerful and the work needing to be done by the group is structured and well defined (e.g., a corporate manager with control over each worker's performance review and merit raise). They also do well in *low-control work situations*, when the leader is not perceived as powerful and the work needing to be done is not clearly defined (e.g., the supervisor of a newly formed group of volunteers). What about relationship-oriented leaders? They are most effective in *moderate-control work situations*. Under these conditions, the wheels are turning fairly smoothly, but important work still needs to be done; the leader who can promote strong relations between individual employees will be the most successful (see Figure 9.5). The contingency theory of leadership has been supported in studies of numerous types of leaders, including business managers, college administrators, military commanders, and postmasters (Ayman, 2002; Chemers, 2000; Van Vugt & DeCremer, 1999; Yukl, 2011).

GENDER AND LEADERSHIP   In Chapter 7, we referenced the television show *Mad Men*, which is about an advertising agency in the 1960s. If you've seen the show, you know that it was not that long ago that businessmen were exactly that: men. Since that time, increasing numbers of women work outside the home, and the U.S. workforce is approximately half female. But are women as likely as men to become leaders in business, politics, and other organizations? Not yet, but this is changing. The barriers between women and high-level advancement are breaking down. In 2008, for example, a woman (Hillary Clinton) came close to winning the

---

Leadership cannot really be taught. It can only be learned.

—Harold Geneen, 1984

Contingency Theory of Leadership

The idea that the effectiveness of a leader depends both on how task oriented or relationship oriented the leader is and on the amount of control the leader has over the group

Task-Oriented Leaders

Leaders who are concerned more with getting the job done than with workers' feelings and relationships

Relationship-Oriented Leaders

Leaders who are concerned more with workers' feelings and relationships

Democratic nomination for president, and another woman (Sarah Palin) ran for vice president on the Republican ticket for the first time; Clinton went on to serve as secretary of state and is considered a presidential front-runner for 2016. Still, though, it is unfortunately the case that the barriers have not completely disappeared. In 2014, only 24 of the chief executive officers of Fortune 500 companies were women, and the boards of directors of U.S. companies included only 17% women (Catalyst, 2014). Things are not much different elsewhere. That 17% figure is actually among the highest in the world; the few countries with higher rates include Norway (41%), Sweden (27%), Finland, (27%), the United Kingdom (21%), and France (18%).

One reason why it is difficult for women to achieve leadership positions is that many people believe that good leaders have *agentic* traits (e.g., assertive, controlling, dominant, independent, self-confident), which are traditionally associated with men. In contrast, women are stereotypically expected to be more *communal* (e.g., concerned with the welfare of others, warm, helpful, kind, affectionate). Thus, if women behave in the way they are "supposed" to behave, they are often viewed as having less leadership potential. But if women succeed in attaining a leadership position and act in ways that leaders are expected to act—namely, in agentic, forceful fashion—they are criticized for not "acting like a woman should" (Brescoll, Dawson, & Uhlmann, 2010; Eagly, Johannesen-Schmidt, & van Engen, 2003; Eagly & Karau, 2002; Koenig, Eagly, Mitchell, & Ristikari, 2011).

Here's another danger that women leaders face: Because they are perceived as being more communal, they are often thought to be better at managing crises, particularly ones involving interpersonal problems, such as a conflict between managers. That might seem like a good thing—trusting women leaders to solve problems—but it has a downside in which women are more likely to be put in precarious, high-risk positions where it is difficult to succeed. Michelle Ryan and her colleagues have called this a "glass cliff" (Ryan, Haslam, Hersby, & Bongiorno, 2011; Ryan, Haslam, Hersby, Kulich, & Atkins, 2008). Even when women have broken through the "glass ceiling" into top leadership positions, they are more likely than men to be put in charge of units that are in crisis and in which the risk of failure is high. Ryan and her colleagues found this to be true in studies of hiring in real-world companies as well as in controlled laboratory studies in which people read descriptions of companies and recommended people for leadership positions. Participants were more likely to recommend a woman when an organizational unit was in crisis and a man when the unit was running smoothly—tendencies that make it more likely that women will fail in their leadership positions.

The better news is that prejudice against women leaders appears to be lessening over time. In a Gallup poll conducted

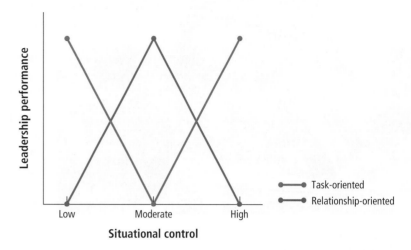

Figure 9.5 Fiedler's Contingency Theory of Leadership

According to Fiedler, task-oriented leaders perform best when situational control is high or low, whereas relationship-oriented leaders perform best when situational control is moderate.

I wonder men dare trust themselves with men.

—William Shakespeare,
The Life of Timon of Athens

If women seeking leadership roles conform to society's expectations about how they ought to behave, by being warm and communal, they are often perceived as having low leadership potential. If they become leaders and act in ways that leaders are expected to act—namely, in agentic, forceful ways—they are often perceived negatively.

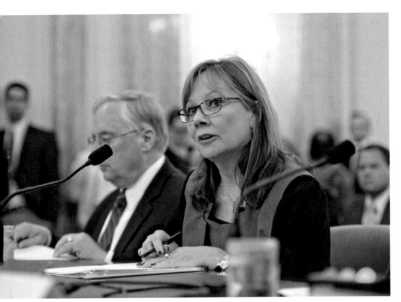

In 2014, Mary Barra became the first female CEO of a major global automaker, in this case General Motors. Within months, she had to announce plans for GM to recall over 11 million cars due to defective design components that the company had known about for nearly 10 years. Could Barra become another example of a woman who broke through a "glass ceiling" only to find herself on a "glass cliff"?

in 1953, 66% of people said that they preferred a man as a boss, and only 5% preferred a woman (25% had no preference). In a similar poll conducted in 2011, 32% preferred a man as a boss, 22% preferred a woman, and 46% had no preference. Further, there is some evidence that people are becoming more accepting of women who act in stereotypically "male" ways (Twenge, 1997) and that there is a growing recognition that effective leaders must be able to act in communal as well as agentic ways (Eagly & Karau, 2002; Koenig et al., 2011).

CULTURE AND LEADERSHIP Most research on leadership has been conducted in Western countries; thus, the question arises as to how much the results apply to leadership in other cultures. For this reason, researchers have recently turned their attention to the kinds of traits people value in leaders and actual leadership styles in different cultures (Aycan, Schyns, Sun, Felfe, & Saher, 2013; Ayman & Korabik, 2010; Eagly & Chin, 2010; Gelfand, Erez, & Aycan, 2007). One ambitious study examined leadership practices and attitudes toward leaders in 62 different countries. The researchers gave questionnaires to 17,000 managers in 951 organizations in those countries, conducted extensive interviews, convened group discussions, and analyzed media content in each country. Not surprisingly, different cultures valued different traits in leaders. For example, autonomous leadership, defined as being independent of one's superiors and keeping one's distance from subordinates (i.e., spending a lot of time working alone), was valued more in most European countries than it was in most Latin American countries. But there was universal agreement about the value of two leadership qualities: charisma and being team oriented (House, Hanges, Javidan, Dorfman, & Gupta, 2004). Questions about cultural differences in leadership are receiving increasing attention because in a global economy, work groups are becoming more diverse and managers from different cultures have increasingly frequent contact.

REVIEW QUESTIONS

1. Which of the following is *not* an example of process loss?
   a. Transactive memory
   b. Group polarization
   c. Failure to share uniquely held information
   d. Groupthink

2. One step that can be taken to reduce the likelihood of groupthink is
   a. putting in place a strong, directive group leader.
   b. taking group votes aloud rather than relying on secret ballot or other anonymous methods.
   c. creating subgroups that meet on their own first before reconvening and sharing the content of their discussions with the group at large.
   d. emphasizing the importance of being unanimous.

3. Walt, Jesse, Mike, and Gus are business partners trying to decide whether they should invest in a risky new direction for their company. Jesse gets the feeling that his partners are leaning toward the risky option. In order to convince his partners that he is a valued member of the company and a "good" group member, Jesse speaks up in strong, public terms in favor of the risky decision, and he leaves the meeting even more convinced than he was before that they should take the risk. Jesse's personal shift in the risky direction illustrates the _____ explanation for group polarization.
   a. social comparison
   b. counterattitudinal
   c. persuasive arguments
   d. social facilitation

4. Research on personality type and leadership indicates that
   a. the great person theory is the best explanation for leadership success.

b. people of all different personality types can become successful leaders.

c. the most successful U.S. presidents (as rated by historians) tended to share major personality traits, such as extraversion, openness to new experience, and empathy.

d. most successful leaders embrace agentic traits but avoid communal traits.

5. A _____ leader is one who sets clear, short-term goals and rewards people for meeting them.
  a. contingent
  b. transformational
  c. communal
  d. transactional

See page 621 for the answers.

Conflict and Cooperation

9.4 **What determines the likelihood that individual or group conflict will escalate or be resolved?**

We have already examined how people work together to make decisions; in these situations, group members have a common goal. Often, however, people have incompatible goals, placing them in conflict with each other. This can be true of two individuals, such as romantic partners who disagree about who should clean the kitchen, or two groups, such as a labor union and company management who disagree over wages and working conditions. It can also be true of nations, such as in the long-standing conflict between Israel and its Arab neighbors or between the Shiites, Sunnis, and Kurds in Iraq. The opportunity for interpersonal conflict exists whenever two or more people interact. Sigmund Freud (1930) went so far as to argue that conflict is an inevitable by-product of civilization because the goals and needs of individuals often clash with the goals and needs of their fellow human beings. The nature of conflict and how it can be resolved has been the topic of a great deal of social psychological research (Cohen & Insko, 2008; De Dreu, 2014; Deutsch, 1973; Thibaut & Kelley, 1959).

Many conflicts are resolved peacefully, with little rancor. Couples often find a way to resolve their differences in a mutually acceptable manner, and labor disputes are sometimes settled with a handshake. All too often, however, conflict erupts into open hostilities. The divorce rate in the United States is distressingly high. People sometimes resort to violence to resolve their differences. Warfare between nations remains an all-too-common solution to international disputes. Obviously, it is of great importance to find ways of resolving conflicts peacefully.

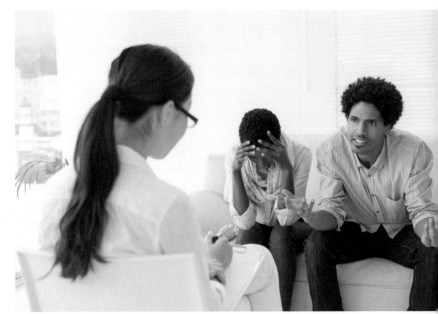

Sometimes people are able to resolve conflicts peacefully, such as a couple that has an amicable divorce. At other times conflicts escalate into rancor and violence. Social psychologists have performed experiments to test ways in which conflict resolution is most likely to occur.

Social Dilemmas

One of the reasons why we have conflicts in the first place is because very often, what is best for an individual is not always best for the group as a whole. Consider a publishing venture by the novelist Stephen King. He wrote two installments of a novel called *The Plant* and posted them on the Internet, asking readers to pay $1 per installment. The deal he offered was simple: If at least 75% of the people who downloaded the installments paid the fee, he would keep writing and posting new installments. If fewer than 75% of the people paid, he would stop writing, and people would never get the rest of the novel.

Social Dilemma

A conflict in which the most beneficial action for an individual will, if chosen by most people, have harmful effects on everyone

King had devised a classic **social dilemma**, a conflict in which the most beneficial action for an individual will, if chosen by most people, be harmful to everyone (Van Lange, Joireman, Parks, & Van Dijk, 2013; Weber, Kopelman, & Messick, 2004). It was to any individual's financial advantage to download King's novel free of charge and let other people pay. However, if too many people took this approach, everyone would lose because King said he would stop writing the novel. At first, people acted for the good of all; more than 75% paid for the first installment. As with many other social dilemmas, however, people eventually acted in their own self-interest, to the detriment of everyone. The number of people who paid for later installments dropped below 75%, and King stopped posting new ones, saying on his Web site that the novel was "on hiatus."

The Panera restaurant chain has had more success with this approach. A few years ago, they began opening Panera Cares restaurants, which look and operate like other Paneras except for one thing: People aren't required to pay anything if they don't want to. There are suggested prices for all menu items, but customers are allowed to pay whatever they want. The chief executive officer and founder of the restaurant chain, Ronald Shaich, had a vision in which people in real need could come get a good meal and pay whatever they could afford; the costs would be offset, he hoped, by customers who could afford to pay more than the suggested prices. So far it's working. At the first three Panera Cares restaurants to open—in St. Louis, Detroit, and Portland—about three in five people paid the suggested prices, one in five paid less, and one in five paid more. Those who paid less were usually people who couldn't otherwise afford to eat out, such as a teacher who was laid off after 25 years and low-income families who come in to celebrate a birthday. True, some people have taken advantage of the system, such as three college students who paid $3 for a $40 meal. But enough people have paid more than the suggested price to offset those who pay less. The three stores are self-sustaining (Salter, 2011), and additional Panera Cares locations have since opened in Boston and Chicago. What determines whether people respond selfishly or selflessly in social dilemmas such as these? Social psychologists have attempted to find out by studying such conflicts experimentally, testing both their causes and resolutions in the laboratory.

One of the most common ways of studying social dilemmas in the laboratory is with a game called "the prisoner's dilemma." In each session, two players have to choose one of two options without knowing what the other player will choose. The number of points they win depends on the options chosen by both people. Suppose that you were playing the game with a friend. As shown in the following Try It! exercise, you have to choose Option X or Option Y without knowing which option your friend will choose. Your payoff—the amount of money you win or lose—depends on the choices made by both you and your friend. For example, if both you and your friend choose Option X, you both win $3. If, however, you choose Option Y and your friend chooses Option X, you win $6 and your friend loses $6. Which option would you choose?

Many people begin by choosing Option Y. At worst, you will lose $1, and at best, you will win the highest possible amount, $6. Choosing Option X raises the possibility that both sides will win some money, but it is also a risky choice. If your partner chooses Y while you choose X, you stand to lose a great deal. Because people often do not know how much they can trust their partners, Option Y frequently seems like the safest choice (Rapoport & Chammah, 1965). The dilemma is that both players may come to think this way, ensuring that both sides lose (see the lower right-hand corner of the table in the Try It! exercise).

People's actions in these games seem to mirror many conflicts in everyday life. To find a solution desirable to both parties, people must trust each other. Often they do not, and this lack of trust leads to an escalating series of competitive moves so that in the end no one wins (Insko & Schopler, 1998; Kelley & Thibaut, 1978; Lount,

Zhong, Sivanathan, & Murnighan, 2008). Two countries locked in an arms race, for example, may feel that they cannot afford to disarm out of fear that the other side will take advantage of their weakened position. The result is that both sides add furiously to their stockpile of weapons, neither gaining superiority over the other and both spending money they could use to solve domestic problems (Deutsch, 1973). Such an escalation of conflict is also seen all too often among couples who are divorcing. Sometimes the goal seems more to hurt the other person than to further one's own needs (or the children's). In the end, everyone suffers because, metaphorically speaking, both choose Option Y too often.

TRY IT!

The Prisoner's Dilemma

Your Friend's Options	Your Options	
	Option X	**Option Y**
Option X	You win $3 Your friend wins $3	You win $6 Your friend loses $6
Option Y	You lose $6 Your friend wins $6	You lose $1 Your friend loses $1

Play this version of the prisoner's dilemma game with a friend. First, show the table to the friend and explain how the game works: On each trial of the game, you and your friend can choose Option X or Option Y, without knowing what the other will choose. You should each write your choice on folded pieces of paper that are opened at the same time. The numbers in the table represent imaginary money that you and your friend win or lose on each trial. For example, if you choose Option X on the first trial and your friend chooses Option Y, you lose an imaginary $6 and your friend wins an imaginary $6. If both of you choose Option Y, you both lose an imaginary $1. Play the game for 10 trials and keep track of how much each of you wins or loses. Did you and your friend choose the cooperative option (Option X) or the competitive option (Option Y) more often? Why? Did a pattern of trust or mistrust develop over the course of the game?

INCREASING COOPERATION IN THE PRISONER'S DILEMMA   Such escalating conflict, though common, is not inevitable. Many studies have found that when people play the prisoner's dilemma game, they will, under certain conditions, adopt the more cooperative response (Option X), ensuring that both sides end up with a positive outcome. Not surprisingly, if people are playing the game with a friend or a partner with whom they expect to interact in the future, they are more likely to adopt a cooperative strategy that maximizes everyone's profits (Cohen & Insko, 2008). Also, subtly changing the norms about what kind of behavior is expected can have large effects on how cooperative people are. One study found that simply changing the name of a game from the "Wall Street Game" to the "Community Game" increased the percentage of people who played cooperatively from 33% to 71% (Liberman, Samuels, & Ross, 2004). Another study, conducted with Chinese college students in Hong Kong, found that showing people symbols of Chinese culture before the game (e.g., a Chinese dragon) made people more cooperative, whereas showing people symbols of American culture (e.g., an American flag) made them more competitive (Wong & Hong, 2005).

Tit-for-Tat Strategy

A means of encouraging cooperation by at first acting cooperatively but then always responding the way your opponent did (cooperatively or competitively) on the previous trial

---

My own belief is that Russian and Chinese behavior is as much influenced by suspicion of our intentions as ours is by suspicion of theirs. This would mean that we have great influence over their behavior—that, by treating them as hostile, we assure their hostility.

—J. WILLIAM FULBRIGHT,
APRIL 4, 1971

To increase cooperation, you can also try the **tit-for-tat strategy**, a way of encouraging cooperation by at first acting cooperatively but then always responding the way your opponent did (cooperatively or competitively) in the previous trial. This strategy communicates a willingness to cooperate and an unwillingness to sit back and be exploited if the partner does not cooperate. The tit-for-tat strategy is often successful in getting the other person to respond with the cooperative, trusting response (Klapwijk & Van Lange, 2009; Leite, 2011; Messick & Liebrand, 1995; Wubben, De Cremer, & van Dijk, 2009). Using this tactic in the arms race would mean matching not only any military buildup made by an unfriendly nation but also any conciliatory gesture, such as a ban on nuclear testing.

Another proven strategy is to allow individuals rather than opposing groups to resolve a conflict because two individuals who play the prisoner's dilemma are more likely to cooperate with each other than two groups who play the same game (Schopler & Insko, 1999). The reason for this is that people are more likely to assume that another individual is cooperative at heart and can be trusted but that groups will, if given the opportunity, stab us in the back. Does this mean that world leaders would be more cooperative when negotiating one-on-one than when groups of advisers from the two nations meet? Possibly. In 1985, Ronald Reagan and Mikhail Gorbachev, then leaders of the United States and the Soviet Union, met for the first time, in Switzerland, to discuss arms reduction. After formal meetings between the leaders and their aides stalled, Reagan and Gorbachev took a walk to a boathouse, accompanied only by translators. According to some reports, the two men came close to agreeing to dismantle all of their nuclear missiles—until their aides got wind of this "preposterous" idea and squelched it (Korda, 1997).

Using Threats to Resolve Conflict

When involved in a conflict, many of us are tempted to use threats to get the other party to cave to our wishes, believing that we should, in the words of Teddy Roosevelt, "speak softly and carry a big stick." Parents commonly use threats to get their children to behave, and teachers often threaten their students with demerits or a visit to the principal. Threats are commonly used on an international scale as well to further the interests of one nation over another (Turner & Horvitz, 2001).

A classic series of studies by Morton Deutsch and Robert Krauss (1960, 1962) indicates that threats are not an effective means of reducing conflict. These researchers developed a game in which two participants imagined that they were in charge of trucking companies named Acme and Bolt. The goal of each company was to transport merchandise as quickly as possible to a destination. The participants were paid 60 cents for each "trip" but had 1 cent subtracted for every second it took them to make the trip. The most direct route for each company was over a one-lane road that only one truck could travel at a time. This placed the two companies in direct conflict, as seen in Figure 9.6. If Acme and Bolt both tried to take the one-lane road, neither truck could pass, and both would lose money. Each company could take an alternate route, but this was much longer, guaranteeing that they would lose at least 10 cents per trial.

After a while, most participants worked out a solution that allowed both trucks to make a modest amount of money. They took turns waiting until the other party crossed the one-lane road, then they would take that route as well. In another version of the study, the researchers gave Acme a gate that could be lowered over the one-lane road, thereby blocking Bolt from using that route. You might think that using force—the gate—would increase Acme's profits because all Acme had to do was to threaten Bolt to "stay off the one-lane road or else." In fact, quite the opposite

---

Figure 9.6 The Deutsch and Krauss Trucking Game

Deutsch and Krauss (1962) studied cooperation (and the lack thereof) by asking participants to play a trucking game. In the game, players earned money by driving from one point to another as quickly as possible. As in the image below, the shortest route in their game required crossing a one-lane road, but both companies could not use this road at the same time. When players were given gates they could use to restrict the other player's use of the one-lane road, both companies made even less money.

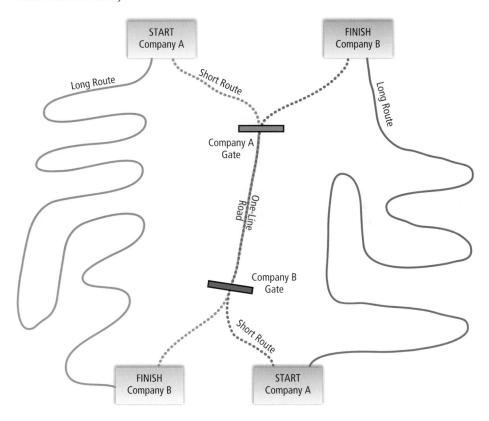

happened. When one side had the gate, both participants lost more than when neither side had the gate—as seen in the left panel of Figure 9.7. This figure shows the total amount earned or lost by both sides (Acme earned slightly more than Bolt when it had the gate but earned substantially more when neither side had a gate). Bolt did not like being threatened and often retaliated by parking its truck on the one-lane road, blocking the Acme truck's progress. Meanwhile, seconds ticked away, and both sides lost money.

What would happen if the situation were more equitable, with both sides having gates? Surely they would learn to cooperate very quickly, recognizing the stalemate that would ensue if both of them used their gates—right? To the contrary (as you can see in the left panel of Figure 9.7), both sides lost even more money in the bilateral threat condition than in any of the others. Here, the owners of both trucking companies threatened to use their gates and did so with great frequency.

EFFECTS OF COMMUNICATION   There is a way in which the Deutsch and Krauss trucking game does not approximate real life: The two sides were not allowed to communicate with each other. Would the two adversaries have worked out their differences if they could have talked them over? To find out, Deutsch and Krauss

Figure 9.7 Results of the Trucking Game Studies

The left-hand panel shows the amount of money the participants made (summed over Acme and Bolt) when they could not communicate. When threats were introduced by giving one ("unilateral threat") or both sides ("bilateral threat") a gate, both sides lost more money. The right-hand panel shows the amount of money the participants made when they were required to communicate in every trial. Once again, giving them gates reduced their winnings.

(Based on data in Deutsch & Krauss, 1962)

ran a version of their study in which the participants were required to communicate through an intercom on every trial. Surely if people talked to each other, they would cooperate more. But as seen in the right panel of Figure 9.7, no dramatic increase in profits occurred. Making people communicate reduced losses somewhat in the unilateral threat condition when Acme alone had the gate but failed to increase cooperation in either of the two other conditions (no threat, bilateral threat). Overall, requiring people to communicate did not raise profits dramatically. Why not?

The problem with the communication in the trucking studies is that it did not foster trust. In fact, people used the opportunity to threaten each other. Krauss and Deutsch demonstrated this fact in a later version of their trucking study in which they specifically instructed people on how to communicate, telling them to work out a solution that was fair to both parties (i.e., one that they would be willing to accept if they were in the other person's shoes). Under these conditions, verbal communication did increase the amount of money both sides won because it fostered trust instead of adding fuel to the competitive fires (Deutsch, 1973; Deutsch, Coleman, & Marcus, 2011; Krauss & Deutsch, 1966).

Negotiation and Bargaining

In the laboratory games we have discussed so far, people's options are limited. They have to choose Option X or Y in the prisoner's dilemma, and they have only a couple of ways of getting their truck to its destination in the trucking game. In everyday life, we often have a wide array of options. Consider two people haggling over the price of a car. Both the buyer and the seller can give in to all of the other's demands, to some of them, or to none of them. Either party can walk away from the deal at any time. Given that there is considerable latitude in how people can resolve the conflict, communication between the parties becomes all the more important. By talking, bargaining, and negotiating, people can arrive at a satisfactory settlement. **Negotiation** is a form of communication between opposing sides in a conflict in which offers and counteroffers are made and a solution occurs only when both parties agree (De Dreu, 2010; Menon, Sheldon, & Galinsky, 2014; Thompson, Wang, & Gunia, 2010). How successful are people at negotiating mutually beneficial solutions?

One limit to successful negotiation is that people often assume that they are locked in a conflict in which only one party can come out ahead. They don't realize that a solution favorable to both parties is available. A couple getting a divorce, for example, might find it impossible to reach a financial settlement until they realize that they have different priorities. Perhaps it is most important to one person to keep the furniture and the season tickets to the orchestra, whereas the other wants the china and the vintage collection of vinyl records. This type of compromise, called an **integrative solution**, is an outcome to a conflict whereby the parties make trade-offs on issues according to their different interests; each side concedes the most on issues that are unimportant to it but are important to the other side.

It might seem that such integrative solutions would be easy to achieve. After all, the two parties simply have to sit down and figure out which issues are the most important to each. However, people often find it difficult to identify integrative solutions (Moran & Ritov, 2007; Thompson, 1997). For example, the more people have at stake in a negotiation, the more biased their perceptions of their opponent. They will tend to distrust proposals made by the other side and to overlook interests they have in common (O'Connor & Carnevale, 1997; Ross & Ward, 1995). This is one reason why people often use neutral mediators to solve labor disputes, legal battles, and divorce proceedings: Mediators are often in a better position to recognize that there are mutually agreeable solutions to a conflict (Carnevale, 1986; Kressel & Pruitt, 1989; Ross & LaCroix, 1996).

The *style* of communication is also critical to developing trust during negotiation. It appears that trust is more easily established in old-fashioned face-to-face negotiations than in electronic communications such as e-mail, instant messaging, texting, and videoconferencing. The modern techniques have many advantages, of course, but one disadvantage is that it is harder to get to know people and learn to trust them. A meta-analysis of several studies found that negotiations conducted over electronic media were more hostile and resulted in lower profits than face-to-face negotiations (Stuhlmacher & Citera, 2005).

The bottom line? When you are negotiating with someone, it is important to keep in mind that integrative solutions are often available. Try to gain the other side's trust, communicate your own interests in an open manner and try taking the other person's perspective (Trötschel, Hüffmeier, Loschelder, Schwartz, & Gollwitzer, 2011). Remember that the way you construe the situation is not necessarily the same as the way the other party construes it. You may well discover that the other side communicates its interests more freely as a result, increasing the likelihood that you will find a solution beneficial to both parties.

Negotiation

A form of communication between opposing sides in a conflict in which offers and counteroffers are made and a solution occurs only when both parties agree

---

Yet there remains another wall. This wall constitutes a psychological barrier between us, . . . [a] barrier of distorted and eroded interpretation of every event and statement. . . . I ask, why don't we stretch our hands with faith and sincerity so that together we might destroy this barrier?

—FORMER EGYPTIAN PRESIDENT ANWAR AL-SADAT, SPEAKING BEFORE THE ISRAELI KNESSET, 1977

Integrative Solution

A solution to a conflict whereby the parties make trade-offs on issues, with each side conceding the most on issues that are unimportant to it but important to the other side

Neutral mediators often help solve labor disputes, legal battles, and divorce proceedings. Mediators can be in a better position to recognize that there are mutually agreeable solutions to a conflict.

REVIEW QUESTIONS

1. When it comes to social dilemmas,
   a. an individual who adopts a cooperative strategy will always be more profitable than one who is selfish.
   b. the most beneficial course of action for an individual will, if chosen by most people, be harmful to all in the long run.
   c. one always has to win, and one side always has to lose.
   d. laboratory studies cannot be useful in understanding the escalation and persistence of group conflicts.

2. Consider the prisoner's dilemma. You will receive the worst possible outcome for yourself as an individual if
   a. you are cooperative and so is your partner.
   b. you are cooperative but your partner is selfish.
   c. you are selfish and so is your partner.
   d. you are selfish but your partner is cooperative.

3. Two fishing companies, Hufflepuff and Ravenclaw, use the same body of water to catch fish. Both companies are considering building dams that would allow them to cut off the water supply and prevent the other company from fishing. Research on the power of threats indicates that if both companies build a dam and gain the ability to prevent the other from fishing,
   a. conflict will decrease because each side has equal threat capacity.
   b. conflict will increase because each side has equal threat capacity.
   c. conflict will increase slightly, but not as much as it would if only one side built a dam and had threat capacity.
   d. conflict will increase, but only if communication between the two companies is prevented.

4. A(n) _____ solution is an outcome to a negotiation in which each side concedes on issues that are unimportant to it but are important to the other side.
   a. tit-for-tat
   b. transactive
   c. integrative
   d. communal

5. According to Sigmund Freud, _____ is an inevitable by-product of civilization.
   a. negotiation
   b. cooperation
   c. conflict
   d. psychology

See page 622 for the answers.

Summary

9.1 What are groups, and why do people join them?

- **What Is a Group?** A **group** consists of two or more (usually more) people who interact with each other and are interdependent.

  - **Why Do People Join Groups?** The *need to belong* to groups may be innate. Groups also allow us to accomplish difficult objectives, serve as a source of information about the social world, and are an important part of our social identities. People are very sensitive to rejection from groups and do what they can to avoid it. Groups also make people feel distinctive from members of other groups.

  - **The Composition and Functions of Groups** Groups tend to consist of homogeneous members, in part because groups have *social norms* that people are expected to obey. Groups also have well-defined social roles, shared expectations about how people are supposed to behave. People can get so far into a social role that their personal identities and personalities get lost. Group cohesiveness, qualities of a group that bind members together and promote liking between members, is another important property of groups that influences the group's performance. So does a group's composition, with diversity sometimes negatively associated with group morale but positively associated with a range of performance outcomes.

9.2 In what ways do individuals perform differently when others are around?

- **Individual Behavior in a Group Setting** Research has compared the performance of people who are by themselves versus in groups.

  - **Social Facilitation: When the Presence of Others Energizes Us** When people's individual efforts on a task can be evaluated, the mere presence of others leads to social facilitation: Their performance is enhanced on simple tasks but impaired on complex tasks.

  - **Social Loafing: When the Presence of Others Relaxes Us** When people's individual efforts *cannot* be evaluated, the mere presence of others leads to relaxation and social loafing: Performance is impaired on simple or unimportant tasks but enhanced on complex tasks.

- **Gender and Cultural Differences in Social Loafing: Who Slacks Off the Most?** Social loafing is more prevalent among men than women and more prevalent in Western than Asian cultures.

- **Deindividuation: Getting Lost in the Crowd** The mere presence of others can also lead to more serious consequences such as deindividuation, the loosening of normal constraints on behavior when people are in crowds.

9.3 Are two (or more) heads better than one in decision making, and how do leaders shape group outcomes?

- **Group Decisions: Are Two (or More) Heads Better Than One?** Research has compared how people make decisions when they are by themselves versus in groups.

  - **Process Loss: When Group Interactions Inhibit Good Problem Solving** Groups make better decisions than individuals if they are good at pooling independent ideas and listening to the expert members of the group. Often, however, process loss occurs, which is any aspect of group interaction that inhibits good decision making. For example, groups often focus on the information they have in common and fail to share unique information. Tightly knit, cohesive groups are also prone to groupthink, which occurs when maintaining group cohesiveness and solidarity becomes more important than considering the facts in a realistic manner.

  - **Group Polarization: Going to Extremes** Group polarization causes individuals to become more extreme in their attitudes than they were before group discussions; in this manner, group decisions can be more risky or more cautious than individual decisions, depending on which direction the individual members were initially leaning.

  - **Leadership in Groups** There is little support for the great person theory, which argues that good leadership is a matter of having the right personality traits. Leaders adopt specific kinds of leadership styles, such as transactional or transformational. Leadership effectiveness is a function of both the kind of person a leader is and the nature of the work situation. Although strides have been made, women are still underrepresented in leadership positions. Women who become leaders often face a "glass cliff" whereby they are put in charge of work units that are in crisis and in which the risk of failure is high. Further, there is a double bind for women leaders: If they conform to societal expectations about how they ought to behave, by being warm and communal, they are often perceived as having low leadership potential. If they succeed in attaining a leadership position and act in ways that leaders are expected to act—namely, in agentic, forceful ways—they are often perceived negatively for not "acting like a woman should."

9.4 What determines the likelihood that individual or group conflict will escalate or be resolved?

- **Conflict and Cooperation** Research has examined how people resolve conflicts when they have incompatible goals.

  - **Social Dilemmas** These occur when the most beneficial action for an individual will, if chosen by most people, have harmful effects for everyone. A commonly studied social dilemma is the prisoner's dilemma, in which two people must decide whether to look out for only their own interests or for their partner's interests as well. Creating trust is crucial in solving this kind of conflict.

  - **Using Threats to Resolve Conflict** Research has found that using threats tends to escalate rather than resolve conflicts.

  - **Negotiation and Bargaining** When two sides are negotiating and bargaining, it is important to look for an integrative solution whereby each side concedes the most on issues that are unimportant to it but are very important to its adversary.

Test Yourself

1. Why are groups often homogeneous (comprising members who are alike in age, sex, beliefs, and opinions)?

a. People who are already similar to each tend to be drawn to joining the same groups.

b. Evolutionary pressures caused people with similar genes to join groups and people with dissimilar genes to avoid each other.

c. Groups are more productive when they are homogeneous.

d. Social loafing prevents us from seeking out new people and experiences.

2. Social norms are

a. behaviors expected from people who occupy certain positions.

b. behaviors that promote mutual liking and bind members together.

c. a powerful determinant of one's behavior.

d. group members listening to each other's opinions.

3. The presence of others increases physiological arousal. Therefore, one is expected to perform better on a simple task in the _____ and a difficult task in the _____.

a. presence of others; absence of others

b. absence of others; presence of others

c. presence of others; same way

d. absence of others; same way

4. The tendency to engage in social loafing is stronger in _____; it is also stronger in _____.

a. men than women; Asian cultures than Western cultures

b. women than men; Asian cultures than Western cultures

c. men than women; Western cultures than Asian cultures

d. women than men; Western cultures than Asian cultures

5. On his way back from class, Sanjeev encounters an angry mob ready to storm the dining hall to demand better food. Sanjeev likes the food as it is and wants to stop the mob. What would be the most effective solution?

a. Increasing group cohesiveness by inviting the entire mob to his house for tea

b. Passing out blue shirts for everyone to wear

c. Reducing process loss in the group by making sure that its most expert members have the most influence

d. Finding a friend in the group, calling out her name, and talking to her loudly in front of everyone

6. Four psychology students working on a group project together are trying to figure out how they should avoid groupthink when making decisions about their project. Which of these ideas would be the *least* helpful?

a. Bonding by going to see a movie together before starting the project

b. Assigning each group member to be responsible for a different chapter in their textbook so that they cover all the details

c. Having a student who is not in their group review the project

d. Designating a leader to oversee the project, one who is nondirective and encourages people to give honest feedback

7. Jim and Pam, a married couple, are buying a house and have narrowed their choice down to two options. Jim remembers that one house had a beautiful kitchen; Pam, however, remembers that there were roaches in the broom closet. By sharing this information with each other, Pam and Jim are using _____ to avoid _____.

a. mindguards; groupthink

b. social roles; deindividuation

c. transactive memory; process loss

d. subgroups; group polarization

8. Which of the following is most likely to lead to process loss in a committee?

a. All members of the committee listen carefully to each other's opinions.

b. The committee members are good friends and have known each other for years.

c. Individual committee members share information that others lack.

d. The most competent member on any given topic feels free to speak up.

9. Which of the following is true about research on leadership?

a. Female leaders are more likely than male leaders to be put in precarious, high-risk positions where it is difficult to succeed.

b. The best leaders are just born that way.

c. People in all cultures value the same traits in leaders.

d. If a woman succeeds in becoming a leader of an organization and acts in an agentic way, she is evaluated in the same way that male leaders are.

10. When is communication most effective for resolving conflict?

a. When people communicate through electronic means (e.g., over e-mail)

b. When it is required

c. When the stakes are high and both sides of a conflict have the ability to issue threats

d. When a mediator is used

See page 622 for the answers.

Chapter 10
Interpersonal Attraction
From First Impressions to Close Relationships

 ## Chapter Outline and Learning Objectives

What Predicts Attraction?

10.1 How do people decide whom they like and want to get to know better?

The Person Next Door: The Propinquity Effect
Similarity
Reciprocal Liking
Physical Attractiveness
Evolution and Mate Selection

Making Connections in the Age of Technology

10.2 How have new technologies shaped attraction and social connections?

Attraction 2.0: Mate Preference in an Online Era
The Promise and Pitfalls of Online Dating

Love and Close Relationships

10.3 What is love and what gives people satisfaction in close relationships?

Defining Love: Companionship and Passion
Culture and Love
Attachment Styles in Intimate Relationships
This Is Your Brain . . . in Love
Theories of Relationship Satisfaction: Social Exchange and Equity

Ending Intimate Relationships

10.4 What does research demonstrate about romantic breakups?

The Process of Breaking Up
The Experience of Breaking Up

Janie Egan and Chris George are both huge basketball fans. So it comes as no surprise to friends who know the young couple that their first date was going to see second-round NCAA tournament games in nearby Salt Lake City. Janie had gotten tickets from a friend and, in an emoji-filled texting session, she convinced Chris to change his existing plans and go watch basketball with her instead. In truth, it didn't take that much convincing, and two days later they returned to the same arena to see third-round games. Within 7 months they were engaged, and in early 2014, Chris and Janie got married.

There was one bump in the road of this whirlwind romance, however. The first time Chris met Janie's dad, he lied to the man who would eventually become his father-in-law. In fact, Janie forced him to. Because there was one aspect about the past that Janie wanted Chris to hide at all costs from her own parents. One skeleton in Chris's closet that she thought would be too much for her father to bear. What was it that Janie asked Chris to keep secret from her family? That the couple had met on Tinder.

Perhaps you're familiar with Tinder; maybe you've used it on your own phone. Launched in late 2012, the mobile app links to a user's Facebook account and asks for a photo and a brief tagline. Then the matching process begins. You get shown a series of photos of other Tinder users. You simply "swipe" your screen to the right for someone you might be interested in; you "swipe" left if you're not interested. Meanwhile, other users in your area are seeing your photo as well, and if someone whom you've right-swiped does the same to you, the app notifies you both of the match. Whether, where, and how far you take things from there is then up to the two of you.

Chris and Janie aren't the only couple out there to have met on Tinder. According to one of the app's creators, by early 2014, 10 million matches were offered to users per day, with over 1 billion matches since its inception (Ha, 2014). Still, Janie didn't want her parents to know any of this when they first met Chris. It wasn't that they wouldn't understand what Tinder was. Quite the contrary: they were all too familiar with the app. They had been on her case for how much time she spent on it, and they didn't care for some of the other men she had met while using it. Indeed, when Chris showed up to the house that night for their first date, Janie's dad greeted him with, "You aren't one of those Tinder boys, are you?" And so, heeding the warnings of the woman who would one day become his wife, the very first words Chris uttered to his future father-in-law were a lie: "No, sir."

Janie and Chris have since come clean with Mr. Egan. With the whole world, in fact. They have a blog (on which they've also documented their wedding) titled "Right Swiped: The Ultimate Tinder Success Story." As the couple's backstory illustrates, attraction takes many forms and emerges from many places. A college dormitory or party. Happy hour at the local bar. A dance club, the gym, the grocery store . . . and, increasingly these days, online, whether in the form of dating Web sites—like OkCupid, Match.com, or eHarmony—or mobile apps like Tinder, Grindr, How About We, and others. Clearly, interpersonal attraction is something that's often on our minds (and tablets and smart phones). And like much of human nature, it can also be studied scientifically.

This is a good thing too, because many of our assumptions about attraction and falling in love turn out to be false, as we'll discuss throughout this chapter. One such example is the belief that opposites attract: Research offers the clear conclusion that similarity is a stronger predictor of who we're drawn to (Heine, Foster, & Spina, 2009; West et al., 2014). How about the idea that women are pickier than men in selecting mates? This is often true, but not for the reasons you might assume (Finkel & Eastwick, 2009).

Social psychologists even study dating Web sites themselves, as we'll explore in more detail later. (As for Tinder, the app is such a new phenomenon that you'll likely have to wait for the next edition of this book to read about published research on it!) As one example, Eli Finkel and colleagues recently reviewed data regarding online dating and concluded that although the practice has never been more popular than it is today, many of the promises made by these Web sites go unfulfilled. Specifically, the idea of mathematical algorithms that can point users toward ideally compatible mates finds little in the way of empirical support. Sure, more Americans than ever are pairing up via dating Web sites, but the success rate for dates facilitated in this manner is no higher than for dates engineered through more old-fashioned routes, like meeting at a bar or getting fixed up by friends (Finkel et al., 2012).

The compatibility analyses of dating Web sites don't live up to their promises for a variety of reasons, according to Finkel and his colleagues. First, as you read about in Chapter 5, sometimes we don't have a good sense of why we do what we do or what will make us happy. By the same token, we aren't always accurate when it comes to predicting the mate characteristics that will lead to a satisfying relationship. Second, most dating Web site algorithms focus on matching people by personality traits or other stable characteristics. But many of the best predictors of relationship satisfaction—like communication style and sexual compatibility—can't be assessed until people actually get to know each other (Finkel et al., 2012). Thus, some of the basic principles of social psychology—the limitations of self-knowledge and the power of the situation—even apply to the most intimate (and, some would say, mystical) of human processes, such as falling in love and choosing a life partner.

Of course, none of this is to suggest that online dating and Tinder matching will be going away any time soon. Nor that it should. Just like any other way of starting a relationship, sometimes a match made online works out, like it did for Janie and Chris. And sometimes it doesn't. But no matter how persuasive their advertising claims, websites and apps have not cracked the mysterious code of human attraction—they've just given researchers new and exciting directions to pursue in asking questions about the psychology of falling in love. Because make no mistake about it, as magical and romantic a view as many of us hold of love, the experience of falling for someone can still be studied using psychological theories and methods. In this chapter, we will explore what makes us feel attracted to other people, whether as friends or lovers, and how relationships develop and progress, online and in the flesh.

What Predicts Attraction?

10.1 How do people decide whom they like and want to get to know better?

When social psychologist Ellen Berscheid asked people of various ages what made them happy, at or near the top of their lists were making friends and having positive, warm relationships (Berscheid, 1985; Berscheid & Reis, 1998). The absence of meaningful relationships with other people makes people feel lonely, worthless, hopeless, helpless, and powerless (Baumeister & Leary, 1995; Cacioppo & Patrick, 2008; Hartup & Stevens, 1997). In fact, social psychologist Arthur Aron has suggested that a central human motivation is "self-expansion." This is the desire to overlap or blend with another person, so that you have access to that person's knowledge, insights, and experience and thus broaden and deepen your own experience of life (Aron, Aron, & Norman, 2004; Fivecoat et al., 2014). We will begin this chapter by discussing the antecedents of attraction, from the initial liking of people meeting for the first time to the love that develops in close relationships.

The Person Next Door: The Propinquity Effect

Propinquity Effect

The finding that the more we see and interact with people, the more likely they are to become our friends

One of the simplest determinants of interpersonal attraction is *propinquity* (also known as proximity). The people who, by chance, are the ones you see and interact with the most often are the most likely to become your friends and lovers (Berscheid & Reis, 1998).

Now, this might seem obvious. But the striking thing about the positive relationship that exists between proximity and attraction, or the **propinquity effect**, is that it works in a very narrow sense. For example, consider a classic study conducted in a housing complex for married students at MIT. Leon Festinger, Stanley Schachter, and Kurt Back (1950) tracked friendship formation among the couples in the various apartment buildings. One section of the complex, Westgate West, was composed of 17 two-story buildings, each having 10 apartments. Residents had been assigned to apartments at random, and nearly all were strangers when they moved in. The researchers asked residents to name their three closest friends in the complex. Just as the propinquity effect would predict, 65% of the friends mentioned lived in their same building, even though the other buildings were not far away.

Even more striking was the pattern of friendships *within* a building. Each Westgate West building was designed with front doors only 19 feet apart, and the greatest distance between apartment doors was only 89 feet. The researchers found that 41% of the next-door neighbors indicated that they were close friends, 22% of those who lived two doors apart said so, and only 10% of those who lived on opposite ends of the hall indicated that they were close friends.

Festinger and his colleagues (1950) demonstrated that attraction and propinquity rely not only on actual physical distance but also on "functional distance," which refers to aspects of architectural design that determine which people you cross paths with most often. For example, living at the foot of the stairs or near the mailboxes meant that one would see upstairs residents quite often. Sure enough, throughout the complex, residents in such apartments had more upstairs friends than did those who lived in the other first-floor apartments. (You can map out propinquity effects in your own life with the following Try It! exercise.)

TRY IT!
Mapping the Effect of Propinquity in Your Life

Try examining the relationship between your friends and acquaintances and the places where you spend time regularly. Does propinquity help explain who your friends are?

First, pick a physical space to focus on. You could choose your dormitory, your apartment building, or the location where you work. (We'll use a dormitory for our example.) Draw a rough floor plan. Include the location of all the doors, stairs or elevators, bathrooms, common rooms, laundry rooms, and so on. Mark your room with a large X.

Second, think about your close friends on the floor or in the building. Mark their rooms with the number 1. Next, think about whom your not-as-close friends are; mark their rooms with a 2. Finally, think about your acquaintances—people you say hello to or chat with briefly now and then but aren't really close enough to be considered friends. Mark their rooms with a 3.

Now examine the pattern of friendships on your map. Are your friends clustered near your room in physical space? Are the rooms with the numbers 1 and 2 among the closest to your room in physical space? Are they physically closer to your room than the ones with number 3? And what about the dorm rooms that didn't get a number (meaning that you don't really know these people or interact with them)—are these rooms the farthest from yours, on average?

Finally, examine your propinquity map for the presence of functional distance. Do aspects of the architectural design of your dorm make you more likely to cross paths with some residents than others? For example, the location of the bathrooms, kitchen, living rooms, stairs, and mailboxes can play an important role in propinquity and friendship formation. These are all places where you go frequently; when walking there and back, you pass some people's rooms more than others'. Are you more likely to know the people who are located along your path? If so, propinquity has played an important role in determining your relationships!

Your social life likely has more to do with floor plans than you think! The physical layout of a building can play a surprising role in relationship formation. Research indicates that in a residential building like the one pictured here, the closer two people's apartments are, the more likely they are to become friends. And those residents who live near the stairs or elevator are more likely to make friends with people who live on other floors of the building.

Propinquity works because of familiarity, or the **mere exposure effect**: The more exposure we have to a stimulus, the more apt we are to like it (Kawakami & Yoshida, 2014; Moreland & Topolinski, 2010; Zajonc, 1968). In reality, familiarity doesn't usually breed contempt; it breeds liking. We typically associate positive feelings with things that are familiar, like comfort food, songs we remember from childhood, certain corporate logos, and the sound of the local play-by-play announcer's voice. The same is true for the people we encounter. The more often we see certain people, and the more familiar they become, the more friendship blooms. However, there is a caveat: If the person in question is an obnoxious jerk, then, not surprisingly, the more exposure you have, the greater your dislike becomes (Norton, Frost, & Ariely, 2007). But in the absence of negative qualities, familiarity tends to breed attraction and liking (Bornstein, 1989; Moreland & Beach, 1992; Lee, 2001; Reis et al., 2011).

Another good example of the propinquity and mere exposure effects is the college classroom. All semester long, you see the same people. Does this increase your liking for them? Researchers tested this hypothesis with German students by randomly assigning them on the first day of class to permanent seats for the semester (Back, Schmukle, & Egloff, 2008). That first day, they had students rate each member of the class on likability and the extent to which they would like to get to know each other. These initial ratings indicated that students who sat in neighboring seats or in the same row had higher initial attraction scores than those seated far apart. A year later, they asked these students to rate the members of their original class again in terms of how much they liked them, how well they knew

Mere Exposure Effect

The finding that the more exposure we have to a stimulus, the more apt we are to like it

Contrary to popular belief, I do not believe that friends are necessarily the people you like best; they are merely the people who got there first.
—Sir Peter Ustinov, *Dear Me*, 1977

them, and to what degree they were friends. Once again, those who had sat side by side or in the same row the prior semester were significantly more likely to be friends a year later than those who sat far apart. The propinquity effect means that some of our relationships initially blossom because we were "at the right place, at the right time."

Similarity

As we saw, propinquity increases familiarity, which leads to liking. But more than that is needed to fuel a growing friendship or a romantic relationship. (Otherwise, every pair of roommates would be best friends!) That "fuel" is often *similarity*—a match between our interests, attitudes, values, background, or personality and those of another person. As we discussed in Chapter 1, folk wisdom captures this idea in the expression "Birds of a feather flock together" (the concept of *similarity*). But folk wisdom also has another saying, "Opposites attract" (the concept of *complementarity*). Luckily, we don't have to remain forever confused by contradictory advice from old sayings; as mentioned in the opening to this chapter, research evidence demonstrates that it is overwhelmingly similarity and not complementarity that draws people together (Berscheid & Reis, 1998; Heine et al., 2009; McPherson, Smith-Lovin, & Cook, 2001; Montoya & Horton, 2013).

OPINIONS AND PERSONALITY   A large body of research indicates that the more similar someone's opinions are to yours, the more you will like the person (Byrne & Nelson, 1965; Lutz-Zois et al., 2006; Tidwell, Eastwick, & Finkel, 2013). For example, in a classic study, Theodore Newcomb (1961) randomly assigned male students at the University of Michigan to be roommates in a particular dormitory at the start of the school year. Would similarity predict friendship formation? The answer was yes: Men became friends with those who were demographically similar (e.g., shared a rural background), as well as with those who were similar in attitudes and values (e.g., were also engineering majors or also held comparable political views). It's not just attitudes or demographics that are important. Similar personality characteristics also promote liking and attraction. For example, in a study of gay men's relationships, those who scored high on a test of stereotypically male traits desired most of all a partner who was logical—another stereotypically masculine trait. Gay men who scored high on a test of stereotypically female traits desired most of all a partner who was expressive—another stereotypically feminine trait (Boyden, Carroll, & Maier, 1984). Similar personality characteristics are important for heterosexual couples and for friends as well (Gonzaga, Campos, & Bradbury, 2007; Smith et al., 2014; Weaver & Bosson, 2011).

Close friendships are often made in college, in part because of prolonged propinquity.

INTERESTS AND EXPERIENCES   The situations you choose to be in are usually populated by people who have chosen them for similar reasons. You're sitting in a social psychology class, surrounded by people who also chose to take social psychology this semester. You sign up for salsa dance lessons; the others in your class also want to learn Latin dancing. Thus, we choose to enter into certain social situations where we then find similar others. For example, in a study of the patterns of students' friendships that focused on the effects of "tracking" (grouping students by academic ability), researchers found that students were significantly more likely to choose friends from inside their track than from outside it (Kubitschek & Hallinan, 1998). Clearly, propinquity and initial similarity play a role in the formation of these friendships. However, the researchers add that similarity plays yet another role: Over time, students in the same academic track share many of the same experiences, which are different from the experiences of those in other tracks. Thus, new similarities are created and discovered, fueling the friendships. In short, shared experiences promote attraction (Pinel et al., 2006; Pinel & Long, 2012).

APPEARANCE   Similarity also operates when it comes to more superficial considerations. Sean Mackinnon, Christian Jordan, and Anne Wilson (2011) conducted a series of studies examining physical similarity and seating choice. In one study, they simply analyzed the seating arrangement of college students in a library computer lab, making observations multiple times over the course of several different days. Results indicated that, for instance, students who wore glasses sat next to other students with glasses far more often than random chance alone would predict. A second study found the same pattern by hair color.

In a third study, participants arrived at a psychology lab and were introduced to a partner who was already sitting. Handed a chair, they were told to have a seat, at which point the research team secretly measured how close to the partner's chair they put down their own chair. A separate set of researchers later evaluated photos of both the participant and the partner. Pairs judged as more physically similar had sat, on average, closer to each other. Without even realizing it, we are often drawn to those who look like us, to the point where people are even more likely to ask out on dates others who are similar to them in terms of attractiveness level (Taylor et al., 2011; Walster et al., 1966).

GENETICS   People also tend to be drawn toward others who are genetically similar to them. That is, friends tend to have more similar DNA than do strangers. At least, that's the surprising conclusion of recent research conducted by Nicholas Christakis and James Fowler (2014). Their study included close to 2,000 participants, some of whom were friends and some of whom were strangers, and analyzed close to 1.5 million markers of gene variation. Christakis and Fowler (2014) found that participants shared more DNA with their friends than with strangers, to a degree that participants were as genetically similar to their average friend as they would be to someone who shared a great-great-great grandparent. Of course, these data do not prove that our genes *cause* friendships or that our DNA drives people toward certain others. After all, this is a correlational study and not an experiment—researchers certainly can't manipulate and randomly assign participants to genetic conditions. As noted earlier, people tend to make friends with others who live near them, and individuals of similar genetic ancestry may be more likely to share such geographical propinquity. And perhaps certain genetic predispositions—say, an athletic build and good lung capacity—make people more likely to select certain activities and frequent certain locales—say, joining a running club—which means that genetically similar individuals often end up doing the same thing at the same time in the same place. These and other possibilities provide intriguing explanations for Christakis and Fowler's (2014) provocative findings, which certainly suggest interesting interactions between our genetic and social tendencies.

SOME FINAL COMMENTS ABOUT SIMILARITY   Here are two additional points about similarity. First, while similarity is very important in close relationships,

"I don't care if she is a tape dispenser. I love her."

Sam Gross/The New Yorker Collection/ The Cartoon Bank

We often prioritize different characteristics in a romantic partner when looking for a long-term relationship versus a fling. In fact, in recent years many media outlets have suggested that such short-term flings have become more frequent than ever among young people, going so far as to refer to a "hook-up culture" common on many a college campus. But interestingly, research indicates that this is hardly a new development. When researchers compared survey responses of college students from 1988 to 1996 with those from 2004 to 2012, they found no differences in number of sexual partners or frequency of sex reported (Monto & Carey, 2014).

it is important to make a distinction between *actual* similarity and *perceived* similarity (Morry, 2007; Tidwell et al., 2013). In a recent meta-analysis, R. Matthew Montoya and his colleagues found that in long-term relationships, individuals' *beliefs* about how similar they were to another person predicted liking and attraction better than their *actual* similarity did. Thus, feeling similar to another is what's really important—so much so that we will sometimes create beliefs about the similarity between ourselves and intimate others even when they don't exist (Montoya, Horton, & Kirchner, 2008).

Second, a *lack* of similarity does appear to play an important role in one type of relationship. Sometimes when we begin a romantic encounter, we want a serious, committed relationship; but sometimes, we just want a "fling." David Amodio and Carolin Showers (2005) found that whether similarity or complementarity was important depended on the level of commitment that research participants felt toward their romantic partner. If participants wanted a committed relationship, they chose a similar partner; however, if they felt a low level of commitment to the relationship, they favored dissimilar partners. Thus, in low-commitment relationships (i.e., "one-night stands" or "hook-ups"), we may go out of our way to choose someone who is strikingly different from us. A relationship with this sort of person represents more of an adventure, but, as we'll see as we progress through this chapter, relationships based on differences, rather than similarities, can be difficult to maintain.

Reciprocal Liking

Life is to be fortified by many friendships. To love, and to be loved, is the greatest happiness of existence.
—WILLIAM BLAKE, *LOVE TO FAULTS*

We like to be liked. In fact, just knowing that a person likes us fuels our attraction to that individual. Liking is so powerful that it can even make up for the absence of similarity. For example, in one experiment, when a young woman expressed interest in male research participants simply by maintaining eye contact, leaning toward them, and listening attentively, the men expressed great liking for her despite the fact that they knew she disagreed with them on important issues (Gold, Ryckman, & Mosley, 1984). Whether the clues are nonverbal or verbal, perhaps the most crucial determinant of whether we will like person A is the extent to which we believe person A likes us (Berscheid & Walster, 1978; Kenny & La Voie, 1982; Luo & Zhang, 2009; Montoya & Insko, 2008).

Just how powerful is reciprocal liking? According to recent research, powerful enough to neutralize our basic tendency to pay more attention to attractive faces. Nicolas Koranyi and Klaus Rothermund (2012) used a computer program to present a series of opposite-sex faces to German research participants. Immediately after each photo appeared, a geometrical shape was shown that required participants to respond quickly using a keyboard. This procedure also allowed the researchers to measure which faces elicited the most visual attention from the respondents, and the results indicated, as you might predict, that we have a tendency to linger and look longer at good-looking faces.

But not all respondents showed this bias to stare a bit longer at attractive faces. Who was able to break the spell of the pretty face? Participants who had previously been asked to imagine that they had just learned that someone whom they had a crush on also had feelings for them. As the researchers suggest, it makes sense that this type of interest from someone else would disrupt our otherwise default focus on the attractive alternatives out there. Think about it: If our attention were repeatedly hijacked by *every* pretty face that passed by, we'd never get the chance to turn initial interactions into more meaningful, sustained romantic relationships. Basking in the glow of reciprocated liking is enough to stop a wandering eye and convince you, at least for a while, that the grass may not be greener on the other side. And more generally, few factors are stronger predictors of being attracted to someone than finding out that the person is attracted to you.

One indicator of just how important physical appearance is in attraction is our nearly chronic tendency to shift visual attention to attractive others in our immediate vicinity.

Physical Attractiveness

Speaking of pretty faces, propinquity, similarity, and reciprocal liking are not the only predictors of whom we come to like. How important is physical appearance to our first impressions? In field experiments investigating actual behavior (rather than simply what people *say* they will do), people overwhelmingly go for physical attractiveness. For example, in a classic study, Elaine Walster Hatfield and her colleagues (Walster, et al., 1966) randomly matched 752 incoming students at the University of Minnesota for a blind date at a dance during freshman orientation week. Although the students had previously taken a battery of personality and aptitude tests, the researchers paired them up totally at random. On the night of the dance, the couples spent a few hours together dancing and chatting. They then evaluated their date and indicated the strength of their desire to see that person again. Of the many possible characteristics that could have determined whether they liked each other—such as their partner's intelligence, independence, sensitivity, or sincerity—the overriding determinant was physical attractiveness.

What's more, there was no great difference between men and women on this count. This is an interesting point, for several studies have found that men and women pay equal attention to the physical attractiveness of others (Duck, 1994a; Eastwick et al., 2011; Lynn & Shurgot, 1984), but other studies have reported that men value attractiveness more than women do (Buss, 1989; Howard, Blumstein, & Schwartz, 1987; Meltzer et al., 2014). A meta-analysis of many studies found that while both sexes

The finding that we like people who like us suggests that the strategy of "playing hard-to-get" can sometimes backfire. Recent research suggests that the strategy tends to decrease how much another person *likes* you, all the while potentially increasing how much that person *wants* to be with you (Dai, Dong, & Jia, 2014). Consider yourselves warned!

value attractiveness, men value it a bit more (Feingold, 1990); however, this gender difference was greater when men's and women's attitudes were being measured than when their actual behavior was being measured. Thus, it may be that men are more likely than women to *say* that physical attractiveness is important to them, but when it comes to actual behavior, the sexes are fairly similar in how they respond to the physical attractiveness of others. Indeed, across multiple studies, both genders rated physical attractiveness as the single most important characteristic that triggers sexual desire (Graziano et al., 1993; Regan & Berscheid, 1997), a finding that has been observed among straight as well as gay men as well as women (Ha et al., 2012; Sergios & Cody, 1985).

> It is only shallow people who do not judge by appearances.
>
> —OSCAR WILDE,
> *THE PICTURE OF DORIAN GRAY*, 1891

WHAT IS ATTRACTIVE?   Is physical attractiveness "in the eye of the beholder," or do we all share the same notions of what is beautiful and handsome? (For now, let's focus on American culture; we'll get to potential cross-cultural differences in a moment.) From early childhood, the media tell us what is beautiful, and they tell us that beauty is associated with goodness. For example, illustrators of most traditional children's books, as well as Disney movies, have taught us that heroines—and the princes who woo and win them—have a specific look. The female protagonists have small, pert noses; big eyes; shapely lips; blemish-free complexions; and slim, athletic bodies—often rather like Barbie dolls.

Bombarded as we are with media depictions of attractiveness, it is not surprising to learn that we often share criteria for defining beauty (Fink & Penton-Voak, 2002; Tseëlon, 1995; Yan & Bissell, 2014). Michael Cunningham (1986) designed a creative study to determine these standards of beauty. He asked college men to rate the attractiveness of 50 photographs of women, taken from a college yearbook and from an international beauty-pageant program. Cunningham then carefully measured the relative size of the facial features in each photograph. He found that high attractiveness ratings for female faces were associated with large eyes, a small nose, a small chin, prominent cheekbones, high eyebrows, large pupils, and a big smile. Researchers then examined women's ratings of male beauty in the same way (Cunningham, Barbee, & Pike, 1990). They found that male faces with large eyes, prominent cheekbones, a large chin, and a big smile received higher attractiveness ratings.

> She's beautiful and therefore to be woo'd.
>
> —WILLIAM SHAKESPEARE

CULTURAL STANDARDS OF BEAUTY   Are people's perceptions of what is beautiful or handsome similar across cultures? The answer is a surprising yes (Coetzee et al., 2014; Cunningham et al., 1995; Jones & Hill, 1993; Rhodes et al., 2001; Zebrowitz et al., 2012). Even though racial and ethnic groups do vary in their specific facial features, people from a wide range of cultures agree on what is physically attractive in the human face. For example, one review of the literature that has compared how people from various countries, ethnicities, and racial groups rate the attractiveness of photos found that the correlations between participants' ratings were strong, ranging from 0.66 to 0.93 (Langlois & Roggman, 1990). A meta-analysis of several studies by Judith Langlois and her colleagues (2000) also found evidence for cross-cultural agreement in what constitutes a beautiful or handsome face. In short, perceivers across cultural backgrounds think some faces are just better looking than others.

How can we explain these results? Researchers have suggested that humans came to find certain dimensions of faces attractive during the course of our evolution (Langlois & Roggman, 1990; Langlois, Roggman, & Musselman, 1994). For example, we know that even infants prefer photographs of attractive faces to unattractive ones, and infants prefer the same photographs as adults do (Langlois et al., 1991). So what specific facial characteristics do people tend to find attractive? One aspect of beauty that is preferred—in both men and women—is symmetry, where the size, shape, and location of the features on one side of the face match those on the other (Langlois et al., 2000; Little et al., 2008; Rhodes, 2006). Evolutionary psychologists suggest that we're attracted to symmetrical features because they serve as markers of good health and reproductive fitness—that is, facial symmetry is an indicator of "good genes" (Jones et al., 2001; Nedelec & Beaver, 2014).

A series of studies explored this preference by creating composite photographs of faces. Faces were morphed (i.e., combined digitally) to create the mathematical average of the features of multiple faces; ultimately, 32 faces were combined into a single composite. When shown to research participants, composite photographs were judged as more attractive than were all the separate faces that had created them, and this held true for both male and female photographs (Langlois & Roggman, 1990; Langlois et al., 1994). The "averaged" composite face was more attractive because it had lost some of the atypical or asymmetrical variation that was present in the individual faces.

Does this mean that we find "average" faces the most attractive? Clearly not, for we respond to the physical appearance of movie stars and models and consider their looks to be "above average" compared to most humans. So by "average" here we don't mean "average looking," but rather refer to features that appear to be of average size and dimension. David Perret and his colleagues made this point clear in the following study (Perret, May, & Yoshikawa, 1994). They created composite faces of two types: One composite was based on 60 photographs that had each been rated as average in attractiveness. The other composite was based on 60 photographs that had each been rated as highly attractive. Composites of these two types were made using photographs of Caucasian women, Caucasian men, Japanese women, and Japanese men. Research participants in Great Britain and Japan then rated all the composite faces for attractiveness. The researchers found that the composites of highly attractive faces were rated as significantly more attractive than the composites of average attractiveness faces. Japanese and British participants showed the same pattern when judging the faces, reinforcing the idea that similar perceptions of facial attractiveness exist cross-culturally (Perrett et al., 1994). Of course, it's also worth nothing that this study only included two cultures, leaving unanswered the question of whether people from, say, Borneo or Egypt or El Salvador would respond the same way.

Photography models represent facial standards of beauty for men and women.

Physical attractiveness of composite faces. Langlois and Roggman (1990) created composites of faces using a computer. Pictured here is the first step in the process: The first two women's photos are merged to create the "composite person" at the far right. This composite person has facial features that are the mathematical average of the facial features of the two original women.

THE POWER OF FAMILIARITY   In the end, the crucial variable on which much of interpersonal attraction hinges may actually be familiarity. We've seen that "averaging" faces together produces one face that looks typical, familiar, and physically attractive (see also Halberstadt & Rhodes, 2000). Research has also uncovered an even more startling familiarity effect: When participants rated the attractiveness of faces, they preferred those faces that most resembled their own! The researchers morphed a picture of each participant's face (without the participant's knowledge) with one of a person of the opposite sex. When presented with this photo of their opposite-sex "clone," participants gave it high ratings of attractiveness (Little & Perrett, 2002). Familiarity also underlies many of the other concepts we've discussed thus far: propinquity (people we see frequently become familiar through mere exposure), similarity (people who are similar to us will also seem familiar to us), and reciprocal liking (people who like each other get to know and become familiar with each other). All of these factors predicting attraction may be thought of as different examples of our basic preference for the comfortable, familiar, and safe over the unknown and unfamiliar.

ASSUMPTIONS ABOUT ATTRACTIVE PEOPLE   It's important to realize that beauty matters—even when it shouldn't. We're attracted to that which is beautiful, and this can lead to inequity in everyday life. A particularly chilling example of the unfair benefit of beauty was discovered by Lina Badr and Bahia Abdallah (2001), who rated the facial physical attractiveness and health status of premature infants born in hospitals in Beirut, Lebanon. They found that physical attractiveness significantly predicted the health outcomes of these infants above and beyond factors such as their medical condition. The more attractive the infant, the more quickly he or she gained weight and the shorter his or her stay in the hospital. The reason? Neonatal nurses responded more to the "prettier" infants and gave them better care.

Physical attractiveness is associated with a variety of benefits. People of above-average looks tend to earn 10% to 15% more than those of below-average appearance (French, 2002; Judge, Hurst, & Simon, 2009; Mobius & Rosenblat, 2006). College professors perceived as attractive tend to receive higher student evaluation ratings (Rinolo et al., 2006). Attractiveness even helps win elections. Niclas Berggren and his colleagues (2010) presented photographs of Finnish political candidates to research participants in many other countries (who would have no prior knowledge of these candidates) and asked them to rate the politicians on a variety of attributes, including attractiveness. They found that the ratings of attractiveness were the best predictors of the actual number of votes each candidate had gotten in the real elections. A higher beauty rating predicted an increase of between 2.5 and 2.8 percentage points in the vote total for female candidates and between 1.5 and 2.1 percentage points for male candidates, amounts that could tip the balance of a close election (Berggren, Jordahl, & Poutvaara, 2010).

Many studies have found that physical attractiveness affects the attributions people make about others (and vice versa). This tendency provides a specific example of what psychologists refer to more generally as the **halo effect** (Forgas, 2011; Thorndike, 1920). The halo effect is a cognitive bias in which the perception that an individual possesses one positive characteristic makes us more likely to believe that he or she also possesses other (even unrelated) positive characteristics. Specifically, when it comes to attractiveness, we tend to attribute to beautiful people other good qualities, including some that have nothing to do with their looks, buying into a "what is beautiful is good" stereotype (Ashmore & Longo, 1995; Dion, Berscheid, & Walster, 1972; Lemay, Clark, & Greenberg, 2010; Zebrowitz & Franklin, 2014). Meta-analyses have revealed that physical attractiveness has its largest effect on attributions related to social competence: The beautiful are thought

---

Beauty is a greater recommendation than any letter of introduction.
    —ARISTOTLE, FOURTH CENTURY B.C.

Oh, what vileness human beauty is, corroding, corrupting everything it touches.
    —ORESTES, 408 B.C.

Halo Effect

A cognitive bias by which we tend to assume that an individual with one positive characteristic also possesses other (even unrelated) positive characteristics to be more sociable, extroverted, and popular than the less attractive (Eagly et al., 1991; Feingold, 1992b). They are also seen as more sexual, happier, and more assertive. The "halo" provided by being good-looking extends to the online realm as well: One study of dating websites found that those users who posted more attractive photos were also rated as having written more attractive profile descriptions (Brand et al., 2012).

Do these stereotypes about the beautiful operate across cultures? The answer appears to be yes (Anderson, Adams, & Plaut, 2008; Chen, Shaffer, & Wu, 1997). For example, college students in South Korea were asked to rate a number of yearbook photographs (Wheeler & Kim, 1997). Both male and female participants thought the more physically attractive people would also be more socially skilled, friendly, and well adjusted— the same group of traits that North American participants thought went with physical attractiveness (see Table 10.1). But Korean and North American students differed in some of the other traits they assigned to the beautiful, highlighting differences in what is considered important in each culture (Markus et al., 1996; Triandis, 1995). For the American and Canadian students—who live in more individualistic cultures that value independence, individuality, and self-reliance—the "beautiful" stereotype included traits of personal strength. These traits were not part of the Korean "beautiful" stereotype. Instead, for these students, who live in a more collectivistic culture that values harmonious group relations, the "beautiful" stereotype included integrity and concern for others (see Table 10.1).

Interestingly, the stereotype that the beautiful are particularly gifted in the area of social competence has some research support. That is, highly attractive people *do* actually develop good social interaction skills and report having more satisfying interactions with others than do less-attractive people (Feingold, 1992b; Langlois

It's no coincidence that in children's movies, the hero is traditionally attractive and the villain ugly. In addition to finding it pleasing to look at attractive others, we also tend to assume that "what is beautiful is good."

Table 10.1 Culture and the "What Is Beautiful Is Good" Stereotype

The "what is beautiful is good" stereotype has been explored in both individualistic cultures (e.g., North America) and collectivistic cultures (e.g., Asia). Male and female participants in the United States, Canada, and South Korea rated photographs of people with varying degrees of physical attractiveness. Responses indicated that some of the traits that make up the stereotype are the same across cultures, while other traits associated with the stereotype are different in the two cultures. In both cultures, the physically attractive are seen as having more of the characteristics that are valued in that culture than do the less physically attractive.

Traits Shared in the Korean, American, and Canadian Stereotype		
sociable	extraverted	likable
happy	popular	well-adjusted
friendly	mature	poised
sexually warm/responsive		
Additional Traits Present in the American and Canadian Stereotype		
strong	assertive	dominant
Additional Traits Present in the Korean Stereotype		
sensitive	empathic	generous
honest	trustworthy	

(Based on Eagly, Ashmore, Makhhijani, & Longo, 1991; Feingold, 1992b; Wheeler & Kim, 1997)

et al., 2000; Meier et al., 2010; Reis et al., 1982). Why does this "kernel of truth" emerge in the stereotype? A leading explanation is that because the beautiful, from a young age, receive a great deal of attention that in turn helps them develop good social skills. You probably recognize the self-fulfilling prophecy at work here (see Chapter 3): Our expectations of people can affect how they actually come to behave. If others always treat you as if they expect you to be socially proficient (whether because of your physical appearance or otherwise), this then provides you with ample opportunities to actually develop superior social skills.

Can a "regular" person be made to act like a "beautiful" one through the self-fulfilling prophecy? To find out, researchers gave college men a photo and a packet of information about a woman with whom they were about to have a phone conversation (Snyder, Tanke, & Berscheid, 1977). But the photograph was rigged; at random, the men were either given a photo that a previous group of raters had judged to be attractive or one that a previous group had rated as unattractive. In both cases, this photo was *not* of the actual woman they were about to speak with. The experimental purpose of the photograph was to invoke the men's stereotype that "what is beautiful is good"—to test the possibility that a woman would be more likable, poised, and fun to talk to if her male conversation partner believed she was attractive. Again, the prediction here was not just that the men would *perceive* the woman as more fun to talk to when they thought she was attractive, but that the men's beliefs about her appearance would actually change the reality of how the woman behaved.

Did the researchers find evidence of an attractiveness-based self-fulfilling prophecy? In short, yes! The men who thought they were talking to an attractive woman responded to her in a warmer, more sociable manner than the men who thought they were talking to an unattractive woman. And the men's behavior actually influenced how the women behaved: When independent observers listened to a tape recording of only the woman's half of the conversation (without knowing anything about the photograph the men had seen), they rated the women whose male part-ners thought they were physically attractive as more confident, animated, and warm than they rated those women whose male partners thought they were unattractive. In other words, because the male partner thought he was talking to an attractive woman, he spoke to her in a way that brought out her most sparkling qualities. Subsequent studies have found similar results with the gender roles reversed (Andersen & Bem, 1981), reminding us that it is a myth that physical attractiveness only affects how men perceive women. Indeed, meta-analyses that have examined hundreds of studies have found that physical attractiveness is also an important factor how men are perceived and treated (Eagly et al., 1991; Feingold, 1992b; Langlois et al., 2000; Zhang et al., 2014).

Evolution and Mate Selection

The poet Robert Browning asked, "How do I love thee? Let me count the ways." For psychologists, the question is *"Why* do I love thee?" Some researchers believe that the answer lies in an evolutionary approach to mate selection. The basic tenet of evolu-tionary biology is that an animal's "fitness" is measured by its reproductive success (i.e., its capability to pass on genes to the next generation). Reproductive success is not just part of the game; it *is* the game. This biological concept has been applied to social behavior by some psychologists, who define **evolutionary psychology** as the attempt to explain social behavior in terms of genetic factors that have evolved over time according to the principles of natural selection. For example, as detailed earlier, one explanation for people's tendency to find symmetrical faces more attractive is that symmetry indicates positive health and "good genes."

Evolutionary Psychology

The attempt to explain social behavior in terms of genetic factors that have evolved over time according to the principles of natural selection

EVOLUTION AND SEX DIFFERENCES Evolutionary psychology also makes some particularly interesting (and controversial) predictions regarding sex differences in mate preference. Specifically, evolutionary psychologists argue that men and women have very different agendas when it comes to mate selection, due to their differing roles in producing (and raising) offspring. For females, reproduction is costly in terms of time, energy, and effort: They must endure the discomforts of pregnancy, the risks of childbirth, and, traditionally, theirs is the primary responsibility for caring for the infant until maturity. Reproducing, then, is serious business, so females, the theory goes, must consider carefully when and with whom to reproduce. In comparison, reproduction is a low-cost, short-term investment for males. The evolutionary approach to mate selection concludes that reproductive success for the two sexes translates into two very different behavior patterns: Throughout the animal world, males' reproductive success is measured by the *quantity* of their offspring. They pursue frequent pairings with many females in order to maximize their number of surviving progeny. In contrast, females' reproductive success lies in successfully raising each of their offspring to maturity. They pair less frequently and only with carefully chosen males, because the cost to them of raising and ensuring the survival of each offspring is so high (Griffith, Pryke, & Buettemer, 2011; Symons, 1979).

Now, what does all of this have to do with how people fall in love? David Buss and his colleagues argue that the evolutionary approach explains the different strategies and tendencies of men and women in romantic relationships (Buss, 1985, 1988a; Buss & Schmitt, 1993). Buss (1988b) argues that finding (and keeping) a mate requires one to display resources—the aspects of oneself that will appear attractive to potential mates. He proposes that, across millennia, human beings have been selected through evolution to respond to certain external cues in the opposite sex. Women, facing high reproductive costs, will look for a man who can supply the resources and support she needs to raise a child. Men will look for a woman who appears capable of reproducing successfully. More precisely, the argument goes, men will respond to the physical appearance of women because age and health denote reproductive fitness, and women will respond to the economic and career achievements of men because these variables represent resources they and their offspring need (Buss, 1988b).

Many studies have provided support for these predictions. For example, Buss and colleagues (Buss, 1989; Buss et al., 1990) asked more than 9 thousand adults in 37 countries how desirable various characteristics were in a marriage partner. In general, women valued ambition, industriousness, and earning capacity in a potential mate more than the men did. The men valued physical attractiveness in a mate more than the women did. It should be noted, however, that the top characteristics on both men's and women's lists were the same: honesty, trustworthiness, and a pleasant personality (Buss & Barnes, 1986; Hatfield & Sprecher, 1995; Regan & Berscheid, 1997; Sprecher, Sullivan, & Hatfield, 1994). Further evidence for the importance of reproductive considerations in human attraction comes from more recent research that has examined the relationship between a woman's menstrual cycle, her perceptions of potential mates, and how potential mates view her. For example, Kelly Gildersleeve and colleagues (2014) conducted a meta-analysis that examined 50 studies and found reliable support for the hypothesis that as they near ovulation and peak fertility, women tend to exhibit greater preference for men who exhibit outward signs of reproductive fitness: a symmetrical face, a masculine face (e.g., sharp, pronounced jawline), and a muscular physique (Gildersleeve, Haselton, & Fales, 2014).

Men seek to propagate widely, whereas women seek to propagate wisely.

—Robert Hinde

Research has linked perceptions of attractiveness to reproductive concerns. For example, as ovulation nears, women tend to rate as more attractive men with highly masculine faces and body types (Gildersleeve et al., 2014).

... when 'such things happened' it was undoubtedly foolish of the man, but somehow always criminal of the woman.

—EDITH WHARTON,
THE AGE OF INNOCENCE, 1920

ALTERNATE PERSPECTIVES ON SEX DIFFERENCES The evolutionary approach to attraction and love has inspired its share of debate. For example, one could argue that evolutionary advantages to having multiple sexual partners should not be limited to men, but should also apply to women. With multiple partners, females would increase the odds of getting resources for their offspring, as well as benefit from genetic diversity. Females could choose an attractive male with "good genes" with whom to procreate and another male with whom to raise the offspring (Campbell, 2002; Gangestad & Simpson, 2000). It may also be the case that men value physical attractiveness in a partner not because of evolved tendencies, but simply because they have been taught by society to value it—that they have been conditioned by decades of advertising, media images, and other cultural messages to value beauty in women and to have a more recreational approach to sex than women do (Hatfield & Rapson, 1993; Lefkowitz et al., 2014). Similarly, research has found that in some situations, women value physical attractiveness just as much as men—specifically, when they are considering a potential sexual partner as opposed to a potential marriage partner (Regan & Berscheid, 1997; Simpson & Gangestad, 1992).

Other researchers offer additional arguments that the preference for different qualities in a mate can be explained without resorting to evolutionary principles: Around the world, women typically have less power, status, wealth, and other resources than men do. Therefore, in many societies women need to rely on men to achieve economic security, and they must consider this characteristic when choosing a husband (Rosenblatt, 1974). To test this hypothesis, Steven Gangestad (1993) correlated the extent to which women in several countries had access to financial resources and the extent to which women reported male physical attractiveness as an important variable in a mate. His results revealed that the more economic power women had in a given culture, the more highly women prioritized a man's physical attractiveness.

As you can see, when discussing human mate preference, it is often difficult to disentangle "nature" (inborn preferences) from "nurture" (cultural norms and gender roles). When we hear about sex differences related to mate selection and attraction, our first instinct is often to turn to biological or evolutionary explanations (Conley et al., 2011). But a closer look often reveals that many of these differences are also attributable to situational factors. Take, for instance, the proposition that women are pickier than men when it comes to selecting a mate. Indeed, whether you look at online dating, speed-dating events, or old-fashioned face-to-face date requests, research indicates that women are significantly more discriminating about who they'll go out with than men are (Clark & Hatfield, 1989; Hitsch, Hortaçsu, & Ariely, 2010; Schützwohl et al., 2009). This makes sense from an evolutionary perspective. The argument would be that women *have* to be picky because they can't afford to make mistakes; unlike men, their fertility window is relatively narrow across the lifespan, and each decision to reproduce requires more time and resources.

But consider the provocative results of a speed-dating study conducted by Eli Finkel and Paul Eastwick (2009). College students in this research had brief conversations with a dozen different opposite-sex individuals. In these speed-dating sessions, the women remained seated while the men in attendance rotated in a circle, spending 4 minutes with each prospective dating partner before moving on to the next person. After each of the 12 women had been visited by each of the 12 men, all participants completed a questionnaire assessing their attraction to these potential mates (and later, from the comfort of their own homes, they recorded on the study website whether or not they'd be interested in seeing each person again). Once again, women were more selective than men, reporting lower levels of romantic desire and identifying fewer prospective mates that they'd like to get to know better.

But an interesting thing happened when the researchers made a minor tweak to the speed-dating situation. In a second set of dating events, they had men and women swap roles. Now the men remained seated and the women rotated around—a simple modification, but one that stood regular dating protocol on its head. Instead of women sitting still while male suitors paraded in a circle, now the men remained stationary as women approached them. The "dates" themselves were still the same: 4-minute conversations after which both parties were asked for their impressions. But from a situational standpoint, this was traditional dating in reverse (Conley et al., 2011). And in this bizarro dating world where women did the approaching, women were no longer pickier than men. If anything, the female participants now reported more chemistry with their partners and identified more prospective mates that they wanted to see again.

Finkel and Eastwick's (2009) results suggest that the sex differences in mate selectivity do not simply reflect evolution or biology, but are also attributable to the established dating paradigm in most societies, in which men are the approachers and women the approachees. Being approached gives you control in the world of dating, regardless of sex or gender; being approached also means feeling in demand and having options. And so it is that, as with many aspects of human nature, we need both "nature" and "nurture" explanations to fully understand the psychology of attraction and mate selection.

REVIEW QUESTIONS

1. Which of the following examples best illustrates how functional distance plays a role in the propinquity effect?
   a. Bart doesn't like his next-door neighbor, primarily because of his habit of playing loud music that makes it difficult to get to sleep at night.
   b. Marge, whose cubicle is right next to both the kitchen and the elevator, is one of the most popular people in the entire office.
   c. Homer prefers to take the stairs rather than the elevator because it decreases his likelihood of running into people he finds annoying.
   d. Lisa made more friends in her sophomore-year dorm than in her freshman-year dorm.

2. The _____ suggests that the more times we encounter someone or something, the more we tend to like it.
   a. evolutionary perspective
   b. halo effect
   c. mere exposure effect
   d. reciprocal liking effect

3. Similarity in terms of which of the following dimensions has been found to predict increased attraction?
   a. attitudes
   b. attractiveness level
   c. genetics
   d. All of the above

4. Which of the following statements about perceptions of physical attractiveness is true?
   a. Asymmetrical faces are typically viewed as more attractive because they are so distinctive.
   b. Large cross-cultural differences emerge in terms of what is seen as physically attractive in the human face.
   c. The more someone looks like us, the less attractive we typically find him or her to be.
   d. Perceivers tend to believe that someone who is attractive also possesses a range of other (unrelated) positive characteristics.

5. Which of the following is *not* identified as a major predictor of attraction in long-term romantic relationships?
   a. similarity
   b. reciprocity
   c. complementarity
   d. propinquity

6. Research indicates that a face's symmetry is a reliable predictor of how attractive it is seen to be. An evolutionary psychology explanation for this finding would be that
   a. symmetrical faces remind us of ourselves and therefore elicit positive feelings.
   b. symmetry is a sign of health and that a potential mate has good genes.
   c. "Western" cultures place a greater emphasis on physical attractiveness than do "Eastern" cultures.
   d. All of the above

7. Men and women differ in their approach while selecting a mate for themselves. According to the evolutionary perspective, what are the specific characteristics that men and women favor while making this decision?
   a. Men tend to favor trustworthiness while women favor a pleasant personality.
   b. Women tend to favor physical attractiveness while men favor industriousness.
   c. Men tend to favor reproductive capability while women favor men with resources.
   d. Women tend to favor earning capacity of men while men favor ambitious women.

See page 622 for the answers.

Making Connections in the Age of Technology

10.2 How have new technologies shaped attraction and social connections?

As we have detailed, psychologists have studied attraction for decades now. And as is the case with any topic in social psychology, it is reasonable to ask whether research findings observed generations ago still apply to tendencies in the modern age. In particular, as illustrated by our opening example of Tinder couple Janie and Chris George, we now live in an era in which much social interaction is not of the face-to-face variety, but rather takes place via text, Twitter, Snapchat, Instagram, interactive gaming, virtual reality, and probably even newer technologies and apps developed since this sentence was typed. How do principles, processes, and theories of attraction and social connection play out in this constantly evolving technological landscape? This section provides some initial answers to this question, but clearly there is no shortage of interesting future research directions available to social psychologists interested in studying interpersonal attraction.

One thing's for sure: a time-traveler from just 15 to 20 years ago would barely recognize much of what passes for social interaction today. In our smartphone era, it isn't unusual to see a group out to a meal, faces (and thumbs) buried in devices, perhaps all the while carrying on a conversation of sorts with others at the table. The opportunities presented by these amazing handheld technologies are plentiful, allowing us to get work done as we commute, stay in touch with loved ones an ocean away, and locate a nearby spot for coffee and dessert before the waiter has even brought the check for dinner. But are there also social costs to an increasingly smartphone-tethered existence? Research suggests that there might be. Consider a recent field experiment in which researchers visited coffee shops and cafes in the Washington D.C. area, observed 100 real-life interactions between pairs of people, and then asked the individuals involved questions about the conversation they just had. Among pairs who had at least one mobile device (e.g., smartphone, laptop, tablet) present during the conversation, ratings of connectedness to and empathy for the other person were significantly lower than they were among pairs who interacted in the absence of such a device (Misra et al., 2014).

This finding is a correlational one, though. Maybe it's a certain type of person who always keeps a smartphone nearby and doesn't invest as much in face-to-face conversation. Perhaps you're saying to yourself, *I'm not like that; even when I have my phone, I'm engaged with the people around me.* Perhaps. But experiments have also demonstrated a

As amazing as the technologies are, mobile devices like smartphones can also impair our feelings of social connectedness to others during the course of face-to-face interaction.

causal link between the presence of a mobile device and decreased social connection. In one such experiment, Andrew Pryzbylski and Netta Weinstein (2013) brought pairs of strangers into their lab for a 10-minute conversation. Half of these conversations took place with a mobile phone or tablet sitting on the small table between them; in another condition, there was no phone present. The researchers found that the mere presence of the mobile device decreased participants' feelings of trust, closeness, and empathy with their conversation partner. These effects were particularly pronounced when the pairs were instructed to discuss a personally meaningful topic, a scenario that, in the absence of a phone, would be expected to foster a sense of closeness among strangers meeting for the first time (Pryzbylski & Weinstein, 2013).

We're not suggesting or expecting that you toss your smartphone upon learning about these data—to be honest, your authors aren't giving up theirs either. But these findings do give pause for thought. If the mere presence of a phone that isn't even yours can impair aspects of social interaction, just imagine how distracting our own devices can be, even when they aren't actively ringing, chiming, or buzzing! Technologies like these are here to stay, and there's no question that this is a good thing on the whole. But social psychological research does provide additional support for the emerging movement to unplug once in a while and force ourselves to take periodic vacations from our phones, tablets, and computers (Huffington, 2014).

Attraction 2.0: Mate Preference in an Online Era

One way to explore how our rapidly developing technological world affects processes of attraction and relationship formation is to revisit some of the classic findings regarding propinquity, similarity, and familiarity, examining how these factors operate in the Internet age. For example, consider how propinquity operates in an era when physical distance no longer creates the same obstacles to interaction that it once did (Chan & Cheng, 2004; Dodds, Muhamad, & Watts, 2003). Jure Leskovec and Eric Horvitz conducted a study testing just how connected we are to other people in the modern world. They examined "degrees of separation," a measure of social distance between people: You are one degree away from everyone you know, two degrees away from everyone they know, and so on. These researchers analyzed an instant-messaging network, looking at who sent messages to whom and calculating how many different people in a "chain" it would take, on average, to connect two random users to each other. After making calculations for 30 billion conversations among 240 million people, they found that the average length of a "chain" needed to connect any two people was seven, and that 90% of pairs could be connected in no more than eight "hops" (Leskovec & Horvitz, 2007). This research demonstrates empirically what many of us now take for granted: in the modern world, there aren't nearly as many degrees of separation between strangers as there once were, putting a whole new spin on the relationship between propinquity and attraction that we discussed earlier.

Similarity continues to have value in technologically driven relationships. We have already discussed the tendency to be attracted to people of similar appearance, right down to people being attracted to others who are the same *level* of physical attractiveness as they are. Recent research indicates that this tendency to be drawn to comparable others who are "in our own league" is also evident when relationships go online. Lindsay Taylor and colleagues (2011) assessed the popularity of over 3,000 heterosexual users of a dating Web site, testing the hypothesis that profiles would be most popular among other users who shared the same attractiveness level. They defined popularity as the number of opposite-sex individuals who sent unsolicited messages to a particular profile. To increase the validity of this measure, the researchers did not count messages sent in response to contact initiated by the user him or herself (or subsequent messages sent during an ongoing exchange), meaning that there was no way for the users in the study to increase their own popularity count once they posted a profile.

Taylor and colleagues (2011) found that users who qualified as popular contacted other popular users at a rate greater than would be expected by chance—a finding that probably does not surprise you. After all, who wouldn't want to reach out to the popular potential mates? The less popular users of the site, that's who. The researchers also found that users lower in popularity contacted other low-popularity users more often. A follow-up study with over 1 million users produced a comparable result: People tend to select (and be selected by) others with similar levels of popularity, and this tendency to try to "match up" with mates of comparable popularity was no different for men than for women. As the researchers concluded, "one reason that established couples tend to be similar is that matching is at play from the earliest stages of dating" (Taylor et al., 2011, p. 952).

And what about familiarity? As you will recall, research has demonstrated that familiarity typically promotes attraction, to the point where even mere exposure to an object or person increases liking. But you may also recall that mere exposure works in the opposite direction when the additional encounters reveal negative characteristics of the object or person in question—a conclusion supported by another study of online dating. In this research, Michael Norton and colleagues (2007) gave a survey to participants both before and after going on a date. Pre-date, all that participants knew about their partner was what they had read on a website profile, so their ratings of how much knowledge they had about their partner increased post-date. But their ratings of how much they liked their partner *decreased* after the date. Why? Because the more familiar participants became with their partner during the date, the more they realized that some aspects of their initial impression (based on an

One question surrounding attraction is how tendencies regarding mate preference that have evolved over generations play out in the modern era of Internet dating, speed-dating events, and Facebook.

ambiguous dating website profile) turned out to be inaccurate. As they obtained additional information during the date itself, they came to appreciate all their incompatibilities and dissimilarities, which in turn decreased average liking ratings (Norton et al., 2007; see Finkel et al., 2015).

The Promise and Pitfalls of Online Dating

According to a recent review of online dating reports, by the end of the last decade, "more new romantic relationships had begun online than through any means other than meeting through friends" (Finkel et al., 2012, p. 11). Participation on dating websites and apps is at an all-time high and attitudes toward internet dating have never been more positive than they are today. These developments are understandable, particularly given that dating websites advertise three primary services: (1) aggregating a large number of profiles for browsing, (2) providing opportunity for communication with potential mates, and (3) matching users based on analyses of compatibility (Finkel et al., 2012).

Clearly, online dating services have a lot to offer those who are looking for love (Blackhart, Fitzpatrick, & Williamson, 2014). Still, some of the promise of online dating is tempered by psychological research findings. For example, as discussed in the opening of this chapter, the dating Web site algorithms used to match potential mates by compatibility do not lead to higher relationship success rates than older, lower-tech methods of matching such as the fix-up among friends or getting to know someone through mutual activities. Furthermore, just how honest are people when they post profiles and photos on dating websites anyway? Norton and colleagues (2007) found that learning more about a partner during a date often makes you like that person less than you did when you had only seen a profile, suggesting that perhaps the profiles aren't too accurate to begin with.

Catalina Toma and Jeffrey Hancock have conducted a series of investigations to assess these questions regarding online dating profiles. Some of their research examines potential differences in how men and women describe themselves online. In one study, they interviewed 84 online daters, presenting them with a printout of their own dating profile and asking them how accurate they believed they were in describing their height, weight, and age (Toma, Hancock, & Ellison, 2008). Of course, the researchers were able to compare these self-assessments of accuracy to objective measures of participants' actual height, weight, and age. Results indicated that a full 81% of participants provided inaccurate information in their profile for at least one characteristic, with the most lies coming about weight, followed by age, then height. Interestingly, no gender differences emerged: Men and women were equally likely to try to stretch the truth. Participants' self-reported estimates of their profile accuracy were reasonably good predictors of actual accuracy, indicating that the discrepancies observed did not result from unconscious tendencies to view the self through rose-colored glasses, but rather intentional efforts to fudge facts.

"On the Internet, nobody knows you're a dog."

Peter Steiner/The New Yorker Collection/The Cartoon Bank

Fundamentally speaking, man is what he hides.

—ANDRÉ MALRAUX,
THE WALNUT TREES OF ALTENBURG, 1948

A slightly different pattern emerges from analysis of photos used in dating profiles. Here, Hancock and Toma (2009) found that distortions are often less conscious, especially among women. Following a similar procedure to their previous study, the researchers interviewed online daters about how accurate they believed their profile photo to be. They then had a separate group of college students look at a series of two images side by side: (1) each participant's dating profile photo and (2) a photo taken of the participant during the recent interview. The college students were asked to evaluate how accurate a depiction the profile photograph was of the participant's current physical appearance. In total, 32% of profile photographs were judged to be deceptive or misleading, and females' photos were found to be less accurate than males'. Common inaccuracies included daters looking thinner in the profile photo than they currently do, having more hair in the profile photo than they do now, or using profile photos that were retouched or airbrushed. Unlike with written profiles, users' self-assessed accuracy ratings were not reliable predictors of the actual accuracy of their photo (as rated by the students), particularly among female daters.

In light of these inaccuracies—both intentional and unintentional—what's a lovelorn Internet dater to do? Luckily, the same research techniques that uncovered these inaccurate profiles and photos can also be used to identify which potential online mates are the most (and least) honest. Specifically, Toma and Hancock (2012) suggest three giveaways that the profile you're checking out online may not pass a reality check. First, deceptive profiles tend to have fewer first-person pronouns like *I* and *me*. The researchers explain that this is one way for those who lie or exaggerate to distance themselves psychologically from their half-truths. Second, deceptive profiles make more use of negations, or negative turns of phrase (e.g., "not judgmental" instead of "open-minded"; "not averse to taking risks" instead of "adventurous"). Third, deceptive profiles simply include fewer total words than accurate profiles. Stretching the truth is hard work and cognitively demanding; the fewer inaccurate statements you put in your profile, the fewer fabrications you have to remember later on when you meet someone in person. In short, online dating offers users a much larger pool of potential mates than do more traditional methods that are constrained by personal contacts and physical geography. At the same time, in some important respects, dating sites and apps sometimes fall short of the promises they make to users.

REVIEW QUESTIONS

1. Research on the influence of mobile phone technology on social interaction indicates that
   a. contrary to what some critics believe, the availability of mobile phones and smartphones has no negative effect on social engagement.
   b. men are more easily distracted by the presence of a mobile phone during a conversation than are women.
   c. even if a mobile phone isn't being used during a conversation, it can still pose a distraction that comes at the expense of social engagement.
   d. while laptops and tablet computers can be distracting during face-to-face interaction, smartphones are not.

2. One measure of the social distance between people is known as
   a. degrees of separation.
   b. social engagement.
   c. mate preference.
   d. halo effect.

3. Research on the effectiveness of dating websites indicates that
   a. Web sites using mathematical algorithms to match couples by compatibility are far more successful than more traditional ways of meeting a partner such as getting fixed up by friends.
   b. people tend to send messages to fellow website users whose attractiveness and popularity levels are similar to their own.

    c. these sites are very popular among gay and lesbian users, but not among heterosexuals.

    d. the more you find out about someone you met online the more you tend to like that person.

4. Which of the following statements is true regarding how people tend to represent themselves in online dating profiles?

    a. Misrepresentation in online profiles tends to be of both the intentional and unintentional varieties.

    b. Deceptive web profiles tend to be longer and more detailed than accurate profiles.

    c. There are no gender differences in how men and women represent themselves online.

    d. The vast majority of people post inaccurate or misleading photos of themselves in online profiles.

See page 622 for the answers.

Love and Close Relationships

10.3 **What is love and what gives people satisfaction in close relationships?**

By this point in the chapter, you have learned enough about attraction to make a favorable first impression the next time you meet someone. Suppose you want Sophia to like you. You should hang around her so that you become familiar, emphasize your similarity to her, and let her know you enjoy her company. But what if you want to do more than make a good impression? What if you want to have a close friendship or a romantic relationship?

Until recently, social psychologists had little to say in answer to this question—research on attraction focused almost exclusively on first impressions. Why? Primarily because long-term relationships are much more difficult to study scientifically than first impressions are. As we saw in Chapter 2, random assignment to different conditions is the hallmark of an experiment. When studying first impressions, a researcher can randomly assign you to a get-acquainted session with someone who is similar or dissimilar to you. But a researcher can't randomly assign you to the similar or dissimilar "lover" condition and make you have a relationship! In addition, the feelings and intimacy associated with close relationships can be difficult to measure. Psychologists face a daunting task when trying to analyze such complex feelings as love and passion.

> Love is something so divine, Description would but make it less; 'Tis what I feel, but can't define, 'Tis what I know, but can't express.
>
> —Beilby Porteus

Defining Love: Companionship and Passion

Despite the difficulties inherent to studying close relationships, social psychologists have made interesting discoveries about the nature of love, how it develops, and how it flourishes. Let's begin with perhaps the most difficult question: What, exactly, is love? Early attempts to define love distinguished between liking and loving, showing that, as you might expect, love is something different from "lots of liking"—and not just in terms of sexual desire (Rubin, 1970; Sternberg, 1987).

For Shakespeare's Romeo and Juliet, love was passionate, turbulent, and full of longing; same goes for the Bella, Edward, and Jacob triangle of the *Twilight* series. Your grandparents, if they've remained married for a long time, probably exemplify a calmer, more tranquil (and probably less supernatural) kind of love. We use the word *love* to describe all of these relationships, though each one seems to be of a different kind (Berscheid & Meyers, 1997; Fehr, 2013; Fehr & Russell, 1991; Vohs & Baumeister, 2004).

Social psychologists have recognized that a good definition of love must include the passionate, giddy feelings of romantic love as well as the deep,

> Try to reason about love, and you will lose your reason.
>
> —French Proverb

This scene from the *Twilight* saga exemplifies the early stages of passionate love.

Companionate Love

The feelings of intimacy and affection we have for someone that are not accompanied by passion or physiological arousal

Passionate Love

An intense longing we feel for a person, accompanied by physiological arousal

Love is or it ain't. Thin love ain't love at all.

— TONI MORRISON

long-term devotion of married couples, lifelong friends, or siblings. In defining love, then, we generally distinguish between *companionate love* and *passionate love* (Hatfield & Rapson, 1993; Hatfield & Walster, 1978). **Companionate love** consists of feelings of intimacy and affection we have for someone that are not accompanied by passion or physiological arousal. People can experience companionate love in nonsexual close friendships, or in romantic relationships in which they experience great feelings of intimacy but not as much of the heat and passion as they once felt.

Passionate love involves an intense longing for another person, characterized by the experience of physiological arousal—the feeling of shortness of breath and a thumping heart in someone's presence (Fisher, 2004; Ratelle et al., 2013; Regan & Berscheid, 1999). When things are going well (the other person loves us too), we feel great fulfillment and ecstasy. When things are not going well (our love is unrequited), we feel great sadness and despair. Cross-cultural research indicates that American couples tend to value passionate love more than Chinese couples do, and Chinese couples tend to value companionate love more than American couples do (Gao, 1993; Jankowiak, 1995; Ting-Toomey & Chung, 1996). In comparison, the Taita of Kenya, in East Africa, value both equally; they conceptualize romantic love as a combination of companionate and passionate love. The Taita consider this the best kind of love, and achieving it is a primary goal in their society (Bell, 1995). Reviewing the anthropological research on 166 societies, William Jankowiak and Edward Fischer (1992) found evidence for passionate love in 147 of them, as you can see in Table 10.2.

Elaine Hatfield and Susan Sprecher (1986) developed a questionnaire to measure passionate love. As measured by this scale, passionate love consists of strong, uncontrollable thoughts; intense feelings; and overt acts toward the target of one's affection. Find out if you are experiencing (or have experienced) passionate love by filling out the questionnaire in the Try It! exercise on the following page.

Table 10.2 Cross-Cultural Evidence for Passionate Love Based on Anthropological Research in 166 Societies

Cultural Area	Passionate Love Present	Passionate Love Absent
Mediterranean	22 (95.7%)	1 (4.3%)
Sub-Saharan Africa	20 (76.9%)	6 (23.1%)
Eurasia	32 (97.0%)	1 (3.0%)
Insular Pacific	27 (93.1%)	2 (6.9%)
North America	24 (82.8%)	5 (17.2%)
South and Central America	22 (84.6%)	4 (15.4%)

(Based on data from Jankowiak & Fischer, 1992)

TRY IT!

Passionate Love Scale

These items ask you to describe how you feel when you are passionately in love. Think of the person whom you love most passionately right now. If you are not in love right now, think of the last person you loved passionately. If you have never been in love, think of the person you came closest to caring for in that way. Choose your answers as you remember how you felt when your feelings were the most intense.

For each of the 15 items, choose the number between 1 and 9 that most accurately describes your feelings. The answer scale ranges from 1 (not at all true) to 9 (definitely true). Write the number you choose next to each item.

```
1    2    3    4    5    6    7    8    9
↑              ↑                    ↑
Not at all true    Moderately true    Definitely true
```

1. I would feel deep despair if _____ left me.
2. Sometimes I feel I can't control my thoughts; they are obsessively on _____.
3. I feel happy when I am doing something to make _____ happy.
4. I would rather be with _____ than anyone else.
5. I'd get jealous if I thought _____ were falling in love with someone else.
6. I yearn to know all about _____.
7. I want _____ —physically, emotionally, mentally.
8. I have an endless appetite for affection from _____.
9. For me, _____ is the perfect romantic partner.
10. I sense my body responding when _____ touches me.
11. _____ always seems to be on my mind.
12. I want _____ to know me—my thoughts, my fears, and my hopes.
13. I eagerly look for signs indicating _____'s desire for me.
14. I possess a powerful attraction for _____.
15. I get extremely depressed when things don't go right in my relationship with _____.

Scoring: Add up your scores for the 15 items. The total score can range from a minimum of 15 to a maximum of 135. The higher your score, the more your feelings for the person reflect passionate love; the items to which you gave a particularly high score reflect those components of passionate love that you experience most strongly.

(Adapted from Elaine Hatfield and Richard L. Rapson, "Passionate love in intimate relationships", in Bert S. Moore, Alice M. Isen. Affect and Social Behavior, Cambridge University Press, 1990, p. 146.)

Culture and Love

The process of finding a romantic partner varies across the world. For example, in villages in Nepal, dating is forbidden, and even casual meetings between young men and women are considered inappropriate. Traditionally, a future spouse is chosen by one's parents, who focus on the potential mate's social standing: family, caste, and economic resources. In these arranged marriages, the bride and groom often speak to each other for the first time on their wedding day. It is not unusual for the bride to cry during the ceremony and for the groom to look stunned and resigned (Goode, 1999). But despite what might seem an inauspicious beginning, many of these unions turn out to be successful, especially considering the high divorce rate of unarranged marriages in the United States. That said, others might point out that the freedom to even consider seeking a divorce in an unhappy marriage is also something that varies by culture.

Beyond differences in custom and ceremony, cultures also differ with regard to how people think about, define, and experience love. As we have discussed throughout this book, Western and Eastern cultures vary with respect to how they conceptualize the needs of individuals, groups, and societies (Kim & Markus, 1999; Markus, Kitayama, & Heiman, 1996; Triandis, 1995). Social psychologists have noted that, while romantic love is deemed an important, even crucial, basis for marriage in individualistic societies, it is less emphasized in collectivistic ones. In individualistic societies, romantic love is a heady, highly personal experience. One immerses oneself in the new partner, virtually ignoring friends and family for a while. The decision regarding whom to become involved with or marry is for the most part a personal one. In comparison, in collectivistic societies, the individual in love must consider the wishes of family and other group members, which sometimes includes agreeing to an arranged marriage (Dion & Dion, 1993; Kamble et al., 2014; Levine et al., 1995). Interestingly, though, in recent decades Western ways of finding a partner have begun to permeate collectivistic cultures through the media (Hatfield & Rapson, 2002). In Nepal, for example, prospective brides and grooms now write each other letters, getting to know each other a bit before the wedding (Goode, 1999).

How romantic love is defined varies across individualistic and collectivistic cultures. Researchers have found that Canadian college students' attitudes about love vary depending on their ethnocultural background: In comparison to other Canadians, Asian Canadian respondents are significantly more likely to identify with a companionable, friendship-based romantic love, a "style of love that would not disrupt a complex network of existing family relationships" (Dion & Dion, 1993, p. 465). Other researchers have found that in West African settings, relationships with one's parents, siblings, and other relatives are seen as more important and consequential than the more recent relationship one has formed with a spouse. In many areas of West Africa, married couples do not live together in the same house, nor do they expect to sleep together every night. In stark contrast to the pattern of intimate relationships in individualistic cultures, their connection and obligation to their extended family members takes precedence over those to their spouse (Adams, Anderson, & Adonu, 2004). As another example of cross-cultural research, college students in 11 countries around the world were asked, "If a man (woman) had all the qualities you desired, would you marry this person if you were not in love with him (her)?" This study found that marrying for love was most important to participants in Westernized countries (e.g., the United States, Brazil, England, and Australia) and of least importance to participants in Asian countries (e.g., India, Pakistan, and Thailand; Levine et al., 1995).

The results of these studies indicate that the concept of romantic love is culturally specific (Dion & Dion, 1996; Hatfield & Rapson, 2002; Hatfield & Sprecher, 1995; Li et al., 2010). We all love, but we do not necessarily all love in the same way—or at least we don't describe it in the same way (Landis & O'Shea, 2000). For example, the Japanese use the word *amae* as an extremely positive emotional state in which one is a totally passive love object, indulged and taken care of by one's romantic partner, much like a mother-infant relationship. Amae has no equivalent word in English or in any other Western language; the closest is the word *dependency*, an emotional state that Western cultures consider unhealthy in adult relationships (Dion & Dion, 1993; Doi, 1988; Farrer, Tsuchiya, & Bagrowicz, 2008).

Similarly, the Chinese concept of *gan qing* differs from the Western view of romantic love. Gan qing is achieved by helping and working for another person; for example, a "romantic" act would be fixing someone's bicycle or helping someone learn new material (Gao, 1996). In Korea, a special kind of relationship is expressed by the concept of *jung*. Much more than "love," jung is what ties two people together. Couples in new relationships may feel strong love for each other, but they have not yet developed jung—that takes time and mutual experiences. Interestingly, jung can develop in negative relationships too—for example, between business rivals who dislike each other. Jung may unknowingly grow over time, with the result that they will feel that a strange connection exists between them (Kline, Horton, & Zhang, 2008; Lim & Choi, 1996).

Some researchers have studied what lyrics in popular American and Chinese love songs reveal about the experience of love in each culture (Rothbaum & Tsang, 1998). Finding that the Chinese love songs had significantly more references to suffering and to negative outcomes than the American love songs, the researchers looked to the Chinese concept of *yuan* for explanation. *Yuan* is the belief that interpersonal relations are predestined. According to the traditional Chinese Buddhist belief in *karma*, fate determines what happens in a relationship. The romantic partners have little control over this process (Goodwin, 1999). If a relationship is not working, it cannot be saved; one must accept fate and the suffering that accompanies it (Rothbaum & Tsang, 1998). Although Chinese songs were sadder than American ones, there was no difference in the intensity with which love was described in the two countries. The researchers found that love in Chinese songs was as "passionate and erotic" as love expressed in American songs.

Thus, it appears that romantic love is nearly universal in the human species, but cultural rules alter how that emotional state is experienced, expressed, and remembered (Higgins et al., 2002; Jackson et al., 2006). As one final example, Shuangyue Zhang and Susan Kline (2009) found two major differences in American and Chinese dating couples' decisions to marry. When describing how they would decide whether or not to marry their partners, Chinese students placed a heavier emphasis on two concepts central to their collectivistic culture: *xiao* (the obedience and devotion shown by children to their parents) and *guanxi* (relationships as a network of connections). In contrast, American students placed importance on receiving support, care, and "living a better life." As Robert Moore (1998) noted in summarizing his research in the People's Republic of China, "Young Chinese do fall deeply in love and experience the same joys and sorrows of romance as young Westerners do. But they do so according to standards that require . . . the individual [to] sacrifice personal interests for the sake of the family . . . This means avoiding fleeting infatuations, casual sexual encounters, and a dating context [where] family concerns are forgotten" (p. 280).

Although people all over the world experience love, how love is defined can vary across cultures.

Attachment Styles in Intimate Relationships

Much as the culture in which we grow up shapes how we think about and experience love, so do our interactions in the early years of life with parents or caregivers. Specifically, one approach to examining intimate relationships among adults focuses on **attachment styles** and draws on the groundbreaking work of John Bowlby (1969, 1973, 1980) and Mary Ainsworth (Ainsworth et al., 1978) concerning how infants form bonds with their primary caregivers (usually their mothers or fathers).

Ainsworth and her colleagues (1978) identified three types of relationships between infants and their caregivers. They did so by creating a situation in which a caregiver briefly left his or her infant in an unfamiliar room with a stranger before returning. The infant's reactions upon separation and reunion with the parent were observed. Infants with a **secure attachment style** cry and show signs of distress when their parent leaves the room and are quite happy when he or she returns. These infants tend to trust their caregivers, show positive emotions when interacting with them, and are not particularly worried about abandonment. Infants with an **avoidant attachment style** do not react much at their parent's departure or return. They desire to be close to their caregiver but learn to suppress this need, as if they know that such attempts will be rejected, sometimes by a caregiver who is aloof, distant, or busy. Infants with an **anxious/ambivalent attachment style** seem distressed even before the parent leaves

Attachment Styles

The expectations people develop about relationships with others based on the relationship they had with their primary caregiver when they were infants

Secure Attachment Style

An attachment style characterized by trust, a lack of concern with being abandoned, and the view that one is worthy and well liked

Avoidant Attachment Style

An attachment style characterized by difficulty developing intimate relationships because previous attempts to be intimate have been rebuffed

Anxious/Ambivalent Attachment Style

An attachment style characterized by a concern that others will not reciprocate one's desire for intimacy, resulting in higher-than-average levels of anxiety

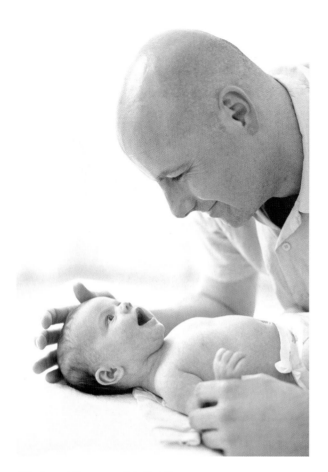

Attachment theory predicts that the attachment style we learn as infants and young children stays with us throughout life and generalizes to all of our relationships with other people.

the room and can be difficult to soothe even upon the parent's return, their response often a mixture of anger and indifference. These infants are unusually anxious, sometimes owing to an inability to predict when and how their caregivers will respond to their needs.

The key assumption of attachment theory is that the particular attachment style we learn in infancy becomes our working model or schema (as we discussed in Chapter 3) for what all relationships are like. These early relationship schemas typically stay with us throughout life and generalize to adult relationships with other people (Fraley & Shaver, 2000; Konrath et al., 2014; Mikulincer et al., 2009). Thus, people who as children had a secure relationship with their parents or caregivers are better able to develop mature, lasting relationships as adults; people who had avoidant relationships with their parents are less able to trust others and find it difficult to develop close, intimate relationships; and people who had anxious/ambivalent relationships with their parents want to become close to their adult partners but often worry that their partners will not return their affections (Collins & Feeney, 2000; Rholes, Simpson & Friedman, 2006; Simpson et al., 2007). This has been borne out in numerous studies using questionnaires to measure adults' attachment styles and analyzing correlations between attachment style and the quality of their adult romantic relationships. For example, in one study researchers asked adults to choose one of the three statements shown in Table 10.3, according to how they typically feel in romantic relationships (Hazan & Shaver, 1987). Each statement was designed to capture one of the three kinds of attachment styles we described.

When researchers correlate adults' responses to questions about attachment style with their answers to questions about their current relationships, they find results consistent with an attachment theory perspective (Feeney, Cassidy, & Ramos-Marcuse, 2008; Feeney, Noller, & Roberts, 2000; Hazan & Shaver, 1994a). For example, securely attached individuals tend to have the most enduring romantic relationships of the three attachment types. They experience the highest level of commitment to relationships as well as the highest level of satisfaction with their relationships. The anxious/ambivalently attached individuals have the most short-lived romantic

---

Table 10.3 Measuring Adult Attachment Styles

As part of a survey of attitudes toward love published in a newspaper, people were asked to choose the statement that best described their romantic relationships. The attachment style each statement was designed to measure and the percentage of people who chose each alternative are indicated.

Secure style	56%	"I find it relatively easy to get close to others and am comfortable depending on them and having them depend on me. I don't often worry about being abandoned or about someone getting too close."
Avoidant style	25%	"I am somewhat uncomfortable being close to others; I find it difficult to trust them completely, difficult to allow myself to depend on them. I am nervous when anyone gets close, and often love partners want me to be more intimate than I feel comfortable being."
Anxious style	19%	"I find that others are reluctant to get as close as I would like. I often worry that my partner doesn't really love me or won't stay with me. I want to merge completely with another person, and this desire sometimes scares people away."

(Adapted from Hazan & Shaver, 1987)

relationships. They enter into relationships the most quickly, often before they know their partner well. One study conducted at a marriage license bureau found that anxious men acquired marriage licenses after a shorter courtship than did either secure or avoidant men (Senchak & Leonard, 1992). They are also the most upset and angriest of the three types when their love is not reciprocated. The third group, avoidant individuals, is the least likely to enter into a relationship and the most likely to report never having been in love. They maintain their emotional distance and have the lowest level of commitment to their relationships of the three types (Campbell et al., 2005; Collins et al., 2006; Feeney & Noller, 1990; Keelan, Dion, & Dion, 1994).

It is important to note, however, that attachment theory does not suggest that people who had unhappy relationships with their parents are doomed to repeat this same kind of unhappy relationship with everyone they ever meet, or that secure attachment as an infant guarantees a healthy adult love life (Simms, 2002). Some researchers have recontacted their research participants months or years after their original studies and asked them to take the attachment-style scale again. They have found that 25% to 30% of participants change from one attachment style to another (Feeney & Noller, 1996; Kirkpatrick & Hazan, 1994). People can and do change; their experiences in relationships can help them learn new ways of relating to others than what they experienced as children (Baldwin & Fehr, 1995). Moreover, other research suggests that, at any given time, the attachment style that people display is the one that is called into play by their partner's behavior and the type of relationship that they've created as a couple. Thus, people can respond to situational variables in their relationships, displaying a more secure attachment style in one relationship and a more anxious one in another, or evolving in their attachment style within one relationship as time goes by (Fraley, 2002; Hadden et al., 2014; Simpson et al., 2003).

> In my very own self, I am part of my family.
>
> —D. H. LAWRENCE

This Is Your Brain . . . in Love

Falling in love is an extraordinary feeling—you are giddy, euphoric, full of energy, and more or less obsessed with your new beloved. These powerful emotions, experienced by people in many different cultures with many different early childhood experiences, suggest that romantic love may have evolved as a primary component of the human mating system. Is something special happening in our brains when we fall in love?

To find out, a team of researchers recruited college students in the greater New York area who described themselves as currently being "intensely in love" (Aron et al., 2005). They asked these research participants to bring two photographs to the experimental session: one of their beloved and one of an acquaintance of the same age and sex as their beloved. After filling out some questionnaires (including the Try It! Passionate Love Scale on page 34\7), the participants were ready for the main event. They slid into a functional MRI (fMRI) scanner, which records increases and decreases in blood flow in the brain, thus indicating which regions of the brain have changes in neural activity at any given time. While the participant was in the scanner, the experimenters alternated projecting on a screen one photograph and then the other, interspersed with a mathematical distraction task.

The researchers found that two specific areas, deep within the brain, showed evidence of increased activation when participants looked at the photograph of their romantic partner, but not when they looked at the photograph of their acquaintance (or when they engaged in the math task). Furthermore, those participants who self-reported higher levels of romantic love showed greater activation in these areas when looking at their beloved than those who reported lower levels (Aron et al., 2005). These two brain areas were the ventral tegmental area (VTA) and the caudate nucleus,

Falling in love predicts increased activation in a reward center of the brain that is also activated by eating chocolate.

which communicate with each other as part of a circuit. A great deal is already known about what causes these areas of the brain to fire and what kind of processing they do—and now, this knowledge can be applied to the experience of passionate love.

Specifically, prior research has found that the VTA becomes active when we engage in rewarding behaviors, such as, for example, when people ingest cocaine—a drug that induces feelings of pleasure, euphoria, restlessness, sleeplessness, and loss of appetite (reactions that, wouldn't you know it, are also reminiscent of falling in love). The VTA, rich in the neurotransmitter dopamine, also fires when people eat chocolate. Thus, the VTA and the caudate nucleus constitute a major reward and motivation center of the brain. For example, fMRI studies of gamblers' brains as they gamble show greatly increased activity in these dopamine-rich areas when they win—a rewarding and motivating event (Aron et al., 2005). Thus, when people say that falling in love is "addictive," "like a drug," or "like winning the lottery," they're right. All these experiences predict greater activation in the same areas of the brain: dopamine-rich centers of pleasure, reward, and motivation (Bartels & Zeki, 2000, 2004; Fisher, 2004; Scheele et al., 2013).

Theories of Relationship Satisfaction: Social Exchange and Equity

So far, we've examined how cultural expectations and personal attachment styles predict the ways in which you define and experience love, and how those experiences operate at the level of the brain. But what aspects of your actual relationships influence relationship satisfaction? What factors determine how happy you are with your current mate or with your "love life" more generally? We turn now to theories of relationship satisfaction in the attempt to provide empirically based answers to these most intimate of questions.

SOCIAL EXCHANGE THEORY   Many of the variables we discussed above as antecedents of attraction can be thought of as examples of social rewards. It is pleasing to have our attitudes validated; thus, the more similar a person's attitudes are to ours, the more rewarded we are by spending time together. Likewise, it is rewarding to be around someone who likes us, particularly when that person is physically attractive. In other words, the more social rewards (and the fewer costs) a person provides us with, the more we like the person. The flip side of this equation is that if a relationship costs (e.g., in terms of emotional turmoil) far more than it gives (e.g., in terms of validation or praise), chances are that it will not last.

This simple notion that relationships operate on an economic model of costs and benefits, much like other marketplaces, has been expanded by researchers into complex theories of social exchange (Blau, 1964; Cook et al., 2013; Kelley & Thibaut, 1978; Thibaut & Kelley, 1959). **Social exchange theory** holds that how people feel about a relationship will depend on their perceptions of the rewards they receive from it, their perceptions of the costs they incur, their beliefs regarding what kind of relationship they deserve, and the probability that they could find a better relationship with someone else. In essence, we "buy" the best relationship we can get—one that gives us the most value for our emotional dollar based on the options on the table. The basic concepts of social exchange theory are reward, cost, outcome, and comparison level.

What, after all, is our life but a great dance in which we are all trying to fix the best going rate of exchange?
—MALCOLM BRADBURY, 1992

Social Exchange Theory
The idea that people's feelings about a relationship depend on their perceptions of its rewards and costs, the kind of relationship they deserve, and their chances for having a better relationship with someone else

Rewards are the gratifying aspects of a relationship that make it worthwhile and reinforcing. They include the kinds of personal characteristics and behaviors of our relationship partner that we have already discussed, and our ability to acquire external resources by virtue of knowing this person (e.g., gaining access to money, status, activities, or other interesting people; Lott & Lott, 1974). For example, in Brazil, friendship is openly used as an exchange value. Brazilians will readily admit that they need a *pistolão* (literally, a big, powerful handgun), meaning that they need a person who will use personal connections to help them get what they want (Rector & Neiva, 1996). Costs are, obviously, the other side of the coin, and all friendships and romantic relationships have some costs attached, such as putting up with those annoying habits and characteristics of the other person. The outcome of the relationship is a direct comparison of its rewards and costs; you can think of it as a mathematical formula where outcome equals rewards minus costs. If you come up with a negative number, your relationship is not in good shape.

In addition to rewards and costs, how satisfied you are with your relationship depends on another variable: your **comparison level**, or what you *expect* the outcome of your relationship to be in terms of costs and rewards (Kelley & Thibaut, 1978; Thibaut & Kelley, 1959). Over time, you have amassed a long history of relationships with others, and this history has led you to have certain expectations as to what your current and future relationships should be like. Some people have a high comparison level, expecting lots of rewards and few costs in their relationships. If a given relationship doesn't match this lofty expected comparison level, they quickly will grow unhappy and unsatisfied. In contrast, people who have a low comparison level would be happy in the same relationship because they expect their relationships to be difficult and costly.

Finally, your satisfaction with a relationship also depends on your perception of the likelihood that you could replace it with a better one—or your **comparison level for alternatives**. As the saying goes, there are plenty of fish in the sea. Could a relationship with a different person give you a better outcome than your current one? People who have a high comparison level for alternatives—either because they believe the world is full of fabulous people dying to meet them or because they know of one particular fabulous person dying to meet them—are more likely to take the plunge, change things up, and hit the market for a new friend or lover. People with a low comparison level for alternatives will be more likely to stay in a costly relationship, because, in their mind, what they have may not be great, but it's better than what they expect they could find elsewhere (Etcheverry, Le, & Hoffman, 2013; Lehmiller & Agnew, 2006; Simpson, 1987).

Social exchange theory has received a great deal of empirical support. Friends and romantic couples often do pay attention to the costs and rewards in their relationships, and these perceptions predict how positively people feel about the status of the relationship (Bui, Peplau, & Hill, 1996; Rusbult, 1983; Rusbult, Martz, & Agnew, 1998). Such findings have been observed for intimate relationships in cultures as different as Taiwan and the Netherlands (Le & Agnew, 2003; Lin & Rusbult, 1995; Rusbult & Van Lange, 1996; Van Lange et al., 1997). Generally speaking, when relationships are seen as offering a lot of rewards, people report feeling happy and satisfied.

However, many people do not leave their partners even when they are dissatisfied and their other alternatives look bright. Research indicates that we need to consider at least one additional factor to understand close relationships: a person's level of investment in the relationship (Carter et al., 2013; Goodfriend & Agnew, 2008; Rusbult et al., 2001). In her **investment model** of close relationships, Caryl Rusbult (1983) defines *investment* as anything people have put into a relationship that will be lost if they leave it. Examples include tangible things, such as financial resources, possessions, and property, as well as intangible things, such as the emotional welfare of

Comparison Level

People's expectations about the level of rewards and costs they are likely to receive in a particular relationship

Comparison Level for Alternatives

People's expectations about the level of rewards and costs they would receive in an alternative relationship

Love is often nothing but a favorable exchange between two people who get the most of what they can expect, considering their value on the personality market.

—Erich Fromm, *The Sane Society*, 1955

Investment Model

The theory that people's commitment to a relationship depends not only on their satisfaction with the relationship, but also on how much they have invested in the relationship that would be lost by ending it one's children, the time and emotional energy spent building the relationship, and the sense of personal integrity that will be lost if one gets divorced. As seen in Figure 10.1, the greater the investment individuals have in a relationship, the less likely they are to leave, even when satisfaction is low and other alternatives look promising. In short, to predict whether people will stay in an intimate relationship, we need to know (1) how satisfied they are with the relationship, (2) what they think of their alternatives, and (3) how great their investment in the relationship is.

To test this model, Rusbult (1983) asked college students involved in heterosexual dating relationships to fill out questionnaires over the course of 7 months. Every 3 weeks, people answered questions about each of the components of the model shown in Figure 10.1. Rusbult also kept track of whether the students stayed in the relationships or broke up. As you can see in Figure 10.2, satisfaction, alternatives, and investments all predicted how committed people were to the relationship and whether it lasted. (The higher the number on the scale, the more each factor predicted the commitment to and length of the relationship.) Subsequent studies have found results similar to those shown in Figure 10.2 for married couples of diverse ages, lesbian and gay couples, nonsexual friendships, and residents of both the United States and Taiwan (Kurdek, 1992; Lin & Rusbult, 1995; Rusbult, 1991; Rusbult & Buunk, 1993).

Does the same model hold for destructive relationships? To find out, Rusbult and a colleague interviewed women who had sought refuge at a shelter for victims of domestic abuse, asking them about their abusive romantic relationships (Rusbult & Martz, 1995). Why had these women stayed in these relationships, even to the point where some of them returned to an abusive partner after leaving the shelter? As the theory predicts, feelings of commitment to the abusive relationship were greater among women who had poorer economic alternatives to the relationship or were

---

Figure 10.1 The Investment Model of Commitment

People's commitment to a relationship depends on several variables. First, their *satisfaction* with the relationship is based on their comparing their *rewards* to their costs and determining if the outcome exceeds their general expectation of what they should get in a relationship (or *comparison level*). Next, their *commitment* to the relationship depends on three variables: how *satisfied* they are, how much they feel they have *invested* in the relationship, and whether they have good *alternatives* to this relationship. These commitment variables in turn predict how stable the relationship will be. For example, a woman who feels her relationship has more costs and fewer rewards than she considers acceptable would have low satisfaction. If she also felt she had little invested in the relationship and an attractive person had just asked her for a date, she would have a low level of commitment. The end result is low stability; most likely, she will break up with her current partner.

(Adapted from Rusbult, 1983)

Figure 10.2 A Test of the Investment Model

This study examined the extent to which college students' satisfaction with a relationship, their comparison level for alternatives, and their investment in the relationship predicted their commitment to the relationship and their decision about whether to break up with their partner. The higher the number, the more each variable predicted commitment and breakup, independent of the two other variables. All three variables were good predictors of how committed people were and whether or not they broke up.

(Adapted from Rusbult, 1983)

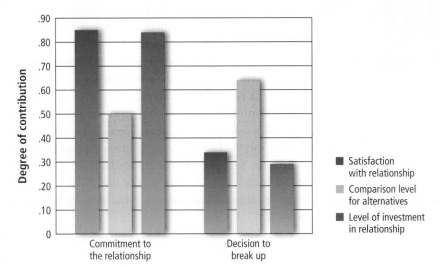

more heavily invested in the relationship. In long-term relationships, then, commitment is based on more than just the amount of rewards and costs a partner elicits; it also depends on people's perceptions of their investments in, satisfaction with, and alternatives to the relationship.

EQUITY THEORY   Some researchers have criticized social exchange theory for ignoring an essential variable in relationships—the notion of fairness, or equity. Proponents of **equity theory** argue that people don't engage in relationships the way they do board games, doing anything they can to end up with the most reward in the bank. We aren't just out to get the most rewards for the least cost, the argument goes: We are also concerned about equity or the idea that the rewards and costs we experience should be roughly equal to those of the other person involved (Kalmijn & Monden, 2012; Walster, Walster, & Berscheid, 1978). Indeed, these theorists describe equitable relationships as the happiest and most stable, whereas, inequitable relationships result in one person feeling overbenefited (getting a lot of rewards, incurring few costs, having to devote little time or energy to the relationship) and the other feeling underbenefited (getting few rewards, incurring a lot of costs, having to devote a lot of time and energy to the relationship).

According to equity theory, both underbenefited and overbenefited partners should feel uneasy about this state of affairs, and both should be motivated to restore equity to the relationship. This makes sense for the underbenefited person—after all, who wants to feel miserable and unappreciated? But why should the overbenefited individual want to give up what social exchange theory indicates is a cushy deal, lots of rewards for little cost and little work? Theorists argue that equity is a powerful social norm and that people will eventually feel uncomfortable and guilty if they keep getting more than they deserve in a relationship. Still, being overbenefited isn't as bad as being underbenefited, and research has indicated that inequity is perceived as *more* of a problem by the underbenefited individual (Buunk & Schaufeli, 1999; Guerrero, La Valley, & Farinelli, 2008; Sprecher & Schwartz, 1994).

Equity Theory

The idea that people are happiest with relationships in which the rewards and costs experienced by both parties are roughly equal

Close relationships can have either exchange or communal properties. Family relationships are typically communal.

Exchange Relationships

Relationships governed by the need for equity (i.e., for an equal ratio of rewards and costs)

Of course, this whole notion of equity implies that partners in a relationship are keeping track of who is benefiting how much and who is getting shortchanged. Some might suggest that many people in happy relationships don't spend so much time and energy keeping tabs on contributions and benefits in this manner. Indeed, the more we get to know someone, the more reluctant we are to believe that we are simply exchanging favors or expecting immediate compensation for every kind gesture. Sure, in casual relationships, we trade "in kind"—you lend someone your class notes, she buys you lunch. But in intimate relationships, we're trading different types of resources, so even if we wanted to, determining whether or not equity has been achieved becomes difficult. Does taking out your significant other to a nice dinner one night balance out the fact that you had to work late the previous two nights and couldn't spend time together? In other words, long-term, intimate relationships may be governed by a looser give-and-take notion of equity rather than a rigid tit-for-tat strategy (Kollack, Blumstein, & Schwartz, 1994; Laursen & Hartup, 2002; Vaananen et al., 2005).

According to Margaret Clark and Judson Mills (1993), interactions between new acquaintances are governed by equity concerns and are called **exchange relationships**. As you can see in Figure 10.3, in exchange relationships, people keep track of who is contributing what and feel taken advantage of when they feel they are putting more into the relationship than they are getting out of it. In comparison, longer-term interactions between close friends, family members, and romantic partners are governed less by an equity norm and more by a desire to help each other

Figure 10.3 Exchange Versus Communal Relationships

Exchange Relationships are governed by

Equity Concerns:
(a) We like to be repaid immediately for our favors.
(b) We feel exploited when our favors are not returned.
(c) We keep track of who is contributing what to the relationship.
(d) Being able to help the person has no effect on our mood.

Communal Relationships are governed by

Responsiveness to the Other's Needs:
(a) We do <u>not</u> like to be repaid immediately for our favors.
(b) We do <u>not</u> feel exploited when our favors are not repaid.
(c) We do <u>not</u> keep track of who is contributing to the relationship.
(d) Being able to help the person puts us in a good mood.

as needed. In these **communal relationships**, people give in response to the other's needs, regardless of whether they get paid back (Abele & Brack, 2013; Clark & Mills, 1993; Mills & Clark, 2011; Vaananen et al., 2005). In this manner, communal interactions are the hallmark of long-term, intimate relationships. Research comparing heterosexual couples to same-sex couples has found that they are equally committed and communal in their relationships: if anything, gay men and lesbians report greater compatibility and less conflict than heterosexual couples do (Balsam et al., 2008; Roisman et al., 2008).

Are people in communal relationships completely unconcerned with equity? Not necessarily. As we saw earlier, people do feel distressed if they believe their intimate relationships are inequitable (Canary & Stafford, 2001; Walster et al., 1978); however, equity takes on a somewhat different form in communal relationships than it does in less intimate ones. In communal relationships, the partners are more relaxed about what constitutes equity at any given time, believing that things will eventually balance out and a rough kind of equity will be achieved over the long run (Lemay & Clark, 2008; Lemay, Clark, & Feeney, 2007). If this doesn't happen—if they continue to feel that there is an imbalance—the relationship may ultimately end.

Communal Relationships

Relationships in which people's primary concern is being responsive to the other person's needs

---

Friendship is a scheme for the mutual exchange of personal advantages and favors.

—FRANÇOIS DE LA ROCHEFOUCAULD,
MAXIMS, 1665

REVIEW QUESTIONS

1. Whereas _____ love is characterized by feelings of intimacy and affection, _____ love tends to include intense longing and physiological arousal.
   a. platonic; romantic
   b. tranquil; sexual
   c. companionate; passionate
   d. empty; erotic

2. The positive emotional state when one is indulged and taken care of by one's romantic partner is known as
   a. yuan
   b. gan qing
   c. amae
   d. jung

3. Which attachment style below is best captured by the following sentiment: "I am uncomfortable being close to others and find it difficult to trust people completely. I am nervous when anyone gets close, and often my partners want me to be more intimate than I feel comfortable being."
   a. secure attachment style
   b. avoidant attachment style
   c. anxious/ambivalent attachment style
   d. exchange attachment style

4. The regions of the brain that exhibit signs of increased activity when someone thinks about feelings of romantic love are the same regions that exhibit signs of increased activity when a person

   a. sleeps.
   b. ingests cocaine.
   c. cries.
   d. is anxious about being the focus of attention.

5. Although her boyfriend treats her well, always puts her needs first, and doesn't demand much in the way of relationship effort from her, Courtney feels unsatisfied with the relationship because a little voice in her head keeps telling her there must be an even better mate out there for her somewhere. Courtney seems to have
   a. a high comparison level.
   b. a low comparison level.
   c. a low comparison level for alternatives.
   d. a high sense of investment.

6. Equity theory suggests that if a relationship is not equitable
   a. the overbenefited individual will still be satisfied with it.
   b. both the underbenefited and the overbenefited individuals will still be satisfied with it.
   c. both the underbenefited and the overbenefited individuals will be unsatisfied with it.
   d. it will transition from a communal relationship to an exchange relationship.

See page 622 for the answers.

Ending Intimate Relationships

10.4   What does research demonstrate about romantic breakups?

The American divorce rate is nearly 50% and has been for the past few decades (Kennedy & Ruggles, 2014; National Center for Health Statistics, 2005). An examination of data from 58 societies, taken from the *Demographic Yearbook of the United Nations*, indicates that the majority of separations and divorces occur around the fourth year of marriage (Fisher, 2004). And, of course, countless romantic relationships between unmarried individuals end every day. After many years of studying what love is and how it blooms, social psychologists are now beginning to explore the end of the story—how it dies.

> Love is like war; easy to begin but very hard to stop.
>
> —H. L. MENCKEN

The Process of Breaking Up

Ending a romantic relationship is one of life's more painful experiences. Researchers continue to examine what prompts couples to break up and the disengagement strategies they use to do so (Baxter, 1986; Femlee, Sprecher, & Bassin, 1990; Frazier & Cook, 1993; Rusbult & Zembrodt, 1983; Sprecher, Zimmerman, & Fehr, 2014). For example, Steve Duck (1982) reminds us that relationship dissolution is not a single event but a process with many steps (see Figure 10.4). Duck theorizes that there are four stages to dissolving a relationship, ranging from the intrapersonal (the individual thinks a lot about his or her dissatisfaction with the relationship) to the dyadic (the individual discusses the breakup with the partner) to the social (the breakup is announced to other people) and back to the intrapersonal (the individual recovers from the breakup and forms an internal account of how and why it happened). In terms of the last stage in the process, John Harvey and his colleagues (Harvey, 1995; Harvey, Flanary, & Morgan, 1986) have found that the honest version of "why the relationship ended" that we present to close friends can be very different from the official version that we present to coworkers or neighbors.

Why relationships end has been studied from several angles (Bui et al., 1996; Drigotas & Rusbult, 1992). For example, Caryl Rusbult has identified four types of behavior that occur in troubled relationships (Rusbult, 1987; Rusbult & Zembrodt, 1983). The first two are destructive behaviors: actively harming the relationship (e.g., abusing the partner, threatening to break up, actually leaving) and passively allowing the relationship to deteriorate (e.g., refusing to deal with problems, ignoring the partner or spending less time together, putting no energy into the relationship). The other two responses are positive, constructive behaviors: actively trying to improve the relationship (e.g., discussing problems, trying to change, going to a therapist) and passively remaining loyal to the relationship (e.g., waiting and hoping that the situation will improve, being supportive rather than fighting, remaining optimistic). Rusbult and her colleagues have found that destructive behaviors harm a relationship a lot more than constructive behaviors help it. When one partner acts destructively and the other partner responds constructively to save the relationship, a common pattern, the relationship is likely to continue, but when both partners act destructively, the relationship typically ends (Rusbult, Johnson, & Morrow, 1986; Rusbult, Yovetich, & Verette, 1996).

Another approach to studying why relationships end considers what attracted the people to each other in the first place. For example, in one study, college men and women were asked to focus on a former romantic relationship to list the qualities that first attracted them to the person and the characteristics they ended up

Figure 10.4 Steps in Dissolving Close Relationships

(Based on Duck, 1982)

Breakdown: Dissatisfaction with the relationship

↓

Threshold: "I can't stand this anymore"

↓

Intrapersonal phase

Focus on partner's behavior
Assess adequacy of partner's behavior
Depict and evaluate negative aspects of being in the relationship
Consider the costs of withdrawal
Assess positive aspects of alternative relationships
Face the "express my thoughts/repress my thoughts" dilemma

↓

Threshold: "I'd be justified in withdrawing"

↓

Dyadic phase

Face the "confront the issue/avoid the issue" dilemma
Confront partner
Negotiate and discuss "our relationship"
Attempt repair of relationship and reconciliation
Assess costs of withdrawal or reduced intimacy for both partners

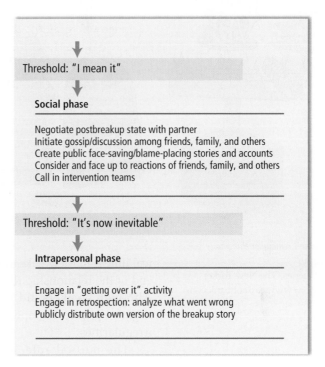

Threshold: "I mean it"

↓

Social phase

Negotiate postbreakup state with partner
Initiate gossip/discussion among friends, family, and others
Create public face-saving/blame-placing stories and accounts
Consider and face up to reactions of friends, family, and others
Call in intervention teams

↓

Threshold: "It's now inevitable"

↓

Intrapersonal phase

Engage in "getting over it" activity
Engage in retrospection: analyze what went wrong
Publicly distribute own version of the breakup story

disliking the most about the person (Femlee, 1995, 1998a). Thirty percent of these breakups were examples of "fatal attractions." The very qualities that were initially so attractive became the very reasons why the relationship ended. For example, "He's so unusual and different" became "He and I have nothing in common." "She's so exciting and unpredictable" became "I can never count on her." This type of breakup reminds us again of the importance of similarity between partners to successful relationships.

If a romantic relationship is in bad shape, can we predict who will end it? Much has been made about the tendency in heterosexual relationships for women to end relationships more often than men. Research has found, however, that neither sex ends romantic relationships more frequently than the other (Akert, 1998; Hagestad & Smyer, 1982; Rusbult et al., 1986). A better predictor of whether and when a relationship will end seems to be how a couple deals with conflict. All relationships go through conflict, but not all couples handle it the same way. In studies of newlyweds, John Gottman and his colleagues have found that when discussing issues related to relationship conflict, those couples whose communication shows signs of contempt, sarcasm, and criticism are more likely to break up (and break up sooner) than other couples (Gottman, 2014; Gottman & Levenson, 2002). Couples better able to weather the storms of conflict are those who wait to calm down before hashing out a disagreement and those who exhibit an ability to listen without automatically getting defensive.

The Experience of Breaking Up

Can we predict the different ways people will feel when their relationship ends? One key is the role people play in the decision to end the relationship (Helgeson, 1994; Lloyd & Cate, 1985). For example, Robin Akert asked 344 college-age men

"Somehow I remember this one differently."
Steve Duenes/The New Yorker Collection/www.cartoonbank.com.

and women to complete a questionnaire about their most important romantic relationship that had ended. One question asked to what extent they or their partner had been responsible for the decision to break up. Participants who indicated a high level of responsibility for the decision were labeled "breakers"; those who reported a low level of responsibility, "breakees"; and those who shared the decision making with their partners about equally, "mutuals."

Akert found that the role people played in the decision to end the relationship was the single most powerful predictor of their breakup experiences. Not surprisingly, breakees were miserable; they reported high levels of loneliness, depression, and anger, and virtually all reported experiencing physical illness in the weeks after the breakup. Of the three groups, breakers found the end of the relationship the least upsetting, the least painful, and the least stressful. Although breakers did report feeling guilty and unhappy, they had the fewest negative physical symptoms (39%), such as headaches, stomachaches, and sleeping irregularities.

The mutual role, which carries with it a component of shared decision-making, helped individuals avoid some of the negative emotional and physical reactions to breaking up. Mutuals were not as upset or hurt as breakees, but they were more affected than the breakers. Some 60% of the mutuals reported physical symptoms, indicating that a mutual conclusion to a romantic relationship is a more stressful experience than simply deciding to end it on one's own. Finally, gender played a role in the emotional and physical responses of the respondents, with women reporting somewhat more negative reactions to breaking up than men.

Do people want to stay friends once they break up? It depends on the role played in the breakup as well as gender. Akert (1998) found that heterosexual men are not particularly interested in remaining friends with their ex-girlfriends when they are in either the breaker or the breakee role; overall, women are more interested in remaining friends, hoping to reshape the intimate relationship into a platonic friendship, especially when they are the breakees. Finally, more recent research suggests that investment also plays a role in post-breakup interactions, as couples with higher rates of satisfaction and investment during the course of their relationship are also more likely to remain friends afterward (Tan et al., 2014).

REVIEW QUESTIONS

1. Which of the following is an example of an intrapersonal stage to relationship dissolution?

a. The breakup is announced to other people.

b. One member of the couple thinks a lot about his or her relationship dissatisfaction.

c. One member of the couple discusses the potential breakup with the other person.

d. The couple decides to get back together.

2. Which of the following findings regarding gender differences and breakups in heterosexual relationships is true?
  a. Men tend to be more likely than women to display contempt and sarcasm during a breakup.
  b. Women tend to be more likely than men to want to remain friends after a breakup.
  c. Men tend to be more likely to be breakers than breakees.
  d. Women tend to be more likely than men to initiate a relationship breakup.

3. Research on "fatal attractions" suggests that
  a. the same qualities that first draw us to a person can, with time, become qualities that contribute to breaking up.
  b. heterosexual couples are more likely than homosexual couples to remain friends after a breakup.
  c. constructive behaviors help a relationship more than destructive behaviors harm it.
  d. so-called "mutual" breakups are often the most emotionally disruptive type of relationship dissolution.

See page 622 for the answers.

Summary

10.1 How do people decide whom they like and want to get to know better?

- **What Predicts Attraction?**

  - **The Person Next Door: The Propinquity Effect** In the first part of this chapter, we discussed the variables that cause initial attraction between two people. One such variable is physical proximity, or the **propinquity effect**: People who you come into contact with the most are the most likely to become your friends and lovers. This occurs because of the **mere exposure effect**: Exposure to a stimulus increases liking for it.

  - **Similarity** Similarity between people, whether in attitudes, values, demographic characteristics, physical appearance, and even genetics is also a powerful predictor of attraction and liking. Similarity is more associated with attraction than complementarity, the idea that opposites attract, especially for long-term relationship formation.

  - **Reciprocal Liking** In general, we like others who behave as if they like us.

  - **Physical Attractiveness and Liking** Physical attractiveness also plays an important role in liking. People from different cultures perceive facial attractiveness quite similarly. The "what is beautiful is good" stereotype is an example of a **halo effect**, the tendency to believe that an individual who possesses on positive characteristic also possesses other, unrelated positive traits. Specifically, people assume that physical attractiveness is associated with a variety of other desirable traits, sometimes leading to self-fulfilling prophecies.

  - **Evolution and Mate Selection** Evolutionary psychology explains love in terms of genetic factors that have evolved over time according to the principles of natural selection. According to this perspective, which is not without its critics, men and women are attracted to different characteristics because this maximizes their reproductive success.

10.2 How have new technologies shaped attraction and social connections?

- **Making Connections in the Age of Technology**

  - New technologies provide social psychologists with new questions to ask about attraction and relationships, including whether smartphones and other mobile devices can undermine social connectedness.

  - **Attraction 2.0: Mate Preference in an Online Era** Basic predictors of attraction such as propinquity, similarity, and familiarity manifest themselves differently in the modern era of text messages, the Internet, and social media.

  - **The Promise and Pitfalls of Online Dating** Online dating expands your pool of potential mates, but carries its own risks, including unproven compatibility algorithms and deceptive profile descriptions and photos.

10.3 What is love and what gives people satisfaction in close relationships?

- **Love and Close Relationships**

  - **Defining Love: Companionship and Passion** One definition of love makes a distinction between **companionate love**, feelings of intimacy that are not accompanied by intense longing and arousal, and **passionate love**, feelings of intimacy that are accompanied by intense longing and arousal.

  - **Culture and Love** Although love is a universal emotion, there are cultural variations in the practice and definition of love. Love has a somewhat different emphasis in collectivistic and individualistic cultures.

- **Attachment Styles in Intimate Relationships** People's past relationships with their caregivers are significant predictors of the quality of their close relationships as adults. There are three types of attachment relationships: **secure**, **avoidant**, and **anxious/ambivalent**.

- **This Is Your Brain . . . in Love** The experience of falling in love can also be examined at the level of the brain. Functional Magnetic Resonance Imaging studies indicate that thinking about someone with whom you are in love leads to greater activation in regions of the brain also activated by other pleasurable rewards.

- **Theories of Relationship Satisfaction: Social Exchange and Equity Social Exchange Theory** states that how people feel about their relationship depends on their perception of the rewards they receive and the costs they incur. In order to determine whether people will stay in a relationship, we need to know their **comparison level** (expectations about the outcomes of their relationship), their **comparison level for alternatives** (expectations about how happy they would be in other relationships), as well as their **investment** in the relationship. **Equity theory** states that the most important determinant of satisfaction is that both parties feel comparably rewarded by the relationship. People are less likely to track costs and rewards in **communal relationships** than in **exchange relationships**.

10.4 What does research demonstrate about romantic breakups?

- **Ending Intimate Relationships**
  - **The Process of Breaking Up** Strategies for responding to problems in a romantic relationship include both constructive and destructive behaviors. The breaking-up process is often composed of stages.
  - **The Experience of Breaking Up** A powerful variable that predicts how a person will weather the breakup is the role he or she plays in the decision to terminate the relationship.

Test Yourself

1. Sam has his eye on Julie and wants her to like him. According to research in social psychology, which of the following is *least* likely to work?
   a. Emphasizing how similar their attitudes are
   b. Arranging to work with her on a class project so that he can spend time with her
   c. Emphasizing that they have complementary personalities and that opposites attract
   d. Making himself look as physically attractive as he can

2. Which of the following is a benefit of online dating?
   a. The ability to achieve propinquity with a wider range of people
   b. Mathematical formulas that are highly effective at creating compatibility matches
   c. People tend to be more honest about themselves online
   d. With online dating, there's no such thing as potential mates feeling "out of your league"

3. Which of the following is *false*?
   a. People in communal relationships tend to keep track of who is contributing what to the relationship.
   b. People find "average" faces to be more attractive than unusual faces.
   c. People like others who like them.
   d. The more we see and interact with people, the more we will like them.

4. Katie and Madeline are dating. According to the *investment model of close relationships*, which of the following will influence their commitment to the relationship?
   a. Their satisfaction with the relationship
   b. Their level of investment in the relationship
   c. The availability and quality of alternative partners
   d. All of the above

5. _____ style is characterized by difficulty to form close relationships because of having been rejected in previous attempts to form such relations.
   a. Reciprocal attachment
   b. Avoidant attachment
   c. Anxious/ambivalent attachment
   d. Secure attachment

6. Which of the following statements regarding attachment style is true?
   a. Few if any individuals change their attachment style once they reach adulthood.
   b. A majority of adults have been found to exhibit an avoidant attachment style.
   c. The attachment style that adults display is shaped by their partner's behavior and the type of relationship they've created as a couple.
   d. Your attachment style as an infant typically has little to do with the attachment style you have in your adult relationships.

7. Marquel and Eric have been friends since the beginning of the school year. According to equity theory, their friendship will suffer if

a. Eric is much more likely to help Marquel out when he needs it than Marquel is to help Eric.

b. Eric has a "makeover" and suddenly becomes far more attractive than Marquel.

c. Eric and Marquel stop having similar interests.

d. Eric and Marquel are romantically interested in the same person.

8. Elliot worries that his girlfriend doesn't really love him and he smothers her with attention. According to attachment theory, Elliot probably has a(n) _____ attachment style, because when he was an infant, his caregivers were _____.

a. avoidant; aloof and distant

b. secure; responsive to his needs

c. communal; smothering but very open

d. anxious/ambivalent; inconsistent and overbearing

9. You are considering breaking up with your significant other after 1 month of being a couple. While the relationship gives you lots of rewards and has few costs, you have recently met someone new whom you anticipate will give you even more rewards for even fewer costs. Your dilemma stems from the fact that you have a _____ and a _____.

a. low comparison level; high comparison level for alternatives

b. high comparison level; high comparison level for alternatives

c. low comparison level; low comparison level for alternatives

d. high comparison level; low equity level

10. According to research, who among the following tend to find the end of a relationship as the least stressful and upsetting?

a. Breakers

b. Breakees

c. Mutuals

d. Avoidants

See page 622 for the answers.

Chapter 11
Prosocial Behavior
Why Do People Help?

 Chapter Outline and Learning Objectives

Basic Motives Underlying Prosocial Behavior: Why Do People Help?

11.1 What are the basic motives that determine whether people help others?

Evolutionary Psychology: Instincts and Genes
Social Exchange: The Costs and Rewards of Helping
Empathy and Altruism: The Pure Motive for Helping

Personal Qualities and Prosocial Behavior: Why Do Some People Help More than Others?

11.2 What are some personal qualities that influence whether a given individual will help?

Individual Differences: The Altruistic Personality
Gender Differences in Prosocial Behavior
Cultural Differences in Prosocial Behavior
Religion and Prosocial Behavior
The Effects of Mood on Prosocial Behavior

Situational Determinants of Prosocial Behavior: When Will People Help?

11.3 In what situations are people more likely, or less likely, to help others?

Environment: Rural versus Urban
Residential Mobility
The Number of Bystanders: The Bystander Effect
Effects of the Media: Video Games and Music Lyrics

How Can Helping Be Increased?

11.4 What can be done to promote prosocial behavior?

Increasing the Likelihood That Bystanders Will Intervene
Increasing Volunteerism
Positive Psychology, Human Virtues, and Prosocial Behavior

September 11, 2001, was truly a day of infamy in American history, with terrible loss of life at the World Trade Center, the Pentagon, and the field in Pennsylvania where United Airlines flight 93 crashed. It was also a day of incredible courage and sacrifice by people who did not hesitate to help their fellow human beings. Many people lost their lives while helping others, including 403 New York firefighters and police officers who died trying to rescue people from the World Trade Center.

Many of the heroes of September 11 were ordinary citizens who found themselves in extraordinary circumstances. Imagine that you were working in the World Trade Center towers when they were hit by the planes and how strong the desire would be to flee and seek personal safety. This is exactly what William Wik's wife urged him to do when he called her from the 92nd floor of the South Tower shortly after the attacks. "No, I can't do that; there are still people here," he replied (Lee, 2001, p. 28). Wik's body was found in the rubble of the South Tower after it collapsed; he was wearing work gloves and holding a flashlight.

Abe Zelmanowitz worked on the 27th floor of the North Tower and could easily have walked down the stairs to safety when the plane struck the floors above. Instead, he stayed behind with his friend Ed Beyea, a quadriplegic, waiting for help to carry him down the stairs. Both died when the tower collapsed.

Rick Rescorla was head of security for the Morgan Stanley brokerage firm. After the first plane hit the North Tower, Rescorla and the other employees in the South Tower were instructed to remain at their desks. Rescorla, who had spent years studying the security of the towers, had drilled his employees repeatedly on what to do in an emergency like this—find a partner, avoid the elevators, and evacuate the building. He invoked this plan immediately, and when the plane hit the South Tower, he was on the 44th floor supervising the evacuation, yelling instructions through a bullhorn. After most of the Morgan Stanley employees made it out of the building, Rescorla decided to do a final sweep of the offices to make sure no one was left behind, and he perished when the South Tower collapsed. Rescorla is credited with saving the lives of the 3,700 employees he guided to safety (Stewart, 2002).

And then there were the passengers on United flight 93. Based on phone calls made from the plane in the fateful minutes after it was hijacked, it appears that several passengers, including Todd Beamer, Jeremy Glick, and Thomas Burnett—all fathers of young children—stormed the cockpit and struggled with the terrorists. They could not prevent the plane from crashing, killing everyone on board, but they did prevent the plane from carrying out its likely mission: crashing into the White House or the U.S. Capitol.

Basic Motives Underlying Prosocial Behavior: Why Do People Help?

11.1 What are the basic motives that determine whether people help others?

How can we explain acts of great self-sacrifice and heroism when people are also capable of acting in uncaring, heartless ways? In this chapter, we will consider the major causes of **prosocial behavior**—any act performed with the goal of benefiting another person (Batson, 2012; Penner et al., 2005). We are particularly concerned with prosocial behavior that is motivated by **altruism**, which is the desire to help another person even if it involves a cost to the helper. Someone might act in a prosocial way out of self-interest, hoping to get something in return. Altruism is helping purely out of the desire to benefit someone else, with no benefit (and often a cost) to oneself; the heroes of September 11, who gave their lives while helping strangers, are a clear example of altruism.

Prosocial Behavior

Any act performed with the goal of benefiting another person

Altruism

The desire to help another person even if it involves a cost to the helper

We begin by considering the basic origins of prosocial behavior and altruism: Is the willingness to help a basic impulse with genetic roots? Must it be taught and nurtured in childhood? Is there a pure motive for helping? Or do people typically help only when there is something in it for them? Let's see how psychologists have addressed these centuries-old questions (Keltner, Kogan, Piff, & Saturn, 2014; McCullough & Tabak, 2010; Piliavin, 2009; Tomasello & Vaish, 2013).

Evolutionary Psychology: Instincts and Genes

According to Charles Darwin's (1859) theory of evolution, natural selection favors genes that promote the survival of the individual (see Chapter 10). Any gene that furthers our survival and increases the probability that we will produce offspring is likely to be passed on from generation to generation. Genes that lower our chances of survival, such as those causing life-threatening diseases, reduce the chances that we will produce offspring and thus are less likely to be passed on. Evolutionary biologists such as E. O. Wilson (1975) and Richard Dawkins (1976) have used these principles of evolutionary theory to explain such social behaviors as aggression and altruism. Several psychologists have pursued these ideas, spawning the field of *evolutionary psychology*, which is the attempt to explain social behavior in terms of genetic factors that have evolved over time according to the principles of natural selection (Buss, 2005; Neuberg, Kenrick, & Schaller, 2010; Tooby & Cosmides, 2005). In Chapter 10, we discussed how evolutionary psychology attempts to explain love and attraction; here we discuss its explanation of prosocial behavior (Rand & Nowak, 2013; Simpson & Beckes, 2010).

Darwin realized early on that there was a problem with evolutionary theory: How can it explain altruism? If people's overriding goal is to ensure their own survival, why would they ever help others at a cost to themselves? It would seem that over the course of human evolution altruistic behavior would disappear, because people who acted that way would, by putting themselves at risk, produce fewer offspring than would people who acted selfishly. Genes promoting selfish behavior should be more likely to be passed on—or should they?

Kin Selection

The idea that behaviors that help a genetic relative are favored by natural selection

According to evolutionary psychology, prosocial behavior occurs in part because of kin selection.

KIN SELECTION   One way that evolutionary psychologists attempt to resolve this dilemma is with the notion of **kin selection**, the idea that behaviors that help a genetic relative are favored by natural selection (Breed, 2014; Hamilton, 1964; Vasey & VanderLaan, 2010). People can increase the chances that their genes will be passed along not only by having their own children, but also by ensuring that their genetic relatives have children. Because a person's blood relatives share some of his or her genes, the more that person ensures their survival, the greater the chances that his or her genes will flourish in future generations. Thus, natural selection should favor altruistic acts directed toward genetic relatives.

In one study, for example, people reported that they would be more likely to help genetic relatives than nonrelatives in life-and-death situations, such as a house fire. People did not report that they would be more likely to help genetic relatives when the situation was non-life-threatening, which supports the idea that people are most likely to help in ways that ensure the survival of their own genes. Interestingly, both males and females, and both American and Japanese participants, followed this rule of kin selection in life-threatening situations, suggesting that kin selection is not limited to one gender or a particular culture (Burnstein, Crandall, & Kitayama, 1994).

Of course, in this study people reported what they thought they would do; this doesn't prove that in a real fire they would indeed be more likely to save their sibling than their cousin. Anecdotal evidence from real emergencies, however, is consistent with these results. Survivors of a fire at a vacation complex reported that when they became aware that there was a fire, they were much more likely to search for family members before exiting the building than they were to search for friends (Sime, 1983).

Evolutionary psychologists are not suggesting that people consciously weigh the biological importance of their behavior before deciding whether to help. According to evolutionary theory, however, kin selection may have become ingrained in human behavior, and as a result the genes of people who help their relatives are more likely to survive than the genes of people who do not (Archer, 2013; Vasey & VanderLaan, 2010).

THE RECIPROCITY NORM   To explain altruism, evolutionary psychologists also point to the **norm of reciprocity**, which is the expectation that helping others will increase the likelihood that they will help us in the future. The idea is that as human beings were evolving, a group of completely selfish individuals, each living in his or her own cave, would have found it more difficult to survive than a group that had learned to cooperate. Of course, if people cooperated too readily, they might have been exploited by an adversary who never helped in return. Those who were most likely to survive, the argument goes, were people who developed an understanding with their neighbors about reciprocity: "I will help you now, with the agreement that when I need help, you will return the favor." Because of its survival value, such a norm of reciprocity may have become genetically based (Gray, Ward, & Norton, 2014; Halali, Bereby-Meyer, & Meiran, 2014; Trivers, 1971; Zhang & Epley, 2009). Some researchers suggest that the emotion of *gratitude*—the positive feelings that are caused by the perception that one has been helped by others—evolved in order to regulate reciprocity (Algoe, 2012; Algoe, Fredrickson, & Gable, 2013; Bartlett & DeSteno, 2006; Grant & Gino, 2010). That is, if someone helps us, we feel gratitude, which motivates us to return the favor in the future. The following Try It! describes how the reciprocity norm has been studied using economic games.

> Altruism based on kin selection is the enemy of civilization. If human beings are to a large extent guided to favor their own relatives and tribe, only a limited amount of global harmony is possible.
> —E. O. Wilson, 1978

Norm of Reciprocity
The expectation that helping others will increase the likelihood that they will help us in the future

> Let him who neglects to raise the fallen, fear lest, when he falls, no one will stretch out his hand to lift him up.
> —Saadi, *The Orchard*, 1257

TRY IT!
The Dictator Game

Imagine that you take part in the following study: An experimenter gives you 10 one dollar bills and says that you can keep all of the money or donate some of it to the next participant, whom you will never meet. The experimenter leaves you by yourself, with the instructions to put whatever amount you want to give to the next participant (if any) in a sealed envelope, after which you can leave. How much, if anything, would you donate?

This procedure, called the Dictator Game, has been used in dozens of studies to study human generosity. Although it would be in people's self-interest to keep all the money, most people donate some of it to the anonymous stranger they will never meet—on

average, about $2.80 (Engel, 2010). In other words, people act altruistically in this situation, by helping another person at some cost to themselves. Now imagine a slight twist in the game: When you arrive, the experimenter gives you an envelope containing money that a participant in another room sent to you as part of the Dictator Game. That is, the other person was given $10 and told that he/she could keep it all or give some of it to you, and the amount he/she donated—let's say it was $4.00—is in your hands.

Now the experimenter gives you an additional $10 and asks you to keep it or give some of it to that same participant in the next room. By the way, you will never meet this person, and the experimenter will never know how much you gave—after you make your decision you will leave without seeing the other participant. How much of the $10, if anything, will you give to the other participant?

If your answer was $4.00—the same amount that the other participant gave you—you answered like most people in a study that followed this exact procedure. In that study, almost all participants gave the person in the next room the same amount that that person had given them, or close to it (Ben-Ner, Putterman, Kong, & Magan, 2004). Thus, if the person had given you $4, you likely gave them $4 back, whereas if he/she had given you $1, you likely give them that much back. This study illustrates how sensitive people are to the *reciprocity norm*; we help others to the same degree that they help us.

GROUP SELECTION   Classic evolutionary theory argues that natural selection operates on individuals: People who have traits that make them more likely to survive are more likely to reproduce and pass those traits on to future generations. Some argue that natural selection also operates at the group level. Imagine two neighboring villages, for example, that are often at war with each other. Village A is made up entirely of selfish individuals who refuse to put themselves at risk to help the village. Village B, on the other hand, has selfless sentries who put their lives at risk by alerting their comrades of an invasion. Which *group* is more likely to win the war and pass on its genes to later generations? The one with the selfless (altruistic) sentries, of course. Even though the *individual* sentries in Village B are at risk and likely to be captured and killed, their selfless behavior increases the likelihood that their *group* will survive—namely, the group that values altruism. Though the idea of group selection is controversial and not supported by all biologists, it has prominent proponents (Rand & Nowak, 2013; Wilson, Van Vugt, & O'Gorman, 2008; Wilson & Wilson, 2007).

In sum, evolutionary psychologists believe that people help others because of factors that have become ingrained in our genes. As we saw in Chapter 10, evolutionary psychology is a challenging and creative approach to understanding prosocial behavior, though it has its critics (Batson, 2011; Buller, 2005; Caporael & Brewer, 2000; Confer et al., 2010; Panksepp & Panksepp, 2000; Wood & Eagly, 2002). How, for example, can evolutionary theory explain why complete strangers sometimes help each other, even when there is no reason for them to assume that they share some of the same genes or that their favor will ever be returned? It seems absurd to say that the heroes of September 11, who lost their lives while saving others, somehow calculated how genetically similar they were to the others before deciding to help. Further, just because people are more likely to save family members than strangers from a fire does not necessarily mean that they are genetically programmed to help genetic relatives. It may simply be that they cannot bear the thought of losing a loved one and therefore go to greater lengths to save the ones they love over people they have never met. We turn now to other possible motives behind prosocial behavior that do not necessarily originate in people's genes.

Social Exchange: The Costs and Rewards of Helping

Although some social psychologists disagree with evolutionary approaches to prosocial behavior, they share the view that altruistic behavior can be based on self-interest. In fact, *social exchange theory* (see Chapter 10) argues that much of what we do stems from the desire to maximize our rewards and minimize our costs (Cook & Rice, 2003; Homans, 1961; Lawler & Thye, 1999; Thibaut & Kelley, 1959). The difference from evolutionary approaches is that social exchange theory doesn't trace this desire back to our evolutionary roots, nor does it assume that the desire is genetically based. Social exchange theorists assume that just as people in an economic marketplace try to maximize the ratio of their monetary profits to their monetary losses, people in their relationships with others try to maximize the ratio of social rewards to social costs.

Helping can be rewarding in a number of ways. As we saw with the norm of reciprocity, it can increase the likelihood that someone will help us in return. Helping someone is an investment in the future, the social exchange being that someday someone will help us when we need it. Helping can also relieve the personal distress of a bystander. Considerable evidence indicates that people are aroused and disturbed when they see another person suffer and that they help at least in part to relieve their own distress (Dovidio, 1984; Dovidio et al., 1991; Eisenberg & Fabes, 1991). By helping others, we can also gain such rewards as social approval from others and increased feelings of self-worth.

The other side of the coin, of course, is that helping can be costly. Helping decreases when the costs are high, such as when it would put us in physical danger, result in pain or embarrassment, or simply take too much time (Dovidio et al., 1991; Piliavin et al., 1981; Piliavin, Piliavin, & Rodin, 1975). Perhaps Abe Zelmanowitz, who stayed behind with his friend Ed Beyea in the World Trade Center, found the prospect of walking away and letting his friend die too distressing. Basically, social exchange theory argues that true altruism, in which people help even when doing so is costly to them, does not exist. People help when the benefits outweigh the costs.

If you are like many of our students, you may think this is an overly cynical view of human nature. Is true altruism, motivated only by the desire to help someone else, really such a mythical act? Must we trace all prosocial behavior, such as large charitable gifts made by wealthy individuals, to the self-interest of the helper? Well, a social exchange theorist might reply, there are many ways in which people can obtain gratification, and we should be thankful that one way is by helping others. After all, wealthy people could decide to get their pleasure solely from lavish vacations, expensive cars, and meals at fancy restaurants. We should applaud their decision to give money to the disadvantaged, even if, ultimately, it is just a way for them to feel good about themselves. Prosocial acts are doubly rewarding in that they help both the giver and the recipient of the aid. Thus, it is to everyone's advantage to promote and praise such acts.

Still, many people are dissatisfied with the argument that all helping stems from self-interest. How can it explain why people give up their lives for others, as many of the heroes of September 11 did? According to some social psychologists, people do have hearts of gold and sometimes help only for the sake of helping.

Study: Cavemen helped disabled

United Press International
NEW YORK—The skeleton of a dwarf who died about 12,000 years ago indicates that cave people cared for physically disabled members of their communities , a researcher said yesterday.

The skeleton of the 3-foot-high youth was initially discovered in 1963 in a cave in southern Italy but was lost to anthropologists until American researcher David W. Frayer reexamined the remains and reported his findings in the British journal Nature.

Frayer, a professor of anthropology at the University of Kansas at Lawrence, said in a telephone interview that the youth "couldn't have taken part in normal hunting of food or gathering activities so

he was obviously cared for by others."

Archaeologists have found the remains of other handicapped individuals who lived during the same time period, but their disabilities occurred when they were adults, Frayer said.

"This is the first time we've found someone who was disabled since birth . . . .", Frayer said. He said there was no indication that the dwarf, who was about 17 at the time of his death, had suffered from malnutrition or neglect.

He was one of six individuals buried in the floor of a cave and was found in a dual grave in the arms of a woman, about 40 years old.

This touching story of early hominid prosocial behavior is intriguing to think about in terms of different theories of prosocial behavior. Evolutionary psychologists might argue that the caregivers helped the dwarf because he was a relative and that people are programmed to help those who share their genes (kin selection). Social exchange theory would maintain that the dwarf's caregivers received sufficient rewards from their actions to outweigh the costs of caring for him. The empathy-altruism hypothesis would hold that the caregivers helped out of strong feelings of empathy and compassion for him—an interpretation supported by the article's final paragraph.

> I once saw a man out of courtesy help a lame dog over a stile, and [the dog] for requital bit his fingers.
> —WILLIAM CHILLINGWORTH

> What seems to be generosity is often no more than disguised ambition.
> —FRANÇOIS DE LA ROCHEFOUCAULD, *MAXIMS*, 1665

Empathy and Altruism: The Pure Motive for Helping

C. Daniel Batson (1991) is the strongest proponent of the idea that people often help purely out of the goodness of their hearts. Batson acknowledges that people sometimes help others for selfish reasons, such as to relieve their own distress at seeing another person suffer. But he also argues that people's motives are sometimes purely altruistic, in that their only goal is to help the other person, even if doing so involves

Empathy

The ability to put oneself in the shoes of another person and to experience events and emotions (e.g., joy and sadness) the way that person experiences them

some cost to them. Pure altruism is likely to come into play, he maintains, when we feel **empathy** for the person in need of help, putting ourselves in the shoes of another person and experiencing events and emotions the way that person experiences them (Batson, 2011; Batson, Ahmad, & Stocks, 2011).

Suppose that while you are food shopping, you see a man holding a baby and a bag full of diapers, toys, and rattles. As he reaches for a box of Wheat Chex, the man drops the bag, and everything spills onto the floor. Will you help him pick up his things? According to Batson, it depends first on whether you feel empathy for him. If you do, you will help, regardless of what you have to gain. Your goal will be to relieve the other person's distress, not to gain something for yourself. This is the crux of Batson's **empathy-altruism hypothesis**: When we feel empathy for another person, we will attempt to help that person for purely altruistic reasons, regardless of what we have to gain.

Empathy-Altruism Hypothesis

The idea that when we feel empathy for a person, we will attempt to help that person for purely altruistic reasons, regardless of what we have to gain

If you do not feel empathy, Batson says, social exchange concerns come into play. What's in it for you? If there is something to be gained, such as obtaining approval from the man or from onlookers, you will help the man pick up his things. If you will not profit from helping, you will go on your way without stopping. Batson's empathy-altruism hypothesis is summarized in Figure 11.1.

Batson and his colleagues would be the first to acknowledge that it can be very difficult to isolate the exact motives behind complex social behaviors. If you saw someone help the man pick up his possessions, how could you tell whether the person was acting out of empathic concern or to gain some sort of reward, such as relieving his own distress? Consider a famous story about Abraham Lincoln. One day, while riding in a coach, Lincoln and a fellow passenger were debating the very question we are considering: Is helping ever truly altruistic? Lincoln argued that helping always stems from self-interest, whereas his fellow passenger took the view that true altruism exists. Suddenly, the men were interrupted by the screeching of a pig that was trying

Figure 11.1 Empathy-Altruism Theory

to save her piglets from drowning in a creek. Lincoln ordered the coach to stop, jumped out, ran down to the creek, and lifted the piglets to the safety of the bank. When he returned, his companion said, "Now, Abe, where does selfishness come in on this little episode?" "Why, bless your soul, Ed," Lincoln replied. "That was the very essence of selfishness. I should have had no peace of mind all day had I gone on and left that suffering old sow worrying over those pigs. I did it to get peace of mind, don't you see?" (Sharp, 1928, p. 75).

As this example illustrates, an act that seems truly altruistic is sometimes motivated by self-interest. How, then, can we tell which is which? Batson and his colleagues have devised a series of clever experiments to unravel people's motives (Batson, Ahmad, & Stocks, 2004; Batson & Powell, 2003). Imagine that you were an introductory psychology student in one of these studies (Toi & Batson, 1982). You are asked to evaluate some tapes of new programs for the university radio station, one of which is called *News from the Personal Side*. There are lots of different pilot tapes for this program, and you are told that only one person will be listening to each tape. The one you hear is an interview with a student named Carol Marcy. She says she was in a bad automobile accident in which both of her legs were broken and talks about how hard it has been to keep up with her class work as a result of the accident, especially because she is still in a wheelchair. Carol says she is especially concerned about how far she has fallen behind in her Introductory Psychology class and mentions that she will have to drop the class unless she can find another student to tell her what she has missed.

After you listen to the tape, the experimenter hands you an envelope marked "To the student listening to the Carol Marcy pilot tape." The experimenter says she doesn't know what's in the envelope but was asked by the professor supervising the research to hand it out. You open the envelope and find a note from the professor, saying that he was wondering if the student who listened to Carol's tape

> It is one of the beautiful compensations of this life that no one can sincerely try to help another without helping himself.
> —CHARLES DUDLEY WARNER, 1873

Helping behavior is common in virtually all species of animals, and sometimes it even crosses species lines. In August 1996, a 3-year-old boy fell into a pit containing seven gorillas, at the Brookfield, Illinois, zoo. Binti, a 7-year-old gorilla, immediately picked up the boy. After cradling him in her arms, she placed the boy near a door where zookeepers could get to him. Why did she help? Evolutionary psychologists would argue that prosocial behavior is selected for and thus becomes part of the genetic makeup of the members of many species. Social exchange theorists would argue that Binti had been rewarded for helping in the past. In fact, because she had been rejected by her mother, she had received training in parenting skills from zookeepers, in which she was rewarded for caring for a doll (Bils & Singer, 1996).

would be willing to help her out with her psychology class. Carol was reluctant to ask for help, he says, but because she is so far behind in the class, she agreed to write a note to the person listening to her tape. The note asks if you could meet with her and share your Introductory Psychology lecture notes.

As you have probably guessed, the point of the study was to look at whether people agreed to help Carol and to pit two motives against each other: empathy versus self-interest. The researchers varied how much empathy people felt toward Carol by telling different participants to adopt different perspectives when listening to the tape. In the high-empathy condition, people were told to try to imagine how Carol felt about what had happened to her and how it had changed her life. In the low-empathy condition, people were told to try to be objective and not be concerned with how Carol felt. As expected, people in the high-empathy condition reported feeling more empathy for Carol than people in the low-empathy condition did.

The researchers looked at self-interest by varying how costly it would be *not* to help Carol. In one condition, participants learned that she would start coming back to class the following week and happened to be in the same psychology section as they were; thus, they would see her every time they went to class and would be reminded that she needed help. This was the high-cost condition because it would be unpleasant to refuse to help Carol and then run into her every week in class. In the low-cost condition, people learned that Carol would be studying at home and would not be coming to class; therefore, they would never have to face her in her wheelchair and feel guilty about not helping her.

According to the empathy-altruism hypothesis, people should have been motivated purely by altruistic concerns and helped regardless of the costs—if empathy was high (see Figure 11.1). As you can see from the right side of Figure 11.2, this prediction was confirmed: In the high-empathy condition, about as many people agreed to help when they thought they would see Carol in class as when they thought they would not see her in class. This suggests that people had Carol's interests in mind and not their own. But in the low-empathy condition many more people agreed to help when they thought they would see Carol in class than when they thought they would not see her in class (see the left side of Figure 11.2). This suggests that when empathy was low, social exchange concerns came into play, in that people based their decision to help on the costs and benefits to themselves. They helped when it was in their interests to do so (i.e., when they would see Carol in her wheelchair and feel guilty for not helping), but not otherwise (i.e., when they thought they would never see her again). These results suggest that true altruism exists when people experience empathy toward the suffering of another.

To sum up, we've identified three basic motives underlying prosocial behavior, each of which has its supporters and critics:

1. Helping is an instinctive reaction to promote the welfare of those genetically similar to us (evolutionary psychology).
2. The rewards of helping often outweigh the costs, so helping is in our self-interest (social exchange theory).
3. Under some conditions, powerful feelings of empathy and compassion for the victim prompt selfless giving (the empathy-altruism hypothesis).

Figure 11.2 Altruism versus Self-Interest

Under what conditions did people agree to help Carol with the work she missed in her introductory psychology class? When empathy was high, people helped regardless of the costs and rewards (i.e., regardless of whether they would encounter her in their psychology class). When empathy was low, people were more concerned with the rewards and costs for themselves—they helped only if they would encounter Carol in their psychology class and thus feel guilty about not helping.

(Adapted from Toi & Batson, 1982)

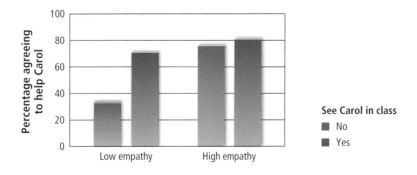

REVIEW QUESTIONS

1. Which of the following is the best example of altruistic behavior?

    a. Julie puts a dollar in the church collection basket because everyone else donates.

    b. Robert volunteers at his son's school to help out his class.

    c. Jawal anonymously donates $100 to a homeless shelter.

    d. Mary helps her husband with the dishes with the hope that he will cook dinner more often.

2. Evolutionary psychology would have the most trouble explaining which of the following incidents?

    a. When Jane was in a building that caught on fire, she let everyone else exit before her, even though she didn't know them.

    b. Bob risks his life to save his nephew who was drowning.

    c. Nancy runs in front of a moving car to keep her daughter from being hit.

    d. When Kareem was put in the unfortunate situation of saving his cousin or his son in a boating accident, he chose to save his son.

3. According to social exchange theory, which of the following people is most likely to give money to a homeless person?

    a. Erin, who feels empathy for the homeless person.

    b. Bill, who wants to impress his date by helping the homeless person.

    c. Jack, who is related to the homeless person.

    d. Kate, who has a genetic predisposition for helping people.

4. According to Batson's empathy-altruism theory, which of the following people is most likely to give money to a homeless person?

    a. Erin, who feels empathy for the homeless person.

    b. Bill, who wants to impress his date by helping the homeless person.

    c. Jack, who is related to the homeless person.

    d. Both Erin and Bill.

See page 621 for the answers.

Personal Qualities and Prosocial Behavior: Why Do Some People Help More Than Others?

11.2 What are some personal qualities that influence whether a given individual will help?

If basic human motives fully explained prosocial behavior, why are some people so much more helpful than others? Clearly, we need to consider the personal qualities that distinguish the helpful person from the selfish one.

> On reflecting at dinner that he had done nothing to help anybody all day, he uttered these memorable and praiseworthy words: "Friends, I have lost a day."
>
> —SUETONIUS, *LIVES OF THE TWELVE CAESARS*, FIRST CENTURY A.D.

Some people have more of an altruistic personality than others. Taylor Swift and Beyoncé, for example, have topped lists of "Most Generous Celebreties" for helping to raise money for charities. Personality, however, is not the whole story; the nature of the social situation also determines whether people help.

Individual Differences: The Altruistic Personality

Throughout history individuals have stood out for their incredibly altruistic acts, such as those who sheltered Jews during World War II, saving them from the death camps, often at great risk to themselves (Oliner & Oliner, 1988). The heroes of September 11 are other examples—selfless, caring people who gave their lives to save others. It is natural to assume that such people have an **altruistic personality**, the qualities that cause an individual to help others in a wide variety of situations (Boer & Fischer, 2013; Davis, 1983; Eisenberg, Spinrad, & Sadovsky, 2006; Penner & Orom, 2010).

Clearly some people have more of an altruistic personality than others, and psychologists have developed instruments to measure this quality. Go ahead and fill out the empathic concern questionnaire in the Try It! exercise below, to see where you fall on this dimension.

Even if you have a high score on this measure, though, research shows that when it comes to predicting how helpful people actually are, personality is not the full story

Altruistic Personality

The qualities that cause an individual to help others in a wide variety of situations

TRY IT!

Empathic Concern

Instructions: The following statements inquire about your thoughts and feelings in a variety of situations. For each item, indicate how well it describes you by circling the appropriate number next to the statement. Please read each item carefully before responding. Answer as honestly as you can.

	Does Not Describe Me Very Well				Describes Me Very Well
1. I often have tender, concerned feelings for people less fortunate than me.	1	2	3	4	5
2. Sometimes I don't feel very sorry for other people when they are having problems.	1	2	3	4	5
3. When I see someone being taken advantage of, I feel kind of protective toward them.	1	2	3	4	5
4. Other people's misfortunes do not usually disturb me a great deal.	1	2	3	4	5
5. When I see someone being treated unfairly, I sometimes don't feel very much pity for them.	1	2	3	4	5
6. I am often quite touched by things that I see happen.	1	2	3	4	5
7. I would describe myself as a pretty soft-hearted person.	1	2	3	4	5

Scoring: On some of the questions a high score reflects low sympathy, so we first need to "reverse score" your answers to those questions. First, reverse your answers to Questions 2, 4, and 5. That is, if you answered 1 change it to 5, if you answered 2 change it to a 4, if you answered 3 keep it the same, if you answered 4 change it to a 2, and if you answered 5 change it to a 1. Now sum your answers to all the items and divide by 7 to get your average score.

Interpretation: These questions, from a scale by Davis (1983), are a measure of empathic concern (your feelings of sympathy for other people in need). The higher your score, the more empathic concern you expressed.

Empathy and Your Age: Research shows that your score might be a function of how old you are.

Recall that in Chapter 5, we saw that narcissism has increased in college students over the past few decades. Unfortunately, people's empathic concern has decreased during that same time period (Konrath, O'Brien, & Hsing, 2011). Why has empathy decreased? No one knows for sure, though the authors speculate that it might have to do with the increase in the amount of time people spend on personal technology and media, to the extent that that decreases the amount of time people spend in meaningful, face-to-face interactions with others. The increase in reality television shows might also play a role, to the extent that they portray narcissistic people concerned mostly with themselves.

(Batson, 1998; Eisenberg, Hofer, Sulik, & Liew, 2014; Piliavin & Charng, 1990). We need to consider several other critical factors as well, such as the situational pressures that are affecting people, their gender, the culture in which they grew up, how religious they are, and even their current mood (Graziano et al., 2007).

Gender Differences in Prosocial Behavior

Consider two scenarios. In one, someone performs a dramatic, heroic act, like storming the cockpit of United flight 93 to fight the terrorists. In the other, someone is involved in a long-term helping relationship, such as assisting a disabled neighbor with chores around the house. Are men or women more likely to help in each situation?

The answer is males in the first situation and females in the second (Eagly, 2009; Eagly & Crowley, 1986; Eagly & Koenig, 2006; Einolf, 2011). In virtually all cultures, norms prescribe different traits and behaviors for males and females, learned as boys and girls are growing up. In Western cultures, the male sex role includes being chivalrous and heroic; females are expected to be nurturing and caring and to value close, long-term relationships. Indeed, of the 7000 people who received medals from the Carnegie Hero Fund Commission for risking their lives to save a stranger, 91% have been men. In contrast, women are more likely than men to provide social support to their friends and to engage in volunteer work that involves helping others (Eagly & Koenig, 2006; McGuire, 1994; Monin, Clark, & Lemay, 2008; Volunteering in the United States, 2013). Cross-cultural evidence suggests the same pattern. In a survey of adolescents in seven countries, more girls than boys reported doing volunteer work in their communities (Flanagan et al., 1998).

Whereas men are more likely to perform chivalrous and heroic acts, women are more likely to be helpful in long-term relationships that involve greater commitment.

Cultural Differences in Prosocial Behavior

Suppose you find out that a student at your university needs help because she lost all of her possessions in a fire at her apartment building. She has no insurance and very little money, so a call goes out to donate to a fund to help her buy clothes and other necessities. Would you donate money? Well, let's take this example a little further: Suppose that in one case the student was very similar to you; she is of the same race and has a similar background. Alternatively, suppose that she is a member of a different cultural group. Perhaps you grew up in the United States and she is an international student, or vice versa. Would this make a difference in your willingness to help her?

On the one hand, there is ample evidence that people often favor their **in-groups**, or the groups with which they identify as a member, and discriminate against members of **out-groups**, defined as groups with which they do not identify. Indeed, as we will see in Chapter 13, there is a long history of discrimination and prejudice against out-group members, including those of other races, cultures, and genders, as well as people with different sexual orientations. But on the other hand, people often go out of their way to help out-group members. People donate to charities that help disadvantaged strangers and rise to the occasion when an individual is in need, even if he or she belongs to a different group.

Recent research resolves this conundrum. It turns out that people often do help both in-group and out-group members, but for different reasons. We are more likely to feel empathy toward members of our in-groups who are in need. Thus, if the student who lost her possessions in the apartment fire is a member of your in-group, you will probably feel empathy for her, and the more empathy you feel, the more likely you are to help. We tend to help out-group members for a different reason—we do so, to put it bluntly, when there is something in it for us, such as making us feel good about ourselves or making a good impression on others. Sound familiar? Recall that Batson's empathy-altruism theory posits two routes to helping others: When we feel empathy, we help regardless

In-Group

The group with which an individual identifies as a member

Out-Group

Any group with which an individual does not identify

of whether there is something in it for us, but when we don't feel empathy, we help only if there is something in it for us (see Figure 11.1). Research on intergroup helping suggests that we are more likely to take the first route when the person in need is an in-group member, but more likely to take the second route when the person in need is an out-group member (van Leeuwen & Täuber, 2010; Stürmer & Snyder, 2010).

More generally, are there differences in cultural values that make people in one culture more likely to help than people in another culture? One such value is *simpatía*. Prominent in Spanish-speaking countries, simpatía refers to a range of social and emotional traits, including being friendly, polite, good-natured, pleasant, and helpful toward others (interestingly, it has no direct English translation). One study tested the hypothesis that helping would be higher in cultures that value simpatía than in cultures that do not (Levine, 2003; Levine, Norenzayan, & Philbrick, 2001; Ramírez-Esparza, Chung, Sierra-Otero, & Pennebaker, 2012). The researchers staged helping incidents in large cities in 23 countries and observed what people did. In one scenario, for example, a researcher posing as a blind person stopped at a busy intersection and observed whether pedestrians offered help in crossing or informed the researcher when the light turned green.

If you look at Table 11.1, you'll see that the percentage of people who helped (averaged across the different incidents) in countries that value simpatía was higher

Table 11.1 Helping in 23 Cities

In 23 cities around the world, researchers observed how many people helped in three situations: helping a person with a leg brace who dropped a pile of magazines, helping someone who did not notice that he or she had dropped a pen, and helping a blind person across a busy intersection. The percentages in the table are averaged across the three situations. The cities in boldface are in countries that have the cultural value of *simpatía*, which prizes friendliness, politeness, and helping others.

City	Percent Helping
Rio de Janeiro, Brazil	**93**
San José, Costa Rica	**91**
Lilongwe, Malawi	86
Calcutta, India	83
Vienna, Austria	81
Madrid, Spain	**79**
Copenhagen, Denmark	78
Shanghai, China	77
Mexico City, Mexico	**76**
San Salvador, El Salvador	**75**
Prague, Czech Republic	75
Stockholm, Sweden	72
Budapest, Hungary	71
Bucharest, Romania	69
Tel Aviv, Israel	68
Rome, Italy	63
Bangkok, Thailand	61
Taipei, Taiwan	59
Sofia, Bulgaria	57
Amsterdam, Netherlands	54
Singapore	48
New York, United States	45
Kuala Lumpur, Malaysia	40

(Based on Levine, Norenzayan, & Philbrick, 2001)

than in countries that did not, 83% to 66%. The researchers noted that these results are only suggestive, because the five Latin American and Spanish countries differed from the others in ways other than the value they placed on simpatía. And some countries not known for their simpatía had high rates of helping. Nevertheless, if a culture strongly values friendliness and prosocial behavior, people may be more likely to help strangers on city streets (Janoff-Bulman & Leggatt, 2002).

Religion and Prosocial Behavior

Most religions teach some version of the Golden Rule, urging us to do unto others as we would have others do unto us. Are religious people more likely to follow this advice than nonreligious people? That is, do religious people engage in more prosocial behavior?

There is no doubt that people *believe* the answer is yes. There is a pervasive stereotype that religious people are more moral and feel more empathy toward others than nonreligious people do (Galen, 2012). In a survey conducted in the United States, for example, people reported that the only group they disliked more than Muslims was atheists (Edgell, Gerteis, & Hartmann, 2006). The question of whether religious people are *actually* more empathic, however, has been the subject of much debate (Bloom, 2012; Brooks, 2006; Galen, 2012; Putnam & Campbell, 2010).

The answer, it turns out, is a qualified yes—but it doesn't appear to be related to religion per se. A very important feature of religion is that it binds people together and creates strong social bonds—and as a result, religious people are more likely to help than other people are if the person in need of help shares their beliefs (Galen, 2012; Graham & Haidt, 2010). When it comes to helping strangers, however, such as donating blood, or tipping a waiter or waitress, religious people are no more helpful than nonreligious people (Batson, Schoenrade, & Ventis, 1993; Galen, 2012; Preston, Ritter, & Hernandez, 2010). This is likely another example of in-group favoritism, which, as we saw in the previous section on cultural differences in helping, means that people feel more empathy toward in-group than out-group members. Thus, it may not be religiosity per se that causes people to be more helpful, but rather that people are more helpful toward people who belong to the same groups they do.

For example, imagine that you were organizing a community service project and were looking for volunteers to help you clean up a park on a Saturday morning. Would you be more likely to get volunteers by going to a community church and asking members of the congregation to help, or by asking members of a local softball team, none of whom happen to be religious? The answer is that neither group will be more likely to volunteer than the other, unless you happen to be a member of that group. Thus, if you belong to the church but not the softball team, then definitely ask your fellow parishioners to help; but if you are the shortstop on the softball team but don't belong to the church, then definitely ask your teammates.

The Effects of Mood on Prosocial Behavior

It turns out that it also matters what mood the parishioners or softball players are in. Whether people are in good, bad, or neutral moods can have surprising effects on how helpful they will be.

EFFECTS OF POSITIVE MOODS: FEEL GOOD, DO GOOD In a classic study, researchers wanted to see whether people's mood influenced the likelihood that they would help a stranger in a real world setting (Isen & Levin, 1972). To find out, they staged a helping opportunity at a shopping mall, whereby a man "accidentally" dropped a manila folder full of papers in front of stranger who was by him- or

"As every enquiry which regards religion is of the utmost importance, there are two questions in particular which challenge our attention, to wit, that concerning its foundation in reason, and that concerning its origin in human nature."

—David Hume (1757)

herself. The researchers then observed whether the stranger stopped and helped the man pick up the papers. But how did they experimentally manipulate the stranger's mood? They did so in a clever way, namely by leaving a dime in the coin-return slot of a public telephone at the mall and then waiting for someone to find it. (Note that when this study was done there were no cell phones, so people relied on pay phones, and also that 10 cents then would be like finding 50 cents today.) Half of the time the research assistant dropped the folder in front of a stranger who had just found the planted dime, and thus had just gotten a temporary mood boost, and half of the time he dropped the folder in front of a stranger who had just used the phone without a planted dime. Now, it might not seem like finding a dime would influence people's moods very much, or affect their likelihood of helping a stranger, but the results were dramatic: Only 4% of the people who did not find a dime helped the man pick up his papers, whereas a whopping 84% of the people who found a dime stopped to help.

This "feel good, do good" effect has been replicated many times with different ways of boosting people's moods (including giving positive feedback on a test, giving gifts, and playing cheerful music; North, Tarrant, & Hargreaves, 2004) and with many different ways of measuring helping (e.g., whether people help someone find a lost contact lens, tutor another student, donate blood, or help coworkers on the job; Carlson, Charlin, & Miller, 1988; Isen, 1999; Kayser et al., 2010).

Being in a good mood can increase helping for three reasons. First, good moods make us look on the bright side of life. That is, when we're in a good mood, we tend to see the good side of other people, giving them the benefit of the doubt. A victim who might normally seem clumsy or annoying will, when we are feeling cheerful, seem like a decent, needy person who is worthy of our help (Carlson et al., 1988; Forgas & Bower, 1987). Second, helping other people is an excellent way of prolonging our good mood. If we see someone who needs help, then being a Good Samaritan spawns even more good feelings, and we can walk away feeling terrific. In comparison, not helping when we know we should is a surefire "downer," deflating our good mood (Clark & Isen, 1982; Isen, 1987; Lyubomirsky, Sheldon, & Schkade, 2005). Finally, good moods increase the amount of attention we pay to ourselves, and this factor in turn makes us more likely to behave according to our values and ideals (see Chapter 3). Because most of us value altruism and because good moods increase our attention to this value, good moods increase helping behavior (Carlson et al., 1988; Salovey & Rodin, 1985). So, if you are trying to get volunteers for your community service project, try to catch people when they are in a good mood.

FEEL BAD, DO GOOD   Should you avoid asking people to help when they are in a bad mood? Given that feeling happy leads to greater helping, it might seem that feeling sad would lower it. Surprisingly, however, sadness can also lead to an increase in helping, because when people are sad, they are motivated to engage in activities that make them feel better. And, because helping others is rewarding, it can lift people out of the doldrums. Thus, you might also have luck asking people to help with your community service project if they are in sad moods (as opposed to neutral moods; Carlson & Miller, 1987; Cialdini & Fultz, 1990; Kayser et al., 2010; Wegener & Petty, 1994).

Another kind of bad mood also increases helping: feeling guilty (Ahn, Kim, & Aggarwal, 2014; Xu, Bègue, & Bushman, 2012). People often act on the idea that good deeds cancel out bad deeds. When they have done something that has made them feel guilty, helping another person balances things out, reducing their guilty feelings. For example, one study found that Catholic churchgoers were more likely to donate money to charities before attending confession than afterward, presumably because confessing to a priest reduced their guilt (Harris, Benson, & Hall, 1975).

If you want others to be happy, practice compassion. If you want to be happy, practice compassion.
—THE DALAI LAMA

REVIEW QUESTIONS

1. Which of the following is true?
   a. People with high scores on tests of altruism are *not* that much more likely to help another person than people with low scores.
   b. People with high scores on tests of altruism *are* much more likely to help another person than people with low scores.
   c. If a person has an altruistic personality, then they are quite likely to overcome situational pressures preventing them from helping someone.
   d. The genes for an altruistic personality have been identified by evolutionary psychologists.

2. Your friend needs assistance in hosting a party; you help her because _____. You assist your elderly neighbor in crossing the road; you help because _____
   a. it makes you feel good; you empathize with her
   b. it makes you feel good; it makes an impression
   c. you empathize with her; it makes you feel good
   d. it makes an impression; it makes you feel good

3. Which of the following does not explain why people in a good mood are more likely to help others?
   a. It makes us behave according to our ideals.
   b. It prolongs one's good mood.
   c. It makes us see the bright side of life.
   d. It tends to pass on to others.

4. Which person is *least* likely help a blind person cross the street?
   a. Marco, who is having a normal day and is in a neutral mood.
   b. Silvi, who just got an A on a paper and is thus in a good mood.
   c. Olvia, who just got a D on a paper and is thus feeling sad.
   d. Brandon, who just cheated on his girlfriend and is thus feeling guilty.

See page 622 for the answers.

Situational Determinants of Prosocial Behavior: When Will People Help?

11.3   In what situations are people more likely, or less likely, to help others?

Personality, gender, culture, and mood all contribute a piece to the puzzle of why people help others, but they do not complete the picture. To understand more fully why people help, we also need to consider the social situation in which people find themselves.

> Do not wait for extraordinary circumstances to do good actions; try to use ordinary situations.
> —JOHN PAUL RICHTER, 1763

Environment: Rural versus Urban

Here's another helping scenario for you. Suppose you are walking down the street one day when you see a man suddenly fall down and cry out with pain. He rolls up his pants leg, revealing a bandaged shin that is bleeding heavily. What would you do? When this event was staged in small towns, about half the people who walked by stopped and offered to help the man. But in large cities, only 15% of passersby stopped to help (Amato, 1983). Other studies have found that people in small towns are more likely to help when asked to find a lost child, give directions, and return a lost letter. Increased helping in small towns has been found in several countries, including the United States, Canada, Israel, Australia, Turkey, Great Britain, and the Sudan (Hedge & Yousif, 1992; Oishi, 2014; Steblay, 1987).

Why are people more likely to help in small towns? One possibility is that people who grow up in a small town are more likely to internalize altruistic values. If this were the case, people who grew up in small towns would be more likely to help, even if they were visiting a big city. Alternatively, the immediate surroundings might be the key and not people's internalized values. Stanley Milgram (1970), for example, suggested that people living in cities are constantly bombarded with stimulation and that they keep to themselves in order to avoid being overwhelmed by it. According to this **urban overload hypothesis**, if you put urban dwellers in a calmer, less stimulating

Urban Overload Hypothesis

The theory that people living in cities are constantly bombarded with stimulation and that they keep to themselves to avoid being overwhelmed by it

People are less helpful in big cities than in small towns, not because of a difference in values, but because the stress of urban life causes them to keep to themselves.

environment, they would be as likely as anyone else to reach out to others. Research has supported the urban overload hypothesis more than the idea that living in cities makes people less altruistic by nature. Thus, to predict whether people will help, it is more important to know whether they are currently in a rural or urban area than it is to know where they happened to grow up (Levine et al., 1994; Steblay, 1987).

Residential Mobility

> In the United States, a man will carefully construct a home in which to spend his old age and sell it before the roof is on. . . . He will settle in one place only to go off elsewhere shortly afterwards with a new set of desires.
> —ALEXIS DE TOCQUEVILLE, 1835

In many areas of the world, it is common for people to move far away from where they were raised (Hochstadt, 1999). In the year 2000, for example, nearly one in five Americans (18%) were living in a different state than they were in 1995 ("Migration and Geographic Mobility," 2003), and in many urban areas, fewer than half of the residents were living in the same house as they were in 1995 (Oishi et al., 2007). As it turns out, people who have lived for a long time in one place are more likely to engage in prosocial behaviors that help their community. Residing in one place leads to a greater attachment to the community, more interdependence with one's neighbors, and a greater concern with one's reputation in the community (O'Brien, Gallup, & Wilson, 2012; Oishi, 2014; Tahlheim & Oishi, 2014). For all these reasons, long-time residents are more likely to engage in prosocial behaviors. Shigehiro Oishi and colleagues (2007), for example, found that people who had lived for a long time in the Minneapolis-St. Paul area were more likely to purchase "critical habitat" license plates, compared to people who had recently moved to the area. (These license plates cost an extra $30 a year and provide funds for the state to purchase and manage natural habitats.)

Perhaps it is not surprising that people who have lived in one place for years feel more of a stake in their community. Oishi and his colleagues (2007) also found, though, that this increase in helping can arise quite quickly, even in a one-time laboratory setting. Imagine that you are in a study in which you are playing a trivia contest against four other students, where the winner will win a $10 gift certificate. The experimenter says that people in the group can help each other if they want, but that doing so might lower the helper's chances of winning the prize. As the game progresses, one of your fellow group members keeps sighing and commenting that he doesn't know the answers to the questions. Would you offer him some help or let him continue to struggle on his own?

The answer, it turns out, depends on how long you have been in the group with the struggling student. The study by Oishi and colleagues involved a total of four tasks; the trivia contest was the last one. Half of the participants remained together and worked on all the tasks throughout the study, whereas the other half switched to a new group after each task. Thus, in the former condition people had more of an opportunity to get to know each other and form a sense of community, whereas the latter group was more analogous to moving from one community to another. As the researchers predicted, people in the "stable community" condition were more likely to help their struggling companion than were people in the "transient" group condition. Another reason that people might be less helpful in big cities, then, is that residential mobility is higher in cities than in rural areas. People are more likely to have just moved to a city and thus feel less of a stake in the community.

The Number of Bystanders: The Bystander Effect

Remember Kitty Genovese from Chapter 2? She is the woman who was brutally murdered in New York City while many of her neighbors did nothing to help. As we discussed in Chapter 2, it now appears that newspaper accounts of the neighbors' reactions were not entirely accurate. But, unfortunately, incidents similar to this, where bystanders fail to help someone in need, are all too common. On March 11, 2011, in Bethesda, Maryland, Jayna Murray was brutally murdered by a coworker inside the clothing store where they worked. Two employees in an Apple store next door heard the murder through the walls, including cries for help from Murray, but did nothing to help (Johnson, 2011). In October of 2011 in Southern China, a 2-year-old girl was run over by two vans, minutes apart, and lay in the street dying. Neither car stopped, and a dozen people walked or rode past the girl without offering help (Branigan, 2011). In September of 2013 in Philadelphia, a transit police officer was beaten by a man he was trying to arrest, in front of more than a dozen onlookers, none of whom intervened or called 911 (Ubinas, 2013).

Why did the bystanders fail to come to the aid of a fellow human being who was in dire need of help? We have just discussed one possibility, namely that the passersby kept to themselves because they were overloaded with urban stimulation (all of the events took place in large cities). Although this may be part of the reason, these kinds of failures to help are not limited to big cities. In Fredericksburg, Virginia, for example, a town of 28,000 residents, a convenience store clerk was beaten in front of customers, who did nothing to help, even after the assailant had fled and the clerk lay bleeding on the floor (Hsu, 1995).

Maybe the answer is that people are just too afraid or cowardly to do anything. That was the premise of the movie *Kick-Ass*, in which the main character, a nerdy high school student who gets picked on by bullies, decides to become a superhero to help those in need. Unlike superheroes in comic books he doesn't have any super powers, but donning a costume and assuming an alternative identity gives him the courage to confront bullies and bad guys. But as entertaining as the movie is, it misses a key social psychological point: Often, the fact that many people fail to help in emergencies is not because of who they are, but because of the nature of the social situation.

Bibb Latané and John Darley (1970), two social psychologists who taught at universities in New York at the time of the Kitty Genovese murder, were the first to propose this idea and put it to the test. The key situational variable, they thought, might be the number of bystanders who witness an emergency. Paradoxically, they reasoned, the greater the number of bystanders who observe an emergency, the less likely any one of them is to help. In each of the three brutal incidents we described earlier, more than one bystander witnessed the emergency, and this may have been the key to why no one intervened.

In a series of now-classic experiments, Latané and Darley (1970) found support for this hypothesis. Think back to the seizure experiment we discussed in Chapter 2. In that study, people sat in individual cubicles, participating in a group discussion of college life (over an intercom system) with students in other cubicles. One of the other students suddenly had a seizure, crying out for help, choking, and finally falling silent. There was actually only one real participant in the study. The other "participants," including the one who had the seizure, were prerecorded voices. The point of the study was to see whether the real participant would attempt to help the seizure victim by trying to find him or by summoning the experimenter or whether, like Kitty Genovese's neighbors, the person would simply sit there and do nothing.

As Latané and Darley anticipated, the answer depended on how many people the participant thought witnessed the emergency. When people believed they were the only ones listening to the student having the seizure, most of them (85%) helped within 60 seconds. By 2 1/2 minutes, 100% of the people who thought they were the only bystander had offered assistance (see Figure 11.3). In comparison, when the research participants believed there was one other student listening, fewer helped— only 62% within 60 seconds; helping occurred more slowly when there were two bystanders and never reached 100%, even after 6 minutes, when the experiment was ended. Finally, when the participants believed there were four other students listening in addition to themselves, the percentage of people who helped dropped even more dramatically. Only 31% helped in the first 60 seconds, and after 6 minutes only 62% had offered help. Dozens of other studies, conducted in the laboratory and in the field, have found the same thing: The greater the number of bystanders who witness an emergency, the less likely any one of them is to help the victim—a phenomenon called the **bystander effect** (Fischer et al., 2011).

Why is it that people are less likely to help when others are present? Latané and Darley (1970) developed a five-step tree that describes how people decide whether to intervene in an emergency (see Figure 11.4). Part of this description is an explanation of how the number of bystanders can make a difference. But let's begin with the first step—whether people notice that someone needs help.

Bystander Effect

The finding that the greater the number of bystanders who witness an emergency, the less likely any one of them is to help

NOTICING AN EVENT   If you are hurrying down a crowded street, you might not notice that someone has collapsed in a doorway. Obviously, if people don't notice that an emergency situation exists, they will not intervene and offer to help. What determines whether people notice an emergency? John Darley and Daniel Batson (1973) demonstrated that something as seemingly trivial as how much of a hurry people are in can make more of a difference than what kind of people they are. These researchers conducted a study that mirrored the parable of the Good Samaritan, wherein many passersby failed to stop to help a man lying unconscious at the side of the road. The research participants were people we might think would be extremely altruistic— seminary students preparing to devote their lives to the ministry. The students were asked to walk to another building, where the researchers would record them making a brief speech. Some were told that they were late and should hurry to keep their appointment. Others were told that there was no rush because the assistant in the other building was running a few minutes behind schedule. As they walked to the other building, each of the students passed a man who was slumped in a doorway. The man (an accomplice of the experimenters) coughed and groaned as each student walked by. Did the seminary students stop and offer to help him? If they were not in a hurry, most of them (63%) did. If they were hurrying to keep their appointment, however, only 10% stopped to help. Many of the students who were in a hurry did not even notice the man.

Surely if people were deeply religious, they would be less influenced by such a small matter as how hurried they were. Surprisingly, though, Darley and Batson (1973) found that the seminary students who were the most religious were no more likely to help than those who were the least religious. What about if they were thinking about

Figure 11.3 Bystander Intervention: The Presence of Bystanders Reduces Helping

When people believed they were the only one witnessing a student having a seizure, when they were the lone bystander, most of them helped him immediately, and all did so within a few minutes. When they believed that someone else was listening as well, that there were two bystanders, they were less likely to help and did so more slowly. And when they believed that four others were listening, that there were five bystanders, they were even less likely to help.

(Based on Darley & Latané, 1968)

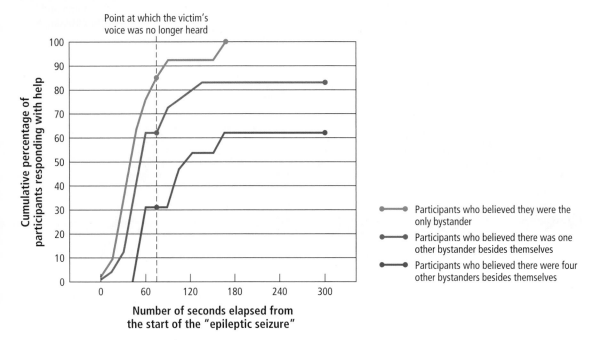

helping people in need? The researchers also varied the topic of the speech they asked the students to give. Some were asked to discuss the kinds of jobs seminary students preferred; others were asked to discuss the parable of the Good Samaritan. You might think that seminary students who were thinking about the parable of the Good Samaritan would be especially likely to stop and help a man slumped in a doorway, given the similarity of this incident to the parable, but the topic of the speech made little difference in whether they helped. Students in a hurry were unlikely to notice the man and help, even if they were very religious and about to give a speech about the Good Samaritan.

INTERPRETING THE EVENT AS AN EMERGENCY Even if people do notice someone slumped in a doorway, they might not stop and help. The next determinant of helping is whether the bystander interprets the event as an emergency—as a situation where help is needed (see Figure 11.4). Sometimes, of course, there is little doubt that an emergency has occurred, such as when we witness a car accident and see that people have been seriously injured. Under these circumstances, the number of bystanders is less likely to matter, because people know that help is needed (Fischer et al., 2011). Often, however, the situation is more ambiguous.

Is the person in the doorway drunk or seriously ill? Did the scream we just heard come from someone having a good time at a party or is someone being attacked? If people assume that what they witnessed is not an emergency, then obviously they will not help.

In ambiguous situations such as these, the number of bystanders makes a difference in a curious way: The greater the number of people who witness an emergency, the less likely they are to *know* that it is an emergency. To understand why, think back to our discussion of informational social influence in Chapter 8. This type of social influence occurs when we use other people to help us define reality. Suppose, for example, that you are sitting in class one day and notice that some White vapor or smoke is

Figure 11.4 Bystander Intervention Decision Tree: Five Steps to Helping in an Emergency

Latané and Darley (1970) showed that people go through five decision-making steps before they help someone in an emergency. If bystanders fail to take any one of the five steps, they will not help. Each step is outlined here, along with the possible reasons why people decide not to intervene.

(Based on Darley & Latané, 1968)

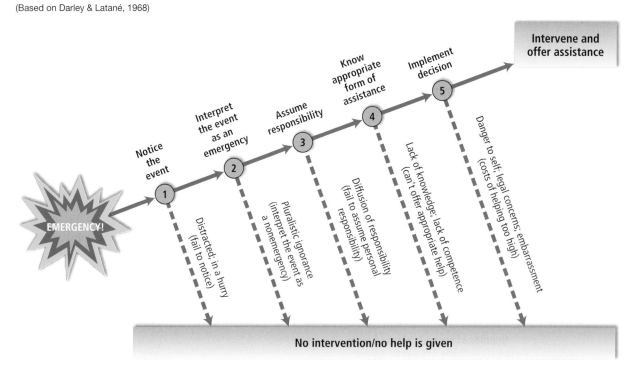

coming out of an air conditioning vent. Because you aren't sure what to make of this, you do what comes naturally to us all—you look around and see how other people are responding. You notice that the person to your left is looking at the vent and doesn't seem at all concerned, so you conclude that there is nothing to worry about. "Probably just some water vapor from the air conditioning system," you think. As we saw in Chapter 8, using other people to help us interpret an ambiguous event is often a good strategy. The danger is that no one may know exactly what is going on, and mistakenly assume that everyone else does. For example, the guy sitting to your left in the class may look unconcerned because he saw that *you* weren't panicking. Emergencies are often confusing and sudden events, and bystanders tend to freeze, watching with blank expressions as they try to figure out what is happening (Van den Bos & Linds, 2013). When they glance at each other, they see an apparent lack of concern on the part of everyone else. This results in a state of **pluralistic ignorance**, wherein people think that everyone else is interpreting a situation in a certain way, when in fact they are not.

This White-smoke scenario is taken from another classic experiment by Latané and Darley (1970) and illustrates the dangers of pluralistic ignorance. Again, imagine you were a participant and arrive at the appointed time for a study of people's attitudes toward the problems of urban life. A sign tells you to fill out a questionnaire while you're waiting for the study to begin, so you take a seat and get started. Then you notice something odd: White smoke is trickling into the room through a small vent in the wall. Before long, the room is so filled with smoke that you can barely see the questionnaire. What will you do?

In fact, there was no real danger—the experimenters were pumping smoke into the room to see how people would respond to this potential emergency. Not surprisingly, when people were alone, most of them took action. Within 2 minutes, 50% of the participants left the room and found the experimenter down the hall, reporting that

Pluralistic Ignorance

The case in which people think that everyone else is interpreting a situation in a certain way, when in fact they are not there may have been a fire in the building; by 6 minutes, 75% of the participants had left the room to alert the experimenter.

But what would happen if people were not alone? Given that 75% of the participants who were by themselves reported the smoke, it would seem that the larger the group, the greater the likelihood that someone would report the smoke. In fact, this can be figured mathematically: If there is a 75% chance that any one person will report the smoke, then there is a 98% chance that at least one person in a three-person group will do so.

To find out if there really is safety in numbers, Latané and Darley (1970) included a condition in which three participants took part at the same time. Everything was identical except that three people sat in the room as the smoke began to seep in. Surprisingly, in only 12% of the three-person groups did someone report the smoke within 2 minutes, and in only 38% of the groups did someone report the smoke within 6 minutes. In the remaining groups, the participants sat there filling out questionnaires even when they had to wave away the smoke with their hands to see what they were writing. What went wrong?

Emergency situations can be confusing. Does this man need help? Have the bystanders failed to notice him, or has the behavior of the others led each of them to interpret the situation as a nonemergency—an example of pluralistic ignorance?

Unsure whether the smoke signaled an emergency, participants used each other as a source of information. If the people next to you glance at the smoke and then continue filling out their questionnaires, you will feel reassured that nothing is wrong; otherwise, why would they be acting so unconcerned? The problem is that they are probably looking at you as well, and if you seem untroubled, they too are reassured that everything is OK. In short, each group member is reassured because they assume that everyone else knows more about what's going on than they do. And when the event is ambiguous—as when smoke is coming from a vent—people in groups will convince each other that nothing is wrong, resulting in potentially tragic cases of pluralistic ignorance (Clark & Word, 1972; Solomon, Solomon, & Stone, 1978).

ASSUMING RESPONSIBILITY Sometimes it is obvious that an emergency is occurring, such as when the bystanders in Philadelphia witnessed the transit officer being attacked by a man he was trying to arrest. That they did nothing indicates that even if we interpret an event as an emergency, we have to decide that it is *our* responsibility, not someone else's, to do something about it. Here again the number of bystanders is a crucial variable.

Think back to the Latané and Darley (1968) seizure experiment in which participants believed they were the only one listening to the student while he had a seizure. The responsibility was totally on their shoulders. If they didn't help, no one would, and the student might die. As a result, in this condition most people helped almost immediately, and all helped within a few minutes.

But what happens when there are many witnesses? A **diffusion of responsibility** occurs: Each bystander's sense of responsibility to help decreases as the number of witnesses increases. Because other people are present, no single bystander feels a strong personal responsibility to act. Recall from our earlier discussion that helping often entails costs: We might be putting ourselves in danger or end up looking foolish by overreacting or doing the wrong thing. Why should we risk these costs when many other people who can help are present? The problem is that everyone is likely to feel the same way, making all the bystanders less likely to help. This is particularly true if people cannot tell whether someone else has already intervened. When participants in the seizure experiment believed that other students were witnesses as well, they couldn't tell whether another student had already helped, because the intercom system allowed only the voice of the student having the seizure to be transmitted. Each student probably assumed that he or she did not have to help, thinking that surely someone else had already done so. The same is true in many real-life emergencies; when we

Diffusion of Responsibility

The phenomenon wherein each bystander's sense of responsibility to help decreases as the number of witnesses increases drive by a car accident on the highway, for example, we assume that someone else has already called 911.

KNOWING HOW TO HELP   Even if people have made it this far in the helping sequence, another condition must still be met (Step 4 in Figure 11.4): They must decide what kind of help is appropriate. Suppose that on a hot summer day you see a woman collapse in the street. No one else seems to be helping, so you decide it is up to you. But what should you do? Has the woman had a heart attack? Is she suffering from heat-stroke? Should you call an ambulance, administer CPR, or try to get her out of the sun? If people don't know what form of assistance to give, obviously they will be unable to help.

DECIDING TO IMPLEMENT THE HELP   Finally, even if you know exactly what kind of help is appropriate, there are still reasons why you might decide not to intervene. For one thing, you might not be qualified to deliver the right kind of help. Even if the woman is complaining of chest pains, indicating a heart attack, you may not know how to give her CPR. Or you might be afraid of making a fool of yourself, of doing the wrong thing and making matters worse, or even of placing yourself in danger by trying to help. Consider the fate of three television network technicians who in 1982 saw a man beating a woman in a New York parking lot, tried to intervene, and were shot and killed by the assailant. Even when we know what kind of intervention is needed, we have to weigh the costs of trying to help.

What about helping in situations that are not emergencies? The Latané and Darley model applies here as well. Consider an Internet chat room in which someone needs help figuring out how to use the software. Are people less likely to help each other as the number of people in the chat room increases? Researchers in one study entered chat groups on Yahoo! Chat where 2 to 19 people were discussing a wide variety of topics (Markey, 2000). The researchers posed as either a male or female participant and typed this request for help: "Can anyone tell me how to look at someone's profile?" (p. 185). The message was addressed either to the group as a whole or to one randomly selected person in the chat room. Then the researchers timed how long it took someone in the group to respond to the request for help.

When the request was addressed to the group as a whole, Latané and Darley's results were replicated closely: The more people there were in the chat room, the longer it took for anyone to respond to the request for help. But when the request was directed to a specific person, that person responded quickly, regardless of the size of the group. These results suggest that the diffusion of responsibility was operating. When a general request for help is made, a large group makes people feel that they do not have much responsibility to respond. When addressed by name, though, people are more likely to feel a responsibility to help, even when many others are present (van Bommel, van Prooijen, Elffers, & Van Lange, 2012).

Effects of the Media: Video Games and Music Lyrics

When we think about the effects of the media on behavior, we usually think about negative influences, such as whether violence on television or playing violent video games makes people more aggressive. There are indeed such negative effects, which we discuss in Chapter 12. But can the opposite also occur, such that seeing people act in prosocial ways or playing prosocial video games makes people more cooperative? Recent research suggests that it can.

Tobias Greitemeyer and his colleagues have conducted a number of studies that follow the same procedure: First, participants come into the lab and play a video game for about 10 minutes. Half are randomly assigned to play a game that involves proso-cial acts, such as *Lemmings*, in which the goal is to care for a group of small beings and save them by helping them find the exit out of different worlds. The other half play a neutral video game such as *Tetris*, where the goal is to rotate falling geometric figures so that they cover the bottom of the screen. Participants then take part in what they think is an unrelated study, in which they are given the opportunity to help someone. The helping opportunities include relatively easy actions such as helping an experimenter pick up a cup of pencils that he or she accidentally knocked over, more time-consuming commitments such as volunteering to participate in future studies without compensation; and potentially dangerous actions such as helping a female experimenter when an ex-boyfriend enters the room and starts harassing her. As seen in Figure 11.5, people who had just played a prosocial video game were more likely to help in all of these ways than were people who had just played a neutral video game (Greitemeyer & Osswald, 2010; Prot et al., 2014).

It isn't just prosocial video games that can make people more helpful—listening to songs with prosocial lyrics works too. Studies have found that people who listen to songs such as Michael Jackson's *Heal the World* or the Beatles' *Help* are more likely to help someone than people who listened to songs with neutral lyrics such as the Beatles' *Octopus's Garden* (Greitemeyer, 2009, 2011; North et al., 2004).

Why does playing a prosocial video game or listening to prosocial song lyrics make people more cooperative? It works in at least two ways: by increasing people's empathy toward someone in need of help and increasing the accessibility of thoughts about helping others (Greitemeyer, Osswald, & Brauer, 2010). So, if you ever find yourself in need of help and see someone approaching who is listening to an MP3 player, hope that he or she is listening to music with prosocial lyrics!

Does music with prosocial lyrics influence other types of prosocial behavior, such as agreeing to go on a date with someone? If you have your eye on someone special, consider this study, which took research on song lyrics one step further (Guéguen, Jacob, & Lamy, 2010). The study was conducted in France, and the participants were female college students who were not dating anyone. When a participant arrived for the study, she was ushered into a waiting room where music happened to be playing on a sound system. For half of the participants it was a romantic song called "Je l'aime à mourir" (which loosely translates as "I love her to death"), while for the others it was a song with neutral lyrics ("L'heure du thé," or "tea time"). After a few minutes, the participant was taken to another room where she performed a consumer taste test with another participant, who happened to be a male student of average attractiveness. During a break, the man asked for the woman's phone number. "I think you are very nice and I was wondering if you would give me your phone number," he said. "I'll phone you later and we can have a drink together somewhere next week" (Guéguen, Jacob, & Lamy, 2010, p. 305). Were the women who had just listened to the romantic song more likely to say yes? Indeed they were; 52% who had listened to "Je l'aime à mourir" gave the man their number, whereas only 30% of the women who had listened to "L'heure du thé" did so.

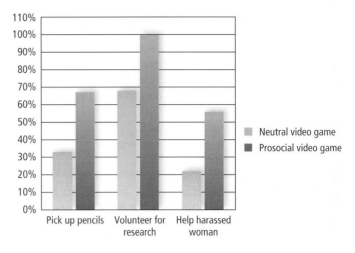

Figure 11.5 Effects of Playing Prosocial Video Games on the Likelihood of Helping

(Based on Greitemeyer & Osswald, 2010)

Legend:
- Neutral video game
- Prosocial video game

What are the effects of playing prosocial video games (such as *Lemmings*) on people's behavior? Research shows that those who have just played a prosocial video game are more likely to help others than are people who have just played a neutral video game.

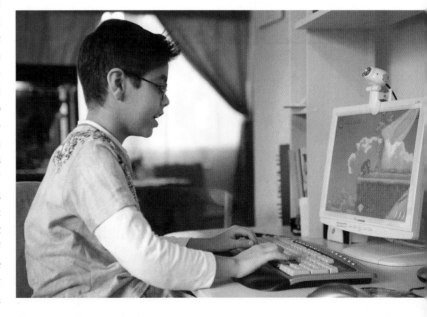

REVIEW QUESTIONS

1. Which of the following people is most likely to agree to help clean up a park in a large city?
   a. Brian, who just moved to that city.
   b. Rachel, who grew up in a small town.
   c. Jiaying, who has lived in that city her entire life.
   d. David, who just played a violent video game.
2. Which one of the following is *not* part of the Bystander Intervention Decision Tree?
   a. Having an altruistic personality
   b. Interpreting an event as an emergency
   c. Assuming responsibility
   d. Knowing the appropriate form of assistance
3. A woman collapses at a bus stop. Jane suspects it to be a heat stroke and understands that immediate intervention is required, but she may not intervene. What could be the likely cause?

a. Jane is very sure about the situation.
b. Jane is experiencing the standing effect.
c. Jane does not feel qualified to help.
d. Jane is a longtime resident of the area.

4. A person who plays a prosocial video game or listens to a prosocial song is likely to be more cooperative. What could be the possible reasons for this behavior?
   a. Increase in accessibility of helping thoughts; enhancement of their mood.
   b. Increase in their empathy; increase in accessibility of helping thoughts.
   c. Increase in their integrity; enhancement of their mood.
   d. Increase in accessibility of pleasant thoughts; feeling compelled to do a good deed.

See page 622 for the answers

How Can Helping Be Increased?

11.4   What can be done to promote prosocial behavior?

We would all be better off if prosocial behavior were more common than it is. How can we get people, when faced with an emergency, to act more like Abe Zelmanowitz and less like Kitty Genovese's neighbors?

Before addressing this question, we should point out that people do not always want to be helped. Imagine that you are sitting in a coffee shop and are trying to figure out how to upload a video from your cell phone to a social media site such as Vine. You're having trouble getting it to work when a guy you know saunters over, looks over your shoulder for a few minutes and then says, "You have a lot to learn. Let me show you how to do it." How would you react? You might feel gratitude, but you will probably also feel some resentment. His offer of help comes with a message: "You are too stupid to figure this out for yourself." Because receiving help can make people feel inadequate and dependent, they do not always react positively when someone offers them aid. People do not want to appear incompetent, so they often decide to suffer in silence, even if doing so lowers their chances of successfully completing a task (Alvarez & Van Leeuwen, 2011; Halabi, Nadler, & Dovidio, 2013).

Nevertheless, the world would be a better place if more people helped those in need. How can we increase everyday acts of kindness, such as looking out for an elderly neighbor or volunteering to read to kids at the local school? The answer to this question lies in our discussion of the causes of prosocial behavior. For example, we saw that several personal characteristics of potential helpers are important, and promoting those factors can increase the likelihood that these people will help (Clary et al., 1994; Snyder, 1993). But even kind, altruistic people will fail to help if certain situational constraints are present, such as being in an urban environment or witnessing an emergency in the presence of numerous bystanders.

> When death, the great reconciler, has come, it is never our tenderness that we repent of, but our severity.
> —George Eliot (Marian Evans), *Adam Bede*, 1859

Increasing the Likelihood That Bystanders Will Intervene

There is evidence that simply being aware of the barriers to helping in an emergency can increase people's chances of overcoming those barriers. A few years ago at Cornell University, several students intervened to prevent another student from committing suicide. As is often the case with emergencies, the situation was very confusing, and at first the bystanders were not sure what was happening or what they should do. The student who led the intervention said that she was reminded of a lecture she had heard on bystander intervention in her introductory psychology class a few days before and realized that if she didn't act, no one would (Savitsky, 1998). Or consider an incident at Vassar College not long ago where students saw someone being attacked by a mugger. As so often happens with incidents like this, most of the bystanders did nothing, probably because they assumed that somebody else had already called the police. One of the students, however, immediately called the campus police because she was struck by how similar the situation was to the studies on bystander intervention she had read about in her social psychology course—even though she had taken the class more than a year earlier (Coats, 1998).

Why did this person help, even when several other bystanders witnessed the same emergency and didn't help? Perhaps this person learned about the barriers to bystander intervention in a social psychology class.

These are not controlled experiments, of course, and we cannot be certain that these helpful people were spurred on by what they had learned in their psychology classes. Fortunately, this question has been addressed experimentally (Beaman et al., 1978). The researchers randomly assigned students to listen to a lecture about Latané and Darley's (1970) bystander intervention research or a lecture on an unrelated topic. Two weeks later, all the students participated in what they thought was a completely unrelated sociology study, during which they came across a student lying on the floor. Was he in need of help? Had he fallen and injured himself, or was he simply a student who had fallen asleep after pulling an all-nighter? As we have seen, when in an ambiguous situation such as this one, people look to see how other people are reacting. Because an accomplice of the experimenter (posing as another participant) intentionally acted unconcerned, the natural thing to do was to assume that nothing was wrong. This is exactly what most participants did if they had not heard the lecture about bystander intervention research; in this condition, only 25% of them stopped to help the student. However, if the participants had heard the lecture about bystander intervention, 43% stopped to help the student. Thus, knowing how we can be unwittingly influenced by others can by itself help overcome this type of social influence and make us more likely to intervene in a possible emergency.

Another approach is simply to remind ourselves that it can be important to overcome our inhibitions and do the right thing. When people find themselves in situations that are surprising and difficult to understand—which is certainly the case when emergencies arise—they naturally "freeze" and try to make sense of what is happening around them (van den Bos & Lind, 2013). This is particularly likely to happen when people are in public and worry about "doing the wrong thing" in front of others. They might want to help, but the natural tendency is to freeze while they try to figure out what is happening and see what other people do.

Maybe people who are concerned about doing the wrong thing in public would be more likely to help if they thought about times in the past when they overcame their inhibitions. To test that hypothesis, Kees van den Bos and colleagues (2009) asked people to fill out one of two versions of a questionnaire. In the disinhibition condition, people wrote about times when they had acted in an uninhibited way despite what other people thought. In the control condition, people wrote about how they behaved on normal days. Next the researchers staged a helping situation to see which group of people was most likely to come to the aid of someone in need. As they predicted, it was the people in the disinhibition condition. In one study, for example, 53% of individuals who had filled out the disinhibition questionnaire helped a man pick up pens that he dropped as he was rushing to catch a train, compared to only 7% of individuals in the control condition. As natural as it is to hang back and do nothing in situations such as this one, reminding ourselves of times in the past when we overcame our inhibitions can make us more likely to help (Van den Bos & Linds, 2013).

Increasing Volunteerism

There are many important kinds of prosocial behavior besides intervening in emergencies, including volunteerism and community service. Social psychologists have studied this kind of helping as well, wherein people commit to helping strangers on a more long-term basis (Mannino, Snyder, & Omoto, 2011; Penner, 2004; Piliavin, 2010).

Surveys of Western European and North American countries have found that many people engage in volunteer work, with the highest rate in the United States (47%; Ting & Piliavin, 2000). Of course, that means that even in the United States more than half of the population is not volunteering, raising the question of how to increase people's willingness to spend time helping others. Some institutions have responded by requiring their members to perform community service. Some high schools, colleges, and businesses, for example, require their students or employees to engage in volunteer work.

These programs have the benefit of increasing the pool of volunteers available to help community organizations such as homeless shelters, medical clinics, and day-care centers. But the question arises as to the effect of such "mandatory volunteerism" on the motivation of the people who do the helping. Many of these organizations assume that they are increasing the likelihood that their members will volunteer in the future, even after they leave the organizations. That is, making people volunteer is assumed to foster volunteerism by enlightening people about its benefits.

As we discussed in Chapter 5, however, giving people strong external reasons for performing an activity can actually undermine their intrinsic interest in that activity. This is called the *overjustification effect*: People see their behavior as caused by compelling extrinsic reasons (e.g., being required to do volunteer work), making them underestimate the extent to which their behavior was caused by intrinsic reasons (e.g., that they like to do volunteer work). Consistent with this research, the more that people feel they are volunteering because of external requirements, the less likely they are to volunteer freely in the future (Batson et al., 1978; Bringle, 2005; Kunda & Schwartz, 1983; Stukas, Snyder, & Clary, 1999). The moral is that organizations should be careful about how heavy-handedly they impose requirements to volunteer. If people feel that they are complying only because they have to, they may actually become less likely to volunteer in the future. Encouraging people to volunteer while preserving the sense that they freely choose to do so has been shown to increase people's sense of well-being and their intentions to volunteer again in the future (Piliavin, 2008; Stukas et al., 1999).

If you are the person doing the volunteering, you might be interested in how other people will view your actions. In general, people will think highly you if you volunteer to help others, unless, that is, they perceive that you are doing it out of self-interest. Suppose, for example, that you learned that Justin spends five hours a week volunteering at a homeless shelter. "What a nice guy," you would probably think. "He really cares about people who are down on their luck." But what if we told you that one reason that Justin volunteers is because he has a romantic interest in Alicia, another volunteer, and wants to hang out with her? How much do you like Justin now? Probably not so much, according to research by Newman and Cain (2014). They found that people were judged especially harshly when they appeared to be doing something charitable (e.g., volunteering in the shelter) but were actually acting in their own self-interest (e.g., wanting to spend time with Alicia). Note that this is not entirely logical, because it is possible that Justin has two motives—he wants to get to know Alicia, yes, but he also cares deeply about the homeless. But when people attribute a kind act to self-interest, they subtract out the kindness and focus on the self-interest. So, if you are in Justin's

An increasing number of schools and businesses are requiring people to perform community service. These programs can actually lower interest in volunteering if people feel they are helping because of an external requirement. Encouraging people to volunteer while preserving the sense that they freely choose to do so is likely to increase people's intentions to volunteer again in the future.

shoes, the last thing you want to do is to tell Alicia that you volunteered in order to spend time with her!

Positive Psychology, Human Virtues, and Prosocial Behavior

In this chapter we have seen many reasons why people come to the aid of their fellow human beings—and why they might fail to do so. By now you know that this is an example of the social psychological approach, which focuses on the power of social influence in shaping human behavior. Something as seemingly inconsequential as the number of bystanders who witness an emergency can have a large effect on whether people help.

It is worth contrasting the social psychological approach to one called *positive psychology* (Mills, Fleck, & Kozikowski, 2013; Seligman, 2002; Waterman, 2013). This field began as a counterpoint to clinical psychology, which focuses on mental disorders such as depression and anxiety. In addition to focusing on what can go wrong with human functioning, positive psychologists say, we should seek to understand human strength and virtue—all that can go right and contribute to a happy, fulfilling life. Many psychologists have adopted this approach and now focus on such topics as the nature of healthy human functioning, how to define and categorize human strengths, and how to improve people's lives (Lopez & Snyder, 2009).

Although the positive psychology movement has been a useful corrective to the emphasis on mental illness in clinical psychology and has led to many fascinating research programs, it is important to point out that it makes different assumptions from the social psychological approach (McNulty & Fincham, 2012). The topic of this chapter, prosocial behavior, is an excellent example of these differences. How can helping behavior be increased? The positive psychologist focuses on qualities of the person, and would seek to increase human virtues such as empathy and altruism. But, as we have seen in this chapter, helping behavior often depends more on the nature of the social situation than the personalities of the people in that situation. Thus, social psychologists believe that it is best to focus on the conditions under which people help or fail to help their fellow humans, such as the five steps of Latané and Darley's (1970) helping model, the role of video games and the media, and the conditions that foster volunteerism. By so doing, we can help ensure that all of us receive the help we need when we need it.

REVIEW QUESTIONS

1. Jack notices an elderly man struggling with his baggage at the airport. He decides to give him a hand with his luggage but the man promptly refuses to take help and says that he can handle it himself. Which of the following explains why people may not always like being helped?
   a. Majority of the people like to do their tasks themselves.
   b. Taking help may not be ideal.
   c. Taking help may make people feel incompetent.
   d. Taking help would mean interdependence.

2. On his way to work, Bob witnesses a boy being beaten up by a group of men. The boy was bleeding profusely. In which of the following scenarios is Bob likely to help?
   a. Bob reminds himself to overcome his inhibitions and do the right thing.
   b. Bob makes eye contact with fellow passengers.
   c. Bob has plenty of spare time.
   d. Bob calls up his friend and narrates the incident.

3. Rita enjoys baking cookies every Sunday for children in an orphanage. She gets immense satisfaction by looking at the children's happy faces. Off late, her family has started coaxing her to start baking on a large scale for other children in the neighborhood and charge money for her cookies. Rita seems to be losing interest in baking and does not feel like doing it anymore. Which of the following best explains this situation?
   a. Bystander effect
   b. Pluralistic ignorance
   c. Halo effect
   d. Overjustification effect

See page 622 for the answers.

Summary

11.1 What are the basic motives that determine whether people help others?

- **Basic Motives Underlying Prosocial Behavior: Why Do People Help?** This chapter examined the causes of **prosocial behavior**, acts performed with the goal of benefiting another person. What are the basic origins of prosocial behavior?

  - **Evolutionary Psychology: Instincts and Genes** Evolutionary theory explains prosocial behavior in four ways. The first is **kin selection**, the idea that behaviors that help a genetic relative are favored by natural selection. The second is the **norm of reciprocity**, which is the expectation that helping others will increase the likelihood that they will help us in the future. The third is *group selection*, the idea that social groups with altruistic members are more likely to survive in competition with other groups.

  - **Social Exchange: The Costs and Rewards of Helping** Social exchange theory argues that prosocial behavior is not necessarily rooted in our genes. Instead, people help others in order to maximize social rewards and minimize social costs.

  - **Empathy and Altruism: The Pure Motive for Helping** People can be motivated by **altruism**, the desire to help another person even if it involves a cost to the helper. According to the **empathy-altruism hypothesis**, when people feel **empathy** toward another person (they experience events and emotions the other person experiences), they attempt to help that person purely for altruistic reasons.

11.2 What are some personal qualities that influence whether a given individual will help?

- **Personal Qualities and Prosocial Behavior: Why Do Some People Help More Than Others?** Basic motives are not all there is to understanding prosocial behavior—personal qualities matter as well.

  - **Individual Differences: The Altruistic Personality** Although some people have altruistic personalities that make them more likely to help others, we need to consider several other critical factors when predicting who will help and who will not.

  - **Gender Differences in Prosocial Behavior** In many cultures, the male sex role includes helping in chivalrous and heroic ways, whereas the female sex role includes helping in close, long-term relationships.

- **Cultural Differences in Prosocial Behavior** People are willing to help both **in-group** and **out-group** members, but for different reasons. People are more likely to feel empathy toward members of their in-groups who are in need, and the more empathy they feel, the more likely they are to help. People help out-group members for a different reason: They do so when they have something to gain, such as feeling good about themselves or making a good impression on others.

- **Religion and Prosocial Behavior** There is a pervasive stereotype that religious people are more moral and engage in more prosocial behavior than nonreligious people. When it comes to actual behavior, it is true that religious people are more likely to help than other people are *if* the person in need of help shares their beliefs, but religious people are not more likely to help strangers. This is an example of in-group favoritism, in that people show preference to in-group members over out-group members. Thus, it may not be religiosity per se that causes people to be more helpful, but rather that people are more helpful toward people who belong to the same groups they do.

- **The Effects of Mood on Prosocial Behavior** People are more likely to help if they are in especially good moods, but also if they are in especially bad moods.

11.3 In what situations are people more likely, or less likely, to help others?

- **Situational Determinants of Prosocial Behavior: When Will People Help?** To understand why people help others, we also need to consider the nature of the social situation.

  - **Environment: Rural versus Urban** People are less likely to help in dense, urban settings because of the **urban overload hypothesis**—the idea that people living in cities are constantly bombarded with stimulation and that they keep to themselves in order to avoid being overwhelmed by it.

  - **Residential Mobility** People who have lived for a long time in one place are more likely to engage in prosocial behaviors than are people who have recently moved to an area.

  - **The Number of Bystanders: The Bystander Effect** To help in an emergency, people must meet five conditions: They must notice the event, interpret it as an emergency, assume responsibility, know how to help, and implement their decision to help. As the number of bystanders who witness an emergency increases, the more difficult it is to meet two of these conditions—interpreting the event as an emergency and assuming responsibility. This produces the **bystander effect**: The larger the number of bystanders, the less likely any one of them is to help.

- **Effects of the Media: Video Games and Music Lyrics** Playing a prosocial video game or listening to a song with prosocial lyrics makes people more likely to help others in a variety of ways.

11.4 **What can be done to promote prosocial behavior?**

- **How Can Helping Be Increased?** Prosocial behavior can be increased in a number of ways.

  - **Increasing the Likelihood That Bystanders Will Intervene** Research shows that teaching people about the barriers to bystander intervention increases the likelihood that they will help in

emergencies. Reminding people of times they acted in uninhibited ways can work as well.

- **Increasing Volunteerism** Organizations that encourage their employees to engage in volunteer work should be careful about how they do so. If people feel that they are volunteering only because they have to, they may actually become less likely to volunteer in the future. Encouraging people to volunteer while preserving the sense that they freely choose to do so has been shown to increase people's sense of well-being and their intentions to volunteer again in the future.

- **Positive Psychology and Prosocial Behavior** A new subfield called positive psychology focuses on qualities of the person and seeks to increase human virtues such as empathy and altruism. The social psychological approach, however, holds that helping behavior often depends more on the nature of the social situation than the personalities of the people in that situation.

Test Yourself

1. Which of the following is *not* a way in which evolutionary theory explains prosocial behavior?

   a. social exchange
   b. kin selection
   c. the reciprocity norm
   d. group selection

2. Brian rescues a bird that is stuck in a broken window and is badly injured. He takes the bird to a vet, where proper medical attention is given to it. Brian takes good care of the bird till it is fit to fly again. According to the social exchange theory, why do people help others?

   a. People often get distressed to see others in trouble and help others at least in part to relieve their own distress.
   b. When people feel empathy toward others, they help if there is something in it for them.
   c. Helping others gives a sense of joy and uplifts one's mood, which spills over to other activities.
   d. Helping is an innate reaction that surfaces when we see others in distress.

3. Research on prosocial behavior finds that religious people:

   a. help others more than nonreligious people do in virtually all ways.
   b. show more compassion toward needy strangers than do nonreligious people.
   c. are more likely to help than other people are if the person in need of shares their beliefs, but are not more likely to help strangers.
   d. actually help others less than do nonreligious people.

4. Betty has won the best student award in her class. It is a proud moment for her. Nevertheless she is in a sad mood because her best friend, who helped her during the semester, did not get good grades. On her way back, Betty comes across a man who looks pale and hungry. How likely is Betty to help the man?

   a. Very likely; helping the man will make her look good.
   b. Very unlikely; she may not even notice the man.
   c. Very likely; helping the man may uplift her mood.
   d. Very unlikely; she is feeling miserable and in no mood to help.

5. Luke listened to a lecture in his history class that he found very confusing, but at the end of the class when the professor asked whether there was

anything students didn't understand, Luke didn't raise his hand. Because no other hands were raised, Luke assumed that other students had understood the material and that he just didn't pay enough attention. In fact, many students hadn't understood the material and were in the same situation as Luke. This is an example of:

a. empathy-altruism hypothesis.

b. reciprocity norm.

c. social exchange.

d. pluralistic ignorance.

6. Which of the following is *not* a reason why being in a good mood tends to increase prosocial behavior?

a. Good moods make us view situations more positively, and thus we are more likely to give people the benefit of the doubt.

b. Helping prolongs good moods.

c. Good moods make us pay more attention to the possible rewards for helping.

d. Good moods increase how much attention we pay to ourselves, which makes us more likely to act according to our values.

7. Which of the following is true?

a. Listening to song lyrics with prosocial lyrics makes people more helpful.

b. If we want someone to say yes when we ask for a date, it doesn't really work to have him or her listen to a song with romantic lyrics.

c. Playing prosocial video games has no effect on how helpful people will be.

d. Playing violent video games makes people more helpful.

8. Meghan lives in a single room in a college dormitory. Late one night, she hears a scream coming from just outside her dorm. She is pretty sure that the person needs help because the person yelled, "Help me! I think I broke my leg!" Meghan goes back to sleep, only to find out the next day that the person was on the ground for 45 minutes before someone helped. Which of the following best explains why Meghan didn't help?

a. Informational influence

b. A diffusion of responsibility

c. She didn't interpret it as an emergency

d. Pluralistic ignorance

9. Which of the following is true about prosocial behavior?

a. How often people have moved from one place to another influences how helpful they are.

b. There is no effect of personality on prosocial behavior.

c. Being in a bad mood decreases prosocial behavior.

d. Being in a good mood decreases prosocial behavior.

10. It's a busy day at the motor vehicles office and many people are waiting for their turn. As one man gets up to leave, he accidentally drops a folder he was carrying and papers go everywhere. Which person is *least* likely to help him pick up the papers?

a. Meghan, who was just thinking about times in her past when she acted in uninhibited ways.

b. Joe, who is taking social psychology and heard a lecture about Latané and Darley's decision tree earlier in the week.

c. Michael, who is feeling guilty because he should be home helping his roommates clean their apartment.

d. Maggie, who is very religious but doesn't know the man who dropped the papers.

See page 621 for the answers.

Chapter 12
Aggression
Why Do We Hurt Other People?
Can We Prevent It?

 ## Chapter Outline and Learning Objectives

Is Aggression Innate, Learned, or Optional?

12.1 How do evolutionary, cultural, and learning explanations of aggression differ?

The Evolutionary View
Culture and Aggression
Gender and Aggression
Learning to Behave Aggressively
Some Physiological Influences

Social Situations and Aggression

12.2 What are some situational and social causes of aggression and sexual assault?

Frustration and Aggression
Provocation and Reciprocation

Weapons as Aggressive Cues
Putting the Elements Together: The Case of Sexual Assault

Violence and the Media

12.3 Does observing violence increase violence?

Studying the Effects of Media Violence
The Problem of Determining Cause and Effect

How to Decrease Aggression

12.4 How can aggression be diminished?

Does Punishing Aggression Reduce Aggression?
Catharsis and Aggression
What Are We Supposed to Do with Our Anger?
Disrupting the Rejection-Rage Cycle

The mass murder at Columbine High School in Littleton, Colorado, casts a long shadow in American culture. There, in 1999, Eric Harris and Dylan Klebold, feeling disrespected by their classmates and armed with assault weapons, went on a rampage, killing a teacher and 12 of their fellow students. They then turned their guns on themselves. As horrendous as it was, the death toll could have been much higher. The two shooters had made a videotape prior to the massacre in which they announced that they had prepared and planted 95 explosive devices (fortunately, due to a technical error, these failed to go off). The videotape shows the perpetrators gleefully predicting that, before the day was over, they would have killed 250 people.

Since then, dozens of troubled teenagers have apparently used Columbine as a template for revenge against the classmates they believe have taunted, bullied, or rejected them; some researchers even call this the "Columbine effect." For example, in 2014, John David LaDue was thwarted just before carrying out a similar rampage at his high school in Waseca, Minnesota. LaDue, who confessed that he "idolized" Eric Harris, had planned his attack to take place on the fifteenth anniversary of the Columbine massacre.

In the aftermath of every mass shooting, the country invariably seeks someone to blame. Were the parents at fault? Does our country make weapons too easily accessible? Does the media show too much violence, influencing viewer behavior in real life? Were all of the shooters crazy? Obviously, anyone who commits mass murder is not emotionally stable, but mental illness itself cannot explain most of these tragic outbursts; most mentally ill people, after all, are not mass murderers.

The violence that human beings inflict on one another comes in all too many varieties: mass shootings, fistfights and brawls, murder, sexual coercion and rape, and domestic abuse. In this chapter, we will try to understand some of the diverse causes of aggression. Are human beings innately aggressive? You almost never hear about a woman going on a shooting rampage; does that mean men are innately more aggressive than women? Can healthy people be inspired to commit violence by watching violent characters in films or playing violent video games? Can a society, a school, or a parent do anything to reduce aggression? If so, specifically what?

Needless to say, social psychologists don't have all the answers, but we do have some of them. By the time you get to the end of this chapter, we hope you will have gained some insight into these issues.

Is Aggression Innate, Learned, or Optional?

12.1 How do evolutionary, cultural, and learning explanations of aggression differ?

Aggression

Intentional behavior aimed at causing physical harm or psychological pain to another person

For social psychologists, **aggression** is defined as intentional behavior aimed at causing either physical or psychological pain. It should not be confused with assertiveness, even though most people loosely refer to others as "aggressive" if they stand up for their rights, write letters to the editor complaining about real or imagined injustices, or are supremely ambitious. Some people would say that a woman who speaks her mind or disagrees with a male coworker is being "aggressive." But true aggression involves the intent to harm another. The action might be physical or verbal; it might succeed in its goal or not. If someone throws a beer bottle at your head and you duck so that the bottle misses you, it was still an aggressive act. The important thing is the intention. By the same token, if a drunk driver unintentionally runs you down while you're attempting to cross the street, that is not an act of aggression, even though the damage would be far greater than that caused by the beer bottle that missed. "Violence" is an extreme form of aggression, as in acts of war, murder, and assault.

It is also useful to distinguish between types of aggression (Berkowitz, 1993). **Hostile aggression** is an act of aggression stemming from feelings of anger and is aimed at inflicting pain or injury. In **instrumental aggression**, there is an intention to hurt the other person, but the hurting takes place as a means to some goal other than causing pain. In a professional football game, a defensive lineman will usually do whatever it takes to thwart his opponent (the blocker) and tackle the ball carrier. This typically includes intentionally inflicting pain on his opponent if doing so is useful in helping him get the blocker out of the way so that he can get to the ball carrier. This is instrumental aggression. By contrast, if he believes his opponent has been playing dirty, he might become angry and go out of his way to hurt his opponent, even if doing so does not increase his chances of tackling the ball carrier. This is hostile aggression.

Today, social psychologists and other scientists have made great strides in understanding the biological, social, cultural, and situational causes of aggressive behavior. But they emphasize that the fact that aggression has many complex causes, and that it comes in many forms, from direct assault to indirect cruelty, neither excuses it nor means it is inevitable. Nor does it mean that such behavior cannot be altered, as we will discuss at the end of this chapter.

The Evolutionary View

It seems obvious that men are more aggressive than women. More than 90% of all mass murders (defined as killing at least four people in one location) are committed by men (Hillshafer, 2013). Men are more likely than women to get into spontaneous, unprovoked acts of "picking a fight" with a stranger, join in a flash mob bent on destruction and looting, and commit crimes of violence (murder, aggravated assault, rape). But as we will see, this fact doesn't necessarily mean that women are the shy, retiring, peaceful sex.

Evolutionary psychologists argue that physical aggression is genetically programmed into men because it enables them to defend their group and perpetuate their genes. In cultures all over the world—as diverse as the United States, Switzerland, and Ethiopia—male aggressiveness starts in childhood: Little boys are far more likely than little girls to go in for "nonplayful" pushing, shoving, and hitting (Deaux & La France, 1998; Maccoby & Jacklin, 1974). Males are theorized to aggress for two reasons: first, to establish dominance over other males and secure the highest possible status and, second, males aggress out of sexual jealousy to ensure that their mate is not having sex with other men, thereby ensuring their own paternity (Buss, 2004, 2005; Kaighobadi, Shackelford, & Goetz, 2009). When females behave aggressively, in the evolutionary view, it is generally to protect their offspring. Do not get in the way of a mother bear—or, for that matter, a mother bird.

It is commonly believed that the hormone that fuels male aggression is testosterone, which both sexes have, although in higher proportion in males. Laboratory animals whose testosterone is removed become less aggressive, and those injected with testosterone become more aggressive (Moyer, 1983; Sapolsky, 1998). Testosterone levels are significantly higher among prisoners convicted of violent crimes than among those convicted of nonviolent crimes (Dabbs, 2000; Dabbs, Carr, Frady, & Riad, 1995). However, it's easy (and wrong) to get carried away, for example, with claims that men suffer from "testosterone poisoning." Most of the studies have been correlational, which suggests that causality can (and does) flow in both directions: That is, testosterone itself can slightly increase aggression, but being in an aggressive, competitive, or sexual situation increases the production of testosterone (Mazur, Booth, & Dabbs, 1992; Thompson, Dabbs, & Frady, 1990).

Man's inhumanity to man makes countless thousands mourn.
—ROBERT BURNS

Hostile Aggression

Aggression stemming from feelings of anger and aimed at inflicting pain or injury

Instrumental Aggression

Aggression as a means to some goal other than causing pain

Boys are more likely than girls, the world over, to roughhouse and pummel each other. Is this evidence of hostile or instrumental aggression—or just of physical play?

When people say that aggression is "natural," they often point to our primate relatives. Chimpanzees (top) are indeed pretty belligerent and aggressive, but bonobos (bottom) would rather make love than war.

AGGRESSION IN OTHER ANIMALS To determine the extent to which aggressiveness is innate or learned, some scientists have turned to experiments with nonhuman species. Consider the common belief that cats will instinctively stalk and kill rats. More than a half century ago, biologist Zing Yang Kuo (1961) performed a simple experiment: He raised a kitten in the same cage with a rat. Not only did the cat refrain from attacking the rat, but the two became close companions. When given the opportunity, the cat refused either to chase or to kill other rats; thus, the benign behavior was not confined to his one buddy but generalized to rats the cat had never met.

Although this experiment is charming, it fails to prove that aggressive behavior is not instinctive in cats; it merely demonstrates that early experience can override it. What if an organism grows up without any contact with other organisms? Will it or won't it show aggressive tendencies? It turns out that rats raised in isolation, without any experience in fighting other rats, will attack a fellow rat when one is introduced into the cage; the isolated rats use the same pattern of threat and attack that experienced rats use (Eibl-Eibesfeldt, 1963). So even though aggressive behavior can be modified by experience, as shown by Kuo's experiment, some kinds of aggressive behavior apparently do not need to be learned.

We can gain still greater insight into our own biological heritage by observing the behavior of those animals with whom we have the most genetic similarity. Our closest relatives in the animal kingdom are two primates: the chimpanzees and the bonobos. Both species have 98% of their DNA in common with human beings. The chimpanzee is known for its aggressive behavior; the females too can be pretty mean (Watts, Muller, Amsler, Mbabazi, & Mitani, 2006). It is the only nonhuman species in which groups of male members hunt and kill other members of their own kind—indeed, at about the same rate that humans in hunter-gatherer societies kill each other (Wrangham, Wilson, & Muller, 2006). Based on the research on chimps, we might conclude that humans, especially males, are genetically programmed for aggressive behavior.

However, living across the river from the chimpanzees and out of their reach are the bonobos, our equally close genetic relative. Unlike the chimp, the bonobo is known for its nonaggressive behavior. In fact, bonobos are often referred to as the "make love, not war" ape. Prior to engaging in activities that could otherwise lead to conflict, bonobos have sex, an activity that functions to diffuse potential conflict (De Waal, 1995). Thus, when the group arrives at a feeding ground, they first enjoy some sexual play and then proceed to eat peacefully. In contrast, when chimps arrive at a feeding ground, they compete aggressively for the food. Also, unlike the chimps, bonobos form female-dominated societies, keeping males in line and often behaving with remarkable sensitivity to others in their group (Parish & de Waal, 2000).

Unfortunately, the bonobo way of life is rare in the animal kingdom. The near universality of aggression strongly suggests that aggressiveness has evolved and has been maintained because it has survival value (Buss, 2004; Lore & Schultz, 1993). At the same time, nearly all organisms also seem to have evolved strong inhibitory mechanisms that enable them to suppress aggression when it is in their best interests to do so. Aggression is determined by the animal's previous experiences as well as by the specific social context in which the animal finds itself.

Culture and Aggression

Most social psychologists, therefore, believe that aggression is an optional strategy: We humans are born with the *capacity* for aggressive behavior, but how, whether, when, and where we express it is learned and depends on our circumstances and culture (Berkowitz, 1993). Males all over the world have testosterone, after all, but their rates of aggression and violence vary dramatically. Likewise, we seem to have an inborn tendency to respond to certain provocative stimuli by striking out against the perpetrator, but whether we actually do so depends on a complex interplay between these innate tendencies, a variety of learned inhibitory responses, and the precise nature of the social situation. You may be really, really angry if a police officer stops you for speeding, but it is likely that you will control your temper—and your behavior.

Thus, although many animals, from insects to apes, will usually attack another animal that invades their territory, we cannot conclude that human beings are similarly programmed to protect their territory and behave aggressively in response to specific stimuli. Three major lines of evidence support this view: studies of cultures across time, studies across cultures, and laboratory experiments.

CHANGES IN AGGRESSION ACROSS TIME AND CULTURES   Within a given culture, changing social conditions frequently lead to significant changes in aggressive behavior. Consider the Iroquois of North America. For hundreds of years, the Iroquois lived peacefully as a hunting nation, without fighting other tribes. But in the seventeenth century, barter with the newly arrived Europeans brought the Iroquois into direct competition with the neighboring Hurons over furs, which dramatically increased in value because they could now be traded for manufactured goods. A series of skirmishes with the Hurons ensued, and within a short time, the Iroquois developed into ferocious warriors. It would be hard to argue that they became ferocious warriors because of some innate aggressive impulse; rather, their aggressiveness almost certainly came about because a social change produced increases in competition (Hunt, 1940).

It works in the other direction, too. Psychologist Steven Pinker (2011) has gathered evidence showing that war, crime, torture, and murder—though unquestionably still prevalent—have actually been steadily declining over the centuries. Genocidal eruptions such as the Holocaust and contemporary wars are interruptions on a trajectory showing that violence has declined in the family, in neighborhoods, and between nations. We now live in an era, Pinker argues, that is less violent, less cruel, and more peaceful than any previous period of human history. Where these changes have occurred, they did so not as a result of a change in "human nature" but because of the civilizing processes of settled communities and nation-states, the rising belief in human rights, and the human capacity for empathy and reason. Many societies that were once warlike—such as the Scandinavians or Portuguese—have become the most peaceful on the planet. "Violence as entertainment" now takes place on movie screens and not in gladiator arenas where actual people were once torn apart to the cheers of audiences.

Moreover, not all societies have been equally warlike. Cultures embedded with cooperative, collectivist values have had lower levels of aggression than European societies (Bergeron & Schneider, 2005). Certain tribes, such as the Lepchas of Sikkim, the Pygmies of Central Africa, and the Arapesh of New Guinea, live in apparent peace and harmony, with acts of aggression being extremely rare (Baron & Richardson, 1994). In close-knit cultures that depend on cooperation for the group's survival, anger and aggression are considered dangerous and disruptive, and an offender will be ostracized or punished. When men live in cultures that lack internal and external threats to their survival—and, admittedly, not many cultures are so blessed—they are not raised to be aggressive, sex differences are minimized, and cooperation is encouraged (Gilmore, 1990; Kimmel, 2012).

For example, the forest Teduray, a hunter-gatherer culture in the Philippine rain forest, have established institutions and norms specifically designed to prevent aggression among themselves. In their societies, people are expected to pay special attention to the effect of their actions on the feelings of others. When a situation arises, such as adultery, in which there is significant risk that anger will lead to violence, specific members of a Teduray village work to placate the injured individuals. The Teduray

The early economies of the American South and West created a "culture of honor" in which a man was literally quick on the trigger if he thought another man was about to smear his reputation—or steal his cattle.

believe that human beings are aggressive by nature but do all they can to reduce its expression within their group. They will, however, behave aggressively to protect themselves from aggression from outsiders (Schlegel, 1998).

CULTURES OF HONOR   Perhaps the strongest evidence against the notion that "men are naturally aggressive because of their testosterone" comes from experiments showing how cultural norms and expectations literally "get inside" people, causing them to behave differently under similar provocation.

For example, in the United States, there are some major regional differences in aggressive behavior and in the kinds of events that trigger violence. Homicide rates for males from the South and Southwest are substantially higher than those for White northern males, especially in rural areas. Richard Nisbett (1993) hypothesized that the higher rates of violence derive from economic causes: The higher rates occur in cultures that were originally based on herding, in contrast to cultures based on agriculture. Why would this be so? People who depend economically on agriculture tend to develop cooperative strategies for survival. But people who depend on their herds are extremely vulnerable; their livelihoods can be lost in an instant by the theft of their animals. To reduce the likelihood of theft, Nisbett theorized, herders learn to be hyperalert to any threatening act (real or perceived) and respond to it immediately with force. This would explain why cattle rustling and horse thievery were capital crimes in the Old West and why Mediterranean and Middle Eastern herding cultures even today place a high value on male aggressiveness. And indeed, when Nisbett looked at agricultural practices *within* the South, he found that homicide rates were more than twice as high in the hills and dry plains areas (where herding occurs) as in farming regions.

The emphasis on aggressiveness and vigilance in herding communities fosters, in turn, a *culture of honor* in which even small disputes put a man's reputation for toughness on the line, requiring him to respond aggressively to restore his status (Cohen, 1998). Although the herding economy has become much less important in the South and West, the legacy of its culture of honor remains. These regions have rates of honor-related homicides (such as murder to avenge a perceived insult to one's family) that are five times higher than in other regions of the country. High school students in culture-of-honor states are far more likely than students from other states to bring a weapon to school and to use that weapon. These states have more than twice as many school shootings per capita than do other states (Brown, Osterman, & Barnes, 2009). Whereas Pinker (2011) found that violence declines in democracies that allow the government to manage justice and determine the proper punishment for offenders—thereby removing the burden of revenge from individual citizens—men in cultures of honor tend to distrust governments and believe they are the ones who have the obligation to retaliate, personally and sometimes violently. Cultures of honor also have higher rates of domestic violence. Both sexes in such cultures believe it is appropriate for a man to physically assault a woman if he believes she is threatening his honor and reputation by being unfaithful or leaving him (Vandello & Cohen, 2008).

In a series of experiments with southern and northern students at the University of Michigan, Nisbett and his colleagues demonstrated how a culture of honor manifests itself in the cognitions, emotions, behaviors, and even physiological reactions of its young men. Each participant was "accidentally" bumped into by the experimenter's confederate, who then insulted him by calling him a denigrating name. Compared with northern White males, who tended to shrug off the insult, southerners were more likely to think their masculine reputation was threatened, became more upset (as shown by a rise in cortisol levels in their bloodstream), were more physiologically primed for aggression (as shown by a rise in testosterone levels), became more cognitively primed for aggression, and were ultimately more likely to retaliate aggressively against the confederate when given the chance (Cohen, Nisbett, Bowdle, & Schwarz, 1996).

The research on cultures of honor suggests that male aggression ("don't mess with me") is encouraged when it fulfills a powerful part of the male role and identity. When "being a man" is defined by competitiveness and strength, men are constantly trying to "prove" their masculinity and status in displays of aggression (Bosson & Vandello, 2011).

Gender and Aggression

If women aren't very likely to get into fistfights, start riots, or shoot someone to defend their family's reputation, does that mean that they are inherently less aggressive than men? Gender differences are obvious in the larger social world; in the private world of families and relationships, gender differences aren't always so clear.

PHYSICAL AGGRESSION   Most cases of *extreme* violence in the family are perpetrated by men: For example, 8 in 10 murderers who kill a family member are male. And when men beat up their victims, they inflict more serious injury than women abusers do. According to the Centers for Disease Control's national survey of violence between partners, women have a significantly higher lifetime prevalence of severe physical violence by an intimate partner (24.3%) compared to men (13.8%) (Breiding, Chen, & Black, 2014; see Figure 12.1). But when it comes to hitting, slapping, throwing objects, and battering, women, dare we say, don't pull their punches. In a study of nearly 500 first-year American college women who reported their experiences with violence with their boyfriends, most reported reciprocal abuse (Testa, Hoffman, & Leonard, 2011). A few years ago, a review of more than 200 studies of community samples found no significant gender differences in the percentage of men and women who are physically aggressive with their partners (Straus, 2011). The causes are the

Figure 12.1 Lifetime Prevalence of Physical Violence by an Intimate Partner

(U.S. Women and Men, NISVS 2010)

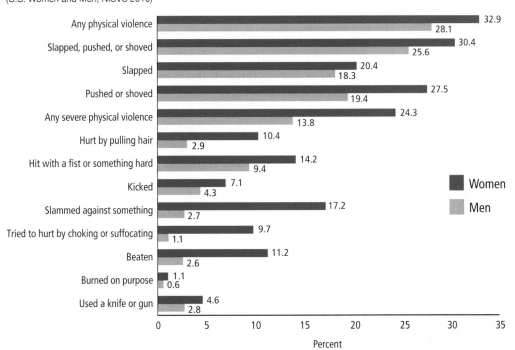

same for both parties—including sexual jealousy, anger, to get partner's attention, revenge for perceived emotional abuse, and self-defense (Langhinrichsen-Rohling, Misra, Selwyn, & Rohling, 2012).

When it comes to forms of physical aggression that are less violent than destruction and killing, therefore, there is often great overlap between males and females. Indeed, in some studies that compared young boys and girls in levels of physical aggression, most of the boys and girls were similarly nonaggressive; the sex difference was due primarily to a small number of extremely aggressive boys (Archer, 2004). Among adults, the sex difference in the willingness to inflict physical harm often vanishes when both sexes feel provoked and entitled to retaliate (Matlin, 2012). One meta-analysis of 64 separate experiments found that although men are more aggressive than women under ordinary circumstances, the gender difference shrinks when men and women are insulted and when women are given the same chance to retaliate aggressively—especially when others are unaware of their gender (Bettencourt & Miller, 1996). Adult women do not differ from men, on average, in their willingness to yell, be verbally abusive, humiliate or punish their children, and express aggression in similar ways (Archer, 2004).

Just as male aggression is influenced by culture, so is female aggression. The rate of the physical abuse of women, through beatings, stabbings, and hitting, is highest in cultures that regard such abuse as a male prerogative and a legitimate means of asserting power and control over women—as we see in countries such as Afghanistan and Nigeria, where girls can be murdered just for wanting to attend school (Eisenstat & Bancroft, 1999; Levy, 2008). Yet in one international study, women from Australia and New Zealand showed greater evidence of aggressiveness than men from Sweden and Korea (Archer & McDaniel, 1995). In a cultural community that admires physical aggression, both sexes may rely on violent tactics: Female teenage members of Mexican American gangs in Los Angeles carry any kind of weapon they can get hold of, from bats to guns, and told a researcher that they had joined not only for social support but for revenge (Harris, 1994). A study of all known female suicide bombers throughout the world since 1981 (including Afghanistan, Israel, Iraq, India, Lebanon, Pakistan, Russia, Somalia, Sri Lanka, and Turkey) found that "the main motives and circumstances that drive female suicide bombers are quite similar to those that drive men"—loyalty to their country or religion, anger at being occupied by a foreign military, and revenge for loved ones killed by the enemy (O'Rourke, 2008).

> Nothing is more costly, nothing is more sterile, than revenge.
> —Winston Churchill

RELATIONAL AGGRESSION Physical aggression is not the only way that people harm one another. Girls and women are more likely than males to commit *relational aggression*—harming another person through the manipulation of relationships, usually in such covert acts as backbiting, spreading false rumors about the target person, shunning or excluding that person, or, to use an ugly contemporary term, "slut-shaming" (Archer, 2004; Blakemore, Berenbaum, & Liben, 2009; Coie et al., 1999; Hess, 2014; McFadyen-Ketchum, Bates, Dodge, & Pettit, 1996; Richardson, 2014). "Mean girls" have been the subject of books, TV shows, and even a movie of that title. Phoebe Prince, a 15-year-old Irish girl living in Massachusetts, was targeted by a group known as the Mean Girls after she had a brief relationship with a popular boy at her school. Seven girls and two boys began a relentless campaign against her of verbal assault (including calling her "Irish slut" and "whore" on Facebook and other social media) and threats of bodily harm. After 4 months of being slandered and harassed, Prince committed suicide.

The average gender difference in relational aggression starts early: In one study of 3- to 5-year-old children playing in groups of

Males and females can be equally aggressive when aggression is defined as intending to harm another person. But women are more likely than men to indulge in "relational aggression"—backbiting, shunning, or spreading false rumors about their target.

three, the kids were instructed to use a crayon to color in a picture on a White sheet of paper. Three crayons were provided, but only one was a color (orange), and the other two were White. Naturally, the children all wanted the orange crayon. The boys used physical aggression to get it, hitting or pushing the child who had the orange crayon. The girls used relational aggression, spreading rumors about the child with the orange crayon or ignoring her to make her cry (Ostrov, Woods, Jansen, Casas, & Crick, 2004).

One especially harmful form of relational aggression is online bullying. Physical bullying, in which a stronger person intentionally humiliates or physically abuses a weaker one, has long been a fact of school life, and cyberbullying simply translates that impulse into a newer technology (Rivers, Chesney, & Coyne, 2011). Cyberbullying ranges from the less severe (prank calls and mild insults on instant messaging) to extremely severe acts (posting unpleasant or sexual photos on Web sites; sending a target photos or videos of threatening, violent scenes; and widely distributing insults, nasty text messages, rumors, and ugly accusations). It may be a one-time impulsive act or a planned campaign of harassment. According to a review prepared for the government on Child Safety and Online Technologies, the greatest source of danger that teenagers face on the Internet does not come from pornography (which many teens themselves, usually older boys, seek out) or even from predatory adults, let alone from sexting. The report found that the most frequent threats that minors face, both online and offline, are bullying and harassment, most often by peers (Palfrey, boyd [*sic*], & Sacco, 2010).

What is your own experience with gender differences in physical and relational aggression? See the Try It!

TRY IT!
Do Women and Men Differ in Their Responses?

During lunch break, Lydia purposefully sprays soda onto Julianne's new shirt. Now Julianne, a girl in rage, wishes to aggress against Lydia for what she has done. Given what you know about gender and aggression, try to write a scenario of how Julianne may go about accomplishing her goal. What type of aggression will she be using? What if Julianne were *Julian* — a boy? Would this change your predictions about the scenario? If so, how?

Learning to Behave Aggressively

Most of us take our cues from other people. If we want to know whether aggressive behavior is okay, we will look to see what others are doing or what others are saying about it—and whether they get away with it or are punished. We learn, almost unconsciously, what our culture's rules are and what the norms are for men and women. Either way, those situations can shape, direct, encourage, or suppress people's individual wishes to behave aggressively or peacefully.

Social-cognitive learning theory holds that we learn social behavior, from aggression to altruism, in large part by observing others and imitating them—a process called *observational learning*. But observational learning in human beings cannot be fully understood without taking into account the thought processes and perceptions of the learner; that's the "cognitive" part of social-cognitive learning theory (Mischel & Shoda, 1995). It's the reason that you and a friend can see the same vampire movie and one of you thinks it's stupid and the other thinks it's funny.

Social-Cognitive Learning Theory

The theory that people learn social behavior (e.g., aggression or altruism) in large part through observation and imitation of others and by cognitive processes such as plans, expectations, and beliefs

Children have never been very good at listening to their elders, but they have never failed to imitate them.

—JAMES BALDWIN, *NOBODY KNOWS MY NAME*

Children are especially susceptible to observational learning. In a classic series of experiments, Albert Bandura and his associates demonstrated the power of social learning on children's aggressive behavior (Bandura, Ross, & Ross, 1961, 1963). Their basic procedure was to have an adult knock around a plastic, air-filled Bobo doll, the kind that bounces back after it's been knocked down. The adult would smack the doll around with the palm of a hand, strike it with a mallet, kick it, and yell aggressive things at it. The kids were then allowed to play with the doll. In these experiments, the children imitated the aggressive adults and treated the doll in almost exactly the same ways, as you can see in Figure 12.2. Some of them went beyond mere imitation, coming up with inventive new forms of beating up the doll. Children who did not see the aggressive adult in action almost never unleashed any aggression against the hapless doll. This research offers strong support for the social learning of aggressive behavior—the power of watching and imitating the behavior of others.

In general, the more respected a person or institution is, the greater their influence as a role model. Brad Bushman and his colleagues (2007) explored the impact of religiously sanctioned stories of violence. They found that when a violent story was attributed to the Bible and when, in that story, God sanctioned the violence, the reader was more likely to behave aggressively afterward. The effect held for nonreligious as well as religious participants. Sports are another hallowed institution, in which the more aggressive players usually achieve the greatest fame and the highest salaries, and the more aggressive teams win more games. It usually doesn't pay to be a gentle soul. Famed baseball manager Leo Durocher once said, "Nice guys finish last," and the data bear him out. In professional hockey, those players most frequently sent to the penalty box for overly aggressive play also scored the most goals and earned the highest salaries (McCarthy & Kelly, 1978). To the extent that athletes serve as role models for children and adolescents, what is being modeled is that fame and fortune go hand in hand with excessive aggressiveness.

Figure 12.2 The Bobo Doll Experiment

Children learn aggressive behavior through imitation. In this classic study, the experimenter modeled some rather violent treatment of the doll—and the children imitated her perfectly.

Similarly, when children watch their parents or other adults they admire yelling, kicking, and acting in other aggressive ways, that is the behavior they will copy. One of the main predictors of whether women will commit physical aggression against their male partners, for example, is their having grown up in a household where they saw their mothers hitting their fathers (Testa et al., 2011).

What happens if we reverse things and expose children to nonaggressive models— to people who, when provoked, express themselves in a restrained, rational, pleasant manner? This question has been tested in several experiments (Baron, 1972; Donnerstein & Donnerstein, 1976; Vidyasagar & Mishra, 1993). Children first watched youngsters behaving peacefully even when provoked. Later, when the children were put in a situation in which they themselves were provoked, they were much less likely to respond aggressively than were children who had not seen the nonaggressive models.

Some Physiological Influences

It is hardly news that when people are drunk, hot, or in considerable pain, they are more likely to lash out at others, getting into fights and quarrels, than if they feel completely fine, sipping lemonade on a cool spring day. But why does the chance of aggression increase under these physical influences? Does it always?

THE EFFECTS OF ALCOHOL   As most college students know, alcohol is a social lubricant that lowers our inhibitions against acting in ways frowned on by society, including acts of aggression (Desmond, 1987; Taylor & Leonard, 1983). The link between alcohol and aggressive behavior has been well documented, and it appears even among people who have not been provoked and who do not usually behave aggressively when sober (Bailey & Taylor, 1991; Bushman & Cooper, 1990; Graham, Osgood, Wells, & Stockwell, 2006). This might explain why fistfights frequently break out in bars and nightclubs and why family violence is often associated with alcohol abuse.

Why can alcohol increase aggressive behavior? Alcohol reduces anxiety and lowers social inhibitions, making us less cautious than we usually are (MacDonald, Zanna, & Fong, 1996). But it is more than that. By impairing the part of the brain involved in planning and controlling behavior, alcohol also disrupts the way we usually process information (Bushman, 1997; Bushman & Cooper, 1990; Hanson, Medina, Padula, Tapert, & Brown, 2011). This is why intoxicated people often respond to the most obvious aspects of a social situation and tend to miss the subtleties. If you are sober and someone steps on your toe, you would notice that the person didn't do it on purpose. But if you were drunk, you might miss the subtlety of the situation and respond as if that person had purposely stomped on your foot. If you and the offender are males, you might slug him. This response is typical of the kinds of ambiguous situations that men tend to interpret as provocative, especially under the influence of alcohol (Pedersen, Vasquez, Bartholow, Grosvenor, & Truong, 2014). Laboratory experiments demonstrate that when individuals drink enough alcohol to make them legally drunk, they tend to respond more violently to provocations than do people who have ingested little or no alcohol (Bushman, 1997; Lipsey, Wilson, Cohen, & Derzon, 1997; Taylor & Leonard, 1983).

There is another way in which alcohol facilitates aggression, however, and this is through what has been called the "think-drink" effect: When people *expect* alcohol to have certain effects on them, it often does (Marlatt & Rohsenow, 1980). Indeed, when people expect that alcohol will "release" their aggressive impulses, they often do become more aggressive—even when they are drinking something nonalcoholic. In a study of 116 men ages 18 to 45, experimenters gave one-third of the men a nonalcoholic drink, one-third a drink targeting a modest blood alcohol level, and one-third a stronger drink targeting a high blood alcohol level. Within each of these three groups, the researchers manipulated the drinkers' expectancies of how much alcohol they were getting. They then measured the men's behavior toward a research

"Oh, that wasn't me talking, it was the alcohol."

Dana Fradon/The New Yorker Collection/ www.cartoonbank.com.

confederate who had behaved aggressively toward them. Remarkably, the actual quantity of alcohol that the men drank was less related to their aggressive behavior than their *expectations* were. The more alcohol the men believed they were drinking, the more aggressively they behaved toward the confederate (Bègue et al., 2009).

Of course, alcohol does have potent physiological effects on cognition and behavior. But those effects interact with what people have learned about alcohol, such as whether it provides an excuse to behave aggressively (or, as we will see, sexually) and how they expect to feel after imbibing (Davis & Loftus, 2004).

THE EFFECTS OF PAIN AND HEAT If an animal is in pain and cannot flee the scene, it will almost invariably attack; this is true of rats, mice, hamsters, foxes, monkeys, crayfish, snakes, raccoons, alligators, and a host of other creatures (Azrin, 1967; Hutchinson, 1983). In those circumstances, animals will attack members of their own species, members of different species, or anything else in sight, including stuffed dolls and tennis balls. Do you think this is true of human beings as well? You probably will say yes. Most of us feel a flash of irritation when we hit our thumb with a hammer and know the feeling of wanting to lash out at the nearest available target. Indeed, in a series of experiments, students who underwent the pain of having their hand immersed in very cold water were far more likely to act aggressively against other students than were those who had not suffered the pain (Berkowitz, 1983).

Other forms of bodily discomfort—such as heat, humidity, air pollution, crowds, and offensive odors—also lower the threshold for aggressive behavior (Stoff & Cairns, 1997). During the late 1960s and early 1970s, when tensions in the United States ran high over the war in Vietnam and the rise of the civil rights movement, national leaders worried about "the long, hot summer." The phrase was a code for the fear that the summer's heat would cause simmering tensions to explode. Their fears were justified. An analysis of disturbances in 79 cities between 1967 and 1971 found that riots were far more likely to occur on hot days than on cold ones (Carlsmith & Anderson, 1979) (see Figure 12.3).

Similarly, in major American cities from Houston, Texas, to Des Moines, Iowa, the hotter it is on a given day or a given average year, the greater the likelihood that violent crimes will occur (Anderson, 2012; Anderson, Anderson, Dorr, DeNeve, & Flanagan, 2000; Rotton & Cohn, 2004). Smaller "crimes" increase, too: In the desert city of Phoenix, Arizona, drivers in non–air-conditioned cars are more likely to honk their horns in traffic jams than drivers in air-conditioned cars (Kenrick & MacFarlane, 1986). Even on the baseball field, heat and hostility go together. In major league baseball games when the temperature rises above 90 degrees, significantly more batters are hit by pitched balls, and pitchers are more likely to intentionally retaliate against a batter when the pitcher's teammates have been hit by the opposing team earlier in the game (Larrick, Timmerman, Carton, & Abrevaya, 2011).

As you know by now, one must be cautious about interpreting events that take place outside the laboratory. The scientist in you might be tempted to ask whether increases in aggression are due to the temperature itself or merely to the fact that more people are apt to be outside (getting in one another's way) on hot days than on cold or rainy days. So how might we determine that it's the heat causing the aggression and not merely the greater opportunity for contact? We can bring the phenomenon into the laboratory. In one such experiment, students took the same test under different conditions: Some worked in a room at normal room temperature, while others worked in a room where the temperature reached 90 degrees (Griffitt & Veitch, 1971). The students in the hot room not only reported feeling more aggressive but also

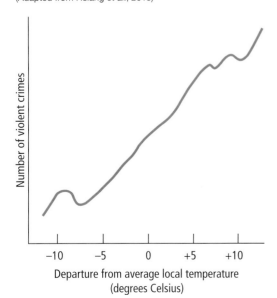

Figure 12.3 The Long, Hot Summer

Warm temperatures predict an increased likelihood of violent crime and other aggressive acts.

(Adapted from Hsiang et al., 2013)

Number of violent crimes

−10   −5   0   +5   +10

Departure from average local temperature
(degrees Celsius)

expressed more hostility toward a stranger whom they were asked to describe and evaluate. Similar results have been reported by a number of investigators (Anderson, 2012; Anderson et al., 2000; Rule, Taylor, & Dobbs, 1987).

If heat increases hostility, does that mean that global warming might have an effect on aggression as well? The answer appears to be yes. An analysis of 60 studies—including data going back to 10,000 B.C. and covering all world regions—found that warmer temperatures substantially increase the risk of many types of conflict, from domestic violence, murder, and rape to riots and civil wars (Hsiang, Burke, & Miguel, 2013). Craig Anderson (2012), the world's leading expert on the effects of climate on aggression, maintains that global warming produces a major increase in the rate of violent crime for three reasons. One involves the effects of uncomfortable heat itself on irritability and aggression. A second involves the indirect effects of global warming on the economic and social factors known to put children and adolescents at risk for becoming violent: poverty, poor prenatal and childhood nutrition, broken families, low IQ, growing up in violent neighborhoods, poor education, and living in a disorganized and unstable neighborhood. And a third involves the effects of rapid climate change on populations whose livelihoods and survival are at risk as a result of droughts, flooding, famine, and war.

REVIEW QUESTIONS

1. From a social-psychological perspective, a problem with evolutionary theories of aggression is that they fail to account for
   a. different levels of testosterone among men.
   b. different rates of aggression across cultures.
   c. genetic influences on behavior.
   d. differences between bonobos and chimpanzees.

2. Herding communities are known to emphasize aggressiveness and vigilance. This fosters a
   a. culture of cooperation.
   b. culture of honor.
   c. culture of adultery.
   d. culture of anger.

3. Which of the following statements about gender differences in aggression is true?
   a. In families, almost all acts of physical aggression are committed by men.
   b. Girls are more likely than boys to express aggressive feelings indirectly, as by shunning or slandering a target.
   c. Gender differences in physical aggression increase when men and women are insulted.
   d. Because violence is so rare in women, female suicide bombers are much crazier than males who carry out these attacks.

4. After watching his teenage brother beat up a classmate in a fistfight and walk away with the admiration of their friends, a little boy takes a swipe at another boy in the playground. He has acquired this behavior through a process of
   a. cognitive learning.
   b. parental support.
   c. playing violent video games.
   d. observational learning.

5. What does the "think-drink" effect refer to?
   a. If you think you'd like a drink, you'll get one.
   b. If you think alcohol releases your anger, it will.
   c. If you think alcohol is harmful, you won't drink.
   d. If you think alcohol is healthy, you'll drink too much.

See page 622 for the answers.

Social Situations and Aggression

12.2   What are some situational and social causes of aggression and sexual assault?

Imagine that your friend Kevin is driving you to the airport so that you can fly home for the Christmas holidays. Kevin has picked you up a bit later than you feel comfortable with; he accuses you of being overly anxious and assures you that he knows the route well and that you will arrive there with plenty of time to spare. Halfway to the airport, you are standing still in bumper-to-bumper traffic. Kevin assures you that there is plenty of time, but this time he sounds less confident.

Is road rage an inevitable outcome of frustration with fellow drivers? If so, how come not every driver gets as angry as this woman?

Frustration-Aggression Theory

The theory that frustration—the perception that you are being prevented from attaining a goal—increases the probability of an aggressive response

Many experiences in daily life are frustrating—and can lead to aggression.

After 10 more minutes, your palms are sweating. You open the car door and survey the road ahead: Not a car is moving as far ahead as you can see. You get back in the car, slam the door, and glare at Kevin. He smiles lamely and says, "How was I supposed to know there would be so much traffic?" Should he be prepared to duck?

Frustration and Aggression

As this all-too-familiar story suggests, frustration is a major cause of aggression. Frustration occurs when a person is thwarted on the way to an expected goal or gratification. All of us have felt frustrated from time to time—at least three or four times a week, if not three or four times a day! According to **frustration-aggression theory**, people's perception that they are being prevented from attaining a goal will increase the probability of an aggressive response (Dollard, Doob, Miller, Mowrer, & Sears, 1939). This is especially true when the frustration is unpleasant, unwelcome, and uncontrollable.

Several things can increase frustration and, accordingly, will increase the probability that some form of aggression will occur. One such factor involves your closeness to the goal or the object of your desire. The closer the goal, the greater the expectation of pleasure that is thwarted; the greater the expectation, the more likely the aggression. In one field experiment, a confederate cut in line in front of people who were waiting in a variety of places—for movie tickets, outside crowded restaurants, and at the checkout counter of a supermarket. On some occasions, the confederate cut in front of the second person in line; at other times, in front of the twelfth person. The results were clear: The people standing right behind the intruder were much more aggressive when the confederate cut into the second place in line (Harris, 1974).

However, frustration does not always produce aggression. Rather, it seems to produce anger or annoyance and a *readiness* to aggress if other things about the situation are conducive to aggressive behavior (Berkowitz, 1989, 1993; Gustafson, 1989). What are those other things? Well, an obvious one would be the size and strength of the person responsible for your frustration as well as that person's ability to retaliate. It is undoubtedly easier to become impatient and rude with an incompetent customer-service person who is miles away and has no idea who you are than to take out your anger against your frustrator if he turned out to be the middle linebacker of the Green Bay Packers and was staring you right in the face. Similarly, if the frustration is understandable, legitimate, and unintentional, the tendency to aggress will be reduced. In one experiment, when a confederate "unwittingly" sabotaged his teammates' effort to solve a problem because his hearing aid had stopped working, the teammates' resulting frustration did not lead to a measurable degree of aggression (Burnstein & Worchel, 1962).

We want to emphasize that frustration is not the same as deprivation: Children who don't have toys do not aggress more than children who do. In the toy experiment, frustration and aggression occurred because the children had every reason to expect to play with the toys, and their reasonable expectation was thwarted; this thwarting was what caused the children to behave destructively.

On a national scale also, thwarted expectations combined with frustration can produce riots and revolutions. Social scientists have found that it is often not *absolute* deprivation that creates anger and aggression but *relative* deprivation, which occurs when people see a discrepancy between what they have and what they expect to have (Moore, 1978). For example, in 1967 and 1968, nationwide race riots occurred in the middle of rising expectations and increased social spending to fight poverty. The most serious riots did not erupt in the geographic areas of greatest poverty; instead, they exploded in Los Angeles and Detroit, where things were not nearly as bad for African Americans as they were in most other large urban centers. But conditions were bad relative to the rioters' perception of how White people were doing and relative to the positive changes many African Americans had a right to expect.

A similar phenomenon occurred in Eastern Europe in 1991, when serious rebellion against the Soviet Union took place only after the government had loosened the chains controlling the population. And research on contemporary suicide bombers in the Middle East, including Mohamed Atta, who led the 9/11 attack on the World Trade Center, or the Tsarnaev brothers, who bombed the Boston marathon in 2013, shows that they usually have no psychopathology and are often quite educated and affluent (Krueger, 2007; Sageman, 2008; Silke, 2003). But they were motivated by anger over the perceived discrepancy between what they had and what they felt their nation and religion were entitled to. Thus, an important cause of aggression is relative deprivation: the perception that you (or your group) have less than you deserve, less than what you have been led to expect, or less than what people similar to you have.

> Evils which are patiently endured when they seem inevitable become intolerable when once the idea of escape from them is suggested.
> —ALEXIS DE TOCQUEVILLE

Provocation and Reciprocation

Suppose you are working at your part-time job behind the counter, flipping hamburgers in a crowded fast-food restaurant. Today, you are working harder than usual because the other short-order cook went home sick, and the customers are lining up at the counter, clamoring for their burgers. In your eagerness to speed up the process, you spin around too fast and knock over a large jar of pickles that smashes on the floor just as the boss enters the workplace. "Boy, are you clumsy!" he shouts. "I'm gonna dock your pay $10 for that one; grab a broom and clean up, you moron! I'll take over here!" You glare at him. You'd love to tell him what he can do with this lousy job.

Aggression frequently stems from the need to reciprocate after being provoked by aggressive behavior from another person. Although the Christian plea to "turn the other cheek" is wonderful advice, most people don't take it, as has been demonstrated in countless experiments in and out of the laboratory. In one experiment, participants prepared an advertisement for a new product; their ad was then evaluated and criticized by an accomplice of the experimenter. In one condition, the criticism, though strong, was done in a gentle and considerate manner ("I think there's a lot of room for improvement"); in the other condition, the criticism was given in an insulting manner ("I don't think you could be original if you tried"). When provided with an opportunity to retaliate, those people who were criticized harshly were far more likely to do so than those in the "gentle criticism" condition (Baron, 1988).

But even when provoked, people do not always reciprocate, as social-cognitive learning theory would predict. Why? Because we often pause to ask ourselves whether the provocation was intentional. When we are convinced it was unintentional or if there are mitigating circumstances, most of us will not reciprocate (Kremer & Stephens, 1983). But to curtail an aggressive response, we must be aware of those mitigating circumstances at the time of the provocation. In one study, students were insulted by the experimenter's assistant. Half of them were first told that the assistant was upset after receiving an unfair low grade on a chemistry exam; the other students received this information only after the insult was delivered. All subjects later had an opportunity to retaliate by choosing the level of unpleasant noise with which to zap the assistant. Those students who knew about the mitigating circumstances before being insulted delivered weaker bursts of noise (Johnson & Rule, 1986). Why the difference? At the time of the insult, the informed students simply did not take it personally and therefore felt no need to retaliate. This interpretation is bolstered by evidence of their physiological arousal: At the time of the insult, the heart rates of the insulted students did not increase as rapidly if they knew about the assistant's unhappy state of mind beforehand.

To help you identify your own triggers and responses to provocation, take this Try It!

TRY IT!

Insults and Aggression

Think about the last time you felt insulted by another person. Note down your answers to these questions:
- Who insulted you?
- What were the circumstances?
- Did you take it personally or not?

- How did you respond—with anger, patience, amusement, or something else?

How do your answers relate to the material you have just finished reading?

Weapons as Aggressive Cues

Certain stimuli seem to impel us to action. Is it conceivable that the mere presence of an aggressive stimulus—an object that is associated with aggressive responses—might increase the probability of aggression?

Weapons Effect

The increase in aggression that can occur because of the mere presence of a gun or other weapon

In a classic experiment, Leonard Berkowitz and Anthony Le Page (1967) purposely angered college students by insulting them. Some of the students were in a room in which a gun was left lying around (ostensibly from a previous experiment) and others in a room in which a neutral object (a badminton racket) was substituted for the gun. Participants were then given the opportunity to administer what they believed were electric shocks to a fellow college student. Those individuals who had been angered in the presence of the gun administered stronger electric shocks than those angered in the presence of the racket (see Figure 12.4). The presence of a gun seems to trigger—so to speak—an aggressive response when a person is already primed to respond that way because of frustration or anger (Anderson, Benjamin, & Bartholow, 1998).

This provocative finding, which has been replicated many times in the United States and Europe, is now referred to as the **weapons effect**—an increase in aggression that can occur because of the mere presence of a gun or other weapon (Frodi, 1975; Turner & Leyens, 1992). The effect is physiological as well as psychological: Male college students asked to interact with a gun for 15 minutes show higher testosterone levels than do students playing a children's game for the same amount of time (Klinesmith, Kasser, & McAndrew, 2006). Such findings point to a conclusion opposite to the familiar slogan often used by opponents of gun control, that "guns don't kill; people do." As Leonard Berkowitz (1981) put it, "The finger pulls the trigger, but the trigger may also be pulling the finger."

Violence, especially involving guns, is a major part of American society, so it is no wonder that it plays a major role in the expectations and fantasies of American children. When teenagers from the

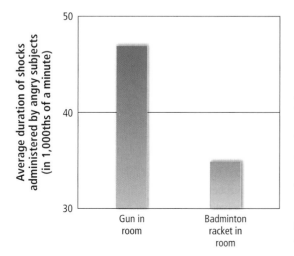

Figure 12.4 The Trigger Can Pull the Finger

Aggressive cues, such as weapons, tend to increase levels of aggression.

(Based on Berkowitz & Le Page, 1967)

United States and 10 other countries were asked to read stories involving conflict among people and to predict the outcome of the conflict, American teenagers were more likely than teenagers from other countries to anticipate a violent conclusion (Archer, 1994; Archer & McDaniel, 1995). And those conclusions were far more likely to be "lethal, gun-laden and merciless" (Archer, 1994).

Putting the Elements Together: The Case of Sexual Assault

One of the most troubling kinds of aggression is sexual assault, which can take many forms. Although "rape" is an upsetting word to many people, it is important to define it so that everyone agrees on what it means—and so that the law can reflect that meaning. (For example, the law used to exempt married men, who were legally allowed to have forcible sex with their wives.) In 2013, the Department of Justice revised the definition of *rape* to include the penetration of any bodily orifice with any part of the body or with any object, without the consent of the victim. Sexual assault is the broader term, including various other acts, but lack of consent remains the key criterion. In this section, we will consider how social psychologists draw on various kinds of evidence to help understand this phenomenon.

MOTIVATIONS FOR RAPE   Some men commit rape out of a desire to dominate, humiliate, or punish their victims. This motive is apparent among soldiers who rape captive women during war and then often kill them (Olujic, 1998) and among men who rape other men, usually by anal penetration (King & Woollett, 1997). The latter form of rape often occurs in youth gangs, where the intention is to humiliate rival gang members, and in prison, where the motive, in addition to the obvious sexual one, is to conquer and degrade the victim. Men can be sexually assaulted and raped by women also, although many men are ashamed to admit it (Stemple & Meyer, 2014).

When most people think of a "rapist," they imagine a violent stranger or a serial predator. Some rapists are exactly that. They are often unable to empathize with women, may feel hostility and contempt toward women, and feel entitled to have sexual relations with whatever woman they choose. This may be why sexual violence is often committed by high-status men, including sports heroes, high school and college athletic stars, powerful politicians, and celebrities, who could easily find consenting sexual partners. They equate feelings of power with sexuality, angrily accuse women of provoking them, and endorse rape myths, such as "women want to be raped" (Forbes, Adams-Curtis, Pakalka, & White, 2006; Malamuth, Linz, Heavey, Barnes, & Acker, 1995; Nunes, Hermann, & Ratcliffe, 2013; Thompson, Koss, Kingree, Goree, & Rice, 2011).

But the fact is that about 85% of all rapes or attempted rapes—being forced to engage in sexual acts against one's will—occur between people who know each other; the victim may even be having a relationship with the assailant (Koss, 2011; McMullin & White, 2006). Rape may occur as a result of *physical force* (having sex under actual or threatened violence), or through *incapacitation*: having sex with a victim who has been induced into a blackout with Rohypnol ("roofies"), who is drunk or otherwise drugged, or who has passed out (Breiding, Chen, & Black, 2014).

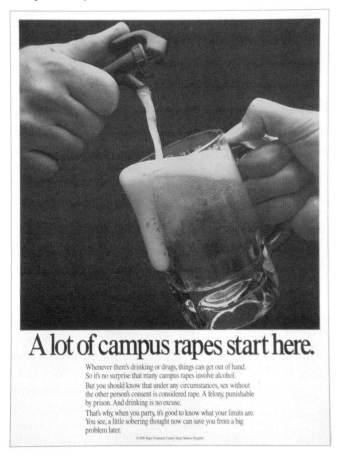

A lot of campus rapes start here.

Whenever there's drinking or drugs, things can get out of hand. So it's no surprise that many campus rapes involve alcohol. But you should know that under any circumstances, sex without the other person's consent is considered rape. A felony, punishable by prison. And drinking is no excuse.

That's why, when you party, it's good to know what your limits are. You see, a little sobering thought now can save you from a big problem later.

SEXUAL SCRIPTS AND THE PROBLEM OF CONSENT Everyone understands that a sexual predator who rapes a woman by overt force, threats of violence, or drugs used to render her unconscious has committed a serious crime. But what is going on with the large, additional numbers of women assaulted through "incapacitation" caused by their voluntary enjoyment of alcohol and other drugs? One answer may stem from the different **sexual scripts** that males and females learn as part of their gender roles in American society (Laumann & Gagnon, 1995). Sexual scripts vary according to one's culture, sexual orientation, ethnicity, and geographic region, and they change over time. One dominant script in America for young straight women and men is that the female's role is to resist the male's sexual advances and that the male's role is to be persistent. In films, TV, and magazines, male characters frequently act out this traditional male script; many female characters still play the part of "sex object" and are judged by their sexual conduct (Hust et al., 2014; Kim et al., 2007). (Sexual scripts for gay men and lesbians tend to be more flexible than heterosexual scripts because partners are not following traditional gender roles [Kurdek, 2005].)

Sexual Scripts

Sets of implicit rules that specify proper sexual behavior for a person in a given situation, varying with the person's gender, age, religion, social status, and peer group

The existence of scripts that dictate notions about appropriate sexual behavior may explain why many people are confused or angry over the meaning of the word *no*. The repeated message of antirape groups—"What part of 'no' don't you understand?"—seems obvious. Yet "no" can be as hard for women to say as it is for men to hear: For men who are following traditional sexual scripts, "no" occasionally means "maybe" or "in a little while." Some women, following scripts that say "It's okay to want sex but be careful about saying yes too soon or they'll call you a slut" agree with them. In one survey of high school students, although almost 100% of the males and females agreed that the man should stop his sexual advances as soon as the woman says no, nearly half of those same students also believed that when a woman says no, she doesn't always mean it (Monson, Langhinrichsen-Rohling, & Binderup, 2002). The resulting confusion may also explain why some college women feel they need to drink heavily as a prelude to sex (Cole, 2006; Howard, Griffin, & Boekeloo, 2008; Villalobos, Davis, & Leo, 2015). After all, if they are inebriated, they haven't said "yes," and if they haven't explicitly said "yes," no one can accuse them of being a slut.

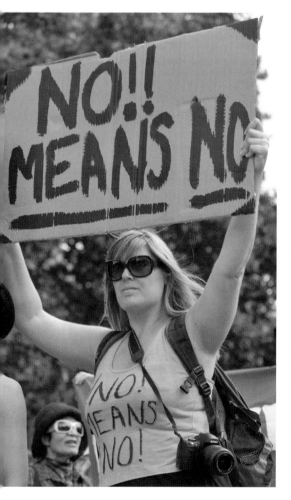

Further complicating matters is that most couples communicate sexual interest and intentions—including a wish *not* to have sex—indirectly through hints, body language, eye contact, and other nonverbal behaviors. The resulting "dance of ambiguity," write psychologist Deborah Davis and her colleagues, "serves to protect both parties": His ego is protected in case she says no, and she can accept without having to explicitly admit it's what she wants or reject the offer without rejecting the suitor. Unfortunately, this scripted dance can lead to what the researchers call "honest false testimony" by both sides: She really thinks he should have known to stop, and he really thinks she gave consent (Villalobos, Davis, & Leo, 2015). For example, studies find that sometimes young women, following a script that says they should "be nice" and not offend or anger the initiator, try to convey "no" without saying no—in nonverbal ways, such as by stepping a few inches back, not resisting but not agreeing, or pretending not to notice the man's advances. For their part, many men are motivated to overinterpret women's nonverbal actions as signs of sexual interest rather than friendly flirting—or just friendliness (La France, Henningssen, Oates, & Shaw, 2009).

As a result of all of these reasons for miscommunication, the sexes often disagree on whether a rape has even occurred (Hamby & Koss, 2003; Villalobos, Davis, & Leo, 2015; Yoffe, 2014). In a nationally representative survey of more than 3,000 Americans ages 18 to 59, nearly one-fourth of the women said that a man, usually a husband or boyfriend, had forced them to do something sexually that they did not want to do, yet only about 3% of the men said that they had ever forced a woman into a sexual act (Laumann, Gagnon, Michael, & Michaels, 1994).

PUTTING THE ELEMENTS TOGETHER   Think now about how the material you have read in this chapter might apply to misunderstandings about sexual consent—and how an understanding of these points might help to reduce date and acquaintance rape:

- The importance of cultural and social norms, which may dictate whether men feel entitled to assault an unwilling woman or whether that would be considered despicable behavior by their peers. Does a college, a fraternity, or a country endorse a "rape culture" that lets men off the hook, especially when the men are athletic heroes? "Boys will be boys," said an Indian politician after two teenage girls had been gang-raped and strangled—an attitude that is by no means unique to India.

- The power of perceptions, expectations, and beliefs, which mediate between an action and a response: "She is flirting with me—she obviously wants it"; "Am I allowed to say I want him to stop, even though we have gone pretty far?"

- The importance of observational learning in shaping what women and men learn is the "right" way to be sexual and popular—primarily through role models, peers, and media images and messages.

- Men don't get to say "testosterone made me do it." Testosterone does fuel aggressive and sexual inclinations (in both sexes) but not in a simple, uncontrollable way. As we saw, it is strongly affected by circumstances, learning, and culture.

- The "think-drink" effect and the role of alcohol in disinhibiting sexual and aggressive responses.

Perhaps the most important step toward reducing date and acquaintance rape is for both sexes to make sure that they are following a script that is in the same play. Women need to learn to express their wishes in a clear, direct way, without worrying about hurting the other person's feelings or making him angry. Most crucially, men need to understand that an intoxicated woman cannot legally consent to sex and that having sex with someone who is incapacitated, even if she chose to get drunk, is unacceptable.

REVIEW QUESTIONS

1. According to frustration-aggression theory,
   a. when people are frustrated, they almost always become aggressive.
   b. when people behave aggressively, they feel frustrated.
   c. frustration increases the likelihood of aggression.
   d. frustration caused by deprivation causes aggression.

2. Noah was counting on his roommate George to help him on moving day, but George never showed up, and Noah is plenty annoyed. What might he say to himself to reduce his wish to retaliate or tell George off?
   a. "That's just his personality; he's always thoughtless."
   b. "I'm a better person than he is."
   c. "I don't need his help anyway."
   d. "I bet George is under a lot of stress about exams this week."

3. What is relative deprivation?
   a. When people feel deprived of having close relatives they can count on
   b. When people live in poverty and feel they have no hope of improvement
   c. When people feel there is an unfair discrepancy between what they have and what they expect to get
   d. When some people earn relatively less than others for doing the same work

4. The "weapons effect" refers to the fact that
   a. many people have an emotional response to seeing a weapon.
   b. the mere presence of a gun can provoke an aggressive response.
   c. the mere presence of a gun makes people feel safer.
   d. some weapons provoke more aggression than others.

5. Which of the following statements about rape is true?

  a. Men who commit rape tend to be mentally ill.

  b. Most rapes are committed by men who attack unknown women.

  c. Most rapes are committed in the context of an acquaintance or ongoing relationship.

  d. Men cannot be raped.

6. According to research, sexual violence is often committed by high-status men. What are the reasons cited for this behavior?

  a. They equate feelings of power with sexuality; they accuse women of provoking them.

  b. Easy accessibility of consenting partners; sexual violence is the norm in high-status men.

  c. Friendly liaison with multiple women; contempt toward women.

  d. Sexual violence is the norm in high-status men; they equate power with sexuality.

7. "Honest false testimony" refers to

  a. an ambiguous situation where a woman thinks that the man should have known when to stop making sexual advances whereas the man thinks that the woman consented.

  b. a clear situation where both the man and the woman honestly make sexual advances toward each other.

  c. an ambiguous situation where a man thinks that the woman got the message to stop making sexual advances whereas the woman thinks the man consented.

  d. a clear situation where either the man or the woman makes sexual advances toward the other.

See page 622 for the answers.

Violence and the Media

12.3   Does observing violence increase violence?

Most American children are immersed in images of violence in television, movies, video games, pop and rap music, music videos, comics, and everywhere on the Internet. Immersed in it? They are marinated in it! They see an unending parade of murders, rapes, beatings, explosions, and bad guys committing brutal acts as well as good guys doing brutal things to catch them. Violence in films has more than doubled since 1950, and gun violence in PG-13-rated films has more than tripled since 1985. In fact, PG-13-rated films now contain as much violence as R-rated films (Bushman, Jamieson, Weitz, & Romer, 2013).

Many people—psychologists as well as the general public—are worried about all the mayhem that children and teenagers observe; they figure there *must* be significant consequences, starting with making guns seem cool and exciting (Bushman & Pollard-Sacks, 2014). For them, it is as obvious as the Bobo doll study that children imitate the violence they see on TV and in the movies and are otherwise affected emotionally by it. If *prosocial* videos can increase helpful behavior in children who watch them (see Chapter 11), surely the far more common antisocial, violent videos can increase antisocial, violent behavior.

For just as many others, though, this is a nonissue. How powerful can media violence be, they ask, if during the same years that gun violence in PG-13 movies tripled, real-world gun violence and overall violent crime by young people decreased to record lows? Besides, they add, media violence consists of cartoon-like stories and images that "everyone knows" are not real. Indeed, that was the reasoning behind the Supreme Court's 2011 decision that video games can be sold to minors no matter how violent the games are, including the popular *Mortal Kombat* and *Grand Theft Auto* series.

And so the debate rages on, and in this section we want to sort through the evidence on both sides and come to what we think is the most sensible resolution.

Studying the Effects of Media Violence

How would you study the possible effects of media violence? Countless stories in the news would seem to provide a compelling answer. For example, several years ago, a man drove his truck through the window of a crowded cafeteria in Killeen, Texas; emerged from the cab; and began shooting people at random, killing 22. In his pocket, police found a ticket stub to *The Fisher King*, a film depicting a deranged man firing a shotgun into a crowded bar, killing several people. Dylan Klebold and Eric Harris, the

Columbine killers, enjoyed the video game *Doom*, and the Columbine murders themselves spurred many copycat acts across the United States (Aronson, 2000). Two teenagers in Tennessee took their guns and went out sniping at passing cars on a freeway, killing one driver, because they wanted to act out their favorite video game, *Grand Theft Auto*. And then there is the case of a man who, having seen a movie showing women dancing on screen, became convinced that all women were immoral and deserved to die. He then committed four brutal rape-murders before he was caught. The film that set him off was *The Ten Commandments*.

But social scientists know that anecdotes, no matter how interesting they may be, are not sufficient to answer the question of the effects of media violence. It's too easy to cherry-pick your examples to make a case either way; you could select examples of kids who play *Grand Theft Auto* and then go off to do their homework and take piano lessons. Accordingly, researchers have conducted experimental and field studies to try to untangle this complicated question.

Does watching violent movies make children and adults numb to what violence really does?

EXPERIMENTAL STUDIES The beauty of the laboratory experiment is that it allows us to determine whether images in the media have any impact at all on the behavior of a random sample of people (see Chapter 2). In such an experiment, the situation is completely controlled; every factor can be held constant except for exposure to violence. The dependent variable, the participant's behavior, can likewise be carefully measured.

Most of the experimental evidence demonstrates that watching violence does increase the frequency of aggressive behavior, angry emotions, and hostile thoughts (Anderson et al., 2003, 2010; Cantor et al., 2001; Greitemeyer & McLatchie, 2011; Huesmann, Dubow, & Yang, 2013). In one early experiment, a group of children watched an extremely violent episode of a police drama. In a control condition, a similar group watched an exciting but nonviolent televised sporting event for the same length of time. Each child was then allowed to play in another room with a group of other children. Those who had watched the violent police drama later behaved far more aggressively with their playmates than did those who had watched the sporting event—the Bobo doll effect (Liebert & Baron, 1972). The research is not consistent, however, and some reviews of the experimental literature have found minimal or no effects (Ferguson, 2009, 2013; Sherry, 2001).

However, actively playing violent video games seems to have a stronger influence: Games that directly reward violence—for example, by awarding points or moving the player to the next level after a "kill"—are especially likely to increase feelings of hostility, aggressive thoughts, and aggressive acts, and this is true not only for American kids but also for those in other nations (Anderson et al., 2010; Carnagey & Anderson, 2005). A meta-analysis of 98 studies, with nearly 37,000 participants, found that both violent video games and prosocial video games have direct effects on their players (Greitemeyer & Mügge, 2014).

Another detrimental consequence of a diet of violence might be numbing people to difficult, violent, or unpleasant events (Thomas, 1982). In one of the earliest experiments on this issue, researchers measured the physiological responses of young men while they were watching a brutal and bloody boxing match (Cline, Croft, & Courrier, 1973). Those who had watched a lot of television in their daily lives seemed relatively indifferent to the mayhem in the ring; they showed little physiological evidence of excitement, anxiety, or other arousal. They were unmoved by the

Television has brought murder back into the home—where it belongs.
—ALFRED HITCHCOCK, 1965

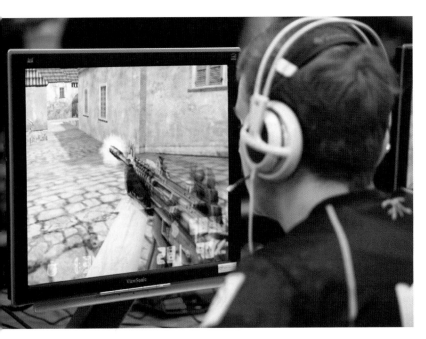

Does playing first-person shooter video games make people more violent or are people who have violent tendencies to begin with drawn to such games? Or could it be both?

violence. But those who watched relatively little TV showed major physiological arousal; the violence really agitated them. Today, that "brutal and bloody boxing match" from a 40-year-old experiment seems tame compared to *Game of Thrones* or *Sons of Anarchy*. The very fact that violence has had to increase in gruesomeness and intensity to get the same reaction from audiences that mild violence once did may be the perfect illustration of the numbing effects of a diet of violence.

Although psychic numbing may protect us from feeling upset, it may also have the unintended effect of increasing our indifference to real victims of violence and others who need help. In one field study, people who had just seen a violent movie took longer to come to the aid of a woman struggling to pick up her crutches than did people who had seen a nonviolent movie or people still waiting to see one of the two movies (Bushman & Anderson, 2009).

And if the person needing help is not "one of us," watch out. When you are playing a violent video game, you are likely to see yourself as the hero who is blasting those evil creatures out of existence. That's fun, as far as it goes, but some research suggests it can go further: Once players get in the habit of dehumanizing the "enemy," that habit can be carried over into how players come to regard real people, not just robots and life-like cartoons. In two experiments in England, researchers found that participants (male and female) who played a violent video game (*Lamers*) were later more likely to dehumanize immigrants to Britain, seeing them as somehow less human and deserving than native Britons, in contrast to the students who played a prosocial version of the game (*Lemmings*) or a neutral game (*Tetris*) (Greitemeyer & McLatchie, 2011; see also Greitemeyer, 2014).

Exposure to media violence, especially playing video games, may have these effects for three reasons: They increase physiological arousal and excitement, they trigger an automatic tendency to imitate the hostile or violent characters, and they *prime* existing aggressive ideas and expectations, making people more likely to act on them (Anderson et al., 2003). Movies and games also model social *scripts*, approved ways of behaving when we are frustrated, angry, or hurt.

LONGITUDINAL STUDIES Taken together, these experiments show that under controlled conditions, media violence has an impact on children and teenagers. The lab allows us to demonstrate that something of significance is happening, but it has a major limitation: Experiments cannot begin to capture the effects on a person who plays video games 20 or 30 hours a week and lives on a steady diet of action and horror films over weeks, months, and years.

To investigate that effect, we need to use longitudinal studies in which children are followed for a year or longer. The researcher has less control over the factors being studied, but it is a better way of determining the effects of what a child is *really* being exposed to. In addition, unlike most laboratory experiments that must use artificial measures of aggression (such as administering fake electric shocks or loud noises to the victim), longitudinal studies can examine seriously aggressive behavior. The disadvantage of this method is that people's lives are full of many other factors that can enhance or mitigate the effects of media violence.

Longitudinal research finds that the more violence children watch, the more aggressively they behave later as teenagers and young adults (Anderson et al., 2003;

Eron, 1987, 2001). For example, one study followed more than 700 families over a period of 17 years. The amount of time spent watching television during adolescence and early adulthood was strongly related to the likelihood of later committing violent acts against others, including assault. This association was significant regardless of parental education, family income, and extent of neighborhood violence (Johnson, Cohen, Smailes, Kasen & Brook, 2002). A more recent study followed 430 elementary-age children in the third to fifth grades over the course of a school year. The investigators measured three types of aggression—verbal, relational, and physical—and exposure to violence in television, movies, and video games. They measured both aggressive and prosocial behaviors in the children twice during the year, interviewing the children's peers and teachers as well as observing the children directly. They found that the children's consumption of media violence early in the school year predicted higher rates of all three kinds of aggression (verbal, relational, and physical) and less prosocial behavior later in the year (Gentile, Coyne, & Walsh, 2011).

The Problem of Determining Cause and Effect

Longitudinal studies find another consequence of watching a heavy dose of media violence: the magnification of danger. If I am watching all this murder and mayhem on the home screen, wouldn't it be logical for me to conclude that it isn't safe to leave the house, especially after dark? That is exactly what many heavy viewers do conclude. Adolescents and adults who watch TV for more than 4 hours per day are more likely than people who watch less than 2 hours per day to have an exaggerated view of the degree of violence taking place outside their own homes, and they have a much greater fear of being personally assaulted (Gerbner, Gross, Morgan, Signorielli, & Shanahan, 2002).

Now, it is possible that watching violence made them fearful. But it is just as likely that they spend a lot of time indoors because they think there is danger in the streets. Then, being at home with nothing to do, they watch a lot of television. As this example illustrates, the greatest challenge involved in trying to interpret the data in most nonexperimental longitudinal studies and survey research is teasing apart cause and effect. The usual assumption has been that watching violence makes people more aggressive, but aggressive people are also drawn to watching violence. Moreover, another entirely independent factor may be causing both. Some children are born with a mental or emotional predisposition toward violence; or learn it as toddlers from the way they are treated by abusive parents or siblings; or in other ways develop aggressiveness as a personality trait. In turn, this trait or predisposition manifests itself in both their aggressive behavior *and* their liking for watching violence or playing aggressive games (Bushman, 1995; Ferguson, 2013).

In an experiment investigating the interaction between temperament and exposure to violence, children watched either a film depicting a great deal of police violence or an exciting but nonviolent film about bike racing. They then played a game of floor hockey. Watching the violent film did increase the number of aggressive acts the children committed during the hockey game—but primarily by those who had previously been rated as highly aggressive by their teachers. These kids hit others with their sticks, threw elbows, and yelled aggressive things at their opponents to a much greater extent than did either the kids rated as nonaggressive who had also watched the violent film or the kids rated as aggressive who had watched the nonviolent film (Josephson, 1987).

Likewise, a few longitudinal studies have shown that exposure to violence in media or video games has the strongest relationship in children who are already predisposed to violence (Anderson & Dill, 2000). Thus, it may be that watching media violence merely serves to give them permission to express their aggressive inclinations (Ferguson & Kilburn, 2009). The same conclusions apply to the research on violent pornography (in contrast to nonviolent erotica). Meta-analyses repeatedly conclude that although there is, for men, a positive correlation between watching violent pornography and hostile, aggressive attitudes toward women, that association is largely due to men who already have high levels of hostility toward women and are predisposed to sexual aggression (Malamuth, Hald, & Koss, 2012).

Taking all this research together, we conclude that frequent exposure to violent media, especially in the form of violent video games, does have an impact on average children and adolescents, but the impact is greatest on those who are already prone to violent behavior. Obviously, most people do not become motivated to behave aggressively or commit an act of violence as a result of what they observe. As social-cognitive learning theory predicts, people's interpretation of what they are watching, their personality dispositions, and the social context can all affect how they respond (Feshbach & Tangney, 2008). Children and teens watch many different programs and movies and have many models to observe besides those they see in the media, including parents and peers. But the fact that some people *are* influenced by violent entertainments, with tragic results, cannot be denied.

One of the leading researchers who study media violence argues that it is "time to move forward with a more sophisticated perspective on media effects that focuses less on moral objections to certain content and more on media consumers and their motivations" (Ferguson, 2014). Given the research just discussed, we think there are at least five distinct reactions that explain why exposure to violence might increase aggression in those vulnerable "media consumers":

1. *If they can do it, so can I.*   When people see characters behaving violently, it may weaken their previously learned inhibitions against violent behavior.

2. *Oh, so that's how you do it!*   When people see characters behaving violently, it might trigger imitation, providing them with ideas as to how they might go about it.

3. *Those feelings I am having must be real anger rather than merely my reaction to a stressful day.*   Watching violence may put people more in touch with their feelings of anger and make an aggressive response more likely through priming. Having recently viewed violence, someone might interpret his or her own feelings of mild irritation as intense anger and then be more likely to lash out.

4. *Ho-hum, another brutal beating. What's on the other channel?*   Watching a lot of mayhem seems to reduce both our sense of horror about violence and our sympathy for the victims, making it easier for us to live with violence and perhaps easier for us to act aggressively.

5. *I had better get him before he gets me!*   If watching a lot of television makes people think the world is a dangerous place, they might be more apt to be hostile to a stranger who approaches them on the street.

Finally, however, let's put this issue in larger perspective. The effects of the media pale in comparison to the biological, social, economic, and psychological factors that are far more powerful predictors of aggressive behavior: a child's genetic predispositions to violence, low feelings of self-control, being socially rejected by peers (which we will discuss further at the end of this chapter), criminal opportunity, being the victim of childhood physical abuse, being in a peer group that endorses and encourages violence, and living in a community where aggression is a way of life (Crescioni & Baumeister, 2009; Ferguson & Kilburn, 2009).

REVIEW QUESTIONS

1. Which of the following statements is true?
   a. Watching violent shows makes most young children likely to imitate them.
   b. Watching violent shows makes some children more likely to imitate them.
   c. Playing violent video games has less of an impact on children than watching violence on TV or in the movies does.
   d. Viewing television violence has no effect on people's response to others in trouble.

2. Once people playing violent video games get into the habit of "dehumanizing the enemy," they may dehumanize people in real life. What is a possible explanation for this?
   a. The player is so engrossed in the virtual world that he/she starts perceiving real people as video game characters.
   b. Violent video games tend to trigger an automatic tendency to imitate the aggressive characters.
   c. All video games trigger a sense of anger in the player, which is manifested in real life.
   d. Violent video games decrease physiological arousal and excitement.

3. Sixteen-years-old Mike often watches violence on television at home. He does not like to venture out after dark. What could be a likely reason?
   a. Mike is aware of his tendency to be violent after dark.
   b. People are more likely to watch violent shows after sunset.
   c. Mike wants to stay away from reality.
   d. Mike has an exaggerated view of the degree of violence taking place outside his house.

4. What does research on children indicate about the relationship between temperament and exposure to violence?
   a. Hyperactive children are drawn more toward violent films.
   b. Highly aggressive children tend to behave violently after watching violent media.
   c. Watching violent media makes children highly aggressive.
   d. Violent media has the same impact on all children.

5. Which of the following is not a reason given by researchers to explain why exposure to violence might increase aggressive behavior?
   a. Observing someone else acting violently may weaken people's inhibitions against violence.
   b. Observing someone else acting violently may trigger an urge to imitate their behavior.
   c. Watching too much violence reduces one's sense of horror about violence and sympathy for victims.
   d. Watching violent movies equips the viewer with essential skills needed to be aggressive.

See page 622 for the answers.

How to Decrease Aggression

12.4   How can aggression be diminished?

"Stop hitting your brother!" "Turn off the TV and go to your room *right now!*" Most parents, trying to curb the aggressive behavior of their children, use some form of punishment. Some deny privileges; others shout, threaten, or use force, believing in the old saying, "Spare the rod and spoil the child." How well does punishment work? On the one hand, you might think that punishing any behavior would reduce its frequency. On the other hand, if the punishment takes the form of an aggressive act, parents who are administering the penalty are actually modeling aggressive behavior—thereby inducing their child to imitate them.

Does Punishing Aggression Reduce Aggression?

Let's consider the complexities of punishment. As we discussed in Chapter 6, several experiments with preschoolers demonstrated that the threat of relatively severe punishment for committing a transgression does not make the transgression less appealing to the child. But the threat of *mild* punishment, of a degree just powerful enough to get the child to stop the undesired activity temporarily, leads the child to try to justify his or her restraint and, as a result, can make the behavior less appealing (Aronson & Carlsmith, 1963; Freedman, 1965).

However, the use of *harsh* punishments to reduce aggression usually backfires; it may put a halt to a child's aggressive behavior in the short term, but children who are

Many tired, exasperated parents punish their children's misbehavior by shouting at them or hitting or grabbing them. But this usually backfires, making the child angry and resentful without stopping the misbehavior. On the contrary, it teaches children what to do when they are tired and exasperated—hit someone.

All punishment is mischief; all punishment itself is evil.

—JEREMY BENTHAM, *PRINCIPLES OF MORALS AND LEGISLATION*, 1789

physically punished tend to become more aggressive and anti-social over time (Durrant & Ensom, 2012). Harsh punishments backfire for several other reasons, too. People may shout things they don't mean or, out of frustration, use severe methods to try to control the behavior of their children. The target of all this noise and abuse is then likely to respond with anxiety or anger rather than with a reaction of "Thanks, I'd better correct that aggressive habit you don't like." In some cases, angry attention may be just what the offender is hoping to get. If a mother yells at her daughter who is throwing a tantrum, the very act of yelling may give her what she wants, namely, a reaction from Mom. More seriously, extreme punishment—physical abuse—is a risk factor in children for the development of depression, low self-esteem, violent behavior, and many other problems (Gershoff, 2002; Widom, DuMont, & Czaja, 2007). And, finally, punishment often fails because it tells the target what not to do, but it does not communicate what the person should do. Spanking a little boy for hitting his sister will not teach him to play cooperatively with her.

Because of these drawbacks, most psychologists believe that harsh punishment is a poor way to eliminate aggressive or other unwanted behavior. In certain cases, for example, when a bully is hitting a classmate, temporary physical restraint is usually called for. But is that the best strategy to keep a bully from behaving aggressively when the adult leaves the room?

USING PUNISHMENT ON VIOLENT ADULTS   The criminal justice system of most cultures administers harsh punishments both as retribution and as a means of deterring violent crimes like murder, manslaughter, and rape. Does the threat of harsh punishments make such crimes less likely? Do people who are about to commit violent crimes say to themselves, "I'd better not do this because if I get caught, I'm going to jail for a long time; I might even be executed"?

Laboratory experiments indicate that punishment can indeed act as a deterrent but only if two conditions are met: Punishment must be (a) prompt and (b) certain (Bower & Hilgard, 1981). It must follow quickly after the aggression occurred, and it must be unavoidable. In the real world, these conditions are almost never met. In most American cities, the probability that a person who commits a violent crime will be apprehended, charged, tried, and convicted is not high. Given the volume of cases in our courts, punishment is delayed by months or even years. Because many things influence crime rates—the proportion of young versus older people in the population, poverty levels, drug policies, discriminatory arrest patterns—the relationship between incarceration rates and crime rates in the United States varies considerably from state to state (King, Maurer, & Young, 2005). Consequently, in the complex world of criminal justice, severe punishment is unlikely to have the kind of deterrent effect that it does in the controlled conditions of the laboratory.

Given these realities, severe punishment is not likely to deter violent crime. Countries that invoke the death penalty for murder do not have fewer murders per capita than those without it. American states that have abolished the death penalty have not had an increase in capital crimes, as some experts predicted (Archer, 1994; Nathanson, 1987). A natural experiment occurred in the United States during a period that began with a national hiatus on the death penalty, resulting from a Supreme Court ruling that it constituted cruel and unusual punishment, and ended with the Court's reversal of that ruling in 1976. There was no indication that the return to capital punishment produced a decrease in homicides (Peterson & Bailey, 1988). Indeed, a study by the National Academy of Sciences demonstrated once again that consistency and certainty of punishment were far more effective deterrents of violent behavior than was severe punishment, including the death penalty (Berkowitz, 1993).

Catharsis and Aggression

Conventional wisdom suggests that one way to reduce feelings of aggression is to do something aggressive. "Get it out of your system" has been common advice for decades: If you are feeling angry, yell, scream, curse, throw a dish at the wall; express the anger, and it won't build up into something uncontrollable. This belief stems from Sigmund Freud's psychoanalytic notion of **catharsis** (Dollard, Doob, Miller, Mowrer, & Sears, 1939; Freud, 1933). Freud held a "hydraulic" idea of aggressive impulses: Unless people were allowed to express ("sublimate") their aggression in harmless or constructive ways, he believed, their aggressive energy would be dammed up, pressure would build, and the energy would seek an outlet, either exploding into acts of extreme violence or manifesting itself as symptoms of mental illness.

Unfortunately, Freud's theory of catharsis has been greatly oversimplified into the notion that people should vent their anger or they will suffer physically and emotionally; by venting that anger, they will become less likely to commit aggressive acts in the future. When we are feeling frustrated or angry, many of us do temporarily feel less tense after blowing off steam by yelling, cursing, or perhaps kicking the sofa. But do any of those actions reduce the chance that we will commit further aggression? Does the notion of catharsis square with the data?

THE EFFECTS OF AGGRESSIVE ACTS ON SUBSEQUENT AGGRESSION Following Freud, many psychoanalysts believed that playing competitive games served as a harmless outlet for aggressive energies. But they were wrong. In fact, the reverse is true: Competitive games often make participants and observers *more* aggressive.

In one demonstration of this fact, the hostility levels of high school football players were measured 1 week before the football season began and 1 week after it ended. If the intense competitiveness and aggressive behavior that are part of playing football serve to reduce the tension caused by pent-up aggression, the players would be expected to show a decline in hostility over the course of the season. Instead, the results showed that feelings of hostility *increased* significantly (Patterson, 1974).

What about watching aggressive games? Will that reduce aggressive behavior? A Canadian sports psychologist tested this proposition by measuring the hostility of spectators at an especially violent hockey game (Russell, 1983). As the game progressed, the spectators became increasingly belligerent; toward the end of the final period, their level of hostility was extremely high and did not return to the pregame level until several hours after the game was over. Similar results have been found among spectators at football games and wrestling matches (Arms, Russell, & Sandilands, 1979; Branscombe & Wann, 1992; Goldstein & Arms, 1971). As with participating in an aggressive sport, watching one also increases aggressive behavior.

Finally, does direct aggression against the source of your anger reduce further aggression? Again, the answer is no (Geen & Quanty, 1977). When people commit acts of aggression, such acts increase the tendency toward future aggression. In an early experiment, college students were paired with another student who was actually a confederate of the experimenters (Geen, Stonner, & Shope, 1975). First, the student was angered by the confederate; during this phase, which involved the exchanging of opinions on various issues, the student was instructed to give an electric shock to the confederate each time the confederate disagreed. (The shocks, of course, were phony.) Next, during a bogus study of "the effects of punishment on learning," the student

Catharsis

The notion that "blowing off steam"—by behaving aggressively or watching others do so—relieves built-up anger and aggressive energy and hence reduces the likelihood of further aggressive behavior

Contrary to the catharsis hypothesis, many fans who watch aggressive sports do not become less aggressive; they may become more aggressive than if they hadn't watched at all.

acted as a teacher while the confederate served as a learner. On the first learning task, some of the students were required to deliver electric shocks to the confederate each time he made a mistake; others merely recorded his errors. On the next task, all the students were given the opportunity to deliver shocks. If a cathartic effect were operating, we would expect the students who had previously given shocks to the confederate to administer fewer and weaker shocks the second time. This didn't happen; in fact, those students who had previously delivered shocks to the confederate expressed even greater aggression when given the subsequent opportunity to attack him.

Outside the lab, in the real world, we see the same phenomenon: Verbal acts of aggression are followed by more of the same. Many people feel worse, both physically and mentally, after an angry confrontation. When people brood and ruminate about their anger, talk to others incessantly about how angry they are, or ventilate their feelings in hostile acts, their blood pressure shoots up, they often feel angrier, and they behave even *more* aggressively later than if they had just let their feelings of anger subside (Bushman, Bonacci, Pedersen, Vasquez, & Miller, 2005). Conversely, when people learn to control their tempers and express anger constructively, they usually feel better, not worse; they feel calmer, not angrier. All in all, the weight of the evidence does not support the catharsis hypothesis (Tavris, 1989).

BLAMING THE VICTIM OF OUR AGGRESSION   Imagine yourself in the experiments just described. After you've administered what you think are shocks to another person or have expressed hostility toward someone you dislike, it becomes easier to do so a second time. Aggressing the first time can reduce your inhibitions against doing it again; in a sense, the aggression is legitimized.

Does this sound familiar? It should. Harming someone sets in motion cognitive processes that are aimed at justifying the act of cruelty. (See Chapter 6.) When you hurt another person, you experience cognitive dissonance: The cognition "I hurt Charlie" is dissonant with the cognition "I am a decent, kind person." A good way for you to reduce dissonance is to convince yourself that hurting Charlie was not a bad thing to do. You can accomplish this by ignoring Charlie's virtues and emphasizing his faults, convincing yourself that Charlie is a bad person who deserved to be hurt. And you would be especially likely to reduce dissonance this way if Charlie were an innocent victim of your aggression. In the experiments described in Chapter 6, participants inflicted either psychological or physical harm on an innocent person who had not hurt them (Davis & Jones, 1960; Glass, 1964). Participants then persuaded themselves that their victims were not nice people and therefore deserved what they got. This certainly reduces dissonance, but it also sets the stage for further aggression because once a person has succeeded in finding reasons to dislike someone, it is easier to harm that victim again.

What happens, though, if the victim isn't totally innocent? What if the victim has done something that did hurt or disturb you and therefore, in your opinion, deserves your retaliation? Here the situation becomes more complex and more interesting. Consider the results of one of the first experiments designed to test the catharsis hypothesis (Kahn, 1966). A young man, posing as a medical technician, took physiological measurements from college students. As he did, he made derogatory remarks about the students, which naturally annoyed them. In one experimental condition, the participants were allowed to vent their hostility by expressing their feelings about the technician to his employer—an action that looked as though it would get the technician into serious trouble, perhaps even cost him his job. In another condition, participants did not have the opportunity to complain about the person who had aroused their anger. Those who were allowed to complain subsequently disliked the technician more than did those who were blocked from expressing their irritation. In other words, expressing aggression did not "get it out of their systems"; rather, it tended to *increase* hostility—even when the target was not simply an innocent victim.

These results suggest that when people are angered, they frequently respond with overkill. In this case, costing the technician his job was much more devastating than the minor offense the man committed with his insult. The overreaction, in turn, produces dissonance in much the same way that hurting an innocent person does: If there is a major discrepancy between what the person did to you and the force of your retaliation, you must justify that discrepancy by deciding that the object of your wrath really did something awful to warrant it.

What Are We Supposed to Do with Our Anger?

If aggression leads to self-justification, which in turn breeds more aggression, what should we do with our angry feelings toward someone? Stifling anger, sulking around the house, and hoping the other person will read our mind doesn't seem to be a good solution, and neither are brooding and ruminating by ourselves, which just prolong and intensify the anger (Bushman et al., 2005; Rusting & Nolen-Hoeksema, 1998). But if keeping our feelings bottled up and expressing them are both harmful, what is the alternative?

"It's truly remarkable, Louis, thirty-seven years next Tuesday and never a cross word between us."

Charles Barsotti/The New Yorker Collection/The Cartoon Bank

First, it is possible to control anger by actively enabling it to dissipate. *Actively enabling* means using such simple devices as counting to 10 (or 100!) before shooting your mouth off. Taking deep breaths or getting involved in a pleasant, distracting activity (working on a crossword puzzle, taking a bike ride, or even doing a good deed) are active ways of enabling the anger to fade away. If this advice sounds suspiciously like something your grandmother could have told you, well, that's because it is! Your grandmother often knows what she is talking about. But there is more to anger than merely controlling it, as you will see.

VENTING VERSUS SELF-AWARENESS   Dissipating anger is not always best for you or for a relationship. If your close friend or partner does something that makes you angry, you may want to express that anger in a way that helps you gain insight into yourself and the dynamics of the relationship. You may also wish to express yourself in a way that solves the problem without escalating it by arousing anger in the other person. But for that to happen, you must express your feelings in a way that is neither hostile nor demeaning.

You can do this (after counting to 10) by calmly stating that you are feeling angry and describing, nonjudgmentally, what you believe the other person did to bring about those feelings. Such a statement in itself will probably make you feel better to have "cleared the air," and because you haven't harmed the target of your anger with verbal or physical abuse, your response will not set in motion the cognitive processes that would lead you to justify your behavior by ridiculing your friend or escalating the argument. It is important that you speak in a way that does not cause your listener to become defensive or counterattack ("You're mad at me? Well, let me tell you where *you're* wrong!"). Instead, you want to speak in a way that invites problem solving ("Look, we seem to have different notions about housework standards. Can we figure out how to resolve this so that I don't get angry about your 'compulsive neatness' and you don't get angry with my being a 'slob'?"). When such feelings are expressed between friends or partners in a straightforward, open, nonpunitive manner, greater mutual understanding and a strengthening of the friendship can result (Christensen, Doss, & Jacobson, 2014).

Although it is probably best to reveal your anger to the friend who provoked it—at least if you are hoping to resolve the problem between you—sometimes the target of your anger is unavailable. Perhaps the person did something to you many years ago, or he or she has died or moved away. Then, research finds, it can be helpful to write down your feelings in a journal. In experiments with people undergoing traumatic events or who had been carrying a burdensome secret they had never shared with anyone, those who were instructed simply to write their "deepest thoughts and feelings" about the event or the secret felt healthier and even had fewer physical illnesses 6 months to a year later than did people who suffered in silence, who wrote about trivial topics, or who wrote about the details of the traumatic events without revealing their own underlying feelings. The benefits of "opening up" are due not to the venting of feeling but primarily to the insights and self-awareness that usually accompany such self-disclosure (Pennebaker, 1990, 2002). For example, one young woman realized that she had been carrying a lot of anger since her childhood over something another child had done to her. When she saw what she had written about the incident, she realized, "My god, we were both just kids." To see whether this technique can help you let go of anger or shame over an unexpressed experience or secret, take the Try It!

TRY IT!
Controlling Your Anger

Are you feeling angry about a personal matter in your life? Try to write your "deepest thoughts and feelings" about the event that has distressed you. Don't censor your feelings or thoughts.

Do this for 20 minutes a day for a few days and then reread what you have written. Can you see the situation differently? Do solutions offer themselves that you hadn't thought of?

TRAINING IN COMMUNICATION AND PROBLEM-SOLVING SKILLS Feeling angry is part of being human. The problem is not anger itself but the expression of anger in harmful ways. Yet we are not born knowing how to express anger or annoyance constructively and nonviolently; we have to learn the right skills. In most societies, it is precisely the people who lack those social skills who are most prone to violent solutions to problems in relationships (Langhinrichsen-Rohling et al., 2012). One way to reduce aggression, then, is to teach people such techniques as how to communicate anger or criticism in constructive ways, how to negotiate and compromise when conflicts arise, and how to apologize when they need to (Christensen et al., 2014).

In a classic experiment, children were allowed to play in groups of four (Davitz, 1952). Some of these groups were taught constructive ways to relate to one another and were rewarded for such behavior; others were rewarded for aggressive or competitive behavior. Next, the children were deliberately frustrated: They were told that they would see some entertaining movies and would be allowed to have fun. The experimenter began to show a movie and hand out candy bars, but then he abruptly stopped the movie at the point of highest interest and took the candy bars away. Now the children were allowed to play freely as the researchers watched. The results? Children who had been taught constructive ways of behaving when they were frustrated or angry were far less aggressive than children in the other group. Many elementary and secondary schools now train students to use nonaggressive strategies for resolving conflict, along with problem-solving skills, emotional control, and conflict resolution (Eargle, Guerra, & Tolan, 1994; Reading, 2008; Wilson & Lipsey, 2007).

Do you remember our discussion of men in "cultures of honor" and how their testosterone levels increase when the men perceive they have been insulted? Even this apparently ingrained response can be permanently modified through education and skills training. For example, in one major longitudinal study, kindergarten boys who were already showing high levels of aggression were randomly assigned to either a 10-year intervention or a control group. The intervention included teaching them to feel more *competent* in managing their emotions, getting along with peers, and succeeding in school. At age 26, more than 10 years after the intervention was over, the young men were brought into a laboratory, where they played a game with a (fictitious) partner who provoked them to anger by stealing points from them. Those who had been in the intervention not only behaved less aggressively when given the chance to retaliate but even showed reduced testosterone reactivity to the provocation (Carré, Iselin, Welker, Hariri, & Dodge, 2014).

What if you are not the person who is feeling angry, but the one who caused it in someone else? How should you apologize in a way that won't make the other person even angrier? Should you say, "Hey, lighten up, it was no big deal!" or "Look, I'm really sorry, I screwed up—let me make it up to you"? Many experiments find that your friend would become even angrier in the first case but not in the second (Baron, 1988, 1990; Ohbuchi & Sato, 1994; Weiner, Amirkhan, Folkes, & Verette, 1987). Typically, any apology sincerely given and in which the perpetrator takes full responsibility is effective. Notice the "sincerely" part and the "full responsibility" part. The bland, token apologies offered by many public figures or corporate leaders when they've been caught doing something illegal or immoral don't count (Smith, 2014).

Of course, the offender must believe that an apology is even necessary, and here we see a gender difference. In a study in which young women and men kept daily diaries noting whether they committed an offense or experienced one, the researchers found that men simply have a higher threshold for what constitutes an offensive action warranting an apology. When everyone was asked to evaluate actual offenses they had experienced in the past or come up with imaginary ones, again the men rated them all as being less severe than women did. You can imagine the unfortunate consequences of this discrepancy in close relationships: A woman might feel angry or slighted that her partner doesn't even notice an offense that she thinks is serious enough to warrant an apology, and the man might feel angry that she is being oversensitive and thin-skinned (Schumann & Ross, 2010).

COUNTERING DEHUMANIZATION BY BUILDING EMPATHY Picture the following scene: A long line of cars is stopped at a traffic light at a busy intersection; the light turns green, and the lead car hesitates for 10 seconds. What happens? Almost inevitably, there will be an eruption of horn honking. In one experiment, when the lead car failed to move after the light turned green, almost 90% of the drivers of the second car honked their horns angrily (Baron, 1976). But if, while the light was still red, a pedestrian was hobbling across the street on crutches, only 57% of the drivers honked their horns. Seeing a person on crutches evoked feelings of empathy, which infused the consciousness of the potential horn honkers and decreased their urge to be aggressive.

As we saw, most people find it difficult to inflict pain on a stranger unless they can find a way to justify it, and the most common way of justifying it is to dehumanize the victim (Caselman, 2007). By building empathy among people, aggressive acts should be more difficult to commit. The research data lend strong

Children who are taught to put themselves in others' shoes often have higher self-esteem, are more generous, and are less aggressive than children who lack skills of empathy.

support to this contention. In one study, students who had been trained to empathize—that is, to take the perspective of the other person—behaved far less aggressively toward that person than did students who had not received the training (Richardson, Hammock, Smith, & Gardener, 1994). In a similar study, Japanese students were told to shock another student as part of an alleged learning experiment (Ohbuchi, Ohno, & Mukai, 1993). In one condition, the "victims" first revealed something personal about themselves; in the other condition, they were not given this opportunity. Participants gave weaker shocks to the victim who had revealed personal information. It's harder to harm a stranger if you have made a personal connection with that person, and this is true whether the stranger is your neighbor, a homeless person, a sales clerk, or a civilian enemy.

Norma Feshbach (1989, 1997), who has pioneered the teaching of empathy in elementary schools, designed a 30-hour empathy-training program for children. The kids had to think hard about questions such as "What would the world look like to you if you were as small as a cat?" and "What birthday present would make each member of your family happiest?" Thinking about the answers expands children's ability to put themselves in another's situation. The children also listened to stories and then retold them from the point of view of each of the different characters in each story. The children played the role of each of the characters, and their performances were videotaped. The children then viewed the tapes and talked about how people look and sound when they express different feelings. At the end of the program, the children not only had learned to be more empathic but also had higher self-esteem, were more generous, and were less aggressive than were students who had not participated in the program.

At first glance, such a program may seem unrelated to academics. Yet role-playing and close analysis of stories is just what students do when putting on a play or analyzing a piece of literature. In reminiscing about his childhood, the Nobel Prize–winning physicist Richard Feynman reported that his father challenged his intellect by asking him to pretend he was a tiny creature living in their living room carpet. To do that, Feynman needed to crawl into the skin of that tiny creature and get a feel for what his life would be like in those circumstances. Such questions also encourage the kind of cognitive flexibility taught in corporate creativity programs. Accordingly, it should not surprise us to learn that students who develop greater empathic ability also tend to have higher academic achievement (Feshbach & Feshbach, 2009).

Disrupting the Rejection-Rage Cycle

At the beginning of this chapter, we described the massacre at Columbine High School and discussed some of the speculations about what might have caused that horrifying event and the many other school shootings like it. Could these tragedies have been prevented?

To be sure, many of the shooters were severely mentally ill. Seung-Hui Cho, who murdered 32 of his fellow students at Virginia Tech University in 2007, had had a lifelong history of mental problems, delusions, and aberrant behavior that had been increasing in the previous year; as a boy, he had written that he wanted to "repeat Columbine" (Hillshafer, 2013). Adam Lanza, who killed 20 children and 6 adults at the Sandy Hook Elementary School in Newtown, Connecticut, in 2012, and Elliot Rodger, who killed 6 people in Santa Barbara, California, in 2014, had a history, since childhood, of mental problems that had recently been worsening. Some investigators have concluded that Harris might have been a psychopath who was easily able to fool adults, including his own psychiatrist; Klebold suffered from major depression (Cullen, 2010). But it would be a mistake to dismiss the Columbine massacre and most other school shootings as being a result of individual pathology and let it go at that. Such an explanation leads nowhere, because Harris and Klebold had been functioning effectively. They were getting good grades, attended class regularly, and did not present serious behavior problems to their parents or to the school authorities. Klebold had even gone to his prom three days earlier. True, they were loners, but so were many other students at Columbine High School; true, they dressed in Goth style, but so did other students.

Thus, to dismiss their horrifying deed as solely the result of mental illness would lead us to miss something of vital importance, something that might help us prevent similar tragedies: the power of the social situation. Elliot Aronson (2000) argued that Harris and Klebold were reacting in an extreme manner to a school atmosphere that creates an environment of exclusion and mockery, making life difficult for a sizable number of students. Most high schools are cliquish places where students are shunned if they belong to the "wrong" ethnic group, come from the poor side of the tracks, wear the "wrong" clothes, or are too short, too fat, too tall, or too smart. After the shootings, Columbine students recalled that Harris and Klebold had been taunted and bullied. Indeed, one student justified this behavior by saying, "Most kids didn't want them there. They were into witchcraft. They were into voodoo. Sure we teased them. But what do you expect with kids who come to school with weird hairdos and horns on their hats? If you want to get rid of someone, usually you tease 'em. So the whole school would call them homos" (Gibbs & Roche, 1999).

In the video they left behind, Harris and Klebold spoke angrily about the insults and bullying they endured at Columbine. "Perhaps now we will get the respect we deserve," said Klebold, brandishing a sawed-off shotgun. Indeed, the motivation behind the vast majority of rampage killings is an attempt to transform feelings of shame, humiliation, and rejection into feelings of pride. Social rejection is the most significant risk factor for teenage suicide, despair, and violence (Crescioni & Baumeister, 2009; Leary, Twenge, & Quinlivan, 2006; Stillman et al., 2009). When a team of researchers investigated 15 school shootings that occurred between 1995 and 2001, they found that in 13 of them, the killers had been angered by bullying and social rejection (Leary, Kowalski, Smith, & Phillips, 2003). In the immediate aftermath of the Columbine massacre, countless young people posted messages online, describing their anguish over being rejected and taunted by their popular classmates. None of these teenagers condoned the shootings, yet their Internet postings revealed a high degree of empathy for the suffering that they assumed Harris and Klebold must have endured. A 16-year-old girl wrote, "I know how they feel. Parents need to realize that a kid is not overreacting all the time they say that no one accepts them. Also, all of the popular conformists need to learn to accept everyone else. Why do they shun everyone who is different?"

Some years ago, the Norwegian government became concerned over the suicides of three young victims of bullying and the attempted suicide of several others. One sixth grader, after having been insulted, mocked, and harassed on a daily basis, was taken to the bathroom by his tormentors, who made him lie face down in the urinal. He went home and tried to kill himself. His parents found him unconscious.

Alarmed, the Norwegian government commissioned psychologist Dan Olweus (1991, 1996) to assess the problem of bullying across the entire nation and develop an intervention that might help reduce it. First, community-wide meetings were held to explain the problem. Parents were given brochures detailing symptoms of victimization. Teachers received training on handling bullying. Students watched

In the past decade, many schools have adopted bullying prevention programs to change norms regarding a form of aggression that can otherwise become dangerously prevalent among adolescents.

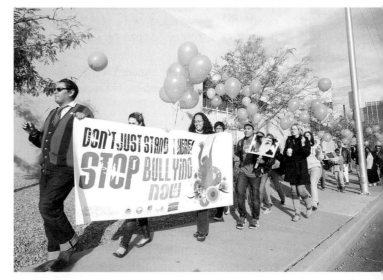

videotapes to evoke sympathy for victims of bullying. Second, students themselves, in their classes, discussed ways to prevent bullying and befriend lonely children. Teachers organized cooperative learning groups and moved quickly to stop name-calling and other forms of aggressive bullying. Principals ensured that lunchrooms, bathrooms, and playgrounds were adequately supervised. Third, if bullying occurred despite these preventive steps, trained counselors intervened, using a combination of mild punishment and intensive therapy with the bully and counseling with the bully's parents. Twenty months after the campaign began, acts of bullying had decreased by half, with improvements at every grade level.

Olweus's "Bullying Prevention Program" has since been imported to America and other countries, inspiring other researchers and school systems to implement many of its elements. These programs have reduced bullying significantly—from 20% to 50%—wherever they have been introduced (Olweus & Limber, 2010; Ttofi & Farrington, 2011).

Research from social psychology shows that it should be possible to make our schools safer, as well as more pleasant and humane, by bringing about a change in the negative, exclusionary social atmosphere and by building empathy among schoolchildren. And, by the way, Columbine High School now has an antibullying program in place.

REVIEW QUESTIONS

1. Suppose you want to reduce the chances that your children will act aggressively toward other people. Which of the following strategies is most likely to work?
   a. Be a good role model; do not be verbally or physically abusive.
   b. Let your children play all the violent video games they want.
   c. Order them to behave nicely with other children and punish them if they don't.
   d. Encourage them to play sports where they can vent their frustrations on the playing field.

2. Tiffany is angry at Whitney for forgetting her birthday. To defuse her anger, Tiffany should
   a. think about other times Whit annoyed her and then confront Whit with all the evidence of what a bad friend she is.
   b. write about her feelings privately for 20 minutes a day for a few days to get some perspective.
   c. post her feelings about Whit on her Facebook page.
   d. get back at Whit by complaining about her to all their mutual friends.

3. Tiffany finally decides she is ready to confront Whitney directly. How should she express her anger (assuming she wants to keep the friendship)?

   a. She should "let it all out" so that she will feel better, and Whit will know exactly how she feels.
   b. She should invite Whitney to play a game of tennis and then really try to clobber her.
   c. She should explain why she feels upset and hurt, as calmly as she can, without blame and accusation.
   d. She should explain why she feels upset and hurt, but let Whit know that she blames her for her thoughtless behavior.

4. Which form of apology is most likely to be accepted and believed?
   a. "If I hurt your feelings, I'm really sorry."
   b. "I'm sorry I hurt your feelings, but look, we were both to blame here."
   c. "I'm really sorry, and I understand what I did wrong; it won't happen again."
   d. "I'm sorry."

5. What is the most significant risk factor for teenage suicide and violence?
   a. Doing poorly in school
   b. Having strict parents
   c. Having a genetic predisposition
   d. Being socially rejected

See page 622 for the answers.

Summary

12.1 How do evolutionary, cultural, and learning explanations of aggression differ?

• **Is Aggression Innate, Learned, or Optional? Aggression** is intentional behavior aimed at doing harm or causing physical or psychological pain to another person. **Hostile aggression** is defined as having as one's goal the harming of another; **instrumental aggression** inflicts harm as a means to some other end.

- **The Evolutionary View** Evolutionary psychologists argue that aggression is genetically programmed into men because it enables them to defend their group and perpetuate their genes; males also aggress out of sexual jealousy to protect their paternity. A hormone involved in male aggression is testosterone (which both sexes have in varying levels), but the aggression-testosterone link is modest, and each affects the other. There is substantial variation in the degree of aggressiveness among human males and also among our two closest animal relatives, chimpanzees and bonobos. Even if aggressive behavior has survival value, nearly all animals have also evolved strong inhibitory mechanisms that enable them to suppress aggression when they need to.

- **Culture and Aggression** Most social psychologists believe that human beings are born with the capacity for aggression, but whether or not it is expressed is influenced by situational and cultural factors and is therefore modifiable. There is a great variation in the levels of aggression across cultures; under some conditions, groups have had to become more aggressive, and under other conditions, they have become more peaceful. Cooperative, collectivist cultures have low levels of aggression, and in the past few centuries, war, murder, and torture have been steadily declining around the world. In *cultures of honor*, however, such as those in the American South and Southwest and in the Middle East, men are raised to respond aggressively to perceptions of threat and disrespect, a response that originated in economic conditions. In such cultures, the rate of physical abuse of women is often higher than elsewhere because such abuse is regarded as a male prerogative. Multiple factors shape whether or not a culture tends to nurture aggressive behavior, including the extent to which male aggression fulfills a central part of the male role and identity.

- **Gender and Aggression** Men and boys are much more likely than women to commit *physical aggression* in provocative situations, to pick fights with strangers, and to commit crimes of violence. However, gender differences in physical aggression are reduced when women are as provoked as men or when cultural norms foster female aggression. Husbands are far more likely to murder their wives than vice versa, but community studies find no significant gender differences in rates of less extreme partner abuse, such as hitting. Girls and women are more likely to commit *relational aggression*, acts that harm another person through manipulation of the relationship (backbiting, spreading rumors, shunning).

- **Learning to Behave Aggressively** Social-cognitive learning theory holds that people often learn social behavior, including aggression, through *observational learning*—observing and imitating others, especially people or institutions they respect. But their actual behavior also depends on their beliefs, perceptions, and interpretations of what they observe.

- **Some Physiological Influences** Alcohol can increase aggressive behavior because it serves as a disinhibitor, reducing a person's inhibitions. Alcohol also disrupts the way people usually process information so that they may respond to the most obvious aspects of a social situation and fail to pick up its subtle elements. But thanks to the "think-drink" effect, when people expect alcohol to have certain effects, it often does. When people are in pain or in a very hot environment, they are more likely to act aggressively.

12.2 What are some situational and social causes of aggression and sexual assault?

- Social Situations and Aggression

  - **Frustration and Aggression** The **frustration-aggression theory** states that frustration can increase the probability of an aggressive response. Frustration is more likely to produce aggression if one is thwarted on the way to a goal in a manner that is either illegitimate or unexpected. Also, *relative deprivation*—the feeling that you have less than what you deserve or less than people similar to you have—is more likely to cause frustration and aggressive behavior than absolute deprivation, as illustrated by protests and revolutions from the civil rights movement to Eastern Europe to the Middle East.

  - **Provocation and Reciprocation** Individuals frequently aggress to reciprocate the aggressive behavior of others. This response is reduced if there are mitigating circumstances or the recipient believes the other person's behavior was unintentional.

  - **Weapons as Aggressive Cues** The mere presence of a gun, an aggressive stimulus, in an otherwise neutral situation increases the degree of aggressive behavior, especially if a person is already feeling angry or frustrated. In a classic study, participants angered in the presence of a gun administered stronger electric shocks to their "victim" than those angered in the same setting in which a tennis racket was substituted for the gun.

- **Putting the Elements Together: The Case of Sexual Assault** Most crimes of rape are committed by assailants known to the victim (acquaintance or date rape). Rape may occur as a result of *physical force* or through *incapacitation*, when the victim has been drugged or is drunk or unconscious. Sexually aggressive males who commit these acts are often unable to empathize with women, may feel hostility and contempt toward women, and feel entitled to have sexual relations with whatever woman they choose. Date rape may also occur because of misunderstandings and ambiguities in the sexual **scripts** that men and women follow regarding sexual norms. Because most couples communicate sexual interest and intentions—including a wish *not* to have sex—indirectly through hints, body language, eye contact, and other nonverbal behaviors, the possibility of misunderstanding one another is greatly increased. The topics in this chapter lend themselves to understanding the factors involved in sexual assault: the importance of social and cultural norms; the power of perceptions and beliefs; the role of observational learning from role models, peers, and the media; why "testosterone made me do it" is an excuse, not an explanation; and the disinhibiting effects of alcohol and the "think-drink" effect.

12.3 Does observing violence increase violence?

- **Violence and the Media**

  - **Studying the Effects of Media Violence** To try to determine what effect all the violence in media and video games might have on children and adults, researchers have conducted laboratory experiments and longitudinal studies. Watching violence is associated with an increase in aggressive behavior, especially in children, but not all studies find a relationship. Exposure to violent pornography, in contrast to nonviolent erotica, increases acceptance of sexual violence toward women; the effects are strongest on men who already have hostile attitudes toward women and are predisposed to behave aggressively with them. In the laboratory, playing violent video games does increase hostile feelings and aggressive behavior and also has a "numbing" effect, increasing people's indifference to the needs of others, especially if the others are not "one of us." Longitudinal studies show that the more television violence observed by children, the greater the amount of violence they exhibit as teenagers and young adults. Viewing violence also exaggerates people's perceptions of danger in the outside world.

  - **The Problem of Determining Cause and Effect** The relationship between media violence and actual aggression, however, is a two-way street: Children who are already predisposed to aggression are more likely to seek out aggressive shows and games to watch and play. The effects of violence in the media have the greatest effect on children already predisposed to violence because of a genetic predisposition, living in a violent family, or a personality trait. And many other factors have a far more powerful influence on aggression, including growing up with violent or otherwise abusive parents, living in a violent community, and being rejected socially.

12.4 How can aggression be diminished?

- **How to Decrease Aggression?**

  - **Does Punishing Aggression Reduce Aggression?** If punishment is itself aggressive, it actually models such behavior to children and may engender greater aggressiveness. Punishment may also enhance the attractiveness of the transgression to the child, get the attention that the child is hoping for, or backfire by making the child anxious and angry. Punishment often fails to reduce aggression because it does not communicate what the target should do, only what he or she should not do. For punishment to serve as a deterrent to misbehavior or criminal acts, it must be both prompt and certain. For that reason, in the complex world of criminal justice, severe punishment is unlikely to deter violent crime.

  - **Catharsis and Aggression** The theory of **catharsis** predicts that venting one's anger or watching others behave aggressively would serve to "get it out of your system" and make people less likely to behave aggressively themselves. Research shows the contrary: Acting aggressively or observing aggressive events or sports increases the likelihood of aggressive behavior in players and fans. Ventilating anger directly toward someone who has insulted or otherwise angered you also increases blood pressure, feelings of anger, and acts of aggression. In turn, because of self-justification and the need to reduce dissonance, each act of "righteous aggression" a person commits increases the likelihood that it will be repeated.

  - **What Are We Supposed to Do with Our Anger?** Venting anger usually causes more harm than good, but stifling serious feelings is often not useful either. It is more effective to become aware of the anger and then to deal with it in ways that are more constructive than yelling or hitting: cooling off; becoming more self-aware (perhaps through writing down your feelings privately); learning to communicate your feelings in a clear but nonjudgmental or insulting way; taking responsibility for acts that anger others, through understanding and apology; learning how to solve the problem that has made you and the other person angry; and strengthening empathic skills.

- **Disrupting the Rejection-Rage Cycle** Social rejection is the most significant risk factor for teenage suicide, despair, and violence. Most of the teenagers who have committed horrifying murders in their schools felt angry and vengeful at having been bullied and rejected by their peers. Changing the structure and atmosphere of schools through awareness, empathy training, and bullying-reduction programs can reduce bullying and improve the lives of children and teenagers.

Test Yourself

1. _____ aggression stems from feelings of anger and is aimed at inflicting pain, whereas _____ aggression serves as a means to some goal other than pain.

   a. Hostile, instrumental
   b. Direct, passive
   c. Instrumental, hostile
   d. Passive, direct

2. What does the research on cultures of honor suggest about the relationship between testosterone and aggression?

   a. It explains why men are more aggressive than women across cultures.
   b. It shows that testosterone and aggression are unrelated.
   c. It shows that culture affects when and why men can be provoked to become aggressive.
   d. It shows that culture has little effect on the basic biology of testosterone in men.

3. *Relational aggression* refers to

   a. behaving violently against one's relations.
   b. the negative effects of aggression on one's relationships.
   c. expressing aggression indirectly by manipulating a relationship.
   d. having sexual relations with the target of one's aggression.

4. In terms of *physical aggression*, men are more likely than women to

   a. engage in public displays of violence.
   b. behave aggressively to defend their honor or status.
   c. hit or slap a spouse or partner.
   d. All of the above.
   e. a and b.

5. Social-cognitive learning theory explains why, when people are provoked,

   a. they respond aggressively if they think aggression is justified.
   b. they respond aggressively if they are tired or hungry.
   c. they automatically respond aggressively.
   d. they seek their friends' opinions of what to do.

6. John has consumed enough alcohol to make him legally drunk. Under which of the following conditions is he most likely to become aggressive?

   a. He is partying with his friends.
   b. A stranger says hello to him.
   c. He is walking to work on a cold winter day.
   d. A stranger bumps into him in a crowded restaurant.

7. What does research suggest is the most reasonable conclusion about the effects of media violence?

   a. They have an effect, but primarily on children already predisposed to aggression.
   b. They have a strong effect, making most young children more aggressive.
   c. They have virtually no effect.
   d. Their effects depend on whether children are watching cartoons, television, or movies.

8. Harsh punishment to control aggressive behavior usually backfires because the children tend to

   a. become more aggressive and antisocial over time.
   b. pass on their aggression to their peers.
   c. get hooked on to violent games to retaliate.
   d. stop defending themselves and get bullied.

9. What does research find about the validity of the catharsis theory?

   a. Supported: It is usually beneficial to ventilate anger and get it out of your system.

b. Supported: Playing or watching violent sports reduces aggression.

c. Disconfirmed: Expressing anger often makes people angrier.

d. Disconfirmed: Acting out anger is healthy for physical but not psychological reasons.

e. a and b.

10. Which of the following concepts holds that blowing off steam reduces the likelihood of further aggressive behavior?

a. Actively enabling

b. Catharsis

c. Psychic numbing

d. Self-awareness

See page 622 for the answers.

Chapter 13
Prejudice
Causes, Consequences, and Cures

 Chapter Outline and Learning Objectives

Defining Prejudice

13.1 What are the three components of prejudice?

The Cognitive Component: Stereotypes
The Affective Component: Emotions
The Behavioral Component: Discrimination

Detecting Hidden Prejudices

13.2 How can we measure prejudices that people don't want to reveal—or that they don't know they hold?

Ways of Identifying Suppressed Prejudices
Ways of Identifying Implicit Prejudices

The Effects of Prejudice on the Victim

13.3 What are some ways that prejudice harms its targets?

The Self-Fulfilling Prophecy
Stereotype Threat

Causes of Prejudice

13.4 What are three aspects of social life that can cause prejudice?

Pressures to Conform: Normative Rules
Social Identity Theory: Us versus Them
Realistic Conflict Theory

Reducing Prejudice

13.5 What are the six conditions that can reduce prejudice?

The Contact Hypothesis
When Contact Reduces Prejudice
Cooperation and Interdependence: The Jigsaw Classroom

Of all the social behaviors we discuss in this book, prejudice is among the most common and the most dangerous. Consider these examples:

- Provoked by the debate over building a mosque near Ground Zero in New York City, a college student stabbed a cabdriver who said he was Muslim, and another man was arrested for entering a mosque and urinating on prayer rugs, all the while shouting anti-Muslim insults. In Florida, a minister of a fringe Christian church urged the burning of Korans. In Tennessee, two Muslim imams were kicked off a plane when the pilot refused to fly with them. They were going to a conference on anti-Muslim prejudice.

- Clothes designer John Galliano was fired by the Christian Dior fashion house after allegedly harassing a couple—a Jewish woman and an Asian man—and using anti-Semitic and racist slurs. Eyewitnesses reported that Galliano said, "Dirty Jewish face, you should be dead" to the woman, and then shouted at her companion, "F***ing Asian bastard, I will kill you." An earlier video posted on YouTube shows Galliano yelling at a different couple, saying "I love Hitler. . . . People like you would be dead. Your mothers, your forefathers, would all be f***ing gassed." (Galliano, who is gay, apparently did not realize that he himself would have been gassed by the Nazis on that count.)

- A survey of African American college graduates looking for jobs in Chicago found that many said they had "Whitened" their résumés. One young woman changed her first name (Tahani) on her application to "T. S.," and others spoke of ways in which they had disguised parts of their identities that they thought signaled their Blackness, such as membership in the African American Business Students Association. The applicants were not being oversensitive. In spite of the widespread perception that affirmative action has given an advantage to Black job candidates, especially those who are college graduates, studies show that they remain at a disadvantage in tough economic times.

None of us emerges completely unscathed by prejudice; it is a problem common to all humankind. When prejudice escalates into extreme hatred, it can lead to brutality, murder, war, and even genocide. During the past half century, social psychologists have contributed greatly to our understanding of the psychological processes underlying prejudice and have begun to identify some possible solutions. What is prejudice? How does it come about? How can it be reduced?

Defining Prejudice

13.1 What are the three components of prejudice?

Prejudice is an attitude—an emotionally powerful one. Attitudes are made up of three components: a cognitive component, involving the beliefs or thoughts (cognitions) that make up the attitude; an affective or emotional component, representing both the type of emotion linked with the attitude (e.g., anger, warmth) and the intensity of the emotion (e.g., mild uneasiness, outright hostility); and a behavioral component, relating to one's actions. (See Chapter 7.) People don't only hold attitudes; they usually act on them as well.

In this context, a **prejudice** is a hostile or negative attitude toward people in a distinguishable group, based *solely* on their membership in that group. Thus, when we say that someone is prejudiced against Black people, we mean that he or she is primed to behave coolly or with hostility toward them and that he or she feels that they are all pretty much the same. The characteristics this individual assigns to Black people are negative and applied to the group as a whole. The individual traits or behaviors of

Prejudice

A hostile or negative attitude toward people in a distinguishable group based solely on their membership in that group; it contains cognitive, emotional, and behavioral components the individual target of prejudice will either go unnoticed or be dismissed. Prejudices have a cognitive element (a stereotype) and can influence behavior (in the form of discrimination).

We are all victims or potential victims of prejudice for no other reason than our membership in an identifiable group, whether on the basis of ethnicity, skin color, religion, gender, age, national origin, sexual orientation, body size, or disability, to name just a few. And it is not only minority groups that are the targets of prejudice at the hands of the dominant majority. Prejudice is a two-way street; it often flows from the minority group to the majority group as well as in the other direction.

To be sure, enormous progress has been made. The numbers of people who admit to believing that Blacks are inferior to Whites, women inferior to men, and gays inferior to straights have been steadily dropping (Weaver, 2008). Fifty years ago, the overwhelming majority of Americans were opposed to racial integration and could not imagine ever voting for any Black candidate, let alone for president of the United States. Many other changes have swept the country. Fifty years ago, few could imagine that it would one day become utterly routine to see female lawyers, doctors, bartenders, Supreme Court justices, astronauts, or marine biologists. Gay men and lesbians lived in fear of anyone discovering their sexual orientation, and few could imagine that same-sex marriage would ever be a possibility, let alone become legal. Inspired by the civil rights movement, the National Association to Advance Fat Acceptance was formed in 1969, "dedicated to ending size discrimination in all of its forms," and Disability Rights Advocates likewise have organized to fight discrimination against anyone with a disability.

And yet it's clear that prejudice continues. Some White Americans regard racism as a zero-sum game in which actions to improve the welfare of minority groups have been at their expense; they feel that the reduction in antiBlack bias has been accompanied by a rise in antiWhite bias (Norton & Sommers, 2011; Wilkins & Kaiser, 2014). Many White people, confronted with information that the country is becoming more ethnically diverse and that the proportion of Whites is declining, respond not with tolerance but with fear and increased prejudice toward Latinos, African Americans, and Asian Americans (Craig & Richeson, 2014). Online, hundreds of thousands of self-identified White nationalists proudly express their contempt for gays, Blacks, Mexicans, and, primarily, Jews (Stephens-Davidowitz, 2014). Sometimes prejudice erupts overtly, as in the stories we described above, along with hate crimes, vandalism, bigoted jokes, or the thoughtless remarks made by some celebrity, sports figure, actor, or politician. Many of its expressions are more subtle, however, having gone underground, as we will see.

> We all decry prejudice, yet all are prejudiced.
> —HERBERT SPENCER, 1873

The Cognitive Component: Stereotypes

The human mind cannot avoid creating categories, putting some people into one group based on certain characteristics and others into another group based on their different characteristics (Brewer, 2007; Dovidio & Gaertner, 2010). Researchers in the field of *social neuroscience* find that creating categories is an adaptive mechanism, one built into the human brain; humans begin creating categories almost as soon as they are born (Cikara & Van Bavel, 2014). Newborns have no preferences for faces of one race or another, but if they live in a "monoracial" world, they will show a preference for faces of their own race by only 3 months of age

"It's a cat calendar, so it may not be all that accurate."

Jack Ziegler/The New Yorker Collection/ The Cartoon Bank

What is this woman's occupation? Most Western non-Muslims hold the stereotype that Muslim women who wear the full-length Black *niqab* must be repressed sexually as well as politically. But Wedad Lootah, a Muslim living in Dubai, United Arab Emirates, is a marriage counselor and sexual activist, and the author of a best-selling Arabic sex manual.

Stereotype

A generalization about a group of people in which certain traits are assigned to virtually all members of the group, regardless of actual variation among the members

(Anzures et al., 2013). If they repeatedly see faces of two or more races, however, they show no preference. This research illustrates a major theme of social-psychological approaches to prejudice: We are born with the ability to notice different categories, but experience shapes that ability, right from the get-go.

Just as we make sense out of the physical world by grouping animals and plants into taxonomies, we make sense out of our social world by grouping people according to characteristics that are important, most notably gender, age, and race. We rely on our perceptions of what people with similar characteristics have been like in the past to help us determine how to react to someone else with the same ones (Andersen & Klatzky, 1987; Macrae & Bodenhausen, 2000). The resulting categories are both useful and necessary, but they have profound consequences. They do not inevitably generate prejudices, but they can be the first step.

FROM CATEGORIES TO STEREOTYPES Close your eyes for a moment and imagine the looks and characteristics of the following people: a high school cheerleader, a compassionate nurse, a Jewish computer scientist, and a Black musician. Our guess is that this task was not difficult. We all walk around with images of various types of people in our heads. Walter Lippmann (1922), a distinguished journalist who was the first to introduce the term *stereotype*, described the distinction between the world "out there" and stereotypes—"the little pictures we carry around inside our heads." Within a given culture, these pictures tend to be remarkably similar. We would be surprised if your image of the cheerleader was anything but a pretty, nonintellectual female. We would also be surprised if the nurse was male, the Jewish computer scientist was female, or the Black musician was playing classical music.

Deep down, we know that there are male cheerleaders and nurses, female Jewish computer programmers, and Black classical musicians. But we tend to categorize according to what we regard as normative. And within a given culture, what people regard as normative is similar, in part because these images are perpetuated and broadcast widely by the media. Stereotyping, however, goes a step beyond simple categorization. A **stereotype** is a generalization about a group of people in which identical characteristics are assigned to virtually all members of the group, regardless of actual variation among the members. The stereotypic quality might be physical, mental, or occupational: blondes are ditzy bimbos, jocks are dumb, engineers are nerds. Blue-collar workers and Wall Street bankers have uncomplimentary stereotypes of each other.

Stereotyping is a cognitive process, and stereotypes can be positive as well as negative. If you like a group, your stereotype will be positive, but if you dislike the group, your stereotype *of the same behavior* will be negative. After all, you can see the same behavior as being stingy or frugal, family loving or clannish, outgoing or pushy (Peabody, 1985). Often, stereotyping is merely a technique that all of us use to simplify how we look at the world—a useful tool in the mental toolbox. Gordon Allport (1954) described stereotyping as "the law of least effort": Because the world is too complicated for us to have a highly differentiated attitude about everything, we maximize our cognitive time and energy by developing elegant, accurate attitudes about some topics while relying on simple, sketchy beliefs for others. There is a neurological basis for the cognitive efficiency of stereotyping; given our limited capacity for processing informa-tion, it allows human beings to behave like "cognitive misers"—to take short-cuts and adopt certain rules of thumb in our attempt to understand other people (Ito & Urland, 2003; Macrae & Bodenhausen, 2000). Information consistent with our notions about a group will be given more attention, will be rehearsed (or recalled) more often, and will therefore be remembered better than information that contradicts those notions. Thus, whenever a member of a group behaves as we expect, the behavior confirms and even strengthens our stereotype; we are not inclined to seek, notice, or remember the "exceptions." Anyone who doesn't fit the stereotype can be considered an exception, so we have no need to change the stereotype.

To the extent that a stereotype is based on experience and accurately identi-fies certain attributes of a group overall, it can be an adaptive, shorthand way of dealing with complex situations (Jussim, Cain, Crawford, Harber, & Cohen, 2009; Lee, McCauley, & Jussim, 2013). However, if the stereotype blinds us to individual differences within a class of people, it can become maladaptive, unfair, and harmful both to the person holding the stereotype and the individuals being lumped into that category. (See the Try It!)

> I will look at any additional evidence to confirm the opinion to which I have already come.
>
> —Lord Molson, British politician

TRY IT!

Stereotypes and Aggression

Close your eyes. Imagine an aggressive construction worker. How is this person dressed, where is this person located, and what, specifically, is this person doing to express aggression? Write your answers, being specific about the person's actions.

Now imagine an aggressive lawyer. How is this person dressed, where is this person located, and what, specifically, is this person doing to express aggression? Write your answers, being specific about the person's actions.

If you are like the experimental participants in one research study, your stereotypes of the construction worker and the lawyer will have influenced the way you have construed the term *aggression*: Most of the study subjects imagined the construction worker using physical aggression and the lawyer using verbal aggression (Kunda, Sinclair, & Griffin, 1997). And, by the way, in your visualization, are the construction worker and lawyer both men? Young? What is their race or ethnicity? Unless you are Asian American, we are pretty sure that neither one of the people you are imagining is Asian American. How come?

WHAT'S WRONG WITH POSITIVE STEREOTYPES?   The abuse of stereotyping's mental shortcuts can be blatant and obvious, as when one ethnic group is considered lazy or another ethnic group is considered violent. But the potential abuse can be more subtle, and it might even involve a stereotype about a positive attribute.

For example, Asian Americans have often been labeled a "model minority," a culture of people who are hardworking, ambitious, and intelligent. But many Asian Americans themselves object to this blanket characterization because it sets up expectations for those who are not interested in academic achievement, who don't like science and math and don't do well in those subjects, and who in general don't appreciate being treated as a category rather than as individuals (Thompson & Kiang, 2010). Moreover, the stereotype lumps together *all* Asian Americans, ignoring differences across Asian cultures (rather like referring to Swedes, Germans, the Irish, the French, and Greeks as all one bunch of "European Americans").

Do you have a stereotype of Asian women, blond women, tattooed women, or muscular women? This woman is all four. Are any or all of those four stereotypes positive or negative for you?

A study of Cambodian, Chinese, Korean, Lao, and Vietnamese students in America found many average differences in values, motivations, and goals across these groups (Lee, 2009).

Or consider the stereotype that "White men can't jump" and its implied corollary that (all) Black men *can* jump. Currently, more than 80% of National Basketball Association (NBA) players are Black, yet African Americans constitute only 13% of the U.S. population. So what here is insulting to the minority? What's wrong is that this assumption obscures the overlap in the distributions—that is, it blurs the fact that many African American kids are not adept at basketball and that many White kids are. (To say that 80% of NBA players are Black does not mean that 80% of all Black men are capable of becoming NBA players.) Thus, a White person who meets a young African American man and is astonished at his ineptitude on the basketball court is, in a real sense, denying him his individuality. He is also insulting him by relegating him to a category of "good athlete" rather than, say, "smart professional." An African American law professor described her evening at an elegant restaurant with her two young sons. The maître d' came by and casually asked her if they would become rappers or ball players. She replied that doctor or lawyer was more likely. "Aiming kind of high, aren't we?" he said (Cashin, 2014).

Experiments have confirmed how embedded this kind of demeaning stereotyping can be. In one experiment, college students listened to a 20-minute audiotape of a college basketball game. They were asked to focus on one of the players, given the name "Mark Flick," and were allowed to look at a folder containing information about him, including a photograph. Half of the participants saw a photo of an African American male; the others saw a photo of a White male. After listening to the game, the students rated Flick's performance. Their ratings reflected the prevailing stereotypes: Students who believed Flick was African American rated him as having more athletic ability and as having played a better game than did those who thought he was White. Those who thought he was White rated him as having greater hustle and greater basketball sense (Stone, Perry, & Darley, 1997).

STEREOTYPES OF GENDER Just about everyone holds stereotypes of women and men—some positive, some negative: Women are more empathic and talkative, men are more competent and aggressive (Kite, Deaux, & Haines, 2008; Matlin, 2012). But, as usual, the stereotypes exaggerate differences between the sexes, ignore differences in personality traits and abilities *within* each gender, and oversimplify (Fine, 2010). Are women really "more empathic" than men? Which women? Empathic toward whom? When women's and men's actual behavior is observed systematically under a variety of conditions, the sexes do not differ in having feelings of empathy or in its expression (Fine, 2010). Some supposed differences disappear on closer inspection. Consider the pop-psych stereotype that women are "more talkative" than men. To test this assumption, psychologists wired up a sample of men and women with voice recorders that tracked their conversations while they went about their daily lives. There was no significant difference in the number of words spoken: Both sexes used about 16,000 words per day on average, with large individual differences among the participants (Mehl, Vazire, Ramírez-Esparza, & Pennebacker, 2007).

Contrasting the stereotypes of women and men might just be a fun game if the stereotypes didn't morph into prejudices, but too often they do. In research involving

15,000 men and women in 19 nations, Peter Glick and Susan Fiske (2001) have found that around the world sexism takes two basic forms, which they call *hostile sexism* and *benevolent sexism*. Hostile sexists hold negative stereotypes of women: Women are inferior to men because they are inherently less intelligent, less competent, less brave, less capable of math and science, and so on. Benevolent sexists hold positive stereotypes of women: Women are kinder than men, more empathic, more nurturing, and so on.

According to Glick and Fiske, both sets of stereotypes are demeaning to women because benevolent sexists, like hostile sexists, assume that women are the weaker sex. Benevolent sexists tend to idealize women romantically, may admire them as wonderful cooks and mothers, and want to protect them when they do not need protection. This type of sexism is affectionate but patronizing, conveying the attitude that women are so wonderful, good, kind, and moral that they should stay at home, away from the aggressiveness and corruption (and power and income) of public life (Glick, 2006). Because benevolent sexism lacks a tone of hostility to women, it doesn't seem like a prejudice to many people. Many women find it alluring to think that they are better than men, and those who endorse benevolent sexism are less motivated to support action for women's equal rights (Becker & Wright, 2011). But both forms of sexism—whether someone thinks women are too good for equality or not good enough—legitimize discrimination against women and can be used to justify relegating them to traditional stereotyped roles (Christopher & Wojda, 2008).

Benevolent sexism can even cost lives—in surprising ways. Here's one. Researchers discovered an interesting mystery: In the years between 1950 and 2012, about twice as many people died in hurricanes named after women than in hurricanes named after men (with the exception of a few outliers like Hurricane Katrina). Curious, the scientists went into the laboratory and asked people to predict the danger and risk of hurricanes with male names (Alexander, Christopher, Victor) or comparable female names (Alexandra, Christina, Victoria). People thought the hurricanes with male names would be more deadly and violent. This finding suggests that people take male-named hurricanes more seriously and so take greater precautions—and are therefore less likely to be killed when the storm arrives (Jung, Shavitt, Viswanathan, & Hilbe, 2014). Even when people are reacting to storms, they apply their stereotypes about men and women. A female-named hurricane seems gentler than a male-named hurricane.

Perhaps you are thinking, "Hey, what about men? There are plenty of negative stereotypes about men too—that they are sexual predators, emotionally heartless, domineering, and arrogant." In fact, when Glick and Fiske completed a 16-nation study of attitudes toward men, they found that many people believe that men are aggressive and predatory and overall just not as warm and kind as women (Glick et al., 2004). This attitude seems hostile to men, the researchers found, but it also reflects and supports gender inequality and prejudice against women by characterizing men as being "naturally" designed for leadership and dominance.

"No, this is not Mel's secretary. This is Mel."

Bacall Aaron/CartoonStock

Gender stereotypes are so influential that people even tend to take less seriously the risks posed by hurricanes given female names.

The Affective Component: Emotions

If you've ever argued with people who hold deep-seated prejudices, you know how hard it is to get them to change their minds. Even people who are usually reasonable about most topics become immune to rational, logical arguments when it comes to the topic of their prejudice. Why is this so? It is primarily the emotional aspect of attitudes that makes a prejudiced person so hard to argue with; logical arguments are not effective in countering emotions. If you have a stereotype of a group that you know little about, and if you are not invested emotionally in that stereotype, you are likely to be open to information that disputes it:

> *You:* Nah, I don't want to visit Norway. I hear everyone there is pretty cold and aloof. I'd be much more comfortable with those expressive Italians.
>
> *Your good friend:* Boy, are you ever wrong! I lived in Norway for 6 years, and it was *fabulous*. The people are helpful, friendly, and smart. Besides, they throw great parties.
>
> *You:* No kidding? I'd better rethink my view of Norwegians! When are we going?

In contrast, the difficulty of using reason to change a prejudice was beautifully illustrated by Gordon Allport (1954) in his landmark book *The Nature of Prejudice*. He reports a dialogue between Mr. X and Mr. Y:

> *Mr. X:* The trouble with the Jews is that they only take care of their own group.
>
> *Mr. Y:* But the record of the Community Chest campaign shows that they gave more generously, in proportion to their numbers, to the general charities of the community than did non-Jews.
>
> *Mr. X:* That shows they are always trying to buy favor and intrude into Christian affairs. They think of nothing but money; that is why there are so many Jewish bankers.
>
> *Mr. Y:* But a recent study shows that the percentage of Jews in the banking business is negligible, far smaller than the percentage of non-Jews.
>
> *Mr. X:* That's just it; they don't go in for respectable business; they are only in the movie business or run nightclubs.

Because Mr. X is emotionally caught up in his beliefs about Jews, his responses are not logical. In effect, the prejudiced Mr. X is saying, "Don't trouble me with facts; my mind is made up." Rather than challenging the data presented by Mr. Y, he distorts the facts so that they support his hatred of Jews, or he simply ignores them and initiates a new line of attack. The prejudiced attitude remains intact, despite the fact that the specific arguments Mr. X began with are now lying in tatters at his feet.

That is the signal that emotional reasoning is at work: It is impervious to logic or evidence. Indeed, many of the stereotypes underlying anti-Semitism are mutually contradictory and constantly shift across generations and nations. Jews were attacked for being communists in Nazi Germany and Argentina, and for being greedy capitalists in the communist Soviet Union. They have been criticized for being too secular and for being too mystical, for being weak and ineffectual and for being powerful enough to dominate the world (Cohen, Jussim, Harber, & Bhasin, 2009).

Throughout this book, we have seen that none of us is 100% reliable when it comes to processing social information that is important to us. The human mind does not tally events objectively; our emotions, needs, and self-concepts get in the way (Fine, 2008; Gilovich, 1991; Westen et al., 2006). That is why a prejudice—a blend of a stereotype and emotional "heat" toward a particular group—is so hard to change. We see only the information that confirms how right we are about "those people" and, like Mr. X, dismiss information that might require us to change our minds.

The mind of a bigot is like the pupil of the eye; the more light you pour upon it, the more it will contract.

—Oliver Wendell Holmes Jr., 1901

The result, as Gordon Allport observed long ago, is that "defeated intellectually, prejudice lingers emotionally." He meant that the emotional component of prejudice, its deep-seated negative feelings, may persist even when a person knows consciously that the prejudice is wrong. Thus, some social psychologists, while welcoming the evidence that *explicit*, conscious prejudices have declined, have turned to more sophisticated measures to see whether *implicit*, unconscious negative feelings between groups have also diminished. (We discuss the difference between implicit and explicit attitudes in Chapter 7.) They maintain that implicit attitudes, being automatic and unintentional, reflect lingering negative feelings that keep prejudice alive below the surface (Dovidio & Gaertner, 2008). We will soon discuss the phenomenon of implicit prejudice and the conditions under which it is activated. For now, what explicit negative feelings do you hold toward some group—perhaps in spite of your wishes not to have those feelings? (See the Try It!)

TRY IT!
Identifying Your Prejudices

Is there some group of people you "can't stand"? Who evokes the strongest prejudice in you? Is it a category defined by their looks, weight, age, occupation, ethnicity, religion, sexual orientation, gender, or race? Think about the factors that cause prejudice: Which one or ones might be contributing to your negative feelings? Think about the changes in experience and attitudes that might reduce your prejudice: What would have to happen before you could let go of it?

The Behavioral Component: Discrimination

Prejudice often leads to **discrimination**, which is unfair treatment of members of a stigmatized group solely because of their membership in that group. The discrimination may be official or subtle. In a culture that relentlessly endorses "thin is beautiful," for example, fat people are often targets of jokes, harassment, and humiliation; they are less likely than slender people to be hired and promoted; and they are less likely to get appropriate medical treatment from their physicians (Finkelstein, DeMuth, & Sweeney, 2007; King, Shapiro, Hebl, Singletary, & Turner, 2006; Miller et al., 2013). Most forms of explicit discrimination in schools and the workplace are now illegal in America, but stereotypes and prejudices can "leak out" and express themselves behaviorally in potent ways, as we can see in the examples of African Americans and women.

Discrimination

Unjustified negative or harmful action toward a member of a group solely because of his or her membership in that group

RACIAL DISCRIMINATION   Consider the fact that Blacks and Whites are not treated equally in the national "war against drugs" (Fellner, 2009). Across the country, relative to their numbers in the general population and among drug offenders, African Americans are disproportionately arrested, convicted, and incarcerated on drug charges (Blow, 2011). A typical illustration comes from a study in Seattle, which is 70% White. The great majority of those who use or sell serious drugs are White, yet almost two-thirds of those who are arrested are Black. Whites constitute the majority of those who use or sell methamphetamine, ecstasy, powder cocaine, and heroin; Blacks are the majority of those who use or sell crack. But the police virtually ignore the White market and concentrate on crack arrests. The researchers said they could not find a "racially neutral" explanation for this difference. The focus on crack offenders did not appear to be related to the frequency of crack transactions compared to other drugs, public safety or health concerns, crime rates, or citizen complaints. The researchers concluded that the police department's drug enforcement efforts reflect racial discrimination—the unconscious impact of race on official perceptions of who is the cause of the city's drug problem (Beckett, Nyrop, & Pfingst, 2006).

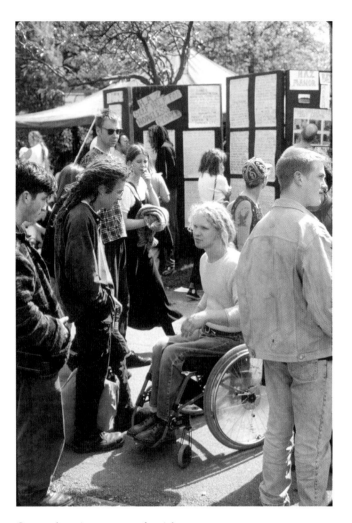

One unobtrusive measure of social distance and "microaggressions" is to notice how people respond, nonverbally, to people with disabilities.

Prejudice can also lead to discrimination through *microaggressions*, defined as the "slights, indignities, and put-downs" that many minorities routinely encounter (Dovidio, Pagotto, & Hebl, 2011; Nadal et al., 2011; Sue, 2010). Derald Sue (2010) offers these examples: A White professor compliments an Asian American graduate student on his "excellent English," although the student has lived in the United States his whole life. A White woman leaving work starts to enter an elevator, sees a Black man inside, covers her necklace with her hand, and "remembers" that she left something at her desk—thereby conveying to her Black coworker that she thinks he is dangerous, a potential thief. Men in a discussion group completely ignore the contributions of the one female member, talking past her and paying attention only to one another. Employers spend less time interviewing people they are uncomfortable with, making less eye contact and being less verbally positive (Hebl, Foster, Bigazzi, Mannix, & Dovidio, 2002).

The behavior of the employers reflects a kind of discrimination measured by *social distance*, a person's reluctance to get "too close" to another group. Measures of social distance can be applied in many settings: Is a straight student as likely to sit next to a gay student as to another straight student? Does a nondisabled woman move away from a woman in a wheelchair? How close will you let "those people" into your social life—work with them, live near them, marry them? A review of decades of representative surveys of the American population—focusing on Hispanics, Whites, Blacks, Jews, and Asians—found that while overt prejudice among all of these groups has declined, most people within each ethnic group are still strongly opposed to virtually all of the other ethnic groups living in their neighborhoods or marrying into their families (Weaver, 2008). But does this fact reflect a true "prejudice" or merely a comfort with and preference for people of one's own religion and ethnicity? Do you or your classmates think that you could choose a life partner of any ethnicity and that your parents would accept that person? Have your parents ever told you that you could marry anyone you loved, *except* . . . ?

GENDER DISCRIMINATION How about gender discrimination, which many people think is no longer a problem in the United States? When science professors at leading universities rated the applications of a student for a laboratory manager position—identical except for a randomly assigned male or female name—they thought the male applicant was significantly more competent than the female applicant. They were more willing to hire him, and they offered him a higher starting salary and more career mentoring than they would offer the female. Women faculty were as likely to show this bias as male faculty were (Moss-Racusin, Dovidio, Brescoll, Graham, & Handelsman, 2012).

The status of women varies around the world, and discrimination varies accordingly. When occupations are segregated by gender, many people form gender stereotypes about the requirements of such careers: Female jobs require kindness and nurturance; male jobs require strength and smarts. These stereotypes, in turn, stifle many people's aspirations to enter a nontraditional career and also create prejudices in employers that motivate them to discriminate (Agars, 2004; Cejka & Eagly, 1999; Eccles, 2011).

When gender ratios change in occupations, so do prejudice and discrimination. In the 1950s and 1960s, when almost all American lawyers, veterinary doctors, pharmacists, real estate agents, and bartenders were male and almost all nurses, elementary school teachers, and child care workers were female, few women aspired to enter the "male" professions, and employers were reluctant to hire them. When job segregation became illegal, however, people's career motivations changed. Today, it is common to see a female lawyer, vet, pharmacist, and bartender. And although women are still a minority in engineering, math, and science, their numbers have been rising: In 1960, women earned only 0.4% of the doctorates in engineering, 5.2% of those in mathematics, and 8.8% of those in the life sciences. But by 2006, according to government statistics, the percentages had jumped to 20.2%, 29.6%, and 51.8%, respectively, and the numbers have risen even more since then. In 2010, 43% of the younger cohorts of people in engineering were women.

As these numbers have increased, the old prejudice that women are not "naturally" suited to engineering, math, and science has been fading, though certainly not everywhere, and discriminatory practices continue. For example, a study of nearly 2,500 women and men in science, engineering, and technology—all of whom had the same levels of aptitude and skill—explored the reasons that many of the women eventually left their jobs, with some abandoning science altogether. The women who left reported feeling isolated (many said they were the only woman in their work group), and two-thirds said they had been sexually harassed (Hewlitt, Luce, & Servon, 2008). Other reasons included being paid less than men for the same work and having working conditions that did not allow them to handle their family obligations. Mothers are still more likely than fathers to reduce their work hours, modify their work schedules, and feel distracted on the job because of child care concerns (Sabattini & Crosby, 2009).

THE ACTIVATION OF PREJUDICE Late one winter evening in the South Bronx, Amadou Diallo, an immigrant from West Africa, took in the night air on the steps of his apartment building. In what was soon to become a fateful encounter, four undercover police officers on patrol turned down Diallo's street. One of the officers noticed Diallo and thought that he looked like sketches of a man who had committed rapes in that area about a year earlier. The officers got out of their car and ordered Diallo to stop as he entered the vestibule of his apartment building. Diallo had no criminal record. He was working long hours as a street vendor and in his spare time was earning high school credits so that he could go to college. When the police approached him, he reached for his wallet, probably so that he could show some identification. Alarmed by the sight of a Black man reaching into his pocket, the four officers did not hesitate. They fired a total of 41 shots at Diallo, killing him instantly.

Roy Delgado/Cartoon Stock

In Florida, George Zimmerman fatally shot Trayvon Martin, an unarmed 17-year-old African American high school student. Zimmerman, who is part Hispanic, was the neighborhood watch coordinator, and he thought Martin was acting suspiciously. He trailed him; a quarrel ensued, and Zimmerman fired. At first, the police declined to arrest Zimmerman because Florida has a "Stand Your Ground" law that allows people to shoot if they feel they are in danger. Nationwide protest led to a full investigation, and Zimmerman was arrested on charges of second-degree murder and manslaughter. A jury acquitted him.

The key term here is "feel they are in danger." Police officers—or, in Zimmerman's case, self-appointed police officers—often make quick decisions under conditions of extreme stress and have little time to stop and analyze whether someone poses a threat. Is that person hiding a wallet or a gun? Is the decision to open fire influenced by the victim's race? Would the officers or Zimmerman have acted any differently if the men they had confronted had been White?

This question led researchers to try to re-create the situation in the laboratory. In one study, White participants saw videos of young men in realistic settings, such as in a park, at a train station, and on a city sidewalk (Correll, Park, Judd, & Wittenbrink, 2002). Half of the men were African American, and half were White. And half of the men in each group were holding a handgun, and half were holding nonthreatening objects, such as a cell phone, wallet, or camera. Participants were instructed to press a button labeled "shoot" if the man in the video had a gun and a button labeled "don't shoot" if he did not. Like a police officer, they had less than a second to make up their minds. Participants won or lost points on each round: They won 5 points for not shooting someone who did not have a gun and 10 points for shooting someone who did have a gun; they lost 20 points if they shot someone who was not holding a gun and lost 40 points if they failed to shoot someone who was holding a gun (which would be the most life-threatening situation for a police officer).

The results? The White participants were especially likely to pull the trigger when the men in the videos were Black, whether or not they were holding a gun. This "shooter bias" meant that people made relatively few errors when a Black

The fatal shootings of Trayvon Martin (left) in Florida in 2012 and Michael Brown (right) in Missouri in 2014 continued a tragic pattern of unarmed African American males being killed because their shooters claimed to have perceived them as dangerous. Research on implicit bias and the activation of prejudice is relevant to the effort to understand and prevent such tragedies.

Figure 13.1 Errors Made in "Shooting" People in a Video Game

Participants played a video game in which they were supposed to "shoot" a man if he was holding a gun and withhold fire if he was holding a harmless object, such as a cell phone. As the graph shows, players' most common error was to "shoot" an unarmed Black man, like the individual pictured below.

(Adapted from Correll, Park, Judd, & Wittenbrink, 2002)

 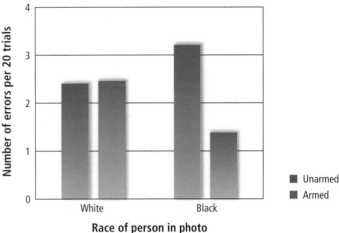

person was actually holding a gun; it also meant, however, that they made the most errors (shooting an unarmed person) when a Black person was not holding a gun (see Figure 13.1). When the men in the picture were White, participants made about the same number of errors whether the men were armed or unarmed. When this experiment was done with police officers, the officers showed the same association between Black men and guns, taking less time to shoot an armed Black man than an armed White man, even when the background situation looked safe and unthreatening. Many variations of these experiments have replicated the basic findings (Correll, Wittenbrink, Park, Judd, & Goyle, 2011; Correll et al., 2007; Eberhardt, Goff, Purdie, & Davies, 2004; Ma & Correll, 2011; Payne, 2001, 2006; Plant & Peruche, 2005).

Prejudices can also be activated when a person is angered or insulted (Rogers & Prentice-Dunn, 1981). White students were told they would be inflicting electric shock on another student, the "learner," whom they were told was either White or African American, as part of an apparent study of biofeedback. The students initially gave a *lower* intensity of shock to Black learners than to White ones—reflecting a desire, perhaps, to show that they were not prejudiced. The students then overheard the learner making derogatory comments about them, which, naturally, made them angry. Now, given another opportunity to inflict electric shock, the students who were working with a Black learner administered *higher* levels of shock than did students who worked with a White learner (see Figure 13.2). The same pattern appears in studies of how English-speaking Canadians behave toward French-speaking Canadians, straights toward gays, non-Jewish students toward Jews, and men toward women (Fein & Spencer, 1997; Maass, Cadinu, Guarnierni, & Grasselli, 2003; Meindl & Lerner, 1985).

These findings suggest that prejudices often lurk just beneath the surface. It doesn't take much to activate them, and once activated, they can have tragic consequences for how we perceive and treat a particular member of an out-group.

Figure 13.2 The Unleashing of Prejudice Against African Americans

Prejudices can be activated when people feel angry or insulted. In this experiment, White participants gave less shock to a Black "learner" than to a White learner when they were feeling fine. But once insulted, the White students gave higher levels to the Black learner.

(Adapted from Rogers & Prentice-Dunn, 1981)

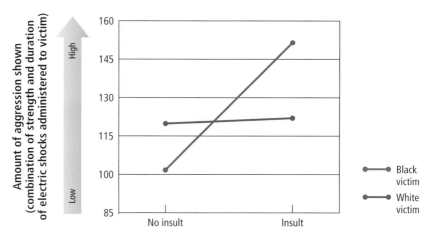

REVIEW QUESTIONS

1. Findings from social neuroscience suggest that
   a. it has been evolutionarily beneficial for the brain to be able to rapidly form categories.
   b. the tendency to form categories and stereotypes is determined largely by experience.
   c. people in some cultures are more likely to form stereotypes than other people.
   d. experience plays almost no role in the ability to notice different categories.

2. A group of delegates from around the world attend a conference on diversity. One of the keynote speakers is a professor from Asia. The delegates are very impressed with the way she delivers the talk. They discuss amongst themselves that being from Asia, the professor must be very good at various other things apart from academics, like following traditions, being creative, and managing her home. Can positive stereotypes be wrong?
   a. No, a positive stereotype will help promote peace and harmony among people.
   b. Yes, a positive stereotype might categorize a person rather than see him/her as an individual.
   c. No, a positive stereotype helps people appreciate the differences across communities.
   d. Yes, a positive stereotype is a complex way of looking at the world.

3. *Benevolent sexism* refers to people who think that women are naturally superior to men in kindness and nurturance.

What does international research show is a consequence of this belief?
   a. Women have higher self-esteem than men.
   b. Men envy women for having more positive traits than they have.
   c. It can legitimize discrimination against women and justify relegating them to traditional roles.
   d. It can cause people to overlook sexism directed against men.

4. In the social-psychological perspective, what is a primary cause of discrimination against women in the workforce?
   a. Women don't want to do the same work that men do.
   b. Women are a small minority of a given occupation.
   c. Women are not as biologically suited to leadership as men.
   d. Women and men are integrated in a given occupation.

5. According to some social psychologists, _____ prejudice may be declining; however, _____ attitudes tend to keep the prejudice alive below the surface.
   a. explicit; implicit
   b. implicit; explicit
   c. explicit; hostile
   d. implicit; hostile

See page 622 for the answers.

Detecting Hidden Prejudices

13.2   How can we measure prejudices that people don't want to reveal—or that they don't know they hold?

When Barack Obama was first elected president, many people hoped the nation was entering a "postracial" era, but before long it became apparent that we're not there yet. Highly prejudiced people realized that it would have been uncool to oppose him on transparently racial grounds, so their prejudice took the form of questioning his nationality and religion: He wasn't born in the United States (he was). He is a Muslim (he is Christian). He wasn't a legitimate citizen (he is). He wasn't, in short, "one of us." A study of nearly 300 students, Black and White, found that for prejudiced Whites, President Obama's perceived "non-Americanism" affected their evaluation of his performance, but not of Vice President Joe Biden's performance (Hehman, Gaertner, & Dovidio, 2011). In effect, these students could say, "I'm not prejudiced against Black people—it's just that Obama isn't really an American *and* is a lousy president." In contrast, Black students and unprejudiced White students could be either supportive or critical of Obama, but belief in his American status was irrelevant to their personal evaluation of him.

The election of America's first African American president was an exhilarating milestone for many Americans, but it awakened implicit prejudices in others.

Now that expressing prejudice is socially unacceptable in most places, people have become more careful about revealing them. Some *suppress* their true feelings out of a sincere motivation to become less prejudiced; others suppress their beliefs to avoid being labeled as racist, sexist, or homophobic (Devine, Plant, Amodio, Harmon-Jones, & Vance, 2002; Plant & Devine, 2009). And some people, as we saw in Chapter 7, hold *implicit* prejudices that they might not even be aware of consciously. Social psychologists have developed a variety of measures to try to identify the prejudices that people don't want to admit—to others or to themselves (De Houwer, Teige-Mocigemba, Spruyt, & Moors, 2009; Fazio, Jackson, Dunton, & Williams, 1995; Olson, 2009).

Ways of Identifying Suppressed Prejudices

One method is to send identical résumés to potential employers, varying only a name that indicates gender (e.g., John or Jennifer), implies race (a name or membership in an African American organization), mentions religious affiliation or sexual orientation, or describes an applicant as obese (Agerström & Rooth, 2011; Luo, 2009). Does the employer show bias in responding?

We saw that the answer is often yes in the case of female applicants, but this method, combined with social media, can reveal other prejudices too. Today, more than a third of U.S. employers check an applicant's Facebook page or other online sources for information they would be prohibited from asking the candidate directly because of state or federal laws. One research team sent out more than 4,000 fabricated résumés to private firms across the country that had posted job openings. They then created fake Facebook pages containing information that the candidate was Muslim or Christian, or gay or straight. The researchers found incredible progress in the acceptance of gay men and lesbians: Employers did not discriminate on the basis of sexual orientation anywhere in the country. But employers in the most conservative states revealed an anti-Muslim bias: Christian applicants were much more likely to get a callback than Muslim applicants were—17% to 2.3% (Acquisti & Fong, 2014).

Because people tend to believe they can't fool a machine, another way of identifying people's explicit but suppressed prejudices calls on technology. An early version of this method was named the *bogus pipeline*. Participants were hooked up to an impressive-looking machine and told it was a kind of lie detector; actually, it was just a pile of electronic hardware that did nothing. Participants were randomly assigned to one of two conditions in which they indicated their attitudes either on a questionnaire (where it was easy to give socially correct responses) or by using the bogus pipeline (where they believed the machine would reveal their true attitudes if they lied). People expressed more racial prejudice when the bogus pipeline was used (Jones & Sigall, 1971; Roese & Jamieson, 1993; Sigall & Page, 1971). Similarly, college men and women expressed almost identically positive attitudes about women's rights and women's roles in society on a questionnaire. When the bogus pipeline was used, however, most of the men revealed their true feelings, which were far less sympathetic to women's issues (Tourangeau, Smith, & Rasinski, 1997). The bogus pipeline has also been used to reveal people's hostility toward Jews and Israel, feelings that would otherwise be masked as socially inappropriate (Cohen et al., 2009).

Ways of Identifying Implicit Prejudices

The methods just described are based on the assumption that people know what they really feel but prefer to hide those feelings from others. But some people may harbor implicit prejudices that are hidden from themselves. Psychologists have developed several ways of measuring implicit prejudice.

Implicit Association Test (IAT)

A test thought to measure unconscious (implicit) prejudices according to the speed with which people can pair a target face (e.g., Black or White, old or young, Asian or White) with a positive or negative association (e.g., the words *honest* or *evil*)

One method that has garnered national and international attention is the **Implicit Association Test (IAT)**, which measures the speed of people's positive and negative associations to a target group (Banaji & Greenwald, 2013; Greenwald, McGhee, & Schwartz, 1998). Here's how it works. You sit at a console and are shown a series of faces you must sort as quickly as you can—pressing a left key for a Black face, say, and a right key for a White face. Now you have to do the same for a series of positive or negative words—press the left key for positive words (such as *triumph*, *joy*, *honest*) and the right key for negative words (such as *devil*, *maggot*, *failure*). Once you've mastered these sorting tasks, the faces and words are combined: Now, as quickly as possible, you must press the left key when you see a Black face or a positive word and the right key when you see a White face or a negative word. You are given a rapid set of combinations: *Black + triumph*, *Black + poison*, *White + peace*, *White + hatred*. The pairings get harder as you go along.

Repeatedly, people respond more quickly when White faces are paired with positive words and when Black faces are paired with negative words. That speed difference is said to be a measure of their implicit attitudes toward African Americans because it's harder for their unconscious minds to link African Americans with positive words. Versions of the IAT have been administered using many target groups, including people who are young or old, male or female, Asian or White, disabled or not, gay or straight, fat or thin. More than 15 million people of all ages and walks of life, all over the world, have taken the test online, in school, or in their workplaces, and most learn that they hold implicit prejudices (Nosek, Greenwald, & Banaji, 2007; Miller et al., 2013).

Typical stimuli used in the IAT to measure implicit racism.

The developers of the IAT, Mahzarin Banaji and Anthony Greenwald (2013), report that people are often surprised and alarmed to be told they have prejudices they are unaware of. Banaji herself, a woman of color who was born and raised in India, says that she "failed" the racial IAT, revealing antiBlack associations that she consciously repudiates. One gay activist they describe was stunned to learn that "her own mind contained stronger gay = bad associations than gay = good associations." Young people have faster reaction times to *old + bad* than to *old + good*, but the great majority of old people do also. And writer Malcolm Gladwell, who is biracial, likewise was shocked by his responses on the IAT. The researchers quote from his interview with Oprah Winfrey: "The person in my life [his mother] who I love more than almost anyone else is Black, and here I was taking a test, which said, frankly, I wasn't too crazy about Black people, you know?" (quoted in Banaji & Greenwald, 2013, p. 57).

Well, not so fast, Malcolm! The IAT could mean you are prejudiced, but it might not. Psychological scientists have debated the ambiguities surrounding interpretations of the test. If Gladwell's response to *Black + good* is a few milliseconds slower than to *Black + bad*, that could mean that he holds an unconscious (implicit) bias. But it could also mean that the IAT is not always measuring what it says it's measuring (De Houwer et al., 2009; Kinoshita & Peek-O'Leary, 2005; Rothermund & Wentura, 2004). Some psychological scientists think it simply captures a cultural association or stereotype, in the same way that people would be quicker to pair *bread + butter* than *bread + avocado*. Thus, old people may really be as biased against other old people as young people are, but it could also be that old and young share the same cultural stereotypes and associations about the elderly (Arkes & Tetlock, 2004; Olson & Fazio, 2004).

One way to judge the IAT's validity is to see if a high score predicts actual behavior toward old people, fat people, African Americans, or any other group. Some studies do show that the higher a person's IAT score, the more likely he or she is to discriminate against the target in some way (Green et al., 2007; Greenwald, Poehlman, Uhlmann, & Banaji, 2009). For example, one study found that Whites who reveal racial bias on the IAT tend to find Blacks less trustworthy (Stanley, Sokol-Hessner, Banaji, & Phelps, 2011), and another found that Whites with high scores don't communicate as warmly with Blacks in professional settings as they would with Whites (Cooper et al., 2012). Overall, however, the evidence linking IAT scores with overt behavior is weak. That means that if any given individual were to take the IAT and get a high score, it doesn't necessarily mean that person is prejudiced.

Moreover, when one team of researchers directly asked people to predict their responses toward five different groups on the Implicit Association Test (IAT), they found that people were "surprisingly accurate"—regardless of whether they were told that implicit attitudes are "true" prejudices or culturally learned associations. The researchers concluded that "the research findings cast doubt on the belief that attitudes or evaluations measured by the IAT necessarily reflect unconscious attitudes" (Hahn, Judd, Hirsh, & Blair, 2014).

Thus, although it is clear that people can and do hold implicit prejudices that govern their behavior in ways they do not always recognize (see Chapter 7), the debate over how best to identify them continues.

REVIEW QUESTIONS

1. What is a *suppressed* prejudice?
   a. A person holds a prejudice without being aware of it.
   b. A person has a tendency to become prejudiced under the right circumstances.
   c. A person knows he or she is prejudiced but chooses not to express it in public.
   d. A person reveals a prejudice subtly, by *implying* a bias rather than saying so outright.

2. What is an *implicit* prejudice?
   a. A person holds a prejudice without being aware of it.
   b. A person has a tendency to become prejudiced under the right circumstances.

   c. A person knows he or she is prejudiced but chooses not to express it in public.
   d. A person reveals a prejudice subtly, by *implying* a bias rather than saying so outright.

3. When people are attached to a "bogus pipeline" or other technological "lie detectors," how does this affect their willingness to admit their prejudices?
   a. They are more likely admit prejudices that they would otherwise suppress.
   b. They are more likely to admit unconscious prejudices.

c. They are less likely to admit any kind of prejudice.

d. They are less likely to reveal sexism but more likely to reveal anti-Semitism.

4. What is one of the main problems with the Implicit Association Test?

a. People can't respond to the pairs of associations rapidly enough.

b. It is pretty good at identifying racism but not other kinds of prejudice.

c. It doesn't have a strong relationship with how people actually behave.

d. It is a better test of explicit prejudice than implicit prejudice.

5. The Implicit Association Test might be measuring implicit prejudice, but what other explanations might account for the findings it produces?

a. It is capturing cultural stereotypes rather than people's real feelings.

b. It reflects actual associations between two traits but not necessarily prejudices.

c. It doesn't measure speed of associations quickly enough.

d. All of the above.

e. a and b.

See page 622 for the answers.

The Effects of Prejudice on the Victim

13.3 What are some ways that prejudice harms its targets?

Thus far, we have been looking at prejudice from the perspective of the perpetrator, but let's shift the focus now to the victim. One common result of being the target of prejudice is a diminution of self-esteem, internalizing society's views of one's group as being inferior, unattractive, or incompetent. Here we will discuss two kinds of self-defeating problems that can occur as a result of those internalized feelings.

The Self-Fulfilling Prophecy

Self-Fulfilling Prophecy

An expectation of one's own or another person's behavior that comes true because of the tendency of the person holding it to act in ways that bring it about.

All other things being equal, if you believe that Amy is not very bright and treat her accordingly, chances are that she will not say a lot of clever things in your presence. This is the well-known **self-fulfilling prophecy**. (See Chapter 3.) How does it work? Given your belief in her low intelligence, you probably will not ask her interesting questions, and you will not listen intently while she is talking; you might even look out the window or yawn. You behave this way because of a simple expectation: Why waste energy paying attention to Amy if she is unlikely to say anything smart or interesting? Your behavior, in turn, is bound to influence Amy's behavior, for if the people she is talking to aren't paying much attention, she will feel uneasy. She will probably clam up and not come out with all the poetry and wisdom within her. Her silence then serves to confirm the belief you had about her in the first place. The circle is closed; the self-fulfilling prophecy is complete. And it is complete for Amy as well: As people continue to ignore her observations, she develops a self-concept that she is stupid and boring.

Researchers demonstrated the relevance of this phenomenon to stereotyping and discrimination in an elegant experiment (Word, Zanna, & Cooper, 1974). White college undergraduates were asked to interview several job applicants, some White, others African American. The White students displayed discomfort and lack of interest when interviewing African American applicants. They sat farther away, tended to stammer, and ended the interview far sooner than when they were interviewing White applicants. Then, in a second experiment, the researchers systematically varied the behavior of the interviewers (actually their confederates) so that it coincided with the way the original interviewers had treated the African American or White interviewees in the first experiment. But in the second experiment, all of the people being interviewed were White. The researchers videotaped the proceedings and had the applicants rated by independent judges. Applicants who were interviewed the way African Americans had been interviewed in the first experiment were judged to be far more nervous and far less effective than those who were interviewed the way White applicants had originally been interviewed. Their behavior, in short, reflected the *interviewer's* expectations (see Figure 13.3).

On a societal level, the insidiousness of the self-fulfilling prophecy goes even further. Suppose that there is a general belief that a particular group is irredeemably uneducable and fit only for low-paying jobs. Why waste educational resources on them? Hence, they are given inadequate schooling. Hence, many drop out and fail to acquire the skills they need for well-paying careers. Hence, they face a limited number of jobs that are available and that they can do. Thirty years later, what do you find? For the most part, members of the targeted group will be severely limited in the jobs available to them and otherwise disadvantaged compared to the rest of the population. "See? I was right all the while," says the bigot. "How fortunate that we didn't waste our precious educational resources on such people!" The self-fulfilling prophecy strikes again.

Stereotype Threat

You might think that victims of prejudice and stereotyping would say, "Hey! I'm smarter than you think! Let me show you!" But too often they don't. Why not?

Various cultural groups in the United States differ, on average, in their academic test performance. Asian Americans as a group perform slightly better than Anglo-Americans, who in turn perform better than African Americans. Why does this occur? There are any number of explanations—economic, cultural, historical, political. But one major contributing factor is clearly situational and stems from the anxiety produced by negative stereotypes. In an illuminating series of experiments, Claude Steele, Joshua Aronson, and their colleagues have demonstrated the power of what

Figure 13.3 An Experiment Demonstrating Self-Fulfilling Prophecies

Stereotype Threat

The apprehension experienced by members of a group that their behavior might confirm a cultural stereotype

they call **stereotype threat** (Aronson, Wilson, & Brewer, 1998; Aronson et al., 1999; Aronson & McGlone, 2009; Steele, 1997; Steele & Aronson, 1995a, b). When African American students find themselves in highly evaluative educational situations, many feel apprehensive about confirming the existing negative cultural stereotype of "intellectual inferiority." In effect, they are saying, "If I perform poorly on this test, it will reflect badly on me and on my race." This extra burden of apprehension in turn interferes with their ability to perform well.

In one of their experiments, Steele and Aronson administered a difficult test (the GRE) individually to African American and White students at Stanford University. Half of the students of each race were led to believe that the investigator was interested in measuring their intellectual ability. The other half were led to believe that the investigator was examining the process of test taking but didn't care about the students' abilities. The results confirmed the researchers' predictions. White students performed equally well (or poorly) regardless of whether or not they believed the test was being used as a diagnostic tool. The African American students who believed their abilities were not being measured performed as well as the White students. But the African American students who thought the test *was* measuring their abilities did not perform as well as the White students or as well as the African Americans in the other group. Steele and Aronson subsequently found that one of the triggers of stereotype threat is the salience of race: If test takers are asked to indicate their race prior to taking the test, Black students perform significantly worse than they would otherwise. This detail has no effect on the performance of White test takers.

The effects of stereotype threat generalize to other performance domains. When a game of miniature golf was framed as a measure of "sport strategic intelligence," Black athletes performed worse than Whites. But when the game was framed as a measure of "natural athletic ability," the pattern reversed, and the Black athletes outperformed the White athletes (Stone, Lynch, Sjomeling, & Darley, 1999).

Stereotype threat applies to gender as well (Spencer, Steele, & Quinn, 1999). The common belief is that men are far better at math than women are. (Actually, the sexes' math skills overlap far more than they diverge [Else-Quest, Hyde, & Linn, 2010].) Accordingly, when women were led to believe that a particular test was designed to show differences in math abilities between men and women, they did not perform as well as men. But in another condition, when women were told that the same test had nothing to do with male-female differences, they performed as well as men. Asian American women do worse on math tests when they are reminded of their gender (stereotype: women are poor at math) than when they

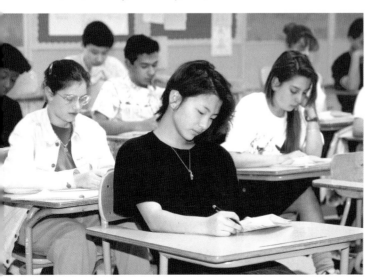

Whether or not you feel "stereotype threat" depends on what category you are identifying with at the time. Asian women do worse on math tests when they see themselves as "women" (stereotype = poor at math) rather than as "Asians" (stereotype = good at math) (Shih, Pittinsky, & Ambady, 1999).

are reminded of their cultural identity (stereotype: Asians are good at math) (Shih, Pittinsky, & Ambady, 1999). The phenomenon applies to White males too: They performed less well on a math exam when they thought they would be compared with Asian males (J. Aronson et al., 1999).

More than 300 studies have shown that stereotype threat can affect the test performance not only of many African Americans and women of any ethnicity, but also of Latinos, low-income people, and the elderly—all of whom perform better when they are not feeling self-conscious about being in a negatively stereotyped group (J. Aronson, 2010; Aronson & McGlone, 2009; Steele, 2010). The more conscious individuals are of the stereotype about their group, the greater is the effect on their performance.

How can the effects of stereotype threat be reversed? Joshua Aronson and his colleagues reasoned in the following way: If merely thinking about a stereotype can harm performance, then some kind of alternative mindset ought to help performance— if it counters the stereotype. In one experimental condition, they reminded the test takers (women and men who were about to take a difficult test of spatial ability) that they were students at a "selective northeastern liberal arts college." This reminder was enough to completely eliminate the male-female gap that occurred in the control condition, in which the test takers were merely reminded of the fact that they were "residents of the Northeast." The "I'm a good student" mindset effectively countered the "women aren't good at math" stereotype, leading to significantly better spatial performance for the female test takers (McGlone & Aronson, 2006). Similar results have been found for advanced calculus students at the university level and with middle school students on actual standardized tests (for a review, see Aronson & McGlone, 2009).

We have discussed *self-affirmation*, the practice of reminding yourself— realistically—of your good qualities or experiences that made you feel successful or proud. Experimental and field studies have found that this practice can help to counteract the effects of feeling stigmatized, disrespected, or incompetent (Cohen, Garcia, Purdie-Vaughns, Apfel, & Brzustoski, 2009; Hall, Zhao, & Shafir, 2014). The reason is that self-affirmation directs a person to focus on important domains other than the stereotyped one. It puts poor performance in that one area into broader perspective—their worth does not depend on performance in one domain alone (Sherman et al., 2013). Other counterstereotype mindsets can enhance performance as well: being reminded that abilities, including intelligence, are improvable rather than fixed; and being informed that anxiety on standardized tests is normal for members of stereotyped groups (Aronson, Fried, & Good, 2002; Aronson & Williams, 2009; Johns, Schmader, & Martens, 2005). An understanding of stereotype threat, then, can itself improve performance on tests and other evaluations.

Now that we have described the universality and consequences of prejudice, it is time to look at some of its causes.

REVIEW QUESTIONS

1. Noah's teachers don't think that Noah is very smart, so they stop paying attention to him or asking him questions. After a few years, Noah decides there is no point trying to do well in school because he's dumb. He has become a victim of
   a. the justification of effort.
   b. a self-fulfilling prophecy.
   c. implicit prejudice.
   d. stereotype threat.

2. Akash, who is Asian American, is taking a math test. Under which of these conditions is he likely to do best?
   a. When he is made aware that an equal number of men and women are taking the test
   b. When he's made aware of his Asian identity
   c. When he's made aware that he is not at a top-notch university
   d. Since Akash is very good at math, none of these conditions will affect his performance

3. What is stereotype threat?
   a. Feeling threatened by prejudices we wish we didn't have
   b. Feeling threatened by stereotypes we hold about other people

c. Feeling threatened by people who confirm our stereotypes
d. Feeling threatened by stereotypes that others hold of our group

4. How can test takers reduce the effects of stereotype threat on their performance?
   a. By reminding themselves of their skills and good qualities
   b. By denying that stereotypes affect them
   c. By studying harder
   d. By blaming cultural prejudices in society

5. Which of these ways of thinking can reduce the power of stereotype threat?
   a. Understanding that people's abilities are pretty fixed, so it's not worth being upset if you don't do well on a test
   b. Being aware that anxiety about taking tests is normal, especially for members of stereotyped groups
   c. Accepting the cultural stereotype as one that is likely to be based on actual group differences
   d. Inflating your confidence in your abilities to counteract others' expectations

See page 622 for the answers.

Causes of Prejudice

13.4   What are three aspects of social life that can cause prejudice?

Prejudice is created and maintained by many forces in the social world. Some operate on the level of the group or institution, which demands conformity to normative standards or rules in the society. Some operate within the individual, such as in the ways we process information and assign meaning to observed events. And some forces operate on whole groups of people, such as the effects of competition, conflict, and frustration.

Pressures to Conform: Normative Rules

In the 1930s, when Thurgood Marshall was a young lawyer working for the National Association for the Advancement of Colored People (NAACP), he was sent to a small town in the South to defend a Black man who was accused of a serious crime. When he arrived, he was shocked and dismayed to learn that the defendant was already dead—lynched by an angry White mob. With a heavy heart, Marshall returned to the railroad station to wait for a train back to New York. While waiting, he noticed a small food stand on the platform. He debated whether to go right up to the front and order a sandwich (as was his legal right) or to go around to the back of the stand (as was the common practice for African Americans in the South at that time). But before he reached the stand, he was approached by a heavyset White man who looked at him suspiciously. Marshall took him to be a lawman of some sort because he walked with an air of authority and had a bulge in his pants pocket that could only have been made by a handgun.

"Hey, boy," the man shouted at Marshall. "What are you doing here?" "I'm just waiting for a train," Marshall replied. The man took a few steps closer, glared at him menacingly, and said, "I didn't hear you. What did you say, boy?"

Marshall realized that his initial reply had not been sufficiently obsequious. "I beg your pardon, sir, but I'm waiting for a train." There was a long silence, during which the man slowly looked Marshall up and down and then said, "And you'd better catch that train, boy—and soon, because in this town, the sun has never set on a live nigger."

As Marshall later recalled, he decided not to get a sandwich at all but to catch the next train out, no matter where it was headed. Besides, somehow he didn't feel hungry anymore (Williams, 1998).

Thurgood Marshall went on to become chief counsel for the NAACP; in 1954, he argued the case of *Brown v. Board of Education* before the U.S. Supreme Court. His victory there put an end to legalized racial segregation in public schools. Subsequently, Marshall was appointed to the Supreme Court, where he served with distinction until his retirement in 1991. We are not sure what became of the man with the bulge in his pocket.

This remarkable story illustrates the enormous power of norms: beliefs held by a society as to what is correct, acceptable, and permissible. When Thurgood Marshall was a young man, racial segregation in hotels, eating places, motion picture theaters, drinking fountains, and toilet facilities was normative in the American South. Yet in Marshall's own lifetime, that norm almost entirely evaporated, and racial segregation is not normative in the South today.

Most people, simply by living in a society where stereotypical information abounds and where discriminatory behavior is the norm, will develop prejudiced attitudes and behave in discriminatory ways to some extent. Under conditions of **institutional discrimination**, when companies and other institutions are legally permitted—or socially encouraged—to

Institutional Discrimination
Practices that discriminate, legally or illegally, against a minority group by virtue of its ethnicity, gender, culture, age, sexual orientation, or other target of societal or company prejudice

Children often learn prejudice from parents and grandparents.

discriminate on the basis of race, gender, or other categories, prejudice will seem normal. If you grow up in a society where few minority group members and women have professional careers and where most people in these groups hold menial jobs, the likelihood of your developing negative attitudes about the inherent abilities of minorities and women will be increased. This will happen without anyone actively teaching you that minorities and women are inferior and without any law or decree banning minorities and women from college faculties, boardrooms, or medical schools. Instead, social barriers create a lack of opportunity for these groups that makes their success unlikely.

As social norms change, often as a result of changing laws and customs, so does prejudice. For decades, prejudice against gay men and lesbians was institutionalized in law and custom, just as segregation was. "Sodomy" (anal sex and certain other forms of sexual behavior, practiced by people of all sexual orientations) was against the law until the Supreme Court struck down state laws against sodomy in 2003. The 1996 Defense of Marriage Act, which had defined marriage as the union of one man and one woman, was ruled unconstitutional in 2013, and by 2014, nearly 60% of all Americans supported same-sex marriage, up from only 27% in 1996. But gay marriage is a nonissue for most young people, whereas it remains highly contentious among many of their elders. Among those aged 18 to 34, 70% support the legalization of same-sex marriage, compared to only 39% of those over age 55 (Newport, 2011).

The tendency to go along with the group to fulfill the group's expectations and gain acceptance is known as **normative conformity**. (See Chapter 8.) An understanding of normative conformity helps explain why people who hold deep prejudices might not act on them, and why people who are not prejudiced might behave in a discriminatory way: They are conforming to the norms of their social groups or institutions. A vivid example of the influence of social norms occurred in a small mining town in West Virginia many decades ago, when racial segregation was rigidly enforced: African American miners and White miners worked together with total integration while they were underground but observed the norms of total segregation while they were above ground (Minard, 1952).

Being a nonconformist is not easy; your friends might reject you, or your employer might fire you. Many people would rather go along with the prevailing view of their friends and culture rather than rock the boat. It's as if people say, "Everybody else thinks Xs are inferior; if I behave warmly toward Xs, people won't like me. They'll say bad things about me. I could lose my job. I don't need the hassle. I'll just go along with everybody else." But what happens to people who think it is important to confront friends or colleagues who make racist or sexist remarks—and, when it actually happens, decide not to, preferring to go along rather than speak up? In a series of experiments, college women were put in a group allegedly to discuss group decision making; one male member (a confederate of the experimenter) repeatedly made sexist remarks. The women who valued confronting—but did not say anything when given the opportunity—later evaluated the confederate *more highly* than women who didn't care about speaking out. Moreover, the self-silencers later decided that confronting guys who make sexist remarks is less important than they originally thought: "I guess what he said wasn't that bad" (Rasinski, Geers, & Czopp, 2013). The crucial message of this research is that silence has a price: It not only affects the target of the racist or sexist remark, who mistakenly assumes everyone else in the room agrees with it. It also affects the people who remain silent. They reduce dissonance by justifying their inaction—and thereby increasing the chance that they won't speak up in the future.

> Prejudices are the props of civilization.
>
> —André Gide, 1939

Normative Conformity

The tendency to go along with the group in order to fulfill the group's expectations and gain acceptance

When the mayor of Latta, South Carolina, fired 20-year force veteran Crystal Moore (below) from her position as police chief in 2014, he made little secret of the fact that it was because of her sexual orientation. But the citizens of Latta were outraged, rallying behind Chief Moore and forcing a vote on a referendum that allowed the town council to reinstate her. By reacting vocally to examples of prejudice in our immediate environment, we have the potential to create norms that combat bias.

Thus, people can conform to the prejudices of others and to the pressures of institutional discrimination without being prejudiced themselves, just as they can suppress their own prejudices when the norms and situation demand. But how do prejudices get "inside" us in the first place and become so difficult to eradicate?

Social Identity Theory: Us versus Them

Each of us develops a personal identity that is based on our particular traits and unique life history. But we also develop a **social identity** based on the groups we belong to, including our national, religious, political, and occupational groups (Brewer & Brown, 1998; Dovidio & Gaertner, 2010; Tajfel, 1982; Tajfel & Turner, 1986). Social identities give us a sense of place and position in the world. It feels good to be part of an "us." But does that mean that we must automatically feel superior to "them"?

ETHNOCENTRISM   The belief that your own culture, nation, or religion is superior to all others is called **ethnocentrism**. It is universal, probably because it aids survival by increasing people's attachment to their own group and their willingness to work on its behalf. It rests on a fundamental category: us. As soon as people have created an "us," however, they perceive everybody else as "not us." The impulse to feel suspicious of "outsiders" seems to be part of a biological survival mechanism inducing us to favor our own family, tribe, or race and to protect our tribe from external threat. But that statement doesn't go far enough, because human beings are also biologically prepared to be friendly, open, and cooperative (Cikara & Van Bavel, 2014; Kappeler & van Schaik, 2006).

Earlier we described the work of social neuroscientists, who investigate which parts of the brain might be involved in forming stereotypes, holding prejudiced beliefs, and feeling disgust, anger, or anxiety about an ethnic or stigmatized group (Harris & Fiske, 2006; Stanley, Phelps, & Banaji, 2008). In one study, when African Americans and Whites saw pictures of each other, activity in the amygdala (the brain structure associated with fear and other negative emotions) was elevated; it was not elevated when people saw pictures of members of their own group. Yet when participants were registering the faces as individuals or as part of a simple visual test rather than as members of the category "Blacks," there was no increased activation in the amygdala. The brain is designed to register differences, it appears, but any negative associations with those differences depend on context and learning (Wheeler & Fiske, 2005). That is why social psychologists strive to identify the *conditions* under which prejudice and hostility toward out-groups are fostered or reduced.

IN-GROUP BIAS   Kurt Vonnegut captured the concept of in-group versus out-group beautifully in his novel *Cat's Cradle*. A woman discovers that a person she has just met casually on a plane is from Indiana. Even though they have almost nothing else in common, a bond immediately forms between them:

> "My God," she said, "are you a Hoosier?"
> I admitted I was.
> "I'm a Hoosier too," she crowed. "Nobody has to be ashamed of being a Hoosier."
> "I'm not," I said. "I never knew anybody who was."

This **in-group bias** refers to the positive feelings and special treatment we give to people we have defined as being part of our in-group; unfortunately, it often leads to unfair treatment of others merely because we have defined them as being in the out-group. Indeed, social psychologists Anthony Greenwald and Thomas Pettigrew (2014) argue that in-group bias is an even more powerful reason for discrimination than outright prejudice and hostility are. People prefer being with others who

---

Social Identity

The part of a person's self-concept that is based on his or her identification with a nation, religious or political group, occupation, or other social affiliation

Ethnocentrism

The belief that one's own ethnic group, nation, or religion is superior to all others

In-Group Bias

The tendency to favor members of one's own group and give them special preference over people who belong to other groups; the group can be temporary and trivial as well as significant

Dressing alike is a way of demonstrating membership in an in-group.

are familiar, who are similar to them in norms and customs, and whom they perceive as being "like them" in other important ways. But this bias can lead to unintended negative outcomes, such as preference for the in-group in hiring and promotion.

To get at the pure, unvarnished mechanisms behind this phenomenon, British social psychologist Henri Tajfel and his colleagues created entities called *minimal groups* (Tajfel, 1982a; Tajfel & Turner, 1986). In their experiments, complete strangers are formed into groups using the most trivial criteria imaginable. For example, in one, British schoolboys were shown a set of slides with varying numbers of dots on them. The boys were asked to guess how many dots there were. The boys were arbitrarily told that they were "overestimators" or "underestimators" and were then asked to work on another task. In this phase, they had a chance to give points to other boys identified as overestimators or underestimators. Although each boy worked alone in his cubicle, almost every single one assigned far more points to boys he thought were like him, an overestimator or an underestimator. As the boys emerged from their rooms, they were asked, "Which were you?" The answers received either cheers or boos from the others.

In short, even when the reasons for differentiation are minimal, being in the in-group makes you want to win against members of the out-group and leads you to treat the latter unfairly, because such tactics build your self-esteem and feeling of "belongingness." When your group does win, it strengthens your feelings of pride and identification with that group. How do you feel about being a student of your university following a winning or losing football season? Robert Cialdini and his colleagues (Cialdini et al., 1976; see also Cialdini, 2009) counted the number of college insignia T-shirts and sweatshirts worn to classes on the Monday following a football game at seven different universities. The results? You guessed it: Students were more likely to wear their university's insignia after victory than after defeat. "We" won. But if our team loses, we say "they" lost.

OUT-GROUP HOMOGENEITY   Besides the in-group bias, another consequence of social categorization is the perception of **out-group homogeneity**, the belief that "they" are all alike (Linville, Fischer, & Salovey, 1989; Quattrone, 1986). In-group members tend to perceive those in the out-group as more similar to each other (homogeneous) than they really are. Does your college have a traditional rival, whether in athletics or academics? If so, as an in-group member, you probably value your institution more highly than you value the rival (thereby raising and protecting your self-esteem), and you probably perceive students at this rival school to be alike than you perceive students at your own college to be.

Consider a study of students in two rival universities: Princeton and Rutgers. The rivalry between these institutions has long been based on athletics, academics, and even social-class consciousness (Princeton is private, and Rutgers is public). Male students at the two schools watched videotaped scenes in which three different young men were asked to make a decision, such as whether he wanted to listen to rock music or classical music while participating in an experiment on auditory perception (Quattrone & Jones, 1980). The participants were told that the man was either a Princeton or a Rutgers student, so for some of them, the student in the videotape was an in-group member and for others an out-group member. Participants had to predict what the man in the videotape would choose. After they saw the man make his choice (e.g., rock or classical music), they were asked to predict what percentage of male students at that institution would make the same choice. Did the predictions vary due to the in-group or the out-group status of the target men?

As you can see in Figure 13.4, the results support the out-group homogeneity hypothesis: When the target person was an out-group member, the participants believed his choice was more predictive of what his peers would choose than when he was an in-group member (a student at their own school). In other words, if you

Out-Group Homogeneity

The perception that individuals in the out-group are more similar to each other (homogeneous) than they really are, as well as more similar than members of the in-group are

Figure 13.4 Judgments About In-Group and Out-Group Members

After watching a target person choose between two alternatives, Rutgers students and Princeton students had to estimate what percentage of students at their school (their in-group) versus their rival school (the out-group) would make the same choice. Students thought that out-group members were more alike, whereas they noticed variation within their own group. This "homogeneity bias" was especially pronounced among Rutgers students (blue line).

(Adapted from Quattrone & Jones, 1980)

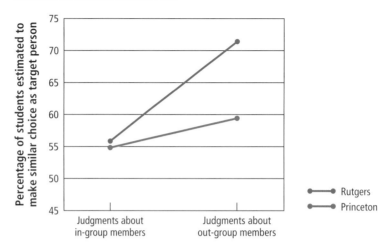

know something about one out-group member, you are more likely to feel you know something about all of them. Similar results have been found in a wide variety of experiments in the United States, Europe, and Australia (Duck, Hogg, & Terry, 1995; Hartstone & Augoustinos, 1995; Judd & Park, 1988; Ostrom & Sedikides, 1992; Park & Rothbart, 1982).

BLAMING THE VICTIM   Try as they might, people who have rarely been discriminated against have a hard time fully understanding what it's like to be a target of prejudice. Well-intentioned members of the majority will sympathize with groups that are targets of discrimination, but true empathy is difficult for those who have routinely been judged on the basis of their own merit and not their racial, ethnic, religious, or other group membership. And when empathy is absent, it is hard to avoid falling into the attributional trap of **blaming the victim** for his or her plight.

Ironically, this tendency to blame victims for their victimization—attributing their predicaments to inherent deficits in their abilities and character—is typically motivated by an understandable desire to see the world as a fair and just place, one where people get what they deserve and deserve what they get. (See Chapter 4.) The stronger a person's belief in a just world, the more likely he or she is to blame the poor and homeless for their own plight, or to blame overweight people for being lazy, rather than consider economic conditions, genetic predispositions, mental illness, lack of opportunities, and so forth (Crandall et al., 2001; Furnham & Gunter, 1984). Similarly, most people, when confronted with evidence of an unfair outcome that is otherwise hard to explain, find a way to blame the victim (Aguiar, Vala, Correia, & Pereira, 2008; Lerner, 1980, 1991; Lerner & Grant, 1990). In one experiment, two people worked equally hard on the same task, and by the flip of a coin, one received a sizable reward, and the other received nothing. After the fact, observers tended to reconstruct what happened and convince themselves that the unlucky person must not have worked as hard.

Most of us are good at reconstructing situations after the fact to support our belief in a just world. It simply requires making a dispositional attribution (it's the victim's fault) rather than a situational one (scary, random events can happen to anyone at any time). In a fascinating experiment, college students who were provided with a

Blaming the Victim

The tendency to blame individuals (make dispositional attributions) for their victimization, typically motivated by a desire to see the world as a fair place description of a young woman's friendly behavior toward a man judged that behavior as completely appropriate (Janoff-Bulman, Timko, & Carli, 1985). Another group of students was given the same description, plus the information that the encounter ended with the young woman being raped by the man. This group rated the young woman's behavior as inappropriate; she was judged as having brought the rape on herself.

How can we account for such harsh attributions? When something bad happens to another person, as when someone is mugged or raped, we will feel sorry for the person but at the same time relieved that this horrible thing didn't happen to us. We will also feel scared that such a thing might happen to us in the future. We can protect ourselves from that fear by convincing ourselves that the person must have done something to cause the tragedy. We feel safer, then, because we believe that *we* would have behaved more cautiously (Jones & Aronson, 1973).

How does the belief in a just world lead to the perpetuation of prejudice? Most of us find it frightening to think that we live in a world where people, through no fault of their own, can be raped, discriminated against, deprived of equal pay for equal work, or denied the basic necessities of life. It is much more reassuring to believe that they brought their fates on themselves. One variation of blaming the victim is the "well-deserved reputation" excuse. It goes something like this: "If the Jews have been victimized throughout their history, they must have been doing something to deserve it." Such reasoning constitutes a demand that members of the out-group conform to more stringent standards of behavior than those the majority have set for themselves.

JUSTIFYING FEELINGS OF ENTITLEMENT AND SUPERIORITY   Prejudices support the in-group's feeling of superiority, its religious or political identity, and the legitimacy of inequality in wealth, status, and power ("our group is entitled to its greater wealth and status because 'those people' are inferior"). Wherever a majority group systematically discriminates against a minority to preserve its power—Whites, Blacks, Muslims, Hindus, Japanese, Hutu, Christians, Jews, you name it—they will claim that their actions are legitimate because the minority is so obviously inferior and incompetent (Jost, Nosek, & Gosling, 2008; Morton, Postmes, Haslam, & Hornsey, 2009; Sidanius, Pratto, & Bobo, 1996). In a series of experiments in Bangladesh, Muslims (who are the majority there) and Hindus (a minority) both revealed strong in-group favoritism, but only the majority Muslims denigrated the minority Hindus (Islam & Hewstone, 1993). Most people who are in dominant positions in their society do not see themselves as being prejudiced; they regard *their* beliefs about the out-group as being perfectly reasonable.

Christian Crandall and Amy Eshleman (2003) argue that most people struggle between their urge to express a prejudice they hold and their need to maintain a positive self-concept as someone who is not a bigot, both in their own eyes and in the eyes of others. But suppressing prejudiced impulses requires constant energy, so people are always on the lookout for information that will enable them to convince themselves that they are justified in disliking a particular out-group. Once they find that justification, they can discriminate all they want and still feel that they are not bigots (thus avoiding cognitive dissonance). Remember the experiments in which supposedly unprejudiced people administered more punishment to the out-group when they had been insulted or angered? They had a justification for their increased aggression: "I'm not a bad or prejudiced person, but he insulted me! She hurt me!" In this way, as Crandall and Eshleman (2003) put it, "Justification undoes suppression, it provides cover, and it protects a sense of egalitarianism and a non-prejudiced self-image."

Many people justify their beliefs, including their prejudiced beliefs, by calling on religious doctrine. For example, it's not uncommon for people to defend their antigay

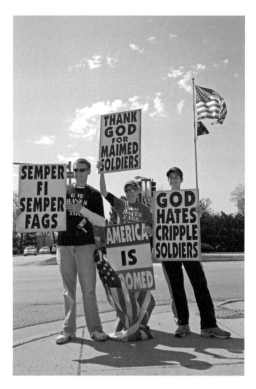

The Bible has been used to promote tolerance and compassion—as well as to justify and inflame many prejudices.

feelings by citing the Bible, either claiming that the Bible prohibits homosexuality or that they are fighting for "family values" rather than against gays and lesbians. The problem with using the Bible in this way is that equally religious people use the Bible to support their belief in acceptance of and equality for gay men and lesbians, and many religious denominations now endorse gay marriage and approve of gay clergy. In their book *What God Has Joined Together: The Christian Case for Gay Marriage*, David Myers and Letha Scanzoni (2006) argued that there are far more verses in the Bible celebrating compassion, love, and justice than the very few that refer vaguely to homosexuality.

Because the Bible is a historical as well as a spiritual document, it has been used to justify many practices that Americans no longer believe in. In the nineteenth century, American slaveholders often quoted the Bible (Exodus 21:7) as a moral justification for slavery. Prominent among these was the Reverend Thornton Stringfellow of Virginia, a distinguished theologian who, in 1841, wrote a treatise designed to "rebut the palpable ignorance" of northerners who were denouncing slavery as a sin. On the contrary, he wrote, "From Abraham's day, until the coming of Christ, a period of two thousand years, this institution found favor with God." He added that Jesus accepted slavery and never spoke out against it. Needless to say, biblical teachings about love and justice have also informed and motivated the proliferation of hospitals, the founding of universities, the fight to abolish slavery, and the modern civil rights movement. As Gordon Allport (1954) wrote, "The role of religion is paradoxical. It makes prejudice and it unmakes prejudice."

Realistic Conflict Theory

Realistic Conflict Theory

The idea that limited resources lead to conflict between groups and result in increased prejudice and discrimination

Finally, one of the most obvious sources of conflict and prejudice is competition—for scarce resources, for political power, and for social status. **Realistic conflict theory** holds that limited resources lead to conflict between groups and result in prejudice and discrimination (Jackson, 1993; Sherif, 1966; White, 1977). For example, many young people rightfully complain about the stereotypes and prejudices that some old people hold toward them. But they too may be ageist, regarding old people as incompetent, irrelevant, stubborn, foolish, or stingy. In today's economic climate, intergenerational tensions have grown, with some young people feeling resentful that the old are getting more of society's benefits and opportunities than they deserve. Both old and young now complain that they are victims of age discrimination (North & Fiske, 2012).

On a national level, weak leaders and governments often select a minority group to use as a scapegoat—"those people are the reason for all our problems." This is an effort to unify their citizens ("us") against "them" and thereby distract everyone's attention from "our" failures to run the country (Staub, 1999). In many of the Eastern European countries that emerged following the fall of the former Soviet Union in 1991, new freedoms were accompanied by increased feelings of nationalism that in turn intensified feelings of rancor and prejudice against out-groups. In the Baltic states and the Balkans, the rise in nationalistic feelings led to the outbreak of hostility and war among Serbs, Muslims, and Croats; Azerbaijanis and Armenians; and other groups. In 2011, the Serbian general Ratko Mladic was finally arrested on charges of committing war crimes and genocide, including the execution of more than 7,000 Muslims at Srebrenica during the Serbian war of the 1990s. Mladic had made the Muslims the scapegoat as a way of unifying Serbians and solidifying his power.

ECONOMIC AND POLITICAL COMPETITION   In his classic study of prejudice in a small industrial town, John Dollard (1938) was among the first to document the relationship between discrimination and economic competition. At first, there was no discernible hostility toward the new German immigrants who had arrived in the town; prejudice flourished, however, as jobs grew scarce. Local Whites became hostile and aggressive toward the newcomers. They began to express scornful, derogatory opinions about the Germans, to whom the native White people felt superior. "The chief element in the permission to be aggressive against the Germans," wrote Dollard, "was rivalry for jobs and status in the local woodenware plants."

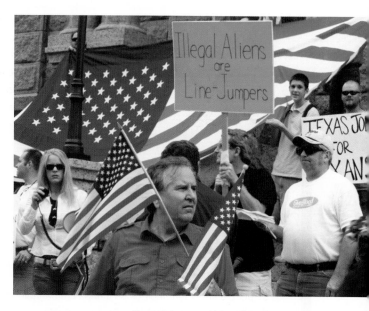

Economic competition drives a good deal of prejudice. When unemployment rises, so does resentment against minorities.

Similarly, the prejudice, violence, and negative stereotyping directed against Chinese immigrants in the United States fluctuated wildly throughout the nineteenth century as a result of changes in economic competition. Chinese people who joined the California gold rush, competing directly with White miners, were described as "depraved and vicious," "gross gluttons," and "bloodthirsty and inhuman" (Jacobs & Landau, 1971). Only a few years later, however, when they were willing to accept backbreaking work as laborers on the transcontinental railroad—work that few White Americans were willing to do—they were regarded as sober, industrious, and law abiding. They were so highly regarded that Charles Crocker, one of the great tycoons financing the railroad, wrote, "They are equal to the best White men. . . . They are very trusty, very intelligent, and they live up to their contracts." At the end of the Civil War, former soldiers flooded into an already tight job market. This influx of labor was immediately followed by an increase in negative attitudes toward the Chinese: The stereotype changed to criminal, conniving, crafty, and stupid.

Today, Mexicans are viewed in the same way the Chinese were, particularly the Mexican migrant workers whose labor is needed in many American states but who are perceived as costing American workers their jobs. As competition—real and imagined—has increased, violence against Latinos has risen as well, and Mexicans and other Latinos have become the main focus of White anger about illegal immigration. These changes in the target of a majority group's anger suggest that when times are tough and resources are scarce, in-group members will feel more threatened by the out-group. Accordingly, incidents of prejudice, discrimination, and violence toward out-group members will increase.

In a classic experiment, Muzafer Sherif and his colleagues (1961) tested group conflict theory using the natural environment of a Boy Scout camp called Robber's Cave. The participants in the camp were healthy 12-year-old boys who were randomly assigned to one of two groups, the Eagles or the Rattlers. Each group stayed in its own cabin; the cabins were located quite a distance apart to reduce contact between the two groups. The boys were placed in situations designed to increase the cohesiveness of their own group, such as going hiking and swimming, working together on building projects, and preparing group meals.

After feelings of cohesiveness developed within each group, the researchers set up a series of competitive activities in which the two groups were pitted against each other—in football, baseball, and tug-of-war, where prizes were awarded to the winning team. These competitive games aroused feelings of conflict and tension between the two groups. The investigators created other situations to further intensify the conflict: A camp party was arranged, but each group was told that it started at a different time, thereby ensuring that the Eagles would arrive well before the Rattlers. Also, the refreshments at the party consisted of two different kinds of food. Half the food was fresh, appealing, and appetizing, while the other half was squashed, ugly, and unappetizing.

As you'd expect, the early-arriving Eagles ate well, and the late-coming Rattlers were not happy with what they found. They began to curse the Eagles for being greedy. Because the Eagles believed they deserved what they got (first come, first served), they resented the name-calling and responded in kind. Name-calling escalated into food throwing, and within a short time punches were thrown and a full-scale riot ensued.

The investigators did manage to reduce the hostility between the two groups, and we will tell you how they did it at the end of this chapter.

REVIEW QUESTIONS

1. According to realistic conflict theory, prejudice and discrimination are likely to increase when
   a. a country has a history of racism.
   b. people who hold stereotypes about a target group are frustrated.
   c. people know that their close friends are prejudiced.
   d. people are competing for jobs and security.
   e. prejudice is explicit rather than implicit.

2. Rebecca is covering her college's football game against its archrival for the school newspaper. At the game, she interviews six students from her college but decides she needs to interview only one student from the rival school to represent their view of the game. Rebecca is demonstrating
   a. in-group bias.
   b. out-group homogeneity.
   c. entitlement.
   d. blaming the victim.

3. Following are some explanations of prejudice that social psychologists investigate. Which one doesn't fit?
   a. Pressures to conform
   b. Ethnocentrism
   c. Realistic economic conflicts

   d. The need for catharsis
   e. Institutional discrimination

4. Most people are caught between the struggle to express their prejudice and the need to maintain a positive self-image. To relieve themselves from the discomfort experienced by suppressing their prejudice, people tend to
   a. resort to self-talk to convince themselves that suppressing is important.
   b. look for information to justify their prejudice.
   c. try to befriend a member of the group they are prejudiced against.
   d. hold a prejudiced attitude toward a group without harboring any feelings of resentment.

5. The Robber's Cave study created hostility between two groups of boys by
   a. putting them in competitive situations with prizes for the winners.
   b. allowing them to freely express their feelings of anger.
   c. randomly giving one group more privileges.
   d. letting the boys set their own rules and games.

See page 622 for the answers.

Reducing Prejudice

13.5   What are the six conditions that can reduce prejudice?

Sometimes subtle, sometimes brutally overt, prejudice is ubiquitous. The good news of declining prejudicial attitudes, greater tolerance, and an end to legal discrimination seems always to be followed by eruptions of hostility, conflict, and hatred toward the target group of the moment. Does this mean that prejudice is an essential aspect of human social interaction and will therefore always be with us? We social psychologists do not take such a pessimistic view. We tend to agree with Henry David Thoreau that "it is never too late to give up our prejudices." People can change. But how? What can we do to reduce this noxious aspect of human social behavior?

One logical step might be to provide people with accurate information that refutes their stereotypes, but by now you know it is not that simple. During and after World War II, most Anglo-Americans thought that Japanese Americans were unpatriotic, potential traitors to the Allied cause. The U.S. government had uprooted the Japanese Americans living on the West Coast and dispatched them to internment camps for the duration of the war. What if those prejudiced Americans learned that the most highly decorated American combat unit in World War II was composed solely of

Japanese Americans? Would this information have affected their attitude toward their fellow citizens?

Not necessarily. As we saw in discussing stereotypes earlier, when people are presented with an example or two that seems to refute their existing stereotype, most of them do not change their general belief. In one experiment, some people presented with this kind of disconfirming evidence actually *strengthened* their stereotypical belief because the disconfirming evidence challenged them to come up with additional reasons for holding on to their prejudice (Kunda & Oleson, 1997). When you offer people only two or three strong disconfirming pieces of evidence, participants can dismiss them as "the exceptions that prove the rule." That's why the most fervent racist or anti-Semite can say, "but some of my best friends are . . ."

Because stereotypes and prejudice are based on false information, for many years social activists believed that education was the answer: All we needed to do was expose people to the truth, and their prejudices would disappear. But, as we saw earlier, this expectation proved to be naive. Because of the underlying emotional aspects of prejudice, as well as some of the cognitive ruts we get into, stereotypes based on misinformation are difficult to modify merely by providing people with the facts. But there is hope. Repeated contact with members of an out-group can modify stereotypes and prejudice (Webber & Crocker, 1983). But mere contact is not enough; it must be a special kind of contact. What exactly does this mean?

After the attacks on the World Trade Center and the Pentagon on September 11, 2001, scapegoating of Muslims increased.

The Contact Hypothesis

In 1954, when the U.S. Supreme Court outlawed segregated schools, social psychologists were excited and optimistic. They believed that desegregating the schools—increasing the contact between White children and Black children—would increase the self-esteem of minority children and herald the beginning of the end of prejudice. This view came to be called the *contact hypothesis*.

There was good reason for this optimism because not only did it make sense theoretically, but empirical evidence also supported the power of contact among races (Van Laar, Levin, & Sidanius, 2008). As early as 1951, Morton Deutsch and Mary Ellen Collins examined the attitudes of White Americans toward African Americans in two public housing projects that differed in their degree of racial integration. In one, Black and White families had been randomly assigned to separate buildings in the same project. In the other project, Black and White families lived in the same building. After several months, White residents in the integrated project reported a greater positive change in their attitudes toward Black neighbors than residents of the segregated project did, even though the former had not chosen to live in an integrated building initially (Deutsch & Collins, 1951). Similarly, when White southerners joined the U.S. Army—after army units became integrated in the early 1950s—their racism gradually decreased (Pettigrew, 1958; Watson, 1950).

The contact hypothesis has been supported by many studies in the laboratory and in the real world: young people's attitudes toward the elderly, healthy people's attitudes toward the mentally ill, nondisabled children's attitudes toward the disabled, and straight people's prejudices toward gay men and lesbians (Herek & Capitanio, 1996; Pettigrew & Tropp, 2006; Wilner, Walkley, & Cook, 1955).

Today's multiethnic college campuses are a living laboratory of the contact hypothesis. White students who have roommates, friends, and relationships across racial and ethnic lines tend to become less prejudiced and find commonalities across group borders (Van Laar et al., 2008). Cross-group friendships benefit minorities and reduce their prejudices too. Minority students who join ethnic student organizations tend to develop, over time, not only an even stronger ethnic identity but also an increased sense of ethnic victimization. Just like White students who live in White fraternities and sororities, they come to feel that they have less in common with other ethnic groups (Sidanius, Van Laar, Levin, & Sinclair, 2004). But a longitudinal study of Black and Latino students at a predominantly White university found that friendships with White students increased their feelings of belonging and reduced their feelings of dissatisfaction with the school. This was especially true for students who had been feeling insecure and sensitive about being rejected as members of a minority (Mendoza-Denton & Page-Gould, 2008) (see Figure 13.5).

Although contact between ethnic groups is generally a good thing, the desegregation of schools did not work as smoothly as most knowledgeable people had expected. Far from producing the hoped-for harmony, school desegregation frequently led to tension and turmoil in the classroom. In his analysis of the research examining the impact of desegregation, Walter Stephan (1978, 1985) was unable to find a single study demonstrating a significant increase in self-esteem among African American children, and 25% of the studies showed a significant decrease in their self-esteem following desegregation. Prejudice was not reduced either. Stephan (1978) found that in 53% of the studies prejudice actually increased; in 34% of the studies, no change in prejudice occurred. And if you had taken an aerial photograph of the school yards of most desegregated schools, you would have found almost no integration: White kids tended to cluster with White kids, Black kids tended to cluster with Black kids, Hispanic kids tended to cluster with Hispanic kids, and so on (Aronson & Gonzalez, 1988; Aronson & Thibodeau, 1992; Schofield, 1986). Clearly, in this instance, mere contact did not work as anticipated.

What went wrong? Why did desegregated housing work better than desegregated schools? To answer these questions, we need to take a closer look at the contact hypothesis and the conditions under which it is effective—or ineffective. Clearly, not all kinds of contact will reduce prejudice and raise self-esteem; sometimes, contact can

---

Figure 13.5 The Impact of Cross-Ethnic Friendships on Minority Students' Well-Being

In a longitudinal study of minority Black students at a predominantly White university, many Black students at first felt dissatisfied and excluded from school life. But the more White friends they made, the higher their sense of belonging (orange bar) and satisfaction with the university (red bar). This finding was particularly significant for minority students who had been the most sensitive to rejection and who had felt the most anxious and insecure about being in a largely White school. The study was later replicated with minority Latino students.

(Based on Mendoza-Denton & Page-Gould, 2008)

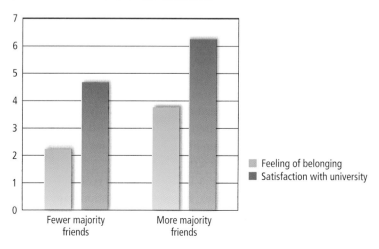

make intergroup relations more hostile and even increase prejudice (Saguy, Tausch, Dovidio, Pratto, & Singh, 2011). In the South, Blacks and Whites have had a great deal of contact, dating back to the time when Africans first arrived on American shores; however, prejudice flourished nonetheless. Obviously, the *kind* of contact they were having, as master and slave, was not the kind that would reduce prejudice.

Gordon Allport (1954) observed that contact can reduce prejudice only when three conditions are met: both groups are of equal status; both share a common goal that generates awareness of their shared interests and common humanity; and their contact is supported by law or local custom (social norms). Note that in the housing study, as with the U.S. Army recruits, the two groups were of equal status, and no obvious conflict existed between them—but this was not true in the schools. Decades of research have substantiated Allport's early claim. But in the intervening years, researchers have identified three additional conditions. Let's see what they are.

When Contact Reduces Prejudice

In the Robber's Cave study, the Eagles and the Rattlers, under conditions of conflict and competition, became prejudiced and hostile toward each other. Once that happened, the cat was out of the bag. Removing the conflict and the competition did not restore harmony. Bringing the two groups together in neutral situations actually *increased* their hostility and distrust. The boys in these two groups quarreled with each other even when they were just sitting around watching a movie together (Sherif et al., 1961). But then the researchers staged several events to try to reduce the hostilities they had created, and their findings tell us a great deal about what contact can and cannot do. Sherif's research and subsequent studies have clarified the conditions that must be met if contact is to reduce prejudice between two formerly hostile groups:

1. *Both sides must depend on each other to accomplish their goals.* Sherif created conditions of **interdependence**, placing the two groups of boys in situations where they needed one another to get something that was important to both sides. One time, the investigators set up an emergency situation by damaging the water supply system; the only way the system could be repaired was if all the Rattlers and Eagles cooperated immediately. On another occasion, the camp truck broke down while the boys were on a camping trip. To get the truck going again, it was necessary for all of them to work in harmony to pull it up a steep hill.

2. *Both sides must pursue a common goal.* The boys now shared the same goals, which could be achieved only if all the boys pulled together, regardless of whether they were Eagles or Rattlers. Eventually, these first two conditions succeeded in reducing the hostile feelings and negative stereotyping between the two sets of campers. After these cooperative situations were introduced, the number of boys who said their closest friend was in the other group increased (see Figure 13.6).

3. *Both sides must have equal status.* At the boys' camp and in the public housing project, the group members were much the same in terms of status and power. No one was the boss, and no one was the less powerful employee. When status is unequal, interactions can easily follow stereotypical patterns. The whole point of contact is to allow people to learn that their stereotypes are inaccurate; contact and interaction should lead to disconfirmation of negative, stereotyped beliefs. If status is unequal between the groups, their interactions will be shaped by that status difference—the bosses will act like stereotypical bosses, the employees like stereotypical subordinates—and no one will learn new, disconfirming information about the other group (Pettigrew, 1969; Wilder, 1984).

4. *Both sides must get to know each other in a friendly, informal setting* where they can interact on a one-to-one basis—discovering shared interests, having meals together, hanging out casually. Simply placing two groups in "contact" in a room

Interdependence

The situation that exists when two or more groups need to depend on one another to accomplish a goal that is important to each of them

Figure 13.6 How Cooperation Fosters Intergroup Relations

When the Eagles and the Rattlers were in competition, few of the boys in each group had friends from the other side. Intergroup tensions were eased only after the boys had to cooperate to get shared privileges and the boys began to make friends across "enemy lines."

(Based on data in Sherif, Harvey, White, Hood, & Sherif, 1961)

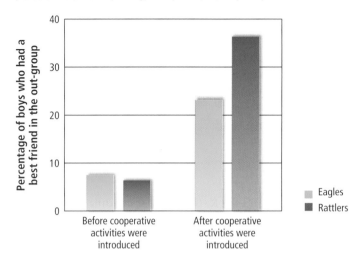

where they remain segregated will do little to promote their understanding or knowledge of each other (Brewer & Miller, 1984).

5. *Both sides must be exposed to multiple members of the other group, not just one token.* In this way, the individual learns that the out-group members in that informal setting are typical of their group; otherwise, the stereotype can be maintained by labeling that one token as the outstanding exception (Wilder, 1984). When discrimination against women in the workforce became illegal, it was common for a single (brave!) woman to be hired in a field that was otherwise almost entirely male. An early study of male police officers assigned female partners in Washington, D.C., found that although the men were satisfied with their female partners' performance, they still opposed hiring women police officers. Their stereotypes about women's ability to do police work hadn't changed; the stereotypes they held matched those of male officers with male partners (Milton, 1971). Why? The men assigned a female partner simply perceived her as an exception.

6. *Both sides must know that the social norms of their group, institution, and community promote and support equality.* Social norms wield great power; here they can be harnessed to motivate people to reach out to members of the out-group (Allport, 1954; Amir, 1976; Wilder, 1984). If a boss or professor creates and reinforces a norm of acceptance and tolerance at work or in the classroom, group members will change their behavior to fit the norm.

To sum up, two groups are more likely to reduce their reciprocal stereotyping, prejudice, and discriminatory behavior when six conditions of contact are met: Both sides are interdependent; they share a common goal; they have equal status; they have opportunities for informal contact with one another; there are multiple members of each group; and the larger social norms promote equality.

WHERE DESEGREGATION WENT WRONG Knowing now what conditions must exist for contact to work, we can better

When women first began to work as peers with male police officers, they were often seen as the exception to the existing stereotype of women. Under what conditions will contact in the workplace reduce prejudice?

understand the problems that occurred when schools were first desegregated. Imagine a typical scenario. Carlos, a Mexican American sixth grader, has been attending schools in an underprivileged neighborhood his entire life. Because the schools in his neighborhood were not well equipped or well staffed, his first 5 years of education were somewhat deficient. Suddenly, without much warning or preparation, he is bused to a school in a predominantly White, middle-class neighborhood.

As most students know from experience, the traditional classroom is a highly competitive environment. The typical scene involves the teacher asking a question; immediately, several hands go into the air as the children strive to show the teacher that they know the answer. When a teacher calls on one child, several others groan because they've missed an opportunity to show the teacher how smart they are. If the child who is called on hesitates or comes up with the wrong answer, there is a renewed and intensified flurry of hands in the air, perhaps even accompanied by whispered, derisive comments directed at the student who failed. Carlos finds he must compete against White, middle-class students who have had better preparation than he and who have been reared to hold White, middle-class values, which include working hard in pursuit of good grades, raising one's hand enthusiastically whenever the teacher asks a question, and so on. In effect, Carlos has been thrust into a highly competitive situation for which he is unprepared and in which payoffs are made for abilities he has not yet developed. He is virtually guaranteed to lose. After a few failures, Carlos, feeling defeated, humiliated, and dispirited, stops raising his hand and can hardly wait for the bell to ring to signal the end of the school day.

In the typical desegregated classroom, the students were not of equal status and were not pursuing common goals. We might say that they were in a tug-of-war on an uneven playing field; no wonder the self-esteem of minority children plummeted following desegregation (Stephan, 1978). Given the competitive atmosphere of the classroom, it is likely that the situation would have exacerbated whatever stereotypes existed before desegregation. Given that the minority kids were not prepared for the competitiveness of the classroom, some of the White kids quickly concluded that the minority kids were stupid, unmotivated, and sullen, just as they had suspected (Wilder & Shapiro, 1989). For their part, the minority kids might conclude that the White kids were arrogant show-offs. The self-fulfilling prophecy strikes again.

How could we change the atmosphere of the classroom so that it comes closer to Allport's prescription for the effectiveness of contact? How could we get White students and minority students to be of equal status, interdependent, and in pursuit of common goals?

Cooperation and Interdependence: The Jigsaw Classroom

In 1971, Austin, Texas, desegregated its schools. Within just a few weeks, African American, White, and Mexican American children were in open conflict; fistfights broke out in the corridors and school yards. Austin's school superintendent called on Elliot Aronson, then a professor at the University of Texas, to find a way to create a more harmonious environment. After spending a few days observing the dynamics of several classrooms, Aronson and his graduate students were reminded of the situation that existed in the camp experiment of Sherif and colleagues (1961). With the findings of that study in mind, they developed a technique that created an interdependent classroom atmosphere designed to place the students of various racial and ethnic groups in pursuit of common goals. They called it the **jigsaw classroom** because it resembled the assembling of a jigsaw puzzle (Aronson, 1978; Aronson & Bridgeman, 1979; Aronson & Gonzalez, 1988; Aronson & Patnoe, 1997; Walker & Crogan, 1998; Wolfe & Spencer, 1996).

Jigsaw Classroom

A classroom setting designed to reduce prejudice and raise the self-esteem of children by placing them in small, multiethnic groups and making each child dependent on the other children in the group to learn the course material

Two are better than one because they have a good reward for their toil. For if they fail, one will lift up his fellow, but woe to him who is alone when he falls and has not another to lift him up.

—Ecclesiastes 4:9–12

Here is how the jigsaw classroom works: Students are placed in diverse six-person learning groups. The day's lesson is divided into six segments, and each student is assigned one segment of the written material. Thus, if the students are to learn the life of Eleanor Roosevelt, her biography is broken into six parts and distributed to the six students, each of whom has possession of a unique and vital part of the information, which, like the pieces of a jigsaw puzzle, must be put together before anyone can view the whole picture. Each student must learn his or her own section and teach it to the other members of the group, who do not have any other access to that material. Therefore, if Debbie wants to do well on the exam about the life of Eleanor Roosevelt, she must pay close attention to Carlos (who is reciting on Roosevelt's girlhood years), to Shamika (who is reciting on Roosevelt's years in the White House), and so on.

Unlike the traditional classroom, where students are competing against each other, the jigsaw classroom has students depending on each other. In the traditional classroom, if Carlos, because of anxiety and discomfort, is having trouble reciting, the other students can easily ignore him or put him down in their zeal to show the teacher how smart they are. But in the jigsaw classroom, if Carlos is having trouble reciting, it is now in the best interests of the other students to be patient, make encouraging comments, and even ask friendly, probing questions to make it easier for Carlos to bring forth the knowledge that only he has.

Through the jigsaw process, the children begin to pay more attention to each other and to show respect for each other. A child such as Carlos would respond to this treatment by simultaneously becoming more relaxed and more engaged; this would inevitably produce an improvement in his ability to communicate. After a couple of weeks, the other students were struck by their realization that Carlos was a lot smarter than they had thought he was. They began to like him. Carlos began to enjoy school more and began to see the Anglo students in his group not as tormentors, but as helpful and responsible teammates. In turn, as he began to feel increasingly comfortable in class and started to gain more confidence in himself, Carlos's academic performance began to improve. As his academic performance improved, so did his self-esteem. The vicious circle had been broken; the elements that had been causing a downward spiral were changed, and the spiral moved upward.

The formal data gathered from the jigsaw experiments confirmed the observations of the experimenters and the teachers: Compared to students in traditional classrooms, students in jigsaw groups became less prejudiced and liked their groupmates more, both within and across ethnic boundaries. Children in the jigsaw classrooms did better on exams, had higher self-esteem, and began to like school better than did the children in traditional classrooms. Finally, the jigsaw children became more truly integrated: In the school yard, there was far more intermingling among ethnic groups than on the grounds of schools using more traditional classroom techniques.

When the classroom is structured so that students of various ethnic groups work together cooperatively, prejudice decreases and self-esteem increases.

WHY DOES JIGSAW WORK? One reason for the success of this technique is that the process of participating in a cooperative group breaks down in-group versus out-group perceptions and allows the individual to develop the cognitive category of "oneness" (Gaertner, Mann, Dovidio, & Murrell, 1990). In addition, the cooperative strategy places people in a "favor-doing" situation. In Chapter 6, we discussed an experiment demonstrating that people who act in a way that benefits others subsequently come to feel more favorable toward the people they helped (Leippe & Eisenstadt, 1998).

Jigsaw learning produces positive outcomes for another reason: It encourages the development of empathy. In the competitive classroom, the goal is to show the teacher how smart you are. You don't have to pay much attention to the other students in your classroom. But to participate effectively in the jigsaw classroom, you have to pay close attention to whichever member of the group is reciting. In doing so, the participants learn how to approach each classmate in a way that is tailored to fit his or her special needs. Alicia may learn that Carlos is a bit shy and needs to be prodded gently, while Trang is so talkative that she might need to be reined in occasionally. Peter can be joked with, but Darnell responds only to serious suggestions.

If our analysis is sound, it should follow that working in jigsaw groups would lead to the sharpening of a child's general empathic ability, a change that will reduce the tendency to rely on stereotypes. To test this notion, Diane Bridgeman conducted a clever experiment with 10-year-old children. Just prior to her experiment, half of the children had spent 2 months participating in jigsaw classes and the other half in traditional classrooms. Bridgeman (1981) showed the children a series of cartoons aimed at testing their ability to put themselves in the shoes of the cartoon characters. In one cartoon, the first panel shows a little boy looking sad as he waves good-bye to his father at the airport. In the next panel, a letter carrier delivers a package to the boy. In the third panel, the boy opens the package, finds a toy airplane inside, and bursts into tears. Bridgeman asked the children why they thought the little boy burst into tears at the sight of the airplane. Nearly all of the children could answer correctly: because the toy airplane reminded him of how much he missed his father. Then Bridgeman asked the crucial question: "What did the letter carrier think when he saw the boy open the package and start to cry?"

The children in the control group thought that the letter carrier would know the boy was sad because the gift reminded him of his father leaving. But those who had participated in the jigsaw classroom responded differently. They had developed the ability to take the perspective of the letter carrier—to put themselves in his shoes—and they realized that he would be confused at seeing the boy cry over receiving a nice present because he hadn't witnessed the farewell scene at the airport. Offhand, this might not seem important. Who cares whether kids have the ability to figure out what is in the mind of a cartoon character? We should all care. The extent to which children can develop the ability to see the world from the perspective of another human being has profound implications for empathy, generosity, and learning to get along with others (Todd, Bodenhausen, Richeson, & Galinsky, 2011). (To find out if the jigsaw method will benefit you, see the Try It!)

When we develop the ability to understand what another person is going through, it increases the probability that our heart will open to that person. Once our heart opens to another person, it becomes almost impossible to feel prejudice against that person, to bully that person, to humiliate that person.

TRY IT!
Jigsaw-Type Group Study

The next time a quiz is coming up in one of your courses, try to organize a handful of your classmates into a jigsaw-type group for purposes of studying for the quiz.

Assign each person a segment of the reading. That person is responsible for becoming the world's greatest expert on that material. That person will organize the material into a report that will be given to the rest of the group. The rest of the group will feel free to ask questions to make sure they fully understand the material. At the end of the session, ask the group members the following questions:

1. Compared to studying alone, was this more or less enjoyable?
2. Compared to studying alone, was this more or less efficient?
3. How are you feeling about each of the people in the group, compared to how you felt about them prior to the session?
4. Would you like to do this again?

You should realize that this situation is probably less influential than the jigsaw groups described in this book. Why?

THE GRADUAL SPREAD OF COOPERATIVE AND INTERDEPENDENT LEARNING The jigsaw approach was first tested in 1971; since then, educational researchers have developed a variety of similar cooperative techniques (J. Aronson, 2010; Cook, 1985; Johnson & Johnson, 1987; Slavin & Cooper, 1999). The striking results that Aronson and his colleagues obtained years ago in Austin have now been replicated in hundreds of classrooms, for children of all ages and in many regions of the country and abroad (Hänze & Berger, 2007; Jurgen-Lohmann, Borsch, & Giesen, 2001; Sharan, 1980; Walker & Crogan, 1998). This method is now generally accepted as one of the most effective ways of improving relations between ethnic groups, increasing acceptance of stigmatized individuals such as people with mental illness, building empathy, and improving instruction (Desforges et al., 1991; Deutsch, 1997; McConahay, 1981; Slavin, 1996). What began as a simple experiment in one school system is slowly becoming an important force in public education. Unfortunately, the operative word in the preceding sentence is *slowly*. The educational system, like all other bureaucracies, tends to resist change.

But it is a goal worth pursuing. It is impossible to overstate the power that a simple change in the classroom structure can have on the life of a child. Some three decades ago, Elliot Aronson, the inventor of the jigsaw classroom, received a letter from a college student. He has saved it all these years, as an eloquent reminder that under all the scientific research and statistical analyses, there are living, breathing human beings who are affected every day by prejudice and by how the social situation treats them—individuals who can rise and flourish when the classroom structure makes it possible for them to do so. Here is the letter in its entirety:

> Dear Professor Aronson:
>
> I am a senior at _____ University. Today I got a letter admitting me to the Harvard Law School. This may not seem odd to you, but let me tell you something. I am the 6th of 7 children my parents had—and I am the only one who ever went to college, let alone graduate, or go to law school.
>
> By now, you are probably wondering why this stranger is writing to you and bragging to you about his achievements. Actually, I'm not a stranger although we never met. You see, last year I was taking a course in social psychology and we were using a book you wrote, *The Social Animal*, and when I read about prejudice and jigsaw it all sounded very familiar—and then, I realized that I was in that very first class you ever did jigsaw in—when I was in the 5th grade. And as I read on, it dawned on me that I was the boy that you called Carlos. And then I remembered you when you first came to our classroom and how I was scared and how I hated school and how I was so stupid and didn't know anything. And you came in—it all came back to me when I read your book—you were very tall—about 6 1/2 feet—and you had a big Black beard and you were funny and made us all laugh.
>
> And, most important, when we started to do work in jigsaw groups, I began to realize that I wasn't really that stupid. And the kids I thought were cruel became my friends and the teacher acted friendly and nice to me and I actually began to love school, and I began to love to learn things and now I'm about to go to Harvard Law School.
>
> You must get a lot of letters like this but I decided to write anyway because let me tell you something. My mother tells me that when I was born I almost died. I was born at home and the cord was wrapped around my neck and the midwife gave me mouth to mouth and saved my life. If she was still alive, I would write to her too, to tell her that I grew up smart and good and I'm going to law school. But she died a few years ago. I'm writing to you because, no less than her, you saved my life too.
>
> Sincerely,
> "Carlos"

REVIEW QUESTIONS

1. Increasing contact between groups will reduce prejudice if all of the following conditions are met except one. Which one?
   a. Interdependence
   b. Higher status of the minority group
   c. Opportunity for informal contacts
   d. Out-group consists of many individuals, not just one token
   e. Social norms of equality

2. What strategy does the Robber's Cave study suggest for reducing hostility between groups?
   a. Sharing social norms
   b. Being together in the same environment
   c. Working together in pursuit of common goals
   d. Playing fun competitive games like tug-of-war

3. Why did early attempts at desegregation fail to reduce prejudice between ethnic groups?
   a. The students were given equal status.
   b. The minority students were usually unprepared to compete academically.
   c. The minority students didn't try hard enough to make friends.

   d. The majority students shared the same goals as the minority students.

4. What is the key feature of the jigsaw classroom?
   a. Kids of different ethnicities need each other to solve problems.
   b. Kids of different ethnicities have a chance to show their individual talents.
   c. Minority kids get to work in their own language and preferred pace.
   d. Teachers stop calling on individual students.

5. What is one of the main reasons that the jigsaw method is effective?
   a. It requires kids to behave in polite and empathic ways.
   b. It sets clear rules for good behavior.
   c. It allows kids to express their real feelings toward one another.
   d. It breaks down in-group versus out-group perceptions and stereotypes.

See page 622 for the answers.

Summary

13.1 What are the three components of prejudice?

- **Defining Prejudice** Prejudice is a widespread phenomenon, present in all societies of the world. What varies across societies are the particular social groups that are the victims of prejudice and the degree to which societies enable or discourage discrimination. Social psychologists define **prejudice** as a hostile or negative attitude toward a distinguishable group of people based solely on their group membership. It contains cognitive, emotional, and behavioral components.

- **The Cognitive Component: Stereotypes** A **stereotype** is a generalization about a group of people in which identical characteristics are assigned to virtually all members of the group, regardless of actual variation among the members. A stereotype may be positive or negative, and it can be a useful, adaptive mental tool to organize the social world. However, by obliterating individual differences within a group of people, it can become maladaptive and unfair both to the person holding the stereotype and to the target. Even positive stereotypes of a group can be limiting and demeaning to members. Modern stereotypes of gender—which can take the form of *hostile sexism*

or *benevolent sexism*—justify discrimination against women and their relegation to traditional roles.

- **The Affective Component: Emotions** The deep emotional aspect of prejudice is what makes a prejudiced person so hard to argue with; logical arguments are not effective in countering emotions. This is the reason that prejudices can linger unconsciously long after a person wishes to be rid of them.

- **The Behavioral Component: Discrimination** An unjustified negative or harmful action directed toward members of a group solely because of their membership in that group is a sign of **discrimination**. Examples include police focus on Black drug users rather than on the much larger number of White drug users; *microaggressions*, the small insults and put-downs that many members of minority groups experience; and *social distance*, a nonverbal measure of how people respond to groups that are different from their own. Gender discrimination is fostered when women are a small minority within a profession and employers' prejudices justify treating them differently and paying them less than men. When people are stressed, angry, have suffered a blow to their self-esteem, or otherwise are not in full control of their conscious intentions, they often behave with greater aggression or hostility toward a stereotyped target than toward members of their own group.

13.2 How can we measure prejudices that people don't want to reveal—or that they don't know they hold?

- **Detecting Hidden Prejudices** Because of a shift in normative rules about prejudice, many people have learned to hide their prejudices in situations where they might be labeled as racist, sexist, anti-Semitic, homophobic, and so on. Accordingly, researchers have developed unobtrusive measures to identify suppressed prejudices, such as sending out identical résumés that vary only the applicant's name or another identifying feature to see whether employers are biased against a particular group; or using the "bogus pipeline," in which participants believe a machine is registering their real attitudes. A popular method of identifying unconscious (implicit) prejudices is the **Implicit Association Test (IAT)**, a measure of the speed of people's associations between a target group and negative attributes. However, controversy exists about what the IAT actually measures and whether it predicts prejudiced behavior.

13.3 What are some ways that prejudice harms its targets?

- **The Effects of Prejudice on the Victim**
  - **The Self-Fulfilling Prophecy** The prevalence of stereotypes and prejudices can create a **self-fulfilling prophecy** both for members of the majority and for victims of prejudice.
  - **Stereotype Threat** One cause of the average difference in academic performance is **stereotype threat**, the anxiety that some groups feel when a stereotype about their group is activated—for example, that women are not as good at math as men, that Asian people are smarter than White people, or that old people are less mentally competent than young people.

13.4 What are three aspects of social life that can cause prejudice?

- **Causes of Prejudice** Three aspects of social life that increase the likelihood of prejudice are conformity to social rules, the importance of social identities and "us-them" thinking, and realistic conflict over resources or power.
  - **Pressures to Conform: Normative Rules** Institutional discrimination reflects society's norms. Normative conformity, or the desire to be accepted

and fit in, leads many people to go along with stereotyped beliefs and their society's dominant prejudices and not challenge them. As norms change, so, often, does prejudice.

- **Social Identity: Us versus Them** Prejudice is enabled by the human tendency to organize people into in-groups and out-groups. It begins with **ethnocentrism**, the universal human inclination to see our own groups as superior to all others, and the need for a **social identity**, the part of the self-concept based on our membership in groups that are important to us. Ethnocentrism may originally have served as a survival mechanism inducing people to favor their own families and tribes, but human beings are also biologically designed to be friendly and cooperative. Social psychologists therefore strive to identify the conditions under which intergroup prejudice is fostered or reduced. Ethnocentrism and "us-them" categorization leads to **in-group bias** (the tendency to treat members of our own group more positively than members of the out-group) and **out-group homogeneity** (the mistaken perception that "they" are all alike). One common out-group attribution is **blaming the victim** for one's own prejudices and discriminatory behavior. Blaming the victim also promotes the in-group's feelings of superiority, its religious or political identity, and the legitimacy of its power.

- **Realistic Conflict Theory** According to **realistic conflict theory**, prejudice is the inevitable by-product of real conflict between groups for limited resources, whether involving economics, power, or status. Competition for resources leads to denigration of and discrimination against the competing out-group, as happened with Chinese immigrants in the nineteenth century and as happens with Mexican and other Latino immigrants today. Scapegoating is a process whereby frustrated and angry people tend to displace their aggression from its real source to a convenient target—an out-group that is disliked, visible, and relatively powerless.

13.5 What are the six conditions that can reduce prejudice?

- **Reducing Prejudice** Prejudice may be universal, but social psychologists have investigated many of the conditions under which intergroup hostility can be reduced and better relationships fostered. It is not enough simply to provide prejudiced people with information that they are stereotyping the out-group; they will often cling even more tightly to their beliefs.

- **The Contact Hypothesis** According to the *contact hypothesis*, the most important way to reduce prejudice between racial and ethnic groups is through contact, bringing in-group and out-group members together. Such contact has been shown to be effective in many situations, from integrating housing projects and the military to fostering friendships across ethnic lines at universities. However, mere contact is not enough and can even exacerbate existing negative attitudes.

- **When Contact Reduces Prejudice** For contact between two groups to be truly successful in reducing prejudice, six conditions must be met: interdependence; a common goal; equal status; the opportunity for informal contact; the chance to interact with multiple members of the out-group rather than one "token"; and social norms of equality.

- **Cooperation and Interdependence: The Jigsaw Classroom** The **jigsaw classroom** is a form of cooperative learning in which children from different ethnic groups must cooperate in order to learn a lesson. It has been shown to improve minority students' self-esteem and performance, increase empathy, and promote intergroup friendships.

Test Yourself

1. A *prejudice* is

a. a hostile attitude toward members of a group, based solely on their membership in that group.

b. a feeling held by members of a majority group toward members of a minority group.

c. generally unaffected by societal events.

d. usually acquired in childhood and lasts a lifetime.

2. A *stereotype* is

a. the cognitive form of a prejudice.

b. a negative impression of a group of people.

c. always inaccurate.

d. a cognitive summary that can be positive or negative.

3. "Hostile sexists" think women are inferior to men; "benevolent sexists" think women are superior to men. What do they have in common? Both

a. reveal a dislike of women.

b. legitimize discrimination against women.

c. share an underlying admiration for women.

d. share an underlying dislike of men.

4. When Gordon Allport said that "defeated intellectually, prejudice lingers emotionally," what did he mean?

a. You can't argue intellectually with a prejudiced person.

b. A prejudiced person cannot intellectually defend his or her attitude.

c. A person's implicit prejudices may decline while explicit prejudices remain.

d. A person's explicit prejudices may decline while implicit prejudices remain.

5. Which of the following measures of unconscious prejudice describes the IAT?

a. A person's keeping greater distance from a member of a group he or she dislikes

b. A person's slower associations between a target image and positive words than with negative words

c. A person's making subtle slights and put-downs about a target person

d. A group's ignoring the comments and contributions of its lone minority member

6. According to the realistic conflict theory, which of the following leads to conflict between groups and increases prejudice and discrimination?

a. Excess resources

b. Lack of information

c. Lack of stability

d. Limited resources

7. What is stereotype threat?

a. Some members of a majority group feel threatened by minorities.

b. Some members of a stereotyped group feel anxious when they are made aware of a stereotype about them.

c. Some members of a majority group threaten a minority by stereotyping them.

d. Some members of a minority group threaten to retaliate against the stereotypes they find unfair.

8. Which of the following describes a consequence of in-group bias?

a. A self-fulfilling prophecy

b. Feelings of inadequacy about our own in-group

c. A tendency to discriminate against members of an out-group

d. A greater vulnerability to stereotype threat

9. Early attempts at desegregation often failed to reduce prejudice between ethnic groups. What is the primary reason the contact hypothesis didn't work?

   a. The students remained angry with each other.

   b. Each group felt superior to the other.

   c. The minority students didn't have equal status, and equality wasn't valued.

   d. The majority students didn't try to make friends with the minority students.

10. What is the main social psychological mechanism that makes the jigsaw classroom effective?

   a. It requires cooperation in pursuit of shared goals.

   b. It relies on ethnocentrism.

   c. It emphasizes individual achievement to demonstrate minority competence.

   d. It measures and overcomes implicit prejudices.

See page 622 for the answers.

Social Psychology in Action 1
Using Social Psychology to Achieve a Sustainable and Happy Future

 ## Chapter Outline and Learning Objectives

Applied Research in Social Psychology

SPA1.1 **How can we apply social psychological principles to improve people's lives?**

Capitalizing on the Experimental Method
Social Psychology to the Rescue

Using Social Psychology to Achieve a Sustainable Future

SPA1.2 **How can social psychology help the world's people to live in a sustainable manner?**

Conveying and Changing Social Norms

Keeping Track of Consumption
Introducing a Little Competitiveness
Inducing Hypocrisy
Removing Small Barriers to Achieve Big Changes

Happiness and a Sustainable Lifestyle

SPA1.3 **How can we apply social psychology to make people happier?**

What Makes People Happy?
Do People Know What Makes Them Happy?

When Jankel Aleman drives to work at an electronics store in Miami, Florida, he is sure to bring with him some plastic bags and rubber bands, which he uses to cover his shoes as he walks from his car to the store. Otherwise, his feet would be soaked by the sea water that often comes through drains and floods the street in front of the store. As sea levels rise flooding is increasingly common on the streets of Miami—even on sunny days—and efforts to prevent the city from becoming an underwater metropolis will likely cost billions of dollars (Davenport, 2014).

Miami is in worse shape than other coastal cities in the United States, because it rests on porous limestone that allows sea water to bubble up through drains and into the streets. But rising sea levels threatens other cities as well. In Norfolk, Virginia, the congregation of the United Church of Norfolk became fed up with walking through water to get to church and decided to relocate to higher ground. "I don't know many churches that have to put the tide chart on their Web site," said Reverend Jennifer Slade, which she does so that members of the congregation know whether there will be sea water lapping at the entrance to the sanctuary (Montgomery, 2014, p. A1). The U.S. Naval Station in Norfolk will be increasingly vulnerable to storms in the next few decades and could be underwater for days if a big storm hits (Cahn, 2013). The navy is already in the process of raising each of its 12 piers at a cost of millions of dollars.

Global warming has been a controversial topic and Americans have been slow to embrace it as an important issue. As the effects of climate change affect people's lives, however, they are becoming increasingly convinced: more than half of Americans now believe that climate change is a serious problem (Dugan, 2014; Rudman, McLean, & Bunzl, 2013). "We are past the point of debating the existence of climate change and are now focusing on adapting to current and future threats," said Miami's mayor, Philip Levine (Davenport, 2014).

To review some basic facts, Planet Earth has always had a supply of "greenhouse" gases that capture heat from the sun and keep the earth warm. But ever since the Industrial Revolution in the eighteenth century, humans have been adding to these gases—chiefly carbon dioxide (CO_2), which is released when we burn fossil fuels (e.g., in power plants, factories, and automobiles). The amount of CO_2 we are now releasing far exceeds the amount that the earth can absorb naturally. As a result, global temperatures are on the rise. For example, 13 of the 14 hottest years ever recorded have occurred since the beginning of this century (Johnson, 2014). Shelf ice in Antarctica and Greenland has been melting at an alarming rate. Experts estimate that sea levels will rise an additional 1–4 feet by the end of the century, though some argue that the increase will be much higher (Melillo, Richmond, & Yohe, 2014). Further, many scientists believe that the frequency and severity of hurricanes is getting worse because of a rise in ocean temperatures. By some estimates, deaths attributable to global warming have already reached 300,000 people a year (Vidal, 2009).

Unfortunately, global warming is not the only environmental problem that human beings are causing. We are using up the world's oil, coal, fresh water, and other nonrenewable natural resources at a precipitous rate. Where to put all of our trash is another problem. In 1987, a barge called the *Mobro 4000* set out from New York City in search of a place to dump its cargo of trash, because landfills in that area were overflowing. It made ports of call in North

Rising sea levels due to global warming are already impacting American cities, including Miami, FL and Norfolk, VA.

Carolina, Florida, Alabama, Mississippi, Louisiana, Mexico, Belize, and the Bahamas, but no one was willing to dump New York's trash in their landfills. Finally, after a 6,000-mile voyage, the *Mobro 4000* returned home, and local authorities convinced a landfill outside of New York City to incinerate and bury the trash. Where else is our trash going? In the 1990s, researchers discovered that a huge patch of the Pacific Ocean (an area larger than the United States, by some estimates) has become an enormous garbage dump; similar "trash vortex" areas have since been identified in other areas of the world's oceans (Lovett, 2010). The problem is that a great deal of plastic material is produced, and it is then discarded into rivers and oceans near coastlines. Because the plastic is not biodegradable, it floats along currents into the ocean, which has become the final resting place for used toothbrushes, disposable cigarette lighters, plastic bags, and umbrella handles ("Plastic oceans," 2008).

The root cause of all of these environmental problems is that there are so many of us; the world-wide human population is 7.2 billion and counting. As seen in Figure SPA-1.1, the human population was relatively constant until the Industrial Revolution, at which point people began to reproduce like crazy. Around that time, English clergyman Thomas Malthus warned that the human population was expanding so rapidly that soon there would not be enough food to feed everyone. Malthus was wrong about when such a calamity would occur, chiefly because of technological advances in agriculture that have vastly improved grain yields. But he was right that, as the food supply has dwindled, the number of malnourished people in the world has increased. By some estimates, one out of every eight people in the world today is hungry ("Hunger," n.d.). Malthus's timing may have been a little off, but many scientists fear that his predictions are becoming truer every day.

In 1987, a barge called the *Mobro 4000* left New York City in search of a place to dump its load of trash. After traveling 6,000 miles and finding no takers, it returned to New York and dumped it in an overflowing landfill outside of the city.

Figure SPA-1.1 The Growth of World Population

The size of the human race increased only very gradually until the Industrial Revolution in the eighteenth century. It has been growing exponentially ever since.

"Gentlemen, it's time we gave some serious thought to the effects of global warming."

Mick Stevens/The New Yorker Collection/
The Cartoon Bank

What can we do? Basically, there are three solutions: First, we can try to curb population growth. The good news is that the rate of growth has slowed in the past few decades, although the population is still rapidly expanding ("Population Growth Rate," n.d.). Second, we can hope that improved technology bails us out—such as the development of more-efficient grains and renewable energy sources including wind and solar power. Although advances are being made in these areas, they are unlikely to solve environmental problems on their own. Third, people can adopt a more sustainable lifestyle by using fewer of the world's resources. This is easier said than done, of course; no one likes to be told that they have to consume less, and entrenched habits are hard to change. But if change we must, how can we encourage people to act in more environmentally responsible ways?

By now you know that this is a classic social psychological question. In earlier chapters, we talked about how people form and change attitudes, how people are influenced by other people's behavior, the power of social norms, and so on. We turn now to a general discussion of how social psychology can be used to address social and psychological problems, followed by a specific discussion of research on how to get people to adopt more-sustainable lifestyles. Then, in the following chapters, we discuss two other major areas of applied social psychological research—namely, health and the law.

Applied Research in Social Psychology

SPA1.1 How can we apply social psychological principles to improve people's lives?

Since its inception, the field of social psychology has been interested in applying what it knows to solve practical problems. Kurt Lewin (1946), generally recognized as the founder of empirical social psychology, made three key points:

- Social psychological questions are best tested with the experimental method.
- These studies can be used to understand basic psychological processes and to develop theories about social influence.
- Social psychological theories and methods can be used to address pressing social problems.

We have already touched on these issues elsewhere in the book. In Chapter 2 we saw the importance of using the experimental method to test causal hypotheses, and in subsequent chapters we saw how social psychological research has increased our understanding of important theoretical questions, such as how people think about themselves and the social world, respond to social influence, change their attitudes, and help and hurt their fellow humans. Much of this research also dealt directly with important applied issues, such as school violence, racism, bystander intervention, and decision making. To many of us in the field, the beauty of social psychology is that by its very nature it addresses both basic and applied questions about human behavior. Research on stereotyping and prejudice, for example, investigates basic theoretical questions about the ways in which people form impressions of each other, as well as applied questions about how stereotyping and prejudice can be reduced.

As we discussed in Chapter 2, though, a distinction can still be made between *basic research* that is concerned primarily with theoretical issues and *applied research* that is concerned primarily with addressing specific real-world problems. Although much of the research we have discussed so far has touched on practical problems, it falls squarely in the category of basic research. As Kurt Lewin (1951) said, "There is nothing so practical as a good theory," by which he meant that to solve difficult social problems, we must first understand the underlying psychological dynamics of human nature and social influence. Increasingly, though, social psychologists are conducting studies designed specifically to address practical problems. In fact, social psychologists are better equipped to study applied problems than researchers in many other disciplines, for reasons we now discuss.

Capitalizing on the Experimental Method

One of the most important lessons of social psychology is the value of conducting experiments to answer questions about social influence. Nowhere is this more important than in finding ways to solve applied questions, such as getting people to reduce energy consumption. Only by conducting experiments (as opposed to observational or correlational studies; see Chapter 2) can we hope to discover which solutions will work the best.

Most people seem to understand this lesson in other domains, such as research on medical treatments. Suppose that a chemist found a new compound that seems to be an effective pain killer; the initial studies with animals look very promising, but studies with people have not yet been conducted. Should we allow a drug company to go ahead and market the drug to people? Not so fast, most of us would think. Who knows how safe the drug is for humans—it might turn out to have dangerous side effects, as seems to have been the case with the pain killer Vioxx and the psoriasis drug Raptiva. There should be extensive clinical trials in humans, in which people are randomly assigned to receive the new drug or a placebo, to see whether it really does reduce pain and whether it has any serious side effects. Indeed, federal law requires extensive testing and approval by the FDA before drugs become available to the public.

We have laxer standards when it comes to testing psychological and social "treatments." If someone wants to try a new energy conservation technique, a new educational initiative, or a program to reduce prejudice, they can usually do so without a lot of rigorous testing of the intervention. A company might try a new program to reduce energy usage or institute a mandatory diversity training program, for example, before such techniques have been tested experimentally.

Well, you might think, what's the harm? Trying a new energy conservation program hardly puts people at risk, and we certainly don't want to inhibit innovation by subjecting people to cumbersome testing guidelines. And can't we find out whether these interventions work simply by interviewing people afterward or seeing whether their behavior changes (e.g., if they use less energy after the conservation program)? Unfortunately, it's not so simple. It is difficult to test the effectiveness of an intervention without a randomly assigned control group, and failing to conduct such tests can have serious consequences.

ASSESSING THE EFFECTIVENESS OF INTERVENTIONS   As an example, consider a psychological intervention that has been widely implemented across the world to help people who have experienced traumatic events, such as rescue workers who witness multiple deaths in a natural disaster or plane crash. The basic idea of the program, called Critical Incident Stress Debriefing (CISD), is to bring people together as soon as possible after the trauma for a 3- to 4-hour session in which participants describe their experiences in detail and discuss their emotional reactions to the events. This cathartic experience is supposed to prevent later psychiatric symptoms, including post-traumatic stress disorder (PTSD). Numerous fire and police departments have made CISD the treatment of choice for officers who witness terrible human tragedies.

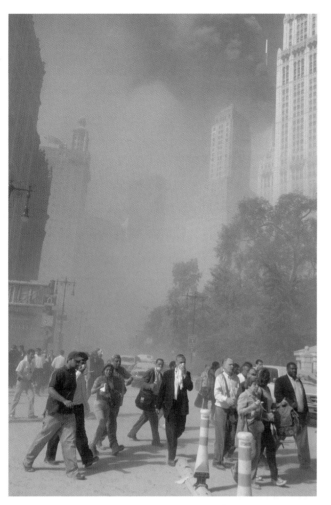

Following the September 11, 2001, terrorists attacks, more than 9,000 counselors rushed to New York City to help survivors deal with the trauma and stress and prevent post-traumatic stress disorder. Many used a technique called Critical Incident Stress Debriefing. Was this technique adequately tested before it was widely used? Does it work or actually do harm? (See the text for the answer.)

It is also widely used with civilians who experience traumatic events. Following the September 11, 2001, terrorist attacks, more than 9,000 counselors rushed to New York City to help survivors deal with the trauma and stress and prevent post-traumatic stress disorder, many using psychological debriefing techniques.

Psychological debriefing makes sense, doesn't it? An ounce of prevention is worth a pound of cure, and getting people to openly discuss their reactions to traumas rather than bottling them up seems like a good thing. "Seems like" and "really is" are not the same thing, however, and an interesting thing about CISD is that it was widely implemented before social scientists conducted rigorous tests of its effectiveness. Once they did, by randomly assigning some people to undergo CISD and others to an untreated control condition, and then giving everyone a battery of psychological measures—the results were not encouraging. In a comprehensive review of the literature, Harvard psychologist Richard McNally and his colleagues concluded that there is "no convincing evidence" that psychological debriefing techniques prevent post-traumatic stress disorders (McNally, Bryant, & Ehlers, 2003, p. 72).

POTENTIAL RISKS OF SOCIAL INTERVENTIONS   Even if CISD doesn't work as well as people said it did, what's the big deal? Surely getting people together to talk about their experiences can't do any harm. But here's another problem with social and psychological interventions: People use common sense to assess their effectiveness, and common sense is sometimes wrong. Not only has CISD been found to be ineffective at preventing PTSD, it may in fact do harm. In one study, participants who had been severely burned and admitted to the hospital were randomly assigned to receive CISD or to be a part of a control group that did not. All participants completed various psychological measures over the next several months and were interviewed at home by a researcher who was unaware of whether they had undergone CISD. The results were sobering: Thirteen months after the intervention, the CISD group had a significantly *higher* incidence of post-traumatic stress disorder, scored *higher* on psychological measures of anxiety and depression, and reported significantly *less* contentedness with their lives (Carlier, Voerman, & Gersons, 2000). Similar results have been found in studies testing the effectiveness of CISD with emergency workers. In their review of the literature, McNally and colleagues (2003) noted that "some evidence suggests that it [CISD] may impede natural recovery" and recommended that "for scientific and ethical reasons, professionals should cease compulsory debriefing of trauma-exposed people" (p. 72).

It turns out that right after a traumatic event, when people are experiencing considerable negative emotions, may not be the best time to focus on the event and discuss it with others. Instead, as we will see in Chapter SPA-2, people are often quite resilient when left alone (Bonanno, 2004). Forcing people to talk about and relive traumatic experiences may make them more likely to remember those experiences later (Paterson, Whittle, & Kemp, 2014). If people don't succeed in recovering on their own, they might do better to let some time pass before reliving the trauma, at a point when they have distance from it and can think about the event more objectively (Pennebaker, 2001).

Think of the consequences of implementing CISD so widely before it was adequately tested. Not only has it been a colossal waste of time, effort, and money, but also thousands of police, fire, and rescue workers have been forced to undergo a debriefing procedure that may have harmed more of them than it helped. If this were a medical intervention, there would be a huge public outcry (followed by the inevitable lawsuits).

Social Psychology to the Rescue

Social psychologists are in a unique position to find solutions to applied problems and to avoid fiascos such as the widespread use of CISD. First, the field of social psychology is a rich source of theories about human behavior that people can draw upon to devise solutions to problems. Second, and of equal importance, social psychologists know how to perform rigorous experimental tests of these solutions to see if they work (Walton, 2014; Wilson, 2011). We will see many examples of such applied research in the next two chapters. We return now to the issue with which we began this chapter: how to get people to act in ways that will help ensure a sustainable future.

REVIEW QUESTIONS

1. Why is social psychology in a unique position to find solutions to pressing social problems?
   a. Unlike other disciplines, social psychology doesn't rely on the experimental method.
   b. Social psychology can employ Kurt Lewin's three key points as a means of using applied research to solve social problems.
   c. Social psychology theories, such as CISD, have widespread use and effectiveness in solving societal issues.
   d. Social psychology can rely on observations and correlational studies to enhance societal well-being.

2. As a means of reducing racial stereotyping at the workplace, Adam organized a series of mandatory diversity trainings for his employees. However, a year later he finds that his employees still show hostility toward their colleagues belonging to other races. Which of the following options best answers why Adam wasn't able to use social psychology to improve his employees' behavior?
   a. He didn't employ the experimental method to understand hostility at his workplace.
   b. He used basic research instead of applied research to solve a social problem.
   c. He didn't test the intervention experimentally before implementing it.
   d. He didn't conduct a survey asking for his employees' opinion on whether the initiative would be successful.

3. Why might Critical Incident Stress Debriefing (CISD) prove ineffective even though it seems like a good idea to talk to someone about a trauma that you have just experienced?
   a. CISD may impede natural recovery.
   b. People experience considerable negative emotions right after a traumatic event and that's not the best time to talk about it.
   c. People are more resilient when they are left on their own and can talk to someone, if need be, after they have objectively assessed their emotions.
   d. All of the above are true.

See page 622 for the answers.

Using Social Psychology to Achieve a Sustainable Future

SPA1.2 How can social psychology help the world's people to live in a sustainable manner?

Social psychologists have adopted a variety of approaches to get people to act in more–environmentally responsible ways. The approaches were inspired by social psychological theories and used the experimental method to see if they were successful (Oskamp, 2000; Schultz & Kaiser, 2012; Stern, 2011; Swim, Clayton, & Howard, 2011).

Conveying and Changing Social Norms

One approach to getting people to behave more environmentally responsibly is to remind them of social norms, the rules a group has for the acceptable behaviors, values, and beliefs of its members. As we discussed in Chapter 8, people follow two kinds of norms: *injunctive norms*, which are people's perceptions of what behaviors are approved or disapproved of by others, and *descriptive norms*, those that are people's perceptions of how people actually behave. If people believe that a certain kind of behavior is strongly frowned upon by their social group and they observe that others are obeying the norm, they are likely to follow the norm as well (Cialdini, 2012; Jacobson, Mortensen, & Cialdini, 2011).

Robert Cialdini and his colleagues have illustrated the power of social norms in encouraging people to act in environmentally friendly ways. Take littering, for example. Throwing trash on the ground may not seem to be all that serious a matter. Although billboards implore us to "keep America beautiful," many people seem to think it isn't a big deal to leave their paper cup at the side of the road instead of in a trash barrel. Unfortunately, those paper cups add up. Americans discard 51 billion pieces of trash on roadsides each year, and it costs over $11 billion per year to clean up that litter ("Litter Prevention," n.d.).

In Chapter 8, we discussed a field experiment by Reno and his colleagues (1993) in which an experimental accomplice conveyed an injunctive norm against littering, by picking up a fast-food bag that had been discarded on the ground. The researchers hypothesized that seeing the accomplice pick up the bag would be a vivid reminder of the injunctive norm—that littering is bad and other people disapprove of it—and hence would lower people's inclination to litter. They were right; almost no one who saw the accomplice pick up the fast-food bag took a handbill that had been placed on the windshield of their car and tossed it on the ground. In a control condition, in which there was no bag on the ground and the accomplice simply walked by, 37% threw the handbill on the ground.

What is the best way to communicate *descriptive* norms against littering? The most straightforward way, it would seem, would be to clean up all the litter in an environment, to illustrate that "no one litters here." In general, this is true: The less litter there is in an environment, the less likely people are to litter (Huffman et al., 1995; Krauss, Freedman, & Whitcup, 1978; Reiter & Samuel, 1980).

There is, however, an interesting exception to this finding. Cialdini, Reno, and Kallgren (1990) figured that seeing one conspicuous piece of litter on the ground spoiling an otherwise clean environment would be a better reminder of descriptive norms than seeing a completely clean environment. The single piece of trash sticks out like a sore thumb, reminding people that no one has littered here except one thoughtless person. In contrast, if there is no litter on the ground, people might be less likely to think about what the descriptive norm is. Ironically, then, littering may be more likely to occur in a totally clean environment than in one containing a single piece of litter.

To test this hypothesis, the researchers stuffed students' mailboxes with handbills and then observed from a hidden vantage point how many of the students dropped the handbills on the floor (Cialdini et al., 1990). In one condition, the researchers cleaned up the mailroom so that there were no other pieces of litter to be seen. In another condition, they placed one very noticeable piece of litter on the floor—a hollowed-out piece of watermelon. In a third condition, they not only

> We live in an environment whose principal product is garbage.
> —Russell Baker, 1968

"Help!"

Mick Stevens/The New Yorker Collection/ The Cartoon Bank

put the watermelon rind on the floor, but also spread out dozens of discarded handbills. As predicted, the lowest rate of littering occurred in the condition where there was a single piece of trash on the floor (see Figure SPA-1.2). The single violation of a descriptive norm highlighted the fact that no one had littered but the one doofus who had dropped the watermelon rind on the floor. Now that people's attention was focused on the descriptive norm against littering, virtually none of the students littered. The highest percentage of littering occurred when the floor was littered with lots of handbills; here it was clear that there was a descriptive norm in favor of littering, and many of the students followed suit.

Another way of conveying descriptive norms is simply to tell people what most others do—particularly in situations in which you can't directly observe others' behavior. If you have ever stayed in a hotel, for example, you might have seen a sign asking you to reuse your towels, because washing towels every day wastes environmental resources (e.g., water and electricity). Do these appeals work? Not as much as conveying a descriptive norm about what people *actually* do. Researchers found that the standard appeal to help the environment worked less well than one that said, "Join your fellow guests in helping to save the environment" and went on to communicate that 75% of guests reuse their towels (Goldstein, Cialdini, & Griskevicius, 2008). The simple message that "other people do it" can be enough to get people to do the right thing (Nolan et al., 2008). See the Try It! below for an example of how you might apply this study to getting people to recycle more.

Figure SPA-1.2 Descriptive Norms and Littering

Who littered the least—people who saw that no one else had littered, people who saw one piece of litter on the floor, or people who saw several pieces of litter? As shown in the figure, it was people who saw one piece of litter. Seeing the single piece of litter was most likely to draw people's attention to the fact that most people had not littered, making people less likely themselves to litter.

(Based on Cialdini, Reno, & Kallgren, 1990)

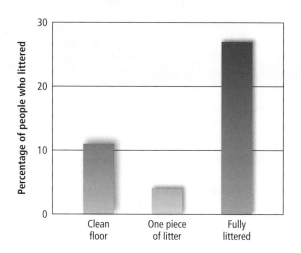

TRY IT!

Reducing Littering with Descriptive Norms

Can you think of ways of getting people to act in more environmentally friendly ways, based on the findings of the Goldstein et al. (2008) hotel study? For example, suppose that you decided to make a sign to put in a dormitory, urging people to recycle their bottles and cans. Based on what you have read so far, which of these signs do you think would work the best?

(a) "Help to save the environment—recycle your bottles and cans."
(b) "Join your fellow students in helping to save the environment—75% of residents of this dorm recycle their bottles and cans."

(c) "Many people in this dorm don't recycle their bottles and cans. You can do better!"

The correct answer is (b) because it conveys a descriptive norm that most people are recycling, which can motivate others to conform to that norm. Option (c) could have a negative effect, because it conveys the descriptive norm that most people *don't* recycle, and others might conform to that norm.

Clearly, drawing people's attention to both injunctive and descriptive norms can nudge them into acting in more environmentally responsible ways. But what happens when there are no norms for acting in the proper way, or even norms for behaving in the opposite manner? Suppose, for example, that you are a member of a fraternity or sorority in which many people drive gas-guzzling SUVs. Perhaps that is the vehicle of choice for you and your peers; maybe it's even a sign of status and prestige. No one likes to "break the rules," and though you might have been thinking about trading in your Jeep Grand Cherokee for a smaller car with a hybrid engine, you worry about what your friends will say.

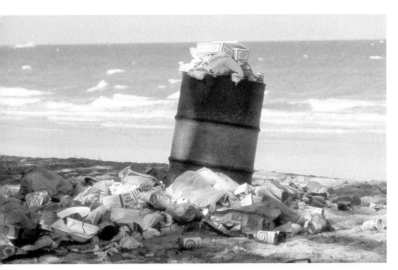

Besides being unsightly, litter can cost millions of dollars to clean up. Social psychologists have found that emphasizing different kinds of social norms against littering is an effective way to prevent it.

But would it really be so bad? Sometimes people overestimate the consequences of violating an injunctive norm—in other words, how much your friends would really care if you traded in your SUV. Research shows that college students overestimate other injunctive norms, such as what their friends think about drinking alcohol. Many college students believe that their peers are more in favor of drinking than they actually are (Neighbors et al., 2008; Prince & Carey, 2010). The same might be true about cars; people might not care as much as you think about what kind of car you drive.

Even if your friends would look disparagingly at your purchase of a hybrid car, someone has to be the first to change an injunctive norm. As we saw in Chapter 8, it is easier to buck the tide if we can get just one other person to go along with us, so you might first try to convince a friend who is looking to buy a car to consider a hybrid. If this doesn't work, just go for it. You might be surprised by how much you alone can change a norm, especially if you keep reminding people how much you are saving on gas and that SUVs are not nearly as safe as people think they are (Gladwell, 2005).

Keeping Track of Consumption

A problem with some types of consumption is that it is not easy for people to keep track of how much of a resource they are using—such as gas, electricity, or water. During a drought, for example, people may be asked to conserve water, but it is not easy for them to monitor how many gallons a month they are using. One pair of researchers reasoned that making it easy for people to keep track of their water consumption would make it easier for them to act on their concern for the greater good (Van Vugt & Samuelson, 1999). They compared two communities in the Hampshire region of England during a severe drought in the summer of 1995. The houses in one community had been equipped with water meters that allowed residents to monitor how much water they were consuming. The houses in the other community did not have meters. As expected, when people felt that the water shortage was severe, those in the metered houses consumed less water than those in the unmetered houses.

What if we got people to keep track of the energy they were saving, rather than the energy they were consuming? For example, what if we asked drivers to keep track of the miles they *avoided* driving, by walking, riding a bike, taking public transportation, or getting a ride with a friend? Making people more mindful of opportunities to avoid driving might make them more willing to leave their car at home. To find out, Graham, Koo, and Wilson (2011) asked college students to keep track of the number of miles they avoided driving and to record that figure on a Web site every other day for 2 weeks. As predicted, students who kept track of the miles they saved drove their cars less than did students in a control group who did not keep track of the miles they saved. This finding is consistent with research showing that simply keeping track of one's behavior is the first step to changing it.

Graham and colleagues (2011) also examined whether there would be an added benefit to giving the students different kinds of feedback about the miles they saved. After students entered how many miles they had avoided driving, some received feedback about how much money they had saved on gas and maintenance costs. Others received feedback about savings in air pollution (e.g., how many carbon dioxide and hydrocarbon emissions weren't emitted). Some got both kinds of feedback. It turned out that this latter group—the one that learned both how much money they had saved and how much pollution wasn't emitted—was especially likely to avoid driving their cars. Keeping track of one's behavior that avoids environmental damage and receiving concrete feedback about the savings, then, turned out to be an effective way to get college students to drive their cars less. (If you would like to try this on your own, you can download a spreadsheet with instructions how to use it at people.virginia .edu/~tdw/Driving.file.htm.)

Introducing a Little Competitiveness

Other researchers have demonstrated that a little competitiveness helps people conserve energy in the workplace (Siero et al., 1996). At one unit of a factory in the Netherlands, the employees were urged to engage in energy-saving behaviors. For example, announcements were placed in the company magazine asking people to close windows during cold weather and to turn off lights when leaving a room. In addition, the employees got weekly feedback on their behavior; graphs were posted that showed how much they had improved their energy-saving behaviors, such as how often they had turned off the lights. This intervention resulted in modest improvement. By the end of the program, for example, the number of times people left the lights on decreased by 27%.

Another unit of the factory took part in an identical program, with one difference: In addition to receiving weekly feedback on their own energy-saving actions, they got to see how the other unit was doing. The researchers hypothesized that this social comparison information would motivate people to do better than their colleagues in the other unit. As seen in Figure SPA-1.3, they were right. By the end of the program, the number of times people left lights on had decreased by 61%. Engaging people's competitive spirit can have a large impact on their behavior (Staats, Harland, & Wilke, 2004).

Inducing Hypocrisy

In many areas of the world, fresh water is becoming an increasingly scarce resource. Part of the reason is population growth in areas that have limited water supplies, such as the southwestern United States. Another cause is droughts, which are becoming increasingly frequent as the temperature of the earth rises. In 1975, 10% to 15% of the earth was drought stricken; by 2005, that figure was closer to 30% ("Drought's growing reach," 2005). One study estimates that by the middle of this century, a third of the counties in the continental United States will be at high risk for water shortages ("Climate change, water, and risk," 2010). It is thus important to find ways to encourage people to conserve water, especially when drought conditions exist.

Several years ago, when California was experiencing severe water shortages, administrators at one campus of the University of California realized that an enormous amount of water was being wasted by students using the university athletic facilities. The administrators posted signs in the shower rooms of the gymnasiums, exhorting students to conserve water by taking briefer, more efficient showers. The signs appealed to the

Figure SPA-1.3 Effects of Comparative Feedback on Energy-Saving Behaviors

Two units of a factory were urged to conserve energy and received feedback about how their unit was doing. Only one of the units, however, received comparative feedback about how it was doing relative to the other unit. As seen in the graph, this second unit improved its behavior the most, especially by turning off lights more.

(Based on Siero, Bakker, Dekker, & Van Den Burg, 1996)

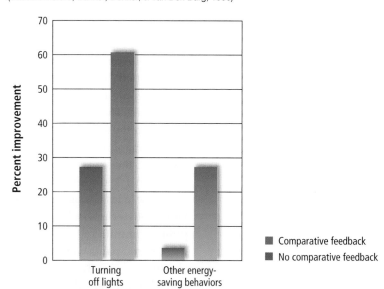

Many parts of the United States are experiencing extreme drought conditions, and many more will as global warming increases. What are some ways that social psychology can be used to increase water conservation?

In an age where man has forgotten his origins and is blind even to his most essential needs for survival, water along with other resources has become the victim of his indifference.
—RACHEL CARSON,
THE SILENT SPRING, 1962

students' conscience by urging them to take brief showers and to turn off the water while soaping up. The administrators were confident that the signs would be effective, because the vast majority of students at this campus were ecology minded and believed in preserving natural resources. However, systematic observation revealed that fewer than 15% of the students complied with the conservation message on the posted signs.

The administrators were puzzled; perhaps the majority of the students hadn't paid attention to the signs. After all, a sign on the wall is easy to ignore. So they made each sign more obtrusive, putting it on a tripod at the entrance to the showers so that the students needed to walk around the sign in order to get into the shower room. Although this increased compliance slightly (19% turned off the shower while soaping up), it apparently made a great many students angry; the sign was continually being knocked over and kicked around, and a large percentage of students took inordinately long showers, apparently as a reaction against being told what to do. The sign was doing more harm than good, puzzling the administrators even more. Time to call in the social psychologists.

Elliot Aronson and his students (Dickerson et al., 1992) decided to apply a technique called "the hypocrisy procedure," which they had successfully used before to get people to increase their use of condoms (see a description of this study in Chapter 6). The procedure involved intercepting female students who were on their way from the swimming pool to the women's shower room, introducing the experimental manipulations, and then having a female research assistant casually follow them into the shower room to time their showers. Experimental manipulations in one condition asked research participants to respond to a brief questionnaire about their water use, a task designed to make them mindful of how they sometimes wasted water while showering. In another condition, research participants were asked to make a public commitment, exhorting others to take steps to conserve water. Specifically, these participants were asked to sign their names to a public poster that read, "Take shorter showers. Turn shower off while soaping up. If I can do it, so can *you*!" In this crucial condition—the "hypocrisy" condition—the participants were not only made mindful of their own wasteful behavior, but they also had to indicate publicly (on the poster) that they were practicing water conservation, even though up to this point they weren't. In short, they were made aware that they were preaching behavior they themselves were not practicing.

Just as in the condom study described in Chapter 6, those participants who were made to feel like hypocrites changed their behavior so that they could feel good about themselves. In this case, they took briefer showers than participants in the other conditions. The hypocrisy procedure has been found to increase other environmentally sound practices as well, such as recycling (Fried & Aronson, 1995).

Removing Small Barriers to Achieve Big Changes

Sometimes the best way to change people's behavior is simply to make it easy for them to do so. Consider recycling. To reduce the amount of trash that ends up in landfills, many cities are encouraging their residents to recycle materials such as glass, paper, and aluminum. But as you know, it can be inconvenient to do so; in some areas, you have to load your car with boxes of cans and bottles and drop them off at a recycling center, which might be several miles from your house. Other cities have curbside recycling, whereby a truck picks up recycling materials that you set out at the curb on a designated day, but in some places you have to remember to separate your cans and bottles from the rest of the trash and find a place to store them until the pickup day. We thus have a classic *social dilemma*, which as we saw in Chapter 9, is a conflict in which the easiest action for an individual (in this case, not bothering to recycle) will, if chosen by most people, have harmful effects on everyone. As you might imagine, several social psychologists have turned their attention to ways of getting people to recycle more.

There have been two general approaches to this problem. First, some psychologists have focused on changing people's attitudes (namely in a proenvironment direction), because doing so often leads to changes in behavior (e.g., recycling more; see Chapter 7). Several studies have found that people's attitudes toward recycling are in fact good predictors of their recycling behaviors, suggesting that a mass media campaign that targets people's attitudes is a good way to go (Knussen, Yule, & MacKenzie, 2004; Oskamp et al., 1998; Schwab, Harton, & Cullum, 2014).

Sometimes, however, we fail to act consistently with our attitudes, despite our best intentions. Perhaps the recycling center is too far away or we just can't find the time to sort our trash, even though we know we should. Kurt Lewin (1947), one of the founders of social psychology, made the observation that big social changes can sometimes occur by removing small barriers from people's environments (Ross & Nisbett, 1991). When it comes to recycling, it might be better simply to make it hassle free, such as instituting curbside recycling, than to try to change people's attitudes toward the environment. A number of studies have found this to be true. Increasing the number of recycling bins in a community, instituting curbside recycling, and allowing residents to mix materials instead of having to sort them have all been found to increase people's recycling behaviors (Domina & Koch, 2002; Ludwig, Gray, & Rowell, 1998; Schultz, Oskamp, & Mainieri, 1995).

Consider a natural experiment that was conducted in Fairfax County, Virginia (Guagnano, Stern, & Dietz, 1995). Curbside recycling had recently begun in the county, but only about a quarter of the residents had received plastic bins for collecting their recyclable materials. Others had to find their own containers in which to put their bottles and cans. Now, it might seem as if this would not be much of an impediment to recycling; if people really cared about the environment, they should be able to find their own box. As Lewin argued, however, sometimes little barriers have big effects, and, indeed, the people who had the bins were much more likely to recycle.

The researchers also measured people's attitudes toward recycling, to see if those with positive attitudes were more likely to recycle than those who were not. Interestingly, people's attitudes predicted behavior only when they did *not* possess a recycling bin. When there was a barrier preventing easy compliance (e.g., people had to search through the garage to find a suitable box), only those with positive attitudes made the effort to circumvent the barrier. When there was no barrier (e.g., people had a convenient container provided by the county), attitudes did not matter as much. In this latter case, people were likely to conform even if they did not have strong proenvironmental attitudes. One study, for example, found that providing office workers with a recycling box that they could keep next to their desks dramatically increased the amount of paper they recycled (Holland, Aarts, & Langendam, 2006). The simple convenience of putting paper in a box next to their desk—as opposed to taking it to a central location—was enough to alter people's behavior. There may be, however, a downside to convenience: one study found that when a recycling bin for paper towels was placed in a public restroom, people used more paper towels. Thus, when recycling is easy people will do it, but they may also consume more of the product they are recycling (Catlin & Wang, 2013). The moral? Keep a recycling bin handy, but resist the temptation to increase consumption of recyclable products.

Of course, we can't make every behavior easy to perform. How else can we nudge people into doing the right thing? The same study found that it works to get people to form **implementation intentions**, which are people's specific plans about where, when, and how they will fulfill a goal (Gollwitzer & Oettingen, 2011). The researchers also measured the extent to which people recycled plastic cups, which had to be taken to a central location (that is, the workers did not have boxes in their offices in which they could deposit used cups). Workers in the implementation intention condition were first asked to visualize and write down exactly when, where, and how they would recycle their cups, whereas workers in a control condition were not. People in the former condition recycled nearly four times as many cups as those in the latter, suggesting that the best-laid plans of mice and men often go awry (to paraphrase the poet Robert Burns), *unless* we first visualize how we are going to make those plans come true.

Now that you have read about several approaches for changing people's behavior in ways that help the environment, you are in a position to try them out yourself.

Implementation Intentions

People's specific plans about where, when, and how they will fulfill a goal

REVIEW QUESTIONS

1. Suppose that where you work, people often fail to recycle. In the copy room, for example, there is both a recycling box and a trash bin, and many people put used paper in the trash instead of the recycling box. Which of the following is *most* likely to get people to recycle more?

   a. Put up a sign that says, "Many of you are putting paper in the trash—please recycle it instead."

   b. Put up a sign that says, "Please recycle. We're already doing better than other units in the company, but there is room to improve."

   c. Set an example by cleaning up the copy room and putting all the paper that was in the trash bin into the recycling box.

   d. Put all the paper that was in the trash bin into the recycling box, except for one big, noticeable paper product (e.g., a poster) into the trash bin.

2. Suppose there is a drought in your area and you want to get college students living in a dorm to use less water. Which of the following is *least* likely to work?

   a. Put up signs in public areas of the dorm urging students to conserve water.

   b. Install devices that show students exactly how much water they used when they took showers.

   c. Start a competition with a neighboring dormitory to see who can conserve the most water in the next month.

   d. Ask students to complete a questionnaire that makes them mindful of times they wasted water, then ask them to sign a public poster endorsing the idea of taking shorter showers.

3. Suppose that there is a college dormitory in which it is difficult for the residents to recycle, because students have to carry their recyclable materials to a bin that is far away from the dorm. Which of the following residents of the dorm is *least* likely to recycle?

a. Alex, who is strongly in favor of recycling.

b. Heather, who doesn't care that much about recycling, but whose roommate agrees to take her recycling goods to the bin, if Heather will put them in a box in their room.

c. Savannah, who is only moderately in favor of recycling, and believes that most of the other students in the dorm don't care much about it either.

d. Eugene, who is only moderately in favor of recycling, but decides to write down exactly when, where, and how he would take his recyclable materials to the bin outside the dorm.

See page 622 for the answers.

Happiness and a Sustainable Lifestyle

SPA1.3   How can we apply social psychology to make people happier?

The research we have been discussing thus far might seem sobering or even depressing. There are lots of environmental problems, and drastic steps are necessary to prevent them. We need to cut back on our use of energy, buy less, recycle more, and in general tighten our belts. This doesn't sound like a recipe for a happy life, does it? Actually, it might be. We end this chapter on an optimistic note by discussing research showing that consumption isn't nearly as important to happiness as people often assume. It is entirely possible to adopt a sustainable lifestyle and be a very happy person (Kjell, 2011).

What Makes People Happy?

A good place to start is with the question of what makes people happy. Philosophers and psychologists have debated this question for centuries, and there is no simple answer that applies to everyone. For one thing, part of the recipe for happiness is outside of our control. Most psychologists agree, for example, that happiness is partly genetic; some of us are born with a happier temperament than are others (Lykken & Tellegen, 1996). Further, we can't control all the outside circumstances that impact our happiness, such as political upheavals or crushing environmental disasters (Inglehart & Klingemann, 2000). Nonetheless, research shows that there are things that people *can* control that influence their happiness. Four of the most important factors are having satisfying relationships with other people, becoming engaged in something you love, pursuing experiences more than things, and helping others.

Very happy people are more likely to spend time with other people and are more satisfied with their relationships than are less-happy people.

SATISFYING RELATIONSHIPS   Perhaps the best predictor of whether someone is happy is the quality of his or her social relationships. In one study, for example, extremely happy college students were compared to their less-happy peers, and the main thing that set them apart was that happy people spent more time with other people and were more satisfied with their relationships (Diener & Biswas-Diener, 2008; Diener & Seligman, 2004). Now, being a good social psychologist, you know that this is a correlational finding and that there are three possible explanations for it: Good social relationships make people happy, happy people are more likely to have good relationships, or a third variable, such as being extraverted, makes people happier and more likely to have good relationships. These possibilities are not mutually exclusive; in fact, we suspect that all three are true. But researchers generally agree that having high-quality relationships is a major source of happiness (Baumeister & Leary, 1995; Diener & Biswas-Diener, 2008; Diener & Oishi, 2005; Siedlecki, Salthouse, Oishi, & Jeswani, 2014).

In fact, even a brief positive interaction with a stranger can improve people's mood, as shown in a study that randomly assigned customers entering a coffee shop to one of two conditions. Half were asked to have a brief, friendly conversation with the cashier, whereas the other half were asked to minimize conversation with the cashier and make their interaction as efficient as possible (Sandstron & Dunn, 2014). Then, as they were leaving the store, all participants completed a questionnaire on which they rated their mood and how connected they felt to other people at that moment. Those who had been asked to have a brief chat with the cashier were in a significantly better mood and felt more connected to other people than those who were asked to have an efficient interaction. So, the next time you are in a store or restaurant, exchange a few pleasant words with the salesperson or waitperson—you will likely feel better as a result.

Things won are done; joy's soul lies in the doing.

—Shakespeare, *Troilus and Cressida*, i.ii.287

FLOW: BECOMING ENGAGED IN SOMETHING YOU ENJOY   Think back to a time when you worked very hard to achieve a highly valued goal and your efforts paid off. Perhaps you were on a sports team that won a championship or in an orchestra that performed a concert to rave reviews. Now think back to when you were the happiest: Was it after you achieved the goal or while you were working toward the goal? In a sport, for example, did you feel happiest when the game ended and you were the champion, or when you were playing well and your team was ahead but you didn't know for sure whether you would win? Although it can be gratifying to have our dreams come true, there is evidence that people are happier when they are working at something they enjoy and making progress (Haidt, 2006).

There are a couple of reasons for this. First, when people are working toward a goal, they are often in a highly desired state called *flow*, which occurs when people are "lost" in a task that is challenging but attainable (Csikszentmihalyi, 1997; Csikszentmihalyi & Nakamura, 2010). Flow is what people feel when they are highly absorbed in a task and have the sense that they are making progress, such as when they are playing sports, engaged in creative activities such as writing, composing, or performing, or simply working on an enjoyable puzzle. Flow is such a pleasurable and absorbing state that people often lose track of how much time has passed and exactly where they are. When people achieve their goal—the game is over or they complete a work of art—the flow stops. People may be very gratified with what they have accomplished, but they are no longer "lost" in the pursuit of their goal (Keller & Bless, 2008).

Second, when people are working toward a goal but are not certain that they will obtain it, it is hard to think about anything else. The uncertainty about the outcome focuses their attention on the task, and other matters fade from view. After a goal is obtained, however, people's thoughts invariably turn to other matters—such as how much homework they have and the fact that they need to do their laundry. People usually adapt quickly to their successes, in the sense that sooner or later their accomplishment comes to seem normal, perhaps even expected, and not something that they think about all that much (Wilson & Gilbert, 2008). In short, pursuing something in an enjoyable way often makes us happier than getting it.

ACCUMULATE EXPERIENCES, NOT THINGS   You may have noticed an important omission from our recipe for happiness—wealth. Surely it is the case that people who make a lot of money are happier than those who don't? Well, the story here is not as straightforward as you might think (Diener, Tay, & Oishi, 2013; Dunn, Gilbert, & Wilson, 2011). It is true that people who are very poor and have trouble getting food and shelter are less happy than others. After people have the basic necessities of

Helping others increases happiness more than does spending money on material things for ourselves.

life, however, having more money doesn't increase happiness much at all (Diener & Seligman, 2004; Kahneman & Deaton, 2010).

One reason for this is that it is not material things that make people happy. In fact, people who are materialistic—those who place a high value on money and possessions—are *less* happy than people who are not as concerned with money and possessions (Banerjee & Dittmar, 2008; Nickerson et al., 2003). In contrast, research shows that over time, experiences make people happier than things. By "experiences" we mean activities that people engage in such as concerts, vacations, and family gatherings, as opposed to material possessions such as clothing, jewelry, cars, and electronic gadgets. People are happier when they think about past experiences they have had than when they think about material things they have purchased (Howell & Guevarra, 2013; Van Boven & Gilovich, 2003).

There are at least two reasons why experiences bring more happiness than things. First, experiences tend to bind us to other people more than do possessions; we go to concerts with other people, for example, whereas we are more likely to play with the newest electronic gadget by ourselves. And, as we saw, interactions with other people make us happy. Second, we are more likely to view experiences as expressions of who we truly are. That is, going to concerts and plays and movies are better ways of expressing our preferences and identities than are buying things, which makes the former more satisfying (Carter & Gilovich, 2012). The moral is that there is no need to be materialistic to be happy; having nice experiences will work better.

HELPING OTHERS   Instead of having experiences or buying things, we could use our time and money to help other people—which research shows is another important ingredient of happiness. We saw evidence for this in a study we discussed in Chapter 5, in which people who were given $20 and asked to spend it on another person ended up happier than people who were given $20 and asked to spend it on themselves (Dunn, Aknin, & Norton, 2008). Why does helping others increase happiness? One reason is that helping increases positive interactions with other people. Spending $20 on a gift for ourselves is nice but doesn't do much for our social life, whereas taking a friend out for lunch connects us more to another person. Another reason is that helping others makes us feel like good people—that is, it improves our self-image (Dunn, Aknin, & Norton, 2014). Now that you know about some ways to increase happiness, see if you can apply them to your own life in the Try It! Exercise below.

TRY IT!

Applying the Research to Your Own Life

This chapter describes four ways in which people can become happier. Can you apply these to your own life?

Satisfying Relationships: In what ways could you spend high-quality time with your friends and loved ones?

Flow: How could you increase the amount of time you spend on "flow" activities?

Experiences instead of Things: How could you spend more time on satisfying experiences and less on accumulating material possessions?

Helping Others: What are some concrete ways in which you could help other people?

Do People Know What Makes Them Happy?

Affective Forecasting

The extent to which people can predict the intensity and duration of their emotional reactions to future events

Although each of us knows what makes us happy to some extent, research on **affective forecasting**—the extent to which people can predict the intensity and duration of their emotional reactions to future events—has found that we haven't figured it out completely (Gilbert, 2007; Gilbert & Wilson, 2007; Wilson & Gilbert, 2003). When it comes to understanding the recipe for happiness, sometimes we even get it backward.

When we talk with our undergraduate advisees about their career plans, for example, many of them mention that their goal is to make a lot of money. There is nothing wrong with wanting to achieve a comfortable lifestyle, of course. But as we have discussed, money itself does not make people happy, especially if it breeds materialism.

We also saw that one of the best predictors of happiness is having satisfying social relationships. And yet Americans are becoming increasingly isolated from each other. (Putnam, 2000). In 1985, about 75% of the people surveyed said they had a close friend with whom they could talk about their problems, but by 2004, only half the people said they had such a friend (Vedantam, 2006).

In short, people often strive for things that are unlikely to make them happier (e.g., earning lots of money) and overlook things that will make them happier (e.g., spending time with close friends and loved ones). And, ironically, striving for money and more consumption is a source of many environmental problems, whereas the things that really make people happy (e.g., social relationships) are not. When it comes to achieving a sustainable lifestyle, the kinds of changes we may need to make can be done without sacrificing the things that truly make people happy.

Suppose, for example, you could choose between two lives. In Life A, you live in a huge house in the suburbs and earn $500,000 a year, which you spend on lots of nice things: beautiful furniture, expensive cars, designer clothes. The downside is that you have a long commute to a job you don't really enjoy very much; you are an attorney, say, and spend most of your time researching how large corporations can pay fewer taxes. In Life B, you live in an apartment and earn $50,000 a year. You don't own a car; most days you ride your bicycle or walk the short distance to your job as a teacher. You can't wait to get to work each morning because you love what you do, especially when you see your efforts to help kids pay off. You have lots of friends at the school where you teach, as well as a tightly knit group of friends from college with whom you get together nearly every weekend. You have many interests and hobbies that keep you busy; you recently started taking salsa dance lessons, for example, and you volunteer with a literacy group that helps adults improve their reading skills.

These are extreme examples, of course, and you might argue that we have stacked the deck in favor of Life B (there is no reason, for example, why our tax attorney couldn't take salsa lessons as well). But we hope the point is clear: Life B includes the recipe for happiness—namely, lots of satisfying social relationships, plenty of flow experiences (at work and during leisure time), and ample opportunities to help others. Life A satisfies none of these things. Further, Life A is much less sustainable than Life B in terms of the amount of resources a person living it would consume—the energy required to heat and cool the huge house, the gasoline needed to commute to work, the resources needed to produce all the consumer items the person buys. The environmental problems we face are severe, but the good news is that we can meet the challenges without sacrificing the things that make us truly happy.

REVIEW QUESTIONS

1. Chantal wins $5,000 in the lottery. Which of the following ways of spending the money will make her the happiest, according to social psychological research?
   a. Buying a new wardrobe of clothes
   b. Taking her three closest friends on a vacation in the Caribbean
   c. Buying new furniture for her apartment
   d. Buying a new TV and sound system for her apartment

2. Which of the following is true, based on social psychological research?
   a. The things that make people happy tend to be bad for the environment.
   b. The more money people earn, the happier they tend to be.
   c. It is possible to adopt a lifestyle that is good for the environment without sacrificing the things that make us happy.

   d. The cars that people enjoy owning the most tend to get the worst gas mileage.

3. According to social psychological research, which of the following people is likely to be *least* happy?
   a. Nicole, who works 60 hours a week on a tedious job and makes $300,000 a year.
   b. Rasia, who mentors underprivileged teens.
   c. Navin, who is passionate about his hobby and spends hours working on it.
   d. Rebecca, who is very close to her family and has a tight-knit group of friends who she spends a lot of time with.

See page 622 for the answers.

Summary

SPA1.1 How can we apply social psychological principles to improve people's lives?

- **Applied Research in Social Psychology** By its very nature, social psychology addresses both basic and applied questions about human behavior. Social psychologists have conducted a good deal of applied research on important social and psychological issues, such as how people can adopt a more sustainable lifestyle.

  - **Capitalizing on the Experimental Method** One of the most important lessons of social psychology is the value of conducting experiments to answer questions about social influence. This is important when testing the effectiveness of interventions designed to solve an applied problem. Some interventions have backfired and had negative effects because they were not adequately tested.

  - **Social Psychology to the Rescue** Social psychologists are in a unique position to find solutions

to applied problems. First, the field of social psychology is a rich source of theories about human behavior that people can draw upon to devise solutions to problems. Second, social psychologists know how to perform rigorous experimental tests of these solutions to see if they work.

SPA1.2 How can social psychology help the world's people to live in a sustainable manner?

- **Using Social Psychology to Achieve a Sustainable Future** The human population is expanding at an exponential rate, with severe environmental consequences. Famine and malnutrition are spreading, natural resources are being depleted, and global warming is an alarming, immediate problem. Social psychologists have devised several approaches to encourage people to adopt a more sustainable lifestyle.

- **Conveying and Changing Social Norms** One approach is to remind people of both *injunctive* and *descriptive* norms against environmentally damaging acts, such as littering. For example, communicating descriptive norms—that other people act in environmentally friendly ways—has been shown to reduce the extent to which passersby litter and increase the extent to which hotel-room guests reuse their towels.

- **Keeping Track of Consumption** One simple technique is to make it easier for people to know how much energy they are using, for example, by providing them with water meters that are easy to read. College students who kept track of the number of miles they avoided driving their cars (e.g., by walking or taking the bus) drove their cars less.

- **Introducing a Little Competitiveness** Units in a company that were competing with each other to conserve energy were more successful than units that were encouraged to save but did not compete.

- **Inducing Hypocrisy** It works to arouse dissonance in people by making them feel that they are not practicing what they are preaching—for example, that even though they believe in water conservation, they are taking long showers.

- **Removing Small Barriers to Achieve Big Changes** Removing barriers that make proenvironmental behaviors difficult, such as instituting curbside recycling and providing people with recycling bins, has been shown to be effective. It also helps to get people to form **implementation intentions**, which are people's specific plans about where, when, and how they will fulfill a goal, such as the goal to recycle.

SPA1.3 How can we apply social psychology to make people happier?

- **Happiness and a Sustainable Lifestyle** It is possible to adopt a sustainable lifestyle and be a happy person.

  - **What Makes People Happy?** Happiness is partly a matter of the temperament with which we are born and partly a matter of environmental conditions outside of our control, such as the political stability of the government. Four things we can control also influence our happiness: the quality of our social relationships, opportunities for "flow" experiences, pursuing experiences instead of things, and helping others. Further, people who are materialistic—those who place a high value on money and possessions—tend to be less happy than people who place less value on money and possessions.

  - **Do People Know What Makes Them Happy?** When it comes to understanding the recipe for happiness, some people get it backward: They focus too much on wealth and materialism, and too little on social relationships, flow, and helping others. The moral is that people can achieve a sustainable lifestyle without sacrificing the things that make people truly happy.

Test Yourself

1. According to what you read in this chapter, in which of the following areas is social psychology research of least help to us?

   a. Making people happier

   b. Improving people's lives by using applied research to solve societal problems

   c. Helping people adopt a more sustainable lifestyle

   d. Understanding the underlying causes of mental health issues

2. Which of the following is the *most* effective way of getting people to recycle more?

   a. Informing people that recycling helps in the conservation of resources for future generations

   b. Allowing people to drop all recyclable material in one container instead of sorting it first

   c. Finding ways in which technology can help decompose materials faster

   d. Asking people to download an app that tracks their recycling efforts

3. Lina has moved to a new country and notices that, unlike her hometown, people casually throw garbage on the streets here. She is trying to figure out the norms about environmental conservation in the new country. Which of the following is an example of an *injunctive norm*?

   a. Lina believes that most people throw garbage on the streets for convenience.

   b. Lina believes that most people would not disapprove of her if she littered on the streets.

   c. Lina believes that only some people do not throw garbage on the streets.

   d. Lina believes that most people throw garbage on the streets because of a lack of disposal bins.

4. According to what you read in this chapter, which of these strategies could you employ if you wanted students living in dorms to use less water?

a. Install a water meter that shows them up-to-date consumption when they wash their dishes or take a shower.

b. Put up posters stressing the importance of water conservation.

c. Put up posters emphasizing the effects of drought across the world.

d. Measure students' attitude toward water conservation.

5. Based on the research conducted by Cialdini, Reno, and Kallgren (1990), which of the following is an effective way to ensure that people don't litter in public transport?

a. Leave several pieces of litter on the bus or train floor.

b. Post signs stating rules of using public transport.

c. Make sure that the bus or train compartment is clean, with only one container of food lying on the floor.

d. All of the above.

6. Mr. Gean has noticed that his students leave the classroom messy when they leave. He wants his students to tidy up the classroom before they go home every day. What can Mr. Gean do to ensure that his students act more responsibly?

a. Ask his students to sign a "responsibility pledge," then assess their own actions against what they signed.

b. Clean up the classroom himself after the students leave every day.

c. Put up a sign stating rules of responsible behavior in the classroom.

d. Ask a few students to volunteer for tidying up the classroom every day.

7. Which of the following is a possible explanation for why experiences make people happier than material possessions?

a. Experiences can involve shopping for material possessions that help people express who they are.

b. Experiences help people imagine positive future emotions.

c. Experiences help people bond with others and express who they truly are.

d. Experiences such as going to work every day help people achieve materialistic goals.

8. What do we know about affective forecasting?

a. People can accurately predict the intensity and duration of their future emotions.

b. People are becoming increasingly connected to close friends, which improves affective forecasting.

c. People often strive for things that will make them happier (e.g., buying a house) and forego those things that will not make them happy (e.g., meeting new people).

d. People are not very effective at getting the recipe of happiness right.

See page 622 for the answers.

Social Psychology in Action 2
Social Psychology and Health

 ## Chapter Outline and Learning Objectives

Stress and Human Health

SPA2.1 **How is stress defined and what effect does it have on our health?**

Resilience

Effects of Negative Life Events

Perceived Stress and Health

Feeling in Charge: The Importance of Perceived Control

Coping with Stress

SPA2.2 **What can people do to cope and recover after a stressful experience?**

Gender Differences in Coping with Stress

Social Support: Getting Help from Others

Reframing: Finding Meaning in Traumatic Events

Prevention: Promoting Healthier Behavior

SPA2.3 **How can we apply social psychology to help people live healthier lives?**

Joanne Hill suffered an unimaginable amount of loss over a 4-year period. It started when her husband, Ken, died of heart failure at the age of 55. Shortly after that Hill lost her brother, stepfather, mother, aunt, two uncles, two cousins, her cousin's partner, her stepmother, and, finally, her son, who died suddenly of a heart attack at the age of 38. Joanne helped care for several of these loved ones before they died, including her mother, who suffered from Alzheimer's and breast cancer, her brother, who died of lung cancer, and her aunt, who died of liver cancer. "Everyone I loved seemed to need help," she said (Hill, 2002, p. 21).

How could anyone endure so much loss? Surely any one of these tragedies would stop us in our tracks, and suffering so many in such a short time would surely push most of us to the breaking point, taking a severe toll on our physical and emotional well-being. But rather than crawl under a rock, Joanne made it through what she calls her "locust years" with remarkable strength, grace, and resilience. She was the executor of several of her relatives' estates and dealt successfully with complicated legal issues. She provided help and support to numerous friends and family members. She also went back to college, traveled to Europe, and wrote a book about her experiences. Life is "filled with both bright sunny places and dark stormy times," she says. "Within each I looked for the golden nuggets of wisdom and truth that helped me grow stronger, happier and healthier" (Hill, n.d.).

Maybe Joanne is one of those rare people born with a huge reservoir of inner strength, allowing her to weather any storm. But she didn't always find it easy to deal with life's slings and arrows. She had struggled with depression in childhood and beyond, was addicted to prescription medication early in her marriage, and suffered from debilitating physical ailments—so many that she had difficulty buying life insurance. "Today," she reports in her book, "in spite of one trauma after another for several years, I am healthy in body and whole in mind. Not because of Lady Luck, but because I decided to make different choices" (p. 153). Hill attributes her survival to a series of "rainbow remedies" that she learned, through hard experience, to apply to her life.

This chapter is concerned with the application of psychology to physical and mental health, which is a flourishing area of research. We will focus primarily on topics that connect social psychology and health: how people cope with stress in their lives, the relationship between their coping styles and their physical and mental health, and how we can get people to behave in healthier ways. Along the way we will return to Joanne Hill's story, discuss her "rainbow remedies," and see that at least some of them are backed up by research in social psychology and health.

People are surprisingly resilient in the face of stressful events. Studies of reactions to the 9/11 terrorist attacks, for example, have found that relatively few people showed long-term signs of depression or other mental health problems.

Stress and Human Health

SPA2.1 How is stress defined and what effect does it have on our health?

There is more to our physical health than germs and disease—we also need to consider the amount of stress in our lives and how we deal with that stress (Chida & Hamer, 2008; Ganzel, Morris, & Wethington, 2010; Inglehart, 1991; Park, 2010; Segerstrom & O'Connor, 2012; Taylor, 2015). Early research in this area documented some extreme cases in which people's health was influenced by stress. Consider these examples, reported by psychologist W. B. Cannon (1942):

- A New Zealand woman eats a piece of fruit and then learns that it came from a forbidden supply reserved for the chief. Horrified, her health deteriorates, and the next day she dies—even though it was a perfectly fine piece of fruit.

- A man in Africa has breakfast with a friend, eats heartily, and goes on his way. A year later, he learns that his friend had made the breakfast from a wild hen, a food strictly forbidden in his culture. The man immediately begins to tremble and is dead within 24 hours.

- An Australian man's health deteriorates after a witch doctor casts a spell on him. He recovers only when the witch doctor removes the spell.

These examples probably sound bizarre, like something you would read in *Ripley's Believe It or Not*. But let's shift to the present in the United States, where many similar cases of sudden death occur following a psychological trauma. When people undergo a major upheaval in their lives, such as losing a spouse, declaring bankruptcy, or being forced to resettle in a new culture, their chance of dying increases (Morse, Martin, & Moshonov, 1991). Soon after a major earthquake in the Los Angeles area on January 17, 1994, there was an increase in the number of people who died suddenly of heart attacks (Leor, Poole, & Kloner, 1996). And many people experienced psychological and physical problems after the terrorist attacks on September 11, 2001 (Neria, DiGrande, & Adams, 2011; Silver et al., 2002). One study measured the heart rates of a sample of adults in New Haven, Connecticut, the week after the attacks. Compared to a control group of people studied before the attacks, the post–September 11 sample showed lower heart rate variability, which is a risk factor for sudden death (Gerin et al., 2005; Lampert et al., 2002). On the other hand, as we will see in a moment, studies of the long-term effects of the 9/11 attacks have found relatively little evidence of prolonged negative reactions. What exactly are the effects of stress on our psychological and physical health, and how can we learn to cope most effectively?

Resilience

The first thing to note is that humans are remarkably resilient. To be sure, we all must contend with the blows that life deals us, including day-to-day hassles and major, life-altering events. And although it is true that such events can have negative effects on psychological and physical health, many people, such as Joanne Hill, cope with them extremely well. Researchers have examined people's reactions over time to major life events, including the death of loved ones and the 9/11 terrorist attacks. The most common response to such traumas is **resilience**, which can be defined as mild, transient reactions to stressful events, followed by a quick return to normal, healthy functioning (Bonanno, 2005; Bonanno, Westphal, & Mancini, 2011; Galatzer-Levy, Bonanno, Bush, & LeDoux, 2013; Kalisch, Müller, & Tüscher, 2015).

Resilience

Mild, transient reactions to stressful events, followed by a quick return to normal, healthy functioning

Take life's most difficult challenge—dealing with the loss of a loved one. For years, mental health professionals assumed that the "right" way to grieve was to go through an intense period of sadness and distress, in which people confronted and worked through their feelings, eventually leading to acceptance of the loss. People who did not show symptoms of extreme distress were said to be in a state of denial that would lead to greater problems down the road. When researchers looked systematically at how people respond to the death of loved ones, however, an interesting fact emerged: Many people never experienced significant distress and recovered quickly (Bookwala, 2014; Wortman & Silver, 1989). Studies of bereaved spouses, for example, typically find that fewer than half show signs of significant, long-term distress (Bonanno, Boerner, & Wortman, 2008; Bonanno et al., 2005). The remainder, like Joanne Hill, show no signs of depression and are able to experience positive emotions.

Although one might think that such people are in a state of denial, or that they were never very attached to their spouses, there is little evidence to support these possibilities. Rather, there is increasing evidence that although life's traumas can be quite painful, many people have the resources to recover from them quickly. The same pattern has been found in people's responses to other highly stressful events, such as emergency workers' reactions to the bombing of the federal building in Oklahoma City in 1995 and New Yorkers' reactions to the 9/11 terrorist attacks. Surprisingly few people show prolonged, negative reactions to these tragedies (Dekel et al, 2013; Seery et al., 2008; Updegraff, Silver, & Holman, 2008). Nonetheless, some people do have severe negative reactions to stressful events. What determines whether people bounce back quickly or buckle under stress?

Effects of Negative Life Events

Among the pioneers in research on stress is Hans Selye (1956, 1976), who defined *stress* as the body's physiological response to threatening events. Selye focused on how the human body adapts to threats from the environment, regardless of the source—be it a psychological or physiological trauma. Later researchers have examined what it is about a life event that makes it threatening. Holmes and Rahe (1967), for example, suggested that stress is the degree to which people have to change and readjust their lives in response to an external event. The more change that is required, the greater the stress we experience. For example, if a spouse or partner dies, just about every aspect of a person's life is disrupted, leading to a great deal of stress. Holmes and Rahe's definition of stress applies to happy events as well if the event causes big changes in one's daily routine. Getting married is a happy occasion, but it can also be stressful because of the planning involved and the potential for family friction, such as Uncle Harry drinking too much and making a fool of himself on the dance floor again.

What makes life stressful for college students? To find out, researchers made a long list of potential stressors and had college students rate how often they had experienced them and how stressful they were (Renner & Mackin, 1998). You can take an abridged version of this stress inventory in the Try It! exercise on the next page. How did you do? Studies have shown that the higher people score on stress inventories such as this one, the worse their mental and physical health (Armata & Baldwin, 2008; Dohrenwend, 2006; Seta, Seta, & Wang, 1990).

Some of these events or situations are happy, yet they cause stress. Which might cause you to experience stress?

TRY IT!

The College Life Stress Inventory

Instructions: Copy the "stress rating" number into the right column for any event that has happened to you in the past year; then add these scores.

Event	Stress Rating	Your Score
Being raped	100	_____
Finding out that you are HIV-positive	100	_____
Death of a close friend	97	_____
Death of a close family member	96	_____
Contracting a sexually transmitted disease (other than AIDS)	94	_____
Concerns about being pregnant	91	_____
Finals week	90	_____
Concerns about your partner being pregnant	90	_____
Oversleeping for an exam	89	_____
Flunking a class	89	_____
Having a boyfriend or girlfriend cheat on you	85	_____
Ending a steady dating relationship	85	_____
Serious illness in a close friend or family member	85	_____
Financial difficulties	84	_____
Writing a major term paper	83	_____
Being caught cheating on a test	83	_____
Drunk driving	82	_____
Cheating on your boyfriend or girlfriend	77	_____
Negative consequences of drinking or drug use	75	_____
Depression or crisis in your best friend	73	_____
Difficulties with parents	73	_____
Competing or performing in public	69	_____
Difficulties with a roommate	66	_____
Job changes (applying, new job, work hassles)	65	_____
Declaring a major or concerns about future plans	65	_____
A class you hate	62	_____
Drinking or use of drugs	61	_____
Starting a new semester	58	_____
Going on a first date	57	_____
Maintaining a steady dating relationship	55	_____
Commuting to campus or work, or both	54	_____
Peer pressures	53	_____
Being away from home for the first time	53	_____
Concerns about your appearance	52	_____
Getting straight A's	51	_____
Making new friends; getting along with friends	47	_____
Falling asleep in class	40	_____
Sum of Your Score		_____

LIMITS OF STRESS INVENTORIES It may seem obvious that the more stress people are experiencing, the more likely they are to feel anxious and get sick. But the findings aren't all that straightforward. One problem, as you may have recognized, is that most studies in this area use correlational designs, not experimental designs. Just because life changes are correlated with health problems does not mean that the life changes caused the health problems (see Chapter 2 on correlation and causality). Some researchers have argued persuasively for the role of "third variables," whereby certain kinds of people are more likely to be experiencing difficult life changes and to report that they are ill (Schroeder & Costa, 1984; Watson & Pennebaker, 1989). According to these researchers, it is not life changes that cause health problems. Instead, people with certain personality traits, such as the tendency to experience negative moods, are more likely to experience life difficulties and to have health problems.

Another problem with measures such as the College Life Stress Inventory is that they focus on stressors experienced by the middle class and underrepresent stressors experienced by the poor and members of minority groups. Variables such as poverty and racism are potent causes of stress (Gibbons, Gerrard, & Cleveland, 2004; Jackson et al., 1996; Lick, Durso, & Johnson, 2013; Myers, 2009). Moreover, the way in which these variables influence health is not always obvious. It might not surprise you to learn that the more racism minority groups experience, the worse their health. It might come as more of a surprise to learn that majority groups who express the most racist attitudes also experience diminished health (Jackson & Inglehart, 1995). Racism is often associated with hostility and aggression, and there is evidence that hostility is related to health problems such as coronary heart disease. Clearly, to understand the relationship between stress and health, we need to understand better such community and cultural variables as poverty and racism.

Perceived Stress and Health

There is another problem with measures such as the College Life Stress Inventory: They violate a basic principle of social psychology—namely, that subjective situations have more of an impact on people than objective situations (Dohrenwend, 2006; Griffin & Ross, 1991). Of course, some situational variables are hazardous to our health regardless of how we interpret them (Jackson & Inglehart, 1995; Taylor, Repetti, & Seeman, 1997). Children growing up in smog-infested areas such as Los Angeles and Mexico City, for example, have been found to have physiological and psychological deficits, compared to children who grow up in less-polluted areas (Calderón-Garcidueñas & Torres-Jardón, 2012; Ferguson et al., 2013; Peters et al., 1999). Nonetheless, some environmental events are open to interpretation and seem to have negative effects only on people who construe these events in certain ways. To some students, writing a term paper is a major hassle; for others, it's a minor inconvenience (or even an enjoyable challenge). For some people, a major life change such as getting divorced is a liberating escape from an abusive relationship; for others, it is a devastating personal failure (Crum, Salovey, & Achor, 2013; Yeager et al., 2014). As recognized by Richard Lazarus (1966, 2000) in his pioneering work on stress, it is subjective, not objective, stress that causes problems. An event is stressful for people only if they interpret it as stressful; thus, we can define **stress** as the negative feelings and beliefs that occur whenever people feel unable to cope with demands from their environment (Lazarus & Folkman, 1984).

Consider the number of losses Joanne Hill experienced in a 4-year period. According to research on life events, she should have been experiencing a great deal of stress—enough to put her at great risk for severe physical problems. The fact that she made it through with grace and strength suggests that there are limits to trying to predict people's reactions from a count of the number of stressful events in their lives. We need to take into account how different people *interpret* disruptions and challenges in their lives.

Adopting the right attitude can convert a negative stress into a positive one.

—HANS SELYE (1978)

Stress

The negative feelings and beliefs that arise whenever people feel unable to cope with demands from their environment

Studies using the subjective definition of stress confirm the idea that negative life experiences are bad for our health. In fact, stress caused by negative interpretations of events can directly affect our immune systems, making us more susceptible to disease. Consider the common cold. When people are exposed to the virus that causes a cold, only 20% to 60% of them become sick. Is it possible that stress is one determinant of who will be in this category? To find out, researchers asked volunteers to spend a week at a research institute in southern England (Cohen, Tyrrell, & Smith, 1991, 1993). As a measure of stress, the participants listed recent events that had had a negative impact on their lives. (Consistent with our definition of stress, the participants listed only events they *perceived* as negative.)

The researchers then gave participants nasal drops that contained either the virus that causes the common cold or saline (salt water). The participants were subsequently quarantined for several days so that they had no contact with other people. The results? The more stress people were experiencing, the more likely they were to catch a cold from the virus (see Figure SPA-2.1).

Among people who reported the least amount of stress, about 27% came down with a cold. This rate increased steadily the more stress people reported, topping out at a rate of nearly 50% in the group that was experiencing the most stress. This effect of stress was found even when several other factors that influence catching a cold were taken into account, such as the time of year people participated and the participants' age, weight, and gender. This study, along with others like it, shows that the more stress people experience, the lower their immunity to disease (Cohen et al., 2008; Marsland, Bachen, & Cohen, 2012; O'Leary, 1990).

You may have noticed that the Cohen and colleagues study used a correlational design; this must make us cautious about its interpretation. The amount of stress people were experiencing was measured and correlated with the likelihood that people caught a cold. It is possible that stress itself did not lower people's immunity but rather that some third variable did. For example, maybe having a pessimistic outlook on life lowers people's immunity and increases the likelihood that they will experience stress. It would have been ethically impermissible, of course, to conduct an experimental study in which people were randomly assigned to a condition in which they experienced a great deal of prolonged stress. There are studies, however, in which people's immune responses are measured before and after undergoing mildly stressful tasks in the laboratory, such as solving mental arithmetic problems continuously for 6 minutes or giving speeches on short notice. Even relatively mild stressors such as these can lead to a suppression of the immune system (Cacioppo, 1998; Cacioppo et al., 1998).

The finding that stress negatively affects health raises an important question: What exactly is it that makes people perceive a situation as stressful? One important determinant is the amount of control they believe they have over the event.

Feeling in Charge: The Importance of Perceived Control

"There are times in life when we feel so out of control that helplessness and hopelessness become constant companions," writes Joanne Hill. "But choice, like breath, is something that is part of us. *We always have a choice*" (Hill, 2002, p. 128). Research shows, however, that some people feel this way more than others. For example, suppose you read a series of statements and had to choose the one in each pair that you thought was more true, such as "people's misfortunes result from mistakes they make" versus "many of the unhappy

Figure SPA-2.1 Stress and the Likelihood of Catching a Cold

People were first exposed to the virus that causes the common cold and then isolated. The greater the amount of stress they were experiencing, the greater the likelihood that they caught a cold from the virus.

(Based on Cohen, Tyrrell, & Smith, 1991)

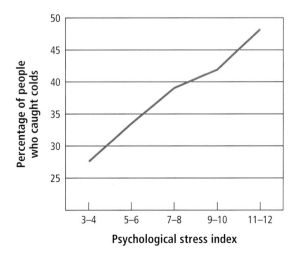

things in people's lives are partly due to bad luck." Which of these two do you think is more true? These statements are part of a test of **internal-external locus of control** (Levenson, 1981; Rotter, 1966), which is the tendency to believe that things happen because we control them versus believing that good and bad outcomes are out of our control. The first statement above reflects an internal locus of control, which is the belief that people can control their fates. The second statement reflects an external locus of control, which is the belief that our fates are more a matter of happenstance.

Research by Jean Twenge and her colleagues (Twenge, Gentile, & Campbell, 2015; Twenge, Zhang, & Im, 2004) has found that between the years 1960 and 2002, college students in the United States have scored more and more on the external end of the locus-of-control scale. That is, as seen in Figure SPA-2.2, college students are becoming more convinced that good and bad things in life are outside of their control. The reasons for this trend are not entirely clear; it may be part of an increased sense of alienation and distrust among younger generations in the United States (Fukuyama, 1999; Putnam, 2000).

Whatever the reasons, recent research suggests that feelings of control are not something that we either have or do not have. These feelings vary from day to day; on some days, like Leonard DiCaprio's character in the movie *Titanic*, people feel like they are the "King of the World!", whereas other days, they feel like they are butting their heads against the wall to no avail. These beliefs are important, because on the days that people feel like the King of the World they engage in healthier behaviors such as exercising and eating well (Ryon & Gleason, 2014). More generally, having a sense of **perceived control**—defined as the belief that we can influence our environment in ways that determine whether we experience positive or negative outcomes—is associated with good physical and mental health (Frazier et al., 2011; Infurna, Ram, & Gerstorf, 2013; Leotti, Iyengar, & Ochsner, 2010; Roepke & Grant, 2011; Thompson, 1999).

If people become seriously ill, feeling in control is especially important. Shelley Taylor and her colleagues (Taylor, Lichtman, & Wood, 1984; Taylor, 2015) interviewed women with breast cancer and found that many of them believed they could control whether their cancer returned. Here is how one man described his wife: "She got books, she got pamphlets, she studied, she talked to cancer patients. She found out everything that was happening to her and she fought it. She went to war with it. She calls it 'taking in her covered wagons and surrounding it'" (quoted in Taylor, 1989, p. 178). The researchers found that women who believed their cancer was controllable were better adjusted psychologically (Folkman & Moskowitz, 2000). Similar results have been found with people who have other kinds of medical issues, such as those who underwent a coronary angioplasty because of diseased arteries. Those who had a high sense of control over their futures were less likely to experience subsequent heart problems than people with a low sense of control (Helgeson, 2003; Helgeson & Fritz, 1999). Joanne Hill recognized this lesson; one of her rainbow remedies is that the "Power of Choice is an empowering remedy that truly makes the difference whether we survive and thrive, or wither and die" (Hill, n.d.).

INCREASING PERCEIVED CONTROL IN NURSING HOMES
Some of the most dramatic effects of perceived control have been found in studies of older people in nursing homes. Many people who end up in nursing homes and hospitals feel they have lost control of their lives (Raps et al., 1982; Sherwin & Winsby, 2011). People are often placed in long-term care facilities

Internal-External Locus of Control

The tendency to believe that things happen because we control them versus believing that good and bad outcomes are out of our control

Perceived Control

The belief that we can influence our environment in ways that determine whether we experience positive or negative outcomes

Figure SPA-2.2 Beliefs in Internal-External Locus of Control in College Students Over Time

As seen in the graph, in the past 50 years there is a trend whereby college students in the United States endorse more external beliefs about locus of control. This means that they increasingly believe that good and bad things in life are outside of their control.

(Data from Twenge, Zhang, & Im, 2004)

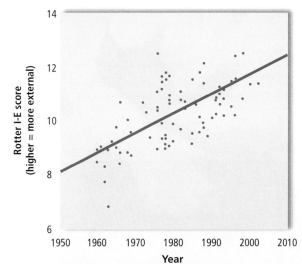

against their wishes and, when there, have little say in what they do, whom they see, or what they eat. Two psychologists believed that boosting their feelings of control would help such people (Langer & Rodin, 1976). They asked the director of a nursing home in Connecticut to convey to the residents that, contrary to what they might think, they had a lot of responsibility for their own lives. Here is an excerpt of his speech:

> Take a minute to think of the decisions you can and should be making. For example, you have the responsibility of caring for yourselves, of deciding whether or not you want to make this a home you can be proud of and happy in. You should be deciding how you want your rooms to be arranged—whether you want it to be as it is or whether you want the staff to help you rearrange the furniture. You should be deciding how you want to spend your time. . . . If you are unsatisfied with anything here, you have the influence to change it. . . . These are just a few of the things you could and should be deciding and thinking about now and from time to time every day. (Langer & Rodin, 1976, pp. 194–195)

The director went on to say that a movie would be shown on two nights the next week and that the residents should decide which night they wanted to attend. Finally, he offered each resident a gift of a house plant, emphasizing that it was up to the resident to decide whether to take one (they all did) and to take care of it. The director also gave a speech to residents assigned to a comparison group. This speech was different in one crucial way: All references to making decisions and being responsible for oneself were deleted. He emphasized that he wanted the residents to be happy, but he did not say anything about the control they had over their lives. He said that a movie would be shown on two nights the next week but that the residents would be assigned to see it on one night or the other. He gave plants to these residents as well but said that the nurses would take care of the plants.

Nursing home residents who have a sense of control over their lives have been found to do better, both physically and psychologically.

The director's speech might not seem like a major change in the lives of the residents. The people in the induced-control group heard one speech about the responsibility they had for their lives and were given one plant to water. That doesn't seem like very strong stuff, does it? But to an institutionalized person who feels helpless and constrained, even a small boost in control can have a dramatic effect. Indeed, the residents in the induced-control group became happier and more active than residents in the comparison group (Langer & Rodin, 1976). Most dramatically of all, the intervention improved the residents' health and reduced the likelihood that they would die in the next year and a half (Rodin & Langer, 1977). Eighteen months after the director's speech, 15% of the residents in the induced-control group had died, compared to 30% in the comparison condition (see the left side of Figure SPA-2.3).

Another researcher increased feelings of control in residents of nursing homes in a different way (Schulz, 1976). Undergraduates visited the residents of a North Carolina nursing home once a week for 2 months. In the induced-control condition, the residents decided when their visits would occur and how long they would last. In a randomly assigned comparison condition, it was the students, not the residents, who decided when the visits would occur and how long they would last. Thus, the residents received visits in both conditions, but in only one could they control the visits' frequency and duration. This may seem like a minor difference, but again, giving the residents some semblance of control over their lives had dramatic effects. After 2 months, those in the induced-control condition were happier, healthier, more active, and taking fewer medications than those in the comparison group.

The researchers returned to the nursing home several months later to assess the long-term effects of their intervention, including its effect on mortality rates. Based on the results of the Langer and Rodin (1976) study,

---

Figure SPA-2.3 Perceived Control and Mortality

In two studies, elderly residents in nursing homes were made to feel more in control of their lives. In one (Rodin & Langer, 1977), the intervention endured over time, so that people continued to feel in control. As seen on the left side of the figure, this intervention had positive effects on mortality rates. Those who received it were more likely to be alive 18 months later than those who did not. In the other study (Schulz & Hanusa, 1978), the intervention was temporary. Being given control and then having it taken away had negative effects on mortality rates, as seen on the right side of the figure.

(Based on Rodin & Langer, 1977; Schulz & Hanusa, 1978)

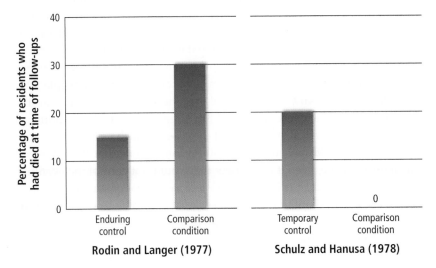

we might expect that the residents who could control the students' visits would be healthier and more likely still to be alive than the residents who could not. But there is a crucial difference between the two studies: The residents in the Langer and Rodin study were given an enduring sense of control, whereas the residents in the Schulz study experienced control and then lost it. That is, Langer and Rodin's participants could continue to choose which days to participate in different activities, continue to take care of their plant, and continue to feel that they could make a difference in what happened to them, even after the study ended. By contrast, when Schulz's study was over, the student visits ended. The residents who could control the visits suddenly had that control removed.

Unfortunately, Schulz's intervention had an unintended effect: After the program ended, the people in the induced-control group did worse (Schulz & Hanusa, 1978). Compared to people in the comparison group, they were more likely to have experienced deteriorating health and zest for life, and they were more likely to have died (see the right side of Figure SPA-2.3). This study has sobering implications for the many college-based volunteer programs in which students visit residents of nursing homes, prisons, and mental hospitals. These programs might be beneficial in the short run but do more harm than good after they end.

DISEASE, CONTROL, AND WELL-BEING   We end this discussion with some words of caution. First, the relationship between perceived control and distress is more important to members of Western cultures than to members of Asian cultures. Research shows that Asians report that perceived control is less important to them than Westerners do and that there is less of a relationship between perceived control and psychological distress among Asians than Westerners (Cheng, Cheung, Chio, & Chan, 2013; Sastry & Ross, 1998). In Western cultures, where individualism and personal achievement are prized, people are more likely to be distressed if they feel that they cannot personally control their destinies. A lowered sense of control is less of an issue in Asian cultures, because Asians place greater value on collectivism and putting the social group ahead of individual goals.

Second, even in Western societies, there is a danger in exaggerating the relationship between perceived control and health. Social critic Susan Sontag (1978, 1988) perceptively observed that when a society is plagued by a deadly but poorly understood disease, such as tuberculosis in the nineteenth century and AIDS today, the illness is often blamed on some kind of human frailty, such as a lack of faith, a moral weakness, or a broken heart. As a result, people may blame themselves for their illnesses, even to the point where they do not seek effective treatment. Even though it helps people to feel that they are in control of their illnesses, the downside of this strategy is that if they do not get better, they may blame themselves for failing to recover. Tragically, diseases such as cancer can be fatal no matter how much control a person feels. It only adds to the tragedy if people with serious diseases feel a sense of moral failure, blaming themselves for a disease that is unpredictable and incurable.

For people living with serious illnesses, keeping some form of control has benefits, even when their health is failing. Researchers have found that when people who are seriously ill with cancer or AIDS felt no control over the disease, many of them still believed they could control the consequences of the disease, such as their emotional reactions and some of the physical symptoms of the disease, such as how tired they felt. And the more people felt they could control the consequences of their disease, the better adjusted they were, even if they knew they could not control the eventual course of their illness. In short, it is important to feel in control of something, even if it is not the disease itself. Maintaining such a sense of control is likely to improve one's psychological well-being, even if one's health fails (Heckhausen & Schulz, 1995; Morling & Evered, 2006; Thompson, 2002).

REVIEW QUESTIONS

1. Michael's roommate has come down with a cold. In which of the following circumstances is Michael most likely to catch his roommate's cold?
   a. Michael's girlfriend just broke up with him, but he knew it was coming and doesn't view it as all that bad a thing.
   b. Michael's goldfish just died, which he views as a very negative event.
   c. Michael hasn't been exercising very much lately.
   d. It doesn't matter what is going on in Michael's life; all that matters is whether he is exposed to the virus that causes the cold.

2. Which of the following is true?
   a. Someone who is are exposed to the cold virus is almost certainly going to come down with a cold.
   b. For people with serious diseases such as cancer, it doesn't matter how much control they feel they have over the disease or its consequences.

   c. If a college student experiences one or more of the stressful life events at the top of the College Life Stress Inventory, he or she will almost certainly get sick.
   d. Many people who experience the death of a loved one do not experience severe distress and recover quickly.

3. Which of the following is true? In the last 60 years or so, college students have:
   a. scored more on the external end of the locus-of-control scale.
   b. scored more on the internal end of the locus-of-control scale.
   c. scored higher on a measure of resiliency.
   d. scored lower on a measure of resiliency.

4. Which of the following is most associated with good health?
   a. low perceived control
   b. low perceived stress
   c. a small number of negative life events
   d. low resiliency

See page 622 for the answers.

Coping with Stress

SPA2.2 What can people do to cope and recover after a stressful experience?

Coping Styles

The ways in which people react to threatening events

No one always feels in control, of course, and sometimes it is difficult to avoid being pessimistic after something bad happens. The death of a loved one, an acrimonious divorce, and the loss of a job are extremely stressful events. Considerable research indicates that people exhibit various reactions, or **coping styles**, in the face of such events (Aspinwall & Taylor, 1997; Lazarus & Folkman, 1984; Lehman et al., 1993; Moos & Holahan, 2003; Taylor, 2015). We examine a few coping styles here, beginning with research on gender differences in the ways people respond to stress.

Gender Differences in Coping with Stress

If you have ever been to a dog park, you know that dogs respond in one of two ways when they are attacked: Sometimes they respond in kind, and a dogfight occurs, with owners scrambling to remove their dogs from the melee. Other times, the dog who is attacked will take off as fast as it can, tail between its legs. Walter Cannon (1932) termed this the **fight-or-flight response**, defined as responding to stress by either attacking the source of the stress or fleeing from it. For years, the fight-or-flight response has been viewed as the way in which all mammals respond to stress. When under threat, mammals are energized by the release of hormones such as norepinephrine and epinephrine, and, like the dogs in the park, they either go on the attack or retreat as quickly as they can.

That, at least, has been the accepted story for many years. Shelley Taylor and her colleagues (Taylor, 2012; Taylor et al., 2000; Taylor & Master, 2011) pointed out that there is another way to deal with stress, namely the **tend-and-befriend response**. Instead of fighting or fleeing, people can respond to stress with nurturing activities designed to protect oneself and one's offspring (tending) and creating social networks that provide protection from threats (befriending). Although both men and women exhibit the tend-and-befriend response (von Dawans et al., 2012), it is especially prevalent in women. Why? Taylor and her colleagues argue that the fight-or-flight response does not work well for females because they typically play a greater role in caring for children. Fighting is not always a good option for a pregnant female or one tending offspring. Similarly, fleeing is difficult when an adult is responsible for the care of young children or in the later months of pregnancy. Indeed, research shows that when under stress the hormone oxytocin is released, which is sometimes called the "bonding hormone," because it is associated with the desire to be close to other people. And, whereas both men and women have oxytocin, its effects are enhanced by the presence of estrogen, a female hormone (Taylor, 2012).

We should be careful not to oversimplify gender differences such as these. Although gender differences in coping do exist, the magnitude of these differences is not very large (Tamres et al., 2002). Further, seeking social support can benefit both women and men—as seen in the next section.

Social Support: Getting Help from Others

Joanne Hill could not have gotten through her "locust years" without the support of a good many family members and friends. When she got the devastating news that her son had died, she was at a gathering of the National Speakers Association (NSA). Joanne turned immediately to her friend Mitchell, a man who had survived both a motorcycle accident and a plane crash. Although badly scarred and wheelchair bound, Mitchell had overcome his adversity and become a successful public speaker. On that terrible day, he held Joanne's hand, shared her grief, and rode with her to the airport. Others helped too: The president of the NSA and her husband took charge of the travel arrangements, and Barbara, a woman Joanne had met just a couple of days earlier at the convention, insisted on accompanying her home.

Females are somewhat more likely than males to develop intimate friendships, cooperate with others, and focus their attention on social relationships, particularly when under stress. This is called a *tend-and-befriend* coping strategy.

Fight-or-Flight Response

Responding to stress by either attacking the source of the stress or fleeing from it

Tend-and-Befriend Response

Responding to stress with nurturing activities designed to protect oneself and one's offspring (tending) and creating social networks that provide protection from threats (befriending)

Friendship is a sheltering tree.
—Samuel Taylor
Coleridge (1772–1834)

Social Support

The perception that others are responsive and receptive to one's needs

Social support, perceiving that others are responsive and receptive to one's needs, is very helpful for dealing with stress (Hostinar, Sullivan, & Gunnar, 2014; Lakey & Orehek, 2011; Lam & Dickerson, 2013; Taylor, 2015). But researchers have wondered: Does social support help people physically as well as emotionally? There is some evidence that it does. Studies have shown that interventions designed to increase social support and decrease stress in cancer patients improve the functioning of their immune systems (Andersen et al., 2004; Antoni & Lutgendorf, 2007; McGregor et al., 2004; Weihs, Enright, & Simmens, 2008). And, social support seems to prolong the lives of healthy people as well. In a study of a large sample of American men and women in the years 1967 to 1969, those with a low level of social support were significantly more likely to die over the next dozen years than people with a high level of social support (House, Robbins, & Metzner, 1982), a finding that has been replicated in a number of other studies (Holt-Lunstad, Smith, & Layton, 2010). To get an idea of the amount of social support you feel is available in your life, complete the Try It! exercise that follows.

TRY IT!
Social Support

This list contains statements that may or may not be true about you. For each statement that is probably true about you, circle T; for each that is probably not true about you, circle F.

You may find that many of the statements are neither clearly true nor clearly false. In these cases, try to decide quickly whether probably true (T) or probably false (F) is more descriptive of you. Although some questions will be difficult to answer, it is important that you pick one alternative or the other. Circle only one of the alternatives for each statement.

Read each item quickly but carefully before responding. This is not a test, and there are no right or wrong answers.

1.	There is at least one person I know whose advice I really trust.	T	F
2.	There is really no one I can trust to give me good financial advice.	T	F
3.	There is really no one who can give me objective feedback about how I'm handling my problems.	T	F
4.	When I need suggestions for how to deal with a personal problem, I know there is someone I can turn to.	T	F
5.	There is someone I feel comfortable going to for advice about sexual problems.	T	F
6.	There is someone I can turn to for advice about handling hassles over household responsibilities.	T	F
7.	I feel that there is no one with whom I can share my most private worries and fears.	T	F
8.	If a family crisis arose, few of my friends would be able to give me good advice about how to handle it.	T	F
9.	There are very few people I trust to help solve my problems.	T	F
10.	There is someone I could turn to for advice about changing my job or finding a new one.	T	F

(Scoring instructions appear on page 622).

(Adapted from Cohen, Mermelstein, Kamarack, & Hoberman, 1985)

Though it may seem obvious that social support is beneficial, it turns out that there are some interesting qualifications in when and how it helps. First, when things are tough, the kind of social support we get matters. To illustrate, imagine that you are struggling in one of your classes and attend a study session for the final exam. Sarah, a friend of yours in the group, greets you by saying, "I know you aren't doing very well in this class, so how about if we all focus on the material you don't understand and give you an extra hand?" On the one hand, you appreciate the support and extra help. But who likes being singled out as the person who "isn't doing very well"? As we saw in Chapter 11, people don't like receiving help when it comes with the message "you are too incompetent to do it yourself." Now suppose that Sarah was a little more subtle in her support. She knows that you are having trouble with the material in the last chapter of the textbook, but rather than singling you out, she says, "A lot of us are struggling with the material in Chapter 16—I know I am. How about if we focus on that?" She steers help your way without singling you out or communicating that you are incompetent.

Research has demonstrated that the latter kind of help, which is called *invisible support*, is much more effective. This kind of support provides people with assistance without sending the message that they are incapable of doing it themselves. The former type of help, which is called *visible support*, is a two-edged sword, because it singles out beneficiaries as needy and as people who can't help themselves. The moral? If you have a friend who is under a great deal of stress, find a way to help him or her unobtrusively without making a big deal of it (Bolger & Amarel, 2007; Girme, Overall, & Simpson, 2013; Maisel & Gable, 2009).

Second, social support operates differently in different cultures. Who do you think is more likely to seek support from other people when things get tough: members of Western cultures that stress individualism and independence, or members of East Asian cultures that stress collectivism and interdependence? It might seem as though cultures that stress collectivism would be more likely to seek help from each other, but research has found just the opposite: When under stress, members of East Asian cultures are *less* likely to seek social support than are members of Western cultures (Chen, Kim, Mojaverian, & Morling, 2012; Kim, Sherman, & Taylor, 2008; Mojaverian & Kim, 2013; Taylor et al., 2007). The reason? Members of collectivistic cultures are concerned that seeking support from others will disrupt the harmony of the group and open them up to criticism from others.

Does this mean that members of collectivistic cultures receive less support from others and benefit less from it when they do receive it? Not at all. The main difference is in *how* people in different cultures seek and obtain social support. Because members of collectivistic cultures are concerned with upsetting group harmony and criticism from others, they are less likely to ask directly for help in a way that shows they are having problems. For example, they are less likely to say to a friend, "Hey, I'm having a hard time here. Can you give me a hand?" They do benefit from interacting with supportive others, as long as they do not have to disclose that they are having problems (Kim et al., 2008).

Reframing: Finding Meaning in Traumatic Events

When something traumatic happens to you, is it best to try to bury it as deep as you can and never talk about it, or to spend time thinking about the event and discuss it with others? Although folk wisdom has long held that it is best to open up, only recently has this assumption been put to the test. James Pennebaker and his colleagues (Pennebaker, 1990, 1997, 2004; Sloan et al., 2008; Smyth, Pennebaker, & Arigo, 2012) have conducted a number of interesting experiments on the value of writing about traumatic events. Pennebaker and Beale (1986), for example, asked college students to write, for 15 minutes on each of 4 consecutive nights, about a traumatic event that had happened to them. Students in a control condition wrote for the same amount of time about a trivial event. The traumas that people chose to write about included tragedies such as rape and the death of a sibling.

Not surprisingly writing about these events was upsetting, at least in the short run: Students who wrote about traumas reported more-negative moods and showed

If he wrote it he could get rid of it. He had gotten rid of many things by writing them.

—ERNEST HEMINGWAY,
FATHERS AND SONS (1933)

greater increases in blood pressure. But there were dramatic long-term benefits: The same students were less likely to visit the student health center during the next 6 months, and they reported having fewer illnesses. Similarly, first-year college students who wrote about the problems of entering college, survivors of the Holocaust who wrote about their World War II experiences, and patients who had had a heart attack and wrote about it improved their health over the several months after putting their experiences in writing (Pennebaker, Barger, & Tiebout, 1989; Pennebaker, Colder, & Sharp, 1990; Willmott et al., 2011).

What is it about opening up that leads to better health? People who write about negative events construct a more meaningful narrative or story that reframes the event. Pennebaker (1997) has analyzed the hundreds of pages of writing his participants provided and found that the people who improved the most were those who began with rather incoherent, disorganized descriptions of their problem and ended with coherent, organized stories that explained the event and gave it meaning. Subsequent research has shown that reframing is especially likely to occur when people take a step back and write about a negative life event like an observer would, rather than immersing themselves in the event and trying to relive it (Kross & Ayduk, 2011; Kross et al., 2014). The result? Once people have reframed a traumatic event in this way, they think about it less and are less likely to try to suppress thoughts about it when it does come to mind. Trying to suppress negative thoughts can lead to a preoccupation with those very thoughts, because the act of trying not to think about them can actually make us think about them more, leading to intrusive memories (Wegner, 1994).

You may recall that in Chapter SPA-1 we discussed an intervention called Critical Incident Stress Debriefing (CISD), in which people who have witnessed a horrific event are asked to relive the event as soon as possible in a 3- to 4-hour session, describing their experiences in detail and discussing their emotional reactions to the event. As we saw, CISD has been shown, in well-controlled studies, *not* to be beneficial. But why does writing about an event help people recover when reliving it in a CISD session does not? One reason appears to be the timing. The writing exercise works best if enough time has passed to allow people to gain a new perspective on the incident. In contrast, right after the event occurs is not a good time to try to relive it, reframe it, or understand it in a different way. In fact, one problem with CISD is that it can solidify memories of the bad things that occurred, rather than helping people

Research by James Pennebaker (1990) shows that there are long-term health benefits to writing or talking about one's personal traumas, particularly if enough time has passed to allow people to gain a new perspective on the traumatic events.

to reframe them. Thus, if you would like to try the writing exercise, allow some time to pass to make it easier to gain some perspective on what happened to you. You can find instructions about how to do the exercise on the Writing and Health section of James Pennebaker's Web site: homepage.psy.utexas.edu/homepage/Faculty/Pennebaker/Home2000/WritingandHealth.html

In sum, research shows that humans are often remarkably resilient in the face of adversity, particularly if they can maintain a sense of control. Seeking social support can help. If people continue to be troubled by the memories of stressful events, it may help to use Pennebaker's writing technique to help make sense of what happened and what it means.

REVIEW QUESTIONS

1. What does dealing with stress using the tend-and-befriend response entail?
   a. Forgetting the effects of the stressful event
   b. Attacking the source of stress or fleeing from it
   c. Engaging in nurturing activities and developing friendships that provide protection from the threats or stressors
   d. Accepting the stressor as a means of dealing with it

2. Under which of the following cultural conditions is social support likely to be most effective?
   a. If you belong to an individualistic culture and somebody offers you invisible support
   b. If you belong to a collectivistic culture and you ask someone for support
   c. If you belong to a collectivistic culture and somebody offers you visible support
   d. If you belong to an individualistic culture and somebody offers you visible support

3. Which of the following is an effective alternative to Critical Incident Stress Debriefing (CISD) in helping people deal with stress after they have experienced a traumatic event?
   a. Writing about the traumatic event instead of talking about it, right after experiencing it
   b. Talking about the event with as many people as possible
   c. Writing about the traumatic event after some time has passed so that one can gain new perspective on it
   d. Repressing the event and forgetting about it

See page 623 for the answers.

Prevention: Promoting Healthier Behavior

SPA2.3 How can we apply social psychology to help people live healthier lives?

According to the World Health Organization, more than half of the deaths worldwide are due to preventable chronic diseases (Reardon, 2011). The same is true in the United States, where tobacco use remains the number one cause of preventable deaths. What is number two? It might surprise you to learn that it is obesity, an area in which Americans are not doing such a good job (see Table SPA-2.1). More than 1 in 3 Americans are obese, which is associated with such health problems as high blood pressure, diabetes, heart disease, and cancer of the breast, prostate, and colon ("Adult obesity," 2011).

Another problem is alcohol consumption. Binge drinking, defined as five or more drinks in a short period of time for men and four or more for women (Wechsler & Austin, 1998), is a problem on many college campuses. Binge drinkers are at heightened risk for a number of health problems, including high blood pressure, heart disease, liver disease, meningitis, and sexually transmitted diseases. They are also more likely to be in car accidents, die by drowning, have unwanted pregnancies,

Table SPA2.1 Behavioral Causes of Health Problems in the United States

Behavior	Health Risks	How Are Americans Doing?
Tobacco Use	Cigarette smoking accounts for more than 480,000 deaths each year in the U.S.*	18% of adults in the U.S. smoke cigarettes*
Overeating (Obesity)	Obese people are at a higher risk for heart disease, diabetes, some forms of cancer, gynecological problems, and erectile dysfunction**	More than a third of American adults are obese; 17% of American children are obese*
Excessive Alcohol Use	Excessive drinking causes 88,000 deaths each year*	17% of Americans binge drink at least four times a month*
Lack of Exercise	Regular exercise can help prevent heart disease, diabetes, and some cancers*	52% of adults in the U.S. do not meet recommendations for exercise*
Poor Diet	Poor diets have been linked to a number of diseases, such as heart disease, some forms of cancer, and diabetes*	38% of adults in the U.S. eat fruit less than once a day, and 23% eat vegetables less than once a day*
Unsafe Sex	About 15,000 Americans with HIV die each year*	More than one million people in the U.S. are HIV-positive*
Exposure to Sun, Indoor Tanning Rays	More than 60,000 adults in the U.S. are diagnosed with melanomas of the skin each year*	Only 58% of adults reported that they regularly protect themselves from the sun by using sunscreen, wearing protective clothing, or avoiding the sun*

*Center for Disease Control and Prevention (2014)
**Mayo Clinic (n.d.)

experience domestic violence, and have difficulty performing sexually (Naimi et al., 2003; "Quick stats," 2008).

More than 35 million people worldwide are currently infected with the HIV virus, and in 2012, 1.6 million people died of AIDS ("Global Health Observatory," n.d.). Most cases are in Sub-Saharan Africa, although no continent is free of the disease. Most of these cases could have been avoided if people had used condoms during sexual intercourse. Fortunately, the use of condoms is increasing in the United States; one survey found that among teenagers, 80% of males used a condom the first time they had sex. But that means that 20% did not (Martinez, Copen, & Abma, 2011). And although condom use is increasing in some African countries, in others it is decreasing ("Global report," 2013).

Many serious health problems are preventable, including those resulting from unsafe sex, smoking, and overeating.

We realize that we have just maligned what many people consider to be the chief pleasures of life: sex, eating, drinking, and smoking. Health problems resulting from these behaviors are prevalent precisely because they are so pleasurable—in some cases (e.g., smoking), addictive. It is thus a challenge to find ways to change people's attitudes and behaviors in ways that lead to better health habits. How might we do so?

By now you know that this is a classic social psychological question. It should be possible to put theories into action theories of attitude change and social influence to help people to act in healthier ways. Indeed, there is a great deal of research on this very issue, and social psychologists have had considerable success in designing programs to get people to use condoms, quit smoking, drink less, and engage in a variety of preventive behaviors, such as using sunscreen (Klein, Rothman, & Cameron, 2013; Noar, Benac, & Harris, 2007; Taylor, 2015). Many of these programs use principles covered elsewhere in this text—for example, the attitude-change techniques discussed in Chapter 7 and social norms techniques described in Chapters 8 and SPA1. For example, one study found that women living in Phoenix, Arizona, had incorrect perceptions of injunctive norms about sun exposure: They overestimated how much other women thought that tanned skin was attractive, and underestimated how much other women approved of protecting skin from the sun. Researchers found that correcting these misperceptions caused women to protect themselves more from the sun by using sunscreen and wearing protective clothing (Reid & Aiken, 2013). Perhaps you can think of ways to adopt some of these approaches in your own life. Behavior change isn't easy, but armed with the social psychological techniques you have learned in this book, we are convinced that you can do it.

"Maybe we shouldn't have kicked all our bad habits."
www.CartoonStock.com

REVIEW QUESTIONS

1. Which of the following is *true*?
   a. The use of condoms is increasing worldwide.
   b. Most people meet the daily recommended guidelines of exercise.
   c. Most of the chronic health problems listed in this chapter are caused by pleasurable behaviors such as eating, drinking, sex, and smoking.
   d. Overeating is not problematic as it does not directly contribute to chronic health problems.

2. Which of the following is *false*?
   a. Protection from the sun is a growing concern as the prevalence of skin cancer is increasing.
   b. Reid and Aiken (2013) found that women overestimate how much other women think tanned skin is attractive.
   c. Reid and Aiken (2013) found that women underestimate how much other women approve of sun protection.
   d. Attitudes about sun protection are easy to change by spreading awareness about skin cancer statistics.

See page 623 for the answers.

Summary

SPA2.1 How is stress defined and what effect does it have on our health?

- **Stress and Human Health** The relationship between stress and human health has received a great deal of attention from social psychologists.

  - **Resilience** People have been found to be surprisingly resilient when they experience negative events, often showing only mild, transient reactions, followed by a quick return to normal, healthy functioning.

  - **Effects of Negative Life Events** Nonetheless, stressful events can have debilitating effects on people's psychological and physical health. Some studies calculate the number of stressful events people are experiencing and use that to predict their health.

- **Perceived Stress and Health** Stress is best defined as the negative feelings and beliefs that arise when people feel unable to cope with demands from their environment. The more stress people experience, the more likely they are to get sick (e.g., catch a cold).

- **Feeling in Charge: The Importance of Perceived Control** People perceive negative events as stressful if they feel they cannot control them.

In the last 40 years, college students have increasingly adopted an external locus of control, which is the tendency to believe that good and bad outcomes are out of their control. The less control people believe they have, the more likely it is that the event will cause them physical and psychological problems. For example, the loss of control experienced by many older people in nursing homes can have negative effects on their health.

SPA2.2 **What can people do to cope and recover after a stressful experience?**

- **Coping with Stress** Coping styles refer to the ways in which people react to stressful events.

  - **Gender Differences in Coping with Stress** There are two ways of responding to stress. One is the **fight-or-flight reaction**, which involves attacking the source of the stress or fleeing from it. Another is the **tend-and-befriend reaction**, which involves nurturing activities designed to protect oneself and one's offspring (tending) and creating social networks that provide protection from threats (befriending). Although both men and women exhibit the tend-and-befriend response, it is especially prevalent in women.

- **Social Support: Getting Help from Others** Social support—the perception that other people are responsive to one's needs—is beneficial for men and women. The form of social support, however, is important. People react better to invisible than visible support. People from individualistic cultures react well when they directly ask for support, whereas people from collectivistic cultures react well when they get support without disclosing that they are having problems.

- **Reframing: Finding Meaning in Traumatic Events** Other researchers focus on ways of coping with stress that everyone can adopt. Several studies show that reframing traumatic events, by writing or talking about one's problems, has long-term health benefits.

SPA2.3 **How can we apply social psychology to help people live healthier lives?**

- **Prevention: Promoting Healthier Behavior** It also important to find ways to help people change their health habits more directly. Numerous studies have used social psychological techniques to do so, such as correcting people's beliefs about injunctive norms.

Test Yourself

1. After her husband died, Rachel did not experience significant distress. Within a few weeks she had returned to her usual activities and regained a cheerful outlook on life. Which is most true, according to research discussed in this chapter?

   a. Rachel's lack of distress indicates the likelihood of poor psychological adjustment.

   b. Because Rachel did not experience extreme grief, she was probably in a troubled marriage and did not love her husband very much.

   c. Although life's traumas can be quite painful, many people have the resources to recover from them quickly.

   d. Rachel is showing "delayed grief syndrome" and will probably experience grief later.

2. Bob's grandmother died recently, and he just found out that his girlfriend cheated on him. He is also in the middle of final exams. According to research on stress and health, which is true?

   a. Because Bob is experiencing so many negative life events, he will almost certainly get sick.

   b. These life events will be stressful for Bob only if he interprets them as stressful—in other words, if he feels unable to cope with the events.

   c. When under stress, a person's immune system is stimulated. Therefore, Bob is less likely to get sick now than he normally would.

   d. If Bob feels more in control of these events than he really is, he is especially likely to get sick.

3. Lindsay does an internship at a nursing home. According to research discussed in this chapter, which of the following would be most likely to benefit the residents?

   a. Lindsay encourages the residents to talk to her about any stressful issues in their lives.

   b. Lindsay allows the residents to choose what time she will come to visit them, and when her internship ends, she decides to keep visiting the residents when they ask her to.

   c. Lindsay allows the residents to choose what time she will come to visit them, but when her internship ends, she doesn't visit the nursing home anymore.

   d. Lindsay gives the residents a plant and makes sure to water it for them.

4. Which of the following is true about research on social support?

a. Social support of all kinds has been found to be beneficial to people in all cultures.

b. If you are thinking of helping someone, it is better to give them invisible rather than visible social support.

c. If you are thinking of helping someone, it is better to given them visible rather than invisible social support.

d. Members of East Asian cultures are more likely to seek help from others than are members of Western cultures.

5. Which of the following is true about gender differences in coping with stress?

a. Both men and women equally exhibit the tend-and-befriend response.

b. Women tend to exhibit the tend-and-befriend stress response more than men.

c. Men tend to exhibit the fight-or-flight stress response less than women.

d. Seeking social support tends to help women more than men.

6. Kate has had a hard time getting over her parents' divorce. According to social psychological research, which of the following would probably help Kate the most?

a. She should spend 15 minutes a night on four consecutive nights writing about her feelings about the divorce.

b. She should try to attribute the divorce to internal, global, stable things about herself.

c. She should avoid talking about the divorce with her closest friends because it would probably just depress them.

d. She should focus on the fact that she has low self-efficacy to improve her relationship with her parents.

7. According to research, which of the following is false?

a. Poor diets have been linked to a number of diseases including AIDS.

b. More than half the deaths worldwide are due to preventable chronic diseases.

c. Obesity is the number two cause of preventable deaths in the US.

d. Tobacco use is the number one cause of preventable deaths in the US.

8. Based on the chapter, which of the following could be an effective way of encouraging students to eat healthy?

a. Increase campaigns on eating boiled food across schools.

b. Point out to students that they cannot control what they eat.

c. Point out to students that most people don't realize how much they eat.

d. Point out to students how much people would approve of them if they had healthy eating habits.

See page 623 for the answers.

Social Psychology in Action 3
Social Psychology and the Law

 ## Chapter Outline and Learning Objectives

Eyewitness Testimony

SPA3.1 **What does psychology indicate about the accuracy of eyewitness testimony?**

Why Are Eyewitnesses Often Wrong?
Judging Whether Eyewitnesses Are Mistaken
The Recovered Memory Debate

Juries: Group Processes in Action

SPA3.2 **Does social psychology help explain how juries make decisions?**

How Jurors Process Information During the Trial
Confessions: Are They Always What They Seem?
Deliberations in the Jury Room

You be the jury. You decide how you would vote after hearing the following testimony from an actual case in Texas. On a cold, dark November night, police officer Robert Wood and his partner spotted a car driving with its headlights off. Wood signaled the car to pull over, got out, and walked up to the driver's side. He intended only to tell the driver to turn on his lights, but he never got the chance. Before Wood could even speak, the driver pointed a handgun at Wood and shot him, killing him instantly. Wood's partner emptied her revolver at the car as it sped away, but the killer escaped.

A month later, the police picked up a suspect, 16-year-old David Harris. Harris admitted that he had stolen a neighbor's car and revolver the day before the murder, that this same car was the one Officer Wood had pulled over that night, and that he was in the car when the shooting occurred. Harris denied, however, that he was the one who shot Wood. He said he had picked up a hitchhiker by the name of Randall Adams and had let Adams drive. It was Adams, he claimed, who reached under the seat, grabbed the revolver, and shot the officer. When the police questioned Randall Adams, he admitted that he had gotten a ride from David Harris but said that Harris had dropped him off at his motel 3 hours before the murder occurred. It was Harris, he claimed, who must have been the murderer.

Who was telling the truth? It was Harris's word against Adams's—until the police found three eyewitnesses who corroborated Harris's story. Emily and Robert Miller testified that they drove by just before Officer Wood was shot. Though it was very dark, they said they got a good look at the driver of the car, and both identified him as Randall Adams. "When he rolled down the window, that's what made his face stand out," said Robert Miller. "He had a beard, mustache, kind of dishwater blond hair" (Morris, 1988). Indeed, Randall Adams fit the Millers' description; David Harris, on the other hand, was clean-shaven (see the photos on the right). Michael Randell, a salesman, also happened to be driving by right before the murder and claimed to have seen two people in the car. He, too, said the driver had long hair and a mustache, matching the appearance of Randall Adams.

Who do you think committed this murder, an actual crime that took place in 1976? The jury believed the eyewitnesses and convicted Adams, sentencing him to death. However, as Adams languished in jail, waiting for the courts to hear his appeals, several experts began to doubt that he was guilty. New evidence came to light (largely because of a documentary made about the case, *The Thin Blue Line*), and it is now almost certain that David Harris was the actual murderer. Harris was later convicted of another murder and, while on death row, strongly implied that he, not Randall Adams, had shot Officer Wood. Finally, an appeals court overturned Adams's conviction. He was a free man—but only after spending 12 years in prison for a crime he did not commit.

If Adams was innocent, why had eyewitnesses said that the driver of the car had long hair and a mustache? And why did the jury believe them? How common are such miscarriages of justice? In this chapter, we will discuss the answers to these questions, focusing on the role social psychological processes play in the legal system.

Let's begin with a brief review of the American justice system. When someone commits a crime and the police arrest a suspect, a judge or a grand jury decides whether there is enough evidence to press formal charges. If there is, lawyers for the defense and the prosecution gather evidence and negotiate with each other. As a result of these negotiations, the defendant often pleads guilty to a lesser charge. Fewer than 10% of cases actually go to a trial in which a jury decides the defendant's fate (Edkins, 2011). (There are also civil trials, where one party, the plaintiff, brings a complaint against another, the defendant, for violating the former's rights in some way.)

Social psychologists have studied the legal system a great deal in recent years, both because it offers an excellent applied setting in which to study basic psychological processes and because of its immense importance in daily life (Greene & Heilbrun, 2013; Kovera & Borgida, 2010). If you, through no fault of your own, become the

Randall Adams (top) and David Harris (bottom). The fact that eyewitnesses said the murderer had long hair and a mustache was the main reason Adams was convicted of murdering Officer Wood.

accused in a criminal case, what do you need to know to convince the system of your innocence? If you ever find yourself seated on a jury, how might your expertise in social psychology help you to make a better, more informed decision in the case? We will begin our discussion with eyewitness testimony, the most troubling aspect of the Randall Adams story.

Eyewitness Testimony

SPA3.1 **What does psychology indicate about the accuracy of eyewitness testimony?**

Randall Adams was convicted largely because of the eyewitnesses who identified him, even though in other ways the case against him was weak. Unfortunately, wrongful convictions based on faulty eyewitness identification are not uncommon. According to the Innocence Project (www.innocenceproject.org), there have been more than 325 cases in which someone has been exonerated with DNA evidence after being convicted of a crime—often, like Randall Adams, after already having spent many years in prison. In approximately 75% of these cases, the conviction was based, at least in part, on faulty eyewitness testimony. Sometimes, as in Randall Adams's case, *multiple* eyewitnesses got it wrong. In short, one of the most common causes of an innocent person being convicted of a crime is an erroneous eyewitness (Brewer & Wells, 2011; Wells & Hasel, 2008; Pezdek, 2012; Wells, 2014).

Why Are Eyewitnesses Often Wrong?

The problem is that our minds are not like video cameras or DVRs, which can record an event, store it over time, and play it back later with perfect accuracy. To be an accurate eyewitness, a person must successfully complete three stages of memory processing: acquisition, storage, and retrieval of the events witnessed. **Acquisition** refers to the process whereby people notice and pay attention to information in their environment. Because people cannot perceive everything that is happening around them, they acquire only a subset of the information. **Storage** is the process by which people maintain in memory information they have acquired. **Retrieval** refers to the process by which people recall information stored in their memories (see Figure SPA-3.1). Eyewitnesses can be inaccurate because of difficulties that arise at any of these three stages.

ACQUISITION   The amount of information about a crime that people take in at the acquisition stage is limited by several factors, such as how much time they have to watch an event and the nature of the viewing conditions. As obvious as this may sound, people sometimes overlook how these factors can limit eyewitness reports of crimes. Crimes usually occur under the very conditions that make acquisition difficult: quickly, unexpectedly, under poor viewing conditions (e.g., at night), and under considerable stress. These conditions certainly describe the scene of the murder of Officer Wood. Eyewitnesses were driving down a dimly lit road, past a pulled-over car, when the unexpected happened—shots were fired and a police officer fell to the ground.

When eyewitnesses are the victims of a crime, they are usually terribly afraid, and this alone can make it difficult to take in everything that is happening. The more stress people are under, the worse their memory for people involved in and the details of a crime (Deffenbacher, Bornstein, & Penrod, 2004; Morgan et al., 2013). Another reason why victims of crimes have a poor memory for a suspect is that they focus their attention mostly on any weapon they see and less on the suspect's features (Fawcett et al., 2013; Pickel, 2007; Saunders, 2009). If someone points a gun at you and demands your money, your attention is likely to be more on the gun than on what color the robber's eyes are.

Acquisition

The process by which people notice and pay attention to information in their environment

Storage

The process by which people maintain in memory information they have acquired from the environment

Retrieval

The process by which people recall information stored in their memories

Figure SPA-3.1 Acquisition, Storage, and Retrieval

To be an accurate eyewitness, people must complete three stages of memory processing. Errors may creep in at each of the three stages.

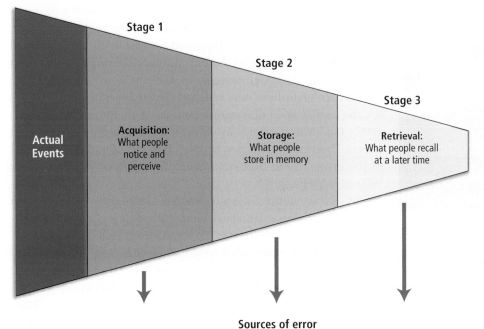

Stage 1

Stage 2

Stage 3

Actual Events

Acquisition: What people notice and perceive

Storage: What people store in memory

Retrieval: What people recall at a later time

Sources of error

- Poor viewing conditions
- People see what they expect to see
- Focus on weapons
- Own-race bias
- Change blindness

- Misleading questions
- Source monitoring errors

- "Best guess" problem in lineup identification
- Negative effects of verbalization

The information witnesses notice and pay attention to is also influenced by what they expect to see. Consider our friend Alan, a social psychologist who is an expert on social perception. One Sunday, Alan was worried because his neighbor, a frail woman in her 80s, did not appear for church. After knocking on her door repeatedly and receiving no response, Alan jimmied open a window and searched her house. Soon his worst fears were realized: The woman was lying dead on the floor of her bedroom.

Shaken, Alan went back to his house and telephoned the police. A detective spent a great deal of time in the woman's house, after which he asked Alan some pointed questions, such as whether he had noticed any suspicious activity in the past day or two. Alan was confused by this line of questioning and finally burst out, "Why are you asking me these questions? Isn't it obvious that my neighbor died of old age? Shouldn't we be notifying her family?" Now it was the detective's turn to look puzzled. "Aren't you the one who discovered the body?" he asked. Alan said he was. "Well," said the detective, "didn't you notice that her bedroom had been ransacked, that there was broken glass everywhere, and that there was a belt tied around her neck?"

It turned out that Alan's neighbor had been strangled by a man who had come to spray her house for insects. There had been a fierce struggle, and the fact that the woman was murdered could not have been more obvious. But Alan saw none of the signs. He was worried that his elderly neighbor had passed away. When he discovered that she had in fact died, he was quite upset, and the furthest thing from his mind was that she had been murdered. As a result, he saw what he expected and failed to see what he did not expect. When the police later showed him photographs of the crime scene, he felt as though he had never been there. He recognized almost nothing.

When an actual perceptual fact is in conflict with expectation, expectation may prove a stronger determinant of perception and memory than the situation itself.

—Gordon Allport and Leo Postman, 1947

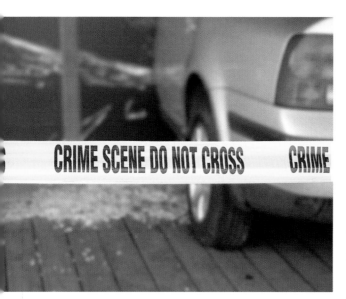

A variety of factors combine to limit the amount (and accuracy) of information that eyewitnesses acquire when they are present during the commission of a crime.

Own-Race Bias

The tendency for people to be better at recognizing faces of their own race than those of other races

Research has confirmed that people are poor at noticing the unexpected. In one study, participants watched a videotape of two teams passing a basketball back and forth and counted the number of times one team passed the ball to the other. Thirty-five seconds into the film, something weird happened: A woman wearing a gorilla costume walked into the middle of the basketball game, turned toward the camera, thumped her chest, and then walked away. Meanwhile, the basketball players continued with their passing game. Although it seems as if everyone would notice such a bizarre interruption, only half did. The other half simply didn't see the gorilla at all (Chabris & Simons, 2010; Simons & Chabris, 1999). Given that crimes are almost always highly unexpected events, it is no surprise that people often fail to notice key details in the crime scene (Rensink, 2002; Simons & Ambinder, 2005; Wilford & Wells, 2010).

Even if we notice a person or event, we might not remember it very well if we are unfamiliar with it. For example, people are better at recognizing faces that are of the same race as they are, a phenomenon known as **own-race bias** (or sometimes referred as the cross-race effect). Whites are better at recognizing White faces than Black or Asian faces, Blacks are better at recognizing Black than White faces, and Asians are better at recognizing Asian than White faces (Brigham et al., 2007; Johnson & Fredrickson, 2005; Levin, 2000; McGuire & Pezdek, 2014). One study found a similar effect with age: College students were better at recognizing faces of people their own age than faces of middle-aged people, whereas middle-aged people were better at recognizing faces of people their own age than faces of college students (Wright & Stroud, 2002).

One reason for the own-race bias is that people have more contact with members of their own race, allowing them to learn better how to distinguish one individual from another (Meissner & Brigham, 2001). Another is that when people examine same-race faces, they often pay close attention to individuating features that distinguish that face from others, such as the height of the cheekbones or the contour of the forehead. When people examine different-race faces, however, they are drawn more to features that distinguish that face from their own race, rather than individuating features (Hugenberg et al., 2010; Levin, 2000). Daniel Levin, a researcher who has investigated this hypothesis, puts it like this: "When a White person looks at another White person's nose, they're likely to think to themselves, 'That's John's nose.' When they look at a Black person's nose, they're likely to think, 'That's a Black nose'" (quoted in Carpenter, 2000, p. 44). Because people usually have less experience with features that characterize individuals of other races, they find it more difficult to tell members of that race apart.

STORAGE In the preceding discussion of acquisition, we have seen that several variables limit what people perceive and thus what they are able to store in their memories. After a piece of information is in memory, it might seem as if it stays there, unaltered like a photograph in an album, until we recall it at a later time. In reality, few of us have photographic memories. Memories, like printed photographs, fade with age. Further, it is tempting to believe that a picture, once stored, cannot be altered or retouched, and that details cannot be added to or subtracted from the image. If the shooter we saw was clean-shaven, surely we will not pencil in a mustache at some later time, right? Hence, the fact that the witnesses who testified at the Randall Adams trial remembered that the driver of the car had long hair and a mustache seems like pretty incriminating evidence against Randall Adams.

Unfortunately, however, memories are far from indelible. People can get mixed up about where they heard or saw something; memories in one "album" can get confused with memories in another. As a result, people can have quite inaccurate recall about what they saw. This is the conclusion reached after years of research on **reconstructive memory**: the distortion of memories of an event by information encountered after the event occurred (Blank & Launay, 2014; Loftus, 1979, 2005; McDonald & Hirt, 1997). According to this research, information we obtain after witnessing an event can change our memories of the event.

In one classic study, Elizabeth Loftus showed students 30 slides depicting different stages of an automobile accident. The content of one slide varied; some students saw a car stopped at a stop sign, and others saw the same car stopped at a yield sign. After the slide show, the students were asked several questions about the car accident they had "witnessed." The key question varied how the traffic sign was described. In one version, the question asked, "Did another car pass the red Datsun while it was stopped at the stop sign?" In the other version, the question was "Did another car pass the red Datsun while it was stopped at the yield sign?" Thus, for half the participants, the question described the traffic sign as they had in fact seen it. But for the other half, the wording of the question subtly introduced new information—that they had seen a stop sign, when in fact they had seen a yield sign. Would this small change (akin to what might occur when witnesses are being questioned by police investigators or attorneys) influence people's memories of the actual event?

All the students were shown the two pictures (reproduced below) and asked which one they had originally seen. Most people (75%) who were asked about the sign they had actually seen chose the correct picture; that is, if they had seen a stop sign and were asked about a stop sign, most of them correctly identified the stop sign photograph (note that 25% still got it wrong, making a crucial mistake on what would seem to be an easy question). However, of those who had received the misleading question, only 41% chose the correct photograph (Loftus, Miller, & Burns, 1978).

In subsequent experiments, Loftus and her colleagues found that misleading questions could change people's minds about how fast a car was going, whether broken glass was at the scene of an accident, whether a traffic light was green or red, and—of relevance to the Randall Adams trial—whether or not a suspect had a mustache (Loftus, 1979). Her studies show that the way in which the police and lawyers question witnesses can change the witnesses' reports about what they saw. (Indeed, there is some suspicion that in the Randall Adams case the police may have led the witnesses by asking questions that implicated Adams and not Harris. At the time of the murder, Harris was a juvenile and could not receive the death penalty for killing a police officer; Adams was in his thirties and was eligible for the death

Reconstructive Memory
The process whereby memories of an event become distorted by information encountered after the event occurred

Give us a dozen healthy memories, well-formed, and . . . we'll guarantee to take any one at random and train it to become any type of memory we might select—hammer, screwdriver, wrench, stop sign, yield sign, Indian chief—regardless of its origin or the brain that holds it.
—Elizabeth Loftus and Hunter Hoffman, 1989

Students saw one of these pictures and then tried to remember whether they had seen a stop sign or a yield sign. Many of those who heard leading questions about the street sign made mistaken reports about which sign they had seen.

(From Loftus, Miller, & Burns, 1978.)

Source Monitoring

The process whereby people try to identify the source of their memories

penalty, allowing them to pursue the most severe of penalties for someone who they believed had killed one of their colleagues.)

Misleading questions can cause a problem with **source monitoring**, the process people use to try to identify the basis for their memories (Hyman et al., 2014; Johnson, Verfaellie, & Dunlosky, 2008; Qin, Ogle, & Goodman, 2008). In the Loftus studies, for example, people who saw a stop sign but received the misleading question about a yield sign then had two different pieces of information in memory—the stop sign and the yield sign. This is all well and good as long as they could remember where these memories came from: the stop sign from the accident they saw earlier and the yield sign from the question they were asked later. The problem is that people often get mixed up about where they heard or saw something, mistakenly believing, for instance, that the yield sign looks familiar because they saw it during the slide show. This process is similar to the misattribution effects we discussed in Chapter 5, when people are unsure about what has caused their arousal. It's easy to get confused about the source of our memories as well. When information gets stored in memory, it is not always well "tagged" as to where it came from.

The implications for legal testimony are sobering. Eyewitnesses who are asked misleading questions often report seeing things that were not really there. In addition, eyewitnesses might be confused as to why a suspect looks familiar. It is likely, for example, that the eyewitnesses in the Randall Adams trial saw pictures of Adams in the newspaper before they testified about what they saw the night of the murder. When asked to remember what they saw that night, they might have become confused because of a source monitoring error, recalling Adams's photo from the newspaper—depicting a man with long hair and a mustache—rather than thinking about what they actually saw on the night of the shooting.

RETRIEVAL   Suppose you are an eyewitness to a crime. The police have arrested a suspect and want to see if you identify him or her as the person you saw commit the crime. Typically, the police arrange a lineup or photo array at the police station, where you will be asked whether one of several people is the perpetrator. You might be asked to look through a one-way mirror at a live lineup of the suspect and some foils (people known not to have committed the crime); more likely, you would view a series of photographs of the suspect and the foils. In either case, if you identify the suspect as the perpetrator, that suspect is likely to be charged and convicted of the crime. After all, if an eyewitness saw the suspect commit the crime and subsequently picked him out of a lineup, that's pretty good evidence that the suspect is the guilty party, isn't it? Well, maybe not.

Just as there are problems with acquisition and storage of information, so too can there be problems with how people retrieve information from their memories (Brewer & Wells, 2011; Malpass, Tredoux, & McQuiston-Surrett, 2007; Wells & Quinlivan, 2009). Unfortunately, a number of things other than the image of a person that is stored in memory can influence whether eyewitnesses will pick someone out of a lineup. For example, witnesses often choose the person in a lineup who most resembles the criminal, a major problem if the actual perpetrator isn't actually in the lineup!

In short, eyewitnesses who view a photo array or live lineup often complete the task much the same way as a student takes a multiple-choice test: they use a process of elimination. This means that, just like in a multiple-choice test, a variety of seemingly trivial factors have the potential to greatly influence performance, including who is administering the test, the instructions given to the test-taker, and the other response options available for each question. To avoid this process-of-elimination guessing, as well as other problems with lineup identifications, social psychologists have made several recommendations about how the police should conduct lineups. These are summarized in Table SPA-3.1.

Table SPA-3.1 Research-Based Recommendations for How to Conduct Lineups

Recommendation	Why It Is Important
Make sure everyone in the lineup resembles the witness's description of the suspect.	Doing so minimizes the possibility that the witness will simply choose the person who looks most like the culprit relative to the other photos available (Fitzgerald, Oriet, & Price, 2014; Wells et al., 1998).
Tell the witnesses that the person suspected of the crime may or may not be in the lineup.	If witnesses assume that the culprit is present, they are much more likely to choose the person who looks most like the culprit, rather than saying that they aren't sure if the person is there. As a result, false identifications are less likely to occur when people are instructed that the culprit may or may not be in the lineup (Clark, 2005; Steblay, 1997; Wells et al., 1998, 2000).
Make sure that the police officer administering the lineup does not know which person in the lineup is the suspect.	This avoids the possibility that the person will (intentionally or unintentionally) communicate to the witness who the suspect is (Greene & Evelo, 2014; Wells et al., 1998).
If using photographs of people, present the pictures sequentially, one at a time, instead of simultaneously, or all at once.	Doing so makes it more difficult for witnesses to compare all the pictures and choose the one that most resembles the criminal even when the criminal is not actually in the lineup (Lindsay & Wells, 1985; Meissner, Tredoux, & Parker, 2005; Steblay, Dysart, Fulero, & Lindsay, 2001), though recent research suggests that such a procedure may also make eyewitnesses less likely to identify *anyone* in the lineup, even the actual perpetrator (Dobolyi, & Dodson, 2013; Gronlund, Wixted, & Mickes, 2014).
Avoid using composite face programs (computer programs designed to reconstruct a suspect's face according to witnesses' descriptions).	Typically, the faces that witnesses generate with these programs do not look much like the actual suspect. Also, research shows that people who give descriptions for computer-generated facial images subsequently have a worse memory for the suspect than people who do not (Wells, Charman, & Olson, 2005; Wells & Hasel, 2007). Focusing on specific features of a face, such as what the chin looked like, appears to interfere with people's original memory for the face.
Don't count on witnesses knowing whether their selections were biased.	To determine whether a witness's selection was biased, attorneys or judges sometimes ask them, for example, "Do you think your choice of suspect was influenced by how the pictures were presented or what the police told you?" Unfortunately, people don't have sufficient access to their thought processes to detect whether they were biased (Charman & Wells, 2008; Nisbett & Wilson, 1977).

Judging Whether Eyewitnesses Are Mistaken

Suppose you are a member of a jury who is listening to a witness describe a suspect. How can you tell whether the witness's memory is accurate or whether the witness is making one of the mistakes in memory we have just documented? It might seem that the answer to this question is straightforward: Pay careful attention to how confident the witness is. Consider the case of Jennifer Thompson, who was raped when she was a 22-year-old college student. During the rape, Thompson reports, she "studied every single detail on the rapist's face" to help her identify him. She was determined that if she survived, she was going to make sure he was caught and went to prison. After the ordeal, she went to the police station and looked through hundreds of police photos. When she saw Ronald Cotton's picture, she knew right away that he was the rapist. "I knew this was the man. I was completely confident. I was sure."

The police brought Cotton in and put him in a lineup, and Thompson picked him out without hesitation. Certain that Cotton was the man who had raped her, she testified against him in court. "I was sure. I knew it. I had picked the right guy." On the basis of her convincing testimony, Cotton was sentenced to life in prison.

A few years later, the police asked Thompson to go to court and look at another man, Bobby Poole, who had been bragging in prison that he had committed the rape. Some people thought that Poole looked a lot like Cotton, others that they bore only a passing resemblance to one another. When asked if she recognized Poole, Thompson replied, "I have never seen him in my life. I have no idea who he is."

As the years passed, and Cotton remained in jail for the rape, DNA testing became more widely available. The police decided to see if evidence from the case matched Cotton's or Poole's DNA. In 1995, 11 years after the crime, the police informed Thompson of the results: "I was standing in my kitchen when the detective and the district attorney visited. They were good and decent people who were trying to do their jobs—as I had done mine, as anyone would try to do the right thing. They told me: 'Ronald Cotton didn't rape you. It was Bobby Poole.'" (Thompson, 2000, p. 15). Cotton was released from prison after serving 11 years for a crime he did not commit.

This example illustrates that eyewitness confidence is not always a good indicator of eyewitness accuracy. In fact, numerous studies have shown that witnesses' confidence is inconsistently related to their accuracy (Charman, Wells, & Joy, 2011; Douglass & Pavletic, 2012; Eisenstadt & Leippe, 2010). When law enforcement officials and jurors assume that a witness who is very confident is also correct, they can make serious mistakes.

Why isn't confidence always a sign of accuracy? One reason is that the things that influence people's confidence are not necessarily the same things that influence their accuracy. After identifying a suspect, for example, a person's confidence increases if he or she finds out that other witnesses identified the same suspect and decreases if he or she finds out that other witnesses identified a different suspect (Busey et al., 2000). Of course, this change in confidence doesn't influence the accuracy of the actual identification made earlier. Therefore, just because a witness is confident does not mean that he or she is accurate, as the cases of Randall Adams and Ronald Cotton illustrate so tragically. However, confidence in combination with another way of responding might indeed suggest that people are accurate—namely, if people identify a face quickly.

RESPONDING QUICKLY In a study by David Dunning and Lisa Beth Stern (1994), participants watched a film in which a man stole some money from a woman's wallet; they then tried to identify the thief in a photo lineup. Some participants were able to make their choices quickly, saying that the perpetrator's face just "popped out" at them. Others needed to take their time, deliberately comparing one face to another. Who was more likely to correctly identify the thief? It turned out to be the fast responders, for whom the man's face "popped out." We should thus be more willing to believe a witness who says, "I knew it was the defendant as soon as I saw him in the lineup" than one who says, "I compared everyone in the lineup to each other, thought about it, and decided it was the defendant"—particularly if the first witness made his or her judgment in 10 seconds or less (Dunning & Perretta, 2002). Of course, being quick does not guarantee being accurate: we saw with the example of Jennifer Thompson that even when eyewitnesses make judgments quickly, and are very confident in their judgments, they can still be incorrect. But, witnesses who respond quickly are more likely to be correct than those who think about it for awhile.

THE PROBLEM WITH VERBALIZATION It might seem that another way to improve the accuracy of eyewitness identification would be to tell people to write down a description of the suspect as soon as they can, to help them remember what they saw. Studies by Jonathan Schooler and Tonya Engstler-Schooler (1990), however, show that trying to put an image of a face into words can actually make people's memory worse. They showed students a film of a bank robbery and asked some of the students to write detailed descriptions of the robber's face (the verbalization condition). The others spent the same amount of time completing an unrelated task (the no-verbalization condition). All students then tried to identify the robber from

> No subjective feeling of certainty can be an objective criterion for the desired truth.
> —Hugo Münsterberg, *On the Witness Stand*, 1908

Time and again, research studies demonstrate that being an accurate eyewitness and correctly identifying a perpetrator from a lineup is much more challenging than we assume it to be.

a photo lineup of eight faces. The results? Only 38% of the people in the verbalization condition correctly identified the robber, compared to 64% of the people in the no-verbalization condition. Schooler and Engstler-Schooler (1990; see also Chin & Schooler, 2008) suggest that trying to put a face into words is difficult and impairs memory for that face. Using the word *squinty* to describe a robber's eyes, for example, might be a general description of what his eyes looked like but probably does not capture the subtle contours of his eyes, eyelids, eyelashes, eyebrows, and upper cheeks. When you see the photo lineup, you look for eyes that are squinty, and doing so interferes with your attention to the finer details of the faces.

POST-IDENTIFICATION FEEDBACK   Yet another factor that can influence an eyewitness's confidence is feedback after an identification is made. Note that in Table SPA-3.1, one recommendation for improving lineup procedure is making sure that the person administering the lineup does not know who the suspect is. Keeping the lineup administrator "blind" in this fashion guarantees that nothing he or she says or does will affect who the eyewitness chooses or how confident the eyewitness becomes in that identification. Consider the dangers of the alternative: Laura Smalarz and Gary Wells (2014) conducted a two-part study in which college students were asked to be eyewitnesses and watch a video of a theft at an airport. In the first phase of the study, eyewitnesses were asked to identify the culprit from a six-photo array (because they had made the video, the researchers also knew whether the eyewitnesses were accurate or inaccurate in making an identification). In the second phase, the eyewitnesses recorded video testimony in which they described what they had seen and the identification that they had made; these videos were then shown to a separate group of participants, who you could think of as the equivalent of jurors, whose job it was to determine whether each eyewitness had made a correct identification. In a baseline condition, these Phase II observers were, indeed, significantly more likely to believe the testimony of accurate versus inaccurate eyewitnesses. That's good! We would hope that observers, such as jurors, would be able to differentiate between accurate and inaccurate eyewitnesses.

But in another condition of the study, the Phase II observers became unable to tell which eyewitnesses had

Understandably, jurors place a great deal of weight on how confident an eyewitness appears to be when they assess the accuracy of his or her memory. But various factors, including post-identification feedback, can inflate the confidence of even erroneous eyewitnesses.

gotten the identification right. This was the condition in which the eyewitnesses had received positive feedback immediately after making their identification. Specifically, eyewitnesses in this condition made a selection from the photo array, at which point the administrator in charge of things had remarked, "Good job, you got the suspect." Smalarz and Wells (2014) found that this simple comment (which was made regardless of whether or not the eyewitness was actually correct) inflated eyewitness's confidence in the reliability of their memory. It also made it next-to-impossible for outside observers to figure out which eyewitnesses were accurate and which ones weren't, a finding with sobering implications for jurors who have to make such determinations in real trials.

To sum up, several factors can contribute to making eyewitness testimony inaccurate, leading to all too many false identifications. Research suggests that perhaps the United States legal system should rely less on eyewitness testimony than it now does. For example, in the legal systems of some countries, a suspect cannot be convicted on the basis of a sole eyewitness; at least two independent witnesses are needed. Of course, adopting this more stringent standard in the effort to curtail false convictions would also raise the risk that some guilty people go free. The following Try It! exercise provides an opportunity to see how accurate you and your friends are at eyewitness testimony and to illustrate some of the pitfalls of human memory.

TRY IT!
The Accuracy of Eyewitness Testimony

Try this demonstration with a group of friends who you know will be gathered in one place, such as a dorm room or an apartment. The idea is to stage an incident in which someone comes into the room suddenly, acts in a strange manner, and then leaves. Your friends will then be asked to recall as much as they can about this person, to see if they are good eyewitnesses. Here are some specific instructions about how you might do this.

1. Take one friend, whom we will call the actor, into your confidence before you do this exercise. Ideally, the actor should be a stranger to the people who will be the eyewitnesses. The actor should suddenly rush into the room where you and your other friends are gathered and act in a strange (but nonthreatening) manner. For example, the actor could hand someone a flower and say, "The flower man cometh!" Or he or she could go up to each person and say something unexpected, like "Meet me in Moscow at the mosque." Ask the actor to hold something in his or her hand during this episode, such as a pencil, shoelace, or banana.

2. *Important note:* The actor should not act in a violent or threatening way or make the eyewitnesses uncomfortable. The goal is to act in unexpected and surprising ways, not to frighten people.

3. After a few moments, the actor should leave the room. Inform your friends that you staged this event as a demonstration of eyewitness testimony and that, if they are willing, they should try to remember in as much detail as possible what occurred. Ask them to write down answers to these questions:
   a. What did the actor look like? Write down a detailed description.
   b. What did the actor say? Write down his or her words as best as you can remember.
   c. How much time did the actor spend in the room?
   d. Did the actor touch anyone? If yes, whom?
   e. What was the actor holding in his or her hand?

4. After all participants have answered these questions, ask them to read their answers aloud. How much did they agree? How accurate were people's answers? Discuss with your friends why they were correct or incorrect in their descriptions.

Note: This demonstration will work best if you have access to a video camera and can record the actor's actions. That way, you can play back the video to assess the accuracy of the eyewitnesses' descriptions. If you cannot video record it, keep track of how much time elapsed, so that you can judge the accuracy of people's time estimates.

The Recovered Memory Debate

Sometimes an eyewitness is also a victim. One form of memory that has received a great deal of attention is the case in which a person recalls having been the victim of a crime, typically sexual abuse, after many years of not consciously remembering the crime. Not surprisingly, the accuracy of such **recovered memories** has been hotly debated (McNally, 2003; Pezdek & Banks, 1996; Schooler & Eich, 2000).

One infamous case occurred in 1988 in Olympia, Washington, when Paul Ingram's daughters accused him of sexual abuse, satanic rituals, and murder—events they claimed to have suddenly recalled years after they occurred. The police could find no evidence for the crimes, and Ingram initially denied that they had ever taken place. Eventually, though, after a series of interviews that included hypnosis, he became convinced that he too had repressed his past behavior and must have committed the crimes, even though he could not remember having done so. According to experts who have studied this case, Ingram's daughters made their allegations after returning from a group religious retreat intended to encourage women to reveal past incidents of satanic abuse. They genuinely believed that the ritualistic abuse had occurred, as did Ingram himself, but they were wrong. What they thought they remembered were actually false memories (Wright, 1994).

Indeed, in the 1980s and 1990s, some psychotherapists came to believe that traumatic events like these are routinely "repressed" and can be retrieved in therapy through hypnosis, "dream analysis," and other suggestive techniques. This coincided with a nationwide epidemic of claims: people going into therapy and coming out making charges that their fathers, daycare workers, teachers, or other adults had routinely abused them for years, only for the abuse to then be forgotten. With so many cases being brought, psychological scientists began to examine the assumptions of recovered-memory therapy by doing empirical research, and they found that many assumptions about recovered memories were simply wrong. Traumas are not usually repressed; on the contrary, most sufferers have difficulty forgetting them. They found that memories are not stored perfectly in the brain, but are subject to confabulation, distortion, and social influence (e.g., Loftus, Garry, & Hayne, 2008; McNally & Geraerts, 2009; Ofshe & Watters, 1994; Schooler, 1999).

This research led to the notion of **false memory syndrome**: People recalling past traumatic experiences that are objectively false but that they believe to be true (Kihlstrom, 1996). Extensive evidence now exists that people can acquire vivid memories of events that never occurred, especially if another person—such as a psychotherapist—suggests that the events occurred (Loftus et al., 2008; Meyersburg et al., 2009; Schooler & Eich, 2000). In addition to numerous laboratory demonstrations of false memories, evidence from everyday life also indicates that memories of

Recovered Memories

Recollections of a past event, such as sexual abuse, that have been forgotten or repressed

'Tis with our judgments as our watches, None go just alike, yet each believes his own.
—ALEXANDER POPE,
ESSAY ON CRITICISM, 1711

False Memory Syndrome

Remembering a past traumatic experience that is objectively false but is nevertheless accepted by the person as true

In 1988, Paul Ingram was accused by his daughters of sexual abuse, satanic rituals, and murder. His daughters claimed to have suddenly recalled these events years after they occurred, but what they thought they remembered were actually false memories.

Figure SPA-3.2 Corroborating Evidence for Remembered Childhood Sexual Abuse

People who reported that they had been sexually abused in childhood were divided into three groups: those who had never forgotten the abuse, those who had recovered a memory of the abuse outside of psychotherapy, and those who had recovered a memory of the abuse in psychotherapy. All participants reported whether there was any corroborating evidence of the abuse, such as the perpetrator confessing. As seen here, people who recovered memories of abuse in psychotherapy were less likely to report corroborating evidence.

(Based on Geraerts et al., 2007)

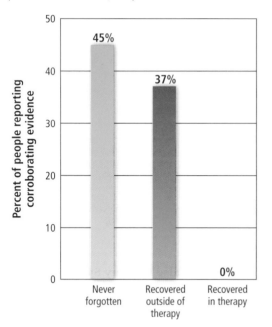

abuse can be false. Often, these memories are contradicted by objective evidence (e.g., no evidence of satanic murders found in the Ingram case); sometimes people who suddenly acquire such memories decide later that the events never occurred; and sometimes the memories are so bizarre (e.g., alien abduction) as to strain credibility. Accordingly, psychotherapists have to consider that the risk of suggesting past abuse is implanting false memories rather than helping clients remember real events.

In one examination of such memories, Elke Geraerts and her colleagues (2007) placed advertisements in the newspaper to recruit people who reported having memories of childhood sexual abuse. The researchers divided the sample into two groups: those who had continuous memories (that is, they had never forgotten their abuse) and those who believed they had recovered a memory of abuse (that is, they said there was a time when they had no memory of being a victim of abuse but later came to recall that they had been abused). This second group was further divided into those who recovered their memory of abuse outside of psychotherapy and those who did so in psychotherapy. All participants were asked to report any knowledge they had of corroborating evidence for the abuse, such as whether other individuals had reported being abused by the same perpetrator or if the perpetrator had confessed to the abuse. Although not perfect, the reported existence of corroborating information gives some indication related to the likelihood that the memories were accurate.

As seen in Figure SPA-3.2, people whose memories of sexual abuse had been recovered in therapy were *least* likely to be able to provide corroborating evidence of the abuse. In fact, no one in this group could do so. Does this prove that everyone who recovered a memory of abuse with the help of a psychotherapist was incorrect and that no such abuse occurred? Certainly not; in cases like these, we can't be 100% sure how accurate memories are. But these results do suggest that claims of abuse cannot be simply taken on faith, especially if they are the result of suggestions from others. Of course, sexual abuse and other childhood traumas *are* a terrible problem and *are* more common than we would like to think. But the scientific evidence now shows quite clearly that abuse is not usually repressed, and suggests that it can be dangerous for therapists to repeatedly encourage clients with no memory of abuse to consider the possibility that they were victimized.

REVIEW QUESTIONS

1. Which of the following is *not* one of the stages of memory processing?
   a. storage
   b. retrieval
   c. schema
   d. acquisition

2. Marina and Jay have been asked to serve as eyewitnesses to a hit-and-run case that they encountered on their way to work. When the law enforcement agent asks Marina the speed at which the car hit the victim, she estimates that the car was traveling at a very high speed, which caused the victim to be thrown at a distance. However, when the agent asks Jay the speed at which the car bumped into the victim, Jay estimates that the car was navigating the busy neighborhood very slowly. What could be the reason for the discrepancy in the speeds reported by Marina and Jay?
   a. There was a retrieval error in their memory.
   b. They encountered misleading questions.
   c. There was a storage error in their respective memories.
   d. They experienced change blindness.

3. The recommendation that the police investigator who administers a lineup should not know which person is the suspect is
   a. not supported by psychological research findings.
   b. intended to prevent post-identification feedback.
   c. likely to make the own-race bias worse.
   d. the best solution to the problems caused by witness verbalization.

4. Which of the following statements about eyewitness memory is true?
   a. Jurors often have a difficult time determining whether or not an eyewitness is accurate.
   b. The best indicator of an eyewitness' accuracy is his or her confidence.
   c. Eyewitnesses who take their time and look at all the photographs presented to them before making an identification tend to be more accurate then those who make a judgment quickly.
   d. When presenting photographs to an eyewitness, the recommendation is that police show all of the photos at once instead of presenting them one at a time.

5. Researchers who have studied recovered memories of abuse have found that
   a. all supposedly recovered memories are false.
   b. false memory syndrome does not exist.
   c. memories recovered outside of psychotherapy are more likely to have corroborating evidence than memories recovered in a psychotherapy setting.
   d. hypnosis is an effective way to prevent people from coming to believe in what turn out to be false memories.

See page 623 for the answers.

Juries: Group Processes in Action

SPA3.2   **Does social psychology help explain how juries make decisions?**

The right to be tried by a jury of one's peers has a long tradition in English and American law. Trial by jury was an established institution in England at the beginning of the seventeenth century, and the people who founded the first permanent English settlement in North America—at Jamestown, Virginia—carried this tradition with them (although, it should be noted, this right was not granted to Native Americans or other nonWhites, nor to a few rebellious English settlers who were summarily hanged).

Despite this tradition, the jury system has often come under attack. In the Randall Adams trial, it is now clear that the jury reached the wrong decision. One study found that judges who presided over criminal jury trials disagreed with the verdict rendered by the jury a full 25% of the time (Kalven & Zeisel, 1966). Recent observers have also criticized the jury system, questioning the ability of jurors to understand complex evidence and reach a dispassionate verdict (Arkes & Mellers, 2002; Bornstein & Greene, 2011). As noted by a former dean of the Harvard Law School, "Why should anyone think that 12 persons brought in from the street, selected in various ways for their lack of general ability, should have any special capacity for deciding controversies between persons?" (Kalven & Zeisel, 1966, p. 5).

Of course, the jury system also has its staunch supporters, and few people on either side of the debate argue that it should be abolished. Sometimes juries seem to "get it wrong," but individual judges deciding cases would also be susceptible to many of the biased perceptions and decision processes we have discussed in previous chapters. And allowing citizens to participate in important decisions such as these also can boost public perceptions of how fair our legal system is. The point is that the jury system is not a perfect system and many researchers continue to devote their efforts to better understanding the ways in which it sometimes goes awry and how the process can be improved in the future (Desmarais & Read, 2011; Devine, 2012; Semmler, Brewer, & Douglass, 2012; Sommers & Marotta, 2014).

> A court is no better than each . . . of you sitting before me on this jury. A court is only as sound as its jury, and a jury is only as sound as the [people] who make it up.
>
> —HARPER LEE, *TO KILL A MOCKINGBIRD*, 1960

How Jurors Process Information During the Trial

How do individual jurors think about the evidence they hear during a trial? As we saw in Chapter 3, people often construct theories and schemas to interpret the world around them, and the same is true of jurors (Hart, 1995; Smith, 1991; Weinstock, 2011). Some psychologists have proposed a **story model** for jury decision-making, namely that as

Story Model
The theory that jurors try to fit the evidence they hear at trial into a coherent story, and ultimately reach a verdict that best fits the story they have created

"Your Honor, we're going to go with the prosecution's spin."

Mike Twohy/The New Yorker Collection/The Cartoon Bank

jurors hear evidence in case, they decide on one story that best explains everything they hear. They then try to fit this story to the possible verdicts they are allowed to render, and if one of those verdicts fits well with their preferred story, they are likely to vote to convict on that charge (Hastie, 2008; Hastie & Pennington, 2000). The story model has important implications for how lawyers present their cases. Lawyers typically present the evidence in one of two ways. One is *story order*, in which they present the evidence in the sequence in which the events occurred, corresponding as closely as possible to the story they want the jurors to believe. Another is called *witness order*, in which attorneys present witnesses in the sequence they think will have the greatest impact, even if this means that events are described out of order. For example, a lawyer might save his or her best witness for last so that the trial ends on a dramatic, memorable note, even if this witness describes events that occurred early on in the alleged criminal incident.

If you were a lawyer, in which order would you present the evidence? You can probably guess which order researchers in this area hypothesized would be the most successful. If jurors are ultimately swayed by the story or schema they think best explains the sequence of events, the best strategy should be to present the evidence in story order, not witness order. To test their hypothesis, researchers asked mock jurors to listen to a simulated murder trial and varied the order in which the prosecuting and defense attorneys presented their cases (Pennington & Hastie, 1988). In one condition, both used story order, whereas in another condition, both used witness order. In other conditions, one attorney used story order and the other used witness order.

The results provided clear and dramatic support for the story-order strategy. As seen in Table SPA-3.2, when the prosecutor used story order and the defense used witness order, the jurors were most likely to believe the prosecutor—78% voted to convict the defendant. When the prosecutor used witness order and the defense used story order, the tables were turned—only 31% voted to convict. One reason the conviction rate in felony trials in America is so high—approximately 80%—may be that in real trials prosecutors are more likely to present evidence in story order. If you are a budding lawyer, remember this when you are preparing for your first trial!

Confessions: Are They Always What They Seem?

Imagine that you are a member of a jury at a murder trial. The prosecution presents what seems to be ironclad evidence—namely, a videotape of the defendant confessing to the crime. "OK, yes," you hear the defendant say, "I was the one who pulled the trigger."

Table SPA-3.2 How Should Lawyers Present a Case?

A lawyer can present a case in a variety of ways. This study found that story order, in which a lawyer presents the evidence in the order that corresponds most closely to the story he or she wants the jurors to believe, works best.

	Percentage of People Voting to Convict the Defendant	
	Defense Evidence	
Prosecution Evidence	**Story Order**	**Witness Order**
Story order	59%	78%
Witness order	31%	63%

(Adapted from Pennington & Hastie, 1988.)

More than likely, you would vote to convict. Why would the defendant admit to the crime if he was innocent? And many cases never go to trial, because the defendant pleads guilty after confessing to the crime.

Confessions, however, are not always what they seem. Consider the high-profile case of the Central Park jogger, a woman who was raped and brutally beaten while jogging in New York City in 1989. The victim, who suffered a fractured skull and traumatic brain injuries, was in a coma for several days, and when she awoke, she had no memory of the attack. Despite her inability to point to a perpetrator, the police arrested five teenagers, all either African American or Hispanic, who had been in the park that night. The boys confessed to the crime and ultimately provided lurid details of what had happened. Four of the confessions were videotaped and played at the trial, and largely on this basis, all of the teenagers were convicted and given long prison sentences.

The only problem is that, 13 years later, as detailed in Ken Burns's documentary *The Central Park Five*, it became clear that the boys were innocent. Another man, in prison for three rapes and a murder, confessed to the crime, admitting he had acted alone. His DNA matched samples recovered from the victim (none of the teenagers' DNA matched), and he gave details of the crime scene that were known only to the police. In 2002, a judge vacated the convictions of all five boys.

If the boys were innocent, then why did they confess to the crime? Unfortunately, the police interrogation process can go wrong in ways that elicit false confessions, even to the point where innocent suspects come to believe that they actually committed the crime (Gudjonsson et al., 2014; Hasel & Kassin, 2012; Kassin et al., 2010; Narchet, Meissner, & Russano, 2011). One problem is that police investigators are often convinced that the suspect is guilty, and this belief biases how they conduct the interrogation. They ask leading questions, isolate suspects and put them under considerable stress, and sometimes make false promises. The suspects in the Central Park jogger case, for example, were questioned for up to 30 hours, and the police detectives implied that they could go home if they would sign a confession. After many hours of prolonged interrogation, innocent people can become so psychologically fatigued that they don't know what to think and may even come to believe that they are guilty. This may seem relatively unproblematic to you if the suspect really is guilty, and if the techniques succeed in making him or her confess. However, people—even trained investigators—are not very good at telling whether someone is lying, which means that innocent

The problem with some confessions is that they are not autobiographical at all, but false.

people are sometimes subjected to these techniques as well. In fact, in a large number of cases in which DNA evidence has exonerated defendants who have been falsely convicted of a crime, the defendant has confessed ("False confessions," 2006).

One solution to the problem of false confessions is requiring that interrogations be videotaped, so a jury can view the recording and judge for itself whether the defendant was coerced into admitting things he or she didn't do. In 2003, Illinois became the first state to pass a law requiring that all police interrogations of homicide suspects be electronically recorded; other states have since followed suit. Although this is a step forward, it raises another potential problem. Almost all videos of interrogations focus on the suspect, rather than on the interrogator asking the questions. Well, you might wonder, what's wrong with that?

As we noted in Chapter 4, the problem is that viewers tend to think that whoever the camera is focused on is more in charge of the situation than they

"For me, a confession is much too autobiographical."

Frank Cotham/The New Yorker Collection/The Cartoon Bank

People sometimes confess to crimes they did not commit, when they are subjected to long, stressful interrogations.

actually are. Some studies have showed people a video of the same confession from different camera angles—similar to what we discussed earlier in the book regarding how the angle at which you see a speaker affects your impressions of who has control over the conversation—and then asked them to judge how voluntary or coerced the confession appeared to be. People thought that the confession was most voluntary (i.e., the least coerced) when the camera focused on the suspect; here, people had the sense that the suspect was in charge of what was happening. When the camera showed both the suspect and the interrogator, people thought the confession was less voluntary. And when the camera focused only on the interrogator, people thought the confession was the most coerced (Lassiter, 2010). Remember, everyone heard the same confession; all that differed was their visual perspective. In part because of this research, some states are now beginning to require that both the suspect and the questioner be shown in videotaped interviews.

Deliberations in the Jury Room

As any trial lawyer can tell you, the crucial part of the jury process occurs out of sight, when jurors deliberate in the attempt to reach a unanimous verdict. Even if most jurors are inclined to vote in one direction, there might be a persuasive minority able to change the other jurors' minds. Sometimes this can be a minority of one, as in the classic movie *Twelve Angry Men*. When the film begins, a jury has just finished listening to the evidence in a murder case, and all the jurors except one are ready to vote to convict the defendant. But over the course of the next 90 minutes, the lone holdout, played by Henry Fonda, persuades his peers that there is reason to doubt that the young Hispanic defendant is guilty. At first, the other jurors pressure Fonda to change his mind (using techniques of normative and informational conformity, as discussed in Chapter 8), but in the end, reason triumphs, and the other jurors come to see that Fonda is right.

As entertaining as this movie is, research indicates that it does not reflect the reality of most jury deliberations (Bornstein & Greene, 2011; Kalven & Zeisel, 1966; MacCoun, 1989). In the Randall Adams trial, for example, a majority of the 12-person jury (7 men and 5 women) initially voted to convict Adams. After 8 hours of deliberations, the majority prevailed: The holdouts changed their minds, and the jury voted unanimously to convict. In a study of more than 200 juries in actual criminal trials, researchers found that in 97% of the cases the jury's final decision was the same as the one favored by a majority of the jurors on the initial vote (Kalven & Zeisel, 1966). Thus, just as we saw in Chapter 8 on the subject of conformity, majority opinion usually carries the day, bringing dissenting jurors into line.

If jury deliberation is stacked toward the initial majority opinion, why not just abandon the deliberation process, letting the jury's initial vote determine a defendant's guilt or innocence? For at least two reasons, this would not be a good idea. First, forcing jurors to reach a unanimous verdict makes them consider the evidence more carefully rather than simply assuming that their initial impressions of the case were correct (Hastie, Penrod, & Pennington, 1983; Sommers, 2006). Second,

In the 1954 movie *Twelve Angry Men*, Henry Fonda convinces all of his fellow jurors to change their minds about a defendant's guilt. In real life, however, it is rare for a minority of one to convince the rest of the jurors to change their minds.

even if the jury minority seldom succeeds in persuading the majority to change its mind about guilt or innocence, minorities often do change people's minds about how guilty a person is. In criminal trials, juries may have some discretion about the type of guilty verdict they can reach. In a murder trial, for example, they can often decide whether to convict the defendant of first-degree murder, second-degree murder, or manslaughter. One study found that people on a jury who have a minority point of view often convince fellow jurors to change their minds about the specific charge on which to convict (Pennington & Hastie, 1990). Thus, while a minority of jurors is less likely to convince a majority of jurors to change a verdict from first-degree murder to not guilty, these jurors might well convince the others to switch from first-degree to second-degree murder.

REVIEW QUESTIONS

1. Research indicates that _____ tends to be the most persuasive way of presenting evidence to a jury.
   a. witness order
   b. schema order
   c. blind order
   d. story order
2. Police responded to a robbery report at Mr. Olivier's house. Mr. Olivier claims that when he got home from work, his front door was open and his valuables were missing. Police immediately took photographs of the house. A neighbor later claimed witnessing a man break into the house. Which of the following ways of presenting evidence to a jury was described in the previous sentences?
   a. Chronological order
   b. Evidence order
   c. Witness order
   d. Story order
3. When it comes to jury decision-making, minority influence
   a. never occurs.
   b. is more effective in 12-person juries than in 6-person juries.
   c. can be more effective in changing which charge the jury convicts on as opposed to actually changing the jury's verdict from, say, guilty to not guilty.
   d. works best when done in witness order.

See page 623 for the answers.

Summary

SPA3.1 What does psychology indicate about the accuracy of eyewitness testimony?

- **Eyewitness Testimony** Eyewitness testimony is often of questionable accuracy because of the way people naturally observe and remember unexpected events.

  - **Why Are Eyewitnesses Often Wrong?** A number of factors bias the **acquisition**, **storage**, and **retrieval** of what people observe, sometimes leading to the false identification of criminals. For example, research on **own-race bias** shows that people find it more difficult to recognize members of other races than members of their own race. Research on **reconstructive memory** indicates that errors in **source monitoring** can occur when people become confused about where they saw or heard something. Recognizing the problems people have retrieving information from memory, social psychology research has contributed to new guidelines for how police lineups should be conducted.

- **Judging Whether Eyewitnesses Are Mistaken** There is no surefire way of telling whether a witness is making an accurate or inaccurate identification, although there is some evidence that people who identify a suspect from an array of pictures within 10 seconds *and* express very high confidence in their choice are especially likely to be correct. Post-identification feedback from a lineup administrator can inflate an eyewitness's confidence, making it even harder for jurors to determine whether or not the witness's memory is accurate.

- **The Recovered Memory Debate** Although **recovered memories** may be accurate in some instances, they can also be the result of **false memory syndrome**, whereby people come to believe that a memory is true when it actually is not. False memories are especially likely to occur when another person, such as a psychotherapist, plants the suggestion that an event likely occurred.

SPA3.2 Does social psychology help explain how juries make decisions?

- **Juries: Group Processes in Action** Juries are of particular interest to social psychologists, because the way they reach verdicts is directly relevant to social psychological research on group processes and social interaction. Jurors are susceptible to the same kinds of biases and social pressures we have documented in earlier chapters (though it's only fair to note that so, too, are individual judges).

  - **How Jurors Process Information During the Trial** According to the **story model** of jury decision-making, during a trial, jurors attempt to make sense out of the testimony and often decide on one story that explains all of the evidence. Juries are thus most swayed by lawyers who present the evidence in a way that tells a consistent story.

- **Confessions: Are They Always What They Seem?** The interrogation techniques used by the police can sometimes produce false confessions. The video recording of interrogations is a safeguard against this, although focusing the camera solely on the suspect increases the likelihood that viewers will think he or she voluntarily confessed.

- **Deliberations in the Jury Room** During deliberations, jurors with minority views are often pressured into conforming to the view of the majority; thus, verdicts usually correspond to the initial feelings of the majority of jurors.

Test Yourself

1. Which of the following is *least* true about eyewitness testimony?

   a. Jurors and law enforcement professionals rely heavily on eyewitness testimony when they are deciding whether someone is guilty.

   b. Jurors tend to overestimate the accuracy of eyewitnesses.

   c. People are better at recognizing faces of people of their own race than faces of people of different races.

   d. Writing down a description of someone you saw will make it easier for you to recognize that person later.

2. Gloria was working the night shift at a convenience store. A man came in, pulled out a gun, and demanded that Gloria give him all the money in the cash register. When the police interview Gloria about the crime, which of the following will she most likely be able to tell them?

   a. The size of the gun the man had

   b. The type of clothes the man wore

   c. The height of the man

   d. The color of the man's eyes

3. Following a murder, police have arrested a suspect and asked three eyewitnesses to identify the suspect from a photo array. Based on social psychology research, in which of the following situations is the eyewitness' selection least likely to be accurate?

   a. When the witnesses were told that the suspect may or may not be in the lineup photographs

   b. When the witnesses were shown the photographs one at a time, as opposed to all at once

   c. When the lineup included photographs of people who did not resemble the witnesses' description of the suspect

   d. When the police officer administering the lineup did not know which person in the lineup was the suspect

4. Which of the following is *not* a recommendation that social psychologists have made about how the police should conduct lineups?

   a. Make sure everyone in the lineup resembles the witness's description of the suspect.

   b. Tell the witness that the person suspected of the crime may or may not be in the lineup.

   c. Before seeing the lineup, have the witness reconstruct the face of the suspect, using face-composite computer programs.

   d. Don't assume that witnesses know whether their selections were biased.

5. Research has supported which of the following statements about recovered memories?

   a. False memory syndrome does not exist.

   b. People who recover memories of sexual abuse in psychotherapy are almost always correct that the abuse really occurred.

   c. There may be instances in which people do suddenly remember traumatic events that really did occur.

   d. Judges are more likely to believe them than are juries.

6. Which of the following recommendations have social psychologists made to the legal profession?

   a. The police should try as hard as they can to get suspects to confess to a crime, because if the suspects confess, they are surely guilty.

   b. Lawyers should present witnesses in the sequence they think will have the greatest impact, even if this means that events of the case are described out of order.

c. The police should videotape all interrogations and make sure that the camera angle shows both the interrogator and the suspect.

d. Hypnosis is a useful way for producing accurate eyewitness memories.

7. According to social psychology, why might police interrogations elicit false confessions from suspects?

a. They might ask suspects leading questions.

b. They might make false promises, encouraging suspects to confess to a crime.

c. They might isolate suspects and put them under stressful conditions, which leads them to confess.

d. All of the above can lead to false confessions from suspects.

8. Which of the following is *most true* about research on social psychology and the law?

a. In police interrogations, people sometimes confess to a crime they did not commit and even come to believe that they did commit the crime.

b. When jury deliberations begin, if a couple of jurors disagree with everyone else, they are easily able to persuade the majority to change from a guilty to a not-guilty verdict.

c. People have pretty good memories for events they witness, and it is hard to convince them that they saw something they did not.

d. If a witness picks a suspect out of a lineup and is extremely confident that he or she has identified the right person, then he or she is almost certainly correct.

9. One explanation for why eyewitnesses might be confident in an inaccurate identification is

a. the story model.

b. post-identification feedback.

c. own-race bias.

d. recovered memory.

10. Raj is having trouble remembering whether he actually saw a White van speeding away from the scene of the bank robbery or whether he just heard other people talking about a White van. Raj is having difficulty with

a. composite memory.

b. verbalization effects.

c. storage.

d. source monitoring.

See page 623 for the answers.

Glossary

Accessibility   The extent to which schemas and concepts are at the forefront of people's minds and are therefore likely to be used when making judgments about the social world

Acquisition   The process by which people notice and pay attention to information in their environment

Affect Blends   Facial expressions in which one part of the face registers one emotion while another part of the face registers a different emotion

Affective Forecasting   The extent to which people can predict the intensity and duration of their emotional reactions to future events

Affective Forecasts   People's predictions about how they will feel in response to a future emotional event

Affectively Based Attitude   An attitude based more on people's feelings and values than on their beliefs about the nature of an attitude object

Aggression   Intentional behavior aimed at causing physical harm or psychological pain to another person

Altruism   The desire to help another person even if it involves a cost to the helper

Altruistic Personality   The qualities that cause an individual to help others in a wide variety of situations

Analytic Thinking Style   A type of thinking in which people focus on the properties of objects without considering their surrounding context; this type of thinking is common in Western cultures

Anxious/Ambivalent Attachment Style   An attachment style characterized by a concern that others will not reciprocate one's desire for intimacy, resulting in higher-than-average levels of anxiety

Applied Research   Studies designed to solve a particular social problem

Archival Analysis   A form of the observational method in which the researcher examines the accumulated documents, or archives, of a culture (e.g., diaries, novels, magazines, and newspapers)

Attachment Styles   The expectations people develop about relationships with others based on the relationship they had with their primary caregiver when they were infants

Attitude Accessibility   The strength of the association between an attitude object and a person's evaluation of that object, measured by the speed with which people can report how they feel about the object

Attitude Inoculation   Making people immune to attempts to change their attitudes by initially exposing them to small doses of the arguments against their position

Attitudes   Evaluations of people, objects, and ideas

Attribution Theory   A description of the way in which people explain the causes of their own and other people's behavior

Automatic Thinking   Thinking that is nonconscious, unintentional, involuntary, and effortless

Availability Heuristic   A mental rule of thumb whereby people base a judgment on the ease with which they can bring something to mind

Avoidant Attachment Style   An attachment style characterized by difficulty developing intimate relationships because previous attempts to be intimate have been rebuffed

Base Rate Information   Information about the frequency of members of different categories in the population

Basic Dilemma of the Social Psychologist   The trade-off between internal and external validity in conducting research; it is very difficult to do one experiment that is both high in internal validity and generalizable to other situations and people

Basic Research   Studies that are designed to find the best answer to the question of why people behave as they do and that are conducted purely for reasons of intellectual curiosity

Behaviorally Based Attitude   An attitude based on observations of how one behaves toward an object

Behaviorism   A school of psychology maintaining that to understand human behavior, one need only consider the reinforcing properties of the environment

Belief in a Just World   A form of defensive attribution wherein people assume that bad things happen to bad people and that good things happen to good people

Belief Perseverance   The tendency to stick with an initial judgment even in the face of new information that should prompt us to reconsider

Bias Blind Spot   The tendency to think that other people are more susceptible to attributional biases in their thinking than we are

Blaming the Victim   The tendency to blame individuals (make dispositional attributions) for their victimization, typically motivated by a desire to see the world as a fair place

Bystander Effect   The finding that the greater the number of bystanders who witness an emergency, the less likely any one of them is to help

Catharsis   The notion that "blowing off steam"—by behaving aggressively or watching others do so—relieves built-up anger and aggressive energy and hence reduces the likelihood of further aggressive behavior

Causal Theories   Theories about the causes of one's own feelings and behaviors; often we learn such theories from our culture (e.g., "absence makes the heart grow fonder")

Central Route to Persuasion   The case in which people have both the ability and the motivation to elaborate on a persuasive communication, listening carefully to and thinking about the arguments presented

Classical Conditioning   The phenomenon whereby a stimulus that elicits an emotional response is repeatedly paired with a neutral stimulus that does not, until the neutral stimulus takes on the emotional properties of the first stimulus

Cognitive Dissonance   The discomfort that people feel when two cognitions (beliefs, attitudes) conflict, or when they behave in ways that are inconsistent with their conception of themselves

Cognitively Based Attitude   An attitude based primarily on people's beliefs about the properties of an attitude object

Communal Relationships   Relationships in which people's primary concern is being responsive to the other person's needs

Companionate Love   The feelings of intimacy and affection we have for someone that are not accompanied by passion or physiological arousal

Comparison Level for Alternatives   People's expectations about the level of rewards and costs they would receive in an alternative relationship

Comparison Level   People's expectations about the level of rewards and costs they are likely to receive in a particular relationship

Conformity A change in one's behavior due to the real or imagined influence of other people

Consensus Information Information about the extent to which other people behave the same way toward the same stimulus as the actor does

Consistency Information Information about the extent to which the behavior between one actor and one stimulus is the same across time and circumstances

Construal The way in which people perceive, comprehend, and interpret the social world

Contingency Theory of Leadership The idea that the effectiveness of a leader depends both on how task oriented or relationship oriented the leader is and on the amount of control the leader has over the group

Controlled Thinking Thinking that is conscious, intentional, voluntary, and effortful

Coping Styles The ways in which people react to threatening events

Correlational Method The technique whereby two or more variables are systematically measured and the relationship between them (i.e., how much one can be predicted from the other) is assessed

Correlation Coefficient A statistical technique that assesses how well you can predict one variable from another—for example, how well you can predict people's weight from their height

Counterattitudinal Advocacy Stating an opinion or attitude that runs counter to one's private belief or attitude

Counterfactual Thinking Mentally changing some aspect of the past as a way of imagining what might have been

Covariation Model A theory that states that to form an attribution about what caused a person's behavior, we systematically note the pattern between the presence or absence of possible causal factors and whether the behavior occurs

Cover Story A description of the purpose of a study, given to participants, that is different from its true purpose and is used to maintain psychological realism

Cross-Cultural Research Research conducted with members of different cultures, to see whether the psychological processes of interest are present in both cultures or whether they are specific to the culture in which people were raised

Debriefing Explaining to participants, at the end of an experiment, the true purpose of the study and exactly what transpired

Deception Misleading participants about the true purpose of a study or the events that will actually transpire

Decode To interpret the meaning of the nonverbal behavior other people express, such as deciding that a pat on the back was an expression of condescension and not kindness

Deindividuation The loosening of normal constraints on behavior when people can't be identified (such as when they are in a crowd)

Dependent Variable The variable a researcher measures to see if it is influenced by the independent variable; the researcher hypothesizes that the dependent variable will depend on the level of the independent variable

Descriptive Norms People's perceptions of how people actually behave in given situations, regardless of whether the behavior is approved or disapproved of by others

Diffusion of Responsibility The phenomenon wherein each bystander's sense of responsibility to help decreases as the number of witnesses increases

Discrimination Unjustified negative or harmful action toward a member of a group solely because of his or her membership in that group

Display Rules Culturally determined rules about which nonverbal behaviors are appropriate to display

Distinctiveness Information Information about the extent to which one particular actor behaves in the same way to different stimuli

Door-in-the-Face Technique Social influence strategy in which first asking people for a large request that they will probably refuse makes them more likely to agree later to a second, smaller request

Downward Social Comparison Comparing ourselves to people who are worse than we are with regard to a particular trait or ability

Elaboration Likelihood Model A model explaining two ways in which persuasive communications can cause attitude change: *centrally*, when people are motivated and have the ability to pay attention to the arguments in the communication, and *peripherally*, when people do not pay attention to the arguments but are instead swayed by surface characteristics

Emblems Nonverbal gestures that have well-understood definitions within a given culture; they usually have direct verbal translations, such as the OK sign

Empathy The ability to put oneself in the shoes of another person and to experience events and emotions (e.g., joy and sadness) the way that person experiences them

Empathy-Altruism Hypothesis The idea that when we feel empathy for a person, we will attempt to help that person for purely altruistic reasons, regardless of what we have to gain

Encode To express or emit nonverbal behavior, such as smiling or patting someone on the back

Equity Theory The idea that people are happiest with relationships in which the rewards and costs experienced by both parties are roughly equal

Ethnocentrism The belief that one's own ethnic group, nation, or religion is superior to all others

Ethnography The method by which researchers attempt to understand a group or culture by observing it from the inside, without imposing any preconceived notions they might have

Evolutionary Psychology The attempt to explain social behavior in terms of genetic factors that have evolved over time according to the principles of natural selection

Evolutionary Theory A concept developed by Charles Darwin to explain the ways in which animals adapt to their environments

Exchange Relationships Relationships governed by the need for equity (i.e., for an equal ratio of rewards and costs)

Experimental Method The method in which the researcher randomly assigns participants to different conditions and ensures that these conditions are identical except for the independent variable (the one thought to have a causal effect on people's responses)

Explicit Attitudes Attitudes that we consciously endorse and can easily report

External Attribution The inference that a person is behaving a certain way because of something about the situation he or she is in; the assumption is that most people would respond the same way in that situation

External Justification A reason or an explanation for dissonant personal behavior that resides outside the individual (e.g., to receive a large reward or avoid a severe punishment)

External Validity The extent to which the results of a study can be generalized to other situations and to other people

Extrinsic Motivation The desire to engage in an activity because of external rewards or pressures, not because we enjoy the task or find it interesting

False Memory Syndrome   Remembering a past traumatic experience that is objectively false but is nevertheless accepted by the person as true

Fear-Arousing Communication   Persuasive message that attempts to change people's attitudes by arousing their fears

Field Experiments   Experiments conducted in natural settings rather than in the laboratory

Fight-or-Flight Response   Responding to stress by either attacking the source of the stress or fleeing from it

Fixed Mind-Set   The idea that we have a set amount of an ability that cannot change

Foot-in-the-Door Technique   Social influence strategy in which getting people to agree first to a small request makes them more likely to agree later to a second, larger request

Frustration-Aggression Theory   The theory that frustration—the perception that you are being prevented from attaining a goal—increases the probability of an aggressive response

Fundamental Attribution Error   The tendency to overestimate the extent to which other people's behavior is due to internal, dispositional factors and to underestimate the role of situational factors

Gender Roles   Societal beliefs—such as those conveyed by media and other sources—regarding how men and women are expected to behave

Gestalt Psychology   A school of psychology stressing the importance of studying the subjective way in which an object appears in people's minds rather than the objective, physical attributes of the object

Great Person Theory   The idea that certain key personality traits make a person a good leader, regardless of the situation

Group Cohesiveness   Qualities of a group that bind members together and promote liking between them

Group Polarization   The tendency for groups to make decisions that are more extreme than the initial inclinations of their members

Groupthink   A kind of decision process in which maintaining group cohesiveness and solidarity is more important than considering the facts in a realistic manner

Group   Two or more people who interact and are interdependent in the sense that their needs and goals cause them to influence each other

Growth Mind-Set   The idea that our abilities are malleable qualities that we can cultivate and grow

Halo Effect   A cognitive bias by which we tend to assume that an individual with one positive characteristic also possesses other (even unrelated) positive characteristics

Heuristic–Systematic Model of Persuasion   An explanation of the two ways in which persuasive communications can cause attitude change: either systematically processing the merits of the arguments or using mental shortcuts or heuristics

Hindsight Bias   The tendency for people to exaggerate, after knowing that something occurred, how much they could have predicted it before it occurred

Holistic Thinking Style   A type of thinking in which people focus on the overall context, particularly the ways in which objects relate to each other; this type of thinking is common in East Asian cultures (e.g., China, Japan, and Korea)

Hostile Aggression   Aggression stemming from feelings of anger and aimed at inflicting pain or injury

Hypocrisy Induction   The arousal of dissonance by having individuals make statements that run counter to their behaviors and then reminding them of the inconsistency between what they advocated and their behavior; the purpose is to lead individuals to more responsible behavior

Idiosyncrasy Credits   The tolerance a person earns, over time, by conforming to group norms; if enough credits are earned, the person can, on occasion, deviate from the group without retribution

Impact Bias   The tendency to overestimate the intensity and duration of one's emotional reactions to future negative events

Implementation Intentions   People's specific plans about where, when, and how they will fulfill a goal

Implicit Association Test (IAT)   A test thought to measure unconscious (implicit) prejudices according to the speed with which people can pair a target face (e.g., Black or White, old or young, Asian or White) with a positive or negative association (e.g., the words *honest* or *evil*)

Implicit Attitudes   Attitudes that exist outside of conscious awareness

Impression Management   The attempt by people to get others to see them as they want to be seen

In-Group   The group with which an individual identifies as a member

In-Group Bias   The tendency to favor members of one's own group and give them special preference over people who belong to other groups; the group can be temporary and trivial as well as significant

Independent Variable   The variable a researcher changes or varies to see if it has an effect on some other variable

Independent View of the Self   A way of defining oneself in terms of one's own internal thoughts, feelings, and actions and not in terms of the thoughts, feelings, and actions of other people

Informational Social Influence   Relying on other people as a source of information to guide our behavior; we conform because we believe that others' interpretation of an ambiguous situation is correct and can help us choose an appropriate course of action

Informed Consent   Agreement to participate in an experiment, granted in full awareness of the nature of the experiment, which has been explained in advance

Ingratiation   The process whereby people flatter, praise, and generally try to make themselves likable to another person, often of higher status

Injunctive Norms   People's perceptions of what behaviors are approved or disapproved of by others

Institutional Discrimination   Practices that discriminate, legally or illegally, against a minority group by virtue of its ethnicity, gender, culture, age, sexual orientation, or other target of societal or company prejudice

Institutional Review Board (IRB)   A group made up of at least one scientist, one nonscientist, and one member not affiliated with the institution that reviews all psychological research at that institution and decides whether it meets ethical guidelines; all research must be approved by the IRB before it is conducted

Instrumental Aggression   Aggression as a means to some goal other than causing pain

Insufficient Punishment   The dissonance aroused when individuals lack sufficient external justification for having resisted a desired activity or object, usually resulting in individuals devaluing the forbidden activity or object

Integrative Solution   A solution to a conflict whereby the parties make trade-offs on issues, with each side conceding the most on issues that are unimportant to it but important to the other side

Interdependence   The situation that exists when two or more groups need to depend on one another to accomplish a goal that is important to each of them

Interdependent View of the Self   A way of defining oneself in terms of one's relationships to other people, recognizing that one's behavior is often determined by the thoughts, feelings, and actions of others

Interjudge Reliability   The level of agreement between two or more people who independently observe and code a set of data; by showing that two or more judges independently come up with the same observations, researchers ensure that the observations are not the subjective, distorted impressions of one individual

Internal-External Locus of Control   The tendency to believe that things happen because we control them versus believing that good and bad outcomes are out of our control

Internal Attribution   The inference that a person is behaving in a certain way because of something about the person, such as attitude, character, or personality

Internal Justification   The reduction of dissonance by changing something about oneself (e.g., one's attitude or behavior)

Internal Validity   Making sure that nothing besides the independent variable can affect the dependent variable; this is accomplished by controlling all extraneous variables and by randomly assigning people to different experimental conditions

Intrinsic Motivation   The desire to engage in an activity because we enjoy it or find it interesting, not because of external rewards or pressures

Introspection   The process whereby people look inward and examine their own thoughts, feelings, and motives

Investment Model   The theory that people's commitment to a relationship depends not only on their satisfaction with the relationship, but also on how much they have invested in the relationship that would be lost by ending it

Jigsaw Classroom   A classroom setting designed to reduce prejudice and raise the self-esteem of children by placing them in small, multiethnic groups and making each child dependent on the other children in the group to learn the course material and do well in the class

Judgmental Heuristics   Mental shortcuts people use to make judgments quickly and efficiently

Justification of Effort   The tendency for individuals to increase their liking for something they have worked hard to attain

Kin Selection   The idea that behaviors that help a genetic relative are favored by natural selection

Lowballing   An unscrupulous strategy whereby a salesperson induces a customer to agree to purchase a product at a low cost, subsequently claims it was an error, and then raises the price; frequently, the customer will agree to make the purchase at the inflated price

Mere Exposure Effect   The finding that the more exposure we have to a stimulus, the more apt we are to like it

Meta-Analysis   A statistical technique that averages the results of two or more studies to see if the effect of an independent variable is reliable

Minority Influence   The case where a minority of group members influences the behavior or beliefs of the majority

Misattribution of Arousal   The process whereby people make mistaken inferences about what is causing them to feel the way they do

Narcissism   The combination of excessive self-love and a lack of empathy toward others

Natural Selection   The process by which heritable traits that promote survival in a particular environment are passed along to future generations; organisms with those traits are more likely to produce offspring

Negotiation   A form of communication between opposing sides in a conflict in which offers and counteroffers are made and a solution occurs only when both parties agree

Nonverbal Communication   The way in which people communicate, intentionally or unintentionally, without words; nonverbal cues include facial expressions, tone of voice, gestures, body position and movement, the use of touch, and gaze

Normative Conformity   The tendency to go along with the group in order to fulfill the group's expectations and gain acceptance

Normative Social Influence   Going along with what other people do in order to be liked and accepted by them; we publicly conform with the group's beliefs and behaviors but do not always privately accept them

Norm of Reciprocity   The expectation that helping others will increase the likelihood that they will help us in the future

Observational Method   The technique whereby a researcher observes people and systematically records measurements or impressions of their behavior

Operant Conditioning   The phenomenon whereby behaviors we freely choose to perform become more or less frequent, depending on whether they are followed by a reward or punishment

Out-Group   Any group with which an individual does not identify

Out-Group Homogeneity   The perception that individuals in the out-group are more similar to each other (homogeneous) than they really are, as well as more similar than members of the in-group are

Overconfidence Barrier   The fact that people usually have too much confidence in the accuracy of their judgments

Overjustification Effect   The tendency for people to view their behavior as caused by compelling extrinsic reasons, making them underestimate the extent to which it was caused by intrinsic reasons

Own-Race Bias   The tendency for people to be better at recognizing faces of their own race than those of other races

Passionate Love   An intense longing we feel for a person, accompanied by physiological arousal

Perceived Control   The belief that we can influence our environment in ways that determine whether we experience positive or negative outcomes

Perceptual Salience   The seeming importance of information that is the focus of people's attention

Performance-Contingent Rewards   Rewards that are based on how well we perform a task

Peripheral Route to Persuasion   The case in which people do not elaborate on the arguments in a persuasive communication but are instead swayed by more superficial cues

Persuasive Communication   A message advocating a particular side of an issue

Pluralistic Ignorance   The case in which people think that everyone else is interpreting a situation in a certain way, when in fact they are not

Postdecision Dissonance   Dissonance aroused after making a decision, typically reduced by enhancing the attractiveness of the chosen alternative and devaluating the rejected alternatives

Prejudice   A hostile or negative attitude toward people in a distinguishable group based solely on their membership in that group; it contains cognitive, emotional, and behavioral components

Primacy Effect   When it comes to forming impressions, the first traits we perceive in others influence how we view information that we learn about them later

Priming   The process by which recent experiences increase the accessibility of a schema, trait, or concept

Private Acceptance   Conforming to other people's behavior out of a genuine belief that what they are doing or saying is right

Probability Level (*p*-value)   A number calculated with statistical techniques that tells researchers how likely it is that the results of their experiment occurred by chance and not because of the independent variable or variables; the convention in science, including social psychology, is to consider results *significant* (trustworthy) if the probability level is less than 5 in 100 that the results might be due to chance factors and not the independent variables studied

Process Loss   Any aspect of group interaction that inhibits good problem solving

Propaganda   A deliberate, systematic attempt to advance a cause by manipulating mass attitudes and behaviors, often through misleading or emotionally charged information

Propinquity Effect   The finding that the more we see and interact with people, the more likely they are to become our friends

Prosocial Behavior   Any act performed with the goal of benefiting another person

Psychological Realism   The extent to which the psychological processes triggered in an experiment are similar to psychological processes that occur in everyday life

Public Compliance   Conforming to other people's behavior publicly without necessarily believing in what the other people are doing or saying

Random Assignment to Condition   A process ensuring that all participants have an equal chance of taking part in any condition of an experiment; through random assignment, researchers can be relatively certain that differences in the participants' personalities or backgrounds are distributed evenly across conditions

Random Selection   A way of ensuring that a sample of people is representative of a population by giving everyone in the population an equal chance of being selected for the sample

Reactance Theory   The idea that when people feel their freedom to perform a certain behavior is threatened, an unpleasant state of resistance is aroused, which they can reduce by performing the prohibited behavior

Realistic Conflict Theory   The idea that limited resources lead to conflict between groups and result in increased prejudice and discrimination

Reasons-Generated Attitude Change   Attitude change resulting from thinking about the reasons for one's attitudes; people assume that their attitudes match the reasons that are plausible and easy to verbalize

Reconstructive Memory   The process whereby memories of an event become distorted by information encountered after the event occurred

Recovered Memories   Recollections of a past event, such as sexual abuse, that have been forgotten or repressed

Relationship-Oriented Leaders   Leaders who are concerned more with workers' feelings and relationships

Replications   Repeating a study, often with different subject populations or in different settings

Representativeness Heuristic   A mental shortcut whereby people classify something according to how similar it is to a typical case

Resilience   Mild, transient reactions to stressful events, followed by a quick return to normal, healthy functioning

Retrieval   The process by which people recall information stored in their memories

Schemas   Mental structures people use to organize their knowledge about the social world around themes or subjects and that influence the information people notice, think about, and remember

Sexual Scripts   Sets of implicit rules that specify proper sexual behavior for a person in a given situation, varying with the person's gender, age, religion, social status, and peer group

Secure Attachment Style   An attachment style characterized by trust, a lack of concern with being abandoned, and the view that one is worthy and well liked

Self-Affirmation   In the context of dissonance theory, a way of reducing dissonance by reminding oneself of one or more of one's positive attributes

Self-Awareness Theory   The idea that when people focus their attention on themselves, they evaluate and compare their behavior to their internal standards and values

Self-Concept   The overall set of beliefs that people have about their personal attributes

Self-Esteem   People's evaluations of their own self-worth—that is, the extent to which they view themselves as good, competent, and decent

Self-Fulfilling Prophecy   An expectation of one's own or another person's behavior that comes true because of the tendency of the person holding it to act in ways that bring it about

Self-Handicapping   The strategy whereby people create obstacles and excuses for themselves so that if they do poorly on a task, they can avoid blaming themselves

Self-Perception Theory   The theory that when our attitudes and feelings are uncertain or ambiguous, we infer these states by observing our behavior and the situation in which it occurs

Self-Persuasion   A long-lasting form of attitude change that results from attempts at self-justification

Self-Serving Attributions   Explanations for one's successes that credit internal, dispositional factors and explanations for one's failures that blame external, situational factors

Social-Cognitive Learning Theory   The theory that people learn social behavior (e.g., aggression or altruism) in large part through observation and imitation of others and by cognitive processes such as plans, expectations, and beliefs

Social Cognition   How people think about themselves and the social world; more specifically, how people select, interpret, remember, and use social information to make judgments and decisions

Social Comparison Theory   The idea that we learn about our own abilities and attitudes by comparing ourselves to other people

Social Dilemma   A conflict in which the most beneficial action for an individual will, if chosen by most people, have harmful effects on everyone

Social Exchange Theory   The idea that people's feelings about a relationship depend on their perceptions of its rewards and costs, the kind of relationship they deserve, and their chances for having a better relationship with someone else

Social Facilitation   When people are in the presence of others and their individual performance can be evaluated, the tendency to perform better on simple tasks and worse on complex tasks

Social Identity   The part of a person's self-concept that is based on his or her identification with a nation, religious or political group, occupation, or other social affiliation

Social Impact Theory   The idea that conforming to social influence depends on the group's importance, immediacy, and the number of people in the group

Social Influence   The effect that the words, actions, or mere presence of other people have on our thoughts, feelings, attitudes, or behavior

Social Loafing   When people are in the presence of others and their individual performance cannot be evaluated, the tendency to perform worse on simple or unimportant tasks but better on complex or important tasks

Social Norms The implicit or explicit rules a group has for the acceptable behaviors, values, and beliefs of its members

Social Perception The study of how we form impressions of and make inferences about other people

Social Psychology The scientific study of the way in which people's thoughts, feelings, and behaviors are influenced by the real or imagined presence of other people

Social Roles Shared expectations in a group about how particular people are supposed to behave

Social Support The perception that others are responsive and receptive to one's needs

Social Tuning The process whereby people adopt another person's attitudes

Source Monitoring The process whereby people try to identify the source of their memories

Stereotype Threat The apprehension experienced by members of a group that their behavior might confirm a cultural stereotype

Stereotype A generalization about a group of people in which certain traits are assigned to virtually all members of the group, regardless of actual variation among the members

Storage The process by which people maintain in memory information they have acquired from the environment

Story Model The theory that jurors try to fit the evidence they hear at trial into a coherent story, and ultimately reach a verdict that best fits the story they have created

Stress The negative feelings and beliefs that arise whenever people feel unable to cope with demands from their environment

Subliminal Messages Words or pictures that are not consciously perceived but may nevertheless influence judgments, attitudes, and behaviors

Surveys Research in which a representative sample of people are asked (often anonymously) questions about their attitudes or behavior

Task-Contingent Rewards Rewards that are given for performing a task, regardless of how well the task is done

Task-Oriented Leaders Leaders who are concerned more with getting the job done than with workers' feelings and relationships

Tend-and-Befriend Response Responding to stress with nurturing activities designed to protect oneself and one's offspring (tending) and creating social networks that provide protection from threats (befriending)

Terror Management Theory The theory that holds that self-esteem serves as a buffer, protecting people from terrifying thoughts about their own mortality

Theory of Planned Behavior The idea that people's intentions are the best predictors of their deliberate behaviors, which are determined by their attitudes toward specific behaviors, subjective norms, and perceived behavioral control

Thin-Slicing Drawing meaningful conclusions about another person's personality or skills based on an extremely brief sample of behavior

Tit-for-Tat Strategy A means of encouraging cooperation by at first acting cooperatively but then always responding the way your opponent did (cooperatively or competitively) on the previous trial

Transactional Leaders Leaders who set clear, short-term goals and reward people who meet them

Transactive Memory The combined memory of a group that is more efficient than the memory of the individual members

Transformational Leaders Leaders who inspire followers to focus on common, long-term goals

Two-Factor Theory of Emotion The idea that emotional experience is the result of a two-step self-perception process in which people first experience physiological arousal and then seek an appropriate explanation for it

Two-Step Attribution Process Analyzing another person's behavior first by making an automatic internal attribution and only then thinking about possible situational reasons for the behavior, after which one may adjust the original internal attribution

Upward Social Comparison Comparing ourselves to people who are better than we are with regard to a particular trait or ability

Urban Overload Hypothesis The theory that people living in cities are constantly bombarded with stimulation and that they keep to themselves to avoid being overwhelmed by it

Weapons Effect The increase in aggression that can occur because of the mere presence of a gun or other weapon

Yale Attitude Change Approach The study of the conditions under which people are most likely to change their attitudes in response to persuasive messages, focusing on the source of the communication, the nature of the communication, and the nature of the audience

References

Aaker, J. L. (2000). Accessibility or diagnosticity? Disentangling the influence of culture on persuasion processes and attitudes. *Journal of Consumer Research, 26*, 340–357.

Aarts, H., & Dijksterhuis, A. (2003). The silence of the library: Environment, situational norm, and social behavior. *Journal of Personality and Social Psychology, 84*, 18–28.

Aarts, H., & Elliot, A. J. (Eds.). (2012). *Goal-directed behavior*. New York: Taylor & Francis.

ABC News. (2006). Strip-search case closed? http://abcnews.go.com/2020/strip-search-case-closed/story?id=2684890&singlePage=true

Abele, A. E., & Brack, S. (2013). Preference for other persons' traits is dependent on the kind of social relationship. *Social Psychology, 44*, 84–94.

Abelson, R. P., Kinder, D. R., Peters, M. D., & Fiske, S. T. (1982). Affective and semantic components in political person perception. *Journal of Personality and Social Psychology, 42*, 619–630.

Abrams, D., Marques, J. M., Bown, N., & Henson, M. (2000). Pro-norm and anti-norm deviance within and between groups. *Journal of Personality and Social Psychology, 78*, 906–912.

Abrams, D., Palmer, S. B., Rutland, A., Cameron, L., & Van de Vyer, J. (2014). Evaluations of and reasoning about normative and deviant ingroup and outgroup members: Development of the Black sheep effect. *Developmental Psychology, 50*, 258–270.

Abrams, D., Viki, G. T., Masser, B., & Bohner, G. (2003). Perceptions of stranger and acquaintance rape: The role of benevolent and hostile sexism in victim blame and rape proclivity. *Journal of Personality and Social Psychology, 84*, 111–125.

Abrams, D., Wetherell, M., Cochrane, S., Hogg, M. A., & Turner, J. C. (1990). Knowing what to think by knowing who you are: Self-categorization and the nature of norm formation, conformity and group polarization. *British Journal of Social Psychology, 29*, 97–119.

Acquisti, A., & Fong, C. M. (2014, October 26). An experiment in hiring discrimination via online social networks. Available at SSRN: http://ssrn.com/abstract=2031979 or http://dx.doi.org/10.2139/ssrn.2031979

Adams, G., Anderson, S. L., & Adonu, J. K. (2004). The cultural grounding of closeness and intimacy. In D. J. Mashek & A. Aron (Eds.), *Handbook of closeness and intimacy* (pp. 321–342). Mahwah, NJ: Erlbaum.

Adams, R. B., Jr., & Kleck, R. E. (2003). Perceived gaze direction and the processing of facial displays of emotion. *Psychological Science, 14*, 644–647.

Adams, R. B., Jr., Franklin, R. G., Jr., Rule, N. O., Freeman, J. B., Kveraga, K., Hadjikhani, N., et al. (2010). Culture, gaze, and the neural processing of fear expressions. *Social Cognitive and Affective Neuroscience, 5*, 340–348.

Adler, J. (1997, March 22). It's a wise father who knows . . . *Newsweek*, p. 73.

Adult obesity. (2011). Centers for Disease Control and Prevention. Retrieved November 1, 2011, from www.cdc.gov/obesity/data/adult.html

Agars, M. D. (2004). Reconsidering the impact of gender stereotypes on the advancement of women in organizations. *Psychology of Women Quarterly, 28*, 103–111.

Agerström, J., & Rooth, D-O. (2011). The role of automatic obesity stereotypes in real hiring discrimination. *Journal of Applied Psychology, 96*, 790–805.

Aguiar, P., Vala, J., Correia, I., & Pereira, C. (2008). Justice in our world and in that of others: Belief in a just world and reactions to victims. *Social Justice Research, 21*, 50–68.

Ahn, H.-K., Kim, H. J., & Aggarwal, P. (2014). Helping fellow beings: Anthropomorphized social causes and the role of anticipatory guilt. *Psychological Science, 25*(1), 224–229.

Aiello, J. R., & Douthitt, E. A. (2001). Social facilitation from Triplett to electronic performance monitoring. *Group Dynamics: Theory, Research, and Practice, 5*, 163–180.

Ainsworth, M. D. S., Blehar, M. C., Waters, E., & Wall, S. (1978). *Patterns of attachment: A psychological study of the strange situation*. Hillsdale, NJ: Erlbaum.

Ajzen, I. (1985). From intentions to actions: A theory of planned behavior. In J. Kuhl & J. Beckmann (Eds.), *Action control: From cognition to behavior* (pp. 11–39). Heidelberg, Germany: Springer-Verlag.

Ajzen, I., & Fishbein, M. (1980). *Understanding attitudes and predicting social behavior*. Englewood Cliffs, NJ: Prentice Hall.

Ajzen, I., & Sheikh, S. (2013). Action versus inaction: Anticipated affect in the theory of planned behavior. *Journal of Applied Social Psychology, 43*, 155–162.

Akert, R. M. (1998). *Terminating romantic relationships: The role of personal responsibility and gender*. Unpublished manuscript, Wellesley College, Wellesley, MA.

Akert, R. M., Chen, J., & Panter, A. T. (1991). *Facial prominence and stereotypes: The incidence and meaning of face-ism in print and television media*. Unpublished manuscript, Wellesley College, Wellesley, MA.

Aknin, L. B., Sandstrom, G. M., Dunn, E. W., & Norton, M. I. (2011). Investing in others: Prosocial spending for (pro)social change. In R. Biswas-Diener (Ed.), *Positive psychology as social change* (pp. 219–234). New York: Springer. doi:10.1007/978-90-481-9938-9_13

Akrami, N., Hedlund, L., & Ekehammar, B. (2007). Personality scale response latencies as self-schema indicators: The inverted-U effect revisited. *Personality and Individual Differences, 43*, 611–618.

Alaskan village copes with real-life impacts of global climate change. (2008, July 10). *Online News Hour*. Retrieved December 30, 2008, from www.pbs.org/newshour/bb/environment/july-dec08/alaskawarming_07-10.html

Albarracín, D., & Wyer, R. S., Jr. (2001). Elaborative and nonelaborative processing of a behavior-related communication. *Personality and Social Psychology Bulletin, 27*, 691–705.

Albarracín, D., Johnson, B. T., Fishbein, M., & Muellerleile, P. A. (2001). Theories of reasoned action and planned behavior as models of condom use: A meta-analysis. *Psychological Bulletin, 127*, 142–161.

Algoe, S. B. (2012). Find, remind, and bind: The functions of gratitude in everyday relationships. *Social and Personality Psychology Compass, 6*(6), 455–469. doi:10.1111/j.1751–004.2012.00439.x

Algoe, S. B., Fredrickson, B. L., & Gable, S. L. (2013). The social functions of the emotion of gratitude via expression. *Emotion, 13*, 605–609. doi:10.1037/a0032701

Allen, M., Donohue, W. A., & Griffin, A. (2003). Comparing the influence of parents and peers on the choice to use drugs. *Criminal Justice and Behavior, 30*, 163–186.

Allen, V. L. (1965). Situational factors in conformity. In L. Berkowitz (Ed.), *Advances in experimental social psychology* (Vol. 2, pp. 133–175). New York: Academic Press.

Allen, V. L., & Levine, J. M. (1969). Consensus and conformity. *Journal of Personality and Social Psychology, 5*, 389–399.

Allison, P. D. (1992). The cultural evolution of beneficent norms. *Social Forces, 71*, 279–301.

Allmendinger, J., & Hackman, J. R. (1995). The more, the better? A four-nation study of the inclusion of women in symphony orchestras. *Social Forces, 74*, 423–460.

Allport, G. W. (1954). *The nature of prejudice*. Reading, MA: Addison-Wesley.

Allport, G. W. (1985). The historical background of social psychology. In G. Lindzey & E. Aronson (Eds.), *The handbook of social psychology* (3rd ed., Vol. 1, pp. 1–46). New York: McGraw-Hill.

ALSA. (2014). The ALS Association expresses sincere gratitude to over three million donors. Retrieved August 29, 2014, from www.alsa.org/news/media/press-releases/ice-bucket-challenge-082914.html

Alter, A. L., & Darley, J. M. (2009). When the association between appearance and outcome contaminates social judgment: A bidirectional model linking group homogeneity and collective treatment. *Journal of Personality and Social Psychology, 9*, 776–795. doi:10.1037/a0016957

Alvarez, K., & Van Leeuwen, E. (2011). To teach or to tell? Consequences of receiving help from experts and peers. *European Journal of Social Psychology, 41*(3), 397–402. doi:10.1002/ejsp.789

Alvarez, L. (2003, June 22). Arranged marriages get a little rearranging. *The New York Times*, p. 3.

Amato, P. R. (1983). Helping behavior in urban and rural environments: Field studies based on a taxonomic organization of helping episodes. *Journal of Personality and Social Psychology, 45*, 571–586.

Ambady, N., & Rosenthal, R. (1992). Thin slices of expressive behavior as predictors of interpersonal consequences: A meta-analysis. *Psychological Bulletin, 111*, 256–274.

Ambady, N., & Rosenthal, R. (1993). Half a minute: Predicting teacher evaluations from thin slices of nonverbal behavior and physical attractiveness. *Journal of Personality and Social Psychology, 64*, 431–441.

Ambady, N., Bernieri, F. J., & Richeson, J. A. (2000). Toward a histology of social behavior: Judgmental accuracy from thin slices of the behavioral stream. In M. P. Zanna (Ed.), *Advances in experimental social psychology* (Vol. 32, pp. 201–271). San Diego, CA: Academic Press.

Ambady, N., LaPlante, D., Nguen, T., Rosenthal, R., & Levinson, W. (2002). Surgeon's tone of voice: A clue to malpractice history. *Surgery, 132*, 5–9.

The American freshman: National norms for 2005. (2006). Higher Education Research Institute, UCLA. Retrieved June 22, 2006, from www.gseis.ucla.edu/heri/PDFs/ResearchBrief05.PDF

American Psychological Association. (2010). Ethical principles of psychologists and code of conduct. Retrieved March 22, 2010, from www.apa.org/ethics/code/index.aspx

Ames, D. R., & Flynn, F. J. (2007). What breaks a leader: The curvilinear relation between assertiveness and leadership. *Journal of Personality and Social Psychology, 92*, 307–324.

Ames, D. R., & Johar, G. V. (2009). I'll know what you're like when I see how you feel: How and when affective displays influence behavior-based impressions. *Psychological Science, 20*, 586–593.

Amir, I. (1976). The role of intergroup contact in change of prejudice and ethnic relations. In P. A. Katz (Ed.), *Towards the elimination of racism* (pp. 245–308). New York: Pergamon Press.

Amodio, D. M., & Showers, C. J. (2005). 'Similarity breeds liking' revisited: The moderating role of commitment. *Journal of Social and Personal Relationships, 22,* 817–836.

Andersen, B., Farrar, W. B., Golden-Kreutz, D. M., Glaser, R., Emery, C. F., & Crespin, T. R. (2004). Psychological, behavioral, and immune changes after a psychological intervention: A clinical trial. *Journal of Clinical Oncology, 22,* 3570–3580.

Andersen, S. M. (1984). Self-knowledge and social inference: II. The diagnosticity of cognitive/affective and behavioral data. *Journal of Personality and Social Psychology, 46,* 294–307.

Andersen, S. M., & Bem, S. L. (1981). Sex typing and androgyny in dyadic interaction: Individual differences in responsiveness to physical attractiveness. *Journal of Personality and Social Psychology, 41,* 74–86.

Andersen, S. M., & Klatzky, R. L. (1987). Traits and social stereotypes: Levels of categorization in person perception. *Journal of Personality and Social Psychology, 53,* 235–246.

Andersen, S. M., & Ross, L. D. (1984). Self-knowledge and social inference: I. The impact of cognitive/affective and behavioral data. *Journal of Personality and Social Psychology, 46,* 280–293.

Anderson, C. A. (1995). Implicit personality theories and empirical data: Biased assimilation, belief perseverance and change, and covariation detection sensitivity. *Social Cognition, 13,* 25–48.

Anderson, C. A. (1999). Attributional style, depression, and loneliness: A cross-cultural comparison of American and Chinese students. *Personality and Social Psychology Bulletin, 25,* 482–499.

Anderson, C. A. (2012). Climate change and violence. In D. J. Christie (Ed.), *The encyclopedia of peace psychology.* New York: Wiley-Blackwell.

Anderson, C. A., & Bushman, B. J. (1997). External validity of "trivial" experiments: The case of laboratory aggression. *Review of General Psychology, 1,* 19–41.

Anderson, C. A., & Dill, K. E. (2000). Video games and aggressive thoughts, feelings, and behavior in the laboratory and in life. *Journal of Personality and Social Psychology, 78,* 772–790.

Anderson, C. A., Anderson, K. B., Dorr, N., DeNeve, K. M., & Flanagan, M. (2000). Temperature and aggression. In M. P. Zanna (Ed.), *Advances in experimental social psychology* (Vol. 32, pp. 63–133). San Diego, CA: Academic Press.

Anderson, C. A., Benjamin, A. J., Jr., & Bartholow, B. D. (1998). Does the gun pull the trigger? Automatic priming effects of weapon pictures and weapon names. *Psychological Science, 9,* 308–314.

Anderson, C. A., Berkowitz, L., Donnerstein, E., Huesmann, L. R., Johnson, J. D., et al. (2003). The influence of media violence on youth. *Psychological Science in the Public Interest, 4,* 81–110.

Anderson, C. A., Lepper, M. R., & Ross, L. (1980). The perseverance of social theories: The role of explanation in the persistence of discredited information. *Journal of Personality and Social Psychology, 39,* 1037–1049.

Anderson, C. S., Shibuya, A., Ihori, N., Swing, E. L., Bushman, B. J., Sakamoto, A., Rothstein, H. R., & Saleem, M. (2010). Violent video game effects on aggression, empathy, and prosocial behavior in Eastern and Western countries: A meta-analytic review. *Psychological Bulletin, 136,* 151–173.

Anderson, E., Siegel, E., White, D., & Barrett, L. F. (2012). Out of sight but not out of mind: Unseen affective faces influence evaluations and social impressions. *Emotion, 12*(6), 1210–1221. doi:10.1037/a0027514

Anderson, J. R., & Gallup, G. G., Jr. (2011). Do rhesus monkeys recognize themselves in mirrors? *American Journal of Primatology, 73,* 603–606.

Anderson, N. B. (1989). Racial differences in stress-induced cardiovascular reactivity and hypertension: Current status and substantive issues. *Psychological Bulletin, 105,* 89–105.

Anderson, S. L., Adams, G., & Plaut, V. C. (2008). The cultural grounding of personal relationship: The importance of attractiveness in everyday life. *Journal of Personality and Social Psychology, 95,* 352–368.

Anderson, U. S., Perea, E. F., Becker, D. V., Ackerman, J. M., Shapiro, J. R., Neuberg, S. L., & Kenrick, D. T. (2010). I only have eyes for you: Ovulation redirects attention (but not memory) to attractive men. *Journal of Experimental Social Psychology, 46,* 804–808.

Andrade, E. B., & Van Boven, L. (2010). Feelings not forgone: Underestimating affective reactions to what does not happen. *Psychological Science, 21*(5), 706–711.

Angier, N. (2006, January 3). The cute factor. *The New York Times,* pp. D1–D8.

Antoni, M. H., & Lutgendorf, S. (2007). Psychosocial factors and disease progression in cancer. *Current Directions in Psychological Science, 16,* 42–46.

Anzures, G., Quinn, P. C., Pascalis, O., Slater, A. M., Tanaka, J. W., & Lee, K. (2013). Developmental origins of the other-race effect. *Current Directions in Psychological Science, 22,* 173–178.

Apfelbaum, E. P., Phillips, K. W., & Richeson, J. A. (2014). Rethinking the baseline in diversity research: Should we be explaining the effects of homogeneity? *Perspectives on Psychological Science, 9,* 235–244.

Applebome, P. (1991, November 10). Duke: The ex-Nazi who would be governor. *New York Times.* Retrieved February 17, 2015, from http://www.nytimes.com/1991/11/10/us/duke-the-ex-nazi-who-would-be-governor.html

The AP-GfK Poll. (2014, March). Retrieved April 28, 2014, from http://ap-gfkpoll.com/main/wp-content/uploads/2014/03/AP-GfK-March-2014-Poll-Topline-Final_POLITICS1.pdf

Arad, A. (2013). Past decisions do affect future choices: An experimental demonstration. *Organizational Behavior and Human Decision Processes, 121,* 267–277.

Archer, D. (1991). *A world of gestures: Culture and nonverbal communication* [Videotape and manual]. Berkeley: University of California Extension Center for Media and Independent Learning.

Archer, D. (1994). American violence: How high and why? *Law Studies, 19,* 12–20.

Archer, D. (1997a). Unspoken diversity: Cultural differences in gestures. *Qualitative Sociology, 20,* 79–105.

Archer, D. (1997b). *A world of differences: Understanding cross-cultural communication* [Videotape and manual]. Berkeley: University of California Extension Center for Media and Independent Learning.

Archer, D., & Akert, R. M. (1984). Problems of context and criterion in nonverbal communication: A new look at the accuracy issue. In M. Cook (Ed.), *Issues in person perception* (pp. 114–144). New York: Methuen.

Archer, D., & McDaniel, P. (1995). Violence and gender: Differences and similarities across societies. In R. B. Ruback & N. A. Weiner (Eds.), *Interpersonal violent behaviors: Social and cultural aspects* (pp. 63–88). New York: Springer-Verlag.

Archer, D., Iritani, B., Kimes, D. D., & Barrios, M. (1983). Face-ism: Five studies of sex differences in facial prominence. *Journal of Personality and Social Psychology, 45,* 725–735.

Archer, J. (2004). Sex differences in aggression in real-world settings: A meta-analytic review. *Review of General Psychology, 8,* 291–322.

Archer, J. (2013). Can evolutionary principles explain patterns of family violence? *Psychological Bulletin, 139*(2), 403–440. doi:10.1037/a0029114

Archer, J., & Coyne, S. M. (2005). An integrated review of indirect, relational, and social aggression. *Personality and Social Psychology Review, 9,* 212–230.

Arendt, H. (1965). *Eichmann in Jerusalem: A report on the banality of evil.* New York: Viking.

Argyle, M. (1975). *Bodily communication.* New York: International Universities Press.

Argyle, M. (1986). Rules for social relationships in four cultures. *Australian Journal of Psychology, 38,* 309–318.

Arkes, H. R., & Mellers, B. A. (2002). Do juries meet our expectations? *Law and Human Behavior, 26,* 625–639.

Arkes, H., & Tetlock, P. (2004). Attributions of implicit prejudice, or "Would Jesse Jackson 'fail'

the Implicit Association Test?" *Psychological Inquiry, 15,* 257–278.

Arkin, R. M., & Maruyama, G. M. (1979). Attribution, affect, and college exam performance. *Journal of Educational Psychology, 71,* 85–93.

Arkin, R. M., & Oleson, K. C. (1998). Self-handicapping. In J. M. Darley & J. Cooper (Eds.), *Attribution and social interaction: The legacy of Edward E. Jones* (pp. 313–341). Washington, DC: American Psychological Association.

Armata, P. M., & Baldwin, D. R. (2008). Stress, optimism, resiliency, and cortisol with relation to digestive symptoms or diagnosis. *Individual Differences Research, 6,* 123–138.

Arms, R. L., Russell, G. W., & Sandilands, M. L. (1979). Effects on the hostility of spectators of viewing aggressive sports. *Social Psychology Quarterly, 42,* 275–279.

Aron, A., & Aron, E. N. (1996). Self and self-expansion in relationships. In G. J. O. Fletcher & J. Fitness (Eds.), *Knowledge structures in close relationships: A social psychological approach* (pp. 325–344). Mahwah, NJ: Erlbaum.

Aron, A., & Rodriguez, G. (1992). Scenarios of falling in love among Mexican, Chinese, and Anglo-Americans. In A. Aron (Chair), *Ethnic and cultural differences in love.* Symposium conducted at the Sixth International Conference on Personal Relationships, Orono, ME.

Aron, A., & Westbay, L. (1996). Dimensions of the prototype of love. *Journal of Personality and Social Psychology, 70,* 535–551.

Aron, A., Aron, E. N., & Norman, C. (2004). Self-expansion model of motivation and cognition in close relationships and beyond. In M. B. Brewer & M. Hewstone (Eds.), *Self and social identity* (pp. 99–123). Malden, MA: Blackwell Publishing.

Aron, A., Dutton, D. G., Aron, E. N., & Iverson, A. (1989). Experiences of falling in love. *Journal of Social and Personal Relationships, 6,* 243–257.

Aron, A., Fisher, H., Mashek, D. J., Strong, G., Li, H., & Brown, L. L. (2005). Reward, motivation, and emotion systems associated with early-stage intense romantic love. *Journal of Neurophysiology, 94,* 327–337.

Aronson, E. (1969). The theory of cognitive dissonance: A current perspective. In L. Berkowitz (Ed.), *Advances in experimental social psychology* (Vol. 4, pp. 1–34). New York: Academic Press.

Aronson, E. (1978). *The jigsaw classroom.* Beverly Hills, CA: Sage.

Aronson, E. (1997). The theory of cognitive dissonance: The evolution and vicissitudes of an idea. In C. McGarty & S. A. Haslam (Eds.), *The message of social psychology: Perspectives on mind in society* (pp. 20–35). Malden, MA: Blackwell.

Aronson, E. (1998). Dissonance, hypocrisy, and the self-concept. In E. Harmon-Jones & J. S. Mills (Eds.), *Cognitive dissonance theory: Revival with revisions and controversies* (pp. 21–36). Washington, DC: American Psychological Association.

Aronson, E. (1999). *The social animal* (8th ed.). New York: Worth/Freeman.

Aronson, E. (2000). *Nobody left to hate: Teaching compassion after Columbine.* New York: Worth/Freeman.

Aronson, E. (2002). Drifting my own way: Following my nose and my heart. In R. Sternberg (Ed.), *Psychologists defying the crowd: Stories of those who battled the establishment and won* (pp. 132–148). Washington, DC: American Psychological Association.

Aronson, E. (2007). The evolution of cognitive dissonance theory: A personal appraisal. In A. Pratkanis (Ed.), *The science of social influence.* New York: Psychology Press.

Aronson, E. (2008). *The social animal* (11th ed.). New York: W. H. Freeman.

Aronson, E. (2010a). Fear, denial, and sensible action in the face of disasters. *Social Research.*

Aronson, E. (2010b). *Not by chance alone: My life as a social psychologist.* New York: Basic Books.

Aronson, E. (2012). *The social animal.* New York: W. H. Freeman.

Aronson, E., & Bridgeman, D. (1979). Jigsaw groups and the desegregated classroom: In pursuit of common goals. *Personality and Social Psychology Bulletin, 5,* 438–446.

Aronson, E., & Carlsmith, J. M. (1962). Performance expectancy as a determinant of actual performance. *Journal of Abnormal and Social Psychology, 65*, 178–182.

Aronson, E., & Carlsmith, J. M. (1963). Effect of severity of threat in the devaluation of forbidden behavior. *Journal of Abnormal and Social Psychology, 66*, 584–588.

Aronson, E., & Carlsmith, J. M. (1968). Experimentation in social psychology. In G. Lindzey & E. Aronson (Eds.), *The handbook of social psychology* (Vol. 2, pp. 1–79). Reading, MA: Addison-Wesley.

Aronson, E., & Gonzalez, A. (1988). Desegregation, jigsaw, and the Mexican-American experience. In P. A. Katz & D. Taylor (Eds.), *Towards the elimination of racism: Profiles in controversy* (pp. 310–330). New York: Plenum.

Aronson, E., & Linder, D. (1965). Gain and loss of esteem as determinants of interpersonal attractiveness. *Journal of Experimental Social Psychology, 1*, 156–171.

Aronson, E., & Mettee, D. (1968). Dishonest behavior as a function of differential levels of induced self-esteem. *Journal of Personality and Social Psychology, 9*, 121–127.

Aronson, E., & Mills, J. S. (1959). The effect of severity of initiation on liking for a group. *Journal of Abnormal and Social Psychology, 59*, 177–181.

Aronson, E., & Patnoe, S. (1997). *Cooperation in the classroom: The jigsaw method*. New York: Longman.

Aronson, E., & Patnoe, S. (2011). *Cooperation in the classroom: The jigsaw method*. London, England: Pinter & Martin. Available in the U.S. through Amazon Digital Services as a Kindle edition.

Aronson, E., & Thibodeau, R. (1992). The jigsaw classroom: A cooperative strategy for reducing prejudice. In J. Lynch, C. Modgil, & S. Modgil (Eds.), *Cultural diversity in the schools* (pp. 110–118). London: Falmer Press.

Aronson, E., Ellsworth, P. C., Carlsmith, J. M., & Gonzalez, M. H. (1990). *Methods of research in social psychology* (2nd ed.). New York: McGraw-Hill.

Aronson, E., Fried, C., & Stone, J. (1991). Overcoming denial and increasing the intention to use condoms through the induction of hypocrisy. *American Journal of Public Health, 81*, 1636–1638.

Aronson, E., Stephan, C., Sikes, J., Blaney, N., & Snapp, M. (1978). *The jigsaw classroom*. Beverly Hills, CA: Sage.

Aronson, E., Wilson, T. D., & Brewer, M. B. (1998). Experimental methods. In D. T. Gilbert, S. T. Fiske, & G. Lindzey (Eds.), *The handbook of social psychology* (4th ed., Vol. 1, pp. 99–142). New York: McGraw-Hill.

Aronson, J. (2009). Jigsaw, social psychology, and the nurture of human intelligence. In *The scientist and the humanist: A festschrift in honor of Elliot Aronson*. New York: Taylor & Francis.

Aronson, J. (2010). Jigsaw, social psychology, and the nurture of human intelligence. In *The scientist and the humanist: A festschrift in honor of Elliot Aronson*. New York: Taylor & Francis.

Aronson, J. M., Cohen, G., & Nail, P. R. (1999). Self-affirmation theory: An update and appraisal. In E. Harmon-Jones & J. S. Mills (Eds.), *Cognitive dissonance: Progress on a pivotal theory in social psychology* (pp. 127–147). Washington, DC: American Psychological Association.

Aronson, J. M., Lustina, M. J., Good, C., Keough, K., Steele, C. M., & Brown, J. (1999). When White men can't do math: Necessary and sufficient factors in stereotype threat. *Journal of Experimental Social Psychology, 35*, 29–46.

Aronson, J., & McGlone, M. (2009). Stereotype threat. In T. Nelson (Ed.), *The handbook of prejudice, stereotyping, and discrimination* (pp. 153–179). New York: Psychology Press.

Aronson, J., & Williams, J. (2009). *Stereotype threat: Forewarned is forearmed*. Manuscript under review.

Aronson, J., Fried, C. B., & Good, C. (2002). Reducing the effects of stereotype threat on African American college students by shaping theories of intelligence. *Journal of Experimental Social Psychology, 38*, 113–125.

Arsena, A., Silvera, D. H., & Pandelaere, M. (2014). Brand trait transference: When celebrity endorsers acquire brand personality traits. *Journal of Business Research*. Advance online publication. doi: http://dx.doi.org/10.1016/j.jbusres.2014.01.011

Asch, S. E. (1946). Forming impressions of personality. *Journal of Abnormal and Social Psychology, 41*, 258–290.

Asch, S. E. (1951). Effects of group pressure upon the modification and distortion of judgment. In H. Guetzkow (Ed.), *Groups, leadership, and men* (pp. 76–92). Pittsburgh, PA: Carnegie Press.

Asch, S. E. (1955). Opinions and social pressure. *Scientific American, 193*, 31–35.

Asch, S. E. (1956). Studies of independence and conformity: A minority of one against a unanimous majority. *Psychological Monographs, 7* (9, Whole No. 416).

Asch, S. E. (1957). An experimental investigation of group influence. In Walter Reed Army Institute of Research, *Symposium on preventive and social psychiatry* (pp. 15–17). Washington, DC: U.S. Government Printing Office.

Ashmore, R. D., & Longo, L. C. (1995). Accuracy of stereotypes: What research on physical attractiveness can teach us. In Y.-T. Lee, L. J. Jussim, & C. R. McCauley (Eds.), *Stereotype accuracy: Toward appreciating group difference* (pp. 63–86). Washington, DC: American Psychological Association.

Aspinwall, L. G., & Taylor, S. E. (1993). Effects of social comparison direction, threat, and self-esteem on affect, evaluation, and expected success. *Journal of Personality and Social Psychology, 64*, 708–722.

Aspinwall, L. G., & Taylor, S. E. (1997). A stitch in time: Self-regulation and proactive coping. *Psychological Bulletin, 121*, 417–436.

Associated Press. (2002, November 1). Halloween is debated by French. *The Boston Globe*, p. A20.

Augustinova, M., & Ferrand, L. (2012). The influence of mere social presence of Stroop interference: New evidence from the semantically-based Stroop task. *Journal of Experimental Social Psychology, 48*, 1213–1216.

Aune, K. S., & Aune, R. K. (1996). Cultural differences in the self-reported experience and expression of emotions in relationships. *Journal of Cross-Cultural Psychology, 27*, 67–81.

Avolio, B. J., Walumbwa, F. O., & Weber, T. J. (2009). Leadership: Current theories, research, and future directions. *Annual Review of Psychology, 60*, 421–449.

Aycan, Z., Schyns, B., Sun, J., Felfe, J., & Saher, N. (2013). Convergence and divergence of paternalistic leadership: A cross-cultural investigation of prototypes. *Journal of International Business Studies, 44*, 962–969.

Ayman, R. (2002). Contingency model of leadership effectiveness. In L. L. Neider & C. A. Schriesheim (Eds.), *Leadership* (pp. 197–228). Greenwich, CT: Information Age.

Ayman, R., & Korabik, K. (2010). Leadership: Why gender and culture matter. *American Psychologist, 65*(3), 157–170. doi:10.1037/a0018806

Azrin, N. H. (1967, May). Pain and aggression. *Psychology Today*, pp. 27–33.

Back, M. D., Schmukle, S. C., & Egloff, B. (2008). Becoming friends by chance. *Psychological Science, 19*, 439–440.

Badr, L. K., & Abdallah, B. (2001). Physical attractiveness of premature infants affects outcome at discharge from the NICU. *Infant Behavior and Development, 24*, 129–133.

Bailey, D. S., & Taylor, S. P. (1991). Effects of alcohol and aggressive disposition on human physical aggression. *Journal of Research in Personality, 25*(3), 334–342.

Baird, B., Smallwood, J., Fishman, D. J. F., Mrazek, M. D., & Schooler, J. W. (2013). Unnoticed intrusions: Dissociations of meta-consciousness in thought suppression. *Consciousness and Cognition: An International Journal, 22*(3), 1003–1012.

Baldwin, M. W., & Fehr, B. (1995). On the instability of attachment style ratings. *Personal Relationships, 2*, 247–261.

Baldwin, M. W., Keelan, J. P. R., Fehr, B., Enns, V., & Koh-Rangarajoo, E. (1996). Social-cognitive conceptualizations of attachment working models: Availability and accessibility effects. *Journal of Personality and Social Psychology, 71*, 94–109.

Balsam, K. F., Beauchaine, T. P., Rothblum, E. D., & Solomon, S. E. (2008). Three-year follow-up of same-sex couples who had civil unions in Vermont, same-sex couples not in civil unions, and heterosexual married couples. *Developmental Psychology, 44*, 102–116.

Banaji, M. R., & Greenwald, A. G. (2013). *Blindspot: Hidden biases of good people*. New York: Delacorte.

Banaji, M. R., & Heiphetz, L. (2010). Attitudes. In S. T. Fiske, D. T. Gilbert, & G. Lindzey (Eds.), *Handbook of social psychology* (5th ed., Vol. 1, pp. 353–393). Hoboken, NJ: Wiley.

Banas, J. A., & Miller, G. (2013). Inducing resistance to conspiracy theory propaganda: Testing inoculation and metainoculation strategies. *Human Communication Research, 39*, 184–207.

Bandura, A., Ross, D., & Ross, S. (1961). Transmission of aggression through imitation of aggressive models. *Journal of Abnormal and Social Psychology, 63*, 575–582.

Bandura, A., Ross, D., & Ross, S. (1963). Imitation of film-mediated aggressive models. *Journal of Abnormal and Social Psychology, 66*, 3–11.

Banuazizi, A., & Movahedi, S. (1975). Interpersonal dynamics in a simulated prison: A methodological analysis. *American Psychologist, 30*, 152–160.

Bar, M., Neta, M., & Linz, H. (2006). Very first impressions. *Emotion, 6*, 269–278.

Bar-Anan, Y., Wilson, T. D., & Hassin, R. R. (2010). Inaccurate self-knowledge formation as a result of automatic behavior. *Journal of Experimental Social Psychology, 46*(6), 884–894. doi:10.1016/j.jesp.2010.07.007

Bargh, J. A. (1996). Automaticity in social psychology. In E. T. Higgins & A. W. Kruglanski (Eds.), *Social psychology: Handbook of basic principles* (pp. 169–183). New York: Guilford Press.

Bargh, J. A. (2013). Social psychology cares about causal conscious thought, not free will per se. *British Journal of Social Psychology, 52*(2), 228–230. doi:10.1111/bjso.12011

Bargh, J. A., & Pietromonaco, P. (1982). Automatic information processing and social perception: The influence of trait information presented outside of conscious awareness on impression formation. *Journal of Personality and Social Psychology, 43*, 437–449.

Bargh, J. A., Schwader, K. L., Hailey, S. E., Dyer, R. L., & Boothby, E. J. (2012). Automaticity in social-cognitive processes. *Trends in Cognitive Sciences, 16*(12), 593–605. doi:10.1016/j.tics.2012.10.002

Bargh, J. A. (2011). Unconscious thought theory and its discontents: A critique of the critiques. *Social Cognition, 29*, 629–647.

Barkan, R., Ayal, S., Gino, F., & Ariely, D. (2012). The pot calling the kettle Black: Distancing response to ethical dissonance. *Journal of Experimental Psychology: General, 141*, 757–773.

Barker, R., Dembo, T., & Lewin, K. (1941). Frustration and aggression: An experiment with young children. *University of Iowa Studies in Child Welfare, 18*, 1–314.

Barley, S. R., & Bechky, B. A. (1994). In the backrooms of science: The work of technicians in science labs. *Work and Occupations, 21*, 85–126.

Baron, R. A. (1972). Reducing the influence of an aggressive model: The restraining effects of peer censure. *Journal of Experimental Social Psychology, 8*, 266–275.

Baron, R. A. (1976). The reduction of human aggression: A field study on the influence of incompatible responses. *Journal of Applied Social Psychology, 6*, 95–104.

Baron, R. A. (1988). Negative effects of destructive criticism: Impact on conflict, self-efficacy, and task performance. *Journal of Applied Psychology, 73*, 199–207.

Baron, R. A. (1990). Countering the effects of destructive criticism: The relative efficacy of four interventions. *Journal of Applied Psychology, 75*, 235–245.

Baron, R. A. (1997). The sweet smell of . . . helping: Effects of pleasant ambient fragrance on prosocial behavior in shopping malls. *Personality and Social Psychology Bulletin, 23*, 498–503.

Baron, R. A., & Richardson, D. R. (1994). *Human aggression* (2nd ed.). New York: Plenum.

Baron, R. M., & Misovich, S. J. (1993). Dispositional knowing from an ecological perspective. *Personality and Social Psychology Bulletin, 19*, 541–552.

Baron, R. S. (1986). Distraction/conflict theory: Progress and problems. In L. Berkowitz (Ed.), *Advances in experimental social psychology* (Vol. 19, pp. 1–40). Orlando, FL: Academic Press.

Baron, R. S. (2005). So right it's wrong: Groupthink and the ubiquitous nature of polarized group decision making. In M. P. Zanna (Ed.), *Advances in experimental social psychology* (Vol. 37, pp. 219–253). San Diego, CA: Academic Press.

Baron, R. S., Vandello, J. A., & Brunsman, B. (1996). The forgotten variable in conformity research: Impact of task importance on social influence. *Journal of Personality and Social Psychology, 71*, 915–927.

Barrett, L. F., Mesquita, B., & Gendron, M. (2011). Context in emotion perception. *Current Directions in Psychological Science, 20*, 286–290.

Barrouquere, B. (2006, June 15). A call, a hoax, a nationwide search for the man on the phone. *Associated Press*. Retrieved August 25, 2006, from 0-web.lexis-nexis.com

Barsalou, L. W. (2008). Grounded cognition. *Annual Review of Psychology, 59*, 617–645.

Bartels, A., & Zeki, S. (2004). The neural correlates of maternal and romantic love. *Neuroimage, 21*, 1155–1166.

Bartlett, F. C. (1932). *Remembering*. Cambridge, UK: Cambridge University Press.

Bartlett, M. Y., & DeSteno, D. (2006). Gratitude and prosocial behavior: Helping when it costs you. *Psychological Science, 17*, 319–325.

Bass, B. M. (1998). *Transformational leadership: Industry, military, and educational impact*. Mahwah, NJ: Erlbaum.

Batson, C. D. (1991). *The altruism question: Toward a social-psychological answer*. Hillsdale, NJ: Erlbaum.

Batson, C. D. (1993). Communal and exchange relationships: What's the difference? *Personality and Social Psychology Bulletin, 19*, 677–683.

Batson, C. D. (2011). *Altruism in humans*. New York: Oxford University Press.

Batson, C. D. (2012). A history of prosocial behavior research. In A. W. Kruglanski & W. Stroebe (Eds.), *Handbook of the history of social psychology* (pp. 243–264). New York: Psychology Press.

Batson, C. D., & Powell, A. A. (2003). Altruism and prosocial behavior. In T. Millon & M. J. Lerner (Eds.), *Handbook of psychology: Personality and social psychology* (Vol. 5, pp. 463–484). New York: Wiley.

Batson, C. D., Ahmad, N., & Stocks, E. L. (2004). Benefits and liabilities of empathy-induced altruism. In A. G. Miller (Ed.), *The social psychology of good and evil* (pp. 359–385). New York: Guilford.

Batson, C. D., Ahmad, N., & Stocks, E. L. (2011). Four forms of prosocial motivation: Egoism, altruism, collectivism, and principlism. In D. Dunning (Ed.), *Frontiers of social psychology. Social motivation* (pp. 103–126). New York: Psychology Press.

Batson, C. D., Ahmad, N., Lishner, D. A., & Tsang, J. (2002). Empathy and altruism. In C. R. Snyder & S. J. Lopez (Eds.), *Handbook of positive psychology* (pp. 485–498). New York: Oxford University Press.

Batson, C. D., Coke, J. S., Jasnoski, M. L., & Hanson, M. (1978). Buying kindness: Effect of an extrinsic incentive for helping on perceived altruism. *Personality and Social Psychology Bulletin, 4*, 86–91.

Batson, C. D., Polycarpou, M. P., Harmon-Jones, E., Imhoff, H. J., Mitchener, E. C., Bednar, L. L., Klein, T. R., & Highberger, L. (1997). Empathy and attitudes: Can feeling for a member of a stigmatized group improve feelings toward the group? *Journal of Personality and Social Psychology, 72*, 105–118.

Batson, C. D., Sager, K., Garst, E., Kang, M., Rubchinsky, K., & Dawson, K. (1997). Is empathy-induced helping due to self-other merging? *Journal of Personality and Social Psychology, 73*, 495–509.

Batson, C. D., Schoenrade, P., & Ventis, W. L. (1993). *Religion and the individual*. New York: Oxford University Press.

Battle for your brain. (1991, August). *Consumer Reports*, pp. 520–521.

Bauer, I., & Wrosch, C. (2011). Making up for lost opportunities: The protective role of downward social comparisons for coping with regrets across adulthood. *Personality and Social Psychology Bulletin, 37*, 215–228. doi:10.1177/0146167210393256

Baumeister, R. (Ed.). (1993). *Self-esteem: The puzzle of low self-regard*. New York: Plenum.

Baumeister, R. F. (1991). *Escaping the self: Alcoholism, spirituality, masochism, and other flights from the burden of selfhood*. New York: Basic Books.

Baumeister, R. F., & Hetherington, T. F. (1996). Self-regulation failure: An overview. *Psychological Inquiry, 7*, 1–15.

Baumeister, R. F., & Leary, M. R. (1995). The need to belong: Desire for interpersonal attachment as a fundamental human motivation. *Psychological Bulletin, 117*, 497–529.

Baumeister, R. F., & Masicampo, E. J. (2010). Conscious thought is for facilitating social and cultural interactions: How mental simulations serve the animal–culture interface. *Psychological Review, 117*(3), 945–971. doi:10.1037/a0019393

Baumeister, R. F., & Sommer, K. L. (1997). What do men want? Gender differences and two spheres of belongingness: Comment on Cross and Madson (1997). *Psychological Bulletin, 122*, 38–44.

Baumeister, R. F., Campbell, J. D., Krueger, J. I., & Vohs, K. D. (2003). Does high self-esteem cause better performance, interpersonal success, happiness, or healthier lifestyles? *Psychological Science in the Public Interest, 4*, 1–44. doi:10.1111/1529-1006.01431

Baumeister, R. F., Masicampo, E. J., & Vohs, K. D. (2011). Can consciousness cause behavior? *Annual Review of Psychology, 62*, 331–361.

Baumeister, R. F., Schmeichel, B. J., & Vohs, K. D. (2007). Self-regulation and the executive function: The self as controlling agent. In E. T. Higgins & A. W. Kruglanski (Eds.), *Social psychology: Handbook of basic principles* (2nd ed., pp. 516–534). New York: Guilford.

Baumeister, R., Vohs, K., & Tice, D. (2007). The strength model of self-control. *Current Directions in Psychological Science, 16*, 351–355.

Baumgardner, A. H., Lake, E. A., & Arkin, R. M. (1985). Claiming mood as a self-handicap. *Personality and Social Psychology Bulletin, 11*, 349–357.

Baumrind, D. (1964). Some thoughts on ethics of research: After reading Milgram's "Behavioral study of obedience". *American Psychologist, 19*, 421–423.

Baumrind, D. (1985). Research using intentional deception: Ethical issues revisited. *American Psychologist, 40*, 165–174.

Baxter, L. A. (1986). Gender differences in the heterosexual relationship rules embedded in break-up accounts. *Journal of Social and Personal Relationships, 3*, 289–306.

Bayat, M. (2011). Clarifying issues regarding the use of praise with young children. *Topics in Early Childhood Special Education, 31*, 121–128. doi:10.1177/0271121410389339

Beach, S. R. H., Tesser, A., Mendolia, M., & Anderson, P. (1996). Self-evaluation maintenance in marriage: Toward a performance ecology of the marital relationship. *Journal of Family Psychology, 10*, 379–396.

Beaman, A. L., Barnes, P. J., Klentz, B., & McQuirk, B. (1978). Increasing helping rates through informational dissemination: Teaching pays. *Personality and Social Psychology Bulletin, 4*, 406–411.

Beaman, A. L., Klentz, B., Diener, E., & Svanum, S. (1979). Objective self-awareness and transgression in children: A field study. *Journal of Personality and Social Psychology, 37*, 1835–1846.

Beauvois, J., & Joule, R. (1996). *A radical dissonance theory*. London: Taylor & Francis.

Becker, D. V., Kenrick, D. T., Neuberg, S. L., Blackwell, K. C., & Smith, D. M. (2007). The confounded nature of angry men and happy women. *Journal of Personality and Social Psychology, 92*, 179–190.

Becker, J. C., & Wright, S. C. (2011). Yet another dark side of chivalry: Benevolent sexism undermines and hostile sexism motivates collective action for social change. *Journal of Personality and Social Psychology, 101*, 62–77.

Beckett, K., Nyrop, K., & Pfingst, L. (2006). *Race, drugs, and policing: Understanding disparities in drug delivery arrests. Criminology, 44*, 105–137.

Beer, J. S., Chester, D. S., & Hughes, B. L. (2013). Social threat and cognitive load magnify self-enhancement and attenuate self-deprecation. *Journal of Experimental Social Psychology, 49*(4), 706–711. doi:10.1016/j.jesp.2013.02.017

Beer, J., & Ochsner, K. (2006). Social cognition: A multi level analysis. *Brain Research, 1079*, 98–105.

Bègue, L., Subra, B., Arvers, P., Muller, D., Bricout, V., & Zorman, M. (2009). A message in a bottle: Extrapharmacological effects of alcohol on aggression. *Journal of Experimental Social Psychology, 45*, 137–142.

Bell, J. (1995). Notions of love and romance among the Taita of Kenya. In W. Jankowiak (Ed.), *Romantic passion: A universal experience?* (pp. 152–165). New York: Columbia University Press.

Bell, S. T., Kuriloff, P. J., & Lottes, I. (1994). Understanding attributions of blame in stranger-rape and date-rape situations: An examination of gender, race, identification, and students' social perceptions of rape victims. *Journal of Applied Social Psychology, 24*, 1719–1734.

Bem, D. J. (1972). Self-perception theory. In L. Berkowitz (Ed.), *Advances in experimental social psychology* (Vol. 6, pp. 1–62). New York: Academic Press.

Bender, B. (2003, June 15). Scandals rock military academies. *Boston Globe*, p. A10.

Benedetti, P. (2007). Ontario removes video slot machines flashing winning images. *CBC News*. http://www.cbc.ca/news/canada/ontario-removes-video-slot-machines-flashing-winning-images-1.631835

Benjamin Jr, L. T., & Simpson, J. A. (2009). The power of the situation: The impact of Milgram's obedience studies on personality and social psychology. *American Psychologist, 64*, 12–19.

Ben-Ner, A., Putterman, L., Kong, F., & Magan, D. (2004). Reciprocity in a two-part dictator game. *Journal of Economic Behavior and Organization, 53*, 333–352.

Bergeron, N., & Schneider, B. H. (2005). Explaining cross-national differences in peer-directed aggression: A quantitative synthesis. *Aggressive Behavior, 31*, 116–137.

Berggren, N., Jordahl, H., & Poutvaara, P. (2010). The looks of a winner: Beauty and electoral success. *Journal of Public Economics, 94*, 8–15.

Berke, R. L. (2000, September 12). Democrats see, and smell, "rats" in GOP ad. *New York Times on the Web*, www.nytimes.com

Berkowitz, L. (1962). *Aggression: A social psychological analysis*. New York: McGraw-Hill.

Berkowitz, L. (1968, September). Impulse, aggression, and the gun. *Psychology Today*, pp. 18–22.

Berkowitz, L. (1978). Whatever happened to the frustration-aggression hypothesis? *American Behavioral Scientist, 21*, 691–708.

Berkowitz, L. (1983). Aversively simulated aggression. *American Psychologist, 38*, 1135–1144.

Berkowitz, L. (1989). Frustration-aggression hypothesis: Examination and reformulation. *Psychological Bulletin, 106*, 59–73.

Berkowitz, L. (1993). *Aggression: Its causes, consequences, and control*. New York: McGraw-Hill.

Berkowitz, L., & Le Page, A. (1967). Weapons as aggression-eliciting stimuli. *Journal of Personality and Social Psychology, 7*, 202–207.

Bermeitinger, C., Goelz, R., Johr, N., Neumann, M., Ecker, U. K. H., & Doerr, R. (2009). The hidden persuaders break into the tired brain. *Journal of Experimental Social Psychology*, 45(2), 320–326. doi:10.1016/j.jesp.2008.10.001

Berns, G. S., Chappelow, J., Zink, C. F., Pagnoni, G., Martin-Skurski, M. E., & Richards, J. (2005). Neurobiological correlates of social conformity and independence during mental rotation. *Biological Psychiatry*, 58, 245–253.

Berry, J. W. (1967). Independence and conformity in subsistence-level societies. *Journal of Personality and Social Psychology*, 7, 415–418.

Berscheid, E. (1985). Interpersonal attraction. In G. Lindzey & E. Aronson (Eds.), *The handbook of social psychology* (3rd ed., Vol. 3, pp. 413–484). New York: McGraw-Hill.

Berscheid, E., & Meyers, S. A. (1997). The language of love: The difference a preposition makes. *Personality and Social Psychology Bulletin*, 23, 347–362.

Berscheid, E., & Walster, E. (1978). *Interpersonal attraction*. Reading, MA: Addison-Wesley.

Berscheid, E., Boye, D., & Walster, E. (1968). Retaliation as a means of restoring equity. *Journal of Personality and Social Psychology*, 10, 370–376.

Bettencourt, B. A., & Miller, N. (1996). Gender differences in aggression as a function of provocation: A meta-analysis. *Psychological Bulletin*, 119, 422–447.

Bettencourt, B. A., & Sheldon, K. (2001). Social roles as mechanism for psychological need satisfaction within social groups. *Journal of Personality and Social Psychology*, 81, 1131–1143.

Bickman, L. (1974). The social power of a uniform. *Journal of Applied Social Psychology*, 4, 47–61.

Biehl, M., Matsumoto, D., Ekman, P., Hearn, V., Heider, K., Kudoh, T., & Ton, V. (1997). Matsumoto and Ekman's Japanese and Caucasian facial expressions of emotion (JACFEE): Reliability and cross-national differences. *Journal of Nonverbal Behavior*, 21, 3–21.

Biek, M., Wood, W., & Chaiken, S. (1996). Working knowledge, cognitive processing, and attitudes: On the determinants of bias. *Personality and Social Psychology Bulletin*, 22, 547–556.

Biesanz, J. C., Neuberg, S. L., Smith, D. M., Asher, T., & Judice, T. N. (2001). When accuracy-motivated perceivers fail: Limited attentional resources and the reemerging self-fulfilling prophecy. *Personality and Social Psychology Bulletin*, 27, 621–629.

Blackhart, G. C., Fitzpatrick, J., & Williamson, J. (2014). Dispositional factors predicting use of online dating sites and behaviors related to online dating. *Computers in Human Behavior*, 33, 113–118.

Blackhart, G. C., Nelson, B. C., Knowles, M. L., & Baumeister, R. F. (2009). Rejection elicits emotional reactions but neither causes immediate distress nor lowers self-esteem: A meta-analytic review of 192 studies on social exclusion. *Personality and Social Psychology Review*, 13(4), 269–309. doi:10.1177/1088868309346065

Blakemore, J. E. O., Berenbaum, S. A., & Liben, L. S. (2009). *Gender development*. New York: Psychology Press.

Blank, H., & Launay, C. (2014). How to protect eyewitness memory against the misinformation effect: A meta-analysis of post-warning studies. *Journal of Applied Research in Memory and Cognition*, 3, 77–88.

Blascovich, J., Mendes, W. B., Hunter, S. B., & Salomon, K. (1999). Social "facilitation" as challenge and threat. *Journal of Personality and Social Psychology*, 77, 68–77.

Blass, T. (1991). Understanding behavior in the Milgram obedience experiment. *Journal of Personality and Social Psychology*, 60, 398–413.

Blass, T. (2000). *Obedience to authority: Current perspectives on the Milgram paradigm*. Mahwah, NJ: Erlbaum.

Blass, T. (2003). The Milgram paradigm after 35 years: Some things we now know about obedience to authority. *Journal of Applied Social Psychology*, 29, 955–978.

Blau, P. M. (1964). *Exchange and power in social life*. New York: Wiley.

Bless, H., Strack, F., & Walther, E. (2001). Memory as a target of social influence? Memory distortions as a function of social influence and metacognitive knowledge. In J. P. Forgas & W. D. Kipling (Eds.), *Social influence: Direct and indirect processes* (pp. 167–183). Philadelphia: Psychology Press.

Bloom, P. (2012). Religion, morality, evolution. *Annual Review of Psychology*, 63, 179–199. doi:10.1146/annurev-psych-120710-100334

Blow, C. (2011, June 11). Drug bust. *The New York Times*. Op-ed page.

Bochner, S. (1994). Cross-cultural differences in the self-concept: A test of Hofstede's individualism/collectivism distinction. *Journal of Cross-Cultural Psychology*, 25, 273–283.

Bodimeade, H., Anderson, E., La Macchia, S., Smith, J. R., Terry, D. J., & Louis, W. R. (2014). Testing the direct, indirect, and interactive roles of referent group injunctive and descriptive norms for sun protection in relation to the theory of planned behavior. *Journal of Applied Social Psychology*, 44, 739–750.

Boduroglu, A., Shah, P., & Nisbett, R. E. (2009). Cultural differences in allocation of attention in visual information processing. *Journal of Cross-Cultural Psychology*, 40(3), 349–360. doi:10.1177/0022022108331005

Boer, D., & Fischer, R. (2013). How and when do personal values guide our attitudes and sociality? Explaining cross-cultural variability in attitude-value linkages. *Psychological Bulletin*, 139, 1113–1147.

Bohner, G., & Dickel, N. (2011). Attitudes and attitude change. *Annual Review of Psychology*, 62, 391–417. doi:10.1146/annurev.psych.121208.131609

Bolger, N., & Amarel, D. (2007). Effects of social support visibility on adjustment to stress: Experimental evidence. *Journal of Personality and Social Psychology*, 92, 458–475.

Bonanno, G. A. (2005). Resilience in the face of potential trauma. *Current Directions in Psychological Science*, 14, 135–138.

Bonanno, G. A., Moskowitz, J. T., Papa, A., & Folkman, S. (2005). Resilience to loss in bereaved spouses, bereaved parents, and bereaved gay men. *Journal of Personality and Social Psychology*, 88, 827–843.

Bonanno, G. A., Westphal, M., & Mancini, A. D. (2011). Resilience to loss and potential trauma. *Annual Review of Clinical Psychology*, 7, 511–535. doi:10.1146/annurev-clinpsy-032210-104526

Bonanno, G. A., Boerner, K., & Wortman, C. B. (2008). Trajectories of grieving. In M. S. Stroebe, R. O. Hansson, H. Schut, W. Stroebe, & E. Van den Blink (Eds.), *Handbook of bereavement research and practice: Advances in theory and intervention* (pp. 287–307). Washington, DC: American Psychological Association.

Bond, C. F., Jr., & Titus, L. J. (1983). Social facilitation: A meta-analysis of 241 studies. *Psychological Bulletin*, 94, 264–292.

Bond, M. H. (1991). Chinese values and health: A culture-level examination. *Psychology and Health*, 5, 137–152.

Bond, M. H. (1996). Chinese values. In M. H. Bond (Ed.), *The handbook of Chinese psychology* (pp. 208–226). Hong Kong: Oxford University Press.

Bond, M. H. (Ed.). (1988). *The cross-cultural challenge to social psychology*. Newbury Park, CA: Sage.

Bond, R. (2005). Group size and conformity. *Group Processes and Intergroup Relations*, 8, 331–354.

Bond, R. M., Fariss, C. J., Jones, J. J., Kramer, A. D. I., Marlow, C., Settle, J. E., et al. (2012). A 61-million-person experiment in social influence and political mobilization. *Nature*, 489, 295–298.

Bond, R., & Smith, P. B. (1996). Culture and conformity: A meta-analysis of studies using Asch's (1952b, 1956) line judgment task. *Psychological Bulletin*, 119, 111–137.

Bookwala, J. (2014). Spouse health status, depressed affect, and resilience in mid and late life: A longitudinal study. *Developmental Psychology*, 50, 1241–1249.

Boos, M., Schauenberg, B., Strack, M., & Belz, M. (2013). Social validation of shared and non-validation of unshared information in group discussions. *Small Group Research*, 44, 257–271.

Bornstein, B. H., & Greene, E. (2011). Jury decision making: Implications for and from psychology. *Current Directions in Psychological Science*, 20(1), 63–67. doi:10.1177/0963721410397282

Bornstein, R. F. (1989). Exposure and affect: Overview and meta-analysis of research, 1968–1987. *Psychological Bulletin*, 106, 265–289.

Bos, M. W., & Dijksterhuis, A. (2012). Self-knowledge, unconscious thought, and decision making. In S. Vazire & T. D. Wilson (Eds.), *The handbook of self-knowledge*. New York: Guilford.

Bosson, J. K., & Vandello, J. A. (2011). Precarious manhood and its links to action and aggression. *Psychological Science*, 20, 82–86.

Botvin, G. J., & Griffin, K. W. (2004). Life skills training: Empirical findings and future directions. *Journal of Primary Prevention*, 25, 211–232.

Bourgeois, M. J., & Bowen, A. (2001). Self-organization of alcohol-related attitudes and beliefs in a campus housing complex: An initial investigation. *Health Psychology*, 20, 434–437.

Bower, G. H., & Hilgard, E. R. (1981). *Theories of learning* (15th ed.). Englewood Cliffs, NJ: Prentice Hall.

Bowlby, J. (1969). *Attachment and loss: Vol. 1. Attachment*. New York: Basic Books.

Bowlby, J. (1973). *Attachment and loss: Vol. 2. Separation: Anxiety and anger*. New York: Basic Books.

Bowlby, J. (1980). *Attachment and loss: Vol. 3. Loss*. New York: Basic Books.

Boyden, T., Carroll, J. S., & Maier, R. A. (1984). Similarity and attraction in homosexual males: The effects of age and masculinity-femininity. *Sex Roles*, 10, 939–948.

Bradbury, T. N., & Fincham, F. D. (1991). A contextual model for advancing the study of marital relationships. In G. J. O. Fletcher & F. D. Fincham (Eds.), *Cognition in close relationships* (pp. 127–147). Hillsdale, NJ: Erlbaum.

Brakel, T. M., Dijkstra, A., & Buunk, A. P. (2012). Effects of the source of social comparison information on former cancer patients' quality of life. *British Journal of Health Psychology*, 17(4), 667–681. doi:10.1111/j.2044-8287.2012.02064.x

Brand, R. J., Bonatsos, A., D'Orazio, R., & DeShong, H. (2012). What is beautiful is good, even online: Correlations between photo attractiveness and text attractiveness in men's online dating profiles. *Computers in Human Behavior*, 28, 166–170.

Branigan, T. (2011, October 21). Chinese toddler dies after hit-and-run ordeal. *The Guardian*. Retrieved November 21, 2011, from www.guardian.co.uk/world/2011/oct/21/chinese-toddler-dies-hit-and-run

Brannon, L. A., & Brock, T. C. (1994). The subliminal persuasion controversy. In S. Shavitt & T. C. Brock (Eds.), *Persuasion: Psychological insights and perspectives* (pp. 279–293). Needham Heights, MA: Allyn & Bacon.

Branscombe, N. R., & Wann, D. L. (1992). Physiological arousal and reactions to outgroup members during competitions that implicate an important social identity. *Aggressive Behavior*, 18, 85–93.

Branscombe, N. R., Owen, S., Garstka, T. A., & Coleman, J. (1996). Rape and accident counterfactuals: Who might have done otherwise, and would it have changed the outcome? *Journal of Applied Social Psychology*, 26, 1042–1067.

Brauer, M., Judd, C. M., & Gliner, M. D. (1995). The effects of repeated expressions on attitude polarization during group discussions. *Journal of Personality and Social Psychology*, 68, 1014–1029.

Breckler, S. J., & Wiggins, E. C. (1989). On defining attitude and attitude theory: Once more with feeling. In A. R. Pratkanis, S. J. Breckler, & A. G. Greenwald (Eds.), *Attitude structure and function* (pp. 407–427). Hillsdale, NJ: Erlbaum.

Breed, M. D. (2014). Kin and nestmate recognition: The influence of W. D. Hamilton on 50 years of research. *Animal Behaviour*. Advance online publication. doi:10.1016/j.anbehav.2014.02.030

Brehm, J. W. (1956). Postdecision changes in the desirability of alternatives. *Journal of Abnormal and Social Psychology, 52*, 384–389.

Brehm, J. W. (1966). *A theory of psychological reactance.* New York: Academic Press.

Brehm, J. W., & Cohen, A. R. (1962). *Explorations in cognitive dissonance.* New York: Wiley.

Breiding, M. J., Chen J., & Black, M. C. (2014). *Intimate partner violence in the United States—2010.* Atlanta: National Center for Injury Prevention and Control, Centers for Disease Control and Prevention.

Brescoll, V. L., Dawson, E., & Uhlmann, E. L. (2010). Hard won and easily lost: The fragile status of leaders in gender-stereotype-incongruent occupations. *Psychological Science, 21*(11), 1640–1642. doi:10.1177/0956797610384744

Brewer, M. B. (1979). In-group bias in the minimal intergroup situation: A cognitive-motivational analysis. *Psychological Bulletin, 86*, 307–324.

Brewer, M. B. (1991). The social self: On being the same and different at the same time. *Personality and Social Psychology Bulletin, 17*(5), 475–482. doi:10.1177/0146167291175001

Brewer, M. B. (2007). The importance of being we: Human nature and intergroup relations. *American Psychologist, 62*(8), 728–738. doi:10.1037/0003-066X.62.8.728

Brewer, M. B., & Gardner, W. L. (1996). Who is this "we"? Levels of collective identity and self-representations. *Journal of Personality and Social Psychology, 71*, 83–93.

Brewer, M. B., & Miller, N. (1984). Beyond the contact hypothesis: Theoretical perspectives on desegregation. In N. Miller & M. B. Brewer (Eds.), *Groups in contact: The psychology of desegregation* (pp. 281–302). New York: Academic Press.

Brewer, N., & Wells, G. L. (2011). Eyewitness identification. *Current Directions in Psychological Science, 20*, 24–27.

Bridgeman, D. L. (1981). Enhanced role taking through cooperative interdependence: A field study. *Child Development, 52*, 1231–1238.

Brigham, J., Bennett, L., Meissner, C., & Mitchell, T. (2007). The influence of race on eyewitness memory. In R. C. L. Lindsay, D. F. Ross, D. J. Read, & M. P. Toglia (Eds.). *The handbook of eyewitness psychology, Vol. II: Memory for people* (pp. 257–281). Mahwah, NJ: Erlbaum.

Bringle, R. G. (2005). Designing interventions to promote civic engagement. In A. M. Omoto (Ed.), *Processes of community change and social action* (pp. 167–187). Mahwah, NJ: Erlbaum.

Briñol, P., & Petty, R. E. (2003). Over head movements and persuasion: A self-validation analysis. *Journal of Personality and Social Psychology, 4*, 1123–1139.

Briñol, P., & Petty, R. E. (2009). Persuasion: Insights from the self-validation hypothesis. In M. P. Zanna (Ed.), *Advances in experimental social psychology* (Vol. 41, pp. 69–118). New York: Elsevier.

Briñol, P., & Petty, R. E. (2012). Knowing our attitudes and how to change them. In S. Vazire & T. D. Wilson (Eds.), *Handbook of self-knowledge.* New York: Guilford.

Brislin, R. (1993). *Understanding culture's influence on behavior.* Fort Worth, TX: Harcourt Brace.

Brooke, J. (2000, January 20). Canada proposes scaring smokers with pictures on the packs. *New York Times on the Web,* www.nytimes.com

Brooks, A. (2006). *Who really cares? The surprising truth about compassionate conservatism.* New York: Basic Books.

Brophy, J. E. (1983). Research on the self-fulfilling prophecy and teacher expectations. *Journal of Educational Psychology, 75*, 631–661.

Brosch, T., Schiller, D., Mojdehbakhsh, R., Uleman, J. S., & Phelps, E. A. (2013). Neural mechanisms underlying the integration of situational information into attribution outcomes. *Social Cognitive and Affective Neuroscience, 8*, 640–646.

Brown, J. D. (2012). Understanding the better than average effect: Motives (still) matter. *Personality and Social Psychology Bulletin, 38*, 209–219.

Brown, R. (1965). *Social psychology.* New York: Free Press.

Brown, R. P., Osterman, L. L., & Barnes, C. D. (2009). School violence and the culture of honor. *Psychological Science, 20*, 1400–1405.

Bruchmann, K., & Evans, A. T. (2013). Abstract mind-sets and social comparison: When global comparisons matter. *Social Psychological and Personality Science, 4*(4), 427–433. doi:10.1177/1948550612464661

Brummelman, E., Thomaes, S., Orobio de Castro, B., Overbeek, G., & Bushman, B. J. (2014). "That's not just beautiful—that's incredibly beautiful!": The adverse impact of inflated praise on children with low self-esteem. *Psychological Science, 25*, 728–735.

Bruschke, J., & Loges, W. E. (2004). *Free press vs. fair trials: Examining publicity's role in trial outcomes.* Mahwah, NJ: Erlbaum.

Bryan, C. J., Adams, G. S., & Monin, B. (2013). When cheating would make you a cheater: Implicating the self prevents unethical behavior. *Journal of Experimental Psychology: General, 142*, 1001–1005.

Buehler, R., & Griffin, D. W. (1994). Change-of-meaning effects in conformity and dissent: Observing construal processes over time. *Journal of Personality and Social Psychology, 67*, 984–996.

Buehler, R., Griffin, D. W., & Ross, M. (2002). Inside the planning fallacy: The causes and consequences of optimistic time preferences. In T. Gilovich, D. W. Griffin, & D. Kahneman (Eds.), *Heuristics and biases: The psychology of intuitive judgment* (pp. 250–270). New York: Cambridge University Press.

Bugliosi, V. T. (1997). *Outrage: The five reasons why O. J. Simpson got away with murder.* New York: Dell.

Bui, K.-V. T., Peplau, L. A., & Hill, C. T. (1996). Testing the Rusbult model of relationship commitment and stability in a 15-year study of heterosexual couples. *Personality and Social Psychology Bulletin, 22*, 1244–1257.

Bülbül, C., & Menon, G. (2010). The power of emotional appeals in advertising: The influence of concrete versus abstract affect on time-dependent decision. *Journal of Advertising Research, 50*, 169–180.

Bullens, L., van Harreveld, F., Förster, J., & van der Pligt, J. (2013). Reversible decisions: The grass isn't merely greener on the other side; it's also very brown over here. *Journal of Experimental Social Psychology, 49*, 1093–1099.

Buller, D. J. (2005). *Adapting minds: Evolutionary psychology and the persistent quest for human nature.* Cambridge, MA: MIT Press.

Burger, J. M. (1981). Motivational biases in the attribution of responsibility for an accident: A meta-analysis of the defensive-attribution hypothesis. *Psychological Bulletin, 90*, 496–512.

Burger, J. M. (1999). The foot-in-the-door compliance procedure: A multiple-process analysis and review. *Personality and Social Psychology Review, 3*, 303–325.

Burger, J. M. (2009). Replicating Milgram: Would people still obey today? *American Psychologist, 64*, 1–11.

Burnstein, E., & Vinokur, A. (1977). Persuasive argumentation and social comparison as determinants of attitude polarization. *Journal of Experimental Social Psychology, 13*, 315–332.

Burnstein, E., & Worchel, P. (1962). Arbitrariness of frustration and its consequences for aggression in a social situation. *Journal of Personality, 30*, 528–540.

Burnstein, E., Crandall, C. S., & Kitayama, S. (1994). Some neo-Darwinian decision rules for altruism: Weighing cues for inclusive fitness as a function of the biological importance of the decision. *Journal of Personality and Social Psychology, 67*, 773–789.

Busey, T. A., Tunnicliff, J., Loftus, G. R., & Loftus, E. F. (2000). Accounts of the confidence-accuracy relation in recognition memory. *Psychonomic Bulletin and Review, 7*, 26–48.

Bush sought "way" to invade Iraq? (2004, January 11). Retrieved March 8, 2006, from www.cbsnews.com/stories/2004/01/09/60minutes/main592330.shtml

Bush, G. W. (2010). *Decision points.* New York: Crown.

Bushman, B. J. (1995). Moderating role of trait aggressiveness in the effects of violent media on aggression. *Journal of Personality and Social Psychology, 69*, 950–960.

Bushman, B. J. (1997). Effects of alcohol on human aggression: Validity of proposed explanations. In M. Galanter (Ed.), *Recent developments in alcoholism*: Vol. 13. *Alcohol and violence: Epidemiology, neurobiology, psychology, family issues* (pp. 227–243). New York: Plenum.

Bushman, B. J. (2002). Does venting anger feed or extinguish the flame? Catharsis, rumination, distraction, anger, and aggressive responding. *Personality and Social Psychology Bulletin, 28*, 724–731.

Bushman, B. J., & Anderson, C. A. (2009). Comfortably numb: Desensitizing effects of violent media on helping others. *Psychological Science, 20*, 273–277.

Bushman, B. J., & Baumeister, R. F. (2002). Does self-love or self-hate lead to violence? *Journal of Research in Personality, 36*, 543–545.

Bushman, B. J., & Cooper, H. M. (1990). Alcohol and human aggression: An integrative research review. *Psychological Bulletin, 107*, 341–354.

Bushman, B. J., & Pollard-Sacks, D. (2014). Supreme Court decision on violent video games was based on the First Amendment, not scientific evidence. *American Psychologist, 69*, 306–307.

Bushman, B. J., Bonacci, A. M., Pedersen, W. C., Vasquez, E. A., & Miller, N. (2005). Chewing on it can chew you up: Effects of rumination on triggered displaced aggression. *Journal of Personality and Social Psychology, 88*, 969–983.

Bushman, B. J., Jamieson, P. E., Weitz, I., & Romer, D. (2013). Gun violence trends in movies. *Pediatrics, 132*, 1014–1018.

Bushman, B. J., Ridge, R. D., Das, E., Key, C. W., & Busath, G. L. (2007). When God sanctions killing: The effect of scriptural violence on aggression. *Psychological Science, 18*(3), 204–207.

Buss D. (2005). *The handbook of evolutionary psychology.* New Jersey: John Wiley & Sons.

Buss, D. M. (1985). Human mate selection. *American Scientist, 73*, 47–51.

Buss, D. M. (1988a). The evolution of human intra-sexual competition. *Journal of Personality and Social Psychology, 54*, 616–628.

Buss, D. M. (1988b). Love acts: The evolutionary biology of love. In R. J. Sternberg & M. L. Barnes (Eds.), *The psychology of love* (pp. 110–118). New Haven, CT: Yale University Press.

Buss, D. M. (1989). Sex differences in human mate preferences: Evolutionary hypotheses tested in 37 cultures. *Behavioral and Brain Sciences, 12*, 1–49.

Buss, D. M. (2004). *Evolutionary psychology: The new science of the mind* (2nd ed.). Boston: Allyn & Bacon.

Buss, D. M. (Ed.). (2005). *The handbook of evolutionary psychology.* Hoboken, NJ: Wiley.

Buss, D. M., & Kenrick, D. T. (1998). Evolutionary social psychology. In D. T. Gilbert, S. T. Fiske, & G. Lindzey (Eds.), *The handbook of social psychology* (4th ed., Vol. 2, pp. 982–1026). New York: McGraw-Hill.

Buss, D. M., & Schmitt, D. P. (1993). Sexual strategies theory: An evolutionary perspective on human mating. *Psychological Bulletin, 100*, 204–232.

Buss, D. M., & Shackelford, T. K. (1997). From vigilance to violence: Mate retention tactics in married couples. *Journal of Personality and Social Psychology, 72*, 346–361.

Buss, D. M., Abbott, M., Angleitner, A., Biaggio, A., Blanco-Villasenor, A., Bruchon-Schweitzer, M., et al. (1990). International preferences in selecting mates: A study of 37 cultures. *Journal of Cross-Cultural Psychology, 21*, 5–47.

Butler, D., & Geis, F. L. (1990). Nonverbal affect responses to male and female leaders: Implications for leadership evaluations. *Journal of Personality and Social Psychology, 58*, 48–59.

Buunk, B. P., & Gibbons, F. X. (2013). *Health, coping, and well-being: Perspectives from social comparison theory.* New York: Psychology Press.

Buunk, B. P., & Schaufeli, W. B. (1999). Reciprocity in interpersonal relationships: An evolutionary perspective on its importance for health and well-being. In W. Stroebe & M. Hewstone (Eds.), *European review of social psychology* (Vol. 10, pp. 259–291). New York: Wiley.

Buunk, B. P., & Van Yperen, N. W. (1991). Referential comparisons, relational comparisons, and exchange orientation: Their relation to marital satisfaction. *Personality and Social Psychology Bulletin, 17,* 709–717.

Byrne, D., & Clore, G. L. (1970). A reinforcement model of evaluative processes. *Personality, 1,* 103–128.

Byrne, D., & Nelson, D. (1965). Attraction as a linear function of positive reinforcement. *Journal of Personality and Social Psychology, 1,* 659–663.

Cacioppo, J. T. (1998). Somatic responses to psychological stress: The reactivity hypothesis. In M. Sabourin & F. Craik (Eds.), *Advances in psychological science: Biological and cognitive aspects* (Vol. 2, pp. 87–112). Hove, England: Psychology Press.

Cacioppo, J. T., & Cacioppo, S. (2013). Social neuroscience. *Perspectives on Psychological Science, 8,* 667–669. doi:10.1177/1745691613507456

Cacioppo, J. T., & Patrick, W. (2008). *Loneliness: Human nature and the need for social connection.* New York: Norton & Company.

Cacioppo, J. T., Berntson, G. G., Malarkey, W. B., Kiecolt-Glaser, J. K., Sheridan, J. F., Poehlmann, K. M., Burleson, M. H., Ernst, J. M., Hawkley, L. C., & Glaser, R. (1998). Autonomic, neuroendocrine, and immune responses to psychological stress: The reactivity hypothesis. In S. M. McCann & J. M. Lipton (Eds.), *Annals of the New York academy of sciences* (Vol. 840, pp. 664–673). New York: New York Academy of Sciences.

Cacioppo, J. T., Marshall-Goodell, B. S., Tassinary, L. G., & Petty, R. E. (1992). Rudimentary determinants of attitudes: Classical conditioning is more effective when prior knowledge about the attitude stimulus is low than high. *Journal of Experimental Social Psychology, 28,* 207–233.

Cacioppo, J. T., Petty, R. E., Feinstein, J., & Jarvis, B. (1996). Dispositional differences in cognitive motivation: The life and times of individuals low versus high in need for cognition. *Psychological Bulletin, 119,* 197–253.

Cafri, G., & Thompson, J. K. (2004). Measuring male body image: A review of the current methodology. *Psychology of Men and Masculinity, 5,* 18–29.

Cafri, G., Thompson, J. K., Ricciardelli, L., McCabe, M., Smolak, L., & Yesalis, C. (2005). Pursuit of the muscular ideal: Physical and psychological consequences and putative risk factors. *Clinical Psychology Review, 25,* 215–239.

Cahn, D. (2013, November 2). Study: Storms would submerge Norfolk Naval Station. *PilotonLine.com.* Retrieved July 15, 2014, from http://hamptonroads.com/2013/11/study-storms-would-submerge-norfolk-naval-station

Calder, B. J., & Staw, B. M. (1975). Self-perception of intrinsic and extrinsic motivation. *Journal of Personality and Social Psychology, 31,* 599–605.

Calderón-Garcidueñas, L., & Torres-Jardón, R. (2012). Air pollution, socioeconomic status, and children's cognition in megacities: The Mexico City scenario. *Frontiers in Psychology, 3,* Article 217.

Caldwell, M., & Peplau, L. A. (1982). Sex differences in same-sex friendship. *Sex Roles, 8,* 721–733.

Calvillo, D. P. (2013). Rapid recollection of foresight judgments increases hindsight bias in a memory design. *Journal of Experimental Psychology: Learning, Memory, and Cognition, 39,* 959–964.

Cameron, C. D., Brown-Iannuzzi, J. L., & Payne, B. K. (2012). Sequential priming measures of implicit social cognition: A meta-analysis of associations with behavior and explicit attitudes. *Personality and Social Psychology Review, 16*(4), 330–350. doi:10.1177/1088868312440047

Camille, N., Coricelli, G., Sallet, J., Pradat-Diehl, P., Duhamel, J., & Sirigu, A. (2004). The involvement of the orbitofrontal cortex in the experience of regret. *Science, 304,* 1167–1170.

Campbell, A. (2002). *A mind of her own.* New York: Oxford University Press.

Campbell, D. T. (1967). Stereotypes and the perception of group differences. *American Psychologist, 22,* 817–829.

Campbell, D. T., & Stanley, J. C. (1967). *Experimental and quasi-experimental designs for research.* Chicago: Rand McNally.

Campbell, J. D., & Fairey, P. J. (1989). Informational and normative routes to conformity: The effect of faction size as a function of norm extremity and attention to the stimulus. *Journal of Personality and Social Psychology, 57,* 457–468.

Campbell, J., & Stasser, G. (2006). The influence of time and task demonstrability on decision-making in computer-mediated and face-to-face groups. *Small Group Research, 37,* 271–294.

Campbell, L., Simpson, J. A., Boldry, J., & Kashy, D. A. (2005). Perceptions of conflict and support in romantic relationships: The role of attachment anxiety. *Journal of Personality and Social Psychology, 88,* 510–531.

Canary, D. J., & Stafford, L. (2001). Equity in the preservation of personal relationships. In J. Harvey & A. Wenzel (Eds.), *Close romantic relationships: Maintenance and enhancement* (pp. 133–151). Mahwah, NJ: Erlbaum.

Cannon, W. B. (1932). *The wisdom of the body.* New York: Norton.

Cannon, W. B. (1942). "Voodoo" death. *American Anthropologist, 44,* 169–181.

Cantor, J., Bushman, B. J., Huesmann, L. R., Groebel, J., Malamuth, N. M., Impett, E. A., Donnerstein, E., & Smith, S. (2001). Some hazards of television viewing: Fears, aggression, and sexual attitudes. In D. G. Singer & J. L. Singer (Eds.), *Handbook of children and the media* (pp. 207–307). Thousand Oaks, CA: Sage.

Cantril, H. (1940). *The invasion from Mars: A study in the psychology of panic.* New York: Harper & Row.

Capella, M. L., Webster, C., & Kinard, B. R. (2011). A review of the effect of cigarette advertising. *International Journal of Research in Marketing, 28*(3), 269–279. doi:10.1016/j.ijresmar.2011.05.002

Caporael, L. R., & Brewer, M. B. (2000). Metatheories, evolution, and psychology: Once more with feeling. *Psychological Inquiry, 11,* 23–26.

Carey, B. (2006, February 14). In music, others' tastes may help shape your own. *The New York Times,* p. D7.

Carli, L. L. (1999). Cognitive reconstruction, hindsight, and reactions to victims and perpetrators. *Personality and Social Psychology Bulletin, 25,* 966–979.

Carlier, I. V. E., Voerman, A. E., & Gersons, B. P. R. (2000). The influence of occupational debriefing on post-traumatic stress symptomatology in traumatized police officers. *British Journal of Medical Psychology, 73,* 87–98.

Carlsmith, J. M., & Anderson, C. A. (1979). Ambient temperature and the occurrence of collective violence: A new analysis. *Journal of Personality and Social Psychology, 37,* 337–344.

Carlson, M., & Miller, N. (1987). Explanation of the relationship between negative mood and helping. *Psychological Bulletin, 102,* 91–108.

Carlson, M., Charlin, V., & Miller, N. (1988). Positive mood and helping behavior: A test of six hypotheses. *Journal of Personality and Social Psychology, 55,* 211–229.

Carnagey, N. L., & Anderson, C. A. (2005). The effects of reward and punishment in violent video games on aggressive affect, cognition, and behavior. *Psychological Science, 16,* 882–889.

Carnevale, P. J. (1986). Strategic choice in mediation. *Negotiation Journal, 2,* 41–56.

Carney, D., Cuddy, A. J. C., & Yap, A. J. (2010). Power posing: Brief nonverbal displays affect neuroendocrine levels and risk tolerance. *Psychological Science, 21,* 1363–1368.

Carpenter, S. (2000, December). Why do "they all look alike"? *Monitor on Psychology,* pp. 44–45.

Carr, J. L., & VanDeusen, K. M. (2004). Risk factors for male sexual aggression on college campuses. *Journal of Family Violence, 19,* 279–289.

Carré, J. M., Iselin, A. R., Welker, K. M., Hariri, A. R., & Dodge, K. A. (2014). Testosterone reactivity to provocation mediates the effect of early

intervention on aggressive behavior. *Psychological Science, 25,* 1140–1146.

Carroll, J. S., Padilla-Walker, L. M., Nelson, L. J., Olson, C. D., Barry, C. M., & Madsen, S. D. (2008). Generation XXX: Pornography acceptance and use among emerging adults. *Journal of Adolescent Research, 23,* 6–30.

Carter, A. M., Fabrigar, L. R., MacDonald, T. K., & Monner, L. J. (2013). Investigating the interface of the investment model and adult attachment theory. *European Journal of Social Psychology, 43,* 661–672.

Carter, B. (2000, August 24). CBS is surprise winner in ratings contest. *The New York Times,* p. A22.

Carter, B. (2003, May 19). Even as executives scorn the genre, TV networks still rely on reality. *The New York Times,* pp. C1, C7.

Carter, B. (2009, May 19). Upfronts: "Chuck" saved by Subway. *The New York Times.* Retrieved July 1, 2011, from mediadecoder.blogs.nytimes.com/2009/05/19/upfronts-chuck-takes-the-subway/

Carter, T. J., & Gilovich, T. (2012). I am what I do, not what I have: The differential centrality of experiential and material purchases to the self. *Journal of Personality and Social Psychology, 102,* 1304.

Cartwright, D. (1979). Contemporary social psychology in historical perspective. *Social Psychology Quarterly, 42,* 82–93.

Cartwright, D., & Zander, A. (1968). *Group dynamics: Research and theory.* New York: Harper & Row.

Caruso, E. (2008). Use of experienced retrieval ease in self and social judgments. *Journal of Experimental Social Psychology, 44,* 148–155.

Caruso, E. M. (2008). Use of experienced retrieval ease in self and social judgments. *Journal of Experimental Social Psychology, 44*(1), 148–155. doi:10.1016/j.jesp.2006.11.003

Carver, C. S. (2003). Self-awareness. In M. R. Leary & J. P. Tangney (Eds.), *Handbook of self and identity* (pp. 179–196). New York: Guilford Press.

Carver, C. S., & Scheier, M. F. (1981). *Attention and self-regulation: A control-theory approach to human behavior.* New York: Springer-Verlag.

Carver, C. S., & Scheier, M. F. (1998). *On the self-regulation of behavior.* New York: Cambridge University Press.

Caselman, T., (2007). *Teaching children empathy.* New York: YouthLight.

Casey-Campbell, M., & Martens, M. L. (2009). Sticking it all together: A critical assessment of the group cohesion-performance literature. *International Journal of Management Reviews, 11,* 223–246.

Cashin, S. (2014). *Place, not race: A new vision of opportunity in America.* Boston: Beacon Press.

Catalyst. (2014). Changing workplaces, changing lives. Retrieved July 2, 2014, from www.catalyst.org

Catlin, J. R., & Wang, Y. (2013). Recycling gone bad: When the option to recycle increases resource consumption. *Journal of Consumer Psychology, 23,* 122–127.

Cejka, M., & Eagly, A. H. (1999). Gender-stereotypic images of occupations correspond to the sex segregation of employment. *Personality and Social Psychology Bulletin, 25,* 413–423.

Centers for Disease Control and Prevention. (2014). Chronic disease prevention and health promotion. Retrieved August 19, 2014, from http://www.cdc.gov/chronicdisease/index.htm

Centers for Disease Control and Prevention. (2014, January). Current cigarette smoking among adults—United States, 2005–2012. *Morbidity and Mortality Weekly Report.* Retrieved April 26, 2014, from http://www.cdc.gov/mmwr/preview/mmwrhtml/mm6302a2.htm

Centers for Disease Control and Prevention. (n.d.). Retrieved June 6, 2011, from profiles.nlm.nih.gov/ps/access/NNBCPH.pdf

Chabris, C., & Simons, D. (2010). *The invisible gorilla: And other ways our intuitions deceive us.* New York: Harmony.

Chaiken, S. (1980). Heuristic versus systematic information processing and the use of source versus message cues in persuasion. *Journal of Personality and Social Psychology, 39,* 752–766.

Chaiken, S., & Baldwin, M. W. (1981). Affective-cognitive consistency and the effect of salient behavioral information on the self-perception of attitudes. *Journal of Personality and Social Psychology, 41*, 1–12.

Chambers, J. R., & Windschitl, P. D. (2009). Evaluating one performance among others: The influence of rank and degree of exposure to comparison referents. *Personality and Social Psychology Bulletin, 35*, 776–792. doi:10.1177/0146167209333044

Chan, A., & Au, T. K. (2011). Getting children to do more academic work: Foot-in-the-door versus door-in-the-face. *Teaching and Teacher Education, 27*, 982–985.

Chan, D. K.-S., & Cheng, G. H.-L. (2004). A comparison of offline and online friendship qualities at different stages of relationship development. *Journal of Personal and Social Relationships, 21*, 305–320.

Chan, E., & Sengupta, J. (2013). Observing flattery: A social comparison perspective. *Journal of Consumer Research, 40*, 740–758. doi:10.1086/672357

Chang, C., & Chen, J. (1995). Effects of different motivation strategies on reducing social loafing. *Chinese Journal of Psychology, 37*, 71–81.

Chaplin, W. F., Phillips, J. B., Brown, J. D., & Clanton, N. R. (2000). Handshaking, gender, personality, and first impressions. *Journal of Personality and Social Psychology, 79*, 110–117.

Chapman, G. B., & Johnson, E. J. (2002). Incorporating the irrelevant: Anchors in judgments of belief and value. In T. Gilovich, D. W. Griffin, & D. Kahneman (Eds.), *Heuristics and biases: The psychology of intuitive judgment* (pp. 120–138). New York: Cambridge University Press.

Charman, S. D., Wells, G. L., & Joy, S. W. (2011). The dud effect: Adding highly dissimilar fillers increases confidence in lineup identifications. *Law and Human Behavior, 35*(6), 479–500. doi:10.1007/s10979-010-9261-1

Charman, S., & Wells, G. (2007). Applied lineup theory. *The handbook of eyewitness psychology, Vol II: Memory for people* (pp. 219–254). Mahwah, NJ: Erlbaum.

Charman, S., & Wells, G. (2008). Can eyewitnesses correct for external influences on their lineup identifications? The actual/counterfactual assessment paradigm. *Journal of Experimental Psychology: Applied, 14*, 5–20.

Chaxel, A. (2014). The impact of procedural priming of selective accessibility on self-generated and experimenter-provided anchors. *Journal of Experimental Social Psychology, 50*, 45–51.

Check, J. V., & Malamuth, N. M. (1983). Sex role stereotyping and reactions to depictions of stranger versus acquaintance rape. *Journal of Personality and Social Psychology, 45*, 344–356.

Chemers, M. M. (2000). Leadership research and theory: A functional integration. *Group Dynamics: Theory, Research, and Practice, 4*, 27–43.

Chemers, M. M., Watson, C. B., & May, S. T. (2000). Dispositional affect and leadership effectiveness: A comparison of self-esteem, optimism, and efficacy. *Personality and Social Psychology Bulletin, 26*, 267–277.

Chen, J. M., Kim, H. S., Mojaverian, T., & Morling, B. (2012). Culture and social support provision: Who gives what and why. *Personality and Social Psychology Bulletin, 38*, 3–13.

Chen, J., Wu, Y., Tong, G., Guan, X., & Zhou, X. (2012). ERP correlates of social conformity in a line judgment task. *BMC Neuroscience, 13*. doi:10.1186/1471-2202-13-43

Chen, M., & Bargh, J. A. (1997). Nonconscious behavioral confirmation processes: The self-fulfilling consequences of automatic stereotype activation. *Journal of Experimental Social Psychology, 33*, 541–560.

Chen, N. Y., Shaffer, D. R., & Wu, C. H. (1997). On physical attractiveness stereotyping in Taiwan: A revised sociocultural perspective. *Journal of Social Psychology, 137*, 117–124.

Chen, S., & Andersen, S. M. (1999). Relationships from the past in the present: Significant-other representations and transference in interpersonal life. In M. P. Zanna (Ed.), *Advances in experimental social psychology* (Vol. 31, pp. 123–190). San Diego, CA: Academic Press.

Chen, S., & Chaiken, S. (1999). The heuristic-systematic model in its broader context. In S. Chaiken & Y. Trope (Eds.), *Dual-process theories in social psychology* (pp. 73–96). New York: Guilford Press.

Cheng, C., Cheung, S.-F., Chio, J. H.-M., & Chan, M.-P. S. (2013). Cultural meaning of perceived control: A meta-analysis of locus of control and psychological symptoms across 18 cultural regions. *Psychological Bulletin, 139*, 152–188.

Chernyak, N., & Kushnir, T. (2013). Giving preschoolers choice increases sharing behavior. *Psychological Science, 24*, 1971–1979.

Cheung, B. Y., Chudek, M., & Heine, S. J. (2011). Evidence for a sensitive period for acculturation: Younger immigrants report acculturating at a faster rate. *Psychological Science, 22*(2), 147–152. doi:10.1177/0956797610394661

Chiao, J. Y., Hariri, A. R., Harada, T., Mano, Y., Sadato, N., Parrish, T. B., & Iidaka, T. (2010). Theory and methods in cultural neuroscience. *Social Cognitive and Affective Neuroscience, 5*, 356–361.

Chida, Y., & Hamer, M. (2008). Chronic psychosocial factors and acute physiological responses to laboratory-induced stress in healthy populations: A quantitative review of 30 years of investigations. *Psychological Bulletin, 134*, 829–885.

Chin, J., & Schooler, J. (2008). Why do words hurt? Content, process, and criterion shift accounts of verbal overshadowing. *European Journal of Cognitive Psychology, 20*, 396–413.

Choi, I., & Nisbett, R. E. (1998). Situational salience and cultural differences in the correspondence bias and in the actor-observer bias. *Personality and Social Psychology Bulletin, 24*, 949–960.

Choi, I., Dalal, R., Kim-Prieto, C., & Park, H. (2003). Culture and judgment of causal relevance. *Journal of Personality and Social Psychology, 84*, 46–59.

Choi, I., Nisbett, R. E., & Norenzayan, A. (1999). Causal attribution across cultures: Variation and universality. *Psychological Bulletin, 125*, 47–63.

Choi, Y., He, M., & Harachi, T. (2008). Intergenerational cultural dissonance, parent-child conflict and bonding, and youth problem behaviors among Vietnamese and Cambodian immigrant families. *Journal of Youth and Adolescence, 37*, 85–96.

Chou, C., Montgomery, S., Pentz, M., Rohrbach, L., Johnson, C., Flay, B., & MacKinnon, D. P. (1998). Effects of a community-based prevention program in decreasing drug use in high-risk adolescents. *American Journal of Public Health, 88*, 944–948.

Christakis, N. A., & Fowler, J. H. (2014). Friendship and natural selection. *Proceedings of the National Academy of Sciences*. doi:10.1073/pnas.1400825111

Christensen, A., Doss, B., & Jacobson, N. S. (2014). *Reconcilable differences* (2nd ed.). New York: Guilford Press.

Christensen, L. (1988). Deception in psychological research: When is its use justified? *Personality and Social Psychology Bulletin, 14*, 664–675.

Cialdini, R. B. (2009). *Influence: Science and practice* (5th ed.). Upper Saddle River, NJ: Prentice Hall.

Cialdini, R. B. (2012). The focus theory of normative conduct. In P. A. M. Van Lange, A. W. Kruglanski, & E. T. Higgins (Eds.), *Handbook of theories of social psychology* (Vol. 2, pp. 295–312). Thousand Oaks, CA: Sage Publications.

Cialdini, R. B., & Fultz, J. (1990). Interpreting the negative mood-helping literature via "mega"-analysis: A contrary view. *Psychological Bulletin, 107*, 210–214.

Cialdini, R. B., & Goldstein, N. J. (2004). Social influence: Compliance and conformity. *Annual Review of Psychology, 55*, 591–621.

Cialdini, R. B., & Trost, M. R. (1998). Social influence: Social norms, conformity, and compliance. In D. T. Gilbert, S. T. Fiske, & G. Lindzey (Eds.), *The handbook of social psychology* (4th ed., Vol. 2, pp. 151–192). New York: McGraw-Hill.

Cialdini, R. B., Borden, R. J., Thorne, A., Walker, M. R., Freeman, S., & Sloan, L. R. (1976). Basking in reflected glory: Three (football) field studies. *Journal of Personality and Social Psychology, 34*, 366–375.

Cialdini, R. B., Cacioppo, J. T., Basset, R., & Miller, J. (1978). Low-ball procedure for producing compliance: Commitment, then cost. *Journal of Personality and Social Psychology, 36*, 463–476.

Cialdini, R. B., Kallgren, C. A., & Reno, R. R. (1991). A focus theory of normative conduct: A theoretical refinement and reevaluation of the role of norms in human behavior. In M. P. Zanna (Ed.), *Advances in experimental social psychology* (Vol. 24, pp. 201–234). San Diego, CA: Academic Press.

Cialdini, R. B., Reno, R. R., & Kallgren, C. A. (1990). A focus theory of normative conduct: Recycling the concept of norms to reduce littering in public places. *Journal of Personality and Social Psychology, 58*, 1015–1026.

Cialdini, R. B., Vincent, J. E., Lewis, S. K., Catalan, J., Wheeler, D., & Darby, B. L. (1975). Reciprocal concessions procedure for inducing compliance: The door-in-the face technique. *Journal of Personality and Social Psychology, 31*, 206–215.

Cikara, M., & Van Bavel, J. J. (2014). The neuroscience of intergroup relations: An integrative review. *Perspectives on Psychological Science, 9*, 245–274.

Clark, C. J., Luguri, J. B., Ditto, P. H., Knobe, J., Shariff, A. F., & Baumeister, R. F. (2014). Free to punish: A motivated account of free will belief. *Journal of Personality and Social Psychology, 106*, 501–513. doi:10.1037/a0035880

Clark, M. S., & Isen, A. M. (1982). Toward understanding the relationship between feeling states and social behavior. In A. H. Hastorf & A. M. Isen (Eds.), *Cognitive social psychology* (pp. 73–108). New York: Elsevier.

Clark, M. S., & Mills, J. (1993). The difference between communal and exchange relationships: What it is and what it is not. *Personality and Social Psychology Bulletin, 19*, 684–691.

Clark, R. D., III, & Hatfield, E. (1989). Gender differences in receptivity to sexual offers. *Journal of Psychology and Human Sexuality, 2*, 39–55.

Clark, R. D., III, & Maass, A. (1988). The role of social categorization and perceived source credibility in minority influence. *European Journal of Social Psychology, 18*, 347–364.

Clark, R. D., III, & Word, L. E. (1972). Why don't bystanders help? Because of ambiguity? *Journal of Personality and Social Psychology, 24*, 392–400.

Clark, S. E. (2005). A re-examination of the effects of biased lineup instructions in eyewitness identification. *Law and Human Behavior, 29*, 575–604.

Clary, E. G., Snyder, M., Ridge, R. D., Miene, P. K., & Haugen, J. A. (1994). Matching messages to motives in persuasion: A functional approach to promoting volunteerism. *Journal of Applied Social Psychology, 24*, 1129–1149.

Claypool, H. M., Hall, C. E., Mackie, D. M., & Garcia-Marques, T. (2008). Positive mood, attribution, and the illusion of familiarity. *Journal of Experimental Social Psychology, 44*, 721–728.

Climate change, water, and risk: Current water demands are not sustainable. (2010). National Resources Defense Council. Retrieved July 23, 2014, from http://www.nrdc.org/globalwarming/watersustainability/files/WaterRisk.pdf

Cline, V. B., Croft, R. G., & Courrier, S. (1973). Desensitization of children to television violence. *Journal of Personality and Social Psychology, 27*, 360–365.

Coane, J. H., & Balota, D. A. (2009). Priming the holiday spirit: Persistent activation due to extraexperimental experiences. *Psychonomic Bulletin & Review, 16*(6), 1124–1128. doi:10.3758/PBR.16.6.1124

Coats, E. (1998, March 20). Bystander intervention [E-mail response to G. Mumford, Tobacco update]. Retrieved from www.stolaf.edu/cgibin/mailarchivesearch.pl?directory=/home/www/people/huff/SPSP&listname=archive98

Cochran, J. L., & Rutten, T. (1998). *Journey to justice*. New York: Ballantine Books.

Coetzee V., Greeff, J. M., Stephen, I. D., & Perrett, D. I. (2014). Cross-cultural agreement in facial attractiveness preferences: The role of ethnicity and gender. *PLoS ONE, 9,* e99629.

Cogsdill, E. J., Todorov, A. T., Spelke, E. S., & Banaji, M. R. (2014). Inferring character from faces: A developmental study. *Psychological Science.* Retrieved March 25, 2014. doi:10.1177/0956797614523297

Cohen, A. B. (Ed.). (2014). *Culture reexamined: Broadening our understanding of social and evolutionary influences.* Washington, DC: American Psychological Association.

Cohen, A. R. (1962). An experiment on small rewards for discrepant compliance and attitude change. In J. W. Brehm & A. R. Cohen (Eds.), *Explorations in cognitive dissonance* (pp. 73–78). New York: Wiley.

Cohen, A. B. (2014). Introduction. In A. B. Cohen (Ed.), *Culture reexamined: Broadening our understanding of social and evolutionary influences* (pp. 3–10). Washington, DC: American Psychological Association.

Cohen, D. (1998). Culture, social organization, and patterns of violence. *Journal of Personality and Social Psychology, 75*(2), 408–419.

Cohen, D., & Nisbett, R. E. (1996). *Culture of honor: The psychology of violence in the South.* Boulder, CO: Westview Press.

Cohen, D., Hoshino-Browne, E., & Leung, A. (2007). Culture and the structure of personal experience: Insider and outsider phenomenologies of the self and social world. In M. P. Zanna (Ed.), *Advances in experimental social psychology* (Vol. 39, pp. 1–67). San Diego, CA: Elsevier Academic Press.

Cohen, D., Nisbett, R. E., Bowdle, B. F., & Schwarz, N. (1996). Insult, aggression, and the southern culture of honor: An "experimental ethnography." *Journal of Personality and Social Psychology, 70,* 945–960.

Cohen, F., Jussim, L., Harber, K. D., & Bhasin, G. (2009). Modern anti-Semitism and anti-Israeli attitudes. *Journal of Personality and Social Psychology, 97,* 290–306.

Cohen, G. L., Garcia, J., Purdie-Vaughns, V., Apfel, N., & Brzustoski, P. (2009, April 17). Recursive processes in self-affirmation: Intervening to close the minority achievement gap. *Science,* 400–403.

Cohen, J. (2001, January 18). On the Internet, love really is blind. *The New York Times,* pp. E1, E7.

Cohen, R. (1997, October 31). AH-lo-ween: An American holiday in Paris? *The New York Times,* pp. A1, A4.

Cohen, S., Alper, C., Doyle, W., Adler, N., Treanor, J., & Turner, R. (2008). Objective and subjective socioeconomic status and susceptibility to the common cold. *Health Psychology, 27,* 268–274.

Cohen, S., Evans, G. W., Krantz, D. S., Stokols, D., & Kelly, S. (1981). Aircraft noise and children: Longitudinal and cross-sectional evidence on adaptation to noise and the effectiveness of noise abatement. *Journal of Personality and Social Psychology, 40,* 331–345.

Cohen, S., Mermelstein, R., Kamarack, T., & Hoberman, H. (1985). Measuring the functional components of social support. In I. G. Sarason & B. R. Sarason (Eds.), *Social support: Theory, research, and applications* (pp. 73–94). The Hague, Netherlands: Martines Nijhoff.

Cohen, S., Tyrrell, D. A. J., & Smith, A. P. (1991). Psychological stress in humans and susceptibility to the common cold. *New England Journal of Medicine, 325,* 606–612.

Cohen, S., Tyrrell, D. A. J., & Smith, A. P. (1993). Negative life events, perceived stress, negative affect, and susceptibility to the common cold. *Journal of Personality and Social Psychology, 64,* 131–140.

Cohen, T. R., & Insko, C. A. (2008). War and peace: Possible approaches to reducing intergroup conflict. *Perspectives on Psychological Science, 3,* 87–93.

Coie, J. D., Cillessen, A. H. N., Dodge, K. A., Hubbard, J. A., Schwartz, D., Lemerise, E. D., & Bateman, H. (1999). It takes two to fight: A test of relational factors and a method for assessing aggressive dyads. *Developmental Psychology, 35,* 1179–1188.

Cole, T. B. (2006). Rape at U.S. colleges often fueled by alcohol. *Journal of the American Medical Association, 296,* 504–505.

Coleman, M. D. (2010). Sunk cost and commitment to medical treatment. *Current Psychology: A Journal for Diverse Perspectives on Diverse Psychological Issues, 29,* 121–134.

Collins, B. E., & Brief, D. E. (1995). Using person-perception vignette methodologies to uncover the symbolic meanings of teacher behaviors in the Milgram paradigm. *Journal of Social Issues, 51,* 89–106.

Collins, N. L., & Feeney, B. C. (2000). A safe haven: An attachment theory perspective on support seeking and caregiving in intimate relationships. *Journal of Personality and Social Psychology, 78,* 1053–1073.

Collins, N. L., Ford, M. B., Guichard, A. C., & Allard, L. M. (2006). Working models of attachment and attribution processes in intimate relationships. *Personality and Social Psychology Bulletin, 32,* 201–219.

Collins, W. A., & Sroufe, L. A. (1999). Capacity for intimate relationships: A developmental construction. In W. Furman, C. Feiring, & B. B. Brown (Eds.), *Contemporary perspectives on adolescent romantic relationships.* New York: Cambridge University Press.

Confer, J. C., Easton, J. A., Fleischman, D. S., Goetz, C. D., Lewis, D. M. G., Perilloux, C., & Buss, D. M. (2010). Evolutionary psychology: Controversies, questions, prospects, and limitations. *American Psychologist, 65*(2), 110–126. doi:10.1037/a0018413

Conley, T. D., & Ramsey, L. R. (2011). Killing us softly? Investigating portrayals of women and men in contemporary magazine advertisements. *Psychology of Women Quarterly, 35*(3), 469–478. doi:10.1177/0361684311413383

Conley, T. D., Moors, A. C., Matsick, J. L., Ziegler, A., & Valentine, B. A. (2011). Women, men, and the bedroom: Methodological and conceptual insights that narrow, reframe, and eliminate gender differences in sexuality. *Current Directions in Psychological Science, 20,* 296–300.

Conner, M., Rhodes, R. E., Morris, B., McEachan, R., & Lawton, R. (2011). Changing exercise through targeting affective or cognitive attitudes. *Psychology & Health, 26*(2), 133–149. doi:10.1080/08870446.2011.531570

Conway, L. G., III, & Schaller, M. (2005). When authorities' commands backfire: Attributions about consensus and effects on deviant decision making. *Journal of Personality and Social Psychology, 89,* 311–326.

Conway, M., & Ross, M. (1984). Getting what you want by revising what you had. *Journal of Personality and Social Psychology, 47,* 738–748.

Cook, K. (2014). *Kitty Genovese: The murder, the bystanders, the crime that changed America.* New York: W. W. Norton.

Cook, K. S., Cheshire, C., Rice, E. R. W., & Nakagawa, S. (2013). Social exchange theory. In J. DeLamater & A. Ward (Eds.), *Handbook of social psychology.* Netherlands: Springer.

Cook, K., & Rice, E. (2003). Social exchange theory. In J. Delamater (Ed.), *Handbook of social psychology* (pp. 53–76). New York: Kluwer Academic/Plenum.

Cooley, C. H. (1902). *Human nature and social order.* New York: Scribners.

Cooper, J. (1980). Reducing fears and increasing assertiveness: The role of dissonance reduction. *Journal of Experimental Social Psychology, 47,* 738–748.

Cooper, J. (1980). Reducing fears and increasing assertiveness: The role of dissonance reduction. *Journal of Experimental Social Psychology, 16,* 199–287.

Cooper, J. (2010). Riding the D train with Elliot. In M. H. Gonzales, C. Tavris, & J. Aronson (Eds.), *The scientist and the humanist: A festschrift in honor of Elliot Aronson* (pp. 159–174). New York: Psychology Press.

Cooper, J. (2012). Cognitive dissonance theory. In P. Van Lange, A. W. Kruglanski, & E. T. Higgins (Eds.), *Handbook of theories of social psychology* (Vol. 1, pp. 377–397). Thousand Oaks, CA: Sage.

Cooper, J., Bennett, E. A., & Sukel, H. L. (1996). Complex scientific testimony: How do jurors make decisions? *Law and Human Behavior, 20,* 379–394.

Cooper, L. A., Roter, D. L., Carson, K. A., Beach, M. C., Sabin, J. A., et al. (2012). The associations of clinicians' implicit attitudes about race with medical visit communication and patient ratings of interpersonal care. *American Journal of Public Health, 102,* 979–987.

Corcoran, K., & Mussweiler, T. (2009). The efficiency of social comparisons with routine standards. *Social Cognition, 27,* 939–948. doi:10.1521/soco.2009.27.6.939

Cornelis, E., Cauberghe, V., & De Pelesmacker, P. (2014). Regulatory congruence effects in two-sided advertising: The mediating role of processing fluency and processing depth. *European Journal of Marketing, 48,* 1451–1465.

Correll, J., Park, B., Judd, C. M., & Wittenbrink, B. (2002). The police officer's dilemma: Using ethnicity to disambiguate potentially threatening individuals. *Journal of Personality and Social Psychology, 83,* 1314–1329.

Correll, J., Park, B., Judd, C., Wittenbrink, B., Sadler, M., & Keesee, T. (2007). Across the thin blue line: Police officers and racial bias in the decision to shoot. *Journal of Personality and Social Psychology, 92,* 1006–1023.

Correll, J., Wittenbrink, B., Park, B., Judd, C. M., & Goyle, A. (2011). Dangerous enough: Moderating racial bias with contextual threat cues. *Journal of Experimental Social Psychology, 47,* 184–189.

Costanzo, M., & Archer, D. (1989). Interpreting the expressive behavior of others: The interpersonal perceptions task. *Journal of Nonverbal Behavior, 13,* 223–245.

Cottrell, N. B., Wack, K. L., Sekerak, G. J., & Rittle, R. (1968). Social facilitation in dominant responses by the presence of an audience and the mere presence of others. *Journal of Personality and Social Psychology, 9,* 245–250.

Courage, M. L., Edison, S. C., & Howe, M. L. (2004). Variability in the early development of visual self-recognition. *Infant Behavior and Development, 27,* 509–532.

Courbet, D., Fourquet-Courbet, M., Kazan, R., & Intartaglia, J. (2014). The long-term effects of e-advertising: The influence of internet pop-ups viewed at a low level of attention in implicit memory. *Journal of Computer-Mediated Communication, 19,* 274–293.

Craig, M. A., & Richeson, J. A. (2014). More diverse yet less tolerant? How the increasingly diverse racial landscape affects White Americans' racial attitudes. *Personality and Social Psychology Bulletin, 40,* 750–761.

Crandall, C. S., & Eshleman, A. (2003). A justification-suppression model of the expression and experience of prejudice. *Psychological Bulletin, 129*(3), 414–446.

Crandall, C. S., & Greenfield, B. S. (1986). Understanding the conjunction fallacy: A conjunction of effects? *Social Cognition, 4,* 408–419.

Crandall, C. S., D'anello, S., Sakalli, N., Lazarus, E., Wieczorkowska, G., & Feather, N. T. (2001). An attribution-value model of prejudice: Anti-fat attitudes in six nations. *Personality and Social Psychology Bulletin, 27,* 30–37.

Crandall, C. S., Silvia, P. J., N'Gbala, A. N., Tsang, J.-A., & Dawson, K. (2007). Balance theory, unit relations, and attribution: The underlying integrity of Heiderian theory. *Review of General Psychology, 11,* 12–30.

Crescioni, A. W., & Baumeister, R. F. (2009). Alone and aggressive: Social exclusion impairs self-control and empathy and increases hostile cognition. In M. J. Harris (Ed.), *Bullying, rejection, and peer victimization: A social-cognitive neuroscience perspective* (pp. 251–277). New York: Springer.

Creswell, J. D., Bursley, J. K., & Satpute, A. B. (2013). Neural reactivation links unconscious thought to decision making performance. *Social Cognitive and Affective Neuroscience, 8,* 863–869.

Critcher, C. R., & Gilovich, T. (2010). Inferring attitudes from mindwandering. *Personality and Social Psychology Bulletin, 36,* 1255–1266. doi:10.1177/0146167210375434

Cross, S. E., & Madson, L. (1997). Models of the self: Self-construals and gender. *Psychological Bulletin, 122,* 5–37.

Cross, S. E., Bacon, P. L., & Morris, M. L. (2000). The relational-interdependent self-construal and relationships. *Journal of Personality and Social Psychology, 78,* 791–808.

Crowley, A. E., & Hoyer, W. D. (1994). An integrative framework for understanding two-sided persuasion. *Journal of Consumer Research, 20,* 561–574.

Croyle, R. T., & Jemmott, J. B., III. (1990). Psychological reactions to risk factor testing. In J. A. Skelton & R. T. Croyle (Eds.), *The mental representation of health and illness* (pp. 121–157). New York: Springer-Verlag.

Crum, A. J., Salovey, P., & Achor, S. (2013). Rethinking stress: The role of mindsets in determining the stress response. *Journal of Personality and Social Psychology, 104,* 716–733. doi:10.1037/a0031201

Csikszentmihalyi, M. (1997). *Finding flow.* New York: Basic Books.

Csikszentmihalyi, M., & Figurski, T. J. (1982). Self-awareness and aversive experience in everyday life. *Journal of Personality, 50,* 15–28.

Csikszentmihalyi, M., & Nakamura, J. (2010). Effortless attention in everyday life: A systematic phenomenology. In B. Bruya (Ed.), *Effortless attention: A new perspective in the cognitive science of attention and action* (pp. 179–189). Cambridge, MA: MIT Press.

Cullen, D. (2010). *Columbine.* New York: Twelve.

Cunningham, M. R. (1986). Measuring the physical in physical attractiveness: Quasi-experiments on the sociobiology of female facial beauty. *Journal of Personality and Social Psychology, 50,* 925–935.

Cunningham, M. R., Barbee, A. P., & Pike, C. L. (1990). What do women want? Facialmetric assessment of multiple motives in the perception of male facial physical attractiveness. *Journal of Personality and Social Psychology, 59,* 61–72.

Cunningham, M. R., Roberts, A. R., Barbee, A. P., Druen, P. B., & Wu, C. (1995). "Their ideas of beauty are, on the whole, the same as ours": Consistency and variability in the cross-cultural perception of female physical attractiveness. *Journal of Personality and Social Psychology, 68,* 261–279.

Curtiss, S. (1977). *Genie: A psycholinguistic study of a modern-day "wild child."* New York: Academic Press.

Cury, F., Da Fonseca, D., Zahn, I., & Elliot, A. (2008). Implicit theories and IQ test performance: A sequential mediation analysis. *Journal of Experimental Social Psychology, 44,* 783–791.

Dabbs, J. M., Jr. (2000). *Heroes, rogues, and lovers.* New York: McGraw-Hill.

Dabbs, J. M., Jr., Carr, T. S., Frady, R. L., & Riad, J. K. (1995). Testosterone, crime, and misbehavior among 692 male prison inmates. *Personality and Individual Differences, 18,* 627–633.

Dabbs, J. M., Jr., Hargrove, M. F., & Heusel, C. (1996). Testosterone differences among college fraternities: Well-behaved vs. rambunctious. *Personality and Individual Differences, 20,* 157–161.

Dai, X., Dong, P., & Jia, J. S. (2014). When does playing hard to get increase romantic attraction? *Journal of Experimental Psychology: General, 132,* 521–526.

Dalbert, C., & Yamauchi, L. A. (1994). Belief in a just world and attitudes toward immigrants and foreign workers: A cultural comparison between Hawaii and Germany. *Journal of Applied Social Psychology, 24,* 1612–1626.

Darley, J. M. (1992). Social organization for the production of evil. *Psychological Inquiry, 3,* 199–218.

Darley, J. M. (2004). Social comparison motives in ongoing groups. In M. B. Brewer & M. Hewstone (Eds.), *Emotion and motivation* (pp. 281–297). Malden, MA: Blackwell.

Darley, J. M., & Akert, R. M. (1993). *Biographical interpretation: The influence of later events in life on the meaning of and memory for earlier events.* Unpublished manuscript, Princeton University.

Darley, J. M., & Batson, C. D. (1973). From Jerusalem to Jericho: A study of situational and dispositional variables in helping behavior. *Journal of Personality and Social Psychology, 27,* 100–108.

Darley, J. M., & Latané, B. (1968). Bystandar intervention in emergencies: Diffusion of responsibility. *Journal of Personality and Social Psychology, 8,* 377–383.

Dar-Nimrod, I., & Heine, S. J. (2011). Genetic essentialism: On the deceptive determinism of DNA. *Psychological Bulletin, 137,* 800–818.

Darwin, C. R. (1859). *The origin of species.* London: Murray.

Darwin, C. R. (1872). *The expression of the emotions in man and animals.* London: Murray.

Davenport, C. (2014, May 7). Miami finds itself ankle-deep in Climate Change debate. *New York Times.* Retrieved July 15, 2014, from http://www.nytimes.com/2014/05/08/us/florida-finds-itself-in-the-eye-of-the-storm-on-climate-change.html?emc=eta1

Davidson, A. R., & Jaccard, J. J. (1979). Variables that moderate the attitude-behavior relation: Results of a longitudinal survey. *Journal of Personality and Social Psychology, 37,* 1364–1376.

Davidson, L., & Duberman, L. (1982). Friendship: Communication and interactional patterns in same-sex dyads. *Sex Roles, 8,* 809–822.

Davis, A. L., & Fischhoff, B. (2014). Communicating uncertain experimental evidence. *Journal of Experimental Psychology: Learning, Memory, and Cognition, 40,* 261–274.

Davis, C. G., Lehman, D. R., Wortman, C. B., Silver, R. C., & Thompson, S. C. (1995). The undoing of traumatic life events. *Personality and Social Psychology Bulletin, 21,* 109–124.

Davis, D., & Loftus, E. F. (2003). What's good for the goose cooks the gander: Inconsistencies between the law and psychology of voluntary intoxication and sexual assault. In W. T. O'Donohue & E. Levensky (Eds.), *Handbook of forensic psychology* (pp. 997–1032). New York: Elsevier Academic Press.

Davis, K. E., & Jones, E. E. (1960). Changes in interpersonal perception as a means of reducing cognitive dissonance. *Journal of Abnormal and Social Psychology, 61,* 402–410.

Davis, M. H. (1983). Measuring individual differences in empathy: Evidence for a multidimensional approach. *Journal of Personality and Social Psychology, 44,* 113–126.

Davis, M. H., & Stephan, W. G. (1980). Attributions for exam performance. *Journal of Applied Social Psychology, 10,* 235–248.

Davitz, J. (1952). The effects of previous training on post-frustration behavior. *Journal of Abnormal and Social Psychology, 47,* 309–315.

Dawkins, R. (1976). *The selfish gene.* New York: Oxford University Press.

De Bono, K. G., & Snyder, M. (1995). Acting on one's attitudes: The role of a history of choosing situations. *Personality and Social Psychology Bulletin, 21,* 629–636.

De Dreu, C. K. W. (2014). *Social conflict within and between groups.* East Sussex: Psychology Press.

De Dreu, C. K. W., & De Vries, N. K. (Eds.). (2001). *Group consensus and minority influence: Implications for innovation.* Oxford, England: Blackwell Publishers.

De Dreu, C. K. W., & Weingart, L. R. (2003). Task versus relationship conflict, team performance, and team member satisfaction: A meta-analysis. *Journal of Applied Psychology, 88,* 741–749.

De Dreu, C., Nijstad, B., & van Knippenberg, D. (2008). Motivated information processing in group judgment and decision making. *Personality and Social Psychology Review, 12,* 22–49.

De Houwer, J. (2011). Evaluative conditioning: A review of procedure knowledge and mental process theories. In T. Schachtman & S. Reilly (Eds.), *Applications of learning and conditioning.* Oxford, UK: Oxford University Press.

De Houwer, J., Teige-Mocigemba, S., Spruyt, A., & Moors, A. (2009). Implicit measures: A normative analysis and review. *Psychological Bulletin, 135,* 347–368.

de Mooij, M. (2014). International and cross-cultural consumer behavior. In H. Cheng (Ed.), *The handbook of international advertising research* (Vol. 1, pp. 128–148).

De Waal, F. B. M. (1995, March). Bonobo sex and society: The behavior of a close relative challenges assumptions about male supremacy in human evolution. *Scientific American,* 82–88.

Dean, K. E., & Malamuth, N. M. (1997). Characteristics of men who aggress sexually and of men who imagine aggressing: Risk and moderating variables. *Journal of Personality and Social Psychology, 72,* 449–455.

Deaux, K., & LaFrance, M. (1998). Gender. In D. T. Gilbert, S. T. Fiske, & G. Lindzey (Eds.), *The handbook of social psychology.* Boston: McGraw Hill.

Deci, E. L., & Ryan, R. M. (1985). *Intrinsic motivation and self-determination in human behavior.* New York: Plenum.

Deci, E. L., Koestner, R., & Ryan, R. M. (1999a). A meta-analytic review of experiments examining the effects of extrinsic rewards. *Psychological Bulletin, 125,* 627–668.

Deci, E. L., Koestner, R., & Ryan, R. M. (1999b). The undermining effect is a reality after all—extrinsic rewards, task interest, and self-determination: Reply to Eisenberger, Pierce, and Cameron (1999) and Lepper, Henderlong, and Gingras (1999). *Psychological Bulletin, 125,* 692–700.

Dedonder, J., Corneille, O., Yzerbyt, V., & Kuppens, T. (2010). Evaluative conditioning of high-novelty stimuli does not seem to be based on an automatic form of associative learning. *Journal of Experimental Social Psychology, 46(6),* 1118–1121. doi:10.1016/j.jesp.2010.06.004

Deffenbacher, K. A., Bornstein, B. H., & Penrod, S. D. (2004). A meta-analytic review of the effects of high stress on eyewitness memory. *Law and Human Behavior, 28,* 687–706.

Dekel, S., Ein-Dor, T., Gordon, K. M., Rosen, J. B., & Bonanno, G. A. (2013). Cortisol and PTSD symptoms among male and female high-exposure 9/11 survivors. *Journal of Traumatic Stress, 26,* 621–625.

DeMarco, P. (1994, September 28). Dear diary. *The New York Times,* p. C2.

DeMarree, K. G., Loersch, C., Briñol, P., Petty, R. E., Payne, B. K., & Rucker, D. D. (2012). From primed construct to motivated behavior: Validation processes in goal pursuit. *Personality and Social Psychology Bulletin, 38,* 1659–1670.

Dennett, D. C. (1991). *Consciousness explained.* Boston: Little, Brown.

DePaulo, B. M. (1992). Nonverbal behavior and self-presentation. *Psychological Bulletin, 111,* 203–243.

DePaulo, B. M., & Friedman, H. S. (1998). Nonverbal communication. In D. T. Gilbert, S. T. Fiske, & G. Lindzey (Eds.), *The handbook of social psychology* (Vol. 2, 4th ed., pp. 3–40). New York: McGraw-Hill.

DePaulo, B. M., Kenny, D. A., Hoover, C. W., Webb, W., & Oliver, P. (1987). Accuracy of person perception: Do people know what kinds of impressions they convey? *Journal of Personality and Social Psychology, 52,* 303–315.

DePaulo, B. M., Stone, J. L., & Lassiter, G. D. (1985). Deceiving and detecting deceit. In B. R. Schlenker (Ed.), *The self and social life* (pp. 323–370). New York: McGraw-Hill.

Deppe, R. K., & Harackiewicz, J. M. (1996). Self-handicapping and intrinsic motivation: Buffering intrinsic motivation from the threat of failure. *Journal of Personality and Social Psychology, 70,* 868–876.

Dershowitz, A. M. (1997). *Reasonable doubts: The criminal justice system and the O. J. Simpson case.* New York: Touchstone.

Derzon, J. H., & Lipsey, M. W. (2002). A meta-analysis of the effectiveness of mass communication for changing substance-use knowledge, attitudes, and behavior. In W. D. Crano & M. Burgoon (Eds.), *Mass media and drug prevention: Classic and contemporary theories and research* (pp. 231–258). Mahwah, NJ: Erlbaum.

Desforges, D. M., Lord, C. G., Ramsey, S. L., Mason, J. A., Van Leeuwen, M. D., et al. (1991). Effects of structured cooperative contact on changing negative attitudes toward stigmatized social groups. *Journal of Personality and Social Psychology, 60,* 531–544.

Desmarais, S. L., & Read, J. D. (2011). After 30 years, what do we know about what jurors know? A meta-analytic review of lay knowledge regarding eyewitness factors. *Law and Human Behavior, 35*(3), 200–210. doi:10.1007/s10979-010-9232-6

Desmond, E. W. (1987, November 30). Out in the open. *Time,* pp. 80–90.

Desportes, J. P., & Lemaine, J. M. (1998). The sizes of human groups: An analysis of their distributions. In D. Canter, J. C. Jesuino, L. Soczka, & G. M. Stephenson (Eds.), *Environmental social psychology* (pp. 57–65). Dordrecht, Netherlands: Kluwer.

Deutsch, M. (1973). *The resolution of conflict: Constructive and destructive processes.* New Haven, CT: Yale University Press.

Deutsch, M. (1997, April). *Comments on cooperation and prejudice reduction.* Paper presented at the symposium Reflections on 100 Years of Social Psychology, Yosemite National Park, CA.

Deutsch, M., & Collins, M. E. (1951). *Interracial housing: A psychological evaluation of a social experiment.* Minneapolis: University of Minnesota Press.

Deutsch, M., & Gerard, H. G. (1955). A study of normative and informational social influence upon individual judgment. *Journal of Abnormal and Social Psychology, 51,* 629–636.

Deutsch, M., & Krauss, R. M. (1960). The effect of threat upon interpersonal bargaining. *Journal of Abnormal and Social Psychology, 61,* 181–189.

Deutsch, M., & Krauss, R. M. (1962). Studies of interpersonal bargaining. *Journal of Conflict Resolution, 6,* 52–76.

Deutsch, M., Coleman, P. T., & Marcus, E. C. (2011). *The handbook of conflict resolution: Theory and practice.* Hoboken, NJ: Wiley.

Devine, D. J. (2012). *Jury decision making: The state of the science.* New York: NYU Press.

Devine, P. G., Plant, E. A., Amodio, D. M., Harmon-Jones, E., & Vance, S. L. (2002). The regulation of explicit and implicit race bias: The role of motivations to respond without prejudice. *Journal of Personality and Social Psychology, 82*(5), 835–848.

Devos-Comby, L., & Salovey, P. (2002). Applying persuasion strategies to alter HIV-relevant thoughts and behavior. *Review of General Psychology, 6,* 287–304.

DeWall, C. N., & Richman, S. B. (2011). Social exclusion and the desire to reconnect. *Social and Personality Psychology Compass, 5,* 919–932. doi:10.1111/j.1751-9004.2011.00383.x

DeWall, C. N., Pond, R. S., Jr., Campbell, W. K., & Twenge, J. M. (2011, March 21). Tuning in to psychological change: Linguistic markers of psychological traits and emotions over time in popular U.S. song lyrics. *Psychology of Aesthetics, Creativity, and the Arts.* Advance online publication. doi:10.1037/a0023195

Dezecache, G., Conty, L., Chadwick, M., Philip, L., Soussignan, R., Sperber, D., et al. (2013). Evidence for unintentional emotional contagion beyond dyads. *PLoS ONE, 8,* e67371.

Dickerson, C., Thibodeau, R., Aronson, E., & Miller, D. (1992). Using cognitive dissonance to encourage water conservation. *Journal of Applied Social Psychology, 22,* 841–854.

Diener, E. (1980). Deindividuation: The absence of self-awareness and self-regulation in group members. In P. B. Paulus (Ed.), *Psychology of group influence* (pp. 209–242). Hillsdale, NJ: Erlbaum.

Diener, E., & Biswas-Diener, R. (2008). *Happiness: Unlocking the mysteries of psychological wealth.* Boston: Wiley-Blackwell.

Diener, E., & Oishi, S. (2005). The nonobvious social psychology of happiness. *Psychological Inquiry, 16,* 162–167.

Diener, E., & Seligman, M. E. P. (2004). Beyond money: Toward an economy of well-being. *Psychological Science in the Public Interest, 5,* 1–31.

Diener, E., & Wallbom, M. (1976). Effects of self-awareness on antinormative behavior. *Journal of Research in Personality, 10,* 107–111.

Diener, E., Tay, L., & Oishi, S. (2013). Rising income and the subjective well-being of nations. *Journal of Personality and Social Psychology, 104,* 267–276.

Dijksterhuis, A. (2004). Think different: The merits of unconscious thought in preference development and decision making. *Journal of Personality and Social Psychology, 87,* 586–598.

Dijksterhuis, A. (2010). Automaticity and the unconscious. In S. T. Fiske, D. T. Gilbert, & G. Lindzey (Eds.), *Handbook of social psychology* (5th ed., Vol. 1, pp. 228–267). Hoboken, NJ: Wiley.

Dijksterhuis, A., & Nordgren, L. (2006). A theory of unconscious thought. *Perspectives on Psychological Science, 1,* 95–109.

Dijksterhuis, A., & Nordgren, L. F. (2005). *A theory of unconscious thought* (Vol. I, pp. 95–109). University of Amsterdam.

Dijksterhuis, A., & Nordgren, L. F. (2006). A theory of unconscious thought. *Perspectives on Psychological Science, 1,* 95–109.

Dijksterhuis, A., Aarts, H., & Smith, P. K. (2005). The power of the subliminal: On subliminal persuasion and other potential applications. In R. R. Hassin, J. S. Uleman, & J. A. Bargh (Eds.), *The new unconscious* (pp. 77–106). New York: Oxford University Press.

Dill, J. C., & Anderson, C. A. (1995). Effects of frustration justification on hostile aggression. *Aggressive Behavior, 21,* 359–369.

Dillon, S. (2009, 23 January). Study sees an Obama effect as lifting Black test-takers. *The New York Times.*

Dion, K. K., & Dion, K. L. (1993). Individualistic and collectivistic perspectives on gender and the cultural context of love and intimacy. *Journal of Social Issues, 49,* 53–69.

Dion, K. K., & Dion, K. L. (1996). Cultural perspectives on romantic love. *Personal Relationships, 3,* 5–17.

Dion, K. L. (2000). Group cohesion: From "fields of forces" to multidimensional construct. *Group Dynamics, 4,* 7–26.

Dion, K. L., & Dion, K. K. (1993). Gender and ethnocultural comparisons in styles of love. *Psychology of Women Quarterly, 17,* 463–473.

Dion, K., Berscheid, E., & Walster, E. (1972). What is beautiful is good. *Journal of Personality and Social Psychology, 24,* 285–290.

Dionne, E. J. Jr. (2005, June 21). How Cheney fooled himself. *Washington Post,* p. A21.

Dittmar, H., Bond, R., Hurst, M., & Kasser, T. (2014). The relationship between materialism and personal well-being: A meta-analysis. *Journal of Personality and Social Psychology, 107,* 879–924.

Dobbs, M. (2008, June 22). Cool crisis management? It's a myth. Ask JFK. *Washington Post,* pp. B1, B4.

Dobolyi, D. G., & Dodson, C. S. (2013). Eyewitness confidence in simultaneous and sequential lineups: A criterion shift account for sequential mistaken identification overconfidence. *Journal of Experimental Psychology: Applied, 19,* 345–357.

Dodds, D. P., Towgood, K. H., McClure, S., & Olson, J. M. (2011). The biological roots of complex thinking: Are heritable attitudes more complex? (L. G. Conway III, Illus.). *Journal of Personality, 79*(1), 101–134. doi:10.1111/j.1467-6494.2010.00690.x

Dodds, P. S., Muhamad, R., & Watts, D. J. (2003). An experimental study of search in global social networks. *Science, 301,* 827–829.

Dohrenwend, B. (2006). Inventorying stressful life events as risk factors for psychopathology: Toward resolution of the problem of intracategory variability. *Psychological Bulletin, 132,* 477–495.

Doi, T. (1988). *The anatomy of dependence.* New York: Kodansha International.

Dollard, J. (1938). Hostility and fear in social life. *Social Forces, 17,* 15–26.

Dollard, J., Doob, L., Miller, N., Mowrer, O. H., & Sears, R. R. (1939). *Frustration and aggression.* New Haven, CT: Yale University Press.

Domina, T., & Koch, K. (2002). Convenience and frequency of recycling: Implications for including textiles in curbside recycling programs. *Environment and Behavior, 34,* 216–238.

Donnerstein, E. (1980). Aggressive erotica and violence against women. *Journal of Personality and Social Psychology, 39,* 269–277.

Donnerstein, E., & Berkowitz, L. (1981). Victim reactions in aggressive erotic films as a factor in violence against women. *Journal of Personality and Social Psychology, 41,* 710–724.

Donnerstein, E., & Donnerstein, M. (1976). Research in the control of interracial aggression. In R. G. Green & E. C. O'Neal (Eds.), *Perspectives on aggression* (pp. 133–168). New York: Academic Press.

Donnerstein, E., & Linz, D. G. (1994). Sexual violence in the mass media. In M. Costanzo & S. Oskamp (Eds.), *Violence and the law* (pp. 9–36). Thousand Oaks, CA: Sage.

Douglass, A. B., & Pavletic, A. (2012). Eyewitness confidence malleability. In B. L. Cutler (Ed.), *Conviction of the innocent: Lessons from psychological research* (pp. 149–165). Washington, DC: American Psychological Association.

Dovidio, J. F. (1984). Helping behavior and altruism: An empirical and conceptual overview. In L. Berkowitz (Ed.), *Advances in experimental social psychology* (Vol. 17, pp. 361–427). New York: Academic Press.

Dovidio, J. F., & Gaertner, S. L. (1996). Affirmative action, unintentional racial biases, and intergroup relations. *Journal of Social Issues, 52,* 51–75.

Dovidio, J. F., & Gaertner, S. L. (2008). New directions in aversive racism research: Persistence and pervasiveness. In C. Willis-Esqueda (Ed.), *Motivational aspects of prejudice and racism.* Nebraska Symposium on Motivation. New York: Springer Science 1 Business Media.

Dovidio, J. F., & Gaertner, S. L. (2010). Intergroup bias. In S. T. Fiske, D. T. Gilbert, & G. Lindzey (Eds.), *Handbook of social psychology* (5th ed., Vol. 2, pp. 1084–1121). Hoboken, NJ: John Wiley & Sons.

Dovidio, J. F., Kawakami, K., & Gaertner, S. L. (2002). Implicit and explicit prejudice and interracial interaction. *Journal of Personality and Social Psychology, 82,* 62–68.

Dovidio, J. F., Pagotto, L., & Hebl, M. R. (2011). Implicit attitudes and discrimination against people with physical disabilities. In R. L. Wiener & S. L. Willborn (Eds.), *Disability and aging discrimination: Perspectives in law and psychology* (pp. 157–183). New York: Springer Science 1 Business Media.

Dovidio, J. F., Piliavin, J. A., Gaertner, S. L., Schroeder, D. A., & Clark, R. D., III. (1991). The arousal cost-reward model and the process of intervention. In M. S. Clark (Ed.), *Review of personality and social psychology* (Vol. 12, pp. 86–118). Newbury Park, CA: Sage.

Draper, R. (2008). *Dead certain.* New York: Free Press.

Drigotas, S. M., & Rusbult, C. E. (1992). Should I stay or should I go? A dependence model of breakups. *Journal of Personality and Social Psychology, 62,* 62–87.

Du, S., Tao, Y., & Martinez, A. M. (2014). Compound facial expressions of emotion. *Proceedings of the National Academy of Sciences.* doi:10.1073/pnas.1322355111

Duck, J., Hogg, M., & Terry, D. (1995). Me, us, and them: Political identification and the third-person effect in the 1993 Australian federal election. *European Journal of Social Psychology, 25,* 195–215.

Duck, S. W. (1982). A typography of relationship disengagement and dissolution. In S. W. Duck (Ed.), *Personal relationships 4: Dissolving personal relationships* (pp. 1–32). London: Academic Press.

Duck, S. W. (1994a). *Meaningful relationships: Talking, sense, and relating.* Thousand Oaks, CA: Sage.

Dugan, A. (2014). Americans most likely to say global warming is exaggerated: Sixty percent say most scientists believe global warming is occurring. *Gallup Politics.* Retrieved July 25, 2014, from http://www.gallup.com/poll/167960/americans-likely-say-global-warming-exaggerated.aspx

Dunn, E. W., Aknin, L. B., & Norton, M. I. (2014). Prosocial spending and happiness: Using money to benefit others pays off. *Current Directions in Psychological Science, 23,* 41–47.

Dunn, E. W., Aknin, L., & Norton, M. (2008). Spending money on others promotes happiness. *Science, 319,* 1687–1688.

Dunn, E. W., Gilbert, D. T., & Wilson, T. D. (2011). If money doesn't make you happy, then you probably aren't spending it right. *Journal of Consumer Psychology, 21,* 115–125.

Dunning, D., & Perretta, S. (2002). Automaticity and eyewitness accuracy: A 10- to 12-second rule for distinguishing accurate from inaccurate positive identifications. *Journal of Applied Psychology, 87,* 951–962.

Dunning, D., & Stern, L. B. (1994). Distinguishing accurate from inaccurate eyewitness identifications via inquiries about decision processes. *Journal of Personality and Social Psychology, 67,* 818–835.

During blackout, fewer crimes than on a typical NYPD day. (2003, August 16). Retrieved from www.wnbc.com/news/2409267/detail.html

Durrant, J., & Ensom, R. (2012). Physical punishment of children: Lessons from 20 years of research. *Canadian Medical Association Journal, 184,* 1373–1377.

Durrant, R., Ellis, B. J., Nelson, R. J., Mizumori, S. J. Y., & Weiner, I. (Eds.). (2013). *Evolutionary psychology. Handbook of psychology: Behavioral neuroscience* (Vol. 3, 2nd ed., pp. 26–51). New York: John Wiley & Sons.

Dutton, D. G., & Aron, A. P. (1974). Some evidence for heightened sexual attraction under conditions of high anxiety. *Journal of Personality and Social Psychology, 30,* 510–517.

Duval, T. S., & Silvia, P. J. (2001). *Self-awareness and causal attributions: A dual-systems theory.* Boston: Kluwer Academic.

Duval, T. S., & Silvia, P. J. (2002). Self-awareness, probability of improvement, and the self-serving bias. *Journal of Personality and Social Psychology, 82,* 49–61.

Duval, T. S., & Wicklund, R. A. (1972). *A theory of objective self-awareness.* New York: Academic Press.

Dweck, C. S. (2006). *Mindset: The new psychology of success.* New York: Random House.

Dzokoto, V., Wallace, D. S., Peters, L., & Bentsi-Enchill, E. (2014). Attention to emotion and non-Western faces: Revisiting the facial feedback hypothesis. *Journal of General Psychology, 141,* 151–168.

Eagly & Chaiken, 1975; Khan, R. F., & Sutvliàe, A. (2014). Attractive agents are more persuasive. *International Journal of Human-Computer Interaction, 30,* 142–150.

Eagly, A. H. (1987). *Sex differences in social behavior: A social-role interpretation.* Hillsdale, NJ: Erlbaum.

Eagly, A. H. (1995). The science and politics of comparing women and men. *American Psychologist, 50,* 145–158.

Eagly, A. H. (1996). Differences between women and men: Their magnitude, practical importance, and political meaning. *American Psychologist, 51,* 158–159.

Eagly, A. H. (2009). The his and hers of prosocial behavior: An examination of the social psychology of gender. *American Psychologist, 64*(8), 644–658. doi:10.1037/0003-066X.64.8.644

Eagly, A. H., & Chaiken, S. (1975). An attribution analysis of communicator characteristics on opinion change: The case of communicator attractiveness. *Journal of Personality and Social Psychology, 32,* 136–244.

Eagly, A. H., & Chaiken, S. (1993). *The psychology of attitudes.* Fort Worth, TX: Harcourt Brace.

Eagly, A. H., & Chaiken, S. (2007). The advantages of an inclusive definition of attitude. *Social Cognition, 25,* 582–602.

Eagly, A. H., & Chin, J. L. (2010). Diversity and leadership in a changing world. *American Psychologist, 65,* 216–224.

Eagly, A. H., & Crowley, M. (1986). Gender and helping behavior: A meta-analytic review of the social psychological literature. *Psychological Bulletin, 100,* 283–308.

Eagly, A. H., & Diekman, A. B. (2003). The malleability of sex differences in response to changing social roles. In L. G. Aspinwall & U. M. Staudinger (Eds.), *A psychology of human strengths: Fundamental questions and future directions for a positive psychology* (pp. 103–115). Washington, DC: American Psychological Association.

Eagly, A. H., & Karau, S. J. (2002). Role congruity theory of prejudice toward female leaders. *Psychological Review, 109,* 573–598.

Eagly, A. H., & Koenig, A. M. (2006). Social role theory of sex differences and similarities: Implication for prosocial behavior. In K. Dindia & D. J. Canary (Eds.), *Sex differences and similarities in communication* (2nd ed., pp. 161–177). Mahwah, NJ: Erlbaum.

Eagly, A. H., & Steffen, V. J. (2000). Gender stereotypes stem from the distribution of women and men into social roles. In C. Stangor (Ed.), *Stereotypes and prejudice: Essential readings* (pp. 142–160). Philadelphia: Psychology Press.

Eagly, A. H., Ashmore, R. D., Makhijani, M. G., & Longo, L. C. (1991). What is beautiful is good, but . . . : A meta-analytic review of research on the physical attractiveness stereotype. *Psychological Bulletin, 110,* 109–128.

Eagly, A. H., Diekman, A. B., Johannesen-Schmidt, M. C., & Koenig, A. M. (2004). Gender gaps in sociopolitical attitudes: A social psychological analysis. *Journal of Personality and Social Psychology, 87,* 796–816.

Eagly, A. H., Johannesen-Schmidt, M. C., & van Engen, M. L. (2003). Transformational, transactional, and laissez-faire leadership styles: A meta-analysis comparing women and men. *Psychological Bulletin, 129,* 569–591.

Eargle, A., Guerra, N., & Tolan, P. (1994). Preventing aggression in inner-city children: Small group training to change cognitions, social skills, and behavior. *Journal of Child and Adolescent Group Therapy, 4,* 229–242.

Eastwick, P. W., Eagly, A. H., Finkel, E. J., & Johnson, S. E. (2011). Implicit and explicit preferences for physical attractiveness in a romantic partner: A double dissociation in predictive validity. *Journal of Personality and Social Psychology, 101,* 993–1011.

Eberhardt, J. L., Goff, P. A., Purdie, V. J., & Davies, P. G. (2004). Seeing Black: Race, crime, and visual processing. *Journal of Personality and Social Psychology, 87,* 876–893.

Ebert, J. P., & Wegner, D. M. (2011). Mistaking randomness for free will. *Consciousness and Cognition: An International Journal, 20,* 965–971. doi:10.1016/j.concog.2010.12.012

Eccles, J. S. (2011). Understanding women's achievement choices: Looking back and looking forward. *Psychology of Women Quarterly, 35,* 520–516.

Edelman, B. (2009). Red light states: Who buys online adult entertainment? *Journal of Economic Perspectives, 23,* 209–230.

Edgell, P., Gerteis, J., & Hartmann, D. (2006). Atheists as "other": Moral boundaries and cultural membership in American society. *American Sociological Review, 71,* 211–234.

Edkins, V. A. (2011). Defense attorney plea recommendations and client race: Does zealous representation apply equally to all? *Law and Human Behavior, 35,* 413–425.

Edwards, H. (1973, July). The Black athletes: 20th-century gladiators in White America. *Psychology Today,* pp. 43–52.

Edwards, K., & Smith, E. (1996). A disconfirmation bias in the evaluation of arguments. *Journal of Personality and Social Psychology, 71,* 5–24.

Egan, L. C., Santos, L. R., & Bloom, P. (2007). The origins of cognitive dissonance: Evidence from children and monkeys. *Psychological Science, 18,* 978–983.

Egan, P. M., Hirt, E. R., & Karpen, S. C. (2012). Taking a fresh perspective: Vicarious restoration as a means of recovering self-control. *Journal of Experimental Social Psychology, 48*(2), 457–465. doi:10.1016/j.jesp.2011.10.019

Eggleston, M., Wilson, T. D., Lee, M., & Gilbert, D. T. (2014). *Predicting what we will like: Asking a stranger can be as good as asking a friend.* Unpublished manuscript, University of Virginia.

Ehrlinger, J., Gilovich, T., & Ross, L. (2005). Peering into the bias blind spot: People's assessments of bias in themselves and others. *Personality and Social Psychology Bulletin, 31,* 680–692.

Eibl-Eibesfeldt, I. (1963). Aggressive behavior and ritualized fighting in animals. In J. H. Masserman (Ed.), *Science and psychoanalysis:* Vol. 6. *Violence and war* (pp. 8–17). New York: Grune & Stratton.

Einolf, C. J. (2011). Gender differences in the correlates of volunteering and charitable giving. *Nonprofit and Voluntary Sector Quarterly, 40,* 1092–1112.

Eisenberg, N., & Fabes, R. A. (1991). Prosocial behavior and empathy: A multimethod developmental perspective. In M. S. Clark (Ed.), *Review of personality and social psychology* (Vol. 12, pp. 34–61). Newbury Park, CA: Sage.

Eisenberg, N., Hofer, C., Sulik, M. J., & Liew, J. (2014). The development of prosocial moral reasoning and a prosocial orientation in young adulthood: Concurrent and longitudinal correlates. *Developmental Psychology, 50,* 58–70.

Eisenberg, N., Spinrad, T. L., & Sadovsky, A. (2006). Empathy-related responding in children. In M. Killen & J. G. Smetana (Eds.), *Handbook of moral development* (pp. 517–549). Mahwah, NJ: Erlbaum.

Eisend, M. (2010). A meta-analysis of gender roles in advertising. *Journal of the Academy of Marketing Science, 38*(4), 418–440. doi:10.1007/s11747-009-0181-x

Eisenstadt, D., & Leippe, M. R. (2010). Social influences on eyewitness confidence: The social psychology of memory self-certainty. In R. M. Arkin, K. C. Oleson, & P. J. Carroll (Eds.), *Handbook of the uncertain self* (pp. 36–61). New York: Psychology Press.

Eisenstat, S. A., & Bancroft, L. (1999). Domestic violence. *New England Journal of Medicine, 341,* 886–892.

Eitam, B., & Higgins, E. T. (2010). Motivation in mental accessibility: Relevance of a Representation (ROAR) as a new framework. *Social and Personality Psychology Compass, 4*(10), 951–967. doi:10.1111/j.1751-9004.2010.00309.x

Ekman, P. (1965). Communication through nonverbal behavior: A source of information about an interpersonal relationship. In S. S. Tomkins & C. E. Izard (Eds.), *Affect, cognition, and personality* (pp. 390–442). New York: Springer-Verlag.

Ekman, P. (1993). Facial expression and emotion. *American Psychologist, 48,* 384–392.

Ekman, P., & Davidson, R. J. (Eds.). (1994). *The nature of emotion: Fundamental questions.* New York: Oxford University Press.

Ekman, P., & Friesen, W. V. (1971). Constants across cultures in the face and emotion. *Journal of Personality and Social Psychology, 17,* 124–129.

Ekman, P., & Friesen, W. V. (1975). *Unmasking the face.* Englewood Cliffs, NJ: Prentice Hall.

Ekman, P., Friesen, W. V., O'Sullivan, M., Chan, A., Diacoyanni-Tarlatzis, I., Heider, K., et al. (1987). Universals and cultural differences in the judgments of facial expressions of emotions. *Journal of Personality and Social Psychology, 53,* 712–717.

Ekman, P., O'Sullivan, M., & Matsumoto, D. (1991). Confusions about content in the judgment of facial expression: A reply to "Contempt and the relativity thesis." *Motivation and Emotion, 15,* 169–176.

Elfenbein, H. A., & Ambady, N. (2002). On the universality and cultural specificity of emotion recognition: A meta-analysis. *Psychological Bulletin, 128,* 203–235.

Ellemers, N., & Jetten, J. (2013). The many ways to be marginal in a group. *Personality and Social Psychology Review, 17,* 3–21.

Ellis, A. P. J., Porter, C. O. L. H., & Wolverton, S. A. (2008). Learning to work together: An examination of transactive memory system development in teams. In V. I. Sessa & M. London (Eds.), *Work group learning: Understanding, improving and assessing how groups learn in organizations* (pp. 91–115). New York: Erlbaum.

Ellis, J. (2002). *Founding brothers.* New York: Vintage.

Else-Quest, N. M., Hyde, J. S., & Linn, M. C. (2010). Cross-national patterns of gender differences in mathematics: A meta-analysis. *Psychological Bulletin, 136,* 103–127.

El-Shinnawy, M., & Vinze, A. S. (1998). Polarization and persuasive argumentation: A study of decision making in group settings. *Management Information Systems Quarterly, 22,* 165–198.

Emery, S. L., Szczypka, G., Abril, E. P., Kim, Y., & Vera, L. (2014). Are you scared yet? Evaluating fear appeal messages in tweets about the Tips campaign. *Journal of Communication*, 64, 278–295.

Engel, B. (2001). *The power of apology*. New York: Wiley.

Engel, C. (2010). Dictator games: A meta study. Retrieved June 13, 2014, from http://www.coll.mpg.de/pdf_dat/2010_07online.pdf

Englich, B., & Mussweiler, T. (2001). Sentencing under uncertainty: Anchoring effects in the courtroom. *Journal of Applied Social Psychology*, 31, 1535–1551.

Epley, E., & Huff, C. (1998). Suspicion, affective response, and education benefit as a result of deception in psychology research. *Personality and Social Psychology Bulletin*, 24, 759–768.

Epley, N., & Gilovich, T. (2004). Are adjustments insufficient? *Personality and Social Psychology Bulletin*, 30, 447–460.

Epley, N., & Gilovich, T. (2005). When effortful thinking influences judgmental anchoring: Differential effects of forewarning and incentives on self-generated and externally provided anchors. *Journal of Behavioral Decision Making*, 18, 199–212.

Erceg-Hurn, D. M., & Steed, L. G. (2011). Does exposure to cigarette health warnings elicit psychological reactance in smokers? *Journal of Applied Social Psychology*, 41(1), 219–237. doi:10.1111/j.1559-1816.2010.00710.x

Eron, L. D. (2001). Seeing is believing: How viewing violence alters attitudes and aggressive behavior. In A. C. Bohart & D. J. Stipek (Eds.), *Constructive and destructive behavior: Implications for family, school, and society* (pp. 49–60). Washington, DC: American Psychological Association.

Etcheverry, P. E., Le, B., & Hoffman, N. G. (2013). Predictors of friend approval for romantic relationships. *Personal Relationships*, 20, 69–83.

European Commission. (2007). *Decision-making in the Top 50 Publicly Quoted Companies*. Retrieved September 3, 2008, from europa.eu.int/comm/employment_social/women_men_stats/out/measures_out438_en.htm

Fabrigar, L. R., & Petty, R. E. (1999). The role of affective and cognitive bases of attitudes in susceptibility to affectively and cognitively based persuasion. *Personality and Social Psychology Bulletin*, 25, 363–381.

Fabrigar, L. R., Priester, J. R., Petty, R. E., & Wegener, D. T. (1998). The impact of attitude accessibility on elaboration of persuasive messages. *Personality and Social Psychology Bulletin*, 24, 339–352.

False Confessions. (2006). Accessed on June 9, 2006, from www.innocenceproject.org/causes/falseconfessions.php

Farhi, P. (2006, January 21). Deluge shuts down post blog; Ombudsman's column had sparked profane responses. *Washington Post*, p. A08.

Farrer, J., Tsuchiya, H., & Bagrowicz, B. (2008). Emotional expression in tsukiau dating relationships in Japan. *Journal of Social and Personal Relationships*, 25, 169–188.

Fawcett, J. M., Russell, E. J., Peace, K. A., & Christie, J. (2013). Of guns and geese: A meta-analytic review of the 'weapon focus' literature. *Psychology, Crime, and Law*, 19, 35–66.

Fazio, R. H. (1990). Multiple processes by which attitudes guide behavior: The MODE model as an integrative framework. In M. P. Zanna (Ed.), *Advances in experimental social psychology* (Vol. 23, pp. 75–109). San Diego, CA: Academic Press.

Fazio, R. H., & Olson, M. A. (2003). Implicit measures in social cognition research: Their meaning and uses. *Annual Review of Psychology*, 54, 297–327.

Fazio, R. H., Jackson, J. R., Dunton, B. C., & Williams, C. J. (1995). Variability in automatic activation as an unobtrusive measure of racial attitudes: A bona fide pipeline? *Journal of Personality and Social Psychology*, 69, 1013–1027.

Feeney, B. C., Cassidy, J., & Ramos-Marcuse, F. (2008). The generalization of attachment representations to new social situations: Predicting behavior during initial interactions

with strangers. *Journal of Personality and Social Psychology*, 95, 1481–1498.

Feeney, J. A., & Noller, P. (1990). Attachment style as a predictor of adult romantic relationships. *Journal of Personality and Social Psychology*, 58, 281–291.

Feeney, J. A., & Noller, P. (1996). *Adult attachment.* Thousand Oaks, CA: Sage.

Feeney, J. A., Noller, P., & Roberts, N. (2000). Attachment and close relationships. In C. Hendrick & S. S. Hendrick (Eds.), *Close relationships: A sourcebook* (pp. 185–201). Thousand Oaks, CA: Sage.

Feeney, M. (2005, October 25). Rosa Parks, civil rights icon, dead at 92. *Boston Globe*, pp. A1, B8.

Fehr, B. (2001). The life cycle of friendship. In C. Hendrick & S. S. Hendrick (Eds.), *Close relationships: A sourcebook* (pp. 71–82). Thousand Oaks, CA: Sage.

Fehr, B. (2013). The social psychology of love. In J. A. Simpson & L. Campbell (Eds.), *Oxford handbook of close relationships* (pp. 201–233). New York, NY: Oxford University Press.

Fehr, B., & Russell, J. A. (1991). The concept of love viewed from a prototype perspective. *Journal of Personality and Social Psychology*, 60, 425–438.

Fein, S., McCloskey, A. L., & Tomlinson, T. M. (1997). Can the jury disregard that information? The use of suspicion to reduce the prejudicial effects of pretrial publicity and inadmissible testimony. *Personality and Social Psychology Bulletin*, 23, 1215–1226.

Feinberg, J. M., & Aiello, J. R. (2006). Social facilitation: A test of competing theories. *Journal of Applied Social Psychology*, 36, 1087–1109.

Feinberg, M., & Willer, R. (2011). Apocalypse soon? Dire messages reduce belief in global warming by contradicting just-world beliefs. *Psychological Science*, 22, 34–38.

Feingold, A. (1990). Gender differences in effects of physical attractiveness on romantic attraction: A comparison across five research paradigms. *Journal of Personality and Social Psychology*, 59, 981–993.

Feingold, A. (1992a). Gender differences in mate selection preferences: A test of the parental investment model. *Psychological Bulletin*, 112, 125–139.

Feingold, A. (1992b). Good-looking people are not what we think. *Psychological Bulletin*, 111, 304–341.

Felberbaum, M. (2013, March 19). US to revise cigarette warning labels. Retrieved May 22, 2014, from http://bigstory.ap.org/article/apnewsbreak-us-revise-cigarette-warning-labels

Feld, S. L. (1982). Social structural determinants of similarity among associates. *American Sociological Review*, 47, 797–801.

Fellner, J. (2009, June 19). Race, drugs, and law enforcement in the United States. *Stanford Law and Policy Review*, 20, 257–291.

Femlee, D. H. (1995). Fatal attractions: Affection and disaffection in intimate relationships. *Journal of Social and Personal Relationships*, 12, 295–311.

Femlee, D. H. (1998). "Be careful what you wish for . . .": A quantitative and qualitative investigation of "fatal attractions." *Personal Relationships*, 5, 235–253.

Femlee, D. H., Sprecher, S., & Bassin, E. (1990). The dissolution of intimate relationships: A hazard model. *Social Psychology Quarterly*, 53, 13–30.

Fenigstein, A., Scheier, M. F., & Buss, A. H. (1975). Public and private self-consciousness: Assessment and theory. *Journal of Consulting and Clinical Psychology*, 43, 522–527.

Ferguson, C. J. (2009). Media violence effects: Confirmed truth or just another X-File? *Journal of Forensic Psychology Practice*, 9, 103–126.

Ferguson, C. J. (2009). Media violence effects: Confirmed truth or just another X-file? *Journal of Forensic Psychology Practice*, 9, 103–126.

Ferguson, C. J. (2013). Violent video games and the Supreme Court: Lessons for the scientific community in the wake of Brown v. Entertainment Merchants Association. *American Psychologist*, 68, 57–74.

Ferguson, C. J. (2014). A way forward for video game violence research. *American Psychologist*, 69, 307–309.

Ferguson, C. J. , & Kilburn, J. (2009). The public health risks of media violence: A meta-analytic review. *Journal of Pediatrics*, 154, 759–763.

Ferguson, K. T., Cassells, R. C., MacAllister, J. W., & Evans, G. W. (2013). The physical environment and child development: An international review. *International Journal of Psychology*, 48, 437–468.

Fernández-Dols J. M., & Crivelli C. (2013). Emotion and expression: Naturalistic studies. *Emotion Review*, 5, 24–29.

Ferris, T. (1997, April 14). The wrong stuff. *New Yorker*, p. 32.

Feshbach, N. D. (1989). Empathy training and prosocial behavior. In J. Groebel & R. A. Hinde (Eds.), *Aggression and war: Their biological and social bases* (pp. 101–111). New York: Cambridge University Press.

Feshbach, N. D. (1997). Empathy—the formative years: Implications for clinical practice. In A. C. Bohart & L. S. Greenberg (Eds.), *Empathy reconsidered: New directions in psychotherapy* (pp. 33–59). Washington, DC: American Psychological Association.

Feshbach, N. D., & Feshbach, S. (2009). Empathy and education: Social neuroscience. In J. Decety & W. Ickes (Eds.), The social neuroscience of empathy (pp. 85–97). Cambridge, MA: MIT Press.

Feshbach, S., & Tangney, J. (2008). Television viewing and aggression: Some alternative perspectives. *Perspectives on Psychological Science*, 3, 387–389.

Festinger, L. (1954). A theory of social comparison processes. *Human Relations*, 7, 117–140.

Festinger, L. (1957). *A theory of cognitive dissonance.* Stanford, CA: Stanford University Press.

Festinger, L., & Carlsmith, J. M. (1959). Cognitive consequences of forced compliance. *Journal of Abnormal and Social Psychology*, 58, 203–211.

Festinger, L., & Maccoby, N. (1964). On resistance to persuasive communications. *Journal of Abnormal and Social Psychology*, 68, 359–366.

Festinger, L., & Thibaut, J. (1951). Interpersonal communication in small groups. *Journal of Abnormal and Social Psychology*, 46, 92–99.

Festinger, L., Riecken, H. W., & Schachter, S. (1956). *When prophecy fails.* Minneapolis: University of Minnesota Press.

Festinger, L., Schachter, S., & Back, K. (1950). *Social pressures in informal groups: A study of human factors in housing.* New York: Harper.

Fiedler, F. (1967). *A theory of leadership effectiveness.* New York: McGraw-Hill.

Fiedler, K., Walther, E., & Nickel, S. (1999). Covariation-based attribution: On the ability to assess multiple covariations of an effect. *Personality and Social Psychology Bulletin*, 25, 607–622.

Fincham, F. D., Bradbury, T. N., Arias, I., Byrne, C. A., & Karney, B. R. (1997). Marital violence, marital distress, and attributions. *Journal of Family Psychology*, 11, 367–372.

Fine, C. (2008). *A mind of its own: How your brain distorts and deceives.* New York: W.W. Norton.

Fine, C. (2010). *Delusions of gender: The real science behind sex differences.* New York: W.W. Norton.

Fine, G. A., & Elsbach, K. D. (2000). Ethnography and experiment in social psychological theory building: Tactics for integrating qualitative field data with quantitative lab data. *Journal of Experimental Social Psychology*, 36, 51–76.

Fink, B., & Penton-Voak, I. (2002). Evolutionary psychology of facial attractiveness. *Current Directions in Psychological Science*, 11, 154–158.

Finkel, E. J., & Eastwick, P. W. (2009). Arbitrary social norms influence sex differences in romantic selectivity. *Psychological Science*, 20, 1291–1295.

Finkel, E. J., Eastwick, P. W., Karney, B. R., Reis, H. T., & Sprecher, S. (2012). Online dating: A critical analysis from the perspective of psychological science. *Psychological Science in the Public Interest.* doi:10.1177/1529100612436522

Finkel, E. J., Norton, M. I., Reis, H. T., Ariely, D., Caprariello, P. A., Eastwick, P. W., Frost, J. H., & Maniaci, M. R. (2015). When does familiarity promote versus undermine interpersonal attraction? A proposed integrative model from erstwhile adversaries. *Perspectives on Psychological Science, 10,* 3–19.

Finkelstein, L. M., DeMuth, R. L. F., & Sweeney, D. L. (2007). Bias against overweight job applicants: Further explorations of when and why. *Human Resource Management, 46,* 203–222.

Finney, P. D. (1987). When consent information refers to risk and deception: Implications for social research. *Journal of Social Behavior and Personality, 2,* 37–48.

Fischer, P., Krueger, J. I., Greitemeyer, T., Vogrincic, C., Kastenmüller, A., Frey, D., Heene, M., Wicher, M., & Kainbacher, M. (2011). The bystander-effect: A meta-analytic review on bystander intervention in dangerous and non-dangerous emergencies. *Psychological Bulletin, 137*(4), 517–537. doi:10.1037/a0023304

Fischhoff, B. (2007). An early history of hindsight research. *Social Cognition, 25,* 10–13.

Fishbein, M., & Ajzen, I. (2010). *Predicting and changing behavior: The reasoned action approach.* New York: Psychology Press.

Fishbein, M., Chan, D., O'Reilly, K., Schnell, D., Wood, R., Beeker, C., & Cohn, C. (1993). Factors influencing gay men's attitudes, subjective norms, and intentions with respect to performing sexual behaviors. *Journal of Applied Social Psychology, 23,* 417–438.

Fisher, H. (2004). *Why we love: The nature and chemistry of romantic love.* New York: Macmillan.

Fisher, J. D., & Fisher, W. A. (2000). Theoretical approaches to individual-level changes in HIV risk behavior. In J. L. Peterson & C. C. DiClemente (Eds.), *Handbook of HIV prevention* (pp. 3–55). New York: Kluwer Academic /Plenum Press.

Fisher, R. P., & Schreiber, N. (2007). Interview protocols to improve eyewitness memory. In M. P. Toglia, J. D. Read, D. F. Ross, & R. C. L. Lindsay (Eds.), *The handbook of eyewitness psychology,* Vol I: *Memory for events* (pp. 53–80). Mahwah, NJ: Erlbaum.

Fisher, W. A., & Barak, A. (2001). Internet pornography: A social psychological perspective on Internet sexuality. *Journal of Sex Research, 38,* 312–323.

Fiske, S. T., & Taylor, S. E. (2013). *Social cognition: From brains to culture* (2nd ed.). Thousand Oaks, CA: Sage.

Fiske, S. T., Cuddy, A. J. C., & Glick, P. (2006). Universal dimensions of social cognition: Warmth and competence. *Trends in Cognitive Sciences, 11,* 77–83.

Fitzgerald, R. J., Oriet, C., & Price, H. L. (2014). Suspect filler similarity in eyewitness lineups: A literature review and a novel methodology. *Law and Human Behavior.*doi:10.1037/lhb0000095

Fivecoat, H. C., Tomlinson, J. M., Aron, A., & Caprariello, P. A. (2014). Partner support for individual self-expansion opportunities: Effects on relationship satisfaction in long-term couples. *Journal of Social and Personal Relationships.* doi:10.1177/0265407514533767

Flanagan, C. A., Bowes, J. M., Jonsson, B., Csapo, B., & Sheblanova, E. (1998). Ties that bind: Correlates of adolescents' civic commitments in seven countries. *Journal of Social Issues, 54,* 457–475.

Flick, U. (2014). *An introduction to qualitative research methods.* Thousand Oaks, CA: Sage.

Flowers, M. L. (1977). A lab test of some implications of Janis's groupthink hypothesis. *Journal of Personality and Social Psychology, 35,* 888–897.

Fointiat, V., Grosbras, J-M., Michel, S., & Somat, A. (2001). Encouraging young adults to drive carefully. The use of the hypocrisy paradigm. *Promoting Public Health,* Chambery (France), May, 10–12.

Folkman, S., & Moskowitz, J. T. (2000). The context matters. *Personality and Social Psychology Bulletin, 26,* 150–151.

Forbes, G. B., Adams-Curtis, L. E., Pakalka, A. H., & White, K. B. (2006). Dating aggression, sexual coercion, and aggression-supporting attitudes

among college men as a function of participation in aggressive high school sports. *Violence Against Women, 12,* 441–455.

Forer, B. R. (1949). The fallacy of personal validation: A classroom demonstration of gullibility. *Journal of Abnormal and Social Psychology, 44,* 118–123.

Forgas, J. P. (2011). She just doesn't look like a philosopher…? Affective influences on the halo effect in impression formation. *European Journal of Social Psychology, 41,* 812–817.

Forgas, J. P. (2013). Don't worry, be sad! On the cognitive, motivational, and interpersonal benefits of negative mood. *Current Directions in Psychological Science, 22,* 225–232.

Forgas, J. P., & Bower, G. H. (1987). Mood effects on person-perception judgments. *Journal of Personality and Social Psychology, 53,* 53–60.

Förster, J., Liberman, N., & Friedman, R. (2007). Seven principles of goal activation: A systematic approach to distinguishing goal priming from priming of non-goal constructs. *Personality and Social Psychology Review, 11*(3), 211–233.

Forsterling, F. (1989). Models of covariation and attribution: How do they relate to the analogy of analysis of variance? *Journal of Personality and Social Psychology, 57,* 615–625.

Forsyth, D. R., & Burnette, J. (2010). Group processes. In R. F. Baumeister & E. J. Finkel (Eds.), *Advanced social psychology: The state of the science* (pp. 495–534). New York: Oxford.

Fotuhi, O., Fong, G. T., Zanna, M. P., Borland, R., Yong, H., & Cummings, K. M. (2013). Patterns of cognitive dissonance-reducing beliefs among smokers: A longitudinal analysis from the International Tobacco Control (ITC) Four Country Survey. *Tobacco Control: An International Journal, 22,* 52–58.

Fountain, J. W. (1997, May 4). No fare. *Washington Post,* p. F1.

Fouts, G., & Burggraf, K. (1999). Television situation comedies: Female body images and verbal reinforcements. *Sex Roles, 40,* 473–479.

Fox, C. (2006). The availability heuristic in the classroom: How soliciting more criticism can boost your course ratings. *Judgment and Decision Making, 1,* 86–90.

Frager, R. (1970). Conformity and anticonformity in Japan. *Journal of Personality and Social Psychology, 15,* 203–210.

Fraidin, S. N. (2004). When is one head better than two? Interdependent information in group decision making. *Organizational Behavior and Human Decision Processes, 93,* 102–113.

Fraley, R. C. (2002). Attachment stability from infancy to adulthood: Meta-analysis and dynamic modeling of developmental mechanisms. *Personality and Social Psychology Review, 6,* 123–151.

Fraley, R. C., & Shaver, P. R. (2000). Adult romantic attachment: Theoretical developments, emerging controversies, and unanswered questions. *Review of General Psychology, 4,* 132–154.

France: An event not hallowed. (2001, November 1). *The New York Times,* p. A14.

Franklin, B. (1900). *The autobiography of Benjamin Franklin* (J. Bigelow, Ed.). Philadelphia: Lippincott. (Originally published 1868)

Frazier, P. A., & Cook, S. W. (1993). Correlates of distress following heterosexual relationship dissolution. *Journal of Social and Personal Relationships, 10,* 55–67.

Frazier, P., Keenan, N., Anders, S., Perera, S., Shallcross, S., & Hintz, S. (2011). Perceived past, present, and future control and adjustment to stressful life events. *Journal of Personality and Social Psychology, 100,* 749–765. doi:10.1037/a0022405

Freedman, J. L. (1965). Long-term behavioral effects of cognitive dissonance. *Journal of Experimental and Social Psychology, 1,* 145–155.

Freedman, J. L., & Fraser, S. C. (1966). Compliance without pressure: The foot-in-the-door technique. *Journal of Personality and Social Psychology, 4,* 195–202.

Freijy, T., & Kothe, E. J. (2013). Dissonance-based interventions for health behaviour change:

A systematic review. *British Journal of Health Psychology, 18,* 310–337.

Freud, S. (1930). *Civilization and its discontents* (J. Riviere, Trans.). London: Hogarth Press.

Freud, S. (1933). *New introductory lectures on psychoanalysis.* New York: Norton.

Fried, C., & Aronson, E. (1995). Hypocrisy, misattribution, and dissonance reduction: A demonstration of dissonance in the absence of aversive consequences. *Personality and Social Psychology Bulletin, 21,* 925–933.

Friese, M., & Wänke, M. (2014). Personal prayer buffers self-control depletion. *Journal of Experimental Social Psychology, 51,* 56–59.

Frodi, A. (1975). The effect of exposure to weapons on aggressive behavior from a cross-cultural perspective. *International Journal of Psychology, 10,* 283–292.

Fukuyama, F. (1999). *The great disruption: Human nature and the reconstitution of social order.* New York: Free Press.

Fulero, S. M. (2002). Afterword: The past, present, and future of applied pretrial publicity research. *Law and Human Behavior, 26,* 127–133.

Fumento, M. (1997, September 12). Why we need a new war on weight. *USA Weekend,* pp. 4–6.

Funder, D. C. (1995). On the accuracy of personality judgments: A realistic approach. *Psychological Review, 102,* 652–670.

Funder, D. C., & Colvin, C. R. (1988). Friends and strangers: Acquaintanceship, agreement, and the accuracy of personality judgment. *Journal of Personality and Social Psychology, 55,* 149–158.

Furnham, A. (1993). Just world beliefs in twelve societies. *Journal of Social Psychology, 133,* 317–329.

Furnham, A., & Gunter, B. (1984). Just world beliefs and attitudes toward the poor. *British Journal of Social Psychology, 23,* 265–269.

Furnham, A., & Mak, T. (1999). Sex-role stereotyping in television commercials: A review and comparison of fourteen studies done on five continents over 25 years. *Sex Roles, 41,* 413–437.

Furnham, A., & Procter, E. (1989). Beliefs in a just world: Review and critique of the individual difference literature. *British Journal of Social Psychology, 28,* 365–384.

Furnham, A., Richards, S. C., & Paulhus, D. L. (2013). The dark triad of personality: A 10 year review. *Social and Personality Psychology Compass, 7,* 199–216.

Fury, G., Carlson, E. A., & Sroufe, L. A. (1997). Children's representations of attachment relationships in family drawings. *Child Development, 68,* 1154–1164.

Gabbert, F., Memon, A., & Allan, K. (2003). Memory conformity: Can eyewitnesses influence each other's memories for an event? *Applied Cognitive Psychology, 17,* 533–543.

Gabriel, S., & Gardner, W. L. (1999). Are there "his" and "hers" types of interdependence? The implications of gender differences in collective versus relational interdependence for affect, behavior, and cognition. *Journal of Personality and Social Psychology, 77,* 642–655.

Gaertner, S. L., Mann, J. A., Dovidio, J. F., & Murrell, A. J. (1990). How does cooperation reduce intergroup bias? *Journal of Personality and Social Psychology, 59,* 692–704.

Galatzer-Levy, I. R., Bonanno, G. A., Bush, D. E. A., & LeDoux, J. E. (2013). Heterogeneity in threat extinction learning: Substantive and methodological considerations for identifying individual difference in response to stress. *Frontiers in Behavioral Neuroscience, 7,* Article ID 55.

Galdi, S., Arcuri, L., & Gawronski, B. (2008). Automatic mental associations predict future choices of undecided decision makers. *Science, 321,* 1100–1102.

Galen, L. W. (2012). Does religious belief promote prosociality? A critical examination. *Psychological Bulletin, 138,* 876–906.

Gallup, G. (1997). On the rise and fall of self-conception in primates. In J. G. Snodgrass & R. L. Thompson (Eds.), *The self across psychology: Self-recognition, self-awareness, and the self concept* (pp. 73–82). New York: New York Academy of Sciences.

Gallup, G. G., Jr., Anderson, J. R., & Shillito, D. J. (2002). The mirror test. In M. Bekoff & C. Allen (Eds.), *Cognitive animal: Empirical and theoretical perspectives on animal cognition* (pp. 325–333). Cambridge, MA: MIT Press.

Gangestad, S. W. (1993). Sexual selection and physical attractiveness: Implications for mating dynamics. *Human Nature, 4,* 205–235.

Ganzel, B. L., Morris, P. A., & Wethington, E. (2010). Allostasis and the human brain: Integrating models of stress from the social and life sciences. *Psychological Review, 117,* 134–174.

Gao, G. (1993, May). *An investigation of love and intimacy in romantic relationships in China and the United States.* Paper presented at the annual conference of the International Communication Association, Washington, DC.

Gao, G. (1996). Self and other: A Chinese perspective on interpersonal relationships. In W. B. Gudykunst, S. Ting-Toomey, & T. Nishida (Eds.), *Communication in personal relationships across cultures* (pp. 81–101). Thousand Oaks, CA: Sage.

Garcia, L. T., & Milano, L. (1990). A content analysis of erotic videos. *Journal of Psychology and Human Sexuality, 3,* 95–103.

Garcia, S., Stinson, L., Ickes, W. J., Bissonnette, V., & Briggs, S. (1991). Shyness and physical attractiveness in mixed-sex dyads. *Journal of Personality and Social Psychology, 61,* 35–49.

Gardner, W. L., & Gabriel, S. (2004). Gender differences in relational and collective interdependence: Implications for self-views, social behavior, and subjective well-being. In A. H. Eagly, A. E. Beall, & R. J. Sternberg (Eds.), *Psychology of gender* (2nd ed., pp. 169–191). New York: Guilford.

Gardner, W. L., Pickett, C. L., & Brewer, M. B. (2000). Social exclusion and selective memory: How the need to belong influences memory for social events. *Personality and Social Psychology Bulletin, 26,* 486–496.

Gardner, W., & Gabriel, S. (2004). Gender differences in relational and collective interdependence: Implications for self-views, social behavior, and subjective well-being. In A. H. Eagly, A. E. Beall, & R. J. Sternberg (Eds.), *The psychology of gender* (2nd ed., pp. 169–191). New York: Guilford Press.

Gardner, W., & Knowles, M. L. (2008). Love makes you real: Favorite television characters are perceived as "real" in a social facilitation paradigm. *Social Cognition, 26,* 156–168.

Garfinkle, H. (1967). *Studies in ethnomethodology.* Englewood Cliffs, NJ: Prentice Hall.

Gates, H. L., Jr. (1995, October 23). Thirteen ways of looking at a Black man. *New Yorker,* pp. 56–65.

Gawronski, B. (2003a). Implicational schemata and the correspondence bias: On the diagnostic value of situationally constrained behavior. *Journal of Personality and Social Psychology, 84,* 1154–1171.

Gawronski, B. (2003b). On difficult questions and evident answers: Dispositional inference from role-constrained behavior. *Personality and Social Psychology Bulletin, 29,* 1459–1475.

Gawronski, B., & Bodenhausen, G. V. (2012). Self-insight from a dual-process perspective. In S. Vazire, & T. D. Wilson (Eds.), *Handbook of self-knowledge.* New York: Guilford Press.

Gawronski, B., & Payne, B. K. (Eds.). (2010). *Handbook of implicit social cognition: Measurement, theory, and applications.* New York: Guilford Press.

Geen, R. G. (1989). Alternative conceptions of social facilitation. In P. B. Paulus (Ed.), *Psychology of group influence* (2nd ed., pp. 15–51). Hillsdale, NJ: Erlbaum.

Geen, R. G. (1994). Television and aggression: Recent developments in research and theory. In D. Zillmann, J. Bryant, & A. C. Huston (Eds.), *Media, children, and the family: Social scientific, psychodynamic, and clinical perspectives* (pp. 151–162). Hillsdale, NJ: Erlbaum.

Geen, R. G., & Quanty, M. (1977). The catharsis of aggression: An evaluation of a hypothesis. In L. Berkowitz (Ed.), *Advances in experimental social psychology* (Vol. 10, pp. 1–36). New York: Academic Press.

Geen, R. G., Stonner, D., & Shope, G. (1975). The facilitation of aggression by aggression: A study in response inhibition and disinhibition. *Journal of Personality and Social Psychology, 31,* 721–726.

Gelfand, M. J., Chiu, C., & Hong, Y. (Eds.). (2014). *Advances in culture and psychology* (Vol. 4). New York: Oxford University Press.

Gelfand, M. J., Erez, M., Aycan, Z. (2007). Cross-cultural organizational behavior. *Annual Review of Psychology, 58,* 479–514.

Gendron, M., Roberson, D., van der Vyver, J. M., & Barrett, L. F. (2014). Perceptions of emotion from facial expressions are not culturally universal: Evidence from a remote culture. *Emotion, 14,* 251–262.

Gentile, B., Grabe, S., Dolan-Pascoe, B., Twenge, J. M., Wells, B. E., & Maitino, A. (2009). Gender differences in domain-specific self-esteem: A meta-analysis. *Review of General Psychology, 13,* 34–45.

Gentile, D. A., Coyne, S., & Walsh, D. A. (2011). Media violence, physical aggression, and relational aggression in school age children: A short-term longitudinal study. *Aggressive Behavior, 37,* 193–206.

George, J. M. (1990). Personality, affect, and behavior in groups. *Journal of Applied Psychology, 75,* 107–116.

Geraerts, E., Lindsay, D. S., Merckelbach, H., Jelicic, M., Raymaekers, L., Arnold, M. M., & Schooler, J. W. (2009). Cognitive mechanisms underlying recovered-memory experiences of childhood sexual abuse. *Psychological Science, 20*(1), 92–98. doi:10.1111/j.1467-9280.2008.02247.x

Geraerts, E., Schooler, J., Merckelbach, H., Jelicic, M., Hauer, B., & Ambadar, Z. (2007). The reality of recovered memories: Corroborating continuous and discontinuous memories of childhood sexual abuse. *Psychological Science, 18,* 564–568.

Gerard, H. B. (1953). The effect of different dimensions of disagreement on the communication process in small groups. *Human Relations, 6,* 249–271.

Gerard, H. B., & Mathewson, G. C. (1966). The effects of severity of initiation on liking for a group: A replication. *Journal of Experimental Social Psychology, 2,* 278–287.

Gerard, H. B., Wilhelmy, R. A., & Conolley, E. S. (1968). Conformity and group size. *Journal of Personality and Social Psychology, 8,* 79–82.

Gerbner, G., Gross, L., Morgan, M., Signorielli, N., & Shanahan, J. (2002). Growing up with television: Cultivation processes. In J. Bryant & D. Zillmann (Eds.), *Media effects: Advances in theory and research* (pp. 43–67). Mahwah, NJ: Erlbaum.

Gerdes, E. P. (1979). College students' reactions to social psychological experiments involving deception. *Journal of Social Psychology, 107,* 99–110.

Gerin, W., Chaplin, W., Schwartz, J. E., Holland, J., Alter, R., Wheeler, R., Duong, D., & Pickering, T. G. (2005). Sustained blood pressure increase after an acute stressor: The effects of the 11 September 2001 attack on the New York City World Trade Center. *Journal of Hypertension, 23,* 279–284.

Gershoff, E. T. (2002). Parental corporal punishment and associated child behaviors and experiences: A meta-analytic and theoretical review. *Psychological Bulletin, 128,* 539–579.

Gibbons, F. X. (1978). Sexual standards and reactions to pornography: Enhancing behavioral consistency through self-focused attention. *Journal of Personality and Social Psychology, 36,* 976–987.

Gibbons, F. X., Eggleston, T. J., & Benthin, A. C. (1997). Cognitive reactions to smoking relapse: The reciprocal relation between dissonance and self-esteem. *Journal of Personality and Social Psychology, 72,* 184–195.

Gibbons, F. X., Gerrard, M., & Cleveland, M. J. (2004). Perceived discrimination and substance use in African American parents and their children: A panel study. *Journal of Personality and Social Psychology, 86,* 517–529. www.obesity.org/subs/fastfacts/obesity_what2.shtml

Gibbs, N., & Roche, T. (1999, December 20). The Columbine tapes. *Time,* p. 154.

Gibson, B., & Poposki, E. M. (2010). How the adoption of impression management goals alters impression formation. *Personality and Social Psychology Bulletin, 36,* 1543–1554. doi:10.1177/0146167210385008

Gifford, R. (1991). Mapping nonverbal behavior on the interpersonal circle. *Journal of Personality and Social Psychology, 61,* 279–288.

Gigerenzer, G. (2000). *Adaptive thinking: Rationality in the real world.* Oxford: Oxford University Press.

Gigerenzer, G. (2008). Why heuristics work. *Perspectives on Psychological Science, 3,* 20–29.

Gilbert, D. T. (1989). Thinking lightly about others: Automatic components of the social inference process. In J. S. Uleman & J. A. Bargh (Eds.), *Unintended thought* (pp. 189–211). New York: Guilford Press.

Gilbert, D. T. (1991). How mental systems believe. *American Psychologist, 46,* 107–119.

Gilbert, D. T. (1993). The assent of man: Mental representation and the control of belief. In D. M. Wegner & J. W. Pennebaker (Eds.), *The handbook of mental control* (pp. 57–87). Englewood Cliffs, NJ: Prentice Hall.

Gilbert, D. T. (2005). *Stumbling on happiness.* New York: Knopf.

Gilbert, D. T., & Hixon, J. G. (1991). The trouble of thinking: Activation and applications of stereotypical beliefs. *Journal of Personality and Social Psychology, 60,* 509–517.

Gilbert, D. T., & Jones, E. E. (1986). Perceiver-induced constraint: Interpretations of self-generated reality. *Journal of Personality and Social Psychology, 50,* 269–280.

Gilbert, D. T., & Malone, P. S. (1995). The correspondence bias. *Psychological Bulletin, 117,* 21–38.

Gilbert, D. T., & Osborne, R. E. (1989). Thinking backward: Some curable and incurable consequences of cognitive busyness. *Journal of Personality and Social Psychology, 57,* 940–949.

Gilbert, D. T., & Wilson, T. D. (2007). Prospection: Experiencing the future. *Science, 317,* 1351–1354.

Gilbert, D. T., & Ebert, E. J. (2002). Decisions and revisions: The affective forecasting of changeable outcomes. *Journal of Personality and Social Psychology, 82*(4), 503–514.

Gilbert, D. T., Killingsworth, M. A., Eyre, R. N., & Wilson, T. D. (2009). The surprising power of neighborly advice. *Science, 323,* 1617–1619.

Gilbert, D. T., Pelham, B. W., & Krull, D. S. (1988). On cognitive busyness: When person perceivers meet persons perceived. *Journal of Personality and Social Psychology, 54,* 733–740.

Gilbert, S. J. (1981). Another look at the Milgram obedience studies: The role of the gradated series of shocks. *Personality and Social Psychology Bulletin, 4,* 690–695.

Gildersleeve, K., Haselton, M. G., & Fales, M. R. (2014). Do women's mate preferences change across the ovulatory cycle? A meta-analytic review. *Psychological Bulletin.*doi:10.1037/a0035438

Gilmore, D. D. (1990). *Manhood in the making: Cultural concepts of masculinity.* New Haven, CT: Yale University Press.

Gilovich, T. (1991). *How we know what isn't so: The fallibility of human reason in everyday life.* New York: Free Press.

Gilovich, T., & Griffin, D. W. (2002). Introduction: Heuristics and biases, now and then. In T. Gilovich, D. W. Griffin, & D. Kahneman (Eds.), *Heuristics and biases: The psychology of intuitive judgment* (pp. 1–18). New York: Cambridge University Press.

Girl born to Japan's princess. (2001, December 1). *The New York Times,* p. 8.

Girme, Y. U., Overall, N. C., & Simpson, J. A. (2013). When visibility matters: Short-term versus long-term costs and benefits of visible and invisible support. *Personality and Social Psychology Bulletin, 39,* 1441–1454.

Gladue, B. A., Boechler, M., & McCaul, K. D. (1989). Hormonal response to competition in human males. *Aggressive Behavior, 15,* 409–422.

Gladwell, M. (2004, January 12). Big and bad: How the S.U.V. ran over automotive safety. *New Yorker,* p. 28.

Gladwell, M. (2005). *Blink: The power of thinking without thinking*. New York: Little, Brown.

Gladwell, M. (2005, January 12). Big and bad: How the S.U.V. ran over automotive safety. *New Yorker*.

Glasman, L. R., & Albarracín, D. (2006). Forming attitudes that predict future behavior: A meta-analysis of the attitude-behavior relation. *Psychological Bulletin,132*, 778–822.

Glasman, L. R., & Albarracín, D. (2006). Forming attitudes that predict future behavior: A meta-analysis of the attitude-behavior relation. *Psychological Bulletin, 132*, 778–822.

Glass, D. C. (1964). Changes in liking as a means of reducing cognitive discrepancies between self-esteem and aggression. *Journal of Personality, 32*, 531–549.

Gleick, E. (1997, April 7). Planet Earth about to be recycled. Your only chance to survive—leave with us. *Time*, pp. 28–36.

Glick, P. (2006). Ambivalent sexism, power distance, and gender inequality across cultures. In S. Guimond (Ed.), *Social comparison and social psychology: Understanding cognition, intergroup relations, and culture*. New York: Cambridge University Press.

Glick, P., & Fiske, S. (2001). An ambivalent alliance: Hostile and benevolent sexism as complementary justifications for gender inequality. *American Psychologist, 56*, 109–118.

Glick, P., Lameiras, M., Fiske, S. T., Eckes, T., Masser, B., et al. (2004). Bad but bold: Ambivalent attitudes toward men predict gender inequality in sixteen nations. *Journal of Personality and Social Psychology, 86*, 713–728.

Global Health Observatory. (n.d.). World Health Organization. Retrieved August 19, 2014, from "Global statistics," 2011.

Global Report: UNAIDS Report on the Global Aids Epidemic 2013. (2013). Retrieved August 19, 2014, from http://www.unaids.org/en/media/unaids/contentassets/documents/epidemiology/2013/gr2013/UNAIDS_Global_Report_2013_en.pdf

Goethals, G. R., & Darley, J. M. (1977). Social comparison theory: An attributional approach. In J. M. Suls & R. L. Miller (Eds.), *Social comparison processes: Theoretical and empirical perspectives* (pp. 259–278). Washington, DC: Hemisphere/Halsted.

Goffman, E. (1959). *Presentation of self in everyday life*. Garden City, NY: Anchor/Doubleday.

Gold, J. A., Ryckman, R. M., & Mosley, N. R. (1984). Romantic mood induction and attraction to a dissimilar other: Is love blind? *Personality and Social Psychology Bulletin, 10*, 358–368.

Golder, S. A., & Macy, M. W. (2011). Diurnal and season mood vary with work, sleep, and daylength across diverse cultures. *Science, 333*, 1878–1881. doi:10.1126/science.1202775

Goldinger, S. D., Kleider, H. M., Azuma, T., & Beike, D. R. (2003). "Blaming the victim" under memory load. *Psychological Science, 14*, 81–85.

Goldstein, J. H., & Arms, R. L. (1971). Effect of observing athletic contests on hostility. *Sociometry, 34*, 83–90.

Goldstein, N. J., Cialdini, R. B., & Griskevicius, V. (2008). A room with a viewpoint: Using social norms to motivate environmental conservation in hotels. *Journal of Consumer Research, 35*, 472–482.

Gollwitzer, P. M., & Oettingen, G. (2011). Planning promotes goal striving. In K. D. Vohs & R. F. Baumeister (Eds.), *Handbook of self-regulation: Research, theory, and applications* (2nd ed., pp. 162–185). New York: Guilford.

Golumbic, E. Z., Cogan, G. B., Schroeder, C. E., & Poeppel, D. (2013). Visual input enhances selective speech envelope tracking in auditory cortex at a "Cocktail Party." *The Journal of Neuroscience, 33*(4), 1417–1426. doi:10.1523/JNEUROSCI.3675-12.2013

Gonzaga, G. C., Campos, B., & Bradbury, T. (2007). Similarity, convergence, and relationship satisfaction in dating and married couples. *Journal of Personality and Social Psychology, 93*, 34–48.

Good, C., Aronson, J., & Harder, J. (2008). Problems in the pipeline: Women's achievement in high-level math courses. *Journal of Applied Developmental Psychology, 29*, 17–28.

Goode, E. (1999, February 9). Arranged marriage gives way to courtship by mail. *The New York Times*, p. D3.

Goodfriend, W., & Agnew, C. R. (2008). Sunken costs and desired plans: Examining different types of investments in close relationships. *Personality and Social Psychology Bulletin, 34*, 1639–1652.

Goodwin, D. K. (2006). *Team of rivals*. New York: Simon & Schuster.

Goodwin, G. P., Piazza, J., & Rozin, P. (2014). Moral character predominates in person perception and evaluation. *Journal of Personality and Social Psychology, 106*, 148–168.

Goodwin, R. (1999). *Personal relationships across cultures*. New York: Routledge.

Gosling, S. (2008). *Snoop: What your stuff says about you*. London: Profile Books Ltd.

Goto, S. G., Ando, Y., Huang, C., Yee, A., & Lewis, R. S. (2010). Cultural differences in the visual processing of meaning: Detecting incongruities between background and foreground objects using the N400. *Social Cognitive and Affective Neuroscience, 5*, 242–253.

Goto, S. G., Yee, A., Lowenberg, K., & Lewis, R. S. (2013). Cultural differences in sensitivity to social context: Detecting affective incongruity using the N400. *Social Neuroscience, 8*, 63–74.

Gottman, J. M. (2014). *What predicts divorce?: The relationship between marital processes and marital outcomes*. New York, NY: Psychology Press.

Gottman, J. M., & Levenson, R. W. (2002). A two-factor model for predicting when a couple will divorce: Exploratory analyses using 14-year longitudinal data. *Family Process, 41*, 83–96.

Grabe, S., & Hyde, J. S. (2006). Ethnicity and body dissatisfaction among women in the United States: A meta-analysis. *Psychological Bulletin, 132*, 622–640.

Grabe, S., Ward, L. M., & Hyde, J. S. (2008). The role of the media in body image concerns among women: A meta-analysis of experimental and correlational studies. *Psychological Bulletin, 134*, 460–476.

Graham, J., & Haidt, J. (2010). Beyond beliefs: Religion binds individuals into moral communities. *Personality and Social Psychology Review, 14*, 140–150.

Graham, J., Koo, M., & Wilson, T. D. (2011). Conserving energy by inducing people to drive less. *Journal of Applied Social Psychology, 41*, 106–118.

Graham, K., Osgood, D. W., Wells, S., & Stockwell, T. (2006). To what extent is intoxication associated with aggression in bars? A multilevel analysis. *Journal of Studies on Alcohol, 67*, 382–390.

Granberg, D., & Bartels, B. (2005). On being a lone dissenter. *Journal of Applied Social Psychology, 35*, 1849–1858.

Grant, A. M., & Gino, F. (2010). A little thanks goes a long way: Explaining why gratitude expressions motivate prosocial behavior. *Journal of Personality and Social Psychology, 98*(6), 946–955. doi:10.1037/a0017935

Gray, K., & Wegner, D. M. (2010). Torture and judgments of guilt. *Journal of Experimental Social Psychology, 46*, 233–235.

Gray, K., Ward, A. F., & Norton, M. I. (2014). Paying it forward: Generalized reciprocity and the limits of generosity. *Journal of Experimental Psychology: General, 143*(1), 247–254. doi:10.1037/a0031047

Gray, S. (2004, March 30). Bizarre hoaxes on restaurants trigger lawsuits. *Wall Street Journal*, Retrieved June 5, 2006, from online.wsj.com/article_print/SB108061045899868615.html

Graziano, W. G., Habashi, M. M., Sheese, B. E., & Tobin, R. M. (2007). Agreeableness, empathy, and helping: A person × situation perspective. *Journal of Personality and Social Psychology, 93*, 583–599.

Graziano, W. G., Jensen-Campbell, L. A., Shebilske, L. J., & Lundgren, S. R. (1993). Social influence, sex differences, and judgments of beauty: Putting the interpersonal back in interpersonal attraction. *Journal of Personality and Social Psychology, 65*, 522–531.

Green, A. R., Carney, D. R., Pallin, D. J., Ngo, L. H., Raymond, K. L., et al. (2007). Implicit bias among physicians and its prediction of thrombolysis decisions for Black and White patients. *Journal of General Internal Medicine, 22*, 1231–1238.

Greenberg, J., & Musham, C. (1981). Avoiding and seeking self-focused attention. *Journal of Research in Personality, 15*, 191–200.

Greenberg, J., Pyszczynski, T., & Solomon, S. (1982). The self-serving attributional bias: Beyond self-presentation. *Journal of Experimental Social Psychology, 18*, 56–67.

Greenberg, J., Solomon, S., & Pyszczynski, T. (1997). Terror management theory of self-esteem and social behavior: Empirical assessments and conceptual refinements. In M. P. Zanna (Ed.), *Advances in experimental social psychology* (Vol. 29, pp. 61–139). New York: Academic Press.

Greene, D., Sternberg, B., & Lepper, M. R. (1976). Overjustification in a token economy. *Journal of Personality and Social Psychology, 34*, 1219–1234.

Greene, E., & Evelo, A. (2014). Cops and robbers (and eyewitnesses): A comparison of lineup administration by robbery detectives in the U.S. and Canada. *Psychology, Crime, and Law*. doi:10.1080/1068316X.2014.952236

Greene, E., & Helbrun, K. (2013). *Wrightsman's Psychology and the Legal System*. New York: Cengage.

Greenwald, A. G., & Banaji, M. R. (1995). Implicit social cognition: Attitudes, self-esteem, and stereotypes. *Psychological Review, 102*, 4–27.

Greenwald, A. G., McGhee, D. E., & Schwartz, J. L. K. (1998). Measuring individual differences in implicit cognition: The Implicit Association Test. *Journal of Personality and Social Psychology, 74*, 1464–1480.

Greenwald, A. G., Poehlman, T. A., Uhlmann, E. L., & Banaji, M. R. (2009). Understanding and using the Implicit Association Test: III. Meta-analysis of predictive validity. *Journal of Personality and Social Psychology, 97*(1), 17–41. doi:10.1037/a0015575

Greenwald, A. G., Spangenberg, E. R., Pratkanis, A. R., & Eskenazi, J. (1991). Double-blind tests of subliminal self-help audiotapes. *Psychological Science, 2*, 119–122.

Greenwald, A. G., & Pettigrew, T. (2014). With malice toward none and charity for some: Ingroup favoritism enables discrimination. *American Psychologist*. doi:10.1037/a0036056

Greitemeyer, T. (2009). Effects of songs with prosocial lyrics on prosocial behavior: Further evidence and a mediating mechanism. *Personality and Social Psychology Bulletin, 35*(11), 1500–1511. doi:10.1177/0146167209341648

Greitemeyer, T. (2011). Exposure to music with prosocial lyrics reduces aggression: First evidence and test of the underlying mechanism. *Journal of Experimental Social Psychology, 47*(1), 28–36. doi:10.1016/j.jesp.2010.08.005

Greitemeyer, T. (2013). Article retracted, but the message lives on. *Psychonomic Bulletin Review*. Advance online publication. doi:10.3758/s13423-013-0500-6

Greitemeyer, T. (2014). Playing violent video games increases intergroup bias. *Personality and Social Psychology Bulletin, 40*, 70–78.

Greitemeyer, T., & McLatchie, N. (2011). Denying humanness to others: A newly discovered mechanism by which violent video games increase aggressive behavior. *Psychological Science, 22*, 659–665.

Greitemeyer, T., & Mügge, D. O. (2014). Video games do affect social outcomes: A meta-analytic review of the effects of violent and prosocial video game play. *Personality and Social Psychology Bulletin, 40*, 578–589.

Greitemeyer, T., & Osswald, S. (2010). Effects of prosocial video games on prosocial behavior. *Journal of Personality and Social Psychology, 98*(2), 211–221. doi:10.1037/a0016997

Greitemeyer, T., & Schulz-Hardt, S. (2003). Preference-consistent evaluation of information in the hidden profile paradigm: Beyond group-level explanations for the dominance of shared information in group decisions. *Journal of Personality and Social Psychology, 84,* 322–339.

Greitemeyer, T., Osswald, S., & Brauer, M. (2010). Playing prosocial video games increases empathy and decreases schadenfreude. *Emotion, 10*(6), 796–802. doi:10.1037/a0020194

Griffin, D. W., & Ross, L. (1991). Subjective construal, social inference, and human misunderstanding. In L. Berkowitz (Ed.), *Advances in experimental social psychology* (Vol. 24, pp. 319–359). San Diego, CA: Academic Press.

Griffin, D. W., Gonzalez, R., & Varey, C. (2001). The heuristics and biases approach to judgment under uncertainty. In A. Tesser & N. Schwarz (Eds.), *Blackwell handbook of social psychology: Intraindividual processes* (pp. 127–133). Oxford, UK: Blackwell.

Griffin, D., & Kahneman, D. (2003). Judgmental heuristics: Human strengths or human weaknesses? In L. G. Aspinwall & U. M. Staudinger (Eds.), *A psychology of human strengths: Fundamental questions and future directions for a positive psychology* (pp. 165–178). Washington, DC: American Psychological Association.

Griffith, S. C., Pryke, S. R., & Buettemer, W. A. (2011). Constrained mate choice in social monogamy and the stress of having an unattractive partner. *Proceedings of the Royal Society of London, Series B, 278,* 2798–2805.

Griffitt, W., & Veitch, R. (1971). Hot and crowded: influences of population density and temperature on interpersonal affective behavior. *Journal of Personality and Social Psychology, 17*(1), 92–98.

Griggs, R. A., & Whitehead, G. I., III. (2014). Coverage of the Stanford Prison Experiment in introductory social psychology textbooks. *Teaching of Psychology, 41,* 318–324.

Gronlund, S. D., Wixted, J. T., & Mickes, L. (2014). Evaluating eyewitness identification procedures using receiver operating characteristic analysis. *Current Directions in Psychological Science, 23,* 3–10.

Grossbard, J. R., Lee, C. M., Neighbors, C., & Larimer, M. E. (2008). Body image concerns and contingent self-esteem in male and female college students. *Sex Roles, 60,* 198–207.

Guagnano, G. A., Stern, P. C., & Dietz, T. (1995). Influences on attitude-behavior relationships: A natural experiment with curbside recycling. *Environment and Behavior, 27,* 699–718.

Gudjonsson, G. H., Sigurdsson, J. F., Sigurdardottir, A. S., Steinthorsson, H., & Sigurdardottir, V. M. (2014). The role of memory distrust in cases of internalised false confession. *Applied Cognitive Psychology, 28,* 336–348.

Gudykunst, W. B. (1988). Culture and intergroup processes. In M. H. Bond (Ed.), *The cross-cultural challenge to social psychology* (pp. 165–181). Newbury Park, CA: Sage.

Gudykunst, W. B., Ting-Toomey, S., & Nishida, T. (1996). *Communication in personal relationships across cultures.* Thousand Oaks, CA: Sage.

Guéguen, N., Jacob, C., & Lamy, L. (2010). 'Love is in the air': Effects of songs with romantic lyrics on compliance with a courtship request. *Psychology of Music, 38*(3), 303–307. doi:10.1177/0305735609360428

Guenther, C. L., & Alicke, M. D. (2010). Deconstructing the better-than-average effect. *Journal of Personality and Social Psychology, 99,* 755–770. doi:10.1037/a0020959

Guerin, B. (1993). *Social facilitation.* Cambridge: Cambridge University Press.

Guerrero, L. K., La Valley, A. G., & Farinelli, L. (2008). The experience and expression of anger, guilt, and sadness in marriage: An equity theory explanation. *Journal of Social and Personal Relationships, 25,* 699–724.

Guimond, S. (1999). Attitude change during college: Normative or informational social influence? *Social Psychology of Education, 2,* 237–261.

Guimond, S., Chatard, A., Martinot, D., Crisp, R. J., & Redersdorff, S. (2006). Social comparison, self-stereotyping, and gender differences in self-construals. *Journal of Personality and Social Psychology, 90*(2), 221–242.

Guisinger, S., & Blatt, S. J. (1994). Individuality and relatedness: Evolution of a fundamental dialect. *American Psychologist, 49,* 104–111.

Gully, S. M., Devine, D. J., & Whitney, D. J. (1995). A meta-analysis of cohesion and performance: Effects of level of analysis and task interdependence. *Small Groups Research, 26,* 497–520.

Gunn, A. (2013, August 23). I have a character issue. *New York Times.* Retrieved March 17, 2014, from www.nytimes.com/2013/08/24/opinion/i-have-a-character-issue.html

Gustafson, R. (1989). Frustration and successful vs. unsuccessful aggression: A test of Berkowitz's completion hypothesis. *Aggressive Behavior, 15,* 5–12.

Guyll, M., Madon, S., Prieto, L., & Scherr, K. C. (2010). The potential roles of self-fulfilling prophecies, stigma consciousness, and stereotype threat in linking Latino/a ethnicity and educational outcomes. *Journal of Social Issues, 66*(1), 113–130. doi:10.1111/j.1540-4560.2009.01636.x

Ha, A. (2014, March 13). CEO Sean Rad says dating app Tinder has made 1 billion matches. Retrieved July 16, 2014, from http://techcrunch.com/2014/03/13/tinder-1-billion-matches/

Ha, T., van den Berg, J. E. M., Engels, R. C. M. E., & Lichtwarck-Aschoff, A. (2012). Effects of attractiveness and status in dating desire in homosexual and heterosexual men and women. *Archives of Sexual Behavior, 41,* 673–682.

Hadden, B. W., Smith, C. V., & Webster, G. D. (2014). Relationship duration moderates associations between attachment and relationship quality: Meta-analytic support for the temporal adult romantic attachment model. *Personality and Social Psychology Review, 18,* 42–58.

Haddock, G., Maio, G. R., Arnold, K., & Huskinson, T. (2008). Should persuasion be affective or cognitive? The moderating effects of need for affect and need for cognition. *Personality and Social Psychology Bulletin, 34,* 769–778.

Hafer, C. L. (2000). Investment in long-term goals and commitment to just means drive the need to believe in a just world. *Personality and Social Psychology Bulletin, 26,* 1059–1073.

Hafer, C. L., & Begue, L. (2005). Experimental research on just-world theory: Problems, developments, and future challenges. *Psychological Bulletin, 131*(1), 128–167.

Hagestad, G. O., & Smyer, M. A. (1982). Dissolving long-term relationships: Patterns of divorcing in middle age. In S. W. Duck (Ed.), *Personal relationships: Vol. 4. Dissolving personal relationships* (pp. 155–188). London: Academic Press.

Hahn, A., & Gawronski, B. (2014). Do implicit evaluations reflect unconscious atittudes? *Behavioral and Brain Sciences, 37,* 28–29.

Hahn, A., Judd, C. M., Hirsh, H. K., & Blair, I. V. (2014). Awareness of implicit attitudes. *Journal of Experimental Psychology: General, 143,* 1369–1392.

Hahn, R., Fuqua-Whitley, D., Wethington, H., et al. (2008). Effectiveness of universal school-based programs to prevent violent and aggressive behaviour: A systematic review. *Child: Care, Health, & Development, 34,* 139.

Haidt, J. (2006). *The happiness hypothesis: Finding modern truth in ancient wisdom.* New York: Basic Books.

Halabi, S., Nadler, A., & Dovidio, J. F. (2013). Positive responses to intergroup assistance: The roles of apology and trust. *Group Processes & Intergroup Relations, 16*(4), 395–411. doi:10.1177/1368430212453863

Halali, E., Bereby-Meyer, Y., & Meiran, N. (2014). Between self-interest and reciprocity: The social bright side of self-control failure. *Journal of Experimental Psychology: General, 143*(2), 745–754. doi:10.1037/a0033824

Halberstadt, J. B., & Levine, G. L. (1997). *Effects of reasons analysis on the accuracy of predicting basketball games.* Unpublished manuscript, Indiana University.

Halberstadt, J. B., & Rhodes, G. (2000). The attractiveness of nonface averages: Implications for an evolutionary explanation of the attractiveness of average faces. *Psychological Science, 11,* 285–289.

Hald, G. M., Malamuth, N. M., & Yuen, C. (2010). Pornography and attitudes supporting violence against women: Revisiting the relationship in nonexperimental studies. *Aggressive Behavior, 36,* 14–20. doi:10.1002/ab.20328

Hall, C. C., Zhao, J., & Shafir, E. (2014). Self-affirmation among the poor: Cognitive and behavioral implications. *Psychological Science, 25,* 619–625.

Hall, E. T. (1969). *The hidden dimension.* Garden City, NY: Doubleday.

Hall, J. A., Gunnery, S. D., & Andrzejewski, S. A., (2011). Nonverbal emotion displays, communication modality, and the judgment of personality. *Journal of Research in Personality, 45*(1), 77–83.

Hall, J. A., Murphy, N. A., & Schmid Mast, M. (2007). Nonverbal self-accuracy in interpersonal interaction. *Personality and Social Psychology Bulletin, 33,* 1675–1685.

Halliwell, E., & Diedrichs, P. C. (2014). Testing a dissonance body image intervention among young girls. *Health Psychology, 33,* 201–204.

Ham, J., & Vonk, R. (2011). Impressions of impression management: Evidence of spontaneous suspicion of ulterior motivation. *Journal of Experimental Social Psychology, 47,* 466–471. doi:10.1016/j.jesp.2010.12.008

Hamby, S. L., & Koss, M. P. (2003). Shades of gray: A qualitative study of terms used in the measurement of sexual victimization. *Psychology of Women Quarterly, 27,* 243–255.

Hamby, S. L., & Koss, M. P. (2003). Shades of gray: A qualitative study of terms used in the measurement of sexual victimization. *Psychology of Women Quarterly, 27,* 243–255.

Hamilton, D. L. (1981). Illusory correlation as a basis for stereotyping. In D. L. Hamilton (Ed.), *Cognitive processes in stereotyping and intergroup behavior* (pp. 563–571). Hillsdale, NJ: Erlbaum.

Hamilton, V. L., Sanders, J., & McKearney, S. J. (1995). Orientations toward authority in an authoritarian state: Moscow in 1990. *Personality and Social Psychology Bulletin, 21,* 356–365.

Hamilton, W. D. (1964). The genetical evolution of social behavior. *Journal of Theoretical Biology, 7,* 1–52.

Hamm, M. (1999). *Go for the goal: A champion's guide to winning in soccer and life.* New York: HarperCollins.

Han, S., & Shavitt, S. (1994). Persuasion and culture: Advertising appeals in individualistic and collectivistic societies. *Journal of Experimental Social Psychology, 30,* 326–350.

Hancock, J. T., & Toma, C. L. (2009). Putting your best face forward: The accuracy of online dating photographs. *Journal of Communication, 59,* 367–286.

Haney, C., Banks, C., & Zimbardo, P. (1973). Interpersonal dynamics in a simulated prison. *International Journal of Criminology and Penology, 1,* 69–97.

Hansen, E. M., Kimble, C. E., & Biers, D. W. (2000). Actors and observers: Divergent attributions of constrained unfriendly behavior. *Social Behavior and Personality, 29,* 87–104.

Hansen, K., Gerbasi, M., Todorov, A., Kruse, E., & Pronin, E. (2014). People claim objectivity after knowingly using biased strategies. *Personality and Social Psychology Bulletin.* doi:10.1177/0146167214523476

Hanson, K. L., Medina, K. L., Padula, C. B., Tapert, S. F., & Brown, S. A. (2011). Impact of adolescent alcohol and drug use on neuropsychological functioning in young adulthood: 10-year outcomes. *Journal of Child & Adolescent Substance Abuse, 20,* 135–154.

Hänze, M., & Berger, R. (2007). Cooperative learning, motivational effects, and student characteristics: An experimental study comparing cooperative learning and direct instruction in 12th grade physics classes. *Learning and Instruction, 17,* 29–41.

Harackiewicz, J. M. (1979). The effects of reward contingency and performance feedback on intrinsic motivation. *Journal of Personality and Social Psychology, 37,* 1352–1363.

Harackiewicz, J. M. (1989). Performance evaluation and intrinsic motivation processes: The effects of achievement orientation and rewards. In D. M. Buss & N. Cantor (Eds.), *Personality psychology: Recent trends and emerging directions* (pp. 128–137). New York: Springer-Verlag.

Harackiewicz, J. M., & Elliot, A. J. (1993). Achievement goals and intrinsic motivation. *Journal of Personality and Social Psychology, 65,* 904–915.

Harackiewicz, J. M., & Elliot, A. J. (1998). The joint effects of target and purpose goals on intrinsic motivation: A mediational analysis. *Personality and Social Psychology Bulletin, 24,* 675–689.

Harackiewicz, J. M., & Hulleman, C. S. (2010). The importance of interest: The role of achievement goals and task values in promoting the development of interest. *Social and Personality Psychology Compass, 4,* 42–52. doi:10.1111/ j.1751-9004.2009.00207.x

Harackiewicz, J. M., Manderlink, G., & Sansone, C. (1984). Rewarding pinball wizardry: The effects of evaluation and cue value on intrinsic interest. *Journal of Personality and Social Psychology, 47,* 287–300.

Hardin, C. D., & Higgins, E. T. (Eds.). (1996). *Shared reality: How social verification makes the subjective objective.* New York: Guilford Press.

Hare, A. P. (2003). Roles, relationships, and groups in organizations: Some conclusions and recommendations. *Small Group Research, 34,* 123–154.

Harmon-Jones, C., Schmeichel, B. J., Mennitt, E., & Harmon-Jones, E. (2011). The expression of determination: Similarities between anger and approach-related positive affect. *Journal of Personality and Social Psychology, 100,* 172–181.

Harmon-Jones, E., Harmon-Jones, C., & Amodio, D. M. (2012). A neuroscientific perspective on dissonance, guided by the action-based model. In B. Gawronski & F. Strack (Eds.), *Cognitive consistency: A fundamental principle in social cognition* (pp. 47–65). New York: Guilford Press.

Harrigan, J. A., & O'Connell, D. M. (1996). How do you feel when feeling anxious? Facial displays of anxiety. *Personality and Individual Differences, 21,* 205–212.

Harris M. (Ed.). (2009). *Bullying, rejection, and peer victimization: A social-cognitive neuroscience perspective* (pp. 251–277). New York: Springer.

Harris, B. (1986). Reviewing 50 years of the psychology of social issues. *Journal of Social Issues, 42,* 1–20.

Harris, C. R. (2003). A review of sex differences in jealousy, including self-report data, psychophysiological responses, interpersonal violence, and morbid jealousy. *Personality and Social Psychology Review, 7,* 102–128.

Harris, L. T., & Fiske, S. T. (2006). Dehumanizing the lowest of the low: Neuro-imaging responses to extreme outgroups. *Psychological Science, 17,* 847–853.

Harris, M. B. (1974). Mediators between frustration and aggression in a field experiment. *Journal of Experimental and Social Psychology, 10,* 561–571.

Harris, M. B., & Perkins, R. (1995). Effects of distraction on interpersonal expectancy effects: A social interaction test of the cognitive busyness hypothesis. *Social Cognition, 13,* 163–182.

Harris, M. B., Benson, S. M., & Hall, C. (1975). The effects of confession on altruism. *Journal of Social Psychology, 96,* 187–192.

Harris, M. G. (1994). Cholas, Mexican-American girls, and gangs. *Sex Roles, 30,* 289–301.

Harrison, J. A., & Wells, R. B. (1991). Bystander effects on male helping behavior: Social comparison and diffusion of responsibility. *Representative Research in Social Psychology, 19,* 53–63.

Hart, A. J. (1995). Naturally occurring expectation effects. *Journal of Personality and Social Psychology, 68,* 109–115.

Hart, D., & Damon, W. (1986). Developmental trends in self-understanding. *Social Cognition, 4,* 388–407.

Hart, D., & Matsuba, M. K. (2012). The development of self-knowledge. In S. Vazire & T. D. Wilson (Eds.), *The handbook of self-knowledge* (pp. 7–21). New York: Guilford Press.

Hart, W., Albarracín, D., Eagly, A. H., Brechan, I., Lindberg, M. J., & Merrill, L. (2009). Feeling validated versus being correct: A meta-analysis of selective exposure to information. *Psychological Bulletin, 135,* 555–588.

Harter, S. (1993). Causes and consequences of low self-esteem in children and adolescents. In R. F. Baumeister (Ed.), *Self-esteem: The puzzle of low self-regard* (pp. 87–116). New York: Plenum.

Harter, S. (2003). The development of self-representations during childhood and adolescence. In M. R. Leary & J. P. Tangney (Eds.), *Handbook of self and identity* (pp. 610–642). New York: Guilford Press.

Hartstone, M., & Augoustinos, M. (1995). The minimal group paradigm: Categorization into two versus three groups. *European Journal of Social Psychology, 25,* 179–193.

Hartup, W. W., & Stevens, N. (1997). Friendships and adaptation in the life course. *Psychological Bulletin, 121,* 355–370.

Harvey, J. H. (1995). *Odyssey of the heart: The search for closeness, intimacy, and love.* New York: Freeman.

Harvey, J. H., Flanary, R., & Morgan, M. (1986). Vivid memories of vivid loves gone by. *Journal of Personal and Social Relationships, 3,* 359–373.

Hasel, L. E., & Kassin, S. M. (2012). False confessions. In B. L. Cutler (Ed.), *Conviction of the innocent: Lessons from psychological research* (pp. 53–77). Washington, DC: American Psychological Association.

Haslam, S. A., Reicher, S. D., & Platow, M. J. (2013). *The new psychology of leadership: Identity, influence, and power.* East Sussex: Psychology Press.

Hassebrauck, M., & Buhl, T. (1996). Three-dimensional love. *Journal of Social Psychology, 136,* 121–122.

Hassin R. R., Aviezer H., & Bentin S. (2013). Inherently ambiguous: Facial expressions of emotions, in context. *Emotion Review, 5,* 60–65.

Hassin, R. R. (2013). Yes it can: On the functional abilities of the human unconscious. *Perspectives in Psychological Science, 8*(2), 195–207.

Hastie, R. (2008). What's the story? Explanations and narratives in civil jury decisions. In B, H. Bornstein, R. L. Wiener, R. Schopp, & S. L. Willborn (Eds.), *Civil juries and civil justice: Psychological and legal perspectives* (pp. 23–34). New York: Springer.

Hastie, R., & Pennington, N. (2000). Explanation-based decision making. In T. Connolly & H. R. Arkes (Eds.), *Judgment and decision making: An interdisciplinary reader* (2nd ed., pp. 212–228). New York: Cambridge University Press.

Hastie, R., Penrod, S. D., & Pennington, N. (1983). *Inside the jury.* Cambridge, MA: Harvard University Press.

Hatfield, E., & Rapson, R. L. (1993). *Love, sex, and intimacy: Their psychology, biology, and history.* New York: HarperCollins.

Hatfield, E., & Rapson, R. L. (1996). *Love and sex: Cross-cultural perspectives.* Needham Heights, MA: Allyn & Bacon.

Hatfield, E., & Rapson, R. L. (2002). Passionate love and sexual desire: Cultural and historical perspectives. In A. L. Vangelisti, H. T. Reis, & M. A. Fitzpatrick (Eds.), *Stability and change in relationships* (pp. 306–324). New York: Cambridge University Press.

Hatfield, E., & Sprecher, S. (1986). Measuring passionate love in intimate relationships. *Journal of Adolescence, 9,* 383–410.

Hatfield, E., & Sprecher, S. (1995). Men's and women's preferences in marital partners in the United States, Russia, and Japan. *Journal of Cross-Cultural Psychology, 26,* 728–750.

Hatfield, E., & Walster, G. W. (1978). *A new look at love.* Reading, MA: Addison-Wesley.

Hatfield, E., Cacioppo, J. T., & Rapson, R. L. (1993). *Emotional contagion.* New York: Cambridge University Press.

Hatoum, I. J., & Belle, D. (2004). Mags and abs: Media consumption and bodily concerns in men. *Sex Roles, 51,* 397–407.

Haugtvedt, C. P., & Wegener, D. T. (1994). Message order effects in persuasion: An attitude strength perspective. *Journal of Consumer Research, 21,* 205–218.

Hays, C. L. (2003, June 5). Martha Stewart indicted by U.S. on obstruction. *The New York Times,* pp. A1, C4.

Hazan, C., & Shaver, P. (1987). Romantic love conceptualized as an attachment process. *Journal of Personality and Social Psychology, 52,* 511–524.

Hazan, C., & Shaver, P. (1987). Romantic love conceptualized as an attachment process. *Journal of Personality and Social Psychology, 52,* 511–524.

Hazan, C., & Shaver, P. (1994). Deeper into attachment theory. *Psychological Inquiry, 5,* 68–79.

Hazelwood, J. D., & Olson, J. M. (1986). Covariation information, causal questioning, and interpersonal behavior. *Journal of Experimental Social Psychology, 22,* 276–291.

Heatherton, T. F., & Sargent, J. D. (2009). Does watching smoking in movies promote teenage smoking? *Current Directions in Psychological Science, 18,* 63–67.

Hebl, M., Foster, J., Bigazzi, J., Mannix, L., & Dovidio, J. (2002). Formal and interpersonal discrimination: A field study of bias toward homosexual applicants. *Personality and Social Psychology Bulletin, 28,* 815–825.

Heckhausen, J., & Schulz, R. (1995). A life-span theory of control. *Psychological Review, 102,* 284–304.

Hedden, T., Ketey, S., Aron, A., Markus, H. R., & Gabrieli, J. D. E. (2008). Cultural influence on neural substrates of attentional control. *Psychological Science, 19,* 12–17.

Hedge, A., & Yousif, Y. H. (1992). Effects of urban size, urgency, and cost on helpfulness. *Journal of Cross-Cultural Psychology, 23,* 107–115.

Hehman, E., Gaertner, S. L., & Dovidio, J. F. (2011). Evaluations of presidential performance: Race, prejudice, and perceptions of Americanism. *Journal of Experimental Social Psychology, 47,* 430–435.

Heider, F. (1944). Social perception and phenomenal causality. *Psychological Review, 51,* 358–374.

Heider, F. (1958). *The psychology of interpersonal relations.* New York: Wiley.

Heine, S. J. (2010). Cultural psychology. In S. T. Fiske, D. T. Gilbert, & G. Lindzey (Eds.), *Handbook of social psychology* (5th ed., Vol. 2, pp. 1423–1464). Hoboken, NJ: John Wiley.

Heine, S. J., Foster, J. B., & Spina, R. (2009). Do birds of a feather universally flock together? Cultural variation in the similarity-attraction effect. *Asian Journal of Psychology, 12,* 247–258.

Heine, S. J., Kitayama, S., & Lehman, D. R. (2001). Cultural differences in self-evaluation: Japanese readily accept negative self-relevant information. *Journal of Cross-Cultural Psychology, 32,* 434–443.

Heine, S. J., Lehman, D. R., Peng, K., & Greenholtz, J. (2002). What's wrong with cross-cultural comparisons of subjective Likert scales?: The reference-group effect. *Journal of Personality and Social Psychology, 82,* 903–918.

Heine, S. J., Takemoto, T., Moskalenko, S., Lasaleta, J., & Henrich, J. (2008). Mirrors in the head: Cultural variation in objective self-awareness. *Personality and Social Psychology Bulletin. 34,* 879–887.

Heine, S., Proulx, T., & Vohs, K. (2006). The meaning maintenance model: On the coherence of social motivations. *Personality and Social Psychology Review, 10,* 88–110.

Heitland, K., & Bohner, G. (2010). Reducing prejudice via cognitive dissonance: Individual differences in preference for consistency moderate the effects of counter-attitudinal advocacy. *Social Influence, 5,* 164–181.

Helgeson, V. S. (2003). Cognitive adaptation, psychological adjustment, and disease progression among angioplasty patients: 4 years later. *Health Psychology, 22,* 30–38.

Helgeson, V.S., & Fritz, H. L. (1999). Cognitive adaptation as a predictor of new coronary events after percutaneous transluminal coronary angioplasty. *Psychosomatic Medicine, 61,* 488–495.

Helzer, E. G., & Pizarro, D. A. (2011). Dirty liberals! Reminders of physical cleanliness influence moral and political attitudes. *Psychological Science, 22,* 517–522.

Henderlong, J., & Lepper, M. R. (2002). The effects of praise on children's intrinsic motivation: A review and synthesis. *Psychological Bulletin, 128,* 774–795.

Hendrix, K. S., & Hirt, E. R. (2009). Stressed out over possible failure: The role of regulatory fit on claimed self-handicapping. *Journal of Experimental Social Psychology, 45,* 51–59. doi:10.1016/j.jesp.2008.08.016

Henningsen, D., Henningsen, M., Eden, J., & Cruz, M. (2006). Examining the symptoms of group-think and retrospective sensemaking. *Small Group Research, 37,* 36–64.

Henrich, J., Heine, S. J., & Norenzayan, A. (2010). The weirdest people in the world? *Behavioral and Brain Sciences, 33*(2–3), 61–83. doi:10.1017/S0140525X0999152X

Herring, C. (2009). Does diversity pay? Race, gender, and the business case for diversity. *American Sociological Review, 74,* 208–224.

Hersh, S. M. (1970). *My Lai 4: A report on the massacre and its aftermath.* New York: Vintage Books.

Hersh, S. (2004, May 10). Torture at Abu Ghraib. *New Yorker.*

Heschl, A., & Burkart, J. (2006). A new mark test for mirror self-recognition in non-human primates. *Primates, 47,* 187–198.

Hess, A. (2014, May 28). Are you a slut? That depends. Are you rich? *Slate.com.* http://www.slate.com/blogs/xx_factor/2014/05/28/slut_shaming_and_class_a_study_on_how_college_women_decide_who_s_trashy.html

Heunemann, R. L., Shapiro, L. R., Hampton, M. C., & Mitchell, B. W. (1966). A longitudinal study of gross body composition and body conformation and their association with food and activity in the teenage population. *American Journal of Clinical Nutrition, 18,* 325–338.

Hewitt, J., & Alqahtani, M. A. (2003). Differences between Saudi and U.S. students in reaction to same- and mixed-sex intimacy shown by others. *Journal of Social Psychology, 143,* 233–242.

Hewlitt, S. A., Luce, C. B., & Servon, L. J. (2008, June). Stopping the exodus of women in science. *Harvard Business Review, 6,* 22–24, 139.

Hewstone, M., & Jaspars, J. (1987). Covariation and causal attribution: A logical model of the intuitive analysis of variance. *Journal of Personality and Social Psychology, 53,* 663–672.

Hibbard, L. (2011, November 8). Virginia Beach high schools pay students for good grades. *Huffington Post.* Retrieved January 10, 2012, from www.huffingtonpost.com/2011/11/08/high-school-pays-students_n_1082488.html

Higgins, E. T. (1987). Self-discrepancy: A theory relating self and affect. *Psychological Review, 94,* 319–340.

Higgins, E. T. (1989). Self-discrepancy theory: What patterns of self-beliefs cause people to suffer? In L. Berkowitz (Ed.), *Advances in experimental social psychology* (Vol. 22, pp. 93–136). New York: Academic Press.

Higgins, E. T. (1996a). Knowledge application: Accessibility, applicability, and salience. In E. T. Higgins & A. R. Kruglanski (Eds.), *Social psychology: Handbook of basic principles* (pp. 133–168). New York: Guilford Press.

Higgins, E. T. (1996b). The "self-digest": Self-knowledge serving self-regulatory functions. *Journal of Personality and Social Psychology, 71,* 1062–1083.

Higgins, E. T. (1999). Self-discrepancy: A theory relating self and affect. In R. F. Baumeister (Ed.), *The self in social psychology* (pp. 150–181). Philadelphia: Psychology Press.

Higgins, E. T. (2005). Value from regulatory fit. *Current Directions in Psychological Science, 14,* 209–213.

Higgins, E. T., & Bargh, J. A. (1987). Social cognition and social perception. *Annual Review of Psychology, 38,* 369–425.

Higgins, E. T., Bond, R. N., Klein, R., & Strauman, T. (1986). Self-discrepancies and emotional vulnerability: How magnitude, accessibility, and type of discrepancy influence affect. *Journal of Personality and Social Psychology, 51,* 5–15.

Higgins, E. T., Klein, R., & Strauman, T. (1987). Self-discrepancies: Distinguishing among self-states, self-state conflicts, and emotional vulnerabilities. In K. M. Yardley & T. M. Honess (Eds.), *Self and identity: Psychosocial perspectives* (pp. 173–186). New York: Wiley.

Higgins, E. T., Rholes, W. S., & Jones, C. R. (1977). Category accessibility and impression formation. *Journal of Experimental Social Psychology, 13,* 141–154.

Higgins, L. T., Zheng, M., Liu, Y., & Sun, C. H. (2002). Attitudes to marriage and sexual behaviors: A survey of gender and culture differences in China and United Kingdom. *Sex Roles, 46,* 75–89.

Hill, J. K. (2002). *Rainbow remedies for life's stormy times.* South Bend, IN: Moorhill Communications.

Hill, J. K. (n.d.). How I survived the deaths of twelve family members. Retrieved December 21, 2008, from www.resiliencycenter.com/stories/2002stories/0201hill.shtml

Hillshafer, D. (2013). The mass murder problem. *Skeptic, 18,* 24–32.

Hilton, D. J., Smith, R. H., & Kim, S. H. (1995). Process of causal explanation and dispositional attribution. *Journal of Personality and Social Psychology, 68,* 377–387.

Hilton, J. L., Fein, S., & Miller, D. T. (1993). Suspicion and dispositional inference. *Journal of Personality and Social Psychology, 19,* 501–512.

Hinds, M. de C. (1993, October 19). Not like the movie: 3 take a dare and lose. *The New York Times,* pp. A1, A22.

Hirsh, J. B., Galinsky, A. D., & Zhong, C. (2011). Drunk, powerful, and in the dark: How general processes of disinhibition produce both prosocial and antisocial behavior. *Perspectives on Psychological Science, 6,* 415–427.

Hirt, E. R., & McCrea, S. M. (2009). Man smart, woman smarter? Getting to the root of gender differences in self-handicapping. *Social and Personality Psychology Compass, 3,* 260–274. doi:10.1111/j.1751-9004.2009.00176.x

Hirt, E. R., Kardes, F. R., & Markman, K. D. (2004). Activating a mental simulation mind-set through generation of alternatives: Implications for debiasing in related and unrelated domains. *Journal of Experimental Social Psychology, 40,* 374–383.

Hirt, E. R., McCrea, S. M., & Boris, H. I. (2003). "I know you self-handicapped last exam": Gender differences in reactions to self-handicapping. *Journal of Personality and Social Psychology, 84,* 177–193.

Hirt, E. R., Melton, J. R., McDonald, H. E., & Harackiewicz, J. M. (1996). Processing goals, task interest, and the mood-performance relationship: A mediational analysis. *Journal of Personality and Social Psychology, 71,* 245–261.

Hitler, A. (1925). *Mein kampf.* Boston: Houghton Mifflin.

Hitsch, G., Hortaçsu, A., & Ariely, D. (2010). What makes you click? Mate preferences in online dating. *Quantitative Marketing and Economics, 8,* 393–427.

Hochstadt, S. (1999). *Mobility and modernity: Migration in Germany, 1820–1989.* Ann Arbor: University of Michigan Press.

Hodges, B. H., & Geyer, A. L. (2006). A nonconformist account of the Asch experiments: Values, pragmatics, and moral dilemmas. *Personality and Social Psychology Review, 10,* 2–19.

Hoffman, H. G., Granhag, P. A., See, S. T. K., & Loftus, E. F. (2001). Social influences on reality-monitoring decisions. *Memory and Cognition, 29,* 394–404.

Hofmann, W., De Houwer, J., Perugini, M., Baeyens, F., & Crombez, G. (2010). Evaluative conditioning in humans: A meta-analysis. *Psychological Bulletin, 136,* 390–421.

Hogg, M. A. (1992). *The social psychology of group cohesiveness: From attraction to social identity.* London: Harvester-Wheatsheaf.

Hogg, M. A. (1993). Group cohesiveness: A critical review and some new directions. In W. Stroebe & M. Hewstone (Eds.), *European review of social psychology* (Vol. 4, pp. 85–111). Chichester, UK: Wiley.

Hogg, M. A. (2001). A social identity theory of leadership. *Personality and Social Psychology Review, 5,* 184–200.

Hogg, M. A., & Abrams, D. (1988). *Social identifications.* London: Routledge.

Hogg, M. A., Hohman, Z. P., & Rivera, J. E. (2008). Why do people join groups? Three motivational accounts from social psychology. *Social and Personality Psychology Compass, 2* (www.blackwellcompass.com/subject/socialpsychology/).

Hogh-Olessen, H. (2008). Human spatial behavior: The spacing of people, objects and animals in six cross-cultural samples. *Journal of Cognition and Culture, 8,* 245–280.

Holland, R. W., Aarts, H., & Langendam, D. (2006). Breaking and creating habits on the working floor: A field-experiment on the power of implementation intentions. *Journal of Experimental Social Psychology, 42,* 776–783.

Holland, R. W., Meertens, R. M., & Van Vugt, M. (2002). Dissonance on the road: Self-esteem as a moderator of internal and external self-justification strategies. *Personality and Social Psychology Bulletin, 28,* 1713–1724.

Hollander, E. P. (1960). Competence and conformity in the acceptance of influence. *Journal of Abnormal and Social Psychology, 61,* 361–365.

Holmes, T. H., & Rahe, R. H. (1967). The social readjustment rating scale. *Journal of Psychosomatic Research, 11,* 213–218.

Holt-Lunstad, J., Smith, T. B., & Layton, J. B. (2010). Social relationships and mortality risk: A meta-analytic review. *PLoS Medicine, 7*(7), e1000316.

Holtz, R. (2004). Group cohesion, attitude projection, and opinion certainty: Beyond interaction. *Group Dynamics: Theory, Research, and Practice, 8,* 112–125.

Hong, Y., Benet-Martínez, V., Chiu, C., & Morris, M. W. (2003). Boundaries of cultural influence: Construct activation as a mechanism for cultural differences in social perception. *Journal of Cross-Cultural Psychology, 34,* 453–464.

Hong, Y., Wyer, R. S., Jr., & Fong, C. P. S. (2008). Chinese working in groups: Effort dispensability versus normative influence. *Asian Journal of Social Psychology, 11,* 187–195. doi:10.1111/j.1467-839X.2008.00257.x

Hong, Y.-Y., Chiu, C.-Y., & Kung, T. M. (1997). Bringing culture out in front: Effects of cultural meaning system activation on social cognition. In K. Leung, Y. Kashima, U. Kim, & S. Yamaguchi (Eds.), *Progress in Asian social psychology* (Vol. 1, pp. 135–146). Singapore: Wiley.

Hong, Y.-Y., Morris, M. W., Chiu, C.-Y., & Benet-Martinez, V. (2000). Multicultural minds: A dynamic constructivist approach to culture and cognition. *American Psychologist, 55,* 709–720.

Hood, K. B., & Shook, N. J. (2014). Who cares what others think?: The indirect effect of other's attitudes on condom use intentions. *International Journal of Sexual Health, 26,* 282–294.

Hoog, N., Stroebe, W., & de Wit, J. B. F. (2005). The impact of fear appeals on processing and acceptance of action recommendations. *Personality and Social Psychology Bulletin, 31,* 24–33.

Hoorens, V., & Van Damme, C. (2012). What do people infer from social comparisons? Bridges between social comparison and person perception. *Social and Personality Psychology Compass, 6*(8), 607–618. doi:10.1111/j.1751-9004.2012.00451.x

Hope, L., Memon, A., & McGeorge, P. (2004). Understanding pretrial publicity: Predecisional distortion of evidence by mock jurors. *Journal of Experimental Psychology: Applied, 10,* 111–119.

Horcajo, J., Briñol, P., & Petty, R. E. (2014). Multiple roles for majority versus minority source status on persuasion when source status follows the message. *Social Influence, 9,* 37–51.

Hornsey, M. J., Grice, T., Jetten, J., Paulsen, N., & Callan, V. (2007). Group-directed criticisms and recommendations for change: Why newcomers arouse more resistance than old-timers. *Personality and Social Psychology Bulletin, 32,* 1620–1632.

Hornsey, M. J., Jetten, J., McAuliffe, B. J., & Hogg, M. A. (2006). The impact of individualist and collectivist group norms on evaluations of dissenting group members. *Journal of Experimental Social Psychology*, 42, 57–68.

Hornsey, M. J., Majkut, L., Terry, D. J., & McKimmie, B. M. (2003). On being loud and proud: Non-conformity and counter-conformity to group norms. *British Journal of Social Psychology*, 42, 319–335.

Hostinar, C. E., Sullivan, R. M., & Gunnar, M. R. (2014). Psychobiological mechanisms underlying the social buffering of the hypothalamic–pituitary–adrenocortical axis: A review of animal models and human studies across development. *Psychological Bulletin*, 140, 256–282.

House, J. S., Robbins, C., & Metzner, H. L. (1982). The association of social relationships and activities with mortality: Prospective evidence from the Tecumseh Community Health Study. *American Journal of Epidemiology*, 116, 123–140.

House, R. J., Hanges, P. J., Javidan, M., Dorfman, P. W., & Gupta, V. (2004). *Culture, leadership, and organizations: The GLOBE study of 62 societies.* Thousand Oaks, CA: Sage.

Hovland, C. I., & Sears, R. R. (1940). Minor studies in aggression: 6. Correlation of lynchings with economic indices. *Journal of Psychology*, 9, 301–310.

Hovland, C. I., Janis, I. L., & Kelley, H. H. (1953). *Communication and persuasion: Psychological studies of opinion change.* New Haven, CT: Yale University Press.

Howard, D. E., Griffin, M. A., & Boekeloo, B. O. (2008). Prevalence and psychosocial correlates of alcohol-related sexual assault among university students. *Adolescence*, 43, 733–750.

Howard, J. A., Blumstein, P., & Schwartz, P. (1987). Social or evolutionary theories? Some observations on preferences in human mate selection. *Journal of Personality and Social Psychology*, 53, 194–200.

Howell, R. T., & Guevarra, D. A. (2013). Buying happiness: Differential consumption experiences for material and experiential purchases. *Advances in Psychology Research*, 98, 57–69.

Howerton, D. M., Meltzer, A. L., & Olson, M. A. (2012). Honeymoon vacation: Sexual-orientation prejudice and inconsistent behavioral responses. *Basic and Applied Social Psychology*, 34, 146–151.

Hsiang, S. M., Burke, M., & Miguel, E. (2013, September). Quantifying the influence of climate on human conflict. *Science*, 341. doi:10.1126/science.1235367

Hsu, S. S. (1995, April 8). Fredericksburg searches its soul after clerk is beaten as 6 watch. *Washington Post*, pp. A1, A13.

Huesman, L. R., Dubow, E. F., & Yang, G. (2013). Why it is hard to believe that media violence causes aggression. In K. E. Dill (Ed.), *The Oxford handbook of media psychology* (pp. 159–171). Oxford: Oxford University Press.

Huffington, A. (2014). *Thrive: The third metric to redefining success and creating a life of well-being, wisdom, and wonder.* New York, NY: Harmony.

Huffman, K. T., Grossnickle, W. F., Cope, J. G., & Huffman, K. P. (1995). Litter reduction: A review and integration of the literature. *Environment and Behavior*, 27, 153–183.

Hugenberg, K., Young, S. G., Bernstein, M. J., & Sacco, D. F. (2010). The categorization-individuation model: An integrative account of the other-race recognition deficit. *Psychological Review*, 117(4), 1168–1187. doi:10.1037/a0020463

Hui, C. H., & Triandis, H. C. (1986). Individualism-collectivism: A study of cross-cultural researchers. *Journal of Cross-Cultural Psychology*, 17, 225–248.

Hull, J. G., Young, R. D., & Jouriles, E. (1986). Applications of the self-awareness model of alcohol consumption: Predicting patterns of use and abuse. *Journal of Personality and Social Psychology*, 51, 790–796.

Hulleman, C. S., Schrager, S. M., Bodmann, S. M., & Harackiewicz, J. M. (2010). A meta-analytic review of achievement goal measures: Different labels for the same constructs or different constructs with similar labels? *Psychological Bulletin*, 136, 422–449. doi:10.1037/a0018947

Hunger. (n.d.). World Food Programme. Retrieved July 15, 2014, from http://www.wfp.org/hunger

Hunt, G. T. (1940). *The wars of the Iroquois.* Madison: University of Wisconsin Press.

Huntsinger, J., & Sinclair, S. (2010). When it feels right, go with it: Affective regulation of affiliative social tuning. *Social Cognition*, 28, 290–305.

Hurley, D., & Allen, B. P. (1974). The effect of the number of people present in a nonemergency situation. *Journal of Social Psychology*, 92, 27–29.

Hust, S. J. T., Marett, E. G., Ren, C., Adams, P. M., Willoughby, J. F., Lei, M., et al. (2014). Establishing and adhering to sexual consent: The association between reading magazines and college students' sexual consent negotiation. *Journal of Sex Research*, 51, 280–290.

Huston, A., & Wright, J. (1996). Television and socialization of young children. In T. M. MacBeth (Ed.), *Tuning in to young viewers: Social science perspectives on television* (pp. 37–60). Thousand Oaks, CA: Sage.

Hutchinson, R. R. (1983). The pain-aggression relationship and its expression in naturalistic settings. *Aggressive Behavior*, 9, 229–242.

Hütter, M., & Sweldens, S. (2013). Implicit misattribution of evaluative responses: Contingency-unaware evaluative conditioning requires simultaneous stimulus presentations. *Journal of Experimental Psychology: General*, 142(3), 638–643. doi:10.1037/a0029989

Hyde, J. S. (2005). The gender similarities hypothesis. *American Psychologist*, 60, 581–592.

Hyman, I. E., Jr., Roundhill, R. F., Wener, K. M., & Rabiroff, C. A. (2014). Collaboration inflation: Egocentric source monitoring errors following collaborative remembering. *Journal of Applied Research in Memory and Cognition.*doi:10.1016/j.jarmac.2014.04.004

Ibrahim, J. K., & Glantz, S. A. (2007). The rise and fall of tobacco control media campaigns, 1967–2006. *American Journal of Public Health*, 97, 1383–1396.

Ickes, W. J., Patterson, M. L., Rajecki, D. W., & Tanford, S. (1982). Behavioral and cognitive consequences of reciprocal versus compensatory responses to preinteraction expectancies. *Social Cognition*, 1, 160–190.

IJzerman, H., & Semin, G. R. (2010). Temperature perceptions as a ground for social proximity. *Journal of Experimental Social Psychology*, 46(6), 867–873. doi:10.1016/j.jesp.2010.07.015

IJzerman, H., & Semin, G. R. (2010). Temperature perceptions as a ground for social proximity. *Journal of Experimental Social Psychology*, 46, 867–873.

Imada, T., & Kitayama, S. (2010). Social eyes and choice justification: Culture and dissonance revisited. *Social Cognition*, 28, 589–608.

Imhoff, R., & Erb, H. (2009). What motivates non-conformity? Uniqueness seeking blocks majority influence. *Personality and Social Psychology Bulletin*, 35, 309–320.

Imrich, D. J., Mullin, C., & Linz, D. G. (1995). Measuring the extent of prejudicial pretrial publicity in major American newspapers: A content analysis. *Journal of Communication*, 45, 94–117.

Infurna, F. J., Ram, N., & Gerstorf, D. (2013). Level and change in perceived control predict 19-year mortality: Findings from the Americans' changing lives study. *Developmental Psychology*, 49, 1833–1847.

Inglehart, M. R. (1991). *Reactions to critical life events: A social psychological analysis.* New York: Praeger.

Inglehart, R., & Klingemann, H. (2000). Genes, culture, democracy, and happiness. In E. Diener & E. M. Suh (Eds.), *Culture and subjective well-being* (pp. 165–183). Cambridge, MA: MIT Press.

Insko, C. A., & Schopler, J. (1998). Differential trust of groups and individuals. In C. Sedikides & J. Schopler (Eds.), *Intergroup cognition and intergroup behavior* (pp. 75–107). Mahwah, NJ: Erlbaum.

Insko, C. A., Smith, R. H., Alicke, M. D., Wade, J., & Taylor, S. (1985). Conformity and group size: The concern with being right and the concern with being liked. *Personality and Social Psychology Bulletin*, 11, 41–50.

Isen, A. M. (1987). Positive affect, cognitive processes, and social behavior. In L. Berkowitz (Ed.), *Advances in experimental social psychology* (Vol. 20, pp. 203–253). San Diego, CA: Academic Press.

Isen, A. M. (1999). Positive affect. In T. Dalgleish & M. J. Power (Eds.), *Handbook of cognition and emotion* (pp. 521–539). Chichester, UK: Wiley.

Isen, A. M., & Levin, P. A. (1972). Effect of feeling good on helping: Cookies and kindness. *Journal of Personality and Social Psychology*, 21, 384–388.

Isenberg, D. J. (1986). Group polarization: A critical review and meta-analysis. *Journal of Personality and Social Psychology*, 50, 1141–1151.

Islam, M. R., & Hewstone, M. (1993). Intergroup attributions and affective consequences in majority and minority groups. *Journal of Personality and Social Psychology*, 64, 936–950.

Ito, K., Masuda, T., & Li, M. W. (2013). Agency and facial emotion judgment in context. *Personality and Social Psychology Bulletin*, 39, 763–776.

Ito, T. A., & Urland, G. R. (2003). Race and gender on the brain: Electrocortical measures of attention to the race and gender of multiply categorizable individuals. *Journal of Personality and Social Psychology*, 85, 616–626.

Ivanov, B., Pfau, M., & Parker, K. A. (2009). Can inoculation withstand multiple attacks?: An examination of the effectiveness of the inoculation strategy compared to the supportive and restoration strategies. *Communication Research*, 36(5), 655–676. doi:10.1177/0093650209338909

Izard, C. E. (1994). Innate and universal facial expressions: Evidence from developmental and cross-cultural research. *Psychological Bulletin*, 115, 288–299.

Izuma, K., Matsumoto, M., Murayama, K., Samejima, K., Sadato, N., & Matsumoto, K. (2010). Neural correlates of cognitive dissonance and choice-induced preference change. *PNAS Proceedings of the National Academy of Sciences*, 107, 22014–22019.

Jack, R. E., Garrod, O. G., Yu, H., Caldara, R., & Schyns, P. G. (2012). Facial expressions of emotion are not culturally universal. *Proceedings of the National Academy of Sciences*, 109, 7241–7244.

Jackson, J. M., & Williams, K. D. (1985). Social loafing on difficult tasks: Working collectively can improve performance. *Journal of Personality and Social Psychology*, 49, 937–942.

Jackson, J. S., & Inglehart, M. R. (1995). Reverberation theory: Stress and racism in hierarchically structured communities. In S. E. Hobfoll & M. W. De Vries (Eds.), *Extreme stress and communities: Impact and intervention* (pp. 353–373). Dordrecht, Netherlands: Kluwer.

Jackson, J. S., Brown, T. N., Williams, D. R., Torres, M., Sellers, S. L., & Brown, K. (1996). Racism and the physical and mental health status of African Americans: A thirteen-year national panel study. *Ethnicity and Disease*, 6, 132–147.

Jackson, J. W. (1993). Realistic group conflict theory: A review and evaluation of the theoretical and empirical literature. *Psychological Record*, 43, 395–413.

Jackson, L. A. (1992). *Physical appearance and gender: Sociobiological and sociocultural perspectives.* Albany: State University of New York Press.

Jackson, L. A., Hunter, J. E., & Hodge, C. N. (1995). Physical attractiveness and intellectual competence: A meta-analytic review. *Social Psychology Quarterly*, 58, 108–122.

Jackson, T., Chen, H., Guo, C., & Gao, X. (2006). Stories we love by conceptions of love among couples from the People's Republic of China and the United States. *Journal of Cross-Cultural Psychology*, 37, 446–464.

Jacobs, P., & Landau, S. (1971). *To serve the devil* (Vol. 2). New York: Vintage Books.

Jacobson, R. P., Mortensen, C. R., & Cialdini, R. B. (2011). Bodies obliged and unbound: Differentiated response tendencies for injunctive and descriptive social norms. *Journal of Personality and Social Psychology*, 100(3), 433–448. doi:10.1037/a0021470

Jacowitz, K. E., & Kahneman, D. (1995). Measures of anchoring in estimation tasks. *Personality and Social Psychology Bulletin*, 21, 1161–1166.

Jain, S. P., & Posavac, S. S. (2001). Prepurchase attribute verifiability, source credibility, and persuasion. *Journal of Consumer Psychology, 11,* 169–180.

James, L. M., & Olson, J. M. (2000). Jeer pressure: The behavioral effects of observing ridicule of others. *Personality and Social Psychology Bulletin, 26,* 474–485.

James, W. (1890). *The principles of psychology.* New York: Henry Holt.

Janis, I. L. (1972). *Victims of groupthink.* Boston: Houghton Mifflin.

Janis, I. L. (1982). *Groupthink: Psychological studies of policy decisions and fiascoes* (2nd ed.). Boston: Houghton Mifflin.

Janis, I. L., & Feshbach, S. (1953). Effects of fear-arousing communications. *Journal of Abnormal and Social Psychology, 49,* 78–92.

Janis, I. L., & Mann, L. (1977). Decision Making. Copyright © 1977 by The Free Press, a Division of Macmillan Publishing Co., Inc.

Jankowiak, W. R. (1995). Introduction. In W. R. Jankowiak (Ed.), *Romantic passion: A universal experience?* (pp. 1–19). New York: Columbia University Press.

Jankowiak, W. R., & Fischer, E. F. (1992). A cross-cultural perspective on romantic love. *Ethnology, 31,* 149–155.

Janoff-Bulman, R., & Leggatt, H. K. (2002). Culture and social obligation: When "shoulds" are perceived as "wants." *Journal of Research in Personality, 36,* 260–270.

Janoff-Bulman, R., Timko, C., & Carli, L. L. (1985). Cognitive biases in blaming the victim. *Journal of Experimental Social Psychology, 21,* 161–177.

Jecker, J., & Landy, D. (1969). Liking a person as a function of doing him a favor. *Human Relations, 22,* 371–378.

Jehn, K. A., Northcraft, G. B., & Neale, M. A. (1999). Why differences make a difference: A field study of diversity, conflict, and performance in workgroups. *Administrative Science Quarterly, 44,* 741–763.

Jennings, K. (2011, February 16). My puny human brain. *Slate.com.* Retrieved April 18, 2011, from www.slate.com/id/2284721/

Jetten, J., & Hornsey, M. J. (2014). Deviance and dissent in groups. *Annual Review of Psychology, 65,* 461–485.

Job, V., Dweck, C. S., & Walton, G. M. (2010). Ego depletion—Is it all in your head? Implicit theories about willpower affect self-regulation. *Psychological Science, 21,* 1686–1693.

Johansson, P., Hall, L., Skiström, S., & Olsson, A. (2005). Failure to detect mismatches between intention and outcome in a simple decision task. *Science, 310,* 116–119.

Johns, M., Schmader, T., & Martens, A. (2005). Knowing is half the battle: Teaching stereotype threat as a means of improving women's math performance. *Psychological Science, 16,* 175–179.

Johnson, C. (2012). Behavioral responses to threatening social comparisons: From dastardly deeds to rising above. *Social and Personality Psychology Compass, 6*(7), 515–524. doi:10.1111/j.1751-9004.2012.00445.x

Johnson, D. M. (1945). The phantom anesthetist of Mattoon: A field study of mass hysteria. *Journal of Abnormal and Social Psychology, 40,* 175–186.

Johnson, D. W., & Johnson, R. T. (1987). *Learning together and alone: Cooperative, competitive, and individualistic learning* (2nd ed.). Englewood Cliffs, NJ: Prentice Hall.

Johnson, F. L., & Arles, E. J. (1983). Conversational patterns among same-sex pairs of late-adolescent close friends. *Journal of Genetic Psychology, 142,* 225–238.

Johnson, J. G., Cohen, P., Smailes, E. M., Kasen, S., & Brook, J. (2002). Television viewing and aggressive behavior during adolescence and adulthood. *Science, 295,* 2468–2471.

Johnson, K. J., & Fredrickson, B. L. (2005). We all look the same to me: Positive emotions eliminate the own-race bias in face recognition. *Psychological Science, 16,* 875–881.

Johnson, L. B. (1971). *The vantage point: Perspectives of the presidency, 1963–69.* New York: Holt, Rinehart and Winston.

Johnson, M., Verfaellie, M., & Dunlosky, J. (2008). Introduction to the special section on integrative approaches to source memory. *Journal of Experimental Psychology: Learning, Memory, and Cognition, 34,* 727–729.

Johnson, R. D., & Downing, R. L. (1979). Deindividuation and valence of cues: Effects of prosocial and antisocial behavior. *Journal of Personality and Social Psychology, 37,* 1532–1538.

Johnson, T. (2014, March 24). 13 of 14 hottest years on record all occurred in 21st century. *Weather.com.* Retrieved July 15, 2014, from http://www.weather.com/news/science/environment/13-14-hottest-years-record-occurred-21st-century-wmo-20140324

Johnson, T. E., & Rule, B. G. (1986). Mitigating circumstance information, censure, and aggression. *Journal of Personality and Social Psychology, 50,* 537–542.

Jonas, E., Martens, A., Kayser, D. N., Fritsche, I., Sullivan, D., & Greenberg, J. (2008). Focus theory of normative conduct and terror-management theory: The interactive impact of mortality salience and norm salience on social judgment. *Journal of Personality and Social Psychology Bulletin, 95,* 1239–1251.

Jonas, K. J. (2013). Automatic behavior—Its social embedding and individual consequences. *Social and Personality Psychology Compass, 7,* 689–700. doi:10.1111/spc3.12060

Jones, B. C., Little, A. C., Penton-Voak, I. S., Tiddeman, B. P., Burt, D. M., & Perrett, D. I. (2001). Facial symmetry and judgements of apparent health: Support for a "good genes" explanation of the attractiveness-symmetry relationship. *Evolution and Human Behavior, 22,* 417–429.

Jones, C., & Aronson, E. (1973). Attribution of fault to a rape victim as a function of the respectability of the victim. *Journal of Personality and Social Psychology, 26,* 415–419.

Jones, E. E. (1964). *Ingratiation: A social psychological analysis.* New York: Appleton-Century-Crofts.

Jones, E. E. (1979). The rocky road from acts to dispositions. *American Scientist, 34,* 107–117.

Jones, E. E., & Berglas, S. (1978). Control of attributions about the self through self-handicapping strategies: The appeal of alcohol and the role of underachievement. *Personality and Social Psychology Bulletin, 4,* 200–206.

Jones, E. E., & Harris, V. A. (1967). The attribution of attitudes. *Journal of Experimental Social Psychology, 3,* 1–24.

Jones, E. E., & Kohler, R. (1959). The effects of plausibility on the learning of controversial statements. *Journal of Abnormal and Social Psychology, 57,* 315–320.

Jones, E. E., & Nisbett, R. E. (1972). The actor and the observer: Divergent perceptions of the causes of behavior. In E. E. Jones, D. E. Kanouse, H. H. Kelley, R. E. Nisbett, S. Valins, & B. Weiner (Eds.), *Attribution: Perceiving the causes of behavior* (pp. 79–94). Morristown, NJ: General Learning Press.

Jones, E. E., & Pittman, T. S. (1982). Toward a general theory of strategic self-presentation. In J. Suls (Ed.), *Psychological perspectives on the self* (pp. 231–262). Hillsdale, NJ: Erlbaum.

Jones, E. E., & Sigall, H. (1971). The bogus pipeline: A new paradigm for measuring affect and attitude. *Psychological Bulletin, 76,* 349–364.

Jones, E. E., & Wortman, C. B. (1973). *Ingratiation: An attributional approach.* Morristown, NJ: General Learning Press.

Jones, G. (2003, October 2). World oil and gas 'running out.' CNN .com/World. Retrieved June 21, 2006, from edition.cnn.com/2003/WORLD/europe/10/02/global.warming/

Jones, M. (2006, January 15). Shutting themselves in. *The New York Times,* Sec. 6, pp. 46–51.

Jones, M. A., Taylor, V. A., & Reynolds, K. E. (2014). The effect of requests for positive evaluations on customer satisfaction ratings. *Psychology and Marketing, 31,* 161–170.

Jordan, M. (1996, January 15). In Japan, bullying children to death. *Washington Post,* pp. A1, A15.

Jordan, M., & Sullivan, K. (1995, September 8). A matter of saving face: Japanese can rent

mourners, relatives, friends, even enemies to buff an image. *Washington Post,* pp. A1, A28.

Josephson, W. D. (1987). Television violence and children's aggression: Testing the priming, social script, and disinhibition prediction. *Journal of Personality and Social Psychology, 53,* 882–890.

Jost, J. T., Nosek, B. A., & Gosling, S. D. (2008). Ideology: Its resurgence in social, personality, and political psychology. *Perspectives on Psychological Science, 3,* 126–136.

Jostmann, N. B., Lakens, D., & Schubert, T. W. (2009). Weight as an embodiment of importance. *Psychological Science, 20,* 1169–1174. doi:10.1111/j.1467-9280.2009.02426.x

Jowett, G. S., & O'Donnell, V. (1999). *Propaganda and persuasion.* Thousand Oaks, CA: Sage.

Judd, C. M., & Park B. (1988). Out-group homogeneity: Judgments of variability at the individual and group levels. *Journal of Personality and Social Psychology, 54*(5), 778–788.

Judge rules ACLU discrimination suit against Continental Airlines can go forward. (2002). Retrieved from www.aclu.org/RacialEquality/RacialEquality.cfm?ID=10994&c=133

Judge, T. A., & Piccolo, R. F. (2004). Transformational and transactional leadership: A meta-analytic test of their relative validity. *Journal of Applied Psychology, 89,* 755–768.

Judge, T. A., Bono, J. E., Ilies, R., & Gerhardt, M. W. (2002). Personality and leadership: A qualitative and quantitative review. *Journal of Applied Psychology, 87,* 765–780.

Judge, T. A., Colbert, A. E., & Ilies, R. (2004). Intelligence and leadership: A quantitative review and test of theoretical propositions. *Journal of Applied Psychology, 89,* 542–552.

Judge, T. A., Hurst, C. , & Simon, L. S. (2009). Does it pay to be smart, attractive, or confident (or all three)? Relationships among general mental ability, physical attractiveness, core self-evaluations, and income. *Journal of Applied Psychology, 94,* 742–755.

Jung, K., Shavitt, S., Viswanathan, M., & Hilbe, J. M. (2014, June 2). Female hurricanes are deadlier than male hurricanes. *PNAS.* Published ahead of print June 2, 2014. doi:10.1073/pnas.1402786111

Jürgen-Lohmann, J., Borsch, F., & Giesen, H. (2001). Kooperatives Lernen an der Hochschule: Evaluation des Gruppenpuzzles in Seminaren der Pädagogischen Psychologie. *Zeitschrift für Pädagogische Psychologie, 15,* 74–84.

Juslin, P., Winman, A., & Hansson, P. (2007). The naïve intuitive statistician: A naïve sampling model of intuitive confidence intervals. *Psychological Review, 114,* 678–703.

Jussim, L. (2012). *Social perception and social reality: Why accuracy dominates bias and self-fulfilling prophecy.* New York: Oxford University Press.

Jussim, L., Cain, T. R., Crawford, J. T., Harber, K., & Cohen, F. (2009). The unbearable accuracy of stereotypes. In T. Nelson (Ed.), *The handbook of prejudice, stereotyping, and discrimination* (pp. 199–227). New York: Psychology Press.

Jussim, L., Eccles, J., & Madon, S. (1996). Social perception, social stereotypes, and teacher expectations: Accuracy and the quest for the powerful self-fulfilling prophecy. In M. P. Zanna (Ed.), *Advances in experimental social psychology* (Vol. 28, pp. 281–388). doi:10.1016/S0065-2601(08)60240-3

Kahn, J. P. (2003, June 7). How the mighty have fallen. *Boston Globe,* pp. D1, D7.

Kahn, M. (1966). The physiology of catharsis. *Journal of Personality and Social Psychology, 3,* 278–298.

Kahneman, D. (2011). *Thinking, fast and slow.* New York: Farrar, Straus, & Giroux.

Kahneman, D., & Deaton, A. (2010). High income improves evaluation of life but not emotional well-being. *Proceedings of the National Academy of Sciences, 10,* 16489–16493.

Kahneman, D., & Frederick, S. (2002). Representativeness revisited: Attribute substitution in intuitive judgment. In T. Gilovich, D. W. Griffin, & D. Kahneman (Eds.), *Heuristics and biases: The psychology of intuitive judgment* (pp. 49–81). New York: Cambridge University Press.

Kahneman, D., & Tversky, A. (1973). On the psychology of prediction. *Psychological Review, 80,* 237–251.

Kaighobadi, F., Shackelford, T. K., & Goetz, A. T. (2009). From mate retention to murder: Evolutionary psychological perspectives on men's partner-directed violence. *Review of General Psychology, 13,* 327–334.

Kalisch, R., Müller, M. B., & Tüscher, O. (2014). A conceptual framework for the neurobiological study of resilience. *Behavioral and Brain Sciences,* 1–49.

Kallgren, C. A., Reno, R. R., & Cialdini, R. B. (2000). A focus theory of normative conduct: When norms do and do not affect behavior. *Personality and Social Psychology Bulletin, 26,* 1002–1012.

Kalmijn, M., & Monden, C. W. S. (2012). The division of labor and depressive symptoms at the couple level: Effects of equity of specialization? *Journal of Social and Personal Relationships.* doi:10.1177/0265407511431182

Kalven, H., Jr., & Zeisel, H. (1966). *The American jury.* Boston: Little, Brown.

Kamble, S., Shackelford, T. K., Pham, M. N., & Buss, D. M. (2014). Indian mate preferences: Continuity, sex differences, and cultural change across a quarter of a century. *Personality and Individual Differences, 70,* 150–155.

Kameda, T., Takezawa, M., & Hastie, R. (2005). Where do social norms come from?: The example of communal sharing. *Current Directions in Psychological Science, 14*(6), 331–334. doi:10.1111/j.0963-7214.2005.00392.x

Kang, C. (2008). Product placement on TV targeted. *Washington Post.* http://www.washingtonpost.com/wp-dyn/content/article/2008/06/26/AR2008062603632.html

Kang, N., & Kwak, N. (2003). A multilevel approach to civic participation: Individual length of residence, neighborhood residential stability, and their interactive effects with media use. *Communication Research, 30,* 80–106.

Kappas, A. (1997). The fascination with faces: Are they windows to our soul? *Journal of Nonverbal Behavior, 21,* 157–162.

Kappeler, P., & van Schaik, C. P. (Eds.). (2006). *Cooperation in primates and humans: Mechanisms and evolution.* Berlin: Springer.

Karau, S. J., & Williams, K. D. (1993). Social loafing: A meta-analytic review and theoretical integration. *Journal of Personality and Social Psychology, 65,* 681–706.

Karau, S. J., & Williams, K. D. (2001). Understanding individual motivation in groups: The collective effort model. In M. E. Turner (Ed.), *Groups at work—theory and research: Applied social research* (pp. 113–141). Mahwah, NJ: Erlbaum.

Karremans, J. C., Stroebe, W., & Claus, J. (2006). Beyond Vicary's fantasies: The impact of subliminal priming and brand choice. *Journal of Experimental Social Psychology, 42,* 792–798.

Kassin, S. M., Drizin, S. A., Grisso, T., Gudjonsson, G. H., Leo, R. A., & Redlich, A. (2010). Police-induced confessions, risk factors, and recommendations: Looking ahead. *Law and Human Behavior, 34*(1), 49–52. doi:10.1007/s10979-010-9217-5

Katz, D. (1960). The functional approach to the study of attitudes. *Public Opinion Quarterly, 24,* 163–204.

Kauffman, D. R., & Steiner, I. D. (1968). Conformity as an ingratiation technique. *Journal of Experimental Social Psychology, 4,* 404–414.

Kaufman, L. (2009). Utilities turn their customers green with envy. *New York Times.* www.nytimes.com/2009/01/31/science/earth/31compete.html

Kawakami, N., & Yoshida, F. (2014). How do implicit effects of subliminal mere exposure become explicit? Mediating effects of social interaction. *Social Influence.* doi:10.1080/15534510.2014.901245

Kayser, D. N., Greitemeyer, T., Fischer, P., & Frey, D. (2010). Why mood affects help giving, but not moral courage: Comparing two types of prosocial behaviour. *European Journal of Social Psychology, 40*(7), 1136–1157. doi:10.1002/ejsp.717

Keelan, J. P. R., Dion, K. L., & Dion, K. K. (1994). Attachment style and hetereosexual relationships among young adults: A short-term panel study. *Journal of Social and Personal Relationships, 11,* 201–214.

Keller, J., & Bless, H. (2008). Flow and regulatory compatibility: An experimental approach to the flow model of intrinsic motivation. *Personality and Social Psychology Bulletin, 34,* 196–209.

Kelley, H. H. (1950). The warm-cold variable in first impressions of persons. *Journal of Personality, 18,* 431–439.

Kelley, H. H. (1955). The two functions of reference groups. In G. E. Swanson, T. M. Newcomb, & E. L. Hartley (Eds.), *Readings in social psychology* (2nd ed., pp. 410–414). New York: Henry Holt.

Kelley, H. H. (1967). Attribution theory in social psychology. In D. Levine (Ed.), *Nebraska Symposium on Motivation* (Vol. 15, pp. 192–238). Lincoln: University of Nebraska Press.

Kelley, H. H. (1973). The process of causal attribution. *American Psychologist, 28,* 107–128.

Kelley, H. H. (1983). Love and commitment. In H. H. Kelley, E. Berscheid, A. Christensen, J. H. Harvey, T. L. Huston, G. Levinger, et al. (Eds.), *Close relationships* (pp. 265–314). New York: Freeman.

Kelley, H. H., & Thibaut, J. W. (1978). *Interpersonal relations: A theory of interdependence.* New York, NY: Wiley.

Keltner, D., & Shiota, M. N. (2003). New displays and new emotions: A commentary on Rozin and Cohen. *Emotion, 3,* 86–91.

Keltner, D., Kogan, A., Piff, P. K., & Saturn, S. R. (2014). The sociocultural appraisals, values, and emotions (SAVE) framework of prosociality: Core processes from gene to meme. *Annual Review of Psychology, 65,* 425–460.

Kennedy, S., & Ruggles, S. (2014). Breaking up is hard to count: The rise of divorce in the United States, 1980–2010. *Demography, 51,* 587–598.

Kenny, D. A. (1994). Using the social relations model to understand relationships. In R. Erber & R. Gilmour (Eds.), *Theoretical frameworks for personal relationships* (pp. 111–127). Hillsdale, NJ: Erlbaum.

Kenny, D. A., & La Voie, L. (1982). Reciprocity of interpersonal attraction: A confirmed hypothesis. *Social Psychology Quarterly, 45,* 54–58.

Kenrick, D. T., & MacFarlane, S. W. (1986). Ambient temperature and horn honking: A field study of the heat/aggression relationship. *Environment and Behavior, 18,* 179–191.

Kernis, M. H. (2001). Following the trail from narcissism to fragile self-esteem. *Psychological Inquiry, 12,* 223–225.

Kerr, N. L., & Tindale, R. S. (2004). Groups performance and decision making. *Annual Review of Psychology, 55,* 623–655.

Kerr, N., & Levine, J. (2008). The detection of social exclusion: Evolution and beyond. *Group Dynamics: Theory, Research, and Practice, 12,* 39–52.

Kestemont, J., Ma, N., Baetens, K., Clément, N., Van Overwalle, F., & Vandekerckhove, M. (2014). Neural correlates of attributing causes to the self, another person, and the situation. *Social Cognitive and Affective Neuroscience.* doi:10.1093/scan/nsu030

Key, W. B. (1973). *Subliminal seduction.* Englewood Cliffs, NJ: Signet Books.

Key, W. B. (1989). *Age of manipulation: The con in confidence and the sin in sincere.* New York: Henry Holt.

Kiesler, C. A., & Kiesler, S. B. (1969). *Conformity.* Reading, MA: Addison-Wesley.

Kihlstrom, J. F. (1996). The trauma-memory argument and recovered memory therapy. In K. Pezdek & W. P. Banks (Eds.), *The recovered memory/false memory debate* (pp. 297–311). San Diego, CA: Academic Press.

Killian, L. M. (1964). Social movements. In R. E. L. Farris (Ed.), *Handbook of modern sociology* (pp. 426–455). Chicago: Rand McNally.

Kim, H. S., Sherman, D. K., & Taylor, S. E. (2008). Culture and social support. *American Psychologist, 63,* 518–526.

Kim, H., & Markus, H. R. (1999). Deviance or uniqueness, harmony or conformity? A cultural analysis. *Journal of Personality and Social Psychology, 77,* 785–800.

Kim, H., Park, K., & Schwarz, N. (2010). Will this trip really be exciting? The role of incidental emotions in product evaluation. *Journal of Consumer Research, 36*(6), 983–991. doi:10.1086/644763

Kim, J. L., Sorsoli, C. L., Collins, K., Zylbergold, B. A., Schooler, D., & Tolman, D. L. (2007). From sex to sexuality: Exposing the heterosexual script on primetime network television. *Journal of Sex Research, 44,* 145–157.

Kim, U., & Berry, J. W. (1993). *Indigenous psychologies: Research and experience in cultural context.* Newbury Park, CA: Sage.

Kim, U., Triandis, H. C., Kagitcibasi, C., Choi, S. C., & Yoon, G. (Eds.). (1994). *Individualism and collectivism: Theory, method, and applications.* Thousand Oaks, CA: Sage.

Kimel, E. (2001, August 2). Students earn cash for summer reading. *Sarasota Herald Tribune,* p. BV2.

Kimmel, M. (2012). *The gendered society* (5th ed.). New York: Oxford University Press.

Kinder, D. R., & Sears, D. O. (1981). Prejudice and politics: Symbolic racism versus racial threats to the good life. *Journal of Personality and Social Psychology, 40,* 414–431.

King, B., Shapiro, R., Hebl, R., Singletary, L., & Turner, S. (2006). The stigma of obesity in customer service: A mechanism for remediation and bottom-line consequences of interpersonal discrimination. *Journal of Applied Psychology, 91,* 579–593.

King, M., & Woollett, E. (1997). Sexually assaulted males: 115 men consulting a counseling service. *Archives of Sexual Behavior, 26,* 579–588.

King, R. S., Mauer, M., & Young, M. C. (2005). *Incarceration and crime: A complex relationship.* Washington, DC: The Sentencing Project.

Kinoshita, S., Peek-O'Leary, M. (2005). Does the compatibility effect in the race Implicit Association Test reflect familiarity or affect? *Psychonomic Bulletin Review, 12,* 442–452.

Kirkpatrick, L. A., & Hazan, C. (1994). Attachment styles and close relationships: A four-year prospective study. *Personal Relationships, 1,* 123–142.

Kitayama, S., & Cohen, D. (Eds.). (2007). *Handbook of cultural psychology.* New York: Guilford.

Kitayama, S., & Markus, H. R. (1994). Culture and the self: How cultures influence the way we view ourselves. In D. Matsumoto (Ed.), *People: Psychology from a cultural perspective* (pp. 17–37). Pacific Grove, CA: Brooks/Cole.

Kitayama, S., & Uchida, Y. (2003). Explicit self-criticism and implicit self-regard: Evaluating self and friend in two cultures. *Journal of Experimental Social Psychology, 39,* 476–482.

Kitayama, S., & Uchida, Y. (2005). Interdependent agency: An alternative system for action. In R. M. Sorrentino & D. Cohen (Eds.), *Cultural and social behavior: The Ontario Symposium* (Vol. 10, pp. 137–164). Mahwah, NJ: Erlbaum.

Kitayama, S., Chua, H. F., Tompson, S., & Han, S. (2013). Neural mechanisms of dissonance: An fMRI investigation of choice justification. *NeuroImage, 69,* 206–212.

Kitayama, S., Conway, L. G., Pietromonaco, P. R., Park, H., & Plaut, V. C. (2010). Ethos of independence across regions in the United States: The production-adoption model of cultural change. *American Psychologist, 65,* 559–574.

Kitayama, S., Ishii, K., Imada, T., Takemura, K., & Ramaswamy, J. (2006). Voluntary settlement and the spirit of independence: Evidence from Japan's 'northern frontier.' *Journal of Personality and Social Psychology, 91,* 369–384.

Kitayama, S., Markus, H. R., Matsumoto, H., & Norasakkunkit, V. (1997). Individual and collective processes in the construction of the self: Self-enhancement in the United States and self-criticism in Japan. *Journal of Personality and Social Psychology, 72,* 1245–1267.

Kitayama, S., Park, H., Sevincer, A. T., Karasawa, M., & Uskul, A. K. (2009). A cultural task analysis of implicit independence: Comparing North America, Western Europe, and East Asia.

Journal of Personality and Social Psychology, 97, 236–255.

Kite, M. E., Deaux, K., & Haines, E. L. (2008). Gender stereotypes. In F. L. Denmark & M. A. Paludi (Eds.), *Psychology of women: A handbook of issues and theories* (2nd ed., pp. 205–236). Westport, CT: Praeger.

Kjell, O. N. E. (2011). Sustainable well-being: A potential synergy between sustainability and well-being research. *Review of General Psychology, 15*(3), 255–266. doi:10.1037/a0024603

Klapwijk, A., & Van Lange, P. A. M. (2009). Promoting cooperation and trust in "noisy" situations: The power of generosity. *Journal of Personality and Social Psychology, 96,* 83–103.

Klein, R. (2005, November 12). President steps up attack on war critics. *The Boston Globe.* Retrieved March 8, 2006, from www.boston.com/news/nation/washington/articles/2005/11/12/president_steps_up_attack_on_war_critics/

Klein, W. M. P., Rothman, A. J., & Cameron, L. D. (2013). Theoretical innovations in social and personality psychology and implications for health: Introduction to special issue. *Health Psychology, 32,* 457–459.

Kleinjan, M., van den Eijnden, R. J., & Engels, R. C. (2009). Adolescents' rationalizations to continue smoking: The role of disengagement beliefs and nicotine dependence in smoking cessation. *Addictive Behaviors, 34,* 440–445.

Klenke, K. (1996). *Women and leadership: A contextual perspective.* New York: Springer-Verlag.

Klinesmith, J., Kasser, T., & McAndrew, F. T. (2006). Guns, testosterone, and aggression an experimental test of a mediational hypothesis. *Psychological Science, 17,* 568–571.

Klug, W., O'Dwyer, A., Barry, D., Dillard, L., Polo-Neil, H., & Warriner, M. (2011). The burden of combat: Cognitive dissonance in Iraq war veterans. In D. Kelly, S. Howe-Barksdale, & D. Gitelson (Eds.), *Treating young veterans: Promoting resilience through practice and advocacy* (pp. 33–79). New York: Springer.

Kluger, R. (1996). *Ashes to ashes: America's hundred-year cigarette war, the public health, and the unabashed triumph of Philip Morris.* New York: Knopf.

Knapp, M. L., Hall, J. A., & Horgan, T. G. (2014). *Nonverbal communication in human interaction.* Belmont, CA: Wadsworth.

Knobe, J., Buckwalter, W., Nichols, S., Robbins, P., Sarkissian, H., & Sommers, T. (2012). Experimental philosophy. *Annual Review of Psychology, 63,* 81–99.

Knowles, E. D., Morris, M. W., Chiu, C., & Hong, Y. (2001). Culture and the process of person perception: Evidence for automaticity among East Asians in correcting for situational influences on behavior. *Personality and Social Psychology Bulletin, 27,* 1344–1356.

Knox, R., & Inkster, J. (1968). Postdecision dissonance at post time. *Journal of Personality and Social Psychology, 8,* 319–323.

Knussen, C., Yule, F., & MacKenzie, J. (2004). An analysis of intentions to recycle household waste: The roles of past behaviour, perceived habit, and perceived lack of facilities. *Journal of Environmental Psychology, 24,* 237–246.

Koehler, J. J. (1993). The base rate fallacy myth. *Psycoloquy, 4,* 49.

Koehler, J. J. (1996). The base rate fallacy reconsidered: Descriptive, normative, and methodological challenges. *Behavioral and Brain Sciences, 19,* 1–53.

Koehnken, G., Malpass, R. S., & Wogalter, M. S. (1996). Forensic applications of line-up research. In S. L. Sporer, R. S. Malpass, & G. Koehnken (Eds.), *Psychological issues in eyewitness identification* (pp. 205–231). Mahwah, NJ: Erlbaum.

Koenig, A. M., Eagly, A. H., Mitchell, A. A., & Ristikari, T. (2011). Are leader stereotypes masculine? A meta-analysis of three research paradigms. *Psychological Bulletin, 137*(4), 616–642. doi:10.1037/a0023557

Koenig, A. M., Eagly, A. H., Mitchell, A. A., & Ristikari, T. (2011). Are leader stereotypes masculine? A meta-analysis of three research paradigms. *Psychological Bulletin, 137,* 616–642.

Kokkoris, M. D., & Kühnen, U. (2013). Choice and dissonance in a European cultural context: The case of Western and Eastern Europeans. *International Journal of Psychology, 48,* 1260–1266.

Kolbert, E. (2006). *Field notes from a catastrophe: Man, nature, and climate change.* New York: Bloomsbury.

Kollack, P., Blumstein, P., & Schwartz, P., (1994). The judgment of equity in intimate relationships. *Social Psychology Quarterly, 57,* 340–351.

Konrath, S. H., Chopik, W. J., Hsing, C. K., & O'Brien, E. (2014). Changes in adult attachment styles in American college students over time. *Personality and Social Psychology Review.* doi:10.1177/1088868314530516

Konrath, S. H., O'Brien, E. H., & Hsing, C. (2011). Changes in dispositional empathy in American college students over time: A meta-analysis. *Personality and Social Psychology Review, 15,* 180–198.

Koranyi, N., & Rothermund, K. (2012). When the grass on the other side of the fence doesn't matter: Reciprocal romantic interest neutralizes attentional bias towards attractive alternatives. *Journal of Experimental Social Psychology, 48,* 186–191.

Korda, M. (1997, October 6). Prompting the president. *The New Yorker,* p. 88.

Koss, M. P. (2011). Hidden, unacknowledged, acquaintance, and date rape: Looking back, looking forward. *Psychology of Woman Quarterly, 35,* 348–354.

Kouchaki, M., & Smith, I. H. (2014). The morning morality effect: The influence of time of day on unethical behavior. *Psychological Science, 25,* 95–102.

Kovera, M. B., & Borgida, E. (2010). Social psychology and law. In S. T. Fiske, D. T. Gilbert, & G. Lindzey (Eds.), *Handbook of social psychology* (5th ed., Vol. 2, pp. 1343–1385). Hoboken, NJ: John Wiley.

Kowalski, R. M., Giumetti, G. W., Schroeder, A. N., & Lattanner, M. R. (2014). Bullying in the digital age: A critical review and meta-analysis of cyberbullying research among youth. *Psychological Bulletin, 140,* 1073–1137.

Kowert, P. A. (2002). *Groupthink or deadlock: When do leaders learn from their advisors?* Albany: State University of New York Press.

Krakow, A., & Blass, T. (1995). When nurses obey or defy inappropriate physician orders: Attributional differences. *Journal of Social Behavior and Personality, 10,* 585–594.

Kramer, G. P., Kerr, N. L., & Carroll, J. S. (1990). Pretrial publicity, judicial remedies, and jury bias. *Law and Human Behavior, 14,* 409–438.

Krasheninnikova, A., & Schneider, J. M. (2014). Testing problem-solving capacities: Differences between individual testing and social group setting. *Animal Behavior.* doi:10.1007/s10071-014-0744-1

Krauss, R. M., & Deutsch, M. (1966). Communication in interpersonal bargaining. *Journal of Personality and Social Psychology, 4,* 572–577.

Krauss, R. M., Freedman, J. L., & Whitcup, M. (1978). Field and laboratory studies of littering. *Journal of Experimental Social Psychology, 14,* 109–122.

Kremer, J. F., & Stephens, L. (1983). Attributions and arousal as mediators of mitigation's effects on retaliation. *Journal of Personality and Social Psychology, 45,* 335–343.

Kressel, K., & Pruitt, D. G. (1989). A research perspective on the mediation of social conflict. In K. Kressel & D. G. Pruitt (Eds.), *Mediation research: The process and effectiveness of third party intervention* (pp. 394–435). San Francisco: Jossey-Bass.

Krosnick, J. A., & Alwin, D. F. (1989). Aging and susceptibility to attitude change. *Journal of Personality and Social Psychology, 57,* 416–425.

Kross, E., & Ayduk, O. (2011). Making meaning out of negative experiences by self-distancing. *Current Directions in Psychological Science, 20*(3), 187–191. doi:10.1177/0963721411408883

Kross, E., Bruehlman-Senecal, E., Park, J., Burson, A., Dougherty, A., Shablack, H., et al. (2014).

Self-talk as a regulatory mechanism: How you do it matters. *Journal of Personality and Social Psychology, 106,* 304–324.

Krueger, A. B. (2007). *What makes a terrorist: Economics and the roots of terrorism.* Princeton, NJ: Princeton University Press.

Krueger, J., Ham, J. J., & Linford, K. (1996). Perceptions of behavioral consistency: Are people aware of the actor-observer effect? *Psychological Science, 7,* 259–264.

Krull, D. S. (1993). Does the grist change the mill? The effect of the perceiver's inferential goal on the process of social inference. *Personality and Social Psychology Bulletin, 19,* 340–348.

Krull, D. S., & Dill, J. C. (1996). On thinking first and responding fast: Flexibility in social inference processes. *Personality and Social Psychology Bulletin, 22,* 949–959.

Krull, D. S., Loy, M. H., Lin, J., Wang, C., Chen, S., & Zhao, X. (1999). The fundamental correspondence bias in individualist and collectivist cultures. *Personality and Social Psychology Bulletin, 25,* 1208–1219.

Kuan, K. K. Y., Zhong, Y., & Chau. P. Y. K. (2014). Informational and normative social influence in group-buying: Evidence from self-reported and EEG data. *Journal of Management Information Systems, 30,* 151–178.

Kubitschek, W. N., & Hallinan, M. T. (1998). Tracking and students' friendships. *Social Psychology Quarterly, 61,* 1–15.

Kumkale, G. T., & Albarracín, D. (2004). The sleeper eàect in persuasion: A meta-analytic review. *Psychological Bulletin, 130,* 143–172.

Kunda, Z. (1999). *Social cognition: Making sense of people.* Cambridge, MA: MIT Press.

Kunda, Z., & Oleson, K. C. (1997). When exceptions prove the rule: How extremity of deviance determines the impact of deviant examples on stereotypes. *Journal of Personality and Social Psychology, 72,* 965–979.

Kunda, Z., & Schwartz, S. H. (1983). Undermining intrinsic moral motivation: External reward and self-presentation. *Journal of Personality and Social Psychology, 45,* 763–771.

Kunda, Z., Sinclair, L., & Griffin, D. W. (1997). Equal ratings but separate meanings: Stereotypes and the construal of traits. *Journal of Personality and Social Psychology, 72,* 720–734.

Kuo, Z. Y. (1961). *Instinct.* Princeton, NJ: Van Nostrand.

Kurdek, L. A. (1992). Relationship stability and relationship satisfaction in cohabitating gay and lesbian couples: A prospective longitudinal test of the contextual and interdependence models. *Journal of Social and Personal Relationships, 9,* 125–142.

Kurdek, L. A. (2005). What do we know about gay and lesbian couples? *Current Directions in Psychological Science, 14,* 251–254.

Kuykendall, D., & Keating, J. P. (1990). Altering thoughts and judgments through repeated association. *British Journal of Social Psychology, 29,* 79–86.

Kwan, L. Y., & Chiu, C. (2014). Holistic versus analytic thinking explains collective culpability attribution. *Basic and Applied Social Psychology, 36,* 3–8.

La France, B. H., Henningsen, D. D., Oates, A., & Shaw, C. M. (2009). Social-sexual interactions? Meta-analyses of sex differences in perceptions of flirtatiousness, seductiveness, and promiscuousness. *Communication Monographs, 76,* 263–285.

La France, M., Hecht, M. A., & Paluck, E. L. (2003). The contingent smile: A meta-analysis of sex differences in smiling. *Psychological Bulletin, 129,* 305–334.

La Piere, R. T. (1934). Attitudes vs. actions. *Social Forces, 13,* 230–237.

Laird, J. (2007). *Feelings: The perception of self.* New York, Oxford University Press.

Lakey, B., & Orehek, E. (2011). Relational regulation theory: A new approach to explain the link between perceived social support and mental health. *Psychological Review, 118*(3), 482–495. doi:10.1037/a0023477

Lakoff, G., & Johnson, M. (1999). *Philosophy in the flesh: The embodied mind and its challenge to Western thought.* New York: Basic Books.

Lalwani, A. K., & Shavitt, S. (2009). The "me" I claim to be: Cultural self-construal elicits self-presentational goal pursuit. *Journal of Personality and Social Psychology, 97,* 88–102. doi:10.1037/a0014100

Lam, S., & Dickerson, S. S. (2013). Social relationships, social threat, and health. In M. L. Newman & N. A. Roberts (Eds.), *Health and social relationships: The good, the bad, and the complicated* (pp. 19–38). Washington, DC: American Psychological Association.

Lambert, A. J., Burroughs, T., & Nguyen, T. (1999). Perceptions of risk and the buffering hypothesis: The role of just world beliefs and right-wing authoritarianism. *Personality and Social Psychology Bulletin, 25,* 643–656.

Lampert, R., Baron, S. J., McPherson, C. A., & Lee, F. A. (2002). Heart rate variability during the week of September 11, 2001. *Journal of the American Medical Association, 288,* 575.

Landau, M. J., Meier, B. P., & Keefer, L. A. (2010). A metaphor-enriched social cognition. *Psychological Bulletin, 136*(6), 1045–1067. doi:10.1037/a0020970

Landis, D., & O'Shea, W. A. (2000). Cross-cultural aspects of passionate love: An individual differences analysis. *Journal of Cross-Cultural Psychology, 31,* 752–777.

Landman, J. (1993). *Regret: The persistence of the possible.* New York: Oxford University Press.

Lane, K. A., Banaji, M. R., & Nosek, B. A. (2007). Understanding and using the implicit association test: IV: What we know (so far) about the method. In B. Wittenbrink & N. Schwarz (Eds.), *Implicit measures of attitudes* (pp. 59–102). New York: Guilford.

Langer, E. J. (1975). The illusion of control. *Journal of Personality and Social Psychology, 32,* 311–328.

Langer, E. J., & Rodin, J. (1976). The effects of choice and enhanced personal responsibility for the aged: A field experiment. *Journal of Personality and Social Psychology, 34,* 191–198.

Langhinrichsen-Rohling, J., Misra, T. A., Selwyn, C., & Rohling, M. L. (2012). Rates of bi-directional versus unidirectional intimate partner violence across samples, sexual orientations, and race/ethnicities: A comprehensive review. *Partner Abuse, 3,* 199–230.

Langlois, J. H., Kalakanis, L., Rubenstein, A. J., Larson, A., Hallam, M., & Smoot, M. (2000). Maxims or myths of beauty? A meta-analytic and theoretical review. *Psychological Bulletin, 126,* 390–423.

Langlois, J. H., Ritter, J. M., Roggman, L. A., & Vaughn, L. S. (1991). Facial diversity and infant preferences for attractive faces. *Developmental Psychology, 27,* 79–84.

Langlois, J. H., Roggman, L. A., & Musselman, L. (1994). What is average and what is not average about attractive faces? *Psychological Science, 5,* 214–220.

Langlois, J. H., Roggman, L. A., & Rieser-Danner, L. A. (1990). Infants' differential social responses to attractive and unattractive faces. *Developmental Psychology, 26,* 153–159.

Larrick, R. P., Timmerman, T. A., Carton, A. M., & Abrevaya, J. (2011). Temper, temperature, and temptation: Heat-related retaliation in baseball. *Psychological Science, 22,* 423–428.

Larson, J. R., Jr., Christensen, C., Franz, T. M., & Abbott, A. S. (1998). Diagnosing groups: The pooling, management, and impact of shared and unshared case information in team-based medical decision making. *Journal of Personality and Social Psychology, 75,* 93–108.

Lassiter, G. D. (2010). Psychological science and sound public policy: Video recording of custodial interrogations. *American Psychologist, 65*(8), 768–779. doi:10.1037/0003-066X.65.8.768

Lassiter, G. D., Diamond, S. S., Schmidt, H. C., & Elek, J. K. (2007). Evaluating videotaped confessions: Expertise provides no defense against the camera perspective effect. *Psychological Science, 18,* 224–226.

Lassiter, G. D., Geers, A. L., Munhall, P. J., Ploutz-Snyder, R. J., & Breitenbecher, D. L. (2002). Illusory causation: Why it occurs. *Psychological Science, 13,* 299–305.

Lassiter, G. D., Ratcliff, J. J., Ware, L. J., & Irvin, C. R. (2006). Videotaped confessions: Panacea or Pandora's Box? *Law and Policy, 28,* 192–210.

Latané, B. (1981). The psychology of social impact. *American Psychologist, 36,* 343–356.

Latané, B. (1987). From student to colleague: Retracing a decade. In N. E. Grunberg, R. E. Nisbett, J. Rodin, & J. E. Singer (Eds.), *A distinctive approach to psychological research: The influence of Stanley Schachter* (pp. 66–86). Hillsdale, NJ: Erlbaum.

Latané, B., & Bourgeois, M. J. (2001). Successfully simulating dynamic social impact: Three levels of prediction. In J. P. Forgas & K. D. Williams (Eds.), *Social influence: Direct and indirect processes* (pp. 61–76). Philadelphia: Psychology Press.

Latané, B., & Dabbs, J. M. (1975). Sex, group size, and helping in three cities. *Sociometry, 38,* 108–194.

Latané, B., & Darley, J. M. (1968). Group inhibition of bystander intervention. *Journal of Personality and Social Psychology, 10,* 215–221.

Latané, B., & Darley, J. M. (1970). *The unresponsive bystander: Why doesn't he help?* Englewood Cliffs, NJ: Prentice Hall.

Latané, B., & L'Herrou, T. (1996). Spatial clustering in the conformity game: Dynamic social impact in electronic games. *Journal of Personality and Social Psychology, 70,* 1218–1230.

Latané, B., & Nida, S. (1981). Ten years of research on group size and helping. *Psychological Bulletin, 89,* 308–324.

Latané, B., Williams, K., & Harkins, S. (2006). Many hands make light the work: The causes and consequences of social loafing. In J. M. Levine & R. L. Moreland (Eds.), *Small groups* (pp. 297–308). New York: Psychology Press.

Lau, R. R., & Russell, D. (1980). Attributions in the sports pages: A field test of some current hypotheses about attribution research. *Journal of Personality and Social Psychology, 39,* 29–38.

Laumann, E. O., & Gagnon, J. H. (1995). A sociological perspective on sexual action. In R. G. Parker & J. H. Gagnon (Eds.), *Conceiving sexuality: Approaches to sex research in a postmodern world.* New York: Routledge.

Laumann, E. O., Gagnon, J. H., Michael, R. T., & Michaels, S. (1994). *The social organization of sexuality.* Chicago: University of Chicago Press.

Laursen, B., & Hartup, W. W. (2002). The origins of reciprocity and social exchange in friendships. In L. Brett & W. G. Graziano (Eds.), *Social exchange in development: New directions for child and adolescent development* (pp. 27–40). San Francisco: Jossey-Bass/Pfeiffer.

Lawler, E. J., & Thye, S. R. (1999). Bringing emotions into social exchange theory. *Annual Review of Sociology, 25,* 217–244.

Lazarsfeld, P. (Ed.). (1940). *Radio and the printed page.* New York: Duell, Sloan & Pearce.

Lazarus, R. S. (1966). *Psychological stress and the coping process.* New York: McGraw-Hill.

Lazarus, R. S. (2000). Toward better research on stress and coping. *American Psychologist, 55,* 665–673.

Lazarus, R. S., & Folkman, S. (1984). *Stress, appraisal, and coping.* New York: Springer-Verlag.

Le Bon, G. (1895). *The crowd.* London: Unwin.

Le, B., & Agnew, C. R. (2003). Commitment and its theorized determinants: A meta-analysis of the investment model. *Personal Relationships, 10,* 37–57.

Lea, M., & Spears, R. (1995). Love at first byte: Building personal relationships over computer networks. In J. T. Wood & S. W. Duck (Eds.), *Understudied relationships: Off the beaten track* (pp. 197–233). Thousand Oaks, CA: Sage.

Lea, M., Spears, R., & de Groot, D. (2001). Knowing me, knowing you: Anonymity effects on social identity processes within groups. *Personality and Social Psychology Bulletin, 27,* 526–537.

Leary, M. R. (2004a). *The curse of the self: Self-awareness, egotism, and the quality of human life.* New York: Oxford University Press.

Leary, M. R. (2004b). The self we know and the self we show: Self-esteem, self-presentation, and the maintenance of interpersonal relationships. In M. B. Brewer & M. Hewstone (Eds.), *Emotion and motivation* (pp. 204–224). Malden, MA: Blackwell.

Leary, M. R., & Baumeister, R. F. (2000). The nature and function of self-esteem: Sociometer theory. In M. P. Zanna (Ed.), *Advances in experimental social psychology* (Vol. 32, pp. 1–62). San Diego, CA: Academic Press.

Leary, M. R., & Tate, E. B. (2010). The role of self-awareness and self-evaluation in dysfunctional patterns of thought, emotion, and behavior. In J. E. Maddux & J. P. Tangney (Eds.), *Social psychological foundations of clinical psychology* (pp. 19–35). New York: Guilford Press.

Leary, M. R., Kowalski, R. M., Smith, L., & Phillips, S. (2003). Teasing, rejection, and violence: Case studies of the school shootings. *Aggressive Behavior, 29,* 202–214.

Leary, M. R., Twenge, J. M., & Quinlivan, E. (2006). Interpersonal rejection as a determinant of anger and aggression. *Personality and Social Psychology Review, 10,* 111–132.

Leathers, D. G. (1997). *Successful nonverbal communication: Principles and applications.* Needham Heights, MA: Allyn & Bacon.

Lee, A. Y. (2001). The mere exposure effect: An uncertainty reduction explanation revisited. *Personality and Social Psychology Bulletin, 27,* 1255–1266.

Lee, E. (2004). Effects of visual representation on social influence in computer-mediated communication: Experimental tests of the social identity model of deindividuation effects. *Human Communication Research, 30,* 234–259.

Lee, H. (1960). *To kill a mockingbird.* New York: Warner Books.

Lee, R. W. (2001). Citizen heroes. *New American, 17,* 19–32.

Lee, S. J. (2009). *Unraveling the "Model Minority" stereotype: Listening to Asian American youth* (2nd ed.). New York: Teachers College, Columbia University.

Lee, Y., & Seligman, M. E. P. (1997). Are Americans more optimistic than the Chinese? *Personality and Social Psychology Bulletin, 23,* 32–40.

Lee, Y-T., McCauley, C., & Jussim, L. (2013). Stereotypes as valid categories of knowledge and human perceptions of group differences. *Social and Personality Psychology Compass, 7,* 470–486.

Lefkowitz, E. S., Shearer, C. L., Gillen, M. M., & Espinosa-Hernandez, G. (2014). How gendered attitudes relate to women's and men's sexual behaviors and beliefs. *Sexuality and Culture.* doi:10.1007/s12119-014-9225-6

Lehman, D. R., Davis, C. G., De Longis, A., & Wortman, C. B. (1993). Positive and negative life changes following bereavement and their relations to adjustment. *Journal of Social and Clinical Psychology, 12,* 90–112.

Lehman, D. R., Lempert, R. O., & Nisbett, R. E. (1988). The effects of graduate training on reasoning: Formal discipline and thinking about everyday-life events. *American Psychologist, 43,* 431–442.

Lehmiller, J. J., & Agnew, C. R. (2006). Marginalized relationships: The impact of social disapproval on romantic relationship commitment. *Personality and Social Psychology Bulletin, 32,* 40–51.

Leippe, M. R., & Eisenstadt, D. (1994). Generalization of dissonance reduction: Decreasing prejudice through induced compliance. *Journal of Personality and Social Psychology, 67,* 395–413.

Leippe, M. R., & Eisenstadt, D. (1998). A self-accountability model of dissonance reduction: Multiple modes on a continuum of elaboration. In E. Harmon-Jones & J. S. Mills (Eds.), *Cognitive dissonance theory: Revival with revisions and controversies.* Washington, DC: American Psychological Association.

Leite, F. P. (2011). Larger reward values alone are not enough to entice more cooperation. *Thinking & Reasoning, 17*(1), 82–103. doi:10.1080/13546783. 2010.537521

Lemay, E. P., Jr., Clark, M. S., & Greenberg, A. (2010). What is beautiful is good because what is beautiful is desired: Physical attractiveness stereotyping as projection of interpersonal goals. *Personality and Social Psychology Bulletin, 36,* 339–353.

Lemay, E. P., Jr., & Clark, M. S. (2008). How the head liberates the heart: Projection of communal responsiveness guides relationship promotion. *Journal of Personality and Social Psychology, 94*, 647–671.

Lemay, E. P., Jr., Clark, M. S., & Feeney, B. C. (2007). Projection of responsiveness to needs and the construction of satisfying communal relationships. *Journal of Personality and Social Psychology, 92*, 834–853.

Lemieux, R., & Hale, J. L. (1999). Intimacy, passion, and commitment in young romantic relationships: Successfully measuring the triangular theory of love. *Psychological Reports, 85*, 497–503.

Leor, J., Poole, W. K., & Kloner, R. A. (1996). Sudden cardiac death triggered by an earthquake. *New England Journal of Medicine, 334*, 413–419.

Leotti, L. A., Iyengar, S. S., & Ochsner, K. N. (2010). Born to choose: The origins and value of the need for control. *Trends in Cognitive Sciences, 14*, 457–463. doi:10.1016/j.tics.2010.08.001

Lepper, M. R. (1995). Theory by numbers? Some concerns about meta-analysis as a theoretical tool. *Applied Cognitive Psychology, 9*, 411–422.

Lepper, M. R. (1996). Intrinsic motivation and extrinsic rewards: A commentary on Cameron and Pierce's meta-analysis. *Review of Educational Research, 66*, 5–32.

Lepper, M. R., Corpus, J. H., & Iyengar, S. S. (2005). Intrinsic and extrinsic motivational orientations in the classroom: Age differences and academic correlates. *Journal of Educational Psychology, 97*, 184–196.

Lepper, M. R., Greene, D., & Nisbett, R. E. (1973). Undermining children's intrinsic interest with extrinsic reward: A test of the overjustification hypothesis. *Journal of Personality and Social Psychology, 28*, 129–137.

Lepper, M. R., Henderlong, J., & Gingras, I. (1999). Understanding the effects of extrinsic rewards on intrinsic motivation—uses and abuses of meta-analysis: Comment on Deci, Koestner, and Ryan (1999). *Psychological Bulletin, 125*, 669–676.

Lerner, J. S., & Tetlock, P. E. (1999). Accounting for the effects of accountability. *Psychological Bulletin, 125*, 255–275.

Lerner, M. J. (1980). *The belief in a just world: A fundamental decision.* New York: Plenum.

Lerner, M. J. (1991). The belief in a just world and the "heroic motive": Searching for "constants" in the psychology of religious ideology. *International Journal for the Psychology of Religion, 1*, 27–32.

Lerner, M. J. (1998). The two forms of belief in a just world. In L. Montada & M. J. Lerner (Eds.), *Responses to victimization and belief in a just world.* (pp. 247–269). New York: Plenum Press.

Lerner, M. J., & Grant, P. R. (1990). The influences of commitment to justice and ethnocentrism on children's allocations of pay. *Social Psychology Quarterly, 53*, 229–238.

Lerner, M. J., & Miller, D. T. (1978). Just world research and the attribution process: Looking back and ahead. *Psychological Bulletin, 85*, 1030–1051.

Leskovec, J., & Horvitz, E. (2007). *Worldwide buzz: Planetary-scale views on an instant-messaging network* (Vol. 60). Technical report, Microsoft Research.

Leung, K. (1996). Beliefs in Chinese culture. In M. H. Bond (Ed.), *The handbook of Chinese psychology* (pp. 247–262). Hong Kong: Oxford University Press.

Levenson, H. (1981). Differentiating between internality, powerful others, and chance. In H. M. Lefcourt (Ed.), *Research with the locus of control construct* (Vol. 1, pp. 15–63). New York, NY: Academic Press.

Leventhal, H., Watts, J. C., & Pagano, F. (1967). Effects of fear and instructions on how to cope with danger. *Journal of Personality and Social Psychology, 6*, 313–321.

Levett, L. M. (2013). Co-witness information influences whether a witness is likely to choose from a lineup. *Legal and Criminological Psychology, 18*, 168–180.

Levin, D. T. (2000). Race as a visual feature: Using visual search and perceptual discrimination tasks to understand face categories and the cross-race recognition deficit. *Journal of Experimental Psychology: General, 129*, 559–574.

Levine, J. M., & Moreland, R. L. (1998). Small groups. In D. T. Gilbert, S. T. Fiske, & G. Lindzey (Eds.), *The handbook of social psychology* (4th ed., Vol. 2, pp. 415–469). New York: McGraw-Hill.

Levine, J. M., & Russo, E. M. (1987). Majority and minority influence. In C. Hendrick (Ed.), *Group processes: Review of personality and social psychology* (Vol. 8, pp. 13–54). Newbury Park, CA: Sage.

Levine, J. M., Higgins, E. T., & Choi, H.-S. (2000). Development of strategic norms in groups. *Organizational Behavior and Human Decision Processes, 82*, 88–101.

Levine, J. M., Moreland, R. L., & Choi, S. (2001). Group socialization and newcomer innovation. In M. Hogg & S. Tindale (Eds.), *Blackwell handbook of social psychology: Group processes* (pp. 86–106). Oxford, England: Blackwell Publishers.

Levine, R. A., & Campbell, D. T. (1972). *Ethnocentrism: Theories of conflict, ethnic attitudes, and group behavior.* New York: Wiley.

Levine, R. V. (2003). The kindness of strangers: People's willingness to help someone during a chance encounter on a city street varies considerably around the world. *American Scientist, 91*, 226–233.

Levine, R. V., Martinez, T. S., Brase, G., & Sorenson, K. (1994). Helping in 36 U.S. cities. *Journal of Personality and Social Psychology, 67*, 69–82.

Levine, R. V., Norenzayan, A., & Philbrick, K. (2001). Cross-cultural differences in helping strangers. *Journal of Cross-Cultural Psychology, 32*, 543–560.

Levine, R., Sato, S., Hashimoto, T., & Verma, J. (1995). Love and marriage in eleven cultures. *Journal of Cross-Cultural Psychology, 26*, 554–571.

Levine, S. S., Apfelbaum, E. P., Bernard, M., Bartelt, V. L., Zajac, E. J., & Stark, D. (2015). Ethnic diversity deflates price bubbles. *Proceedings of the National Academy of Sciences.* doi:10.1073/pnas.1407301111

Levitan, L. C., & Visser, P. S. (2008). The impact of the social context on resistance to persuasion: Effortful versus effortless responses to counterattitudinal information. *Journal of Experimental Social Psychology, 44*, 640–649.

Levy, B. (2008). *Women and violence.* Berkeley, CA: Seal Press.

Levy, D. A., & Nail, P. R. (1993). Contagion: A theoretical and empirical review and reconceptualization. *Genetic, Social, and General Psychology Monographs, 119*, 233–284.

Lévy-Leboyer, C. (1988). Success and failure in applying psychology. *American Psychologist, 43*, 779–785.

Lewin, K. (1943). Defining the "field at a given time." *Psychological Review, 50*, 292–310.

Lewin, K. (1946). Action research and minority problems. *Journal of Social Issues, 2*, 34–46.

Lewin, K. (1947). Frontiers in group dynamics. *Human Relations, 1*, 5–41.

Lewin, K. (1948). *Resolving social conflicts: Selected papers in group dynamics.* New York: Harper.

Lewin, K. (1951). Problems of research in social psychology. In D. Cartwright (Ed.), *Field theory in social science* (pp. 155–169). New York: Harper.

Lewin, K., Lippit, R., & White, R. K. (1939). Patterns of aggressive behavior in experimentally created social climates. *Journal of Social Psychology, 10*, 271–301.

Lewis, C. C. (1995). *Educating hearts and minds: Reflections on Japanese preschool and elementary education.* Cambridge: Cambridge University Press.

Lewis, G. J., Kandler, C., & Riemann, R. (2014). Distinct heritable influences underpin in-group love and out-group derogation. *Social Psychology and Personality Science, 5*, 407–4013.

Lewis, K., Belliveau, M., Herndon, B., & Keller, J. (2007). Group cognition, membership change, and performance: Investigating the benefits and detriments of collective knowledge.

Organizational Behavior and Human Decision Processes, 103, 159–178.

Lewis, M., & Ramsay, D. (2004). Development of self-recognition, personal pronoun use, and pretend play during the 2nd year. *Child Development, 75*, 1821–1831.

Lewis, R. S., Goto, S. G., & Kong, L. (2008). Culture and context: East Asian American and European American differences in P3 event-related potential. *Personality and Social Psychology Bulletin, 34*, 623–634.

Li, Y. J., Johnson, K. A., Cohen, A. B., Williams, M. J., & Knowles, E. D. (2012). Fundamental(ist) attribution error: Protestants are dispositionally focused. *Journal of Personality and Social Psychology, 102*, 281–290.

Li, Z., Connolly, J., Jiang, D., Pepier, D., & Craig, W. (2010). Adolescent romantic relationships in China and Canada: A cross-national comparison. *International Journal of Behavioral Development, 34*, 113–120.

Liberman, A., & Chaiken, S. (1992). Defensive processing of personally relevant health messages. *Personality and Social Psychology Bulletin, 18*, 669–679.

Liberman, V., Samuels, S. M., & Ross, L. D. (2004). The name of the game: Predictive power of reputations versus situational labels in determining Prisoner's Dilemma Game moves. *Personality and Social Psychology Bulletin, 30*, 1175–1185.

Lick, D. J., Durso, L. E., & Johnson, K. L. (2013). Minority stress and physical health among sexual minorities. *Perspectives on Psychological Science, 8*, 521–548.

Lieberman, M. D. (2013). *Social: Why our brains are wired to connect.* New York: Crown.

Lieberman, M. D., & Rosenthal, R. (2001). Why introverts can't always tell who likes them: Multitasking and nonverbal decoding. *Journal of Personality and Social Psychology, 80*, 294–310.

Liebert, R. M., & Baron, R. A. (1972). Some immediate effects of televised violence on children's behavior. *Developmental Psychology, 6*, 469–475.

Lilienfeld, S. O., & Byron, R. B. (2013). Your brain on trial. *Scientific American Mind, 23*, 44–53.

Liljenquist, K. A., Zhong, C., & Galinsky, A. D. (2010). The smell of virtue: Clean scents promote reciprocity and charity. *Psychological Science, 21*, 381–383.

Lim, T.-S., & Choi, H.-S. (1996). Interpersonal relationships in Korea. In W. B. Gudykunst, S. Ting-Toomey, & T. Nishida (Eds.), *Communication in personal relationships across cultures* (pp. 122–136). Thousand Oaks, CA: Sage.

Lin, Y. H. W., & Rusbult, C. E. (1995). Commitment to dating relationships and cross-sex friendships in America and China. *Journal of Social and Personal Relationships, 12*, 7–26.

Lindsay, R. C. L., & Wells, G. L. (1985). Improving eyewitness identifications from lineups: Simultaneous versus sequential lineup presentation. *Journal of Applied Psychology, 70*, 556–564.

Linville, P. W., Fischer, G. W., & Salovey, P. (1989). Perceived distributions of characteristics of in-group and out-group members: Empirical evidence and a computer simulation. *Journal of Personality and Social Psychology, 57*, 165–188.

Linz, D. G., Donnerstein, E., & Penrod, S. (1984). The effects of multiple exposures to filmed violence against women. *Journal of Communication, 34*, 130–147.

Lippmann, W. (1922). *Public opinion.* New York: Free Press.

Lipsey, M. W., Wilson, D. B., Cohen, M. A., & Derzon, J. H. (1997). Is there a causal relationship between alcohol use and violence? A synthesis of evidence. In M. Galanter (Ed.), *Recent developments in alcoholism*: Vol. 13. *Alcohol and violence: Epidemiology, neurobiology, psychology, and family issues* (pp. 245–282). New York: Plenum.

Litter prevention (n.d.). Keep America Beautiful. Retrieved September 5, 2011, from www.kab.org/site/PageServer?pagename=focus_litter_prevention#COSTS

Little, A. C., & Perrett, D. I. (2002). Putting beauty back in the eye of the beholder. *Psychologist*, 15, 28–32.

Little, A. C., Jones, B. C., Waitt, C., Tiddeman, B. P., Feinberg, D. R., Perrett, D. I., Apicella, C. L., & Marlowe, F. W. (2008). Symmetry is related to sexual dimorphism in faces: Data across culture and species. *PLoS One*, 3, e2106.

Livesley, W. J., & Bromley, D. B. (1973). *Person perception in childhood and adolescence.* New York: Wiley.

Livingston, R. W., & Pearce, N. A. (2009). The teddy-bear effect: Does having a baby face benefit Black chief executive officers? *Psychological Science*, 22, 1478–1483.

Livingston, R. W., & Pearce, N. A. (2009). The teddy-bear effect: Does having a baby face benefit Black chief executive officers? *Psychological Science*, 20, 1229–1236.

Lloyd, S. A., & Cate, R. M. (1985). The developmental course of conflict in dissolution of premarital relationships. *Journal of Social and Personal Relationships*, 2, 179–194.

Lockwood, P., Shaughnessy, S. C., Fortune, J. L., & Tong, M.-O. (2012). Social comparisons in novel situations: Finding inspiration during life transitions. *Personality and Social Psychology Bulletin*, 38(8), 985–996. doi:10.1177/0146167212447234

Lodish, L. M., Abraham, M., Kalmenson, S., Lievelsberger, J., Lubetkin, B., Richardson, B., & Stevens, M. E. (1995). How TV advertising works: A meta-analysis of 389 real-world split-cable TV advertising experiments. *Journal of Marketing Research*, 32, 125–139.

Loersch, C., & Payne, B. K. (2011). The situated inference model: An integrative account of the effects of primes on perception, behavior, and motivation. *Perspectives on Psychological Science*, 6(3), 234–252. doi:10.1177/1745691611406921

Loftus, E. F. (1979). *Eyewitness testimony.* Cambridge, MA: Harvard University Press.

Loftus, E. F. (1993). The reality of repressed memories. *American Psychologist*, 48, 518–537.

Loftus, E. F. (2005). Planting misinformation in the human mind: A 30-year investigation of the malleability of memory. *Learning and Memory*, 12, 361–366.

Loftus, E. F., Garry, M., & Hayne, H. (2008). Repressed and recovered memory. In E. Borgida & S. T. Fiske (Eds.), *Beyond common sense: Psychological science in the courtroom* (pp. 177–194). Malden, MA: Blackwell.

Loftus, E. F., Miller, D. G., & Burns, H. J. (1978). Semantic integration of verbal information into a visual memory. *Journal of Experimental Psychology: Human Learning and Memory*, 4, 19–31.

Lonner, W., & Berry, J. (Eds.). (1986). *Field methods in cross-cultural research.* Beverly Hills, CA: Sage.

Lonsdale, A. J., & North, A. C. (2012). Musical taste and the representativeness heuristic. *Psychology of Music*, 40, 131–142.

Lord, C. G., Lepper, M. R., & Preston, E. (1984). Considering the opposite: A corrective strategy for social judgment. *Journal of Personality and Social Psychology*, 47, 1231–1243.

Lore, R. K., & Schultz, L. A. (1993). Control of human aggression. *American Psychologist*, 48, 16–25.

Lorenz, K. (1966). *On aggression* (M. Wilson, Trans.). New York: Harcourt Brace.

Lott, A. J., & Lott, B. E. (1961). Group cohesiveness, communication level, and conformity. *Journal of Abnormal and Social Psychology*, 62, 408–412.

Lott, A. J., & Lott, B. E. (1974). The role of reward in the formation of positive interpersonal attitudes. In T. L. Huston (Ed.), *Foundations of interpersonal attraction* (pp. 171–189). New York: Academic Press.

Lount, R. B., Jr., & Wilk, S. L. (2014). Working harder or hardly working? Posting performance eliminates social loafing and promotes social laboring in workgroups. *Management Science*, 60, 1098–1106.

Lount, R. B., Jr., Zhong, C.-B., Sivanathan, N., & Murnighan, J. K. (2008). Getting off on the wrong foot: The timing of a breach and the restoration of trust. *Personality and Social Psychology Bulletin*, 34(12), 1601–1612. doi:10.1177/0146167208324512

Lovett, R. A. (2010, March 2). Huge garbage patch found in Atlantic too. *National Geographic News.* National Geographic Society. Retrieved March 8, 2012, from news.nationalgeographic.com/news/2010/03/100302-new-ocean-trash-garbage-patch/

Ludwig, T. D., Gray, T. W., & Rowell, A. (1998). Increasing recycling in academic buildings: A systematic replication. *Journal of Applied Behavior Analysis*, 31, 683–686.

Lumsdaine, A. A., & Janis, I. L. (1953). Resistance to "counterpropaganda" produced by one-sided and two-sided "propaganda" presentations. *Public Opinion Quarterly*, 17, 311–318.

Luo, M. (2009, December 1). In job hunt, college degree can't close racial gap. *The New York Times*, p. 1.

Luo, S., & Zhang, G. (2009). What leads to romantic attraction: Similarity, reciprocity, security, or beauty? Evidence from a speed dating study. *Journal of Personality*, 77, 933–964.

Lupien, S. P., Seery, M. D., & Almonte, J. L. (2010). Discrepant and congruent high self-esteem: Behavioral self-handicapping as a preemptive defensive strategy. *Journal of Experimental Social Psychology*, 46, 1105–1108. doi:10.1016/j.jesp.2010.05.022

Lutz-Zois, C. J., Bradley, A. C., Mihalik, J. L., & Moorman-Eavers, E. R. (2006). Perceived similarity and relationship success among dating couples: An idiographic approach. *Journal of Social and Personal Relationships*, 23, 865–880.

Lykken, D., & Tellegen, A. (1996). Happiness is a stochastic phenomenon. *Psychological Science*, 7, 186–189.

Lynn, M., & Shurgot, B. A. (1984). Responses to lonely hearts advertisements: Effects of reported physical attractiveness, physique, and coloration. *Personality and Social Psychology Bulletin*, 10, 349–357.

Lyubomirsky, S., Caldwell, N. D., & Nolen-Hoeksema, S. (1993). Effects of ruminative and distracting responses to depressed mood on retrieval of autobiographical memories. *Journal of Personality and Social Psychology*, 75, 166–177.

Lyubomirsky, S., Sheldon, K. M., & Schkade, D. (2005). Pursuing happiness: The architecture of sustainable change. *Review of General Psychology*, 9, 111–131.

Ma, D. S., & Correll, J. (2011). Target prototypicality moderates racial bias in the decision to shoot. *Journal of Experimental Social Psychology*, 47, 391–396.

Maass, A., & Clark, R. D., III. (1984). Hidden impact of minorities: Fifteen years of research. *Psychological Bulletin*, 95, 428–450.

Maass, A., Cadinu, M., Guarnieri, G., & Grasselli, A. (2003). Sexual harassment under social identity threat: The computer harassment paradigm. *Journal of Personality and Social Psychology*, 85, 853–870.

Maccoby, E. E., & Jacklin, C. N. (1974). *The psychology of sex differences.* Stanford, CA: Stanford University Press.

MacCoun, R. J. (1989). Experimental research on jury decision-making. *Science*, 244, 1046–1050.

MacDonald, T. K., Zanna, M. P., & Fong, G. T. (1996). Why common sense goes out the window: Effects of alcohol on intentions to use condoms. *Personality and Social Psychology Bulletin*, 22, 763–775.

Mackie, D. M. (1987). Systematic and nonsystematic processing of majority and minority persuasive communications. *Journal of Personality and Social Psychology*, 53, 41–52.

MacKinnon, C. (1993, July–August). Turning rape into pornography: Postmodern genocide. *Ms.*, pp. 24–30.

Mackinnon, S. P., Jordan, C. H., & Wilson, A. E. (2011). Birds of a feather sit together: Physical similarity predicts seating choice. *Personality and Social Psychology Bulletin*, 37, 879–892.

Maclean, N. (1983). *A river runs through it.* Chicago: University of Chicago Press.

MacNeil, M. K., & Sherif, M. (1976). Norm change over subject generations as a function of arbitrariness of prescribed norms. *Journal of Personality and Social Psychology*, 34, 762–773.

Macrae, C. N., & Bodenhausen, G. V. (2000). Social cognition: Thinking categorically about others. *Annual Review of Psychology*, 51, 93–120.

Madon, S., Guyll, M., Buller, A. A., Scherr, K. C., Willard, J., & Spoth, R. (2008). The mediation of mothers' self-fulfilling effects on their children's alcohol use: Self-verification, informational conformity, and modeling processes. *Journal of Personality and Social Psychology*, 95(2), 369–384. doi:10.1037/0022-3514.95.2.369

Madon, S., Guyll, M., Scherr, K. C., Willard, J., Spoth, R., & Vogel, D. L. (2013). The role of the self-fulfilling prophecy in young adolescents' responsiveness to a substance use prevention program. *Journal of Applied Social Psychology*, 43, 1784–1798.

Madon, S., Guyll, M., Spoth, R. L., Cross, S. E., & Hilbert, S. J. (2003). The self-fulfilling influence of mother expectations on children's underage drinking. *Journal of Personality and Social Psychology*, 84(6), 1188–1205. doi:10.1037/0022-3514.84.6.1188

Madon, S., Jussim, L., & Eccles, J. (1997). In search of the powerful self-fulfilling prophecy. *Journal of Personality and Social Psychology*, 72, 791–809. doi:10.1037/0022-3514.72.4.791

Madon, S., Willard, J., Guyll, M., & Scherr, K. C. (2011). Self-fulfilling prophecies: Mechanisms, power, and links to social problems. *Social and Personality Psychology Compass*, 5(8), 578–590. doi:10.1111/j.1751-9004.2011.00375.x

Magaro, P. A., & Ashbrook, R. M. (1985). The personality of societal groups. *Journal of Personality and Social Psychology*, 48, 1479–1489.

Main, M., Kaplan, N., & Cassidy, J. (1985). Security in infancy, childhood, and adulthood: A move to the level of representation. In T. Bretherton & E. Waters (Eds.), *Growing points of attachment theory and research. Monographs of the Society for Research on Child Development*, 50, 66–104.

Maio, G. R., Olson, J. M., Allen, L., & Bernard, M. M. (2001). Addressing discrepancies between values and behavior: The motivating effect of reasons. *Journal of Experimental Social Psychology*, 37, 104–117.

Maisel, N. C., & Gable, S. L. (2009). The paradox of received social support: The importance of responsiveness. *Psychological Science*, 20(8), 928–932. doi:10.1111/j.1467-9280.2009.02388.x

Major, B., & Gramzow, R. H. (1999). Abortion as stigma: Cognitive and emotional implications of concealment. *Journal of Personality and Social Psychology*, 77, 735–745.

Malamuth, N. M. (1981). Rape fantasies as a function of exposure to violent sexual stimuli. *Archives of Sexual Behavior*, 10, 33–47.

Malamuth, N. M., Addison, T., & Koss, M. (2000). Pornography and sexual aggression: Are there reliable effects and can we understand them? *Annual Review of Sex Research* 11, 26–91.

Malamuth, N. M., Hald, G., & Koss, M. (2012). Pornography, individual differences in risk and men's acceptance of violence against women in a representative sample. *Sex Roles*, 66, 427–439.

Malamuth, N. M., Linz, D. G., Heavey, C. L., Barnes, G., & Acker, M. (1995). Using the confluence model of sexual aggression to predict men's conflict with women: A 10-year follow-up study. *Journal of Personality and Social Psychology*, 69, 353–369.

Malle, B. F., & Knobe, J. (1997). Which behaviors do people explain? A basic actor-observer asymmetry. *Journal of Personality and Social Psychology*, 72, 288–304.

Malloy, T. E. (2001). Difference to inference: Teaching logical and statistical reasoning through on-line interactivity. *Behavior Research Methods, Instruments, and Computers*, 33, 270–273.

Malpass, R. S., Tredoux, C. G., & McQuiston-Surrett, D. (2007). Lineup construction and lineup fairness. *The handbook of eyewitness psychology, Vol II: Memory for people* (pp. 155–178). Mahwah, NJ: Lawrence Erlbaum.

Manning, M. (2009). The effects of subjective norms on behaviour in the theory of planned behaviour: A meta-analysis. *British Journal of Social Psychology, 48*(4), 649–705. doi:10.1348/014466608X393136

Mannino, C. A., Snyder, M., & Omoto, A. M. (2011). Why do people get involved? Motivations for volunteerism and other forms of social action. In D. Dunning (Ed.), *Frontiers of social psychology. Social motivation* (pp. 127–146). New York: Psychology Press.

Mannix, E., & Neale, M. A. (2005). What differences make a difference? The promise and reality of diverse teams in organizations. *Psychological Science in the Public Interest, 6,* 31–55.

Manstead, A. S. R. (1997). Situations, belongingness, attitudes, and culture: Four lessons learned from social psychology. In G. McGarty & H. S. Haslam (Eds.), *The message of social psychology: Perspectives on mind and society* (pp. 238–251). Oxford, UK: Blackwell.

Marien, H., Custers, R., Hassin, R. R., & Aarts, H. (2012). Unconscious goal activation and the hijacking of the executive function. *Journal of Personality and Social Psychology, 103,* 399–415.

Marion, R. (1995, August). The girl who mewed. *Discover,* pp. 38–40.

Markey, P. M. (2000). Bystander intervention in computer-mediated communication. *Computers in Human Behavior, 16,* 183–188.

Markman, K. D., Karadogan, F., Lindberg, M. J., & Zell, E. (2009). Counterfactual thinking: Function and dysfunction. In K. D. Markman, W. M. P. Klein, & J. A. Suhr (Eds.), *Handbook of imagination and mental simulation* (pp. 175–193). New York: Psychology Press.

Markoff, J. (2011, February 16). Computer wins on "Jeopardy!": Trivial, it's not. *The New York Times.* Retrieved April 18, 2011, from www.nytimes.com/2011/02/17/science/17jeopardy-watson.html?pagewanted=2

Marks, J. L., Lam, C. B., & McHale, S. M. (2009). Family patterns of gender role attitudes. *Sex Roles, 61*(3–4), 221–234. doi:10.1007/s11199-009-9619-3

Markus, H. R. (1977). Self-schemata and processing information about the self. *Journal of Personality and Social Psychology, 35,* 63–78.

Markus, H. R., & Kitayama, S. (1991). Culture and the self: Implications for cognition, emotion, and motivation. *Psychological Review, 98,* 224–253.

Markus, H. R., & Kitayama, S. (2010). Cultures and selves: A cycle of mutual constitution. *Perspectives on Psychological Science, 5*(4), 420–430. doi:10.1177/1745691610375557

Markus, H. R., & Zajonc, R. B. (1985). The cognitive perspective in social psychology. In G. Lindzey & E. Aronson (Eds.), *Handbook of social psychology* (3rd ed., Vol. 1, pp. 137–230). New York: McGraw-Hill.

Markus, H. R., Kitayama, S., & Heiman, R. J. (1996). Culture and "basic" psychological principles. In E. T. Higgins & A. W. Kruglanski (Eds.), *Social psychology: Handbook of basic principles* (pp. 857–913). New York: Guilford Press.

Marlatt, G. A., & Rohsenow, D. J. (1980). Cognitive processes in alcohol use: Expectancy and the balanced placebo design. In N. K. Mello (Ed.), *Advances in substance abuse* (Vol. 1). Greenwich, CT: JAI Press.

Marlowe, D., & Gergen, K. J. (1970). Personality and social behavior. In K. J. Gergen & D. Marlowe (Eds.), *Personality and social behavior* (pp. 1–75). Reading, MA: Addison-Wesley.

Marques, J., Abrams, D., & Serodio, R. (2001). Being better by being right: Subjective group dynamics and derogation of in-group deviants when generic norms are undermined. *Journal of Personality and Social Psychology, 81,* 436–447.

Marqusee, M. (2005, November 9). A name that lives in infamy. *The Guardian.* Available online at www.guardian.co.uk/world/2005/nov/10/usa.iraq

Marsland, A., Bachen, E. A., & Cohen, S. (2012). Stress, immunity, and susceptibility to upper respiratory infectious disease. In A. Baum, T. A. Revenson, & J. Singer (Eds.), *Handbook of health*

psychology (2nd ed., pp. 717–738). New York, NY: Psychology Press.

Martin, A. J., Berenson, K. R., Griffing, S., Sage, R. E., Madry, L., Bingham, L. E., & Primm, B. J. (2000). The process of leaving an abusive relationship: The role of risk assessments and decision certainty. *Journal of Family Violence, 15,* 109–122.

Martin, L. L., & Tesser, A. (1996). Some ruminative thoughts. In R. S. Wyer, Jr. (Ed.), *Advances in social cognition* (Vol. 9, pp. 1–47). Hillsdale, NJ: Erlbaum.

Martin, N. G., Eaves, L. J., Heath, A. R., Jardine, R., Feingold, L. M., & Eysenck, H. J. (1986). Transmission of social attitudes. *Proceedings of the National Academy of Science, 83,* 4364–4368.

Martin, P. Y., & Marrington, S. (2005). Morningness–eveningness orientation, optimal time-of-day and attitude change: Evidence for the systematic processing of a persuasive communication. *Personality and Individual Differences, 39,* 367–377.

Martin, R. (2013). *Difficult men: Behind the scenes of a creative revolution: From The Sopranos and The Wire to Mad Men and Breaking Bad.* New York: Penguin.

Martinez, G., Copen, C. E., & Abma J. C. (2011). Teenagers in the United States: Sexual activity, contraceptive use, and childbearing, 2006–2010 National Survey of Family Growth. National Center for Health Statistics. *Vital Health Statistics, 23*(31). Retrieved November 1, 2011, from www.cdc.gov/nchs/data/series/sr_23/sr23_031.pdf

Martinez, L. (2012, January 11). U.S. Marines allegedly urinate on Taliban corpses. *ABC News.* Available online at: http://abcnews.go.com/Blotter/marines-allegedly-urinate-taliban-corpes/story?id=15341700#.T1GNRcxLWpc

Martinie, M. A., & Fointiat, V. (2006). Self-esteem, trivialization, and attitude change. *Swiss Journal of Psychology, 65,* 221–225.

Masicampo, E. J., & Ambady, N. (2014). Predicting fluctuations in widespread interest: Memory decay and goal-related memory accessibility in Internet search trends. *Journal of Experimental Psychology: General, 143,* 205–214.

Mason, M. F., & Morris, M. W. (2010). Culture, attribution and automaticity: A social cognitive neuroscience view. *Social Cognitive and Affective Neuroscience, 5,* 292–306.

Masuda, T., & Nisbett, R. E. (2006). Culture and change blindness. *Cognitive Science: A Multidisciplinary Journal, 30,* 381–399.

Masuda, T., Ellsworth, P. C., & Mesquita, B. (2008). Placing the face in context: Cultural differences in the perception of facial emotion. *Journal of Personality and Social Psychology, 94*(3), 365–381.

Matlin, M. W. (2012). *Psychology of women* (7th ed.). Belmont, CA: Wadsworth.

Matsumoto, D., & Ekman, P. (1989). American-Japanese differences in intensity ratings of facial expressions of emotion. *Motivation and Emotion, 13,* 143–157.

Matsumoto, D., & Hwang, H. S. (2010). Judging faces in context. *Social and Personality Psychology Compass, 4,* 393–402.

Matsumoto, D., & Kudoh, T. (1993). American-Japanese cultural differences in attributions of personality based on smiles. *Journal of Nonverbal Behavior, 17,* 231–243.

Matsumoto, D., & Willingham, B. (2006). The thrill of victory and the agony of defeat: Spontaneous expressions of medal winners of the 2004 Athens Olympic games. *Journal of Personality and Social Psychology, 91,* 568–581.

Matsumoto, D., Willingham, B., & Olide, A. (2009). Sequential dynamics of culturally moderated facial expressions of emotion. *Psychological Science, 20,* 1269–1274.

Mayo Clinic. (n.d.). Diseases and conditions. Retrieved August 19, 2014, from http://www.mayoclinic.org/diseases-conditions

Mazur, A., Booth, A., & Dabbs, J. M. (1992). Testosterone and chess competition. *Social Psychology Quarterly, 55,* 70–77.

McAlister, A., Perry, C., Killen, J. D., Slinkard, L. A., & Maccoby, N. (1980). Pilot study of smoking,

alcohol, and drug abuse prevention. *American Journal of Public Health, 70,* 719–721.

McAllister, H. A. (1996). Self-serving bias in the classroom: Who shows it? Who knows it? *Journal of Educational Psychology, 88,* 123–131.

McArthur, L. Z. (1972). The how and what of why: Some determinants and consequences of causal attribution. *Journal of Personality and Social Psychology, 22,* 171–193.

McCauley, C. (1989). The nature of social influence in groupthink: Compliance and internalization. *Journal of Personality and Social Psychology, 57,* 250–260.

McClellan, S. (2008). *What happened: Inside the Bush White House and Washington's culture of deception.* New York: Public Affairs.

McClellan, S. (2009). *What happened: Inside the Bush White House and Washington's culture of deception.* New York: PublicAffairs.

McConahay, J. B. (1981). Reducing racial prejudice in desegregated schools. In W. D. Hawley (Ed.), *Effective school desegregation.* Beverly Hills, CA: Sage.

McConahay, J. B. (1986). Modern racism, ambivalence, and the Modern Racism Scale. In J. F. Dovidio & S. L. Gaertner (Eds.), *Prejudice, discrimination, and racism: Theory and research* (pp. 91–125). New York: Academic Press.

McConnell, A. R., & Brown, C. M. (2010). Dissonance averted: Self-concept organization moderates the effect of hypocrisy on attitude change. *Journal of Experimental Social Psychology, 46,* 361–366.

McCrea, S., Hirt, E., & Milner, B. (2008). She works hard for the money: Valuing effort underlies gender differences in behavioral self-handicapping. *Journal of Experimental Social Psychology, 44,* 292–311.

McCullough, M. E., & Tabak, B. A. (2010). Prosocial behavior. In R. F. Baumeister & E. J. Finkel (Eds.), *Advanced social psychology: The state of the science* (pp. 263–302). New York: Oxford University Press.

McDonald, H. E., & Hirt, E. R. (1997). When expectancy meets desire: Motivational effects in reconstructive memory. *Journal of Personality and Social Psychology, 72,* 5–23.

McFadyen-Ketchum, S. A., Bates, J. E., Dodge, K. A., & Pettit, G. S. (1996). Patterns of change in early childhood aggressive-disruptive behavior: Gender differences in predictions from early coercive and affectionate mother-child interactions. *Child Development, 67,* 2417–2433.

McGlone, M., & Aronson, J. (2006). Social identity salience and stereotype threat. *Journal of Applied Developmental Psychology, 27,* 486–493.

McGregor, B., Antoni, M., Boyers, A., Alferi, S., Cruess, D., Kilbourn, K., et al. (2004). Cognitive behavioral stress management increases benefit finding and immune function among women with early stage breast cancer. *Journal of Psychosomatic Research, 54,* 1–8.

McGuire, A. M. (1994). Helping behaviors in the natural environment: Dimensions and correlates of helping. *Personality and Social Psychology Bulletin, 20,* 45–56.

McGuire, M., & Pezdek, K. (2014). Birds of a feather get misidentified together: High entativity decreases recognition accuracy for groups of other-race faces. *Legal and Criminological Psychology.* doi:10.1111/lcrp.12066

McGuire, W. J. (1964). Inducing resistance to persuasion. In L. Berkowitz (Ed.), *Advances in experimental social psychology* (Vol. 1, pp. 192–229). New York: Academic Press.

McGuire, W. J. (1968). Personality and susceptibility to social influence. In E. F. Borgatta & W. W. Lambert (Eds.), *Handbook of personality theory and research* (pp. 1130–1187). Chicago: Rand McNally.

McKown, C., & Weinstein, R. (2008). Teacher expectations, classroom context, and the achievement gap. *Journal of School Psychology, 46*(3), 235–261. doi:10.1016/j.jsp.2007.05.001

McLeod, P. L. (2013). Distributed people and distributed information: Vigilant decision-making in virtual teams. *Small Group Research, 44,* 627–657.

McLeod, P. L., Lobel, S. A., & Cox, T. H., Jr. (1996). Ethnic diversity and creativity in small groups. *Small Group Research, 27*, 248–264.

McMillan, W., Stice, E., & Rohde, P. (2011). High- and low-level dissonance-based eating disorder prevention programs with young women with body image concerns: An experimental trial. *Journal of Consulting and Clinical Psychology, 79*, 129–134.

McMullin, D., & White, J. W. (2006). Long-term effects of labeling a rape experience. *Psychology of Women Quarterly, 30*, 96–105.

McNally, R. J. (2003). *Remembering trauma.* Cambridge, MA: Harvard University Press.

McNally, R. J., & Geraerts, E. (2009). A new solution to the recovered memory debate. *Perspectives on Psychological Science, 4*(2), 126–134. doi:10.1111/j.1745-6924.2009.01112.x

McNally, R. J., Bryant, R. A., & Ehlers, A. (2003). Does early psychological intervention promote recovery from posttraumatic stress? *Psychological Science in the Public Interest, 4*, 45–79.

McNulty, J. K., & Fincham, F. D. (2012). Beyond positive psychology? Toward a contextual view of psychological processes and well-being. *American Psychologist, 67*(2), 101–110. doi:10.1037/a0024572

McNulty, J. K., O'Mara, E. M., & Karney, B. R. (2008). Benevolent cognitions as a strategy of relationship maintenance: "Don't sweat the small stuff" . . . But it is not all small stuff. *Journal of Personality and Social Psychology, 94*, 631–646.

McPherson, J. M. (1983). The size of voluntary associations. *American Sociological Review, 61*, 1044–1064.

McPherson, M., Smith-Lovin, L., & Cook, J. M. (2001). Birds of a feather: Homophily in social networks. *Annual Review of Sociology, 27*, 415–444.

Medvec, V. H., Madey, S. F., & Gilovich, T. (1995). When less is more: Counterfactual thinking and satisfaction among Olympic medalists. *Journal of Personality and Social Psychology, 69*, 603–610.

Meeus, W. H. J., & Raaijmakers, Q. A. W. (1995). Obedience in modern society: The Utrecht studies. *Journal of Social Issues, 51*, 155–175.

Mehl, M. R., Vazire, S., Ramírez-Esparza, N., & Pennebacker, J. W. (2007). Are women really more talkative than men? *Science, 317*, 82.

Meier, B. P., Robinson, M. D., Carter, M. S., & Hinsz, V. B. (2010). Are sociable people more beautiful? A zero-acquaintance analysis of agreeableness, extraversion, and attractiveness. *Journal of Research in Personality, 44*, 293–296.

Meier, B. P., Schnall, S., Schwarz, N., & Bargh, J. A. (2012). Embodiment in social psychology. *Topics in Cognitive Science, 4*, 705–716.

Meindl, J. R., & Lerner, M. J. (1985). Exacerbation of extreme responses to an out-group. *Journal of Personality and Social Psychology, 47*, 71–84.

Meissner, C. A., & Brigham, J. C. (2001). Thirty years of investigating the own-race bias in memory for faces: A meta-analytic review. *Psychology, Public Policy, and Law, 7*, 3–35.

Meissner, C. A., Tredoux, C. G., & Parker, J. F. (2005). Eyewitness decisions in simultaneous and sequential lineups: A dual-process signal detection theory analysis. *Memory and Cognition, 33*, 783–792.

Melara, R. D., De Witt-Rickards, T. S., & O'Brien, T. P. (1989). Enhancing lineup identification accuracy: Two codes are better than one. *Journal of Applied Psychology, 74*, 706–713.

Melillo, J. M., Richmond, T. C., & Yohe, G. W. (Eds.). (2014). Climate change impacts in the United States: The Third National Climate Assessment. U.S. Global Change Research Program, 841 pp. doi:10.7930/J0Z31WJ2.

Meltzer, A. L., McNulty, J. K., Jackson, G. L., & Karney, B. R. (2014). Sex differences in the implications of partner physical attractiveness for the trajectory of marital satisfaction. *Journal of Personality and Social Psychology, 106*, 418–428.

Mendoza-Denton, R., & Page-Gould, E. (2008). Can cross-group friendships influence minority students' well-being at historically White universities? *Psychological Science, 19*, 933–939.

Menon, T., Morris, M. W., Chiu, C., & Hong, Y. (1999). Culture and the construal of agency: Attribution to individual versus group dispositions. *Journal of Personality and Social Psychology, 76*, 701–717.

Menon, T., Sheldon, O. J., & Galinsky, A. D. (2014). Barriers to transforming hostile relations: Why friendly gestures can backfire. *Negotiation and Conflict Management Research, 7*, 17–37.

Merkle, C., & Weber, M. (2011). True overconfidence: The inability of rational information processing to account for apparent overconfidence. *Organizational Behavior and Human Decision Processes, 116*(2), 262–271. doi:10.1016/j.obhdp.2011.07.004

Messick, D., & Liebrand, W. B. G. (1995). Individual heuristics and the dynamics of cooperation in large groups. *Psychological Review, 102*, 131–145.

Meston, C. M., & Frohlich, P. F. (2003). Love at first fright: Partner salience moderates roller-coaster-induced excitation transfer. *Archives of Sexual Behavior, 32*(6), 537–544.

Metcalfe, J. (1998). Cognitive optimism: Self-deception or memory-based processing heuristics? *Personality and Social Psychology Review, 2*, 100–110.

Meyersburg, C. A., Bogdan, R., Gallo, D. A., & McNally, R. J. (2009). False memory propensity in people reporting recovered memories of past lives. *Journal of Abnormal Psychology, 118*(2), 399–404. doi:10.1037/a0015371

Mezulis, A. H., Abramson, L. Y., Hyde, J. S., & Hankin, B. L. (2004). Is there a universal positivity bias in attributions? A meta-analytic review of individual, developmental, and cultural differences in the self-serving attributional bias. *Psychological Bulletin, 130*(5), 711–747.

Migration and geographic mobility in metropolitan and nonmetropolitan America, 1995–2000 (2003). United States Census Bureau. Accessed on April 16, 2006, at www.census.gov/prod/2003pubs/censr-9.pdf

Mikulincer, M., Shaver, P. R., Sapir-Lavid, Y., & Avihou-Kanza, N. (2009). What's inside the minds of securely and insecurely attached people? The secure-base script and its associations with attachment-style dimensions. *Journal of Personality and Social Psychology, 97*, 615–633.

Milgram, S. (1961). Nationality and conformity. *Scientific American, 205*, 45–51.

Milgram, S. (1963). Behavioral study of obedience. *Journal of Abnormal and Social Psychology, 67*, 371–378.

Milgram, S. (1969, March). The lost letter technique. *Psychology Today*, pp. 30–33, 67–68.

Milgram, S. (1974). *Obedience to authority: An experimental view.* New York: Harper & Row.

Milgram, S. (1976). Obedience to criminal orders: The compulsion to do evil. In T. Blass (Ed.), *Contemporary social psychology: Representative readings* (pp. 175–184). Itasca, IL: Peacock.

Milgram, S. (1977). *The individual in a social world.* Reading, MA: Addison-Wesley.

Milgram, S., & Sabini, J. (1978). On maintaining urban norms: A field experiment in the subway. In A. Baum, J. E. Singer, & S. Valins (Eds.), *Advances in environmental psychology* (Vol. 1, pp. 9–40). Hillsdale, NJ: Erlbaum.

Mill, J. S. (1843). *A system of logic ratiocinative and inductive.* London.

Miller, A. G. (1986). *The obedience experiments: A case study of controversy in social science.* New York: Praeger.

Miller, A. G. (1995). Constructions of the obedience experiments: A focus upon domains of relevance. *Journal of Social Issues, 51*, 33–53.

Miller, A. G. (2009). Reflections on 'Replicating Milgram' (Burger, 2009). *American Psychologist, 64*, 20–27.

Miller, A. G., Ashton, W., & Mishal, M. (1990). Beliefs concerning the features of constrained behavior: A basis for the fundamental attribution error. *Journal of Personality and Social Psychology, 59*, 635–650.

Miller, A. G., Collins, B. E., & Brief, D. E. (1995). Perspectives on obedience to authority: The legacy of the Milgram experiments. *Journal of Social Issues, 51*, 1–19.

Miller, A. G., Jones, E. E., & Hinkle, S. (1981). A robust attribution error in the personality domain. *Journal of Experimental Social Psychology, 17*, 587–600.

Miller, C. E., & Anderson, P. D. (1979). Group decision rules and the rejection of deviates. *Social Psychology Quarterly, 42*, 354–363.

Miller, C. H., Lane, L. T., Deatrick, L. M., Young, A. M., & Potts, K. A. (2007). Psychological reactance and promotional health messages: The effects of controlling language, lexical concreteness, and the restoration of freedom. *Human Communication Research, 33*, 219–240.

Miller, C. T. (1982). The role of performance-related similarity in social comparison of abilities: A test of the related attributes hypothesis. *Journal of Experimental Social Psychology, 18*, 513–523.

Miller, D. P., Jr., Spangler, J. G., Vitolins, M. Z., Davis, S. W., Ip, E. H., et al. (2013). Are medical students aware of their anti-obesity bias? *Academic Medicine, 88*, 978–982.

Miller, D. T., & Prentice, D. A. (1996). The construction of social norms and standards. In E. T. Higgins & A. W. Kruglanski (Eds.), *Social psychology: Handbook of basic principles* (pp. 799–829). New York: Guilford Press.

Miller, D. T., & Ross, M. (1975). Self-serving biases in the attribution of causality: Fact or fiction? *Psychological Bulletin, 82*, 213–225.

Miller, D., & Taylor, B. (2002). Counterfactual thought, regret, and superstition: How to avoid kicking yourself. In T. Gilovich, D. Griffin, & D. Kahneman (Eds.), *Heuristics and biases: The psychology of intuitive judgement* (pp. 367–378). New York: Cambridge University Press.

Miller, J. G. (1984). Culture and the development of everyday social explanation. *Journal of Personality and Social Psychology, 46*, 961–978.

Miller, J. G., & Boyle, J. P. (2013). Culture and social psychology. In H. Tennen, J. Suls, & I. B. Weiner (Eds.), *Handbook of psychology, Vol. 5: Personality and social psychology* (2nd ed., pp. 507–528). Hoboken, NJ: John Wiley & Sons.

Miller, N., & Campbell, D. T. (1959). Recency and primacy in persuasion as a function of the timing of speeches and measurements. *Journal of Abnormal and Social Psychology, 59*, 1–9.

Miller, P. V. (2002). The authority and limitation of polls. In J. Manza, F. L. Cook, & B. I. Page (Eds.), *Navigating public opinion* (pp. 221–231). New York: Oxford University Press.

Mills, J. (1958). Changes in moral attitudes following temptation. *Journal of Personality, 26*, 517–531.

Mills, M. J., Fleck, C. R., & Kozikowski, A. (2013). Positive psychology at work: A conceptual review, state-of-practice assessment, and a look ahead. *Journal of Positive Psychology, 8*(2), 153–164. doi:10.1080/17439760.2013.776622

Mills, M. S., & Clark. J. R. (2011). A theory of communal (and exchange) relationships. In P. A. M. Van Lange, A. W. Kruglanski, & E. T. Higgins (Eds.), *Handbook of theories of social psychology* (Vol. 2, pp. 232–250). Los Angeles, CA: Sage.

Milton, K. (1971). *Women in policing.* New York: Police Foundation Press.

Minard, R. D. (1952). Race relations in the Pocahontas coal field. *Journal of Social Issues, 8*, 29–44.

Mischel, W. (1968). *Personality and assessment.* New York: Wiley.

Mischel, W., & Shoda, Y. (1995). A cognitive affective system theory of personality: Reconceptualizing situations, dispositions, dynamics, and invariance in personality structures. *Psychological Review, 102*, 246–268.

Misra, S., Cheng, L., Genevie, J., & Yuan, M. (2014). The iPhone effect: The quality of in-person social interactions in the presence of mobile devices. *Environment and Behavior.* doi:10.1177/0013916514539755

Mitchell, J., Heatherton, T., Kelley, W., Wyland, C., Wegner, D., & Macrae, C. (2007). Separating sustained from transient aspects of cognitive control during thought suppression. *Psychological Science, 18*, 292–297.

Miyamoto, Y. (2013). Culture and analytic versus holistic cognition: Toward multilevel analyses of cultural influences. *Advances in Experimental Social Psychology, 47*, 131–188.

Miyamoto, Y., & Kitayama, S. (2002). Cultural variation in correspondence bias: The critical role of attitude diagnosticity of socially constrained behavior. *Journal of Personality and Social Psychology, 83*, 1239–1248.

Miyamoto, Y., Nisbett, R. E., & Masuda, T. (2006). Culture and the physical environment: Holistic versus analytic perceptual affordances. *Psychological Science, 17*, 113–119.

Modigliani, A., & Rochat, F. (1995). The role of interaction sequences and the timing of resistance in shaping obedience and defiance to authority. *Journal of Social Issues, 51*, 107–123.

Moghaddam, F. M., Taylor, D. M., & Wright, S. (1993). *Social psychology in cross-cultural perspective.* New York: Freeman.

Mojaverian, T., & Kim, H. S. (2013). Interpreting a helping hand: Cultural variation in the effectiveness of solicited and unsolicited social support. *Personality and Social Psychology Bulletin, 39*, 88–99.

Mojzisch, A., & Schulz-Hardt, S. (2010). Knowing others' preferences degrades the quality of group decisions. *Journal of Personality and Social Psychology, 98*(5), 794–808. doi:10.1037/a0017627

Mok, A., & Morris, M. W. (2010). An upside to bicultural identity conflict: Resisting groupthink in cultural ingroups. *Journal of Experimental Social Psychology, 46*(6), 1114–1117. doi:10.1016/j.jesp.2010.05.020

Monin, J., Clark, M., & Lemay, E. (2008). Communal responsiveness in relationships with female versus male family members. *Sex Roles, 59*, 176–188.

Monson, C. M.; Langhinrichsen-Rohling, J. (2002). Sexual and nonsexual dating violence perpetration: Testing an integrated perpetrator typology, *Violence and Victims, 17*(4), 403–428(26). Springer Publishing Company

Montemayor, R., & Eisen, M. (1977). The development of self-conceptions from childhood to adolescence. *Developmental Psychology, 13*, 314–319.

Montgomery, L. (2014, June 1). Evidence of climate change laps at Norfolk's feet. *Washington Post*, pp. A1, A9.

Monto, M. A., & Carey, A. G. (2014). A new standard of sexual behavior? Are claims associated with the hookup culture" supported by general social survey data? *Journal of Sex Research, 51*, 605–615.

Montoya, R. M., & Horton, R. S. (2013). A meta-analytic investigation of the processes underlying the similarity-attraction effect. *Journal of Social and Personal Relationships, 30*, 64–94.

Montoya, R. M., & Insko, C. A. (2008). Toward a more complete understanding of the reciprocity of liking effect. *European Journal of Social Psychology, 38*, 477–498.

Montoya, R. M., Horton, R. S., & Kirchner, J. (2008). Is actual similarity necessary for attraction? A meta-analysis of actual and perceived similarity. *Journal of Social and Personal Relationships, 25*, 889–922.

Moore, B., Jr. (1978). *Injustice: The social bases of obedience and revolt.* White Plains, NY: Sharpe.

Moore, J. S., Graziano, W. G., & Millar, M. C. (1987). Physical attractiveness, sex role orientation, and the evaluation of adults and children. *Personality and Social Psychology Bulletin, 13*, 95–102.

Moore, R. L. (1998). Love and limerance with Chinese characteristics: Student romance in the PRC. In V. C. de Munck (Ed.), *Romantic love and sexual behavior* (pp. 251–283). Westport, CT: Praeger.

Moors, A., & De Houwer, J. (2006). Automaticity: A theoretical and conceptual analysis. *Psychological Bulletin, 132*, 297–326.

Moos, R. H., & Holahan, C. J. (2003). Dispositional and contextual perspectives on coping: Toward an integrative framework. *Journal of Clinical Psychology, 59*, 1387–1403.

Mor, N., Doane, L. D., Adam, E. K., Mineka, S., Zinbarg, R. E., Griffith, J. W., . . . Nazarian, M. (2010). Within-person variations in self-focused attention and negative affect in depression and

anxiety: A diary study. *Cognition and Emotion, 24*, 48–62. doi:10.1080/02699930802499715

Moran, J. M., Jolly, E., & Mitchell, J. O. (2014). Spontaneous mentalizing predicts the fundamental attribution error. *Journal of Cognitive Neuroscience, 26*, 569–576.

Moran, S., & Ritov, I. (2007). Experience in integrative negotiations: What needs to be learned? *Journal of Experimental Social Psychology, 43*, 77–90.

Moreland, R. L. (1987). The formation of small groups. In C. Hendrick (Ed.), *Review of personality and social psychology* (Vol. 8, pp. 80–110). Newbury Park, CA: Sage.

Moreland, R. L. (1999). Transactive memory: Learning who knows what in work groups and organizations. In L. L. Thompson & J. M. Levine (Eds.), *Shared cognition in organizations: The management of knowledge* (pp. 3–31). Mahwah, NJ: Erlbaum.

Moreland, R. L. (2010). Are dyads really groups? *Small Group Research, 41*(2), 251–267. doi:10.1177/1046496409358618

Moreland, R. L., & Beach, S. R. (1992). Exposure effects in the classroom: The development of affinity among students. *Journal of Experimental Social Psychology, 28*, 255–276.

Moreland, R. L., & Topolinski, S. (2010). The mere exposure phenomenon: A lingering melody by Robert Zajonc. *Emotion Review, 2*, 329–339.

Morgan, C. A. III, Southwick, S., Steffian, G., Hazlett, G. A., & Loftus, E. F. (2013). Misinformation can influence memory for recently experienced, highly stressful events. *International Journal of Law and Psychiatry, 36*, 11–17.

Morin, A. (2011). Self-awareness Part 1: Definition, measures, effects, functions, and antecedents. *Social and Personality Compass, 5*, 807–823.

Morin, R. (2002, March 3). Bias and babies. *Washington Post*, p. B5.

Morling, B., & Evered, S. (2006). Secondary control reviewed and defined. *Psychological Bulletin, 132*, 269–296.

Morling, B., & Lamoreaux, M. (2008). Measuring culture outside the head: A meta-analysis of individualism-collectivism in cultural products. *Personality and Social Psychology Review, 12*, 199–221.

Morris, E. (Director). (1988). *The thin blue line* [Film]. New York: HBO Videos.

Morris, M. W., & Peng, K. (1994). Culture and cause: American and Chinese attributions for social and physical events. *Journal of Personality and Social Psychology, 67*, 949–971.

Morris, W. N., & Miller, R. S. (1975). The effects of consensus-breaking and consensus-preempting partners on reduction of conformity. *Journal of Experimental Social Psychology, 11*, 215–223.

Morry, M. M. (2007). The attraction-similarity hypothesis among cross-sex friends: Relationship satisfaction, perceived similarities, and self-serving perceptions. *Journal of Social and Personal Relationships, 24*, 117–138.

Morry, M. M., & Staska, S. L. (2001). Magazine exposure: Internalization, self-objectification, eating attitudes, and body satisfaction in male and female university students. *Canadian Journal of Behavioural Science, 33*, 269–279.

Morse, D. R., Martin, J., & Moshonov, J. (1991). Psychosomatically induced death relative to stress, hypnosis, mind control, and voodoo: Review and possible mechanisms. *Stress Medicine, 7*, 213–232.

Morton, T. A., Postmes, T., Haslam, S. A., & Hornsey, M. J. (2009). Theorizing gender in the face of social change: Is there anything essential about essentialism? *Journal of Personality and Social Psychology, 96*, 653–664.

Moscovici, S. (1985). Social influence and conformity. In G. Lindzey & E. Aronson (Eds.), *Handbook of social psychology* (3rd ed., Vol. 2, pp. 347–412). New York: McGraw-Hill.

Moscovici, S. (1994). Three concepts: Minority, conflict, and behavioral style. In S. Moscovici, A. Mucchi-Faina, & A. Maass (Eds.), *Minority influence* (pp. 233–251). Chicago: Nelson-Hall.

Moscovici, S., & Nemeth, C. (1974). Minority influence. In C. Nemeth (Ed.), *Social psychology:*

Classic and contemporary integrations (pp. 217–249). Chicago: Rand McNally.

Moscovici, S., Mucchi-Faina, A., & Maass, A. (Eds.). (1994). *Minority influence.* Chicago: Nelson-Hall.

Moss-Racusin, C. A., Dovidio, J. F., Brescoll, V. L., Graham, M. J., & Handelsman, J. (2012). Science faculty's subtle gender biases favor male students. *PNAS, 109*, 16474–16479.

Mostert, M. P. (2010). Facilitated communication and its legitimacy—Twenty-first century developments. *Exceptionality, 18*(1), 31–41. doi:10.1080/09362830903462524

Mucchi-Faina, A., & Pagliaro, S. (2008). Minority influence: The role of ambivalence toward the source. *European Journal of Social Psychology, 38*, 612–623.

Muchnik, L., Aral, S., & Taylor, S. J. (2013). Social influence bias: A randomized experiment. *Science, 341*, 647–651.

Mullen, B. (1986). Atrocity as a function of lynch mob composition: A self-attention perspective. *Personality and Social Psychology Bulletin, 12*, 187–197.

Mullen, B., & Cooper, C. (1994). The relation between group cohesiveness and performance: An integration. *Psychological Bulletin, 115*, 210–227.

Mullen, B., Brown, R., & Smith, C. (1992). Ingroup bias as a function of salience, relevance, and status: An integration. *European Journal of Social Psychology, 22*, 103–122.

Mullen, B., Rozell, D., & Johnson, C. (2001). Ethnophaulisms for ethnic immigrant groups: The contributions of group size and familiarity. *European Journal of Social Psychology, 31*, 231–246.

Muller, D., & Butera, F. (2007). The focusing effect of self-evaluation threat in coaction and social comparison. *Journal of Personality and Social Psychology, 93*, 194–211.

Muller, D., Atzeni, T., & Fabrizio, B. (2004). Coaction and upward social comparison reduce the illusory conjunction effect: Support for distraction-conflict theory. *Journal of Experimental Social Psychology, 40*, 659–665.

Muraven, M., Tice, D. M., & Baumeister, R. F. (1998). Self-control as limited resource: Regulatory depletion patterns. *Journal of Personality and Social Psychology, 74*, 774–789.

Murr, A., & Smalley, S. (2003, March 17). White power, minus the power. *Newsweek*, pp. 42–45.

Murray, A. A., Wood, J. M., & Lilienfeld, S. O. (2012). Psychopathic personality traits and cognitive dissonance: Individual differences in attitude change. *Journal of Research in Personality, 46*, 525–536.

Murstein, B. I. (1970). Stimulus value role: A theory of marital choice. *Journal of Marriage and the Family, 32*, 465–481.

Mushquash, A. R., Stewart, S. H., Sherry, S. B., Mackinnon, S. P., Antony, M. M., & Sherry, D. L. (2011). Heavy episodic drinking among dating partners: A longitudinal actor-partner interdependence model. *Psychology of Addictive Behaviors*. Available online. doi:10.1037/a0026653

Mussweiler, T., & Förster, J. (2000). The sex-aggression link: A perception-behavior dissociation. *Journal of Personality and Social Psychology, 79*, 507–520.

Mussweiler, T., & Strack, F. (1999). Comparing is believing: A selective accessibility model of judgmental anchoring. In W. Stroebe & M. Hewstone (Eds.), *European review of social psychology* (Vol. 10, pp. 135–167). Chichester, UK: Wiley.

Mussweiler, T., Strack, F., & Pfeiffer, T. (2000). Overcoming the inevitable anchoring effect: Considering the opposite compensates for selective accessibility. *Personality and Social Psychology Bulletin, 260*, 1142–1150.

Myers, D. G., & Scanzoni, L. D. (2006). *What God has joined together: The Christian case for gay marriage.* Harper Collins: San Francisco.

Myers, H. F. (2009). Ethnicity- and socio-economic status-related stresses in context: An integrative review and conceptual model. *Journal of Behavioral Medicine, 32*(1), 9–19. doi:10.1007/s10865-008-9181-4

Nadal, K., Griffin, K. E., Vargas, V. M., Issa, M., Lyons, O. B., & Tobio, M. (2011). Processes and struggles with racial microaggressions from the White American perspective: Recommendations for workplace settings. In M. A. Paludi, C. A. Paludi, Jr., & E. R. DeSouza (Eds.), *Praeger handbook on understanding and preventing workplace discrimination* (pp. 155–180). Santa Barbara, CA: Praeger/ABC-CLIO.

Nail, P. R. (1986). Toward an integration of some models and theories of social response. *Psychological Bulletin, 100*, 190–206.

Nail, P. R., McDonald, G., & Levy, D. A. (2000). Proposal of a four-dimensional model of social response. *Psychological Bulletin, 126*, 454–470.

Nail, P. R., Misak, J. E., & Davis, R. M. (2004). Self-affirmation versus self-consistency: A comparison of two competing self-theories of dissonance phenomena. *Personality and Individual Differences, 36*, 1893–1905.

Naimi, T., Brewer, B., Mokdad, A., Serdula, M., Denny, C., & Marks, J. (2003). Binge drinking among U.S. adults. *Journal of the American Medical Association, 289*, 70–75.

Narchet, F. M., Meissner, C. A., & Russano, M. B. (2011). Modeling the influence of investigator bias on the elicitation of true and false confessions. *Law and Human Behavior, 35*(6), 452–465. doi:10.1007/s10979-010-9257-x

Nasco, S. A., & Marsh, K. L. (1999). Gaining control through counter-factual thinking. *Personality and Social Psychology Bulletin, 25*, 556–568.

Natanovich, G., & Eden, D. (2008). Pygmalion effects among outreach supervisors and tutors: Extending sex generalizability. *Journal of Applied Psychology, 93*(6), 1382–1389. doi:10.1037/a0012566

Nathanson, S. (1987). *An eye for an eye? The morality of punishing by death.* Totowa, NJ: Rowman & Littlefield.

National Center for Health Statistics. (2005). Marriage and divorce. Retrieved September 19, 2006, from www.cdc.gov/nchs/fastats/divorce.html2

National Center for Vital Statistics. (2001). *Crime facts at a glance.* Retrieved from Bureau of Justice Statistics, www.ojp.usdoj.gov/bjs/glance/hmrt.htm

National Oceanic and Atmospheric Administration. (2011, January 12). 2010 tied for warmest year on record. U.S. Department of Commerce. Retrieved August 14, 2011, from www.noaanews.noaa.gov/stories2011/20110112_globalstats.html

Naughton, F., Eborall, H., & Sutton, S. (2012). Dissonance and disengagement in pregnant smokers. *Journal of Smoking Cessation, 8*, 24–32.

Nedelec, J. L., & Beaver, K. M. (2014). Physical attractiveness as a phenotypic marker of health: An assessment using a nationally representative sample of American adults. *Evolution and Human Behavior.* doi:10.1016/j.evolhumbehav.2014.06.004

Neighbors, C., O'Connor, R. M., Lewis, M. A., Chawla, N., Lee, C. M., & Fossos, N. (2008). The relative impact of injunctive norms on college student drinking: The role of reference group. *Psychology of Addictive Behaviors, 22*, 576–581.

Nel, E., Helmreich, R., & Aronson, E. (1969). Opinion change in the advocate as a function of the persuasibility of his audience: A clarification of the meaning of dissonance. *Journal of Personality and Social Psychology, 12*, 117–124.

Nelson, D. E., Bland, S., Powell-Griner, E., Klein, R., Wells, H. E., Hogelin, G., & Marks, J. S. (2002). State trends in health risk factors and receipt of clinical preventive services among US adults during the 1990s. *Journal of the American Medical Association, 287*, 2659–2667.

Nelson, M. R., (2008). The hidden persuaders: Then and now. *Journal of Advertising, 37*, 113–126. doi:10.2753/JOA0091-3367370109

Nelson, S. (Writer, Producer, Director). (2010). *Freedom riders* [motion picture]. United States: American Experience (Public Broadcasting Service: WGBH, Boston). Available from http://www.pbs.org/wgbh/americanexperience/freedomriders/

Nemeth, C. J., & Chiles, C. (1988). Modeling courage: The role of dissent in fostering

independence. *European Journal of Social Psychology, 18*, 275–280.

Neria, Y., DiGrande, L., & Adams, B. G. (2011). Posttraumatic stress disorder following the September 11, 2001, terrorist attacks: A review of the literature among highly exposed populations. *American Psychologist, 66*(6), 429–446. doi:10.1037/a0024791

Nes, L. S., & Segerstrom, S. C. (2006). Dispositional optimism and coping: A meta-analytic review. *Personality and Social Psychology Review, 10*, 235–251.

Nestler, S., Blank, H., & Egloff, B. (2010). Hindsight ≠ hindsight: Experimentally induced dissociations between hindsight components. *Journal of Experimental Psychology: Learning, Memory, and Cognition, 36*(6), 1399–1413. doi:10.1037/a0020449

Neuberg, S. L. (1988). Behavioral implications of information presented outside of awareness: The effect of subliminal presentation of trait information on behavior in the prisoner's dilemma game. *Social Cognition, 6*, 207–230.

Neuberg, S. L., Kenrick, D. T., & Schaller, M. (2010). Evolutionary social psychology. In S. T. Fiske, D. T. Gilbert, & G. Lindzey (Eds.), *Handbook of social psychology* (5th ed., Vol. 2, pp. 761–796). Hoboken, NJ: John Wiley.

Newcomb, T. M. (1961). *The acquaintance process.* New York: Holt, Rinehart and Winston.

Newman, A. A. (2009, February 18). The body as billboard: Your ad here. *The New York Times,* p. B3. Retrieved June 6, 2011, from www.nytimes.com/2009/02/18/business/media/18adco.html

Newman, G. E., & Cain, D. M. (2014). Tainted altruism: When doing something good is evaluated worse than doing no good at all. *Psychological Science, 25*, 648–655.

Newman, L. S. (1996). Trait impressions as heuristics for predicting future behavior. *Personality and Social Psychology Bulletin, 22*, 395–411.

Newman, L. S., & Bakina, D. A. (2009). Do people resist social-psychological perspectives on wrongdoing? Reactions to dispositional, situational, and interactionist explanations. *Social Influence, 4*, 256–273.

Newport, F. (2011, May 20). For first time, majority of Americans favor legal gay marriage. *Gallup.* www.gallup.com/poll/147662/first-time-majority-americans-favor-legal-gay-marriage.aspx

Nichols, S. (2011). Experimental philosophy and the problem of free will. *Science, 331*(6023), 1401–1403. doi:10.1126/science.1192931

Nicholson, I. (2011). "Torture at Yale": Experimental subjects, laboratory torment, and the "rehabilitation" of Milgram's "Obedience to Authority." *Theory and Psychology, 21*, 737–761.

Nicholson, N., Cole, S. G., & Rocklin, T. (1985). Conformity in the Asch situation: A comparison between contemporary British and U.S. university students. *British Journal of Social Psychology, 24*, 59–63.

Nickerson, C., Schwarz, N., Diener, E., & Kahneman, D. (2003). Zeroing in on the dark side of the American Dream: A closer look at the negative consequences of the goal for financial success. *Psychological Science, 14*, 531–536.

Nielsen, K., & Cleal, B. (2011). Under which conditions do middle managers exhibit transformational leadership behaviors?—An experience sampling method study on the predictors of transformational leadership behaviors. *Leadership Quarterly, 22*(2), 344–352. doi:10.1016/j.leaqua.2011.02.009

The NIMH Multisite HIV Prevention Trial Group (1998, June 19). The NIMH Multisite HIV Prevention Trial: Reducing sexual HIV risk behavior. *Science, 280*, 1889–1894.

The NIMH Multisite HIV Prevention Trial Group (2001). Social-cognitive theory mediators of behavior change in the National Institute of Mental Health Multisite HIV Prevention Trial. *Health Psychology, 20*, 369–376.

Nisbett, R. E. (1993). Violence and U.S. regional culture. *American Psychologist, 48*, 441–449.

Nisbett, R. E. (2003). *The geography of thought: How Asians and Westerners think differently . . . and why.* New York: Free Press.

Nisbett, R. E. (2009). *Intelligence and how to get it: Why schools and cultures count.* New York: W.W. Norton.

Nisbett, R. E., & Cohen, D. (1996). *Culture of honor: The psychology of violence in the South.* Boulder, CO: Westview Press.

Nisbett, R. E., & Masuda, T. (2003). Culture and point of view. *Proceedings of the National Academy of Sciences, 100*, 11163–11170.

Nisbett, R. E., & Ross, L. (1980). *Human inference: Strategies and shortcomings of human judgment.* Englewood Cliffs, NJ: Prentice Hall.

Nisbett, R. E., & Wilson, T. D. (1977). Telling more than we can know: Verbal reports on mental processes. *Psychological Review, 84*, 231–259.

Nisbett, R. E., Caputo, C., Legant, P., & Marecek, J. (1973). Behavior as seen by the actor and by the observer. *Journal of Personality and Social Psychology, 27*, 154–164.

Nisbett, R. E., Fong, G. T., Lehman, D. R., & Cheng, P. W. (1987). Teaching reasoning. *Science, 238*, 625–631.

Nisbett, R. E., Peng, K., Choi, I., & Norenzayan, A. (2001). Culture and systems of thought: Holistic vs. analytic cognition. *Psychological Review, 108*, 291–310.

Nixon, R. M. (1990). *In the arena: A memoir of victory, defeat, and renewal.* New York: Simon & Schuster.

Noar, S. M., Benac, C. N., & Harris, M. S. (2007). Does tailoring matter? Meta-analytic review of tailored print health behavior change interventions. *Psychological Bulletin, 133*, 673–693.

Nolan, J., Schultz, P., Cialdini, R., Goldstein, N., & Griskevicius, V. (2008). Normative social influence is underdetected. *Personality and Social Psychology Bulletin, 34*, 913–923.

Nordgren, L. F., Bos, M. W., Dijksterhuis, A. (2011). The best of both worlds: Integrating conscious and unconscious thought best solves complex decisions. *Journal of Experimental Social Psychology, 47*, 509–511.

Norenzayan, A., & Heine, S. J. (2005). Psychological universals: What are they and how can we know? *Psychological Bulletin, 131*, 763–784.

Norenzayan, A., & Nisbett, R. E. (2000). Culture and causal cognition. *Current Direction in Psychological Science, 9*, 132–135.

Norenzayan, A., Choi, I., & Peng, K. (2007). Perception and cognition. In S. Kitayama & D. Cohen (Eds.), *Handbook of cultural psychology* (pp. 569–594). New York: Guilford.

Normand, A., & Croizet, J.-C. (2013). Upward social comparison generates attentional focusing when the dimension of comparison is self-threatening. *Social Cognition, 31*(3), 336–348.

North, A. C., Tarrant, M., & Hargreaves, D. J. (2004). The effects of music on helping behavior: A field study. *Environment and Behavior, 36*, 266–275.

North, M. S., & Fiske, S. T. (2012). An inconvenienced youth? Ageism and its potential intergenerational roots. *Psychological Bulletin, 138*, 982–997.

Norton, M. I., & Sommers, S. R. (2011). Whites see racism as a zero-sum game that they are now losing. *Perspectives on Psychological Science, 6*, 215–218.

Norton, M. I., Frost, J. H., & Ariely, D. (2007). Less is more: The lure of ambiguity, or why familiarity breeds contempt. *Journal of Personality and Social Psychology, 92*, 97–105.

Nosek, B. A., Greenwald, A. G., & Banaji, M. R. (2005). Understanding and using the implicit association test: II. Method variables and construct validity. *Personality and Social Psychology Bulletin, 31*, 166–180.

Nosek, B. A., Greenwald, A. G., & Banaji, M. R. (2007). The Implicit Association Test at 7: A methodological and conceptual review. In J. A. Bargh (Ed.), *Social psychology and the unconscious.* New York: Psychology Press.

Nowak, A., Szamrej, J., & Latané, B. (1990). From private attitude to public opinion: A dynamic theory of social impact. *Psychological Review, 97,* 362–376.

The number of people who say they have no one to confide in has risen. *Washington Post*, p. A3.

Nunes, K. L., Hermann, C. A., & Ratcliffe, K. (2013). Implicit and explicit attitudes toward rape are associated with sexual aggression. *Journal of Interpersonal Violence, 28,* 2657–2675.

O'Brien, D. T., Gallup, A. C., & Wilson, D. S. (2012). Residential mobility and prosocial development within a single city. *American Journal of Community Psychology, 50,* 26–36.

O'Brien, S. (2004, May 21). Researcher: It's not bad apples, it's the barrel. Retrieved January 20, 2005, from CNN.com, www.cnn.com/2004/US/05/21/zimbarbo.access/J

O'Connor, K. M., & Carnevale, P. J. (1997). A nasty but effective negotiation strategy: Misrepresentation of a common-value issue. *Personality and Social Psychology Bulletin, 23,* 504–515.

O'Gorman, R., Wilson, D. S., & Miller, R. R. (2008). An evolved cognitive bias for social norms. *Evolution and Human Behavior, 29,* 71–78.

O'Leary, A. (1990). Stress, emotion, and human immune function. *Psychological Bulletin, 108,* 363–382.

O'Rourke, L. (2008, August 2). Behind the woman behind the bomb. *The New York Times*, Op-ed page.

O'Sullivan, C. S., & Durso, F. T. (1984). Effects of schema-incongruent information on memory for stereotypical attributes. *Journal of Personality and Social Psychology, 47,* 55–70.

Obesity and overweight. (2011). National Center for Health Statistics, Center for Disease Control and Prediction. Retrieved March 13, 2011, from www.cdc.gov/nchs/fastats/overwt.htm

Ochsner, K. (2007). Social cognitive neuroscience: Historical development, core principles, and future promise. In A. W. Kruglanski & E. T. Higgins (Eds.), *Social psychology: Handbook of basic principles* (2nd ed., pp. 39–66). New York: Guilford.

Oettingen, G. (2012). Future thought and behaviour change. *European Review of Social Psychology, 23,* 1–63.

Ofshe, R., & Watters, E. (1994). *Making monsters: False memories, psychotherapy, and sexual hysteria.* New York: Scribner.

Ogloff, J. R. P., & Vidmar, N. (1994). The impact of pretrial publicity on jurors: A study to compare the relative effects of television and print media in a child sex abuse case. *Law and Human Behavior, 18,* 507–525.

Ohbuchi, K., & Sato, K. (1994). Children's reactions to mitigating accounts: Apologies, excuses, and intentionality of harm. *Journal of Social Psychology, 134,* 5–17.

Ohbuchi, K., Ohno, T., & Mukai, H. (1993). Empathy and aggression: Effects of self-disclosure and fearful appeal. *Journal of Social Psychology, 133,* 243–253.

Oikawa, M., Aarts, H., & Oikawa, H. (2011). There is a fire burning in my heart: The role of causal attribution in affect transfer. *Cognition and Emotion, 25*(1), 156–163. doi:10.1080/02699931003680061

Oishi, S. (2014). Socioecological psychology. *Annual Review of Psychology, 65,* 581–609.

Oishi, S., Rothman, A. J., Snyder, M., Su, J., Zehm, K., Hertel, A. W., et al. (2007). The socioecological model of procommunity action: The benefits of residential stability. *Journal of Personality and Social Psychology, 93,* 831–844.

Oishi, S., Schimmack, U., & Colcombe, S. J. (2003). The contextual and systematic nature of life satisfaction judgments. *Journal of Experimental Social Psychology, 39,* 232–247.

Oishi, S., Wyer, R. S., & Colcombe, S. J. (2000). Cultural variation in the use of current life satisfaction to predict the future. *Journal of Personality and Social Psychology, 78,* 434–445.

Oliner, S. P., & Oliner, P. M. (1988). *The altruistic personality: Rescuers of Jews in Nazi Europe.* New York: The Free Press.

Olmsted, L. (2012, April 10). James Bond ditches martinis for beer - 007 fans cry sell out. *Forbes.* Retrieved May 1, 2014, from http://www.forbes.com/sites/larryolmsted/2012/04/10/james-bond-ditches-martinis-for-beer-007-fans-cry-sell-out/

Olson, J. M., Vernon, P. A., Harris, J. A., & Jang, K. L. (2001). The heritability of attitudes: A study of twins. *Journal of Personality and Social Psychology, 80*(6), 845–860.

Olson, J., & Stone, J. (2005). The influence of behavior on attitudes. In D. Albarracín, B. T. Johnson, & M. P. Zanna (Eds.), *The handbook of attitudes* (pp. 223–271). Mahwah, NJ: Erlbaum.

Olson, M. A. (2009). Measures of prejudice. In T. Nelson (Ed.), *The handbook of prejudice, stereotyping, and discrimination.* New York: Psychology Press.

Olson, M. A., & Fazio, R. H. (2004). Reducing the influence of extrapersonal associations on the implicit association test: Personalizing the IAT. *Journal of Personality and Social Psychology, 86,* 653–667.

Olujic, M. (1998). Embodiment of terror: Gendered violence in peacetime and wartime in Croatia and Bosnia-Herzegovina. *Medical Anthropology Quarterly, 12,* 31–50.

Olweus, D. (1991). Bully/victim problems among schoolchildren: Basic facts and effects of a school-based intervention program. In D. Pepler & K. Rubin (Eds.), *The development and treatment of childhood aggression* (pp. 411–448). Hillsdale, NJ: Erlbaum.

Olweus, D. (1996). Bullying at school: Knowledge base and an effective intervention program. In C. Ferris & T. Grisso (Eds.), *Understanding aggressive behavior in children* (pp. 265–276). New York: New York Academy of Sciences.

Olweus, D. (2003). Prevalence estimation of school bullying. *Aggressive Behavior 29,* 239–268.

Olweus, D., & Limber, S. P. (2010). Bullying in school: Evaluation and dissemination of the Olweus Bullying Prevention Program. *American Journal of Orthopsychiatry, 80,* 124–134.

The Ontario Symposium (Vol. 5, pp. 3–39). Hillsdale, NJ: Erlbaum.

Orizio, R. (2003). *Talk of the devil: Encounters with seven dictators.* New York: Walker & Company.

Orvis, B. R., Cunningham, J. D., & Kelley, H. H. (1975). A closer examination of causal inference: The role of consensus, distinctiveness, and consistency information. *Journal of Personality and Social Psychology, 32,* 605–616.

Oskamp, S. (2000). A sustainable future for humanity? How can psychology help? *American Psychologist, 55,* 496–508.

Oskamp, S., Burkhardt, R. I., Schultz, P. W., Hurin, S., & Zelezny, L. (1998). Predicting three dimensions of residential curbside recycling: An observational study. *Journal of Environmental Education, 29,* 37–42.

Osofsky, M. J., Bandura, A., & Zimbardo, P. G. (2005). The role of moral disengagement in the execution process. *Law and Human Behavior, 29,* 371–393.

Ostrom, T., & Sedikides, C. (1992). Out-group homogeneity effects in natural and minimal groups. *Psychological Bulletin, 112,* 536–552.

Ostrov, J. M., Woods, K. E., Jansen, E. A., Casas, J. F., & Crick, N. R. (2004). An observational study of delivered and received aggression, gender, and social-psychological adjustment in preschool. *Early Childhood Research Quarterly, 19,* 355–371.

Oyserman, D., & Lee, S. (2008). Does culture influence what and how we think? Effects of priming individualism and collectivism. *Psychological Bulletin, 134,* 311–342.

Pachur, T., Hertwig, R., & Steinmann, F. (2012). How do people judge risks: Availability heuristic, affect heuristic, or both? *Journal of Experimental Psychology: Applied, 18,* 314–330.

Packer, D. J. (2008). Identifying systematic disobedience in Milgram's obedience experiments: A meta-analytic review. *Perspectives on Psychological Science, 3,* 301–304.

Packer, D. J. (2009). Avoiding groupthink: Whereas weakly identified members remain silent, strongly identified members dissent about collective problems. *Psychological Science, 20*(5), 546–548. doi:10.1111/j.1467-9280.2009.02333.x

Page, S. (2008). *The difference: How the power of diversity creates better groups, firms, schools, and societies.* Princeton, NJ: Princeton University Press.

Palfrey, J., Boyd, D., & Sacco, D. (2010). *Enhancing child safety and online technologies.* The Berkman Center for Internet & Society at Harvard University. Durham, NC: Carolina Academic Press. Available online http://www.cap-press.com/pdf/1997.pdf

Palmer, J., & Loveland, J. (2008). The influence of group discussion on performance judgments: Rating accuracy, contrast effects, and halo. *Journal of Psychology: Interdisciplinary and Applied, 142,* 117–130.

Panksepp, J., & Panksepp, J. (2000). The seven sins of evolutionary psychology. *Evolution and Cognition, 6,* 108–131.

Parish, A. R., & de Waal, F. B. M. (2000). The other closest living relative: How bonobos (*pan paniscus*) challenge traditional assumptions about females, dominance, inter- and intrasexual interactions and hominid evolution. *Proceedings of the New York Academy of Sciences, 907,* 97–113.

Parish, A. R., de Waal, F. B. M., & Haig, D. (2000). The other "closest living relative": How bonobos (*Pan paniscus*) challenge traditional assumptions about females, dominance, intra- and intersexual interactions, and hominid evolution. *Annals of the New York Academy of Sciences, 907,* 97–113.

Park, B., & Rothbart, M. (1982). Perception of outgroup homogeneity and levels of social categorization: Memory for the subordinate attributes of in-group and out-group members. *Journal of Personality and Social Psychology, 42,* 1051–1068.

Park, C. L. (2010). Making sense of the meaning literature: An integrative review of meaning making and its effects on adjustment to stressful life events. *Psychological Bulletin, 136,* 257–301.

Park, H. S., & Smith, S. W. (2007). Distinctiveness and influence of subjective norms, personal descriptive and injunctive norms, and societal descriptive and injunctive norms on behavioural intent: A case of two behaviours critical to organ donation. *Human Communication Research, 33,* 194–218.

Parkinson, B. (2013). Contextualizing facial activity. *Emotion Review, 5,* 97–103.

Pascual, A., & Guéguen, N. (2005). Foot-in-the-door and door-in-the-face: A comparative meta-analytic study. *Psychological Reports, 96,* 122–128.

Pascual, A., Guéguen, N., Pujos, S., & Felonneau, M. (2013). Foot-in-the-door and problematic requests: A field experiment. *Social Influence, 8,* 46–53.

Patel, R., & Parmentier, M. J. C. (2005). The persistence of traditional gender roles in the information technology sector: A study of female engineers in India. *Information Technologies and International Development, 2,* 29–46.

Paterson, H. M., Whittle, K., & Kemp, R. I. (2014). Detrimental effects of post-incident debriefing on memory and psychological responses. *Journal of Police and Criminal Psychology.* Advance online publication. doi:10.1007/s11896-014-9141-6

Patrick, C. J., & Iacono, W. G. (1989). Psychopathy, threat, and polygraph test accuracy. *Journal of Applied Psychology, 74,* 347–355.

Patterson, A. (1974, September). *Hostility catharsis: A naturalistic quasi-experiment.* Paper presented at the annual meeting of the American Psychological Association, New Orleans.

Paulus, P. B., McCain, G., & Cox, V. (1981). Prison standards: Some pertinent data on crowding. *Federal Probation, 15,* 48–54.

Payne, B. K. (2001). Prejudice and perception: The role of automatic and controlled processes in misperceiving a weapon. *Journal of Personality and Social Psychology, 81,* 181–192.

Payne, B. K. (2006). Weapon bias: Split-second decisions and unintended stereotyping. *Current Directions in Psychological Science, 15,* 287–291.

Payne, B. K., & Gawronski, B. (2010). A history of implicit social cognition: Where is it coming from? Where is it now? Where is it going? In B. Gawronski & B. K. Payne (Eds.), *Handbook of implicit social cognition: Measurement, theory, and applications* (pp. 1–15). New York: Guilford.

Payne, B. K., Burkley, M. A., & Stokes, M. B. (2008). Why do implicit and explicit attitude tests diverge? The role of structural fit. *Journal of Personality and Social Psychology, 94,* 16–31.

Peabody, D. (1985). *National characteristics.* Cambridge, England: Cambridge University Press.

Peace in the Middle East may be impossible: Lee D. Ross on naive realism and conflict resolution. *American Psychological Society Observer, 17,* 9–11.

Pechmann, C., & Knight, S. J. (2002). An experimental investigation of the joint effects of advertising and peers on adolescents' beliefs and intentions about cigarette consumption. *Journal of Consumer Research, 29,* 5–19.

Pedersen, W. C., Vasquez, E. A., Bartholow, B. D., Grosvenor, M., & Truong, A. (2014). Are you insulting me? Exposure to alcohol primes increases aggression following ambiguous provocation. *Personality and Social Psychology Bulletin, 40,* 1037–1049.

Pelonero, C. (2014). *Kitty Genovese: A true account of a public murder and its private consequences.* New York: Skyhorse Publishing.

Peltokorpi, V. (2008). Transactive memory systems. *Review of General Psychology, 12*(4), 378–394. doi:10.1037/1089-2680.12.4.378

Pennebaker, J. W. (1990). *Opening up: The healing powers of confiding in others.* New York: Morrow.

Pennebaker, J. W. (1997). Writing about emotional experiences as a therapeutic process. *Psychological Science, 8,* 162–166.

Pennebaker, J. W. (2001). Dealing with a traumatic experience immediately after it occurs. *Advances in Mind-Body Medicine, 17,* 160–162.

Pennebaker, J. W. (2002). Writing, social processes, and psychotherapy: From past to future. In S. J. Lepore & J. M. Smyth (Eds.), *The writing cure: How expressive writing promotes health and emotional well-being.* Washington, DC: American Psychological Association.

Pennebaker, J. W. (2004). Theories, therapies, and taxpayers: On the complexities of the expressive writing paradigm. *Clinical Psychology: Science and Practice, 11,* 138–142.

Pennebaker, J. W., & Beale, S. K. (1986). Confronting a traumatic event: Toward an understanding of inhibition and disease. *Journal of Abnormal Psychology, 95,* 274–281.

Pennebaker, J. W., & Francis, M. E. (1996). Cognitive, emotional, and language processes in disclosure. *Cognition and Emotion, 10,* 601–626.

Pennebaker, J. W., & Sanders, D. Y. (1976). American graffiti: Effects of authority and reactance arousal. *Personality and Social Psychology Bulletin, 2,* 264–267.

Pennebaker, J. W., Barger, S. D., & Tiebout, J. (1989). Disclosure of traumas and health among Holocaust survivors. *Psychosomatic Medicine, 51,* 577–589.

Pennebaker, J. W., Colder, M., & Sharp, L. K. (1990). Accelerating the coping process. *Journal of Personality and Social Psychology, 58,* 528–537.

Penner, L. A. (2000). The causes of sustained volunteerism: An interactionist perspective. *Journal of Social Issues, 58,* 447–467.

Penner, L. A. (2004). Volunteerism and social problems: Making things better or worse? *Journal of Social Issues, 60*(3), 645–666.

Penner, L. A., & Orom, H. (2010). Enduring goodness: A person-by-situation perspective on prosocial behavior. In M. Mikulincer & P. R. Shaver (Eds.), *Prosocial motives, emotions, and behavior: The better angels of our nature* (pp. 55–72). Washington, DC: American Psychological Association. doi:10.1037/12061-003

Penner, L. A., Dovidio, J. F., Piliavin, J. A., & Schroeder, D. A. (2005). Prosocial behavior: Multilevel perspectives. *Annual Review of Psychology, 56,* 365–392.

Pennington, J., & Schlenker, B. R. (1999). Accountability for consequential decisions: Justifying ethical judgments to audiences. *Personality and Social Psychology Bulletin, 25,* 1067–1081.

Pennington, N., & Hastie, R. (1988). Explanation-based decision making: Effects of memory

structure on judgment. *Journal of Experimental Psychology: Learning, Memory, and Cognition, 14,* 521–533.

Pennington, N., & Hastie, R. (1990). Practical implications of psychological research on juror and jury decision making. *Personality and Social Psychology Bulletin, 16,* 90–105.

Perkins, H. W. (2007). Misperceptions of peer drinking norms in Canada: Another look at the "reign of error" and its consequences among college students. *Addictive Behaviors, 32,* 2645–2656.

Perkins, H., Haines, M. P., & Rice, R. (2005). Misperceiving the college drinking norm and related problems: A nationwide study of exposure to prevention information, perceived norms and student alcohol misuse. *Journal of Studies on Alcohol and Drugs, 66,* 470–478.

Perlstein, L. (1999, November 14). The sweet rewards of learning: Teachers motivate students with tokens for fries and candy. *Washington Post,* pp. A1, A14.

Perrett, D. I., May, K. A., & Yoshikawa, S. (1994). Facial shape and judgments of female attractiveness. *Nature, 368,* 239–242.

Perry, G. (2013). *Behind the shock machine: The untold story of the notorious Milgram psychology experiments.* New York: New Press.

Persuasion: Insights from the self-validation hypothesis. In M. P. Zanna (Ed.), *Advances in experimental social psychology* (Vol. 41, pp. 69–118). New York: Elsevier.

Peters, J. M., Avol, E., Gauderman, W. J., Linn, W. S., Navidi, W., London, S. J., Margolis, H., Rappaport, E., Vora, H., Gong, H. Jr., & Thomas, D. C. (1999). A study of twelve Southern California communities with differing levels and types of air pollution: II. Effects on pulmonary function. *American Journal of Respiratory and Critical Care Medicine, 159,* 768–775.

Peterson, A. A., Haynes, G. A., & Olson, J. M. (2008). Self-esteem differences in the effects of hypocrisy induction on behavioral intentions in the health domain. *Journal of Personality, 76,* 305–322.

Peterson, R. D., & Bailey, W. C. (1988). Murder and capital punishment in the evolving context of the post-Furman era. *Social Forces, 66,* 774–807.

Petrie, K. J., Booth, R. J., & Pennebaker, J. W. (1998). The immunological effects of thought suppression. *Journal of Personality and Social Psychology, 75,* 1264–1272.

Petroselli, D. M., & Knobler, P. (1998). *Triumph of justice: Closing the book on the Simpson saga.* New York: Crown.

Pettigrew, T. F. (1958). Personality and sociocultural factors and intergroup attitudes: A cross-national comparison. *Journal of Conflict Resolution, 2,* 29–42.

Pettigrew, T. F. (1969). Racially separate or together? *Journal of Social Issues, 25,* 43–69.

Pettigrew, T. F. (1979). The ultimate attribution error: Extending Allport's cognitive analysis of prejudice. *Personality and Social Psychology Bulletin, 5,* 461–476.

Pettigrew, T. F. (1985). New Black-White patterns: How best to conceptualize them? *Annual Review of Sociology, 11,* 329–346.

Pettigrew, T. F. (1989). The nature of modern racism in the United States. *Revue Internationale de Psychologie Sociale, 2,* 291–303.

Pettigrew, T. F. (in press). Final reflections. In U. Wagner, L. Tropp, G. Finchilescu, & C. Tredoux (Eds.), *Emerging research directions for improving intergroup relations: Building on the legacy of Thomas F. Pettigrew.* Oxford, England: Blackwell.

Pettigrew, T. F., & Tropp, L. R. (2006). A meta-analytic test of intergroup contact theory. *Journal of Personality and Social Psychology, 90,* 751–783.

Pettigrew, T. F., Jackson, J. S., Brika, J. B., Lemaine, G., Meertens, R. W., Wagner, U., & Zick, A. (1998). Outgroup prejudice in Western Europe. *European Review of Social Psychology, 8,* 241–273.

Petty, R. E. (1995). Attitude change. In A. Tesser (Ed.), *Advanced social psychology* (pp. 195–255). New York: McGraw-Hill.

Petty, R. E., & Briñol, P. (2012). The elaboration likelihood model. In P. A. M. Van Lange, A.

Kruglanski, & E. T. Higgins (Eds.), *Handbook of theories of social psychology* (Vol. 1, pp. 224–245). London: Sage.

Petty, R. E., & Briñol, P. (2015). Emotion and persuasion: Cognitive and meta-cognitive processes impact attitudes. *Cognition and Emotion, 1.*

Petty, R. E., & Brock, T. C. (1981). Thought disruption and persuasion: Assessing the validity of attitude change experiments. In R. E. Petty, T. M. Ostrom, & T. C. Brock (Eds.), *Cognitive responses in persuasion* (pp. 55–79). Hillsdale, NJ: Erlbaum.

Petty, R. E., & Cacioppo, J. T. (1986). *Communication and persuasion: Central and peripheral routes to attitude change.* New York: Springer-Verlag.

Petty, R. E., & Krosnick, J. A. (2014). *Attitude strength: Antecedents and consequences.* New York: Psychology Press.

Petty, R. E., & Wegener, D. T. (1999). The elaboration likelihood model: Current status and controversies. In S. Chaiken & Y. Trope (Eds.), *Dual-process theories in social psychology* (pp. 41–72). New York: Guilford Press.

Petty, R. E., & Wegener, D. T. (1999). The elaboration likelihood model: Current status and controversies. In S. Chaiken & Y. Trope (Eds.), *Dual-process theories in social psychology* (pp. 37–72). New York: Guilford Press.

Petty, R. E., & Wegener, D. T. (2014). Thought systems, argument quality, and persuasion. In R. S. Wyer, Jr., & T. K. Srull (Eds.), *Advances in social cognition* (Vol. IV, pp. 147–161). New York: Psychology Press.

Petty, R. E., Barden, J., & Wheeler, S. C. (2009). The Elaboration Likelihood Model of persuasion: Developing health promotions for sustained behavioral change. In R. J. DiClemente, R. A. Crosby, & M. C. Kegler (Eds.), *Emerging theories in health promotion practice and research* (2nd ed., pp. 185–214). San Francisco: Jossey-Bass.

Petty, R. E., Cacioppo, J. T., & Goldman, R. (1981). Personal involvement as a determinant of argument-based persuasion. *Journal of Personality and Social Psychology, 41,* 847–855.

Petty, R. E., Cacioppo, J. T., Strathman, A. J., & Priester, J. R. (2005). To think or not to think: Exploring two routes to persuasion. In T. C. Brock & M. C. Green (Eds.), *Persuasion: Psychological insights and perspectives.* Thousand Oaks, CA: Sage Publications, Inc.

Pezdek, K. (2012). Fallible eyewitness memory and identification. In B. L. Cutler (Ed.), *Conviction of the innocent: Lessons from psychological research* (pp. 105–124). Washington, DC: American Psychological Association.

Pezdek, K., & Banks, W. P. (Eds.). (1996). *The recovered memory/false memory debate.* San Diego, CA: Academic Press.

Phelan, J. E., & Rudman, L. A. (2010). Prejudice toward female leaders: Backlash effects and women's impression management dilemma. *Social and Personality Psychology Compass, 4*(10), 807–820. doi:10.1111/j.1751-9004.2010.00306.x

Phillip, A. (2014, April 29). The latest social media "challenge" is dangerous, but probably won't be around for long. *Washington Post.* Retrieved May 26, 2014, from www.washingtonpost.com/news/post-nation/wp/2014/04/29/the-latest-social-media-challenge-is-dangerous-but-probably-wont-be-around-for-long

Phillips, A. G., & Silva, P. J. (2005). Self-awareness and the emotional consequences of self-discrepancies. *Personality & Social Psychology Bulletin, 31,* 703–713.

Phillips, K. W., Mannix, E. A., Neale, M. A., & Gruenfeld, D. H. (2004). Diverse groups and information sharing: The effects of congruent ties. *Journal of Experimental Social Psychology, 40,* 495–510.

Picazo, C., Gamero, N., Zornoza, A., & Peiró, J. M. (2014). Testing relations between group cohesion and satisfaction in project teams: A cross-level and cross-lagged approach. *European Journal of Work and Organizational Psychology.* doi:10.1080/1359432X.2014.894979

Pickel, K. (2007). Remembering and identifying menacing perpetrators: Exposure to violence and the weapon focus effect. In R. C. L. Lindsay, D. F. Ross, J. D. Read, & M. P. Toglia (Eds.), *The handbook of eyewitness psychology*, Vol. II: *Memory for people* (pp. 339–360). Mahwah, NJ: Erlbaum.

Pickett, C. L., & Gardner, W. L. (2005). The social monitoring system: Enhanced sensitivity to social cues as an adaptive response to social exclusion. In K. D. Williams, J. P. Forgas, J. P., & W. von Hippel (Eds.), *The social outcast: Ostracism, social exclusion, rejection, and bullying* (pp. 213–226). New York: Psychology Press.

Pickett, C. L., Silver, M. D., & Brewer, M. B. (2002). The impact of assimilation and differentiation needs on perceived group importance and judgments of ingroup size. *Personality and Social Psychology Bulletin, 28*, 546–558.

Piliavin, I. M., Piliavin, J. A., & Rodin, J. (1975). Costs, diffusion, and the stigmatized victim. *Journal of Personality and Social Psychology, 32*, 429–438.

Piliavin, J. A. (2008). Long-term benefits of habitual helping: Doing well by doing good. In B. A. Sullivan, M. Snyder, & J. L. Sullivan (Eds.), *Cooperation: The political psychology of effective human interaction* (pp. 241–258). Malden, MA: Blackwell.

Piliavin, J. A. (2009). Altruism and helping: The evolution of a field: The 2008 Cooley-Mead Presentation. *Social Psychology Quarterly, 72*(3), 209–225. doi:10.1177/019027250907200305

Piliavin, J. A. (2010). Volunteering across the life span: Doing well by doing good. In S. Stürmer & M. Snyder (Eds.), *The psychology of prosocial behavior: Group processes, intergroup relations, and helping* (pp. 157–172). Oxford, UK: Wiley-Blackwell.

Piliavin, J. A., & Charng, H. (1990). Altruism: A review of recent theory and research. *Annual Review of Sociology, 16*, 27–65.

Piliavin, J. A., & Piliavin, I. M. (1972). The effect of blood on reactions to a victim. *Journal of Personality and Social Psychology, 23*, 253–261.

Piliavin, J. A., Dovidio, J. F., Gaertner, S. L., & Clark, R. D., III. (1981). *Emergency intervention.* New York: Academic Press.

Pinel, E. C., & Long, A. E. (2012). When I's meet: Sharing subjective experience with someone from the outgroup. *Personality and Social Psychology Bulletin, 38*, 296–307.

Pinel, E. C., Long, A. E., Landau, M. J., Alexander, K., & Pyszczynski, T. (2006). Seeing I to I: A pathway to interpersonal connectedness. *Journal of Personality and Social Psychology, 90*, 243–257.

Pinker, S. (2011). *The better angels of our nature.* New York: Penguin.

Pitt, R. N. (2010). "Killing the messenger": Religious Black gay men's neutralization of anti-gay religious messages. *Journal for the Scientific Study of Religion, 49*, 56–72.

Plant, E. A., & Devine, P. G. (1998). Internal and external motivation to respond without prejudice. *Journal of Personality and Social Psychology, 75*, 811–832.

Plant, E. A., & Devine, P. G. (2009). The active control of prejudice: Unpacking the intentions guiding control efforts. *Journal of Personality and Social Psychology, 96*, 640–652.

Plant, E. A., & Peruche, B. M. (2005). The consequences of race for police officers' responses to criminal suspects. *Psychological Science, 16*, 180–183.

Plastic oceans. (2008, November 13). Spencer Michels, reporter. *The Newshour with Jim Lehrer,* Public Broadcasting System.

Pleban, R., & Tesser, A. (1981). The effects of relevance and quality of another's performance on interpersonal closeness. *Social Psychology Quarterly, 44*, 278–285.

PollingReport.com. (2003, July 31). President Bush: Job ratings. Retrieved from www.pollingreport.com/BushJob.htm

Pomfret, J. (2005, November 20). Student turns body into billboard as the Shirtless Guy. *Washington Post,* p. A2.

Pope, H. G., Jr., Olivardia, R., Gruber, A. J., & Borowiecki, J. (1999). Evolving ideals of male body image as seen through action toys. *International Journal of Eating Disorders, 26*, 65–72.

Pope, H. G., Jr., Phillips, K. A., & Olivardia, R. (2000). *The Adonis complex: The secret crisis of male body obsession.* New York: Freeman.

Population Growth Rate. (n.d.). The World Bank Group. Retrieved July 15, 2014, from http://www.worldbank.org/depweb/english/modules/social/pgr/print.html

Posada, S., & Colell, M. (2007). Another gorilla (Gorilla gorilla gorilla) recognizes himself in a mirror. *American Journal of Primatology, 69*(5), 576–583.

Postmes, T., & Spears, R. (1998). Deindividuation and antinormative behavior: A meta-analysis. *Psychological Bulletin, 123*, 238–259.

Powledge, F. (1991). *Free at last? The civil rights movement and the people who made it.* Boston: Little, Brown.

Pratarelli, M. E. (2012). When human nature confronts the need for a global environmental ethics. *Journal of Social, Evolutionary, and Cultural Psychology, 6*, 384–403.

Pratkanis, A. R. (1992). The cargo-cult science of subliminal persuasion. *Skeptical Inquirer, 16*, 260–272.

Pratkanis, A. R., Greenwald, A. G., Leippe, M. R., & Baumgardner, M. H. (1988). In search of reliable persuasion eàects: III. The sleeper eàect is dead: long live the sleeper eàect. *Journal of Personality and Social Psychology, 54*, 203–218.

Predicting sporting events: Accuracy as a function of reasons analysis, expertise, and task difficulty. Unpublished manuscript, Research Institute on Addictions, Buffalo, NY.

Preston, J. L., Ritter, R. S., & Hernandez, J. I. (2010). Principles of religious prosociality: A review and reformulation. *Social and Personality Psychology Compass, 4*(8), 574–590. doi:10.1111/j.1751-9004.2010.00286.x

Prevalence of overweight and obesity among adults: United States, 2003–2004. National Center for Health Statistics. Retrieved December 30, 2008, from www.cdc.gov/nchs/products/pubs/pubd/hestats/overweight/overwght_adult_03.htm

Prince, M. A., & Carey, K. B. (2010). The malleability of injunctive norms among college students. *Addictive Behaviors, 35*, 940–947.

Pronin, E., & Kugler, M. B. (2011). People believe they have more free will than others. *Proceedings of the National Academy of Sciences.*

Pronin, E., Berger, J., & Moluki, S. (2007). Alone in a crowd of sheep: Asymmetric perceptions of conformity and their roots in an introspection illusion. *Journal of Personality and Social Psychology, 92*, 585–595. doi:10.1037/0022-3514.92.4.585

Pronin, E., Gilovich, T., & Ross, L. (2004). Objectivity in the eye of the beholder: Divergent perceptions of bias in self versus others. *Psychological Review, 111*, 781–799.

Pronin, E., Lin, D. Y., & Ross, L. (2002). The bias blind spot: Perceptions of bias in self versus others. *Personality and Social Psychology Bulletin, 28*, 369–381.

Proost, K., Schreurs, B., De Witte, K., & Derous, E. (2010). Ingratiation and self-promotion in the selection interview: The effects of using single tactics or a combination of tactics on interviewer judgments. *Journal of Applied Social Psychology, 40*(9), 2155–2169. doi:10.1111/j.1559-1816.2010.00654.x

Prot, S., Gentile, D. A., Anderson, C. A., Suzuki, K., Swing, E., Lim, K. M., et al. (2014). Long-term relations among prosocial-media use, empathy, and prosocial behavior. *Psychological Science, 25*(2), 358–368.

Pryor, J. B., Reeder, G. D., & Monroe, A. E. (2012). The infection of bad company: Stigma by association. *Journal of Personality and Social Psychology, 102*, 224–241.

Przybylski, A. K., & Weinsten, N. (2013). Can you connect with me now? How the presence of mobile communication technologies influences face-to-face conversation quality. *Journal of Social and Personal Relationships, 30*, 237–246.

Puente, M. (2005, March 2). Rent this space: Bodies double as billboards. USA Today.com. Retrieved December 23, 2005, from www.usatoday.com/life/lifestyle/2005-03-02-body-ads_x.htm

Pulfrey, C., Darnon, C., & Butera, F. (2013). Autonomy and task performance: Explaining the impact of grades on intrinsic motivation. *Journal of Educational Psychology, 105*, 39–57. doi:10.1037/a0029376

Purdham, T. S. (1997, March 28). Tapes left by cult suggest comet was the sign to die. *The New York Times,* p. A2.

Putnam, R. D. (2000). *Bowling alone: The collapse and revival of American community.* New York: Simon & Schuster.

Putnam, R. D., & Campbell, D. E. (2010). *American grace: How religion divides and unites us.* New York, NY: Simon & Schuster.

Pyszczynski, T., Greenberg, J., Solomon, S., Arndt, J., & Schimel, J. (2004). Why do people need self-esteem? A theoretical and empirical review. *Psychological Bulletin, 130*, 435–468.

Qin, J., Kimel, S., Kitayama, S., Wang, X., Yang, X., & Han, S. (2011). How choice modifies preference: Neural correlates of choice justification. *NeuroImage, 55*, 240–246.

Qin, J., Ogle, C., & Goodman, G. (2008). Adults' memories of childhood: True and false reports. *Journal of Experimental Psychology: Applied, 14*, 373–391.

Quattrone, G. A. (1982). Behavioral consequences of attributional bias. *Social Cognition, 1*, 358–378.

Quattrone, G. A. (1986). On the perception of a group's variability. In S. Worchel & W. G. Austin (Eds.), *Psychology of intergroup relations* (2nd ed.). Chicago: Nelson-Hall.

Quattrone, G. A., & Jones, E. E. (1980). The perception of variability within ingroups and outgroups: Implications for the law of small numbers. *Journal of Personality and Social Psychology, 38*, 141–152.

Quick stats binge drinking. (2008). Department of Health and Human Services, Center for Disease Control and Prevention. Retrieved December 30, 2008, from www.cdc.gov/alcohol/quickstats/binge_drinking.htm

Quinn, A., & Schlenker, B. R. (2002). Can accountability produce independence? Goals as determinants of the impact of accountability on conformity. *Personality and Social Psychology Bulletin, 28*, 472–483.

Quoidbach, J., Dunn, E. W., Petrides, K. V., & Mikolajczak, M. (2010). Money giveth, money taketh away: The dual effect of wealth on happiness. *Psychological Science, 21*(6), 759–763.

Rajaram, S., & Pereira-Pasarin, L. P. (2010). Collaborative memory: Cognitive research and theory. *Perspectives on Psychological Science, 5*(6), 649–663. doi:10.1177/1745691610388763

Ramirez, A. (2005, December 2). New Yorkers take a tribute standing up. *The New York Times,* p. B1.

Ramírez-Esparza, N., Chung, C. K., Sierra-Otero, G., & Pennebaker, J. W. (2012). Cross-cultural constructions of self-schemas: Americans and Mexicans. *Journal of Cross-Cultural Psychology, 43*(2), 233–250. doi:10.1177/0022202110385231

Ramsey, S. J. (1981). The kinesics of femininity in Japanese women. *Language Sciences, 3,* 104–123.

Rand, D. G., & Nowak, M. A. (2013). Human cooperation. *Trends in Cognitive Sciences, 17*(8), 413–425. doi:10.1016/j.tics.2013.06.003

Ranganath, K. A., & Nosek, B. A. (2008). Implicit attitude generalization occurs immediately, explicit attitude generalization takes time. *Psychological Science, 19*, 249–254.

Rapoport, A., & Chammah, A. M. (1965). *Prisoner's dilemma: A study in conflict and cooperation.* Ann Arbor: University of Michigan Press.

Raps, C. S., Peterson, C., Jonas, M., & Seligman, M. E. P. (1982). Patient behavior in hospitals: Helplessness, reactance, or both? *Journal of Personality and Social Psychology, 42*, 1036–1041.

Rasinzki, H. M., Geers, A. L., & Czopp, A. M. (2013). "I guess what he said wasn't that bad": Dissonance in nonconfronting targets of prejudice. *Personality and Social Psychology Bulletin, 39*, 856–869.

Raskin, R., & Terry, H. (1988). A principle-components analysis of the Narcissistic Personality Inventory and further evidence of its construct validity. *Journal of Personality and Social Psychology, 54*, 890–902.

Ratelle, C. F., Carbonneau, N., Vallerand, R. J., & Mageau, G. (2013). Passion in the romantic sphere: A look at relational outcomes. *Motivation and Emotion, 37*, 106–120.

Ratliff, K. A., & Oishi, S. (2013). Gender differences in implicit self-esteem following a romantic partner's success or failure. *Journal of Personality and Social Psychology, 105*(4), 688–702. doi:10.1037/a0033769

Reading, R. (2008). Effectiveness of universal school-based programs to prevent violent and aggressive behaviour: A systematic review. *Child: Care, Health and Development, 34,* 139.

Reardon, S. (2011, April 27). Preventable chronic diseases are now the world's biggest killers. *ScienceInsider.* Retrieved August 19, 2014, from http://news.sciencemag.org/2011/04/preventable-chronic-diseases-are-now-worlds-biggest-killers

Rector, M., & Neiva, E. (1996). Communication and personal relations in Brazil. In W. B. Gudykunst, S. Ting-Toomey, & T. Nishida (Eds.), *Communication in personal relationships across cultures* (pp. 156–173). Thousand Oaks, CA: Sage.

Redlawsk, D. P. (2002). Hot cognition or cool consideration? Testing the effects of motivated reasoning on political decision making. *Journal of Politics, 64,* 1021–1044.

Regan, P. C., & Berscheid, E. (1997). Gender differences in characteristics desired in a potential sexual and marriage partner. *Journal of Psychology and Human Sexuality, 9,* 25–37.

Regan, P. C., & Berscheid, E. (1999). *Lust: What we know about human sexual desire.* Thousand Oaks, CA: Sage.

Reid, A. E., & Aiken, L. S. (2013). Correcting injunctive norm misperceptions motivates behavior change: A randomized controlled sun protection intervention. *Health Psychology, 32,* 551–560.

Reis, H. T., & Gosling, S. D. (2010). Social psychological methods outside the laboratory. In S. T. Fiske, D. T. Gilbert, & G. Lindzey (Eds.), *Handbook of social psychology* (5th ed., Vol. 1, pp. 82–114). Hoboken, NJ: John Wiley.

Reis, H. T., & Judd, C. M. (Eds.). (2000). *Handbook of research methods in social and personality psychology.* New York: Cambridge University Press.

Reis, H. T., & Patrick, B. C. (1996). Attachment and intimacy: Component processes. In E. T. Higgins & A. W. Kruglanski (Eds.), *Social psychology: Handbook of basic principles* (pp. 523–563). New York: Guilford Press.

Reis, H. T., Maniaci, M. R., Caprariello, P. A., Eastwick, P. W., & Finkel, E. J. (2011). Familiarity does indeed promote attraction in live interaction. *Journal of Personality and Social Psychology, 101,* 557–570.

Reis, H. T., Wheeler, L., Speigel, N., Kernis, M. H., Nezlek, J., & Perri, M. (1982). Physical attractiveness in social interaction: 2. Why does appearance affect social experience? *Journal of Personality and Social Psychology, 43,* 979–996.

Reisman, J. M. (1990). Intimacy in same-sex friendships. *Sex Roles, 23,* 65–82.

Reiter, S. M., & Samuel, W. (1980). Littering as a function of prior litter and the presence or absence of prohibitive signs. *Journal of Applied Social Psychology, 10,* 45–55.

Renaud, J. M., & McConnell, A. R. (2002). Organization of the self-concept and the suppression of self-relevant thoughts. *Journal of Experimental Social Psychology, 38,* 79–86.

Renner, M. J., & Mackin, R. S. (1998). A life stress instrument for classroom use. *Teaching of Psychology, 25,* 46–48.

Reno, R. R., Cialdini, R. B., & Kallgren, C. A. (1993). The transsituational influence of social norms. *Journal of Personality and Social Psychology, 64,* 104–112.

Rensink, R. A. (2002). Change detection. *Annual Review of Psychology, 53,* 245–277.

Rentfrow, P. J., & Gosling, S. D. (2006). Message in a ballad: The role of music preferences in interpersonal perception. *Psychological Science, 17,* 236–242.

Rentfrow, P. J., & Gosling, S. D. (2006). Message in a ballad: The role of music preferences in interpersonal perception. *Psychological Science, 17,* 236–242.

Rexrode, C. (2011, November 3). Twitter changes business of celebrity endorsements. *USA Today.*

Retrieved December 22, 2011, from www.usatoday.com/tech/news/story/2011-11-03/celebrity-twitter-endorsements/51058228/1

Rhodes, G. (2006). The evolutionary psychology of facial beauty. *Annual Review of Psychology, 57,* 199–226.

Rhodes, G., Yoshikawa, S., Clark, A., Lee, K., McKay, R., & Akamatsu, S. (2001). Attractiveness of facial averageness and symmetry in non-Western cultures: In search of biologically based standards of beauty. *Perception, 30,* 611–625.

Rhodes, N., & Wood, W. (1992). Self-esteem and intelligence affect influenceability: The mediating role of message reception. *Psychological Bulletin, 111,* 156–171.

Rhodewalt, F., Sanbonmatsu, D. M., Tschanz, B., Feick, D. L., & Waller, A. (1995). Self-handicapping and interpersonal trade-offs: The effects of claimed self-handicaps on observers' performance evaluations and feedback. *Personality and Social Psychology Bulletin, 21,* 1042–1050.

Rholes, W. S., Simpson, J. A., & Friedman, M. (2006). Avoidant attachment and the experience of parenting. *Personality and Social Psychology Bulletin, 32,* 275–285.

Richard, F. D., Bond, C. F., Jr., & Stokes-Zoota, J. J. (2001). 'That's completely obvious . . . and important": Lay judgments of social psychological findings. *Personality and Social Psychology Bulletin, 27,* 497–505.

Richardson, D. S. (2014). Everyday aggression takes many forms. *Psychological Science, 23,* 220–224.

Richardson, D., Hammock, G., Smith, S., & Gardner, W. (1994). Empathy as a cognitive inhibitor of interpersonal aggression. *Aggressive Behavior, 20,* 275–289.

Richmond, V. P., & McCroskey, J. C. (1995). *Nonverbal behavior in interpersonal relations.* Needham Heights, MA: Allyn & Bacon.

Richter, C. P. (1957). On the phenomenon of sudden death in animals and man. *Psychosomatic Medicine, 19,* 191–198.

Riggs, J. M., & Gumbrecht, L. B. (2005). Correspondence bias and American sentiment in the wake of September 11, 2001. *Journal of Applied Social Psychology, 35*(1), 15–28.

Ringelmann, M. (1913). Recherches sur les moteurs animés: Travail de l'homme [Research on driving forces: Human work]. *Annales de l'Institut National Agronomique,* series 2, *12,* 1–40.

Rinolo, R. C., Johnson, K. C., Sherman, T. R., & Misso, J. A. (2006). Hot or not? Do professors perceived as physically attractive receive higher student evaluations? *Journal of General Psychology, 133,* 19–35.

Riordan, C. A. (1978). Equal-status interracial contact: A review and revision of a concept. *International Journal of Intercultural Relations, 2,* 161–185.

Rise, J., Sheeran, P., & Hukkelberg, S. (2010). The role of self-identity in the theory of planned behavior: A meta-analysis. *Journal of Applied Social Psychology, 40*(5), 1085–1105. doi:10.1111/j.1559-1816.2010.00611.x

Risen, J. L., & Gilovich, T. (2007). Target and observer differences in the acceptance of questionable apologies. *Journal of Personality and Social Psychology, 92,* 418–433.

Rivers, I., Chesney, T., & Coyne, I. (2011). Cyberbullying. In C. P. Monks & I. Coyne (Eds.), *Bullying in different contexts* (pp. 211–230). New York: Cambridge University Press.

Robins, R. W., & Beer, J. S. (2001). Positive illusions about the self: Short-term benefits and long-term costs. *Journal of Personality and Social Psychology, 80,* 340–352.

Robins, R. W., & Schriber, R. A. (2009). The self-conscious emotions: How are they experienced, expressed, and assessed? *Social and Personality Psychology Compass, 3,* 887–898.

Robins, R. W., Spranca, M. D., & Mendelson, G. A. (1996). The actor-observer effect revisited: Effects of individual differences and repeated social interactions on actor and observer attributions. *Journal of Personality and Social Psychology, 71,* 375–389.

Rodin, J., & Langer, E. J. (1977). Long-term effects of a control-relevant intervention with the institutional aged. *Journal of Personality and Social Psychology, 35,* 897–902.

Rodrigo, M. F., & Ato, M. (2002). Testing the group polarization hypothesis by using logit models. *European Journal of Social Psychology, 32,* 3–18.

Roepke, S. K., & Grant, I. (2011). Toward a more complete understanding of the effects of personal mastery on cardiometabolic health. *Health Psychology, 30,* 615–632. doi:10.1037/a0023480

Roesch, S. C., & Amirkhan, J. H. (1997). Boundary conditions for self-serving attributions: Another look at the sports pages. *Journal of Applied Social Psychology, 27,* 245–261.

Roese, N. J. (1997). Counterfactual thinking. *Psychological Bulletin, 121,* 133–148.

Roese, N. J., & Jamieson, D. W. (1993). Twenty years of bogus pipeline research: A critical review and meta-analysis. *Psychological Bulletin, 114,* 363–375.

Roese, N. J., & Olson, J. M. (1997). Counterfactual thinking: The intersection of affect and function. In M. P. Zanna (Ed.), *Advances in experimental social psychology* (Vol. 29, pp. 1–59). San Diego, CA: Academic Press.

Rogers, R. (1983). Cognitive and physiological processes in fear appeals and attitude change: A revised theory of protection motivation. In J. T. Cacioppo & R. E. Petty (Eds.), *Social psychophysiology: A sourcebook* (pp. 153–176). New York: Guilford Press.

Rogers, R., & Prentice-Dunn, S. (1981). Deindividuation and anger-mediated interracial aggression: Unmasking regressive racism. *Journal of Personality and Social Psychology, 41,* 63–73.

Rogers, T. B., Kuiper, N. A., & Kirker, W. S. (1977). Self-reference and the encoding of personal information. *Journal of Personality and Social Psychology, 35,* 677–688.

Rohrer, J. H., Baron, S. H., Hoffman, E. L., & Swander, D. V. (1954). The stability of autokinetic judgments. *Journal of Abnormal and Social Psychology, 49,* 595–597.

Roisman, G. I., Clausell, E., Holland, A., Fortuna, K., & Elieff, C. (2008). Adult romantic relationships as contexts of human development: A multimethod comparison of same-sex couples with opposite-sex dating, engaged, and married dyads. *Developmental Psychology, 44,* 91–101.

Romero-Canyas, R., Downey, G., Reddy, K. S., Rodriguez, S., Cavanaugh, T. J., & Pelayo, R. (2010). Paying to belong: When does rejection trigger ingratiation? *Journal of Personality and Social Psychology, 99*(5), 802–823. doi:10.1037/a0020013

Rooney, B. (2012, January 25). Apple tops Exxon as most valuable company. *CNN Money Markets.* Available at http://money.cnn.com/2012/01/25/markets/apple_stock/?hpt=hp_t2

Rosenberg, L. A. (1961). Group size, prior experience, and conformity. *Journal of Abnormal and Social Psychology, 63,* 436–437.

Rosenberg, M. J., Davidson, A. J., Chen, J., Judson, F. N., & Douglas, J. M. (1992). Barrier contraceptives and sexually transmitted diseases in women: A comparison of female-dependent methods and condoms. *American Journal of Public Health, 82,* 669–674.

Rosenblatt, P. C. (1974). Cross-cultural perspectives on attraction. In T. L. Huston (Ed.), *Foundations of interpersonal attraction* (pp. 79–99). New York: Academic Press.

Rosenthal, A. M. (1964). *Thirty-eight witnesses.* New York: McGraw-Hill.

Rosenthal, R. (1994). Interpersonal expectancy effects: A 30-year perspective. *Current Directions in Psychological Science, 3,* 176–179.

Rosenthal, R., & Jacobson, L. (1968/2003). *Pygmalion in the classroom: Teacher expectation and pupils' intellectual development* (revised ed.). Norwalk, CT: Crown..

Rosh, L., Offermann, L. R., & Van Diest, R. (2012). Too close for comfort? Distinguishing between team intimacy and team cohesion. *Human Resource Management Review, 22,* 116–127.

Ross, L. (1977). The intuitive psychologist and his shortcomings: Distortions in the attribution process. In L. Berkowitz (Ed.), *Advances in experimental social psychology* (Vol. 10, pp. 173–220). Orlando, FL: Academic Press.

Ross, L. (1998). Comment on Gilbert. In J. M. Darley & J. Cooper (Eds.), *Attribution and social interaction* (pp. 53–66). Washington, DC: American Psychological Association.

Ross, L. (2010). Dealing with conflict: Experiences and experiments. In M. H. Gonzales, C. Tavris, & J. Aronson (Eds.), *The scientist and the humanist: A festschrift in honor of Elliot Aronson* (pp. 39–66). New York: Psychology Press.

Ross, L., & Nisbett, R. E. (1991). *The person and the situation: Perspectives of social psychology.* New York: McGraw-Hill.

Ross, L., & Ward, A. (1995). Psychological barriers to dispute resolution. In M. P. Zanna (Ed.), *Advances in experimental social psychology* (Vol. 27, pp. 255–304). San Diego, CA: Academic Press.

Ross, L., Amabile, T. M., & Steinmetz, J. L. (1977). Social roles, social control, and biases in social perception. *Journal of Personality and Social Psychology, 35,* 485–494.

Ross, L., Lepper, M. R., & Hubbard, M. (1975). Perseverance in self-perception and social perception: Biased attributional processes in the debriefing paradigm. *Journal of Personality and Social Psychology, 32,* 880–892.

Ross, M., & Wilson, A. E. (2003). Autobiographical memory and conceptions of self: Getting better all the time. *Current Directions in Psychological Science, 12,* 66–69.

Ross, W., & La Croix, J. (1996). Multiple meanings of trust in negotiation theory and research: A literature review and integrative model. *International Journal of Conflict Management, 7,* 314–360.

Rothbaum, F., & Tsang, B. Y.-P. (1998). Lovesongs in the United States and China: On the nature of romantic love. *Journal of Cross-Cultural Psychology, 29,* 306–319.

Rothermund, K., & Wentura, D. (2004). Underlying processes in the Implicit Association Test: Dissociating salience from associations. *Journal of Experimental Psychology: General, 133,* 139–165.

Rotter, J. B. (1966). Generalized expectancies for internal versus external control of reinforcement. *Psychological Monographs, 80,* 1–28 (Whole No. 609).

Rotton, J., & Cohn, E. G. (2004). Outdoor temperature, climate control, and criminal assault: The spatial and temporal ecology of violence. *Environment & Behavior, 36,* 276–306.

Rubin, Z. (1970). Measurement of romantic love. *Journal of Personality and Social Psychology, 16,* 265–273.

Rudman, L. A. (1998). Self-promotion as a risk factor for women: The costs and benefits of counterstereotypical impression management. *Journal of Personality and Social Psychology, 74,* 629–645.

Rudman, L. A., McLean, M. C., & Bunzl, M. (2013). When truth is personally inconvenient, attitudes change: The impact of extreme weather on implicit support for green politicians and explicit climate-change beliefs. *Psychological Science, 24,* 2290–2296.

Rudman, L., Phelan, J., & Heppen, J. (2007). Developmental sources of implicit attitudes. *Personality and Social Psychology Bulletin, 33,* 1700–1713.

Ruiter, R. A. C., Abraham, C., & Kok, G. (2001). Scary warnings and rational precautions: A review of the psychology of fear appeals. *Psychology and Health, 16,* 613–630.

Rule, B. G., Taylor, B. R., & Dobbs, A. R. (1987). Priming effects of heat on aggressive thoughts. *Social Cognition, 5,* 131–143.

Rule, N. O., & Ambady, N. (2010). First impressions of the face: Predicting success. *Social and Personality Psychology Compass, 4,* 506–516.

Rule, N. O., Ambady, N., & Hallett, K. C. (2009). Female sexual orientation is perceived accurately, rapidly, and automatically from the face and its features. *Journal of Experimental Social Psychology, 45,* 1245–1251.

Rule, N. O., Ambady, N., Adams, R. B., Jr., & Macrae, C. N. (2008). Accuracy and awareness in the perception and categorization of male sexual orientation. *Journal of Personality and Social Psychology, 95,* 1019–1028.

Rule, N. O., Krendl, A. C., Ivcevic, Z., & Ambady, N. (2013). Accuracy and consensus in judgments of trustworthiness from faces: Behavioral and neural correlates. *Journal of Personality and Social Psychology, 104,* 409–426.

Rusbult, C. E. (1983). A longitudinal test of the investment model: The development (and deterioration) of satisfaction and commitment in heterosexual involvements. *Journal of Personality and Social Psychology, 45,* 101–117.

Rusbult, C. E. (1987). Responses to dissatisfaction in close relationships: The exit-voice-loyalty-neglect model. In D. Perlman & S. W. Duck (Eds.), *Intimate relationships: Development, dynamics, and deterioration* (pp. 209–237). Newbury Park, CA: Sage.

Rusbult, C. E. (1991). *Commitment processes in close relationships: The investment model.* Paper presented at the annual meeting of the American Psychological Association, San Francisco.

Rusbult, C. E., & Buunk, B. P. (1993). Commitment processes in close relationships: An interdependence analysis. *Journal of Social and Personal Relationships, 10,* 175–204.

Rusbult, C. E., & Martz, J. M. (1995). Remaining in an abusive relationship: An investment model analysis of nonvoluntary dependence. *Personality and Social Psychology Bulletin, 21,* 558–571.

Rusbult, C. E., & Van Lange, P. A. M. (1996). Interdependence processes. In E. T. Higgins & A. W. Kruglanski (Eds.), *Social psychology: Handbook of basic principles* (pp. 564–596). New York: Guilford Press.

Rusbult, C. E., & Zembrodt, I. M. (1983). Responses to dissatisfaction in romantic involvements: A multidimensional scaling analysis. *Journal of Experimental Social Psychology, 19,* 274–293.

Rusbult, C. E., Johnson, D. J., & Morrow, G. D. (1986). Impact of couple patterns of problem solving on distress and nondistress in dating relationships. *Journal of Personal and Social Psychology, 50,* 744–753.

Rusbult, C. E., Martz, J. M., & Agnew, C. R. (1998). The investment model scale: Measuring commitment level, satisfaction level, quality of alternatives, and investment size. *Personal Relationships, 5,* 357–391.

Rusbult, C. E., Olsen, N., Davis, N. L., & Hannon, P. (2001). Commitment and relationship maintenance mechanisms. In J. H. Harvey & A. Wenzel (Eds.), *Close romantic relationships: Maintenance and enhancement* (pp. 87–113). Mahwah, NJ: Erlbaum.

Rusbult, C. E., Yovetich, N. A., & Verette, J. (1996). An interdependence analysis of accommodation processes. In G. J. O. Fletcher & J. Fitness (Eds.), *Knowledge structures in close relationships: A social psychological approach* (pp. 63–90). Mahwah, NJ: Erlbaum.

Rushton, J. P. (1989). Genetic similarity, human altruism, and group selection. *Behavioral and Brain Sciences, 12,* 503–559.

Russell, G. W. (1983). Psychological issues in sports aggression. In J. H. Goldstein (Ed.), *Sports violence* (pp. 157–181). New York: Springer-Verlag.

Rusting, C. L., & Nolen-Hoeksema, S. (1998). Regulating responses of anger: Effects of rumination and distraction on angry mood. *Journal of Personality and Social Psychology, 74,* 790–803.

Ryan, B., Jr. (1991). *It works! How investment spending in advertising pays off.* New York: American Association of Advertising Agencies.

Ryan, M. K., Haslam, S. A., Hersby, M. D., & Bongiorno, R. (2011). Think crisis–think female: The glass cliff and contextual variation in the think manager–think male stereotype. *Journal of Applied Psychology, 96*(3), 470–484. doi:10.1037/a0022133

Ryan, M. K., Haslam, S. A., Hersby, M. D., Kulich, C., & Atkins, C. (2008). Opting out or pushed off the edge? The glass cliff and the precariousness of women's leadership positions. *Social and Personality Psychology Compass, 2,* www.blackwell-compass.com/subject/socialpsychology/

Ryan, R. M., & Deci, E. L. (2000). Intrinsic and extrinsic rewards: Classic definitions and new directions. *Current Educational Psychology, 25,* 54–67.

Rydell, R. J., & Durso, G. R. O. (2012). Can I borrow a feeling? Spillover of negative arousal from inconsistent information during attitude formation diminishes perceptions of well-being. *Journal of Experimental Social Psychology, 48*(2), 575–578. doi:10.1016/j.jesp.2011.10.018

Ryon, H. S., & Gleason, M. E. J. (2014). The role of locus of control in daily life. *Personality and Social Psychology Bulletin, 40,* 121–131.

Sabattini, L., & Crosby, F. (2009). Work ceilings and walls: Work-life and "family-friendly" policies. In M. Barreto, M. Ryan, & M. Schmitt (Eds.), *The glass ceiling in the 21st century: Understanding barriers to gender equality.* Washington, DC: American Psychological Association.

Sacks, O. (1987). *The man who mistook his wife for a hat and other clinical tales.* New York: Harper & Row.

Saffer, H. (2002). Alcohol advertising and youth. *Journal of Studies on Alcohol, 14,* 173–181.

Sagarin, B. J., & Wood, S. E. (2007). Resistance to influence. In A. R. Pratkanis (Ed.), *Frontiers of social psychology. The science of social influence: Advances and future progress* (pp. 321–340). New York: Psychology Press.

Sageman, M. (2008). *Leaderless jihad: Terror networks in the twenty-first century.* Philadelphia: University of Pennsylvania Press.

Saguy, T., Tausch, N., Dovidio, J. F., Pratto, F., & Singh, P. (2011). Tension and harmony in intergroup relations. In P. R. Shaver & M. Mikulincer (Eds.), *Human aggression and violence: Causes, manifestations, and consequences* (Herzilya series on personality and social psychology, pp. 333–348). Washington, DC: American Psychological Association.

Sakai, H. (1999). A multiplicative power-function model of cognitive dissonance: Toward an integrated theory of cognition, emotion, and behavior after Leon Festinger. In E. Harmon-Jones & J. S. Mills (Eds.), *Cognitive dissonance: Progress on a pivotal theory in social psychology* (pp. 120–138). Washington, DC: American Psychological Association.

Sakurai, M. M. (1975). Small group cohesiveness and detrimental conformity. *Sociometry, 38,* 340–357.

Salganik, M. J., Dodds, P. S., & Watts, D. J. (2006). Experimental study of inequality and unpredictability in an artificial cultural market. *Science, 311,* 854–856.

Salili, F. (1996). Learning and motivation: An Asian perspective. *Psychology and Developing Societies, 8,* 55–81.

Salovey, P., & Rodin, J. (1985). Cognitions about the self: Connecting feeling states and social behavior. In P. Shaver (Ed.), *Self, situations, and social behavior: Review of personality and social psychology* (Vol. 6, pp. 143–166). Beverly Hills, CA: Sage.

Salter, J. (2011, May 6). Pay-what-you-want Panera called a success. *USA Today.* Retrieved July 12, 2011, from www.usatoday.com/money/industries/food/2011-05-16-panera-pay-what-you-can_n.htm

Sampson, R. J. (1988). Local friendship ties and community attachment in mass society: A multilevel systemic model. *American Sociological Review, 53,* 766–779.

Sandberg, S. (2013). *Lean in: Women, work, and the will to lead.* New York: Knopf.

Sandstorm, G. M., & Dunn, E. W. (2014). Is efficiency overrated? Minimal social interactions lead to belonging and positive affect. *Social Psychological and Personality Science, 5,* 437–442.

Sanfey, A. G., Stallen, M., & Chang, L. J. (2014). Norms and expectations in social decision-making. *Trends in Cognitive Sciences, 18,* 172–174.

Sanger, D. E. (1993, May 30). The career and the kimono. *New York Times Magazine,* pp. 18–19.

Sanna, L. J., Meier, S., & Wegner, E. A. (2001). Counterfactuals and motivation: Mood as input to affective enjoyment and preparation. *British Journal of Social Psychology, 40,* 235–256.

Sapolsky, R. (1998). *The trouble with testosterone.* New York: Scribner.

Sarche, J. (2003, June 22). For new female cadets, an Air Force Academy in turmoil. *The Boston Globe,* p. A12.

Sastry, J., & Ross, C. E. (1998). Asian ethnicity and the sense of personal control. *Social Psychology Quarterly, 61,* 101–120.

Saunders, J. (2009). Memory impairment in the weapon focus effect. *Memory & Cognition, 37*(3), 326–335. doi:10.3758/MC.37.3.326

Savitsky, K. (1998). Embarrassment study [E-mails]. Society for Personal and Social Psychology e-mail list archive. Retrieved from www.stolaf.edu/cgi-bin/mailarchivesearch.pl?directory=/home/www/people/huff/SPSP&listname=archive98

Schachter, S. (1951). Deviation, rejection, and communication. *Journal of Abnormal and Social Psychology, 46,* 190–207.

Schachter, S. (1959). *The psychology of affiliation.* Stanford, CA: Stanford University Press.

Schachter, S. (1964). The interaction of cognitive and physiological determinants of emotional state. In L. Berkowitz (Ed.), *Advances in experimental social psychology* (Vol. 1, pp. 49–80). New York: Academic Press.

Schachter, S., & Singer, J. E. (1962). Cognitive, social, and physiological determinants of emotional states. *Psychological Review, 69,* 379–399.

Schachter, S., & Singer, J. E. (1979). Comments on the Maslach and Marshall-Zimbardo experiments. *Journal of Personality and Social Psychology, 37,* 989–995.

Schacter, D. L., Benoit, R. G., De Brigard, F., & Szpunar, K. K. (2013). Episodic future thinking and episodic counterfactual thinking: Intersections between memory and decisions. *Neurobiology of Learning and Memory.* doi:10.1016/j.nlm.2013.12.008

Schafer, M., & Crichlow, S. (1996). Antecedents of groupthink: A quantitative study. *Journal of Conflict Resolution, 40,* 415–435.

Schaller, M., Asp, C. H., Rosell, M. C., & Heim, S. J. (1996). Training in statistical reasoning inhibits formation of erroneous group stereotypes. *Personality and Social Psychology Bulletin, 22,* 829–844.

Scheele, D., Wille, A., Kendrick, K. M., Stoffel-Wagner, B., Becker, B., Güntürkün, O., et al. (2013). Oxytocin enhances brain reward system responses in men viewing the face of their female partner. *Proceedings of the National Academy of Sciences, 110,* 20308–20313.

Scheier, M. S., Carver, C. S., & Bridges, M. W. (2001). Optimism, pessimism, and psychological well-being. In E. C. Chang (Ed.), *Optimism and pessimism* (pp. 189–216). Washington, DC: American Psychological Association.

Schemo, D. J. (2003, July 12). Ex-superintendent of Air Force Academy is demoted in wake of rape scandal. *The New York Times,* p. A7.

Scherr, K. C., Madon, S., Guyll, M., Willard, J., & Spoth, R. (2011). Self-verification as a mediator of mothers' self-fulfilling effects on adolescents' educational attainment. *Personality and Social Psychology Bulletin, 37*(5), 587–600. doi:10.1177/0146167211399777

Schimel, J., & Greenberg, J. (2013). The birth and death of belonging. In C. N. DeWall (Ed.), *The Oxford handbook of social exclusion* (pp. 286–300). New York: Oxford University Press.

Schlegel, R. J., Hicks, J. A., Arndt, J., & King, L. A. (2009). Thine own self: True self-concept accessibility and meaning in life. *Journal of Personality and Social Psychology, 96*(2), 473–490. doi:10.1037/a0014060

Schlegel, S. (1998). *Wisdom from a rainforest: The spiritual journey of an anthropologist.* Athens: University of Georgia Press.

Schlenker, B. R. (2003). Self-presentation. In M. R. Leary & J. P. Tangney (Eds.), *Handbook of self and identity* (pp. 492–518). New York: Guilford.

Schlenker, B. R., & Weingold, M. F. (1989). Self-identification and accountability. In R. A. Giacalone & P. Rosenfeld (Eds.), *Impression management in the organization* (pp. 21–43). Hillsdale, NJ: Erlbaum.

Schmeichel, B. J., & Baumeister, R. F. (2004). Self-regulatory strength. In R. F. Baumeister & K D. Vohs (Eds.), *Handbook of self-regulation: Research, theory, and applications* (pp. 84–98). New York: Guilford.

Schmeichel, B. J., Gailliot, M. T., Filardo, E.-A., McGregor, I., Gitter, S., & Baumeister, R. F. (2009). Terror management theory and self-esteem revisited: The roles of implicit and explicit self-esteem in mortality salience effects. *Journal of Personality and Social Psychology, 96*(5), 1077–1087. doi:10.1037/a0015091

Schmitt, B. H., Gilovich, T., Goore, N., & Joseph, L. (1986). Mere presence and social facilitation: One more time. *Journal of Experimental Social Psychology, 22,* 228–241.

Schofield, J. W. (1986). Causes and consequences of the color-blind perspective. In J. F. Dovidio & S. L. Gaertner (Eds.), *Prejudice, discrimination, and racism* (pp. 231–253). Orlando, FL: Academic Press.

Scholten, L., van Knippenberg, D., Nijstad, B. A., & De Dreu, C. K. W. (2007). Motivated information processing and group decision-making: Effects of process accountability on information processing and decision quality. *Journal of Experimental Social Psychology, 43,* 539–552.

Schooler, J. W. (1999). Seeking the core: The issues and evidence surrounding recovered accounts of sexual trauma. In L. M. Williams & V. L. Banyard (Eds.), *Trauma and memory* (pp. 203–216). Thousand Oaks, CA: Sage.

Schooler, J. W., & Eich, E. (2000). Memory for emotional events. In E. Tulving & F. I. M. Craik (Eds.), *The Oxford handbook of memory* (pp. 379–392). Oxford, UK: Oxford University Press.

Schooler, J. W., & Engstler-Schooler, T. Y. (1990). Verbal overshadowing of visual memories: Some things are better left unsaid. *Cognitive Psychology, 22,* 36–71.

Schopler, J., & Insko, C. A. (1999). The reduction of the interindividual-intergroup discontinuity effect: The role of future consequences. In M. Foddy & M. Smithson (Eds.), *Resolving social dilemmas: Dynamic, structural, and intergroup aspects* (pp. 281–293). Bristol, PA: Taylor & Francis.

Schriber, R. A., & Robbins, R. W. (2012). Self-knowledge: An individual differences perspective. In S. Vazire & T. D. Wilson (Eds.), *The handbook of self-knowledge* (pp. 105–127). New York: Guilford Press.

Schroeder, D. H., & Costa, P. T., Jr. (1984). Influence of life event stress on physical illness: Substantive effects or methodological flaws? *Journal of Personality and Social Psychology, 46,* 853–863.

Schultz, P. W., & Kaiser, F. G. (2012). Promoting pro-environmental behavior. In S. D. Clayton (Ed.), *Oxford library of psychology. The Oxford handbook of environmental and conservation psychology* (pp. 556–580). doi:10.1093/oxfordhb/9780199733026.013.0029.

Schultz, P. W., Nolan, J. M., Cialdini, R. B., Goldstein, N. J., & Griskevicius, V. (2007). The constructive, destructive, and reconstructive power of social norms. *Psychological Science, 18,* 429–434.

Schultz, P. W., Oskamp, S., & Mainieri, T. (1995). Who recycles and when? A review of personal and situational factors. *Journal of Environmental Psychology, 15,* 105–121.

Schulz, R. (1976). Effects of control and predictability on the physical and psychological well-being of the institutionalized aged. *Journal of Personality and Social Psychology, 33,* 563–573.

Schulz, R., & Hanusa, B. H. (1978). Long-term effects of control and predictability-enhancing interventions: Findings and ethical issues. *Journal of Personality and Social Psychology, 36,* 1202–1212.

Schuman, H., & Kalton, G. (1985). Survey methods. In G. Lindzey & E. Aronson (Eds.), *Handbook of social psychology* (3rd ed., Vol. 1, pp. 635–697). New York: McGraw-Hill.

Schumann, K., & Ross, M. (2010). Why women apologize more than men: Gender differences in thresholds for perceiving offensive behavior. *Psychological Science, 21,* 1649–1655.

Schützwohl, A. (2004). Which infidelity type makes you more jealous? Decision strategies in a forced-choice between sexual and emotional infidelity. *Evolutionary Psychology, 2,* 121–128.

Schützwohl, A., Fuchs, A., McKibbin, W. F., & Schackelford, T. K. (2009). How willing are you to accept sexual requests from slightly unattractive to exceptionally attractive imagined requestors? *Human Nature, 20,* 282–293.

Schwab, N. (2014). Social influence constrained by the heritability of attitudes. *Personality and Individual Differences, 66,* 54–57.

Schwab, N., Harton, H. C., & Cullum, J. G. (2014). The effects of emergent norms and attitudes on recycling behavior. *Environment and Behavior, 46,* 403–422.

Schwartz, J. (2003, June 7). Shuttle tests seem to back foam theory in accident. *The New York Times,* p. A1.

Schwartz, J., & Wald, M. L. (2003, June 7). NASA's failings go beyond foam hitting shuttle, panel says. *The New York Times,* p. A1.

Schwarz, N., & Vaughn, L. A. (2002). The availability heuristic revisited: Ease of recall and content of recall as distinct sources of information. In T. Gilovich, D. W. Griffin, & D. Kahneman (Eds.), *Heuristics and biases: The psychology of intuitive judgment* (pp. 103–119). New York: Cambridge University Press.

Schwarz, N., Bless, H., & Bohner, G. (1991). Mood and persuasion: Affective states influence the processing of persuasive communications. *Advances in Experimental Social Psychology, 24,* 161–199.

Schwarz, N., Bless, H., Strack, F., Klumpp, G., Rittenauer-Schatka, H., & Simmons, A. (1991). Ease of retrieval as information: Another look at the availability heuristic. *Journal of Personality and Social Psychology, 61,* 195–202.

Schwarz, N., Groves, R. M., & Schuman, H. (1998). Survey methods. In D. T. Gilbert, S. T. Fiske, & G. Lindzey (Eds.), *The handbook of social psychology* (4th ed., Vol. 1, pp. 143–179). New York: McGraw-Hill.

Schwinger, M., Wirthwein, L., Lemmer, G., & Steinmayr, R. (2014). Academic self-handicapping and achievement: A meta-analysis. *Journal of Educational Psychology.* Advance online publication. doi:10.1037/a0035832

Scott, J. E., & Cuvelier, S. J. (1993). Violence and sexual violence in pornography: Is it increasing? *Archives of Sexual Behavior, 22,* 357–371.

Scott, J. P. (1958). *Aggression.* Chicago: University of Chicago Press.

Sedikides, C., & Anderson, C. A. (1994). Causal perceptions of intertrait relations: The glue that holds person types together. *Personality and Social Psychology Bulletin, 21,* 294–302.

Sedikides, C., Gaertner, L., & Yoshiyasu, T. (2003). Pancultural self-enhancement. *Journal of Personality and Social Psychology, 84,* 60–79.

Seery, M., Silver, R., Holman, E., Ence, W., & Chu, T. (2008). Expressing thoughts and feelings following a collective trauma: Immediate responses to 9/11 predict negative outcomes in a national sample. *Journal of Consulting and Clinical Psychology, 76,* 657–667.

Segerstrom, S. C., & O'Connor, D. B. (2012). Stress, health and illness: Four challenges for the future. *Psychology & Health, 27,* 128–140.

Seligman, M. E. P. (2002). Positive psychology, positive prevention, and positive therapy. In C. R. Snyder & S. J. Lopez (Eds.), *Handbook of positive psychology* (pp. 3–9). New York: Oxford University Press.

Selye, H. (1956). *The stress of life.* New York: McGraw-Hill.

Selye, H. (1976). *Stress in health and disease.* Woburn, MA: Butterworth.

Semmler, C., Brewer, N., & Douglass, A. B. (2012). Jurors believe eyewitnesses. In B. L. Cutler (Ed.), *Conviction of the innocent: Lessons from psychological research* (pp. 185–209). Washington, DC: American Psychological Association.

Senchak, M., & Leonard, K. E. (1992). Attachment styles and marital adjustment among newlywed couples. *Journal of Social and Personal Relationships*, 9, 51–64.

Sengupta, J., & Fitzsimons, G. J. (2004). The effect of analyzing reasons on the stability of brand attitudes: A reconciliation of opposing predictions. *Journal of Consumer Research*, 31, 705–711.

Senko, C., Durik, A., & Harackiewicz, J. (2008). Historical perspectives and new directions in achievement goal theory: Understanding the effects of mastery and performance–approach goals. In J. Y. Shah & W. L. Gardner (Eds.), *Handbook of motivation science* (pp. 100–113). New York: Guilford.

Seppa, N. (1997). Children's TV remains steeped in violence. *APA Monitor*, 28, 36.

Sergios, P. A., & Cody, J. (1985). Physical attractiveness and social assertiveness skills in male homosexual dating behavior and partner selection. *Journal of Social Psychology*, 125, 505–514.

Seta, J. J., Seta, C. E., & Wang, M. A. (1990). Feelings of negativity and stress: An averaging-summation analysis of impressions of negative life experiences. *Personality and Social Psychology Bulletin*, 17, 376–384.

Shackleford, T. K. (2005). An evolutionary psychological perspective on cultures of honor. *Evolutionary Psychology*, 3, 381–391.

Shah, A. K., & Oppenheimer, D M.. (2008). Heuristics made easy: An effort-reduction framework. *Psychological Bulletin*, 134, 207–232.

Sharan, S. (1980). Cooperative learning in small groups. *Review of Educational Research*, 50, 241–271.

Shariff, A., & Norenzayan, A. (2007). God is watching you: Priming god concepts increases prosocial behavior in an anonymous economic game. *Psychological Science*, 18, 803–809.

Sharma, D., Booth, R., Brown, R., & Huguet, P. (2010). Exploring the temporal dynamics of social facilitation in the Stroop task. *Psychonomic Bulletin & Review*, 17(1), 52–58. doi:10.3758/PBR.17.1.52

Sharp, F. C. (1928). *Ethics*. New York: Century.

Sharpe, D., Adair, J. G., & Roese, N. J. (1992). Twenty years of deception research: A decline in subjects' trust? *Personality and Social Psychology Bulletin*, 18, 585–590.

Shavitt, S. (1989). Operationalizing functional theories of attitude. In A. R. Pratkanis, S. J. Breckler, & A. G. Greenwald (Eds.), *Attitude structure and function* (pp. 311–337). Hillsdale, NJ: Erlbaum.

Shavitt, S. (1990). The role of attitude objects in attitude function. *Journal of Experimental Social Psychology*, 26, 124–148.

Shaw, J. I., & Skolnick, P. (1995). Effects of prohibitive and informative judicial instructions on jury decision making. *Social Behavior and Personality*, 23, 319–325.

Shaw, P., Eisend, M., & Tan, Y. (2014). Gender-role portrayals in international advertising. In H. Cheng (Ed.), *The handbook of international advertising research*, (Vol. 1, pp. 299–312).

Shepperd, J. A., & Taylor, K. M. (1999). Social loafing and expectancy-value theory. *Personality and Social Psychology Bulletin*, 25, 1147–1158.

Shepperd, J. A., Klein, W. M. P., Waters, E. A., & Weinstein, N. D. (2013). Taking stock of unrealistic optimism. *Perspectives on Psychological Science*, 8(4), 395–411. doi:10.1177/1745691613485247

Shepperd, J., Malone, W., & Sweeny, K. (2008). Exploring causes of the self-serving bias. *Social and Personality Psychology Compass*, 2, 895–908.

Sherif, M. (1936). *The psychology of social norms*. New York: Harper.

Sherif, M. (1966). *In common predicament: Social psychology of intergroup conflict and cooperation*. Boston: Houghton Mifflin.

Sherif, M., Harvey, O. J., White, J., Hood, W., & Sherif, C. W. (1961). *Intergroup conflict and cooperation: The robber's cave experiment*. Norman: Institute of Intergroup Relations, University of Oklahoma.

Sherman, D. K., Hartson, K. A., Binning, K. R., Purdie-Vaughns, V., Garcia, J., Taborsky-Barba, S., et al. (2013). Deflecting the trajectory and changing the narrative: How self-affirmation

affects academic performance and motivation under identity threat. *Journal of Personality and Social Psychology*, 104, 591–618.

Sherrod, D. R., & Cohen, S. (1979). Density, personal control, and design. In A. Baum & J. R. Aiello (Eds.), *Residential crowding and design* (pp. 217–227). New York: Plenum.

Sherry, J. L. (2001). The effects of violent video games on aggression: A meta-analysis. *Human Communication Research*, 27, 409–431.

Sherwin, S., & Winsby, M. (2011). A relational perspective on autonomy for older adults residing in nursing homes. *Health Expectations: An International Journal of Public Participation in Health Care & Health Policy*, 14, 182–190.

Shestakova, A., Rieskamp, J., Tugin, S., Ossadtchi, A., Krutitskaya, J., & Klucharev, V. (2013). Electrophysiological precursors of social conformity. *Social Cognitive and Affective Neuroscience*, 8, 756–763.

Shih, M., Pittinsky, T. L., & Ambady, N. (1999). Stereotype susceptibility: Identity salience and shifts in quantitative performance. *Psychological Science*, 10, 80–83.

Shiller, R. J. (2008, November 2). Challenging the crowd in whispers, not shouts. *The New York Times*, p. BU5. Retrieved July 9, 2011, from www.nytimes.com/2008/11/02/business/02view.html?pagewanted=1&_r=1&ref=business

Shipp, E. R. (2005, October 25). Rosa Parks, 92, Intrepid pioneer of civil rights movement, is dead. *The New York Times*, pp. A1, C18.

Shotland, R. L., & Straw, M. K. (1976). Bystander response to an assault: When a man attacks a woman. *Journal of Personality and Social Psychology*, 34, 990–999.

Shteynberg, G. (2010). A silent emergence of culture: The social tuning effect. *Journal of Personality and Social Psychology*, 99, 683–689.

Shupe, L. M. (1954). Alcohol and crimes: A study of the urine alcohol concentration found in 882 persons arrested during or immediately after the commission of a felony. *Journal of Criminal Law and Criminology*, 33, 661–665.

Sidanius, J., Pratto, F., & Bobo, L. (1996). Racism, conservatism, affirmative action, and intellectual sophistication: A matter of principled conservatism or group dominance? *Journal of Personality and Social Psychology*, 70, 476–490.

Sidanius, J., Van Laar, C., Levin, S., & Sinclair, S. (2004). Ethnic enclaves and the dynamics of social identity on the college campus: The good, the bad, and the ugly. *Journal of Personality and Social Psychology*, 87, 96–110.

Siedlecki, K. L., Salthouse, T. A., Oishi, S., & Jeswani, S. (2014). The relationship between social support and subjective well-being across age. *Social Indicators Research*, 117, 561–576.

Siero, F. W., Bakker, A. B., Dekker, G. B., & Van Den Burg, M. T. C. (1996). Changing organizational energy consumption behavior through comparative feedback. *Journal of Environmental Psychology*, 16, 235–246.

Sigall, H., & Page, R. (1971). Current stereotypes: A little fading, a little faking. *Journal of Personality and Social Psychology*, 18, 247–255.

Sigelman, J. D., & Johnson, P. (2008). Left frontal cortical activation and spreading of alternatives: Tests of the action-based model of dissonance. *Journal of Personality and Social Psychology*, 94, 1–15.

Silke, A. (Ed.). (2003). *Terrorists, victims, and society: Psychological perspectives on terrorism and its consequences*. New York: Wiley.

Silver, N. (2012, November 10). Which polls fared best (and worst) in the 2012 presidential race. *New York Times*. Retrieved April 14, 2014, from http://fivethirtyeight.blogs.nytimes.com/2012/11/10/which-polls-fared-best-and-worst-in-the-2012-presidential-race/?_php=true&_type=blogs&_r=0

Silver, R., Holman, E. A., McIntosh, D. N., Poulin, M., & Gil-Rivas, V. (2002). Nationwide longitudinal study of psychological responses to September 11. *Journal of the American Medical Association*, 2882, 1235–1244.

Silverstein, B., Peterson, B., & Perdue, L. (1986). Some correlates of the thin standard of bodily

attractiveness for women. *International Journal of Eating Disorders*, 5, 895–906.

Silvia, P. J., & Abele, A. E. (2002). Can positive affect induce self-focused attention? Methodological and measurement issues. *Cognition and Emotion*, 16, 845–853.

Sime, J. D. (1983). Affiliative behavior during escape to building exits. *Journal of Environmental Psychology*, 3, 21–41.

Simmons, R. E., & Scheepers, L. (1996). Winning by a neck: Sexual selection in the evolution of giraffe. *The American Naturalist*, 148, 771–786.

Simms, L. J. (2002). The application of attachment theory to individual behavior and functioning in close relationships: Theory, research, and practical applications. In J. H. Harvey & A. Wenzel (Eds.), *A clinician's guide to maintaining and enhancing close relationships* (pp. 63–80). Mahwah, NJ: Erlbaum.

Simon, H. A. (1990). A mechanism for social selection and successful altruism. *Science*, 250, 1665–1668.

Simons, D. J., & Chabris, C. F. (1999). Gorillas in our midst: Sustained inattentional blindness for dynamic events. *Perception*, 28, 1059–1074.

Simons, D. J., & Levin, D. T. (2005). Change blindness: Theory and consequences. *Current Directions in Psychological Science*, 14, 44–48.

Simons, D., & Ambinder. M. (2005). Change blindness: Theory and consequences. *Current Directions in Psychological Science*, 14, 44–48.

Simonton, D. K. (1984). *Genius, creativity, and leadership: Historiometric inquiries*. Cambridge, MA: Harvard University Press.

Simonton, D. K. (1985). Intelligence and personal influence in groups: Four nonlinear models. *Psychological Review*, 92, 532–547.

Simonton, D. K. (1987). *Why presidents succeed: A political psychology of leadership*. New Haven, CT: Yale University Press.

Simonton, D. K. (1998). Historiometric methods in social psychology. *European Review of Social Psychology*, 9, 267–293.

Simonton, D. K. (2001). Predicting presidential performance in the United States: Equation replication on recent survey results. *Journal of Social Psychology*, 141, 293–307.

Simpson, J. (2010). A tiller in the greening of relationship science. In M. H. Gonzales, C. Tavris, & J. Aronson (Eds.), *The scientist and the humanist: A festschrift in honor of Elliot Aronson* (pp. 203–210). New York: Psychology Press.

Simpson, J. A. (1987). The dissolution of romantic relationships: Factors involved in relationship stability and emotional distress. *Journal of Personality and Social Psychology*, 53, 683–692.

Simpson, J. A., & Beckes, L. (2010). Evolutionary perspectives on prosocial behavior. In M. Mikulincer & P. R. Shaver (Eds.), *Prosocial motives, emotions, and behavior: The better angels of our nature* (pp. 35–53). Washington, DC: American Psychological Association. doi:10.1037/12061-002

Simpson, J. A., & Gangestad, S. W. (1992). Sociosexuality and romantic partner choice. *Journal of Personality*, 60, 31–51.

Simpson, J. A., Collins, W. A., Tran, S., & Haydon, K. C. (2007). Attachment and the experience and expression of emotions in romantic relationships: A developmental perspective. *Journal of Personality and Social Psychology*, 92, 355–367.

Simpson, J. A., Rholes, W. S., Campbell, L., & Wilson, C. L. (2003). Changes in attachment orientations across the transition to parenthood. *Journal of Experimental Social Psychology*, 39, 317–331.

Sinaceur, M., Thomas-Hunt, M. C., Neale, M. A., O'Neill, O. A., & Haag, C. (2010). Accuracy and perceived expert status in group decisions: When minority members make majority members more accurate privately. *Personality and Social Psychology Bulletin*, 3, 423–437.

Sinclair, R. C., Hoffman, C., Mark, M. M., Martin, L. L., & Pickering, T. L. (1994). Construct accessibility and the misattribution of arousal: Schachter and Singer revisited. *Psychological Science*, 5, 15–19.

Sinclair, S., & Lun, J. (2010). Social tuning of ethnic attitudes. In B. Mesquita, L. Feldman Barrett, &

E. R. Smith (Eds.), *The mind in context* (pp. 214–229). New York: Guilford Press.

Sinclair, S., Lowery, B. S., Hardin, C. D., & Colangelo, A. (2005). Social tuning of automatic racial attitudes: The role of affiliative motivation. *Journal of Personality and Social Psychology, 89*(4), 583–592.

Singelis, T. M. (1994). The measurement of independent and interdependent self-construals. *Personality and Social Psychology Bulletin, 20,* 580–591.

Skinner, B. F. (1938). *The behavior of organisms: An experimental analysis.* New York: Appleton-Century-Crofts.

Skinner, E. A. (1996). A guide to constructs of control. *Journal of Personality and Social Psychology, 71,* 549–570.

Skitka, L. J. (2002). Do the means always justify the ends, or do the ends sometimes justify the means? A value protection model of justice reasoning. *Personality and Social Psychology Bulletin, 28,* 588–597.

Skorinko, J. L., & Sinclair, S. A. (2013). Perspective taking can increase stereotyping: The role of apparent stereotype confirmation. *Journal of Experimental Social Psychology, 49,* 10–18.

Slavin, R. E. (1996). Cooperative learning in middle and secondary schools. (Special section: Young adolescents at risk.) *Clearing House, 69,* 200–205.

Slavin, R. E., & Cooper, R. (1999). Improving intergroup relations: Lessons learned from cooperative learning programs. *Journal of Social Issues, 55,* 647–663.

Slepian, M. L., Bogart, K. B., & Ambady, N. (2014). Thin-slice judgments in the clinical context. *Annual Review of Clinical Psychology, 10,* 16.1–16.23.

Slevec, J. H., & Tiggemann, M. (2011). Predictors of body dissatisfaction and disordered eating in middle-aged women. *Clinical Psychology Review, 31*(4), 515–524. doi:10.1016/j.cpr.2010.12.002

Sloan, D., Marx, B., Epstein, E., & Dobbs, J. (2008). Expressive writing buffers against maladaptive rumination. *Emotion, 8,* 302–306.

Sloan, D., Marx, B., Epstein, E., & Dobbs, J. (2008). Expressive writing buffers against maladaptive rumination. *Emotion, 8,* 302–306.

Slovic, P., Fischhoff, B., & Lichtenstein, S. (1976). Cognitive processes and societal risk taking. In J. S. Carroll & J. Payne (Eds.), *Cognition and social behavior* (pp. 165–184). Hillsdale, NJ: Erlbaum.

Smalarz, L., & Wells, G. L. (2014). Post-identification feedback to eyewitness impairs evaluators' abilities to discriminate between accurate and mistaken testimony. *Law and Human Behavior, 38,* 194–202.

Smith, C. V., Hadden, B. W., Webster, G. D., Jonason, P. K., Gessekman, A. N., & Crysel, L. C. (2014). Mutually attracted or repulsed? Actor-partner interdependence models of Dark Triad traits and relationship outcomes. *Personality and Individual Differences, 67,* 35–41.

Smith, M. B., Bruner, J., & White, R. W. (1956). *Opinions and personality.* New York: Wiley.

Smith, N. (2014). *Justice through apologies: Remorse, reform, and punishment.* New York: Cambridge University Press.

Smith, S. S., & Richardson, D. (1983). Amelioration of deception and harm in psychological research: The important role of debriefing. *Journal of Personality and Social Psychology, 44,* 1075–1082.

Smith, V. L. (1991). Prototypes in the courtroom: Lay representation of legal concepts. *Journal of Personality and Social Psychology, 61,* 857–872.

Smyth, J. M., Pennebaker, J. W., & Arigo, D. (2012). What are the health effects of disclosure? In A. Baum, T. A. Revenson, & J. Singer (Eds.), *Handbook of health psychology* (2nd ed., pp. 175–191). New York: Psychology Press.

Snodgrass, M., Shevrin, H., & Abelson, J. A. (2014). Extremely rigorous subliminal paradigms demonstrate unconscious influences on simple decisions. *Behavioral and Brain Sciences, 37,* 39–40.

Snyder, C. R., & Higgins, R. L. (1988). Excuses: Their effective role in the negotiation of reality. *Psychological Bulletin, 104,* 23–35.

Snyder, C. R., & Lopez, S. J. (2009). *Oxford handbook of positive psychology.* New York: Oxford University Press.

Snyder, K. E., Malin, J. L., Dent, A. L., & Linnenbrink-Garcia, L. (2014). The message matters: The role of implicit beliefs about giftedness and failure experiences in academic self-handicapping. *Journal of Educational Psychology, 106*(1), 230–241.

Snyder, M. (1984). When belief creates reality. In L. Berkowitz (Ed.), *Advances in experimental social psychology* (Vol. 18, pp. 247–305). Orlando, FL: Academic Press.

Snyder, M. (1993). Basic research and practical problems: The promise of a "functional" personality and social psychology. *Personality and Social Psychology Bulletin, 19,* 251–264.

Snyder, M., & DeBono, K. G. (1989). Understanding the functions of attitudes: Lessons from personality and social behavior. In A. R. Pratkanis, S. J. Breckler, & A. G. Greenwald (Eds.), *Attitude structure and function* (pp. 361–381). Hillsdale, NJ: Lawrence Erlbaum.

Snyder, M., Tanke, E. D., & Berscheid, E. (1977). Social perception and interpersonal behavior: On the self-fulfilling nature of social stereotypes. *Journal of Personality and Social Psychology, 35,* 656–666.

Solomon, L. Z., Solomon, H., & Stone, R. (1978). Helping as a function of number of bystanders and ambiguity of emergency. *Personality and Social Psychology Bulletin, 4,* 318–321.

Sommers, S. (2011). *Situations matter: Understanding how context transforms your world.* New York: Riverhead.

Sommers, S. R. (2006). On racial diversity and group decision-making: Identifying multiple effects of racial composition on jury deliberations. *Journal of Personality and Social Psychology, 90,* 597–612.

Sommers, S. R., & Marotta, S. A. (2014). Racial disparities in legal outcomes: On policing, charging decisions, and criminal trial proceedings. *Policy Insights from Behavioral and Brain Sciences, 1,* 103–111.

Sommers, S., & Kassin, S. (2001). On the many impacts of inadmissible testimony: Selective compliance, need for cognition, and the over-correction bias. *Personality and Social Psychology Bulletin, 27,* 1368–1377.

Son Hing, L. S., Li, W., & Zanna, M. P. (2002). Inducing hypocrisy to reduce prejudicial responses among aversive racists. *Journal of Experimental Social Psychology, 38,* 71–78.

Sontag, S. (1978). *Illness as metaphor.* New York: Farrar, Straus & Giroux.

Sontag, S. (1988). *AIDS and its metaphors.* New York: Farrar, Straus & Giroux.

Sorenson, T. C. (1966). *Kennedy.* New York: Bantam Books.

Sorhagen, N. S. (2013). Early teacher expectations disproportionately affect poor children's high school performance. *Journal of Educational Psychology, 105,* 465–477.

Sorkin, R. D., Hays, C. J., & West, R. (2001). Signal-detection analysis of group decision making. *Psychological Review, 108,* 183–203.

Sorrentino, R. M., & Hancock, R. D. (2014). Information and affective value: A case for the study of individual difference and social influence. In M. P. Zanna, J. M. Olson, & C. P. Herman (Eds.), *Social influence: The Ontario Symposium* (Vol. 5, pp. 247–268). New York: Psychology Press.

Spanier, G. B. (1992). Divorce: A comment about the future. In T. L. Orbuch (Ed.), *Close relationship loss: Theoretical approaches* (pp. 207–212). New York: Springer-Verlag.

Spears, T. (2008). Newspaper readers 'rational' thinkers. *Vancouver Sun,* p. A16.

Spelke, E. S. (2005). Sex differences in intrinsic aptitude for mathematics and science? *American Psychologist, 60,* 950–958.

Spencer, S. J., Steele, C. M., & Quinn, D. M. (1999). Stereotype threat and women's math performance. *Journal of Experimental Social Psychology, 35,* 4–28.

Spina, R. R., Ji, L.-J., Guo, T., Zhang, Z., Li, Y., & Fabrigar, L. (2010). Cultural differences in the representativeness heuristic: Expecting a correspondence in magnitude between cause and effect. *Personality and Social Psychology Bulletin, 36*(5), 583–597. doi:10.1177/0146167210368278

Spink, K. S., Ulvick, J. D., Crozier, A. J., & Wilson, K. S. (2014). Group cohesion and adherence in unstructured exercise groups. *Psychology of Sport and Exercise, 15,* 293–298.

Sprecher, S., & Schwartz, P. (1994). Equity and balance in the exchange of contributions in close relationships. In M. J. Lerner & G. Mikula (Eds.), *Entitlement and the affectional bond: Justice in close relationships* (pp. 11–42). New York: Plenum.

Sprecher, S., Sullivan, Q., & Hatfield, E. (1994). Mate selection preference: Gender differences examined in a national sample. *Journal of Personality and Social Psychology, 66,* 1074–1080.

Sprecher, S., Zimmerman, C., & Fehr, B. (2014). The influence of compassionate love on strategies used to end a relationship. *Journal of Social and Personal Relationships, 31,* 697–705.

Staats, H., Harland, P., & Wilke, H. A. M. (2004). Effecting durable change: A team approach to improve environmental behavior in the household. *Environment and Behavior, 36,* 341–367.

Stanley, D. A., Sokol-Hessner, P., Banaji, M. R., & Phelps, E. A. (2011). Implicit race attitudes predict trustworthiness judgments and economic trust decisions. *Proceedings of the National Academy of Sciences, 108,* 7710–7715.

Stanley, D., Phelps, E., & Banaji, M. (2008). The neural basis of implicit attitudes. *Current Directions in Psychological Science, 17,* 164–170.

Stanovich, K. E., West, R., & Toplak, M. E. (2013). Myside bias, rational thinking, and intelligence. *Psychological Science, 22,* 259–264.

Stasser, G. (2000). Information distribution, participation, and group decision: Explorations with the DISCUSS and SPEAK models. In D. R. Ilgen & C. L. Hulin (Eds.), *Computational modeling of behavior in organizations: The third scientific discipline* (pp. 135–161). Washington, DC: American Psychological Association.

Stasser, G., & Titus, W. (1985). Pooling of unshared information in group decision making: Biased information sampling during discussion. *Journal of Personality and Social Psychology, 48,* 1467–1478.

Stasser, G., Stewart, D. D., & Wittenbaum, G. M. (1995). Expert roles and information exchange during discussion: The importance of knowing who knows what. *Journal of Experimental and Social Psychology, 31,* 244–265.

Staub, E. (1974). Helping a distressed person: Social, personality, and stimulus determinants. In L. Berkowitz (Ed.), *Advances in experimental social psychology* (Vol. 7, pp. 293–341). New York: Academic Press.

Staub, E. (1989). *The roots of evil: The origins of genocide and other group violence.* New York: Cambridge University Press.

Staub, E. (1999). The roots of evil: Social conditions, culture, personality, and basic human needs. *Personality and Social Psychology Review, 3,* 179–192.

Steblay, N. M. (1987). Helping behavior in rural and urban environments: A meta-analysis. *Psychological Bulletin, 102,* 346–356.

Steblay, N. M. (1997). Social influence in eyewitness recall: A meta-analytic review of lineup instruction effects. *Law and Human Behavior, 21,* 283–297.

Steblay, N. M., Besirevic, J., Fulero, S. M., & Jimenez-Lorente, B. (1999). The effects of pretrial publicity on juror verdicts: A meta-analytic review. *Law and Human Behavior, 23,* 219–235.

Steblay, N. M., Dysart, J., Fulero, S. M., & Lindsay, R. C. L. (2001). Eyewitness accuracy rates in sequential and simultaneous lineup presentations: A meta-analytic comparison. *Law and Human Behavior, 25,* 459–473.

Steele, C. M. (1988). The psychology of self-affirmation: Sustaining the integrity of the self. In L. Berkowitz (Ed.), *Advances in experimental social psychology* (Vol. 21, pp. 261–302). New York: Academic Press.

Steele, C. M. (1992, April). Race and the schooling of Black Americans. *Atlantic*, pp. 68–78.

Steele, C. M. (1997). A threat in the air: How stereotypes shape intellectual ability and performance. *American Psychologist*, 52, 613–629.

Steele, C. M., & Aronson, J. M. (1995a). Stereotype threat and the intellectual test performance of African-Americans. *Journal of Personality and Social Psychology*, 69, 797–811.

Steele, C. M., & Aronson, J. M. (1995b). Stereotype vulnerability and intellectual performance. In E. Aronson (Ed.), *Readings about the social animal* (7th ed.). New York: Freeman.

Steele, C. M., (2010). *Whistling Vivaldi: And other clues to how stereotypes affect us.* New York: W.W. Norton & Co.

Steele, C. M., Hoppe, H., & Gonzales, J. (1986). *Dissonance and the lab coat: Self-affirmation and the free-choice paradigm.* Unpublished manuscript, University of Washington.

Steele, C. M., Spencer, S. J., & Aronson, J. M. (2002). Contending with group image: The psychology of stereotype and social identity threat. In M. P. Zanna (Ed.), *Advances in experimental social psychology* (Vol. 34, pp. 379–440). San Diego, CA: Academic Press.

Steele, C. M., Spencer, S. J., & Josephs, R. A. (1992). *Seeking self-relevant information: The effects of self-esteem and stability of the information.* Unpublished manuscript, University of Michigan.

Steele, J. R., & Ambady, N. (2006). "Math is Hard!" The effect of gender priming on women's attitudes. *Journal of Experimental Social Psychology*, 42(4), 428–436. doi:10.1016/j.jesp.2005.06.003

Steiner, I. D. (1972). *Group process and productivity.* New York: Academic Press.

Stemple, L., & Meyer, I. H. (2014). The sexual victimization of men in America: New data challenge old assumptions. *American Journal of Public Health*, 104, e19–e26.

Stephan, W. G. (1978). School desegregation: An evaluation of predictions made in *Brown v. Board of Education. Psychological Bulletin*, 85, 217–238.

Stephan, W. G. (1985). Intergroup relations. In G. Lindzey & E. Aronson (Eds.), *Handbook of social psychology* (3rd ed., Vol. 2, pp. 599–658). New York: McGraw-Hill.

Stephens-Davidowitz, S. (2014, July 12). The data of hate. *New York Times*, op-ed.

Stern, P. C. (2011). Contributions of psychology to limiting climate change. *American Psychologist*, 66(4), 303–314. doi:10.1037/a0023235

Sternberg, R. J. (1986). A triangular theory of love. *Psychological Review*, 93, 119–135.

Sternberg, R. J. (1987). Liking versus loving: A comparative evaluation of theories. *Psychological Bulletin*, 102, 331–345.

Sternberg, R. J. (1988). *The triangle of love.* New York: Basic Books.

Sternberg, R. J. (1997). Construct validation of a triangular love scale. *European Journal of Social Psychology*, 27, 313–335.

Sternberg, R. J., & Vroom, V. (2002). The person versus the situation in leadership. *Leadership Quarterly*, 13, 301–323.

Stewart, D. D., & Stasser, G. (1995). Expert role assignment and information sampling during collective recall and decision making. *Journal of Personality and Social Psychology*, 69, 619–628.

Stewart, G. L., Dustin, S. L., Barrick, M. R., & Darnold, T. C. (2008). Exploring the handshake in employment interviews. *Journal of Applied Psychology*, 93, 1139–1146.

Stewart, J. (2011). *Tangled webs: How false statements are undermining America.* New York: Penguin.

Stewart, J. B. (2002). *Heart of a soldier.* New York: Simon & Schuster.

Stice, E., Marti, C. N., Spoor, S., Presnell, K., & Shaw, H. (2008). Dissonance and healthy weight eating disorder prevention programs: Long-term effects from a randomized efficacy trial. *Journal of Consulting and Clinical Psychology*, 76, 329–340.

Stice, E., Rohde, P., Shaw, H., & Gau, J. (2011). An effectiveness trial of a selected dissonance-based eating disorder prevention program for female high school students: Long-term effects. *Journal of Consulting and Clinical Psychology.* Advance online publication. doi:10.1037/a0024351

Stice, E., Shaw, H., Burton, E., & Wade, E. (2006). Dissonance and healthy weight eating disorders prevention programs: A randomized efficacy trial. *Journal of Consulting and Clinical Psychology*, 74, 263–275.

Stillman, T. F., Baumeister, R. F., Lambert, N. M., Crescioni, A. W., DeWall, C. N., & Fincham, F. D. (2009). Alone and without purpose: Life loses meaning following social exclusion. *Journal of Experimental Social Psychology*, 45, 686–694.

Stinson, D. A., Logel, C., Shepherd, S., & Zanna, M. P. (2011). Rewriting the self-fulfilling prophecy of social rejection: Self-affirmation improves relational security and social behavior up to 2 months later. *Psychological Science*, 22(9), 1145–1149. doi:10.1177/0956797611417725

Stoff, D. M., & Cairns, R. B. (Eds.). (1997). *Aggression and violence: Genetic, neurobiological, and biosocial perspectives.* Mahwah, NJ: Erlbaum.

Stone, J., Aronson, E., Crain, A. L., Winslow, M. P., & Fried, C. (1994). Inducing hypocrisy as a means of encouraging young adults to use condoms. *Personality and Social Psychology Bulletin*, 20, 116–128.

Stone, J., Lynch, C. I., Sjomeling, M., & Darley, J. M. (1999). Stereotype threat effects on Black and White athletic performance. *Journal of Personality and Social Psychology*, 77, 1213–1227.

Stone, J., Perry, Z., & Darley, J. (1997). "White men can't jump": Evidence for perceptual confirmation of racial stereotypes following a basketball game. *Basic and Applied Social Psychology*, 19, 291–306.

Storbeck, J., & Clore, G. L. (2008). Affective arousal as information: How affective arousal influences judgments, learning, and memory. *Social and Personality Psychology Compass*, 2(5), 1824–1843. doi:10.1111/j.1751-9004.2008.00138.x

Stormo, K. J., Lang, A. R., & Stritzke, W. G. K. (1997). Attributions about acquaintance rape: The role of alcohol and individual differences. *Journal of Applied Social Psychology*, 27, 279–305.

Storms, M. D. (1973). Videotape and the attribution process: Reversing actors' and observers' points of view. *Journal of Personality and Social Psychology*, 27, 165–175.

Story, L. (2007, January 15). Anywhere the eye can see, it's likely to see an ad. *The New York Times.* Retrieved July 12, 2011, from www.nytimes.com/2007/01/15/business/media/15everywhere.html?scp=1&sq=anywhere%20the%20eye%20can%20see&st=cse

Stouffer, S. A., Suchman, E. A., De Vinney, L. C., Star, S. A., & Williams, R. M., Jr. (1949). *The American soldier: Adjustment during army life* (Vol. 1). Princeton, NJ: Princeton University Press.

Strack, F., & Mussweiler, T. (2003). Heuristic strategies for judgment under uncertainty: The enigmatic case of anchoring. In G. V. Bodenhausen (Ed.), *Foundations of social cognition: A festschrift in honor of Robert S. Wyer Jr.* (pp. 79–95). Mahwah, NJ: Erlbaum.

Strack, F., Martin, L., & Stepper, S. (1988). Inhibiting and facilitating conditions of the human smile: A nonobtrusive test of the facial feedback hypothesis. *Journal of Personality and Social Psychology*, 54, 768–777.

Strahan, E. J., Spencer, S. J., & Zanna, M. P. (2002). Subliminal priming and persuasion: Striking while the iron is hot. *Journal of Experimental Social Psychology*, 38, 556–568.

Straus, M. (2011). Gender symmetry and mutuality in perpetration of clinical-level partner violence: Empirical evidence and implications for prevention and treatment. *Aggression and Violent Behavior*, 16, 279–288.

Strick, M., Dijksterhuis, A., Bos, M. W., Sjoerdsma, A., van Baaren, R. B., & Nordgren, L. F. (2011). A meta-analysis on unconscious thought effects. *Social Cognition*, 29, 738–763.

Stringfellow, T. (1841). A brief examination of scripture testimony on the institution of slavery. *Religious Herald.* Available on Internet.

Strohminger, N., & Nichols, S. (2014). The essential moral self. *Cognition*, 131, 159–171.

Stuhlmacher, A. F., & Citera, M. (2005). Hostile behavior and profit in virtual negotiation: A

meta-analysis. *Journal of Business and Psychology*, 20, 69–93.

Stukas, A. A., Snyder, M., & Clary, E. G. (1999). The effects of "mandatory volunteerism" on intentions to volunteer. *Psychological Science*, 10, 59–64.

Sturman, E. D. (2012). Dehumanizing just makes you feel better: The role of cognitive dissonance in dehumanization. *Journal of Social, Evolutionary, and Cultural Psychology*, 6, 527–531.

Stürmer, S., & Snyder, M. (2010). Helping "us" versus "them": Towards a group-level theory of helping and altruism within and across group boundaries. In S. Stürmer & M. Snyder (Eds.), *The psychology of prosocial behavior: Group processes, intergroup relations, and helping* (pp. 33–58). Oxford, UK: Wiley-Blackwell.

Suddendorf, T., & Butler, D. L. (2013). The nature of visual self-recognition. *Trends in Cognitive Sciences*, 17(3), 121–127. doi:10.1016/j.tics.2013.01.004

Sue, D. W. (2010). *Microaggressions in everyday life: Race, gender, and sexual orientation.* Hoboken, NJ: John Wiley & Sons.

Suls, J. M., & Fletcher, B. (1983). Social comparison in the social and physical sciences: An archival study. *Journal of Personality and Social Psychology*, 44, 575–580.

Suls, J. M., & Miller, R. L. (Eds.). (1977). *Social comparison processes: Theoretical and empirical perspectives.* Washington, DC: Hemisphere/Halstead.

Suls, J. M., & Wheeler, L. (Eds.). (2000). *Handbook of social comparison: Theory and research.* New York: Kluwer/Plenum.

Suls, J., Martin, R., & Wheeler, L. (2000). Three kinds of opinion comparison: The Triadic Model. *Personality and Social Psychology Review*, 4, 219–237.

Summers, G., & Feldman, N. S. (1984). Blaming the victim versus blaming the perpetrator: An attributional analysis of spouse abuse. *Journal of Social and Clinical Psychology*, 2, 339–347.

Surian, L., Caldi, S., & Sperber, D. (2007). Attribution of beliefs by 13-month-old infants. *Psychological Science*, 18, 580–586.

Surowiecki, J. (2004). *The wisdom of crowds: Why the many are smarter than the few and how collective wisdom shapes business, economies, societies and nations.* New York: Doubleday.

Susskind, J. M., Lee, D. H., Cusi, A., Feiman, R., Grabski, W., & Anderson, A. K. (2008). Expressing fear enhances sensory acquisition. *Nature Neuroscience*, 11, 843–850.

Swann, W. B., Jr. (1990). To be adored or to be known? The interplay of self-enhancement and self-verification. In E. T. Higgins & R. M. Sorrentino (Eds.), *Handbook of motivation and cognition* (Vol. 2, pp. 404–448). New York: Guilford Press.

Swann, W. B., Jr. (1996). *Self-traps: The elusive quest for higher self-esteem.* New York: Freeman.

Swann, W. B., Jr., & Pelham, B. W. (1988). *The social construction of identity: Self-verification through friend and intimate selection.* Unpublished manuscript, University of Texas, Austin.

Swim, J. K., Borgida, E., Maruyama, G., & Myers, D. G. (1989). Joan McKay vs. John McKay: Do gender stereotypes bias evaluations? *Psychological Bulletin*, 105, 409–429.

Swim, J. K., Clayton, S., & Howard, G. S. (2011). Human behavioral contributions to climate change: Psychological and contextual drivers. *American Psychologist*, 66(4), 251–264. doi:10.1037/a0023472

Symons, D. (1979). *The evolution of human sexuality.* New York: Oxford University Press.

Tahlheim, T., & Oishi, S. (2014). Residential mobility affects self-concept, group support, and happiness of individuals and communities. In P. J. Rentfrow (Ed.), *Geographical psychology: Exploring the interaction of environment and behavior* (pp. 219–239). Washington, DC: American Psychological Association.

Tajfel, H. (1982). Social psychology of intergroup relations. *Annual Review of Psychology*, 33, 1–39.

Tajfel, H., & Turner, J. C. (1979). An integrative theory of social contact. In W. Austin & S. Worchel (Eds.), *The social psychology of intergroup relations* (pp. 162–173). Monterey, CA: Brooks/Cole.

Tajfel, H., & Turner, J. C. (1986). The social identity theory of intergroup behavior. In S. Worchel & W. G. Austin (Eds.), *Psychology of intergroup relations*. Chicago: Nelson-Hall.

Takaku, S. (2006). Reducing road rage: An application of the dissonance-attribution model of interpersonal forgiveness. *Journal of Applied Social Psychology, 36*, 2362–2378.

Tan, K., Agnew, C. R., VanderDrift, L. E., & Harvey, S. M. (2014). Committed to us: Predicting relationship closeness following nonmarital romantic relationship breakup. *Journal of Social and Personal Relationships*. doi:10.1177/0265407514536293

Tang, S., & Hall, V. (1995). The overjustification effect: A meta-analysis. *Applied Cognitive Psychology, 9*, 365–404.

Tang, Y., Newman, L. S., & Huang, L. (2014). How people react to social-psychological accounts of wrongdoing: The moderating effects of culture. *Journal of Cross-Cultural Psychology, 45*, 752–763.

The tangled web of porn in the office. (2008, December 8). *Newsweek*. Retrieved March 21, 2011, from www.newsweek.com/2008/11/28/the-tangled-web-of-porn-in-the-office.html

Tannen, D. (2001). *You just don't understand: Men and women in conversation*. New York: Harper.

Taras, V., Sarala, R., Muchinsky, P., Kemmelmeier, M., Singelis, T. M., Avsec, A., et al. (2014). Opposite ends of the same stick? Multi-method test of the dimensionality of individualism and collectivism. *Journal of Cross-Cultural Psychology, 45*, 213–245.

Taşdemir, N. (2011). The relationships between motivations of intergroup differentiation as a function of different dimensions of social identity. *Review of General Psychology, 15*(2), 125–137. doi:10.1037/a0022816

Tavris, C., & Aronson, E. (2007). *Mistakes were made (but not by me)*. New York: Harcourt.

Tavris, C. (1989). *Anger: The misunderstood emotion* (Rev. ed.). New York: Touchstone.

Taylor, L. S., Fiore, A. T., Mendelsohn, G. A., & Cheshire, C. (2011). "Out of my league": A real-world test of the matching hypothesis. *Personality and Social Psychology Bulletin, 37*, 942–954.

Taylor, L. S., Fiore, A. T., Mendelsohn, G. A., & Cheshire, C. (2011). "Out of my league": A real-world test of the matching hypothesis. *Personality and Social Psychology Bulletin, 37*, 942–954.

Taylor, S. E. (2012). Tend and befriend theory. In P. A. M. Van Lange, A. W. Kruglanski, & E. T. Higgins (Eds.), *Handbook of theories of social psychology* (Vol. 1, pp. 32–49). Thousand Oaks, CA: Sage Publications.

Taylor, S. E. (2015). Social cognition and health. In M. Mikulincer, P. R. Shaver, E. Borgida, & J. A. Bargh (Eds.), *APA handbooks in psychology. APA handbook of personality and social psychology, Vol. 1. Attitudes and social cognition* (pp. 339–361). Washington, DC: American Psychological Association.

Taylor, S. E., & Brown, J. (1988). Illusion and well-being: A social psychological perspective on mental health. *Psychological Bulletin, 103*, 193–210.

Taylor, S. E., & Brown, J. D. (1994). Positive illusions and well-being revisited: Separating fact from fiction. *Psychological Bulletin, 116*, 21–27.

Taylor, S. E., & Fiske, S. T. (1975). Point of view and perceptions of causality. *Journal of Personality and Social Psychology, 32*, 439–445.

Taylor, S. E., & Master, S. L. (2011). Social responses to stress: The tend-and-befriend model. In R. J. Contrada & A. Baum (Eds.), *The handbook of stress science: Biology, psychology, and health* (pp. 101–109). New York: Springer.

Taylor, S. E., Klein, L. C., Lewis, B. P., Gruenewald, T. L., Gurung, R. A. R., & Updegraff, J. A. (2000). Biobehavioral responses to stress in females: Tend-and-befriend, not fight-or-flight. *Psychological Review, 107*, 411–429.

Taylor, S. E., Lichtman, R. R., & Wood, J. V. (1984). Attributions, beliefs about control, and adjustment to breast cancer. *Journal of Personality and Social Psychology, 46*, 489–502.

Taylor, S. E., Repetti, R. L., & Seeman, T. (1997). Health psychology: What is an unhealthy environment and how does it get under the skin? *Annual Review of Psychology, 48*, 411–447.

Taylor, S. E., Welch, W., Kim, H. S., Sherman, D. K. (2007). Cultural differences in the impact of social support on psychological and biological stress responses. *Psychological Science, 18*, 831–837.

Taylor, S. P., & Leonard, K. E. (1983). Alcohol and human physical aggression. In R. G. Geen & E. Donnerstein (Eds.), *Aggression: Theoretical and empirical reviews* (pp. 77–101). New York: Academic Press.

Tesser, A. (1993). The importance of heritability in psychological research: The case of attitudes. *Psychological Review, 100*, 129–142.

Tesser, A. (2003). Self-evaluation. In M. R. Leary & J. P. Tangney (Eds.), *Handbook of self and identity* (pp. 275–290). New York: Guilford Press.

Tesser, A., & Paulus, D. (1983). The definition of self: Private and public self-evaluation management strategies. *Journal of Personality and Social Psychology, 44*, 672–682.

Tesser, A., Campbell, J. D., & Mickler, S. (1983). The role of social pressure, attention to the stimulus, and self-doubt in conformity. *European Journal of Social Psychology, 13*, 217–233.

Testa, M., Hoffman, J. H., & Leonard, K. E. (2011). Female intimate partner violence perpetration: Stability and predictors of mutual and nonmutual aggression across the first year of college. *Aggressive Behavior, 37*, 362–373.

Tetlock, P. E. (2002). Theory-driven reasoning about plausible pasts and probable futures in world politics. In T. Gilovich, D. W. Griffin, & D. Kahneman (Eds.), *Heuristics and biases: The psychology of intuitive judgment* (pp. 749–762). New York: Cambridge University Press.

Tetlock, P. E., Peterson, R. S., McGuire, C., Chang, S., & Field, J. (1992). Assessing political group dynamics: A test of the groupthink model. *Journal of Personality and Social Psychology, 63*, 403–425.

Teves, O. (2002, May 28). WHO warns Asia 25% of youth will die from smoking without curbed advertising. *Associated Press*.

Theus, K. T. (1994). Subliminal advertising and the psychology of processing unconscious stimuli: A review. *Psychology and Marketing, 11*, 271–290.

Thibaut, J. W., & Kelley, H. H. (1959). *The social psychology of groups*. New York: Wiley.

Thomas, M. H. (1982). Physiological arousal, exposure to a relatively lengthy aggressive film, and aggressive behavior. *Journal of Research in Personality, 16*, 72–81.

Thomas, W. I. (1928). *The child in America*. New York: Knopf.

Thompson, J. (2000, June 18). I was certain, but I was wrong. *The New York Times*, p. D15.

Thompson, L. (1995). They saw a negotiation: Partisanship and involvement. *Journal of Personality and Social Psychology, 68*, 839–853.

Thompson, L. (1997). *The mind and heart of the negotiator*. Upper Saddle River, NJ: Prentice Hall.

Thompson, L. L., Wang, J., & Gunia, B. C. (2010). Negotiation. *Annual Review of Psychology, 61*, 491–515. doi:10.1146/annurev.psych.093008.100458

Thompson, M. P., Koss, M. P., Kingree, J. B., Goree, J., & Rice, J. (2011). Prospective mediational model of sexual aggression among college men. *Journal of Interpersonal Violence, 26*, 2716–2734.

Thompson, S. C. (1999). Illusions of control: How we overestimate our personal influence. *Current Directions in Psychological Science, 8*, 187–190.

Thompson, S. C. (2002). The role of personal control in adaptive functioning. In C. R. Snyder & S. J. Lopez (Eds.), *Handbook of positive psychology* (pp. 202–213). London: Oxford University Press.

Thompson, T. L., & Kiang, L. (2010). The model minority stereotype: Adolescent experiences and links with adjustment. *Asian American Journal of Psychology, 1*, 119–128.

Thompson, W. M., Dabbs, J. M., Jr., & Frady, R. L. (1990). Changes in saliva testosterone levels during a 90-day shock incarceration program. *Criminal Justice and Behavior, 17*, 246–252.

Thorndike, E. L. (1920). A constant error in psychological ratings. *Journal of Applied Psychology, 4*, 25–29.

Thornton, D., & Arrowood, A. J. (1966). Self-evaluation, self-enhancement, and the locus of social comparison. *Journal of Experimental Social Psychology, 1*(Suppl.), 40–48.

Tidikis, V., & Ash, I. K. (2013). Working in dyads and alone: Examining process variables in solving insight problems. *Creativity Research Journal, 25*, 189–198.

Tidwell, N. D., Eastwick, P. W., & Finkel, E. J. (2013). Perceived, not actual, similarity predicts initial attraction in a live romantic context: Evidence from the speed dating paradigm. *Personal Relationships, 20*, 199–215.

Timaeus, E. (1968). Untersuchungen zum sogenannten konformen Verhalten [Research into so-called conforming behavior]. *Zeitschrift für Experimentelle und Angewandte Psychologie, 15*, 176–194.

Tindale, R. S. (1993). Decision errors made by individuals and groups. In N. J. Castellan Jr. (Ed.), *Individual and group decision making* (pp. 109–124). Hillsdale, NJ: Erlbaum.

Tindale, R. S., Munier, C., Wasserman, M., & Smith, C. M. (2002). Group processes and the Holocaust. In L. S. Newman & R. Erber (Eds.), *Understanding genocide: The social psychology of the Holocaust* (pp. 143–161). New York: Oxford University Press.

Ting, J. C., & Piliavin, J. A. (2000). Altruism in comparative international perspective. In J. Phillips, B. Chapman, & D. Stevs (Eds.), *Between state and market: Essays on Charities Law and Policy in Canada* (pp. 51–105). Kingston, Montreal: McGill-Queens University Press.

Ting-Toomey, S., & Chung, L. (1996). Cross-cultural interpersonal communication: Theoretical trends and research directions. In W. B. Gudykunst, S. Ting-Toomey, & T. Nishida (Eds.), *Communication in personal relationships across cultures* (pp. 237–261). Thousand Oaks, CA: Sage.

Todd, A. R., Bodenhausen, G. V., Richeson, J. A., & Galinsky, A. D. (2011). Perspective taking combats automatic expressions of racial bias. *Journal of Personality and Social Psychology, 100*, 1027–1042.

Todd, P. M., Penke, L., Fasolo, B., & Lenton, A. P. (2007). Different cognitive processes underlie human mate choices and mate preferences. *Proceedings of the National Academy of Sciences, 104*, 15011–15016.

Todorov, A., Said, C. P., Engell, A., & Oosterhof, N. N. (2008). Understanding evaluation of faces on social dimensions. *Trends in Cognitive Sciences, 12*, 455–460.

Toi, M., & Batson, C. D. (1982). More evidence that empathy is a source of altruistic motivation. *Journal of Personality and Social Psychology, 43*, 281–292.

Toma, C. L., & Hancock, J. T. (2012). What lies beneath: The linguistic traces of deception in online dating profiles. *Journal of Communication, 62*, 78–97.

Toma, C. L., Hancock, J. T., & Ellison, N. B. (2008). Separating fact from fiction: An examination of deceptive self-presentation in online dating profiles. *Personality and Social Psychology Bulletin, 34*, 1023–1036.

Toma, C., & Butera, F. (2009). Hidden profiles and concealed information: Strategic information sharing and use in group decision making. *Personality and Social Psychology Bulletin, 35*(6), 793–806. doi:10.1177/0146167209333176

Tomasello, M., & Vaish, A. (2013). Origins of human cooperation and morality. *Annual Review of Psychology, 64*, 231–255.

Tooby, J., & Cosmides, L. (2005). Conceptual foundations of evolutionary psychology. In D. M. Buss (Ed.), *The handbook of evolutionary psychology* (pp. 5–67). Hoboken, NJ: Wiley.

Tourangeau, R., Smith, T., & Rasinski, K. (1997). Motivation to report sensitive behaviors on surveys: Evidence from a bogus pipeline experiment. *Journal of Applied Social Psychology*, 27, 209–222.

Tracy, J. L., & Matsumoto, D. (2008). The spontaneous expression of pride and shame: Evidence for biologically innate nonverbal displays. *Proceedings of the National Academy of Sciences*, 105, 11655–11660.

Tracy, J. L., & Robins, R. W. (2004). Putting the self into self-conscious emotions: A theoretical model. *Psychological Inquiry*, 15, 103–125.

Trappey, C. (1996). A meta-analysis of consumer choice and subliminal advertising. *Psychology and Marketing*, 13, 517–530.

Trends in cigarette smoking among high school students: United States, 1991–2002. (2002). *Centers for Disease Control, Morbidity and Mortality Weekly Report*, 51, 409–412.

Triandis, H. C. (1989). The self and social behavior in differing cultural contexts. *Psychological Review*, 96, 506–520.

Triandis, H. C. (1994). *Culture and social behavior*. New York: McGraw-Hill.

Triandis, H. C. (1995). *Individualism and collectivism*. Boulder, CO: Westview Press.

Trivers, R. L. (1971). The evolution of reciprocal altruism. *Quarterly Review of Biology*, 46, 35–57.

Trivers, R. L. (1985). *Social evolution*. Menlo Park, CA: Benjamin-Cummings.

Trötschel, R., Hüffmeier, J., Loschelder, D. D., Schwartz, K., & Gollwitzer, P. M. (2011). Perspective taking as a means to overcome motivational barriers in negotiations: When putting oneself into the opponent's shoes helps to walk toward agreements. *Journal of Personality and Social Psychology*, 101, 771–790. doi:10.1037/a0023801

Tsai, J. L. (2007). Ideal affect: Cultural causes and behavioral consequences. *Perspectives on Psychological Science*, 2, 242–259.

Tsai, J. L., Knutson, B., & Fung, H. (2006). Cultural variation in affect valuation. *Journal of Personality and Social Psychology*, 90, 288–307.

Tseëlon, E. (1995). *The presentation of woman in everyday life*. Thousand Oaks, CA: Sage.

Ttofi, M. M., & Farrington, D. P. (2011). Effectiveness of school-based programs to reduce bullying: A systematic and meta-analytic review. *Journal of Experimental Criminology*, 7, 27–56.

Tucker, P., Pfefferbaum, B., Doughty, D. B., Jones, D. E., Jordan, F. B., & Nixon, S. J. (2002). Body handlers after terrorism in Oklahoma City: Predictors of posttraumatic stress and other symptoms. *American Journal of Orthopsychiatry*, 72, 469–475.

Turner, C., & Leyens, J. (1992). The weapons effect revisited: The effects of firearms on aggressive behavior. In P. Suedfeld & P. E. Tetlock (Eds.), *Psychology and social policy* (pp. 201–221). New York: Hemisphere.

Turner, F. J. (1932). *The significance of sections in American history*. New York: Henry Holt.

Turner, J. C. (1982). Towards a cognitive redefinition of the social group. In H. Tajfel (Ed.), *Social identity and intergroup relations* (pp. 15–40). Cambridge: Cambridge University Press.

Turner, M. E., & Horvitz, T. (2001). The dilemma of threat: Group effectiveness and ineffectiveness under adversity. In M. E. Turner (Ed.), *Groups at work: Theory and research* (pp. 445–470). Mahwah, NJ: Erlbaum.

Turner, M., Pratkanis, A., Probasco, P., & Leve, C. (2006). Threat, cohesion, and group effectiveness: Testing a social identity maintenance perspective on groupthink. *Small Groups* (pp. 241–264). New York: Psychology Press.

Tversky, A., & Kahneman, D. (1973). Availability: A heuristic for judging frequency and probability. *Cognitive Psychology*, 5, 207–232.

Tversky, A., & Kahneman, D. (1974). Judgment under uncertainty: Heuristics and biases. *Science*, 185, 1124–1131.

Twenge, J. M. (1997). Attitudes toward women, 1970–1995: A meta-analysis. *Psychology of Women Quarterly*, 21, 35–51.

Twenge, J. M. (2009). Change over time in obedience: The jury's still out, but it might be decreasing. *American Psychologist*, 64, 28–31.

Twenge, J. M., & Campbell, W. K. (2009). *The narcissism epidemic*. New York: Free Press.

Twenge, J. M., & Foster, J. D. (2010). Birth cohort increases in narcissistic personality traits among American college students, 1982–2009. *Social Psychological and Personality Science*, 1, 99–106.

Twenge, J. M., Campbell, W. K., & Gentile, B. (2013). Changes in pronoun use in American books and the rise of individualism, 1960–2008. *Journal of Cross-Cultural Psychology*, 44, 406–415.

Twenge, J. M., Konrath, S., Foster, J. D., Campbell, W. K., & Bushman, B. J. (2008). Egos inflating over time: A cross-temporal meta-analysis of the Narcissistic Personality Inventory. *Journal of Personality*, 76, 875–902. doi:10.1111/j.1467-6494.2008.00507.x

Twenge, J. M., Zhang, L., & Im, C. (2004). It's beyond my control: A cross-temporal meta-analysis of increasing externality in locus of control, 1960–2002. *Personality and Social Psychology Review*, 8, 308–319.

Twenge. J. M., Gentile, B., & Campbell, W. K. (2015). Birth cohort differences in personality. In Mikulincer, M., Shaver, P. R., Cooper, M. L., & Larsen, R. J. (Eds.), *APA handbook of personality and social psychology, Volume 4: Personality processes and individual differences* (pp. 535–551). Washington, DC: American Psychological Association.

U.S. Department of Justice. (2000). *Violence by intimates*. Washington, DC: Bureau of Justice Statistics.

Ubinas, H. (2013, September 24). Smile, we've apparently lost our sense of civic duty. *Philly.com*. Retrieved April 22, 2014, from http://www.philly.com/philly/columnists/20130924_Smile__we_ve_apparently_lost_our_sense_of_civic_duty_.html

Ulloa, J. L., Puce, A., Hugueville, L., & George, N. (2014). Sustained neural activity to gaze and emotion perception in dynamic social scenes. *Social Cognitive and Affective Neuroscience*, 9, 350–357.

Updegraff, J., Silver, R., & Holman, E. (2008). Searching for and finding meaning in collective trauma: Results from a national longitudinal study of the 9/11 terrorist attacks. *Journal of Personality and Social Psychology*, 95, 709–722.

Uziel, L. (2010). Look at me, I'm happy and creative: The effect of impression management on behavior in social presence. *Personality and Social Psychology Bulletin*, 36(12), 1591–1602. doi:10.1177/0146167210386239

Uzzell, D. (2000). Ethnographic and action research. In G. M. Breakwell, S. Hammond, & C. Fife-Schaw (Eds.), *Research methods in psychology* (2nd ed., pp. 326–337). Thousand Oaks, CA: Sage.

Vaananen, A., Buunk, B. P., Kivimaki, M., Pentti, J., & Vahtera, J. (2005). When is it better to give than to receive: Long-term health effects of perceived reciprocity in support exchange. *Journal of Personality and Social Psychology*, 89, 176–193.

Vala Jorge, P., Cicero, C.-L., & Rui C. (2009). Is the attribution of cultural differences to minorities an expression of racial prejudice? *International Journal of Psychology*, 44 (1), 20–28.

Vallone, R. P., Griffin, D. W., Lin, S., & Ross, L. (1990). The overconfident prediction of future actions and outcomes by self and others. *Journal of Personality and Social Psychology*, 58, 582–592.

van Bommel, M., van Prooijen, J.-W., Elffers, H., & Van Lange, P. A. M. (2012). Be aware to care: Public self-awareness leads to a reversal of the bystander effect. *Journal of Experimental Social Psychology*, 48(4), 926–930. doi:10.1016/j.jesp.2012.02.011

Van Boven, L., & Gilovich, T. (2003). To do or to have? That is the question. *Journal of Personality and Social Psychology*, 85, 1193–1202.

van de Ven, N., Zeelenberg, M., & Pieters, R. (2011). Appraisal patterns of envy and related emotions. *Motivation and Emotion*, 36, 195–204.

van de Vijver, F., & Leung, K. (1997). *Methods and data analyses for cross-cultural research*. Thousand Oaks, CA: Sage.

Van den Bos, K., & Lind, E. A. (2013). On sense-making reactions and public inhibition of benign social motives: An appraisal model of prosocial behavior. *Advances in Experimental Social Psychology*, 48, 1–58.

Van den Bos, K., Müller, P. A., & van Bussel, A. A. L. (2009). Helping to overcome intervention inertia in bystander's dilemmas: Behavioral disinhibition can improve the greater good. *Journal of Experimental Social Psychology*, 45, 873–878.

van der Zwaluw, C. S., Kleinjan, M., Lemmers, L., Spijkerman, R., & Engels, R. (2013). Longitudinal associations between attitudes towards binge drinking and alcohol–free drinks, and binge drinking behavior in adolescence. *Addictive Behaviors*, 38, 2110–2114.

van Knippenberg, D., van Ginkel, W. P., & Homan, A. C. (2013). Diversity mindsets and the performance of diverse teams. *Organizational Behavior and Human Decision Processes*, 121, 183–193.

Van Laar, C., Levin, S., & Sidanius, J. (2008). Ingroup and outgroup contact: A longitudinal study of the effects of cross-ethnic friendships, dates, roommate relationships and participation in segregated organizations. In U. Wagner, L. R. Tropp, G. Finchilescu, & C. Tredoux (Eds.), *Improving intergroup relations: Building on the legacy of Thomas F. Pettigrew*. Malden, MA : Blackwell.

Van Laar, C., Sidanius, J., & Levin, S. (2008). Ethnic related curricula and intergroup attitudes in college: Movement towards and away from the ingroup. *Journal of Applied Social Psychology*, 38 (6), 1601–1638

Van Lange, P. A. M., Joireman, J., Parks, C. D., & Van Dijk, E. (2013). The psychology of social dilemmas: A review. *Organizational Behavior and Human Decision Processes*, 120, 125–141.

Van Lange, P. A. M., Rusbult, C. E., Drigotas, S. M., Arriaga, X. B., Witcher, B. S., & Cox, C. L. (1997). Willingness to sacrifice in close relationships. *Journal of Personality and Social Psychology*, 72, 1373–1395.

van Leeuwen, E., & Täuber, S. (2010). The strategic side of out-group helping. In S. Stürmer & M. Snyder (Eds.), *The psychology of prosocial behavior: Group processes, intergroup relations, and helping* (pp. 81–99). Oxford, UK: Wiley-Blackwell.

Van Reijmersdal, E., Neijens, P., & Smit, E. G. (2009). A new branch of advertising: Reviewing factors that influence reactions to product placement. *Journal of Advertising Research*, 49(4), 429–449. doi:10.2501/S0021849909091065

Van Vugt, M. (2006). Evolutionary origins of leadership and followership. *Personality and Social Psychology Review*, 10(4), 354–371.

Van Vugt, M., & De Cremer, D. (1999). Leadership in social dilemmas: The effects of group identification on collective actions to provide public goods. *Journal of Personality and Social Psychology*, 76, 587–599.

Van Vugt, M., & Samuelson, C. (1999). The impact of personal metering in the management of a natural resource crisis: A social dilemma analysis. *Personality and Social Psychology Bulletin*, 25, 731–745.

Vandello, J. A., & Cohen, D. (2008). Culture, gender, men's intimate partner violence. *Social and Personality Psychology Compass*, 2(2), 652–667.

Vandello, J. A., Cohen, D., & Ransom, S. (2008). U.S. Southern and Northern differences in perceptions of norms about aggression: Mechanisms for the perpetuation of a culture of honor. *Journal of Cross-Cultural Psychology*, 39(2), 162–177.

Vansteenkiste, M., Smeets, S., Soenens, B., Lens, W., Matos, L., & Deci, E. L. (2010). Autonomous and controlled regulation of performance-approach goals: Their relations to perfectionism and educational outcomes. *Motivation and Emotion*, 34(4), 333–353. doi:10.1007/s11031-010-9188-3

Varnum, M. E. W., & Kitayama, S. (2011). What's in a name? Popular names are less common on frontiers. *Psychological Science*, 22, 176–183.

Varnum, M. E. W., Grossmann, I., Kitayama, S., & Nisbett, R. E. (2010). The origin of cultural differences in cognition: The social orientation hypothesis. *Current Directions in Psychological Science*, 19(1), 9–13. doi:10.1177/0963721409359301

Vasey, P. L., & VanderLaan, D. P. (2010). An adaptive cognitive dissociation between willingness to help kin and nonkin in Samoan Fa'afafine. *Psychological Science, 21*(2), 292–297. doi:10.1177/0956797609359623

Vazire, S., & Wilson, T. D. (Eds.). (2012). *Handbook of self-knowledge*. New York: Guilford Press.

Vedantam, S. (2006, June 23). Social isolation growing in U.S.

Verwijmeren, T., Karremans, J. C., Stroebe, W., & Wigboldus, D. (2011), The workings and limits of subliminal advertising: The role of habits. *Journal of Consumer Psychology, 21*, 206–213. doi:10.1016/j.jcps.2010.11.004

Vidal, J. (2009). Global warming causes 300,000 deaths a year, says Kofi Annan thinktank. *CommonDreams.org*. Retrieved August 14, 2011, from www.commondreams.org/headline/2009/05/29

Vidyasagar, P., & Mishra, H. (1993). Effect of modelling on aggression. *Indian Journal of Clinical Psychology, 20*, 50–52.

Villalobos, J. G., Davis, D., & Leo, R. A. (2015). His story, her story: Sexual miscommunication, motivated remembering, and intoxication as pathways to honest false testimony regarding sexual consent. In R. Burnett (Ed.), *Vilified: Wrongful allegations of person abuse*. Oxford: Oxford University Press.

Visscher, T. L. S., & Seidell, J. C. (2001). The public health impact of obesity. *Annual Review of Public Health, 22*, 355–375.

Viswesvaran, C., & Deshpande, S. P. (1996). Ethics, success, and job satisfaction: A test of dissonance theory in India. *Journal of Business Ethics, 10*, 487–501.

Vohs, K. D., & Baumeister, R. F. (2004). Sexual passion, intimacy and gender. In D. J. Mashek & A. Aron (Eds.), *Handbook of closeness and intimacy* (pp. 189–200). Mahwah, NJ: Erlbaum.

Vohs, K. D., & Baumeister, R. F. (Eds.). (2011). *Handbook of self-regulation*. New York: Guilford.

Vohs, K. D., Baumeister, R. F., & Schmeichel, B. J. (2012). Motivation, personal beliefs, and limited resources all contribute to self-control. *Journal of Experimental Social Psychology, 48*, 943–947.

Vohs, K. D., & Schooler, J. W. (2008). The value of believing in free will: Encouraging a belief in determinism increases cheating. *Psychological Science, 19*, 49–54.

Volunteering in the United States. (2013). Bureau of Labor Statistics, United States Department of Labor. Retrieved June 14, 2014, from http://www.bls.gov/news.release/volun.nr0.htm

von Dawans, B., Fischbacher, U., Kirschbaum, C., Fehr, E., & Heinrichs, M. (2012). The social dimension of stress reactivity: Acute stress increases prosocial behavior in humans. *Psychological Science, 23*, 651–660.

von Wittich, D., & Antonakis, J. (2011). The KAI cognitive style inventory: Was it personality all along? *Personality and Individual Differences, 50*(7), 1044–1049. doi:10.1016/j.paid.2011.01.022

Vrijheid, M., Dolk, H., Armstrong, B., Abramsky, L., Bianchi, F., Fazarinc, I., et al. (2002). Chromosomal congenital anomalies and residence near hazardous waste landfill sites. *Lancet, 359*, 320–322.

Wakefield, M., Flay, B., & Nichter, M. (2003). Role of the media in influencing trajectories of youth smoking. *Addiction, 98*(Suppl. 1), Special issue: Contexts and adolescent tobacco use trajectories, 79–103.

Walker, I., & Crogan, M. (1998). Academic performance, prejudice, and the jigsaw classroom: New pieces to the puzzle. *Journal of Community and Applied Social Psychology, 8*, 381–393.

Wallach, M. A., Kogan, N., & Bem, D. J. (1962). Group influences on individual risk taking. *Journal of Abnormal and Social Psychology, 65*, 75–86.

Walster, E. (1966). Assignment of responsibility for an accident. *Journal of Personality and Social Psychology, 3*, 73–79.

Walster, E., & Festinger, L. (1962). The effectiveness of "overheard" persuasive communication. *Journal of Abnormal and Social Psychology, 65*, 395–402.

Walster, E., Aronson, V., Abrahams, D., & Rottman, L. (1966). Importance of physical attractiveness in dating behavior. *Journal of Personality and Social Psychology, 5*, 508–516.

Walster, E., Walster, G. W., & Berscheid, E. (1978). *Equity: Theory and research*. Needham Heights, MA: Allyn & Bacon.

Walther, E., & Langer, T. (2010). For whom Pavlov's bell tolls: Processes underlying evaluative conditioning. In J. P. Forgas, J. Cooper, & W. D. Crano (Eds.), *The Sydney symposium of social psychology. The psychology of attitudes and attitude change* (pp. 59–74). New York: Psychology Press.

Walther, E., Bless, H., Strack, F., Rackstraw, P., Wagner, D., & Werth, L. (2002). Conformity effects in memory as a function of group size, dissenters and uncertainty. *Applied Cognitive Psychology, 16*, 793–810.

Walton, G. M. (2014). The new science of wise interventions. *Current Directions in Psychological Science, 23*, 73–82.

Wang, O., & Ross, M. (2007). Culture and memory. In S. Kitayama & D. Cohen (Eds.), *Handbook of cultural psychology* (pp. 645–667). New York: Guilford.

Warneken, F., & Tomasello, M. (2008). Extrinsic rewards undermine altruistic tendencies in 20-month-olds. *Developmental Psychology, 44*(6), 1785–1788. doi:10.1037/a0013860

Warner, J. (2001, December 23). Laughter auditions: How I learned how to be a professional laugher. *LA Weekly Blogs*. Available at: blogs.laweekly.com/arts/2011/12/how_to_be_a_professional_laugh.php

Waston, J. B. (1925). *Behaviorism*. New York: Norton.

Waterman, A. S. (Ed.). (2013). *The best within us: Positive psychology perspectives on eudaimonia*. Washington, DC, US: American Psychological Association.

Watkins, E. R. (2008). Constructive and unconstructive repetitive thought. *Psychological Bulletin, 134*(2), 163–206. doi:10.1037/0033-2909.134.2.163

Watkins, E. R., & Nolen-Hoeksema, S. (2014). A habit-goal framework of depressive rumination. *Journal of Abnormal Psychology, 123*, 24–24.

Watson, D. (1982). The actor and the observer: How are their perceptions of causality divergent? *Psychological Bulletin, 92*, 682–700.

Watson, D., & Pennebaker, J. W. (1989). Health complaints, stress, and distress: Exploring the central role of negative affectivity. *Psychological Review, 96*, 234–254.

Watson, J. (1950). Some social and psychological situations related to change in attitude. *Human Relations, 3*, 15–56.

Watson, R. I. (1973). Investigation into deindividuation using a cross-cultural survey technique. *Journal of Personality and Social Psychology, 25*, 342–345.

Watson, W. E., Johnson, L., Kumar, K., & Critelli, J. (1998). Process gain and process loss: Comparing interpersonal processes and performance of culturally diverse and non-diverse teams across time. *International Journal of Intercultural Relations, 22*, 409–430.

Wattenberg, M. P. (1987). The hollow realignment: Partisan change in a candidate-centered era. *Public Opinion Quarterly, 51*, 58–74.

Watts, D. P., Muller, M., Amsler, S. J., Mbabazi, G., & Mitani, J. C. (2006, February). Lethal intergroup aggression by chimpanzees in Kibale National Park, Uganda. *American Journal of Primatology, 68*, (2), 161–180.

Wax, E. (2008). In India, new opportunities for women draw anger and abuse from men. *Washington Post*, p. A11.

Weaver, C. N. (2008). Social distance as a measure of prejudice among ethnic groups in the United States. *Journal of Applied Social Psychology, 38*, 778–795.

Weaver, J. R., & Bosson, J. K. (2011). I feel like I know you: Sharing negative attitudes of others promotes feelings of familiarity. *Personality and Social Psychology Bulletin, 37*, 481–491.

Webber, R., & Crocker, J. (1983). Cognitive processes in the revision of stereotypic beliefs. *Journal of Personality and Social Psychology, 45*, 961–977.

Weber, E. U., & Johnson, E. J. (2009). Mindful judgment and decision making. *Annual Review of Psychology, 60*, 53–85. doi:10.1146/annurev.psych.60.110707.163633

Weber, E. U., Bockenholt, U., Hilton, D. J., & Wallace, B. (1993). Determinants of diagnostic hypothesis generation: Effects of information, base rates, and experience. *Journal of Experimental Psychology: Learning, Memory, and Cognition, 19*, 1151–1164.

Weber, J. M., Kopelman, S., & Messick, D. M. (2004). A conceptual review of decision making in social dilemmas: Applying a logic of appropriateness. *Personality and Social Psychology Review, 8*, 281–307.

Weber, N., Brewer, N., Wells, G., Semmler, C., & Keast, A. (2004). Eyewitness identification accuracy and response latency: The unruly 10-12-second rule. *Journal of Experimental Psychology: Applied, 10*, 139–147.

Webster, D. M. (1993). Motivated augmentation and reduction of the overattributional bias. *Journal of Personality and Social Psychology, 65*, 261–271.

Wechsler, H., & Austin, S. B. (1998). Binge drinking: The five/four measure. *Journal of Studies of Alcohol, 59*, 122–124.

Wechsler, H., Lee, J. E., Kuo, M., Siebring, M., Nelson, T. F., & Lee, H. (2002). Trends in college binge drinking during a period of increased prevention efforts: Findings from 4 Harvard School of Public Health college alcohol study surveys, 1993–2001. *Journal of American College Health, 50*, 203–217.

Weeden, J., & Sabini, J. (2005). Physical attractiveness and health in Western societies: A review. *Psychological Bulletin, 131*, 635–653.

Wegener, D. T., & Petty, R. E. (1994). Mood management across affective states: The hedonic contingency hypothesis. *Journal of Personality and Social Psychology, 66*, 1034–1048.

Wegener, D. T., & Petty, R. E. (1995). Flexible correction processes in social judgment: The role of naive theories in corrections for perceived bias. *Journal of Personality and Social Psychology, 68*, 36–51.

Wegner, D. M. (1986). Transactive memory: A contemporary analysis of the group mind. In B. Mullen & G. R. Goethals (Eds.), *Theories of group behavior* (pp. 185–208). New York: Springer-Verlag.

Wegner, D. M. (1989). *White bears and other unwanted thoughts: Suppression, obsession, and the psychology of mental control*. New York: Viking.

Wegner, D. M. (1992). You can't always think what you want: Problems in the suppression of unwanted thoughts. In M. P. Zanna (Ed.), *Advances in experimental social psychology* (Vol. 25, pp. 193–225). San Diego, CA: Academic Press.

Wegner, D. M. (1994). Ironic processes of mental control. *Psychological Review, 101*, 34–52.

Wegner, D. M. (1995). A computer network model of human transactive memory. *Social Cognition, 13*, 319–339.

Wegner, D. M. (2002). *The illusion of conscious will*. Cambridge, MA: MIT Press.

Wegner, D. M. (2004). Precis of the illusion of conscious will. *Behavioral & Brain Sciences, 27*, 649–659.

Wegner, D. M. (2011). Setting free the bears: Escape from thought suppression. *American Psychologist, 66*(8), 671–680. doi:10.1037/a0024985

Wegner, D. M., Ansfield, M., & Pilloff, D. (1998). The putt and the pendulum: Ironic effects of the mental control of action. *Psychological Science, 9*, 196–199.

Wegner, D. M., Fuller, V. A., & Sparrow, B. (2003). Clever hands: Uncontrolled intelligence in facilitated communication. *Journal of Personality and Social Psychology, 85*, 5–19.

Wegner, D. M., Sparrow, B., & Winerman, L. (2004). Vicarious agency: Experiencing control over the movements of others. *Journal of Personality and Social Psychology, 86*, 838–848.

Wegner, D. M., Wenzlaff, R., Kerker, M., & Beattie, A. E. (1981). Incrimination through innuendo: Can media questions become public answers? *Journal of Personality and Social Psychology, 40*, 822–832.

Wehrens, M. J. P. W., Kuyper, H., Dijkstra, P., Buunk, A. P., & Van Der Werf, M. P. C. (2010). The long-term effect of social comparison on academic performance. *European Journal of Social Psychology*, *40*(7), 1158–1171. doi:10.1002/ejsp.706

Wehrle, T., Kaiser, S., Schmidt, S., & Scherer, K. R. (2000). Studying the dynamics of emotional expression using synthesized facial muscle movements. *Journal of Personality and Social Psychology*, *78*, 105–119.

Weihs, K. L., Enright, T. M., & Simmens, S. J. (2008). Close relationships and emotional processing predict decreased mortality in women with breast cancer: Preliminary evidence. *Psychosomatic Medicine*, *70*(1), 117–124. doi:10.1097/PSY.0b013e31815c5cf

Weiner, B. (1985). "Spontaneous" causal thinking. *Psychological Bulletin*, *97*, 74–84.

Weiner, B. (2008). Reflections on the history of attribution theory and research. *Social Psychology*, *39*, 151–156.

Weiner, B., Amirkhan, J., Folkes, V. S., & Verette, J. A. (1987). An attributional analysis of excuse giving: Studies of a naive theory of emotion. *Journal of Personality and Social Psychology*, *52*, 316–324.

Weinstock, M. (2011). Knowledge-telling and knowledge-transforming arguments in mock jurors' verdict justifications. *Thinking & Reasoning*, *17*(3), 282–314. doi:10.1080/13546783.2011.575191

Wells, G. L. (1984). The psychology of lineup identifications. *Journal of Applied Social Psychology*, *14*, 89–103.

Wells, G. L. (1993). What do we know about eyewitness identification? *American Psychologist*, *48*, 553–571.

Wells, G. L. (2014). Eyewitness identification: Probative value, criterion shifts, and policy regarding the sequential lineup. *Current Directions in Psychological Science*, *23*, 11–16.

Wells, G. L., & Bradfield, A. L. (1998). "Good, you identified the suspect": Feedback to eyewitness reports distorts their reports of the witnessing experience. *Journal of Applied Social Psychology*, *83*, 360–376.

Wells, G. L., & Hasel, L. (2007). Facial composite production by eyewitnesses. *Current Directions in Psychological Science*, *16*, 6–10.

Wells, G. L., & Hasel, L. (2008). Eyewitness identification: Issues in common knowledge and generalization. In E. Borgida & S. T. Fiske (Eds.), *Beyond common sense: Psychological science in the courtroom* (pp. 159–176). Malden : Blackwell.

Wells, G. L., & Luus, C. A. E. (1990). Police lineups as experiments: Social methodology as a framework for properly conducted lineups. *Personality and Social Psychology Bulletin*, *16*, 106–117.

Wells, G. L., & Quinlivan, D. S. (2009). Suggestive eyewitness identification procedures and the Supreme Court's reliability test in light of eyewitness science: 30 years later. *Law and Human Behavior*, *33*, 1–24.

Wells, G. L., Charman, S. D., & Olson, E. A. (2005). Building face composites can harm lineup identification performance. *Journal of Experimental Psychology: Applied*, *11*, 147–156.

Wells, G. L., Malpass, R. S., Lindsay, R. C. L., Fisher, R. P., Turtle, J. W., & Fulero, S. M. (2000). From the lab to the police station. *American Psychologist*, *55*, 581–598.

Wells, G. L., Olson, E. A., & Charman, S. D. (2002). The confidence of eyewitnesses in their identifications from lineups. *Current Directions in Psychological Science*, *11*, 151–154.

Wells, W. D. (Ed.). (1997). *Measuring advertising effectiveness*. Mahwah, NJ: Erlbaum.

Wenzlaff, R. M., & Bates, D. E. (2000). The relative efficacy of concentration and suppression strategies of mental control. *Personality and Social Psychology Bulletin*, *26*, 1200–1212.

Werth, L., & Foerster, J. (2002). Implicit person theories influence memory judgments: The circumstances under which metacognitive knowledge is used. *European Journal of Social Psychology*, *32*, 353–362.

West, S., Jett, S. E., Beckman, T., & Vonk, J. (2010). The phylogenetic roots of cognitive dissonance. *Journal of Comparative Psychology*, *124*, 425–432.

West, T. V., Magee, J. C., Gordon, S. H., & Gullett, L. (2014). A little similarity goes a long way: The effects of peripheral but self-revealing similarities on improving and sustaining interracial relationships. *Journal of Personality and Social Psychology*, *107*, 81–100.

Westen, D. (2007). *The political brain: The role of emotion in deciding the fate of the nation*. New York: Public Affairs Books.

Westen, D., Kilts, C., Blagov, P., et al. (2006). The neural basis of motivated reasoning: An fMRI study of emotional constraints on political judgment during the U.S. presidential election of 2004. *Journal of Cognitive Neuroscience*, *18*, 1947–1958.

Weyant, J. M. (1996). Application of compliance techniques to direct-mail requests for charitable donations. *Psychology and Marketing*, *13*, 157–170.

Wheeler, D. L., Jacobson, J. W., Paglieri, R. A., & Schwartz, A. A. (1993). An experimental assessment of facilitated communication. *Mental Retardation*, *31*, 49–59.

Wheeler, L., & Kim, Y. (1997). What is beautiful is culturally good: The physical attractiveness stereotype has different content in collectivistic cultures. *Personality and Social Psychology Bulletin*, *23*, 795–800.

Wheeler, L., Koestner, R., & Driver, R. (1982). Related attributes in the choice of comparison others: It's there, but it isn't all there is. *Journal of Experimental Social Psychology*, *18*, 489–500.

Wheeler, M. E., & Fiske, S. T. (2005). Controlling racial prejudice: Social-cognitive goals affect amygdala and stereotype activation. *Psychological Science*, *16*, 56–63.

Wheeler, S. C., & DeMarree, K. G. (2009). Multiple mechanisms of prime-to-behavior effects. *Social and Personality Psychology Compass*, *3*(4), 566–581. doi:10.1111/j.1751-9004.2009.00187.x

Wheeler, S. C., Briñol, P., & Hermann, A. D. (2007). Resistance to persuasion as self-regulation: Ego-depletion and its effects on attitude change processes. *Journal of Experimental Social Psychology*, *43*, 150–156.

White, J. (2007). Abu Ghraib officer cleared of detainee abuse; verdict means no one in army's upper ranks will be imprisoned for the 2003 mistreatment in Iraq. *Washington Post*, p. A05.

White, J. W., Donat, P. L. N., & Humphrey, J. A. (1995). An examination of the attitudes underlying sexual coercion among acquaintances. *Journal of Psychology and Human Sexuality*, *8*, 27–47.

White, K. M., Smith, J. R., Terry, D. J., Greenslade, J. H., & McKimmie, B. M. (2009). Social influence in the theory of planned behaviour: The role of descriptive, injunctive, and in-group norms. *British Journal of Social Psychology*, *48*, 135–158.

White, P. A. (2002). Causal attribution from covariation information: The evidential evaluation model. *European Journal of Social Psychology*, *32*, 667–684.

White, R. K. (1977). Misperception in the Arab-Israeli conflict. *Journal of Social Issues*, *33*, 190–221.

Whittaker, J. O., & Meade, R. D. (1967). Social pressure in the modification and distortion of judgment: A cross-cultural study. *International Journal of Psychology*, *2*, 109–113.

Wicker, A. W. (1969). Attitudes versus actions: The relationship between verbal and overt behavioral responses to attitude objects. *Journal of Social Issues*, *25*, 41–78.

Widom, C. S., DuMont, K., & Czaja, S. J. (2007). A prospective investigation of major depressive disorder and comorbidity in abused and neglected children grown up. *Archives of General Psychiatry*, *64*(1), 49–56.

Wilder, D. A. (1984). Intergroup contact: The typical member and the exception to the rule. *Journal of Experimental Psychology*, *20*, 177–194.

Wilder, D. A. (1986). Social categorization: Implications for creation and reduction of intergroup bias. In L. Berkowitz (Ed.), *Advances in experimental social psychology* (Vol. 19, pp. 291–355). New York: Academic Press.

Wilder, D. A., & Shapiro, P. N. (1989). Role of competition-induced anxiety in limiting the beneficial impact of positive behavior by an out-group member. *Journal of Personality and Social Psychology*, *56*, 60–69.

Wilford, M. M., & Wells, G. L. (2010). Does facial processing prioritize change detection? Change blindness illustrates costs and benefits of holistic processing. *Psychological Science*, *21*(11), 1611–1615. doi:10.1177/0956797610385952

Wilkins, C. L., & Kaiser, C. R. (2014). Racial progress as a threat to the status hierarchy: Implications for perceptions of anti-White bias. *Psychological Science*, *25*, 439–446.

Willard, J., Madon, S., Guyll, M., & Spoth, R. (in press). Self-efficacy as a moderator of positive and negative self-fulfilling prophecy effects: Mothers' beliefs and children's alcohol use. *European Journal of Social Psychology*.

Willard, J., Madon, S., Guyll, M., Scherr, K. C., & Buller, A. A. (2012). The accumulating effects of shared expectations. *European Journal of Social Psychology*, *42*, 497–508. doi:10.1002/ejsp.874

Williams, J. (1998). *Thurgood Marshall: American revolutionary*. New York: Times Books.

Williams, K. D., & Nida, S. A. (2011). Ostracism: Consequences and coping. *Current Directions in Psychological Science*, *20*, 71–75.

Williams, L. E., & Bargh, J. A. (2008). Experiencing physical warmth promotes interpersonal warmth. *Science*, *322*(5901), 606–607. doi:10.1126/science.1162548

Williams, P. (2001). *How to be like Mike: Life lessons about basketball's best*. Deerfield Beach, FL: Health Communications.

Williams, T. P., & Sogon, S. (1984). Group composition and conforming behavior in Japanese students. *Japanese Psychological Research*, *26*, 231–234.

Willis, J., & Todorov, A. (2006). First impressions: Making up your mind after a 100-ms exposure to a face. *Psychological Science*, *17*, 592–598.

Willis, J., & Todorov, A. (2006). First impressions: Making up your mind after a 100-ms exposure to a face. *Psychological Science*, *17*, 592–298.

Willmott, L., Harris, P., Gellaitry, G., Cooper, V., & Horne, R. (2011). The effects of expressive writing following first myocardial infarction: A randomized controlled trial. *Health Psychology*, *30*(5), 642–650. doi:10.1037/a0023519

Wilner, D., Walkley, R., & Cook, S. (1955). *Human relations in interracial housing*. Minneapolis: University of Minnesota Press.

Wilson, A. E., & Ross, M. (2000). The frequency of temporal-self and social comparisons in people's personal appraisals. *Journal of Personality and Social Psychology*, *78*, 928–942.

Wilson, C. (2011, February 15). Jeopardy, Schmeopardy: Why IBM's next target should be a machine that plays poker. *Slate.com*. Retrieved April 18, 2011, from www.slate.com/id/2285035/

Wilson, D. K., Purdon, S. E., & Wallston, K. A. (1988). Compliance in health recommendations: A theoretical overview of message framing. *Health Education Research*, *3*, 161–171.

Wilson, D. S. (1997). Altruism and organism: Disentangling the themes of multilevel selection theory. *American Naturalist*, *150*, S122–S134.

Wilson, D. S., & Wilson E. O. (2007, November 3). Survival of the selfless. *New Scientist*, pp. 42–46.

Wilson, D. S., Van Vugt, M., & O'Gorman, R. (2008). Multilevel selection theory and major evolutionary transitions: Implications for psychological science. *Current Directions in Psychological Science*, *17*, 6–9.

Wilson, E. O. (1975). *Sociobiology: The new synthesis*. Cambridge, MA: Belknap Press.

Wilson, I. (2014, April 10). Dangerous "polar plunge" trend causes concern for N.H. school districts. *Concord Monitor*. Retrieved May 26, 2014, from www.concordmonitor.com/news/11495396-95/dangerous-polar-plunge-trend-causes-concern-for-nh-school-districts

Wilson, J. (2005). *The politics of truth: A diplomat's memoir*. New York: PublicAffairs.

Wilson, S. J., & Lipsey, M. W. (2007). School-based interventions for aggressive and disruptive behavior: Update of a meta-analysis. *American Journal of Preventive Medicine, 33*, S130–S143.

Wilson, T. D. (2002). *Strangers to ourselves: Discovering the adaptive unconscious*. Cambridge, MA: Harvard University Press.

Wilson, T. D. (2011). *Redirect: The surprising new science of psychological change*. New York: Little, Brown.

Wilson, T. D., & Bar-Anan, Y. (2008). The unseen mind. *Science, 321*, 1046–1047.

Wilson, T. D., & Brekke, N. (1994). Mental contamination and mental correction: Unwanted influences on judgments and evaluations. *Psychological Bulletin, 116*, 117–142.

Wilson, T. D., & Dunn, E. W. (2004). Self-knowledge: Its limits, value and potential for improvement. *Annual Review of Psychology, 55*, 493–518.

Wilson, T. D., & Gilbert, D. T. (2003). Affective forecasting. In M. P. Zanna (Ed.), *Advances in experimental social psychology* (Vol. 35, pp. 345–411). San Diego, CA: Academic Press.

Wilson, T. D., & Gilbert, D. T. (2008). Explaining away: A model of affective adaptation. *Perspectives on Psychological Science, 3*, 370–386.

Wilson, T. D., & Kraft, D. (1993). Why do I love thee? Effects of repeated introspections about a dating relationship on attitudes toward the relationship. *Personality and Social Psychology Bulletin, 19*, 409–418.

Wilson, T. D., & Linville, P. W. (1982). Improving the academic performance of college freshmen: Attribution therapy revisited. *Journal of Personality and Social Psychology, 42*, 367–376.

Wilson, T. D., & Linville, P. W. (1985). Improving the performance of college freshmen using attributional techniques. *Journal of Personality and Social Psychology, 49*, 287–293.

Wilson, T. D., Aronson, E., & Carlsmith, K. (2010). The art of laboratory experimentation. In S. Fiske, D. Gilbert, & G. Lindzey (Eds.), *Handbook of social psychology* (5th ed., pp. 49–79). New York: Wiley.

Wilson, T. D., Dunn, D. S., Kraft, D., & Lisle, D. J. (1989). Introspection, attitude change, and attitude-behavior consistency: The disruptive effects of explaining why we feel the way we do. In L. Berkowitz (Ed.), *Advances in experimental social psychology* (Vol. 19, pp. 123–205). Orlando, FL: Academic Press.

Wilson, T. D., Gilbert, D. T., & Wheatley, T. (1998). Protecting our minds: The role of lay beliefs. In V. Yzerbyt, G. Lories, & B. Dardenne (Eds.), *Metacognition: Cognitive and social dimensions* (pp. 171–201). New York: Russell Sage Foundation.

Wilson, T. D., Hodges, S. D., & La Fleur, S. J. (1995). Effects of introspecting about reasons: Inferring attitudes from accessible thoughts. *Journal of Personality and Social Psychology, 69*, 16–28.

Wilson, T. D., Houston, C. E., & Meyers, J. M. (1998). Choose your poison: Effects of lay beliefs about mental processes on attitude change. *Social Cognition, 16*, 114–132.

Wilson, T. D., Houston, C. E., Etling, K. M., & Brekke, N. C. (1996). A new look at anchoring effects: Basic anchoring and its antecedents. *Journal of Experimental Psychology: General, 125*, 387–402.

Wilson, T. D., Laser, P. S., & Stone, J. I. (1982). Judging the predictors of one's own mood: Accuracy and the use of shared theories. *Journal of Experimental Social Psychology, 18*, 537–556.

Wilson, T. D., Lindsey, S., & Schooler, T. Y. (2000). A model of dual attitudes. *Psychological Review, 107*, 101–126.

Wilson, T. D., Lisle, D., Schooler, J. W., Hodges, S. D., Klaaren, K. J., & La Fleur, S. J. (1993). Introspecting about reasons can reduce post-choice satisfaction. *Personality and Social Psychology Bulletin, 19*, 331–339.

Wilton, C., & Campbell, M. A. (2001). An exploration of the reasons why adolescents engage in traditional and cyber bullying. *Journal of Educational Sciences and Psychology, 1*, 101–109.

Wilton, C., & Campbell, M. A. (2011). An exploration of the reasons why adolescents engage in traditional and cyber bullying. *Journal of Educational Sciences and Psychology, 1*, 101–109.

Winslow, R. W., Franzini, L. R., & Hwang, J. (1992). Perceived peer norms, casual sex, and AIDS risk prevention. *Journal of Applied Social Psychology, 22*, 1809–1827.

Wiseman, C. V., Gray, J. J., Mosimann, J. E., & Ahrens, A. H. (1992). Cultural expectations of thinness in women: An update. *International Journal of Eating Disorders, 11*, 85–89.

Wiseman, M. C., & Moradi, B. (2010). Body image and earing disorder symptoms in sexual minority men: A test and extension of objectification theory. *Journal of Counseling Psychology, 57*, 154–166.

Wittenbaum, G. M., & Moreland, R. L. (2008). Small-group research in social psychology: Topics and trends over time. *Social and Personality Psychology Compass, 2* (www.blackwell-compass.com/subject/socialpsychology/).

Wittenbaum, G. M., & Park, E. S. (2001). The collective preference for shared information. *Current Directions in Psychological Science, 10*, 72–75.

Wittenbrink, B., Judd, C. M., & Park, B. (1997). Implicit racial stereotypes and prejudice and their relationships with questionnaire measures: We know what we think. *Journal of Personality and Social Psychology, 72*, 262–274.

Wojciszke, B. (2005). Affective concomitants of information on morality and competence. *European Psychologist, 10*, 60–70.

Wolf, S. (2014). Majority and minority influence: A social impact analysis. In M. P. Zanna, J. M. Olson, & C. P. Herman (Eds.), *Social influence: The Ontario Symposium* (Vol. 5, pp. 207–236). New York: Psychology Press.

Wolfe, C., & Spencer, S. (1996). Stereotypes and prejudice: Their overt and subtle influence in the classroom. *American Behavioral Scientist, 40*, 176–185.

Wolfson, A. (2005). A hoax most cruel. *The Courier-Journal*, October 9. Retrieved June 5, 2006, from www.courier-journal.com/apps/pbcs.d11/article?Date=20051009&category=NEWS01

Wong, E. M., Galinsky, A. D., & Kray, L. J. (2009). The counterfactual mind-set: A decade of research. In K. D. Markman, W. M. P. Klein, & J. A. Suhr (Eds.), *Handbook of imagination and mental simulation* (pp. 161–174). New York: Psychology Press.

Wong, R. Y., & Hong, Y. (2005). Dynamic influences of culture on cooperation in a Prisoner's Dilemma game. *Psychological Science, 16*, 429–434.

Wood, J. V., Taylor, S. E., & Lichtman, R. R. (1985). Social comparison in adjustment to breast cancer. *Journal of Personality and Social Psychology, 49*, 1169–1183.

Wood, J. V., Perunovic, W.Q.E., & Lee, J. W. (2009). Positive self-statements: Power for some, peril for others. *Psychological Science, 20*, 860–866.

Wood, W. (1982). Retrieval of attitude-relevant information from memory: Effects on susceptibility to persuasion and on intrinsic motivation. *Journal of Personality and Social Psychology, 42*, 798–810.

Wood, W. (1987). Meta-analytic review of sex differences in group performance. *Psychological Bulletin, 102*, 53–71.

Wood, W., & Eagly, A. H. (2002). A cross-cultural analysis of the behavior of women and men: Implications for the origins of sex differences. *Psychological Bulletin, 128*, 699–727.

Wood, W., & Quinn, J. M. (2003). Forewarned and forearmed? Two meta-analytic syntheses of forewarnings of influence appeals. *Psychological Bulletin, 129*, 119–138.

Wood, W., Lundgren, S., Ouellette, J. A., Busceme, S., & Blackstone, T. (1994). Minority influence: A meta-analytic review of social influence processes. *Psychological Bulletin, 115*, 323–345.

Wood, W., Pool, G. J., Leck, K., & Purvis, D. (1996). Self-definition, defensive processing, and influence: The normative impact of majority and minority groups. *Journal of Personality and Social Psychology, 71*, 1181–1193.

Woodward, B. (2004). *Plan of attack*. New York: Simon & Schuster.

Woodward, B. (2006). *State of denial*. New York: Simon & Schuster.

Word, C. O., Zanna, M. P., & Cooper, J. (1974). The nonverbal mediation of self-fulfilling prophecies in interracial interaction. *Journal of Experimental Social Psychology, 10*, 109–120.

Wortman, C. B., & Silver, R. C. (1989). The myths of coping with loss. *Journal of Consulting and Clinical Psychology, 57*, 349–357.

Wrangham, R. W., Wilson, M. L., & Muller, M. N. (2006). Comparative rates of violence in chimpanzees and humans. *Primates, 47*, 14–26.

Wright, E. F., Lüüs, C. E., & Christie, S. D. (1990). Does group discussion facilitate the use of consensus information in making causal attributions? *Journal of Personality and Social Psychology, 59*, 261–269.

Wright, L. (1994). *Remembering Satan*. New York: Knopf.

Wright, P. J., & Arroyo, A. (2013). Internet pornography and U.S. women's sexual behavior: Results from a national sample. *Mass Communication & Society, 16*, 617–638. doi:10.1080/15205436.2012.754045

Wubben, M. J. J., De Cremer, D., & van Dijk, E. (2009). How emotion communication guides reciprocity: Establishing cooperation through disappointment and anger. *Journal of Experimental Social Psychology, 45*(4), 987–990. doi:10.1016/j.jesp.2009.04.010

Wyer, R. S., & Srull, T. K. (1989). *Memory and cognition in its social context*. Hillsdale, NJ: Erlbaum.

Xu, H., Bègue, L., & Bushman, B. J. (2012). Too fatigued to care: Ego depletion, guilt, and prosocial behavior. *Journal of Experimental Social Psychology, 48*(5), 1183–1186.

Xu, K., Nosek, B., & Greenwald, A. G. (2014). Psychology data from the Race Implicit Association Test on the Project Implicit Demo website. *Journal of Open Psychology Data, 2*, e3.

Xygalatas, D., Mitkidis, P., Fischer, R., Reddish, P., Skewes, J., Geertz, A. W., et al. (2013). Extreme rituals promote prosociality. *Psychological Science, 24*, 1602–1605.

Yamada, A., Fukuda, H., Samejima, K., Kiyokawa, S., Ueda, K., Noba, S., et al. (2014). The effect of an analytical appreciation of colas on consumer beverage choice. *Food Quality and Preference, 34*, 1–4.

Yan, Y., & Bissell, K., (2014). The globalization of beauty; How is ideal beauty influenced by globally published fashion and beauty magazines? *Journal of Intercultural Communication Research.* doi:10.1080/17475759.2014.917432

Yeager, D. S., Johnson, R., Spitzer, B. J., Trzesniewski, K. H., Powers, J., & Dweck, C. S. (2014). The far-reaching effects of believing people can change: Implicit theories of personality shape stress, health, and achievement during adolescence. *Journal of Personality and Social Psychology, 106*, 867–884.

Yeager, D. S., Pauneska, D., Walton, G. M., & Dweck, C. S. (2014). *How can we instill productive mindsets at scale? A review of the evidence and an initial R&D agenda*. White paper prepared for the White House Meeting on Excellence in Education: The Importance of Academic Mindsets. Retrieved May 23, 2014, from www.stanford.edu/~gwalton/home/Welcome_files/YeagerPauneskuWaltonDweck%20-%20White%20House%20R%26D%20agenda%20-%205-9-13.pdf

Yoffe, E. (2014, December 7). The college rape overcorrection. *Slate.com.* http://www.slate.com/articles/double_x/doublex/2014/12/college_rape_campus_sexual_assault_is_a_serious_problem_but_the_efforts.html

Young, A. I., & Fazio, R. H. (2013). Attitude accessibility as a determinant of object construal and evaluation. *Journal of Experimental Social Psychology, 49*, 404–418.

Youth and tobacco use. (2014). Center for Disease Control and Prevention. Retrieved August 19, 2014, from http://www.cdc.gov/tobacco/data_statistics/fact_sheets/youth_data/tobacco_use/index.htm

Yuki, M., & Brewer, M. (2014). *Culture and group processes*. New York: Oxford University Press.

Yukl, G. (2011). Contingency theories of effective leadership. In A. Bryman, D. L. Collinson, K. Grint, B. Jacksin, & M. Uhl-Bien (Eds.), *The Sage handbook of leadership* (pp. 286–298). Thousand Oaks, CA: Sage.

Zajonc, R. B. (1965). *Social facilitation*. Research Center for Group Dynamics, Institute for Social Research, University of Michigan.

Zajonc, R. B. (1968). Attitudinal effects of mere exposure. *Journal of Personality and Social Psychology*, 9, 1–27.

Zajonc, R. B. (1980). Feeling and thinking: Preferences need no inferences. *American Psychologist*, 35, 151–175.

Zajonc, R. B., Heingartner, A., & Herman, E. M. (1969). Social enhancement and impairment of performance in the cockroach. *Journal of Personality and Social Psychology*, 13, 83–92.

Zanna, M. P., & Rempel, J. K. (1988). Attitudes: A new look at an old concept. In D. Bar-Tal & A. W. Kruglanski (Eds.), *The social psychology of knowledge* (pp. 315–334). Cambridge, England: Cambridge University Press.

Zanot, E. J., Pincus, J. D., & Lamp, E. J. (1983). Public perceptions of subliminal advertising. *Journal of Advertising*, 12, 39–45.

Zebrowitz, L. A., & Franklin, R. G., Jr. (2014). The attractiveness halo effect and the babyface stereotype in older and younger adults: Similarities, own-age accentuation, and older adult positivity effects. *Experimental Aging Research*, 40, 375–393.

Zebrowitz, L. A., & Montepare, J. M. (2008). Social psychological face perception: Why appearance matters. *Social and Personality Psychology Compass*, 2, 1497–1517.

Zebrowitz, L. A., Wang, R., Bronstad, P. M., Eisenberg, D., Undurraga, E., Reyes-García, V., et al. (2012). First impressions from faces among US and culturally isolated Tsimane' people in the Bolivian rainforest. *Journal of Cross-Cultural Psychology*, 43, 119–134.

Zentall, S. R., & Morris, B. J. (2010). "Good job, you're so smart": The effects of inconsistency of praise type on young children's motivation. *Journal of Experimental Child Psychology*, 107(2), 155–163. doi:10.1016/j.jecp.2010.04.015

Zhang, D., Lowry, P. B., Zhou, L., & Fu, X. (2007). The impact of individualism-collectivism, social presence, and group diversity on group decision making under majority influence. *Journal of Management Information Systems*, 23, 53–80.

Zhang, H., You, J., Teng, F., & Chan, D. K. (2014). Differential roles of physical attractiveness and earning capability in explaining sense of power among dating individuals in China: A gender comparison. *Sex Roles*, 70, 343–355.

Zhang, Q., & Covey, J. (2014). Past and future implications of near-misses and their emotional consequences. *Experimental Psychology*, 61, 118–126.

Zhang, S., & Kline, S. L. (2009). Can I make my own decision? A cross-cultural study of perceived social network influence in mate selection. *Journal of Cross-Cultural Psychology*, 40, 3–23.

Zhang, Y., & Epley, N. (2009). Self-centered social exchange: Differential use of costs versus benefits in prosocial reciprocity. *Journal of Personality and Social Psychology*, 97(5), 796–810. doi:10.1037/a0016233

Zhong, C.-B., & Leonardelli, G. J. (2008). Cold and lonely: Does social exclusion literally feel cold? *Psychological Science*, 19(9), 838–842. doi:10.1111/j.1467-9280.2008.02165.x

Zhong, C.-B., & Liljenquist, K. (2006). Washing away your sins: Threatened morality and physical cleansing. *Science*, 313, 1451–1452.

Zhu, Y., & Han, S. (2008). Cultural differences in the self: From philosophy to psychology and neuroscience. *Social and Personality Psychology Compass*, 2, 1799–1811.

Zillmann, D. (1978). Attributions and misattributions of excitatory reactions. In J. H. Harvey, W. Ickes, & R. F. Kidd, (Eds.), *New directions in attribution research* (Vol. 2). Hillsdale, NJ: Erlbaum.

Zimbardo, P. G. (1970). The human choice: Individuation, reason, and order versus deindividuation, impulse, and chaos. In W. J. Arnold & D. Levine (Eds.), *Nebraska Symposium on Motivation* (Vol. 17; pp. 237–307). Lincoln: University of Nebraska Press.

Zimbardo, P. G. (2007). *The Lucifer effect: Understanding how good people turn evil*. New York: Random House.

Zimbardo, P., & Andersen, S. (1993). Understanding mind control: Exotic and mundane mental manipulations. *Recover from cults: Help for victims of psychological and spiritual abuse*, pp. 104–125.

Zimbardo, P., Weisenberg, M., Firestone, I., & Levy, B. (1965). Communicator effectiveness in producing public conformity and private attitude change. *Journal of Personality*, 33, 233–255.

Zimmer, B. (2009, October 25). On language: Ms.: The origins of the title, explained. *The New York Times*.

Zimmerman, M. (2008, March 12). Competitive to a fault. *Men's Health*. Retrieved April 30, 2014, from www.menshealth.com/fitness/integrity-and-character-derek-jeter

Credits

Photo Credits

Chapter 1 Page **21**: Bikeriderlondon/ Shutterstock; Page **24**: Stockbyte/Getty Images; Page **25**: STR New/Reuters; Page **27**: Glow Images; Page **28**: Paul Chesley/National Geographic Creative; Page **31**: Vacclav/Shutterstock; Page **33t**: Interfoto/Alamy; Page **33b**: The Drs. Nicholas and Dorothy Cummings Center for the History of Psychology, The University of Akron; Page **34**: Shawn Thew/EPA/Newscom; Page **35**: Karen Zebulon; Page **36**: Thomas Kienzle/EPA/Newscom; Page **37**: Newscom; Page **38l**: Felix Choo/Alamy; Page **38r**: Lenscap/Alamy; Page **39**: ProMotion/Fotolia; Page **40**: Villerot/Age Fotostock.

Chapter 2 Page **43**: Indranil Mukhereee/AFP/Getty Images; Page **46**: Kyodo/Newscom; Page **49**: Pixellover RM 8/Alamy; Page **51**: Franklin D. Roosevelt Presidential Library & Museum; Page **52**: Monkey Business/Fotolia; Page **57**: Africa Studio/Fotolia; Page **59**: Megapress/Alamy; Page **64**: Mark Harmel/Science Source; Page **65**: ScienceCartoonsPlus .com.

Chapter 3 Page **71**: Landov; Page **73**: Sean Nel/Shutterstock; Page **75**: National Archives and Records Administration; Page **76**: 88studio/Shutterstock; Page **80**: Monkey Business/Fotolia; Page **82**: Gina Sanders/Fotolia; Page **84**: Feedough/Getty Images; Page **86**: Darren Baker/Alamy; Page **91**: Masuda and Nisbett (2006); Page **95**: Bernd Wittenbrink, Joshua Correll et al © 2002; Page **97**: Nikola Solic/Reuters.

Chapter 4 Page **104**: AMC, Ursula Coyote/AP Images; Page **108bl**: TIPS Images/AGE Fotostock; Page **108tr**: PhotosIndia.com RM 18/Alamy; Page **108tl**: OJenny/Shutterstock; Page **108bm**: Ollyy/Shutterstock; Page **108br**: Maksym Bondarchuk/Shutterstock; Page **108tm**: Pathdoc/Fotolia; Page **109b**: White House Photo/Alamy; Page **109t**: Associated Sports Photography/Alamy; Page **110t**: The Paul Ekman Group, LLC; Page **110b**: The Paul Ekman Group, LLC; Page **111tr**: Andres Rodriguez/Fotolia; Page **111tl**: Pressmaster/Shutterstock; Page **111m**: Victor Tongdee/Shutterstock; Page **111bl**: Carol Beckwith & Angela Fisher/HAGA/The Image Works; Page **111br**: Sisse Brimerg/National Geographic; Page **113**: Jared Milgrim/Everett Collection Inc/Alamy; Page **114**: Isabella Vosmikova/FOX/Everett Collection; Page **116**: Media Rights Capital/Album/Newscom; Page **119**: Minerva Studio/Fotolia; Page **121**: Bettmann/Corbis; Page **122**: Bebeto Matthews/AP Images; Page **125**: Patrick Pleul/dpa/picture-alliance/Newscom; Page **127**: Oxford/Getty Images; Page **130**: Masuda and Nisbett (2006); Page **132**: Steve Vidler/Superstock; Page **133tl**: trubach/Shutterstock; Page **133tr**: Lissandra Melo/Shutterstock; Page **133br**: Izmael/Shutterstock; Page **133bl**: bigredlynx/Shutterstock; Page **133**: violetkaipa/Shutterstock; Page **134**: PCN Black/PCN Photography/Alamy.

Chapter 5 Page **139**: PCN Photography/Alamy; Page **141**: Eddie Lawrence/DK Images; Page **142**: Tsugufumi Matsumoto/Pool/AP Images; Page **149**: Patricia Schlein/PS3 WENN Photos/Newscom; Page **151**: Pearson; Page **152**: PEANUTS © 1995 Peanuts Worldwide LLC. Dist. By UNIVERSAL UCLICK. Reprinted with permission. All rights reserved.; Page **154**: SALLY FORTH © King Features Syndicate, Inc. World Rights reserved.; Page **158**: Omika/Fotolia; Page **167l**: Lee Corkran/Sygma/Corbis; Page **167r**: Library of Congress Prints and Photographs Division; Page **168**: Craig Ruttle/Alamy; Page **171**: SuperStock/Alamy.

Chapter 6 Page **177**: Aaron Horowitz/Flirt/Corbis; Page **180**: Powell John/Prisma/Agefotostock; Page **181**: JackF/Fotolia; Page **184**: Jeff Greenberg/Alamy; Page **185**: Industrieblick/Fotolia; Page **186**: Glow Images; Page **189**: moodboard/Fotolia; Page **190**: Shariff Che'Lah/Fotolia; Page **192**: Splash News/Newscom; Page **193**: Shannon Fagan/The Image Bank/Getty Images; Page **197**: Krasyuk/Fotolia; Page **198**: Library of Congress Prints and Photographs Division Washington [LC-USZC4-7214]; Page **200**: Library of Congress Prints and Photographs Division [LC-USZ62-40764]; Page **202tl**: The Durango Herald/AP Images; Page **202tr**: The Denver Post/AP Images; Page **202bl**: Department of Motor Vehicles/AP Images; Page **202br**: Tribune Newspapers/AP Images; Page **203**: Rodger Mallison/The Fort Worth Star-Telegram/AP Images.

Chapter 7 Page **208**: Pictorial Press Ltd/Alamy; Page **209**: Keith Johnson/Deseret Morning News/AP Images; Page **211**: J Pat Carter/AP Images; Page **216**: Hero Images/Getty Images; Page **219**: NASA Photo/Alamy; Page **222**: Elizabeth Goodenough/Everett Collection/Alamy; Page **226**: UPI/FDA/Landov; Page **227**: Henry Martin/The New Yorker Collection/The Cartoon Bank; Page **228**: DarkOne/Shutterstock; Page **231**: Handout/Mct/Newscom; Page **232**: The Advertising Archives; Page **233**: Bill Greenblat/Newsmakers/Getty Images; Page **234**: American Association of Advertising Agencies; Page **236**: General Mills/AP Images; Page **237**: best_age_model/Fotolia; Page **240**: Jaimie Trueblood/Screen Gems/Everett Collection; Page **241**: Reuters.

Chapter 8 Page **246**: Rich Carey/Shutterstock; Page **249**: ZUMA Press/Newscom; Page **251**: Jeremy Bembaron/Sygma/Corbis; Page **253**: Flirt/SuperStock; Page **254**: Library of Congress Prints and Photographs Division [LC-USZ62-119765]; Page **255**: Eric James/NASA Images; Page **257**: U.S. Dept. of Defense; Page **258**: Anna Daren; Page **259**: Reproduced with permission. Copyright © 2015 Scientific American, Inc. All rights reserved.; Page **262**: Jeff Greenberg "0 people images"/Alamy; Page **263**: Suntzulynn for LE/Splash News/Newscom; Page **267**: Aflo Co., Ltd./Alamy; Page **270**: Joe Belanger/Shutterstock; Page **271**: Craig Steven Thrasher/Alamy; Page **274**: Enviromantic/Getty Images; Page **275**: Pictorial Press Ltd/Alamy; Page **277t**: Prisma Bildagentur AG/Alamy; Page **277bl**: Alexandra Milgram; Page **277br**: Alexandra Milgram; Page **283**: Keith McIntyre/Shutterstock.

Chapter 9 Page **289**: Kevin Lamarque/Reuters; Page **291**: Monkey Business/Fotolia; Page **292**: Philip G. Zimbardo, Inc.; Page **293**: Philip G. Zimbardo, Inc.; Page **297**: wavebreakmedia/Shutterstock; Page **300**: PhotoAlto/Alamy; Page **301**: Library of Congress Prints and Photographs Division [LC-USZ62-138224]; Page **302**: Elnur Amikishiyev/123RF; Page **306**: Henry Martin/The New Yorker Collection/The Cartoon Bank; Page **307**: Andy Dean Photography/Shutterstock; Page **308**: Chuck Nacke/Alamy; Page **309**: File/AP Images; Page **311**: Everett Collection Inc/Alamy; Page **312**: US Senate/Alamy; Page **313**: WavebreakmediaMicro/Fotolia; Page **319**: Tom McCarthy/PhotoEdit.

Chapter 10 Page **323**: Shutterstock; Page **327**: Shutterstock; Page **329**: Sam Gross/The New Yorker Collection/The Cartoon Bank; Page **330**: Dmitriy Shironosov/123RF; Page **331t**: Radius Images/Getty Images; Page **331b**: Samuel R. Sommers; Page **333t**: Trinette Reed/Blend/Glow Images; Page **333b**: Dr. Judith Langlois; Page **335**: WALT DISNEY PICTURES/Album/Newscom; Page **337**: Allstar Picture Library/Alamy; Page **341**: nyul/Fotolia; Page **342**: Peter Scholey/SuperStock; Page **343**: Peter Steiner/The New Yorker Collection/The Cartoon Bank; Page **346**: AF archive/Alamy; Page **349t**: imageBROKER/Alamy; Page **349b**: vario images GmbH & Co.KG/Alamy; Page **350**: Ian Hooton/DK Images; Page **352**: Tomasz Trojanowski/Shutterstock; Page **356**: Monkey Business Images/Shutterstock.

Chapter 11 Page **364**: Suzanne Plunkett/AP Images; Page **366**: wavebreakmedia/Shutterstock; Page **369**: United Press International; Page **371**: AP Images; Page **373l**: HRC WENN Photos/Newscom; Page **373r**: Zelig Shaul/ACE Pictures/Newscom; Page **379**: Toa555/Fotolia; Page **380**: Blend Images/Glow Images; Page **385**: Magnum Photos, Inc.; Page **387**: Kuttig - People/Alamy; Page **389**: Cancan Chu/Getty Images; Page **390**: Jim West/Alamy.

Chapter 12 Page **395**: Sipa Press/Sipa USA; Page **397**: Catherine Ursillo/Science Source; Page **398**: Karl Ammann/Nature Picture Library; Page **400**: Scott Griessel/Fotolia; Page **402**: Universal Images Group/SuperStock; Page **404**: Courtesy of Albert Bandura; Page **405**: Dana Fradon/The New Yorker Collection/The Cartoon Bank; Page **408b**: Digital Vision/Getty Images; Page **408t**: pathdoc/Fotolia; Page **411**: Bill Aron/PhotoEdit; Page **412**: Andreas Gebert/EPA/Newscom; Page **415**: Theartofphoto/Fotolia LLC; Page **416**: Jochen Tack/Alamy; Page **420**: Robert Brenner/PhotoEdit; Page **421**: Science Source; Page **423**: Charles Barsotti/The New Yorker Collection/The Cartoon Bank;

Page 425: igor/Fotolia; Page 426: Michael Pole/Comet/Corbis; Page 427: Junfu Han/Zumapress/Newscom.

Chapter 13 Page 433: Lon C. Diehl/PhotoEdit; Page 435: Jack Ziegler/The New Yorker Collection/The Cartoon Bank; Page 436: Bryan Denton/Corbis; Page 438: Eva Serrabassa/Getty Images; Page 439: Jeff Schmaltz/NASA Images; Page 442: Sally and Richard Greenhill/Alamy; Page 443: Roy Delgado/Cartoon Stock; Page 444r: Splash News/Corbis; Page 444l: BRIAN BLANCO/EPA/Newscom; Page 447: 2009 Owen DB/Black Star/Newscom; Page 448: William Cunningham; Page 452: Gary Conner/PhotoEdit; Page 454: Ross Taylor/The Herald/AP Images; Page 455: Jeffrey Collins/AP Images; Page 456: Cultura Creative (RF)/Alamy; Page 460: Jim Ward/Alamy; Page 461: Richard W. Rodriguez/MCT/Landov; Page 463: David Taylor Photography/Alamy; Page 466: Jonathan Nourok/PhotoEdit; Page 468: Pearson Education.

SPA 1 Page 475: Chuck Beckley/The Daily News/AP Images; Page 476: Rob O'Neal/The Key West Citizen/AP Images; Page 477: David Bookstaver/AP Images; Page 478: Mick Stevens/The New Yorker Collection/The Cartoon Bank; Page 480: Michel Setboun/Glow Images;

Page 482: Mick Stevens/The New Yorker Collection/The Cartoon Bank; Page 484: Pearson Education; Page 486: dracozlat/Fotolia; Page 489: Monkey Business Images/Shutterstock; Page 491: Monkey Business Images/Shutterstock.

SPA 2 Page 496: darknightsky/Fotolia; Page 497: Thomson Reuters (Markets) LLC; Page 499tl: Adam Gregor/Shutterstock; Page 499bl: Elena Rooraid/PhotoEdit; Page 499br: Wladimir Wetzel/Fotolia; Page 499tr: Robert Brenner/Photo Edit; Page 504: Monkey Business Images/Shutterstock; Page 507: Monkey Business/Fotolia; Page 510: AntonioDiaz/Fotolia LLC; Page 512: Alexvav/Shutterstock; Page 513: CartoonStock.

SPA 3 Page 516: Blair Seitz/Newscom; Page 517: Dallas Morning News; Page 520: Shi Yali/Shutterstock; Page 521: Elizabeth Loftus; Page 525t: Divewonder/Fotolia; Page 525b: Junial Enterprises/Shutterstock; Page 527: Steve Bloom; Page 530: Mike Twohy/The New Yorker Collection/The Cartoon Bank; Page 531: Frank Cotham/The New Yorker Collection/The Cartoon Bank; Page 532t: Spencer Grant/PhotoEdit; Page 532b: Photos 12/Alamy.

Text Credits

Chapter 1 Page 29: Data from "The name of the game: Predictive power of reputations versus situational labels in determining Prisoner's Dilemma Game moves," by Verda Liberman, Steven M Samuels, and Lee Ross. Personality and Social Psychology Bulletin, 30.9, pp. 1175–85.; Page 29: Source: Lewin, K., Defining the 'field at a given time.', Psychological Review, Vol 50(3), May 1943, 292–310.; Page 29: Source: Fritz Heider, The Psychology of Interpersonal relations, Hillsdale (New Jersey): Lawrence Erlbaum Associates, cop. 1943; Page 29: Source: Ross, L. (2010). Dealing with conflict: Experiences and experiments. In M. H. Gonzales, C. Tavris, & J. Aronson (Eds.), The scientist and the humanist: A festschrift in honor of Elliot Aronson (pp. 39–66). New York: Psychology Press.; Page 36: Festinger, L (Ed.). (1980). Retrospections on Social Psychology. New York: Oxford University Press.

Chapter 2 Page 44: Source: MacKinnon, C. (1993, July-August). Turning rape into pornography: Postmodern genocide. Ms., pp. 24–30.; Page 46: Source: Festinger, L. (1980) "Looking Backward." In L. Festinger (Ed.), Retrospections on Social Psychology (pp. 236–254). Oxford: Oxford University Press.; Page 46: Source: Darley, J. M., & Latané, B. (1968). Bystandar intervention in emergencies: Diffusion of responsibility. Journal of Personality and Social Psychology, 8, 377–383; Page 52: Source: Nisbett, R. E., & Wilson, T. D. (1977). Telling more than we can know: Verbal reports on mental processes. Psychological Review, 84, 231–259; Page 54: Source: P.L. Kapitza, Experiment, theory, and practice: articles and addresses, Springer Science & Business Media, 30-Apr-1980 – Philosophy - 429 pages; Page 55: Source: Darley, J. M., & Latané, B. (1968). Bystandar intervention in emergencies: Diffusion of responsibility. Journal of Personality and Social Psychology, 8, 377–383; Page 61: Source: Lewin, K. (1951). Problems of research in social psychology. In D. Cartwright (Ed.), Field theory in social science (pp. 155–169). New York: Harper; Page 67: Source: Adapted from APA Ethical Principles of Psychologists and Code of Conduct, 2010.

Chapter 3 Page 72: Source: Markoff, J. (2011, February 16). Computer wins on "Jeopardy!": Trivial, it's not. The New York Times. Retrieved April 18, 2011, from www.nytimes.com/2011/02/17/science/17jeopardy-watson.html?pagewanted=2; Page 72: Source: Dunn, A. (1997). If Deep Blue Wrote Hamlet Would It Change the Endgame? New York Times, May 14.; Page 73: Source: George Robert Gissing, The private papers of Henry Ruecroft, New York: Dutton, 1903.; Page 74: Source: George Santayana, The sense of beauty, New York: C. Scribner's Sons, 1896; Page 54 –55: Source: Oliver W Sacks, The man who mistook his wife for a hat, New York: Harper & Row, 1987; Page 76: Source: Norman Maclean, A river runs through it, and other stories, Chicago: University of Chicago Press, 1976.; Page 78: Source: Based on data in Higgins, E. T., Rholes, W. S., & Jones, C. R. (1977). Category accessibility and impression formation. Journal of Experimental Social Psychology, 13, 141–154.; Page 79: Source: George Eliot (Mary Ann Evans Cross), 1871; Page 80: Source: Figure adapted from R. Rosenthal and L. Jacobson: Pygmalion in the Classroom: Teacher Expectation and Pupils' Intellectual Development. Holt, Rinehart, Winston, © 1968.: Reprinted with permission of R. Rosenthal.; Page 81: Source: Arthur Conan Doyle, The adventures of Sherlock Holmes, London: George Newnes, Ltd., 1892; Page 81: Source: The principles of psychology, William James (1890). London: Macmillan, 1890.; Page 83: Source: Eneas Sweetland Dallas, The Gay Science, Chapman and Hall, 1866; Page 86: Source: Marion, R. (1995, August). The girl who mewed. Discover, pp. 38–40; Page 87: Source: Fox, C. (2006). The availability heuristic in the classroom: How soliciting more criticism can boost your course ratings. Judgment and Decision Making, 1, 86–90; Page 87: Source: Based on Schwarz, N., Bless, H., Strack, F., Klumpp, G., Rittenauer-Schatka, H., & Simmons, A. (1991). Ease of retrieval as information: Another look at the availability heuristic. Journal of Personality and Social Psychology, 61, 195–202.; Page 89: Source: Forer, B. R. (1949). The fallacy of personal validation: A classroom demonstration of gullibility. Journal of Abnormal and Social Psychology, 44, 118–123; Page 93: Source: William James; Page 95: Source: Vos, K and Schooler, J. (2008). The Value of Believing in Free Will. Psychological Science, 19(1), 51.; Page 96: Source: Roese, N. J., & Olson, J. M. (1997). Counterfactual thinking: The intersection of affect and function. In M. P. Zanna (Ed.), Advances in experimental social psychology (Vol. 29, pp. 1–59). San Diego, CA: Academic Press; Page 97: Source: Forty Thousand Quotations: Prose and Poetical, comp. by Charles Noel Douglas. New York: Halcyon House, 1917.; Page 98: Source: Lehman, D. R., Lempert, R. O., & Nisbett, R. E. (1988). The effects of graduate training on reasoning: Formal discipline and thinking about everyday-life events. American Psychologist, 43, 431–442; Page 98: Source: "The Crack-Up", part one of The Crack-Up, by F. Scott Fitzgerald, as originally published inEsquire, February 1936.; Page 99: Source: Figure from "Teaching Reasoning," by Nisbett, Fong, Lehman, Cheng. Science, 238, pp. 625–631. Copyright © 1987 by the American Association for the Advancement of Science. Permission conveyed through Copyright Clearance Center, Inc.

Chapter 4 Page 105: Source: DeMarco, P. (1994, September 28). "Dear diary." The New York Times, p. C2.; Page 106: Source: Emerson, Ralph Waldo. The Conduct of Life. Boston: Ticknor and Fields, reprinted by Forgotten Books, [1860].; Page 112: Source: Archer, D. (1997a). Unspoken diversity: Cultural differences in gestures. Qualitative Sociology, 20, 79–105.; Page 112: Source: Tracy and Matsumoso's (2008), University of British Columbia. "Olympic Athlete Study Shows That Pride And Shame Are Universal And Innate Expressions." ScienceDaily. ScienceDaily, 12 August 2008. www.sciencedaily.com/releases/2008/08/080811200018.htm.; Page 113: Source: Gosling, S. (2008). Snoop: What your stuff says about you. London: Profile Books Ltd.; Page 114: Source: Jorge Luis Borges (1992), This Craft of Verse, Harvard University Press.; Page 117: Source: John Le Carré (1989), The Russia house, Knopf.; Page 119: Source: Kelley, H. H. (1967). Attribution theory in social psychology. In D. Levine (Ed.), Nebraska Symposium on Motivation (Vol. 15, pp. 192–238). Lincoln: University of Nebraska Press.; Page 120: Source: Based on Hoffman, C., Lau, I., & Johnson, D. R. (1986). The linguistic relativity of person cognition: An English-Chinese comparison. Journal of Personality and Social Psychology, 51, 1097–1105.; Page 121: Source: Feeney, M. (2005, October 25). Rosa Parks, civil rights icon, dead at 92. Boston Globe, pp. A1, B8.; Page 121: Source: Ramirez, A. (2005, December 2). New Yorkers take a tribute standing up.The New York Times, p. B1.; Page 122: Source: Based on Jones, E. E., & Harris, V. A. (1967).

The attribution of attitudes. Journal of Experimental Social Psychology, 3, 1–24.; Page **123**: Source: Epictetus (1904). Discourses, New York D. Appleton and Company.Translated by George Long; Page **124**: Source: Adapted from Taylor, S. E., & Fiske, S. T. (1975). Point of view and perceptions of causality. Journal of Personality and Social Psychology, 32, 439–445.; Page **124**: Source: Based on Taylor, S. E., & Fiske, S. T. (1975). Point of view and perceptions of causality. Journal of Personality and Social Psychology, 32, 439–445.; Page **125**: Source: Quattrone, G. A. (1982). Behavioral consequences of attributional bias. Social Cognition, 1, 358–378.; Page **128**: Source: Based on Pronin, E., Lin, D. Y., & Ross, L. (2002). The bias blind spot: Perceptions of bias in self versus others. Personality and Social Psychology Bulletin, 28, 369–381.; Page **132**: Source: Vladimir Nabokov (1989). Pale Fire, Vintage International.; Page **134**: Source: Markus et al., 2006. Going for the Gold, Association for Psychological Science. P. 123.

Chapter 5 Page **140**: Source: Hamm, M. (1999). Go for the goal: A champion's guide to winning in soccer and life. New York: HarperCollins.; Page **140**: Source: Zimmerman, M. (2008, March 12). Competitive to a fault. Men's Health. Retrieved April 30, 2014 from: http://www.menshealth.com/fitness/integrity-and-character-derek-jeter; Page **141**: Source: Montemayor, R., & Eisen, M. (1977). The development of self-conceptions from childhood to adolescence. Developmental Psychology, 13, 314–319.; Page **141**: Source: Montemayor, R., & Eisen, M. (1977). The development of self-conceptions from childhood to adolescence. Developmental Psychology, 13, 314–319.; Page **142**: Source: Girl born to Japan's princess. (2001, December 1). New York Times, p. 28.; Page **142**: Source: Data from Strohminger, N. & Nichols, S. (2014). The essential moral self. Cognition, 131, 159–171.; Page **143**: Source: Adapted from Singelis, T. M. (1994). The measurement of independent and interdependent self-construals. Personality and Social Psychology Bulletin, 20, 580–591.; Page **144**: Source: Kitayama, S., & Markus, H. R. (1994). Culture and the self: How cultures influence the way we view ourselves. In D. Matsumoto (Ed.), People: Psychology from a cultural perspective (pp. 17–37). Pacific Grove, CA: Brooks/Cole.; Page **144**: Source: Based on From Varnum, M. E. W., & Kitayama, S. (2011). What's in a name? Popular names are less common on frontiers. Psychological Science, 22, 176–183.; Page **145**: Source: William James, 1890; Page **146**: Source: Frederich Nietzsche (1961). Thus spoke Zarathustra, Harmondsworth: Penguin Books.; Page **146**: Source: Fyodor Dostoyevsky (1864). Notes from the Underground, Auckland: Floating Press.; Page **146**: Source: Based on Carver, C. S., & Scheier, M. F. (1981). Attention and self-regulation: A control-theory approach to human behavior. New York: Springer-Verlag.; Page **147**: Source: Dame Edith Sitwell, The Observer (30 April 1950); Page **147**: Source: Fenigstein, A., Scheier, M. F., & Buss, A. H. (1975). Public and private self-consciousness: Assessment and theory. Journal of Consulting and Clinical Psychology, 43, 522–527.; Page **148**: Source: Immanuel Kant (1948). The Moral Law: Groundwork og the Metaphysic of Moral, Taylor & Francis Ltd; Page **148**: Source: Richard Russo (1997). Straight man, New York: Random House.; Page **151**: Source: Virginia Hamilton Adair; Page **153**: Source: Bill Russell (1979). Second wind: the memoirs of an opinionated man, New York: Random House.; Page **153**: Adapted from Greene, D., Sternberg, B., & Lepper, M. R. (1976). Overjustification in a token economy. Journal of Personality and Social Psychology, 34, 1219–1234.; Page **156**: Source: Schachter, S., & Singer, J. E. (1962). Cognitive, social, and physiological determinants of emotional states. Psychological Review, 69, 379–399.; Page **157**: Source: Norman Maclean (1976). A River Runs Through It, University of Chicago Press.; Page **158**: Source: Based on Dutton, D. G., & Aron, A. P. (1974). Some evidence for heightened sexual attraction under conditions of high anxiety. Journal of Personality and Social Psychology, 30, 510–517.; Page **159**: Source: P D James (1992). The children of men, London: Faber and Faber.; Page **162**: Source: Adapted from Sinclair, S., Lowery, B. S., Hardin, C. D., & Colangelo, A. (2005). Social tuning of automatic racial attitudes: The role of affiliative motivation. Journal of Personality and Social Psychology, 89(4), 583–592.; Page **161**: Source: Wilde, O. (1996). De Profundis. Mineola, NY: Dover.; Page **162**: Source: Sinclair, S., Lowery, B. S., Hardin, C. D., & Colangelo, A. (2005). Social tuning of automatic racial attitudes: The role of affiliative motivation. Journal of Personality and Social Psychology, 89(4), 583–592.; Page **165**: Source: Friese, M. & Wänke, M. (2014). Personal prayer buffers self-control depletion. Journal of Experimental Social Psychology, 51, 56–59.; Page **166**: Source: Charles Dickens, 1843; Page **169**: Source: De La Rochefoucauld, F. (1871). Reflections; or Sentences and Moral Maxims. Scribner, Welford and Company; Page **171**: Source: Raskin, R., & Terry, H. (1988). A principle-components analysis of the Narcissistic Personality Inventory and further evidence of its construct validity. Journal

of Personality and Social Psychology, 54, 890–902.; Page **172**: Source: Based on Twenge, J. M., & Foster, J. D. (2010). Birth cohort increases in narcissistic personality traits among American college students, 1982–2009. Social Psychological and Personality Science, 1, 99–106.

Chapter 6 Page **178**: Source: Ferris, T. (1997, April 14). The wrong stuff. New Yorker, p. 52.; Page **180**: Source: Naughton, F., Eborall, H., & Sutton, S. (2012). Dissonance and disengagement in pregnant smokers. Journal of Smoking Cessation, 8, 24–32.; Page **180**: Source: Steele, C. M. (1988). The psychology of self-affirmation: Sustaining the integrity of the self. In L. Berkowitz (Ed.), Advances in experimental social psychology (Vol. 21, pp. 261–302). New York: Academic Press.; Page **180**: Source: Pitt, R. N. (2010). "Killing the messenger": Religious Black gay men's neutralization of anti-gay religious messages. Journal for the Scientific Study of Religion, 49, 56–72.; Page **182**: Source: Murray, A.A., Wood, J.M., & Lilienfeld, S.O. (2012). Psychopathic personality traits and cognitive dissonance: Individual differences in attitude change. Journal of Research in Personality, 46, 525–536.; Page **182**: Source: Leo Tolstoy (2006). The Kreutzer Sonata, Modern Library (first published 1889).; Page **187**: Source: Created by Carol Tavris. Used by permission.; Page **190**: Source: Based on Aronson, E., & Mills, J. S. (1959). The effect of severity of initiation on liking for a group. Journal of Abnormal and Social Psychology, 59, 177–181.; Page **195**: Source: Based on data in Freedman, J. L. (1965). Long-term behavioral effects of cognitive dissonance. Journal of Experimental and Social Psychology, 1, 145–155.; Page **197**: Source: Based on data in Jecker, J., & Landy, D. (1969). Liking a person as a function of doing him a favor. Human Relations, 22, 371–378.; Page **197**: Source: Takaku, S. (2006). Reducing road rage: An application of the dissonance- attribution model of interpersonal forgiveness. Journal of Applied Social Psychology, 36, 2362–2378.; Page **198**: Source: Leo Tolstoy (1983). War and peace, New York: Modern Library (first published 1869).; Page **198**: Source: Franklin, B. (1900). The autobiography of Benjamin Franklin (J. Bigelow, Ed.). Philadelphia: Lippincott. (Originally published 1868); Page **200**: Source: Moliè're (1908). The misanthrope, London: G. Bell and Sons (first published 1666).; Page **203**: Source: Nixon, R. M. (1990). In the arena: A memoir of victory, defeat, and renewal. New York: Simon & Schuster.; Page **204**: Source: Tavris, C. & Aronson, E. (2007). Mistakes were made (but not by me). New York: Harcourt.

Chapter 7 Page **209**: Source: Newman, A. A. (2009, February 18). The body as billboard: Your ad here. The New York Times (p. B3). Retrieved June 6, 2011, from www.ny-times.com/2009/02/18/business/media/18adco.html; Page **211**: Source: MARK TWAIN, A CONNECTICUT YANKEE IN KING ARTHUR'S COURT, 1885. Charles L. Webster.; Page **213**: Source: GRAHAM WALLAS, THE ART OF THOUGHT, 1926, Harcourt, Brace and Company.; Page **215**: Source: FRANÇOIS DE LA ROCHEFOUCAULD, MAXIMS, 1665, St. Augustine's Press, 2001.; Page **217**: Source: FRANÇOIS DE LA ROCHEFOUCAULD, MAXIMS, 1665, St. Augustine's Press, 2001.; Page **217**: Source: Data from Ajzen, I. (1985). From intentions to actions: A theory of planned behavior. In J. Kuhl & J. Beckmann (Eds.), Action control: From cognition to behavior (pp. 11–39). Heidelberg, Germany: Springer-Verlag.; Page **217**: Source: Adapted from Davidson, A. R., & Jaccard, J. J. (1979). Variables that moderate the attitude-behavior relation: Results of a longitudinal survey. Journal of Personality and Social Psychology, 37, 1364–1376.; Page **219**: Source: RICHARD COHEN, 1991, Washington Post.; Page **219**: Source: JUNIUS, (December 19, 1769), Harry Sampson Woodfall.; Page **220**: Source: ARISTOTLE (2012), RHETORIC, Courier Corporation.; Page **224**: Source: Based on data in Petty, R. E., Cacioppo, J. T., & Goldman, R. (1981). Personal involvement as a determinant of argument-based persuasion. Journal of Personality and Social Psychology, 41, 847–855.; Page **224**: Source: Patmore, C. (1866). Angel in the House. London & Cambridge.; Page **224**: Source: Chen, S., & Chaiken, S. (1999). The heuristic-systematic model in its broader context. In S. Chaiken & Y. Trope (Eds.), Dual-process theories in social psychology (pp. 73–96) New York: Guilford Press; Page **226**: Source: Adapted from Leventhal, H., Watts, J. C., & Pagano, F. (1967). Effects of fear and instructions on how to cope with danger. Journal of Personality and Social Psychology, 6, 313–321.; Page **228**: Source: JONATHAN SWIFT, Quoted in Maturin Murray Ballou in his Treasury of thought (1872); Page **229**: Source: Based on data in Shavitt, S. (1990). The role of attitude objects in attitude function. Journal of Experimental Social Psychology, 26, 124–148.; Page **229**: Figure adapted from Briñol, P. & Petty, R. E (2003). Overt head movements and persuasion: A self-validation analysis. Journal of Personality and Social Psychology, 84, 1123–1139.; Page **230**: Source: Don Draper, 1960. Inside the mind of Don Draper - understanding his marketing philosophy, Guardian News and Media.; Page **231**: Source: GEORGE NORMAN DOUGLAS, SOUTH WIND, 1917; Page **231**: Source: Battle for your brain. (1991, August). Consumer Reports, pp. 520–; Page **541**.; Page **235**: Source: Don Draper, 1960. Inside the mind of Don Draper - understanding his marketing philosophy, Guardian News and Media.; Page **236**: Source: Based on data in Furnham, A., & Mak, T. (1999). Sex-role stereotyping in television commercials: A review and comparison of fourteen studies done on five continents over 25 years. Sex Roles, 41, 413–437.; Page **239**: Source: CHARLES DUDLEY WARNER, BACKLOG STUDIES, 1873, Boston: J.R. Osgood and Co.; Page **240**: Source: The Iliad of Homer, translated by Mr. Pope. 6 volumes. London: Printed by W. Bowyer, for Bernard Lintot, 1715-20.

Chapter 8   Page **247**: Source: Wolfson, A. (2005). "A hoax most cruel." The Courier-Journal, October 9. Retrieved June 5, 2006, from www.courier-journal.com/apps/pbcs.d11/article?Date=20051009&category=NEWS01 p. 23; Page **247–248**: Source: Wolfson, A. (2005). "A hoax most cruel." The Courier-Journal, October 9. Retrieved June 5, 2006, from www.courier-journal.com/apps/pbcs.d11/article?Date=20051009&category=NEWS01, p. 27; Page **248**: Source: Wolfson, A. (2005). "A hoax most cruel." The Courier-Journal, October 9. Retrieved June 5, 2006, from www.courier-journal.com/apps/pbcs.d11/article?Date=20051009&category=NEWS01; Page **248**: Source: THOMAS FULLER, Gnomologia, adagies and proverbs, wise sentences and witty sayings... collected by Thomas Fuller, London: B. Barker, 1732.; Page **248**: Source: MARK TWAIN, The tragedy of Pudd'nhead Wilson: and the comedy Those extraordinary twins, Hartford, Conn.: American Pub. Co., 1894.; Page **252**: Source: Data from Sherif, M. (1936). The psychology of social norms. New York: Harper.; Page **252**: Source: CHARLES DICKENS, PICKWICK PAPERS; Page **253**: Source: BENJAMIN FRANKLIN AT THE SIGNING OF THE DECLARATION OF INDEPENDENCE, 1776; Page **254**: Source: Cantril, H. (1940). The invasion from Mars: A study in the psychology of panic. New York: Harper & Row p. 115; Page **254**: Source: THORNTON WILDER, THE MATCHMAKER; Page **257**: Source: Wilson, I., (2014, April 10). Dangerous 'polar plunge' trend causes concern for N.H. school districts. Concord Monitor. Retrieved May 26, 2014: http://www.concordmonitor.com/news/11495396-95/dangerous-polar-plunge-trend-causes-concern-for-nh-school-districts; Page **258**: Source: MARK TWAIN, The Gorky Incident, published in the New York sun, April 15, 1906; Page **259**: Source: Adapted from Asch, S. E. (1956). Studies of independence and conformity: A minority of one against a unanimous majority. Psychological Monographs, 7 (9, Whole No. 416).; Page **260**: Source: Adapted from Asch, S. E. (1957). An experimental investigation of group influence. In Walter Reed Army Institute of Research, Symposium on preventive and social psychiatry (pp. 15–17). Washington, DC: U.S. Government Printing Office.; Page **260**: Source: Asch, S. E. (1956). Studies of independence and conformity: A minority of one against a unanimous majority. Psychological Monographs, 7 (9, Whole No. 416); Page **260**: Source: ROBERT BOLT, A MAN FOR ALL SEASONS; Page **260**: Source: Moscovici, S. (1985). Social influence and conformity. In G. Lindzey & E. Aronson (Eds.), Handbook of social psychology (3rd ed., Vol. 2, pp. 347–412). New York: Random House. p. 369; Page **263**: Source: Machiavelli, Niccolò (1958), "The Prince", Machiavelli:The Chief Works and Others 1. Translated by Allan Gilbert; Page **265**: Source: Based on Asch, S. E. (1955). Opinions and social pressure. Scientific American, 193, 31–35.; Page **266**: Source: Markus, H. R., & Kitayama, S. (1991). Culture and the self: Implications for cognition, emotion, and motivation. Psychological Review, 98, 224–253., p. 244; Page **268**: Source: Berry, J. W. (1967). Independence and conformity in subsistence-level societies. Journal of Personality and Social Psychology, 7, 415–418., p. 437; Page **268**: Source: ADAM CLAYTON POWELL, Adam by Adam: The Autobiography of Adam Clayton Powell, Jr., 1st ed., Carol Publishing Group, 1994.; Page **270**: Source: TESS ONWUEME, Three Plays. Detroit: Wayne State University Press. 1993; Page **271**: Source: Adapted from Reno, R. R., Cialdini, R. B., & Kallgren, C. A. (1993). The transsituational influence of social norms. Journal of Personality and Social Psychology, 64, 104–112.; Page **274**: Source: Jowett, G. S., & O'Donnell, V. (1999). Propaganda and persuasion. Thousand Oaks, CA: Sage., p. 26; Page **275**: Source: Ervin Staub. The Roots of Evil: The Origins of Genocide and Other Group Violence. Cambridge University Press, 1989 p. 123; Page **275**: Source: Jowett, G. S., & O'Donnell, V. (1999). Propaganda and persuasion. Thousand Oaks, CA: Sage., p. 262; Page **275**: Source: CHARLOTTE PERKINS GILMAN. Human Work. New York: McClure, Philips & Co. 1904.; Page **278**: Source: Based on Milgram, S. (1963). Behavioral study of obedience. Journal of Abnormal and Social Psychology, 67, 371–378.; Milgram, S. (1974). Obedience to authority: An experimental view. New York: Harper & Row.; Page **279**: Source: Dion,

Milgram, S. (1963). Behavioral study of obedience. Journal of Abnormal and Social Psychology, 67, 371–378., p. 397; Page **279**: Source: Milgram, S. (1974). Obedience to authority: An experimental view. New York: Harper & Row., p. 76; Page **280**: Source: Data from Milgram, S. (1974). Obedience to authority: An experimental view. New York: Harper & Row.; Page **281**: Source: C. P. SNOW. Public Affairs. London: Macmillan, 1971.; Page **283**: Source: Osofsky, M. J., Bandura, A., & Zimbardo, P. G. (2005). The role of moral disengagement in the execution process. Law and Human Behavior, 29, 371–393, p. 406.

Chapter 9   Page **290**: Source: Woodward, B. (2004). Plan of attack. New York: Simon & Schuster. p. 399; Page **293**: Source: quoted in O'Brien, S. (2004, May 21). Researcher: It's not bad apples, it's the barrel. Retrieved on January 20, 2005, from CNN.com, www.cnn.com/2004/US/05/21/zimbarbo.access/J; Page **294**: Source: Desmond Tutu. In Africa, a step backward on human rights. Friday, March 12, 2010. The Washington Post; Page **295**: Source: KARL MARX. Das Kapital: a critique of political economy.Norwalk, Ct.: The Easton Press. 1922; Page **296**: Source: Based on data in Zajonc, Heingartner, & Herman, 1969; Page **299**: Source: JOHN RUSKIN. Sesame and lilies: three lectures. Philadelphia: Altemus, 1892.; Page **301**: Source: RUDYARD KIPLING, "IF," 1909; Page **303**: Source: JOHN DRYDEN, ABSALOM AND ACHITOPHEL, 1682; Page **305**: Source: Sorenson, T. C. (1966). Kennedy. New York: Bantam Books.; Page **306**: Source: Janis, I. L. (1982). Groupthink: Psychological studies of policy decisions and fiascoes (2nd ed.). Boston: Houghton Mifflin. p. 52; Page **306**: Source: Based on data in Janis, I. L., Mann, L (1977). Decision Making. Copyright © 1977 by The Free Press, a Division of Macmillan Publishing Co., Inc.; Page **307**: Source: RALPH WALDO EMERSON, SOCIETY AND SOLITUDE, 1870; Page **307**: Source: McClellan, S. (2008). What happened: Inside the Bush White House and Washington's culture of deception. New York: Public Affairs., p. 148; Page **309**: Source: RALPH WALDO EMERSON, ESSAYS, HISTORY, 1841; Page **310**: Source: Geneen, H. and Alvin Moscow (1984). Managing. Garden City, NY: Doubleday.; Page **311**: Source: WILLIAM SHAKESPEARE, THE LIFE OF TIMON OF ATHENS; Page **316**: Source: Based on J. WILLIAM FULBRIGHT, APRIL 4, 1971; Page **317**: Source: Data from "Studies of interpersonal bargaining," by Morton Deutsch and Robert M. Krauss. Journal of Conflict Resolution, 6, pp. 52–76. Copyright © 1962 by Sage. Reprinted with permission.; Page **318**: Source: Based on data in Deutsch, M., & Krauss, R. M. (1962). Studies of interpersonal bargaining. Journal of Conflict Resolution, 6, 52–76.; Page **319**: Source: FORMER EGYPTIAN PRESIDENT ANWAR AL-SADAT, SPEAKING BEFORE THE ISRAELI KNESSET, 1977.

Chapter 10   Page **327**: Source: SIR PETER USTINOV, DEAR ME, 1977; Page **330**: Source: WILLIAM BLAKE, LOVE TO FAULTS; Page **332**: Source: OSCAR WILDE, THE PICTURE OF DORIAN GRAY, 1891; Page **332**: Source: WILLIAM SHAKESPEARE. History of Henry VI, Part I. Act V; Page **334**: Source: Aristotle, Apothegms, 330 B.C; Page **334**: Source: Euripides. Matthew Wright (trans). (2008). Orestes. Bristol Classical Press.; Page **335**: Sources: Based on Eagly, A. H., Ashmore, R. D., Makhijani, M. G., & Longo, L. C. (1991). What is beautiful is good, but . . .: A meta-analytic review of research on the physical attractiveness stereotype. Psychological Bulletin, 110, 109–128.; Feingold, A. (1992b). Good-looking people are not what we think. Psychological Bulletin, 111, 304–341. Wheeler, L., & Kim, Y. (1997). What is beautiful is culturally good: The physical attractiveness stereotype has different content in collectivistic cultures. Personality and Social Psychology Bulletin, 23, 795–800.; Page **337**: Source: Hinde, R. A. (1984), Why do the sexes behave differently in close relationships? Journal of Social and Personal Relationships, I, 471–501.; Page **338**: Source: EDITH WHARTON, THE AGE OF INNOCENCE, 1920; Page **342**: Source: Taylor, S. E., & Master, S. L. (2011). Social responses to stress: The tendand-befriend model. In R. J. Contrada & A. Baum (Eds.), The handbook of stress science: Biology, psychology, and health (pp. 101–109). New York: Springer. p. 972; Page **343**: Source: Finkel, E. J., Eastwick, P. W., Karney, B. R., Reis, H. T., & Sprecher, S. (2012). Online dating: A critical analysis from the perspective of psychological science. Psychological Science in the Public Interest. doi:10.1177/1529100612436522 p. 31; Page **344**: Source: ANDRÉ MALRAUX, THE WALNUT TREES OF ALTENBURG, 1948; Page **345**: Source: BEILBY PORTEUS (1731–1808); Page **345**: Source: Anton Chekhov, Russian dramatist & short story author (1860 - 1904); Page **346**: Source: TONI MORRISON; Page **346**: Source: Data from Jankowiak, W. R., & Fischer, E. F. (1992). A cross-cultural perspective on romantic love. Ethnology, 31, 149–155.; Page **347**: Source: Based on Elaine Hatfield and Richard L. Rapson, "Passionate love in intimate relationships", in Bert S. Moore, Alice M. Isen. Affect and Social Behavior, Cambridge University Press, 1990, p. 166.; Page **348**: Source: Dion,

K. K., & Dion, K. L. (1993). Individualistic and collectivistic perspectives on gender and the cultural context of love and intimacy. Journal of Social Issues, 49, 53–69., p. 485; Page **349**: Source: Moore, R. L. (1998). Love and limerance with Chinese characteristics: Student romance in the PRC. In V. C. de Munck (Ed.), Romantic love and sexual behavior (pp. 251–283). Westport, CT: Praeger.; Page **350**: Source: Adapted from Hazan, C., & Shaver, P. (1987). Romantic love conceptualized as an attachment process. Journal of Personality and Social Psychology, 52, 511–524.; Page **351**: Source: Lawrence, D.H. (2002). Apocalypse. Cambridge University Press.; Page **352**: Source: MALCOLM BRADBURY, 1992; Page **353**: Source: ERICH FROMM, THE SANE SOCIETY, 1955; Page **354**: Source: Adapted from Rusbult, C. E. (1983). A longitudinal test of the investment model: The development (and deterioration) of satisfaction and commitment in heterosexual involvements. Journal of Personality and Social Psychology, 45, 101–117.; Page **355**: Source: Adapted from Rusbult, C. E. (1983). A longitudinal test of the investment model: The development (and deterioration) of satisfaction and commitment in heterosexual involvements. Journal of Personality and Social Psychology, 45, 101–117.; Page **356**: Source: FRANÇOIS DE LA ROCHEFOUCAULD, MAXIMS, 1665; Page **359**: Source: Data from Duck, S. W. (1982). A typography of relationship disengagement and dissolution. In S. W. Duck (Ed.), Personal relationships 4: Dissolving personal relationships (pp. 1–32). London: Academic Press.; Page **358**: Source: Henry Louis Mencken, Heliogabalus: a buffoonery in three acts (New York: Knopf, 1920).

Chapter 11 Page **365**: Source: Lee, A. Y. (2001). The mere exposure effect: An uncertainty reduction explanation revisited. Personality and Social Psychology Bulletin, 27, 1255–1266; Page **367**: Source: Edward O. Wilson(1978). On Human Nature. Harvard University Press.; Page **368**: Source: Sa'di: The Bustan of Sadi (London: John Murray, 1911), trans. by A. Hart Edwards; Page **369**: Source: William Chillingworth (12 October 1602 – 30 January 1644) controversial English churchman.; Page **369**: Sources: FRANÇOIS DE LA ROCHEFOUCAULD, [Maximes.] Maxims. Translated with an introduction by L.W. Tancock. 1959. Penguin Books.; Page **371**: Sources: Frank Chapman Sharp, Ethics, New York, London, Century [©1928]; Page **371**: Sources: CHARLES DUDLEY WARNER(1873).Backlog studies. Boston: J.R. Osgood and Co.; Page **372**: Source: Adapted from Toi, M., & Batson, C. D. (1982). More evidence that empathy is a source of altruistic motivation. Journal of Personality and Social Psychology, 43, 281–292.; Page **373**: Sources: SUETONIUS, LIVES OF THE TWELVE CAESARS, FIRST CENTURY A.D; Page **376**: Source: Adapted from Levine, R. V., Norenzayan, A., & Philbrick, K. (2001). Cross-cultural differences in helping strangers. Journal of Cross-Cultural Psychology, 32, 543–560.; Page **377**: Sources:David Hume; Andrew Millar (1757), Four dissertations: I. The natural history of religion. II. Of the passions. III. Of tragedy. IV. Of the standard of taste. London: Printed for A. Millar, in the Strand; Page **378**: Sources: Dalai Lama and Howard Cutler (1998). The Art of Happiness. Easton Press; Page **379**: Source: Jean Paul Richter (1763–1825); Page **380**: Source: ALEXIS DE TOCQUEVILLE, 1835. Democracy in America. Saunders and Otley (London); Page **383**: Source: Based on Darley, J. M., & Latané, B. (1968). Bystandar intervention in emergencies: Diffusion of responsibility. Journal of Personality and Social Psychology, 8, 377–383.; Page **385**: Sources: Markey, P. M. (2000). Bystander intervention in computer-mediated communication. Computers in Human Behavior, 16, 183–188; Page **387**: Source: Data from Latané, B., & Darley, J. M. (1970). The unresponsive bystander: Why doesn't he help? Englewood Cliffs, NJ: Prentice Hall.; Page **387**: Sources: Guéguen, N., Jacob, C., & Lamy, L. (2010). 'Love is in the air': Effects of songs with romantic lyrics on compliance with a courtship request. Psychology of Music, 38(3), 303–307. doi:10.1177/0305735609360428; Page **388**: Sources: George Eliot (Marian Evans), Adam Bede, 1859. Edinburgh; London: William Blackwood and Sons.

Chapter 12 Page **397**: Sources: ROBERT BURNS, Man Was Made to Mourn: A Dirge, 1784; Page **401**: Source: Figure 2.1 from p. 15 here: http://www.futureswithoutviolence.org/userfiles/CDC_Intimate%20Partner%20Violence%20in%20the%20US%20%282010%29.pdf; Page **402**: Sources: O'Rourke, L. (2008, August 2). Behind the woman behind the bomb. The New York Times, Op-ed; Page **402**: Sources: Winston Churchill, The river war: an historical account of the reconquest of the Soudan, 1st ed. published 1899 in 2 volumes; Page **403**: Source: ENHANCING CHILD SAFETY AND ONLINE TECHNOLOGIES: FINAL REPORT OF THE INTERNET SAFETY TECHNICAL TASK FORCE TO THE MULTI-STATE WORKING GROUP ON SOCIAL NETWORKING OF STATE ATTORNEYS GENERAL OF THE UNITED STATES December 31, 2008; Page **404**: Source: James Baldwin,

Nobody knows my name, New York: Dial Press, 1961; Page **409**: Sources: ALEXIS DE TOCQUEVILLE, The Old Regime and the Revolution, Harper & brothers, 1856; Page **406**: © Pearson Education, Inc.; Page **410**: Source: Based on data in Berkowitz, L., & Le Page, A. (1967). Weapons as aggression-eliciting stimuli. Journal of Personality and Social Psychology, 7, 202–207.; Page **410**: Sources: Berkowitz L, Cochran ST, Embree MC, Physical pain and the goal of aversively stimulated aggression, J Pers Soc Psychol. 1981 Apr;40(4):687–700.; Page **411**: Sources: Archer, D. (1994). American violence: How high and why? Law Studies, 19, 12–20; Page **415**: Sources: Alfred Hitchcock, National Observer 15 August 1966.; Page **418**: Source: Ferguson, C. J. (2014). A way forward for video game violence research. American Psychologist, 69, 307–309; Page **420**: Sources: Jeremy Bentham, An introduction to the principles of morals and legislation: printed in the year 1780, and now first published, London: T. Payne, 1789.; Page **427**: Sources: Gibbs, N., & Roche, T. (1999, December 20). The Columbine tapes. Time, p. 174.

Chapter 13 Page **435**: Sources: HERBERT SPENCER, Social Statics; Or, The Conditions Essential to Human Happiness Specified, & the First of Them Developed, D. Appleton & Company, 1873; Page **437**: Sources:Lord Molson, British Politician (1903-1991). Carol Tavris and Elliot Aronson, Mistakes Were Made.; Page **438**: Sources: Cashin, S. (2014). Place, not race: A new vision of opportunity in America. Boston, MA: Beacon; Page **440**: Source: Allport, G. W. (1954). The nature of prejudice. Reading, MA: Addison-Wesley.; Page **440**: Sources: OLIVER WENDELL HOLMES, JR., 1901; Page **441**: Sources: Fellner, J. (2009, June 19). Race, drugs, and law enforcement in the United States. Stanford Law and Policy Review, 20, 257–291; Page **445**: Source: Based on Correll, J., Park, B., Judd, C. M., & Wittenbrink, B. (2002). The police officer's dilemma: Using ethnicity to disambiguate potentially threatening individuals. Journal of Personality and Social Psychology, 83, 1314–1329.; Page **446**: Source: Adapted from Rogers, R., & Prentice-Dunn, S. (1981). Deindividuation and anger-mediated interracial aggression: Unmasking regressive racism. Journal of Personality and Social Psychology, 41, 63–73; Page **449**: Sources: Banaji, M. R., & Greenwald, A. G. (2013). Blindspot: Hidden biases of good people. New York: Delacorte; Page **454**: Sources: Williams, J. (1998). Thurgood Marshall: American revolutionary. New York: Times Books; Page **455**: Source: André Gide, 1947. The counterfeiters.ew York: Vintage Books A Division of Random House; Page **456**: Source: Kurt Vonnegut. Cat's Cradle: A Novel. Random House Publishing Group, 04-Nov-2009; Page **458**: Source: Adapted from Quattrone, G. A., & Jones, E. E. (1980). The perception of variability within ingroups and outgroups: Implications for the law of small numbers. Journal of Personality and Social Psychology, 38, 141–152.; Page **459**: Sources: Crandall, C. S., & Eshleman, A. (2003). A justification-suppression model of the expression and experience of prejudice. Psychological Bulletin, 129(3), 414–446; Page **460**: Source: Reverend Thornton Stringfellow, 1850.A brief Examination of Scripture Testimony on ... Slavery, etc.; Page **460**: Sources: Allport, G. W. (1954). The nature of prejudice. Reading, MA: Addison-Wesley; Page **461**: Sources: Dollard, J. (1938). Hostility and fear in social life. Social Forces, 17, 15–26; Page **464**: Source: Based on Mendoza-Denton, R., & Page-Gould, E. (2008). Can cross-group friendships influence minority students' well-being at historically White universities? Psychological Science, 19, 933–939.; Page **466**: Source: Based on data in Sherif, M., Harvey, O. J., White, J., Hood, W., & Sherif, C. W. (1961). Intergroup conflict and cooperation: The robber's cave experiment. Norman: Institute of Intergroup Relations, University of Oklahoma.; Page **468**: Source: The Holy Bible New International Version, Containing the Old Testament and The New Testament. (1978). Zondervan Publishing House.

SPA 1 Page **483**: Source: Based on Cialdini, R. B., Reno, R. R., & Kallgren, C. A. (1990). A focus theory of normative conduct: Recycling the concept of norms to reduce littering in public places. Journal of Personality and Social Psychology, 58, 1015–1026.; Page **485**: Source: Based on Siero, F. W., Bakker, A. B., Dekker, G. B., & Van Den Burg, M. T. C. (1996). Changing organizational energy consumption behavior through comparative feedback. Journal of Environmental Psychology, 16, 235–246.; Page **476**: Source: Montgomery, L. (2014, June 1). Evidence of climate change laps at Norfolk's feet. Washington Post (p. A1, A9).; Page **476**: Source: Davenport, C. (2014, May 7). Miami finds itself ankle-deep in Climate Change debate. New York Times. Retrieved July 15, 2014 from: http://www.nytimes.com/2014/05/08/us/florida-finds-itself-in-the-eye-of-the-storm-on-climate-change.html?emc=eta1; Page **479**: Source: Lewin, K. (1951). Problems of research in social psychology. In D. Cartwright (Ed.), Field theory in social science (pp. 155–169). New York: Harper.; Page **480**: Source: McNally, R. J., Bryant, R. A., & Ehlers, A. (2003). Does early psychological intervention promote recovery from posttraumatic stress? Psycho- logical Science in the Public Interest, 4, 45–79.; Page **480**: Source: McNally, R. J., Bryant, R. A., & Ehlers, A. (2003). Does early psychological intervention promote recovery from posttraumatic stress? Psycho- logical Science in the Public Interest, 4, 45–79.; Page **482**: Source: RUSSELL BAKER, 1968, Pittsburgh Post-Gazette - Feb 22, 1968.; Page **483**: Source: Goldstein, N. J., Cialdini, R. B., & Griskevicius, V. (2008). A room with a viewpoint: Using social norms to motivate environmental conservation in hotels. Journal of Consumer Research, 35, 472–482.; Page **486**: Source: RACHEL CARSON, THE SILENT SPRING, 1962, Houghton Mifflin Harcourt Trade & Reference Publishers,; Page **486**: Source: Dickerson, C., Thibodeau, R., Aronson, E., & Miller, D. (1992). Using cognitive dissonance to encourage water conservation. Journal of Applied Social Psychology, 22, 841–854.; Page **491**: Source: Shakespeare, Troilus And Cressida, I.Ii.287.

SPA 2 Page **497**: Source: Hill, J. K. (2002). Rainbow remedies for life's stormy times. South Bend, IN: Moorhill Communications.; Pages 477–478: Source: Cannon, W. B. (1942). "Voodoo" death. American Anthropologist, 44, 169–181.; Page **501**: Source: HANS SELYE (1978), Overcoming the Fear of Fear: How to Reduce Anxiety Sensitivity, New Harbinger Publications.; Page **502**: Source: Hill, J. K. (2002). Rainbow remedies for life's stormy times. South Bend, IN: Moorhill Communications.; Page **502**: Source: Based on Cohen, S., Tyrrell, D. A. J., & Smith, A. P. (1991). Psychological stress in humans and susceptibility to the common cold. New England Journal of Medicine, 325, 606–612.; Page **503**: Source: Data from Twenge, J. M., Zhang, L., & Im, C. (2004). It's beyond my control: A cross-temporal meta-analysis of increasing externality in locus of control, 1960–2002. Personality and Social Psychology Review, 8, 308–319.; Page **503**: Source: Levenson, H. (1981). Differentiating between internality, powerful others, and chance. In H. M. Lefcourt (Ed.), Research with the locus of control construct (Vol. 1, pp. 15–63). New York, NY: Academic Press; Page **503**: Source: Taylor, 1989. Adjustment to threatening events: A theory of cognitive adaptation.American Psychologist, Vol 38(11), Nov 1983, 1161–1173. p. 198; Page **503**: Source: Hill, J. K. (2002). Rainbow remedies for life's stormy times. South Bend, IN: Moorhill Communications.; Page **504**: Source: Langer, E. J., & Rodin, J. (1976). The effects of choice and enhanced personal responsibility for the aged: A field experiment. Journal of Personality and Social Psychology, 34, 191–198.; Page **505**:

Source: Based on Rodin, J., & Langer, E. J. (1977). Long-term effects of a control-relevant intervention with the institutional aged. Journal of Personality and Social Psychology, 35, 897–902.; Schulz, R., & Hanusa, B. H. (1978). Long-term effects of control and predictability-enhancing interventions: Findings and ethical issues. Journal of Personality and Social Psychology, 36, 1202–1212.; Page **507**: Source: SAMUEL TAYLOR COLERIDGE (1772–1834); Page **509**: Source: ERNEST HEMINGWAY, FATHERS AND SONS (1933), Dt. Taschenbuch-Verl.; Page **508**: Source: Adapted from Cohen, S., Mermelstein, R., Kamarack, T., & Hoberman, H. (1985). Measuring the functional components of social support. In I. G. Sarason & B. R. Sarason (Eds.)., Social support: Theory, research, and applications (pp. 73–94). The Hague, Netherlands: Martines Nijhoff.

SPA 3 Page **517**: Source: Morris, E. (Director). (1988). The thin blue line [Film]. New York: HBO Videos.; Page **519**: Source: Allport, G. and Postman, L.J. (1947) The Psychology of Rumor. New York: H. Holt and Company.; Page **520**: Source: Carpenter, S. (2000, December). Why do "they all look alike"? Monitor on Psychology, pp. 44–45.; Page **521**: Source: ELIZABETH LOFTUS AND HUNTER HOFFMAN, 1989, "Misinformation and Memory, The Creation of New Memories," Journal of Experimental Psychology: General 118(1):100–104 (March 1989).; Page **524**: Source: Thompson, J. (2000, June 18). "I was certain, but I was wrong." The New York Times, p. D15.; Page **524**: Source: HUGO MÜNSTERBERG, ON THE WITNESS STAND, 1908. McClure Company..; Page **524**: Source: Dunning, D., & Perretta, S. (2002). Automaticity and eyewitness accuracy: A 10- to 12-second rule for distinguishing accurate from inaccurate positive identifications. Journal of Applied Psychology, 87, 951–962.; Page **527**: Source: ALEXANDER POPE, ESSAY ON CRITICISM, 1711. W. Lewis,.; Page **528**: Source: Based on Geraerts, E., Schooler, J., Merckelbach, H., Jelicic, M., Hauer, B., & Ambadar, Z. (2007). The reality of recovered memories: Corroborating continuous and discontinuous memories of childhood sexual abuse. Psychological Science, 18, 564–568.; Page **529**: Source: Kalven, H., Jr., & Zeisel, H. (1966). The American jury. Boston: Little, Brown.; Page **529**: Source: HARPER LEE, TO KILL A MOCKINGBIRD, 1960; Page **530**: Source: Adapted from Pennington, N., & Hastie, R. (1988). Explanation-based decision making: Effects of memory structure on judgment. Journal of Experimental Psychology: Learning, Memory, and Cognition, 14, 521–533.

Name Index

A

Aaker, J. L., 238
Aarts, H., 82, 234
Abbott, A. S., 305
Abdallah, B., 334
Abele, A. E., 146
Abelson, J. A., 234
Abelson, R. P., 211
Abma, J. C., 512
Abraham, C., 226
Abrams, D., 128, 257, 263, 265, 267, 292
Abrevaya, J., 406
Achor, S., 501
Acker, M., 411
Adair, J. G., 66
Adams, B. G., 498
Adams, G., 335, 348
Adams, G. S., 183
Adams-Curtis, L. E., 411
Adonu, J. K., 348
Agars, M. D., 443
Agerström, J., 447
Aggarwal, P., 378
Agnew, C. R., 353
Aguiar, P., 127, 458
Ahmad, N., 370, 371
Ahn, H.-K., 378
Aiello, J. R., 297
Aiken, L. S., 513
Ainsworth, M. D. S., 349
Ajzen, I., 215, 216, 217
Akert, R. M., 107, 359, 360
Aknin, L. B. 172, 491
Albarracín, D., 216, 218, 221
Alexander, K., 439
Alicke, M. D., 161
Allan, K., 254
Allen, B. P., 61
Allen, M., 240
Allen, V. L., 255, 266
Allison, P. D., 255
Allmendinger, J., 295
Almonte, J. L., 168
Alter, A. L., 294
Alvarez, L., 388
Alwin, D. F., 221
Amabile, T. M., 123
Amarel, D., 517
Amato, P. R., 379
Ambadar, Z., 528
Ambady, N., 76, 108, 113, 114, 214, 452
Ambinder, M., 520
Ames, D. R., 117, 309
Amir, I., 466
Amirkhan, J. H., 126
Amodio, D. M., 188, 330, 447
Andersen, B., 508
Andersen, S. M., 76, 150, 307
Anderson, A. K., 335
Anderson, C. A., 61, 63, 97, 115, 134, 406, 407, 415, 416, 418

Anderson, C. S., 63
Anderson, D. C., 406, 407, 415
Anderson, E., 348
Anderson, J. R., 141
Anderson, K. B., 406
Anderson, P. D., 258
Anderson, S. L., 335, 348
Ando, Y., 131
Andrade, E. B., 97
Andrzejewski, S. A., 106
Antonakis, J., 309
Antoni, M. H., 508
Anzures, G., 436
Apfelbaum, E. P., 293, 294
Arad, A., 187
Aral, S., 253
Archer, D., 107, 112, 402, 411, 420
Archer, J., 367, 402
Arcuri, L., 214
Arendt, H., 276
Argyle, M., 110
Ariely, D., 196, 327, 338
Arigo, D., 509
Arkes, H., 449
Arkes, H. R., 529
Arkin, R. M., 168
Armata, P. M., 499
Arms, R. L., 421
Arndt, J., 170
Aron, A., 325, 351
Aron, A. P., 157, 158
Aron, E. N., 325
Aronson, E., 25, 31, 36, 37, 44, 58, 60, 66, 178, 181, 182, 190, 192, 194, 196, 202, 204, 226, 415, 419, 427, 452, 453, 459, 464, 467, 470, 486, 487
Aronson, J. M., 451, 452, 470
Arrowood, A. J., 160
Arroyo, A., 53
Arsena, A., 122
Asch, S. E., 259, 260, 261, 262, 265, 266, 267, 268, 286, 288
Ash, I. K., 304
Ashmore, R. D., 115, 334, 335
Ashton, W., 122
Aspinwall, L. G., 161, 507
Atkins, C., 111
Ato, M., 308
Atzeni, T., 298
Au, T. K., 274
Augoustinos, M., 458
Augustinova, M., 297
Aune, K. S., 110
Aune, R. K., 110
Austin, S. B., 511
Aviezer, H., 110
Avolio, B. J., 309
Ayal, S., 196
Aycan, Z., 312
Ayduk, O., 510
Ayman, R., 310, 312
Azrin, N. H., 406

B

Bachen, E. A., 502
Back, K., 326
Back, M. D., 327
Badr, L. K., 334
Bagrowicz, B., 348
Bailey, D. S., 405
Bailey, W. C., 420
Bakina, D. A., 131
Bakker, A. B., 485
Baldwin, D. R., 499
Baldwin, M. W., 150, 351
Balota, D. A., 76
Balsam, K. F., 357
Banaji, M. R., 59, 210, 213, 456, 448
Banas, J. A., 239
Bancroft, L., 402
Bandura, A., 283, 404
Banerjee, R., 491
Banks, C., 292
Banks, W. P., 522
Banuazizi, A., 292
Bar, M., 113
Bar-Anan, Y., 148, 157
Barbee, A. P., 332
Barden, J., 221
Barger, S. D., 510
Bargh, J. A., 73, 74, 77, 79, 83, 84, 95, 234
Barkan, R., 196
Barley, S. R., 292
Barnes, C. D., 400
Barnes, G., 411
Barnes, M. L., 337, 411
Baron, R. A., 405, 415, 425
Baron, R. M., 123
Baron, R. S., 253, 261, 262, 298, 307
Barrett, L. F., 109, 110
Barrouquere, B., 247, 248
Barsalou, L. W., 84
Bartels, A., 352
Bartels, B., 266
Bartholow, B. D., 405, 410
Bartlett, F. C., 74, 90
Bartlett, M. Y., 367
Bass, B. M., 309
Bassin, E., 358
Batson, C. D., 61, 365, 368, 369, 370, 371, 372, 375, 377, 382, 390
Bauer, I., 161
Baumeister, R. F., 36, 93, 95, 146, 164, 165, 170, 172, 258, 291, 325, 345, 418, 427, 490
Baumgardner, A. H., 168
Baumgardner, M. H., 221
Baumrind, D., 284
Baxter, L. A., 358
Beach, S. R., 327
Beale, S. K., 509
Beaman, A. L., 146, 389
Bearman, S. K., 237
Beauvois, J., 188
Beaver, K. M., 333

Bechky, B. A., 292
Becker, D. V., 107
Becker, J. C., 439
Beckes, L., 366
Beckett, K., 441
Beer, J. S., 126, 160
Bègue, L., 127, 378, 406
Bell, J., 346
Bell, S. T., 128
Belle, D., 238
Belliveau, M., 272, 305
Bem, D. J., 150, 182, 213, 308
Bem, S. L., 336
Benac, C. N., 513
Benedetti, P., 233
Benet-Martínez, V., 133
Benjamin, A. J., 410
Benjamin, L. T., Jr., 283, 284
Benson, S. M., 378
Benthin, A. C., 179
Bentin, S., 110
Bereby-Meyer, Y., 367
Berenbaum, S. A., 402
Berger, J., 248
Berger, R., 470
Bergeron, N., 399
Berggren, N., 334
Berglas, S., 168
Berke, R. L., 233
Berkowitz, L., 57, 397, 398, 406, 408,
    410, 421
Bermeitinger, C., 234
Berns, G. S., 260, 261
Berry, J. W., 63, 267, 268
Berscheid, E., 115, 200, 325, 326, 328,
    331, 332, 334, 336, 337, 338, 345,
    346, 355
Bettencourt, B. A., 292, 402
Biehl, M., 108
Biek, M., 181
Bils, 371
Binderup, T., 412
Bissell, K., 332
Biswas Diener, R., 489, 490
Black, M. C., 401, 411
Blackhart, G. C., 291, 343
Blackstone, T., 268
Blackwell, K. C., 107
Blakemore, J. E. O., 402
Blank, H., 44, 521
Blascovich, J., 298
Blass, T., 276, 279, 281, 283, 284
Blatt, S. J., 267
Blau, P. M., 352
Bless, H., 227, 490
Bloom, P., 188, 377
Blow, C., 441
Blumstein, P., 331, 356
Bobo, L., 459
Bochner, S., 142
Bodenhausen, G. V., 213, 436,
    437, 469
Bodimeade, H., 272
Boduroglu, A., 92
Boekeloo, B. O., 412
Boer, D., 374
Boerner, K., 498
Bogart, K. B., 113
Bohner, G., 128, 193, 210, 227

Bonacci, A. M., 422
Bonanno, G. A., 480, 498
Bond, C. F., Jr., 44, 297
Bond, M. H., 63, 133
Bond, R., 260, 265, 267
Bond, R. M., 269, 270
Bongiorno, R., 311
Bookwala, J., 498
Booth, A., 397
Boothby, E. J., 73
Borgida, E., 517
Boris, H. I., 168
Bornstein, B. H., 518, 529, 532
Bornstein, R. F., 327
Borsch, F., 470
Bos, M. W., 83
Bosson, J. K., 328
Botvin, G. J., 241
Bourgeois, M. J., 265
Bowdle, B. F., 401
Bowen, A., 265
Bower, G. H., 378, 420
Bowlby, J., 349
Boyd, D., 403
Boyden, T., 328
Boye, D., 200
Boyle, J. P., 63
Brack, S., 357
Bradbury, T. N., 118, 328
Brakel, T. M., 161
Brand, R. J., 335
Branigan, T., 381
Brannon, L. A., 234
Branscombe, N. R., 96, 421
Brauer, M., 309, 387
Breckler, S. J., 211
Breed, M. D., 366
Brehm, J. W., 184, 241
Breiding, M. J., 401, 411
Brekke, N., 231
Brescoll, V. L., 311, 442
Breslau, N., 499
Brewer, M. B., 58, 290, 291, 368, 435, 452,
    522, 529
Brewer, N., 518
Bridgeman, D. L., 467, 469
Bridges, M. W., 171
Brief, D. E., 281, 282
Brigham, J., 520
Brigham, J. C., 520
Bringle, R. G., 390
Briñol, P., 214, 225, 227, 229, 240, 268
Brislin, R., 237
Brock, T. C., 224, 234
Bromley, D. B., 141
Brook, J., 417
Brooks, A., 377
Brophy, J. E., 80
Brosch, T., 125
Brown, C. M., 180
Brown, J. D., 170
Brown, R. P., 308, 400, 456
Brown, S. A., 405
Bruchmann, K., 160
Brummelman, E., 183
Bruner, J., 211, 212
Brunsman, B., 253
Bryan, C. J., 183
Bryant, R. A., 480
Buehler, R., 97

Buffardi, L. E., 171
Bui, K.-V. T., 353, 358
Bülbül, C., 211
Buller, A. A., 78
Buller, D. J., 368
Bunzl, M., 476
Burger, J. M., 127, 274, 284, 285
Burggraf, K., 237
Burkart, J., 141
Burkley, M. A., 214, 240
Burnette, J., 290
Burns, H. J., 521
Burnstein, E., 308, 367, 408
Bursley, J. K., 83
Busceme, S., 268
Busey, T. A., 524
Bush, D. E. A., 498
Bush, G. W., 203
Bushman, B. J., 61, 171, 172, 378, 405, 414, 416,
    417, 422, 423
Buss, A. H., 147
Buss, D. M., 331, 337, 366, 397, 398
Butera, F., 153, 298, 304
Butler, D. L., 141
Buunk, A. P., 161
Buunk, B. P., 160, 354, 355
Byrne, D., 328
Byrne, S., 118
Byron, R. B., 115

C

Cacioppo, J. T., 64, 212, 221, 222, 224, 232, 254,
    325, 502
Cafri, G., 237
Cain, D. M., 390
Cain, T. R., 437
Cairns, R. B., 406
Calder, B. J., 153
Caldi, S., 117
Caldwell, M., 97
Callan, V., 266
Calvillo, D. P., 44
Cameron, C. D., 257
Cameron, L. D., 513
Camille, N., 96
Campbell, A., 338
Campbell, D. E., 377
Campbell, D. T., 57
Campbell, J., 305
Campbell, J. D., 255
Campbell, L., 351
Campbell, M. A., 258
Campbell, W. K., 171, 172, 503
Campos, B., 328
Canary, D. J., 357
Cannon, W. B., 497, 507
Cantor, J., 415
Cantril, H., 254, 255
Capella, M. L., 231
Capitanio, J. P., 463
Caporael, L. R., 368
Carey, A. G., 330
Carey, K. B., 484
Carli, L. L., 459
Carlier, I. V. E., 480
Carlsmith, J. M., 60, 192, 194, 406, 419
Carlsmith, K., 44
Carlson, M., 378
Carnagey, N. L., 415
Carnevale, P. J., 319

Carney, D., 116
Carr, J. L., 53
Carré, J. M., 425
Carroll, J. S., 44, 328
Carter, T. J., 491
Cartwright, D., 290
Caruso, E. M., 86, 87
Carver, C. S., 145, 146, 164, 171
Casas, J. F., 403
Caselman, T., 425
Casey-Campbell, M., 293
Cashin, S., 438
Cassidy, J., 350
Catalyst., 311
Cate, R. M., 359
Catlin, J. R., 488
Cejka, M., 443
Chabris, C. F., 520
Chaiken, S., 150, 181, 210, 216, 221, 224, 225, 226, 227, 232
Chambers, J. R., 161
Chammah, A. M., 314
Chan, A., 274
Chan, D. K.-S., 341
Chan, E., 160
Chan, M.-P. S., 505
Chang, C., 300
Chang, L. J., 257, 291
Chaplin, W., 116
Charlin, V., 378
Charman, S. D., 523, 524
Charng, H., 375
Chau. P. Y. K., 251
Chaxel, A., 76
Chemers, M. M., 309, 310
Chen, J. M., 509
Chen, J., 260, 300, 401, 411
Chen, M., 79
Chen, N. Y., 335
Chen, S., 76
Cheng, C., 505
Cheng, G. H.-L., 341
Cheng, P. W., 99
Chernyak, N., 199
Chesney, T., 403
Chester, D. S., 160
Cheung, B. Y., 92
Cheung, S.-F., 505
Chiao, J. Y., 64
Chida, Y., 497
Chiles, C., 266
Chin, J. L., 525, 312
Chio, J. H.-M., 505
Chiu, C., 63, 117, 131, 133
Chiu, C.-Y., 129, 133
Choi, H.-S., 253, 348
Choi, I., 94, 133
Choi, S. C., 267, 268
Choi, Y., 188
Chou, C., 241
Christakis, N. A., 329
Christensen, A., 423, 424
Christensen, L., 66
Christie, S. D., 120
Christopher, A. N., 439
Chudek, M., 92
Chung, C. K., 376
Chung, L., 346
Cialdini, R. B., 185, 248, 251, 252, 255, 258, 260, 270, 271, 274, 378, 457, 482, 483

Cikara, M., 434, 456
Citera, M., 319
Clanton, N. R., 116
Clark, C. J., 95
Clark, J. R., 357
Clark, M. S., 357, 375, 378
Clark, R. D., III., 338
Clark, S. E., 523
Clary, E. G., 388, 390
Claus, J., 234
Claypool, H. M., 227
Clayton, S., 481
Cleal, B., 309
Cleveland, M. J., 501
Cline, V. B., 415
Clore, G. L., 227
Coane, J. H., 76
Coats, E., 389
Cochrane, S., 265
Cody, J., 332
Coetzee, V., 332
Cohen, A. B., 123, 187
Cohen, A. R., 192
Cohen, D., 63, 400, 401
Cohen, F., 437
Cohen, P., 417
Cohen, R., 251
Cohen, S., 502
Cohen, T. R., 313, 315
Cohn, E. G., 224
Coie, J. D., 402
Colangelo, A., 161, 162
Colbert, A. E., 309
Colcombe, S. J., 77, 134
Colder, M., 510
Cole, T. B., 412
Colell, M., 141
Coleman, M. D., 190
Coleman, P. T., 318
Collins, B. E., 281, 282
Collins, M. E., 463
Collins, N. L., 350, 351
Confer, J. C., 368
Conley, T. D., 236, 338, 339
Conner, M., 228
Conway, L. G., III., 282
Conway, M., 190
Cook, J. M., 328
Cook, K. S., 46, 352
Cook, S. W., 358, 463
Cooley, C. H., 161
Cooper, C., 293
Cooper, H. M., 405
Cooper, J., 196, 197, 450
Cooper, R., 470
Copen, C. E., 512
Corpus, J. H., 152
Correia, I., 127, 458
Correll, J., 444, 445
Cosmides, L., 366
Costa, P. T., Jr., 501
Courrier, S., 415
Covey, J., 96
Cox, T. H., 294
Coyne, I., 403
Coyne, S., 417
Craig, M. A., 435
Crandall, C. S., 98, 117, 367, 458, 459
Crawford, J. T., 437
Crescioni, A. W., 418, 427

Creswell, J. D., 83
Crick, N. R., 403
Critcher, C. R., 151
Crivelli, C., 107
Crocker, J., 461, 463
Croft, R. G., 415
Crogan, M., 467, 470
Croizet, J.-C., 160
Crosby, F., 443
Crowley, M., 375
Croyle, R. T., 181
Crozier, A. J., 293
Crum, A. J., 501
Cruz, M., 307
Csikszentmihalyi, M., 490
Cuddy, A. J. C., 115, 116
Cullen, D., 426
Cullum, J. G., 487
Cunningham, J. D., 120
Cunningham, M. R., 332
Cury, F., 154
Custers, R., 82
Czaja, S. J., 420
Czopp, A. M., 455

D

Dabbs, J. M., 61, 397
Da Fonseca, D., 154
Dai, X., 331
Dalbert, C., 135
Damon, W., 141
Darley, J., 46, 54, 55, 56, 58, 59, 60, 61, 63, 66, 160, 282, 291, 294, 381, 382, 384, 385, 438, 452
Dar-Nimrod, I., 95
Darnold, T. C., 116
Darnon, C., 153
Darwin, C. R., 63
Davidson, A. J., 52
Davidson, A. R., 217
Davidson, R. J., 114
Davies, P. G., 445
Davis, A. L., 44
Davis, C. G., 96
Davis, D., 412
Davis, K. E., 200
Davis, M. H., 374
Davitz, J., 424
Dawkins, R., 366
Dawson, E., 311
Dawson, K., 117
Deaton, A., 491
Deaux, K., 237, 397, 438
DeBono, K. G., 211, 216
Deci, E. L., 152, 153
De Cremer, D., 316
De Dreu, C. K. W., 268, 294, 304, 305, 313, 319
Deffenbacher, K. A., 518
de Groot, D., 301
De Houwer, J., 74, 211, 447, 449
Dekel, S., 499
Dekker, G. B., 485
De Marco, P., 105
DeMarree, K. G., 76, 82
de Mooij, M., 238
DeMuth, R. L. F., 441
Den Burg, M. T. C., 485
DeNeve, K. M., 406
Dennett, D. C., 24
DePaulo, B. M., 117

Deppe, R. K., 168
Derous, E., 167
Derzon, J. H., 231, 405
Desforges, D. M., 470
Desmarais, S. L., 529
Desmond, E. W., 405
Desportes, J. P., 291
DeSteno, D., 367
Deutsch, M., 251, 257, 258, 313, 315, 316, 317, 318, 463, 470
Devine, D. J., 293, 529
Devine, P. G., 214, 447
De Vries, N. K., 268
de Waal, F. B. M., 398
DeWall, C. N., 95, 171, 172, 291
de Wit, J. B. F., 226
De Witte, K., 167
Dezecache, G., 254
Dickel, N., 210
Dickerson, C., 486
Dickerson, S. S., 508
Diedrichs, P. C., 193
Diekman, A. B., 237
Diener, E., 146, 301, 489, 490, 491
Dietz, T., 487
DiGrande, L., 498
Dijksterhuis, A., 73, 83, 234, 250
Dijkstra, A., 161
Dijkstra, P., 161
Dill, K. E., 418
Dion, K., 115, 293, 334, 348, 351
Dittmar, H., 491
Dobbs, A. R., 407
Dobolyi, D. G., 523
Dodds, D. P., 210
Dodds, P. S., 341
Dodge, K. A., 402, 425
Dodson, C. S., 523
Dohrenwend, B., 499, 501
Doi, T., 348
Dollard, J., 408, 421, 461
Domina, T., 487
Dong, P., 331
Donnerstein, E., 57, 405
Donnerstein, M., 405
Donohue, W. A., 240
Dorr, N., 406
Doss, B., 423
Douglas, J. M., 52
Douglass, A. B., 524, 529
Douthitt, E. A., 297
Dovidio, J. F., 214, 369, 388, 435, 441, 442, 447, 456, 465, 468
Downing, R. L., 302
Draper, R., 36
Drigotas, S. M., 358
Driver, R., 160
Du, S., 109
Dubow, E. F., 415
Duck, J., 458
Duck, S. W., 331, 419
Dugan, A., 476
DuMont, K., 420
Dunlosky, J., 522
Dunn, E. W., 72, 147, 149, 172, 181, 490, 491
Dunning, D., 524
Durrant, J., 420
Durrant, R., 64
Durso, G. R. O., 157

Durso, L. E., 501
Dutton, D. G., 157, 158
Duval, T. S., 127, 145
Dweck, C. S., 154, 165
Dyer, R. L., 73
Dysart, J., 523
Dzokoto, V., 229

E
Eagly, A. H., 115, 210, 216, 221, 237, 300, 311, 312, 334, 335, 336, 368, 375, 443
Eargle, A., 424
Eastwick, P. W., 324, 328, 331, 338
Eberhardt, J. L., 445
Ebert, E. J., 181, 184
Ebert, J. P., 94
Eborall, H., 180
Eccles, J. S., 80, 443
Edelman, B., 49
Eden, D., 79
Eden, J., 307
Edgell, P., 377
Edkins, V. A., 517
Edwards, K., 181
Egan, L. C., 188
Egan, P. M., 165
Eggleston, M., 163
Eggleston, T. J., 179
Egloff, B., 44, 327
Ehlers, A., 480
Ehrlinger, J., 33
Eibl-Eibesfeldt, I., 398
Eich, E., 527
Einolf, C. J., 375
Eisen, M., 141
Eisenberg, N., 369, 374, 375
Eisend, M., 236
Eisenstadt, D., 193, 468, 524
Eisenstat, S. A., 402
Eitam, B., 76
Ekman, P., 108, 109, 110, 112, 114
Elfenbein, H. A., 108
Ellemers, N., 292
Elliot, A. J., 82, 152, 154, 190, 194, 196, 427, 467, 470, 486
Ellis, A. P. J., 305
Ellis, B. J., 64
Ellison, N. B., 343
Elsbach, K. D., 48
Else-Quest, N. M., 452
El-Shinnawy, M., 308
Emery, C. F., 226
Engel, C., 367
Engels, R. C., 180
Engen, M. L., 311
Engstler-Schooler, T. Y., 524, 525
Enright, T. M., 508
Ensom, R., 420
Epley, E., 66
Epley, N., 367
Erb, H., 268
Erceg, D. M., 242
Erez, M., 312
Eron, L. D., 52, 417
Eshleman, A., 459
Etcheverry, P. E., 353
Evans, A. T., 160

Evelo, A., 523
Evered, S., 506

F
Fabes, R. A., 369
Fabrigar, L. R., 224, 228
Fabrizio, B., 298
Fairey, P. J., 265
Farinelli, L., 355
Farrer, J., 348
Farrington, D. P., 428
Fawcett, J. M., 518
Fazio, R. H., 214, 216, 447, 449
Feeney, B. C., 350
Feeney, J. A., 351
Feeney, M., 121
Fehr, B., 345, 351, 358
Fein, S., 125, 445
Feinberg, J. M., 298
Feinberg, M., 226
Feingold, A., 332, 335, 336
Feld, S. L., 294
Feldman, N. S., 128
Fellner, J., 441
Felonneau, M., 274
Femlee, D. H., 358, 359
Fenigstein, A., 147
Ferguson, C. J., 415, 417, 418, 501
Fernández-Dols, J. M., 107
Ferrand, L., 297
Ferris, T., 178
Feshbach, N. D., 426
Feshbach, S., 226, 418, 426
Festinger, L., 35, 45, 48, 160, 178, 192, 221, 263, 326
Fiedler, F., 309
Fiedler, K., 120
Field, P., 307
Fincham, F. D., 118, 391
Fine, C., 178, 438, 440
Fine, G. A., 48
Fink, B., 332
Finkel, E. J., 324, 325, 328, 338, 339, 343
Finkelstein, L. M., 441
Finney, P. D., 66
Fischer, E. F., 346
Fischer, G. W., 457
Fischer, P., 382, 383
Fischer, R., 374
Fischhoff, B., 44
Fishbein, M., 215, 216, 265
Fisher, H., 346, 352, 358
Fiske, S., 123, 439
Fiske, S. T., 37, 114, 115, 124, 456, 460
Fitzgerald, R. J., 523
Fitzsimons, G. J., 149
Flanagan, C. A., 375
Flanagan, M., 406
Flanary, R., 358
Flay, B., 240
Fleck, C. R., 391
Fletcher, B., 160
Flick, U., 48
Flowers, M. L., 307
Flynn, F. J., 309
Foerster, J., 115
Folkman, S., 501, 503, 507
Fong, C. P. S., 300
Fong, G. T., 99, 405, 447

Forbes, G. B., 411
Forer, B. R., 89
Forgas, J. P., 227, 334, 378
Förster, J., 57, 82, 184
Forsterling, F., 120
Forsyth, D. R., 290
Foster, J. B., 324, 442
Foster, J. D., 171, 172
Fotuhi, O., 180
Fouts, G., 237
Fowler, J. H., 329
Fox, C., 87
Frady, R. L., 397
Frager, R., 267
Fraidin, S. N., 305
Fraley, R. C., 350, 351
Franklin, B., 198
Franklin, R. G., Jr., 334
Fraser, S. C., 274
Frazier, P. A., 358, 503
Frederick, S., 88
Fredrickson, B. L., 367, 520
Freedman, J. L., 195, 273, 274,
    419, 482
Freijy, T., 197
Freud, S., 313, 421
Fried, C. B., 196, 453, 487
Friedman, M., 350
Friedman, R., 82
Friese, M., 165
Friesen, W. V., 108, 109, 110, 112
Fritz, H. L., 503
Frodi, A., 410
Frohlich, P. F., 158
Frost, J. H., 327
Fu, X., 267
Fukuyama, F., 503
Fulero, S. M., 523
Fuller, V. A., 94
Fultz, J., 378
Furnham, A., 134, 135, 171, 236, 458

G

Gabbert, F., 254
Gable, S. L., 367, 509
Gaertner, S. L., 214, 435, 441, 447, 456, 468
Gagnon, J. H., 412
Galatzer-Levy, I. R., 498
Galdi, S., 214
Galen, L. W., 377
Galinsky, A. D., 84, 96, 302, 319, 469
Gallup, A. C., 380
Gallup, G., 140, 141, 159, 380
Gangestad, S. W., 338
Ganzel, B. L., 497
Gao, G., 346, 348
Garcia, J., 453
Gardner, W. L., 291, 298
Garfinkle, H., 263
Garry, M., 527
Gawronski, B., 73, 122, 213, 214
Geen, R. G., 296, 297, 421
Geers, A. L., 123, 455
Gelfand, M. J., 63, 312
Gendron, M., 109, 110
Gentile, B., 172, 503
Gentile, D. A., 417
George, J. M., 294
Geraerts, E., 527, 528

Gerard, H. B., 34, 167, 235
Gerard, H. G., 251, 257, 258
Gerbasi, M., 128
Gerbner, G., 417
Gerdes, E. P., 66
Gerin, W., 498
Gerrard, M., 501
Gershoff, E. T., 420
Gersons, B. P. R., 480
Gerstorf, D., 503
Gerteis, J., 377
Geyer, A. L., 267
Gibbons, F. X., 146, 160, 179, 501
Gibbs, N., 427
Gibson, B., 167
Giesen, H., 470
Gifford, R., 106
Gigerenzer, G., 85
Gilbert, D. T., 24, 25, 120, 122, 123, 125, 163,
    164, 181, 184, 490, 492
Gilbert, S. J., 282
Gilmore, D. D., 399
Gilovich, T., 33, 85, 97, 125, 128, 151, 178, 297,
    440, 491
Gingras, I., 152
Gino, F., 196, 367
Girme, Y. U., 509
Giumetti, G. W., 258
Gladwell, M., 114, 449, 484
Glantz, S. A., 231
Glasman, L. R., 216
Glass, D. C., 422
Gleason, M. E. J., 503
Glick, P., 115, 439
Goethals, G. R., 160, 182
Goff, P. A., 445
Goffman, E., 127, 167
Gold, J. A., 330
Golder, S. A., 49
Goldman, R., 222, 224
Goldstein, J. H., 421
Goldstein, N. J., 251, 252, 260, 483
Gollwitzer, P. M., 166, 319
Gonzaga, G. C., 328
Gonzalez, A., 464, 467
Good, C., 453
Goode, E., 347, 348
Goodfriend, W., 353
Goodman, G., 522
Goodwin, G. P., 142
Goodwin, R., 349
Goree, J., 411
Gosling, S. D., 44, 113, 255, 459
Goto, S. G., 131
Gottman, J. M., 359
Goyle, A., 445
Grabe, S., 237
Graham, J., 377, 484
Graham, K., 405
Graham, M. J., 442
Granberg, D., 266
Grant, A. M., 367
Grant, I., 503
Grant, P. R., 458
Gray, K., 200, 367
Gray, S., 247
Gray, T. W., 487
Graziano, W. G., 332, 375
Green, A. R., 449

Greenberg, A., 334
Greenberg, J., 127, 146, 170
Greene, D., 153
Greene, E., 517, 523, 529, 532
Greenfield, B. S., 98
Greenwald, A. G., 213, 214, 221, 234, 448,
    449, 456
Greitemeyer, T., 115, 386, 387, 415, 416
Griffin, A., 240
Griffin, D. W., 85, 240, 437, 501
Griffin, K. W., 241
Griffin, M. A., 412
Griffitt, W., 406
Griggs, R. A., 292
Griskevicius, V., 252, 483
Gronlund, S. D., 523
Grossbard, J. R., 237
Grosvenor, M., 405
Groves, R. M., 52
Gruenfeld, D. H., 294
Guagnano, G. A., 487
Gudjonsson, G. H., 531
Gudykunst, W. B., 63, 110
Guéguen, N., 274, 387
Guenther, C. L., 161
Guerin, B., 296
Guerra, N., 424
Guerrero, L. K., 355
Guevarra, D. A., 491
Guimond, S., 265
Guisinger, S., 267
Gully, S. M., 293
Gunia, B. C., 319
Gunnery, S. D., 106
Gunter, B., 458
Gupta, V., 312
Gustafson, R., 408
Guyll, M., 78

H

Ha, A., 324
Ha, T., 332
Haag, C., 268
Hackman, J. R., 295
Hadden, B. W., 351
Haddock, G., 228
Hafer, C. L., 127
Hagestad, G. O., 359
Hahn, A., 213, 449
Haidt, J., 108, 377, 490
Hailey, S. E., 73
Haines, E. L., 237, 438
Haines, M. P., 272
Halabi, S., 388
Halali, E., 367
Halberstadt, J. B., 149, 334
Hald, G. M., 53, 418
Hall, C. C., 378, 453
Hall, E. T., 110
Hall, J. A., 106
Hall, V., 153
Hallett, K. C., 113
Hallinan, M. T., 328
Halliwell, E., 193
Ham, J., 167
Hamby, S. L., 412
Hamer, M., 497
Hamilton, V. L., 279, 281
Hamilton, W. D., 384

Hamm, M., 140, 154
Hammock, G., 426
Han, S., 130, 238
Hancock, J. T., 343, 344
Hancock, R. D., 250
Handelsman, J., 442
Haney, C., 292
Hansen, K., 128
Hanson, K. L., 405
Hanusa, B. H., 505
Hänze, M., 470
Harachi, T., 188
Harackiewicz, J. M., 152, 153, 168
Harber, K., 437
Harber, K. D., 440
Hardin, C. D., 161, 162
Hare, A. P., 292
Hargreaves, D. J., 378
Hariri, A. R., 425
Harkins, S., 300
Harland, P., 485
Harmon-Jones, C., 109
Harmon-Jones, E., 109, 188, 447
Harrigan, J. A., 109
Harris, L. T., 456
Harris, M. B., 378, 408
Harris, M. G., 402
Harris, M. S., 513
Harris, V. A., 122, 123, 125
Harrison, J. A., 61
Hart, A. J., 529
Hart, D., 141
Hart, W., 181
Harter, S., 141
Hartmann, D., 377
Harton, H. C., 487
Hartstone, M., 458
Hartup, W. W., 325, 356
Harvey, J. H., 358
Harvey, O. J., 466
Hasel, L. and L. E., 518, 523, 531
Haslam, S. A., 309, 311, 459
Hassin, R. R., 74, 82, 110, 148, 157
Hastie, R., 291, 530, 532, 533
Hatfield, E., 254, 331, 337, 338, 346, 348
Hatoum, I. J., 238
Hauer, B., 528
Haugtvedt, C. P., 221
Hayne, H., 527
Haynes, G. A., 197
Hays, C. J., 304
Hazan, C., 350, 351
He, M., 188
Heatherton, T. F., 240
Heavey, C. L., 411
Hebl, M. R., 442
Hecht, M. A., 110
Heckhausen, J., 506
Hedden, T., 131
Hedge, A., 379
Hehman, E., 447
Heider, F., 33, 106, 117, 119, 122, 123
Heiman, R. J., 248, 347
Heine, S. J., 63, 74, 91, 92, 95, 324, 328
Heingartner, A., 296
Heiphetz, L., 210
Heitland, K., 193
Helgeson, V. S., 359, 503
Helmreich, R., 192

Helzer, E. G., 84
Henderlong, J., 152
Hendrix, K. S., 168
Henley, N. M., 110
Henningsen, D., 307
Henningsen, M., 307
Henrich, J., 63
Henson, M., 263
Heppen, J., 214
Herek, G. M., 463
Herman, E. M., 296
Hermann, A. D., 240
Hermann, C. A., 411
Hernandez, J. I., 377
Herndon, B., 272, 305
Herring, C., 294
Hersby, M. D., 311
Hersh, S. M., 250, 293
Hertwig, R., 86
Heschl, A., 141
Hetherington, T. F., 165
Hewstone, M., 120, 459
Hibbard, L., 151
Higgins, E. T., 76, 77, 78, 161, 164, 253, 349
Higgins, R. L., 127
Hilgard, E. R., 420
Hill, C. T., 353
Hill, J., 497, 501, 502, 503, 507
Hill, J. K., 497, 503
Hillshafer, D., 397, 426
Hilton, D. J., 120
Hilton, J. L., 125
Hinkle, S., 122
Hirsh, J. B., 302
Hirt, E. R., 97, 152, 165, 168, 169, 521
Hitler, A., 274, 275
Hitsch, G., 338
Hixon, J. G., 125
Hoberman, H., 508
Hochstadt, S., 380
Hodge, C. N., 115
Hodges, B. H., 267
Hodges, S. D., 149
Hoffman, J. H., 401
Hoffman, N. G., 353
Hogg, M., 458
Hogg, M. A., 263, 265, 291, 293
Hohman, Z. P., 291
Holahan, C. J., 507
Holland, R. W., 488
Hollander, E. P., 265
Holman, E., 499
Holmes, T. H., 499
Holt-Lunstad, J., 508
Holtz, R., 224
Homan, A. C., 294
Homans, G. C., 368
Hong, Y., 63, 129, 131, 300, 315
Hong, Y.-Y., 133
Hood, K. B., 218
Hoog, N., 226
Hoorens, V., 160
Horcajo, J., 268
Horgan, T. G., 106
Hornsey, M. J., 262, 263, 266, 292, 459
Hortaçsu, A., 338
Horton, R. S., 328, 330, 348
Horvitz, E., 341, 342
Horvitz, T., 316
House, J. S., 508

House, R. J., 312
Houston, C. E., 231
Hovland, C. I., 220
Howard, D. E., 412
Howard, G. S., 481
Howard, J. A., 331
Howell, R. T., 491
Hsing, C., 374
Hsu, S. S., 381
Huang, C., 131
Huang, L., 131
Hubbard, M., 115
Huesmann, L. R., 415
Huff, C., 66
Huffington, A., 341
Huffman, K. T., 482
Hüffmeier, J., 319
Hugenberg, K., 520
Hughes, B. L., 160
Hukkelberg, S., 218
Hull, J. G., 146
Hulleman, C. S., 152
Hunt, G. T., 399
Hunter, J. E., 115
Hunter, S. B., 298
Huntsinger, J., 161
Hurley, D., 61
Hurst, C., 334
Hust, S. J. T., 412
Hutchinson, R. R., 406
Hütter, M., 157
Hwang, H. S., 110
Hyde, J. S., 237, 452
Hyman, I. E. Jr., 561

I

Ibrahim, J. K., 231
Ijzerman, H., 84, 291
Ilies, R., 309
Im, C., 503
Imada, T., 188
Imhoff, R., 268
Infurna, F. J., 503
Inglehart, M. R., 497, 501
Inglehart, R., 489
Inkster, J., 184
Insko, C. A., 260, 313, 314, 315, 316, 331
Iselin, A. R., 425
Isen, A. M., 377, 378
Isenberg, D. J., 309
Islam, M. R., 459
Ito, K., 92
Ito, T. A., 437
Ivanov, B., 239
Iyengar, S. S., 152, 503
Izard, C. E., 108
Izuma, K., 188

J

Jaccard, J. J., 217
Jacklin, C. N., 397
Jackson, J. M., 300
Jackson, J. S., 501
Jackson, J. W., 460
Jackson, L. A., 115
Jackson, T., 349
Jacob, C., 387
Jacobs, P., 461
Jacobson, L., 38

Jacobson, N. S., 423
Jacobson, R. P., 270, 482
Jain, S. P., 221
James, L. M., 257
James, W., 93, 145
Jamieson, D. W., 448
Jamieson, P. E., 414
Janis, I. L., 220, 226, 305, 306
Jankowiak, W. R., 346
Janoff-Bulman, R., 377, 459
Jansen, E. A., 403
Jaspars, J., 120
Jecker, J., 198
Jehn, K. A., 295
Jelicic, M., 528
Jemmott, J. B., III, 189
Jeswani, S., 490
Jetten, J., 263, 266, 292
Jia, J. S., 331
Job, V., 165
Johannesen-Schmidt, M. C., 237, 311
Johar, G. V., 117
Johns, M., 453
Johnson, C., 49, 160
Johnson, D. J., 358
Johnson, D. W., 470
Johnson, E. J., 93
Johnson, J. G., 417
Johnson, K. A., 123
Johnson, K. J., 520
Johnson, K. L., 501
Johnson, L. B., 203
Johnson, M., 84, 522
Johnson, R. D., 302
Johnson, R. T., 470
Johnson, T. E., 410
Jolly, E., 125
Jonas, E., 272
Jonas, K. J., 73, 74
Jones, C., 459
Jones, C. R., 77, 78
Jones, E. E., 122, 123, 125, 167, 168, 181, 200,
    242, 258, 332, 333, 422, 448, 457, 458
Jordahl, H., 334
Jordan, C., 329
Jordan, M., 169, 258
Josephson, W. D., 417
Jost, J. T., 459
Jostmann, N. B., 84
Joule, R., 188
Jouriles, E., 146
Jowett, G. S., 274, 275
Joy, S. W., 524
Judd, C. M., 44, 309, 444, 445, 449, 458
Judge, T. A., 309, 334
Jürgen-Lohmann, J., 470
Juslin, P., 97
Jussim, L., 79, 80, 437, 440

K

Kagitcibasi, C., 267
Kahn, M., 422
Kahneman, D., 85, 86, 88, 491
Kaiser, C. R., 435
Kaiser, F. G., 481
Kaiser, S., 107
Kalisch, R., 498
Kallgren, C. A., 258, 270, 271, 272, 482, 483
Kalmijn, M., 355
Kalton, G., 52

Kalven, H., Jr., 529, 532
Kamarack, T., 508
Kamble, S., 348
Kameda, T., 291
Kandel, D. B., 240
Kandler, C., 214
Kang, C., 239
Kappas, A., 107
Kappeler, P., 456
Karasawa, M., 248
Karau, S. J., 300, 311, 312
Kardes, F. R., 97
Karney, B. R., 118
Karpen, S. C., 165
Karremans, J. C., 234
Kasen, S., 417
Kassin, S. M., 531
Katz, D., 212
Kauffman, D. R., 168
Kaufman, L., 273
Kawakami, K., 214
Kawakami, N., 327
Kayser, D. N., 378
Keating, J. P., 212
Keefer, L. A., 84
Keelan, J. P. R., 351
Keller, J., 272, 305, 490
Kelley, H. H., 106, 118, 119, 120, 220, 251, 257,
    313, 314, 352, 353, 368
Keltner, D., 108, 109, 366
Kemp, R. I., 480
Kennedy, S., 358
Kenny, D. A., 331
Kenrick, D. T., 64, 107, 366, 406
Kernis, M. H., 183
Kerr, N., 291
Kerr, N. L., 290, 304
Key, W. B., 233
Kiang, L., 437
Kiesler, C. A., 250
Kiesler, S. B., 250
Kihlstrom, J. F., 527
Kilburn, J., 418
Killian, L. M., 254
Kim, H. J., 227, 248, 347, 378
Kim, H. S., 509
Kim, S. H., 120
Kim, U., 267
Kim, Y., 335
Kimmel, M., 399
Kinard, B. R., 231
King, B., 441
King, M., 411
King, R. S., 420
Kingree, J. B., 411
Kinoshita, S., 449
Kirchner, J., 330
Kirkpatrick, L. A., 351
Kitayama, S., 63, 129, 133, 134, 142, 143, 144,
    188, 248, 266, 347, 367
Kite, M. E., 237, 438
Kjell, O. N. E., 489
Klapwijk, A., 316
Klatzky, R. L., 436
Kleck, R. E., 110
Klein, W. M. P., 171, 513
Kleinjan, M., 179
Klenke, K., 309
Klentz, B., 146
Klinesmith, 410

Klingemann, H., 489
Kloner, R. A., 498
Klug, W., 200
Kluger, R., 209
Knapp, M. L., 106, 107
Knight, S. J., 231
Knobe, J., 93
Knowles, E. D., 123
Knowles, M. L., 291, 298
Knox, R., 184
Knussen, C., 487
Koch, K., 487
Koehler, J. J., 88
Koenig, A. M., 237, 311, 312, 375
Koestner, R., 152, 160
Kogan, N., 308
Kohler, R., 181
Kok, G., 226
Kokkoris, M. D., 188
Kollack, P., 356
Kong, L., 131
Konrath, S. H., 171, 350, 374
Koo, M., 484
Kopelman, S., 314
Korabik, K., 312
Koranyi, N., 331
Korda, M., 316
Koss, M. P., 411, 412, 418
Kothe, E. J., 197
Kouchaki, M., 165
Kovera, M. B., 517
Kowalski, R. M., 258, 427
Kozikowski, A., 391
Kraft, D., 149
Krakow, A., 281
Krasheninnikova, A., 297
Krauss, R. M., 317, 318, 482
Kray, L. J., 96
Kremer, J. F., 409
Kressel, K., 319
Krosnick, J. A., 210, 216, 221
Kross, E., 510
Krueger, A. B., 409
Krueger, J. I., 170
Krull, D. S., 125, 133
Kruse, E., 128
Kuan, K. K. Y., 251
Kubitschek, W. N., 328
Kühnen, U., 188
Kulich, C., 311
Kunda, Z., 390, 437, 463
Kung, T. M., 133
Kuo, Z. Y., 398
Kurdek, L. A., 354, 412
Kuriloff, P. J., 128
Kushnir, T., 199
Kuykendall, D., 212
Kuyper, H., 161
Kwan, L. Y., 117

L

La Croix, J., 319
La Fleur, S. J., 149
La France, B. H., 412
La France, M., 110, 397
Laird, J., 151
Lake, E. A., 168
Lakens, D., 84
Lakoff, G., 84

Lalwani, A. K., 169
Lam, C. B., 237
Lam, S., 508
Lambert, G., 232
Lamoreaux, M., 134
Lamp, E. J., 233
Lampert, R., 498
Lamy, L., 387
Landau, S., 461
Landau, M. J., 84
Landis, D., 348
Landy, D., 198
Lane, K. A., 59
Lang, A. R., 127
Langendam, D., 488
Langer, E. J., 61, 94, 504, 505
Langer, T., 211
Langhinrichsen-Rohling, J., 402,
    412, 424
Langlois, J. H., 332, 335–336
LaPiere, R., 215, 216, 217
LaPlante, D., 114
Larrick, R. P., 406
Larson, J. R., Jr., 305
Laser, P. S., 148
Lassiter, G. D., 117, 123, 124, 125, 532
Latané, B., 46, 49, 54, 55, 56, 58, 59, 60, 61,
    63, 65, 66, 264, 265, 300, 381, 382, 384, 385,
    386, 389, 391
Lattanner, M. R., 258
Lau, R. R., 126
Laumann, E. O., 412, 413
Launay, C., 521
Laursen, B., 356
La Valley, A. G., 355
La Voie, L., 331
Lawler, E. J., 368
Layton, J. B., 508
Lazarus, R. S., 501, 507
Le Bon, G., 254
Le Page, A., 410
Le, B., 353
Lea, M., 301
Leary, M. R., 146, 258, 291, 325,
    427, 490
Leck, K., 268
LeDoux, J. E., 498
Lee, A. Y., 365
Lee, C. M., 142
Lee, E., 302
Lee, H., 529
Lee, K., 327, 365
Lee, R. W., 438
Lee, S. J., 142, 438
Lee, Y., 134
Lee, Y-T., 437
Leggatt, H. K., 377
Lehman, D. R., 99, 507
Lehmiller, J. J., 353
Leippe, M. R., 193, 468, 524
Leite, F. P., 316
Lemaine, J. M., 291
Lemay, E., 334, 357, 375
Lemay, Jr, E. P., 334, 357, 375
Lemmer, G., 168
Leo, R. A., 412
Leonard, K. E., 351, 405
Leonardelli, G. J., 291
Leor, J., 498

Le Page, A., 410
Leotti, L. A., 503
Lepper, M. R., 97, 115, 152, 153
Lerner, M. J., 127, 445, 458
Leskovec, J., 341, 342
Leung, K., 63, 133
Levenson, H., 503
Levenson, R. W., 359
Leventhal, H., 226
Levett, L. M., 254
Levin, D. T., 520
Levin, P. A., 377
Levin, S., 463
Levine, G. L., 149
Levine, J. M., 266, 291, 293
Levine, R. V., 376, 380
Levine, S. S., 295
Levinson, W., 114
Levitan, L. C., 240
Levy, B., 402
Levy, D. A., 254, 258
Lewin, K., 33, 40, 61, 290, 478, 479, 487
Lewis, G. J., 210
Lewis, K., 272, 305
Lewis, M. A., 131, 141
Lewis, R. S., 131
Leyens, J., 410
L'Herrou, T., 265
Li, M. W., 92
Li, W., 193
Li, Y. J., 123
Li, Z., 348
Liben, L. S., 402
Liberman, A., 226
Liberman, N., 82
Liberman, V., 30, 31, 315
Lichtman, R. R., 161, 503
Lick, D. J., 501
Lieberman, M. D., 64
Liebert, R. M., 415
Liebrand, W. B. G., 316
Lilienfeld, S. O., 115, 182
Liljenquist, K. A., 84
Lim, T.-S., 348
Limber, S. P., 428
Lin, D. Y., 126
Lin, Y. H. W., 354
Lind, E. A., 389
Linder, D., 25
Lindsay, R. C. L., 523
Lindsey, S., 149, 213
Linn, M. C., 452
Linville, P. W., 457
Linz, D. G., 411
Linz, H., 113
Lippmann, W., 436
Lipsey, M. W., 231, 405, 424
Little, A. C., 334
Livesley, W. J., 141
Livingston, R. W., 113
Lloyd, S. A., 359
Lobel, S. A., 294
Lodish, L. M., 231
Loersch, C., 82
Loftus, E. F., 521, 522
Long, A. E., 329
Longo, L. C., 334, 335
Lonner, W., 63
Lonsdale, A. J., 88

Lopez, S. J., 391
Lord, C. G., 97, 99
Lore, R. K., 398
Loschelder, D. D., 319
Lott, A. J., 353
Lott, B. E., 353
Lottes, I., 128
Lount, R. B., Jr., 300, 314
Loveland, J., 308
Lovett, R. A., 477
Lowery, B. S., 161, 162
Lowry, P. B., 267
Ludwig, T. D., 487
Lun, J., 161
Lundgren, S., 268
Luo, M., 447
Luo, S., 331
Lupien, S. P., 168
Lutgendorf, S., 508
Lutz-Zois, C. J., 328
Lüüs, C. E., 120
Lykken, D., 489
Lynn, M., 331
Lyubomirsky, S., 97, 378

M
Ma, D. S., 445
Maass, A., 268, 445
Maccoby, E. E., 397
Maccoby, N., 221
MacCoun, R. J., 532
MacDonald, T. K., 405
MacFarlane, S. W., 406
MacKenzie, J., 487
Mackie, D. M., 225
Mackin, R. S., 499
MacKinnon, C., 44
Maclean, N., 76, 157
Macrae, C. N., 113, 436, 437
Macy, M. W., 49
Madey, S. F., 97
Madon, S., 78, 79, 80
Maier, R. A., 328
Mainieri, T., 487
Maio, G. R., 211
Maisel, N. C., 509
Majkut, L., 262
Mak, T., 236
Makhijani, M. G., 115, 335
Malamuth, N., M., 53, 411, 418
Malloy, T. E., 98
Malone, P. S., 122, 123
Malone, W., 127
Malpass, R. S., 522
Mancini, A. D., 498
Manderlink, G., 153
Mann, J. A., 468
Mann, L., 306
Manning, M., 218
Mannino, C. A., 390
Mannix, E. A., 294
Mannix, L., 442
Manstead, A. S. R., 291
Marcus, E. C., 318
Marion, R., 86
Markey, P. M., 386
Markman, K. D., 96, 97
Markoff, J., 72
Marks, J. L., 237

Markus, H. R., 37, 74, 87, 114, 129, 134, 142, 144, 248, 266, 267, 335, 347
Marlatt, G. A., 405
Marotta, S. A., 529
Marques, J., 263, 292
Marqusee, M., 250
Marrington, S., 225
Marsh, K. L., 97
Marsland, A., 502
Martens, A., 453
Martens, M. L., 293
Martin, J., 498
Martin, L. L., 76, 229
Martin, N. G., 210
Martin, P. Y., 225
Martin, R., 160
Martinez, A. M., 109
Martinez, E., 237
Martinez, G., 512
Martinez, L., 250
Martinez, V., 133
Martz, J. M., 353, 354
Masicampo, E. J., 76, 93, 95
Mason, M. F., 126, 131
Masser, B., 128
Master, S. L., 507
Masuda, T., 91, 130, 131
Mathewson, G. C., 37, 190
Matlin, M. W., 402, 438
Matsuba, M. K., 141
Matsumoto, D., 108, 109, 110
Maurer, M., 420
Maxwell, 257
May, K. A., 333
May, S. T., 309
Mazur, A., 397
McAlister, A., 241
McAllister, H. A., 126
McArthur, L. Z., 120
McAuliffe, B. J., 263
McCarthy, J. F., 404
McCauley, C., 307, 437
McClellan, S., 36, 203, 307
McConahay, J. B., 470
McConnell, A. R., 180, 182
McCrea, S. M., 168, 169
McCroskey, J. C., 110
McCullough, M. E., 366
McDaniel, P., 402, 411
McDonald, G., 258
McDonald, H. E., 521
McFadyen-Ketchum, S. A., 402
McGhee, D. E., 448
McGlone, M., 452, 453
McGraw, A. P., 181
McGregor, B., 508
McGuire, A. M., 375
McGuire, M., 520
McGuire, W. J., 239
McHale, S. M., 237
McKearney, S. J., 279
McKimmie, B. M., 262, 270
McKown, C., 80
McLatchie, N., 415, 416
McLean, M. C., 476
McLeod, P. L., 294, 304
McMillan, W., 193
McMullin, D., 411
McNally, R. J., 480, 527

McNulty, J. K., 118, 391
McPherson, J. M., 291, 328
McQuiston-Surrett, D., 522
Meade, R. D., 266
Medina, K. L., 405
Medvec, V. H., 97
Meeus, W. H. J., 279
Mehl, M. R., 438
Meier, B. P., 84
Meindl, J. R., 445
Meiran, N., 367
Meissner, C. A., 520, 531
Mellers, B. A., 181, 529
Memon, A., 254
Mendes, W. B., 298
Mendoza-Denton, R., 464
Mennitt, E., 109
Menon, G., 211
Menon, T., 129, 130, 319
Merckelbach, H., 528
Merkle, C., 97
Mermelstein, R., 508
Mesquita, B., 92, 110
Messick, D., 314, 316
Meston, C. M., 158–159
Metcalfe, J., 97
Mettee, D., 182
Metzner, H. L., 508
Meyer, I. H., 411
Meyers, J. M., 231
Meyers, S. A., 345
Meyersburg, C. A., 527
Mezulis, A. H., 133
Michaels, S., 413
Mickes, L., 523
Mickler, S., 255
Mikulincer, M., 350
Milgram, S., 263, 266, 277, 278, 279, 280, 283, 284, 285, 379
Mill, J. S., 88
Miller, A. G., 122, 279, 282, 284, 285
Miller, C. E., 257
Miller, C. H., 242
Miller, C. T., 160
Miller, D., 96
Miller, D. G., 521
Miller, D. P., 441
Miller, D. T., 126, 127, 257, 279
Miller, G., 239
Miller, J., 132
Miller, J. D., 171
Miller, J. G., 63
Miller, N., 378, 402
Miller, P. V., 96
Miller, R. R., 250
Miller, R. S., 266
Mills, J. S., 37, 187, 190, 356, 357
Mills, M. J., 391
Mills, M. S., 357
Milner, B., 168, 169
Milton, K., 466
Minard, R. D., 455
Mischel, W., 403
Mishal, M., 122
Mishra, H., 405
Misovich, S. J., 123
Misra, S., 340
Misra, T. A., 402
Mitchell, A. A., 311

Mitchell, J. O., 125
Miyamoto, Y., 91, 133
Mizumori, S. J. Y., 64
Modigliani, A., 282
Moghaddam, F. M., 267
Mojaverian, T., 509
Mojdehbakhsh, R., 125
Mojzisch, A., 305
Mok, A., 307
Molouki, S., 248
Monden, C. W. S., 355
Monin, B., 183
Monin, J., 375
Monroe, A. E., 285
Monson, C. M., 412
Montemayor, R., 141
Montepare, J. M., 113
Monto, M. A., 330
Montoya, R. M., 328, 330, 331
Moore, B., Jr., 409
Moore, R. L., 349
Moors, A., 74, 447
Moos, R. H., 507
Mor, N., 145
Moradi, B., 237
Moran, J. M., 125
Moran, S., 319
Moreland, R. L., 268, 290, 291, 293, 294, 305, 327
Morgan, C. A. III, 518
Morgan, M., 358
Morin, A., 145
Morling, B., 134, 506, 509
Morris, E., 517
Morris, M. W., 126, 129, 131, 133, 307
Morris, P. A., 497
Morris, W. N., 266
Morry, M. M., 237, 330
Morse, D. R., 498
Mortensen, C. R., 270, 482
Morton, T. A., 459
Moscovici, S., 260, 268
Moshonov, J., 498
Moskowitz, J. T., 503
Mosley, N. R., 330
Moss-Racusin, C. A., 442
Mostert, M. P., 94
Movahedi, S., 292
Moyer, K. E., 397
Mucchi-Faina, A., 268
Muchnik, L., 253
Mügge, D. O., 415
Muhamad, R., 341
Mukai, H., 426
Mullen, B., 49, 293, 301
Muller, D., 298
Müller, M. B., 498
Muller, M. N., 398
Muraven, M., 165
Murnighan, J. K., 315
Murphy, N. A., 106
Murr, A., 166
Murray, A. A., 182
Murray, Jayna, 381
Murrell, A. J., 468
Musham, C., 146
Mushquash, A. R., 265
Musselman, L., 332
Mussweiler, T., 57, 97

Myers, D. G., 460
Myers, H. F., 501

N

Nadal, K., 442
Nadler, A., 388
Nail, P. R., 254, 258, 260
Naimi, T., 512
Nakamura, J., 490
Narchet, F. M., 531
Nasco, S. A., 97
Natanovich, G., 79
Nathanson, S., 420
Naughton, F., 180
Neale, M. A., 268, 294, 295
Nedelec, J. L., 333
Neighbors, C., 484
Neijens, P., 240
Neiva, E., 353
Nel, E., 192
Nelson, D., 328
Nelson, M. R., 234
Nelson, R. J., 64
Nelson, S., 249
Nemeth, C., 268
Nemeth, C. J., 266
Neria, Y., 498
Nes, L. S., 171
Nestler, S., 44
Neta, M., 113
Neuberg, S. L., 64, 107, 234, 366
Newcomb, T. M., 161, 328
Newman, A. A., 209
Newman, G. E., 390
Newman, L. S., 123, 131
Newport, F., 455
N'Gbala, A. N., 117
Nguen, T., 114
Nichols, S., 142, 284
Nicholson, I., 284
Nichter, M., 240
Nickel, S., 120
Nickerson, C., 491
Nida, S., 61, 258
Nielsen, K., 309
Nijstad, B., 304–305
Nisbett, R. E., 25, 32, 37, 52, 63, 85, 88, 91, 92,
    98, 99, 122, 123, 127, 130, 133, 142, 148, 400,
    401, 487, 523
Nishida, T., 110
Nixon, R. M., 203
Noar, S. M., 513
Nolan, J., 252, 262, 483
Nolen-Hoeksema, S., 97, 423
Noller, P., 350, 351
Nordgren, L. F., 83
Norenzayan, A., 63, 82, 91, 92,
    133, 376
Norman, C., 325
Normand, A., 160
North, A. C., 378, 387
North, M. S., 460
Northcraft, G. B., 295
Norton, M., 172, 327, 342, 343, 367, 435
Nosek, B. and B. A., 59, 214, 448, 459
Nowak, A., 265
Nowak, M. A., 366, 368
Nunes, K. L., 411
Nyrop, K., 441

O

O'Brien, D. T., 380
O'Brien, E. H., 374
Ochsner, K., 64, 503
O'Connell, D. M., 109
O'Connor, D. B., 497
O'Connor, K. M., 319
O'Donnell, V., 274, 275
Oettingen, G., 166, 488
Offermann, L. R., 293
Ofshe, R., 527
Ogle, C., 522
O'Gorman, R., 250, 368
Ohbuchi, K., 425, 426
Ohno, T., 426
Oikawa, H., 157
Oikawa, M., 157
Oishi, S., 49, 77, 134, 160, 379, 380, 490
O'Leary, A., 502
Oleson, K. C., 168, 463
Oliner, P. M., 374
Oliner, S. P., 374
Olivardia, R., 237
Olson, E. A., 523
Olson, J. M., 97, 151, 197, 210, 214, 257
Olson, M. A., 447
Olujic, M., 411
Olweus, D., 427, 428
O'Mara, E. M., 118
Omoto, A. M., 390
O'Neill, O. A., 268
Oppenheimer, D. M., 85
Orehek, E., 508
Oriet, C., 523
Orizio, R., 201
Orom, H., 374
O'Rourke, L., 402
Orvis, B. R., 120
Osborne, R. E., 125
O'Shea, W. A., 348
Oskamp, S., 481, 487
Osofsky, M. J., 283
Osswald, S., 387
Osterman, L. L., 400
Ostrom, T., 458
Ostrov, J. M., 403
O'Sullivan, M., 109
Ouellette, J. A., 268
Overall, N. C., 509
Oyserman, D., 142

P

Pachur, T., 86
Packer, D. J., 284, 307
Padula, C. B., 405
Pagano, F., 226
Page, R., 448
Page, S., 294
Page-Gould, E., 464
Pagliaro, S., 268
Pagotto, L., 442
Pakalka, A. H., 411
Palfrey, J., 403
Palmer, J., 308
Palmer, S. B., 257
Paluck, E. L., 110
Pandelaere, M., 122
Panksepp, J., 368
Parish, A. R., 398

Park, B., 458
Park, C. L., 497
Park, E. S., 304
Park, H. S., 133, 218, 248
Park, K., 227
Parker, J. F., 523
Parker, K. A., 239
Parkinson, B., 110
Pascual, A., 274
Paterson, H. M., 480
Patnoe, S., 31, 467
Patrick, W., 325
Patterson, A., 421
Pauneska, D., 154
Pavletic, A., 524
Payne, B. K., 73, 82, 213–214, 448
Peabody, D., 436
Pearce, N. A., 113
Pechmann, C., 231
Pedersen, W. C., 405, 422
Peek-O'Leary, M., 449
Pelham, B. W., 125
Pelonero, C., 46
Peltokorpi, V., 305
Peng, K., 92
Pennebacker, J. W., 438
Pennebaker, J. W., 241, 376, 424, 480,
    501, 509, 510
Penner, L. A., 365, 374, 390
Pennington, N., 530, 532, 533
Penrod, S. D., 518, 532
Penton-Voak, I., 332
Peplau, L. A., 353
Pereira, C., 127, 458
Pereira-Pasarin, L. P., 305
Perkins, H., 272
Perkins, H. W., 272
Perlstein, L., 151
Perrett, D. I., 333, 334
Perretta, S., 524
Perry, G., 284
Perry, Z., 438
Peruche, B. M., 445
Perunovic, W. Q. E., 183
Peters, J. M., 501
Peterson, A. A., 197
Peterson, R. D., 420
Peterson, R. S., 307
Pettigrew, T. F., 456, 463, 465
Pettit, G. S., 402
Petty, R. E., 210, 214, 216, 221, 222, 224, 225,
    226, 227, 228, 229, 232, 268, 378
Pezdek, K., 518, 520, 527
Pfau, M., 239
Pfeiffer, T., 97
Pfingst, L., 441
Phelan, J., 167, 214
Phelps, E. A., 125, 449, 456
Philbrick, K., 376
Philip, L., 476
Phillips, A. G., 145
Phillips, K. A., 237
Phillips, S., 427
Piazza, J., 142
Piccolo, R. F., 309
Pickel, K., 518
Pickett, C. L., 291, 293
Pieters, R., 109
Pietromonaco, P., 234, 248

Piff, P. K., 366
Pike, C. L., 332
Piliavin, I. M., 369
Piliavin, J. A., 61, 366, 369, 375, 390
Pincus, J. D., 233
Pinel, E. C., 329
Pinker, S., 399, 400
Pitt, R. N., 180
Pittinsky, T. L., 452
Pittman, T. S., 167
Pizarro, D. A., 84
Plant, E. A., 445, 447
Platow, M. J., 309
Plaut, V. C., 248, 335
Pligt, J., 184
Poehlman, T. A., 449
Pollard-Sacks, D., 414
Pond, R. S., 171, 172
Pool, G. J., 268
Poole, W. K., 498
Pope, H. G., Jr., 237
Poposki, E. M., 167
Porter, C. O. L. H., 305
Posada, S., 141
Posavac, S. S., 221
Postman, L., 519
Postmes, T., 301, 459
Poutvaara, P., 334
Powell, A. A., 371
Powledge, F., 249
Pratarelli, M. E., 181
Pratkanis, A. R., 221, 234, 307
Pratto, F., 459, 465
Prentice, D. A., 257
Prentice-Dunn, S., 445, 446
Presnell, K., 237
Preston, E., 97
Preston, J. L., 377
Price, H. L., 523
Prince, M. A., 484
Procter, E., 135
Pronin, E., 33, 126, 128, 248
Proost, K., 167
Prot, S., 387
Proulx, T., 74
Pruitt, D. G., 319
Pryor, J. B., 285
Puente, M., 219
Pujos, S., 274
Pulfrey, C., 153
Purdie, V. J., 445
Purdie-Vaughns, V., 453
Purvis, D., 268
Putnam, R. D., 377, 492, 503
Pyszczynski, T., 127, 170

Q

Qin, J., 188, 522
Quanty, M., 421
Quattrone, G. A., 125, 457, 458
Quinlivan, D. S., 522
Quinlivan, E., 427
Quinn, D. M., 452
Quinn, J. M., 240

R

Raaijmakers, Q. A. W., 279
Rahe, R. H., 499
Rajaram, S., 305

Ram, N., 503
Ramirez, A., 121
Ramírez-Esparza, N., 376, 438
Ramos-Marcuse, F., 350
Ramsay, D., 141
Ramsey, L. R., 236
Ramsey, S. J., 110
Rand, D. G., 366, 368
Ranganath, K. A., 214
Rapoport, A., 314
Rapson, R. L., 254, 338, 346, 348
Rasinski, K., 448
Rasinski, H. M., 455
Raskin, R., 171
Ratcliffe, K., 411
Ratliff, K. A., 160
Read, J. D., 529
Reading, R., 424
Reckman, R. F., 182
Rector, M., 353
Redlawsk, D. P., 211
Reeder, G. D., 285
Regan, P. C., 332, 337, 338, 346
Reicher, S. D., 309
Reid, A. E., 513
Reis, H. T., 44, 325, 326, 327,
    328, 336
Reiter, S. M., 482
Rempel, J. K., 210, 211
Renner, M. J., 499
Renfrow, P. J., 255
Reno, R. R., 258, 270, 272, 482
Rensink, R. A., 520
Repetti, R. L., 501
Rexrode, C., 222
Reynolds, K. E., 242
Rhodes, G., 332, 333, 334
Rhodes, N., 221
Rhodewalt, F., 168
Rholes, W. S., 77, 78, 350
Rice, E. R. W., 272, 368
Rice, J., 411
Richard, F. D., 44
Richards, S. C., 171
Richardson, D., 66, 399, 402, 426
Richeson, J. A., 293, 435, 469
Richman, S. B., 291
Richmond, T. C., 476
Richmond, V. P., 110
Richter, C. P., 61
Riecken, H. W., 48
Riemann, R., 210
Ringelmann, M., 299
Rise, J., 218
Risen, J. L., 125
Ristikari, T., 311
Ritov, I., 319
Ritter, R. S., 377
Rivera, J. E., 291
Rivers, I., 403
Robbins, C., 508
Roberts, N., 350
Robins, R. W., 109, 126, 171
Rochat, F., 282
Roche, T., 427
Rodin, J., 61, 369, 378, 504, 505
Rodrigo, M. F., 308
Rodriguez, 193
Roepke, S. K., 503

Roesch, S. C., 126
Roese, N. J., 66, 96, 97, 448
Rogers, R., 226, 445, 446
Roggman, L. A., 332, 333
Rohde, P., 193
Rohling, M. L., 402
Rohsenow, D. J., 405
Roisman, G. I., 357
Romer, D., 414
Romero-Canyas, R., 167
Rooney, B., 248
Rooth, D-O., 447
Rosenberg, M. J., 52
Rosenblatt, P. C., 338
Rosenthal, R., 39, 78, 79, 80, 114
Rosh, L., 293
Ross, C. E., 505
Ross, D., 404
Ross, L., 30, 31, 32, 33, 37, 85, 88, 97, 122, 123,
    126, 127, 128, 148, 181, 315, 319, 425, 487,
    501, 505
Ross, M., 32, 91, 97, 126, 190
Ross, S., 404
Ross, W., 319
Rothbart, M., 458
Rothbaum, F., 348, 349
Rothermund, K., 331, 449
Rothman, A. J., 513
Rotter, J. B., 503
Rotton, J., 406
Rowell, A., 487
Rozell, D., 49
Rozin, P., 142
Rubin, Z., 345
Rudman, L., 214
Rudman, L. A., 167, 237, 476
Ruggles, S., 358
Ruiter, R. A. C., 226
Rule, B. G., 407, 410
Rule, N. O., 113
Rusbult, C. E., 353, 354, 355,
    358, 359
Russano, M. B., 531
Russell, D., 126
Russell, G. W., 421
Russell, J. A., 345
Russo, Richard, 148
Rusting, C. L., 423
Rutland, A., 257
Ryan, B., Jr., 231
Ryan, M. K., 311
Ryan, R. M., 152, 153
Ryckman, R. M., 330
Rydell, R. J., 157
Ryon, H. S., 503

S

Sabattini, L., 443
Sabini, J., 237, 263
Sacco, D., 403
Sacks, O., 74
Sadovsky, A., 374
Saffer, H., 231
Sagarin, B. J., 240
Sageman, M., 409
Saguy, T., 465
Sakai, H., 188
Salomon, K., 298
Salovey, P., 378, 457, 501

Salter, J., 314
Samuel, W., 482
Samuels, S. M., 30, 31, 315
Samuelson, C., 484
Sandberg, S., 237
Sanders, D. Y., 241
Sanders, J., 279
Sandilands, M. L., 421
Sanfey, A. G., 257, 291
Sansone, C., 153
Santos, L. R., 188
Sapolsky, R., 397
Sargent, J. D., 240
Sastry, J., 505
Sato, K., 425
Satpute, A. B., 83
Saunders, J., 518
Savitsky, K., 389
Scanzoni, L. D., 460
Schachter, S., 48, 155, 156, 258, 263, 292, 326
Schaller, M., 64, 98, 282, 366
Schaufeli, W. B., 355
Scheele, D., 352
Scheepers, L., 64
Scheier, M. F., 146, 147, 164
Scheier, M. S., 171
Scherr, K. C., 78
Schiller, D., 125
Schimel, J., 170
Schimmack, U., 77
Schkade, D., 378
Schlegel, R. J., 76
Schlegel, S., 400
Schlenker, B. R., 167
Schmader, T., 453
Schmeichel, B. J., 109, 164, 165, 170
Schmitt, B. H., 297
Schmitt, D. P., 337
Schmukle, S. C., 327
Schnall, S., 84
Schneider, B. H., 399
Schneider, J. M., 297
Schoenrade, P., 377
Schofield, J. W., 464
Schooler, J. W., 524, 525, 527, 528
Schooler, T. Y., 149, 213, 524, 527
Schopler, J., 314, 316
Schreurs, B., 167
Schriber, R. A., 109, 171
Schroeder, A. N., 258
Schroeder, D. H., 501
Schubert, T. W., 84
Schultz, L. A., 398
Schultz, P. W., 270, 273, 481, 487
Schulz, R., 61, 504, 505, 506
Schulz-Hardt, S., 305
Schuman, H., 52
Schumann, K., 425
Schützwohl, A., 338
Schwab, N., 210, 487
Schwader, K. L., 73
Schwartz, D., 390
Schwartz, J. L. K., 448
Schwartz, K., 319
Schwartz, P., 331, 355
Schwartz, S. H., 390
Schwarz, N., 52, 84, 86, 87, 227, 401
Schyns, B., 312
Schyns, P. G., 109
Sears, D. O., 221

Sears, R. R., 408, 421
Sedikides, C., 115, 458
Seeman, T., 501
Seery, M., 499
Seery, M. D., 168
Segerstrom, S. C., 171, 497
Seligman, M. E. P., 61, 134, 391, 489, 491
Selwyn, C., 402
Selye, H., 499, 501
Semin, G. R., 84, 291
Semmler, C., 529
Senchak, M., 351
Sengupta, J., 149, 160
Sergios, P. A., 332
Serodio, R., 263, 292
Seta, C. E., 499
Seta, J. J., 499
Sevincer, A. T., 248
Shackelford, T. K., 397
Shaffer, D. R., 335
Shafir, E., 453
Shah, A. K., 85
Shah, P., 98
Shanahan, J., 417
Shapiro, P. N., 467
Shapiro, R., 441
Sharan, S., 470
Shariff, A., 82
Sharma, D., 297
Sharp, F. C., 371
Sharp, L. K., 510
Sharpe, D., 66
Shaver, P., 350
Shavitt, S., 169, 228, 238, 439
Shaw, C. M., 412
Shaw, P., 236
Sheeran, P., 218
Sheikh, S., 215, 216
Sheldon, K. M., 292, 378
Sheldon, O. J., 319
Shepperd, J. A., 171, 300
Sherif, C. W., 465, 466
Sherif, M., 251, 252, 460, 461, 466, 467
Sherman, D. K., 453, 509
Sherry, J. L., 415
Sherwin, S., 503
Shestakova, A., 261
Shevrin, H., 234
Shih, M., 452
Shiller, R. J., 307
Shillito, D. J., 141
Shiota, M. N., 109
Shipp, E. R., 121
Shoda, Y., 403
Shook, N. J., 218
Shope, G., 421
Shotland, R. L., 61
Showers, C. J., 330
Shteynberg, G., 161
Shurgot, B. A., 331
Sidanius, J., 459, 463, 464
Siero, F. W., 485
Sierra-Otero, G., 376
Sigall, H., 448
Silke, A., 409
Silva, P. J., 145
Silver, M. D., 293
Silver, N., 52
Silver, R. C., 498, 499

Silvera, D. H., 122
Silvia, P. J., 117, 127, 145, 146
Sime, J. D., 367
Simmens, S. J., 508
Simmons, R. E., 64
Simms, L. J., 351
Simon, L. S., 334
Simons, D. J., 520
Simonton, D. K., 309
Simpson, J., 36
Simpson, J. A., 283, 284, 338, 350, 351, 353, 366, 509
Sinaceur, M., 268
Sinclair, L., 437
Sinclair, S., 161, 162
Singelis, T. M., 143
Singer, 371
Singer, J. E., 156, 157
Singh, P., 465
Sivanathan, N., 315
Skinner, B. F., 32
Skorinko, J. L., 161
Slavin, R. E., 470
Slepian, M. L., 113, 114
Slevec, J. H., 237
Sloan, D., 509
Smailes, E. M., 417
Smalarz, L., 525, 526
Smalley, S., 166
Smit, E. G., 240
Smith, A. P., 502
Smith, C. A., 107
Smith, C. M., 275
Smith, C. V., 328, 425
Smith, D. M., 107
Smith, E., 181
Smith, I. H., 165
Smith, J. R., 425
Smith, L., 427
Smith, M. B., 211, 212
Smith, N., 427
Smith, P. B., 260, 267
Smith, P. K., 234
Smith, R. H., 120, 260
Smith, S. S., 66
Smith, S. W., 218
Smith, T., 448
Smith, T. B., 508
Smith-Lovin, L., 328
Smyer, M. A., 359
Smyth, J. M., 509
Snodgrass, M., 234
Snyder, C. R., 127, 391
Snyder, M., 80, 211, 216, 336, 376, 388, 390
Sogon, S., 267
Solomon, H., 385
Solomon, L. Z., 385
Solomon, S., 127, 170
Sommers, S. and S. R., 262, 294, 435, 529
Son Hing, L. S., 193
Sontag, S., 506
Sorenson, T. C., 305
Sorhagen, N. S., 79, 80
Sorkin, R. D., 304
Sorrentino, R. M., 250
Sparrow, B., 94
Spears, R., 301
Spelke, E. S., 113
Spencer, S., 467
Spencer, S. J., 234, 445, 452

Sperber, D., 117
Spina, R. R., 88, 324
Spink, K. S., 293
Spinrad, T. L., 374
Sprecher, S., 337, 346, 348, 355, 358
Srull, T. K., 76
Staats, H., 485
Stafford, L., 357
Stallen, M., 257, 291
Stanley, D. A., 449, 456
Stanley, J. C., 57
Stanovich, K. E., 180
Staska, S. L., 237
Stasser, G., 304, 305
Staub, E., 60, 275, 276, 460
Staw, B. M., 153
Steblay, N. M., 379, 380, 523
Steed, L. G., 242
Steele, C. M., 180, 451, 452
Steele, J. R., 214
Steffen, V. J., 237
Steiner, I. D., 168, 304
Steinmann, F., 86
Steinmayr, R., 168
Steinmetz, J. L., 123
Stemple, L., 411
Stephan, W. G., 464, 467
Stephens, L., 409
Stepper, S., 229
Stern, L. B., 524
Stern, P. C., 481, 487
Sternberg, B., 153
Sternberg, R. J., 345
Stevens, N., 325
Stewart, D. D., 305
Stewart, J. B., 203, 365
Stice, E., 193, 237
Stillman, T. F., 427
Stinson, D. A., 78
Stocks, E. L., 370, 371
Stoff, D. M., 406
Stokes, M. B., 214
Stokes-Zoota, J. J., 44
Stone, J., 117, 148, 151, 196, 438
Stone, R., 385
Stonner, D., 421
Storbeck, J., 227
Stormo, K. J., 127
Story, L., 209
Stouffer, S. A., 220
Strack, F., 97, 229
Strack, M., 309
Strahan, E. J., 234
Straus, M., 401
Straw, M. K., 61
Stringfellow, T., 460
Stritzke, W. G. K., 127
Stroebe, W., 226, 234
Strohminger, N., 142
Stuhlmacher, A. F., 319
Stukas, A. A., 390
Sturman, E. D., 201
Stürmer, S., 376
Suddendorf, T., 141
Sue, D. W., 442
Sullivan, K., 169
Sullivan, Q., 337
Sullivan, R. M., 508
Suls, J. M., 160
Summers, G., 128

Surian, L., 117
Surowiecki, J., 304
Susskind, J. M., 108
Sutton, S., 180
Swander, D. V., 252
Sweeney, D. L., 441
Sweeny, K., 127
Sweldens, S., 157
Swim, J. K., 481
Symons, D., 337
Szamrej, J., 265
Szpunar, K. K., 96

T
Tabak, B. A., 366
Tahlheim, T., 380
Tajfel, H., 456, 457
Takaku, S., 197
Takezawa, M., 291
Tamres, L. K., 507
Tan, Y., 236
Tang, S., 153
Tang, Y., 131
"The Tangled Web of Porn," 2008, 44
Tangney, J., 418
Tanke, E. D., 336
Tao, Y., 109
Tapert, S. F., 405
Taras, V., 143
Tarrant, M., 378
Tasdemir, N., 291
Tate, E. B., 146
Täuber, S., 376
Tavris, C., 36, 187, 202, 204, 422
Tay, L., 490
Taylor, B. R., 96, 407
Taylor, D. M., 267
Taylor, K. M., 300
Taylor, L., 342
Taylor, S. E., 37, 114, 123, 124, 161, 170, 260, 329, 503, 507
Taylor, S. J., 253
Taylor, S. P., 405
Taylor, V. A., 242
Tellegen, A., 489
Terry, D. J., 262, 270, 458
Terry, H., 171
Tesser, A., 76, 210, 255
Testa, M., 401, 405
Tetlock, P. E., 96, 307, 449
Teves, O., 210
Theus, K. T., 234
Thibaut, J. W., 263, 313, 314, 352, 353, 368
Thibodeau, R., 464
Thomas, M. H., 415
Thomas, W. I., 251
Thomas-Hunt, M. C., 268
Thompson, J., 524
Thompson, J. K., 237
Thompson, L. L., 319
Thompson, M. P., 411
Thompson, S. C., 503
Thompson, T. L., 437
Thompson, W. M., 397
Thorndike, E. L., 334
Thornton, D., 160
Thye, S. R., 368
Tice, D. M., 165
Tidikis, V., 304

Tidwell, N. D., 328, 330
Tiebout, J., 510
Tiggemann, M., 237
Timaeus, E., 267
Timko, C., 459
Tindale, R. S., 275, 290, 304
Ting, J. C., 390
Ting-Toomey, S., 110, 346
Titus, L. J., 297
Titus, W., 304
Todd, A. R., 469
Todorov, A., 113, 115, 128
Toi, M., 371, 372
Tolan, P., 424
Toma, C., 304, 343, 344
Tomasello, M., 152, 366
Tong, G., 260
Tong, M.-O., 160
Tooby, J., 366
Toplak, M. E., 180
Topolinski, S., 327
Tourangeau, R., 448
Tracy, J. L., 109, 110
Trappey, C., 234
Tredoux, C. G., 522, 523
Triandis, H. C., 63, 142, 188, 267, 335, 347
Trivers, R. L., 367
Tropp, L. R., 463
Trost, M. R., 255
Trötschel, R., 319
Truong, A., 405
Tsang, B. Y.-P., 348, 349
Tsang, J.-A., 117
Tseëlon, E., 332
Tsuchiya, H., 348
Ttofi, M. M., 428
Turner, C., 410
Turner, F. J., 248
Turner, J. C., 456, 457
Turner, M. E., 307, 316
Turner, S., 441
Tüscher, O., 498
Tversky, A., 85, 86, 88
Twenge, J. M., 171, 172, 285, 312, 427, 503
Tyrrell, D. A. J., 502

U
Uchida, Y., 134, 142
Uhlmann, E. L., 311, 449
Uleman, J. S., 125
Ulvick, J. D., 293
Updegraff, J., 499
Urland, G. R., 437
Uskul, A. K., 248
Uziel, L., 167

V
Vaananen, A., 356, 357
Vaish, A., 366
Vala, J., 127, 458
Vallone, R. P., 97
Van Bavel, J. J., 435, 456
Van Boven, L., 97, 491
Vance, S. L., 447
Van Damme, C., 160
Vandello, J. A., 253, 400, 401
Van den Bos, K., 384, 389
Van Den Burg, M. T. C., 485

VanderLaan, D. P., 366, 367
Van Der Werf, M. P. C., 161
van der Zwaluw, C. S., 180
VanDeusen, K. M., 53
van de Ven, N., 109
van de Vijver, F., 63
Van Diest, R., 293
van Dijk, E., 316
van Ginkel, W. P., 294
van Knippenberg, D., 294, 304, 305
Van Laar, C., 463, 464
Van Lange, P. A. M., 314, 316, 353, 386
Van Leeuwen, E., 388
Van Reijmersdal, E., 240
van Schaik, C. P., 456
Vansteenkiste, M., 152
Van Vugt, M., 309, 310, 368, 484
Varnum, M. E. W., 92, 143, 144
Vasey, P. L., 366, 367
Vasquez, E. A., 405, 422
Vaughn, L. A., 86
Vazire, S., 147, 438
Vedantam, S., 492
Veitch, R., 406
Ventis, W. L., 377
Verette, J., 358, 425
Verfaellie, M., 522
Verwijmeren, T., 234
Vidal, J., 476
Vidyasagar, P., 405
Villalobos, J. G., 412
Vinokur, A., 308
Vinze, A. S., 308
Visser, P. S., 240
Voerman, A. E., 480
Vohs, K. D., 74, 93, 95, 164, 165,
  170, 345
von Dawans, B., 507
Vonk, R., 167
von Wittich, D., 309

W

Wade, J., 260
Wakefield, M., 240
Walker, I., 467, 470
Walkley, R., 463
Wallach, M. A., 308
Wallbom, M., 146
Walsh, D. A., 417
Walster, E., 115, 127, 200, 221, 329, 331, 334,
  355, 357
Walster, G. W., 346
Walther, E., 120, 211, 255
Walton, G. M., 154, 165, 481
Walumbwa, F. O., 309
Wang, J., 319
Wang, M. A., 499
Wang, O., 91
Wang, Y., 488
Wänke, M., 165
Wann, D. L., 421
Ward, A. F., 31, 319, 367
Ward, L. M., 237
Warneken, F., 152
Warner, J., 262
Waterman, A. S., 391
Watkins, E. R., 97
Watson, C. B., 309
Watson, D., 501
Watson, J., 463

Watson, R. I., 301
Watson, W. E., 304
Wattenberg, M. P., 211
Watters, E., 527
Watts, D. J., 341
Watts, D. P., 398
Watts, J. C., 226
Wax, E., 237
Weaver, C. N., 435, 442
Weaver, J. R., 328
Webber, R., 463
Weber, E. U., 86, 93
Weber, J. M., 314
Weber, M., 97
Weber, T. J., 309
Webster, C., 231
Webster, D. M., 126
Wechsler, H., 511
Weeden, J., 237
Wegener, D. T., 221, 225, 378
Wegner, D. and D. M., 94, 95, 148, 165, 200,
  305, 462, 510
Wehrens, M. J. P. W., 161
Wehrle, T., 107
Weihs, K. L., 508
Weiner, B., 105, 117, 425
Weiner, I., 64
Weingart, L. R., 294
Weinstein, N. D., 171
Weinstein, R., 80
Weinsten, N., 341
Weinstock, M., 529
Weiss, W., 221
Weitz, I., 414
Welker, K. M., 425
Wells, G. L., 518, 520, 522, 523
Wells, R. B., 61
Wells, W. D., 231
Wentura, D., 449
Werth, L., 115
West, R., 180, 304
West, S., 188
West, T, V., 324
Westen, D., 188, 211, 440
Westphal, M., 498
Wetherell, M., 265
Wethington, E., 497
Weyant, J. M., 185
Wheeler, D. L., 94
Wheeler, L., 160, 335
Wheeler, M. E., 456
Wheeler, S. C., 76, 221, 240
Whitcup, M., 482
White, 411
White, J. W., 411, 466
White, K. B., 411
White, K. M., 270
White, P. A., 120
White, R. K., 460
White, R. W., 211
Whitehead, G. I., 292
Whitney, D. J., 293
Whittaker, J. O., 266
Whittle, K., 480
Wicker, A. W., 215
Wicklund, R. A., 145
Widom, C. S., 420
Wiggins, E. C., 211
Wilder, D. A., 465, 466, 467
Wilford, M. M., 520

Wilhelmy, R. A., 265
Wilk, S. L., 300
Wilke, H. A. M., 485
Wilkins, C. L., 435
Willard, J., 78
Willer, R., 226
Williams, J., 453
Williams, K. D., 258, 300
Williams, L. E., 84
Williams, M. J., 123
Williams, T. P., 267
Williamson, G. M., 343
Willis, J., 113, 115
Willmott, L., 510
Wilner, D., 463
Wilson, A. E., 161
Wilson, A., 328
Wilson, C., 72
Wilson, D. S., 250, 368
Wilson, E. O., 366, 367
Wilson, J., 203
Wilson, K. S., 293
Wilson, M. L., 398
Wilson, S. J., 424
Wilson, T. D., 25, 44, 52, 58, 61, 147, 148, 149,
  151, 157, 164, 181, 213, 231, 484, 490, 492,
  523
Wilton, C., 258
Windschitl, P. D., 161
Winerman, L., 94
Winman, A., 97
Winsby, M., 503
Wiseman, C. V., 237
Wiseman, M. C., 237
Wittenbaum, G. M., 290, 304, 305
Wittenbrink, B., 391
Wixted, J. T., 523
Wojciszke, B., 115
Wojda, M. R., 439
Wolf, S., 265
Wolfe, C., 467
Wolfson, A., 247, 248
Wolverton, S. A., 305
Wong, E. M., 96
Wong, R. Y., 315
Wood, J. V., 161, 503
Wood, S. E., 240
Wood, W., 150, 181, 221, 268,
  300, 368
Woods, K. E., 403
Woodward, B., 36, 290
Woollett, E., 411
Worchel, P., 408
Word, C. O., 450
Word, L. E., 385
Wortman, C. B., 167, 498
Wrangham, R. W., 398
Wright, E. F., 120
Wright, L., 527
Wright, P. J., 53
Wright, S., 267, 439
Wrosch, C., 161
Wu, C. H., 335
Wu, Y., 260
Wyer, R. S., 76, 134, 221, 300

X

Xu, H., 378
Xu, K., 214
Xygalatas, D., 190

Y

Yamada, A., 149
Yamaguchi, K., 240
Yamauchi, L. A., 135
Yan, Y., 332
Yang, G., 415
Yap, A. J., 116
Yeager, D. S., 154, 501
Yee, A., 131
Yoon, G., 267
Yoshida, F., 327
Yoshikawa, S., 333
Young, A. I., 216
Young, M. C., 420
Young, R. D., 146
Yousif, Y. H., 379
Yovetich, N. A., 358

Yuen, C., 53
Yuki, M., 290
Yukl, G., 310
Yule, F., 487

Z

Zahn, I., 154
Zajonc, R. B., 37, 114, 296, 297, 298, 327
Zander, A., 290
Zanna, M. P., 193, 210, 211, 234, 405, 450
Zanot, E. J., 233
Zebrowitz, L. A., 113, 332, 334
Zeelenberg, M., 109
Zeisel, H., 529, 532
Zeki, S., 352
Zembrodt, I. M., 358
Zhang, D., 267

Zhang, G., 331
Zhang, H., 336
Zhang, L., 503
Zhang, Q., 96
Zhang, S., 349
Zhang, Y., 367
Zhao, J., 453
Zhong, C., 84, 291, 302, 315
Zhong, Y., 251
Zhou, L., 267
Zhu, Y., 130
Zillmann, D., 157, 159
Zimbardo, P. and P. G., 196, 283, 292, 293, 301, 307
Zimmer, B., 268
Zimmerman, C., 358
Zimmerman, M., 140

Subject Index

A

Abraham Biggs suicide, 22, 25
Abu Ghraib prison abuse, 249–250, 293
Accessibility
    attitudes, 216
    schemas, 76–77
Accuracy. *See also* Eyewitness testimony
    eyewitness testimony, 523–526
    need to be accurate, 35–39
Acquisition process, 518–520
Activating implicit prejudices, 443–446
Adams, Randall. *See* Randall Adams case
Advertising
    alcohol abuse and, 231
    culture and, 238
    gender stereotypes, 236–238
    product placement, 239–240
    subliminal, 232–234
    television, 236
    working of, 231–232
Advocacy, counterattitudinal, 191–193
Affect blends, 109
Affective component, of prejudice, 440–441,
        471
Affective forecasting, 163, 492–493
Affectively based attitudes, 210–213, 228
Afghanistan, 25, 63, 402
African Americans. *See also* Prejudice
    King, Martin Luther, Jr. and, 309
    lynchings, 301
    Obama and, 447
    prejudice against, 445
Aggression, 285, 395–431. *See also* Bullying;
        Massacres; Violence
    alcohol abuse and, 405–406
    anger management, 423–426
    in animals, 398, 406
    blaming the victim, 422–423
    Bobo Doll experiment, 404, 415
    catharsis and, 421–423
    Columbine High School massacre, 396,
        426–428
    cultural argument, 399–400, 429
    defined, 396
    evolutionary argument, 386–387
    frustration and, 408–409, 429
    gender differences, 401–403, 429
    genes, 397–398, 428
    historical, 399
    instrumental, 397, 428
    in intimate relationships, 405–406
    learning, 403–405, 429
    microaggressions, 442
    modeling nonaggressive
        behavior, 424
    physical, 396, 401–403, 428
    physiological influences on, 405–408, 429
    punishment and, 427–428
    reduction strategies, 419–428
    relational, 402–403, 429
    riots, 406, 407, 3881
    road rage, 408

scapegoating, 463, 472
social learning theory and,
        403–405, 429
social situations and, 407–414, 428–429
sports and, 421, 430
testosterone levels, 397, 398, 400, 401
Aggressive cues, weapons as, 410–411
Aggressive stimulus, 410, 429
AIDS, 512
Air pollution, 484, 501
Alcohol abuse
    advertising and, 231
    aggression and, 405–406
    binge drinking, 272
    boomerang effect and, 272
    escaping the self and, 146
    schemas and, 76
    think-drink effect, 413
Allport, Gordon, 519
Al-Sadat, Anwar, 319
Altruism
    defined, 365
    empathy-altruism hypothesis, 369–372, 392
    Lincoln and, 370–371
    self-interest *versus*, 370–373, 392
Altruistic personality, 374–375, 392
Amadou Diallo case, 443
American Cancer Society, 229
American Psychological Association ethical
        principles, 65–67
American South, culture of honor, 400, 429
Analytic thinking style, 91–92,
        130–131
Anger. *See also* Aggression
    apologizing for, 424
    communication skills and, 424–425
    managing, 423–426
    scapegoating, 463, 472
    venting *versus* self-awareness,
        421, 430
Animals
    aggression in, 398, 406
    bonobos, 398, 429
    cats, 398
    chimpanzees, 398, 429
    dogs, fight-or-flight response, 507
    fight-or-flight response, 507
    gorilla, prosocial behavior, 371
    rats, 398
Anti-Semitism, 33, 275, 440
Anxious/ambivalent attachment style,
        349–351
Apology, anger management
        and, 424
Appearance, similarity and, 329
Applewhite, Marshall, 249
Applied research
    defined, 61
    improve people's lives, 478–481, 493
Arapesh people, 399
Archival analysis, 49, 68
Aristotle, 92, 334

Arranged marriages, 347, 348
Asch line-judgment studies, 258–261
Asian cultures. *See* East Asian cultures
Attachment styles, 349–351, 361, 362
Attitude(s)
    accessibility, 216
    affectively based, 210–213, 228
    behaviorally based, 210, 213
    classical conditioning, 211–212
    cognitively based, 210–213, 228
    definition, 210
    explicit, 213–214
    implicit, 213–214
    inoculation, 239
    kinds of, 210
    operant conditioning, 211–212
    predicting behaviors, 216–218
    specific, 217
    theory of planned behavior, 216–218
Attitude change
    body and, 229–230
    cognitive dissonance theory, 219–220
    emotion and, 225–229
    long-lasting, 225
    personal relevance effects, 224
    persuasive communication, 220–225
    reasons-generated, 149
    Yale Attitude Change approach, 220–221
Attitude inoculation, 239
Attraction. *See* Interpersonal attraction
Attractive faces, 331–336
Attractiveness. *See* Beauty
Attributional biases, 125, 128–129, 133–135
Attributions. *See also* Fundamental attribution
        error
    bias blind spot, 128–129
    covariation model, 118–120
    external, 118
    internal, 117
    internal *vs.* external, 118–120
    just-world belief, 458
    process of, 117–118
    self-serving, 126–128
    social perception and, 117–129
    two-step process, 125–126
Attribution theory, 117
Autokinetic effect, 251
Automatic thinking
    body and mind, metaphors of, 83–84
    decision making, 83
    definition, 74
    description, 72
    goal pursuit, 82–83
    with schemas, 74–76, 78
Availability heuristics, 85–87
Avoidant attachment style, 349–351

B

Baker, Russell, 482
Bargaining, 318–319
Barge, *Mobro 4000,* 476–477
Barnum effect, 89

Base rate information, 88
Basic research, 61
Beamer, Todd, 365
Beauty
    attractive faces, 331–336
    competence and, 335
    cultural differences, 332–333
    physical attractiveness, 331–336
    stereotypes, 334–336
Behavior. *See also* Environmentally
    responsible behavior; Prosocial behavior;
    Sepcific behavior
    attitude and, 210, 213
    causal theories and, 148
    individual, in groups, 295–302
Behavioral component, of prejudice, 441–446,
    471
Behaviorally based attitudes, 210, 213
Behavioral self-handicapping, 168
Behaviorism, 32, 45
Belief in a just world, 127
Belief perseverance, 115
Ben Franklin effect, 197–199
Beyea, Ed, 365, 369
Bias blind spot, 128–129
Biases. *See also* Prejudice
    attributional, 125, 128–129, 133–135
    correspondence, 122
    hindsight, 44
    impact, 181
    own-race, 520
Bible, 460
Biden, Joe, 447
Big Blue computers, 72
Biggs, Abraham, Jr., 22, 25
"Birds of a feather flock together,", 26, 328
Blake, William, 331
Blaming the victim, 422–423, 458–459, 472
Blind date study, 331
Bobo Doll experiment, 404, 415
Bogus pipeline, 447–448, 472
Bonobos, 398, 429
Boomerang effect, 272–273
Boy Scout camp, 461
Bradbury, Malcolm, 352
Brain. *See also* Social neuroscience
    cognitive dissonance in, 187–188
    fMRIs, 64, 351–352
    love and, 351–352
Breaking up, 358–361
Brown v. Board of Education, 454
Buddhism, 92, 130, 349
Bullying. *See also* Aggression
    Columbine massacre,
      396, 426–427
    Facebook and, 39
    punishment and, 427–428
    reducing, 427–428, 431
Burnett, Thomas, 365
Burns, Ken, 531
Burns, Robert, 397
Bush, George H. W., 112
Bush, George W., 232–233, 257, 290,
    293, 307
Bystander effect
    Chinese 2-year-old girl, death, 381
    defined, 382
    diffusion of responsibility, 46, 384, 385–386
    Kitty Genovese case, 46, 381–382, 388

    pluralistic ignorance, 383–385
    prosocial behavior, 381–387
Bystander Intervention Decision Tree, 384

C

Carbon dioxide emissions, 476, 484
Carol Marcy experiment, 371
Castro, Fidel, 122, 305
Categorization, social, 457, 472
Catharsis, 421–423, 479
Cats, rats and, 398
Causal theories, 148
Causation, correlation compared to, 52–53, 68
The Central Park Five, 531
Central Park rape, 531
Central route to persuasion, 220–222
Cheating pyramid, 187
Chess, 45, 308
Childhood sexual abuse, 528
Children. *See also* Bullying
    Bobo Doll experiment, 404, 415
    forbidden-toy experiment, 195
    gorilla and, 371
    insufficient punishment, 194
    intrinsic *versus* extrinsic motivation studies,
      151–154
    jigsaw classroom, 467–470, 473
    media violence and, 414–418
    modeling nonaggressive
      behavior, 424
    praising, 32, 183
    reading programs, 151–154
Chillingworth, William, 369
Chimpanzees, 398, 429
China. *See also* Collectivistic cultures; East
    Asian cultures
    fundamental attribution error
      study, 132–133
    gan qing concept, 349
    2-year-old girl, death, 381
    yuan concept, 349
Chocolate, love and, 351–352
Christianity
    Bible and, 460
    Golden Rule, 377
    homosexuality and, 460
    scapegoating and, 463, 472
CISD (Critical Incident Stress Debriefing),
    479–481, 510
Cities study, prosocial behavior, 376
Classical conditioning, 211–212
Clinton, Hillary, 310
Coal, oil, water depletion, 476
Cocaine, 352, 441
Cockroaches experiment, 296–300
Cognitive component, of prejudice, 435–439
Cognitive dissonance
    attitude change, 219–220
    in brain, 187–188
    culture aspects, 187–188
    decisions and, 183–187
    definition, 178
    final thoughts on, 201–204
    Heaven's Gate massacre, 201–202
    hypocrisy induction and, 196–197,
      485–487, 494
    immoral decision, 186–187
    impact bias, 181
    irrevocability of decision, 185–186

    lowballing, 185–186
    overcoming, 203–204
    politics and, 202–203
    postdecision dissonance, 184
    rationalizing and, 180
    reduction, 179
    self-affirmation, 180
    self-concept, 182–183
Cognitively based attitudes,
    210–213, 228
Cold, stress and, 502
Coleridge, Samuel Taylor, 507
Collectivistic cultures
    cognitive dissonance and, 188
    groups, 266–268
    interdependent view of self, 300
    love, 351–352
    normative social influence, 266–268
    passionate love, 345–346
College Life Stress Inventory, 500–501
Columbine High School massacre, 396,
    426–428
Common sense
    "birds of a feather flock together," 26, 328
    CISD, 480, 510
    folk wisdom, 25, 328, 509
    naive realism, 33
    "opposites attract,", 26, 324, 328, 361
    social psychology compared to, 24–26, 40
Communal relationships, 357, 361
Communication. *See also* Persuasion
    anger and, 424–425
    negotiation, 318–319
Community or Wall Street game,
    30–31, 315
Companionate love, 345, 361
Comparison, social comparison theory,
    308, 485
Comparison level, interpersonal attraction,
    352–354, 362
Comparison level for alternatives, 352–354,
    362
Competence, 334, 335
Competition. *See also* Sports
    economic, prejudice and, 460–461
    environmentally responsible behavior and,
      485, 494
    prisoner's dilemma game, 30–31, 314–315,
      318, 321
Computers
    Big Blue, 72
    Watson Supercomputer, 72
Condoms, STDs and, 52
Confessions, 530–532
Conformity. *See also* Groups; Norms
    Abu Ghraib prison abuse,
      249–250, 293
    Asch line-judgment studies, 258–261
    autokinetic effect, 251
    contagion effect, 254
    definition, 250
    group size effects, 265
    Heaven's Gate massacre, 249
    idiosyncrasy credits, 265
    importance of being accurate, 253–254,
      261–263
    informational social influence,
      254–255, 383
    McDonald's incident, 247–248

Conformity (*Continued*)
  minority influence, 268
  normative, 454–456, 472
  obedience, 276–285
  prejudice and, 454–456, 472
  private acceptance, 252
  public compliance, 252
  social impact theory, 264–265
  social norms, 257
Confucianism, 92
Consensus information, 119
Consistency information, 119
Construals
  defined, 32, 41
  described, 32–34
  source of, 35–39
Contact hypothesis, 463–465, 473
Contagion effect, 254
Contingency theory of leadership, 310
Control
  internal-external locus of, 503
  perceived control, 502–506
Controlled thinking
  counterfactual thoughts, 96–97
  definition, 72, 93
  drawbacks of, 93
  free will and, 93–95
  overconfidence barrier, 97–99
Convincing myself, 181–182
Cooperation
  group conflict and, 312–319
  jigsaw classroom, 467–470, 473
  prisoner's dilemma game, 30–31, 314–315,
    318, 321
Cooperative learning, 428, 470, 473
Coping, with stress, 506–511, 514
Coping styles, 506–507
Correlation, causation compared to,
    52–53, 68
Correlational method, 47, 50–54, 68
Correlation coefficient, 50
Correspondence bias. *See* Fundamental
    attribution error
Cotton, Ronald, 523–524
Counterattitudinal advocacy,
    191–193
Counterfactual thinking, 96–97
Covariation model
  causal attributions, 120
  consensus information, 119
  consistency information, 119
  definition, 119
  description, 118–119
  distinctiveness information, 119
  Kelley's theory, 119
Cover story, 58
Critical Incident Stress Debriefing (CISD),
    479–481, 510
Cross-cultural differences, social psychology
    and, 28
Cross-cultural research
  defined, 63
  importance of, 28, 40
  passionate love, 345–346
Cuba, 305, 307
Cues, aggressive objects as, 410–411
Cultural argument, aggression, 399–400,
    429
Cultural determinants, 90–91

Cultural differences. *See also* Collectivistic
    cultures;
    Cross-cultural research; East
    Asian cultures; East Asiancultures;
    Individualistic cultures; Western cultures
  advertising, 238
  aggression, 399–400, 429
  beauty, 332–333
  cognitive dissonance, 187–188
  facial expressions, 107–110
  fundamental attribution error, 131–133
  gender roles, 236
  holistic *vs.* analytic thinking, 91–92
  impression management, 169
  leadership, 312
  love, 347–349
  nonverbal communication, 111
  other attributional biases, 133–135
  passionate love, 345–346
  prosocial behavior, 375–377
  self-knowledge, 144
  social cognition, 90–92
  social loafing, 300–301
  social perception and, 129–135
  social psychology and, 63, 68
Cultural truisms, 239
Cultures of honor, aggression and, 399–400,
    429
Cyberbullying, 403

D

Dalai Lama, 378
Darby, Joe, 293
Darwin, Charles, 63–64, 107, 366
Date rape, 430
Dating
  blind date study, 331
  Internet, 324, 325, 335, 338, 339, 343–344
  speed, 338–339
Debriefing
  CISD, 479–481, 510
  experiments, 66, 69
Deception, 66, 283
Deciding to help, bystander intervention
    process, 386–387
Decision making, automatic, 83
Decisions
  Bystander Intervention Decision Tree, 384
  cognitive dissonance and,
    183–187
  in groups, 303–312, 321
  immoral, 186–187
  irrevocability of, 185–186
  jury deliberations, 529–533
Decoding facial expressions, 109–110
Dehumanization
  Abu Ghraib prison abuse, 293
  empathy and, 424–425
  justifying cruelty, 199–201
Deindividuation, 301–302, 321
de La Rochefoucauld, François,
    357, 369
Deliberative prediction behaviors, 216–218
Dependent variables, 54–56, 68
Depletion, of natural resources, 493
Descriptive norms, 270–272,
    482–484, 494
de Tocqueville, Alexis, 380, 409
Trucking Game, 317–318

Diallo, Amadou, 443
Diffusion of responsibility, 46, 384, 385–386.
    See also Bystander effect
Disappointment, overestimation of,
    181–182
Discrimination. *See also* Prejudice
  defined, 441
  drug abuse and, 441
  economic competition and,
    460–461
  institutional, 454–456, 472
  prejudice and, 441–446, 471
  realistic conflict theory, 460–462
  sexism, 439, 446, 450
  social distance, 442, 471
Disease, perceived control and, 505–506
Display rules, 110
Dispositional (internal) attributions
  blaming the victim, 422–423, 458–459, 472
Dissonance. *See* Cognitive dissonance
Dissonance reduction. *See* Cognitive
    dissonance
Distance, social, 442, 471
Distinctiveness information, 119
Distraction, 83
Dogs, fight-or-flight response, 507
Door-in-the-face technique, 274
Dopamine, 352
Downward social comparison, 160–161
Draper, Don, 230–231
Drug usage
  cocaine, 352, 441
  discrimination and, 441
Dryden, John, 303
Duke, David, 166–167

E

Early hominid prosocial behavior, 369
East Asian cultures
  collectivism and, 509
  holistic thinking style, 91
  perceived control and disease, 505–506
  social loafing, 300
Economic competition, prejudice and,
    461–462
Edwards, Edwin, 166
EEG (electroencephalography), 64
Eichmann, Adolf, 277
Elaboration likelihood model, 221, 223
Electroencephalography (EEG), 64
Eliot, George, 388
Emblems, 112
Emerson, Ralph Waldo, 307, 309
Emotions. *See also* Facial expressions
  attitude types, 228–229
  facial expressions, 107–110
  fear-arousing communications, 225–227
  as heuristic, 227
  prejudice and, 440–441
  two-factor theory, 154–157
Empathy
  defined, 370
  dehumanization and, 424–425
Empathy-altruism hypothesis,
    369–372, 392
Empirical science, social psychology as,
    24–25, 40–41, 44–47
Encoding facial expressions, 107
Ending intimate relationships, 358–360

Energy
   conservation, 479, 486, 487
   natural resource depletion, 485–487, 493
   renewable, 478, 494
Enjoying activities, happiness and, 489–492, 490
Environment, prosocial behavior and, 379–380
Environmentally responsible behavior, 478, 482–489
   competition and, 485, 494
   energy conservation, 479, 486
   happiness and sustainable lifestyle, 489–493
   implementation intentions, 488, 494
   inducing hypocrisy, 485–487, 494
   recycling, 487–488, 494
   remove small barriers to achieve big changes, 487–488, 494
   renewable energy, 478
   through social norms, 482–484, 494
Environmental problems
   addressing, 479
   air pollution, 484, 501
   applied research and, 478–481, 493
   carbon dioxide emissions, 476, 484
   global warming, 408–409, 476–478, 493
   greenhouse gases, 476
   littering, 482–484, 494
   natural resource depletion, 476, 486, 493
   plastic materials, 487, 488
   population growth, 477–478, 485
   smog-infested areas, 501
   social psychology and, 39–40, 478–479
   trash vortex areas, oceans, 477
   world hunger, 477
Epinephrine, 507
Equity theory, 355–357
Essay on Criticism, 527
Ethical issues, 65–67
Ethical principles, American Psychological Association, 65–67
Ethnography, 48, 68
Evaluation apprehension, 298, 299, 300, 301
Evolutionary approach to mate selection, 336–339
Evolutionary psychology. *See also* Genes
   defined, 64, 68–69, 336
   mate selection and, 336–339
   natural selection, 366–367, 392
   prosocial behavior and, 366–368
Evolutionary theory
   aggression, 386–387
   Darwin and, 63–64, 366
   defined, 63
   natural selection, 63, 69, 336, 361
Exchange relationships, 356, 362
Experimental method
   improve people's lives, 479–481, 493
   research methodology, 47, 68
Explicit attitudes, 213–214
Exposure, mere exposure effect, 327–328
The Expression of the Emotions in Man and Animals (Darwin), 107
External attributions, 118
External-internal locus of control, 503
External justification, 191, 196
External validity, 58, 68

Extrinsic motivation, 151–152
Eye contact, 111
Eyewitness testimony. *See also* Bystander effect; Memory
   accuracy studies, 523–526
   Randall Adams case, 517–518, 520, 521–522, 524, 529, 532
   recovered memory debate, 526–528

F
Facebook, 324, 342, 402
Facial expressions
   attractive faces, 331–332
   decoding, 109–110
   of emotion, 107–110
   encoding, 107
   evolution and, 107–109
Facilitated communication, 94–95
False confessions, 531
False memory syndrome, 527–528
Familiarity, 327–328, 334. *See also* Exposure, mere exposure effect
Fear, stereotype threat, 451–453, 472
Fear-arousing communications, 225–227
Feedback, after an identification, 525–526
Feeling in charge, 502–506, 513–514
Feelings. *See also* Emotions; Moods; Stress
   catharsis, 421–423, 479–480
   "telling more than you can know" studies, 52
Female suicide bombers, 402
Field experiments, 59–60
Fight-or-flight response, 507
Financial crisis of 2007, 307
First impressions
   belief perseverance, 115
   lingering influence, 114–115
   nonverbal communication, 115–116
   persistence of, 113
   primacy effect, 115
   thin-slicing, 113
Fischer, Andrew, 209
Fixed mindset, 154
Folk wisdom, 25, 328, 509
Fonda, Henry, 532
Foot-in-the-door technique, 274
Forecasting, affective, 492–493
Forer, Bertram, 89
Franks, Tommy, 290
Free will, 93–95
Freud, Sigmund, 313, 421
Fromm, Erich, 353
Frustration
   aggression and, 408–409
   scapegoating and, 463, 472
Frustration-aggression theory, 408–409
Fulbright, J. William, 316
Functional magnetic resonance imaging (fMRI), 64, 352
Fundamental attribution error
   cultural differences, 131–133
   defined, 30, 41, 122
   people as personality psychologists, 121–123
   perceptual salience, 123–125
   Rosa Parks Day, 121

two-person game, 30
two-step attribution process, 125–126
Furnham, Adrian, 134

G
Gandhi, Mohandas, 249
Garbage dumps, oceans and, 477
Gaze, 111
Gender differences
   aggression, 401–403, 429
   leadership, 310–312
   prosocial behavior, 375
   relational interdependence, 300
   sex differences, 337
   social loafing, 299–300
   stress management, 507, 514
Gender roles, 236
Gender stereotypes, 236–238
Geneen, Harold, 310
Genes. *See also* Evolutionary psychology
   aggression, 397–398, 428
   facial attractiveness, 333
   instincts and, 366–368
   prosocial behavior, 366–368
Genovese, Kitty, 46, 54, 58, 68, 381, 382, 388
Gestalt psychology, 32
Gide, Andrew, 455
Girl, Interrupted (Kaysen), 77
Gladwell, Malcolm, 114
Glick, Jeremy, 365
Global warming, 407, 476–477, 493
Goal pursuit, automatic, 82–83
Golden Rule, 377
Gorbachev, Mikhail, 316
Gore, Al, 232
Gorilla, prosocial behavior, 371
Great person theory, 309, 321
Greenhouse gases, 476
Group cohesiveness, 293, 305–307, 321
Group conflict theory, 461
Group polarization, 307–309
Groups, 289–319. *See also* Conformity; In-groups; Out-groups
   benefits of, 290–291
   collectivistic culture, 266–268
   composition of, 291–295
   conflict, 313–319
   contact hypothesis, 463–465, 473
   cooperation, 313–319
   decisions, 303–312, 321
   defined, 290
   deindividuation, 301–302, 321
   functions of, 291–295
   groupthink, 321
   individual behavior in, 295–302
   interdependence, 465, 473
   jury deliberations, 529–533
   leadership in, 309–312
   minimal, 457
   minority influence, 268
   normative conformity, 454–456, 472
   process loss, 303–312, 321
   reasons for joining, 290–291
   roles, 292–293, 321
   scapegoating and, 463, 472
   social dilemmas, 313–316, 321, 487
   social facilitation, 296–298, 300, 321

Groups (*Continued*)
social loafing, 299–300, 321
social norms, 257
transactive memory, 305
Group selection, prosocial behavior and, 368, 392
Groupthink, 305–307, 321
Growth, of world population, 477–478, 485
Growth mindset, 154

H
Hale-Bopp Comet, 178
Hamm, Mia, 154
Hand gestures, 111
"Hand-purse" gesture, 111
Happiness
causes of, 489–492
enjoying activities and, 490
money and, 490–491
relationships and, 489–490
sustainable lifestyle and, 489–493
Harris, David, 517
Harris, Eric, 396, 402, 414, 426–427. *See also* Columbine High School massacre
Hazing, 22, 36–37
Head gestures, 111
Head nodding, 111
Health
feeling in charge, 502–506
fight-or-flight response, 507
Joanne Hill case, 497, 498, 501–502, 503
nursing homes, 503–505
preventing illness, 511–513, 514
reframing traumatic events, 509–511
resilience and, 480, 498–499
social support, 507–509
stress impacts, 497–506
stress management, 506–511
tend-and-befriend response, 507
Heaven's Gate massacre, 201–202, 249
Hemingway, Ernest, 509
Heuristics
availability, 85–87
judgmental, 85
representativeness, 88–89
in social cognition, 85
Heuristic–systematic model of persuasion, 227
Hikikomori, 258
Hill, Joanne, 497, 498, 501–502, 503
Hinde, Robert, 337
Hindsight bias, 44
Hitler, Adolf, 274–275, 434
HIV virus, 512
Holistic thinking style, 91–92, 130–131
Holmes, Oliver Wendall, 440
Holocaust, 276, 510
Homeless people, 304, 426, 458
Homogeneity, out-group, 457–458
Homosexuality
communal relationships, 357, 361
contact hypothesis, 463
investment model of commitment, 354–355
Justification-Suppression Model of Prejudice, 459
lesbians, 354, 357, 435, 447, 455, 460, 463
microaggressions, 442
prejudice, 435
religion and, 460

same-sex marriage, 435, 455
sexual scripts, 412
similarity and, 328
Honor, cultures of, 400–401, 429
Hostile aggression, 397, 428
Hunger, world, 477
Hurons, 399
Hussein, Saddam, 202
Hybrid cars, SUVs and, 484
Hypocrisy induction, 196–197, 485–487, 494
Hypotheses. *See also* Theories
contact hypothesis, 463–465, 473
empathy-altruism hypothesis, 369–372, 392
research methodology, 26, 44–47, 68
theories and, 26, 44–47, 68
urban overload, 379–380

I
Idiosyncrasy credits, 265
Immoral decision, 186–187
Impact bias, 181
Implausible arguments, 181
Implementation intentions, 488, 494
Implicit Association Test (IAT), 448–449, 472
Implicit attitudes, 213–214
Implicit prejudices, 448–449, 472
Impression management, 144
culture in, 169
definition, 167
description of, 166–167
ingratiation, 167
self-handicapping, 168–169
Improve people's lives, applied research, 478–481, 493
Increasing prosocial behavior, 388–391
Independent variables, 54–56, 68
Independent view of the self, 142
Individual behavior, in groups, 296–298
Individual differences, 26, 40–41
Individualistic cultures
love, 347–348
passionate love, 345–346
perceived control and disease, 505–506
social loafing, 300
Industrial Revolution, 209
Inflicted insight, 284
Informational social influence, 383
ambiguous situations, 255
autokinetic effect, 251
being accurate, importance of, 253–254
conformity, 254–255
contagion effect, 254
crisis situations, 255
definition, 251
obedience, 280–281
private acceptance, 252
public compliance, 252
Informed consent, 66, 69, 283
Ingram, Paul, 527
Ingratiation, 167
In-groups
defined, 375
in-group *versus* out-group concept, 456–457
prosocial behavior, 375–376, 392
Injunctive norms, 270–272, 482–484, 494
Innocence Project, 518
Instincts, prosocial behavior and, 366–368

Institutional discrimination, 454–456, 472
Institutionalized racism, 454–456, 472
Institutionalized sexism, 455
Institutional review board (IRB), 66–67, 69
Instrumental aggression, 397, 428
Insufficient punishment, 194
Integrative solution, 319, 321
Interdependence, 465, 473
jigsaw classroom, 467–470, 473
Interdependent view of self, 142–143, 300
Interjudge reliability, 48
Internal attributions, 117
Internal-external locus of control, 503
Internal justification, 191, 196
Internal validity, 56, 68
Internet
cyberbullying, 403
dating, 324, 325, 335, 338, 339, 343–344
deindividuation on, 302
mate preference in online era, 341–343
pornography and, 44
Internment camps, 462
Interpersonal attraction, 323–363
anxious/ambivalent attachment style, 349–351
attachment styles, 349–352, 362
avoidant attachment style, 349–351
brain research and, 351–352
comparison level, 352–354, 362
evolutionary approach to mate selection, 336–339
familiarity, 327–328, 329, 334, 362
Internet dating, 324, 325, 335, 338–339, 343–344, 361
mere exposure effect, 327–328
opposites attract, 26, 324, 328
physical attractiveness, 331–336
prediction of, 325–339
propinquity effect, 326–328, 331, 334, 361
reciprocal liking, 330–331, 334
relationship satisfaction theories, 352–357
secure attachment style, 349–351
sex differences, 337–339
social exchange theory, 352–355, 362
speed dating, 338–339
Interpreting event as emergency, bystander intervention process, 384, 385–386
Interventions, trauma and, 479–481
Intimate relationships, 345–357
arranged marriages, 347, 348
attachment styles, 349–352, 362
communal relationships, 357, 361
comparison level, 352–354, 361, 362
comparison level for alternatives, 352–354, 362
ending, 358–360
equity theory, 355–357, 362
exchange relationships, 356, 362
investment model, 353, 362
relationship satisfaction theories, 352–357
Intrinsic motivation, 151–152
Introspection
causal theories, 148
consequences of, 148–149
definition, 145
reasons-generated attitude change, 149
self-awareness theory, 145–147

Investment model of commitment, 352–357, 362
Invisible support, 509
Iraq
    Abu Ghraib prison abuse, 293
    U.S. invasion of, 290
Iroquois, 399
Irrevocability of decision, 185–186

J

James, LeBron, 257
James, Williams, 81
Japan
    conformity and, 266–268
    hikikomori, 258
Jennings, Ken, 72
Jeter, Derek, 154
Jigsaw classroom, 467–470, 473
Jobs, Steve, 310
Jones, Jim, 22, 25, 26–27, 30
Jonestown massacre, 22, 25, 26–27, 30
Judgmental heuristics, 85
Jung concept, 348
Jury deliberations, 529–533
Justification
    of kindness, 197–199
    overjustification effect, 152–153, 390
    self-esteem approach and, 36–37, 41
Justification of effort (self-justification)
    cruelty, 199–201
    description of, 189–191
    external, 191, 196
    good deeds, 197–199
    internal, 191, 196
    obedience, 282
    punishment, 193–194
Justification-Suppression Model of Prejudice, 459
Just-world belief, 127

K

Kallgren, Carl, 270
Kapista, Peter L., 54
Karma, 349. *See also* Just-world belief
Kasparov, Gary, 72
Kaysen, Susanna, 77
Kelly's Covariation Model, 119
Kennedy, John F., 305, 306, 307
King, Martin Luther, Jr, 309
King, Stephen, 310, 313
Kin selection, 366–367
Kipling, Rudyard, 266, 268
Kitty Genovese murder, 46, 54, 58, 68, 381, 382, 388
Klebold, Dylan, 396, 414, 426–427
Knowing how to help, bystander intervention process, 386
Korsakov's syndrome, 74
Ku Klux Klan, 166, 301

L

Lady Gaga, 257
Landon, Alf, 51
Larry Mayes case, 204
Law, 517–533. *See also* Eyewitness testimony
    jury deliberations, 529–533
    polygraphs, 447

Randall Adams case, 517–518, 520, 521–522, 524, 529, 532
Lawrence, D. H., 351
Leadership, 309–312, 321
Learning
    aggression, 403–405, 429
    cooperative, 428, 470, 473
    jigsaw classroom, 467–470, 473
Lee, Harper, 265, 268, 529
Lepchas, 399
Lesbians, 354, 357, 435, 447, 455, 460, 463
Lie detector test, 447
Life events, negative, 499
Liking
    physical attractiveness and, 331–336, 337
    reciprocal, 330–331, 334
Lincoln, Abraham, 370–371
Lineups. *See also* Eyewitness testimony
    accuracy studies, 523–526
    recommendations for conducting, 523
Literary Digest poll, 51–52
Littering, 482–484, 494
Loafing, social, 299–300, 320
Locus of control, internal-external, 503
Locust years, 507
Long-lasting attitude change, 225
Lootah, Wedad, 436
Loss of personal responsibility, 282–283
Love, 345–351. *See also* Interpersonal attraction; Intimate relationships
    arranged marriages, 347, 348
    brain and, 347
    chocolate and, 352
    companionate, 345–346
    defining, 345–346
    passionate, 346, 349, 361
Lowballing, 185–186
Lucky Charms, Quaker granola and, 38
Lynchings, 267, 301, 454

M

Machiavelli, Niccolò, 309
Magnetic resonance imaging, functional, 64, 352
Malthus, Thomas, 477
Marriages
    arranged, 347, 348
    same-sex, 435, 455
Marshall, Thurgood, 454
Marx, Karl, 296
Massacres. *See also* Holocaust
    Columbine High School, 396, 426–428
    Heaven's Gate, 201–202
    Jim Jones, 22, 25, 26–27, 30
    My Lai, 250, 277
Materialism, happiness and, 491
McDonald's incident, 247–248
Measuring implicit prejudices, 448–449, 472
Media. *See also* Video games
    prosocial behavior and, 386–387
Memory
    acquisition process, 518–520
    false memory syndrome, 527–528
    reconstructive, 521
    recovered, 526–528

retrieval process, 518, 519, 522
source monitoring, 522
storage process, 518, 519, 520–522
transactive, 305
Mencken, H. L., 358
Mental shortcuts, 85–89
Mental strategies, 85–89
Mere exposure effect, 327–328, 334
Meta-analysis, 60–61
Microaggressions, 442
Miller, Robert, 517
Mind control. *See* Subliminal advertising
Mindsets
    fixed, 154
    growth, 154
    motivations and, 154
Minimal groups, 457
Minority influence, 268
Misattribution of arousal, 157–159
Mobro 4000 barge, 476–477
Modeling nonaggressive behavior, 424
Modern racism, 448–449
Money, happiness and, 490–491
Moods
    negative, 501
    prosocial behavior and, 377–378, 392
    "telling more than you can know" studies, 52
Morrison, Toni, 346
Mortality, perceived control and, 505
Motivation
    extrinsic, 151–152
    intrinsic, 151–152
    mindsets and, 154
Music lyrics, prosocial behavior and, 386–387
Muslims, 199, 201, 436
My Lai massacre, 250, 277

N

Naive realism, 33
Narcissism, 171–173
Natural resources, depletion, 476, 486, 493
Natural selection, 63, 69, 336, 366–367
The Nature of Prejudice (Allport), 440
Nazi regime
    anti-Semitism, 33, 440
    Gestalt psychologists and, 32
    Hitler and, 434
    Holocaust, 510
    propaganda, 274–275
Negative life events, 499, 513
Negative moods, 501
Negotiation, 314–315, 318–319, 321
Neuroscience. *See* Social neuroscience
Neurotransmitters, 28, 352
New York Stock Exchange, 91
New York Times, 105
Nonaggressive behavior, modeling, 424
Nonrenewable natural resource depletion, 476, 493
Nonverbal communication
    culture and the channels of, 110–112
    definition, 106
    facial-expressions, 107–110
    first impressions, 113–116
    importance of, 107
Normative conformity, 454–456, 472

Normative social influence
  Asch line-judgment studies, 258–261
  being accurate, importance of, 261–263
  collectivistic group culture, 266–268
  consequences of resisting, 263–264
  definition, 258
  idiosyncrasy credits, 265
  minority influence, 268
  obedience, 279–280
  social impact theory, 264–265
  social norms, 257
Norms
  to change behavior, 272–273
  descriptive, 482–484, 494
  environmentally responsible behavior
    and, 482–484, 494
  injunctive, 482–484
  littering and, 482–484, 494
  prejudice and, 454–456, 472
  reciprocity, 367, 392
North Tower, 365. *See also* September 11th
    terrorist attacks
Noticing an event, bystander intervention,
    384–385
Nursing homes, perceived control in,
    503–505

O
Obama, Barack, 52, 109, 447
Obedience
  aggression, 285
  conformity, 276–285
  informational social influence,
    280–281
  loss of personal responsibility,
    282–283
  normative social influence,
    279–280
  reasons for, 281–283
  research studies, 283–285
  self-justification, 282
Observational method, 47, 48–49, 68
Oil, water, coal depletion, 476
"OK" sign, 111
Online dating, promise and pitfalls in,
    343–344
Operant conditioning, 211–212
Opinions, similarity and, 328
"Opposites attract,", 26, 324, 328
Orestes, 334
Oscar case, 22, 36–37
Out-groups
  defined, 375
  groupthink, 306
  homogeneity, 457–458
  vs. in-group, 456
  prosocial behavior, 375
Overcoming dissonance, 203–204
Overconfidence barrier, 97–99
Overjustification effect, 152–153, 390
Owada, Masako, 142
Own-race bias, 520

P
Pacific Ocean, garbage dump, 477
Palin, Sarah, 311
Panera Cares restaurant chain, 314
Parks, Rosa, 121
Passionate love, 345–346, 349, 361

Passionate Love Scale, 347, 351
Peer pressure, 240–241
Pentagon attacks, 463. *See also* September 11th
    terrorist attacks
Peoples Temple massacre, 22
Perceived behavioral control, 218
Perceived control, 502–506
Perceived similarity, 63, 330
Perceptual salience
  definition, 123
  effects of, 124
  manipulating, 124
Performance-contingent rewards, 153
Peripheral route to persuasion, 220–222
Personality
  altruistic, 374–375, 392
  individual differences, 26, 41
  leadership and, 309
  similarity and, 328
Personality psychology
  defined, 26
  social psychology compared to, 26–29
Personality tests, representativeness
    heuristics and, 89
Personal observations, hypotheses and,
    46–47
Personal qualities, prosocial behavior,
    373–378, 392
Personal space, 111
Persuasion
  ability to pay attention, 224–225
  central route to, 220–222
  confidence effects, 229
  elaboration likelihood model, 221, 223
  heuristic–systematic model of, 227
  ingratiation, 167
  long-lasting attitude change, 225
  motivation to pay attention, 222–224
  peer pressure, 240–241
  peripheral route to, 220–222
  reactance theory, 241–242
  self-persuasion, 194–195
  strategies for, 239–242
Philosophy, social psychology and, 24–26
Physical aggression, 396, 401–403, 428
Physical attractiveness. *See also* Beauty
  liking and, 331–336
Physiological influences, on aggression,
    405–408, 429
Pipeline, bogus, 447–448, 472
Planned behavior, theory of, 216–217
The Plant (King, S.), 313
Plastic materials, 477, 487, 488
Plato, 92
Plausible arguments, 181
Pluralistic ignorance, 383–385
Polarization, group, 307–309
Polar plunges, 256–257
Poole, Bobby, 524
Pope, Alexander, 527
Population growth, 477–478
Pornography
  defining, 49
  Internet and, 44
  violence and, 44, 49, 50, 53, 57, 61, 418, 430
Porteus, Belby, 345
Positive psychology, 391, 392
Postdecision dissonance, 184
Post-identification feedback, 525–526

Post-traumatic stress disorder, 479, 480
Power of social situation, 29–35, 41
Predicting behaviors, attitudes, 216–218
Prejudice, 433–473
  activating implicit prejudices, 443–446
  affective component, 440–441, 471
  African Americans, 445
  behavioral component, 441–446, 471
  blaming the victim, 458–459, 472
  causes of, 454–462
  cognitive component, 435–439
  components, 435–439, 471
  conformity and, 454–456, 472
  cooperative learning, 470, 473
  defined, 435–436
  discrimination and, 441–446, 471
  economic competition and, 460–461
  effects on victim, 450–453
  emotions and, 440–441
  examples, 434
  homosexuality, 435
  implicit, 448–449, 472
  institutional discrimination, 454–456, 472
  jigsaw classroom, 467–470, 473
  Justification-Suppression Model of
    Prejudice, 459
  measuring implicit prejudices, 448–449, 472
  microaggressions, 442
  modern racism, 448–449
  The Nature of Prejudice, 440
  normative conformity and, 454–456, 472
  out-group homogeneity, 457–458, 472–473
  realistic conflict theory, 460–462, 472
  reduction strategies, 463, 472
  religion and, 460
  scapegoating, 463, 472
  self-fulfilling prophecies and, 450–453, 472
  sexism, 439, 446, 450
  social categorization, 456–457
  stereotypes and, 435–436, 471, 478
Preserving natural resources, 486
Prevention, health and, 511–513, 514
Pride, 109
Primacy effect, 115
Priming effects
  body and mind, metaphors of, 83–84
  definition, 77–78
Prisoner's dilemma, 30–31, 314–315
Prisons
  Abu Ghraib prison abuse, 293
  Zimbardo study, 293
Probability level (p-value), 56
Process loss, 303–312, 321
Product placement, 239–240
Propaganda, 274–275
Propinquity effect, 326–328, 331, 334
Prosocial behavior, 364–394. *See also*
    Altruism; Bystander effect; Empathy
  bystander effect, 381–387
  cities study, 376
  cultural differences, 375–377
  defined, 365–366
  early hominid, 369
  empathy-altruism hypothesis, 369–372, 392
  environment and, 379–380
  evolutionary psychology and, 366–368
  gender differences, 375
  genes, 366–368, 392
  Golden Rule, 377

gorilla, 371
group selection, 368, 392
increasing, 388–389
in-groups, 375–376, 392
instincts, 366–368
kin selection, 366–367, 392
media and, 386–387
moods and, 377–378, 392
music lyrics and, 386–387
out-groups, 375–376, 392
personal qualities, 373–378, 392
positive psychology, 391, 392
reciprocity norm, 367, 392
religion and, 377, 382, 384, 392
self-interest, 348–352, 392
September 11th terrorist attacks, 365, 369, 374, 381, 388
situational determinants of, 379–387
social exchange theory, 368–369, 392
video games, 386–387, 393
volunteerism, 390
Prosocial video games, 386–387, 393, 416
Proximity, 326. *See also* Propinquity effect
Psychological distress, 284
Psychological intervention techniques, trauma and, 479–481
Psychological realism, 58
Psychology
Gestalt, 32
personality, 26–29
positive, 391, 392
Punishment
aggression reduction through, 419–420
forbidden toy experiment, 195
insufficient, 194
in justification, 193–194
tangible rewards, 195–196
Pygmies, 399

Q

Quaker granola, Lucky Charms and, 38

R

Racism
institutionalized, 454–456, 472
modern, 448–449
Randall Adams case, 517–518, 520, 521–522, 524, 529, 532
Random assignment to condition, 56
Random selection, 51
Rape
Amadou Diallo case, 443
blame the victim, 458–459, 472
in *To Kill a Mockingbird*, 268
motivations for, 411
pornography and, 44, 53, 57
reframing event, 509
Ten Commandments film and, 415
Rats, cat and, 398
Reactance theory, 241–242
Reagan, Ronald, 316
Realism, psychological, 58
Realistic conflict theory, 460–462, 472
Reasons-generated attitude change, 149
Reciprocation, 330–331, 334
Reciprocity norm, 367, 392
Reconstructive memory, 521

Recovered memories, 526–528
Recycling, 487–488, 494
Reduction strategies
aggression, 419–428
anger, 423–426
bullying, 427–428
Reframing traumatic events, 509–511, 514
Rejection-rage cycle, disrupting, 426–428
Relational aggression, 402–403, 429
Relational interdependence, 300
Relationship-oriented leadership, 310, 311
Relationships. *See also* Intimate relationships
attachment styles, 349–351, 362
communal, 357, 361
comparison level, 352–354, 361
comparison level for alternatives, 352–354, 361
equity theory, 355–357, 362
exchange, 356, 362
happiness and, 489–490
investment model, 352–357, 361
Relationship satisfaction theories, 352–357
Religion. *See also* Christianity; September 11th terrorist attacks
Bible and, 460
Buddhism, 349
Golden Rule, 377
Muslims, 436
Peoples Temple massacre, 22
prejudice and, 460
prosocial behavior and, 377, 382, 392
Renewable energy sources, 478
Reno, Raymond, 270
Replications, 60–61, 68
Reported self-handicapping, 168
Representativeness heuristics
base rate information, 88
definition, 88
personality tests and, 89
Research
empirical science and, 24–25, 40–41, 44–47
new frontiers, 62–65, 68–69
Research methodology
correlational method, 47, 50–54, 68
experimental method, 47, 54–62, 68
hypotheses, 26, 44–47, 68
research quiz, 45
summary of methods, 47
theories, 26, 44–47, 68
Resilience, 480, 498–499, 513
Responsibility, diffusion of, 46, 384, 385–386
Retrieval process, 518, 519, 522
Rewards
performance-contingent, 153
task-contingent, 153
Richter, John Paul, 379
Riots, 406, 407, 419
Road rage, 408
Roles (social roles)
defined, 292–293
groups, 292–293, 320
violating, 292
Roosevelt, Eleanor, 468

Roosevelt, Franklin, 51, 167
Roosevelt, Teddy, 316
Ruskin, John, 299
Rutter, Brad, 72

S

Sacks, Oliver, 74
Same-sex marriage, 435, 455
Scanzoni, Letha, 460
Scapegoating, 463, 472
Schemas
accessibility, 76–77
automatic thinking with, 74–76
cultural determinants, 90–91
definition, 74
priming effects, 77–78
Schlesinger, Arthur, 306
Science, social psychology and, 25–26
Secure attachment style, 349–351
Self
executive function of, 164–166
functions of, 144
independent view of the, 142
interdependent view of, 300
interdependent view of the, 142–143
key attributes of, 141–142
Self-affirmation, 180
Self-awareness
theory, 145–147
venting *versus*, 421, 430
Self-concept
cultural influences, 142–144
definition, 141
development of, 140–142
dissonance and, 182–183
Self-control, 144
executive function of the self, 164–166
thought suppression, 164–165
Self-enhancement, 169
Self-esteem, 144
African American children, 183
approach, 36–37, 41
definition, 170
jigsaw classroom, 467–470, 473
pros and cons of, 170–173
terror management theory, 170
Self-focus, 146
Self-focused attention, 146
Self-fulfilling prophecies, 38
beauty and competence, 335
defined, 79, 450
first and second graders percentages, 80
jigsaw classroom and, 467–470, 473
prejudice and, 450–453, 472
Self-perpetuating cycle of, 78–79
Self-handicapping
behavioral, 168
definition, 168
reported, 168
Self-interest
altruism *versus*, 368–372, 392
prosocial behavior, 368–372, 392
relationship satisfaction, 352–355, 361
Self-justification. *See* Justification of effort (self-justification)

Self-knowledge, 144
Self-perception theory, 150–151
Self-persuasion
    definition, 195
    lasting effects, 194–195
Self-serving attributions, 126–128
September 11th terrorist attacks
    Pentagon attacks, 463
    prosocial behavior, 369, 374, 381
    psychological debriefing, 480
    Rescorla and, 365
    resilience and, 498
    United Airlines Flight, 365
    World Trade Center towers, 365,
      369, 463
    Zelmanowitz and, 365, 369, 388
Sex differences, 337. *See also* Gender
    differences
Sexism, 439, 446, 450
Sexual abuse, childhood, 528
Sexual assault, 411–413
Sexual scripts, 412, 430
    and the problem of consent, 412–413
Shaich, Ronald, 314
Shakespeare, William, 144, 311, 332,
    345, 490
"Shooting people" video game experiment,
    445
Similarity, 63, 328
Situational determinants, of prosocial
    behavior, 379–387
Smog-infested areas, 501
Social categorization, 456–457
Social cognition
    controlled, 93–99
    cultural differences, 90–92
    defined, 37–38
    definition, 72–73
    kinds of, 73
Social cognition approach, 37–40, 41
Social comparison theory, 160–161,
    308, 485
Social competence, 334, 335
Social dilemmas, 313–316, 321, 487
Social distance, 442, 471
Social exchange theory
    prosocial behavior, 368–372, 392
    relationship satisfaction,
      352–354, 362
Social facilitation, 296–298, 300, 320
Social impact theory, 264–265
Social influence
    defined, 23, 40
    descriptive norms, 270–272
    door-in-the-face technique, 274
    foot-in-the-door technique, 274
    informational, 250–255, 383
    injunctive norms, 270–272
    normative, 256–268
    obedience, 276–285
    propaganda, 274–275
    strategies for, 269–275
    tactics of, 273–275
Social intervention techniques, trauma and,
    479–481
Social learning theory, aggression and,
    403–405, 429
Social loafing, 299–300, 320
Social neuroscience

holistic and analytical thinking styles, 131
    new frontiers, 64, 69
Social norms, 257
Social perception
    attributions and, 117–129
    cultural differences, 129–135
    definition, 106
    nonverbal communication, 106–116
Social problems, social psychology and,
    38–40, 41, 478–479
Social psychology
    common sense compared to, 24–26
    cultural differences and, 28, 63, 68
    defined, 23, 40
    as empirical science, 24–25, 40, 44–47
    environmental problems and, 39–40
    goal of, 28
    introduction, 21–42
    personality psychology compared to, 26–29
    philosophy and, 24
    science and, 25–26
    social problems and, 38–40, 41
    sociology compared to, 26–29
Social situations
    aggression and, 407–413, 429
    power of, 29–32, 40
Social support, 507–509, 514
Social tuning, 161–163
Sociology, social psychology and, 26–29
Sodomy, 455
Source monitoring, 522
South, culture of honor in, 400
South Korea
    beauty stereotype, 335
    jung concept, 348, 349
South Tower, 365. *See also* September 11th
    terrorist attacks
Speed dating, 338–339
Spencer, Herbert, 435
Spinoza, Benedict, 24
Split cable market tests, 231
Spontaneous predicting behaviors, 216
Sports
    aggression and, 421–422
    stereotype threat and, 451–453, 472
STDs (sexually transmitted diseases), 52
Stereotypes. *See also* Prejudice
    beauty, 334–335
    prejudice and, 435–436, 471, 478
    sexism, 439, 446, 450
Stereotype threat, 451–453, 472
Storage process, 518, 519, 520–522
Story model, 529–530
Story order, 530
Stress
    College Life Stress Inventory, 500–501
    coping styles, 506–507
    coping with, 506–511
    Critical Incident Stress Debriefing,
      479–481
    defined, 501
    fight-or-flight response, 507
    health and, 497–506
    post-traumatic stress disorder,
      479, 480
    psychological intervention techniques,
      479–481
    reframing traumatic events, 509–511
    resilience and, 480, 498–499

Selye on, 499
    social support, 507–509
    tend-and-befriend response, 507
Subjective norms, 218
Subliminal advertising
    debunking the claims, 233–234
    form of mind control, 232–234
    laboratory evidence, 234
Subliminal messages, 233
Sugar, Lucky Charms-Quaker granola study,
    38
Suicide
    Abraham Biggs case, 22, 25
    Jim Jones massacre, 22, 25, 26–27, 30
Suicide bombers, 30, 402, 409. *See also*
    September 11th terrorist attacks
Summers, Donna Jean, 247–248
Supercomputer, Watson, 72
Support, social, 507–509
Supreme Court decisions, 303, 414,
    420, 463
Surveys, 50–52
Sustainable lifestyle, happiness and,
    489–493
SUVs, hybrid cars and, 484

T
Taguba, Antonio, 293
Taliban regime, 63
Taoism, 92, 130
Task-contingent rewards, 153
Task-oriented leadership, 310
Technology, making connections in age,
    340–344
Teduray people, 399
Television advertising, 236
"Telling more than you can know" studies, 52
Ten Commandments film, rape incident and,
    415
Tend-and-befriend response, 507
Terrorism. *See also* September 11th terrorist
    suicide bombers, 30, 402, 409
Terror management theory, 170
Testosterone levels, 397, 398, 400, 401
Theories
    attribution theory, 117
    causal theories, 148
    equity theory, 355–356, 362
    frustration-aggression theory, 408–409
    great person theory, 309
    group conflict theory, 460–462, 472
    Kelley's theory, 119
    Lewin on, 61, 479
    planned behavior, 216–218
    reactance theory, 241–242
    realistic conflict theory, 460–462, 472
    relationship satisfaction theories, 352–357
    research methodology, 26, 44–47, 68
    self-awareness theory, 145–147
    self-perception theory, 150–151
    social comparison theory, 308, 485
    social exchange theory, 352–357, 362,
      368–372, 392
    social impact theory, 264–265
    social learning theory, 403–405, 429
    terror management theory, 170
    "There is nothing so practical as a good
      theory,", 479
    two-factor theory, 154–157

Theory of planned behavior, 216–218
"There is nothing so practical as a good theory,", 61
The Thin Blue Line, 517
Thinking
    analytic thinking style, 91–92, 130–131
    automatic, 73–84
    controlled, 72, 93–99
    groupthink, 305–307, 321
    holistic thinking style, 91–92, 130–131
Thompson, Jennifer, 523, 524
Thought suppression, 164–165
Threat, stereotype, 451–453, 472
Thumbs-up gesture, 111
Tit-for-tat strategy, 316, 356
To Kill a Mockingbird, 268, 529
Torture
    Abu Ghraib prison abuse, 293
    deindividuation and, 268
Touching, 111
Tracy, Jessica, 109
Transactive memory, 305
Transformational leadership, 309, 321
Trash
    littering, 482–484
    recycling, 487–488
    trash vortex areas, oceans, 477
Trauma
    Critical Incident Stress Debriefing, 479–481
    reframing traumatic events, 509–511
    social intervention techniques, 479–481
Trucking game, 317–318
Turn the other cheek, 409
Twelve Angry Men, 532
Twilight saga, 346
2-year-old Chinese girl, death, 381
Two-factor theory of emotion, 154–157
Two-step attribution process, 125–126

U

Unconscious thinking, 91
United Airlines Flight, 365

United States (U.S.). *See also* Individualistic cultures; Iraq; September 11th terrorist attacks
    Bush, George W. and, 36, 290, 307
    internment camps, 462
    Obama and, 36, 52, 447
Upward social comparison, 160–161
Urban overload hypothesis, 379–380
U.S. Food and Drug Administration, 225
Ustinov, Peter, 327

V

Values, 23
Variables
    dependent, 54–56, 68
    independent, 54–56, 68
Venting, self-awareness *versus,* 421, 430
Vicary, James, 233
Video games
    prosocial, 386–387, 393, 416
    "shooting people" video game experiment, 445
    violent, 63, 386–387, 393, 396, 403, 445
Vietnam War, 192, 199, 255
    prolonging of, 36
Violating roles, 292
Violence. *See also* Aggression; Massacres; Nazi regime; Rape; September 11th terrorist attacks
    in media, 414–418, 430
    pornography and, 44, 49, 50, 53, 57, 61, 418, 430
    religion and, 414
    riots, 406, 407, 419
    road rage, 408
    video games, 63, 386–387, 393, 396, 403, 414–418, 430, 445
Vioxx, 479
Volunteerism, prosocial behavior, 390
Vonnegut, Kurt, 456

W

Wall Street or Community game, 30–31, 315. *See also* Prisoner's dilemma

Warner, Charles Dudley, 371
Washington, Kerry, 257
Water
    conservation, 487, 494
    natural resource depletion, 476, 494
    trash vortex areas, oceans, 477
Watson supercomputer, 72
Weapons, as aggressive cues, 410–411
Weapons of mass destruction, 202–203
Wegner, Daniel, 94
Weiner, Anthony, 167
Welles, Orson, 254
Wells, H. G., 254
Western cultures
    analytic thinking style, 91
    personality psychologists, 133
Westgate West Building study, 326
What God Has Joined Together: The Christian Case for Gay Marriage (Myers & Scanzoni), 460
Wik, William, 365
Wilde, Oscar, 332
Witness order, 530
Women. *See also* Beauty; Gender differences
    head-to-toe covering, 63
    lesbians, 354, 357, 447, 455, 460, 463
    sexism, 439, 446, 450
    suicide bombers, 402, 409
Wood, Robert, 517
World hunger, 477
World Trade Center attacks, 365, 369, 374, 381. *See also* September 11th terrorist attacks
World War II, 462, 510. *See also* Nazi regime
Wozniak, Stephen, 310

Y

Yale Attitude Change approach, 220–221

Z

Zelmanowitz, Abe, 365, 369, 388
Zimbardo study, 293

Answer Key

CHAPTER 1

Answers to Review Questions on p. 29:

1. b   3. c   5. c
2. a   4. a

Answers to Review Questions on p. 34:

1. a   3. b   5. d
2. c and d   4. a

Answers to Review Questions on p. 39:

1. b   2. a   3. b and c

Test Yourself on p. 41:

1. a   5. c   9. b, d
2. d   6. a   10. e
3. b   7. d
4. b and c   8. c

CHAPTER 2

Answers to Review Questions on p. 47:

1. c   2. b and c   3. b

Answers to Review Questions on p. 62:

1. a   4. a and d   7. c
2. c   5. b   8. a
3. d   6. c

Answers to Review Questions on p. 65:

1. a   2. c   3. c

Answers to Review Questions on p. 67:

1. c   2. c   3. a and c

Test Yourself on p. 69:

1. d   5. c   8. a, b,
2. c   6. c and d   and d
3. c   7. c   9. a and d
4. d   10. c

Answers to Try It! on p. 45:

1. In studies conducted by Stanley Milgram (1974), up to 65% of participants administered what they thought were near-lethal shocks to another subject. (In fact, no real shocks were administered; see Chapter 8.)

2. (c) Rewarding people for doing something they enjoy will typically make them like that activity less in the future (see Chapter 5).
3. (b) False; groups often make worse decisions than individuals (see Chapter 9).
4. (a) Under most circumstances, repeated exposure increases liking for a stimulus (see Chapter 10).
5. (a) More (see Chapter 6).
6. (b) People who are in good moods or bad moods are more likely to help others than people in neutral moods, though for different reasons (see Chapter 11).
7. (a) Research has found that when women think there are sex differences on a test, they do worse, because of the added threat of confirming a stereotype about their gender. When women were told that there were no gender differences in performance on the test, they did as well as men (see Chapter 13).
8. (b) There is no evidence that subliminal messages in advertising have any effect; considerable evidence shows that normal advertising is quite effective (see Chapter 7).
9. (a) (Playing violent video games increases the likelihood that people will act aggressively (see Chapter 12).
10. (b) People given the heavy clipboard thought that student opinion should be weighed the most (see Chapter 3).

Answers to Try It! on p. 53:

1. There could be a third factor—increased daily exercise due to walking the dog. While pets may help reduce blood pressure and reduce depression and loneliness, other factors such as taking more frequent walks outside might actually be responsible.
2. Not necessarily. Though it seems obvious that Instagram distracts them from their studies, there might be other factors involved. For example, students who spend less time studying may be more interested in spending time on social media. Alternately, those who are good at taking photographs that others admire may have weaker skills in more traditional academic subjects.

3. Probably not—it's just that people who are more extroverted are more likely to post more pictures of themselves than people who are introverted.
4. Not necessarily. There is likely a third factor involved, which is the presence of a school psychologist, who is more likely to notice and diagnose these learning disabilities. In other words, children in public schools may be equally likely to have a learning disability but less likely to have it identified by school staff.
5. It is also possible that this correlation is actually something else: that people who own guns are more likely to use one web browser over another. People who own guns may be more anxious about security and privacy and thus choose a web browser that offers better privacy. People who own guns are more likely to commit murder due to the availability of a weapon.
6. Not likely. There is likely a third variable at play. A study found that optimists tend to be more successful in their careers. They also tend to think they have more time left to complete a task (like travel to work) than they really do. Additionally, people with Type B personalities have been shown to be less accurate in assessing time. They also tend be more optimistic and to be more creative.
7. Can certain Eastern religious beliefs stave off heart attacks? Not necessarily, but switching to a vegetarian diet would drastically reduce most peoples' risk of heart attack. There may be other factors that coincide which could explain the relationship, such as stress reduction due to meditation or certain outlooks on life.
8. It is very unlikely that one has to do with the other; this may be a simple random convergence in math. Due to sociopolitical factors, the number of pirates began to steadily decrease around the time of the Industrial Revolution. The increasing human population and lifestyle changes that followed this same period are thought by most experts to be responsible for the increase in global temperatures.
9. It is possible that playing this game makes people more likely to act aggressively. However, it is also likely

that young people who are aggressive are more drawn to violent video games. In addition, it is difficult to pin the blame on one particular game when the shooters were likely exposed to graphic violence in other games as well as from TV and movies.

10. Probably not—people who are more intelligent tend to have a larger vocabulary. Contrary to popular belief, people who swear more often have a bigger vocabulary than people who purposefully try to limit their swearing. As for the neatness of one's desk, people who are more intelligent may just focus on their work rather than on keeping their space tidy.

Note: For more examples on correlation and causation, see http://jfmueller. faculty.noctrl.edu/100/correlation_ or_-causation.htm

CHAPTER 3

Answers to Review Questions on p. 81:

1.	c	3.	d	5.	b
2.	a	4.	a		

Answers to Review Questions on p. 90:

1.	b	3.	a	5.	a
2.	c	4.	d		

Answers to Review Questions on p. 92:

1.	b	3.	b	5.	c
2.	a	4.	d		

Answers to Review Questions on p. 100:

1.	b	3.	c	5.	d
2.	b	4.	a		

Test Yourself on p. 102:

1.	a	5.	d	9.	d
2.	d	6.	c	10.	b
3.	c	7.	a		
4.	b	8.	a		

Answers to Try It! on p. 89:

1. The correct answer is (b), the third letter. Tversky and Kahneman (1974) found that most people thought that the answer was (a), the first letter. Why do people make this mistake? Because, say Tversky and Kahneman, they find it easier to think of examples of words that begin with *r*. By using the availability heuristic, they assume that the ease with which they can bring examples to

mind means that such words are more common.

2. The correct answer is (b). Slovic, Fischhoff, and Lichtenstein (1976) found that most people think that (a) is correct (accidents). Why do people make this error? Again, it's the availability heuristic: Accidental deaths are more likely to be reported by the media, so people find it easier to bring to mind examples of such deaths than deaths from strokes.

3. The correct answer is (c). Both outcomes are equally likely, given that the outcomes of coin flips are random events. Tversky and Kahneman (1974) argue that, due to the representativeness heuristic, people expect a sequence of random events to "look" random. That is, they expect events to be representative of their conception of randomness. Many people, therefore, choose HTTHTH because this sequence is more representative of people's idea of randomness than HHHTTT. In fact, the chance that either sequence will occur is 1 out of 2^6 times, or 1 in 64. As another illustration of this point, if you were to buy a lottery ticket with four numbers, would you rather have the number 6957 or 1111? Many people prefer the former number because it seems more "random" and thus more likely to be picked. In fact, both numbers have a 1 in 1,000 chance of being picked.

4. The correct answer is (b). Many people choose (c) because they think that after five tails in a row, heads is more likely "to even things out." This is called the gambler's fallacy, which is the belief that prior random events (e.g., five tails in a row) have an influence on subsequent random events. Assuming that the coin is fair, prior tosses have no influence on future ones. Tversky and Kahneman (1974) suggest that the gambler's fallacy is due in part to the representativeness heuristic: Five tails and one head seems more representative of a chance outcome than six tails in a row.

Answers to Try It! on p. 96:

These questions are based on ones used by Pronin and Kugler (2010), who found that people tend to believe that they have more free will than do other people. In their study, they asked Princeton undergraduates to predict what would happen in the year after graduation, either to them or to a friend of their choosing. When the students answered the questions about

themselves, they circled "both are possible" 52% of the time, whereas when they answered the questions about a friend, they circled "both are possible" only 36% of the time. In other words, the students seemed to think their friends' actions were more predetermined than were their own.

Answers to Try It! on p. 98:

1. (a) This question assesses methodological reasoning, the recognition that there are several reasons why crime has gone down other than actions taken by the police chief and that a better test of the mayor's claim is to compare the crime rate in Middleopolis with other, similar cities. The other answers might be true, but they don't involve sound methodological reasoning.

2. (a) This question assesses statistical reasoning, the recognition that large samples of information are more likely to reflect true scores and abilities than small samples of information. For example, if you flip a fair coin four times, it is not unusual to get all heads or all tails, but if you flip the coin a thousand times, it is extremely unlikely that you will get all heads or all tails. Applied to this example, this statistical principle says that when baseball players have a small number of at-bats, it is not unusual to see very high (or very low) averages just by chance. By the end of the season, however, when baseball players have hundreds of at-bats, it is highly unlikely that they will have a very high average just by luck. The other answers might also be true, but they don't reflect sound statistical reasoning.

CHAPTER 4

Answers to Review Questions on p. 112:

1.	d		4.	a
2.	c		5.	a
3.	c			

Answers to Review Questions on p. 116:

1.	d		4.	a
2.	b		5.	c
3.	d			

Answers to Review Questions on p. 129:

1.	b		4.	c
2.	d		5.	a
3.	d			

Answers to Review Questions on p. 135:

1. b
2. c
3. a
4. b
5. d

Test Yourself on p. 137:

1. a
2. a
3. c
4. b
5. c
6. c
7. a
8. a
9. c
10. b

CHAPTER 5

Answers to Review Questions on p. 144:

1. c
2. a
3. b
4. a

Answers to Review Questions on p. 150:

1. a
2. d
3. c

Answers to Review Questions on p. 159:

1. b
2. b
3. c
4. b

Answers to Review Questions on p. 164:

1. c
2. c
3. c

Answers to Review Questions on p. 166:

1. d
2. d
3. a

Answers to Review Questions on p. 169:

1. a
2. b
3. c

Answers to Review Questions on p. 173:

1. c
2. d
3. b

Test Yourself on p. 175:

1. a
2. d
3. a
4. d
5. c
6. a
7. b
8. d
9. d
10. c

Answers to Try It! on p. 143:

1. To estimate your degree of interdependence, take the average of your answers to questions 1–5. To estimate your degree of independence, take the average of your answers to questions 6–10. On which measure did you come out higher? Singelis (1994) found

that Asian Americans agreed more with the interdependence than the independence items, whereas Caucasian Americans agreed more with the independence than the interdependence items.

Answers to Try It! on p. 147:

Reverse your answers to questions 2 and 5. If you answered 1 to these questions, change it to a 5; if you answered 2, change it to a 4; and so on. Then add your ratings for all 10 questions. The higher your score, the more likely you are to focus your attention on yourself. Fenigstein, Scheier, and Buss (1975) found that the average score was 26 in a sample of college students.

CHAPTER 6

Answers to Review Questions on p. 189:

1. d
2. c
3. b
4. a
5. a

Answers to Review Questions on p. 204:

1. d
2. d
3. c
4. c
5. a
6. d

Test Yourself on p. 206:

1. d
2. b
3. a
4. b
5. e
6. a
7. d
8. c
9. d
10. c

CHAPTER 7

Answers to Review Questions on p. 214:

1. c
2. a
3. c
4. c
5. b

Answers to Review Questions on p. 218:

1. b
2. a
3. d
4. b
5. b

Answers to Review Questions on p. 230:

1. d
2. c
3. a
4. c
5. c
6. d

Answers to Review Questions on p. 238:

1. c
2. c
3. a
4. b
5. b

Answers to Review Questions on p. 242:

1. b
2. b
3. b
4. d
5. a

Test Yourself on p. 244:

1. b
2. d
3. b
4. c
5. b
6. a
7. b
8. d
9. b
10. b

CHAPTER 8

Answers to Review Questions on p. 250:

1. c
2. d
3. c

Answers to Review Questions on p. 256:

1. a
2. d
3. b
4. c
5. c

Answers to Review Questions on p. 269:

1. b
2. a
3. c
4. a
5. c
6. d

Answers to Review Questions on p. 276:

1. d
2. c
3. a
4. b
5. c

Answers to Review Questions on p. 285:

1. c
2. a
3. d
4. b
5. b

Test Yourself on p. 288:

1. c
2. d
3. b
4. a
5. c
6. b
7. c
8. d
9. b
10. d

CHAPTER 9

Answers to Review Questions on p. 295:

1. d
2. b
3. a
4. b
5. b

Answers to Review Questions on p. 303:

1. b
2. d
3. b
4. c
5. b

Answers to Review Questions on p. 312:

1. a
2. c
3. a
4. b
5. d

Answers to Review Questions on p. 320:

1. b
2. b
3. b
4. c
5. c

Test Yourself on p. 321:

1. a
2. c
3. a
4. c
5. d
6. a
7. c
8. b
9. a
10. d

CHAPTER 10

Answers to Review Questions on p. 339:

1. b
2. c
3. d
4. d
5. c
6. b
7. c

Answers to Review Questions on p. 344:

1. c
2. a
3. b
4. a

Answers to Review Questions on p. 357:

1. c
2. c
3. b
4. b
5. a
6. c

Answers to Review Questions on p. 360:

1. b
2. b
3. a

Test Yourself on p. 362:

1. c
2. a
3. a
4. d
5. b
6. c
7. a
8. d
9. b
10. a

CHAPTER 11

Answers to Review Questions on p. 373:

1. c
2. a
3. b
4. d

Answers to Review Questions on p. 379:

1. a
2. c
3. d
4. a

Answers to Review Questions on p. 388:

1. c
2. a
3. c
4. b

Answers to Review Questions on p. 391:

1. c
2. a
3. d

Test Yourself on p. 393

1. a
2. a
3. c
4. c
5. d
6. c
7. a
8. b
9. a
10. d

CHAPTER 12

Answers to Review Questions on p. 407:

1. b
2. b
3. b
4. d
5. b

Answers to Review Questions on p. 413:

1. c
2. d
3. c
4. b
5. c
6. a
7. a

Answers to Review Questions on p. 419:

1. b
2. b
3. d
4. b
5. d

Answers to Review Questions on p. 428:

1. a
2. b
3. c
4. c
5. d

Test Yourself on p. 431:

1. a
2. c
3. c
4. e
5. a
6. d
7. a
8. a
9. c
10. b

CHAPTER 13

Answers to Review Questions on p. 446:

1. a
2. b
3. c
4. b
5. a

Answers to Review Questions on p. 449:

1. c
2. a
3. a
4. c
5. e

Answers to Review Questions on p. 453:

1. b
2. b

3. d
4. b
5. b

Answers to Review Questions on p. 462:

1. d
2. b
3. d
4. b
5. a

Answers to Review Questions on p. 471:

1. b
2. c
3. b
4. a
5. d

Test Yourself on p. 473:

1. a
2. d
3. b
4. d
5. b
6. d
7. b
8. c
9. c
10. a

SPA 1

Answers to Review Questions on p. 481:

1. b
2. c
3. d

Answers to Review Questions on p. 488:

1. d
2. a
3. c

Answers to Review Questions on p. 493:

1. b
2. c
3. a

Test Yourself on p. 494:

1. d
2. b
3. b
4. a
5. c
6. a
7. c
8. d

SPA 2

Answers to Review Questions on p. 506:

1. b
2. d
3. a
4. b

Answers to Try It! on p. 508:

1. You get 1 point each time you answered true (T) to questions 1, 4, 5, 6, and 10 and 1 point for each time you answered false (F) to questions 2, 3, 7, 8, and 9.
2. This scale was developed to measure what the researchers call appraisal *social support*, or "the perceived availability of someone to talk to about one's problems" (Cohen et al., 1985, pp. 75–76). One of the findings was that when people were not under

stress, those low in social support had no more physical symptoms than people high in social support did. When people were under stress, however, those low in social support had more physical symptoms than did people high in social support. Another finding was that women scored reliably higher on the social support scale than men did. If you scored lower than you would like, you might want to consider reaching out to others more when you are under stress.

Answers to Review Questions on p. 511:

1. c   2. a   3. c

Answers to Review Questions on p. 513:

1. c   2. d

Test Yourself on p. 514:

1. c   5. b
2. b   6. a
3. b   7. a
4. b   8. d

SPA 3
Answers to Review Questions on p. 528:

1. c   3. b   5. c
2. b   4. a

Answers to Review Questions on p. 533:

1. d   2. d   3. c

Test Yourself on p. 534:

1. d   6. c
2. a   7. d
3. c   8. a
4. c   9. b
5. c   10. d